Hemmings'
Vintage Auto Almanac
12TH EDITION

1937 Hupmobile

Publisher & Editor-in-Chief — *Terry Ehrich*	Customer Service — *Carol Dewey, Lisa Knapp,*
Technical Editor — *Dave Brownell*	*Kelly Kwasniak, Amy Mooney, Merri Moore, Kathleen Ryder,*
Managing Editor — *Mary Pat Glover*	*Melissa Telford, Freda Waterman*
Listings Preparation — *Nancy Bianco*	Production Manager — *Edward Heys*
Technical Assistance — *Mary McGuinness &*	Production Staff — *Peg Bakaitis, Nancy Bianco,*
Russell Aminzade	*Wendy Bissonette, Joyce Cipperly, Donna Elwell,*
Retail Sales — *Kathleen Ryder*	*Anita Finney, Karen Gaboury, Chickie Goodine,*
Circulation/Fulfillment Manager — *Heather Hamilton*	*Lucinda Greene-Ensign, Don Hicks, Adelaide Jaquith,*
Circulation/Fulfillment Assistant Manager — *Marian Savage*	*Donna Jones, Paige Kwasniak, Peg Mulligan, Amy Pearson,*
Advertising Sales Manager — *Lesley McFadden*	*Dawn Rogers, Abby Shapiro, Nancy Stearns, Peg Stevens,*
Advertising Sales — *Laurie Mulhern, Tamie Nixon &*	*Bonnie Stratton, Dick Warner, Tracey Watson,*
Randy Shannon	*Carol Wigger, Pat Woodward, Bev Waitekus, Cindy Wright*

Front cover photo credits, left to right:

1930 Studebaker by Dave Brown, 1962 Corvette by John G. Tennyson, 1946 Dodge pickup by Bud Juneau,
Central primary photo, a 1956 Oldsmobile by Roy Query

Back cover photo credits, clockwise from top left:

1951 Studebaker by John & Connie Stanton, 1970 Pontiac Judge by John F. Katz, 1965 AC Cobra 289 by John Matras,
1970 Plymouth Superbird by Allan Weitz, 1925 Kleiber by Arch Brown, 1938 Oldsmobile by Bud Juneau

WHOLESALE INFORMATION:

Dealers, vendors, newsstands:

for wholesale copies of the Twelfth Edition of
Hemmings' Vintage Auto Almanac for resale, contact:
Kathleen Ryder, *Hemmings Vintage Auto Almanac,* PO Box 945, Bennington, Vermont 05201
or phone 1-800-227-4373, Extension 552

A publication from Hemmings Motor News, © 1997
Published in the U.S.A.   Printed in Canada

ISBN 0-917808-17-7
ISSN: 0363-4639
LCCN: 76-649715

CHEVY DUTY PICKUP PARTS

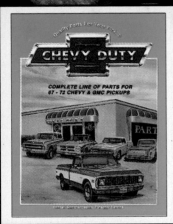

Get your 1947-72 Chevy and GMC truck parts from one of the largest dealers around. We carry only the highest quality new, used, and NOS parts. We have four fully illustrated catalogs, complete with descriptions and prices, for you to order from! Please specify the catalog you'd like us to send: **32.** 47-54; **33.** 55-59; **34.** 60-66; or **35.** 67-72. Catalogs $3.00 each (refundable with your first order).

CHEVY/GMC 6-CYL.

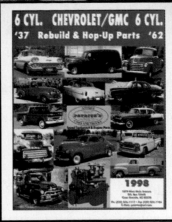

Your rebuild, hop-up parts, engine parts and speed equipment headquarters. One call gets you pistons, rings, gaskets, bearings, oil pumps, etc. Everything for the rebuild. Then, all the finest in nostalgia dress-up and performance: genuine Fenton cast iron headers, econo (steel-tube) headers, Offy heads and intakes, Isky cams, Mallory ignitions. VISA/MC/ Discover/ COD (7 days/week). — Patrick's Antique Cars & Trucks, 520-836-1117. **36.** Catalog FREE.

CHEVYLAND PARTS & ACCESSORIES

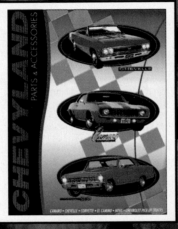

Specializing in restoration parts and accessories for Camaro, Chevelle, El Camino, Nova, and 1967-72 Chevrolet pickup trucks. Toll-free ordering lines available. PH:916-638-3906. **37.** Catalog $4.00.

CLASSIC CHEVY INTERNATIONAL

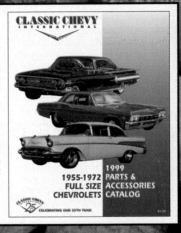

We stock the world's largest inventory of high quality parts for 1955-1972 full-size Chevrolets, including original, modified, reproduction, used, restored, rechromed, and NOS, as well as apparel and accessories. And they're all at the best prices in the industry! PH: 800-456-1957. **38.** 1955-72 Chevrolet catalog $5.00.

CLASSIC INDUSTRIES

Camaro catalog: 580 full color pages! Largest selection of original and reproduction products and accessories ever assembled. Easy-to-read format, thousands of parts, color photos and detailed descriptions. Classic Industries is an Official GM Restoration Parts licensee assuring the highest quality parts for 1967-97 Camaro. 17832 Gothard St., Huntington Beach, CA 92647. PH: 1-888-GM CATALOG. Catalog: **39.** $5.00 (in USA; refundable on first order); **40.** $10.00 (Canada); or **41.** $20.00 (international).

CLASSIC INDUSTRIES

Firebird/Trans Am catalog: 435 full color pages! Largest selection of original and reproduction products and accessories ever assembled. Easy-to-read format, thousands of parts, color photos and detailed descriptions. Classic Industries is an Official GM Restoration Parts licensee assuring the highest quality parts for 1967-97 Firebird & Trans Am. 17832 Gothard St., Huntington Beach, CA 92647. PH: 1-888-GM CATALOG. Catalog: **42.** $5.00 (in USA; refundable on first order); **43.** $10.00 (Canada); or **44.** $20.00 (international).

CLASSIC INDUSTRIES

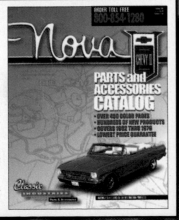

Nova/Chevy II catalog: 400 full color pages! Largest selection of original and reproduction products and accessories ever assembled. Easy-to-read format, thousands of parts, color photos and detailed descriptions. Classic Industries is an Official GM Restoration Parts licensee assuring the highest quality parts for 1962-79 Nova & Chevy II. 17832 Gothard St., Huntington Beach, CA 92647. PH: 1-888-GM CATALOG. Catalog: **45.** $5.00 (in USA; refundable on first order); **46.** $10.00 (Canada); or **47.** $20.00 (international).

CLASSIC MOTORBOOKS

World's largest selection of automotive books and videos. Classic Motorbooks' giant 136-page catalog is filled cover-to-cover with thousands of books and videos on your favorite cars: Packards, Fords, Chevrolets, Duesenbergs, Cadillacs, Mercedes-Benz, Chrysler, Rolls-Royce, Porsche, Ferrari and many more. Plus trucks, tractors, motorcycles, memorabilia, owner's manuals, investment guides, restoration guides, and more! **48.** Catalog $2.00.

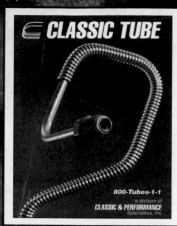

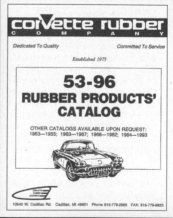
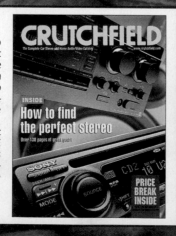

Hemmings' Vintage Auto Almanac

is brought to the collector-car hobby by:

Hemmings Motor News

"The bible" of the collector-car hobby since 1954.
(see full listing on page 532)

The hobby's most authoritative and informative glossy magazine.
(see full listing on page 534)

Hemmings Motor News

Filling Station

Some of our best selling books to help with restoration and maintenance projects.
(see full listing on page 528)

Dear Reader,

Welcome to the *Almanac's* family!

Our *Vintage Auto Almanac* is the world's most complete directory to the old auto hobby. Here are over 2,900 listings for clubs, dealers, vendors, salvage yards, services, and individuals serving the hobbyist. And more, including the most complete listing of old car museums you'll find anywhere.

This edition of the *Almanac* contains 297 listings for Legislative Watch Organizations. These groups were formed to take on the vital chore of protecting the interests of the collector car hobby/industry, a dramatic increase over the six listed in our last edition. From what threats should we be protected? So-called "Clunker Bills" and related governmental actions that threaten to reduce or eliminate the supply of old cars & parts, and bills that would impose additional costs or restrictions on our enjoyment of old cars. Become involved! These important listings begin on page 513.

To old hands, the *Almanac's* excellence is no surprise – it's an offshoot from *Hemmings Motor News* and *Special Interest Autos*, two of the most respected publications in the hobby.

Hemmings Motor News is "the bible" of the collector-car hobby. "*HMN*" has been published monthly since 1954, and now serves over 700,000 readers (paid circulation over 264,000 monthly, average 2.8 readers per copy). We also serve tens of thousands of advertisers worldwide. *Hemmings Motor News* is literally the World's Largest collector-car hobby publication.

HMN is about 98% advertising of collector cars for sale and related items down to the most obscure and hard-to-find parts, literature, services, tools, supplies, and more. During 1996, *HMN* averaged 810 pages per month! That's a fat package for the annual subscription price of just $26.95.

Special Interest Autos magazine is the editorial 'sister' publication to *HMN*. "*SIA*" can help you choose which collector car you want, and tells you all about the collector cars you & your friends already own. *SIA* is unique in the hobby: Each issue features freshly written *driveReports* on at least three collector cars, tracing developmental histories and including complete driving impressions of restored or originial examples of the cars.

SIA's exclusive *comparisonReports* face-off two or three collector cars, of similar vintage & price, against each other – and we pull no punches! To learn which cars are best for

which purposes, read *SIA*.

Edited by David Brownell, a hobbyist and old car writer/editor for over 30 years, SIA features some of the best writing and photography in the collector car field. Dave brings his readers detailed specifications and comparison charts, fascinating facts, tremendous trivia, how-to articles to help you restore & maintain your dreamboat, authoritative advice, nostalgia, entertainment, exclusive interviews with important automotive personalities, and stunning photos (many in color) of your favorite cars. When Dave hires an author or photographer, he makes sure he's got an expert – and Dave's been an editor for old auto magazines longer than anyone else currently in the field.

$19.95 brings you one year (six issues) of *SIA*, with articles and photos you'll simply not find elsewhere.

Hemmings Bookshelf offers a wide & carefully selected list of old car books to aid, educate, and entertain the restorer and enthusiast. Titles offered cover how-to topics, value & investment guides, interchange manuals, marque histories, and more – everything from old farm tractors to '60s and '70s muscle cars, from low-bucks hobby cars to Ferraris & Duesenbergs. We ship promptly, and we refund promptly if you're not satisfied. See our monthly ads in *HMN*.

We welcome visitors to our Bennington, Vermont, offices, and at our Hemmings Motor News Sunoco Filling Station & Store at 216 Main Street (Vermont Route 9) in downtown Bennington, and we're always glad to hear from readers through the mail. Your "feedback" and opinions are desired, because our long-established goal is to make all our publications useful, comprehensive, and a good value for the dollar! Please help us know how we're doing by writing us at PO Box 256, Bennington, Vermont 05201, or by calling us at 1-800-CAR-HERE. Thank you!

Sincerely yours,
Terry Ehrich

Publisher & Editor-in-Chief

CONTENTS

Section One

Specialists by Make and Model 9

Organized alphabetically by marque, this section includes all vendors, dealers and suppliers concerned with specific marques.

A state-by-state index to Section One vendors.

Section Two

Generalists 191

Organized alphabetically by subject, this section lists businesses offering specific types of parts or services for a range of automotive marques.

(Section Two continued)

Tourguide 441

Section Three

Clubs 447

A comprehensive listing of clubs and organizations, divided into sub-sections for multi-marque clubs, marque clubs, registries, specialty clubs, legislative organizations and state or local clubs.

Section Four

Publications & Information Sources 523

Organized alphabetically, this section is a listing of publishers, archivists and libraries which are sources of information for the old-auto hobby.

Section Five

Salvage Yards 537

Organized alphabetically by state, this section lists salvage yards which offer collectible cars and parts.

Section Six

Museums 543

Organized alphabetically by state, this section lists private and public museums or showrooms with vintage cars in their collections.

Section Seven

Useful Lists and Compilations 551

Index

An alphabetical index to every listing in the almanac. 585

Section One:
Specialists by Make & Model

Section One provides a comprehensive roster of specialists in one or a limited number of particular car makes. Marques are presented alphabetically, and vendors offering parts, supplies, literature, services or cars appear alphabetically under every marque in which they specialize. Certain extremely popular models, such as Corvette and Thunderbird, are presented as separate categories following the appropriate main marque category.

The taglines in the right-hand box of each listing offer a quick guide to the primary services or products offered by each marque specialist.

Vendors who specialize in several marques will have an abbreviated listing under each pertinent marque category with a cross reference to the vendor's full listing. This full listing appears under the category of that vendor's most significant concentration.

Hobbyists seeking services or products appropriate to a variety of car marques should also consult Section Two, which lists vendors by general product or service categories.

Brooklands Inc 503 Corporate Square 1500 NW 62nd St Fort Lauderdale, FL 33309 954-776-2748; FAX: 954-772-8383 E-mail: rbiggs@lgc.net	accessories

See full listing in **Section Two** under **accessories**

Cobra Restorers Ltd 3099 Carter Dr Kennesaw, GA 30144 770-427-0020; FAX: 770-427-8658	parts restoration service

See full listing in **Section One** under **Cobra**

Healey Lane 5920 Jones Ave Riverside, CA 92505 800-411-HEALEY (4325) FAX: 909-689-4934	parts restoration service

See full listing in **Section One** under **Austin-Healey**

JWF Restorations Inc 11955 SW Faircrest St Portland, OR 97225-4615 503-643-3225; FAX: 503-646-4009	restoration

AC restoration specialist. 35 years' experience. Partial to full restorations done to street or concours standards.

Ragtops & Roadsters 203 S 4th St Perkasie, PA 18944 215-257-1202; FAX: 215-257-2688	race prep repairs

Open shop only. Monday-Friday 9-5, evenings and Saturday by appointment. Minor repairs to full concours restorations of all British and special interest automobiles. Vintage race car prep and restoration. The more unusual the car the more we enjoy it. Mechanical, engine rebuilds, interior trimming, body and paint refinishing, fabrication.

Alfa Heaven Inc 2698 Nolan Rd Aniwa, WI 54408-9667 715-449-2141	parts

Mail order and open shop. Open Monday-Friday 8 to 5, Saturday by appointment only. Specializing in new & used parts, transmission & brake rebuilding, performance parts, fiberglass repro parts for 1975 thru current models Alfa Romeo. Museum houses mostly Alfa Romeo, but also has one Maserati, a Ferrari and a Lancia. We also have the prototype Giulietta Spyder and specialize in first of Series Alfas. Specializing in 1960s & 1970s Japanese motorcycle parts.

Alfas Unlimited Inc US Rt 44 Norfolk, CT 06058 203-542-5351; FAX: 203-542-5993	engine rebuilding parts restoration service

Repair and restoration shop and mail order parts. Monday-Saturday 10 to 6. Vintage Alfa restorations for racing or street. Also repair shop for modern Alfas. Complete restorations including body, paint, engine and any other mechanical components. Twenty years' experience in Alfas. Many new, NOS and used parts for sale as well as vintage and modern Alfas for sale, for race or street. Member VSCCA, SVRA, AROC.

Caribou Imports Inc 23151-A3 Alcalde Dr Laguna Hills, CA 92653 714-770-3136; FAX: 714-770-0815 E-mail: cariboulh@aol.com	parts

See full listing in **Section One** under **Fiat**

Centerline Products Box 1466 4715 N Broadway Boulder, CO 80306 303-447-0239; FAX: 303-447-0257	cars parts

Mail order and open shop. Monday-Friday 9:30 am-5:30 pm. Specializes in Alfa Romeo parts, new and used and used Alfa cars. Deals in all models, Giulietta, Giulia thru 164.

Concours Cars of Colorado Ltd 2414 W Cucharras St Colorado Springs, CO 80904 719-473-6288	accessories parts service

See full listing in **Section One** under **BMW**

Grand Prix Classics Inc 7456 La Jolla Blvd La Jolla, CA 92037 619-459-3500; FAX: 619-459-3512	racing cars sports cars

See full listing in **Section Two** under **racing**

Marc B Greenwald c/o 6644 San Fernando Rd Glendale, CA 91201 818-956-7933; FAX: 818-956-5160	parts

Mail order only. Italian spare parts for Abarth, Alfa, DeTomaso, Ferrari, Fiat, Iso, Lamborghini, Maserati, as well as many other Italian autos including special bodied autos mfg in Italy.

Healey Lane 5920 Jones Ave Riverside, CA 92505 800-411-HEALEY (4325) FAX: 909-689-4934	parts restoration service

See full listing in **Section One** under **Austin-Healey**

HRE Performance Wheels 2540 Pioneer Ave Vista, CA 92083 619-941-2008; FAX: 619-598-5885	aluminum wheels

See full listing in **Section Two** under **wheels & wheelcovers**

International Auto Parts Inc Rt 29 N PO Box 9036 Charlottesville, VA 22906 800-726-0555, 804-973-0555 FAX: 804-973-2368	accessories parts

Mail order parts and accessories for Alfa Romeo, Fiat, Lancia. 60-page catalog of parts for Italian cars 1956-94. Hours: Monday-Friday 8:30 am to 6 pm and Saturday: 9 am to 3 pm, Eastern time. Parts shipped within 24 hours. Major credit cards accepted. Send $2 (in the US) for catalog, $6 (worldwide).

The Italian Car Registry 3305 Valley Vista Rd Walnut Creek, CA 94598-3943 510-458-1163	information source

See full listing in **Section Four** under **information sources**

Orion Motors European Parts Inc 10722 Jones Rd Houston, TX 77065 800-736-6410; 713-894-1982 FAX: 713-849-1997	parts

Mail order only. All parts for Alfa Romeo, Fiat, Yugo. Direct importer of parts from country of origin and other sources.

Palo Alto Speedometer Inc 718 Emerson St Palo Alto, CA 94301 415-323-0243; FAX: 415-323-4632	instruments

See full listing in **Section One** under **Mercedes-Benz**

Replicarz 99 State St Rutland, VT 05701 802-747-7151 E-mail: replicarz@aol.com	books kits models videos

See full listing in **Section Two** under **racing**

Garry Roberts & Co 922 Sunset Dr Costa Mesa, CA 92627 888-FERRAR; FAX: 714-650-2730	cars parts service

See full listing in **Section One** under **Ferrari**

Scale Autoworks Brady Ward 313 Bridge St #4 Manchester, NH 03104-5045 PH/FAX: 603-623-5925 ext 66	models

See full listing in **Section Two** under **models & toys**

Vintage Restorations The Old Bakery Windmill Street, Tunbridge Wells Kent, TN2 4UU England UK 1892-525-899 FAX: UK 1892-525499	accessories instruments

See full listing in **Section Two** under **instruments**

Victory Autoservices Box 5060, RR 1 W Baldwin, ME 04091 207-625-4581	parts restoration

See full listing in **Section One** under **Austin-Healey**

All American Rambler 11661 Martens River Cir #M Fountain Valley, CA 92708 714-662-7200	manuals parts

Mail order and open shop. Monday-Friday 9-5, Saturday by appointment only. Specializes in parts for 58-63 Rambler Americans. Also tech service manuals for all Ramblers, tail lenses for most Ramblers. Buy, sell, trade. If we don't have it, we will help you find it. Bob (Mr Rambler) Pendleton.

American Parts Depot 409 N Main St West Manchester, OH 45382 513-678-7249; FAX: 513-678-5886	accessories parts

Mail order and open shop. Monday thru Friday 8 am to noon and 1 to 6 pm, Wednesday evenings 7 to 10 pm EST. We supply new, used, reproduction and NOS parts and accessories for AMC and Rambler vehicles. 108 parts cars in stock. Send $5 for our 144 page AMX and Javelin catalog.

American Performance Products 675 S Industry Rd Cocoa, FL 32926 407-632-8299; FAX: 407-632-5119	parts

Mail order and open shop. Monday-Friday 9:30-5:30, Saturday 10 am-3 pm. Specializing in American Motors Corp vehicles parts for AMX, Javelin, Spirit, Gremlin, Hornet and Jeep.

AMX Connection
David Simon
19641 Victory Blvd
Reseda, CA 91335-6621
818-344-4639

literature
parts

Mail order and open shop. Shop open by appointment only.
Dealing in NOS and used parts and original literature for the
1968-70 American Motors AMX. Some 1971-1974 Javelin/AMX
parts and literature available. Also AMC, Nash and Rambler original unused and used shop manuals, owner's manuals, parts
books and sales literature.

Blaser's Auto, Nash, Rambler, AMC
3200 48th Ave
Moline, IL 61265
309-764-3571; FAX: 309-764-1155

NOS parts

Mail order only. We specialize in new old stock Nash, Rambler
and AMC parts for most 1946-1987 model cars. We offer the
largest and most complete stock of parts for these fine cars. Our
52 years of experience makes us the best choice for your one
stop shopping. Now featuring quality reproduction windshield
gaskets for your 1963-1969. Fast shipping worldwide daily. All
orders shipped within 48 hours. Visa, MasterCard, Discover,
American Express and COD accepted. Hours M-F 9-5 pm
Central time. Call today we look forward to helping you.

**Dom Corey Upholstery
& Antique Auto**
1 Arsene Way
Fairhaven Business Park
Fairhaven, MA 02719
508-997-6555

carpets/conv tops
dash covers
door panels
headliners
seats
upholstery

See full listing in **Section Two** under **interiors & interior parts**

Doc & Jessie's Auto Parts
6 Holly Blvd
Scotia, NY 12302
518-346-8553

literature
models
parts

Specializing in AMC memorabilia, literature, scale models, NOS
and hard to find parts, accessory items, V8 motor parts and
1954-1975 AMC/Rambler cars (all models). We buy, sell and
swap AMC. Send SASE for current listing.

Dennis DuPont
77 Island Pond Rd
Derry, NH 03038
603-434-9290

automobilia
literature
parts

See full listing in **Section One** under **Studebaker**

Elliott's Car Radio
313 Linfield Rd
Parkerford, PA 19457
610-495-6360; FAX: 610-495-7723

radio repairs
speaker kits

See full listing in **Section Two** under **radios**

For Ramblers Only
2324 SE 34th Ave
Portland, OR 97214
503-232-0497
E-mail: ramblermac@aol.com

accessories
parts

Mail order and open shop. Weekdays 10 am-2 pm and weekends
10 am-6 pm. Specializing in parts & accessories, NOS & used,
for 58 to 69 Rambler & AMC. Carpets and trunk mats for
Ramblers only. Windshield gaskets for some Ramblers.

Doug Galvin Rambler Parts
7559 Passalis Ln
Sacramento, CA 95829
916-689-3356

parts

Mail order only. Specializing in new and used parts, including
reproduction items and literature for 1958 through 1988
Ramblers and AMCs. No Jeep or Metropolitan.

Hawthorne Appraisals
Box 1332
Coaldale, AB Canada T1M 1N1
403-345-2101

appraisals
parts

See full listing in **Section Two** under **appraisals**

Hidden Valley Auto Parts
21046 N Rio Bravo
Maricopa, AZ 85239
602-252-2122, 602-252-6137
520-568-2945
FAX: 602-258-0951

parts

See full listing in **Section One** under **Chevrolet**

HRE Performance Wheels
2540 Pioneer Ave
Vista, CA 92083
619-941-2008; FAX: 619-598-5885

aluminum wheels

See full listing in **Section Two** under **wheels & wheelcovers**

Jahns Quality Pistons
1360 N Jefferson St
Anaheim, CA 92807
714-579-3795, 800-225-0277
FAX: 714-524-6607

piston rings
pistons

See full listing in **Section Two** under **engine parts**

Kennedy American Inc
7100 State Rt 142 SE
West Jefferson, OH 43162
614-879-7283

parts

Mail order and open shop. Mon-Fri 9 am-6 pm. New, select used
and reproduction parts for American Motors, Rambler, AMX,
Javelin and Jeep vehicles from 1950s to present.

Master Power Brakes
254-1 Rolling Hills Rd
Mooresville, NC 28115
704-664-8866; FAX: 704-664-8862

brake products
conversion kits

See full listing in **Section One** under **Chevelle/Camaro**

Mike's Auto Parts
Box 358
Ridgeland, MS 39158
601-856-7214

bearings
engine parts
NOS parts
windshield wipers

See full listing in **Section One** under **Chrysler**

Garth B Peterson
122 N Conklin Rd
Veradale, WA 99037
509-926-4620 anytime

accessories
parts
radios

See full listing in **Section Two** under **comprehensive parts**

Eddie Stakes' Planet Houston AMX
3400 OCEE #1601
Houston, TX 77063
713-785-1375

parts
parts locator

Mail order only. Specializing in 68-74 AMX & Javelin. Buy, sell, trade, used & NOS parts, literature. Expanded AMC vendors list. Clubs & applications, marketwatch, VIN, paint, trim codes, more. Free parts locator service. Current catalog, $6 US. Call 11 am-1 pm M-F.
AMX files: http://worldwide.net/~stoneji/amc-list.html

Peter Stathes
51 Twin Lawns Ave
Hicksville, NY 11801-1817
516-935-5298, 8-11 pm EST

parts

Mail order only. Specializing in AMC & Rambler vacuum wiper motor rebuilding, door locks, beltline fuzzy window sweeps, rubber window channels, reproduction truss rods. SASE.

Treasure Chest Sales
413 Montgomery
Jackson, MI 49202
517-787-1475

parts

See full listing in **Section One** under **Nash**

Pat Walsh Restorations
Box Q
Wakefield, MA 01880
617-246-5565

literature
rubber parts

See full listing in **Section Two** under **rubber parts**

Webb's Classic Auto Parts
5084 W State Rd 114
Huntington, IN 46750
PH/FAX: 219-344-1714

NOS parts
used parts

Mail order and open shop. Monday-Friday 8 to 5; weekends by appointment. Specialize in NOS, used and repro parts for Rambler and AMC from 1950 and newer. Large line of AMX/Javelin parts. Large selection of technical service manuals and parts books for Nash, Hudson, Rambler, AMC, Jeep and 83-up Renault. Many aftermarket parts available for AMC and other makes. Send SASE with your needs. Discover, VISA, MC and AmEx accepted.

Harold Wenner
5449 Tannery Rd
Schnecksville, PA 18078
610-799-5419

accessories
parts

NOS parts and accessories for AMC, Rambler and Nash.

Wymer Classic AMC
Mark Wymer
340 N Justice St
Fremont, OH 43420
419-332-4291, 8 to 5 pm
419-334-6945 after 5 pm

NOS parts
repairs
used parts

Mail order and open shop. Monday-Friday 8 to 5 EST. An American Motors dealership from 1958/1982. Repairs all AMC and Nash cars. Still has a large supply of NOS and used parts from our AMC, Rambler, Nash salvage yard from 1958-82 and all the specialty tools to repair the cars. Large selection of technical service manuals, service literature, specification books and owner's manuals from 1955 to 1982 for Nash, Hudson, Rambler, AMC, Jeep, Renault, Metropolitan. Can do repair work on Packard cars. Have some Packard literature and memorabilia.

Healey Lane
5920 Jones Ave
Riverside, CA 92505
800-411-HEALEY (4325)
FAX: 909-689-4934

parts
restoration
service

See full listing in **Section One** under **Austin-Healey**

Heinze Enterprise
7914 E Kimsey Ln
Scottsdale, AZ 85257
602-946-5814

instrument
restoration

Mail order and open shop. Free list of items for sale for American Austin, Bantam and Crosley. Also instrument restoration and refacing. Reproducer of vintage auto parts. Mechanical temperature gauge rebuilding. Send SASE for listing.

Gordon Imports Inc
14330 Iseli Rd
Santa Fe Springs, CA 90670-5296
310-802-1608, 714-523-3512
FAX: 310-404-1904

parts

Mail order and business open 8 am to 5:30 pm daily Monday through Friday. Call for weekend hours, special appointments available. Amphicar parts for all years of Amphicars.

Anglia Obsolete
1311 York Dr
Vista, CA 92084
619-630-3136; FAX: 619-630-2953

parts

Mail order only. New, used, reproduction parts for English Fords, 1939-1959, 8 hp and 10 hp cars and commercial vehicles. Models include: 7W, 7Y, Anglia, Prefect, Popular, Thames, E93A Series, 100E Models and some 105E Series.

JAE
375 Pine #26
Goleta, CA 93117
805-967-5767; FAX: 805-967-6183

parts
service
tech info

See full listing in **Section One** under **Lotus**

Kip Motor Company Inc
13325 Denton Dr
Dallas, TX 75234
972-243-0440; FAX: 972-243-2387
E-mail: kipmotor@aol.com

literature
parts
restoration

See full listing in **Section One** under **Austin**

Weld-N-Fab Performance
PO Box 356
Norwalk, IA 50211
515-981-4928

gas pumps
machine work
tractors

Mail order and open shop. Shop open by appointment only. 1948-52 English Ford cars and parts. Anglia, Prefect and Thames parts & Allis Chalmers G tractors bought and sold. Machine shop services, also custom chassis fabrication (drag or street), heliarc, mig welding. Funny cars to sprint cars. 65-70 Chevrolet Impalas. Gas pumps, visible and electric, Ecco Islanders, restoration and parts. Also specializing in custom prototype one-off work.

Dick Ames Stainless Steel Exhaust
3963 Wilshire Cir
Sarasota, FL 34238
813-923-8321; FAX: 813-923-9434

exhaust systems

See full listing in **Section One** under **Jaguar**

Becker Sales
Rear 519 Wyoming Ave
West Pittston, PA 18643
PH/FAX: 717-655-3869

battery master
switches

See full listing in **Section Two** under **batteries**

British Luxury Automotive Parts
257 Niagara St
Toronto, ON Canada M6J 2L7
416-693-8400; FAX: 416-694-3202
Beeper: 416-378-8182

new and used parts

See full listing in **Section One** under **Jaguar**

British Things Inc
515 Ocean Ave
Santa Monica, CA 90402
310-394-4002; FAX: 310-394-3204

badges

See full listing in **Section One** under **Rolls-Royce/Bentley**

British Wiring Inc
20449 Ithaca Rd
Olympia Fields, IL 60461
PH/FAX: 708-481-9050

wiring accessories
wiring harnesses

See full listing in **Section Two** under **electrical systems**

Donovan Motorcar Service
4 Holmes Rd
Lenox, MA 01240
413-499-6000; FAX: 413-499-6699

restoration
service

See full listing in **Section One** under **Jaguar**

Drummond Coach and Paint
531 Raleigh Ave
El Cajon, CA 92020
619-579-7229; FAX: 619-579-2128

painting
restoration

See full listing in **Section One** under **Ferrari**

Euro Coachworks Inc
812 NW 57th St
Ft Lauderdale, FL 33309
954-772-8272; FAX: 954-772-8148

repair & fabrication

See full listing in **Section One** under **Ferrari**

The Fine Car Store
1105 Moana Dr
San Diego, CA 92107
619-223-7766; FAX: 619-223-6838

car dealer

See full listing in **Section One** under **Ferrari**

HK Klassics
Hy Kusnetz
16 Hausmann Ct
Maplewood, NJ 07040
201-761-6642

appraisals

See full listing in **Section Two** under **appraisals**

Lindley Restorations Ltd
Rt 422 RD 3
Pottstown, PA 19464
610-326-8484; FAX: 610-326-3845

parts
sales
service

See full listing in **Section One** under **Jaguar**

The Panel Shop Inc
1785 Barnum Ave
Stratford, CT 06497
203-377-6208; FAX: 203-386-0486

Body parts for:
Aston Martin
Bentley/Rolls-Royce
Ferrari/Lotus

See full listing in **Section Two** under **sheetmetal**

Rolls-Royce of Beverly Hills
11401 West Pico Blvd
Los Angeles, CA 90064
310-477-4262, 800-321-9792
FAX: 310-473-7498

parts

See full listing in **Section One** under **Rolls-Royce/Bentley**

Specialty Car Service Ltd
1330 Ritters Rd
Reading, PA 19606
610-370-0410

parts
restoration
service

See full listing in **Section One** under **Morgan**

Steelwings
229 Railroad Dr
Ivyland, PA 18974
215-322-7420 parts/service
PH/FAX: 215-322-5517 sales

parts
sales
service

Mail order and open shop. Monday-Friday 8 am-5 pm, open most weekends (call to confirm). Specializing in Aston Martin Lagonda. Prewar-current. Large selection of cars for sale. Advice on sales or service freely given.

AUBURN

Auburn's West
3202 NE 185th
Seattle, WA 98155
206-364-1163

parts

Specializing in instrument panels, hood hinges, rubber castings, wood, nameplates, grille mesh, gaskets, plating, runningboard rubber, bearings, cables, top irons, castings, etc. New and used parts for Auburns. Specializing in 1934-36 Auburns. Catalog available.

Cape Cod Classic Cars Pete Harvey PO Box 280 Cataumet, MA 02534 508-548-0660; FAX: 508-457-0660	**car dealer**

See full listing in **Section One** under **Cadillac/LaSalle**

Guild of Automotive Restorers 18237 Woodbine Ave Sharon, ON Canada L0G 1V0 905-895-0035; FAX: 905-895-0036 E-mail: theguild@interhop.com	**restoration** **sales** **service**

See full listing in **Section Two** under **restoration shops**

Interesting Parts Inc Paul TerHorst 27526 N Owens Rd Mundelein, IL 60060 PH/FAX: 847-949-1030	**appraisals** **gaskets** **parts** **storage** **transport**

See full listing in **Section Two** under **comprehensive parts**

Lincoln Highway Packards Main St, PO Box 94 Schellsburg, PA 15559 814-733-4356; FAX: 814-839-4276	**engine rebuilding** **restoration**

See full listing in **Section One** under **Packard**

McLellan's Automotive History Robert McLellan 9111 Longstaff Dr Houston, TX 77031 713-772-3285; FAX: 713-772-3287	**books** **magazines** **programs** **sales literature**

See full listing in **Section Two** under **literature dealers**

Restorations Unlimited Box 1118 Blenheim, ON Canada N0P 1A0 519-676-8455	**metal fabrication** **restoration**

Open shop only. Restores antique, classic and special interest vehicles, specialty being Auburn and Ford products. Specializing in mechanical, wood, metal fabrication for 1931-1935 Auburns.

Austin Works 229 Third St Manhattan Beach, CA 90266 310-372-7985 E-mail: robstu@ix.netcom.com	**parts**

Mail order only. Specializing in parts for 1947-1953 Austin of England. Austin A-40, Dorset (two-door sedan), Devon (four-door sedan) and commercial derivatives (pickup truck, panel delivery van and Countryman estate wagon). Austin A90 Atlantic (convertible and two-door sedan). Austin factory pedal cars (J40 and Pathfinder). Die-cast models and sales literature.

BritBooks 62 Main St Otego, NY 13825 PH/FAX: 607-988-7956	**books**

See full listing in **Section Four** under **books & publications**

British Auto Shoppe Inc 1115 1st Ave Silvis, IL 61282 309-796-2748; FAX: 309-796-2033	**parts** **service**

See full listing in **Section One** under **MG**

Brooklands Inc 503 Corporate Square 1500 NW 62nd St Fort Lauderdale, FL 33309 954-776-2748; FAX: 954-772-8383 E-mail: rbiggs@lgc.net	**accessories**

See full listing in **Section Two** under **accessories**

Don Flye 5 Doe Valley Rd Petersham, MA 01366 508-724-3318	**parts**

See full listing in **Section One** under **Austin-Healey**

Pete Groh 9957 Frederick Rd Ellicott City, MD 21042-3647 410-750-2352	**original British** **keys** **Wilmot Breeden**

See full listing in **Section One** under **Jaguar**

Kip Motor Company Inc 13325 Denton Dr Dallas, TX 75234 972-243-0440; FAX: 972-243-2387 E-mail: kipmotor@aol.com	**literature** **parts** **restoration**

Mail order and open shop. Monday-Friday 9 am-6 pm, Saturday 9 am-12 noon. Parts, service, restoration, manuals & literature, etc, for British orphans: Austin, Berkeley, English Ford, Hillman, Humber, Metropolitan, Morris, Riley, Sunbeam-Talbot, Singer, Triumph Herald, Vauxhall, Vanden Plas, etc. Free catalogs. Complete restoration shop.

Manhattan Mini Inc New York, NY 10036 212-921-8459; FAX: 212-719-5313	**sales**

Specializing in the sale of Austin and Morris Minis.

MG Automotive 3733-C Wilmington Pk Kettering, OH 45429 513-294-7623	**parts** **restoration** **service**

See full listing in **Section One** under **MG**

Mini City Ltd 395 Summit Point Dr Henrietta, NY 14467-9606 716-359-1400; FAX: 716-359-1428	**accessories** **car dealer** **literature** **parts/tools**

Mail order and open shop. Monday-Friday 10 to 6; Saturday 10 to 2. Founded 1967. Parts and accessories for: Austin and Morris Minis and Mini variants (all models and years), Morris Minors 1948-1971, MG 1100 and Austin America. Also complete cars. (NY registered dealer). 128-page Mini parts book, $5. 80-page Morris Minor parts book, $5. British Motor Heritage approved supplier of Austin and Morris parts, including Mini, Morris Minor, MG 1100 and Austin America. Founded 1967.

Mini Mania
31 Winsor St
Milpitas, CA 95035
408-942-5595; FAX: 408-942-5582
E-mail: minimania@aol.com

parts
service

Mail order and open shop. Monday through Friday 8 to 6, Saturday 8 to 2. Mechanical, Performance and restoration parts and services for Austin Minis, Morris Minors, Austin-Healey Sprite, MG Midget, all years. Parts and accessories for all makes and models British made autos. Free separate monthly flyers *Austin Mini*, *Morris Minor*, *Sprite/Midget* and *British Parts Source*.

Mini Registry
395 Summit Point Dr
Henrietta, NY 14467
716-359-1400; FAX: 716-359-1428

See full listing in **Section Three** under **marque clubs**

Mini Store
PO Box 7973
Van Nuys, CA 91409-7973
818-893-1421

cars
repairs
restorations

Open by appointment only. Specializing in restored Minis, restorations of Minis and complete mechanical repairs. Also bench labor available for Austin, Morris Mini, Cooper and Cooper S cars.

Patton Orphan Spares
28 Simon St
Babylon, NY 11702
516-669-2598

parts

See full listing in **Section One** under **Renault**

Seven Enterprises Ltd
716 Bluecrab Rd
Newport News, VA 23606
800-992-7007; FAX: 800-296-3327

accessories
parts

Mail order and open shop. Monday-Friday 9-6, Saturday 9-1. Parts and accessories for Mini Cooper and MGB. Competition parts also for Mini-Mini Coopers 1959-present, MGB 1962-1980.

Victory Autoservices
Box 5060, RR 1
W Baldwin, ME 04091
207-625-4581

parts
restoration

See full listing in **Section One** under **Austin-Healey**

Peter Woodend (Spares)
PO Box 157
Takanini
Auckland New Zealand
PH/FAX: 64-9-298-3393

automobilia
engine parts
gaskets
pistons
wiring harnesses

Mail order only. Specializing in parts and accessories for Austin 7 hp 1923-39 and for other Austin models (Big 7, 8, 10, 12, 14 hp) prior to 1948. Pistons for Austin and other makes, English, continental, USA, all types. Gaskets, all materials including copper, board, copper made to pattern. Other engine parts, rubber, badges, handbooks, manuals, wiring harnesses made to order using period-style braided cable and overbraid, electrical and more for English made cars. $2 US bills for lists.

Absolutely British II
1720 S Grove Ave, Unit A
Ontario, CA 91761
PH/FAX: 909-947-0200

restoration
service

See full listing in **Section Two** under **restoration shops**

**American-Foreign Auto
Electric Inc**
103 Main St
Souderton, PA 18964
215-723-4877

parts
rebuilding

See full listing in **Section Two** under **electrical systems**

The Austin-Healey Store
122 Sheldon St
El Segundo, CA 90245
310-640-3782; FAX: 310-640-3502

parts
restoration
service

Open Monday-Friday 9 am to 5:30 pm. Specializing in competition, service, parts and restoration for Austin-Healey 100-4, 100-6, 3000 1953-1968 and Sprite 1958-1969.

Automotive Artistry
679 W Streetboro St
Hudson, OH 44236
216-650-1503

restoration

See full listing in **Section One** under **Triumph**

Barlow & Co
7 Maple Ave
Newton, NH 03858
603-382-3591; FAX: 603-382-4406

car dealer
restoration

See full listing in **Section Two** under **restoration shops**

BMC Classics
828 N Dixie Freeway
New Smyrna Beach, FL 32168
904-426-6405; FAX: 904-427-4570

parts
repair
restoration

See full listing in **Section One** under **Jaguar**

British Auto Parts Ltd
93256 Holland Ln
Marcola, OR 97454
541-933-2880; FAX: 541-933-2302

parts

See full listing in **Section One** under **Morris**

British Auto Shoppe Inc
1115 1st Ave
Silvis, IL 61282
309-796-2748; FAX: 309-796-2033

parts
service

See full listing in **Section One** under **MG**

British Car Care By Pearson's
745 Orange Ave
Winter Park, FL 32789
407-647-0967

car dealer
parts
repairs
restoration

See full listing in **Section One** under **MG**

British Car Magazine	**periodical**
PO Box 1683	
Los Altos, CA 94023-1683	
415-949-9680; FAX: 415-949-9685	
E-mail: britcarmag@aol.com	

See full listing in **Section Four** under **periodicals**

British Car Specialists	**parts**
2060 N Wilson Way	**repairs**
Stockton, CA 95205	**restoration**
209-948-8767; FAX: 209-948-1030	
E-mail: healeydoc@aol.com	

Specializing in service, repairs, parts, restorations for British cars, MG, Jaguar, Austin-Healey, Triumph, Rover.

British Miles	**accessories**
9278 Old E Tyburn Rd	**literature**
Morrisville, PA 19067	**parts**
215-736-9300; FAX: 215-736-3089	**restoration**

See full listing in **Section One** under **MG**

British Restorations	**car dealer**
4455 Paul St	**restoration**
Philadelphia, PA 19124	
215-533-6696	

See full listing in **Section One** under **Jaguar**

British Wiring Inc	**wiring accessories**
20449 Ithaca Rd	**wiring harnesses**
Olympia Fields, IL 60461	
PH/FAX: 708-481-9050	

See full listing in **Section Two** under **electrical systems**

BritParts Midwest	**parts**
603 Monroe St	**restoration**
LaPorte, IN 46350	**service**
219-324-5474; FAX: 219-324-7541	

Mail order and open shop. Monday-Friday 9 am to 5:30 pm, Saturday 9 am to 2 pm. Specializing in Austin-Healey BN1-BJ8 cars for service, major maintenance, restoration, and holds a comprehensive inventory of parts for these cars. Also carry out the same range of work on other British cars, but stock only engine reconditioning parts with other parts devoted to general servicing. British car engines & transmissions.

Donovan Motorcar Service	**restoration**
4 Holmes Rd	**service**
Lenox, MA 01240	
413-499-6000; FAX: 413-499-6699	

See full listing in **Section One** under **Jaguar**

Doug's British Car Parts	**accessories**
2487 E Colorado Blvd	**parts**
Pasadena, CA 91107	
818-793-2494; FAX: 818-793-4339	

See full listing in **Section One** under **Jaguar**

Eberhardt Service	**parts**
17710 Valley View Ave	
Cleveland, OH 44135-1126	

See full listing in **Section One** under **MG**

Don Flye	**parts**
5 Doe Valley Rd	
Petersham, MA 01366	
508-724-3318	

Mail order and open shop by appointment only. Specializing in

British used parts for Austin-Healey 100-6 thru BJ8, Austin America, MG TD, A, Midget & B, Triumph TR3-TR6.

Fourintune Garage Inc	**restoration**
W63 N147 Washington Ave	
Cedarburg, WI 53012	
414-375-0876	

Open shop, Monday thru Friday, 9-5 CST. Specializes in Austin-Healey restoration.

Harbor Auto Restoration	**restoration**
1504 SW 3rd St	
Pompano Beach, FL 33069	
954-785-7887; FAX: 954-785-7388	

See full listing in **Section Two** under **restoration shops**

Healey Coop	**parts**
400 Harding St	**restorations**
Exeter, PA 18643	**sales**
717-693-2248	**service**

Mail order and open shop. Monday-Friday 9 to 5; Saturday 8 to 12 noon. For 100, 100-6, Mk I, Mk II, Mk III and 3000 models. Ground-up restorations, including acid dipped frames and lacquer painting.

Healey Lane	**parts**
5920 Jones Ave	**restoration**
Riverside, CA 92505	**service**
800-411-HEALEY (4325)	
FAX: 909-689-4934	

Austin-Healey restoration, parts, service, sales for all years and Marks made 53-67.

Healey Surgeons Inc	**parts**
7211 Carroll Ave	**restoration**
Takoma Park, MD 20912	
301-270-8811; FAX: 301-270-8812	

Mail order and open shop. Monday-Friday 9:30-5. Parts and restoration for Austin-Healey 100-4, 100-6, 3000, 1953-1967.

International Restoration Specialist Inc	**parts**
PO Box 1303	**restoration**
Mt Airy, NC 27030	**sales**
910-789-1548	

See full listing in **Section One** under **Jaguar**

Jahns Quality Pistons	**piston rings**
1360 N Jefferson St	**pistons**
Anaheim, CA 92807	
714-579-3795, 800-225-0277	
FAX: 714-524-6607	

See full listing in **Section Two** under **engine parts**

Lindley Restorations Ltd	**parts**
Rt 422 RD 3	**sales**
Pottstown, PA 19464	**service**
610-326-8484; FAX: 610-326-3845	

See full listing in **Section One** under **Jaguar**

MG Automotive	**parts**
3733-C Wilmington Pk	**restoration**
Kettering, OH 45429	**service**
513-294-7623	

See full listing in **Section One** under **MG**

Mini Mania
31 Winsor St
Milpitas, CA 95035
408-942-5595; FAX: 408-942-5582
E-mail: minimania@aol.com

parts
service

See full listing in **Section One** under **Austin**

Mini Motors Classic Coachworks
2775 Cherry Ave NE
Salem, OR 97303
503-362-3187; FAX: 503-375-9609

parts
restoration
sales
service

Mail order and open shop. Monday thru Friday 8-5:30,
evenings/weekends appointments available. Typically 15-20
restorations ongoing. Services: body fabrication, paint, interior,
mechanical service, parts & sales, custom parts casting & manufacturing. In business for 16 years, specializing in British cars
& other collectibles. Our parts business stands out in the fact
that what we use is what we sell, standing behind our service
and products 100%. Ask about our 5-speed transmission conversion for Sprite/Midgets and factory replica hardtops for
Austin-Healey Mk I Sprites.

Moss Motors Ltd
PO Box 847
440 Rutherford St
Goleta, CA 93117
800-235-6954; FAX: 805-692-2525

accessories
parts

See full listing in **Section One** under **MG**

Motorhead Ltd
2811-B Old Lee Highway
Fairfax, VA 22031
800-527-3140; FAX: 703-573-3165

parts
repairs

Parts, repairs and restoration of British sports cars. Please ask
for parts catalogs on MGB, Sprite, Midget, Spitfire, TR6, TR250,
TR7, TR8.

Mr Sport Car Inc
203 E Lincoln
Papillion, NE 68046
402-592-7559

service

See full listing in **Section One** under **Jaguar**

Nisonger Instrument S/S
570 Mamaroneck Ave
Mamaroneck, NY 10543
914-381-1952; FAX: 914-381-1953

gauges

See full listing in **Section Two** under **instruments**

NOS Locators
587 Pawtucket Ave
Pawtucket, RI 02860
401-725-5000

parts

See full listing in **Section One** under **MG**

Omni Specialties
10418 Lorain Ave
Cleveland, OH 44111
800-791-9562; 216-251-2269
FAX: 216-251-6083

parts
restoration
service

See full listing in **Section One** under **MG**

Precision Restoration Service Inc
1551 N Courtney Rd, Ste B-2
Independence, MO 64050
816-461-7500; FAX: 816-461-7504

restoration

See full listing in **Section Two** under **restoration shops**

Ragtops & Roadsters
203 S 4th St
Perkasie, PA 18944
215-257-1202; FAX: 215-257-2688

race prep
repairs

See full listing in **Section One** under **AC**

Scarborough Faire Inc
1151 Main St
Pawtucket, RI 02860
800-556-6300; 401-724-4200
FAX: 401-724-5392

parts

See full listing in **Section One** under **MG**

Sports & Classics
PO Box 1787
512 Boston Post Rd, Dept H
Darien, CT 06820-1787

parts

See full listing in **Section Two** under **body parts**

The Registry
Pine Grove
Stanley, VA 22851
540-778-3728; FAX: 540-778-2402
E-mail: britregstry@aol.com

periodical

See full listing in **Section Four** under **periodicals**

Van Nuys Motors
14422 Oxnard St
Van Nuys, CA 91403
818-988-5455

parts
restoration
sales
service

See full listing in **Section One** under **Mercedes-Benz**

Victoria British Ltd
Box 14991
Lenexa, KS 66285-4991
800-255-0088; 913-599-3299

accessories
parts

See full listing in **Section One** under **MG**

Victory Autoservices
Box 5060
RR 1
W Baldwin, ME 04091
207-625-4581

parts
restoration

Mail order and open shop. Monday-Friday 8-5. Restoration and
parts for post WW II British cars, particularly Austin-Healey,
Jaguar, Alvis, MG, Triumph. Magneto ignitions (new and used) is
a specialty also.

Avanti Auto Service
Rt322, 67 Conchester Hwy
Glen Mills, PA 19342-1506
610-558-9999

repair
restoration

See full listing in **Section One** under **DeTomaso/Pantera**

Motorcar Gallery Inc
715 N Federal Hwy
Fort Lauderdale, FL 33304
954-522-9900; FAX: 954-522-9966

car dealer

See full listing in **Section One** under **Ferrari**

Nostalgic Motor Cars
47400 Avante Dr
Wixom, MI 48393
810-349-4884, 800-AVANTI-1
800-AVANTI-X; FAX: 810-349-0000

car dealer
parts

Mail order and open shop. Avanti dealer, cars and parts. World's largest manufacturer and supplier of 1963-1985 Avanti parts.

Penn Auto Sales Co
Dr Roger Penn
7115 Leesburg Pike, #113
Falls Church, VA 22043
703-538-4388

car dealer
parts
service

Mail order and shop open by appointment only. Avanti sales. All years. Avanti factory franchised dealer since 1970. Parts and service, 1963-1991. Also will provide information on restoration and parts.

Regal International Motor Cars Inc
PO Box 6819
Hollywood, FL 33081
305-989-9777; FAX: 305-989-9778

car dealer

See full listing in **Section One** under **Rolls-Royce/Bentley**

Southwest Avanti Sales & Service
915 W Hatcher
Phoenix, AZ 85021
602-943-6587; FAX: 602-943-3498

parts
repairs
sales

Mail order and open shop. Monday-Saturday 8 to 6. Complete Avanti store. Sales, repairs, parts, restorations of all Avantis, 1963 to 1991.

Studebaker Parts & Locations
228 Marquiss Cir
Clinton, TN 37716
615-457-3002

parts
parts locator

See full listing in **Section One** under **Studebaker**

BITTER

Ed Swart Motors Inc
2675 Skypark Dr Unit 103
Torrance, CA 90505
310-530-9715; FAX: 310-530-9786

cars
parts
restoration

Open shop Monday-Friday 9-6. Specializing in sale of auto parts and race car parts & restoration of Bitter automobiles and Chevron race cars.

Auto Engineering
3661 Sacramento Dr, Unit D
San Luis Obispo, CA 93401
805-544-1041

parts

See full listing in **Section One** under **Volvo**

Bavarian Autosport
275 Constitution Ave
Portsmouth, NH 03801
800-535-2002; FAX: 800-507-2002

accessories
parts

Mail order and open shop. Monday-Friday 9-5:30 and Saturday 9-4. All BMW parts and accessories. Web Site: www.bavauto.com

BCP Sport & Classic Co
10525 Airline Dr
Houston, TX 77037
713-448-4739; FAX: 713-448-0189

parts
service

See full listing in **Section One** under **MG**

Best Deal
8171 Monroe St
Stanton, CA 90680
800-354-9202; FAX: 714-995-5918

accessories
parts

See full listing in **Section One** under **Porsche**

Beverly Hills Motoring Accessories
205 S Robertson Blvd
Beverly Hills, CA 90211
310-657-4880; FAX: 310-659-4664
E-mail: bhma@hollywood.cinenet.net

accessories

See full listing in **Section One** under **Mercedes-Benz**

Blitzen Enterprises Inc
8341 E Evans Rd, Suite 104
Scottsdale, AZ 85260
888-254-8936 toll-free
FAX: 602-991-6301

parts

See full listing in **Section One** under **Mercedes-Benz**

Bud's Parts for Classic Mercedes-Benz
9130 Hwy 5
Douglasville, GA 30134
800-942-8444; FAX: 770-942-8400

parts
restoration
service

See full listing in **Section One** under **Mercedes-Benz**

Concours Cars of Colorado Ltd
2414 W Cucharras St
Colorado Springs, CO 80904
719-473-6288

accessories
parts
service

Mail order and open shop. Monday-Friday 8:30 to 5:30. Dedicated to providing professional service, parts, accessories and modifications on European automobiles. Specializes in Alfa Romeo, BMW, Jaguar and Volvo.

CSI
1100 S Raymond Ave, Suite H
Fullerton, CA 92831
714-879-7955; FAX: 714-879-7310
E-mail: 102263.1046@compuserve.com

accessories
parts

Mail order and open shop. Monday-Friday 9 to 6. Specializing in new and used parts, accessories for BMW and all Japanese marques.

European Parts Specialists Ltd
PO Box 6783
Santa Barbara, CA 93160
805-683-4020; FAX: 805-683-3689

accessories
parts

See full listing in **Section One** under **Mercedes-Benz**

Exotic Wood Dash & Restorations
336 Cottonwood Ave
Hartland, WI 53029
800-900-3274; FAX: 414-367-9474

restoration parts
wood dash overlays

See full listing in **Section One** under **Jaguar**

Foreign Motors West
253 N Main St
Natick, MA 01760
508-655-5350; FAX: 508-651-0178

car sales

See full listing in **Section One** under **Rolls-Royce/Bentley**

Griot's Garage
3500-A 20th St E
Tacoma, WA 98424
800-345-5789; FAX: 206-922-7500
E-mail: griots@aol.com

car care products
paint
tools

See full listing in **Section Two** under **tools**

Hjeltness Restoration Inc
630 Alpine Way
Escondido, CA 92029
619-746-9966; FAX: 619-746-7738

restoration
service

See full listing in **Section Two** under **restoration shops**

IPTC Automotive
300 SW 12th Ave
Pompano Beach, FL 33069
800-277-3806

cars
parts

Specializing in BMWs 82 and up, Mercedes-Benz 80 and up, Porsche 90 and up parts, cars and rebuildables.

JAM Engineering Corp
PO Box 2570
Monterey, CA 93942
408-372-1787; 800-JAM-CORP

carburetors

See full listing in **Section Two** under **carburetors**

Motorcars Ltd
8101 Hempstead
Houston, TX 77008
713-863-9388; FAX: 713-863-8238
E-mail: mcltd@phoenix.net

parts

See full listing in **Section One** under **Jaguar**

Northern Motorsport Ltd
PO Box 508, Rt 5
Wilder, VT 05088
802-296-2099; FAX: 802-295-6599

repair
restoration
sales
service

See full listing in **Section Two** under **restoration shops**

Ottorich
619 Hammond St
Chestnut Hill, MA 02167
617-738-5488

restoration

See full listing in **Section One** under **Mercedes-Benz**

Palo Alto Speedometer Inc
718 Emerson St
Palo Alto, CA 94301
415-323-0243; FAX: 415-323-4632

instruments

See full listing in **Section One** under **Mercedes-Benz**

Peninsula Imports
3749 Harlem Rd
Buffalo, NY 14215
800-263-4538; FAX: 905-847-3021

accessories
parts
trim

Mail order and open shop. Monday-Friday 8-5:30, Saturday 8-2. We specialize in distribution of hard parts, accessories and trim, including starters, alternators, European lighting, Weber carburetors, ignition, fuel system, exhaust, gaskets, filters, radiators, rubber parts, steering wheels, suspension, tops, bras, car covers, transmissions, engines, cams, pistons, bearings, brakes, clutch and hydraulic parts, carpet kits, interior panels, body panels, glass, etc. For Audi, BMW, Mercedes, VW, Porsche, Saab, Volvo, MG, Triumph, Jaguar, Alfa Romeo, Fiat, Ferrari, Lamborghini, Maserati, Honda, Mazda, Hyundai, Toyota, Mitsubishi, Nissan, etc.

John T Poulin Auto Sales/Star Service Center
5th Ave & 111th St
North Troy, NY 12182
518-235-8610

car dealer
parts
restoration service

See full listing in **Section One** under **Mercedes-Benz**

Replicarz
99 State St
Rutland, VT 05701
802-747-7151
E-mail: replicarz@aol.com

books
kits
models
videos

See full listing in **Section Two** under **racing**

Restoration Services
16049 W 4th Ave
Golden, CO 80401
303-271-0356

restoration

See full listing in **Section One** under **Porsche**

Paul Russell & Company
106 Western Ave
Essex, MA 01929
508-768-6919; FAX: 508-768-3523

car dealer
coachbuilding
parts
restoration

See full listing in **Section Two** under **restoration shops**

The Stable Ltd
217 Main St
Gladstone, NJ 07934
908-234-2055; FAX: 908-781-2599

sales
service

See full listing in **Section One** under **Jaguar**

Stephen's Auto Works   parts
433 Meadow Rd
Kings Pk, NY 11754
516-544-1114

Mail order and open shop. Mon-Fri 9-5. Specializing in German car (mechanical) parts for BMW, Mercedes, Porsche. Used engine, transmission, suspension parts. German engine & trans parts. 35 year collection. Porsche, BMW, Mercedes engine parts, cranks, rods, pistons/cyls, reconditioned o/d, used heads, some transmissions or loose parts. Porsche engines/transmissions and suspension parts from 66 to 90s, carburetors, distributors, gearboxes, many rare items, call for needs.

United German Imports   brake parts
4556 Shetland Green   brakes
Alexandria, VA 22312
800-98-BRAKE; FAX: 703-916-1610
E-mail: ugibrakes2@aol.com

See full listing in **Section Two** under **brakes**

Vintage Auto Parts   car dealer
PO Box 323   new & used parts
Temple, PA 19560-0323
610-926-2485, 9 am-noon, 5-7 pm,
answering machine

Mail order or by special appointment. Specializing in BMW 300, 600 and 700, Crosley, Corvair, Citicar (EV), Fiat 500 and 600, Honda 600 and Civic, 1950 Jeepster, Metros, NSU, Panhard, Subaru 360, Trivan, VW II, III, IV and 181 and LeCar. Also Zundapp cycle and NSU. Thousands of new parts for air cooled BMW and Subaru 360 cars. SASE for info. 100 vehicles, restore or parts, no list. Plan on selling out by end of 1997.

Wolf Automotive   car covers
201 N Sullivan   consoles
Santa Ana, CA 92703   steering wheels
800-444-9653, 714-835-2126   tire covers
FAX: 714-835-9653

See full listing in **Section One** under **Chevrolet**

J Wood & Co Auctioneers   auctions
PO Box 852
Searsport, ME 04974
207-548-2113; FAX: 207-548-2888

See full listing in **Section Two** under **auctions & events**

World Upholstery & Trim   carpet kits
PO Box 4857   tops
Thousand Oaks, CA 91359   upholstery kits
800-222-9577; FAX: 818-707-2664
E-mail: worlduph@mail.vcnet.com

See full listing in **Section Two** under **interiors & interior parts**

Bricklin

Bob's Brickyard Inc   parts
399 Washington St
Brighton, MI 48116
810-229-5302

Mail order and open shop. Monday-Friday 9-5. Specializes in 1974-75 Bricklin cars. Full service and mail order parts.

Conte's Corvettes & Classics   leasing
851 W Wheat Rd   parts
Vineland, NJ 08360   sales
609-692-0087; FAX: 609-692-1009   service
E-mail: contes@cybernet.net

See full listing in **Section One** under **Corvette**

DeLorean Literature   collectibles
3116 Welsh Rd   literature
Philadelphia, PA 19136-1810
215-338-6142

See full listing in **Section One** under **DeLorean**

The Gullwing Garage Ltd   appraisals
Bricklin SVI Specialists   literature
5 Cimorelli Dr   parts
New Windsor, NY 12553-6201   service
914-561-0019 anytime

Telephone calls accepted until 10 pm, 7 days a week. Parts service, appraisals, prepurchase assistance literature for Bricklin SVI, 1974-75-76. Over 7,000 original genuine Bricklin parts (74-75-76) with access to thousands more. Aftermarket items such as: consoles, carpet sets, seat covers, fiberglass panels, air scoops, ground affects, gas shocks, antennas, radios, wheels, s/s exhaust pipes. Specializing in air door systems, headlight systems and door glass track system repairs. Prompt, personal, friendly service. Will travel to repair your Bricklin.

Blackhawk Collection   acquisitions
3600 Blackhawk Plaza Cir   sales
Danville, CA 94506-3600
510-736-3444; FAX: 510-736-4375

See full listing in **Section One** under **Duesenberg**

Dragone Classic Motorcars   car dealer
1797 Main St
Bridgeport, CT 06604
203-335-4643; FAX: 203-335-9798

See full listing in **Section Two** under **car dealers**

Guild of Automotive Restorers   restoration
18237 Woodbine Ave   sales
Sharon, ON Canada L0G 1V0   service
905-895-0035; FAX: 905-895-0036
E-mail: theguild@interhop.com

See full listing in **Section Two** under **restoration shops**

Hyannis Restoration   restoration
119 Thornton Dr
Hyannis, MA 02601
508-775-8131; FAX: 508-790-2339

See full listing in **Section One** under **Ferrari**

LMARR Disk Ltd   wheel discs
PO Box 910
Glen Ellen, CA 95442-0910
707-938-9347; FAX: 707-938-3020

See full listing in **Section One** under **Rolls-Royce/Bentley**

Northern Motorsport Ltd PO Box 508 Rt 5 Wilder, VT 05088 802-296-2099; FAX: 802-295-6599	repair restoration sales service

See full listing in **Section Two** under **restoration shops**

Paul Russell & Company 106 Western Ave Essex, MA 01929 508-768-6919; FAX: 508-768-3523	car dealer coachbuilding parts restoration

See full listing in **Section Two** under **restoration shops**

Scale Autoworks Brady Ward 313 Bridge St #4 Manchester, NH 03104-5045 PH/FAX: 603-623-5925 ext 66	models

See full listing in **Section Two** under **models & toys**

Valley Wire Wheel Service 7306 Coldwater Canyon #16 North Hollywood, CA 91605 818-765-3258; FAX: 818-765-8358	wheel restoration wheels

See full listing in **Section Two** under **wheels & wheelcovers**

Vintage Restorations The Old Bakery Windmill Street,Tunbridge Wells Kent, TN2 4UU England UK 1892-525-899 FAX: UK 1892-525499	accessories instruments

See full listing in **Section Two** under **instruments**

Antique & Classic Cars Inc 326 S 2nd St Hamilton, OH 45011 513-844-1146 in OH 800-798-3982 nationwide	bodywork machine work painting parts service

Mail order and open shop. Monday-Friday 9 to 5:30. Services Cadillacs, Packards, Oldsmobiles & Buicks, have a machine shop for engines and drivetrain, will replace rings and grind valves, also can machine parts for old cars. Complete paint and body shop and frame straightening. Painting of old cars. Will use lacquer paint if customer wants it. Also will look for parts for old and unusual cars. Sales of classic cars and some vintage automobiles. Will try and find special classic cars for collectors. (Our 41st year in business).

Antique Automobile Radio Inc 700 Tampa Rd Palm Harbor, FL 34684 800-WE-FIX-AM; 813-785-8733 FAX: 813-789-0283	radio accessories radio parts radio restoration

See full listing in **Section Two** under **radios**

Art's Antique & Classic Auto Services 1985 E 5th St #15 Tempe, AZ 85281 602-899-6068	restoration

Open shop only. Monday-Friday 9-5. Restoration of 50s & 60s General Motors, primarily Buicks.

Auto/Link PO Box 460723 Houston, TX 77056-8723 713-973-1008 713-973-1133 on-line service E-mail: alink@accesscom.net	books

See full listing in **Section Four** under **books & publications**

B & D Motors 1309 Kenwood Cape Girardeau, MO 63701 573-334-3354	rubber parts sheetmetal trim

See full listing in **Section One** under **Chevrolet**

Bicknell Engine Company 7055 Dayton Rd Enon, OH 45323 513-864-5224	repair restoration

Mail order and open shop. Evenings and weekends only. Repair service for antique, classic and special interest cars. Specializing in Buicks and independent make cars from the 20s through early 60s. Services include: engine rebuilding, transmission rebuilding (manual and automatic), any mechanical or electrical work. Buick parts, mostly used, some NOS. Appraisal service.

Big Boy Accessories 581 Kenbridge Dr Carson, CA 90746 310-324-4787	parts

See full listing in **Section One** under **Chevrolet**

Bill's Speed Shop 13951 Millersburg Rd Navarre, OH 44662 330-832-9403; FAX: 330-832-2098	body parts

See full listing in **Section One** under **Chevrolet**

Bob's Automobilia Box 2119 Atascadero, CA 93423 805-434-2963	accessories parts

Mail order only. Parts, accessories for 1920-1953 Buicks. Hubcaps, hood ornaments, floor mats, electrical, interior plastics, rubber. Catalog available.

Boyer's Restorations Skip Boyer 1348 Carlisle Pike Hanover, PA 17331 717-632-0670	parts repairs restorations

Mail order and shop open by appointment only. Exclusively Buick parts, new and used as well as reproductions, servicing primarily 1937 through 1974. Manifolds and machine turned dashes a specialty, as well as interior plastic parts, 1937 through 1950. 1940-42 Buick dash restorations and partial restorations and repairs for 1937 through 1974.

Buick Bonery   parts
6970 Stamper Way
Sacramento, CA 95828
PH/FAX: 916-381-5271

Mail order and open shop. Shop open Monday-Saturday 8 am to
10 pm PST. Specializing in Buick new, used and repro parts.
Full scope stainless restoration for any make. 150+ parts
Buicks, 1936-75. Restored and better Buicks warehoused.

The Buick Nut-Joe Krepps   repro parts
2486 Pacer Ln S
Cocoa, FL 32926-2606
PH/FAX: 407/636-8777

Mail order. Reproductions 1928 thru 1955.

Buick Specialists   parts
PO Box 5368
Kent, WA 98064
206-852-0584

Mail order and open shop. Specialists in 1946-79 Buicks. New,
used and NOS parts for all models.

Cape Cod Classic Cars   car dealer
Pete Harvey
PO Box 280
Cataumet, MA 02534
508-548-0660; FAX: 508-457-0660

See full listing in **Section One** under **Cadillac/LaSalle**

Chevrolet Parts Obsolete   accessories
PO Box 0740   parts
Murrieta, CA 92564-0740
909-279-2833; FAX: 909-279-4013

See full listing in **Section One** under **Chevrolet**

Chrome Masters   chrome plating
1109 W Orange Ave, Unit D   pot metal restoration
Tallahassee, FL 32310
904-576-2100

See full listing in **Section Two** under **plating & polishing**

Classic Buicks Inc   literature
4632 Riverside Dr   parts
Chino, CA 91710-3926
909-591-0283; FAX: 909-627-6094

Mail order and open shop. Shop open Monday-Friday 8 am to 5
pm, Saturday 8 am to 11:30 am. Specializing in parts and literature for 1946 thru 1975 Buicks.

Classic Car Works Ltd   restoration
3050 Upper Bethany Rd
Jasper, GA 30143
770-735-3945

See full listing in **Section Two** under **restoration shops**

Collector Car Appraisals   appraisals
L E Lazarus, Senior Appraiser
PO Box 6732
Rockford, IL 61125
815-229-1258; FAX: 815-229-1238

See full listing in **Section Two** under **appraisals**

Collector Car Buyers   car dealers
4046 11th St
Rockford, IL 61109
815-229-1258; FAX: 815-229-1238

See full listing in **Section Two** under **car dealers**

Collector Car Parts   parts
PO Box 6732
Rockford, IL 61125
815-229-1236; FAX: 815-229-1238

See full listing in **Section Two** under **comprehensive parts**

Collector Cars-U-Can-Afford Ltd   car dealer
4046 11th St
Rockford, IL 61109
815-229-1258; FAX: 815-229-1238

See full listing in **Section One** under **Cadillac/LaSalle**

CR Plastics Inc   bumper filler parts
2790 NE 7th Ave
Pompano Beach, FL 33064
800-551-3155

See full listing in **Section One** under **Cadillac/LaSalle**

Don Cressman   parts
495 Louise Ave N
Listowel, ON Canada N4W 3N5
519-291-1600; FAX: 519-291-1763

See full listing in **Section One** under **Chevrolet**

JB Donaldson Co   castings
2533 W Cypress   steering wheels
Phoenix, AZ 85009   wood parts
602-278-4505; FAX: 602-278-1112

See full listing in **Section Two** under **steering wheels**

ECB, Ed Leek   fiberglass parts
13 Snipe Rd
Key Largo, FL 33037
PH/FAX: 305-451-0864

See full listing in **Section Two** under **fiberglass parts**

Egge Machine Company   babbitting
11707 Slauson Ave   chassis
Santa Fe Springs, CA 90670   motor mounts
310-945-3419 in CA   pistons
800-866-EGGE   valves
FAX: 310-693-1635   wiring harnesses

See full listing in **Section Two** under **engine parts**

Elliott's Car Radio   radio repairs
313 Linfield Rd   speaker kits
Parkerford, PA 19457
610-495-6360; FAX: 610-495-7723

See full listing in **Section Two** under **radios**

Faxon Auto Literature   literature
3901 Carter Ave   manuals
Riverside, CA 92501
800-458-2734; FAX: 909-786-4166

See full listing in **Section Two** under **literature dealers**

Fleetline Automotive   salvage yard
PO Box 291
Highland, NY 12528
914-691-9228

See full listing in **Section Five** under **New York**

Green Valentine Inc
5055 Covington Way
Memphis, TN 38134
901-373-5555; FAX: 901-373-5568

car dealer
woodies

See full listing in **Section Two** under **car dealers**

Harbor Auto Restoration
1504 SW 3rd St
Pompano Beach, FL 33069
954-785-7887; FAX: 954-785-7388

restoration

See full listing in **Section Two** under **restoration shops**

Harnesses Unlimited
PO Box 435
Wayne, PA 19087
610-688-3998

wiring harnesses
wiring supplies

See full listing in **Section Two** under **electrical systems**

J & C's Parts
7127 Ward Rd
North Tonawanda, NY 14120
716-693-4090; FAX: 716-695-7144

parts

We offer new and used 1953-76 Buick stock and high-performance engine parts and services to include engine, carburetor, and distributor rebuilding. Also new and used restoration parts are available for 1965-76 Buicks. We offer distributors and carburetors for 1953-74 GM, Chrysler & Ford cars to include popular and hard-to-find numbers. Electronic ignition conversion service and kits available. ROA, GSCA, BCA member.

King & Queen Mufflers
Box 423
Plumsteadville, PA 18949
PH/FAX: 215-766-8699

exhaust systems

See full listing in **Section Two** under **exhaust systems**

King's Bumper Co Inc
1 Ontario Ave
New Hartford, NY 13413
315-732-8988; FAX: 315-732-2602

chrome plating

See full listing in **Section Two** under **plating & polishing**

Lectric Limited Inc
7322 S Archer Road
Justice, IL 60458
708-563-0400; FAX: 708-458-2662

parts

See full listing in **Section One** under **Corvette**

Legendary Auto Interiors Ltd
121 W Shore Blvd
Newark, NY 14513
800-363-8804; FAX: 800-732-8874

soft trim

See full listing in **Section One** under **Chrysler**

Lloyd's Literature
PO Box 491
Newbury, OH 44065
800-292-2665; 216-338-1527
FAX: 216-338-2222

literature

See full listing in **Section Two** under **literature dealers**

M & H Electric Fabricators Inc
13537 Alondra Blvd
Santa Fe Springs, CA 90670
310-926-9552; FAX: 310-926-9572

wiring harnesses

See full listing in **Section Two** under **electrical systems**

Norman's Classic Auto Radio
7651 Park Blvd
Pinellas Park, FL 33781
813-546-1788

custom sales
radio repairs

See full listing in **Section Two** under **radios**

Old Coach Works Restoration Inc
1206 Badger St
Yorkville, IL 60560
630-553-0414; FAX: 630-553-1053

appraisals
body repairs
restoration

See full listing in **Section Two** under **restoration shops**

Opel GT Source
8030 Remmet Ave, Unit 11
Canoga Park, CA 91304
818-992-7776; FAX: 818-712-9222

parts
service
technical info

See full listing in **Section One** under **Opel**

Opels Unlimited
871 E Lambert Rd #C
La Habra, CA 90631
310-690-1051; FAX: 310-690-3352
E-mail: concept@primenet.com

parts
service

See full listing in **Section One** under **Opel**

Dennis Portka
4326 Beetow Dr
Hamburg, NY 14075
716-649-0921

horns

See full listing in **Section One** under **Corvette**

**Precision Pot Metal/
Bussie Restoration Inc**
1008 Loring Ave #28
Orange Park, FL 32073
904-269-8788

pot metal restoration

See full listing in **Section Two** under **plating & polishing**

David Raine's Springcrafters
425 Harding Hwy
Carney's Point, NJ 08069
609-299-9141; FAX: 609-299-9157

springs
suspension parts

See full listing in **Section Two** under **suspension parts**

Rank & Son Buick-GMC
4200 N Green Bay Ave
Milwaukee, WI 53209
414-372-4000

car dealer
parts

Wally Rank, president. Pierce-Arrow and Buick parts. Collection of 80 antique, classic and special interest cars.

REM Automotive Inc
Box 241, Rt 1, Brandt Rd
Annville, PA 17003
717-838-4242; FAX: 717-838-5091

interior parts

See full listing in **Section Two** under **restoration aids**

Renascence Restoration
219 Park Ave
Beaver Dam, WI 53219
414-887-8285, 6-9 pm

body work
restoration

See full listing in **Section Two** under **restoration shops**

Harry Samuel
65 Wisner St
Pontiac, MI 48342-1066
248-335-1900

carpet
fabrics
interiors
upholstery covers

See full listing in **Section Two** under **interiors & interior parts**

E J Serafin
Valley Rd
Matinecock, NY 11560

manuals

See full listing in **Section One** under **Cadillac/LaSalle**

Tags Backeast
PO Box 581
Plainville, CT 06062
860-747-2942

data plates
trim tags

See full listing in **Section Two** under **special services**

Tom's Classic Parts
5207 Sundew Terr
Tobyhanna, PA 18466
800-832-4073

parts

See full listing in **Section One** under **Chevrolet**

Howard Whitelaw
6067 Richmond Rd
Cleveland (Solon), OH 44139
216-721-6755 days
216-439-2159 evenings & weekends
FAX: 216-721-6758

fenders

See full listing in **Section One** under **MoPar**

Willow Grove Auto Top
43 N York Rd
Willow Grove, PA 19090
215-659-3276

interiors
tops
upholstery

See full listing in **Section Two** under **interiors & interior parts**

Year One Inc
PO Box 129
Tucker, GA 30085
800-YEAR-ONE (932-7663)
770-493-6568 Atlanta & overseas
FAX: 800-680-6806
FAX: 770-496-1949 Atlanta & overseas

parts

See full listing in **Section Two** under **comprehensive parts**

Cadillac

**Aabar's Cadillac & Lincoln
Salvage & Parts**
9700 NE 23rd
Oklahoma City, OK 73141
405-769-3318; FAX: 405-769-9542

parts

Open Monday-Friday 9 to 5:30; some Saturdays 9 to 12. Mainly used parts but some NOS and NORS. 600 cars standing 1938 to 1994, plus many parts off. Satisfaction guaranteed. Credit cards accepted. No negative answers to letters without your enclosing SASE.

Dennis Akerman
19 Gulf Rd Box 107
Sanbornton, NH 03269
800-487-3903; FAX: 603-286-2761
E-mail: cadparts@moe.webstersite.com

hydraulic systems

Open shop by appointment. New and used Cadillac parts and literature, 1937-76. Call, e-mail or fax your requirements. VISA/MC. Fast, courteous service. Ship worldwide.

Antique & Classic Automobiles
Royce A Emerson
Carlisle St, Ext D
Hanover, PA 17331
717-637-8344, 632-9182

car dealer

See full listing in **Section Two** under **car dealers**

Antique & Classic Cars
Rt 15, Box 454
Florence, AL 35633
205-760-0542

car locator

Mail order only. I find antique and classic cars for a finders' fee. My minimum fee is $150 or 3% of the purchase price and $25 deposit for pictures and postage.

Antique Auto Battery Mfg Co
2320 Old Mill Rd
Hudson, OH 44236
800-426-7580; FAX: 216-425-4642

batteries
battery cables

See full listing in **Section Two** under **batteries**

Archive Replacement Parts
211 Cinnaminson Ave
Palmyra, NJ 08065
609-786-0247

parts

Mail order only. Stainless steel water outlet replacements for 1936-48 flathead V8 Cadillac/LaSalle.

**Art's Antique & Classic Auto
Services**
1985 E 5th St #15
Tempe, AZ 85281
602-899-6068

restoration

See full listing in **Section One** under **Buick/McLaughlin**

B & D Motors
1309 Kenwood
Cape Girardeau, MO 63701
573-334-3354

rubber parts
sheetmetal
trim

See full listing in **Section One** under **Chevrolet**

C E Babcock
619 Waterside Way
Sarasota, FL 34242
941-349-4990

41, 42, 46, 47
Cadillac parts

A+ 1941-1947 Cadillac parts (all models): NOS, gently used, remanufactured parts (specialist). 35 years hobbyist accumulation (over 10,000 items) available. Exclusive exact reproduction of 8 pc floorboards, body braces, trunk floors, inner splash guards, stainless and chrome trim parts, battery boxes, rocker panels, special rocker clip, horn parts, large or small, I will assist you or advise. This is not a junk yard. Most parts have been on dry shelves for several years.

Be Happy Automatic Transmission Parts   trans rebuild kits
414 Stivers Rd
Hillsboro, OH 45133
800-416-2862; FAX: 513-442-6133

See full listing in **Section Two** under **transmissions**

Becker Sales   battery master switches
Rear 519 Wyoming Ave
West Pittston, PA 18643
PH/FAX: 717-655-3869

See full listing in **Section Two** under **batteries**

Big Boy Accessories   parts
581 Kenbridge Dr
Carson, CA 90746
310-324-4787

See full listing in **Section One** under **Chevrolet**

Binder's Auto Restoration and Salvage   salvage yard
PO Box 1144, 1 Mile Maud Rd
Palmer, AK 99645
907-745-4670; FAX: 907-745-5510

See full listing in **Section Five** under **Alaska**

Cadillac Auto Display   museum
PO Box 6732
Rockford, IL 61125
815-229-1258; FAX: 815-229-1238

See full listing in **Section Six** under **Illinois**

Cadillac Crazy   parts
PO Box 343
Boyce, VA 22620
703-665-2027 or 703-667-0017

Mail order and open shop. Monday-Saturday 9 to 6, Sunday by appointment. We sell used and NOS mechanical, body, trim, etc. parts for 63-78 Cadillacs. Specializing in the 67-78 Eldorado. We also keep some cars for sale in good restorable condition.

Cadillac Parts & Cars Limited   car dealer literature parts
46 Hardy
Sparks, NV 89431
702-826-8363

Mail order and open shop. Any day by appointment, 8 am to 8 pm. Offers new and good used and reproduction 1938 through 1980 Cadillac parts, manuals, literature and collector cars for sale. Presently have 8,000 square foot facility for parts and maintain 15 to 20 collector car inventory of extra clean, low mileage cars.

California Collectors' Classics (CCC)   parts restoration
PO Box 2281
Irwindale, CA 91706
818-962-6696; FAX: 818-962-7854

Mail order and shop. Specializing in restoration, parts, rebuilding of most major components for Cadillac, Lincoln and Thunderbird 1961-1985. Parts, restoration and service by appointment. Mail order sales, locating and inspection for buyer & seller of cars for sale.

Cape Cod Classic Cars   car dealer
Pete Harvey
PO Box 280
Cataumet, MA 02534
508-548-0660; FAX: 508-457-0660

Open shop by appointment only. Quality collector cars only in good condition for 1930 to 1970 big cars as Cadillac, Packard, Buick. Also classic mahogany runabouts 1920 to 1960. Complete good condition collector. No parts.

Cardillo Classic Cadillac   accessories top boots
351 W 51st St
New York, NY 10019
212-247-1354

Mail order only. Specializing in 1971-76 Eldorado original equipment parade boots, boot hardware and storage bags. Exclusive supplier of conversion kits (from soft boot to parade boot). Master parts books, 1953-79. Specializing in 1959, 60, 65, 71-76 Eldorado California parts. Call anytime for your California connection in New York.

Cars II   parts
6747 Warren Sharon Rd
Brookfield, OH 44403
330-448-2074; FAX: 330-448-1908

Open shop. Monday-Friday 8:00 am to 6:00 pm. Specializes in parts for 57-60 Cadillac Eldorados, 56-62 Corvettes, 66-67 Olds 442.

Chevrolet Parts Obsolete   accessories parts
PO Box 0740
Murrieta, CA 92564-0740
909-279-2833; FAX: 909-279-4013

See full listing in **Section One** under **Chevrolet**

Chewning's Auto Literature
2011 Elm Tree Terr
Buford, GA 30518
770-945-9795

literature
manuals

See full listing in **Section Two** under **literature dealers**

Ed Cholakian Enterprises Inc
dba All Cadillacs of the Forties
12811 Foothill Blvd
Sylmar, CA 91342
818-361-1147; 800-808-1147
FAX: 818-361-9738

museum
parts

Mail order and open shop. Monday-Friday 8 to 5:30; weekends by appointment. Specializing in parts and service for all Cadillacs, 1940-1958. Museum open year round, Monday-Friday 8-5:30. 60 Cadillacs from 1940 through 1958 on display. Many of the cars have been used in movies or on the Discovery Channel and TNN.

See our ad on page 25

Chrome Masters
1109 W Orange Ave, Unit D
Tallahassee, FL 32310
904-576-2100

chrome plating
pot metal restoration

See full listing in **Section Two** under **plating & polishing**

Classic Auto Air Mfg Co
2020 W Kennedy Blvd
Tampa, FL 33606
813-251-4994, 813-251-2356

air conditioning
heating
parts

See full listing in **Section One** under **Mustang**

Cobb's Antique Auto Restoration
717 Western Ave
Washington Court House, OH 43160
614-335-7489

restoration
service

See full listing in **Section Two** under **restoration shops**

Collector Car Appraisals
L E Lazarus, Senior Appraiser
PO Box 6732
Rockford, IL 61125
815-229-1258; FAX: 815-229-1238

appraisals

See full listing in **Section Two** under **appraisals**

Collector Car Buyers
4046 11th St
Rockford, IL 61109
815-229-1258; FAX: 815-229-1238

car dealers

See full listing in **Section Two** under **car dealers**

Collector Cars-U-Can-Afford Ltd
4046 11th St
Rockford, IL 61109
815-229-1258; FAX: 815-229-1238

car dealer

Mail order and open shop. Monday thru Saturday 9 to 5, appointment recommended, no Sunday hours. Cadillac, Packard, Buick and other vehicles from 1940 thru 1969, some others. Over 250 vehicles on hand at all times. No credit check, easy layaway terms available to all.

Colorado Car Collection Inc
3455 F St, Suite 3
Greeley, CO 80631
970-352-3915; FAX: 970-352-4172

car dealer

See full listing in **Section Two** under **car dealers**

Convertible Service
5126-HA Walnut Grove Ave
San Gabriel, CA 91776
800-333-1140, 818-285-2255
FAX: 818-285-9004

convertible parts
top mechanism service

See full listing in **Section Two** under **tops**

The Copper Cooling Works
2455 N 2550 E
Layton, UT 84040
801-544-9939

radiators

See full listing in **Section Two** under **radiators**

CR Plastics Inc
2790 NE 7th Ave
Pompano Beach, FL 33064
800-551-3155

bumper filler parts

Specializing in bumper filler parts, also known as extensions, for Cadillac 1977-1992, rear for Coupe deVille, Sedan deVille, Fleetwood, rear wheel drive. Cadillac Eldorado 1975-1985 front and rear. Cadillac Seville 1976-1985 front and rear. Buick Regal 2-dr 1981-1987 rear. We manufacture them and sell them. ABS plastic, lacquer primed, complete satisfaction guaranteed. The price war continues.

Custom Autosound Mfg
808 W Vermont Ave
Anaheim, CA 92805
800-888-8637; FAX: 714-533-0361
E-mail: carl@globalmark.com

accessories
custom radios
speakers

See full listing in **Section One** under **Chevrolet**

JB Donaldson Co
2533 W Cypress
Phoenix, AZ 85009
602-278-4505; FAX: 602-278-1112

castings
steering wheels
wood parts

See full listing in **Section Two** under **steering wheels**

Driving Passion-1959
7132 Chilton Ct
Clarksville, MD 21029
PH/FAX: 301-596-9078

bumpers
parts
parts locating service

Mail order and open shop. Friday, Saturday, Sunday, 7 am-5 pm. Parts and locating service for all 1959 Cad only including Eldorado and Seville. 1959 Caddy stainless, bumpers and hard to find trim and parts for coupes, conv and 4-doors.

See our ad on page 26

Dylan Bay Auto Museum
1411 4th Ave, #1430
Seattle, WA 98101
206-292-9874; FAX: 206-292-9876
E-mail: cbayley@dylanbay.com

museum

See full listing in **Section Six** under **Washington**

Eaton Detroit Spring Service Co
1555 Michigan Ave
Detroit, MI 48350
313-963-3839; FAX: 313-963-7047
E-mail: ken@eatonsprings.com

bushings
coil springs
leaf springs
shackles
u-bolts

See full listing in **Section Two** under **suspension parts**

ECB, Ed Leek
13 Snipe Rd
Key Largo, FL 33037
PH/FAX: 305-451-0864

fiberglass parts

See full listing in **Section Two** under **fiberglass parts**

Edgerton Classics Ltd
RR 5 Box 199
Canastota, NY 13032
315-697-2722

restoration
woodworking

See full listing in **Section Two** under **restoration shops**

Egge Machine Company
11707 Slauson Ave
Santa Fe Springs, CA 90670
310-945-3419 in CA
800-866-EGGE; FAX: 310-693-1635

babbitting
chassis
motor mounts
pistons
valves

See full listing in **Section Two** under **engine parts**

Elliott's Car Radio
313 Linfield Rd
Parkerford, PA 19457
610-495-6360; FAX: 610-495-7723

radio repairs
speaker kits

See full listing in **Section Two** under **radios**

Extensions Plus Inc
3500 Park Central Blvd N
Pompano Beach, FL 33064
954-978-3362; FAX: 954-978-0630
E-mail: 4star@gate.net

body filler parts

See full listing in **Section Two** under **body parts**

Fan Belt Specialist
PO Box 61195
Denver, CO 80206
800-580-6747; FAX: 303-758-6643

fan belts

Mail order only. Cadillac and LaSalle flathead V8 fan & generator belts, 1940, 1941-48. All belts new, correct dimensions.

Faxon Auto Literature
3901 Carter Ave
Riverside, CA 92501
800-458-2734; FAX: 909-786-4166

literature
manuals

See full listing in **Section Two** under **literature dealers**

FEN Enterprises of New York Inc
PO Box 1559
Wappingers Falls, NY 12590
914-462-5959; 914-462-5094
FAX: 914-462-8450

parts
restoration

Mail order and open shop. Distributor of only the finest Cadillac parts worldwide with full restoration and maintenance facility. Specializing in Cadillacs 1949 thru 1976 (other years upon request).

Fleetline Automotive
PO Box 291
Highland, NY 12528
914-691-9228

salvage yard

See full listing in **Section Five** under **New York**

From Rust To Riches
14200 New Hampshire Ave
Silver Spring, MD 20904
301-384-5856; FAX: 301-989-1866

appraisals
car dealer
repairs
restoration

See full listing in **Section Two** under **restoration shops**

Grand Touring
2785 E Regal Park Dr
Anaheim, CA 92806
714-630-0130; FAX: 714-630-6956

| engine rebuilding |
| machine shop |
| restoration |
| suspension |

See full listing in **Section Two** under **restoration shops**

Harbor Auto Restoration
1504 SW 3rd St
Pompano Beach, FL 33069
954-785-7887; FAX: 954-785-7388

| restoration |

See full listing in **Section Two** under **restoration shops**

Justin Hartley
17 Fox Meadow Ln
West Hartford, CT 06107-1216
860-523-0056 860-604-9950 cellular
FAX: 860-233-8840

| reprinted literature |

Mail order only. Cadillac and LaSalle shop manuals, parts
books, service bulletins, owner`s manuals, body manuals, data
books. 1902 through 1995. Republished full size with care, pride
and love. Prompt delivery. Recommended by Cadillac club judges
and restoration shops. Money-back guarantee. Electronic
improvement of pictures. Layflat binding. Started in 1912.
References in 50 states and worldwide. M/C, Visa, AmEx.

See our ad on page 27

Holcombe Cadillac Parts
2933 Century Ln
Bensalem, PA 19020
215-245-4560; FAX: 215-633-9916

| parts |

Mail order and open shop. Monday-Friday 9 am-5:30 pm.
Specializing in Cadillac parts, NOS, used & reproduction for
1949-1983 Cadillacs, all models. NOS parts a specialty, with
over 11,000 part numbers stocked. We carry a full line of used
body & trim parts. We also carry an extensive inventory of rubber weatherstripping, air conditioning, brake and general
mechanical & electrical parts as well as body fillers.

Honest John's Caddy Corner
PO Box 741
Justin, TX 76247
817-648-3330; FAX: 817-648-9135

| parts |
| restoration |
| service |

Mail order and open shop. Monday-Friday 9 to 5. Parts, sales,
service and restoration for 1941-1979 Cadillacs. Rebuilding, fabrication also available.

Horsepower Sales
100 New South Rd
Hicksville, NY 11801
516-937-3707; FAX: 516-937-3803

| limousines |

See full listing in **Section Two** under **limousine rentals**

Hubcap Mike
26242 Dimension, Ste 150
Lake Forest, CA 92630
714-597-8120; FAX: 714-597-8123

| hubcaps |
| wheelcovers |

See full listing in **Section Two** under **wheels & wheelcovers**

Interesting Parts Inc
Paul TerHorst
27526 N Owens Rd
Mundelein, IL 60060
PH/FAX: 847-949-1030

| appraisals |
| gaskets |
| parts |
| storage |
| transport |

See full listing in **Section Two** under **comprehensive parts**

Jesser's Classic Keys
26 West St, Dept HVA
Akron, OH 44303-2344
330-376-8181; FAX: 330-384-9129

| automobilia |
| keys |

See full listing in **Section Two** under **locks & keys**

John's Auto Classics
6135 N 79 Dr
Glendale, AZ 85303
602-872-8695

| appraisals |

Appraisals for antique, classic and collectibles. Appraisals for
banks, insurance companies & personal use. Specializing in
Cadillacs.

King's Bumper Co Inc
1 Ontario Ave
New Hartford, NY 13413
315-732-8988; FAX: 315-732-2602

| chrome plating |

See full listing in **Section Two** under **plating & polishing**

Lazarus Auto Collection
PO Box 6732
Rockford, IL 61125
815-229-1258; FAX: 815-229-1238

| arcade machines |
| cars |
| jukeboxes |

See full listing in **Section Two** under **car dealers**

Lectric Limited Inc
7322 S Archer Road
Justice, IL 60458
708-563-0400; FAX: 708-458-2662

| parts |

See full listing in **Section One** under **Corvette**

Mainly Convertibles
13805 W Hillsborough Ave
Tampa, FL 33635-9655
813-855-6869; FAX: 813-855-1376

| parts |
| repair |
| restoration |

See full listing in **Section One** under **Lincoln**

Mastermind Inc
32155 Joshua Dr
Wildomar, CA 92595
PH/FAX: 909-674-0509

| parts |
| restoration |

Mail order and open shop, 8:30-5:30. Specializes in restoration
and repro parts for 1957-60 Cadillac Eldorado Broughams. Also
other 50s & 60s Cadillac parts and restoration, stainless molding repair, loads of misc services, expert air suspension rebuilding. Major emphasis and specialization in Eldorado series cars.

McVey's
5040 Antioch, Suite E
Merriam, KS 66203
913-722-0707; FAX: 913-722-1166

| parts |
| trim |

Mail order and open shop. Monday-Friday 8 to 5:30. Brand new,
show quality trim & jewelry items for Cadillacs & LaSalles 1936
to 1969. Specializing in wheelcovers, hubcaps, medallions, hood
& trunk crests, emblems, script & letters, lenses, engine decal &
detail sets, turn signal & gearshift knobs, inside and outside
mirrors (door & rearview), NOS trunk lining material, exhaust
insulation kits, door sill step plates and much more.
MasterCard, Visa welcome. Worldwide shipments daily. Postpaid
catalog $5.

Mid-Jersey Motorama Inc — car dealer
1301 Asbury Ave
PO Box 1395
Asbury Park, NJ 07712
908-775-9885; Beeper: 908-840-6111
FAX: 908-775-9885

Open by appointment. Specializing in Mercedes, Cadillacs, Land Rover, Rolls-Royces, Jaguar, Lincoln.

Midwest Acorn Nut Company — fasteners hardware
256 Minnesota Ave
Troy, MI 48083-4671
800-422-NUTS (6887)
FAX: 810-583-9130

See full listing in **Section Two** under **hardware**

Model Rectifier Corp — die cast models
80 Newfield Ave
Edison, NJ 08837
908-225-2100; FAX: 908-225-0091

Mail order only. Elvis Presley 1955 pink Cadillac, die cast 1/18 scale, licensed by Elvis Presley Enterprises, Graceland and General Motors-Cadillac Division.

Hugh Morrison — parts
1515 Adams
Missouri City, TX 77489
713-499-8282

Mail order only. Specializing in only 1941 Cadillac parts as a semi-retirement activity.

Norman's Classic Auto Radio — custom sales radio repairs
7651 Park Blvd
Pinellas Park, FL 33781
813-546-1788

See full listing in **Section Two** under **radios**

O'Brien High Tech Auto — cellular phone exts & access parts
33 Pheasant Ln
Aliso Viejo, CA 92656
714-583-1780, 800-227-8290
FAX: 714-583-1889
E-mail: ohtind@aol.com

Mail order and open shop. Open 24 hrs. Specializing in rebuilding of fuel injection computers for Cadillac 1976-80, a/c power modules 1980-1989. Cellular phone extensions. Two phones/one line/one phone bill.

OEM Glass Inc — auto glass
PO Box 362, Rt 9 E
Bloomington, IL 61702
309-662-2122; FAX: 309-663-7474

See full listing in **Section Two** under **glass**

Old Air Products — air conditioning
3056 SE Loop 820
Ft Worth, TX 76140
817-551-0602; FAX: 817-568-0037

See full listing in **Section One** under **Corvette**

Old Coach Works Restoration Inc — appraisals body repairs restoration
1206 Badger St
Yorkville, IL 60560
630-553-0414; FAX: 630-553-1053

See full listing in **Section Two** under **restoration shops**

Original Auto Interiors — upholstery
7869 Trumble Rd
Columbus, MI 48063-3915
810-727-2486; FAX: 810-727-4344
E-mail: knight@mich.com

See full listing in **Section Two** under **upholstery**

Piru Cads — cars parts restoration
402 Via Fustero Rd
Box 227
Piru, CA 93040
805-521-1741

Mail order and open shop. Monday-Saturday 10 to 6. Cadillac and LaSalle restoration 1937-70, heavy in 1938-53. Sales also, project cars, plus restored.

Dennis Portka — horns
4326 Beetow Dr
Hamburg, NY 14075
716-649-0921

See full listing in **Section One** under **Corvette**

Precision Pot Metal/ Bussie Restoration Inc — pot metal restoration
1008 Loring Ave #28
Orange Park, FL 32073
904-269-8788

See full listing in **Section Two** under **plating & polishing**

Sam Quinn Cadillac Parts — parts
Box 837
Estacada, OR 97023
503-637-3852

Mail order only. Parts supplier for Cadillac/LaSalle, 1937-77. NOS, rebuilt water pumps 1937-77, parts locater service, MoPar 1952-75. New AC fuel pumps, fender skirts, oil pumps 1949-62. Motor mounts 1954-64. Transmission mounts 1949-up. Ignition parts. Body parts. Locater service.

David Raine's Springcrafters — springs suspension parts
425 Harding Hwy
Carney's Point, NJ 08069
609-299-9141; FAX: 609-299-9157

See full listing in **Section Two** under **suspension parts**

Harry Samuel — carpet fabrics interiors upholstery covers
65 Wisner St
Pontiac, MI 48342-1066
248-335-1900

See full listing in **Section Two** under **interiors & interior parts**

Sea Yachts Inc — parts
2029 N Ocean Blvd #410
Fort Lauderdale, FL 33304
305-561-8389

Mail order only. Collects 1954-58 Cadillacs only as a hobby. Extra parts for sale.

Selco Restoration — parts restoration service
9315 FM 359
Richmond, TX 77469
713-342-9751

Mail order and open shop. Monday-Saturday, flexible hours. Specializes in parts, service and restoration for Cadillacs, 1930s-1960s.

E J Serafin | **manuals**
Valley Rd
Matinecock, NY 11560

Mail order only. Exact reproductions of owner's and shop manuals for 1930, 31, 34, 35, 36, 40, 41, 47, 49, 57, 59, 61 Cadillacs and 1937 Buick.

Dick Shappy Classic Cars | **parts**
26 Katherine Ct
Warwick, RI 02889
401-521-5333; FAX: 401-421-9480

Cadillacs 1930-33 parts. Specializing in V16 but have parts also for 8 and 12 cylinder cars.

Showroom Auto Sales | **car dealer**
960 S Bascom Ave
San Jose, CA 95128
408-554-1550; FAX: 408-554-0550

See full listing in **Section One** under **Mercedes-Benz**

Silverstate Cadillac Parts | **parts**
PO Box 2161
Sparks, NV 89431
702-331-7252; FAX: 702-331-7887

Mail order and open shop. Monday-Friday 8 am to 5 pm by appointment. Specializing in Cadillac parts, NOS, used, reproduction and remanufactured for 1932 through 1985 Cadillacs with 8,000 sq ft of NOS Cadillac parts and over 10,000 different part numbers on hand to service your needs.

Robert H Snyder | **literature**
PO Drawer 821 | **parts**
Yonkers, NY 10702
914-476-8500
FAX: 914-476-8573, business hours

Mail order only. 1941-49 Cadillac Fleetwood Series 75, 76 and 86 only. Free catalog available of revolving inventory of original parts only, principally small trim, garnish, fittings and miscellany. No heavy mechanical parts. Literature and collectibles of every description. All want lists invited.

Southern US Car Export Inc | **repair**
135 Eulon Loop | **restoration**
Raeford, NC 28376 | **sales**
910-875-7534; FAX: 910-875-7731 | **transport**

Mail order and open shop. Mon-Fri 8-5, Sat 9-1. Specialize in 58 Cadillac convertibles. Classic cars, old Mustangs, old pickup trucks (Ford, Chevy). Complete restoration service, repair, automobile brokering, transport and worldwide shipping of all makes and models, mail order parts.

Michael A Stahl | **parts**
PO Box 18036
Huntsville, AL 35804
205-882-6457

Mail order only. Specializing in emblem cover repair kits for 1977-1992 Cadillac, used replacement parts and blower motors for 1981-1983 Delorean.

TA Motor AB | **accessories**
Torpslingan 21 | **parts**
Lulea S 97347 Sweden
+46-920-18888
FAX: +46-920-18821

Mail order and open shop. Shop open Monday-Friday 8 to 5. Specializing in parts and accessories for Cadillacs 1940-1970.

Tom Crook Classic Cars | **car dealer**
27611 42nd Ave S
Auburn, WA 98001
206-941-3454

See full listing in **Section Two** under **car dealers**

Tom's Classic Parts | **parts**
5207 Sundew Terr
Tobyhanna, PA 18466
800-832-4073

See full listing in **Section One** under **Chevrolet**

Town Auto Top and | **convertible repairs**
Restoration Co | **interiors**
78 Bloomfield Ave, PO Box 167
Pine Brook, NJ 07058
201-575-9333; FAX: 201-808-8366

See full listing in **Section Two** under **tops**

U S Oldies & Classics | **car dealer**
Vunt 3 | **parts**
Holsbeek 3220 Belgium
3216446611, FAX: 3216446520

See full listing in **Section Two** under **car dealers**

Valley Wire Wheel Service | **wheel restoration**
7306 Coldwater Canyon #16 | **wheels**
North Hollywood, CA 91605
818-765-3258; FAX: 818-765-8358

See full listing in **Section Two** under **wheels & wheelcovers**

Visual Marketplace Online Inc | **online auto ads**
800 Silverado, Suite 324
La Jolla, CA 92037
619-459-3846; FAX: 619-459-3460
E-mail: pyoung@icreations.com

See full listing in **Section Four** under **information sources**

Waldron's Antique Exhaust Inc | **exhaust systems**
PO Box C 25872 M-86
Nottawa, MI 49075
616-467-7185; FAX: 616-467-9041

See full listing in **Section Two** under **exhaust systems**

West Coast Sheetmetal | **body parts**
Lawrence M Camuso
219 S 20th St
San Jose, CA 95116
408-286-6537

See full listing in **Section Two** under **body parts**

Willow Grove Auto Top | **interiors**
43 N York Rd | **tops**
Willow Grove, PA 19090 | **upholstery**
215-659-3276

See full listing in **Section Two** under **interiors & interior parts**

Woodgrain by Estes | **woodgraining**
7550 Richardson Rd
Sarasota, FL 34240
813-379-3669

See full listing in **Section Two** under **woodgraining**

CHECKER

| **Blackheart Enterprises Ltd** 65 S Service Rd Plainview, NY 11803 516-935-6249; FAX: 516-752-1484 | parts restoration |

Sells Checker taxicab parts. Thousands in stock, mostly all NOS. Reproduction rubber parts. Also restoration and sales. Plastic media blasting. Complete body work and painting, all American cars. Non-destructive paint removal.

| **Bob Hinkley Checker Parts & Cars** Box 14 Newark, NY 14513 716-233-1430 | car dealer parts |

Mail order and open shop by appointment only. Specializing in cars and parts for Checker cars, all models, new and used parts. Cars sold, rented, bought.

| **Pollard Co** Joe Pollard 9331 Johnell Rd Chatsworth, CA 91311 PH/FAX: 818-999-1485 | parts |

Specialize in parts for Checker station wagons and sedans, 1960-1982.

| **Turnpike Checker** Erich Lachmann Jr 495 North St Middletown, NY 10940-4526 914-457-1898; FAX: 914-343-2224 | parts repairs |

Mail order only. Specializing in parts and repairs for 1960 to 1982 Checker taxi cabs and Marathons.

| **4-Speeds by Darrell** PO Box 110 #3 Water St Vermilion, IL 61955 217-275-3743; FAX: 217-275-3515 | transmissions |

See full listing in **Section Two** under **transmissions**

| **A & M SoffSeal Inc** 104 May Dr Harrison, OH 45030 800-426-0902; 513-367-0028, service & info; FAX: 513-367-5506 | rubber parts weatherstripping |

See full listing in **Section Two** under **rubber parts**

| **A-1 Street Rods** 631 E Las Vegas St Colorado Springs, CO 80903 719-632-4920 or 719-577-4588 FAX: 719-634-6577 | parts |

See full listing in **Section Two** under **street rods**

| **Accessoryland Truckin' Supplies** Hwy 151 & 61 S 10723 Rt 61 Dubuque, IA 52003 319-556-5482; FAX: 319-556-9087 | accessories parts |

Mail order and open shop by appointment. Specializing in 1941-59 Chevrolet and GMC truck parts. NOS, reproduction and used. Unity spotlights, fog lights, bracket kits and repair parts for most cars and trucks 1930s to present. Also current custom van and pickup accessories. Established in 1976.

| **Adler's Antique Autos Inc** 801 NY Route 43 Stephentown, NY 12168 518-733-5749 days 518-479-4103 nights | auto preservation Chevrolet parts repair restoration |

See full listing in **Section Two** under **restoration shops**

| **Air Flow Research** 10490 Ilex Ave Pacoima, CA 91331 818-890-0616; FAX: 818-890-0490 | cylinder heads |

Mail order only. Manufacturing aftermarket small block Chevy aluminum cylinder heads for all V8 small block Chevys from 1950 to present.

| **AKH Wheels** 1207 N A St Ellensburg, WA 98926-2522 509-962-3390 | Rallye wheels styled steel wheels vintage aluminum |

See full listing in **Section Two** under **wheels & wheelcovers**

All Chevy/Canadian Impala   parts
404 Allwood Rd
Parksville, BC Canada V9P 1C4
PH/FAX: 604-248-8666

Mail order and open shop. Specializing in reproduction parts for full-size 55-70 Chevy! Impala specialists. Emblems, weatherstrips, interiors, literature, reproduction body parts. Books and manuals.

Muneef Alwan   glass
7400 Crosa Countre Rd   steering wheels
Oroville, CA 95966
916-534-6683

See full listing in **Section One** under **Ford '32-'53**

American Classic Truck Parts   parts
PO Box 50286
Denton, TX 76206
817-497-2456; FAX: 817-497-4439

Mail order only. We stock a very large inventory of antique pick-up parts for Chevy and GMC trucks, 1936-1972. New old stock and reproduction. Weatherstripping, sheetmetal, rubber, trim, emblems, chrome, electrical, wiring, moldings, interior trim, mats, upholstery and much more. We accept VISA, MasterCard, Discover, cash COD, money orders and prepaid checks. Order by FAX, phone or mail. Business hours are 9 to 17:30 CST. Catalogs are free within the USA (we need to know the year and type of truck that you are working on as we have different catalogs). They go bulk mail but if you are in a hurry, send us $2 postage and we'll get you one out first class mail. See our ad on this page.

See our ad on page 31

American Memory Prints   artwork
5935 N Belt W
Belleville, IL 62223
618-235-4788; FAX: 618-235-4899

See full listing in **Section Two** under **artwork**

American Plastic Chrome   replating plastic
1398 Mar Ann Dr
Westland, MI 48185
313-721-1967 days
313-261-4454 eves

See full listing in **Section Two** under **plating & polishing**

Andover Automotive Inc   parts
PO Box 3143   seat belts
Laurel, MD 20709
410-381-6700; FAX: 410-381-6703

See full listing in **Section One** under **Corvette**

Antique & Classic Cars   car locator
Rt 15, Box 454
Florence, AL 35633
205-760-0542

See full listing in **Section One** under **Cadillac/LaSalle**

Antique Auto Battery Mfg Co   batteries
2320 Old Mill Rd   battery cables
Hudson, OH 44236
800-426-7580; FAX: 216-425-4642

See full listing in **Section Two** under **batteries**

Antique Auto Fasteners   fasteners
Guy C Close, Jr & Son   hardware
13426 Valna Dr   hose clamps
Whittier, CA 90602   molding clips
310-696-3307

See full listing in **Section Two** under **hardware**

Antique Automobile Radio Inc   radio accessories
700 Tampa Rd   radio parts
Palm Harbor, FL 34684   radio restoration
800-WE-FIX-AM; 813-785-8733
FAX: 813-789-0283

See full listing in **Section Two** under **radios**

Authentic Automotive   power brakes
529 Buttercup Trail   power steering
Mesquite, TX 75149
972-289-6373

Mail order only. Monday-Friday 9 am to 6 pm CST. Steering, brake and chassis parts for 1953-64 Chevy passenger cars. Specializing in show quality power steering and power brake systems, as well as ps and pb component restorations. Manufacturer of many new reproduction parts that pertain to ps and pb, wholesale and retail. Free catalogs, please state year.

Auto Custom Carpet   carpets
Jeff Moses   floor mats
PO Box 1350, 1429 Noble St
Anniston, AL 36202
800-633-2358; 205-236-1118
FAX: 800-516-8274

Auto Custom Parts Inc, the world's leading manufacturer of aftermarket floor coverings, has a product line covering products from 40s to 90s. Available from ACC is complete line of molded carpet sets, cut and sew carpet sets, vinyl and rubber molded floor coverings, trunk mats and custom floor mats. Furthermore, ACC products meet or exceed OEM specifications.

Auto Etc Neon   signs
PO Box 531992   time pieces
Harlingen, TX 78553
210-425-7487; FAX: 210-425-3025

See full listing in **Section One** under **Corvette**

Auto Hardware Specialties   hardware fasteners
3123 McKinley Ave
Sheldon, IA 51201
712-324-2091; FAX: 712-324-2480

Mail order only. Specializing in original type hardware for 1929-41 GM cars, including: screws, nuts, bolts, molding clips, hinge pins, tube nuts, anchor nuts, step bolts, hose clamps, gas caps and related items. Illustrated catalog $2.

Avanti Auto Service   repair
Rt 322, 67 Conchester Hwy   restoration
Glen Mills, PA 19342-1506
610-558-9999

See full listing in **Section One** under **DeTomaso/Pantera**

B & D Motors   rubber parts
1309 Kenwood   sheetmetal
Cape Girardeau, MO 63701   trim
573-334-3354

Smooth steel runningboards shaped like originals, sheetmetal, rubber, trim and street rod parts for 1934 to 1948 Chevrolets.

B & T Truck Parts   pickup parts
906 E Main St
PO Box 799
Siloam Springs, AR 72761
501-524-5959: FAX: 501-524-5559

See full listing in **Section Two** under **trucks & tractors**

B & W Antique Auto Parts Inc   accessories
4653 Guide Meridian Rd   parts
Bellingham, WA 98227
360-647-4574; FAX: 360-676-0458

See full listing in **Section One** under **Ford '32-'53**

Bay Ridges Classic Chevy   accessories
1362 Poprad Ave   parts
Pickering, ON Canada L1W 1L1
905-839-6169; FAX: 905-420-6613

Authorized dealer for Danchuk Mfg, Ol' 55 & C&P Auto.
Specializing in 1955-57 Chevy parts and accessories, new and
used, including interiors, tires, suspension parts, batteries, car
covers and car care products.

Becker Sales   battery master
Rear 519 Wyoming Ave   switches
West Pittston, PA 18643
PH/FAX: 717-655-3869

See full listing in **Section Two** under **batteries**

Beverly Hills Motoring Accessories   accessories
205 S Robertson Blvd
Beverly Hills, CA 90211
310-657-4880; FAX: 310-659-4664
E-mail: bhma@hollywood.cinenet.net

See full listing in **Section One** under **Mercedes-Benz**

Big Boy Accessories   parts
581 Kenbridge Dr
Carson, CA 90746
310-324-4787

Mail order and open shop. 7 days 8 to 5. Has been selling 1958-
1968 Chevrolet parts for the last three years. Also handles some
GM products.

Bill's Speed Shop   body parts
13951 Millersburg Rd
Navarre, OH 44662
330-832-9403; FAX: 330-832-2098

Mail order and open shop. We are one of the foremost suppliers
of obsolete and current body repair panels. Our main interest is
obsolete panels from 1949-up. Also in stock, a few NOS fenders
and quarters.

Bob's Radio & TV Service/   radios
Vintage Electronics
2300 Broad St
San Lius Obispo, CA 94401
805-543-2946; FAX: 805-782-0803

See full listing in **Section Two** under **radios**

Bow Tie Reproductions   parts
132 S Main St
Germantown, OH 45327
513-855-7478

Specializing in reproduction parts for 1929-32 Chevrolets.

Boyds Hot Rods & Collectable Cars   car dealer
10971 Dale St
Stanton, CA 90680
714-220-9870; FAX: 714-220-9877

Open shop 7 days. Monday-Friday 9 to 6, Saturday 9-4, Sunday
11-4. We sell American cars from hot rods to classic & muscle
cars from 1923 to 1965.

Brasilia Press   models
PO Box 2023
Elkhart, IN 46515
FAX: 219-262-8799

See full listing in **Section Two** under **models & toys**

Rodney Brockman   literature
24862 Ridge Rd   shop manuals
Elwood, IL 60421   signs
815-478-3633

Mail order only. Buys and sells shop manuals, motors, Chilton
books, sales literature, signs and 1955-86 Chevrolet chrome.

Brothers Truck Parts   accessories
5670 Schaefer Ave, Unit G   parts
Chino, CA 91710
800-977-2767, FAX: 909-517-3142
E-mail: brothers96@aol.com

See full listing in **Section Two** under **trucks & tractors**

The Bumper Boyz   bumper repairs
834 E Florence Ave   reconditioning
Los Angeles, CA 90001   sand blasting
213-587-8976, 800-995-1703
FAX: 213-587-2013

Mail order and open shop. 7am to 6 pm PST. Specializing in
reconditioning all makes and models. GM, Ford, Chrysler. Also
foreign bumpers. We repair, sandblast and triple plate bumpers.
We carry accessories, bumper guards, fender wing tips plus
grilles, exchange or outright. We ship nationwide also over seas.

Burrell's Service Inc   parts
PO Box 456
Keego Harbor, MI 48320
810-682-2376

Mail order only. Specializing in service and parts information for
1976-81 Chevy and Ford vans with the Vemco VX4 4-wd conversion.

Butch's Trim   molding
W-224 S-8445 Industrial Ave   polishing
Big Bend, WI 53103   trim restoration
414-679-4883; 414-662-9910 shop

Mail order and open shop. Monday-Saturday 9 to 4. Restoration
of aluminum trim, body side moldings, headlamp bezels, grilles.
Dents & scratches removed. Polishing and anodizing. Stocking
NOS and used for 58 to 67 Chevy.

C & P Chevy Parts
50 Schoolhouse Rd, PO Box 348VA
Kulpsville, PA 19443
215-721-4300, 800-235-2475
FAX: 215-721-4539

| parts |
| restoration supplies |

Mail order and open shop. Monday-Friday 9 to 5. Parts and restoration supplies for 1955-57 Chevrolets and 55-59 Chevrolet truck.

Camaro Specialties
112 Elm St
East Aurora, NY 14052
716-652-7086; FAX: 716-652-2279

| parts |
| restoration |

See full listing in **Section One** under **Chevelle/Camaro**

CARS Inc
1964 W 11 Mile Rd
Berkley, MI 48072
810-398-7100; 810-398-7078

| interior |

Mail order and open shop. Monday-Friday 8:30 am-5:30 pm; Saturday 8:30 am-2 pm. Original style interiors, parts and heavy gauge sheetmetal products for 1955-72 full-size Chevys, 1964-72 Chevelle & El Camino, 1967-76 Camaro, 1962-72 Nova, 1970-72 Monte Carlo, 1955-57 Cameos and 1967-72 Chevy pickups.

Jim Carter's Antique Truck Parts
1500 E Alton
Independence, MO 64055
816-833-1913; FAX: 816-252-3749

| truck parts |

Mail order and open shop. Monday-Friday, 9 am to 5 pm. Specializing in all types of sheetmetal, mechanical, upholstery and bed parts for Chevrolet and GMC trucks, 1934 thru 1972.

See our ad below

If You Have a Mid 30's to Early 70's Chevy or GMC Truck We've Got Your Parts!!!

We specialize in quality parts for the show vehicle as well as the everyday driver. Our trained, experienced crew knows older GM trucks and what you need in their restoration.

Send for FREE Catalog.
$2.50 in stamps is appreciated with your request.
(Please indicate 34-59 or 60-72.)

Personal Service From the Crew at:
Jim Carter Antique Truck Parts
1508 East Alton (23rd St.)
Independence, MO 64055

800-336-1913

John Chambers Vintage Chevrolet
PO Box 35068, Dept VAA
Phoenix, AZ 85069
602-934-CHEV

| parts |

Mail order and open shop by appointment, customer pick-up by appointment. 55, 56 & 57 Chevrolet parts: chrome parts, lenses, wiring harnesses, weatherstripping, sheetmetal, interiors, mechanical items, rubber parts. Large selection of rust-free used parts from the Southwest.

Chernock Motorcars
PO Box 134
Airport Rd
Hazleton, PA 18201
717-455-1752; FAX: 717-455-7585

| trailers |

See full listing in **Section Two** under **trailers**

Chevrolet Parts Obsolete
PO Box 0740
Murrieta, CA 92564-0740
909-279-2833; FAX: 909-279-4013

| accessories |
| parts |

Mail order only. Carries over 50,000 NOS General Motors parts and accessories, 1965 to 1985. For easy access we subscribe to *Parts Voice*. We also purchase discontinued and obsolete GM parts. When calling, please provide part numbers if possible.

Chev's of the 40's
2027 B St
Washougal, WA 98671
360-835-9799; FAX: 360-835-7988

| parts |

Mail order only. Specializing in parts for 1937-1954 Chevrolet cars and trucks.

Chevy Duty Pickup Parts
4319 NW Gateway
Kansas City, MO 64150
816-741-8029; FAX: 816-741-5255
E-mail: chevyduty@aol.com

| pickup parts |

Mail order and open shop. Monday-Friday 9 to 5:30, Saturday 9 to 12. Specializes in parts and restoration supplies for 1947-1972 Chevy and GMC pickups. We have 4 fully illustrated catalogs, complete with descriptions & prices for you to order from.

Chevy Parts Warehouse
13545 Sycamore Ave
San Martin, CA 95046
408-683-2438; FAX: 408-683-2533

| parts |

Mail order and open shop. Monday-Saturday 9 to 5. Specializing in parts for 55-66 passenger, 47-72 pickups, 64-72 Chevelles and El Caminos, 62-74 Novas, 67-73 Camaro.

Chevy Shop
338 Main Ave, Box 75
Milledgeville, IL 61051
815-225-7565

| custom castings |
| parts |

Retail sales of 1933-57 Chevrolet parts. Manufacturer of custom castings in zinc aluminum alloy using spin casting and investment casting techniques. Some iron and aluminum castings (sandcastings) also done. Will custom cast for dealer or individual, one part or many, with painting or plating available also. Catalog $2. Free quotes on parts.

Chewning's Auto Literature
2011 Elm Tree Terr
Buford, GA 30518
770-945-9795

| literature |
| manuals |

See full listing in **Section Two** under **literature dealers**

Ciadella Enterprises | **truck interiors**
3116 S 52nd St | **upholstery**
Tempe, AZ 85282-3212
602-968-4179; FAX: 602-470-0499

Mail order and open shop. Monday-Friday 7 am to 3 pm. Since 1976 Ciadella has been known as the premier source of interior parts for Chevys from 51 thru 69, manufacturers of reproduction and custom interior kits you can install with professional results, known internationally for the highest quality in workmanship and materials used. This year Ciadella introduced several new products, including a custom console, seat foams and springs 55-65, a distinctive custom interior package for full size trucks, Blazers and Suburbans 74-87 and S-10/S-15 trucks and Blazers 74-93.

Classic Auto Air Mfg Co | **air conditioning**
2020 W Kennedy Blvd | **heating**
Tampa, FL 33606 | **parts**
813-251-4994, 813-251-2356

See full listing in **Section One** under **Mustang**

Classic Auto Literature | **data books**
Box 53 Blueback, RR 2 | **literature**
Nanoose Bay, BC Canada V0R 2R0 | **manuals**
250-468-9522 | **models/parts catalog**

See full listing in **Section Two** under **literature dealers**

Classic Auto Restoration | **restoration**
Service Inc
113 National Dr
Rockwall, TX 75087
214-722-9663

Open Monday thru Friday 8 am-5 pm CST. Specializes in Chevrolet 1955-72 cars and pickups. Also Ford and Mustang 1958-68.

The Classic Car Radio Co | **radios**
2718 Koper Dr
Sterling Heights, MI 48310
810-977-7979; info: 810-268-2918
FAX: 810-977-0895

See full listing in **Section Two** under **radios**

Classic Chevy International | **modified parts**
PO Box 607188 | **repro parts**
Orlando, FL 32860-7188 | **used parts**
800-456-1956; FAX: 407-299-3341
E-Mail: cciworld@aol.com

Mail order and open shop. Monday-Friday 8 am-5 pm, Saturday 9-3. Phone orders Monday-Friday 8-11 EST, Saturday 9-6 EST. Specializing in reproduction, modified, used parts and selected restoration services for 1955-66 Chevrolets.

See our ad on this page

Classic Data | **shop manual**
1240 SE Gideon St
Portland, OR 97202
503-234-8617; FAX: 503-234-8618
E-mail: hfreedman@aol.com

Mail order only. Technical shop manual on CD for 55-56-57 Chevrolet.

Classic Industries Inc | **accessories**
Nova/Chevy II Parts and | **parts**
Accessories Catalog
17832 Gothard St
Huntington Beach, CA 92647
800-854-1280 ext 210 toll-free in USA
FAX: 800-300-3081 toll-free

Nova/Chevy II parts and accessories catalog. Over 350 full color pages of the largest selection of original and reproduction products and accessories ever assembled. Easy to read format allows you to choose from literally thousands of different products, each containing a color photo and a brief description. Classic Industries is an official GM Restoration Parts licensee assuring the highest quality parts and accessories for 1962 through 1979 Novas. Call or write for your personal copy today. Cost, $5.

See our ad inside the front cover

Classic Profiles Inc | **artwork**
5770 W Kinnickinnic River Pkwy
West Allis, WI 53219
414-328-9866; FAX: 414-328-1906

See full listing in **Section One** under **Corvette**

Classic Wood Mfg | **wood kits**
1006 N Raleigh St | **wood replacement**
Greensboro, NC 27405
910-691-1344; FAX: 910-273-3074

See full listing in **Section Two** under **woodwork**

Clester's Auto Rubber Seals Inc | **gloveboxes**
PO Box 459 | **headliners**
Cleveland, NC 27013 | **molded rubber parts**
704-637-9979; FAX: 704-636-7390 | **weatherstripping**

See full listing in **Section Two** under **rubber parts**

Cliff's Classic Chevrolet Parts Co	**parts**
619 SE 212nd Ave	
Portland, OR 97233	
503-667-4329; FAX 503-669-4268	

Mail order and open shop. Monday-Saturday 9 am to 5:30 pm. Specializing in 1955-57 Chevrolet passenger car and 1955 2nd Series, 1959 Chevrolet truck parts, new and used. Many rebuilding/restoration services for same.

Coach Builders Muscle Car	**interiors**
Parts & Services	**parts**
PO Box 128	**rust remover**
Baltimore, MD 21087-0128	
410-426-5567	

NOS and reproduction body panels, interiors, convertible & vinyl tops, rechromed bumpers, Oxisolv rust remover & metal conditioner for 55-57 Chevy, Chevelle, Camaro, Impala, Nova, Monte Carlo, GTO, LeMans, Firebird, 442, Cutlass, Charger, Skylark, GS, Roadrunner, GTX, Cuda, Dart. Specializing in the past for the future.

Colorado Car Collection Inc	**car dealer**
3455 F St, Suite 3	
Greeley, CO 80631	
970-352-3915; FAX: 970-352-4172	

See full listing in **Section Two** under **car dealers**

Conte's Corvettes & Classics	**leasing**
851 W Wheat Rd	**parts**
Vineland, NJ 08360	**sales**
609-692-0087; FAX: 609-692-1009	**service**
E-mail: contes@cybernet.net	

See full listing in **Section One** under **Corvette**

Convertible Service	**convertible parts**
5126-HA Walnut Grove Ave	**top mechanism service**
San Gabriel, CA 91776	
800-333-1140, 818-285-2255	
FAX: 818-285-9004	

See full listing in **Section Two** under **tops**

Corvair Haven	**parts**
315 N Prairie St	**service**
Batavia, IL 60510	
630-761-8714	

See full listing in **Section One** under **Corvair**

Grady Cox	**parts**
480 Utah St	
Avery, TX 75554	
903-684-4172, 903-684-3819	

Mail order only. Specializing in new, used and reproduction parts, primarily for 1929-32 Chevrolet but including some items back to 1927. Reproducing inside and outside door handles, window handles, etc. Rebuilding windshield regulators, etc. Want list with SASE appreciated. The best thing we offer is guaranteed satisfaction for thirty days after receipt.

CPX - Doug Martz	**parts**
PO Box 223	
Butler, WI 53007	
414-463-2277; FAX: 414-462-2886	

Mail order and showroom sales. Monday-Friday 9 to 6; Saturday, Sunday & holidays, 9 to 1. Our 20th year as THE major discounter of 1955-75 Chevrolet, Camaro, Chevelle, Nova, Monte Carlo, El Camino parts and accessories, new, used and reproduction. "Why pay more?"

Don Cressman	**parts**
495 Louise Ave N	
Listowel, ON Canada N4W 3N5	
519-291-1600; FAX: 519-291-1763	

Mail order only. Buying and selling mostly NOS parts for GM muscle cars of years 1964 and up for about 10 years. Specializing in parts for 1964 & up for GTOs, Chevelles, Firebirds, Camaros, etc.

Custom Autosound Mfg	**accessories**
808 W Vermont Ave	**custom radios**
Anaheim, CA 92805	**speakers**
800-888-8637; FAX: 714-533-0361	
E-mail: carl@globalmark.com	

Mail order and open shop. Monday-Friday 8 to 5. Custom radios, AM-FM cassettes, CDs, speakers and acc. "No modification fit" for classic Chevys, Fords, MoPar, GM, AMC, Studebaker, Lincoln Mercury, AMC-Nash, DeSoto, Hudson, Kaiser, imports, and more

Custom Classic Cars	**parts**
2046 E 12B Road	**restoration**
Bourbon, IN 46504	
219-342-0399	
E-mail: asmith7112@aol.com	

Mail order and open shop. Monday-Saturday 8:30-5:30. Specializing in 1968-72 Nova and 1969-81 Trans Am and Firebird parts, also restoration of any make or model, 1929-present. Extensive fabrication work, custom concept, complete, partial, chassis, suspension, body, paint & media blasting. Four-man shop dedicated to your needs. Shop rate is very competitive.

Dave's Auto Machine & Parts	**accessories**
Rt 16	**machine work**
Ischua, NY 14743	**parts**
716-557-2402	

Mail order and open shop. Open Monday-Friday 9 to 5 EST. Sometimes closed Friday if at swap meet, please call ahead. Phone hours 10 to 7 EST. Specializing in Chevrolet 1955-72, all models car and truck parts, NOS, used only. Specializing in hp big and small block dated engine parts and accessories, including carbs, manifolds, trans, etc. Machine shop service available.

Dean's Wiper Transmission	**wiper trans service**
Service	
Dean Andrew Rehse	
16367 Martincoit Rd	
Poway, CA 92064	
619-451-1933; FAX: 619-451-1999	

See full listing in **Section One** under **Corvette**

Desert Muscle Cars	**parts**
2853 N Stone Ave	
Tucson, AZ 85705	
520-882-3010; FAX: 520-628-9332	

See full listing in **Section One** under **Chevelle/Camaro**

Digital Design Inc	**t-shirts**
PO Box 139	
Merrick, NY 11566	

See full listing in **Section Two** under **apparel**

Dixie Truck Works	**parts**
10495 Hwy 73 E	
Mount Pleasant, NC 28124	
704-436-2407	

Mail order and open shop. Monday-Friday 4 pm to 8 pm, Saturday 9 am to 5 pm. 38-page catalog lists truck parts for

1942-1982 Chevrolet and GMC trucks. Our complete line of new parts includes rubber parts, bed parts, sheetmetal, chrome moldings, bumpers, grilles, emblems and many other parts. Catalogs are $3.

Dr Jerry 11 Walnut St Farmingdale, NJ 07727 908-938-4375; FAX: 908-919-0476	car dealer

Mail order only. Specializing in sales of classic Chevrolets.

Eagle Wire Products 3308 Valley Forge Dr Knoxville, TN 37920 PH/FAX: 800-977-0030	wire harnesses

See full listing in **Section Two** under **electrical systems**

East Coast Chevy Inc Ol '55 Chevy Parts 4154A Skyron Dr Doylestown, FL 18938 215-348-5568; FAX: 215-348-0560	parts restoration

Mail order and open shop. Monday-Friday 9-5 pm, 1 Saturday per month 9-12 (call first for parts). Complete inventory new, used and reproduction parts (55-57 our specialty). Also restoration services for 1955-57 Chevrolets. Now stocking 1958-70. Personal service, parts restoration and custom work.

Eaton Detroit Spring 1555 Michigan Ave Detroit, MI 48350 313-963-3839; FAX: 313-963-7047 E-mail: ken@eatonsprings.com	bushings coil springs leaf springs shackles u-bolts

See full listing in **Section Two** under **suspension parts**

ECB, Ed Leek 13 Snipe Rd Key Largo, FL 33037 PH/FAX: 305-451-0864	fiberglass parts

See full listing in **Section Two** under **fiberglass parts**

Edwards Bros Brake Parts Inc 14223 Hawthorn Ct Fountain Hills, AZ 85268 602-837-9301, 602-837-9274	power brake kits

See full listing in **Section One** under **Cadillac/LaSalle**

Egge Machine Company 11707 Slauson Ave Santa Fe Springs, CA 90670 310-945-3419 in CA 800-866-EGGE; FAX: 310-693-1635	babbitting chassis motor mounts pistons valves

See full listing in **Section Two** under **engine parts**

Elliott's Car Radio 313 Linfield Rd Parkerford, PA 19457 610-495-6360; FAX: 610-495-7723	radio repairs speaker kits

See full listing in **Section Two** under **radios**

Engineering & Manufacturing Services Box 24362 Cleveland, OH 44124-0362 216-446-1620; FAX: 216-446-9590	sheetmetal

See full listing in **Section One** under **Ford '32-'53**

David J Entler Restorations RD 2, Box 479C Glen Rock, PA 17327 717-235-2112, 8 am to 5 pm Monday thru Friday EST	woodwork

See full listing in **Section Two** under **woodwork**

ETC Every Thing Cars 8727 Clarinda Pico Rivera, CA 90660 310-949-6981	restoration

See full listing in **Section One** under **MoPar**

Experi-Metal Inc 6345 Wall St Sterling Heights, MI 48312 810-977-7800; FAX: 810-977-6981	steel replicas

Mail order and open shop. Monday-Friday 8 am to 5 pm. Manufacture steel replicas of the 1932 Chevrolet roadster, in original gauge steel, made on new dies cast from original gauge parts. Complete line of fenders, aprons, runningboards, 31-32 Chevrolet.

Faxon Auto Literature 3901 Carter Ave Riverside, CA 92501 800-458-2734; FAX: 909-786-4166	literature manuals

See full listing in **Section Two** under **literature dealers**

Fifties Forever Mario Cristelli 206 Division Ave Garfield, NJ 07026 201-478-1306	Chevy specialist

Mail order and showroom. Monday to Friday 9 am-7 pm, Saturday 9 am-4 pm. Complete inventory of new, used and NOS parts for 1955-57 Chevrolet. Also many hard to find items for 1956-67 Corvette. Discounted prices, monthly specials, volume discounts.

John Filiss 45 Kingston Ave Port Jervis, NY 12771 914-856-2942	appraisals

See full listing in **Section Two** under **appraisals**

The Filling Station 990 S Second St Lebanon, OR 97355-3227 541-258-2114; 800-841-6622 FAX: 541-258-6968	literature parts

Mail order and open shop. Monday-Saturday 9 to 5; closed Sunday. Chevrolet and GMC quality reproduction parts for: 1929-64 passenger cars and 1929-72 trucks. Rubber products including: windshield, vent window, door and trunk seals. Chrome items including: mirrors and arms, hood and grille ornaments, door and window handles. Shop manuals, owner's manuals, sales and restoration literature. Brakes, suspensions and much more. Phone orders: 800/841-6622 nationwide.

Fleetline Automotive PO Box 291 Highland, NY 12528 914-691-9228	salvage yard

See full listing in **Section Five** under **New York**

Fowlkes Realty & Auction
500 Hale St
Newman Grove, NE 68758
800-275-5522; FAX: 402-447-6000

| appraisals auctions |

Specializes in the appraisal and auctioning of American made classic and antique automobiles. 15 years' experience. Auctions throughout the Midwest.

George Frechette
14 Cedar Dr
Granby, MA 01033
800-528-5235

| brake cylinder sleeving |

See full listing in **Section Two** under **brakes**

G & L Classics
8225 Taffy Dr
West Chester, OH 45069
513-779-1957

| parts |

Mail order and open shop. Monday-Saturday 9 to 7. 55-57 Chevrolet parts, new & used, bought & sold. Specializes in high-performance parts.

Gus R Garton
401 N 5th St
Millville, NJ 08332
609-825-3618 evenings

| bicycles NOS parts sales literature |

See full listing in **Section One** under **Ford '32-'53**

Gilbert's Early Chevy Pickup Parts
PO Box 1316, 470 Rd 1 NW
Chino Valley, AZ 86323
PH/FAX: 602-636-5337
E-mail: gilb@goodnet.com

| pickup parts |

See full listing in **Section Two** under **trucks & tractors**

Glass Search/LOF
1975 Galaxie Ave
Columbus, OH 43207
800-848-1351; FAX: 614-443-0709

| glass parts |

See full listing in **Section Two** under **glass**

GMC Solutions
Robert English
PO Box 675
Franklin, MA 02038-0675
508-520-3900; FAX: 508-520-7861
E-mail: oldcarkook@aol.com

| literature parts |

See full listing in **Section One** under **GMC**

Golden Gulf Classics Inc
PO Box 490, 22530 Hwy 49
Saucier, MS 39574
601-831-2650

| repairs restorations |

See full listing in **Section One** under **Triumph**

Golden State Pickup Parts Inc
PO Box 1019
Santa Ynez, CA 93460
800-235-5717; 805-686-2020
FAX: 805-686-2040

| truck parts |

Mail order and open shop. Tuesday-Saturday 10-5. Specializes in 1947-1987 truck parts for Chevy & GMC pickups.
See our ad on this page

Goldfield Trim & Upholstery
1267 160th St
Goldfield, IA 50542
515-254-3322

| top installation upholstery |

See full listing in **Section Two** under **interiors & interior parts**

Great Lakes Auto "N" Truck Restoration
PO Box 251
Mayville, MI 48744
517-683-2614

parts

Specializing in 1955-59 Chevy & GMC trucks & parts, Chevrolet Cameo trucks, NOS, used, reproduction, Cameo, Stepside, Fleetside.

Hagerty Classic Insurance
PO Box 87
Traverse City, MI 49685
800-922-4050; FAX: 616-941-8227

insurance

See full listing in **Section Two** under **insurance**

Hampton Coach
6 Chestnut St
PO Box 6
Amesbury, MA 01950
508-388-8047, 888-388-8726
FAX: 508-388-1113

fabrics
top kits
upholstery kits

Mail order and open shop. Monday-Friday 8:30 to 5. We at Hampton Coach have been proudly manfacturing ready to install interior and top kits since 1977 with a worldwide reputation for exceptional quality and service. We currently have kits available for over 200 Chevrolet & Buick models, handcrafted duplicates of the original designs. Free literature with fabric samples available.

Harbor Auto Restoration
1504 SW 3rd St
Pompano Beach, FL 33069
954-785-7887; FAX: 954-785-7388

restoration

See full listing in **Section Two** under **restoration shops**

Harmon's Inc
Hwy 27 N
PO Box 100C
Geneva, IN 46740
219-368-7221
FAX: 219-368-9396

interiors
parts

We are celebrating our 23rd year of bringing our customers the best service, largest variety, guaranteed quality and the fairest prices on Chevrolet restoration parts. In our 1996 catalog, you will find over 16,000 parts for 1955-72 Chevrolet, 1962-72 Nova, 1964-72 Chevelle, 1970-77 Monte Carlo, 1967-80 Camaro and 1947-80 truck. We also offer a wide assortment of accessories for the Chevy enthusiast including books, posters, paints, models and decals. Simply call or write to above address for a free catalog today! Web site: http://www.fwi.com

Hawthorne Appraisals
Box 1332
Coaldale, AB Canada T1M 1N1
403-345-2101

appraisals
parts

See full listing in **Section Two** under **appraisals**

Heavy Chevy Truck Parts
PO Box 650
17445 Heavy Chevy Rd
Siloam Springs, AR 72761
501-524-9575; FAX: 501-524-4873
or 800-317-2277

parts

Mail order and open shop. Tuesday-Friday 8 to 5:30, closed from noon to 1 pm; Saturday 8 to noon. Complete line of parts for 1947-59 Chevrolet and GMC pickups. Call for your free catalog.

Hein's Classic Cars
422 Douglas
Durham, KS 67438
316-732-3335

restoration

See full listing in **Section One** under **Thunderbird**

Hidden Valley Auto Parts
21046 N Rio Bravo
Maricopa, AZ 85239
602-252-2122, 602-252-6137
520-568-2945 FAX: 602-258-0951

parts

Mail order and open shop. Monday through Saturday 8 to 5. Specializing in classic, antique auto and truck parts, 1940s to 80s, American & foreign.

Historic Video Archives
PO Box 189-VA
Cedar Knolls, NJ 07927-0189

videotapes

See full listing in **Section Two** under **automobilia**

Bruce Horkey Cabinetry
Rt 4, Box 188
Windom, MN 56101
507-831-5625; FAX: 507-831-0280

pickup parts

See full listing in **Section Two** under **woodwork**

HRE Performance Wheels
2540 Pioneer Ave
Vista, CA 92083
619-941-2008; FAX: 619-598-5885

aluminum wheels

See full listing in **Section Two** under **wheels & wheelcovers**

Hubcap Mike 26242 Dimension, Ste 150 Lake Forest, CA 92630 714-597-8120; FAX: 714-597-8123	**hubcaps** **wheelcovers**

See full listing in **Section Two** under **wheels & wheelcovers**

William Hulbert Jr PO Box 151 13683 Rt 11 Adams Center, NY 13606 315-583-5765	**radios**

See full listing in **Section Two** under **radios**

Impala Bob's Inc 9006 E Fannin, Dept HVAA12 Mesa, AZ 85207 602-986-0286; FAX: 602-986-3126 order line: 800-209-0678 toll-free FAX: 800-716-6237	**parts** **restoration**

Everything under the sun for your 1958-76 full size Chevrolet. Moldings, emblems, lenses, interior kits, dash pads, convertible parts, weatherstrips, body repair panels, mechanical parts, pre-bent brake and fuel lines, wiring harnesses, radios, original batteries, engine decals, books, etc. Extensive used parts department offering the best in Arizona rust-free and hard to find parts. Show quality restoration services available. Restoration of aluminum grilles, moldings, chrome bumpers and trim a specialty. Send $6 for fully illustrated catalog. Outside USA, please send $10.

See our ad on page 39

Inline Tube 17540 14 Mile Rd Fraser, MI 48026 810-294-4093; FAX: 810-294-7349 E-mail: inline@apk.net	**brake lines** **choke tubes** **fuel lines** **transmission lines** **vacuum lines**

See full listing in **Section Two** under **brakes**

Instrument Services Inc 11765 Main St Roscoe, IL 61073 800-558-2674; FAX: 800-623-6416	**clocks**

See full listing in **Section Two** under **instruments**

J & K Old Chevy Stuff Ship Pond Rd Plymouth, MA 02360 508-224-7616	**car dealer** **parts** **sheetmetal**

Mail order and open shop. Monday-Sunday 8 am to 7 pm. Sells used rot-free Chevy sheetmetal for 1955-69 Chevys including Novas and Chevelles. Also sells used miscellaneous items for 1955-57s and Chevy II Novas. Also buys and sells 1955-69 Chevy cars.

J&M Auto Parts PO Box 778, Dept H Pelham, NH 03076 603-635-3866	**NOS parts** **repro parts**

Mail order and open shop. Shop open by appointment only. NOS and reproduction parts for 1955-79 Chevrolets, including Impalas, Chevelles, Camaros, Novas and Monte Carlos.

Jackson Speaker Service 217 Crestbrook Dr Jackson, MI 49203 517-789-6400	**radio repairs** **speakers**

See full listing in **Section Two** under **radios**

Jefferis Hot Rod Autobody 4130-C Horizon Ln San Luis Obispo, CA 93401 800-807-1937; FAX: 805-543-4757	**windshield glass kit**

See full listing in **Section Two** under **glass**

Jersey Late Greats Inc PO Box 1294 Hightstown, NJ 08520 609-448-0526	**documentation service** **restoration details**

Maintains extensive database of original 58-64 Chevrolets. The only source to have completely decoded the Fisher Body cowl tags from 15 different assembly plants. Documentation service provides when, where and with what options a car was built. Also can provide restoration details which differ between plants and date of production.

JR's Antique Auto 14900 Scherry Ln Claremore, OK 74017 918-342-4398	**chrome parts** **interiors**

Open 8 to 5 Mon-Fri. Manufacturers of body parts for 1930-70s Chevys & Fords. Custom built street rods 1930-1970 Chevys & Fords. Interiors, chrome parts.

J R's Chevy Parts 478 Moe Rd Clifton Park, NY 12065 518-383-5512; FAX: 518-383-2426 E-mail: jrschev@aol.com	**parts**

Mail order only. We specialize in selling parts for 1965-1979 full-size Chevys: Impalas, Caprices, Super Sports, Bel Airs and Biscaynes. We have thousands of parts for these models, NOS and used. Also have same for Chevelle. Catalogs available, $3 each.

KC Wood Mfg 412 Hillside Dr Greensboro, NC 27401 910-274-5496	**wood kits** **wood replacement**

See full listing in **Section Two** under **woodwork**

Kessler's Antique Cars & **Body Shop** 1616 E Main St Olney, IL 62450 618-393-4346	**parts**

Mail order and open shop. Monday-Friday 8 to 5. 1928-48 Chevrolet reproduction parts. Some NOS parts. Please call before you come, we travel a lot to swap meets and we're not always there.

King & Queen Mufflers Box 423 Plumsteadville, PA 18949 PH/FAX: 215-766-8699	**exhaust systems**

See full listing in **Section Two** under **exhaust systems**

King's Bumper Co Inc 1 Ontario Ave New Hartford, NY 13413 315-732-8988; FAX: 315-732-2602	**chrome plating**

See full listing in **Section Two** under **plating & polishing**

Al Knoch Interiors 130 Montoya Rd El Paso, TX 79932 800-880-8080; FAX: 915-581-1545	**carpets interiors tooling services tops**

Mail order and open shop. Monday-Friday 8-5 MST. Specializes in seat covers, carpet, door panels, convertible tops, interiors for Chevrolet Corvette, Camaro and Pontiac Firebird. Manufacturers of original quality interiors, tooling services, dielectric, vacuum forming and foam molding.

Rudy R Koch PO Box 291 Chester Heights, PA 19017 PH/FAX: 610-459-8721	**manuals**

Mail order only. For Chevrolets and Corvettes, Camaros, Chevelles and Monte Carlos. New and original manuals from 1960s. Send SASE for information, state year of manual desired.

Late Great Chevrolet Association 2166 S Orange Blossom Trail Apopka, FL 32703 407-886-1963; FAX: 407-886-7571	**magazine**

See full listing in **Section Four** under **periodicals**

Lee's Classic Chevy Sales 314A Main St Glenbeulah, WI 53023 414-526-3411, 9 am-4 pm Wed-Sat	**accessories literature parts**

Mail order and open shop. Wed-Saturday 9 am to 4 pm. We have operated this business in the same location for 24 years. We take great pride in selling only quality parts that are guaranteed correct with customers all over the world. Parts, accessories and literature for 1955-1956-1957 Chevrolets (all models).

LES Auto Parts PO Box 81 Dayton, NJ 08810 908-329-6128	**parts**

Mail order and open shop. Monday to Saturday 8-5 pm. Specializing in NOS GM parts for Chevrolet Impala, Chevelle, Nova, Camaro, all Pontiacs & Olds & Buick. All car parts 50 to 85.

Lloyd's Literature PO Box 491 Newbury, OH 44065 800-292-2665	**literature**

See full listing in **Section Two** under **literature dealers**

LMC Truck PO Box 14991 Lenexa, KS 66285 800-222-5664; FAX: 913-599-0323	**accessories parts**

Mail order catalog. Monday-Friday 7 to 9, Saturday-Sunday 9 to 5. Restore or repair your 1/2 or 3/4 ton Chevy truck 1947-1987. Our easy to read, fully illustrated free catalogs, fast service and an on-line computer order system make ordering easy. Large supply of parts & accessories include bed kits, body, interior, engine, heating & cooling, suspension, brakes, electrical, and much more.

See our ad on this page

Lord Byron Inc 420 Sackett Point Rd North Haven, CT 06473 203-287-9881; FAX: 203-230-9633	**fender covers**

See full listing in **Section Two** under **car covers**

M & H Electric Fabricators Inc 13537 Alondra Blvd Santa Fe Springs, CA 90670 310-926-9552; FAX: 310-926-9572	**wiring harnesses**

See full listing in **Section Two** under **electrical systems**

Mack Products Box 856 Moberly, MO 65270 816-263-7444	**parts pickup beds**

See full listing in **Section One** under **Ford '32-'53**

Majestic Truck Parts 17726 Dickerson Dallas, TX 75252 214-248-6245	**parts**

Mail order and open shop. Open 365 days a year by appointment. Specializing in 1947-1972 truck parts, new and used for Chev and GMC 1/2, 3/4 and 1 ton pickups, panels, Suburbans, Canopy Express (all truck chassis vehicles).

Manes Truck Parts 9904 E 63rd Terr Raytown, MO 64133 816-358-6745	**parts**

New and used restoration parts with years of technical knowledge. 1967-1972 Chevrolet and GMC trucks.

Marcovicci-Wenz Engineering Inc 33 Comac Loop Ronkonkoma, NY 11779 516-467-9040; FAX: 516-467-9041	**engine parts services**

See full listing in **Section Two** under **racing**

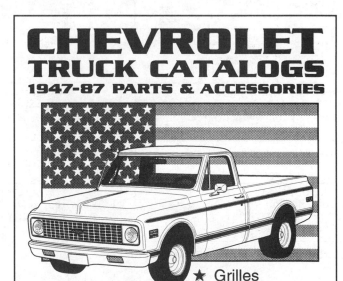

Martz Classic Chevy Parts | parts
RD 1, Box 199B
Thomasville, PA 17364
717-225-1655; FAX: 717-225-3637

Mail order and open shop. Monday-Friday 8 am-5 pm. Specializing in sales of NOS & reproduction parts for 1955-70 full-size Chevrolets, 1962-74 Novas, 1967-81 Camaros & 1964-72 Chevelles.

Master Power Brakes | brake products conversion kits
254-1 Rolling Hills Rd
Mooresville, NC 28115
704-664-8866; FAX: 704-664-8862

See full listing in **Section One** under **Chevelle/Camaro**

Max Neon Design Group | custom face logos neon clocks
19807 Sussex Dr
St Clair Shores, MI 48081-3257
810-773-5000; FAX: 810-772-6224

See full listing in **Section Two** under **automobilia**

Maximliner Inc | cargo mats floor mats
150 E Race St
Troy, OH 45373
513-339-0240; 800-624-2320
FAX: 513-335-5424

See full listing in **Section Two** under **carpets**

James McConville Vintage Chevy Parts | front mats runningboard mats
4205 W 129th St, #22
Hawthorne, CA 90250
310-675-8877 9 am to noon PST

Mail order. 1928-39 Chevy runningboard mats and front mats. SASE for catalog.

McCoy's Memorabilia | memorabilia racing literature
35583 N 1830 E
Rossville, IL 60963-7175
217-748-6513

See full listing in **Section Two** under **literature dealers**

Charlie Merrill | broker car dealer car locator
1041 Kenyon Rd
Twin Falls, ID 83301
208-736-0949

See full listing in **Section Two** under **brokers**

Merv's Classic Chevy Parts | parts
1330 Washington
Iowa Falls, IA 50126
515-648-3168

Mail order and open shop. Specializing in reproduction, NOS & used parts for 55-57 Chevy & 67-72 Chevy pickups

Metro Authentic Finishes | paint
2576B West Point Ave
College Park, GA 30337
404-767-3378

See full listing in **Section One** under **Corvette**

Mid-America Auction Services | auctions
2277 W Hwy 36, Ste 214
St Paul, MN 55113
612-633-9655; FAX: 612-633-3212
E-mail: midauction@aol.com

See full listing in **Section Two** under **auctions & events**

Mike's Chevy Parts | restoration supplies
7716 Deering Ave
Canoga Park, CA 91304
818-346-0070; FAX: 818-713-0715

Mail order and open shop. Monday-Friday 8 to 5; Saturday 9 to 12. Specializing in new, used and reproduction parts for 1955-70 Chevrolets, 1964-72 Chevelles and El Caminos, 1962-74 Novas. Complete frame straightening and front end repair. Antique auto parts and supplies.

Milestone Motorcars | die cast cars models
Mark Tyra
12910 Sunnybrook Dr
Prospect, KY 40059
502-228-5945; FAX: 502-228-1856

See full listing in **Section Two** under **automobilia**

Mike Moran | information
1349 Cleveland Rd
Glendale, CA 91202

Mail order only. Technical information on Vegas, including Cosworth, also Mobil Gas economy runs, gasoline economy devices and unusual engines. SASE required.

Muscle "N" More GM Options & Accessories | accessories factory-installed options
1055 S Pacific Hiwy
Woodburn, OR 97071
503-981-4448

Mail order only. Dealer and factory installed GM options, used and NOS when available. Serving the auto enthusiast with the obsolete hard-to-find parts.

National Chevy Assoc | parts
947 Arcade Street
St Paul, MN 55106
612-778-9522; FAX: 612-778-9686

Mail order and open shop. Monday-Friday 8:30 to 5. Specializing in new, used, NOS parts for 1953-54 Chevrolet. You need our catalog! Catalog and sample newsletter, $5.

National Drivetrain Inc | differential parts transmission parts
3125 S Ashland Ave #201
Chicago, IL 60608
800-507-4327; FAX: 312-376-9135

See full listing in **Section Two** under **transmissions**

New England Mustang Supply Inc | parts accessories
1830 Barnum Ave
Bridgeport, CT 06610
203-333-7454; FAX: 203-332-0880

See full listing in **Section One** under **Mustang**

Charles Noe | broker parts/auto purchases parts/auto sales
64 1/2 Greenwood Ave
Bethel, CT 06801
203-748-4222

See full listing in **Section Two** under **brokers**

Norman's Classic Auto Radio
7651 Park Blvd
Pinellas Park, FL 33781
813-546-1788

custom sales
radio repairs

See full listing in **Section Two** under **radios**

North Yale Auto Parts
Rt 1, Box 707
Sperry, OK 74073
918-288-7218, 800-256-6927 (NYAP)
FAX: 918-288-7223

salvage yard

See full listing in **Section Five** under **Oklahoma**

NOS Reproductions
22425 Sefferlies Rd
RR 3
Komoka, ON Canada N0L 1R0
519-471-2740; FAX: 519-471-7675

parts

See full listing in **Section One** under **MoPar**

Oak Bows
122 Ramsey Ave
Chambersburg, PA 17201
717-264-2602

top bows

See full listing in **Section Two** under **woodwork**

Obsolete Chevrolet Parts Co
524 Hazel Ave
PO Box 68
Nashville, GA 31639
912-686-5812

engine parts
radiators
rubber parts
transmissions

Mail order and open shop. Monday-Friday 8 to 5:30; and
Saturday 8:30 to 12:30. We buy and sell NOS and reproduction
parts for 1929-72 Chevrolet cars and trucks. Large inventory of
mechanical, electrical, weatherstripping, sheetmetal, chrome
and interior parts. We accept MasterCard, VISA, Discover or
COD via UPS. We also accept orders by FAX: 912/686-3056.
Catalogs by mail order only, $2.50 each: 1929-54 car, 1955-57
car, 1958-70 car, 1962-72 Chevelle, Chevy II and Camaro, 1929-
59 truck, 1960-72 truck.

See our ad on this page

OEM Glass Inc
PO Box 362, Rt 9 E
Bloomington, IL 61702
309-662-2122; FAX: 309-663-7474

auto glass

See full listing in **Section Two** under **glass**

**Ol' 55 Chevy Parts/
East Coast Chevy Inc**
4154A Skyron Dr
Doylestown, PA 18901
215-348-5568; FAX: 215-348-0560

custom work
parts
restoration

Mail order and open shop. Monday-Friday 9 to 5; Saturday 9-12
(call first for Saturday). Complete inventory, new, used and
reproduction parts (55-57 our specialty). Also restoration services. For 1955-57 Chevrolets. Now stocking 1958-70. Personal
service.

Old Air Products
3056 SE Loop 820
Ft Worth, TX 76140
817-551-0602; FAX: 817-568-0037

air conditioning

See full listing in **Section One** under **Corvette**

The Old Car Centre
19909 92A Ave
Langley, BC Canada V1M 3B6
604-888-4412, 604-888-4055
FAX: 604-888-7455

parts

See full listing in **Section One** under **Ford '03-'31**

Old Car Parts
109 N 15th St, Box 184
Clear Lake, IA 50428
515-357-5510; FAX: 515-357-3550

parts

Mail order and open shop. Monday-Friday 9 to 5. Basically a
Chevrolet parts house. Mostly mail and phone orders. We handle
NOS and reproduction parts for 1940-54 Chevrolet passenger
car.

Old Car Parts
7525 SE Powell
Portland, OR 97206
503-771-9416; 800-886-7277
FAX: 503-771-1981
E-mail: gsnovak@europa.com

parts

Mail order and open shop. Monday-Friday 9-5. Specializing in
GM parts for Chevrolet cars and pickups 1936-69.

The Old Carb Doctor
Rt 3, Box 338
Drucilla Church Rd
Nebo, NC 28761
800-945-CARB (2272)
704-659-1428

carburetors
fuel pumps

See full listing in **Section Two** under **carburetors**

Old Dominion Mustang | parts
509 S Washington Hwy, Rt 1
Ashland, VA 23005
804-798-3348; FAX: 804-798-5105

See full listing in **Section One** under **Mustang**

Old Tin Australia | salvage yard
PO Box 26
Wendouree, Victoria 3355 Australia
0353-36-1929; FAX: 0353-36-2930

See full listing in **Section Five** under **Australia**

Only Yesterday Classic Autos Inc | cars
19 Valley Rd
Port Washington, NY 11050
516-767-3477; FAX: 212-953-2187

Classic and special interest autos from the 1950s through 1960s. We specialize in Chevys, Corvettes, Fords and Pontiacs. Tell us your interest and we will help you locate what you are looking for.

Original Auto Interiors | upholstery
7869 Trumble Rd
Columbus, MI 48063-3915
810-727-2486; FAX: 810-727-4344
E-mail: knight@mich.com

See full listing in **Section Two** under **upholstery**

Packard Farm | parts
97 N 150 W
Greenfield, IN 46140
317-462-3124, 800-922-1957 orders only; FAX: 317-462-8891

See full listing in **Section One** under **Packard**

The Paddock® Inc | accessories parts
PO Box 30
221 W Main
Knightstown, IN 46148
800-428-4319; FAX: 317-345-2264
E-mail: paddock@indy.net

See full listing in **Section One** under **Mustang**

Paddock West® Inc | accessories parts
1663 Plum Ln
PO Box 8547
Redlands, CA 92375
800-854-8532; FAX: 909-798-1482
E-mail: padwest@msn.com

See full listing in **Section One** under **Mustang**

Palm Springs Obsolete Automotive | parts
653 N Commerical Rd, Unit 10
Palm Springs, CA 92262
619-323-6998; FAX: 619-320-1574

See full listing in **Section One** under **Chevelle/Camaro**

M Parker Autoworks Inc | battery cables harnesses
150 Cooper Rd, Unit C-7
Dept HVAA
West Berlin, NJ 08091
609-753-0350; FAX: 609-753-0353

See full listing in **Section Two** under **electrical systems**

Parts Unlimited Inc | interiors weatherstrips
Todd Bidwell
12101 Westport Rd
Louisville, KY 40245-1789
502-425-3766; FAX: 502-425-0055

Manufacturer of quality interior components for many 1955-81 GM cars and trucks including seat covers, door panels (standard, pre-assembled), headliners, sunvisors, top boots, Windowfelt® brand replacement weatherstrips, package trays/insulation, trunk dividers, arm rest bases/pads, assorted trim products, etc. Also: Chrysler seat upholstery, headliners, Windowfelt®; 1964-73 Ford Mustang Windowfelt®, door panels. All quality products made in USA. Established 1975. Over 500 dealers. Call 800-342-0610 for the dealer nearest you.

Paso Robles Auto Wrecking | salvage yard
5755 Monterey Rd
Paso Robles, CA 93446
800-549-3738; 805-238-3738
805-238-3764

See full listing in **Section Five** under **California**

Passenger Car Supply | parts
102 Cloverdale Rd
Swedesboro, NJ 08085
609-467-7966

Both mail order and open shop. Monday-Friday 10-10, weekends by chance/appt. Full size Chevy resto parts for 1958-75 full size Chevrolet, NOS, used, new and repro, all items.

Patrick's Antique Cars & Trucks | parts
PO Box 10648
Casa Grande, AZ 85230
520-836-1117; FAX: 520-836-1104

Mail order and open shop. Open 7 days a week. Complete engine rebuild parts and speed equipment for 37-62 Chevy/GMC 6s and flathead Ford/Merc V8 32-53. Free catalog (specify Chevy or Ford, please). VISA, MC, COD orders welcome.

PC Automotive Calendars | calendars
PO Box 2002
Madison, WI 53701
608-829-1234

See full listing in **Section Two** under **special services**

Pick-ups Northwest | parts trim
7130 Bickford Ave
Snohomish, WA 98290
360-568-9166; FAX: 360-568-1233

Mail order and open shop. Monday-Friday 9 to 5:30, Saturday 9 to 3. Specializing in weatherstrip, interior, chrome trim, pickup box parts and wood kits for 32-72 Chevy and 32-73 Ford pickup trucks. Restoration or street rod parts.

John E Pirkle | electrical parts
3706 Merion Dr
Augusta, GA 30907
706-860-9047

See full listing in **Section One** under **Corvette**

Jack Podell Fuel Injection Spec	fuel system parts
106 Wakcwa Avc	fuel system rcbuilding
South Bend, IN 46617	
219-232-6430; FAX: 219-234-8632	

See full listing in **Section One** under **Corvette**

Dennis Portka	horns
4326 Beetow Dr	
Hamburg, NY 14075	
716-649-0921	

See full listing in **Section One** under **Corvette**

Power Brake Booster Exchange Inc	brake boosters
4533 SE Division St	
Portland, OR 97206	
503-238-8882	

See full listing in **Section Two** under **brakes**

Precision Pot Metal/	pot metal restoration
Bussie Restoration Inc	
1008 Loring Ave #28	
Orange Park, FL 32073	
904-269-8788	

See full listing in **Section Two** under **plating & polishing**

PRO Antique Auto Parts	parts
50 King Spring Rd	
Windsor Locks, CT 06096	
860-623-8274	

Mail order and open shop. Shop open Monday-Friday 9 to 5. Exclusive distributor of numerous reproduction parts for 1923-1964 Chevrolets. Catalog $3.

R & R Fiberglass & Specialties	body parts
4850 Wilson Dr NW	
Cleveland, TN 37312	
423-476-2270	

See full listing in **Section Two** under **fiberglass parts**

Red Bird Racing	parts
5621 NE Issler St	
Vancouver, WA 98661	
360-694-9929	

Mail order only. Specializing in 1941-48 Chevy chassis update parts. Bolt on Saginaw steering adapters, dropped spindles, Teflon button rear spring kits, f&r tube shock mounting kits, lowering block kits. All Chevy 6-cyl split manifolds, 216-235-261 alternator brackets. GMC & Chevy 6-cyl to Turbo 350-400 kits. Inline and flathead V8 speed parts, Fenton headers, Edmunds style air cleaners.

Reproduction Parts Marketing	parts
#3-1707 Sask Ave	restoration
Saskatoon, SK Canada S7K 1P7	service
306-652-6668; FAX: 306-652-1123	

Mail order and open shop. Monday-Saturday 8-9. Canada's largest stocking GM, Ford and MoPar dealer. All parts are guaranteed to be the finest available and our prices are the lowest. Also handling complete restorations. Parts, service, tech advice, appraisals, locator service.

Restoration Specialties	interiors
John Sarena	restoration
124 North F St	
Lompoc, CA 93436	
805-736-2627	

Open shop only. Monday-Friday 8 am to 5 pm PST. Partial to 1955-57 Chevrolets and one of the authors of the CCCI Restoration & Judging Guidelines Manual. Shares the love of all special interest cars of the 1940s through 1960s and worked with Moss Motors for nine years in designing all of their interior kits. Takes great pride in craftsmanship and it shows in finished interiors. Dealer for CARS reproduction interiors. Specializing in interior restoration, partial restoration for 1955-57 Chevys, American cars of the 1950s and 60s, and English sports cars.

Frank Riley Automotive Art	automotive prints
PO Box 95	
Hawthorne, NJ 07506	
800-848-9459	

See full listing in **Section Two** under **artwork**

Leon J Rocco	accessories
4125 Oak St	parts
Butler, PA 16001	
412-482-4387 after 6 pm	

See full listing in **Section One** under **Chevelle/Camaro**

Rock Valley Antique Auto Parts	gas tanks
Box 352	
Rt 72 and Rothwell Rd	
Stillman Valley, IL 61084	
815-645-2271; FAX: 815-645-2740	

See full listing in **Section One** under **Ford '32-'53**

Rod-1 Shop	street rods
210 Clinton Ave	
Pitman, NJ 08071	
609-228-7631; FAX: 609-582-5770	

See full listing in **Section Two** under **street rods**

Ross' Automotive Machine Co Inc	racing engines
1763 N Main St	rebuilding
Niles, OH 44446	
330-544-4466	

See full listing in **Section Two** under **engine rebuilding**

Saturn Industries	axles
143 Wimborne Rd	instruments
Poole, Dorset BH15 2BCR England	literature
01202-674982; FAX: 01202-668274	repro parts

See full listing in **Section One** under **Ford '03-'31**

SC Automotive	parts
Rt 3 Box 9	restoration
New Ulm, MN 56073	
507-354-1958; FAX: 800-6477-FAX	

1-800-62-SS-409 348-409 parts. Free catalog listing thousands of parts for your 58-64 Chevrolet. Fuel lines, radiators, air cleaners, pistons, valves, rebuild kits, exhaust, decals, moldings/emblems, electrical, accessories, shop and assembly manuals and more. Simply the best. Show Cars, Automotive Inc, Rt 3, Box 09, New Ulm, MN 56073. Information 507-354-1958, FAX: 80064-SS-FAX (77-329). Credit card and CODs accepted.

Chuck Scharf Enterprises — parts
813 S Valley
New Ulm, MN 56073
507-354-4501; FAX: 507-354-4409

Mail order only. Specializing in 348/409 equipped 1958-65 full size Chevrolets. We offer a full line of engine rebuild parts, 8 different engine kits, 348/409 pistons, +.030, +.040, +.060, specially produced 4 core radiators for 348/409 applications, pulleys, fuel lines, detailing items, much more. One call does it all, same day shipping. VISA, M/C, COD orders welcome. Free rebuild catalog.

Scotts Super Trucks — parts
Box 6772
1040 Emma St
Penhold, AB Canada T0M 1R0
403-886-5572; FAX: 403-886-5577

Mail order and open shop. Tuesday-Saturday 10 to 5 MST. We specialize in 67-72 GMC/Chev trucks, but also carry a full line of new & used parts from 1934 to 66 original and custom parts. Everything to restore your classic truck. Also many project trucks for sale, 1935-1972.

Lyn Smith Nova Parts — car dealer / parts
1104 Countryside Ln
Pontiac, IL 61764
815-844-7852

Mail order and open shop. Shop open by appointment only. Specializing in 1962-67 Chevy Nova parts. Have new, used and reproduction items. Also buys and sells Nova cars. Specializing in V8 kits, stick shift set-ups and radiators. Buy, sell, trade Nova parts.

O B Smith Chevy Parts — parts / tires
PO Box 11703
990 New Circle Rd NW
Lexington, KY 40577
606-253-1957; FAX: 606-233-3129

Restoration parts for 55-57 classic Chevrolets and 47-72 Chevrolet pickups. Catalogs, $3 each.

Bob Sottile's Hobby Car — car dealer / restoration
Auto Sales Inc
RD 2, Box 210B, Rt 164
Martinsburg, PA 16662
814-793-4282

See full listing in **Section One** under **Corvette**

Southern US Car Export Inc — repair / restoration / sales / transport
135 Eulon Loop
Raeford, NC 28376
910-875-7534; FAX: 910-875-7731

See full listing in **Section One** under **Cadillac/LaSalle**

Spark Plugs & Stuff — tune-up kits
PO Box 33343
San Diego, CA 92163-3343
619-220-1745

See full listing in **Section Two** under **ignition parts**

Stoudt Auto Sales — parts / sales / service
1350 Carbon St
Reading, PA 19601
800-523-8485 parts orders
610-374-4856 parts; 800-482-3033 sales; 610-375-8595 sales and service; FAX: 610-372-7283

See full listing in **Section One** under **Corvette**

Street-Wise Performance — differentials / parts / rebuild kits / transmissions
Richie Mulligan
105 Creek Rd
Tranquility, NJ 07879
201-786-6668 days
201-786-7133 evenings

See full listing in **Section Two** under **transmissions**

Super Sport Restoration Parts Inc — NOS parts / used parts
7138 Maddox Rd
Lithonia, GA 30058
770-482-9219

Mail order and counter sales. Monday-Friday, 9-6; Saturday, 9-2. Retailer of new, NOS, used & reproduction parts. Parts for 62-75 Chevy II/Nova, 60-75 Impala, 64-75 Chevelle/El Camino, 67-81 Camaro.

Sutton Auto Sounds — radios
3463 Rolling Trail
Palm Harbor, FL 34684-3526
813-787-2717; FAX: 813-789-9215
E-mail: suttonauto@aol.com

See full listing in **Section Two** under **radios**

Bill Thomsen — salvage yard
Rt 4 Box 492
Moneta, VA 24121
540-297-1200

See full listing in **Section Five** under **Virginia**

Tom's Classic Parts — parts
5207 Sundew Terr
Tobyhanna, PA 18466
800-832-4073

Mail order only. NOS and quality used parts for all GM cars, 1960s to present. Parts locating service used.

Tom's Obsolete Chevy Parts — parts
14 Delta Dr
Pawtucket, RI 02860
401-723-7580; FAX: 401-724-7568

Mail order and auto swap meets. New and reproduction 1955-72 Chevrolet parts. Nova, Impala, Chevelle, Camaro. Showroom hours, 1 to 9 pm weekdays, 1 to 5 pm Saturdays.

Top Flite International Inc — fiberglass hardtops
PO Box 505
Winfield, TN 37892
423-569-2460; FAX: 423-569-2525

See full listing in **Section One** under **Chrysler**

Trim Parts Inc — trim items
5161 Wolfpen Pleasant Hill
Milford, OH 45150
513-831-1472; FAX: 513-248-3402

Mail order and open shop. Monday-Friday 8 am- 5pm. Classic GM restoration, reproduction emblems, lenses, scripts & other trim items for classic GM cars and trucks. 55-57 Chevy, 58-72 full size, 67-85 Camaro, 53-82 Corvette, 64-72 Chevelle, 67-69 Firebird, 62-72 Nova, 64-72 El Camino, 70-72 Monte Carlo, GTO, Corvair.

The Truck Shop   parts
PO Box 5035
104 W Marion Ave
Nashville, GA 31639
912-686-3833 info; 912-686-3396
info; 800-245-0556 orders
FAX: 912-686-3531

Mail order and open shop. Mon-Fri, 8 to 5. Chevrolet and GMC truck parts. NOS and reproduction 1927-87. Bed components, weatherstrips, glass channel, hubcaps, handles and controls, headliners, interior parts, emblems and moldings, manuals, mirrors, patch panels, lights, suspension, carpets, mats and much more. Catalog $5.

Ultra Wheel Co   custom wheels
6300 Valley View Ave
Buena Park, CA 90620
714-994-1444; FAX: 714-994-0723

See full listing in **Section Two** under **wheels & wheelcovers**

Unfair Advantage Enterprises   emblems
2219 W Olive Ave #179   trim
Burbank, CA 91506
213-245-8441

See full listing in **Section One** under **Cobra**

Universal Transmission Co   transmission parts
23361 Dequindre Rd
Hazel Park, MI 48030
800-882-4327; FAX: 810-398-2581

See full listing in **Section Two** under **transmissions**

Tom Vagnini   used parts
58 Anthony Rd
RR 3
Pittsfield, MA 01201
413-698-2526

See full listing in **Section One** under **Packard**

Valley Motor Supply   accessories
1402 E Second St   parts
Roswell, NM 88201
505-622-7450

See full listing in **Section One** under **Ford '54-up**

Varco Inc   fitted luggage
8200 S Anderson Rd   trunks
Oklahoma City, OK 73150
405-732-1637

See full listing in **Section One** under **Ford '03-'31**

Vibratech Inc (Fluidampr)   performance parts
11980 Walden Ave
Alden, NY 14004
716-937-3603; FAX: 716-937-4692

See full listing in **Section Two** under **engine parts**

Vintage Books   books
6613 E Mill Plain   literature
Vancouver, WA 98661
360-694-9519; FAX: 360-694-7644
E-mail: vintageb@teleport.com

See full listing in **Section Two** under **literature dealers**

Vintage Ford & Chevrolet Parts of Arizona Inc   parts
3427 E McDowell Rd
Phoenix, AZ 85008
602-275-7990; FAX: 602-267-8439

See full listing in **Section One** under **Ford '54-up**

Vintage Parts 411   books
PO Box 22893
San Diego, CA 92192
800-MOTORHEAD
FAX: 619-560-9900
E-mail: vp411@electriciti.com

See full listing in **Section Four** under **information sources**

Volunteer State Chevy Parts   accessories
Hwy 41 S   parts
Greenbrier, TN 37073
615-643-4583; FAX: 615-643-5100

Mail order and open shop. Monday-Friday (Sat?) 8 am to 6 pm CST. Specializing in obsolete parts and accessories from 1949-72 passenger cars and trucks, includes Chevelle, Chevy II, Camaro, with special emphasis on 1955-67 Impalas, etc.

Waldron's Antique Exhaust Inc   exhaust systems
PO Box C 25872 M-86
Nottawa, MI 49075
616-467-7185; FAX: 616-467-9041

See full listing in **Section Two** under **exhaust systems**

Wale's Antique Chevy Truck Parts   parts
143 Center
Carleton, MI 48117
313-654-8836

Specializing in 1936-72 Chevrolet trucks. Windshield, cab, door & hood rubber. Seals, weatherstrip, headlights, parking lights, taillights. Parts, brackets, outside & inside handles. Bed wood, tailgates, front & side panels. Wear strips, angles, repair panels. Books, manuals. Engine & mechanical parts, fiberglass fenders & runningboards. Hubcaps, trim rings, runningboard step plates. Also rebuilds door handles & refaces & rebuilds gauges. Used parts for 1947-1955 Chevrolet trucks. Send two 32¢ stamps for free catalog, state year of truck.

Weld-N-Fab Performance   gas pumps
PO Box 356   machine work
Norwalk, IA 50211   tractors
515-981-4928

See full listing in **Section One** under **Anglia**

Wheel Vintiques Inc   hubcaps
5468 E Lamona Ave   wheels
Fresno, CA 93727
209-251-6957; FAX: 209-251-1620

Mail order only. Specializing in wheels and hubcaps for 67-82 Corvette, 67-70 Camaro, 65-73 Mustang, all Chevrolet passenger cars 49 and up. All makes and models of street rods.

Ted Williams Enterprises   parts
5615 Rt 45
Lisbon, OH 44432
330-424-9413; FAX: 330-424-9060

Mail order and open shop. Monday 9-8; Tuesday to Friday 9 to 5; Saturday 9 to 2. Call first. NOS and reproduction parts for 1964-72 Chevelles and El Caminos, 1962-72 Nova & Chevy II. Retail and wholesale, mostly mail order, pick up at warehouse available. No show room. COD available. Accepts VISA and MC. UPS daily. Orders shipped same or next business day. In business since 1975.

Willow Grove Auto Top
43 N York Rd
Willow Grove, PA 19090
215-659-3276

| interiors |
| tops |
| upholstery |

See full listing in **Section Two** under **interiors & interior parts**

Wolf Automotive
201 N Sullivan
Santa Ana, CA 92703
800-444-9653, 714-835-2126
FAX: 714-835-9653

| car covers |
| consoles |
| steering wheels |
| tire covers |

Open shop only Monday-Friday 8 to 5. Deals in car covers, nose masks, consoles, steering wheels, shift knobs, tonneau covers, sun tops, cargo covers, tailgate nets, tire covers, for both cars and trucks.

Woodgrain by Estes
7550 Richardson Rd
Sarasota, FL 34240
813-379-3669

| woodgraining |

See full listing in **Section Two** under **woodgraining**

The Woodie Works
Box 346, RR 3
Arlington, VT 05250
802-375-9305

| woodworking |

See full listing in **Section Two** under **woodwork**

Year One Inc
PO Box 129
Tucker, GA 30085
800-YEAR-ONE (932-7663)
770-493-6568 Atlanta & overseas
FAX: 800-680-6806
FAX: 770-496-1949 Atlanta/overseas

| parts |

See full listing in **Section Two** under **comprehensive parts**

CHEVELLE camaro

4-Speeds by Darrell
PO Box 110
#3 Water St
Vermilion, IL 61955
217-275-3743; FAX: 217-275-3515

| transmissions |

See full listing in **Section Two** under **transmissions**

All Chevy/Canadian
404 Allwood Rd
Parksville, BC Canada V9P 1C4
PH/FAX: 604-248-8666

| parts |

See full listing in **Section One** under **Chevrolet**

American Classics Unlimited Inc
Frank Groll-Karen Groll
PO Box 192
Oak Lawn, IL 60454-0192
PH/FAX: 708-424-9223

| automobilia |
| models & toys |
| novelty license plates |
| sales literature |

See full listing in **Section Two** under **models & toys**

American Restorations Unlimited TA
14 Meakin Ave
PO Box 34
Rochelle Park, NJ 07662
201-843-3567; FAX: 201-843-3238
E-mail: amerrest@aol.com

| restoration parts |

See full listing in **Section Two** under **glass**

Auto Custom Carpet
Jeff Moses
PO Box 1350, 1429 Noble St
Anniston, AL 36202
800-633-2358; 205-236-1118
FAX: 800-516-8274

| carpets |
| floor coverings |

See full listing in **Section One** under **Chevrolet**

Auto Decals Unlimited Inc
11259 E Via Linda, Ste 100-201
Scottsdale, AZ 85259
602-860-9800; FAX: 602-860-8370

| decals |
| stripe kits |

See full listing in **Section Two** under **decals**

Benfield's Auto Body
213 Trent St
Kernersville, NC 27284
PH/FAX: 910-993-5772

| body repair |
| paint |

See full listing in **Section Two** under **painting**

Boyds Hot Rods & Collectable Cars
10971 Dale St
Stanton, CA 90680
714-220-9870; FAX: 714-220-9877

| car dealer |

See full listing in **Section One** under **Chevrolet**

Camaro-Heaven
64 River Street
Rochester, NH 03867
800-CAMARO-1; FAX: 603-332-3299

| cars |
| parts |
| salvage yard |

Mail order and open shop. Monday-Friday 9-5, Saturday 9-2. 1967-1997 Camaros & Firebirds parts and cars, new and used.

Camaro Specialties
112 Elm St
East Aurora, NY 14052
716-652-7086; FAX: 716-652-2279

| parts |
| restoration |

Specializing in 66-72 GM muscle cars. We offer new, used, reproduction and southern parts. Now booking restorations for 67-69 Camaros or Firebirds.

CARS Inc
1964 W 11 Mile Rd
Berkley, MI 48072
810-398-7100; 810-398-7078

| interior |

See full listing in **Section One** under **Chevrolet**

Chevy Parts Warehouse
13545 Sycamore Ave
San Martin, CA 95046
408-683-2438; FAX: 408-683-2533

| parts |

See full listing in **Section One** under **Chevrolet**

Ciadella Enterprises
3116 S 52nd St
Tempe, AZ 85282-3212
602-968-4179; FAX: 602-470-0499

| interiors |

See full listing in **Section One** under **Chevrolet**

SAVE $32⁴⁵ A YEAR

AND HAVE HEMMINGS HOME DELIVERED

☞ **97.37% pure collector car advertising** from hobbyists in all 50 states and beyond.

☞ **Averaging over 800 pages per issue** – the world's largest collector-car marketplace.

☞ **The best, most convenient way** to find old cars, body & engine parts, running gear, restoration supplies & services, tools, literature, clubs, rallies, and shows.

Mail your order card today!

Join the hobby – subscribe today!

☑ **YES**, send the next 12 giant issues (one year) of *Hemmings Motor News* for only $26.95 (USA) – save $32.45 off the cover price.

❑ Payment enclosed. ❑ Bill me. (U.S.A. subscriptions only)

Name _____

Address _____

City _____ State _____ Zip _____

Satisfaction guaranteed or your money back on unmailed issues. Allow 4-6 weeks for first issue by 4th class mail. Vermont residents add 5% sales tax. Foreign and Canadian subscriptions must be pre-paid, please call for rates. Prices subject to change.

I04523

Call ext. 550 at 1-800-CAR-HERE (toll-free)
or 802-447-9550, to use your MasterCard, VISA, Discover, or American Express.

Gift Subscriptions $26^{95} U.S.A.

Give gift subscriptions to your collector-car friends, relatives and co-workers.

Order Today!

To use MC/VISA/Discover/AmEx call ext. 550 at 1-800-CAR-HERE (toll-free) or 802-447-9550.

Subscribe and Save!

Classic Industries Inc
Camaro Parts and Accessories
Catalog
17832 Gothard St
Huntington Beach, CA 92647
800-854-1280 toll-free in USA
FAX: 800-300-3081 toll-free

accessories
parts

Camaro parts & accessories catalog. Full color catalog with over 500 pages of origianl and reproduction restoration products and accessories, containing the largest selection of early and late model Camaro parts ever assembled. Classic Industries is an official GM Restoration Parts licensee assuring the highest quality parts for your year and model. Whether you're restoring a 1967 Super Sport Camaro or looking for ground effects and high-performance products for your 1996 Z-28. This catalog is sure to have what you need, cost, $5. Call or write for your personal copy today.

See our ad inside the front cover

Clock Doc®
125 University Ave
Sewanee, TN 37375
800-256-5362; FAX: 615-598-5986

clock repairs
gauge repairs

See full listing in **Section Two** under **instruments**

Coach Builders Muscle Car Parts & Services
PO Box 128
Baltimore, MD 21087-0128
410-426-5567

interiors
parts
rust remover

See full listing in **Section One** under **Chevrolet**

Competitive Automotive Inc
2095 W Shore Rd (Rt 117)
Warwick, RI 02886
401-739-6262, 739-6288
FAX: 401-739-1497

parts
restoration

Mail order and showroom. Monday-Friday, 11 am-8 pm. Gm restoration supplies. Specializing in complete line of 1967-1981 Camaro and Firebird restoration supplies and parts. New, used, reproduction and obscure parts including body panels, trim, mechanical, suspensions, wiring, interior and upholstery, weatherstripping, lenses, convertibles, windows, literature, decals, fasteners, switches, bumpers, braces, grilles, manuals, emblems, headliners, etc.

Conte's Corvettes & Classics
851 W Wheat Rd
Vineland, NJ 08360
609-692-0087; FAX: 609-692-1009
E-mail: contes@cybernet.net

leasing
parts
sales
service

See full listing in **Section One** under **Corvette**

Don Cressman
495 Louise Ave N
Listowel, ON Canada N4W 3N5
519-291-1600; FAX: 519-291-1763

parts

See full listing in **Section One** under **Chevrolet**

Custom Autosound Mfg
808 W Vermont Ave
Anaheim, CA 92805
800-888-8637; FAX: 714-533-0361
E-mail: carl@globalmark.com

accessories
custom radios
speakers

See full listing in **Section One** under **Chevrolet**

Custom Classic Cars
2046 E 12B Road
Bourbon, IN 46504
219-342-0399
E-mail: asmith7112@aol.com

parts
restoration

See full listing in **Section One** under **Chevrolet**

D & R Classic Automotive Inc
30 W 255 Calumet Ave
Warrenville, IL 60563
708-393-0009; FAX: 708-393-1397

parts

Mail order and open shop. Monday-Friday 9-6 Central Time. D & R Classic Automotive is committed to selling the world's best Camaro parts available. Our huge inventory of new, used, discontinued NOS and reproduction parts assures you of getting the right parts you need fast. Whether you are restoring a classic show car or dressing up your daily driver, our knowledgeable staff can help with any technical assistance. We've been selling Camaro parts for 13 years. We've just moved to a new 22,000 sq ft building. All this means you get the correct part fast.

Desert Muscle Cars
2853 N Stone Ave
Tucson, AZ 85705
520-882-3010; FAX: 520-628-9332

parts

Mail order and open shop. Shop open weekdays 9 to 5:30, Saturday 9 to 3. Specializing in restoration supplies and parts for 55-70 Chevrolets, 67-81 Camaro, 64-72 Chevelle, 47-72 Chevrolet trucks, 64-73 Mustangs, all Corvettes. Deals in weatherstripping, interiors, emblems, moldings, decals, books, etc.

Dynatech Engineering
PO Box 1446
Alta Loma, CA 91701-8446
805-492-6134

motor mounts

See full listing in **Section Two** under **suspension parts**

Eagle Wire Products
3308 Valley Forge Dr
Knoxville, TN 37920
PH/FAX: 800-977-0030

wire harnesses

See full listing in **Section Two** under **electrical systems**

ETC Every Thing Cars
8727 Clarinda
Pico Rivera, CA 90660
310-949-6981

restoration

See full listing in **Section One** under **MoPar**

FireAro Restoration Parts Co
935 Hedge Dr
Mississauga, ON Canada L4Y 1E9
PH/FAX: 905-277-3230

accessories
parts

Mail order and open shop. Monday-Saturday hours vary. Specializing in 1967-72 Camaro and Firebird parts and accessories.

Fowlkes Realty & Auction
500 Hale St
Newman Grove, NE 68758
800-275-5522; FAX: 402-447-6000

appraisals
auctions

See full listing in **Section One** under **Chevrolet**

Guldstrand Engineering Inc
11924 W Jefferson Blvd
Culver City, CA 90230
310-391-7108; FAX: 310-391-7424
E-mail: geiauto@aol.com

parts

See full listing in **Section One** under **Corvette**

Harmon's Inc
Hwy 27 N, PO Box 6C
Geneva, IN 46740
219-368-7221
FAX: 219-368-9396

interiors
parts

See full listing in **Section One** under **Chevrolet**

Ken Hicks Promotionals
116 Bethea Rd, Suite 306
Fayetteville, GA 30214
770-460-1654; FAX: 770-460-8956

collectibles
price guide

See full listing in **Section Two** under **automobilia**

J & K Old Chevy Stuff
Ship Pond Rd
Plymouth, MA 02360
508-224-7616

car dealer
parts
sheetmetal

See full listing in **Section One** under **Chevrolet**

J&M Auto Parts
10 Spaulding Hill Rd
Pelham, NH 03076
603-635-3866

NOS parts
repro parts

See full listing in **Section One** under **Chevrolet**

Jackson Speaker Service
217 Crestbrook Dr
Jackson, MI 49203
517-789-6400

radio repairs
speakers

See full listing in **Section Two** under **radios**

JR's Antique Auto
14900 Scherry Ln
Claremore, OK 74017
918-342-4398

chrome parts
interiors

See full listing in **Section One** under **Chevrolet**

Rudy R Koch
PO Box 291
Chester Heights, PA 19017
PH/FAX: 610-459-8721

manuals

See full listing in **Section One** under **Chevrolet**

The Last Precinct Police Museum
Rt 6, Box 345B (62 Highway West)
Eureka Springs, AR 72632
501-253-4948; FAX: 501-253-4949

museum

See full listing in **Section Six** under **Arkansas**

Lectric Limited Inc
7322 S Archer Road
Justice, IL 60458
708-563-0400; FAX: 708-458-2662

parts

See full listing in **Section One** under **Corvette**

LES Auto Parts
PO Box 81
Dayton, NJ 08810
908-329-6128

parts

See full listing in **Section One** under **Chevrolet**

Martz Classic Chevy Parts
RD 1, Box 199B
Thomasville, PA 17364
717-225-1655; FAX: 717-225-3637

parts

See full listing in **Section One** under **Chevrolet**

Master Power Brakes
254-1 Rolling Hills Rd
Mooresville, NC 28115
704-664-8866; FAX: 704-664-8862

brake products
conversion kits

Manufacturer of power boosters and power disc brake conversion kits. Kits available for Fords, Pontiacs, GM cars & trucks. Stainless steel sleeving of 4-piston calipers.

Midwest Acorn Nut Company
256 Minnesota Ave
Troy, MI 48083-4671
800-422-NUTS(6887)
FAX: 810-583-9130

fasteners
hardware

See full listing in **Section Two** under **hardware**

Mike's Chevy Parts
7716 Deering Ave
Canoga Park, CA 91304
818-346-0070; FAX: 818-713-0715

front end repair
parts

See full listing in **Section One** under **Chevrolet**

Muscle Express
509 Commerce Way W #3
Jupiter, FL 33458
800-323-3043 order line
561-744-3043 tech line

parts

At Muscle Express save on all your Camaro & other muscle car needs. Molded carpet, weatherstrip & interior kits, body panels plus more reproduction, used, NOS parts, restorations, installations, UPS daily. Credit cards.

Obsolete Chevrolet Parts Co
524 Hazel Ave
PO Box 68
Nashville, GA 31639
912-686-5812

engine parts
radiators
rubber parts
transmissions

See full listing in **Section One** under **Chevrolet**

OEM Glass Inc
PO Box 362, Rt 9 E
Bloomington, IL 61702
309-662-2122; FAX: 309-663-7474

auto glass

See full listing in **Section Two** under **glass**

Old Dominion Mustang
509 S Washington Hwy, Rt 1
Ashland, VA 23005
804-798-3348; FAX: 804-798-5105

parts

See full listing in **Section One** under **Mustang**

Original Parts Group Inc
17892 Gothard St
Huntington Beach, CA 92647
800-243-8355 US & Canada
714-841-5363; FAX: 714-847-8159

accessories
parts

Mail order and open shop. Monday-Friday 7:30 am to 5 pm, Saturday 10 am to 3 pm PST. Manufacturer and distributor of original and reproduction 64-87 Chevelle & El Camino and 70-88 Monte Carlo parts and accessories: emblems, interior trim, moldings, sheetmetal, electrical, engine parts, dash pads, door panels, seat upholstery, chrome trim parts, weatherstripping, gaskets, body seals, underbody bushings and much more along with an extensive line of obsolete GM items.

See our ad on page 52

Palm Springs Obsolete Automotive
653 N Commerical Rd, Unit 10
Palm Springs, CA 92262
619-323-6998; FAX: 619-320-1574

parts

Mail order and open shop. Monday-Friday 7 to 4:30, Saturday 8 to 12. Manufacture of 55/57 passenger car fan shrouds. Specializing in new, reproduction and used parts for 55/57 pass cars, 64/72 Chevelle & El Camino, 58/72 Impalas. Established in 1980. Catalogs, $3 each in USA and $8 out of country, free with purchase. Please state which model you are working on.

M Parker Autoworks Inc
150 Cooper Rd, Unit C-7
Dept HVAA
West Berlin, NJ 08091
609-753-0350; FAX: 609-753-0353

battery cables
harnesses

See full listing in **Section Two** under **electrical systems**

John E Pirkle
3706 Merion Dr
Augusta, GA 30907
706-860-9047

electrical parts

See full listing in **Section One** under **Corvette**

Power Brake Booster Exchange Inc
4533 SE Division St
Portland, OR 97206
503-238-8882

brake boosters

See full listing in **Section Two** under **brakes**

Rick's First Generation Camaro Parts
120 Commerce Blvd
Bogart, GA 30622
800-359-7717; FAX: 706-548-8581
E-mail: firstgen@negia.net

parts

Mail order and open shop. M-F 9 am-5 pm, Sat 10-2. Restoration parts, new GM, NOS and used parts for 1967-1969 Camaro.

Leon J Rocco
4125 Oak St
Butler, PA 16001
412-482-4387 after 6 pm

accessories
parts

Mail order only. Specializing in accessories and new, used and NOS parts for 50s, 60s, 70s Chevrolet, Camaro, Chevelle, Nova, Corvair. Lights, lenses, bezels, emblems, mirrors, radios, dash knobs, switches, steering wheels, glass triangle Optikleen bottles, door and window handles, misc.

SC Automotive
Rt 3 Box 9
New Ulm, MN 56073
507-354-1958; FAX: 800-6477-FAXS

parts
restoration

See full listing in **Section One** under **Chevrolet**

O B Smith Chevy Parts
PO Box 11703
990 New Circle Rd NW
Lexington, KY 40577
606-253-1957; FAX: 606-233-3129

parts
tires

See full listing in **Section One** under **Chevrolet**

Steve's Camaros
1197 San Mateo Ave
San Bruno, CA 94066
415-873-1890; FAX: 415-873-3670

parts

Mail order and open shop. Monday-Friday 9 am to 6 pm; Saturday 10 am to 3 pm. Specializing in 1967-1969 Camaro parts, new, reproduction; 1970-1981 new and reproduction parts. 1967-69 Pontiac Firebird parts in stock. 1964-1972 Chevelle and El Camino Parts.

Stockton Wheel Service
648 W Fremont St
Stockton, CA 95203
209-464-7771, 800-395-9433
FAX: 209-464-4725

wheel repair

See full listing in **Section Two** under **service shops**

Street-Wise Performance
Richie Mulligan
105 Creek Rd
Tranquility, NJ 07879
201-786-6668 days
201-786-7133 evenings

differentials
parts
rebuild kits
transmissions

See full listing in **Section Two** under **transmissions**

Super Sport Restoration Parts Inc
7138 Maddox Rd
Lithonia, GA 30058
770-482-9219

NOS parts
used parts

See full listing in **Section One** under **Chevrolet**

Sutton Auto Sounds
3463 Rolling Trail
Palm Harbor, FL 34684-3526
813-787-2717; FAX: 813-789-9215
E-mail: suttonauto@aol.com

radios

See full listing in **Section Two** under **radios**

Tabco Inc
11655 Chillicothe Rd
Chesterland, OH 44026-1994
216-729-5151; FAX: 216-729-1251

body parts

See full listing in **Section Two** under **sheetmetal**

Tom's Obsolete Chevy Parts
14 Delta Dr
Pawtucket, RI 02860
401-723-7580; FAX: 401-724-7568

parts

See full listing in **Section One** under **Chevrolet**

THE ESSENTIAL MANUFACTURER DIRECT CATALOG!

#1 IN CHEVELLE & EL CAMINO PARTS FOR 12 YEARS

NO-NONSENSE, PROFESSIONALLY MADE PARTS

TOLL FREE 24 HOURS
1-800-CHEVELLE

Trim Parts Inc 5161 Wolfpen Pleasant Hill Milford, OH 45150 513-831-1472; FAX: 513-248-3402	trim items

See full listing in **Section One** under **Chevrolet**

True Connections 8829 Pembroke Riverside, CA 92503 909-688-6040; FAX: 909-688-4492	parts

Mail order and open shop. Monday-Friday, 9 am-6 pm; Sat 9 am-2 pm. Specializing in 64-72 Chevelle, El Camino & Monte Carlo parts. New, used, repro.

Vibratech Inc (Fluidampr) 11980 Walden Ave Alden, NY 14004 716-937-3603; FAX: 716-937-4692	performance parts

See full listing in **Section Two** under **engine parts**

Volunteer State Chevy Parts Hwy 41 S Greenbrier, TN 37073 615-643-4583; FAX: 615-643-5100	accessories parts

See full listing in **Section One** under **Chevrolet**

Wheel Vintiques Inc 5468 E Lamona Ave Fresno, CA 93727 209-251-6957; FAX: 209-251-1620	hubcaps wheels

See full listing in **Section One** under **Chevrolet**

Ted Williams Enterprises 5615 Rt 45 Lisbon, OH 44432 330-424-9413; FAX: 330-424-9060	parts

See full listing in **Section One** under **Chevrolet**

Year One Inc PO Box 129 Tucker, GA 30085 800-YEAR-ONE (932-7663) 770-493-6568 Atlanta & overseas FAX: 800-680-6806 FAX: 770-496-1949 Atlanta/overseas	parts

See full listing in **Section Two** under **comprehensive parts**

CORVAIR

Big Boy Accessories 581 Kenbridge Dr Carson, CA 90746 310-324-4787	parts

See full listing in **Section One** under **Chevrolet**

Clark's Corvair Parts Inc Rt 2, #400 Mohawk Tr Shelburne Falls, MA 01370 413-625-9776; FAX: 413-625-8498	accessories interiors literature parts

Mail order only. Monday-Friday 8:30-5. Over 24 years supplying

NOS and repro parts, upholstery, carpets, door panels, sheet-metal and accessories for Corvair. Technical assistance by mail or phone. Over 400 page illustrated catalog listing over 10,000 different NOS, used, high-performance and Corvair to VW adapter parts, $5.

Corvair Haven 315 N Prairie St Batavia, IL 60510 630-761-8714	parts service

Mail order and open shop. Monday-Saturday noon to 9. Sells NOS and used parts, rebuilding service and general repair of Chevrolet Corvairs, all makes and models 1960-1969.

Corvair Heaven PO Box 13 Ellenton, FL 34222-0013 813-746-0478; FAX: 813-750-8167	car dealer literature restoration

Mail order and shop hours by appointment. Restoration and repairs on Corvairs only. Parts bought, sold and traded.

Corvair Ranch Inc 1079 Bon-Ox Rd Gettysburg, PA 17325 PH/FAX: 717-624-2805	parts restoration service

Mail order and open shop. Monday-Saturday 8 to 6. Strictly 1960-69 Corvair only parts, service and restoration facility dedicated to the Corvair auto and truck. Parts inventory includes much NOS and repro in many buildings plus a 375 car salvage yard. Also many complete and restorable projects. VISA, MC, Discover, AmEx. UPS daily.

Corvair Underground   parts
PO Box 339
Dundee, OR 97115
503-434-1648, 800-825-8247
FAX: 503-434-1626

Specializes in Corvair parts, new, reproduced, rebuilt and used.
Largest western supplier of Corvair parts. 300 page mail order
catalog for only $5 or a free newsletter. All major credit cards
accepted.

Bill Cotrofeld Automotive Inc   rebuilding service
US Rt 7   repair service
Box 235   restoration
East Arlington, VT 05252
802-375-6782

Corvair repair & restoration shop. Monday-Friday 10 am to 6
pm. Call for Saturday or Sunday hours. Corvair restorations,
repairs and rebuilding services. Call for brochure. "America's
oldest Corvair shop."

See our ad on page 53

Ehrenreich's Corvair Service   parts
1728 Manor Pkwy
Sheboygan, WI 53083-2827
414-458-1170

Used parts. Monday-Saturday call 4-8 pm. Have junked over 75
Corvairs. Member of local and worldwide clubs, Corsa, Corvair
Society of America. Retired.

Joseph A Kastelan   parts
4603 Powell Hwy   sales
Ionia, MI 48846   service
810-296-1871

Mail order and open shop. Monday thru Saturday 8 am-6 pm
EST. Sales, service, parts, appraisals. Corvair club information
for Corvair 1960 thru 1969.

LES Auto Parts   parts
Box 81
Dayton, NJ 08810
908-329-6128

See full listing in **Section One** under **Chevrolet**

Maplewood Motors   restoration
138 Ogunquit Rd
Cape Neddick, ME 03902
207-361-1340

Mail order and open shop. Open by appointment only. Chevrolet
Corvair. Over 40 years in the auto business. Complete mechanical restoration in-house and bodyshop at other location.

Quality Customs   parts
1623 W Broad St   repair
Richmond, VA 23220   restoration
804-358-5674; FAX: 804-353-8168

Mail order and open shop. Monday-Friday 8:30 am to 5 pm EST.
Closed major holidays. A collision repair facility that also performs restoration work on cars from the 1950s and 1960s. We
have a large selection of used parts for Corvairs which we sell by
mail or locally and a smaller selection of new parts to keep our
local customers supplied. We also perform all mechanical and
electrical work on Corvairs.

Safari O-Rings   parts
18131 W Lake Desire Dr SE   repair
Renton, WA 98058
206-255-6751

Mail order and open shop. Supplies Viton O-rings for Corvair
and Corvair related vehicles. Also general repairs for 1960-69
Corvair and Corvair related vehicles.

Silicone Wire Systems   ignition wire sets
3462 Kirkwood Dr
San Jose, CA 95117-1549

Mail order only. Manufactures ignition wire sets for all Corvairs,
street and race. Yellow, blue or black 8mm wire is used with
special snap-in seals and silicone plug boots. Custom wire sets
available. Other colors available.

The Source   machine work/parts
13975 Mira Montana   nos accessories
Del Mar, CA 92014-3113   reproduction
619-259-1520; FAX: 619-259-3843   service/supplies

Open shop by appointment only. Office hours 12-9 pm M-F. The
Source is a supplier of replacement parts (heavy duty, high-performance) and machine shop service center for all Corvair powered vehicles. Corsa (Corvair Society of America) approved. Retail
& wholesale (volume) programs. We have evolved to a reproduction service for replacement parts for all vehicles both vintage
and modern. We are also a bulk sales distributor of most automotive parts and supplies, wholesale only except for Corvair.
Phone or FAX orders anytime. MasterCard & Visa.

Trim Parts Inc   trim items
5161 Wolfpen Pleasant Hill
Milford, OH 45150
513-831-1472; FAX: 513-248-3402

See full listing in **Section One** under **Chevrolet**

Vibratech Inc (Fluidampr)   performance parts
11980 Walden Ave
Alden, NY 14004
716-937-3603; FAX: 716-937-4692

See full listing in **Section Two** under **engine parts**

4-Speeds by Darrell   transmissions
PO Box 110, #3 Water St
Vermilion, IL 61955
217-275-3743; FAX: 217-275-3515

See full listing in **Section Two** under **transmissions**

AM Racing Inc   race prep
PO Box 451   sales
Danvers, MA 01923   vintage racing
PH/FAX: 508-774-4613

See full listing in **Section Two** under **racing**

American Memory Prints   artwork
5935 N Belt W
Belleville, IL 62223
618-235-4788; FAX: 618-235-4899

See full listing in **Section Two** under **artwork**

American Restorations Unlimited TA — restoration parts
14 Meakin Ave
PO Box 34
Rochelle Park, NJ 07662
201-843-3567; FAX: 201-843-3238
E-mail: amerrest@aol.com

See full listing in **Section Two** under **glass**

Andover Automotive Inc — parts, seat belts
PO Box 3143
Laurel, MD 20709
410-381-6700; FAX: 410-381-6703

Mail order and open shop. Monday-Friday 9 to 6. Corvette new, used and NOS parts. Seat belt distributor, retail and wholesale for most classic cars and trucks. We also carry partial sets, webbing, bolt kits, along with related items. Free Corvette parts catalog, specify year.

Antique Cars, Parts & Trains — car dealer, literature, parts, trains
Second & Broad Sts
Millville, NJ 08332
609-825-0200

See full listing in **Section One** under **Ford '03-'31**

Auto Accessories of America Inc — accessories, customizing, gifts & apparel, restoration
PO Box 427
Rt 322
Boalsburg, PA 16827
800-458-3475; FAX: 814-364-9615
Foreign: 814-364-2141

Celebrating 20 years of Corvette satisfaction. Exact reproduction interiors, manufactured on-site in a brand new 55,000 square foot facility. Exquisitely crafted fiberglass. New accessories and innovative new products. Beautiful gifts and apparel. You'll find all this and more at Corvette America. Since 1977. Call today for a free catalog.

Auto Custom Carpet — carpets, floor coverings
Jeff Moses
PO Box 1350, 1429 Noble St
Anniston, AL 36202
800-633-2358; 205-236-1118
FAX: 800-516-8274

See full listing in **Section One** under **Chevrolet**

Auto Etc Neon — signs, time pieces
PO Box 531992
Harlingen, TX 78553
210-425-7487; FAX: 210-425-3025

Mail order only. Nostalgic neon trademark signs and time pieces and licensed gifts for Chevrolet/Corvette owners and enthusiasts home, garage, showroom and business display.

Automotive Artistry — restoration
679 W Streetboro St
Hudson, OH 44236
216-650-1503

See full listing in **Section One** under **Triumph**

Automotive Design Center Inc — chassis, frames
14135 S Harrison
Posen, IL 60469
708-385-8222

Specializing in round tube chassis and frames for 1953-1962 Chevrolet Corvettes. Customer can purchase frame or chassis, or Auto Design will install.

Avanti Auto Service — repair, restoration
Rt 322, 67 Conchester Hwy
Glen Mills, PA 19342-1506
610-558-9999

See full listing in **Section One** under **DeTomaso/Pantera**

B & B Cylinder Head — cylinder heads
320 Washington St
West Warwick, RI 02893
401-828-4900, 800-800-4143

See full listing in **Section Two** under **engine parts**

Bairs Corvettes — parts, service
316 Franklin St
Linesville, PA 16424
814-683-4223; FAX: 814-683-5200

Mail order and open shop. Monday thru Friday 8 am-5 pm. Specializing in parts & service for Corvettes 63-82.

JJ Best & Co — financing
737 Main St, PO Box 10
Chatham, MA 02633
508-945-6000; FAX: 508-945-6006

See full listing in **Section Two** under **consultants**

Blue Ribbon Products — parts
4965 Old House Trail NE
Atlanta, GA 30342
404-843-8414; FAX: 404-252-0688

Mail order and open shop. Mon-Fri 9 am-8 pm, Sat 9 am-noon. New and reproduction parts for 1956-1967 Corvettes. Thousands of parts in stock. Free catalog.

Buds Chevrolet — cars, parts, service
PO Box 128
1415 Commerce Dr
St Marys, OH 45885
800-688-2837; FAX: 419-394-4781

Corvettes, new and used. Over 100 in stock! Also parts and service. Authorized Chevrolet dealership.

Camaro-Heaven — cars, parts, salvage yard
64 River Street
Rochester, NH 03867
800-CAMARO-1; FAX: 603-332-3299

See full listing in **Section One** under **Chevelle/Camaro**

Cars II — parts
6747 Warren Sharon Rd
Brookfield, OH 44403
330-448-2074; FAX: 330-448-1908

See full listing in **Section One** under **Cadillac/LaSalle**

CBS Performance Automotive — ignition systems, performance, products
2605-A W Colorado Ave
Colorado Springs, CO 80904
800-685-1492; FAX: 719-578-9485

See full listing in **Section Two** under **ignition parts**

Chevrolet Parts Obsolete — accessories, parts
PO Box 0740
Murrieta, CA 92564-0740
909-279-2833; FAX: 909-279-4013

See full listing in **Section One** under **Chevrolet**

Chicago Corvette Supply 7322 S Archer Rd Justice, IL 60458 708-458-2500; FAX: 708-458-2662	**parts**

Mail order and open showroom. Monday-Friday 9 am to 6 pm, Saturday 9 am to 1 pm. Specializes in new, reproduction and remanufactured 1953-82 Corvette parts, accessories and books. Also maintain one of the largest inventories of discontinued NOS (new old stock) parts in the nation. Call for our newest catalog.

Chrome Masters 1109 W Orange Ave, Unit D Tallahassee, FL 32310 904-576-2100	**chrome plating** **pot metal** **restoration**

See full listing in **Section Two** under **plating & polishing**

Ciadella Enterprises Inc 3116 S 52nd St Tempe, AZ 85282-3212 602-968-4179; FAX: 602-438-6585	**truck interiors** **upholstery**

See full listing in **Section One** under **Chevrolet**

The Classic Car Radio Co 2718 Koper Dr Sterling Heights, MI 48310 810-977-7979; info: 810-268-2918 FAX: 810-977-0895	**radios**

See full listing in **Section Two** under **radios**

Classic Car Research 29508 Southfield Rd Southfield, MI 48076 810-557-2880; FAX: 810-557-3511	**appraisals** **car locating** **consultant**

See full listing in **Section Two** under **appraisals**

Classic Coachworks 735 Frenchtown Rd Milford, NJ 08848 908-996-3400	**bodywork** **painting** **restoration**

See full listing in **Section Two** under **restoration shops**

Classic Profiles Inc 5770 W Kinnickinnic River Pkwy West Allis, WI 53219 414-328-9866; FAX: 414-328-1906	**artwork**

Specializing in automotive artwork reproducing rear bumpers in 3/4 scale for 1984 to 1996 Corvettes. Thermoplastic piece is 16"x48", battery operated flashing lights, weighs 8 lbs. Makes interesting wallhanging, conversational piece.

Classics 'n More Inc 1001 Ranck Mill Rd Lancaster, PA 17602 717-392-0599; FAX 717-392-2371	**repairs** **restoration**

See full listing in **Section Two** under **restoration shops**

Clock Doc® 125 University Ave Sewanee, TN 37375 800-256-5362; FAX: 615-598-5986	**clock repairs** **gauge repairs**

See full listing in **Section Two** under **instruments**

Composition Materials Co Inc 1375 Kings Hwy E Fairfield, CT 06430 800-262-7763; FAX: 203-335-9728	**plastic media**

See full listing in **Section Two** under **restoration aids**

Conte's Corvettes & Classics 851 W Wheat Rd Vineland, NJ 08360 609-692-0087; FAX: 609-692-1009 E-mail: contes@cybernet.net	**leasing** **parts** **sales** **service**

Mail order and open shop. M-W-F 8-5, T & Thur 8-8, Sat 9-2. Since 1974 Conte's has been serving the needs of Corvette & muscle car enthusiasts with quality Corvette & muscle car sales (20-30 always in stock). New & used parts and expert service ranging from complete mechanical restorations to tune-ups. We sell vehicles on consignment and also take trade-ins. Financing and leasing available on all of our cars. Call, fax or E-mail for an inventory listing. Check out our latest inventory at our web site at: http://www.cyberenet.net/~contes

Corvette & High-Performance Division of Classic & High Performance Inc 2840 Black Lake Blvd SW #D Olympia, WA 98512 360-754-7890	**accessories** **parts**

Mail order and open shop. Tuesday-Saturday 9 to 5:30. Specializing in new and reproduction parts for Corvettes, Camaros, Chevelles and other GM classic cars and trucks. Corvette mechanical service. UPS daily. Major credit cards accepted. Established 1984.

Corvette Central 5865 Sawyer Rd, Dept HM Sawyer, MI 49125 616-426-3342; FAX: 616-426-4108	**accessories** **parts**

Mail order and open shop. Monday-Friday 9 to 6; Saturday 9 to 1. Full line of new, used and reproduction parts for 1953-96 Corvettes. Four catalogs available: 1953-67 parts catalog, 1968-82 parts catalog, 1984-96 parts catalog, 1953-96 accessory catalog.

Corvette Enterprise Brokerage The Power Broker 52 Van Houten Ave Passaic Park, NJ 07055 201-472-7021	**appraiser** **broker** **car locator** **investment** **planning**

Cars shown Monday-Saturday by appointment only. Corvette brokerage offering investment grade classics and new models. SASE for free catalog. Consultations and appraisals. Quality Corvettes always wanted.

Corvette Rubber Company 10640 W Cadillac Rd Cadillac, MI 49601 616-779-2888; FAX: 616-779-9833	**rubber products** **weatherstripping**

Mail order and open shop. Open Monday-Friday 10 to 5. Specializing in weatherstrip and rubber products for 1953-1993 Corvettes.

Corvette Specialties of MD Inc 1912 Liberty Rd Eldersburg, MD 21784 410-795-3180; FAX: 410-795-3247	**parts** **restoration** **service**

Mail order and open shop. Monday-Friday 9 to 5:30. Since 1977, a major supplier of new, used and reproduction parts, specializing in 1956-67. We also offer a restoration service for clocks, gauges, instrument clusters, headlight and wiper motors. Mechanical service and restoration work is also offered at our facility. Tune-ups to frame-off restorations. We service all years.

Corvette World	accessories
RD 9, Box 770, Dept H	parts
Greensburg, PA 15601	
412-837-8600; FAX: 412-837-4420	

Mail order and open shop. Monday-Thursday 9 to 6, Friday 9 to 5, Saturday 9 to 12. Complete line of over 10,000 GM and reproduction parts for 53 and up Corvettes. Call for our 208 page fully illustrated catalog.

County Corvette	restoration
171 Eagleview Blvd	sales
Lionville, PA 19353	service
610-363-0872; FAX: 610-363-5325	

Open shop only. Monday-Friday 8:30-5:30, Saturday 10-2. State of the art restoration, service and sales for Corvettes. Web site: http://www.vettes.com/usa/countypa

CSK Publishing Co Inc	periodical
299 Market St	
Saddle Brook, NJ 07662	
201-712-9300; FAX: 201-712-0990	
E-mail: staff@cskpub.com	

See full listing in **Section Four** under **periodicals**

Custom Autosound Mfg	accessories
808 W Vermont Ave	custom radios
Anaheim, CA 92805	speakers
800-888-8637; FAX: 714-533-0361	
E-mail: carl@globalmark.com	

See full listing in **Section One** under **Chevrolet**

Davies Corvette	customizing
5130 Main St	parts
New Port Richey, FL 34653	restoration
813-842-8000, 800-236-2383	
FAX: 813-846-8216	

Corvette parts & accessories, all years (used & new). "Making Corvettes the best they can be since 1953."

Dean's Wiper Transmission Service	wiper trans service
Dean Andrew Rehse	
16367 Martincoit Rd	
Poway, CA 92064	
619-451-1933; FAX: 619-451-1999	

Specializing in 1953-1962. Rebuilds your broken wiper transmissions. We can restring your broken cables, replace broken parts. Price varies. This is a division of Mary Jo Rohner's Corvette Parts Collection, 1953-1962.

Desert Muscle Cars	parts
2853 N Stone Ave	
Tucson, AZ 85705	
520-882-3010; FAX: 520-628-9332	

See full listing in **Section One** under **Chevelle/Camaro**

M F Dobbins Inc	literature
16 E Montgomery Ave	parts
Hatboro, PA 19040	restoration
215-443-0779	

Mail order and open shop. Corvette service and restoration, parts and literature. Corvette appraisals.

Doug's Corvette Service	race prep
11634 Vanowen St	repairs
North Hollywood, CA 91605	
818-765-9117	

Open shop only. Monday-Friday 8 am-5 pm. Specializing in all mechanical repairs on all year Corvettes. Restoration and race car preparation.

Dr vette	brakes
212 7th St SW	fuel system parts
New Philadelphia, OH 44663	repairs
330-339-3370, 800-878-1022	
orders; FAX: 330-339-6640	

Dr vette has expanded his practice to include treatments for Corvette patients suffering from hardening of power steering componets, tired life-less power boosters, suspension depression, congestive master cylinder failure & clogged proportioning valves. His practice of 15 years continues to specialize in curing fuel & brake illnesses from line rustitis to reconstructive caliper surgery. For Dr vette's catalog of prescribed cures in these critical areas, call 800-878-1022; do it today, feel better tomorrow.

Eagle Wire Products	wire harnesses
3308 Valley Forge Dr	
Knoxville, TN 37920	
PH/FAX: 800-977-0030	

See full listing in **Section Two** under **electrical systems**

EC Products Design Inc	accessories
PO Box 2360	parts
Atascadero, CA 93423	
800-488-5209, 805-466-4703	
international; FAX: 805-466-4782	

Mail order and open shop. Monday-Friday 7:30 am-5 pm, Pacific time. Serves all auto businesses throughout the world that deal in Corvette parts. Business license required, wholesale only. Specializing in parts & accessories for 1953-1996 Corvettes.

Eckler's Quality Parts & Accessories for Corvettes	accessories
PO Box 5637	parts
Titusville, FL 32783	
800-327-4868; FAX: 407-383-2059	

Specializing in parts & accessories for 1953-1996 Corvettes. One 400+ page color catalog for 1953-1996 models, featuring enhancement accessories of every description, plus restoration items including fiberglass body panels, interiors, chassis parts, fuel systems, electrical items, glass, engine parts, exhaust systems in addition to a complete line of gift and apparel items.

Elliott's Car Radio	radio repairs
313 Linfield Rd	speaker kits
Parkerford, PA 19457	
610-495-6360; FAX: 610-495-7723	

See full listing in **Section Two** under **radios**

Elmer's Auto Parts Inc	parts
137 Donovan St	
Webster, NY 14580	
716-872-4402; 800-288-3883	
FAX: 716-872-2519	

Mail order and open shop. Monday-Saturday 9 to 5. Auto parts and salvage Corvette parts, 1953-present. Corvette rebuildable wrecks.

Exotic Wood Dash & Restorations
336 Cottonwood Ave
Hartland, WI 53029
800-900-3274; FAX: 414-367-9474

restoration parts
wood dash overlays

See full listing in **Section One** under **Jaguar**

Fifties Forever
Mario Cristelli
206 Division Ave
Garfield, NJ 07026
201-478-1306

chevy specialist

See full listing in **Section One** under **Chevrolet**

Fowlkes Realty & Auction
500 Hale St
Newman Grove, NE 68758
800-275-5522; FAX: 402-447-6000

appraisals
auctions

See full listing in **Section One** under **Chevrolet**

G & L Classics
8225 Taffy Dr
West Chester, OH 45069
513-779-1957

parts

See full listing in **Section One** under **Chevrolet**

Gemini Racing Systems Inc
7301 W Boston St
Chandler, AZ 85226
800-992-9294, 602-940-9011

race prep
restoration

See full listing in **Section One** under **Mustang**

Guldstrand Engineering Inc
11924 W Jefferson Blvd
Culver City, CA 90230
310-391-7108; FAX: 310-391-7424
E-mail: geiauto@aol.com

parts

Mail order and open shop. Monday to Friday 8 am to 5 pm. GM parts and service, Moog suspension parts, custom made suspension components for Gulstrand only. For Corvettes & Camaros and GM cars, also special built vehicles GS-80/GS-90 for all years 1960 to current. Subscription is $5 each for Corvette suspension manual & parts catalog or Camaro suspension manual & parts catalog.

Ken Hicks Promotionals
116 Bethea Rd, Suite 306
Fayetteville, GA 30214
770-460-1654; FAX: 770-460-8956

collectibles
price guide

See full listing in **Section Two** under **automobilia**

Hubcap Mike
26242 Dimension, Ste 150
Lake Forest, CA 92630
714-597-8120; FAX: 714-597-8123

hubcaps
wheelcovers

See full listing in **Section Two** under **wheels & wheelcovers**

Instrument Services Inc
11765 Main St
Roscoe, IL 61073
800-558-2674; FAX: 800-623-6416

clocks

See full listing in **Section Two** under **instruments**

**International Restoration
Specialist Inc**
PO Box 1303
Mt Airy, NC 27030
910-789-1548

parts
restoration
sales

See full listing in **Section One** under **Jaguar**

Jackson Speaker Service
217 Crestbrook Dr
Jackson, MI 49203
517-789-6400

radio repairs
speakers

See full listing in **Section Two** under **radios**

JR's Antique Auto
14900 Scherry Ln
Claremore, OK 74017
918-342-4398

chrome parts
interiors

See full listing in **Section One** under **Chevrolet**

Kansas City Corvettes Inc
7911 Metcalf
Overland Park, KS 66204
913-648-8118; FAX: 913-648-8114

sales
service

Mail order and open shop. 6 days 9-8 pm. Specializing in Corvette sales and service, 56-95s. Always 60+ units in stock. Restoration shop for all years.

King's Bumper Co Inc
1 Ontario Ave
New Hartford, NY 13413
315-732-8988; FAX: 315-732-2602

chrome plating

See full listing in **Section Two** under **plating & polishing**

Al Knoch Interiors
130 Montoya Rd
El Paso, TX 79932
800-880-8080; FAX: 915-581-1545

carpets
interiors
tooling services
tops

See full listing in **Section One** under **Chevrolet**

Rudy R Koch
PO Box 291
Chester Heights, PA 19017
PH/FAX: 610-459-8721

manuals

See full listing in **Section One** under **Chevrolet**

Lectric Limited Inc
7322 S Archer Road
Justice, IL 60458
708-563-0400; FAX: 708-458-2662

parts

Specializing in wire harnesses, switches, ignition wire sets and T3 headlight bulbs for GM vehicles. Our particular specialty is Corvette.

LES Auto Parts
Box 81
Dayton, NJ 08810
908-329-6128

parts

See full listing in **Section One** under **Chevrolet**

Limited Editions
PO Box 11011
Springfield, IL 62791
217-525-0413; FAX: 217-525-7047

models

See full listing in **Section Two** under **models & toys**

Long Island Corvette Supply Inc
1445 Strong Ave
Copiague, NY 11726-3227
516-225-3000; FAX: 516-225-5030

parts

Mail order and open shop. Monday thru Friday 9-5. Specializing in parts for 63-67 Corvettes. The largest & best stocked manufacturer & distributor of 63-67 Corvette parts. Send $3 for the biggest & best 63-67 Corvette parts catalog.

M & H Electric Fabricators Inc | wiring harnesses
13537 Alondra Blvd
Santa Fe Springs, CA 90670
310-926-9552; FAX: 310-926-9572

See full listing in **Section Two** under **electrical systems**

MAR-K Quality Parts | bed parts
6625 W Wilshire | customizing parts
Oklahoma City, OK 73132 | trim parts
405-721-7945; FAX: 405-721-8906

See full listing in **Section Two** under **trucks & tractors**

Marcel's Corvette Parts | parts
15100 Lee Rd #101
Humble, TX 77396
800-546-2111 order line
713-441-2111 info line
FAX: 713-441-2111

Mail order and open shop. Monday-Friday 9-6 CST. Specializes in 1953-1982 Corvette parts of all kinds. New, NOS, used and reproductions.

Master Power Brakes | brake products
254-1 Rolling Hills Rd | conversion kits
Mooresville, NC 28115
704-664-8866; FAX: 704-664-8862

See full listing in **Section One** under **Chevelle/Camaro**

Metro Authentic Finishes | paint
2576B West Point Ave
College Park, GA 30337
404-767-3378

Mail order only. Monday-Saturday 9 to 6. Specializing in touch up paint (spray cans and bottles) for Corvettes, Camaros, Chevelles, 55-57 Chevrolet. Interior paint and vinyl dye now available for 60s and 70s Corvettes, 67-74 Camaros and 64-72 Chevelles. Eliminates the need for paint mixing, spray guns, air compressors and clean up. Available in all factory colors. Wholesale only, ask your dealer for our paint or call us for the name of the dealer nearest you. Dealer inquiries welcome.

Milestone Motorcars | die cast cars
Mark Tyra | models
12910 Sunnybrook Dr
Prospect, KY 40059
502-228-5945; FAX: 502-228-1856

See full listing in **Section Two** under **automobilia**

Morrison Motor Co | car dealer
1170 Old Charlotte Rd
Concord, NC 28025
704-782-7716; FAX: 704-788-9514

Open shop only. Monday-Saturday 8:30 to 5:30. Auto sales, specializing in Corvettes, all years, collector cars, muscle cars and late model used cars. We've been in business full time since 1970.

Muncie Imports & Classics | repair
4401 St Rd 3 North | restoration
Muncie, IN 47303 | upholstery
800-462-4244; FAX: 317-287-9551

See full listing in **Section One** under **Jaguar**

Muskegon Brake & Dist Co | brakes
848 E Broadway | springs
Muskegon, MI 49444 | suspensions
616-733-0874; FAX: 616-733-0635

See full listing in **Section Two** under **brakes**

OEM Glass Inc | auto glass
PO Box 362, Rt 9 E
Bloomington, IL 61702
309-662-2122; FAX: 309-663-7474

See full listing in **Section Two** under **glass**

Old Air Products | air conditioning
3056 SE Loop 820
Ft Worth, TX 76140
817-551-0602; FAX: 817-568-0037

Mail order and open shop. Monday thru Friday 8:30 am-5 pm. Specilizing in custom air conditioning systems and replacement parts for air conditioning and heating for Corvette, 55-57 Chevy trucks & cars, 72 and back Chevrolet trucks, Ford trucks and cars.

Pacifica Motoring Accessories | accessories
PO Box 2360 | parts
Atascadero, CA 93423
800-488-7671; FAX: 805-466-4782

Mail order and open shop. Monday-Friday 7:30 am to 5 pm, Pacific time. Carries over 10,000 parts and accessories for 1953 to 1996 Corvettes. Call or write for your catalog, $5, refundable with your first order. New catalog coming soon. Call to reserve yours.

M Parker Autoworks Inc | battery cables har-
150 Cooper Rd, Unit C-7 | nesses
Dept HVAA
West Berlin, NJ 08091
609-753-0350; FAX: 609-753-0353

See full listing in **Section Two** under **electrical systems**

PC Automotive Calendars | calendars
PO Box 2002
Madison, WI 53701
608-829-1234

See full listing in **Section Two** under **special services**

JT Piper's Auto Specialties Inc | parts
#2 Water St, Box 140
Vermilion, IL 61955
800-637-6111, orders, nationwide &
Canada
217-275-3743, tech assistance
FAX: 217-275-3515

We have one of the largest inventories of used Corvette parts in the world. Used parts for 1954-86 Corvettes are our specialty, however, we stock a full line of new GM, NOS, discontinued GM and reproduction Corvette parts for the 1954-86 models. All pricing is done over the phone. So just pick up the phone and give us a call: 800-637-6111 for all your 1954-86 Corvette parts needs.

John E Pirkle | electrical parts
3706 Merion Dr
Augusta, GA 30907
706-860-9047

Specializing in starters, alternators, generators, V regulators, relays for Corvette, Chevrolet & GM cars.

Jack Podell Fuel Injection Spec
106 Wakewa Ave
South Bend, IN 46617
219-232-6430; FAX: 219-234-8632

| fuel system parts |
| fuel system |
| rebuilding |

Mail order and open shop. Daily 7-7. Specializing in the rebuilding & restoration of 57-65 Corvette Rochester fuel injection units with over 27 years of satisfied customers worldwide! Units bought, sold, taken in on trade. Massive parts inventory available including steel reproduction air cleaners, restored fi units in stock. Call us first for all your fi needs. Catalog upon request.

Dennis Portka
4326 Beetow Dr
Hamburg, NY 14075
716-649-0921

horns
knock-off wheels

Mail order only. 2 separate businesses. Specializing in rebuilding & sales of GM horns for Corvette & GM cars, 1955-present. Restoration of Corvette aluminum knock-off wheels, enlarged mounting holes remachined to factory specs. Also knock-off wheel wrenches available

Hugo Prado Limited Edition Corvette Art Prints
PO Box 18437
Chicago, IL 60618-0437
PH/FAX: 800-583-7627
E-mail: vetteart@aol.com

fine art prints

Specializes in Limited Edition fine art prints of classic Corvettes & Camaros. 1957 Sebring Corvette, 1960 Roman red Corvette convertible, 1963 tuxedo black Corvette Z06, 1965 tuxedo black Corvette, 1966 rally red Corvette, 1967 marina blue Corvette, 1968 tuxedo black Corvette, 1969 Daytona yellow Corvette, 1967 Camaro SS/RS Indy pace car. 1970 Mulsanne-blue Corvette, 1971 Steel Cities gray Corvette, 1990 bright red ZR-1, 40th Anniversary Corvette. Visit us on the internet at: http://users.aol.com/vetteart/vetteart.htm

Proteam Corvette Sales Inc
PO Box 606
Napoleon, OH 43545-0606
419-592-5086; FAX: 419-592-4242
E-mail: proteam@bright.net

car collection
car dealer

Mail order and open shop. Monday-Saturday 9-5. Corvettes 1954-1985, over 150 in stock, one location. Mostly 1972 and older. Free catalog. Dealers welcomed, worldwide transportation. ProTeam on video, $12.95 pp. Corvettes wanted. Visit our web site for complete comprehensive list of Corvettes for sale: http://www.proteam-corvette.com

RARE Corvettes
Joe Calcagno
Box 1080
Soquel, CA 95073
408-475-4442; FAX: 408-475-1115

cars
parts

Mail order and open shop by appointment. Specializing in Corvette 1956-1962. Complete cars, project cars, Survivors, drivers, show cars. Parts: new reproduced, used original. NOS interiors, technical advice and appraisals.

Repro Parts Mfg
PO Box 3690
San Jose, CA 95156
408-923-2491

parts

Mail order only. Specializing in reproduction and original used parts (body and mechanical) for 1953 to 1957 Corvettes.

Research Project 1956/1957
Michael Hunt
PO Box 5154
Madison, WI 53705

information

Mail order only. Collecting and analyzing 1956-57 Corvette data since 1974. Provides information to owners and restorers, writes articles and is currently assembling a set of information reports. Send SASE.

Rik's Unlimited
3758 Hwy 18 S
Morganton, NC 28655
704-433-6506; FAX: 704-437-7166

accessories
parts

Quality parts and accessories for 63-82 Corvettes: emblems, weatherstrips, interiors, brakes, moldings, suspension, bumpers and much more. Our parts catalog is packed full of illustrations and listings to help find the part you need. We pride ourselves on fast, friendly service, quality parts and competitive pricing. Call or write for catalog (cost $2).

Frank Riley Automotive Art
PO Box 95
Hawthorne, NJ 07506
800-848-9459

automotive prints

See full listing in **Section Two** under **artwork**

Mary Jo Rohner's 1953-1962 Corvette Parts
16367 Martincoit Rd
Poway, CA 92064
619-451-1933; FAX: 619-451-1999

parts

Mail order only. Specializes in new, used and reproduction Corvette parts from 1953-1962. Many rare and hard-to-find parts. Prices lower than the rest.

SC Automotive
Rt 3 Box 9
New Ulm, MN 56073
507-354-1958; FAX: 800-6477-FAXS

parts
restoration

See full listing in **Section One** under **Chevrolet**

Bob Sottile's Hobby Car Auto Sales Inc
RD 2, Box 210B, Rt 164
Martinsburg, PA 16662
814-793-4282

car dealer
restoration

Mail order and open shop. Monday-Friday 9:30 to 8:30, Saturday 9 to 5. Buys, sells, repairs and restores Corvettes. All are clean and original. Have a combined 30 years of Corvette sales and repair and restoration experience. Bob Sottile, the owner, is the manager in charge of all of the business.

Ssnake-Oyl Products Inc
Rt 2, Box 269-6
Hawkins, TX 75765
903-769-4555; 903-769-4552

carpet underlay
firewall insulation
seatbelt restoration

See full listing in **Section Two** under **interiors & interior parts**

Stainless Steel Brakes Corp 11470 Main Rd Clarence, NY 14031 800-448-7722, 716-759-8666 FAX: 716-759-8688, 24 hr	**brake accessories brake fluid/pads disc brakes/rotors parking brake kits power steering parts**

See full listing in **Section Two** under **brakes**

Stencils & Stripes Unlimited Inc 1108 S Crescent Ave #21 Park Ridge, IL 60068 708-692-6893; FAX: 708-692-6895	**NOS decals stripe kits**

See full listing in **Section Two** under **decals**

Still Cruisin' Corvettes 5759 Benford Dr Haymarket, VA 20169 703-754-1960; FAX: 703-754-1222	**appraisals repairs restoration**

Open shop only. Open Monday-Friday 8 am to 5 pm, Saturday 8 am 12 noon. Specializing in restoration or repair of Corvettes 1953 thru 1972 and consultant for pre-purchase. Certified appraiser of all collectible cars. Expert witness for court cases. Sales of original, NOS and reproduction Corvette parts.

Stoudt Auto Sales 1350 Carbon St Reading, PA 19601 800-523-8485 USA for parts dept 800-482-3033 USA for sales dept 610-374-4856 parts information	**parts sales service**

Parts mail order and open shop. Monday-Thursday 9-6; Friday 9-5, Saturday 9-3. Sales dept. Monday-Thursday 9-8; Friday 9-5; Saturday 9-3. Huge selection of new, used and repro parts for all years. Over 6,500 parts in stock. 25 Corvettes in stock. Same location for 36 years. Catalog.

Street-Wise Performance Richie Mulligan 105 Creek Rd Tranquility, NJ 07879 201-786-6668 days, 201-786-7133 evenings	**differentials parts rebuild kits transmissions**

See full listing in **Section Two** under **transmissions**

Strictly Corvettes Inc 1405 Kuser Rd Hamilton, NJ 08619 800-585-0686; FAX: 609-585-6502	**restoration**

Specializing in Corvettes, Pontiac & muscle car restorations for 1953-1996 Corvettes, 55-79 Pontiacs, 60s & 70s muscle cars.

Stripping Technologies Inc 2949 E Elvira Rd Tucson, AZ 85706 800-999-0501; FAX: 520-741-9200 E-mail: sti@stripmaster.com	**paint removal**

See full listing in **Section Two** under **rust removal & stripping**

Trim Parts Inc 5161 Wolfpen Pleasant Hill Milford, OH 45150 513-831-1472; FAX: 513-248-3402	**trim items**

See full listing in **Section One** under **Chevrolet**

U S Oldies & Classics Vunt 3 Holsbeek 3220 Belgium 3216446611, FAX: 3216446520	**car dealer parts**

See full listing in **Section Two** under **car dealers**

Vantage Auto Interiors 11 Fahey St Stamford, CT 06907 203-425-9533; FAX: 203-425-9535	**upholstery**

See full listing in **Section Two** under **interiors & interior parts**

Vibratech Inc (Fluidampr) 11980 Walden Ave Alden, NY 14004 716-937-3603; FAX: 716-937-4692	**performance parts**

See full listing in **Section Two** under **engine parts**

Virginia Vettes Parts & Sales 105 Lindrick St Williamsburg, VA 23188 757-229-0011 FAX: 757-565-1629, 24 hours	**interiors parts**

Mail order and open shop. Saturday 7:30 am to 5 pm. Serves the collector and hobbyist with OEM, reproduction and good used parts. Corvette interiors, carpet, weatherstrip, special fasteners, seat covers and door panels are all made to original specifications. A 6,000-square-foot warehouse of new and used parts. Free catalog showing available parts. Shop location: 5662 Mooretown Road, Williamsburg, VA 23188.

Wild Bill's Corvette & Hi-Performance Center Inc 451 Walpole St Norwood, MA 02062 617-551-8858	**parts rebuilding service**

Mail order and open shop. Monday to Friday 9 am to 6 pm. Specializing in service, parts, consultation, major rebuilding & overhaul for Chevrolet Corvettes 1953 to present. With 16 years' experience concentrating on 1963 to 1982. Member of NCRS.

R L Williams Classic Corvette Parts PO Box 3307 Palmer, PA 18043 610-258-2028; FAX: 610-253-6816	**literature parts**

Specializing in used, reproduction and NOS parts, also literature for 1953 to 1962 Corvettes with catalogues for 1953-55, 1956-57 or 1958-62. Call or write for free catalogue.

Wilson's Classic Auto 417 Kaufman, Rt 150 PO Box 58 Congerville, IL 61729 309-448-2408; FAX: 309-448-2409	**restoration**

See full listing in **Section Two** under **restoration shops**

A & M SoffSeal Inc 104 May Dr Harrison, OH 45030 800-426-0902 513-367-0028, service & info FAX: 513-367-5506	**rubber parts weatherstripping**

See full listing in **Section Two** under **rubber parts**

AARcadia Parts Locating
8294 Allport Ave
Santa Fe Springs, CA 90670
310-698-8067; FAX: 310-696-6505

parts

See full listing in **Section One** under **MoPar**

American Plastic Chrome
1398 Mar Ann Dr
Westland, MI 48185
313-721-1967 days
313-261-4454 eves

replating plastic

See full listing in **Section Two** under **plating & polishing**

Antique Chrysler Parts
5810 Tyler Ave
Export, PA 15632
412-731-4339
FAX: 412-243-4556 anytime

parts

Massive inventory of NOS parts, please send part numbers for wants, 1938-1960.

Antique DeSoto-Plymouth
4206 Burnett Dr
Murrysville, PA 15668
412-733-1818 eves
FAX: 412-243-4556 anytime

MoPar parts

See full listing in **Section One** under **MoPar**

Atlas Motor Parts
10621 Bloomfield St
Unit 32
Los Alamitos, CA 90720
310-594-5560; FAX: 310-936-1398

parts

See full listing in **Section One** under **MoPar**

Benfield's Auto Body
213 Trent St
Kernersville, NC 27284
PH/FAX: 910-993-5772

body repair
paint

See full listing in **Section Two** under **painting**

Andy Bernbaum Auto Parts
315 Franklin St
Newton, MA 02158
617-244-1118

parts

See full listing in **Section One** under **MoPar**

Burchill Antique Auto Parts Inc
PO Box 610637
Port Huron, MI 48061
810-385-3838

parts
technical info

Mail order and open shop. Monday-Saturday 9 am to 12 am. Large stock of new, some used parts. Technical knowledge research available on request. Include SASE with inquiries. Catalogs available for most American made cars, 1920-1961. 810-385-3838 Monday through Friday 9 am to noon.

Classic Auto Air Mfg Co
2020 W Kennedy Blvd
Tampa, FL 33606
813-251-4994, 813-251-2356

air conditioning
heating
parts

See full listing in **Section One** under **Mustang**

Clock Doc®
125 University Ave
Sewanee, TN 37375
800-256-5362; FAX: 615-598-5986

clock repairs
gauge repairs

See full listing in **Section Two** under **instruments**

Collector Car Buyers
4046 11th St
Rockford, IL 61109
815-229-1258; FAX: 815-229-1238

car dealers

See full listing in **Section Two** under **car dealers**

CSK Publishing Co Inc
299 Market St
Saddle Brook, NJ 07662
201-712-9300; FAX: 201-712-0990
E-mail: staff@cskpub.com

periodical

See full listing in **Section Four** under **periodicals**

Lawrence DeSenville
Box 423
1440 Kenilworth
Berwyn, IL 60402
708-788-6759

mechanical parts
trim parts

Mail order and open shop. Specializing in 1930-70 Chrysler Product parts. Also remakes prewar Dodge and Plymouth firewall plates and body and serial number plates.

**Bruce Ebmeier, Obsolete
Parts Depot**
2905 N Osage Ave
Juniata, NE 68955-3002
FAX: 402-751-2566

parts

See full listing in **Section One** under **MoPar**

Edgerton Classics Ltd
RR 5 Box 199
Canastota, NY 13032
315-697-2722

restoration
woodworking

See full listing in **Section Two** under **restoration shops**

ETC Every Thing Cars
8727 Clarinda
Pico Rivera, CA 90660
310-949-6981

restoration

See full listing in **Section One** under **MoPar**

Jay M Fisher
Acken Dr 4-B
Clark, NJ 07066
908-388-6442

radiator caps
sidemount mirrors

See full listing in **Section Two** under **accessories**

Green Valentine Inc
5055 Covington Way
Memphis, TN 38134
901-373-5555; FAX: 901-373-5568

car dealer
woodies

See full listing in **Section Two** under **car dealers**

Hagerty Classic Insurance — insurance
PO Box 87
Traverse City, MI 49685
800-922-4050; FAX: 616-941-8227

See full listing in **Section Two** under **insurance**

Hawthorne Appraisals — appraisals / parts
Box 1332
Coaldale, AB Canada T1M 1N1
403-345-2101

See full listing in **Section Two** under **appraisals**

Hidden Valley Auto Parts — parts
21046 N Rio Bravo
Maricopa, AZ 85239
602-252-2122, 602-252-6137
520-568-2945
FAX: 602-258-0951

See full listing in **Section One** under **Chevrolet**

Imperial Motors — parts
2165 Spencer Creek Rd
Campobello, SC 29322
864-895-3474

Mail order only. Chrysler, Plymouth, Dodge parts only. Chrysler parts 1955-1982. Chrysler, Plymouth, Dodge, Imperial, DeSoto, Barracuda parts. Parting out complete running cars. Rust-free sheetmetal. 30 acres of cars and parts.

Instrument Services Inc — clocks
11765 Main St
Roscoe, IL 61073
800-558-2674; FAX: 800-623-6416

See full listing in **Section Two** under **instruments**

Jeff Johnson Motorsports — accessories / literature / parts
4421 Aldrich Pl
Columbus, OH 43214
614-268-1181; FAX: 614-268-1141

See full listing in **Section One** under **MoPar**

King & Queen Mufflers — exhaust systems
Box 423
Plumsteadville, PA 18949
PH/FAX: 215-766-8699

See full listing in **Section Two** under **exhaust systems**

Kramer Automotive Specialties — body parts / interiors / sheetmetal
PO Box 5
Herman, PA 16039
412-285-5566

See full listing in **Section One** under **MoPar**

L & L Antique Auto Trim — runningboard / moldings
403 Spruce, Box 177
Pierce City, MO 65723
417-476-2871

See full listing in **Section Two** under **special services**

Legendary Auto Interiors Ltd — soft trim
121 W Shore Blvd
Newark, NY 14513
800-363-8804; FAX: 800-732-8874

Mail order. Monday-Friday 8:30 am-5 pm EST. Manufacturers and distributors of the finest quality reproduction interior and exterior soft trim for most 1957-1980 Chrysler, Dodge and Plymouth and 1964-1972 Buick Skylark and GS models. A full color line of OEM quality seat upholstery, door panels, carpets, headliners, convertible tops, boots and well liners are part of an extensive selection of soft trim and interior restoration products. For catalog orders and information, phone toll-free.

Lloyd's Literature — literature
PO Box 491
Newbury, OH 44065
800-292-2665

See full listing in **Section Two** under **literature dealers**

Mainly Convertibles — parts / repair / restoration
13805 W Hillsborough Ave
Tampa, FL 33635
813-855-6869; FAX: 813-855-1376

See full listing in **Section One** under **Lincoln**

David Martin — parts
Box 61
Roosevelt, TX 76874
915-446-4439

Mail order only. Specializes in parts for 1946-47-48 Chryslers, some DeSoto and Dodge.

Mike's Auto Parts — bearings / engine parts / NOS parts / wall calendars
Box 358
Ridgeland, MS 39158
601-856-7214

Mail order. Specializing in Chrysler, AMC/Jeep, GM parts and bearings, universal joints, engine parts, brake parts, ignition parts, spark plugs, 6-volt bulbs, tubular shocks, belts, water pumps, fuel pumps, transmission gears and windshield wipers for all makes. Also collectible wall calendars and memorabilia.

Mitchell Motor Parts Inc — car dealer / parts
1601 Thraikill Rd
Grove City, OH 43123
614-875-4919; FAX: 614-875-9960

See full listing in **Section One** under **MoPar**

Clayton T Nelson — NOS parts
Box 259
Warrenville, IL 60555
708-369-6589

See full listing in **Section One** under **Oldsmobile**

North Yale Auto Parts — salvage yard
Rt 1, Box 707
Sperry, OK 74073
918-288-7218, 800-256-6927 (NYAP)
FAX: 918-288-7223

See full listing in **Section Five** under **Oklahoma**

NS-One   NOS parts
PO Box 2459, Dept VA
Cedar Rapids, IA 52406
319-362-7717

Mail order only. NOS Chrysler product parts. Trim, electricals, minor mechanicals, etc, for late 30s to early 70s. No catalogs, no lists available. Postpaid prices; COD extra. Easy return policy. No SASE, no answer.

Old Air Products   air conditioning
3056 SE Loop 820
Ft Worth, TX 76140
817-551-0602; FAX: 817-568-0037

See full listing in **Section One** under **Corvette**

Older Car Restoration   repro parts
Martin Lum, Owner   restoration
304 S Main St, Box 428
Mont Alto, PA 17237
717-749-3383, 352-7701

See full listing in **Section One** under **MoPar**

Performance Motor Parts   parts
Box 122
West Milton, OH 45383
PH/FAX: 513-698-4259

See full listing in **Section One** under **MoPar**

Plymouth, Dodge, Chrysler,   NOS parts for
DeSoto Parts   DeSoto
935 Limecrest Rd
Pittsburgh, PA 15668
412-733-1818 eves
FAX: 412-243-4556 anytime

See full listing in **Section One** under **DeSoto**

Power Play, Bob Walker   parts
Rt 1 Box 95
Lowgap, NC 27024
910-352-4866; FAX: 910-789-8967

Mail order only. Monday thru Saturday 7 pm-9 pm. Early Hemi engine parts, adaptors and rebuilding for 51 to 58 Chrysler, 52-57 DeSoto and 53-57 Dodge Hemi engines.

REM Automotive Inc   interior parts
Box 241, Rt 1, Brandt Rd
Annville, PA 17003
717-838-4242; FAX: 717-838-5091

See full listing in **Section Two** under **restoration aids**

Restorations By Julius   restoration
22434 Itasca St
Chatsworth, CA 91311
818-882-2866

See full listing in **Section One** under **Plymouth**

Roanoke Motor Co Inc   car dealer
422 N Main
Roanoke, IL 61561
309-923-7171; FAX: 309-923-7332

Chrysler, Dodge and Jeep dealer. Specializing in new and old (late 60s-early 70s) Vipers and various other performance automobiles.

Don Rook   parts
184 Raspberry Ln
Mena, AR 71953
501-394-7555

Mail order and open shop. Open anytime at home. Specializes in parts for Chryslers and Packards of the 40s, 50s and 60s, mostly Chrysler 300s 1955-1971 and specifically 1965 and 1966. Also many Packard parts from 1941-1956, trim and chrome. No heavy and internal mechanical items. Trim and detail pieces only. Some windshields.

R/T Connection   parts
1034 Dover St
Warren, OH 44485
330-399-3959

See full listing in **Section One** under **MoPar**

Paul Slater Auto Parts   parts
9496 85th St N
Stillwater, MN 55082
612-429-4235

See full listing in **Section One** under **Dodge**

Ed Spiegel   literature
Box 402   parts
Murrysville, PA 15668
412-733-1818 evenings

Mail order and open shop. Saturdays 8 to 5. New old stock Chrysler products, parts. Specializing in chrome trim, medallions, fenders and bumpers, thirties through sixties. Lots of literature also. Dodge and Plymouth NOS parts for 1938 to 1958. Satisfaction guaranteed.

Stockton Wheel Service   wheel repair
648 W Fremont St
Stockton, CA 95203
209-464-7771, 800-395-9433
FAX: 209-464-4725

See full listing in **Section Two** under **service shops**

Tire Barn Inc   tires
255 Twinsburg Rd
Northfield, OH 44067
216-467-1284
FAX: 216-467-1289, call first

See full listing in **Section Two** under **tires**

Top Flite International Inc   fiberglass hardtops
PO Box 505
Winfield, TN 37892
423-569-2460; FAX: 423-569-2525

Mail order only. Specializing in removable fiberglass hardtops for Jeep Wrangler, CJ7, CJ5. 1976-current GEO Tracker, Suzuki Sidekick, Isuzu Amigo, all models, years.

Trim Parts Inc   trim items
5161 Wolfpen Pleasant Hill
Milford, OH 45150
513-831-1472; FAX: 513-248-3402

See full listing in **Section One** under **Chevrolet**

U S Oldies & Classics
Vunt 3
Holsbeek 3220 Belgium
3216446611, FAX: 3216446520

car dealer
parts

See full listing in **Section Two** under **car dealers**

Ultra Wheel Co
6300 Valley View Ave
Buena Park, CA 90620
714-994-1444; FAX: 714-994-0723

custom wheels

See full listing in **Section Two** under **wheels & wheelcovers**

Universal Transmission Co
23361 Dequindre Rd
Hazel Park, MI 48030
800-882-4327; FAX: 810-398-2581

transmission parts

See full listing in **Section Two** under **transmissions**

Varco Inc
8200 S Anderson Rd
Oklahoma City, OK 73150
405-732-1637

fitted luggage
trunks

See full listing in **Section One** under **Ford '03-'31**

Vintage Woodworks
PO Box 49
Iola, WI 54945
715-445-3791

upholstery
woodwork

See full listing in **Section Two** under **woodwork**

Weimann's Literature & Collectables
16 Cottage Rd
Harwinton, CT 06791
860-485-0300
FAX: 860-485-1705, 24 hour

literature

See full listing in **Section One** under **Plymouth**

Wheel Vintiques Inc
5468 E Lamona Ave
Fresno, CA 93727
209-251-6957; FAX: 209-251-1620

hubcaps
wheels

See full listing in **Section One** under **Chevrolet**

Willow Grove Auto Top
43 N York Rd
Willow Grove, PA 19090
215-659-3276

interiors
tops
upholstery

See full listing in **Section Two** under **interiors & interior parts**

CITROËN⋀

Proper Motor Cars Inc
1811 11th Ave N
St. Petersburg, FL 33713-5794
813-821-8883; FAX: 813-895-4746

parts
restoration

See full listing in **Section One** under **Rolls-Royce/Bentley**

Brooklands Inc
503 Corporate Square
1500 NW 62nd St
Fort Lauderdale, FL 33309
954-776-2748; FAX: 954-772-8383
E-mail: rbiggs@lgc.net

accessories

See full listing in **Section Two** under **accessories**

Carl's Ford Parts
23219 South ST
Homeworth, OH 44634
PH/FAX: 330-525-7291

muscle parts

See full listing in **Section One** under **Mustang**

CJ Pony Parts Inc
7441 B Allentown Blvd
Harrisburg, PA 17112
800-888-6473; 717-691-5623
FAX: 717-657-9254

parts

See full listing in **Section One** under **Mustang**

Classics 'n More Inc
1001 Ranck Mill Rd
Lancaster, PA 17602
717-392-0599; FAX 717-392-2371

repairs
restoration

See full listing in **Section Two** under **restoration shops**

Cobra Restorers Ltd
3099 Carter Dr
Kennesaw, GA 30144
404-427-0020; FAX: 404-427-8658

parts
restoration
service

Mail order and open shop. Monday-Friday 9 to 6. Largest supplier of parts for Cobra roadsters (replica & original). Restoration & builder of ERA Cobras. Manufactures many parts. Catalog $5.

Collectors Choice LTD
6400 Springfield, Lodi Rd
Dane, WI 53529
608-849-9878; FAX: 608-849-9879

parts
restoration
service

See full listing in **Section One** under **DeTomaso/Pantera**

Drummond Coach and Paint
531 Raleigh Ave
El Cajon, CA 92020
619-579-7229; FAX: 619-579-2128

painting
restoration

See full listing in **Section One** under **Ferrari**

The Fine Car Store
1105 Moana Dr
San Diego, CA 92107
619-223-7766; FAX: 619-223-6838

car dealer

See full listing in **Section One** under **Ferrari**

Gemini Racing Systems Inc
7301 W Boston St
Chandler, AZ 85226
800-992-9294, 602-940-9011

race prep
restoration

See full listing in **Section One** under **Mustang**

Mark Gillett
PO Box 9177
Dallas, TX 75209
PH/FAX: 214-902-9258; 011-525-
559-6240 Mexico City, Mexico
E-mail-autonet@onramp.net

car locator
sales

See full listing in **Section Two** under **car dealers**

Hyannis Restoration
119 Thornton Dr
Hyannis, MA 02601
508-775-8131; FAX: 508-790-2339

restoration

See full listing in **Section One** under **Ferrari**

**International Restoration
Specialist Inc**
PO Box 1303
Mt Airy, NC 27030
910-789-1548

parts
restoration
sales

See full listing in **Section One** under **Jaguar**

JWF Restorations Inc
11955 SW Faircrest St
Portland, OR 97225-4615
503-643-3225; FAX: 503-646-4009

restoration

See full listing in **Section One** under **AC**

Marcovicci-Wenz Engineering Inc
33 Comac Loop
Ronkonkoma, NY 11779
516-467-9040; FAX: 516-467-9041

engine parts
services

See full listing in **Section Two** under **racing**

Milestone Motorcars
Mark Tyra
12910 Sunnybrook Dr
Prospect, KY 40059
502-228-5945; FAX: 502-228-1856

die cast cars
models

See full listing in **Section Two** under **automobilia**

Nisonger Instrument S/S
570 Mamaroneck Ave
Mamaroneck, NY 10543
914-381-1952, FAX: 914-381-1953

gauges

See full listing in **Section Two** under **instruments**

Operations Plus
PO Box 26347
Santa Ana, CA 92799
PH/FAX: 714-962-2776

accessories
parts

Distributor for Unique Motor Cars. Supplier of over 500 Cobra
parts and accessories: body, interior, windshield, lighting, mirrors, hardware, fasteners, steering wheels, fuel, wheels, oil pans,
coolers and adapters, knock-off striking hammers, removable/
reusable static cling vinyl and vintage decals and memorabilia.

Greg Purdy's Mustang Supply
PO Box 784
Forest Hill, MD 21050
410-836-5991

parts

See full listing in **Section One** under **Mustang**

Scarborough Faire Inc
1151 Main St
Pawtucket, RI 02860
800-556-6300; 401-724-4200
FAX: 401-724-5392

parts

See full listing in **Section One** under **MG**

Showroom Auto Sales
960 S Bascom Ave
San Jose, CA 95128
408-554-1550; FAX: 408-554-0550

car dealer

See full listing in **Section One** under **Mercedes-Benz**

Specialty Car Service Ltd
1330 Ritters Rd
Reading, PA 19606
610-370-0410

parts
restoration
service

See full listing in **Section One** under **Morgan**

Unfair Advantage Enterprises
2219 W Olive Ave #179
Burbank, CA 91506
213-245-8441

emblems
trim

Mail order only. Organized to provide exact, high quality emblems and trim pieces for specific automotive markets. Specializing in Cobras, Shelbys 1965-70, Chevrolets 1955, 56, 57.

Visual Marketplace Online Inc
800 Silverado, Suite 324
La Jolla, CA 92037
619-459-3846; FAX: 619-459-3460
E-mail: pyoung@icreations.com

online auto ads

See full listing in **Section Four** under **information sources**

COOPER

Manhattan Mini Inc
New York, NY 10036
212-921-8459; FAX: 212-719-5313

sales

See full listing in **Section One** under **Austin**

Mini Mania
31 Winsor St
Milpitas, CA 95035
408-942-5595; FAX: 408-942-5582
E-mail: minimania@aol.com

parts
service

See full listing in **Section One** under **Austin**

Mini Store
PO Box 7973
Van Nuys, CA 91409-7973
818-893-1421

cars
repairs
restorations

See full listing in **Section One** under **Austin**

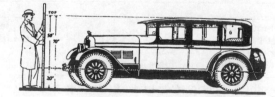

Beckley Auto Restorations Inc | restoration
4405 Capital Ave SW
Battle Creek, MI 49015
616-979-3013

See full listing in **Section Two** under **restoration shops**

J K Howell | parts
455 N Grace St
Lombard, IL 60148
630-495-1949

Mail order only. Full line of new, used, original and reproduction Cord parts and manuals. Catalog available to owners or restorers.

Lincoln Highway Packards | engine rebuilding
Main St, PO Box 94 | restoration
Schellsburg, PA 15559
814-733-4356; FAX: 814-839-4276

See full listing in **Section One** under **Packard**

McLellan's Automotive History | books
Robert McLellan | magazines
9111 Longstaff Dr | programs
Houston, TX 77031 | sales literature
713-772-3285; FAX: 713-772-3277

See full listing in **Section Two** under **literature dealers**

Norm's Custom Shop | interiors
6897 E William St Ext | tops
Bath, NY 14810
607-776-2357; FAX: 607-776-4541

Mail order and open shop. Shop open Monday-Friday 8:30 to 5 pm, Saturday 8:30 to 2 pm. Fabrication and installation of automobile tops and interiors, custom or original design using materials of your choice. Many National winners over the past 34 years.

Seattle Packard | repair
PO Box 2262 | restoration
Seattle, WA 98111
206-726-9625

See full listing in **Section One** under **Packard**

Edwards Crosley Parts | parts
PO Box 632
Mansfield, OH 44901
419-589-5767

Mail order and open shop. Open evenings and weekends. Call before visiting. Shop address: 988 Reed Rd Mansfield, OH 44903.

Heinze Enterprise | instrument
7914 E Kimsey Ln | restoration
Scottsdale, AZ 85257
602-946-5814

See full listing in **Section One** under **American Austin/Bantam**

Service Motors | car dealer
PO Box 116 | parts
Twelve Mile, IN 46988
219-664-3313

Phone hours: 9 to 5 daily. Crosley parts bought, sold and traded. Complete cars for sale. Parts shipped via UPS, COD.

Cushman

Dennis Carpenter Cushman | accessories
Reproductions | parts
PO Box 26398
Charlotte, NC 28221-6398
704-786-8139; FAX: 704-786-8180

Mail order and over the counter sales. Monday-Friday 8 to 5 pm. Manufacture and sell obsolete Cushman motor scooter parts, including body and engine parts, accessories and much more. We also buy and sell all makes of vintage motorbikes and motor scooters. Send $4 for catalog.

Daimler

Arthur W Aseltine | parts
18215 Challenge Cut-Off Rd | research
Forbestown, CA 95941 | restoration
916-675-2773

See full listing in **Section One** under **Stearns-Knight**

Healey Lane | parts
5920 Jones Ave | restoration
Riverside, CA 92505 | service
800-411-HEALEY (4325)
FAX: 909-689-4934

See full listing in **Section One** under **Austin-Healey**

Barry Thorne | manuals
The Old Coach House, Ockley | parts
Surrey RH5 5LS England
01306 713341; FAX: 01306 712168
mobile: 0585-882416

Mail order and open shop. Anytime, any day. For 1959-64 Daimler SP 250s and SP 251s (lhd). Also Daimler 2 1/2 V8 and V8 250. All inquiries answered. Free advice. Worldwide shipping.

Vicarage Jaguars | parts
3952 Douglas Rd | restoration
Miami, FL 33133
305-444-8759; FAX: 305-443-6443

See full listing in **Section One** under **Jaguar**

Banzai Motorworks
6735 Midcities Ave
Beltsville, MD 20705
301-937-5746

pre-purchase
insp/consultation
repairs/restoration
service

Mail order and open shop. Monday-Friday 8:30-6, most Saturdays 10-3. Washington/Baltimore Metro Area's only vintage Datsun shop specializing in Z, 510, 1200, roadster and pickup service, repair, restoration and pre-purchase inspection/consultation. Owner Michael McGinnis has more than 26 years of experience servicing Datsuns. Call or write for vintage Z-car restoration parts catalog.

Stan Chernoff
1215 Greenwood Ave
Torrance, CA 90503
310-320-4554; FAX: 310-328-7867
E-mail: az589@lafn.org

mechanical parts
restoration parts
technical info
trim parts

Mail order only. Specializing in restoration, mechanical and trim parts and technical information for 1963 to 1970 Datsun roadsters, Models SP(L) 310, SP(L) 311 and SR(L) 311.

Classic Datsun Motorsports
402 Olive Ave #A
Vista, CA 92083
PH/FAX: 619-940-6365
E-mail: lescan@cts.com

appraisals
literature
parts
restoration

Specializes in restoration, new and used parts sales, reproduction parts, stickers and a dealership showroom. Datsun roadsters from 1958-1970, 1500, 1600, 2000 and other early cars. Hard to find models of Datsuns, sedans, wagons, pickups. Also has literature, appraisal service and reference materials available.

CSI
1100 S Raymond Ave, Suite H
Fullerton, CA 92831
714-879-7955; FAX: 714-879-7310
E-mail: 102263.1046@compuserve.com

accessories
parts

See full listing in **Section One** under **BMW**.

John's Cars Inc
800 Jaguar Ln
Dallas, TX 75226
214-426-4100; FAX: 214-426-3116

parts
restoration
service

See full listing in **Section One** under **Jaguar**.

Motormetrics
5500 Thomaston Rd
Macon, GA 31204
912-477-6771

used parts

See full listing in **Section One** under **Triumph**.

Motorsport Auto
1139 W Collins Ave
Orange, CA 92667
714-639-2620; 800-633-6331
FAX: 714-639-7460

parts

Mail order and open shop. Monday-Friday 8 am-5 pm, Saturday 10 am-2 pm. Parts and accessories for Datsun 240Z, 260Z, 280Z, 280ZX; Nissan 300ZX. Full line of restoration items for all Z-cars. 144-page catalog now available.

Roadster Restoration
3730 Todrob Ln
Placerville, CA 95667
916-644-6777; FAX: 916-644-7252

restoration parts
service manuals

Mail order only. Supplies a complete line of restoration parts for Datsun roadsters. Engine, mechanical, interior, service manual, weatherstripping, electrical and performance parts for Datsun 1600, 2000 and Fairlady Sports. Also accepts MasterCard and VISA.

Tiger Detailing
PO Box 9875
North Hollywood, CA 91609-1875
PH/FAX: 818-982-1042
E-mail: tygrbeer7@aol.com

accessories
detailing
parts

See full listing in **Section One** under **Sunbeam**.

Tweeks Ltd
8148 Woodland Dr
Indianapolis, IN 46278
317-876-0075; FAX: 317-875-0181

accessories
parts
restoration

See full listing in **Section One** under **Porsche**.

DE LOREAN MOTOR COMPANY

DeLorean Literature
3116 Welsh Rd
Philadelphia, PA 19136-1810
215-338-6142

collectibles
literature

Mail order only. Provides original literature and collectable display items for collectors of DeLorean, Bricklin and 1946-1948 Plymouth material. SASE required.

DeLorean One
20229 Nordhoff St
Chatsworth, CA 91311
818-341-1796; FAX: 818-998-6381

body work
parts
service

Mail order and open shop. Monday-Friday 8 am to 6 pm. Specializes in DeLorean parts, service, bodywork, electrical, suspension and sales for all DeLorean automobiles, 1981 through 1983.

French Stuff
PO Box 39772
Glendale, CA 90039-0772
818-244-2498,
FAX: 818-500-7628

accessories
engine rebuilding
parts
transaxle rebuilding

See full listing in **Section One** under **Renault**.

Michael A Stahl
PO Box 18036
Huntsville, AL 35804
205-882-6457

parts

See full listing in **Section One** under **Cadillac/LaSalle**.

Al Trommers Rare Auto Literature
59 West Front Street, Mailbox #1
Keyport Mini Mall
Keyport, NJ 07735

hubcaps
license plates
literature/records
wheelcovers

See full listing in **Section Two** under **literature dealers**.

Wilson's Classic Auto 417 Kaufman, Rt 150 PO Box 58 Congerville, IL 61729 309-448-2408; FAX: 309-448-2409	restoration

See full listing in **Section Two** under **restoration shops**

DeSoto

Antique DeSoto-Plymouth 4206 Burnett Dr Murrysville, PA 15668 412-733-1818 eves FAX: 412-243-4556 anytime	MoPar parts

See full listing in **Section One** under **MoPar**

Andy Bernbaum Auto Parts 315 Franklin St Newton, MA 02158 617-244-1118	parts

See full listing in **Section One** under **MoPar**

Burchill Antique Auto Parts Inc 4150 24th Ave Fort Gratiot, MI 48059 810-385-3838 after 12/1/93	parts technical info

See full listing in **Section One** under **Chrysler**

Dylan Bay Auto Museum 1411 4th Ave, #1430 Seattle, WA 98101 206-292-9874; FAX: 206-292-9876 E-mail: cbayley@dylanbay.com	museum

See full listing in **Section Six** under **Washington**

Bruce Ebmeier, Obsolete Parts Depot 2905 N Osage Ave Juniata, NE 68955-3002 FAX: 402-751-2566	parts

See full listing in **Section One** under **MoPar**

Jahns Quality Pistons 1360 N Jefferson St Anaheim, CA 92807 714-579-3795, 800-225-0277 FAX: 714-524-6607	piston rings pistons

See full listing in **Section Two** under **engine parts**

David Martin Box 61 Roosevelt, TX 76874 915-446-4439	parts

See full listing in **Section One** under **Chrysler**

Mitchell Motor Parts Inc 1601 Thraikill Rd Grove City, OH 43123 614-875-4919; FAX: 614-875-9960	car dealer parts

See full listing in **Section One** under **MoPar**

Clayton T Nelson Box 259 Warrenville, IL 60555 708-369-6589	NOS parts

See full listing in **Section One** under **Oldsmobile**

NS-One PO Box 2459, Dept VA Cedar Rapids, IA 52406 319-362-7717	NOS parts

See full listing in **Section One** under **Chrysler**

Older Car Restoration Martin Lum, Owner 304 S Main St, Box 428 Mont Alto, PA 17237 717-749-3383, 352-7701	repro parts restoration

See full listing in **Section One** under **MoPar**

Plymouth, Dodge, Chrysler, DeSoto Parts 4206 Burnett Dr Murrysville, PA 15668 412-733-1818 eves; FAX: 412-243-4556 anytime	NOS parts for DeSoto

Mail order only. Large supply of MoPar parts. Strong in DeSoto and Plymouth. Mostly NOS. DeSoto, Plymouth chrome for 1938 to 1965. Send SASE with want list for reply. Satisfaction guaranteed.

Power Play, Bob Walker Rt 1 Box 95 Lowgap, NC 27024 910-352-4866; FAX: 910-789-8967	parts

See full listing in **Section One** under **Chrysler**

R/T Connection 1034 Dover St Warren, OH 44485 330-399-3959	parts

See full listing in **Section One** under **MoPar**

Ed Spiegel Box 402 Murrysville, PA 15668 412-733-1818 evenings	literature parts

See full listing in **Section One** under **Chrysler**

U S Oldies & Classics Vunt 3 Holsbeek 3220 Belgium 3216446611, FAX: 3216446520	car dealer parts

See full listing in **Section Two** under **car dealers**

Weimann's Literature & Collectables 16 Cottage Rd Harwinton, CT 06791 860-485-0300 FAX: 860-485-1705, 24 hour	literature

See full listing in **Section One** under **Plymouth**

DeTomaso PANTERA

Avanti Auto Service	repair
Rt 322, 67 Conchester Hwy	restoration
Glen Mills, PA 19342-1506	
610-558-9999	

Open shop only. Monday-Friday 9 to 6 pm, Saturday 10 to 3 pm. General auto repair serving all makes, models and years. Mechanical restoration, front end alignment, computer service, brakes, shocks, tires, etc. 20 years' experience. Specializing in Pantera, Avanti, Corvette and others.

Collectors Choice LTD	parts
6400 Springfield, Lodi Rd	restoration
Dane, WI 53529	service
608-849-9878; FAX: 608-849-9879	

Mail order and open shop. Monday-Friday 8 am-5 pm. Specializing in DeTomaso Panteras, AC Cobras, GT-40 Fords, Shelbys, Ferraris, Jaguars, Rolls-Royce.

DeTomaso Registry	book
Bill Van Ess	
2306 Post Dr NE	
Belmont, MI 49306	
616-364-1973; FAX: 616-363-2870	

Mail order only. A registry of all the production models from DeTomaso Automobili SpA Modena. Includes all models of the Pantera, Mangusta, Vallelunga, Longchamp and Deauville. 256 pages, includes pictures and history of each model with production figures and running production changes. Current and past owners and history on the remaining cars, etc. A must for anyone with an interest in the cars. $21 postpaid US; $25 postpaid Europe.

Hall Pantera	parts
15337 Garfield Ave	
Paramount, CA 90723	
310-867-3319, 310-531-2629	
FAX: 310-630-8156	

Open shop. Tuesday-Friday 8 am to 5 pm PST. Specializing in DeTomaso parts, Pantera, Mangusta and Vallelunga parts. Ford SVO dealer.

The Italian Car Registry	information source
3305 Valley Vista Rd	
Walnut Creek, CA 94598-3943	
510-458-1163	

See full listing in **Section Four** under **information sources**

Pantera Performance Center	parts
1856 N Park St	restoration
Castle Rock, CO 80104	service
303-660-9897; FAX: 303-660-9159	

Mail order and open shop. Monday-Friday 9-5; evenings/weekends by appointment only. Specializes in parts, service & restoration for DeTomaso Pantera.

Tiger Detailing	accessories
PO Box 9875	detailing
North Hollywood, CA 91609-1875	parts
PH/FAX: 818-982-1042	
E-mail: tygrbeer7@aol.com	

See full listing in **Section One** under **Sunbeam**

Dodge

AARcadia Parts Locating	parts
8294 Allport Ave	
Santa Fe Springs, CA 90670	
310-698-8067; FAX: 310-696-6505	

See full listing in **Section One** under **MoPar**

Antique DeSoto-Plymouth	MoPar parts
4206 Burnett Dr	
Murrysville, PA 15668	
412-733-1818 eves	
FAX: 412-243-4556 anytime	

See full listing in **Section One** under **MoPar**

Barracuda Classic	accessories
1500 Adams Ave, #105-162	parts
Costa Mesa, CA 92626	
PH/FAX: 714-444-2507	

See full listing in **Section One** under **MoPar**

Andy Bernbaum Auto Parts	parts
315 Franklin St	
Newton, MA 02158	
617-244-1118	

See full listing in **Section One** under **MoPar**

Bill's Speed Shop	body parts
13951 Millersburg Rd	
Navarre, OH 44662	
330-832-9403; FAX: 330-832-2098	

See full listing in **Section One** under **Chevrolet**

The Brassworks	radiators
289 Prado Rd	
San Louis Obispo, CA 93401	
800-342-6759; FAX: 805-544-5615	

See full listing in **Section Two** under **radiators**

Burchill Antique Auto Parts Inc	parts
4150 24th Ave	technical info
Fort Gratiot, MI 48061	
810-385-3838	

See full listing in **Section One** under **Chrysler**

Coach Builders Muscle Car	interiors
Parts & Services	parts
PO Box 128	rust remover
Baltimore, MD 21087-0128	
410-426-5567	

See full listing in **Section One** under **Chevrolet**

Conte's Corvettes & Classics	leasing
851 W Wheat Rd	parts
Vineland, NJ 08360	sales
609-692-0087; FAX: 609-692-1009	service
E-mail: contes@cybernet.net	

See full listing in **Section One** under **Corvette**

Lawrence DeSenville
Box 423
1440 Kenilworth
Berwyn, IL 60402
708-788-6759

mech & trim
parts

See full listing in **Section One** under **Chrysler**

Dodge Brothers Club News
17767 Rapids Rd
Hiram, OH 44234
PH/FAX: 216-834-0233

periodical

See full listing in **Section Four** under **periodicals**

Dynatech Engineering
PO Box 1446
Alta Loma, CA 91701-8446
805-492-6134

motor mounts

See full listing in **Section Two** under **suspension parts**

Eaton Detroit Spring Service Co
1555 Michigan Ave
Detroit, MI 48350
313-963-3839; FAX: 313-963-7047
E-mail: ken@eatonsprings.com

bushings
coil springs
leaf springs
shackles
U-bolts

See full listing in **Section Two** under **suspension parts**

Bruce Ebmeier, Obsolete Parts Depot
2905 N Osage Ave
Juniata, NE 68955-3002
FAX: 402-751-2566

parts

See full listing in **Section One** under **MoPar**

ETC Every Thing Cars
8727 Clarinda
Pico Rivera, CA 90660
310-949-6981

restoration

See full listing in **Section One** under **MoPar**

Fitzgerald Motorsports
300 Union Ave
Laconia, NH 03246
800-VIPER-15; 603-524-2311
FAX: 603-528-6334

Viper dealer

Open Monday thru Saturday 9 am-8 pm. Dodge Vipers. We are the largest volume Viper dealer in the USA.

Bruce Horkey Cabinetry
Rt 4, Box 188
Windom, MN 56101
507-831-5625; FAX: 507-831-0280

pickup parts

See full listing in **Section Two** under **woodwork**

Imperial Motors
2165 Spencer Creek Rd
Campobello, SC 29322
864-895-3474

parts

See full listing in **Section One** under **Chrysler**

Jackson Speaker Service
217 Crestbrook Dr
Jackson, MI 49203
517-789-6400

radio repairs
speakers

See full listing in **Section Two** under **radios**

Jeff Johnson Motorsports
4421 Aldrich Pl
Columbus, OH 43214
614-268-1181; FAX: 614-268-1141

accessories
literature
parts

See full listing in **Section One** under **MoPar**

Koller Dodge
1565 W Ogden Ave
Naperville, IL 60540-3906
708-355-3411; FAX: 708-355-3538

restoration parts

Sell original & reproduction high performance and restoration parts for Dodge & Plymouth muscle cars. Mainly 1967-74.

Kramer Automotive Specialties
PO Box 5
Herman, PA 16039
412-285-5566

body parts
interiors
sheetmetal

See full listing in **Section One** under **MoPar**

Legendary Auto Interiors Ltd
121 W Shore Blvd
Newark, NY 14513
800-363-8804; FAX: 800-732-8874

soft trim

See full listing in **Section One** under **Chrysler**

Mack Products
Box 278
Moberly, MO 65270
816-263-7444

parts
pickup beds

See full listing in **Section One** under **Ford '32-'53**

Jim Mallars
5931 Glen St
Stockton, CA 95207
209-477-1702 (9 am-6 pm)

parts

Mail order and open shop. Open by appointment only. For 1915-28 Dodge Brothers 4-cylinder vehicles. New and used parts.

David Martin
Box 61
Roosevelt, TX 76874
915-446-4439

parts

See full listing in **Section One** under **Chrysler**

Mitchell Motor Parts Inc
1601 Thraikill Rd
Grove City, OH 43123
614-875-4919; FAX: 614-875-9960

car dealer
parts

See full listing in **Section One** under **MoPar**

Clayton T Nelson
Box 259
Warrenville, IL 60555
708-369-6589

NOS parts

See full listing in **Section One** under **Oldsmobile**

NOS Reproductions
22425 Sefferlies Rd
RR 3
Komoka, ON Canada N0L 1R0
519-471-2740; FAX: 519-471-7675

parts

See full listing in **Section One** under **MoPar**

NS-One
PO Box 2459, Dept VA
Cedar Rapids, IA 52406
319-362-7717

NOS parts

See full listing in **Section One** under **Chrysler**

Older Car Restoration
Martin Lum, Owner
304 S Main St, Box 428
Mont Alto, PA 17237
717-749-3383, 352-7701

repro parts
restoration

See full listing in **Section One** under **MoPar**

The Paddock® Inc
PO Box 30
221 W Main
Knightstown, IN 46148
800-428-4319; FAX: 317-345-2264
E-mail: paddock@indy.net

accessories
parts

See full listing in **Section One** under **Mustang**

Paddock West® Inc
1663 Plum Ln
PO Box 8547
Redlands, CA 92375
800-854-8532; FAX: 909-798-1482
E-mail: padwest@msn.com

accessories
parts

See full listing in **Section One** under **Mustang**

Performance Motor Parts
Box 122
West Milton, OH 45383
PH/FAX: 513-698-4259

parts

See full listing in **Section One** under **MoPar**

**Plymouth, Dodge, Chrysler,
DeSoto Parts**
935 Limecrest Rd
Pittsburgh, PA 15668
412-733-1818 eves
FAX: 412-243-4556 anytime

NOS parts for
DeSoto

See full listing in **Section One** under **DeSoto**

Power Play, Bob Walker
Rt 1 Box 95
Lowgap, NC 27024
910-352-4866; FAX: 910-789-8967

parts

See full listing in **Section One** under **Chrysler**

R & R Fiberglass & Specialties
4850 Wilson Dr NW
Cleveland, TN 37312
423-476-2270

body parts

See full listing in **Section Two** under **fiberglass parts**

Restorations By Julius
22434 Itasca St
Chatsworth, CA 91311
818-882-2866

restoration

See full listing in **Section One** under **Plymouth**

Roanoke Motor Co Inc
422 N Main
Roanoke, IL 61561
309-923-7171; FAX: 309-923-7332

car dealer

See full listing in **Section One** under **Chrysler**

R/T Connection
1034 Dover St
Warren, OH 44485
330-399-3959

parts

See full listing in **Section One** under **MoPar**

Paul Slater Auto Parts
9496 85th St N
Stillwater, MN 55082
612-429-4235

parts

Mail order and open shop. Shop hours by appointment only. Phone hours are 9 am to 9 pm CST. Specializing in 1966-74 performance Dodge and Plymouth parts (Roadrunner, GTX, Coronet, Super Bee, Charger, Barracuda, Challenger, Dart, Duster, Demon & some others). Excellent quality used my specialty, but also some NOS parts. More items in every week. Call or write me (send SASE) with your needs. Sorry, no list or catalog. I also buy NOS and quality used parts.

Ed Spiegel
4206 Burnett Dr
Murrysville, PA 15668
412-733-1818 evenings

literature
parts

See full listing in **Section One** under **Chrysler**

Stockton Wheel Service
648 W Fremont St
Stockton, CA 95203
209-464-7771, 800-395-9433
FAX: 209-464-4725

wheel repair

See full listing in **Section Two** under **service shops**

Vintage Power Wagons Inc
302 S 7th St
Fairfield, IA 52556
515-472-4665; FAX: 515-472-4824

parts
trucks

Mail order and open shop. Monday-Friday, 8:30 am-5 pm. Specializing in 39-70 Dodge Power Wagons, 4-wd trucks and parts.

**Weimann's Literature &
Collectables**
16 Cottage Rd
Harwinton, CT 06791
860-485-0300
FAX: 860-485-1705, 24 hour

literature

See full listing in **Section One** under **Plymouth**

Year One Inc
PO Box 129
Tucker, GA 30085
800-YEAR-ONE (932-7663)
770-493-6568 Atlanta & overseas
FAX: 800-680-6806
FAX: 770-496-1949 Atlanta/overseas

parts

See full listing in **Section Two** under **comprehensive parts**

Becker Sales Rear 519 Wyoming Ave West Pittston, PA 18643 PH/FAX: 717-655-3869	battery master switches

See full listing in **Section Two** under **batteries**

Blackhawk Collection 3600 Blackhawk Plaza Cir Danville, CA 94506-3600 510-736-3444; FAX: 510-736-4375	acquisitions sales

Specializing in sales and aquisitions as well as exposition sale events for pre and post-war American and European classics, custom-bodied and one-of-a-kind automobiles.

Collector Car Appraisals L E Lazarus, Senior Appraiser PO Box 6732 Rockford, IL 61125 815-229-1258; FAX: 815-229-1238	appraisals

See full listing in **Section Two** under **appraisals**

Collector Car Buyers 4046 11th St Rockford, IL 61109 815-229-1258; FAX: 815-229-1238	car dealers

See full listing in **Section Two** under **car dealers**

Edgerton Classics Ltd RR 5 Box 199 Canastota, NY 13032 315-697-2722	restoration woodworking

See full listing in **Section Two** under **restoration shops**

Leo Gephart Classic Cars 7360 E Acoma Dr, Ste 14 Scottsdale, AZ 85260 602-948-2286, 602-998-8263 FAX: 602-948-2390	car dealer parts

See full listing in **Section Two** under **car dealers**

Grand Touring 2785 E Regal Park Dr Anaheim, CA 92806 714-630-0130; FAX: 714-630-6956	engine rebuilding machine shop restoration suspension

See full listing in **Section Two** under **restoration shops**

Hyannis Restoration 119 Thornton Dr Hyannis, MA 02601 508-775-8131; FAX: 508-790-2339	restoration

See full listing in **Section One** under **Ferrari**

Libbey's Classic Car Restoration Center 137 N Quinsigamond Ave Shrewsbury, MA 01545 PH/FAX: 508-792-1560	bodywork restoration service

See full listing in **Section Two** under **restoration shops**

The McHugh Group 4602 Birch Ct Middletown, MD 21769 301-473-8333; FAX: 301-371-9447	appraisals

See full listing in **Section Two** under **appraisals**

McLellan's Automotive History Robert McLellan 9111 Longstaff Dr Houston, TX 77031 713-772-3285; FAX: 713-772-3287	books magazines programs sales literature

See full listing in **Section Two** under **literature dealers**

Restorations Unlimited II Inc 304 Jandus Rd Cary, IL 60013 847-639-5818	restoration

See full listing in **Section Two** under **restoration shops**

Valley Wire Wheel Service 7306 Coldwater Canyon #16 North Hollywood, CA 91605 818-765-3258; FAX: 818-765-8358	wheel restoration wheels

See full listing in **Section Two** under **wheels & wheelcovers**

Varco Inc 8200 S Anderson Rd Oklahoma City, OK 73150 405-732-1637	fitted luggage trunks

See full listing in **Section One** under **Ford '03-'31**

DURANT

Classic Car Works Ltd 3050 Upper Bethany Rd Jasper, GA 30143 770-735-3945	restoration

See full listing in **Section Two** under **restoration shops**

Larry Blodget Box 753 Rancho Mirage, CA 92270 619-862-1979	models

See full listing in **Section Two** under **models & toys**

Dennis Carpenter Ford Reproductions PO Box 26398 Charlotte, NC 28221 704-786-8139; FAX: 704-786-8180	parts

See full listing in **Section One** under **Ford '54-up**

Edsel Associates
2912 Hunter St
Fort Worth, TX 76112
817-451-2708; FAX: 817-496-8909

brake
suspension
sheetmetal

Mail order, telephone orders and open shop. 1958-60 Edsel parts, new suspension, brake, engine parts, ignition, water/fuel pumps. New and used sheetmetal, interior and exterior trim. SASE for partial list. Keep America beautiful, restore your Edsel.

McCoy's Memorabilia
35583 N 1830 E
Rossville, IL 60963-7175
217-748-6513

memorabilia
racing literature

See full listing in **Section Two** under **literature dealers**

Charlie Sens Antique Auto Museum
2074 Marion Mt Gilead Rd
Marion, OH 43302-8991
614-389-4686; FAX: 614-386-2521

museum

See full listing in **Section Six** under **museums**

Thunderbolt Traders Inc
6900 N Dixie Dr
Dayton, OH 45414-3297
513-890-3344; FAX: 513-890-9403

battery cables

Specializing in battery cables for Edsels 1958, 1959 and 1960. Also fuel additives, real tetraethyl lead, make your own leaded gasoline.

Grand Prix Classics Inc
7456 La Jolla Blvd
La Jolla, CA 92037
619-459-3500; FAX: 619-459-3512

racing cars
sports cars

See full listing in **Section Two** under **racing**

JAE
375 Pine #26
Goleta, CA 93117
805-967-5767; FAX: 805-967-6183

parts
service
tech info

See full listing in **Section One** under **Lotus**

MG Automotive
3733-C Wilmington Pk
Kettering, OH 45429
513-294-7623

parts
restoration
service

See full listing in **Section One** under **MG**

ESSEX

Kenneth Fogarty
Anson Valley Rd
New Vineyard, ME 04956
207-652-2210; FAX: 207-652-2255

literature
parts

Mail order and open shop. Monday to Friday 9 to 5. Essex parts & literature, all models 1919 to 1931. Auto literature, most makes and models 1900 to 1960. Manuals, sales flyers, etc.

Hudson Motor Car Co Memorabilia
Ken Poynter
19638 Huntington
Harper Woods, MI 48225
313-886-9292

literature
memorabilia
novelties
signs

See full listing in **Section One** under **Hudson**

Varco Inc
8200 S Anderson Rd
Oklahoma City, OK 73150
405-732-1637

fitted luggage
trunks

See full listing in **Section One** under **Ford '03-'31**

Facel Vega

Meridian Collision Center Inc
15724 E Meridian
Puyallup, WA 98373-9510
206-848-2364, 800-523-1123
FAX: 206-840-1254

restoration

See full listing in **Section One** under **Marmon**

Ferrari

ABS Exotic Repair Inc
1561 N Federal Hwy
Ft Lauderdale, FL 33304
954-566-7785; FAX: 954-566-7271

parts
service

See full listing in **Section One** under **Mercedes-Benz**

Aero Toy Store
Gary Anzalone
1710 W Cypress Creek Rd
Ft Lauderdale, FL 33309
800-404-2376; FAX: 954-771-3281

acquisitions
sales

Sales and acquisitions for Ferrari, Lamborghini, Aston Martin, Mercedes, race cars and Harleys. Also Porsches, Rolls-Royce and Bentleys.

Bassett's Jaguar	parts
PO Box 245	restoration
Wyoming, RI 02898	service
401-539-3010; FAX: 401-539-7861	upholstery

See full listing in **Section One** under **Jaguar**

Beverly Hills Motoring Accessories	accessories
205 S Robertson Blvd	
Beverly Hills, CA 90211	
310-657-4880; FAX: 310-659-4664	
E-mail: bhma@hollywood.cinenet.net	

See full listing in **Section One** under **Mercedes-Benz**

Francois Bruere	artwork
8 Avenue Olivier Heuze	
LeMans 72000 France	
(33) 02-4377-1877	
FAX: (33) 02-4324-2038	

See full listing in **Section Two** under **artwork**

California Wire Wheel	rechroming
6922 Turnbridge Way	tires
San Diego, CA 92119	tubes
619-698-8255; FAX: 619-589-9032	wheels

See full listing in **Section Two** under **wheels & wheelcovers**

The Checkered Flag Collection	car dealer
PO Box 806	
Millville, NJ 08332	
609-327-1505	

By appointment only. Specializes in investment quality Ferrari, Cobra, Mercedes-Benz and vintage racing cars. For serious collectors.

Classic Auto Concepts	car dealer
1366 S Federal Hwy	
Pompano Beach, FL 33062	
954-781-8440; FAX: 954-781-8449	

See full listing in **Section One** under **Porsche**

Collectors Choice LTD	parts
6400 Springfield, Lodi Rd	restoration
Dane, WI 53529	service
608-849-9878; FAX: 608-849-9879	

See full listing in **Section One** under **DeTomaso/Pantera**

Composition Materials Co Inc	plastic media
1375 Kings Hwy E	
Fairfield, CT 06430	
800-262-7763; FAX: 203-335-9728	

See full listing in **Section Two** under **restoration aids**

Donovan Motorcar Service	restoration
4 Holmes Rd	service
Lenox, MA 01240	
413-499-6000; FAX: 413-499-6699	

See full listing in **Section One** under **Jaguar**

Drummond Coach and Paint	painting
531 Raleigh Ave	restoration
El Cajon, CA 92020	
619-579-7229; FAX: 619-579-2128	

Open shop only. Specializing in Ferrari painting and restoration of paint, interior and chrome for pre-74 Daytonas, 275 GTB 2

and 4 cam, 365, BB, BB512, California Spyders, PF Series II, Lussos. Also other exotics.

Euro Coachworks Inc	repair & fabrication
812 NW 57th St	
Fort Lauderdale, FL 33309	
954-772-8272; FAX: 954-772-8148	

Open shop only. Monday to Friday 8:30 to 5:30 pm. Specializing in Ferrari, Aston Martin, Italian cars for body makers on aluminum. Prototype cars.

See our ad on this page

Exoticars of Hunterdon	machine work
6 Washington St	paint & bodywork
Frenchtown, NJ 08825	restoration service
908-996-4889; FAX: 908-996-6938	welding/fabrication

Ferrari, Maserati and Lamborghini. Racing car preparation. Cars located and inspected worldwide. Expert service and restoration, including paint and bodywork, engine rebuilding, interiors, electrical work, engine compartment detailing and fabrication of parts and pieces no longer available. Basket case to First Place is our specialty.

Ferraris.com	online guide
52 Payn Ave	
Chatham, NY 12037-1427	
PH/FAX: 518-392-7234	
E-mail: editor@ferraris.com	

The Ferraristi's resource. An online guide dedicated to the care, ownership and enjoyment of the marque. Excellent source for those contemplating their 1st Ferrari. Free 24 hours a day. Publication: *Ferraris.com*.

The Fine Car Store | car dealer
1105 Moana Dr
San Diego, CA 92107
619-223-7766
FAX: 619-223-6838

Sale of antique, classic, special interest, collectible, sports and vintage race cars. Specializing in collectible Ferrari, Jaguar & Aston Martin automobiles.

Mark Gillett | car locator
PO Box 9177 | sales
Dallas, TX 75209
PH/FAX: 214-902-9258
011-525-559-6240 Mexico City, Mexico
E-mail-autonet@onramp.net

See full listing in **Section Two** under **car dealers**

Glass Search/LOF | glass parts
1975 Galaxie Ave
Columbus, OH 43207
800-848-1351
FAX: 614-443-0709

See full listing in **Section Two** under **glass**

HK Klassics | appraisals
Hy Kusnetz
16 Hausmann Ct
Maplewood, NJ 07040
201-761-6642

See full listing in **Section Two** under **appraisals**

Offering a Full Range of Services for Antique, Classic and Custom Automobiles

Specializing in:
- *Complete & Partial Restorations*
- *Metal Repair*
- *Welding*
- *Body Work*
- *Painting*
- *Woodworking*
- *Convertible Tops*
- *Interiors*

Whether it's a minor scratch, a tune-up, a torn seat or top, or a major award-winning restoration, our 16 trained professionals can restore your car to perfection.
Call us for an estimate.

Hyannis Restoration

119 Thornton Drive, Hyannis, MA 02601
Sales: (508) 790-2566 • Restorations: (508) 775-8131
Fax: (508) 790-2339

Hyannis Restoration | restoration
119 Thornton Dr
Hyannis, MA 02601
508-775-8131; FAX: 508-790-2339

Open shop only. Monday-Saturday 7 am-5 pm daily, Sunday 7-12. Foreign and American for over 25 years. All makes from Bugattis, Delahaye, AC Cobras, Duesenburgs, Delage, Austin-Healey and on.

See our ad on this page

International Auto Parts Inc | accessories
Rt 29 N | parts
PO Box 9036
Charlottesville, VA 22906
800-726-0555, 804-973-0555
FAX: 804-973-2368

See full listing in **Section One** under **Alfa Romeo**

International Restoration | parts
Specialist Inc | restoration
PO Box 1303 | sales
Mt Airy, NC 27030
910-789-1548

See full listing in **Section One** under **Jaguar**

The Italian Car Registry | information source
3305 Valley Vista Rd
Walnut Creek, CA 94598-3943
510-458-1163

See full listing in **Section Four** under **information sources**

The Klemantaski Collection | books
65 High Ridge Rd, Suite 219 | photography
Stamford, CT 06905
PH/FAX: 203-968-2970
E-mail: klemcoll@aol.com

See full listing in **Section Two** under **photography**

Kreimeyer Co | antennas/glass
3211 N Wilburn Ave | wholesale
Bethany, OK 73008 | parts/radios
405-789-9499; FAX: 405-789-7888 | repair service

See full listing in **Section One** under **Mercedes-Benz**

London Stainless Steel Exhaust | exhaust systems
Centre
249-253 Queenstown Rd
London, SW8 3NP England
011-44-171622-2120
FAX: 011-44-171627-0991
E-mail:101445.341@compuserv.com

See full listing in **Section Two** under **exhaust systems**

Marcovicci-Wenz Engineering Inc | engine parts
33 Comac Loop | services
Ronkonkoma, NY 11779
516-467-9040; FAX: 516-467-9041

See full listing in **Section Two** under **racing**

McAdam Motorcars Ltd 215 Redoubt Rd Yorktown, VA 23692 757-898-7805; FAX: 757-898-9019	restoration

See full listing in **Section Two** under **restoration shops**

The McHugh Group 4602 Birch Ct Middletown, MD 21769 301-473-8333; FAX: 301-371-9447	appraisals

See full listing in **Section Two** under **appraisals**

Milestone Motorcars Mark Tyra 12910 Sunnybrook Dr Prospect, KY 40059 502-228-5945; FAX: 502-228-1856	die cast cars models

See full listing in **Section Two** under **automobilia**

Motorcar Gallery Inc 715 N Federal Hwy Fort Lauderdale, FL 33304 954-522-9900; FAX: 954-522-9966	car dealer

Mail order and open shop. Monday-Saturday 10 am-6:30 pm. Vintage exotic and classic European automobiles of limited production such as Ferrari, Pegaso, Maserati, Lamborghini, Iso, Monteverdi, AC Cobra, Aston Martin, Rolls-Royce, Bentley, mid-year Corvettes, Delage, Delahaye, Talbot-Lago, Facel Vega, Mercedes 300S and 300SL, BMW 503 and 507, etc.

Motorcars International 528 N Prince Ln Springfield, MO 65802 417-831-9999; FAX: 417-863-0777 E-mail: missy@motorcars-intl	accessories cars services tools

Mail order and open shop. Monday-Friday 8-6, Saturday 9-4. Lamborghini dealer. Used car sales of Mecedes, Porsche, Ferrari, BMW, Jaguar. One of America's most respected dealerships. Motorcars offers a full service parts department, service center and detail department. After 18 years of specializing in the sales and service of high line cars, Motorcars has produced a 36 page catalog of over 300 of the hottest motoring accessories available on the market today.

Mr Sport Car Inc 203 E Lincoln Papillion, NE 68046 402-592-7559	service

See full listing in **Section One** under **Jaguar**

Palo Alto Speedometer Inc 718 Emerson St Palo Alto, CA 94301 415-323-0243; FAX: 415-323-4632	instruments

See full listing in **Section One** under **Mercedes-Benz**

Partsource 32 Harden Ave Camden, ME 04843 207-236-9791; FAX: 207-236-6323	parts

Mail order only. Parts importer/distributor. Ferrari parts specialist, 1949-1991. 20 years' experience. Exclusively Ferrari, all models.

Peninsula Imports 3749 Harlem Rd Buffalo, NY 14215 800-263-4538; FAX: 905-847-3021	accessories parts trim

See full listing in **Section One** under **BMW**

Precision Autoworks 2202 Federal Street E Camden, NJ 08105 609-966-0080, NJ FAX: 610-649-3577, PA	restorations

See full listing in **Section One** under **Mercedes-Benz**

Proper Motor Cars Inc 1811 11th Ave N St. Petersburg, FL 33713-5794 813-821-8883; FAX: 813-895-4746	parts restoration

See full listing in **Section One** under **Rolls-Royce/Bentley**

Replicarz 99 State St Rutland, VT 05701 802-747-7151 E-mail: replicarz@aol.com	books kits models videos

See full listing in **Section Two** under **racing**

RM Auto Restoration Ltd 825 Park Ave W Chatham, ON Canada N7M 5J6 519-352-4575; FAX: 519-351-1337	panel fabrication parts restoration

See full listing in **Section Two** under **restoration shops**

Garry Roberts & Co 922 Sunset Dr Costa Mesa, CA 92627 888-FERRAR; FAX: 714-650-2730	cars parts service

Specializing in pre-owned Ferrari, sales, service, restorations for Ferrari.

Scale Autoworks Brady Ward 313 Bridge St #4 Manchester, NH 03104-5045 PH/FAX: 603-623-5925 ext 66	models

See full listing in **Section Two** under **models & toys**

Shelton Dealerships 5740 N Federal Hwy Ford Lauderdale, FL 33308 954-493-5211; FAX: 954-772-2653	accessories leasing parts sales

Mail order and open shop. Monday thru Saturday 8:30 am-5 pm. Factory authorized sales and leasing, full service, parts and accessories for new and preowned Ferrari, Jaguar, Porsche and Land Rover automobiles.

Showroom Auto Sales 960 S Bascom Ave San Jose, CA 95128 408-554-1550; FAX: 408-554-0550	car dealer

See full listing in **Section One** under **Mercedes-Benz**

Spyder Enterprises Inc RFD 1682 Laurel Hollow, NY 11791-9644 516-367-3293 evenings FAX: 516-367-3260	accessories books parts periodicals

See full listing in **Section One** under **Porsche**

The Stable LTD 217 Main St Gladstone, NJ 07934 908-234-2055; FAX: 908-781-2599	sales service

See full listing in **Section One** under **Jaguar**

Tillack & Co Ltd
630 Mary Ann Dr
Redondo Beach, CA 90278
310-316-8760; FAX: 310-376-3392

parts
restoration

See full listing in **Section Two** under **restoration shops**

Valley Wire Wheel Service
7306 Coldwater Canyon #16
North Hollywood, CA 91605
818-765-3258; FAX: 818-765-8358

wheel restoration
wheels

See full listing in **Section Two** under **wheels & wheelcovers**

Vantage Auto Interiors
11 Fahey St
Stamford, CT 06907
203-425-9533; FAX: 203-425-9535

upholstery

See full listing in **Section Two** under **interiors & interior parts**

Vintage Restorations
The Old Bakery
Windmill Street, Tunbridge Wells
Kent, TN2 4UU England
UK 1892-525-899
FAX: UK 1892-525499

accessories
instruments

See full listing in **Section Two** under **instruments**

Bayless Inc
1111 Via Bayless
Marietta, GA 30066-2770
770-928-1446; FAX: 770-928-1342
800-241-1446, order line (US &
Canada)

accessories
parts

Mail order and open shop. Monday-Friday 8 to 5:30. Spare parts
and accessories for Fiats 1953-1989 and Lancia Beta series
1975-82. Distributors of Magneti Marelli electrical components
and Alquati performance parts. Authorized Fiat and Lancia factory parts distributors. Expanded 130 page catalog, $4 ($10
international). Worldwide shipping since 1971.

Caribou Imports Inc
23151-A3 Alcalde Dr
Laguna Hills, CA 92653
714-770-3136; FAX: 714-770-0815
E-mail: cariboulh@aol.com

parts

Mail order and open shop. Shop open Monday-Friday 9:30 am to
5 pm. Supplies parts worldwide for Fiat, Lancia and Maserati
automobiles. Over 22,000 parts are available for immediate shipment. We reproduce parts that the factories have discontinued.
For Fiat Spiders in particular, we are known as "The Spider
Restoration Headquarters".

Celiberti Motors
615 Oak St
Santa Rosa, CA 95404
800-872-3428; FAX: 707-523-1613

parts

Mail order and open shop. Shop open Monday-Friday 8 to 5:30.
Specializing in factory authorized parts, parts rebuilding service,
used parts for Fiat, Lancia, Maserati, Alfa Romeo. Dealers for
AGIP oil. Race winning performance prep and trophy winning
concours preparation.

Bruce Douglas
19150 Rockcliff
Rocky River, OH 44116
216-356-0293

parts

Mail order only. Monday-Friday 9 to 9, Saturday 9 to 5. Fiat 850,
X-1-9, 124, 2000 sports car parts for used, rebuilt, new parts.

Fiat Auto Service
18440 Hart St, Unit J
Reseda, CA 91335
PH/FAX: 818-345-4458

parts
repair
restoration

Specializes in new and used parts. Also full repair & restoration
for Fiats, all makes and models.

Fiat Plus
318-A River St
Santa Cruz, CA 95060
408-423-0218; 800-500-FIAT (orders)
FAX: 408-459-8128

parts
repairs

Mail order and open shop. Monday-Friday 8:30 to 5:30.
Specializes in parts and repairs for Fiat and Lancia. Authorized
Fiat/Lancia parts center. Imports parts as necessary from
Europe. Hard-to-find Fiat parts from 1955 to present. Write or
call for free newsletter.

Giant Auto Wreckers Inc
23944 Pine St
Newhall, CA 91321
805-259-4678; FAX: 805-259-7008

dismantling
hubcaps
wheelcovers

See full listing in **Section Two** under **wheels & wheelcovers**

International Auto Parts Inc
Rt 29 N
PO Box 9036
Charlottesville, VA 22906
800-726-0555, 804-973-0555
FAX: 804-973-2368

accessories
parts

See full listing in **Section One** under **Alfa Romeo**

The Italian Car Registry
3305 Valley Vista Rd
Walnut Creek, CA 94598-3943
510-458-1163

information source

See full listing in **Section Four** under **information sources**

Linearossa International Inc
15281 Barranca Pkwy #A
Irvine, CA 92618
714-727-1201; FAX: 714-727-0603

parts

Mail order and open shop. Monday-Friday 9 to 5. Specializing in
Fiat parts, all years for 500, 600, 850, X19, 124 models.

Motormetrics
5500 Thomaston Rd
Macon, GA 31204
912-477-6771

used parts

See full listing in **Section One** under **Triumph**

Orion Motors European Parts Inc
10722 Jones Rd
Houston, TX 77065
800-736-6410; 713-894-1982
FAX: 713-849-1997

parts

See full listing in **Section One** under **Alfa Romeo**

1903 to 1931

Ace Antique Automotive Since 1963	parts sales
PO Box 81021	
San Diego, CA 92138	
619-702-9084; FAX: 619-702-9178	
East Coast Outlet: 800-995-6626	

See full listing in **Section One** under **Ford '32-'53**

Antique Auto Parts et al	accessories parts
9103 E Garvey Ave	
Rosemead, CA 91770-0458	
818-288-2121; FAX: 818-288-3311	

Mail order only. Phone hours Monday-Friday 9 to 5. Parts and accessories for Ford cars and trucks. SASE required for parts information. Dealer wholesale catalog available.

Antique Auto Parts of Kentucky	parts
PO Box 23070	
Lexington, KY 40523	
606-272-7602	

Mail order and open shop. Open by appointment only. Complete line for Model As, limited number for Model Ts and V8s.

Antique Automotive Engineering Inc	babbitt service engine restoration
3560 Chestnut Pl	
Denver, CO 80216	
303-296-7332; 800-846-7332	

See full listing in **Section Two** under **engine rebuilding**

Antique Cars, Parts & Trains	car dealer literature parts trains
Second & Broad Sts	
Millville, NJ 08332	
609-825-0200	

Open shop. Monday-Saturday 9 to 5. Features Model As and Corvettes. Car dealer, parts, automotive literature and trains for sale. 35 miles west of Atlantic City.

Becker Sales	battery master switches
Rear 519 Wyoming Ave	
West Pittston, PA 18643	
PH/FAX: 717-655-3869	

See full listing in **Section Two** under **batteries**

Bill's Model A Ford	parts restorations
PO Box 220, Rt 611	
Ferndale, PA 18921	
610-847-8030	

Mail order and open shop. Monday-Friday 8 to 5, evenings and weekends by appointment. Evening address: 510 Rt 173, Stewartsville, NJ 08886, PH: 908-479-4479. Weekend address: PO Box 22, Watsontown, PA 17777, PH: 717-538-9544. New and used parts for Model As. Complete or partial restoration services offered. Spin painting of spoke wheels our specialty, call for price quote.

Blough's Automotive Antiques	car dealer
13881 Molly Pitcher Hwy	
Rt 11, Exit 2 off 81	
Greencastle, PA 17225	
804-740-3789, 717-597-3677	

Pennsylvania business, property, licensed salvage yard, all cars, parts and mobile home park, $250,000. No Saturdays.

Bob's Antique Auto Parts Inc	parts
PO Box 2523	
Rockford, IL 61132	
815-633-7244; FAX: 815-654-0761	

Mail order and open shop. Monday-Friday 9-4:30; Saturday 9-12. Specializes in Model T Ford parts, 1903-1927. Quality T parts only. Known as the Model T specialists. Retail catalog upon request, $2. Dealer inquiries invited.

Boyds Hot Rods & Collectable Cars	car dealer
10971 Dale St	
Stanton, CA 90680	
714-220-9870; FAX: 714-220-9877	

See full listing in **Section One** under **Chevrolet**

The Brassworks	radiators
289 Prado Rd	
San Louis Obispo, CA 93401	
800-342-6759; FAX: 805-544-5615	

See full listing in **Section Two** under **radiators**

Bryant's Antique Auto Parts	appraisals parts sheetmetal service
851 Western Ave	
Hampden, ME 04444	
207-862-4019	

Mail order and open shop. Monday-Friday 9 to 5, Saturday by appointment. In business for 25 years. Appraisal within 100 mile area in Maine. Quality Model A & T parts. Call for catalog information.

Calimer's Wheel Shop	wooden wheels
30 E North St	
Waynesboro, PA 17268	
717-762-5056; FAX: 717-762-5021	

See full listing in **Section Two** under **wheels & wheelcovers**

Car-Line Manufacturing & Distribution Inc	chassis parts engine parts sheetmetal
1250 Gulf St	
PO Box 1192	
Beaumont, TX 77701	
409-833-9757; FAX: 409-835-2468	

See full listing in **Section Two** under **sheetmetal**

Class-Tech Corp	wiring harnesses
62935 Layton Ave	
Bend, OR 97701	
800-874-9981	

See full listing in **Section Two** under **electrical systems**

Classic Wood Mfg	wood kits wood replacement
1006 N Raleigh St	
Greensboro, NC 27405	
910-691-1344; FAX: 910-273-3074	

See full listing in **Section Two** under **woodwork**

Classtique Upholstery & Top Co PO Box 278 HK Isanti, MN 55040 612-444-4025; FAX: 612-444-9980	top kits upholstery kits

Mail order and open shop. Specializing in 1914-1931 Ford interior upholstery kits, top kits, etc. Original materials, guaranteed workmanship. $1 requested for samples, advise year & body style, standard or deluxe. Established 1959.

Colorado Car Collection Inc 3455 F St, Suite 3 Greeley, CO 80631 970-352-3915; FAX: 970-352-4172	car dealer

See full listing in **Section Two** under **car dealers**

Tony Copeland Ford Lincoln Mercury 1617 21st St Lewiston, ID 83501 800-821-8174; FAX: 208-746-1543 E-mail: copeland@copelandford.com	parts sales service

See full listing in **Section One** under **Ford '54-up**

Chuck & Judy Cubel PO Box 278 Superior, AZ 85273 PH/FAX: 520-689-2734 eves	wood parts

Top wood and body wood, sold by the piece or the kit. Wood for Fords. Make 2,000 replacement parts for sixty Ford bodies, 1913-1936. Been making new wood for 30 years. Take Visa and MasterCard. Do wood installation. Free illustrated price list. State year and body style.

Darrell's Automotive and Restorations 2639 N Tripp Ave Odessa, TX 79763 915-381-7713	repairs restorations

See full listing in **Section Two** under **fire engines**

Mike Dennis, Nebraska Mail Order 1845 S 48th St Lincoln, NE 68506 402-489-3036; FAX: 402-489-1148	parts Trippe mounting brackets/hardware

See full listing in **Section One** under **Ford '32-'53**

S D Dennis 708 Pineview Dr Valdosta, GA 31602 912-242-3084	rebabbitting

Rebabbitting service Ford As, Bs, and Cs.

Bob Drake Reproductions Inc 1819 NW Washington Blvd Grants Pass, OR 97526 800-221-3673; FAX: 541-474-0099	repro parts

See full listing in **Section One** under **Ford '32-'53**

Early Ford Parts 2948 Summer Ave Memphis, TN 38112 901-323-2179; FAX: 901-323-2195	literature parts

See full listing in **Section One** under **Ford '32-'53**

Ed's Be-Bop Shop 10087 W Co Rd 300 S Medora, IN 47260 812-966-2203	accessories parts restoration

Mail order and open shop. Shop open Monday-Saturday 9 to 5. Specializing in parts and interior restoration for Model A Fords and street rods, new and used parts for early Ford, rod and custom parts and accessories, fuzzy dice, dice valve caps and shifter knobs, headlight shields, air cleaners and carb scoops and other 50s accessories and interior restoration. Send $1 for catalog.

Ezold's Model A Garage 1120 Southampton Rd Westfield, MA 01805 413-562-0273	engine rebuilding restorations

Mail order and open shop. Open Monday-Friday 8 to 5, Saturday 8 to 12, evenings by appointment. Specializing in Model A Fords '28-'31 and V8 engine rebuilding for Fords '32-'53. Complete & partial restorations, carburetors, distributors, water pumps, front and rear end rebuilding.

Ford Obsolete 9107-13 Garvey Ave Rosemead, CA 91770 818-288-2121	parts

Mail order and open shop. Monday-Friday 11 to 5; Saturday 9 to 3. Full line of new and used chassis and engine parts for trucks and Model A, T and V8 Fords. SASE required for information.

Ford Parts Specialists **Div of Joblot Automotive Inc** 98-11 211th St Queens Village, NY 11429 718-468-8585; FAX: 718-468-8686	parts

Mail order and open shop. Monday-Friday 8:30 to 4:30. Over 12,000 different new and rebuilt parts. Specializing in the Ford family of cars and trucks 1928 thru 1969. Engine, brake, transmission and clutch, front and rear end, a full line of rubber, electrical, wiring and ignition. Established in 1956. Three catalogs available: 1928 thru 1948 cars and trucks, 1948/1969 F-1/100 thru F-6/600 trucks, 1949/1969 Ford family of cars. VISA, MC and COD phone or FAX orders accepted.

Freeman's Garage 19 Freeman St Norton, MA 02766 508-285-6500	parts restoration sales service

Mail order and open shop. Weekdays 8:00 to 5:30, Saturday am, some evenings, other times by chance or appointment. Sales, service, parts for 1928-31 Model A & AA Fords. Same location since 1957.

Gaslight Auto Parts Inc PO Box 291 Urbana, OH 43078 513-652-2145; FAX: 513-652-2147	accessories parts

Mail order and open shop. M-F 8:30 am-5 pm. Antique Ford parts, accessories and sheetmetal for Model A, T and early V8.

GF Embossed Notes 11 Caldwell Dr Amherst, NH 03031 603-880-6217; FAX: 603-882-6590	note cards

See full listing in **Section Two** under **automobilia**

Good Old Days Garage Inc
2340 Farley Pl
Birmingham, AL 35226
205-822-4569; FAX: 205-823-1944

engine building
parts
service

Mail order and open shop. Monday-Saturday 8:30 to 10 pm. Parts and service for Model As. Marlar-built engines and T/A/B engine rebuilding a specialty. Uses KR Wilson tools as the Ford repair shops used. Appointment necessary to watch your block poured and align bored.

Herb Griffin
7056 St Hwy 5
Fort Plain, NY 13339
518-568-7813

repair
restoration

Repair and restoration of Model As and other old Fords.

Hancock's Engine Rebuilders and Balancing Service
2885 Cherokee Rd
Athens, GA 30605
706-543-7726

engine rebuilding

Shop open Monday-Friday 9 to 5. For Model Ts, As, Bs, Cs and early V8s.

Harry's Early Ford Parts
6090 Crater Lake Ave, Unit F
Central Point, OR 97502
541-830-3673
800-833-2580, order desk
FAX: 541-830-5105

parts

Mail order and retail sales for 1928-31 Model A Ford parts. Free Model A catalog available.

Earle C Hartshorn
9 Robert St
Walpole, MA 02081
508-688-9319

parts

Mail order only. Used pre-World War II, some Ford & various other parts.

Henry's Model T & A Parts
52 Poole St
Deer Park, Victoria 3023 Australia
03-9363-2869, FAX: 03-9363-5219

parts

Mail order only. Specializing in reproduction parts for Ford Model T & A and early Ford V8 1909-1954. We carry a large range of Model T & A and early Ford V8 parts and distribute Australia wide. Phone orders 7 days a week. Bank card, VISA & MasterCard facilities available.

Hot Rod & Custom Supply
1304 SE 10th St
Cape Coral, FL 33990
941-574-7744; FAX: 941-574-8820

custom parts
engine parts
speed parts

See full listing in **Section One** under **Ford '32-'53**

Howell's Sheetmetal Co
PO Box 792
Nederland, TX 77627
409-727-1999

body panels
sheetmetal

Mail order and open shop. Monday-Friday 8-5; Saturday by appointment. Specializes in reproduction sheetmetal, body panels, seat frames, patches, aprons for 1909-1940 Fords. Custom parts from your patterns other than Ford.

Hudson Wagon Works
Rt 1, Box 28
Bridgewater, IA 50837
515-369-2865;
E-mail: wagonworks@aol.com

hardware
wagon plans

Mail order only. Depot hack plans. Huckster wagon plans and hardware.

Kid Stuff
Larry Machacek
PO Box 515
Porter, TX 77365
713-429-2505

parts
repair
restoration

Shop open Monday-Friday 9 to 4. Specializes in any stage of restoration (particularly the installation of wood) and repair for Model A Fords, 1928-31. Original used parts available for purchase.

Joe Lagana
RD 1, Miller Rd
Canterbury, CT 06331
860-546-6000

parts

Mail order and open shop. Monday-Saturday 9 to 5; other times by appointment. For Model As. No catalogs, send want list.

Lakeview Accessories
PO Box 95
Skaneateles, NY 13152
315-685-7414

nostalgia items

Wholesale supplier of 1928-48 Ford reproduction and 50s nostalgia items. Send SASE and advise what price list you need.

Lang's Old Car Parts
202 School St
Winchendon, MA 01475
800-TPARTS-1; FAX: 508-297-2126

parts

Mail order and retail store. Monday to Friday 8 am to 5:30 pm. Specializing in reproduction, NOS and used parts for Model T Fords 1909-27.

Loyal Ford Mercury Inc
2310 Calumet Dr
New Holstein, WI 53061
414-898-4248; FAX: 414-898-9705

cars
parts

See full listing in **Section One** under **Ford '54-up**

Mac's Antique Auto Parts
1051 Lincoln Ave, PO Box 238
Lockport, NY 14095-0238
716-433-1500 local and foreign
800-777-0948 US and Canada
FAX: 716-433-1172

literature
parts
restoration
supplies

Mail order and store. Monday-Friday 8 to 5:30; Saturday 8 to 12:30 pm. New parts for 1909-72 Fords from Model T to Mustang & 1909-1948 street rods. 14 free catalogs available. Outside US, $5 each. Specify year and model of car to receive correct catalog. Worldwide sales, prompt shipment. MC, VISA, Discover, AmEx, Diners Club, Optima, JCB and COD accepted.

W L Wally Mansfield
Box 237, 526 E 2nd
Blue Springs, NE 68318-0237
402-645-3546

cars
parts
trucks

See full listing in **Section Two** under **comprehensive parts**

Mark Auto Co Inc | **parts**
Layton, NJ 07851 | **restoration supplies**

Mail and phone orders only. Phone orders: 10 am to 2 pm; FAX orders may be sent anytime. No counter service. Model T and A Ford parts. A comprehensive selection of restoration supplies and early Southwind heater parts. Illustrated master catalog free. VISA, MasterCard. Worldwide dealer inquiries welcomed. Wholesale, retail.

McInnes Antique Auto | **parts**
PO Box 653
Niagara-on-the Lake, ON Canada
L0S 1J0
905-468-7779; FAX: 905-468-0759

Mail order and open shop. Open by appointment only. Phone hours: 9 am to 10 pm daily. For 1909-31 Fords. Price list available on request.

Mitchell Manufacturing | **overdrives**
6 Acorn Ct
Novato, CA 94949-6603
800-238-5093

Mail order and open shop. Shop open Monday-Friday 9 am to 5 pm. Specializing in overdrives for 1928-1931 Model A Fords.

C W Moss Ford Parts Inc | **NOS parts**
402 W Chapman Ave | **used parts**
Orange, CA 92666
714-639-3083, Orange
909-629-5223, Pomona
FAX: 714-639-0329

Mail order and open shop. Tuesday-Saturday 8 to 5. Two locations: 967 E Mission, Pomona, CA 91766. New old stock, used and remanufactured parts for 1928-1959 Ford passenger cars and pickups 28-66. Second location: 402 W Chapman Ave, Orange, CA 92666.

Myers Model A Ford Parts & | **parts**
Mustang & Car Trailers
17103 Sterling Rd
Williamsport, MD 21795
301-582-2478

Mail order and open shop. Monday-Friday 5:30 to 9:30 pm, Saturday 8 to 4:30. Sells new and used Model T and A Ford parts and cars. Also Mustang and Ford parts up to 1948.

Northeast Ford | **parts**
Box 66 | **restoration**
Rt 9
E Sullivan, NH 03445
603-847-9956, 800-562-FORD
FAX: 603-847-9691

See full listing in **Section One** under **Ford '54-up**

Oak Bows | **top bows**
122 Ramsey Ave
Chambersburg, PA 17201
717-264-2602

See full listing in **Section Two** under **woodwork**

Obsolete Ford Parts Inc | **parts**
8701 S I-35
Oklahoma City, OK 73149
405-631-3933; FAX: 405-634-6815

See full listing in **Section One** under **Ford '54-up**

The Old Car Centre | **parts**
19909 92A Ave
Langley, BC Canada V1M 3B6
604-888-4412, 888-4055
FAX: 604-888-7455

Mail order and open shop. Monday-Friday 8 to 5; Saturday 10 to 4. 1909-56 Ford cars and pickups, 1937-64 Chev parts. Specializes in 1928-56 Fords. Stock and rod parts. 1955-57 Chevys. A catalog, $3. V8 catalog, $3. 1948-56 Ford pickup catalog, $3. Rod catalog, $3. Chev catalog, $1.50.

Original Falcon, Comet, Ranchero, | **interiors**
Fairlane Interiors | **weatherstripping**
6343 Seaview Ave NW
Seattle, WA 98107-2664
206-781-5230; FAX: 206-781-5046
E-mail: falcons@ix.netcom.com

See full listing in **Section One** under **Ford '54-up**

Original Ford Motor Co Literature | **collectibles**
PO Box 7-AA | **literature**
Hudson, KY 40145-0007
502-257-8642; FAX: 502-257-8643

See full listing in **Section One** under **Ford '32-'53**

Pioneer Valley Model A Ford Inc | **cars**
81 East St | **parts**
Easthampton, MA 01027 | **restoration**
413-584-8400; FAX: 413-584-7605
E-mail: pvma@aol.com

Mail order and open shop. Monday through Friday 8 am to 4:30 pm. Specializing in the sale of new & used parts, repair & complete restoration services for Ford 1928 to 1931, Model A Ford and early V8s to 1940.

The Plasmeter Corporation | **brake drums**
173 Queen Ave SE
Albany, OR 97321
541-928-3233; FAX: 541-928-0596

Specializing in brake drums for Ford Model A 1928-1931.

Precision Babbitt Service | **babbitting**
4681 Lincoln Ave | **engine rebuilding**
Beamsville, ON Canada L0R 1B3
905-563-4364

See full listing in **Section Two** under **babbitting**

The Right Rivet Co | **parts**
5313 John Thomas Dr NE | **rivets**
Albuquerque, NM 87111
505-294-4434

Shop open by appointment, weekends. Mail order T frame rivets, front and rear packet, $12.50 postpaid. Cast runningboard supports, packet $4.50. 1919-1925 demountable wheel kits. Write for brochure. Large inventory original T parts.

Rock Valley Antique Auto Parts | **gas tanks**
Box 352
Rt 72 and Rothwell Rd
Stillman Valley, IL 61084
815-645-2271; FAX: 815-645-2740

See full listing in **Section One** under **Ford '32-'53**

Walter E Rodimon
PO Box 353
Pike, NH 03780
603-989-5557

parts

Mail order. Parts department open by appointment only. Antique original Ford parts bought, sold and traded.

Rootlieb Inc
PO Box 1829
815 S Soderquist
Turlock, CA 95380
209-632-2203; FAX: 209-632-2201

parts

Reproduction parts manufacturer: 1906-37 hoods, 1909-27 fenders, 1909-31 runningboards, 1909-29 splash aprons, Model A and T speedster kits and 1909-16 Model T bodies. Also engine pans. Chevrolet, Ford and MoPar street rod hoods. Free catalog.

S & S Antique Auto
Pine St
Deposit, NY 13754
607-467-2929; FAX: 607-467-2109

parts

See full listing in **Section One** under **Ford '32-'53**

Saturn Industries
143 Wimborne Rd
Poole, Dorset BH15 2BG England
01202-674982; FAX: 01202-668274

axles
instruments
literature
repro parts

Mail order and open shop. Shop open by appointment only. Free price list for individual style and year of car containing complete range of parts used in restoration, building hot rods, street rods, kit cars and customs. Always wanting new suppliers, please send information.

Charlie Sens Antique Auto Museum
2074 Marion Mt Gilead Rd
Marion, OH 43302-8991
614-389-4686; FAX: 614-386-2521

museum

See full listing in **Section Six** under **Ohio**

William Slavik
906 Broadway
Bedford, OH 44146
216-232-8132

keys
locks

See full listing in **Section Two** under **locks & keys**

Smith & Jones Distributing Company Inc
1 Biloxi Square
West Columbia, SC 29170
803-822-8500; FAX: 803-822-8477

parts

Mail order and open shop. Monday thru Friday 8:30 until 5. A complete line of reproduction parts for 1909 through 1931 Ford cars and trucks.

Snyder's Antique Auto Parts Inc
12925 Woodworth Rd
New Springfield, OH 44443
330-549-5313; FAX: 330-549-2211

parts

Mail order and open shop. Monday-Friday 8 to 5; Saturday 8 to 12. 1909-31 Model T and A Ford parts. Also custom builds seat springs for any year or make of vehicle. In business 35 years. Features same day shipping.

Special T's Unlimited Corp
PO Box 146
Prospect Heights, IL 60070
847-255-5494; FAX: 847-391-7082

general repair
parts
restoration
service

Mail order and open shop. Shop address: 103 N Wheeling Rd, Prospect Heights, IL 60070. For Model Ts and As. Also complete street rod parts, service and complete rods built. Also mid-60s MoPar restoration. Specializing in 56-65 Plymouth/Dodge, parts, repair & restoration & high-performance. Replacement "engine tuned" overlays for Sport Fury & Polara 500. Restoration of aluminum headlight rings & trim. Engine turn Swirl Pattern overlays for dash, firewall & trim moldings.

Mike Stein and Ed Stein
31 Gilbert Rd
Southampton, MA 01073
413-527-5129

mech restoration

Mail order and open shop. Monday-Saturday 9 to 7. Specializing in engine, transmission and rear end rebuilding for 1909-27 Model Ts and Model As.

Valley Motor Supply
1402 E Second St
Roswell, NM 88201
505-622-7450

accessories
parts

See full listing in **Section One** under **Ford '54-up**

Valley Obsolete Ford Parts
Kerrville, TX 78029
PH/FAX210-896-3269

accessories
parts

See full listing in **Section One** under **Ford '32-'53**

Varco Inc
8200 S Anderson Rd
Oklahoma City, OK 73150
405-732-1637

fitted luggage
trunks

Mail order and open shop. Monday to Saturday 8 am-6 pm. Manufacturer of racks, reinforcing bands, heater covers for Model A Ford also trunks & fitted luggage for all cars US and foreign. Manufacturer of special size trunks for special interest cars, US & worldwide, also supplier of trunk repair hardware and special trunk racks.

Vintage Speed Parts
9103 E Garvey Ave
Rosemead, CA 91770
818-280-4546

parts

Mail order and open shop. Monday-Friday 12 noon to 5 pm; Saturday 9 to 3. For Model Ts, As, and V8s. SASE required for parts information. Catalog $6. Specify engine, chassis, etc.

Vintage Trunks
5 Brownstone Rd
East Granby, CT 06026
860-658-0353
E-mail: jhdeso@ccmail.monsanto.com

trunks

See full listing in **Section Two** under **trunks**

Pete Watson Enterprises
PO Box 488
Epworth, GA 30541
706-632-7675

car dealer
restoration

See full listing in **Section Two** under **restoration shops**

Wescott's Auto Restyling | body parts
19701 SE Hwy 212
Boring, OR 97009
800-523-6279; FAX: 503-658-2938

See full listing in **Section One** under **Ford '32-'53**

Wilson's Classic Auto | restoration
417 Kaufman, Rt 150
PO Box 58
Congerville, IL 61729
309-448-2408; FAX: 309-448-2409

See full listing in **Section Two** under **restoration shops**

Dave Wilton | engine parts
1344 Manhattan Dr
Paradise, CA 95969
916-872-0122

Mail order only. Manufacturing of alternators, fans for Model A Ford and Rec-A-Co oil & temperature gauges.

Woodgrain by Estes | woodgraining
7550 Richardson Rd
Sarasota, FL 34240
813-379-3669

See full listing in **Section Two** under **woodgraining**

Yesteryear Restorations | repair
387 Nutting Rd | restoration
Jaffrey, NH 03452 | sales
603-532-7469 | transportation

See full listing in **Section One** under **Ford '32-'53**

1932 to 1953

A-1 Street Rods | parts
631 E Las Vegas St
Colorado Springs, CO 80903
719-632-4920 or 719-577-4588
FAX: 719-634-6577

See full listing in **Section Two** under **street rods**

Ace Antique Automotive Since | parts
1963 | sales
PO Box 81021
San Diego, CA 92138
619-702-9084; FAX: 619-702-9178
East Coast Outlet: 800-995-6626

Mail order and open shop by appointment. Specializing in Ford parts for 1928 to 1973. Dealing in classic car sales, parts cars on consignment, in business since 1963, large selection of antiques, classics, exotics.

Muneef Alwan | glass
7400 Crosa Countre Rd | steering wheels
Oroville, CA 95966
916-534-6683

Restoration of customers' steering wheels to show quality condition. Cracks, splits, broken sections, etc, all repaired & wheels painted in factory or custom colors. Also wood rim wheels re-rimmed in walnut, teak or mahogany. Restored Ford banjos 36-

39, also 40-51 wheels in stock, also 35-39 horn rods. Have limited inventory of convertible rear glass, laminated safety 1/8" lightweight, cut to correct sizes, 32-48 Ford, Mercury.

American Memory Prints | artwork
5935 N Belt W
Belleville, IL 62223
618-235-4788; FAX: 618-235-4899

See full listing in **Section Two** under **artwork**

Antique Auto Fasteners | fasteners
Guy C Close, Jr & Son | hardware
13426 Valna Dr | hose clamps
Whittier, CA 90602 | molding clips
310-696-3307

See full listing in **Section Two** under **hardware**

Antique Automobile Radio Inc | radio accessories
700 Tampa Rd | radio parts
Palm Harbor, FL 34684 | radio restoration
800-WE-FIX-AM; 813-785-8733
FAX: 813-789-0283

See full listing in **Section Two** under **radios**

Antique Ford V8 Parts | parts
658 Buckley Hwy | shock absorbers
Union, CT 06076
860-684-3853

Mail order and open shop. Open by appointment only. Specializing in the rebuilding of Ford shock absorbers and shock related parts for 1928-48. Also 1932-48 chassis parts, distributors, starters, generators, fuel pumps, water pumps and brake parts.

ARASCO | parts
PO Box 24, Dept HA10
Newport, KY 41072
606-441-8363

Mail order and open shop. Shop open by appointment only. NOS and used parts for 1942-57 Fords. Auto body replacement panels for all marques. Custom dual and stock exhaust systems for all marques.

Keith Ashley | fiberglass parts
107 W Railroad St, Unit V
St Johns, MI 48879
517-224-6460; FAX: 517-224-9488

Mail order and open shop. Monday-Friday 8:30 am-5 pm. New old stock and fiberglass replacement parts for 1932-56 Ford cars and 1942-66 Ford trucks. Also, 1936 Ford fiberglass bodies for street rods. Cast bronze 1935-36 roadster windshield stanchions.

B & W Antique Auto Parts Inc | accessories
4653 Guide Meridian Rd | parts
Bellingham, WA 98226
360-647-4574; FAX: 360-676-0458

Mail order only. Open Monday-Friday 8 to 5 PST. Specializing in Ford and Chevrolet reproduction and NOS parts and accessories. For all Ford products 1932-72, all GM products 1935-1981.

Benfield's Auto Body | body repair
213 Trent St | paint
Kernersville, NC 27284
PH/FAX: 910-993-5772

See full listing in **Section Two** under **painting**

Blough's Automotive Antiques
13881 Molly Pitcher Hwy
Rt 11, Exit 2 off 81
Greencastle, PA 17225
717-597-3677

car dealer

See full listing in **Section One** under **Ford '03-'31**

Bob's F-100 Parts Co
9372 Mission Blvd
Riverside, CA 92509
909-681-1956; FAX: 909-681-1960

parts

See full listing in **Section One** under **Ford '54-up**

**Bob's Radio & TV Service/
Vintage Electronics**
2300 Broad St
San Lius Obispo, CA 94401
805-543-2946; FAX: 805-782-0803

radios

See full listing in **Section Two** under **radios**

Boyds Hot Rods & Collectable Cars
10971 Dale St
Stanton, CA 90680
714-220-9870; FAX: 714-220-9877

car dealer

See full listing in **Section One** under **Chevrolet**

BPE Precision
9782 Gamble Ave
Garden Grove, CA 92641
714-539-6720; FAX: 714-539-9159

parts

See full listing in **Section One** under **Ford '54-up**

The Brassworks
289 Prado Rd
San Louis Obispo, CA 93401
800-342-6759; FAX: 805-544-5615

radiators

See full listing in **Section Two** under **radiators**

C & G Early Ford Parts
1941 Commercial St, Dept AH
Escondido, CA 92029-1233
619-740-2400
FAX: 619-740-8700

books & decals
chrome accessories
mechanical parts
weatherstripping
wiring

Mail order and open shop. Monday-Friday 9 to 5; Saturday 9 to 3 PST. 1932-70 Ford cars, 1932-70 Ford pickups, 1940-56 Mercury, 1955-66 T-Bird, 1960-70 Falcon and 1962-70 Fairlane. 95%-98% in stock. Orders shipped within 24 hours. Over 200 suppliers, one call gets them all. Catalog, 1932-1956 car and pickup and 1957-1970 car and pickup, $6 each ppd USA, $8 foreign (refundable). Please state year & model.

Chandler Classic Cars
1308 14th St W
Bradenton, FL 34205
813-747-3441; FAX: 813-747-9650

Ford products

See full listing in **Section One** under **Ford '54-up**

Chernock Motorcars
PO Box 134
Airport Rd
Hazleton, PA 18201
717-455-1752; FAX: 717-455-7585

trailers

See full listing in **Section Two** under **trailers**

Class-Tech Corp
62935 Layton Ave
Bend, OR 97701
800-874-9981

wiring harnesses

See full listing in **Section Two** under **electrical systems**

**Tony Copeland Ford Lincoln
Mercury**
1617 21st St
Lewiston, ID 83501
800-821-8174; FAX: 208-746-1543
E-mail: copeland@copelandford.com

parts
sales
service

See full listing in **Section One** under **Ford '54-up**

Chuck & Judy Cubel
PO Box 278
Superior, AZ 85273-0278
520-689-2734

wood parts

See full listing in **Section One** under **Ford '03-'31**

Alan Darr Early Ford Parts
124 E Canyon View Dr
Longview, WA 98632
360-425-2463

accessories
parts

Mail order only. 1932-53. Some original & reproduction parts, accessories, collectibles. New and used flathead speed equipment. No catalog. In business since 1968.

Mike Dennis, Nebraska Mail Order
1845 S 48th St
Lincoln, NE 68506
402-489-3036; FAX: 402-489-1148

parts
Trippe mounting
brackets/hardware

Ford parts 1926 thru 1970, NOS or used. Mercury original parts, 1939-1965. Classic Trippe driving light brackets w/nuts, bolts, wrench.

Dependable RV & Auto Service
2619 Rt 11 N
Lafayette, NY 13084
315-677-5336

parts
restoration
service

See full listing in **Section Two** under **service shops**

Bob Drake Reproductions Inc
1819 NW Washington Blvd
Grants Pass, OR 97526
800-221-3673; FAX: 541-474-0099

repro parts

Mail order and open shop. Shop open Monday-Friday 8 am to 4:30 pm. Specializing in reproduction Ford parts for 1932-1948 automobiles and 1948-1966 pickups.

Early Ford Parts
2948 Summer Ave
Memphis, TN 38112
901-323-2179; FAX: 901-323-2195

literature
parts

Mail order and open store. Monday-Friday 9:30-5:30; Saturday 9-2. New parts for 1928-1959 Ford and Mercury cars and trucks. Catalogs for 1932-1959, $4, specify year and body style. In business full time over 20 years. "Over a million parts." VISA, MasterCard, personal checks accepted.

Early Ford Parts and Service
George and Marion Hibbard
Rt 3, Box 448
Claremont, NH 03743
603-542-6269

engine rebuilding
parts
service

Mail order and open shop. Specializing in Ford engine rebuilding (1928-1948). Parts and service for 1928 through 1948 Ford cars and trucks.

Early Ford Parts Specialist
4223 Arthur
Des Moines, IA 50317
515-265-8043

| parts |

New parts 1932-59. Also trunk and cowl cardboards for 1937-51.

Early Ford V8 Sales Inc
9 Hills Rd
Ballston Lake, NY 12019
518-899-9974; FAX: 518-899-5303

| parts |

Mail order and open shop. Specializing in new, reproduction and NOS original engine, chassis & body parts for Ford 1932-56 passenger & pickup.

Engineering & Manufacturing Services
Box 24362
Cleveland, OH 44124-0362
216-446-1620; FAX: 216-446-9590

| sheetmetal |

Mail order only. Outer body sheetmetal, specialize in under decklid tail pans, fender repair sections for 1935 to 1954 Ford, Mercury cars, 1938 to 1952 Ford pickup trucks, 1935 to 1947 Chevrolet, Pontiac, Oldsmobile.

Fairlane Automotive Specialties
107 W Railroad St
St Johns, MI 48879
517-224-6460; FAX: 517-224-9488

| fiberglass bodies |
| parts |

Mail order and open shop. Monday-Friday 9 am-5 pm. Fairlane Automotive Specialties is the leading manufacturer of high quality replacement panels for Ford trucks (1942-66) and cars (1935-36 and 1941-48). Fairlane is well known for parts that fit like NOS. Check out Fairlanes' selection of truck parts: hoods, tilt front ends, front and rear fenders, runningboards and more! Replacement parts available for cars include: hoods, runningboards, front and rear fenders, dashes, fender skirts and much more. Fairlane also manufactures a superior 36 roadster body.

Ford Obsolete
9107-13 Garvey Ave
Rosemead, CA 91770
818-288-2121

| chassis parts |
| engine parts |

See full listing in **Section One** under **Ford '03-'31**

George Frechette
14 Cedar Dr
Granby, MA 01033
800-528-5235

| brake cylinder |
| sleeving |

See full listing in **Section Two** under **brakes**

Gus R Garton
401 N 5th St
Millville, NJ 08332
609-825-3618 evenings

| bicycles |
| NOS parts |
| sales literature |

Mail order and open shop. Open by appointment only. NOS 1932-75 Ford, Mercury and 1929-60 Chevrolet parts. Send SASE for free sales literature list on Ford V8, Model A, Studebaker or special interest. Also classic balloon bicycles. Genuine Ford, Mercury parts, literature, etc, bought and sold. Specializes in 1929-79 fenders, grilles, bumpers, radiators, etc. Send SASE for list original Schwinn sales literature.

Gaslight Auto Parts Inc
PO Box 291
Urbana, OH 43078
513-652-2145; FAX: 513-652-2147

| accessories |
| parts |

See full listing in **Section One** under **Ford '03-'31**

Leo Gephart Classic Cars
7360 E Acoma Dr, Ste 14
Scottsdale, AZ 85260
602-948-2286, 602-998-8263
FAX: 602-948-2390

| car dealer |
| parts |

See full listing in **Section Two** under **car dealers**

GF Embossed Notes
11 Caldwell Dr
Amherst, NH 03031
603-880-6217; FAX: 603-882-6590

| note cards |

See full listing in **Section Two** under **automobilia**

Green Valentine Inc
5055 Covington Way
Memphis, TN 38134
901-373-5555; FAX: 901-373-5568

| car dealer |
| woodies |

See full listing in **Section Two** under **car dealers**

Hagerty Classic Insurance
PO Box 87
Traverse City, MI 49685
800-922-4050; FAX: 616-941-8227

| insurance |

See full listing in **Section Two** under **insurance**

Half Ton Fun
Bob Selzam
166 Toms River Rd
Jackson, NJ 08527
908-928-9421

| NOS parts |

Mail order and open shop. Specializing in new old stock Ford parts for 1932-56 pickups and trucks, 1932-48 passenger cars (mechanical only) and 1932-53 flathead V8 and 6-cylinder engine and transmission parts.

Haneline Products Co
PO Box 430
Morongo Valley, CA 92256
619-363-6597; FAX: 619-363-7321

| gauges |
| instrument panels |
| stainless parts |
| trim parts |

See full listing in **Section Two** under **instruments**

Bruce Horkey Cabinetry
Rt 4, Box 188
Windom, MN 56101
507-831-5625; FAX: 507-831-0280

| pickup parts |

See full listing in **Section Two** under **woodwork**

Hot Rod & Custom Supply
1304 SE 10th St
Cape Coral, FL 33990
941-574-7744; FAX: 941-574-8820

| custom parts |
| engine parts |
| speed parts |

Specializing in 50s speed and custom parts for Ford/Mercury flathead, speed and custom accessories, flathead air conditioning, engine parts.

Howell's Sheetmetal Co
PO Box 792
Nederland, TX 77627
409-727-1999

| body panels |
| sheetmetal |

See full listing in **Section One** under **Ford '03-'31**

Instrument Services Inc
11765 Main St
Roscoe, IL 61073
800-558-2674; FAX: 800-623-6416

| clocks |

See full listing in **Section Two** under **instruments**

Charles Ivey Speedometer Service 2144 Wallace Dr Wichita, KS 67218 316-683-6765	instruments repair

See full listing in **Section Two** under **instruments**

Janssen's Repair Shop 835 12th Ave Manson, IA 50563 712-469-2308	repairs

Mail order and open shop. Monday-Saturday 8 to 5:30. Post-1921 special interest Fords and all makes of post-1921 classic autos.

Jefferis Auto Body 4130-C Horizon San Luis Obispo, CA 93401 FAX: 805-543-4757	bodywork parts restoration

Mail order and open shop. 1937 Ford parts specialist: known nationally for our 1937-39 Ford windshield conversion kit for all closed cars and trucks. Our V-Butt windshield kit comes in clear, green, dark grey or bronze tint. We have patterns for full car flat glass, 1937 on up, most makes and models. We ship worldwide UPS.

Jefferis Hot Rod Autobody 4130-C Horizon Ln San Luis Obispo, CA 93401 800-807-1937; FAX: 805-543-4757	windshield glass kit

See full listing in **Section Two** under **glass**

Joblot Automotive Inc Ford Parts Specialists 98-11 211th St Queens Village, NY 11429 718-468-8585; FAX: 718-468-8686	parts

Mail order and open shop. Monday-Friday 8:30 to 4:30. Over 12,000 different new and rebuilt parts. Specializing in the Ford family of cars and trucks 1928 thru 1972. Engine, brake, transmission and clutch, front and rear end, a full line of rubber, electrical, wiring and ignition. Established in 1956. Three catalogs available: 1928 thru 1972 cars and trucks, 1948/1972 F-1/100 thru F-6/600 trucks, 1949/1969 Ford family of cars. VISA, MC and COD phone or FAX orders accepted. Dealer inquiries invited.

JR's Antique Auto 14900 Scherry Ln Claremore, OK 74017 918-342-4398	chrome parts interiors

See full listing in **Section One** under **Chevrolet**

K C Obsolete Parts 3343 N 61 Kansas City, KS 66104 PH/FAX: 913-334-9479	parts

Mail order only. Carries a full line of parts for 1948-66 Ford pickups and panels. Full line catalog available for $2.

Kenroy Ford Parts 2 Folwell Ln Mullica Hill, NJ 08062 609-848-4965; FAX: 609-468-2489	NOS parts

See full listing in **Section One** under **Ford '54-up**

Ken's Carburetors 2301 Barnum Ave Stratford, CT 06497 203-375-9340	carburetors distributors parts

Mail order only. Specializing in Ford parts. Mainly rebuilding of flathead carbs and ignition distributors and some NOS & used parts. No body parts. Glass beading services also.

Dale King Obsolete Parts PO Box 1099 Liberty, KY 42539 606-787-5031; FAX: 606-787-2130	parts

See full listing in **Section One** under **Ford '54-up**

Knight Automotive Engineering Inc Kettle Cove Industrial Park 743 Western Ave, Rt 127 Gloucester, MA 01930 508-525-3491	engine rebuilding

See full listing in **Section Two** under **engine rebuilding**

Lakeview Accessories PO Box 95 Skaneateles, NY 13152 315-685-7414	nostalgia items

See full listing in **Section One** under **Ford '03-'31**

LeBaron Bonney Co PO Box 6 6 Chestnut St Amesbury, MA 01913 508-388-3811, 800-221-5408 FAX: 508-388-1113	fabrics interior kits tops

Mail order and open shop. Monday-Friday 8:30 to 5. Duplicate of original interior and top kits for Ford and Mercury 1928/54. Upholstery fabric by the yard for many makes from the early 1920s thru the early 1950s. Kit information for each Ford or Mercury model. Parts and accessories catalog available at $1. Free kit info and catalog.

Loyal Ford Mercury Inc 2310 Calumet Dr New Holstein, WI 53061 414-898-4248; FAX: 414-898-9705	cars parts

See full listing in **Section One** under **Ford '54-up**

Mack Products Box 856 Moberly, MO 65270 816-263-7444	parts pickup beds

Mail order only. Monday-Friday 8 to 5:30. Established in 1973. Die-stamped pickup bed parts, oak bed wood, tailgates. Complete reproduction pickup beds for 1926-72 Fords and 1928-72 Chevrolets. Pickup catalog $1. New items include pickup beds for 1933-47 Dodge, 1941-55 Studebaker and 1933-62 Willys.

Mac's Antique Auto Parts 1051 Lincoln Ave, PO Box 238 Lockport, NY 14095-0238 716-433-1500	literature parts restoration supplies

See full listing in **Section One** under **Ford '03-'31**

Mark's 1941-1948 Ford Parts | **parts**
97 Hoodlum Hill Rd
Binghamton, NY 13905
607-729-1693

Mail order only. Caters to people who feel 1941-1948 Fords are among the best looking Fords ever produced. Deals mainly in used parts from my large assortment of parts cars. Carries vintique reproduction as well. Specializing in NOS, reproduction and used parts for 1941-1948 Ford and Mercury cars. Reproduction catalog $2, NOS parts list $2, free with orders over $100.

Master Power Brakes | **brake products conversion kits**
254-1 Rolling Hills Rd
Mooresville, NC 28115
704-664-8866; FAX: 704-664-8862

See full listing in **Section One** under **Chevelle/Camaro**

Max Neon Design Group | **custom face logos neon clocks**
19807 Sussex Dr
St Clair Shores, MI 48081-3257
810-773-5000; FAX: 810-772-6224

See full listing in **Section Two** under **automobilia**

McDonald Obsolete Parts Company | **body parts chassis parts**
RR 3, Box 94
Rockport, IN 47635
812-359-4965; FAX: 812-359-5555

Mail order only. Specializing in body parts and chassis parts, script glass, spotlights and foglights for 1938-1980 Ford, Mercury, Lincoln and trucks. Inventory is 90% NOS. Also dealers of all major quality reproduced parts.

The McHugh Group | **appraisals**
4602 Birch Ct
Middletown, MD 21769
301-473-8333; FAX: 301-371-9447

See full listing in **Section Two** under **appraisals**

Medicine Bow Motors Inc | **car dealer**
343 One Horse Creek Rd
Florence, MT 59833
406-273-0002

See full listing in **Section Two** under **car dealers**

Melvin's Classic Ford Parts Inc | **parts**
2526 Panola Rd
Lithonia, GA 30058
770-981-2357; FAX: 770-981-6207

See full listing in **Section One** under **Ford '54-up**

Mercury & Ford Molded Rubber | **parts**
12 Plymouth Ave
Wilmington, MA 01887
508-658-8394

See full listing in **Section One** under **Mercury**

Mercury Restorations | **NOS restoration used parts**
Larry Adams
40 Sunset Ridge
Clyde, NC 28721
PH/FAX: 704-452-2049

See full listing in **Section One** under **Mercury**

Miller Obsolete Parts | **parts**
1329 Campus Dr
Vestal, NY 13850
607-722-5371; FAX: 607-729-7645
E-mail: fordpart@spectra.net

Mail order only. New obsolete (NOS) parts. 50s thru 80s Ford, Lincoln, Mercury vehicles.

Monument Motors Inc | **repair restoration used parts**
PO Box 711
Great Barrington, MA 01230
413-637-1017

See full listing in **Section One** under **Mustang**

C W Moss Ford Parts Inc | **NOS parts used parts**
402 W Chapman Ave
Orange, CA 92666
714-639-3083, Orange
909-629-5223, Pomona
FAX: 714-639-0329

See full listing in **Section One** under **Ford '03-'31**

Muck Motor Ford Sales | **parts**
10 Campbell Blvd
Getzville, NY 14068
800-228-6825; FAX: 716-688-5519

See full listing in **Section One** under **Thunderbird**

Narragansett Reproductions | **wire harnesses**
Ed & Miki Pease
107 Woodville Rd, PO Box 51
Wood River Junction, RI 02894
401-364-3839; FAX: 401-364-3830

See full listing in **Section Two** under **electrical systems**

Norman's Classic Auto Radio | **custom sales radio repairs**
7651 Park Blvd
Pinellas Park, FL 33781
813-546-1788

See full listing in **Section Two** under **radios**

Northeast Ford | **parts restoration**
Box 66, Rt 9
E Sullivan, NH 03445
603-847-9956, 800-562-FORD
FAX: 603-847-9691

See full listing in **Section One** under **Ford '54-up**

Oak Bows | **top bows**
122 Ramsey Ave
Chambersburg, PA 17201
717-264-2602

See full listing in **Section Two** under **woodwork**

Obsolete Ford Parts Co | **parts**
PO Box 787
Nashville, GA 31639
912-686-2470, 686-5101
FAX: 912-686-7125

See full listing in **Section One** under **Ford '54-up**

Obsolete Ford Parts Inc | **parts**
8701 S I-35
Oklahoma City, OK 73149
405-631-3933; FAX: 405-634-6815

See full listing in **Section One** under **Ford '54-up**

The Old Car Centre   parts
19909 92A Ave
Langley, BC Canada V1M 3B6
604-888-4412, 604-888-4055
FAX: 604-888-7455

See full listing in **Section One** under **Ford '03-'31**

Old Ford Parts   parts
35 4th Ave N
Algona, WA 98001
206-833-8494; FAX: 206-833-2190

Mail order and open shop. Monday-Thursday 8 am to 6 pm,
Friday-Saturday 8 to 2. Specializing in 32-48 Ford cars and 32-
79 Ford trucks parts. Parts, rubber seals, electrical supplies, ie:
wiring, bulbs, connectors, trim parts, sheetmetal panels,
bumpers, hubcaps, etc.

Old Tin Australia   salvage yard
PO Box 26
Wendouree, Victoria 3355 Australia
0353-36-1929; FAX: 0353-36-2930

See full listing in **Section Five** under **Australia**

Original Falcon, Comet, Ranchero,   interiors
Fairlane Interiors   weatherstripping
6343 Seaview Ave NW
Seattle, WA 98107-2664
206-781-5230; FAX: 206-781-5046
E-mail: falcons@ix.netcom.com

See full listing in **Section One** under **Ford '54-up**

Original Ford Motor Co Literature   collectibles
PO Box 7-AA   literature
Hudson, KY 40145-0007
502-257-8642; FAX: 502-257-8643

Original Ford literature and collectibles. Send SASE with want list.

Patrick's Antique Cars & Trucks   parts
PO Box 10648
Casa Grande, AZ 85230
520-836-1117; FAX: 520-836-1104

See full listing in **Section One** under **Chevrolet**

Pick-ups Northwest   parts
7130 Bickford Ave   trim
Snohomish, WA 98290
360-568-9166; FAX: 360-568-1233

See full listing in **Section One** under **Chevrolet**

Precision Babbitt Service   babbitting
4681 Lincoln Ave   engine rebuilding
Beamsville, ON Canada L0R 1B3
905-563-4364

See full listing in **Section Two** under **babbitting**

PV Antique & Classic Ford   parts
1688 Main St
Tewksbury, MA 01876
508-851-9159; FAX: 508-858-3827

Mail order and open shop. Monday-Friday 9 to 5 pm, Thursday 9
to 9 pm, Saturday 9 to 1. Large inventory in stock of reproduction Model A, 1932-48 early V8, 1948-60 F-100 pickups and
1964 1/2-73 Mustang parts and accessories. We ship UPS daily
and accept MasterCard and VISA on all orders. Toll free: 800-
MSTANGS for ordering only. Any catalog above, $2 or free with
purchase.

R & R Fiberglass & Specialties   body parts
4850 Wilson Dr NW
Cleveland, TN 37312
423-476-2270

See full listing in **Section Two** under **fiberglass parts**

Red's Headers   headers
22950 Bednar Ln   mechanical parts
Fort Bragg, CA 95437-8411
707-964-7733

Mail order and open shop. Monday-Friday 8-4:30. Specializing in
headers, mechanical parts and machine shop services for 28-70
Fords. Headers made and stocked for Model A side valve and
ohv, flathead V8 including V8-60; Y-block Fords 272-312 in
cars, trucks & T-Birds; 289-302 in Falcons/Comets,
Mustangs/Cougars and Fairlanes each diferent. Crankshaft
grinding and balancing, rod work and engine rebuilding for
stock and hot rod Fords, since 1964.

Renner's Corner   engine snubber kits
10320 E Austin   fuel pipes
Manchester, MI 48158   fuel pump kits
313-428-8424; FAX: 313-428-1090   gauge rebuild kits

Mail order only. Specializing in reproduction of 1932 hard-to-
find 4-cylinder and 8-cylinder fuel system parts and repair kits,
4-cylinder engine snubber kits and sidemount spare hardware
kits. Parts exactly as Henry built them.

Restorations Unlimited   metal fabrication
Box 1118   restoration
Blenheim, ON Canada N0P 1A0
519-676-8455

See full listing in **Section One** under **Auburn**

Rock Valley Antique Auto Parts   gas tanks
Box 352
Rt 72 and Rothwell Rd
Stillman Valley, IL 61084
815-645-2271; FAX: 815-645-2740

Deals in stainless steel gas tanks for most antique and street rod
cars and pickups. Makes 31-40 passenger, 41-54 pickup
bumpers for Chevrolet. Offers a full line of 1928-48 reproduction, used and NOS Ford parts. Call or send for our free
brochure.

Rocky Mountain V8 Ford Parts   parts
1124 Clark Cir
Colorado Springs, CO 80915
719-597-8375

Mail order and open shop by appointment. Parts for 1932 to 60s
Ford products. New, used and reproduction. Buy, sell and trade.
Large inventory on hand. Parts cars and trucks in yard.
VISA/MC, UPS, COD. Send your want list.

Rod-1 Shop   street rods
210 Clinton Ave
Pitman, NJ 08071
609-228-7631; FAX: 609-582-5770

See full listing in **Section Two** under **street rods**

Albert A Rogers II   parts
29A Young Rd   storage
Charlton, MA 01507
508-248-3555

Mail order and open shop by appointment only. Specializing in
Ford parts 1933 and 1934. Many NOS, original and reconditioned parts. 33-34 woody wagons a specialty. Storage for
antique cars, safe, secure, heated storage, seasonally or annually. In central Massachusetts.

S & S Antique Auto	**parts**
Pine St	
Deposit, NY 13754	
607-467-2929; FAX: 607-467-2109	

Mail order and open shop. Monday to Saturday 9-6. I specialize in NOS parts, used and repro for Ford cars and trucks.

Sacramento Vintage Ford Parts	**accessories**
4675 Aldona Ln	**parts**
Sacramento, CA 95841	**street rod products**
916-489-3444; FAX: 916-488-3444	

Mail order and open shop. Shop open Monday-Friday 9 to 6, Saturday 9 to 3. Specializing in reproduction parts and accessories for Ford automobiles 1909-1947 and Ford pickups 1928-1966. Plus a complete inventory of street rod products. Catalogs available.

Saturn Industries	**axles**
143 Wimborne Rd	**instruments**
Poole, Dorset BH15 2BCR England	**literature**
01202-674982; FAX: 01202-668274	**repro parts**

See full listing in **Section One** under **Ford '03-'31**

Charlie Sens Antique Auto Museum	**museum**
2074 Marion Mt Gilead Rd	
Marion, OH 43302-8991	
614-389-4686; FAX: 614-386-2521	

See full listing in **Section Six** under **Ohio**

Joe Smith Ford & Hot Rod Parts	**parts**
2140 Canton Rd, Unit C	**service**
Marietta, GA 30066	
800-235-4013; 770-426-9850	
FAX: 770-426-9854	

Mail order and open shop. Monday-Friday 8:30-5:30. 1932-1948 Ford cars, 1932-1952 Ford trucks. Parts and service.

Southside Obsolete	**parts**
6819 James Ave S	
Minneapolis, MN 55423	
612-866-1230	

Mail order and open shop. Monday-Friday 8 to 5. Ford parts 1932-80, NOS or USA, Mercury, Lincoln and truck also. Catalogs $4, please specify. Selling Ford parts since 1970. Largest inventory in USA of NOS genuine Ford.

Dick Spadaro	**fiberglass bodies**
Early Ford Reproductions	**parts**
PO Box 617, 6599 Rt 158 Sharps Rd	
Altamont, NY 12009	
518-861-5367	

Mail order and open shop. Open 9 to 5 pm EST. Ford V8 to 1948 and pickup to 1956. Supplier of quality accessories and replacement parts and sheetmetal repair panels. Dealer for Gibbon fiberglass bodies. Manufacturer of steel 1932 front fenders. NOS and used parts always in stock.

Spark Plugs & Stuff	**tune-up kits**
PO Box 33343	
San Diego, CA 92163-3343	
619-220-1745	

See full listing in **Section Two** under **ignition parts**

Speedway Motors Inc	**parts**
300 Speedway Cir	
Lincoln, NE 68502	
402-474-4411; FAX: 402-477-7476	

See full listing in **Section Two** under **comprehensive parts**

Transport-Nation Collectibles	**artwork**
24040 Camino Del Avion, Ste A-241	**collectibles**
Monarch Beach, CA 92629	
800-474-4404, 714-240-5126	

See full listing in **Section Two** under **artwork**

Truck 'N' Parts	**parts**
9107-9 E Garvey Ave	
Rosemead, CA 91770	
818-288-2121	

Mail order and open shop. Daily 12 to 5. Phone hours 8 to 4:30 daily. For 1932-56 Ford trucks. Catalog RP-2, $6, refundable with purchase.

Ultra Wheel Co	**custom wheels**
6300 Valley View Ave	
Buena Park, CA 90620	
714-994-1444; FAX: 714-994-0723	

See full listing in **Section Two** under **wheels & wheelcovers**

Valley Motor Supply	**accessories**
1402 E Second St	**parts**
Roswell, NM 88201	
505-622-7450	

See full listing in **Section One** under **Ford '54-up**

Valley Obsolete Ford Parts	**parts**
Kerrville, TX 78029	
PH/FAX: 210-896-3269	

Specializing in Ford parts for 1928-1979. We sell Ford parts for Model As, flatheads, Mustangs, Falcons, Fairlanes, Broncos and all other products of Ford Motor Company.

Vintage Ford & Chevrolet Parts of Arizona Inc	**parts**
3427 E McDowell Rd	
Phoenix, AZ 85008	
602-275-7990; FAX: 602-267-8439	

See full listing in **Section One** under **Ford '54-up**

Waldron's Antique Exhaust Parts Inc	**exhaust systems**
PO Box C 25872 M-86	
Nottawa, MI 49075	
616-467-7185; FAX: 616-467-9041	

See full listing in **Section Two** under **exhaust systems**

Wescott's Auto Restyling	**body parts**
19701 SE Hwy 212	
Boring, OR 97009	
800-523-6279; FAX: 503-658-2938	

Mail order and open shop. Monday-Friday 9-5:30; Saturday 9-5 PST. Specializes in fiberglass replacement fenders and bodies and reproduction body parts for 1926-1948 Ford cars and 1926-1956 Ford pickups.

Wheel Vintiques Inc	**hubcaps**
5468 E Lamona Ave	**wheels**
Fresno, CA 93727	
209-251-6957; FAX: 209-251-1620	

See full listing in **Section One** under **Chevrolet**

Wilson's Classic Auto
417 Kaufman, Rt 150
PO Box 58
Congerville, IL 61729
309-448-2408; FAX: 309-448-2409

restoration

See full listing in **Section Two** under **restoration shops**

The Wood N'Carr
3231 E 19th St
Signal Hill, CA 90804
310-498-8730; FAX: 310-985-3360

woodwork
wood parts

See full listing in **Section Two** under **woodwork**

Woodgrain by Estes
7550 Richardson Rd
Sarasota, FL 34240
813-379-3669

woodgraining

See full listing in **Section Two** under **woodgraining**

The Woodie Works
Box 346, RR 3
Arlington, VT 05250
802-375-9305

woodworking

See full listing in **Section Two** under **woodwork**

Yesteryear Restorations
387 Nutting Rd
Jaffrey, NH 03452
603-532-7469

repair
restoration
sales
transportation

Shop open Monday-Friday 8 to 5; call evenings for information or arrangements. Complete or partial restorations for show or driving use of Ford Model A and V8s to 1953. Also general upkeep or maintenance. Brokered selling of your antique or special interest auto. 48 state transportation via open or enclosed carrier arranged.

1954 - up

1958 Thunderbird Convertible Registry
Bill Van Ess
2306 Post Dr NE
Belmont, MI 49306
616-364-1973; FAX: 616-363-2870

book

See full listing in **Section One** under **Thunderbird**

ABC Auto Upholstery & Top Company
1634 Church St
Philadelphia, PA 19124
215-289-0555

upholstery

Mail order and open shop. Monday-Friday 8:30 to 6. Upholstery kits for 1954-59 Fords. NOS vinyls and cloth for most marques, from late forties to early seventies. Over 30,000 yards of NOS cloth and vinyls in stock at all times.

Ace Antique Automotive Since 1963
PO Box 81021
San Diego, CA 92138
619-702-9084; FAX: 619-702-9178
East Coast Outlet: 800-995-6626

parts
sales

See full listing in **Section One** under **Ford '32-'53**

ADHCO Inc
PO Box 2522
Ardmore, OK 73402
405-657-4280; FAX: 405-657-2446

parts
restoration

Mail order only. NOS and reconditioned parts for 55/56 Fords. Also restoration of 55/56 Fords.

AKH Wheels
1207 N A St
Ellensburg, WA 98926-2522
509-962-3390

Rallye wheels
styled steel wheels
vintage aluminum

See full listing in **Section Two** under **wheels & wheelcovers**

American Plastic Chrome
1398 Mar Ann Dr
Westland, MI 48185
313-721-1967 days
313-261-4454 eves

replating plastic

See full listing in **Section Two** under **plating & polishing**

AMK Products
18600 E 96th St
Broken Arrow, OK 74012
918-455-2651; FAX: 918-455-7441

parts

See full listing in **Section One** under **Mustang**

Andover Automotive Inc
PO Box 3143
Laurel, MD 20709
410-381-6700; FAX: 410-381-6703

parts
seat belts

See full listing in **Section One** under **Corvette**

Andy's Classic Mustangs
18502 E Sprague
Greenacres, WA 99016
509-924-9824

parts
service

See full listing in **Section One** under **Mustang**

Donald Antilla
888 Hulls Hill Rd
Southbury, CT 06488
203-264-8301 evenings

supercharger parts

Mail order only. 1957 Ford and Thunderbird supercharger parts bought, sold and traded. Reproductions of hoses, brackets, idlers, fittings. Cast parts machined from ductile iron. Active in 1957 supercharger activities for twenty years.

ARASCO
PO Box 24, Dept HA10
Newport, KY 41072
606-441-8363

parts

See full listing in **Section One** under **Ford '32-'53**

Keith Ashley
107 W Railroad St, Unit V
St Johns, MI 48879
517-224-6460; FAX: 517-224-9488

fiberglass parts

See full listing in **Section One** under **Ford '32-'53**

Auto Custom Carpet Jeff Moses PO Box 1350, 1429 Noble St Anniston, AL 36202 800-633-2358; 205-236-1118 FAX: 800-516-8274	**carpets floor coverings**

See full listing in **Section One** under **Chevrolet**

Auto Krafters Inc PO Box 8 522 S Main St Broadway, VA 22815 703-896-5910; FAX: 703-896-6412	**parts**

Mail order and open shop. Monday-Friday 9-6, Saturday 9-12. Specializing in weatherstrip, interior, exterior, engine, wiring, suspension, brakes, hardware, literature. Specialty, rebuilt ps control valves for 65-73 Mustangs, 67-73 Cougars, 60-70 Falcons, 62-76 Fairlanes/Torinos, 60-70 full size Fords, 58-76 T-Birds, 66-77 Broncos, 53-79 F-100s, 70-77 Mavericks, 60-79 Rancheros. Both new and used parts.

Autowire Division 9109 (Rear) E Garvey Ave Rosemead, CA 91770 818-572-0938; FAX: 818-288-3311	**alternator conversions motors/relays switches**

Mail order and open shop. Monday-Friday 9 to 5. For 1949-68 Fords, Lincolns and Mercurys. Top motors, relays, window regulators, motors and switches, and alternator conversions for all Fords, 6 and 12 volt. Catalog $6, please specify exact year.

B & W Antique Auto Parts Inc 4653 Guide Meridian Rd Bellingham, WA 98227 360-647-4574; FAX: 360-676-0458	**accessories parts**

See full listing in **Section One** under **Ford '32-'53**

Bill's Speed Shop 13951 Millersburg Rd Navarre, OH 44662 330-832-9403; FAX: 330-832-2098	**body parts**

See full listing in **Section One** under **Chevrolet**

Larry Blodget Box 753 Rancho Mirage, CA 92270 619-862-1979	**models**

See full listing in **Section Two** under **models & toys**

Bob's F-100 Parts Co 9372 Mission Blvd Riverside, CA 92509 909-681-1956; FAX: 909-681-1960	**parts**

Mail order and open shop. Monday-Friday 8 to 5, Sunday 10 to 2 (50% of time). Parts for 1948-1967 F-100 pickups. We have every part, original to custom power brakes, window/door locks, frame clips, 9" rear ends, etc. We also do complete restorations. We can build you a rolling chassis or complete truck, stock to pro-street. We do it all!

Boyds Hot Rods & Collectable Cars 10971 Dale St Stanton, CA 90680 714-220-9870; FAX: 714-220-9877	**car dealer**

See full listing in **Section One** under **Chevrolet**

BPE Precision 9782 Gamble Ave Garden Grove, CA 92641 714-539-6720; FAX: 714-539-9159	**parts**

Mail order only. Specializing in 1948-66 Ford F-100 pickup trucks. F-100 parts store/complete line for frame-up restoration of 1948 thru 1966 Ford F-100 pickups. Parts catalog $2.

Brasilia Press PO Box 2023 Elkhart, IN 46515 FAX: 219-262-8799	**models**

See full listing in **Section Two** under **models & toys**

The Bumper Boyz 834 E Florence Ave Los Angeles, CA 90001 213-587-8976, 800-995-1703 FAX: 213-587-2013	**bumper repairs reconditioning sand blasting**

See full listing in **Section One** under **Chevrolet**

Bob Burgess 1955-56 Ford Parts Inc 793 Alpha-Bellbrook Rd Bellbrook, OH 45305 513-426-8041	**parts**

Mail order and open shop. Monday-Saturday 9-6 pm. Specializing in new, used and reproduction parts for 1955-56 Ford, Mercury.

Burrell's Service Inc PO Box 456 Keego Harbor, MI 48320 810-682-2376	**parts**

See full listing in **Section One** under **Chevrolet**

Butch's Trim W-224 S-8445 Industrial Ave Big Bend, WI 53103 414-679-4883; 414-662-9910 shop	**molding polishing trim restoration**

See full listing in **Section One** under **Chevrolet**

C & G Early Ford Parts 1941 Commercial St, Dept AH Escondido, CA 92029-1233 619-740-2400; FAX: 619-740-8700	**books & decals chrome accessories mechanical parts wiring**

See full listing in **Section One** under **Ford '32-'53**

California 55-56-57 T-Birds Neil Schebetta 945 Kensington Dr Fremont, CA 94539-4586 PH/FAX: 510-651-1381	**parts**

See full listing in **Section One** under **Thunderbird**

Carl's Ford Parts 23219 South ST Homeworth, OH 44634 PH/FAX: 330-525-7291	**muscle parts**

See full listing in **Section One** under **Mustang**

Carolina Classics 624 E Geer St Durham, NC 27701 919-682-4211; FAX: 919-682-1286	**truck parts**

Mail order and open shop. Mon-Fri 8-5:30, Sat by appointment. 1948-79 Ford truck parts.

Dennis Carpenter Ford Reproductions PO Box 26398 Charlotte, NC 28221 704-786-8139; FAX: 704-786-8180	parts

Mail order and counter sales. Monday-Friday 8 to 5. Manufacture and sell obsolete Ford car & truck parts. Specializing in weatherstripping, antennas, scuff plates, outside door handles and much more. For 1932/up Ford cars, 1932/79 pickups, 1940/56 Mercury, 1958/66 T-Birds, 1960/70 Falcons and 1962/71 Fairlanes. Catalogs $3, state year and body style.

Chandler Classic Cars 1308 14th St W Bradenton, FL 34205 813-747-3441; FAX: 813-747-9650	Ford products

Specialize in selling Ford products for 1950s & 1960s.

Chewning's Auto Literature 2011 Elm Tree Terr Buford, GA 30518 770-945-9795	literature manuals

See full listing in **Section Two** under **literature dealers**

Class-Tech Corp 62935 Layton Ave Bend, OR 97701 800-874-9981	wiring harnesses

See full listing in **Section Two** under **electrical systems**

Classic Auto 251 SW 5th Ct Pompano Beach, FL 33060 954-786-1687	restoration

See full listing in **Section Two** under **restoration shops**

Classic Auto Air Mfg Co 2020 W Kennedy Blvd Tampa, FL 33606 813-251-4994, 813-251-2356	air conditioning heating parts

See full listing in **Section One** under **Mustang**

Classic Auto Literature Box 53 Blueback, RR 2 Nanoose Bay, BC Canada V0R 2R0 250-468-9522	data books literature/manuals models parts catalog

See full listing in **Section Two** under **literature dealers**

Classic Auto Restoration Service Inc 113 National Dr Rockwall, TX 75087 214-722-9663	restoration

See full listing in **Section One** under **Chevrolet**

Classic Enterprises Box 92 Barron, WI 54812 715-537-5422	sheetmetal

See full listing in **Section One** under **Studebaker**

Classic Ford Sales PO Box 60 E Dixfield, ME 04227 207-562-4443; FAX: 207-562-4576 E-mail: info@classicford.com	salvage yard

See full listing in **Section Five** under **Maine**

Clester's Auto Rubber Seals Inc PO Box 459 Cleveland, NC 27013 704-637-9979; FAX: 704-636-7390	gloveboxes headliners molded rubber parts

See full listing in **Section Two** under **rubber parts**

Clock Doc® 125 University Ave Sewanee, TN 37375 800-256-5362; FAX: 615-598-5986	clock repairs gauge repairs

See full listing in **Section Two** under **instruments**

Bob Cook Classic Auto Parts Inc 2055 Van Cleave Rd, PO Box 600 Murray, KY 42071-0600 502-753-4000, 800-486-1137 FAX: 502-753-4600	new parts NOS parts reproduced parts

Mail and phone orders. Most Ford vehicles 1955-1972. Catalog price refundable, $5.

Tony Copeland Ford Lincoln Mercury 1617 21st St Lewiston, ID 83501 800-821-8174; FAX: 208-746-1543 E-mail: copeland@copelandford.com	parts sales service

Mail order and open shop. Specializing in sales, service & parts for Ford Motor Company products. We have up to 25 specialty, muscle car, restored & street rod vehicles in stock in conjunction with our new & used vehicle inventory.

Walt Dantzler 1567 Bertrand Dr Lafayette, LA 70506 318-234-1344, leave message FAX: 318-233-4113	parts

Mail order and open shop by appointment. NOS Ford and Mercury 1949-up parts. Part time hobbyist. Lists available for SASE.

Dearborn Classics PO Box 1248 Sunset Beach, CA 90742 714-372-3175; FAX: 714-372-3801	accessories restoration parts

The nation's parts source for Ford Ranchero, Falcon, Fairlane and Torino parts and accessories. Moldings, emblems, weatherstripping, interior, engine parts, suspension, brake system and more. Large fully illustrated catalog available or request.

Mike Dennis, Nebraska Mail Order 1845 S 48th St Lincoln, NE 68506 402-489-3036; FAX: 402-489-1148	parts Trippe mounting brackets/hardware

See full listing in **Section One** under **Ford '32-'53**

Bill Denzel dba California Thunderbirds 1507 Arroyo View Dr Pasadena, CA 91103 818-792-0720	parts

See full listing in **Section One** under **Thunderbird**

Greg Donahue Collector Car Restorations Inc 12900 S Betty Pt Floral City, FL 34436 352-344-4329; FAX: 352-344-0015	parts restoration

Phone hours: 9 am to 8 pm, Monday through Saturday. No Sundays or holidays. Shop visits by prior appointment only. 1963/64 Ford Galaxie reproduction and NOS parts including weatherstrip, rubber parts, moldings, carpet, exterior and interior chrome, trim, ornaments, mechanical parts, sheetmetal, wheelcovers and decals, power steering, clectrical, wiring harnesses, seat covers, paints, diagrams and manuals. Current catalog, $5. We have the largest inventory in the US. Also, 100 point concours restorations on all sixties and seventies muscle cars.

Early Ford Parts 2948 Summer Ave Memphis, TN 38112 901-323-2179; FAX: 901-323-2195	literature parts

See full listing in **Section One** under **Ford '32-'53**

Early Ford V8 Sales Inc 9 Hills Rd Ballston Lake, NY 12019 518-899-9974; FAX: 518-899-5303	parts

See full listing in **Section One** under **Ford '32-'53**

Eaton Detroit Spring Service Co 1555 Michigan Ave Detroit, MI 48350 313-963-3839; FAX: 313-963-7047 E-mail: ken@eatonsprings.com	bushings coil springs leaf springs shackles U-bolts

See full listing in **Section Two** under **suspension parts**

Egge Machine Company 11707 Slauson Ave Santa Fe Springs, CA 90670 310-945-3419 in CA 800-866-EGGE FAX: 310-693-1635	babbitting chassis motor mounts pistons valves wiring harnesses

See full listing in **Section Two** under **engine parts**

Daniel A Evans 2850 John St Easton, PA 18045 610-258-9542 after 5:30 pm FAX: 610-252-0370 E-mail: evansd@lafayette.edu	literature parts

Specializing in NOS and restored hard-to-find parts for 1955-57 Thunderbirds. Buy, sell, trade Ford dual quad and supercharger parts. Also original literature and Ford dealership items.

Falcon's Forever PO Box 6531 Albany, CA 94206 510-525-9226; FAX: 510-525-2652	parts

Shop open weekends by appointment. Specializing in hard to find parts for 60-65 Falcons and Comets. This includes rust-free California sheetmetal, moldings, trim and mechanical parts. Also a supply of new rubber parts.

Faxon Auto Literature 3901 Carter Ave Riverside, CA 92501 800-458-2734; FAX: 909-786-4166	literature manuals

See full listing in **Section Two** under **literature dealers**

John Filiss 45 Kingston Ave Port Jervis, NY 12771 914-856-2942	appraisals

See full listing in **Section Two** under **appraisals**

Ford Parts Store 110 Ford Rd, Box 226 Bryan, OH 43506 419-636-2475; FAX: 419-636-8449 E-mail: fordpart@bright.net	parts

Mail and telephone orders only. Monday-Saturday 9 am-9 pm, 24 hour FAX. Since 1978, specializing in 1952-1970 Ford passenger cars. New & reproduction weatherstripping for doors, windshield, convertible tops, roof rails, wire harnesses, trunk mats, carpet, scuff plates, plastic emblems, chrome scripts, owner's & shop manuals. Appears at 18 major swap meets throughout the year. Catalog available, $3.

Ford Reproduction Parts Store 110 Ford Rd, PO Box 226 Bryan, OH 43506-0226 419-636-2475; FAX: 419-636-8449 E-mail: fordpart@bright.net	parts

Mail order only. Since 1978 we have supplied new and reproduction parts and accessories for 1952-1970 Ford cars (Fairlane, Galaxie, Torino, Falcon and Thunderbird) including weatherstripping for doors, windshields, trunk lids and convertible top irons. We offer carpet, decals, trunk mats, scuff plates, plastic and chrome emblems and scripts. See us at major shows throughout the year. Send $3 for our latest catalog.

Fowlkes Realty & Auction 500 Hale St Newman Grove, NE 68758 800-275-5522; FAX: 402-447-6000	appraisals auctions

See full listing in **Section One** under **Chevrolet**

Gemini Racing Systems Inc 7301 W Boston St Chandler, AZ 85226 800-992-9294, 602-940-9011	race prep restoration

See full listing in **Section One** under **Mustang**

Randy Goodling 2046 Mill Rd Elizabethtown, PA 17022-9401 717-367-6700	parts parts locating

See full listing in **Section One** under **Mercury**

Grandpa's Radio Shop 26 Queenston Crescent Kitchener, ON Canada N2B 2V5 519-576-2570	radio restoration

1956 Ford "T" and "C" push-buttons for Town & Country radio. Send check or money order for $47 US or $56 Canadian.

Half Ton Fun Bob Selzam 166 Toms River Rd Jackson, NJ 08527 908-928-9421	NOS parts

See full listing in **Section One** under **Ford '32-'53**

Haneline Products Co PO Box 430 Morongo Valley, CA 92256 619-363-6597; FAX: 619-363-7321	gauges instrument panels stainless parts trim part

See full listing in **Section Two** under **instruments**

Hawthorne Appraisals Box 1332 Coaldale, AB Canada T1M 1N1 403-345-2101	appraisals parts

See full listing in **Section Two** under **appraisals**

Bill Heeley 3621 Mt Olney Ln Olney, MD 20832 301-774-6710	shift levers

Mail order only. Rebuild/restore original Ford shifters from 1962-1973. Generally have at least one of every Ford V8 4-spd shifters in stock. Five to ten of most, have over 20 varieties of rechromed shift levers.

Hein's Classic Cars 422 Douglas Durham, KS 67438 316-732-3335	restoration

See full listing in **Section One** under **Thunderbird**

Hidden Valley Auto Parts 21046 N Rio Bravo Maricopa, AZ 85239 602-252-2122, 602-252-6137 520-568-2945 FAX: 602-258-0951	parts

See full listing in **Section One** under **Chevrolet**

Highway Classics 949 N Cataract Ave, Unit J San Dimas, CA 91702 909-592-8819; FAX: 909-592-4239	parts

Mail order and open shop. Monday-Friday 9 am to 5 pm, Saturday 10 am to 5 pm. Restoration and repair parts for 1960 to 1970 Falcon, 1962 to 1979 Fairlane/Torino, 1967 to 1973 Cougar, 1964 to 1973 Mustang, 1960 to 1967 Comet, 1960 to 1979 Ranchero.

Bill Horton 5804 Jones Valley Dr Huntsville, AL 35802 205-881-6894	vacuum motors

See full listing in **Section One** under **Mercury**

Hot Rod & Custom Supply 1304 SE 10th St Cape Coral, FL 33990 941-574-7744; FAX: 941-574-8820	custom parts engine parts speed parts

See full listing in **Section One** under **Ford '32-'53**

HRE Performance Wheels 2540 Pioneer Ave Vista, CA 92083 619-941-2008; FAX: 619-598-5885	aluminum wheels

See full listing in **Section Two** under **wheels & wheelcovers**

Hubcap Mike 26242 Dimension, Ste 150 Lake Forest, CA 92630 714-597-8120; FAX: 714-597-8123	hubcaps wheelcovers

See full listing in **Section Two** under **wheels & wheelcovers**

Instrument Services Inc 11765 Main St Roscoe, IL 61073 800-558-2674; FAX: 800-623-6416	clocks

See full listing in **Section Two** under **instruments**

JAE 375 Pine #26 Goleta, CA 93117 805-967-5767; FAX: 805-967-6183	parts service tech info

See full listing in **Section One** under **Lotus**

Joe's Auto Sales 5849-190th St E Hastings, MN 55033 612-437-6787	parts

Mail order and open shop. Monday 9 to 5, Tuesday-Friday 8 to 5 & Saturday 8 to 1. Specializing in 1949-86 Ford and Mercury products, sales of used, rebuilt and new parts. We rebuild parts and do some repair work for customers. We rebuild carbs, generators, starters, alternators, steering columns, auto and standard transmissions, rear end 3rd members and power steering control valves.

JR's Antique Auto 14900 Scherry Ln Claremore, OK 74017 918-342-4398	chrome parts interiors

See full listing in **Section One** under **Chevrolet**

Kenroy Ford Parts 2 Folwell Ln Mullica Hill, NJ 08062 609-478-2527; FAX: 609-468-2489	NOS parts

Mail order only. Specializing in NOS Ford parts, all years. 13 years in business. Very low prices, lots of dollar parts sales at flea markets. Ford, Mercury, Lincoln, T-Bird, Mustang and Ford trucks.

Dale King Obsolete Parts PO Box 1099 Liberty, KY 42539 606-787-5031; FAX: 606-787-2130	parts

Specializing in NOS hard to find parts and quality reproductions for Ford, Fairlane, Falcon, Mustang, Ford trucks, Mercury and Comet.

Larry's Thunderbird & Mustang Parts Inc 511 S Raymond Ave Fullerton, CA 92831 714-871-6432; 800-854-0393 orders; FAX: 714-871-1883	parts

See full listing in **Section One** under **Thunderbird**

L B Repair 1308 W Benten Savannah, MO 64485-1549 816-324-3913	restoration

Mail order and open shop. Monday-Saturday 9-7. Specializing in mig welding and subframe installation, all suspension modifications. Special interest: 1953-56 big window Ford pickups and panels. Drop kit installation on late model pickups, low riders, fiberglass repair, economical restorations.

Lincoln Parts International
707 E 4th St, Bldg G
Perris, CA 92570
800-382-1656; 909-657-5588
FAX: 909-657-4758

parts

See full listing in **Section One** under **Lincoln**

Ed Liukkonen
37 Cook Rd
Templeton, MA 01468
508-939-8126

accessories
parts

Mail order only. Sales of NOS genuine FoMoCo parts, 1949/79, for Ford full size, Fairlane, Comet, Mercury, Falcon, Mustang. Some used factory high-performance parts for Ford "muscle cars" also stocked.

Lloyd's Literature
PO Box 491
Newbury, OH 44065
800-292-2665; 216-338-1527
FAX: 216-338-2222

literature

See full listing in **Section Two** under **literature dealers**

Loyal Ford Mercury Inc
2310 Calumet Dr
New Holstein, WI 53061
414-898-4248; FAX: 414-898-9705

cars
parts

Mail order and open shop. Monday-Wednesday 7 am-9 pm, Thursday-Friday 7 am-4 pm, Saturday 8 am-5 pm. Specializing in Ford, Lincoln, Mercury, SVT, Saleen vehicles and parts for most years.

Mac's Antique Auto Parts
1051 Lincoln Ave, PO Box 238
Lockport, NY 14095-0238
716-433-1500

literature
parts
restoration supplies

See full listing in **Section One** under **Ford '03-'31**

The Maverick Connection
137 Valley Dr
Ripley, WV 25271
PH/FAX: 304-372-7825

literature
parts

Mail order only. Specializing in parts & literature for 1970-77 Ford Mavericks & Mercury Comets.

Maximliner Inc
150 E Race St
Troy, OH 45373
513-339-0240; 800-624-2320
FAX: 513-335-5424

cargo mats
floor mats

See full listing in **Section Two** under **carpets**

McDonald Obsolete Parts Company
RR 3, Box 94
Rockport, IN 47635
812-359-4965; FAX: 812-359-5555

body parts
chassis parts

See full listing in **Section One** under **Ford '32-'53**

Melvin's Classic Ford Parts Inc
2526 Panola Rd
Lithonia, GA 30058
770-981-2357; FAX: 770-981-6207

parts

Mail order and showroom. Open Tues-Fri, 9 am-6 pm; Saturday, 9 am-4 pm; closed Sunday & Monday. Specializing in parts for 64-1/2-73 Mustang, 60-70-1/2 Falcon, 62-79 Fairlane, Torino, Ranchero, 49-59 Ford car & T-Bird, 60-72 Ford car & T-Bird, 48-79 Ford trucks.

Mid-America Auction Services
2277 W Hwy 36, Ste 214
St Paul, MN 55113
612-633-9655; FAX: 612-633-3212
E-mail: midauction@aol.com

auctions

See full listing in **Section Two** under **auctions & events**

Miller Obsolete Parts
1329 Campus Dr
Vestal, NY 13850
607-722-5371; FAX: 607-729-7645
E-mail: fordpart@spectra.net

parts

See full listing in **Section One** under **Ford '32-'53**

Monument Motors Inc
PO Box 711
Great Barrington, MA 01230
413-637-1017

repair
restoration
used parts

See full listing in **Section One** under **Mustang**

C W Moss Ford Parts Inc
402 W Chapman Ave
Orange, CA 92666
714-639-3083, Orange
909-629-5223, Pomona
FAX: 714-639-0329

NOS parts
used parts

See full listing in **Section One** under **Ford '03-'31**

Mostly Mustangs Inc
55 Alling St
Hamden, CT 06517
203-562-8804, FAX: 203-562-4891

car dealer
parts sales
restoration

See full listing in **Section One** under **Mustang**

Muck Motor Ford Sales
10 Campbell Blvd
Getzville, NY 14068
800-228-6825; FAX: 716-688-5519

parts

See full listing in **Section One** under **Thunderbird**

Mustang of Chicago Ltd
1321 W Irving Park Rd
Bensenville, IL 60106
708-860-7077
FAX: 708-860-7120, 24 hrs

new & used parts

See full listing in **Section One** under **Mustang**

Mustang Service Center
11610 Vanowen St
North Hollywood, CA 91605
818-765-1196; FAX: 818-765-1349
E-mail: fmustang@primenet.com

parts
service

See full listing in **Section One** under **Mustang**

Mustangs & More
2065 Sperry Ave #C
Ventura, CA 93003
800-356-6573; FAX: 805-642-6468

parts
restoration

See full listing in **Section One** under **Mustang**

Narragansett Reproductions
Ed & Miki Pease
107 Woodville Rd, PO Box 51
Wood River Junction, RI 02894
401-364-3839; FAX: 401-364-3830

wiring harnesses

See full listing in **Section Two** under **electrical systems**

National Drivetrain Inc | differential parts
3125 S Ashland Ave #201 | transmission parts
Chicago, IL 60608
800-507-4327; FAX: 312-376-9135

See full listing in **Section Two** under **transmissions**

Norman's Classic Auto Radio | custom sales
7651 Park Blvd | radio repairs
Pinellas Park, FL 33781
813-546-1788

See full listing in **Section Two** under **radios**

North Yale Auto Parts | salvage yard
Rt 1, Box 707
Sperry, OK 74073
918-288-7218, 800-256-6927 (NYAP)
FAX: 918-288-7223

See full listing in **Section Five** under **Oklahoma**

Northeast Ford | parts
Box 66, Rt 9 | restoration
E Sullivan, NH 03445
603-847-9956, 800-562-FORD
FAX: 603-847-9691

Mail order and open shop. Monday-Friday 8 am-5:30 pm. Ford parts for cars and trucks. Our parts include new, used and quality reproductions from 1928-1979. Catalogues available, from 1932-1979, $3 refundable, must specify year and model. We do inspections and repairs, plus we have a complete restoration facility.

Northwest Classic Falcons Inc | parts
1964 NW Pettygrove St
Portland, OR 97209
503-241-9454; FAX: 503-241-1964

Mail order and open shop. Monday-Thursday 9 am-6 pm. Specializes in new, reproduction, NOS and good used parts for 1960-1970 Falcon and Comet.

See our ad on this page

NOS Only | NOS parts
414 Umbarger Rd, Unit E
San Jose, CA 95111
408-227-2353, 408-227-2354
FAX: 408-227-2355

See full listing in **Section Two** under **comprehensive parts**

Obsolete Ford Parts Co | parts
PO Box 787
Nashville, GA 31639
912-686-2470, 686-5101
FAX: 912-686-7125

Mail order and open shop. Monday-Friday 8 to 5. Comprehensive stock of NOS sheetmetal, trim, chrome, rubber, accessories, literature for 1949-72 Ford, Falcons, Fairlanes, Ford pickups, Comets, Cougars. Customers' requests by phone or mail accepted.

See our ad on page 98

Obsolete Ford Parts Inc | parts
8701 S I-35
Oklahoma City, OK 73149
405-631-3933; FAX: 405-634-6815

Mail order and open shop. Monday-Friday 8-6, Saturday 9-1. Ford parts for 9 different Ford products ranging from 1909 thru 1979. Offer catalogs for: 1909-27 T, 1928-31 A, 1932-48 car and

pickup, 1948-79 Ford truck, 1960-70 Falcon, 1962-72 Fairlane/Torino, 1955-72 T-Bird, 1949-72 full-size car and 1949-72 Mercury.

Joe Odehnal | literature
2722 N Westnedge | parts
Kalamazoo, MI 49004
616-342-5509

Mail order only. New and used parts for 1957-59 Ford retractables. Retractable belt buckles, literature and magazine ads.

Old Air Products | air conditioning
3056 SE Loop 820
Ft Worth, TX 76140
817-551-0602; FAX: 817-568-0037

See full listing in **Section One** under **Corvette**

The Old Car Centre | parts
19909 92A Ave
Langley, BC Canada V1M 3B6
604-888-4412, 888-4055
FAX: 604-888-7455

See full listing in **Section One** under **Ford '03-'31**

The Old Carb Doctor | carburetors
Rt 3, Box 338 | fuel pumps
Drucilla Church Rd
Nebo, NC 28761
800-945-CARB (2272)
704-659-1428

See full listing in **Section Two** under **carburetors**

Old Coach Works Restoration Inc
1206 Badger St
Yorkville, IL 60560
630-553-0414; FAX: 630-553-1053

appraisals
body repairs
restoration

See full listing in **Section Two** under **restoration shops**

Old Dominion Mustang
509 S Washington Hwy, Rt 1
Ashland, VA 23005
804-798-3348; FAX: 804-798-5105

parts

See full listing in **Section One** under **Mustang**

Original Auto Interiors
7869 Trumble Rd
Columbus, MI 48063-3915
810-727-2486; FAX: 810-727-4344
E-mail: knight@mich.com

upholstery

See full listing in **Section Two** under **upholstery**

**Original Falcon, Comet, Ranchero,
Fairlane Interiors**
6343 Seaview Ave NW
Seattle, WA 98107-2664
206-781-5230; FAX: 206-781-5046
E-mail: falcons@ix.netcom.com

interiors
weatherstripping

Mail order and open shop. Shop open Monday-Saturday 10 am to 7 pm. Specializing in new old stock upholstery seat sets as well as produces OEM seat sets, door panels, carpets for 1960 thru 1966 Falcons, Comets and Rancheros, Fairlanes as well as thru the 1970s for Rancheros. These models are Sprints, Futuras, Cyclones, Calientes, Mercury S-22 2 & 4-door sedans, convertibles, with a full range of interior goods and weatherstripping.

Original Ford Motor Co Literature
PO Box 7-AA
Hudson, KY 40145-0007
502-257-8642; FAX: 502-257-8643

collectibles
literature

See full listing in **Section One** under **Ford '32-'53**

Pick-ups Northwest
7130 Bickford Ave
Snohomish, WA 98290
360-568-9166; FAX: 360-568-1233

parts
trim

See full listing in **Section One** under **Chevrolet**

Power Brake Booster Exchange Inc
4533 SE Division St
Portland, OR 97206
503-238-8882

brake boosters

See full listing in **Section Two** under **brakes**

Greg Purdy's Mustang Supply
PO Box 784
Forest Hill, MD 21050
410-836-5991

parts

See full listing in **Section One** under **Mustang**

PV Antique & Classic Ford
1688 Main St
Tewksbury, MA 01876
508-851-9159; FAX: 508-858-3827

parts

See full listing in **Section One** under **Ford '32-'53**

David Raine's Springcrafters
425 Harding Hwy
Carney's Point, NJ 08069
609-299-9141; FAX: 609-299-9157

springs
suspension parts

See full listing in **Section Two** under **suspension parts**

Rapido Group
15930 SW 72nd Ave
Portland, OR 97224
503-620-8400

accessories
parts

See full listing in **Section One** under **Mercury**

Red's Headers
22950 Bednar Ln
Fort Bragg, CA 95437-8411
707-964-7733

headers
mechanical parts

See full listing in **Section One** under **Ford '32-'53**

Regent Trading Corp
Paul Brensilber
15 W 72nd St, Ste 15A
New York, NY 10023
212-873-5582

parts

Mail order only. Specializing in door striker plates for Ford trucks and automobiles, for Ford truck 1953-55, Ford truck 1956, Ford passenger car 1949-56. Also Ford parts.

S & S Antique Auto
Pine St
Deposit, NY 13754
607-467-2929; FAX: 607-467-2109

parts

See full listing in **Section One** under **Ford '32-'53**

Sam's Vintage Ford Parts
5105 Washington
Denver, CO 80216
303-295-1709

parts

Mail order and open shop. Monday-Saturday 9 to 5:30. For V8s, Mustangs and 1949-70 Fords and Mercurys. Also truck parts.

Harry Samuel
65 Wisner St
Pontiac, MI 48342-1066
248-335-1900

carpet
fabrics
interiors
upholstery covers

See full listing in **Section Two** under **interiors & interior parts**

Sixties Ford Parts
639 Glanker St
Memphis, TN 38112
PH/FAX: 901-323-2195, recorder

books
new parts
shop manuals

Mail order only. New parts for 1960-1968 Fords, big Ford, Fairlane, Falcon, Thunderbird, trucks. 90 page catalog, $4, specify year and type of Ford as listed above. In business over 20 years. VISA, MasterCard, personal checks accepted.

So Cal Pickups Inc
6321 Manchester Blvd
Buena Park, CA 90621
714-994-1400; FAX: 714-994-2584

parts

Mail order and open shop. Shop open Tuesday-Friday 9 to 5, Saturday 8 to 3. Specializing in parts for 1953-1956 F-100 pickups. 1948 to 66 Ford pickups parts. 20 years in business, the most complete stock of F-100 parts anywhere. Complete wiring harnesses, hubcaps, complete bed kits, bed sides and fronts, new radiators, power steering, disc and power brake kits, complete weatherstripping, in and outside mirrors, crossmounts, headers, chrome and stock bumpers, grilles, runningboards, stainless steel trim, emblems, monoleaf and stock springs, shop manuals, independent front suspension. We have it all.

Special Interest Cars
451 Woody Rd
Oakville, ON Canada L6K 2Y2
905-844-8063; FAX: 905-338-8063

parts

See full listing in **Section Two** under **comprehensive parts**

Specialty Ford Parts
9103 Garvey Ave
Rosemead, CA 91770
818-280-4546; FAX: 818-288-3311

engine parts
speed parts

A, B, C & V8 Ford engine and speed parts. Catalog, $6 USA.

Specialty Parts/Sanderson Ford
5300 Grand Ave
Glendale, AZ 85301
602-842-8663, 888-364-3673
FAX: 602-842-8876

parts

Mail order and open shop. Monday-Friday 8 to 6; Saturday 8 to 1. Specializing in 1965-73 Mustangs, 1955-66 Thunderbirds, 1960-65 Falcons, 1971-74 Panteras, 1967-73 Cougars, 1953-56 F-100, Motorsport parts and late model 5.0 parts. No catalogs.

Stencils & Stripes Unlimited Inc
1108 S Crescent Ave #21
Park Ridge, IL 60068
708-692-6893; FAX: 708-692-6895

NOS decals
stripe kits

See full listing in **Section Two** under **decals**

Steve's Antiques & Restorations
Steve Verhoeven
5609 S 4300 W
Hooper, UT 84315
801-776-4835

parts
parts locator
POR-15 distributor

Old cars bought, sold or traded. Specializing in locating used parts, reproduction parts, appraisals and restoration work. Intermountain West's POR-15 distributor. Also 1940s, 50s & 60s bicycles. Specializing in Schwinn Stingrays.

Sutton Auto Sounds
3463 Rolling Trail
Palm Harbor, FL 34684-3526
813-787-2717; FAX: 813-789-9215
E-mail: suttonauto@aol.com

radios

See full listing in **Section Two** under **radios**

Tags Backeast
PO Box 581
Plainville, CT 06062
860-747-2942

data plates
trim tags

See full listing in **Section Two** under **special services**

Tech-Art Publications
Jason Houston
Box 753
Ranchero Mirage, CA 92270
619-862-1979

books

See full listing in **Section Four** under **books & publications**

Tee-Bird Products Inc
Box 728
Exton, PA 19341
610-363-1725; FAX: 610-363-2691

parts

Mail order and open shop. Monday-Friday 8 am-5 pm, Saturday morning by appointment. Specializing in a complete line of parts for 1954-59 Ford, with emphasis on 1955-56 cars and 1955-57 Thunderbirds. We have offered prompt service, competitive prices and customer satisfaction since 1973.

Texas Mustang Parts Inc
5774 S University Park Dr
Waco, TX 76706
817-662-2789; FAX: 817-662-0455

parts

See full listing in **Section One** under **Mustang**

Thunderbird, Falcon & Fairlane Connection
728 E Dunlap
Phoenix, AZ 85020
602-997-9285; FAX: 602-997-0624

parts

See full listing in **Section One** under **Thunderbird**

Thunderbird Information eXchange
8421 E Cortez St
Scottsdale, AZ 85260
602-948-3996

newsletter

See full listing in **Section One** under **Thunderbird**

Thunderbird Parts and Restoration
5844 Goodrich Rd
Clarence Center, NY 14032
800-289-2473, 716-741-2866 local
FAX: 716-741-2868

accessories
chrome plating
repairs
restoration parts

See full listing in **Section One** under **Thunderbird**

Thunderbirds East
Andy Lovelace
140 Wilmington W Chester Pike
Chadds Ford, PA 19317
610-358-1021; FAX: 610-558-9615

parts
restoration

See full listing in **Section One** under **Thunderbird**

Tiger Detailing
PO Box 9875
North Hollywood, CA 91609-1875
PH/FAX: 818-982-1042
E-mail: tygrbeer7@aol.com

accessories
detailing
parts

See full listing in **Section One** under **Sunbeam**

Ultra Wheel Co
6300 Valley View Ave
Buena Park, CA 90620
714-994-1444; FAX: 714-994-0723

custom wheels

See full listing in **Section Two** under **wheels & wheelcovers**

Universal Transmission Co
23361 Dequindre Rd
Hazel Park, MI 48030
800-882-4327; FAX: 810-398-2581

transmission parts

See full listing in **Section Two** under **transmissions**

Valley Motor Supply
1402 E Second St
Roswell, NM 88201
505-622-7450

accessories
parts

Mail order and open shop. Monday-Friday 8 to 5. GM, Ford, Chrysler and tractor products. Some parts for all makes, early to present. Many NOS items.

Valley Obsolete Ford Parts
Kerrville, TX 78029
PH/FAX: 210-896-3269

parts

See full listing in **Section One** under **Ford '32-'53**

Vintage Ford & Chevrolet Parts of Arizona Inc
3427 E McDowell Rd
Phoenix, AZ 85008
602-275-7990; FAX: 602-267-8439

parts

Mail order and open shop. Monday-Friday 9-5, Saturday 8-3. Dealing in 28-56 Ford car & truck, 48-72 Ford truck, 47-72 Chevy truck, 65-73 Mustang, street rods. We offer new and used parts.

Gary Vorel
318 78th St
Niagara Falls, NY 14304
716-283-9716, 716-286-4996

parts
service

Mail order only. 1957-1959 Fords and retractables, parts and service. Also 1958-60 Lincoln Continentals, 1972-76 Mark IVs. Engine valves, clutches, light bulbs and ignition parts from 1908-1959. No catalogs. SASE please.

Wheel Vintiques Inc
5468 E Lamona Ave
Fresno, CA 93727
209-251-6957; FAX: 209-251-1620

hubcaps
wheels

See full listing in **Section One** under **Chevrolet**

Dan Williams Toploader Transmissions
206 E Dogwood Dr
Franklin, NC 28734
704-524-9085 noon-midnight
FAX: 704-524-4848

transmissions

Specializing in Ford toploader transmissions. Sales, service, parts. Hurst shifters, Lakewood bellhousings.

MUSTANG

Tom Adams
13211 N 103rd Ave #1
Sun City, AZ 85351
602-933-1777

parts
parts locating

Mail order only. 64-1/2 thru 67 NOS parts, postcards, original sales brochures.

American Memory Prints
5935 N Belt W
Belleville, IL 62223
618-235-4788; FAX: 618-235-4899

artwork

See full listing in **Section Two** under **artwork**

American Restorations Unlimited TA
14 Meakin Ave
PO Box 34
Rochelle Park, NJ 07662
201-843-3567; FAX: 201-843-3238
E-mail: amerrest@aol.com

restoration parts

See full listing in **Section Two** under **glass**

AMK Products
18600 E 96th St
Broken Arrow, OK 74012
918-455-2651; FAX: 918-455-7441

parts

Mail order only. AMK Products offers a comprehensive line of 1965/73 Mustang & Ford fasteners including impossible to find engine fasteners. Items in our fastener kits feature original manufacturer's markings and the correct grade and finish as specified in Ford's assembly manuals. We are also your best source for "True to Original" under the hood detailing items such as voltage regulators, starter solenoids, radiator caps, ignition wires, battery cables and alternators. Catalog available.

Andy's Classic Mustangs
18502 E Sprague
Greenacres, WA 99016
509-924-9824

parts
service

Mail order and open shop. Monday-Saturday 8 to 5. Specializing in Mustangs since 1965. New and used parts. Professional engine rebuilding, carburetors, transmissions, differentials. An authority on Mustangs 65-73 as to original and correct.

Antique & Classic Cars
Rt 15, Box 454
Florence, AL 35633
205-760-0542

car locator

See full listing in **Section One** under **Cadillac/LaSalle**

Antique Auto Electric
9109 (Rear) E Garvey Ave
Rosemead, CA 91770
818-572-0938

repro wiring

See full listing in **Section Two** under **electrical systems**

Auto Craftsmen Restoration Inc
27945 Elm Grove
San Antonio, TX 78261
210-980-4027

appraisals
restoration

See full listing in **Section Two** under **restoration shops**

Auto Custom Carpet
Jeff Moses
PO Box 1350, 1429 Noble St
Anniston, AL 36202
800-633-2358; 205-236-1118
FAX: 800-516-8274

carpets
floor coverings

See full listing in **Section One** under **Chevrolet**

Auto Decals Unlimited Inc
11259 E Via Linda, Ste 100-201
Scottsdale, AZ 85259
602-860-9800; FAX: 602-860-8370

decals
stripe kits

See full listing in **Section Two** under **decals**

Auto Krafters Inc
PO Box 8
522 S Main St
Broadway, VA 22815
703-896-5910; FAX: 703-896-6412

parts

See full listing in **Section One** under **Ford '54-up**

JJ Best & Co
737 Main St, PO Box 10
Chatham, MA 02633
508-945-6000; FAX: 508-945-6006

financing

See full listing in **Section Two** under **consultants**

Larry Blodget
Box 753
Rancho Mirage, CA 92270
619-862-1979

models

See full listing in **Section Two** under **models & toys**

Boss Performance
PO Box 8035
Spokane, WA 99203
509-455-9369, 509-747-6183

automobilia
parts
publications
restoration

Mail order only. Specializes in 1969 and 1970 Boss 429 Mustang performance parts, restoration and publications. Offers NOS and original Boss 429 parts and components. Autolite and Motorcraft automobilia. Large inventory of Ford Boss 429 engine parts.

Tony D Branda Performance
Shelby and Mustang Parts
1434 E Pleasant Valley Blvd
Altoona, PA 16602
814-942-1869; FAX: 814-944-0801

accessories
decals
emblems
sheetmetal
wheels

Mail order and open shop. Open six days a week, 8 to 5:30. Specializing in Shelby and Mustang parts and accessories for 1965-1970 Shelbys, GT-350 and GT-500. Mustang 1965-1992 parts also available. We deal in parts for restoration such as: decals, emblems, aluminum engine dress-up parts, fiberglass, sheetmetal, wheels, etc.

California Pony Cars
1906 Quaker Ridge Pl
Ontario, CA 91761
909-923-2804; FAX: 909-947-8593
E-mail: 105232.3362@compuserv.com

parts

Mail order and open shop. Monday through Friday 7:30 am to 5:30 pm. Specializing in Mustang and high-performance parts for 64-1/2-73 Mustangs.

Canadian Mustang
12844 78th Ave
Surrey, BC Canada V3W 8E7
604-594-2425; FAX: 604-594-9282

parts

Largest and oldest Mustang parts distributor in Canada. Manufacturers, wholesalers and distributors of 1965-73 Mustang parts. Large Canadian mail order catalog.

Carl's Ford Parts
23219 South ST
Homeworth, OH 44634
PH/FAX: 330-525-7291

muscle parts

Mail order only. Specializing in 1960-1970 Ford muscle parts for all Fords& Mercurys. Carburetor rebuilding, parts locating and engine building services for 390, 406, 428, 427 engines.

CBS Performance Automotive
2605-A W Colorado Ave
Colorado Springs, CO 80904
800-685-1492; FAX: 719-578-9485

ignition systems
performance products

See full listing in **Section Two** under **ignition parts**

Central Jersey Mustang
36 Craig St
Edison, NJ 08817
908-572-3939; FAX: 908-985-8653

parts
restoration
service

Mail order and open shop. Monday-Friday 9 to 9, Saturday-Sunday 9 to 5. Specializing in restoration, parts and service for 1964 1/2-1970 Mustangs. Interiors, suspensions, new and used parts, NOS.

CJ Pony Parts Inc
7441 B Allentown Blvd
Harrisburg, PA 17112
800-888-6473; 717-691-5623
FAX: 717-657-9254

parts

Mail order with a store and showroom. Commitment to quality, price and service is the foundation that CJs is built upon. We've been serving the Mustang restorer for 12 years. We carry a complete line of upholstery, weatherstrip, chrome, sheetmetal, wheels, brakes, suspensions, carpet and accessories. One stop shopping from bumper to bumper. Wholesale and body shop discounts available.

Class-Tech Corp
62935 Layton Ave
Bend, OR 97701
800-874-9981

wiring harnesses

See full listing in **Section Two** under **electrical systems**

Classic Auto
251 SW 5th Ct
Pompano Beach, FL 33060
954-786-1687

restoration

See full listing in **Section Two** under **restoration shops**

Classic Auto Air Mfg Co 2020 W Kennedy Blvd Tampa, FL 33606 813-251-4994, 813-251-2356	air conditioning heating parts

Mail order and open shop. Monday-Friday 9:30-6. Manufactures exact factory air replacement parts and complete systems for all pre-1973 cars and trucks. Remanufacturing service on customers' original parts. Specializing in 1965-73 Mustangs and 1949-69 Rolls-Royces and Bentleys and all pre-73 GM auto temp control systems.

Classic Auto Restoration Service Inc 113 National Dr Rockwall, TX 75087 214-722-9663	restoration

See full listing in **Section One** under **Chevrolet**

Classic Coachworks 735 Frenchtown Rd Milford, NJ 08848 908-996-3400	bodywork painting restoration

See full listing in **Section Two** under **restoration shops**

Classic Mustang Inc 24A Robert Porter Rd Southington, CT 06489 800-243-2742; FAX: 203-276-9986	accessories parts

Mail order and open shop. Monday thru Friday 9 to 6, Saturday 9 to 3. Specializing in parts and accessories for 64-73 Mustangs.

Classics 'n More Inc 1001 Ranck Mill Rd Lancaster, PA 17602 717-392-0599; FAX: 717-392-2371	repairs restoration

See full listing in **Section Two** under **restoration shops**

Cobra Restorers Ltd 3099 Carter Dr Kennesaw, GA 30144 770-427-0020; FAX: 770-427-8658	parts restoration service

See full listing in **Section One** under **Cobra**

Composition Materials Co Inc 1375 Kings Hwy E Fairfield, CT 06430 800-262-7763; FAX: 203-335-9728	plastic media

See full listing in **Section Two** under **restoration aids**

Conte's Corvettes & Classics 851 W Wheat Rd Vineland, NJ 08360 609-692-0087; FAX: 609-692-1009 E-mail: contes@cybernet.net	leasing parts sales service

See full listing in **Section One** under **Corvette**

Bob Cook Classic Auto Parts Inc 2055 Van Cleave Rd, PO Box 600 Murray, KY 42071-0600 502-753-4000, 800-486-1137 FAX: 502-753-4600	new parts NOS parts reproduced parts

See full listing in **Section One** under **Ford '54-up**

Tony Copeland Ford Lincoln Mercury 1617 21st St Lewiston, ID 83501 800-821-8174; FAX: 208-746-1543 E-mail: copeland@copelandford.com	parts sales service

See full listing in **Section One** under **Ford '54-up**

Custom Autosound Mfg 808 W Vermont Ave Anaheim, CA 92805 800-888-8637; FAX: 714-533-0361 E-mail: carl@globalmark.com	accessories custom radios speakers

See full listing in **Section One** under **Chevrolet**

Desert Muscle Cars 2853 N Stone Ave Tucson, AZ 85705 520-882-3010; FAX: 520-628-9332	parts

See full listing in **Section One** under **Chevelle/Camaro**

Dynatech Engineering PO Box 1446 Alta Loma, CA 91701-8446 805-492-6134	motor mounts

See full listing in **Section Two** under **suspension parts**

ETC Every Thing Cars 8727 Clarinda Pico Rivera, CA 90660 310-949-6981	restoration

See full listing in **Section One** under **MoPar**

Fowlkes Realty & Auction 500 Hale St Newman Grove, NE 68758 800-275-5522; FAX: 402-447-6000	appraisals auctions

See full listing in **Section One** under **Chevrolet**

Garden State Mustang Inc 160 Horseneck Rd Fairfield, NJ 07004 201-227-0364; FAX: 201-227-0282	bodywork interior work restoration

Mail order and open shop. Monday-Friday 9 to 5; Saturday 10 to 3. Offers full restoration service, mechanical repairs, detailing, interior work, body and unibody repairs, plus a full line of parts, and NOS parts service for 1964 1/2 to 1973 Mustangs, 1974-78 Mustang IIs, 79 and up Mustangs. No catalog. Please call for info.

Gemini Racing Systems Inc 7301 W Boston St Chandler, AZ 85226 800-992-9294, 602-940-9011	race prep restoration

Mail order and open shop. Monday-Friday 9 am-6 pm. Specializing in vintage race car restoration and preparation for Ford GT-40, Cobra, Shelby GT 350, 1965-68 Mustangs, 1963-67 Corvette and late model Mustangs and Corvettes. We are suspension and set-up specialists and fabricate the race and high-performance suspension parts for these cars as well as a full line of other aggressive performance parts.

GF Embossed Notes 11 Caldwell Dr Amherst, NH 03031 603-880-6217; FAX: 603-882-6590	note cards

See full listing in **Section Two** under **automobilia**

Glazier's Mustang Barn Inc | accessories
531 Wambold Rd | parts
Souderton, PA 18964 | restoration
215-723-9674; FAX: 215-723-6277 | service

Mail order and showroom sales. Monday-Friday 8:30 to 5:30; Saturday 9 to 1; other times by appointment. Phone: 800/523-6708. Prize winning restoration shop. Monday-Thursday 8 to 5:30; Friday 8 to 12; other times by appointment. Specializing in 1964-1/2 to 1973 Mustangs and Shelbys. Restorations on other early Fords are considered. Catalog available.

Randy Goodling | parts
2046 Mill Rd | parts locating
Elizabethtown, PA 17022-9401
717-367-6700

See full listing in **Section One** under **Mercury**

Bill Heeley | shift levers
3621 Mt Olney Ln
Olney, MD 20832
301-774-6710

See full listing in **Section One** under **Ford '54-up**

Bill Herndon's Pony Warehouse | accessories
20028 Cinnabar Dr | parts
Gaithersburg, MD 20879
301-977-0309; FAX: 301-977-1573

Mail order only. We specialize in factory original options and accessories for 65-73 Mustangs and Shelbys. We have one of the largest selections of new old stock parts, including hundreds of hard to find reconditioned original parts and the best available reproduction parts. We also have quality reconditioning services available for steering wheels, consoles and radios. Your satisfaction guaranteed. We ship anywhere in the USA, Canada and overseas. Visa/MasterCard. Let us be your number one source for quality parts.

Highway Classics | parts
949 N Cataract Ave, Unit J
San Dimas, CA 91702
909-592-8819; FAX: 909-592-4239

See full listing in **Section One** under **Ford '54-up**

Bill Horton | vacuum motors
5804 Jones Valley Dr
Huntsville, AL 35802
205-881-6894

See full listing in **Section One** under **Mercury**

Hubcap Mike | hubcaps
26242 Dimension, Ste 150 | wheelcovers
Lake Forest, CA 92630
714-597-8120; FAX: 714-597-8123

See full listing in **Section Two** under **wheels & wheelcovers**

Jesser's Classic Keys | automobilia
26 West St, Dept HVA | keys
Akron, OH 44303-2344
330-376-8181; FAX: 330-384-9129

See full listing in **Section Two** under **locks & keys**

Kenroy Ford Parts | NOS parts
2 Folwell Ln
Mullica Hill, NJ 08062
609-848-4965; FAX: 609-468-2489

See full listing in **Section One** under **Ford '54-up**

Dale King Obsolete Parts | parts
PO Box 1099
Liberty, KY 42539
606-787-5031; FAX: 606-787-2130

See full listing in **Section One** under **Ford '54-up**

Larry's Thunderbird & | parts
Mustang Parts Inc
511 S Raymond Ave
Fullerton, CA 92831
714-871-6432; 800-854-0393 orders
FAX: 714-871-1883

See full listing in **Section One** under **Thunderbird**

Ed Liukkonen | accessories
37 Cook Rd | parts
Templeton, MA 01468
508-939-8126

See full listing in **Section One** under **Ford '54-up**

Loyal Ford Mercury Inc | cars
2310 Calumet Dr | parts
New Holstein, WI 53061
414-898-4248; FAX: 414-898-9705

See full listing in **Section One** under **Ford '54-up**

Mac's Antique Auto Parts | literature
1051 Lincoln Ave, PO Box 238 | parts
Lockport, NY 14095-0238 | restoration sup-
716-433-1500 | plies

See full listing in **Section One** under **Ford '03-'31**

Master Power Brakes | brake products
254-1 Rolling Hills Rd | conversion kits
Mooresville, NC 28115
704-664-8866; FAX: 704-664-8862

See full listing in **Section One** under **Chevelle/Camaro**

McDonald Obsolete Parts Company | body parts
RR 3, Box 94 | chassis parts
Rockport, IN 47635
812-359-4965; FAX: 812-359-5555

See full listing in **Section One** under **Ford '32-'53**

Melvin's Classic Ford Parts Inc | parts
2526 Panola Rd
Lithonia, GA 30058
770-981-2357; FAX: 770-981-6207

See full listing in **Section One** under **Ford '54-up**

Miller Obsolete Parts | parts
1329 Campus Dr
Vestal, NY 13850
607-722-5371; FAX: 607-729-7645
E-mail: fordpart@spectra.net

See full listing in **Section One** under **Ford '32-'53**

Monument Motors Inc PO Box 711 Great Barrington, MA 01230 413-637-1017	**repair** **restoration** **used parts**

Mail order and open shop. Monday-Friday 8:30-5 pm, evenings & Sat by appointment. Full service shop performing restoration, modification and general maintenance on Ford/Lincoln/Mercury vehicles, operated by former Ford dealer technician with over 20 years' restoration experience. First generation Mustangs a specialty. Major corrosion & collision damage repairs to Mustang unibodies. Shelby owner & SAAC member since 1979; free estimates, very personal service.

Mostly Mustangs Inc 55 Alling St Hamden, CT 06517 203-562-8804, FAX: 203-562-4891	**car dealer** **parts sales** **restoration**

Mail order and open shop. Monday-Friday 10 am to 9 pm; Saturday 10 am to 5 pm. Sales, restoration and service of Mustangs and sixties and later Ford products. Discounted new and used parts. Free Mustang catalog available.

Muck Motor Ford Sales 10 Campbell Blvd Getzville, NY 14068 800-228-6825; FAX: 716-688-5519	**parts**

See full listing in **Section One** under **Thunderbird**

Mustang Classics 3814 Walnut St Denver, CO 80205 303-295-3140	**parts** **restoration** **sales** **service**

Mail order and open shop. Monday-Friday 9-6. Specializing in parts, service, sales and restoration for 1965-1973 Mustang.

Mustang of Chicago Ltd 1321 W Irving Park Rd Bensenville, IL 60106 708-860-7077 FAX: 708-860-7120, 24 hrs	**new & used parts**

Mail order and open shop. Monday-Friday 9 am to 5 pm, Saturday 8:30 am to 3 pm. Chicagoland's #1 source for 1965-1996 Mustang parts and accessories. Huge inventory of new, used and high performance parts. We are celebrating our 17th year of dedicated and responsible service to our customers. Our experienced staff can assit you with any Ford product you may need. For our 96 Mustang catalog, send $4 and specify year, make and model.

Mustang Service Center 11610 Vanowen St North Hollywood, CA 91605 818-765-1196; FAX: 818-765-1349 E-mail: fmustang@primenet.com	**parts** **service**

Mail order and open shop. Monday-Friday 8-5 pm. Specializing in Ford and Mustang parts and service.

Mustangs & More 2065 Sperry Ave #C Ventura, CA 93003 800-356-6573; FAX: 805-642-6468	**parts** **restoration**

Mail order and open shop. Shop open Monday-Friday 9 to 5:30, Saturday 9 to 1. Specializing in parts and restorations for 1965-94 Mustangs, 1962-73 Fairlanes, 1960-70 Falcons and 1955-57 Thunderbirds. Offers the highest quality parts available, original Ford, reproductions and used, to suit your budget and needs. 25 years of experience in Ford parts and restorations enable us to help you with most of your restoration projects. Quality, service, same day shipping and extensive Ford knowledge are our marks of excellence. Free catalog.

Mustangs Unlimited 185 Adams St Manchester, CT 06040 860-647-1965, FAX: 860-649-1260 E-mail: musunl@connix.com	**accessories** **parts** **repair panels** **restoration**

Mail order and open shop. Monday-Friday 8 to 9 EST, Saturday 8 to 5 EST and Sunday 12 to 5 pm EST. Over 30,000 items available for 1965 to present Mustang, Shelby and 1967 to present Cougar. Quality parts at competitive prices with toll free ordering. Ford Motorsport distributor, catalogs available: 1965-73 Mustang & Shelby, $3; 1974-present Mustang, $3; 1967-present Cougar, $3; 1964-74 suspension catalog, $3; and Motorsport Performance, $5.

Mustangs Unlimited 5182-H Brook Hollow Pkwy Norcross, GA 30071 770-446-1965; FAX: 770-446-3055	**accessories** **parts** **repair panels**

Mail order and open shop. Monday-Friday 8 to 9 EST, Saturday 8 to 5 EST and Sunday 12 to 5 pm EST. Over 30,000 items available for 1965 to present Mustang, Shelby, and 1967 to present Cougar. Quality parts at competitive prices with toll free ordering. Ford Motorsport distributor, catalogs available: 1965-73 Mustang & Shelby, $3; 1974-present Mustang, $3; 1967-present Cougar, $3; 1964-74 suspension catalog, $3; and Motorsport Performance, $5.

New England Mustang Supply Inc 1830 Barnum Ave Bridgeport, CT 06610 203-333-7454; FAX: 203-332-0880	**parts** **accessories**

Mail order and open shop. Monday-Friday 9 to 5:30; except Wednesday 9 to 5; closed Thursday; Saturday 9 to 2. 1965-95 Mustang parts and accessories. Also supplies parts and accessories for classic GM, Ford, MoPar cars and trucks, 1960s to present. Sheetmetal, suspension, soft trim, chrome, weatherstripping and more.

Northeast Ford Box 66, Rt 9 E Sullivan, NH 03445 603-847-9956, 800-562-FORD FAX: 603-847-9691	**parts** **restoration**

See full listing in **Section One** under **Ford '54-up**

Old Dominion Mustang 509 S Washington Hwy, Rt 1 Ashland, VA 23005 804-798-3348; FAX: 804-798-5105	**parts**

Mail order and open shop. Monday-Friday 9-5, Saturday 9-3. Specializing in Mustang and Camaro parts.

Original Falcon, Comet, Ranchero, Fairlane Interiors 6343 Seaview Ave NW Seattle, WA 98107-2664 206-781-5230; FAX: 206-781-5046 E-mail: falcons@ix.netcom.com	**interiors** **weatherstripping**

See full listing in **Section One** under **Ford '54-up**

The Paddock® Inc PO Box 30 221 W Main Knightstown, IN 46148 800-428-4319; FAX: 317-345-2264 E-mail: paddock@indy.net	**accessories** **parts**

Mail order and open shop. Monday-Friday 8-7; Saturday 9-4; Sunday 12-4. Specializing in interior, accessories, sheetmetal, suspension, engine, brake parts & much more for 64-95 Mustang, 67-95 Camaro, 62-74 Dodge/Plymouth, 64-77 Chevelle, 62-79 Nova, 64-74 GTO, 58-76 Impala, 64-77 Cutlass, 70-77 Monte Carlo, 67-95 Firebird, 55-57 Chevy.

Paddock West® Inc 1663 Plum Ln PO Box 8547 Redlands, CA 92375 800-854-8532; FAX: 909-798-1482 E-mail: padwest@msn.com	accessories parts

Mail order and open shop. Monday-Friday 8 to 5, Saturday 9 to 3. Specializing in interior, accessories, sheetmetal, suspension, engine, brake parts and much more for 64-95 Mustang, 67-95 Camaro, 62-74 Dodge/Plymouth, 64-77 Chevelle, 62-79 Nova, 64-74 GTO, 58-76 Impala, 64-77 Cutlass, 70-77 Monte Carlo, 67-95 Firebird, 55-57 Chevy.

Pony Enterprises PO Box L-1007 Langhorne, PA 19047 215-547-2221; FAX: 215-547-7810	fasteners hardware

Specializing in hardware items (nuts, bolts, screws, rubber bumpers, springs, clips, clamps, plugs, straps, etc) for 65-73 Ford Mustangs. We sell items individually packaged in the quantities proper for use or in bulk. We also private label packages for dealers. Wholesale only. Established in 1981.

See our ad on this page

Pony Parts of America 1690 Thomas Paine Pkwy Centerville, OH 45459 513-435-4548	frame rails floor boards

Mail order and open shop. Monday-Friday 7:30 to 6; Saturday 9:30 to 12 noon. Reproduction body parts for Mustangs. Manufacturer of frame rails and floorboards, 1963-1/2 to 1969. Also manufacturer of replacement body panels for Porsche 914 and 911.

Power Brake Booster Exchange Inc 4533 SE Division St Portland, OR 97206 503-238-8882	brake boosters

See full listing in **Section Two** under **brakes**

Greg Purdy's Mustang Supply PO Box 784 Forest Hill, MD 21050 410-836-5991	parts

Mail order only. Good clean used, new, NOS and obsolete parts. 1965-1973 Mustang, as well as other fine Ford products of the 60s and 70s. Specializing in 69-73 Mach I & convertibles. Also a limited supply of NOS Mercury/Ford station wagon taillight lenses from the 60s & early 70s.

PV Antique & Classic Ford 1688 Main St Tewksbury, MA 01876 508-851-9159; FAX: 508-858-3827	parts

See full listing in **Section One** under **Ford '32-'53**

Reproduction Parts Marketing #3-1707 Sask Ave Saskatoon, SK Canada S7K 1P7 306-652-6668; FAX: 306-652-1123	parts restoration service

See full listing in **Section One** under **Chevrolet**

Rode's Restoration 1406 Lohr Rd Galion, OH 44833 419-468-5182; FAX: 419-462-1753	parts restoration

Mail order and open shop. Rebuilders of mid 60 Ford steering components, ie: pumps, control valve, steer gears, slave cylinder, complete power steering conversion kits. Rebuilt date coded 302/289s, 65-67-68-69 engines; welding of Mustang and Fairlane convertibles. Solid welded rolling chassis available, call for detailed quote. Rode's also reproduces unique ps brackets and hoses, Dana products.

Sam's Vintage Ford Parts 5105 Washington Denver, CO 80216 303-295-1709	parts

See full listing in **Section One** under **Ford '54-up**

Southside Obsolete 6819 James Ave S Minneapolis, MN 55423 612-866-1230	parts

See full listing in **Section One** under **Ford '32-'53**

Specialty Parts/Sanderson Ford 5300 Grand Ave Glendale, AZ 85301 602-842-8663, 888-364-3673 FAX: 602-842-8876	parts

See full listing in **Section One** under **Ford '54-up**

Ssnake-Oyl Products Inc
Rt 2, Box 269-6
Hawkins, TX 75765
903-769-4555; 903-769-4552

| carpet underlay firewall insulation seatbelt restoration |

See full listing in **Section Two** under **interiors & interior parts**

Stainless Steel Brakes Corp
11470 Main Rd
Clarence, NY 14031
800-448-7722, 716-759-8666
FAX: 716-759-8688, 24 hr

| brake accessories brake fluid/pads disc brakes/rotors parking brake kits power steering |

See full listing in **Section Two** under **brakes**

Stilwell's Obsolete Car Parts
1617 Wedeking Ave
Evansville, IN 47711
812-425-4794

| body parts interiors parts |

Mail order only. Specializing in 1965-73 Mustang NOS and reproduction parts. Also bumpers, patch panels and upholstery. We stock the finest upholstery and carpets on the market. Catalog $3.

Sutton Auto Sounds
3463 Rolling Trail
Palm Harbor, FL 34684-3526
813-787-2717; FAX: 813-789-9215
E-mail: suttonauto@aol.com

| radios |

See full listing in **Section Two** under **radios**

Tabco Inc
11655 Chillicothe Rd
Chesterland, OH 44026-1994
216-729-5151; FAX: 216-729-1251

| body parts |

See full listing in **Section Two** under **sheetmetal**

Tech-Art Publications
Jason Houston
Box 753
Ranchero Mirage, CA 92270
619-862-1979

| books |

See full listing in **Section Four** under **books & publications**

Texas Mustang Parts Inc
5774 S University Park Dr
Waco, TX 76706
817-662-2789; FAX: 817-662-0455

| parts |

Mail order and open shop. Monday-Friday 8-5:30, Saturday 8-12 noon. Specializing in parts for Ford, Mustangs, years 1964-73 and 1979-1996 with free catalogs for both classic Mustangs and late-model Mustangs.

Thunderbird Parts and Restoration
5844 Goodrich Rd
Clarence Center, NY 14032
800-289-2473, 716-741-2866 local
FAX: 716-741-2868

| accessories chrome plating repairs restoration parts |

See full listing in **Section One** under **Thunderbird**

TJ's Toys
5961 Dry Ridge Rd
Cincinnati, OH 45252
PH/FAX: 513-385-5534

| parts |

Specializing in parts for 1965-73 Mustangs.

TMC (Traction Master Co)
2917 W Olympic Blvd
Los Angeles, CA 90006
213-382-1131

| suspensions |

Mail order and open shop. Monday-Saturday 10 to 3. High performance suspensions for 1964-73 Mustangs. Original supplier to Ford and Shelby, in business since 1953. Free catalog.

TMI Products Inc
191 Granite St
Corona, CA 91719
909-272-1996; 800-624-7960
FAX: 909-272-1584
E-mail: tmiprods@aol.com

| classic car interiors |

See full listing in **Section One** under **Volkswagen**

Vibratech Inc (Fluidampr)
11980 Walden Ave
Alden, NY 14004
716-937-3603; FAX: 716-937-4692

| performance parts |

See full listing in **Section Two** under **engine parts**

Vintage Ford & Chevrolet Parts of Arizona Inc
3427 E McDowell Rd
Phoenix, AZ 85008
602-275-7990; FAX: 602-267-8439

| parts |

See full listing in **Section One** under **Ford '54-up**

Virginia Classic Mustang Inc
PO Box 487
Broadway, VA 22815
540-896-2695; FAX: 540-896-9310

| accessories parts |

Mail order and open shop. Monday-Friday 8 am-6 pm, Saturday 8 am-1 pm. Specializing in parts & accessories for 1964-1/2-73 Mustang. Our 1964-1/2-73 Mustang parts catalog has over 900 photos and 208 pages. Full line of parts available including interior, wheelcovers, weatherstripping, chrome, sheetmetal, engine compartment, suspension, hardware, decals, stereo, literature and detail items. We have been offering super quality parts, fast service and reasonable prices for over 15 years.

Dan Williams Toploader Transmissions
206 E Dogwood Dr
Franklin, NC 28734
704-524-9085 noon-midnight
FAX: 704-524-4848

| transmissions |

See full listing in **Section One** under **Ford '54-up**

Wheel Vintiques Inc
5468 E Lamona Ave
Fresno, CA 93727
209-251-6957; FAX: 209-251-1620

| hubcaps wheels |

See full listing in **Section One** under **Chevrolet**

Wolf Automotive
201 N Sullivan
Santa Ana, CA 92703
800-444-9653, 714-835-2126
FAX: 714-835-9653

| car covers consoles steering wheels tire covers |

See full listing in **Section One** under **Chevrolet**

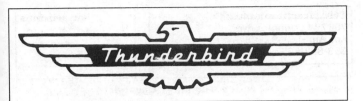

1958 Thunderbird Convertible Registry
Bill Van Ess
2306 Post Dr NE
Belmont, MI 49306
616-364-1973; FAX: 616-363-2870

book

Mail order only. A registry of all the remaining 1958 convertibles. 40 pages of Thunderbird, includes pictures, square Bird history, production figures and running production changes, frame differences between hardtops and convertibles, current and past owners and history on the remaining cars. If you love square Birds, you will enjoy this book. $9.75 postpaid.

AAA Thunderbird Sales
35 Balsam Dr
Dix Hills, NY 11746
516-421-4473

parts

Specializing in 1958 to 1966 Thunderbird sales. Expert electro-hydraulic roof mechanic. Inventory includes twelve convertibles: show cars, drivers, restorables. Also several Ford Skyliner retractable top show cars; original K-H wire wheels and factory tonneau covers. Buy, sell, trade. 40 years' experience in above. Call Jack from 10:00 to midnight, daily and weekends.

Donald Antilla
888 Hulls Hill Rd
Southbury, CT 06488
203-264-8301 evenings

supercharger parts

See full listing in **Section One** under **Ford '54-up**

ARASCO
PO Box 24, Dept HA10
Newport, KY 41072
606-441-8363

parts

See full listing in **Section One** under **Ford '32-'53**

Auto Krafters Inc
PO Box 8
522 S Main St
Broadway, VA 22815
703-896-5910; FAX: 703-896-6412

parts

See full listing in **Section One** under **Ford '54-up**

Auto Parts Exchange
PO Box 736
Reading, PA 19603
610-372-2813, 7-10 am, 7-12 pm
7 days

NORS parts
NOS parts
rebuilt parts
used parts

See full listing in **Section One** under **Lincoln**

B & L Body Shop
104 Brookside
Waynesville, NC 28786-4524
704-456-8277

restoration

See full listing in **Section Two** under **restoration shops**

Ron Baker's Auto Inc
Rt 44
Putnam, CT 06260
860-928-7614, 800-962-9228
FAX: 860-928-0749

parts
service

See full listing in **Section One** under **Lincoln**

Bird Nest
745 SE 9th, PO Box 14865
Portland, OR 97214
503-231-6669
800-232-6378 USA toll-free
FAX: 503-234-2473

parts

Mail order and open shop. Monday-Friday 8 to 5. Specializes in 1958-66 Thunderbird parts. NOS, reproduction and used parts. Parts out approximately one car per week. 19,000-square foot indoor warehouse. Free catalog.

Larry Blodget
Box 753
Rancho Mirage, CA 92270
619-862-1979

models

See full listing in **Section Two** under **models & toys**

Bob's Bird House
124 Watkin Ave
Chadds Ford, PA 19317
215-358-3420; FAX: 215-558-0729

parts

Mail order and retail store. Tuesday-Friday 9 to 5, Saturday 9 to 12. Thunderbird specialist 1958-66, cars, parts. Buy, sell, trade. NOS, NORS, good used and reproduction. Catalog available, $3.

California 55-56-57 T-Birds
Neil Schebetta
945 Kensington Drive
Fremont, CA 94539-4586
PH/FAX: 510-651-1381

parts

Mail order only. Open 7 days, 8 am to 9 pm PST. 55-56-57 Thunderbird parts/car specialists. Real California parts/cars only.

California Continental & T Bird Connection
PO Box 2281
Irwindale, CA 91706
818-962-6696 in CA

consultant
parts
repairs

See full listing in **Section One** under **Lincoln**

California Thunderbirds
Bill Denzel
1507 Arroyo View Dr
Pasadena, CA 91103
818-792-0720

cars
parts

Mail order only. Specializing in new, used & closeout parts plus complete cars for 1955-57 Ford Thunderbirds.

Dennis Carpenter Ford Reproductions
PO Box 26398
Charlotte, NC 28221
704-786-8139; FAX: 704-786-8180

parts

See full listing in **Section One** under **Ford '54-up**

Classic Auto
251 SW 5th Ct
Pompano Beach, FL 33060
954-786-1687

restoration

See full listing in **Section Two** under **restoration shops**

Classic Auto Supply Company Inc
795 High St
PO Box 850
Coshocton, OH 43812
800-374-0914; FAX: 800-513-5806

Thunderbirds

Mail order and open shop. Monday-Friday, 8:30 to 5. Full line parts supplier, restorer and manufacturer of parts for 1955-1957 Thunderbirds. Free 72 page catalog. Shop address: 795 High St, Coshocton, OH 43812. Specializing in 1955-57 Thunderbirds exclusively.

Classic Coachworks
735 Frenchtown Rd
Milford, NJ 08848
908-996-3400

bodywork
painting
restoration

See full listing in **Section Two** under **restoration shops**

Classic Ford Sales
PO Box 60
E Dixfield, ME 04227
207-562-4443; FAX: 207-562-4576
E-mail: info@classicford.com

salvage yard

See full listing in **Section Five** under **Maine**

Classic Sheetmetal Inc
4010 A Hartley St
Charlotte, NC 28206
704-596-5186; FAX: 704-596-3895

body panels
sheetmetal

Mail order and open shop. Monday thru Friday 9-5. Manufacturing sheetmetal body panels for 1955-1971 Thunderbirds.

Classics 'n More Inc
1001 Ranck Mill Rd
Lancaster, PA 17602
717-392-0599; FAX 717-392-2371

repairs
restoration

See full listing in **Section Two** under **restoration shops**

Classique Cars Unlimited
5 Turkey Bayou Rd
PO Box 249
Lakeshore, MS 39558
601-467-9633, FAX: 601-467-9207, MS
800-543-8691, USA

appraisals
parts
repairs
restorations

See full listing in **Section One** under **Lincoln**

Bob Cook Classic Auto Parts Inc
2055 Van Cleave Rd, PO Box 600
Murray, KY 42071-0600
502-753-4000, 800-486-1137
FAX: 502-753-4600

new parts
NOS parts
reproduced parts

See full listing in **Section One** under **Ford '54-up**

Custom Autocraft Inc
2 Flowerfield, Suite 6
St James, NY 11780
PH/FAX: 516-862-7469

restoration
sheetmetal parts

Mail order and open shop. Monday-Friday 8:30 to 5. Specializing in 1955-57 Thunderbirds. Concours quality reproduction sheetmetal (18 ga). Braces, rockers, lower rear quarters, doglegs, floor sections (indentations pressed as original), trunk floors, much more. Buy direct from manufacturer. Doing business since 1974. Stop in, see our parts, compare. Note configuration, easy of fit and quality. Satisfaction guaranteed. Send SASE for free brochure. See us at Carlisle, PA, Spring Q83, Fall Q48-48A.

Custom Autosound Mfg
808 W Vermont Ave
Anaheim, CA 92805
800-888-8637; FAX: 714-533-0361
E-mail: carl@globalmark.com

accessories
custom radios
speakers

See full listing in **Section One** under **Chevrolet**

Bill Denzel
dba California Thunderbirds
1507 Arroyo View Dr
Pasadena, CA 91103
818-792-0720

parts

Mail order only. New, used and closeout parts plus complete cars. 1955-57 Ford Thunderbirds.

Early Ford Parts
2948 Summer Ave
Memphis, TN 38112
901-323-2179; FAX: 901-323-2195

literature
parts

See full listing in **Section One** under **Ford '32-'53**

Daniel A Evans
2850 John St
Easton, PA 18045
610-258-9542 after 5:30 pm
FAX: 610-252-0370
E-mail: evansd@lafayette.edu

literature
parts

See full listing in **Section One** under **Ford '54-up**

GF Embossed Notes
11 Caldwell Dr
Amherst, NH 03031
603-880-6217; FAX: 603-882-6590

note cards

See full listing in **Section Two** under **automobilia**

Randy Goodling
2046 Mill Rd
Elizabethtown, PA 17022-9401
717-367-6700

parts
parts locating

See full listing in **Section One** under **Mercury**

Hein's Classic Cars
422 Douglas
Durham, KS 67438
316-732-3335

restoration

Open Monday-Friday 8 to 5. Small one man shop. Specializing in full or partial restorations as well as mechanical work on 55-57 T-Birds.

Hollywood Classic Motorcars Inc
363 Ansin Blvd
Hallandale, FL 33009
954-454-4641; FAX: 954-457-3801

cars
parts

Mail order and open shop. Monday thru Friday 9 am to 5 pm. Thunderbird parts, 1955 through 1966. Convertible parts such as frames, package trays, limit switches, doors, fenders, hoods, etc. Also sell Thunderbird cars.

Bill Horton
5804 Jones Valley Dr
Huntsville, AL 35802
205-881-6894

vacuum motors

See full listing in **Section One** under **Mercury**

Jim's T-Bird Parts & Service
710 Barney Ave
Winston-Salem, NC 27107
910-784-9363

parts
restoration
service

Mail order and open shop. Monday-Friday 8 am to 5:30 pm. One stop Thunderbird parts and service company. Specializing in parts, service and restoration for 1958-1979 Thunderbirds.

Joblot Automotive Inc
Ford Parts Specialists
98-11 211th St
Queens village, NY 11429
718-468-8585; FAX: 718-468-8686

parts

See full listing in **Section One** under **Ford '32-'53**

JR's Antique Auto
14900 Scherry Ln
Claremore, OK 74017
918-342-4398

chrome parts
interiors

See full listing in **Section One** under **Chevrolet**

Kenroy Ford Parts
2 Folwell Ln
Mullica Hill, NJ 08062
609-848-4965; FAX: 609-468-2489

NOS parts

See full listing in **Section One** under **Ford '54-up**

Dale King Obsolete Parts
PO Box 1099
Liberty, KY 42539
606-787-5031; FAX: 606-787-2130

parts

See full listing in **Section One** under **Ford '54-up**

Larry's Thunderbird and Mustang Parts Inc
511 S Raymond Ave
Fullerton, CA 92831
714-871-6432; 800-854-0393
orders; FAX: 714-871-1883

parts

Mail order and open shop. Monday-Friday 8 am-6 pm, Saturday 9 am-1 pm. Specializing in restoration parts and accessories for 1965-73 Mustangs and 1955-66 Thunderbirds. We have been in business over 25 years supplying Mustang and Thunderbird enthusiasts with extensive product lines of restoration parts. We offer excellent pricing and availability, with most orders shipped out the same day.

See our ad on this page

Lincoln Parts International
707 E 4th St, Bldg G
Perris, CA 92570
800-382-1656; 909-657-5588
FAX: 909-657-4758

parts

See full listing in **Section One** under **Lincoln**

Ed Liukkonen
37 Cook Rd
Templeton, MA 01468
508-939-8126

accessories
parts

See full listing in **Section One** under **Ford '54-up**

Loyal Ford Mercury Inc
2310 Calumet Dr
New Holstein, WI 53061
414-898-4248; FAX: 414-898-9705

cars
parts

See full listing in **Section One** under **Ford '54-up**

Mac's Antique Auto Parts
1051 Lincoln Ave, PO Box 238
Lockport, NY 14095-0238
716-433-1500

literature
parts
restoration
supplies

See full listing in **Section One** under **Ford '03-'31**

Mainly Convertibles
13805 W Hillsborough Ave
Tampa, FL 33635
813-855-6869; FAX: 813-855-1376

parts
repair
restoration

See full listing in **Section One** under **Lincoln**

Bob Marriott
497 Delaware Ave
Delmar, NY 12054

sheetmetal parts
shop manuals

Mail order only. I am a Thunderbird collector (who's gotten carried away with too many cars!). Having found sources for many of the parts I need, I'm making these available to other collectors. Specializing in sheetmetal repair panels and shop manual reprints for 1961-66 Thunderbirds. Send SASE with year for free list.

McDonald Obsolete Parts Company
RR 3, Box 94
Rockport, IN 47635
812-359-4965; FAX: 812-359-5555

body parts
chassis parts

See full listing in **Section One** under **Ford '32-'53**

Midwest Acorn Nut Company
256 Minnesota Ave
Troy, MI 48083-4671
800-422-NUTS(6887)
FAX: 810-583-9130

fasteners
hardware

See full listing in **Section Two** under **hardware**

Miller Obsolete Parts
1329 Campus Dr
Vestal, NY 13850
607-722-5371; FAX: 607-729-7645
E-mail: fordpart@spectra.net

parts

See full listing in **Section One** under **Ford '32-'53**

Muck Motor Ford Sales
10 Campbell Blvd
Getzville, NY 14068
800-228-6825; FAX: 716-688-5519

parts

Mail order and open shop. Monday-Friday, 7-5. Specializing in 58-66 Ford Thunderbird parts.

Mustang Service Center
11610 Vanowen St
North Hollywood, CA 91605
818-765-1196; FAX: 818-765-1349
E-mail: fmustang@primenet.com

parts
service

See full listing in **Section One** under **Mustang**

Mustangs & More
2065 Sperry Ave #C
Ventura, CA 93003
800-356-6573; FAX: 805-642-6468

parts
restoration

See full listing in **Section One** under **Mustang**

Northeast Ford
Box 66, Rt 9
E Sullivan, NH 03445
603-847-9956, 800-562-FORD
FAX: 603-847-9691

parts
restoration

See full listing in **Section One** under **Ford '54-up**

Obsolete Ford Parts Inc
8701 S I-35
Oklahoma City, OK 73149
405-631-3933; FAX: 405-634-6815

parts

See full listing in **Section One** under **Ford '54-up**

Original Falcon, Comet, Ranchero, Fairlane Interiors
6343 Seaview Ave NW
Seattle, WA 98107-2664
206-781-5230; FAX: 206-781-5046
E-mail: falcons@ix.netcom.com

interiors
weatherstripping

See full listing in **Section One** under **Ford '54-up**

Power Brake Booster Exchange Inc
4533 SE Division St
Portland, OR 97206
503-238-8882

brake boosters

See full listing in **Section Two** under **brakes**

Precision Restoration Service Inc
1551 N Courtney Rd, Ste B-2
Independence, MO 64050
816-461-7500; FAX: 816-461-7504

restoration

See full listing in **Section Two** under **restoration shops**

Prestige Thunderbird Inc
10215 Greenleaf Ave
Santa Fe Springs, CA 90670
800-423-4751, 310-944-6237
FAX: 310-941-8677

appraisals
radios
repairs
restorations
tires

Mail order and open shop. Monday-Friday 8:30 to 5:30; Saturday 8:30 to 4. Specializes in 1955-57 Thunderbirds. Offers parts, radios, air conditioners, tires and appraisals, along with restorations and car sales. Parts catalog $2.

Quality Thunderbird Parts & Products Inc
701 Old Crossing Dr
Baltimore, MD 21208
PH/FAX: 410-653-9595

chrome trim parts
NOS parts
used parts

Mail order only or by appointment. Used, refinished and NOS parts for 1964-66 Thunderbirds. Mostly cosmetic and electrical parts and all interior parts. Free 32-page catalog. Immediate response to mail and FAX orders.

Regal Roadsters Ltd
301 W Beltline Hwy
Madison, WI 53713
PH/FAX: 608-273-4141

replicars
restoration

Mail order and open shop. Monday-Friday 8-5. Specializing in the manufacture of the Regal T-Bird and the restoration of domestic and foreign collectibles. The Regal T-Bird is a full size, authentic, fiberglass bodied reproduction of the famed 1955 & 1956 Ford Thunderbird. We manufacture and sell a variety of kits for the hobbyist, ranging from exact reproductions to personalized street rod versions. Also handcraft turnkey Regal T-Birds to your exacting specifications and deliver worldwide.

Frank Riley Automotive Art
PO Box 95
Hawthorne, NJ 07506
800-848-9459

automotive prints

See full listing in **Section Two** under **artwork**

Sixties Ford Parts
639 Glanker St
Memphis, TN 38112
PH/FAX: 901-323-2195, recorder

**books
new parts
shop manuals**

See full listing in **Section One** under **Ford '54-up**

Southside Obsolete
6819 James Ave S
Minneapolis, MN 55423
612-866-1230

parts

See full listing in **Section One** under **Ford '32-'53**

Specialty Parts/Sanderson Ford
5300 Grand Ave
Glendale, AZ 85301
602-842-8663, 888-364-3673
FAX: 602-842-8876

parts

See full listing in **Section One** under **Ford '54-up**

Sunyaks
PO Box 498
Bound Brook, NJ 08805
908-356-0600

**used & NOS parts
and upholstery**

Mail order and open shop. Monday-Saturday 10 am to 10 pm. Specializing in NOS and restored hard to get parts for 1955-1957 Thunderbirds. Over 1,800 items in our catalog. Specializing in convertible top frames, hardtops, original power steering units, power brakes, power windows, and power seat assemblies, dual quads and NASCAR parts along with upholstery and continental kits. Appraisals, and technical help available.

Tags Backeast
PO Box 581
Plainville, CT 06062
860-747-2942

**data plates
trim tags**

See full listing in **Section Two** under **special services**

T-Bird Nest
2550 E Southlake Blvd
Southlake, TX 76092
817-481-1776

**parts
repairs
restoration**

Mail order and open shop. Monday-Friday 8 to 5. Sells parts; repairs and restores 1958-1966 Thunderbirds and other makes. Ships parts. Family business. "We do it all."

T-Bird Sanctuary
9997 SW Avery
Tualatin, OR 97062
503-692-9848, FAX: 503-692-9849

parts

Mail order and open shop. Monday-Friday 8 to 5:30, Saturday 10 to 2, closed Sunday, PST. Comprehensive source for NOS, used and reproduction parts for 1958 to 1979 Thunderbirds. Your T-Bird restoration specialist since 1966. Sheetmetal cut to order. Our parts cars come from the salt-free Northwest and are remarkably well preserved in our mild climate. Same day shipping on most orders. Call in your order on our toll-free parts hotline: 800-275-2661.

T-Bird Specialists
3156 E President St
Tucson, AZ 85714
602-889-8634

**locating service
parts
parts cars
repairs**

Mail order and open shop. Monday-Saturday. One-man shop with knowledge to repair most any problem on 1955-76 T-Birds. Has about 100 parts cars, 1958-76. Also provides locating service for any make and model. Complete service, repairs and parts for 1955-76 Thunderbirds.

T-Birds By Nick
14649 Lanark St, Unit B
Panorama City, CA 91402
818-780-8383; FAX: 818-780-8493

**parts
repair**

Mail order and open shop. Monday-Friday 9 am to 5 pm. Thunderbird parts and repair 1958 to 1966 only.

Tech-Art Publications
Jason Houston
Box 753
Ranchero Mirage, CA 92270
619-862-1979

books

See full listing in **Section Four** under **books & publications**

Tee-Bird Products Inc
Box 728
Exton, PA 19341
610-363-1725; FAX: 610-363-2691

parts

See full listing in **Section One** under **Ford '54-up**

Thunderbird Center
23610 John R St
Hazel Park, MI 48030
810-548-1721; FAX: 810-548-5531
800-562-1955

parts

Monday-Friday 9-5. 1955-56-57 T-Bird parts sales, NOS, used, new repro. Everything you may need.

Thunderbird, Falcon & Fairlane Connection
728 E Dunlap
Phoenix, AZ 85020
602-997-9285; FAX: 602-997-0624

parts

Mail order and open shop. Monday-Friday 8:30 to 5; Saturday 8:30 to 12:30. Offers the finest in new, used and reproduced items for your 58 to 72 T-Birds, 60 to 70 Falcons & Comets and 62 to 69 Fairlanes. Ford authorized dealer. Offers the finest in quality & service. Write for free updated & illustrated Thunderbird catalog. Order number: 800-TTT-BIRD. In business since 1972. Falcon & Fairlane catalogs also available, $3 each.

Thunderbird Headquarters
1080 Detroit Ave
Concord, CA 94518
800-227-2174, US
FAX: 510-689-1771

**accessories
literature
parts
upholstery**

Mail order and open shop. Monday-Friday 8 to 5, Saturday 8 to noon. Specializing in used and new hard parts, rubber weatherstrip, convertible tops, literature including shop and owner's manuals, a complete line of upholstery, carpets and accessories for 1955-1966 Thunderbirds.

Thunderbird Information eXchange
8421 E Cortez St
Scottsdale, AZ 85260
602-948-3996

newsletter

Specializing in the exchange of information about how to enjoy and personalize 1989 and later Thunderbird and Cougar automobiles. The TIX package contains a newsletter with technical tips, want ads, event listings, production figures and model comparisons. The TIX package costs $10 (checks payable to Paul Cornell please).

Thunderbird Parts and Restoration
5844 Goodrich Rd
Clarence Center, NY 14032
800-289-2473, 716-741-2866 local
FAX: 716-741-2868

accesories
chrome plating
repairs
restoration parts

Mail/phone orders and open shop. Monday 8:30 to 8, Tuesday-Friday 8:30 to 5:30, Saturday 9 to 2. Showroom of restoration parts and supplies. Retail/wholesale sales of parts. Repair/restoration facilities. Chrome plating/potmetal restoration available. Specializing in NOS, reproduction, rebuilt and used for Thunderbird, Mustang and performance Ford.

Thunderbirds East
Andy Lovelace
140 Wilmington W Chester Pike
Chadds Ford, PA 19317
610-358-1021; FAX: 610-558-9615

parts
restoration

Mail order and open shop. Monday-Friday 8-5, Saturday 8-12 noon. 1955-56-57 Thunderbirds and 1967 to 80s Thunderbirds for parts, new, used and restorations.

Wilson's Classic Auto
417 Kaufman, Rt 150
PO Box 58
Congerville, IL 61729
309-448-2408; FAX: 309-448-2409

restoration

See full listing in **Section Two** under **restoration shops**

FRANKLIN

Air Cooled Motors
2081 Madelaine Ct
Los Altos, CA 94024
PH/FAX: 415-967-2908
E-mail: zmrmn@aol.com

car dealers
information
restoration

Specializing in the preservation and restoration of Franklin, Zimmerman automobiles.

Hasslen Co
9581 Jeske Ave NW
Annandale, MN 55302
320-274-5576

engine parts

New Franklin gasket sets, engine and trim parts. Series 13 & Series 14 through 16 and Olympic hubcaps. Series 10 reserve and supply fittings. Series 8 through 10 mufflers, belt buckles. Series 16 door handles. Timing chains for most Franklins, porcelain signs and more. Manufactures Franklin parts. Write your needs.

Odyssey Restorations Inc
8080 Central Ave NE
Spring Lake Park, MN 55432
612-786-1518; FAX: 612-786-1524

parts
restoration

See full listing in **Section Two** under **restoration shops**

Seattle Packard
PO Box 2262
Seattle, WA 98111
206-726-9625

repair
restoration

See full listing in **Section One** under **Packard**

A & M SoffSeal Inc
104 May Dr
Harrison, OH 45030
800-426-0902
513-367-0028, service & info
FAX: 513-367-5506

rubber parts
weatherstripping

See full listing in **Section Two** under **rubber parts**

American Classic Truck Parts
PO Box 50286
Denton, TX 76206
817-497-2456; FAX: 817-497-4439

parts

See full listing in **Section One** under **Chevrolet**

American Muscle
PO Box 270543
West Hartford, CT 06127
860-953-2575

parts

Mail order and open shop by appointment only. Monday-Saturday. Provides new & used original GM parts from 70-91 Trans-Ams, IROC Z tuned port injection drivetrains, 5.0 & 5.7, 5-spd & auto, Z-28s, Firebirds & Camaros, including body, interior, parts, motors and transmissions, 4-spd & auto, at prices that won't break you.

B & T Truck Parts
906 E Main St
PO Box 799
Siloam Springs, AR 72761
501-524-5959: FAX: 501-524-5559

pickup parts

See full listing in **Section Two** under **trucks & tractors**

B & W Antique Auto Parts Inc
4653 Guide Meridian Rd
Bellingham, WA 98227
360-647-4574; FAX: 360-676-0458

accessories
parts

See full listing in **Section One** under **Ford '32-'53**

Beverly Hills Motoring Accessories
205 S Robertson Blvd
Beverly Hills, CA 90211
310-657-4880; FAX: 310-659-4664
E-mail: bhma@hollywood.cinenet.net

accessories

See full listing in **Section One** under **Mercedes-Benz**

Brothers Truck Parts
5670 Schaefer Ave, Unit G
Chino, CA 91710
800-977-2767, FAX: 909-517-3142
E-mail: brothers96@aol.com

accessories
parts

See full listing in **Section Two** under **trucks & tractors**

Jim Carter's Antique Truck Parts
1500 E Alton
Independence, MO 64055
816-833-1913; FAX: 816-252-3749

truck parts

See full listing in **Section One** under **Chevrolet**

Chevy Duty Pickup Parts
4319 NW Gateway
Kansas City, MO 64150
816-741-8029; FAX: 816-741-5255
E-mail: chevyduty@aol.com

pickup parts

See full listing in **Section One** under **Chevrolet**

Dixie Truck Works
10495 Hwy 73 E
Mount Pleasant, NC 28124
704-436-2407

parts

See full listing in **Section One** under **Chevrolet**

Eagle Wire Products
3308 Valley Forge Dr
Knoxville, TN 37920
PH/FAX: 800-977-0030

wire harnesses

See full listing in **Section Two** under **electrical systems**

The Filling Station
990 S Second St
Lebanon, OR 97355-3227
541-258-2114; 800-841-6622
FAX: 541-258-6968

literature
parts

See full listing in **Section One** under **Chevrolet**

Fleetline Automotive
PO Box 291
Highland, NY 12528
914-691-9228

parts

See full listing in **Section Five** under **New York**

Gilbert's Early Chevy Pickup Parts
PO Box 1316
470 Rd 1 NW
Chino Valley, AZ 86323
PH/FAX: 602-636-5337
E-mail: gilb@goodnet.com

pickup parts

See full listing in **Section Two** under **trucks & tractors**

GMC Solutions
Robert English
PO Box 675
Franklin, MA 02038-0675
508-520-3900; FAX: 508-520-7861
E-mail: oldcarkook@aol.com

literature
parts

Mail order and open shop. Monday-Friday 9-5. GMC truck parts and literature and factory training films and manuals for 1947-1955 GMC and Chevy trucks, light & medium duty. Accept all credit cars and COD. Ship via UPS daily, worldwide.

Golden State Pickup Parts Inc
PO Box 1019
Santa Ynez, CA 93460
800-235-5717; 805-686-2020
FAX: 805-686-2040

truck parts

See full listing in **Section One** under **Chevrolet**

Hagerty Classic Insurance
PO Box 87
Traverse City, MI 49685
800-922-4050; FAX: 616-941-8227

insurance

See full listing in **Section Two** under **insurance**

Heavy Chevy Truck Parts
PO Box 650
17445 Heavy Chevy Rd
Siloam Springs, AR 72761
501-524-9575; FAX: 501-524-4873
or 800-317-2277

parts

See full listing in **Section One** under **Chevrolet**

HRE Performance Wheels
2540 Pioneer Ave
Vista, CA 92083
619-941-2008; FAX: 619-598-5885

aluminum wheels

See full listing in **Section Two** under **wheels & wheelcovers**

Jahns Quality Pistons
1360 N Jefferson St
Anaheim, CA 92807
714-579-3795, 800-225-0277
FAX: 714-524-6607

piston rings
pistons

See full listing in **Section Two** under **engine parts**

Majestic Truck Parts
17726 Dickerson
Dallas, TX 75252
214-248-6245

parts

See full listing in **Section One** under **Chevrolet**

Manes Truck Parts
9904 E 63rd Terr
Raytown, MO 64133
816-358-6745

parts

See full listing in **Section One** under **Chevrolet**

Maximliner Inc
150 E Race St
Troy, OH 45373
513-339-0240; 800-624-2320
FAX: 513-335-5424

cargo mats
floor mats

See full listing in **Section Two** under **carpets**

Muscle "N" More GM Options & Accessories
1055 S Pacific Hwy
Woodburn, OR 97071
503-981-4448

accessories
factory-installed
options

See full listing in **Section One** under **Chevrolet**

Scotts Super Trucks
Box 6772
1040 Emma St
Penhold, AB Canada T0M 1R0
403-886-5572; FAX: 403-886-5577

parts

See full listing in **Section One** under **Chevrolet**

Stainless Steel Brakes Corp
11470 Main Rd
Clarence, NY 14031
800-448-7722, 716-759-8666
FAX: 716-759-8688, 24 hr

brake accessories
brake fluid/pads
disc brakes/rotors
parking brake kits
power steering

See full listing in **Section Two** under **brakes**

Tags Backeast
PO Box 581
Plainville, CT 06062
860-747-2942

data plates
trim tags

See full listing in **Section Two** under **special services**

Tom's Classic Parts
5207 Sundew Terr
Tobyhanna, PA 18466
800-832-4073

parts

See full listing in **Section One** under **Chevrolet**

Trim Parts Inc
5161 Wolfpen Pleasant Hill
Milford, OH 45150
513-831-1472; FAX: 513-248-3402

trim items

See full listing in **Section One** under **Chevrolet**

The Truck Shop
PO Box 5035
104 W Marion Ave
Nashville, GA 31639
912-686-3833 or 912-686-3396 info
800-245-0556 orders
FAX: 912-686-3531

parts

See full listing in **Section One** under **Chevrolet**

Ultra Wheel Co
6300 Valley View Ave
Buena Park, CA 90620
714-994-1444; FAX: 714-994-0723

custom wheels

See full listing in **Section Two** under **wheels & wheelcovers**

George Zaha
615 Elizabeth
Rochester, MI 48307
810-651-0959 evenings

FM conversions
radio
speakers

See full listing in **Section Two** under **radios**

GRAHAM

Bill McCall
721 Verna Trail N
Fort Worth, TX 76108
817-246-2988

consultant
parts locator

Mail order only. Works with owners of 1932 to 1935 Graham cars to find information, literature and NOS, used or reproduction parts to assist in the restoration of these beautiful automobiles.

B & B Cylinder Head
320 Washington St
West Warwick, RI 02893
401-828-4900, 800-800-4143

cylinder heads

See full listing in **Section Two** under **engine parts**

Boyds Hot Rods & Collectable Cars
10971 Dale St
Stanton, CA 90680
714-220-9870; FAX: 714-220-9877

car dealer

See full listing in **Section One** under **Chevrolet**

Francois Bruere
8 Avenue Olivier Heuze
LeMans 72000 France
(33) 02-4377-1877
FAX: (33) 02-4324-2038

artwork

See full listing in **Section Two** under **artwork**

Cars II
6747 Warren Sharon Rd
Brookfield, OH 44403
330-448-2074; FAX: 330-448-1908

parts

See full listing in **Section One** under **Cadillac/LaSalle**

Charleston Custom Cycle
211 Washington St
Charleston, IL 61920
217-345-2577

parts

Mail order and open shop. Monday-Friday 10 am to 6 pm, Saturday 10 am to 3 pm. Specializing in NOS parts for Harley-Davidson motorcycles, snowmobiles, golf carts, 1948-1984.

Classic Trim Inc
Mick Stamm
3401 S 1st St
Abilene, TX 79605-1708
915-676-8788

collectibles
trim
upholstery

See full listing in **Section Two** under **motorcycles**

Egge Machine Company
11707 Slauson Ave
Santa Fe Springs, CA 90670
310-945-3419 in CA
800-866-EGGE
FAX: 310-693-1635

accessories
parts

See full listing in **Section Two** under **engine parts**

H D Garage
Barry Brown
18 Dumas St
Hull, QC Canada J8Y 2M6
819-771-8504; FAX: 819-771-2502
E-mail: cc708@freenet.carleton.ca

art work
literature
motorcycles

See full listing in **Section Two** under **motorcycles**

Indian Joe Martin's Antique Motorcycle Parts
PO Box 3156
Chattanooga, TN 37404
615-698-1787

parts

See full listing in **Section Two** under **motorcycles**

Kick-Start Motorcycle Parts Inc
PO Box 9347
Wyoming, MI 49509
616-245-8991

parts

Mail order only. Specializing in rebuilding, replacement and restoration parts for Harley-Davidson flathead and Knucklehead machines, 1929 thru 1973.

Mid-America Auction Services
2277 W Hwy 36, Ste 214
St Paul, MN 55113
612-633-9655; FAX: 612-633-3212
E-mail: midauction@aol.com

auctions

See full listing in **Section Two** under **auctions & events**

Moto Italia
13960 Hwy 9
Boulder Creek, CA 95006
PH/FAX: 408-338-3340

parts

Mail order and open shop. Shop open Monday, Wednesday, Friday 8 to 6; Tuesday and Thursday 12 to 6, Saturday 9 to 4. Specializing in parts for Harley-Davidson motorcycles made in Italy from 1961-78. Model Sprints and two-strokes from 50cc to 250cc.

TK Performance Inc
1508 N Harlan Ave
Evansville, IN 47711
812-422-6820; FAX: 812-422-5282

engine building
machine work
restoration

Mail order and open shop. Monday thru Friday 8-5, Saturday 9-2. Complete engine and chassis component building for Harley-Davidsons, all years, makes and models. Ground-up restorations, custom fabricating and machining of parts, complete fabrication of drag bikes and custom show pieces.

Transport-Nation Collectibles
24040 Camino Del Avion, Ste A-241
Monarch Beach, CA 92629
800-474-4404, 714-240-5126

artwork
collectibles

See full listing in **Section Two** under **artwork**

Vehicles In Motion
1000 W Crosby #100
Carrollton, TX 75006
214-242-2453; FAX: 214-446-1919

directory
purchasing guide

America's National Motorcycle Auction Co. Auction held every 90 days in Dallas, Texas. Finance company repos and consignments. Call or write for information.

J Wood & Co Auctioneers
PO Box 852
Searsport, ME 04974
207-548-2113; FAX: 207-548-2888

auctions

See full listing in **Section Two** under **auctions & events**

Blackhawk Collection
3600 Blackhawk Plaza Cir
Danville, CA 94506-3600
510-736-3444; FAX: 510-736-4375

acquisitions
sales

See full listing in **Section One** under **Duesenberg**

RAU Restoration
2027 Pontius Ave
Los Angeles, CA 90025
PH/FAX: 310-445-1128

woodwork

See full listing in **Section Two** under **woodwork**

600 Headquarters, Miles Chappell
PO Box 1262
Felton, CA 95018
408-335-2208 shop

advice
newsletter
parts
service

Mail order and open shop by appointment everyday (7 days). Specializing in 1970-72 Honda 600 sedan & coupe new & used parts, service, advice, newsletter. Send $3 for sample of newsletter and parts list or $20 for 1 year subscription & parts lists. Make checks to Miles Chappell.

CSI
1100 S Raymond Ave, Suite H
Fullerton, CA 92831
714-879-7955; FAX: 714-879-7310
E-mail: 102263.1046@compuserve.com

accessories
parts

See full listing in **Section One** under **BMW**

J Wood & Co Auctioneers
PO Box 852
Searsport, ME 04974
207-548-2113; FAX: 207-548-2888

auctions

See full listing in **Section Two** under **auctions & events**

Wm Albright's Vintage Coach
16593 Arrow Blvd
Fontana, CA 92335
909-823-9168, 909-823-0690

car dealer
NOS & repro parts
tires
used parts

Mail order and open shop. Open by appointment only. Specializing in Hudson convertibles. 25 years same business. Also Remington wide white tires. 35 Hudson-Essex-Terraplane cars in inventory. Hudson built cars and parts, restore, buy and sell.

Brasilia Press
PO Box 2023
Elkhart, IN 46515
FAX: 219-262-8799

models

See full listing in **Section Two** under **models & toys**

Burchill Antique Auto Parts Inc
4150 24th Ave
Fort Gratiot, MI 48061
810-385-3838

parts
technical info

See full listing in **Section One** under **Chrysler**

Guild of Automotive Restorers
18237 Woodbine Ave
Sharon, ON Canada L0G 1V0
905-895-0035; FAX: 905-895-0036
E-mail: theguild@interhop.com

restoration
sales
service

See full listing in **Section Two** under **restoration shops**

Hudson Motor Car Co Memorabilia
Ken Poynter
19638 Huntington
Harper Woods, MI 48225
313-886-9292

literature
memorabilia
novelties
signs

Mail order only. Collector of anything pertaining to Hudsons, Essex, Terraplanes and Dovers. Trade and sell duplicates.

Jesser's Classic Keys
26 West St, Dept HVA
Akron, OH 44303-2344
330-376-8181; FAX: 330-384-9129

automobilia
keys

See full listing in **Section Two** under **locks & keys**

K-GAP
Automotive Parts
PO Box 3065
Santa Fe Springs, CA 90670
FAX: 714-523-0403

repro parts

Hudson, Essex, Terraplane authentic reproduction parts, made in the USA, featuring the products of Metro Moulded Parts. Weatherstrip, runningboard mats, lenses, accessories for 1929-57. For catalog of parts available, send $2 (refundable with order).

Garth B Peterson
122 N Conklin Rd
Veradale, WA 99037
509-926-4620 anytime

accessories
parts
radios

See full listing in **Section Two** under **comprehensive parts**

Don Robertson
2411 Gardner St
Elliston, VA 24087
540-268-2837

car dealer
parts

Hudson cars and parts.

Seattle Packard
PO Box 2262
Seattle, WA 98111
206-726-9625

repair
restoration

See full listing in **Section One** under **Packard**

Webb's Classic Auto Parts
5084 W State Rd 114
Huntington, IN 46750
PH/FAX: 219-344-1714

NOS parts
used parts

See full listing in **Section One** under **AMC**

Harold Wenner
5449 Tannery Rd
Schnecksville, PA 18078
610-799-5419

accessories
parts

See full listing in **Section One** under **AMC**

John J Coven
1172 W 18th Pl
Eugene, OR 97402
541-687-1488

literature

Mail order only. Sells and collects Hupmobile literature, sells runningboard moldings. Will consider production of hard to find items if enough requests are received. At present have only one style of molding, 4 ribs on top, plain on side, extruded aluminum, polished and anodized, very nice, sample on request.

Charles Noe
64 1/2 Greenwood Ave
Bethel, CT 06801
203-748-4222

broker
parts/auto purchases
parts/auto sales

See full listing in **Section Two** under **brokers**

Tire Barn Inc
255 Twinsburg Rd
Northfield, OH 44067
216-467-1284
FAX: 216-467-1289, call first

tires

See full listing in **Section Two** under **tires**

Jerry Greer's Indian Engineering
8400 Monroe, #3
Stanton, CA 90680
714-826-9940

parts
restoration service

Mail order and open shop. Indian motorcycle restorations, repairs, rebuilds, machining, welding, fabrication, plating, painting, parts manufacturer, accessories, literature and apparel. Motorcycle appraisals, consignment sales, consultation, movie advisor.

H D Garage
Barry Brown
18 Dumas St
Hull, QC Canada J8Y 2M6
819-771-8504; FAX: 819-771-2502
E-mail: cc708@freenet.carleton.ca

art work
literature
motorcycles

See full listing in **Section Two** under **motorcycles**

Indian Joe Martin's Antique Motorcycle Parts
PO Box 3156
Chattanooga, TN 37404
615-698-1787

parts

See full listing in **Section Two** under **motorcycles**

Indian Motorcycle Supply Inc   **parts**
PO Box 207
Sugar Grove, IL 60554
630-466-4601; FAX: 630-466-4219

Mail order. Parts for Indian motorcycles.

Kiwi Indian Parts   **parts**
17399 Sage Ave
Riverside, CA 92504
909-780-5400; FAX: 909-780-7722

Manufacturers of reproduction parts for Indian motorcycles.
Web site: http://www.kiwi-indian.com

J Wood & Co Auctioneers   **auctions**
PO Box 852
Searsport, ME 04974
207-548-2113; FAX: 207-548-2888

See full listing in **Section Two** under **auctions & events**

ABS Exotic Repair Inc   **parts**
1561 N Federal Hwy   **service**
Ft Lauderdale, FL 33304
954-566-7785; FAX: 954-566-7271

See full listing in **Section One** under **Mercedes-Benz**

American-Foreign Auto Electric Inc   **parts**
103 Main St   **rebuilding**
Souderton, PA 18964
215-723-4877

See full listing in **Section Two** under **electrical systems**

Dick Ames Stainless Steel Exhaust   **exhaust systems**
3963 Wilshire Cir
Sarasota, FL 34238
813-923-8321; FAX: 813-923-9434

Mail order only. Specializing in stainless steel exhaust systems
made in England for Jaguar, Aston Martins and Morgans. See
monthly ads in Hemmings. Also stock Volvo P1800s.

Antique & Classic Car Restoration   **restoration**
Hwy 107, Box 368
Magdalena, NM 87825

See full listing in **Section Two** under **restoration shops**

Ashton Keynes Vintage   **restoration**
Restorations Ltd   **coachbuilding**
A Keith Bowley
Ashton Keynes, Swindon
Wilshire England
01285/861-288
FAX: 01285/860-604

See full listing in **Section One** under **Rolls-Royce/Bentley**

Atlantic Enterprises   **steering assemblies**
221 Strand Industrial Dr
Little River, SC 29566
803-399-7565; FAX: 803-399-4600

See full listing in **Section Two** under **chassis parts**

Automotive Artistry   **restoration**
679 W Streetboro St
Hudson, OH 44236
216-650-1503

See full listing in **Section One** under **Triumph**

G W Bartlett Co Inc   **convertible tops**
1912 N Granville Ave   **interiors**
Muncie, IN 47303   **rubber seals**
800-338-8034, US & Canada
FAX: 317-289-1251

For twelve years we have been manufacturers and suppliers of
original specification Jaguar interiors, individual Jaguar interior
components, rubber seals, convertible tops, top boots, tonneaus,
top frame wood components and seat frame wood components.
Our product line includes most post WW II Jaguars, from the XK
120s to the XJ6 SIII saloons. We use only genuine Connolly
leather, genuine Hardura, 100% deep pile wool carpet, wool
moquette and Jaguar specification ICI vinyls along with well
researched patterns to produce with confidence the most accurate original specification Jaguar interiors available anywhere.

BAS Ltd Jaguar Trim Specialist   **interior parts**
250 H St, Unit 8110
Blaine, WA 98231
800-661-5377; FAX: 206-332-0984

Mail order only. Specializing in interior products from the smallest
seal to complete interior kits for all Jaguar motor cars, XK to XJ.

Bassett's Jaguar   **parts**
PO Box 245   **restoration**
Wyoming, RI 02898   **service**
401-539-3010; FAX: 401-539-7861   **upholstery**

Mail order and open shop. Monday to Friday 8 to 5. Specializing
in parts, upholstery, restoration & service for Jaguars 1949 to
present. We also offer our services on other exotic types of cars.

BCP Sport & Classic Co   **parts**
10525 Airline Dr   **service**
Houston, TX 77037
713-448-4739; FAX: 713-448-0189

See full listing in **Section One** under **MG**

Best of Britain   **car dealer**
RR 1, Box 33   **restoration**
South Ryegate, VT 05069
802-429-2266

Shop open 7 days, 9 to 5. Licensed dealer, handling XKEs exclusively. Purchases, sales and complete restoration for XKE Series
I, II, III.

BMC Classics   **parts**
828 N Dixie Freeway   **repair**
New Smyrna Beach, FL 32168   **restoration**
904-426-6405; FAX: 904-427-4570

Mail order and open shop. Mon-Fri 8-5:30, Sat 8-12.
Restorations, repairs, service, parts for Jaguars, Austin-Healey,
Triumph, Mercedes, Porsche from the 1950s until 1970s.

BritBooks   **books**
62 Main St
Otego, NY 13825
PH/FAX: 607-988-7956

See full listing in **Section Four** under **books & publications**

British Auto Parts Ltd
93256 Holland Ln
Marcola, OR 97454
541-933-2880; FAX: 541-933-2302

| | parts |

See full listing in **Section One** under **Morris**

British Auto Shoppe Inc
1115 1st Ave
Silvis, IL 61282
309-796-2748; FAX: 309-796-2033

| | parts |
| | service |

See full listing in **Section One** under **MG**

British Auto/USA
92 Londonderry Tpke
Manchester, NH 03104
603-622-1050

	restoration
	parts
	upholstery

Mail order and open shop. Monday-Friday 8:30 to 5. Full-scale restoration facility specializing in Jaguars from postwar to present day. Extensive inventory of Jaguar parts and accessories, and in-house manufacturer of top quality upholstery for Jaguar, Rolls-Royce and most British cars.

British Car Care By Pearson's
745 Orange Ave
Winter Park, FL 32789
407-647-0967

	car dealer
	parts
	repairs
	restoration

See full listing in **Section One** under **MG**

British Car Magazine
PO Box 1683
Los Altos, CA 94023-1683
415-949-9680; FAX: 415-949-9685
E-mail: britcarmag@aol.com

| | periodical |

See full listing in **Section Four** under **periodicals**

British Car Specialists
2060 N Wilson Way
Stockton, CA 95205
209-948-8767; FAX: 209-948-1030
E-mail: healeydoc@aol.com

	parts
	repairs
	restoration

See full listing in **Section One** under **Austin-Healey**

British Luxury Automotive Parts
257 Niagara St
Toronto, ON Canada M6J 2L7
416-693-8400; FAX: 416-694-3202
Beeper: 416-378-8182

| | new and used parts |

Specializing in Jaguar, Rolls-Royce, Aston Martin, Lotus and Range Rover. Alternative source of new or pre-owned parts, accessories and performance. Used parts of all kinds from engine, a/c, suspension, electrical, body and interior trim. We have leather and wooden pieces that will match yours better than new. Wheels used and new, spoke, disc and alloy in many sizes. All wheels are available as 1 or sets of 4. Please feel free to call for any piece however small. We will be most happy to serve you.

British Miles
9278 Old E Tyburn Rd
Morrisville, PA 19067
215-736-9300; FAX: 215-736-3089

	accessories
	literature
	parts
	restoration

See full listing in **Section One** under **MG**

British Motor Co
3825 W 11th Ave
Eugene, OR 97402
800-995-1895; FAX: 541-485-8544

| | engine rebuilding |

Mail order and open shop. Monday-Friday 8 am to 5:30 pm. Specializing in all Jaguar model engine rebuilding. At BMC we understand your desire for the best workmanship available. We use factory parts and commit the time and care necessary to do a superior engine rebuild. Please call if you would like references from some of our satisfied customers.

British Restorations
4455 Paul St
Philadelphia, PA 19124
215-533-6696

| | car dealer |
| | restoration |

Open shop only. Monday-Friday 8 am to 6 pm. Total restoration, including body, mechanical, wood, interior, etc., of all sports and classic cars. Specializing in Jaguars from 1948-1987. Also buys and sells sports and classic cars.

British T Shop Inc
165 Rt 82
Oakdale, CT 06370
860-889-0178; FAX: 860-889-6096

	car dealer
	parts
	service

See full listing in **Section One** under **MG**

British Things Inc
515 Ocean Ave
Santa Monica, CA 90402
310-394-4002; FAX: 310-394-3204

| | badges |

See full listing in **Section One** under **Rolls-Royce/Bentley**

British Wiring Inc
20449 Ithaca Rd
Olympia Fields, IL 60461
PH/FAX: 708-481-9050

| | wiring accessories |
| | wiring harnesses |

See full listing in **Section Two** under **electrical systems**

BritParts Midwest
603 Monroe St
LaPorte, IN 46350
219-324-5474; FAX: 219-324-7541

	parts
	restoration
	service

See full listing in **Section One** under **Austin-Healey**

Brooklands Inc
503 Corporate Square
1500 NW 62nd St
Fort Lauderdale, FL 33309
954-776-2748; FAX: 954-772-8383
E-mail: rbiggs@lgc.net

| | accessories |

See full listing in **Section Two** under **accessories**

Francois Bruere
8 Avenue Olivier Heuze
LeMans 72000 France
(33) 02-4377-1877
FAX: (33) 02-4324-2038

| | artwork |

See full listing in **Section Two** under **artwork**

Bud's Parts for Classic Mercedes-Benz
9130 Hwy 5
Douglasville, GA 30134
800-942-8444; FAX: 770-942-8400

	parts
	restoration
	service

See full listing in **Section One** under **Mercedes-Benz**

California Wire Wheel
6922 Turnbridge Way
San Diego, CA 92119
619-698-8255; FAX: 619-589-9032

	rechroming
	tires
	tubes
	wheels

See full listing in **Section Two** under **wheels & wheelcovers**

CARS (Computer Aided Resale System)
2724 Cove View Dr N
Jacksonville, FL 32257
904-448-0633; FAX: 904-448-0623

car dealer

See full listing in **Section Two** under **car dealers**

Classic Auto Concepts
1366 S Federal Hwy
Pompano Beach, FL 33062
954-781-8440; FAX: 954-781-8449

car dealer

See full listing in **Section One** under **Porsche**

Classic Car Works Ltd
3050 Upper Bethany Rd
Jasper, GA 30143
770-735-3945

restoration

See full listing in **Section Two** under **restoration shops**

Collectors Choice LTD
6400 Springfield, Lodi Rd
Dane, WI 53529
608-849-9878; FAX: 608-849-9879

parts
restoration
service

See full listing in **Section One** under **DeTomaso/Pantera**

Composition Materials Co Inc
1375 Kings Hwy E
Fairfield, CT 06430
800-262-7763; FAX: 203-335-9728

plastic media

See full listing in **Section Two** under **restoration aids**

Concours Cars of Colorado Ltd
2414 W Cucharras St
Colorado Springs, CO 80904
719-473-6288

accessories
parts
service

See full listing in **Section One** under **BMW**

Tom Crook Classic Cars
27611 42nd Ave S
Auburn, WA 98001
206-941-3454

car dealer

See full listing in **Section Two** under **car dealers**

Crow Engineering Jaguar Engines
433 Tremont St
Taunton, MA 02780
800-537-4146

engine rebuilding

Mail order and open shop. Seven days per week, 365 days per year, 25 hours per day. Jaguar from XKSS to XJ220. We rebuild your engine at your home or business. No need to mail your engine away or send your car out to be done. We do it all at your place.

Dave's Auto Restoration
2285 Rt 307 E
Jefferson, OH 44047
PH/FAX: 216-858-2227

upholstery

See full listing in **Section Two** under **interiors & interior parts**

Deters Restorations
6205 Swiss Garden Rd
Temperance, MI 48182-1020
313-847-1820

restoration

See full listing in **Section Two** under **restoration shops**

Doc's Jags
125 Baker Rd
Lake Bluff, IL 60044
847-367-5247; FAX: 847-367-6363

appraisals
interiors
restoration

Open shop only. Monday thru Sunday by appointment. Largest classic Jaguar selection for sale in the world. All conditions, all models. We restore and maintain all Jaguars. We have many National show winners resulting from our restorations. There are always 80 letters of reference available. Insurance appraisals are available as well as "expert witness" testimony. We also sell the finest Jaguar Connolly leather interiors in the world. We do NOT sell parts.

Doctor Jaguar Inc
740 W 16th St
Costa Mesa, CA 92627
714-646-2816; FAX: 714-574-8097

restoration
service

Mail order and open shop. Monday-Friday 8:30-5:30 PST. Service, restoration and used parts for all years Jaguar.

Donovan Motorcar Service
4 Holmes Rd
Lenox, MA 01240
413-499-6000; FAX: 413-499-6699

restoration
service

Mail order and open shop. Specializing in service and restoration for all British & European motor cars.

Doug's British Car Parts
2487 E Colorado Blvd
Pasadena, CA 91107
818-793-2494; FAX: 818-793-4339

accessories
parts

Mail order and open shop Monday-Saturday, 8:30 am to 6 pm. Specializing in new and used auto parts and accessories including Jaguar XK 120 & Mk VII through XKE; 3.8 Mk II, XJ6, 12, S; MG T Series through MGA to MGB, Midget, Triumph TR2-8, Spitfire, GT6, Austin-Healey 100-4/3000 Mk III BJ8; Rover 2000 TC, 3500S & 1980 3500, Sunbeam Alpine & Hillman.

Eddie's Restorations
4725 Rt 30
Elwood, NJ 08217
609-965-2211

restoration

Shop open Monday-Friday 9 am to 5 pm. Restorations on classic imports, Jaguar XK 120, XK 140, XK 150 and XKE in particular, to factory new specifications, using new metal panels and new parts for rebuilding mechanical components.

Exotic Wood Dash & Restorations
336 Cottonwood Ave
Hartland, WI 53029
800-900-3274; FAX: 414-367-9474

restoration parts
wood dash overlays

Mail order only. Exotic wood dash overlays and restoration parts. We offer genuine wood dash kits for over 600 different cars, trucks and motorcycles. All kits come with a 3 year warranty and are easily installed using the instructions provided with each kit.

The Fine Car Store
1105 Moana Dr
San Diego, CA 92107
619-223-7766; FAX: 619-223-6838

car dealer

See full listing in **Section One** under **Ferrari**

GAHH Inc
8116 Lankershim Blvd
North Hollywood, CA 91605
818-767-6242; FAX: 818-767-2786

auto interiors
convertible tops

See full listing in **Section One** under **Mercedes-Benz**

Grand Prix Classics Inc
7456 La Jolla Blvd
La Jolla, CA 92037
619-459-3500; FAX: 619-459-3512

racing cars
sports cars

See full listing in **Section Two** under **racing**

Pete Groh
9957 Frederick Rd
Ellicott City, MD 21042-3647
410-750-2352

original British
keys
Wilmot Breeden

Mail order only. Specializing in original British keys for Austin-Healey, Austin, Hillman, Jaguar, Morris, MG, Singer, Triumph, Vauxhall, Nash, Metropolitan. British keys for FA, FP and FS, original, also keys cut by code, need three digit number. Cost: original, $12; cut by code, $6; double sided cut, $9.

Harbor Auto Restoration
1504 SW 3rd St
Pompano Beach, FL 33069
954-785-7887; FAX: 954-785-7388

restoration

See full listing in **Section Two** under **restoration shops**

International Restoration Specialist Inc
PO Box 1303
Mt Airy, NC 27030
910-789-1548

parts
restoration
sales

Mail order and open shop. Mon-Fri 8-5 EST. Sell, buy, restore parts for all Jag, Ferrari, Mercedes-Benz, Austin-Healey, Corvette, Cobra. An established top quality vintage restorer and sales brokerage firm. Best known for Jaguar, we perform ground-up restorations on all marques. We consistently receive National honors, including Grand National 1st Place AACA, Regional British Car Best of Show, JCNA Regional and National Concours awards and prestigious invitational appearances. Full or partial restorations, street to concours level, sales or purchases. When it comes to automotive investments you need to call Lloyd.

Italy's Famous Exhaust
2711 183rd St
Redondo Beach, CA 90278
PH/FAX: 310-542-5432
E-mail: http://famous@earthlink.com

exhaust systems
wheels

See full listing in **Section Two** under **exhaust systems**

Jaguar Cars Inc Archives
555 MacArthur Blvd
Mahwah, NJ 07430
201-818-8144; FAX: 201-818-0281

literature sales
research

See full listing in **Section Four** under **information sources**

Jaguar of Puerto Rico Inc
PO Box 13055
San Juan, PR 00908-3055
787-723-5177; FAX: 787-723-9488

car dealer
parts
service

Open shop only. Monday-Friday 8 to 6. New Jaguar sales. Used Jaguar parts and service. Selected classic restorations. Sales of new Range Rovers.

Jahns Quality Pistons
1360 N Jefferson St
Anaheim, CA 92807
714-579-3795, 800-225-0277
FAX: 714-524-6607

piston rings
pistons

See full listing in **Section Two** under **engine parts**

John's Cars Inc
800 Jaguar Ln
Dallas, TX 75226
214-426-4100; FAX: 214-426-3116

parts
restoration
service

Mail order and open shop. Monday-Friday 8 to 6. Jaguar XJ series, service, parts, restoration, V8 conversions and kits for DIY conversions XJ, E-type, TR7, Z car, etc. Rebuilt steering racks, water pumps, brake boosters, etc.
Web site: www.johnscars.com

Georges B Karakolev
228 Rt 221
Napierville, QC Canada J0J 1L0
PH/FAX: 514-245-0028

car dealer
parts
restoration

See full listing in **Section Two** under **restoration aids**

Chuck Konesky
110 Stolle Rd
Elma, NY 14059
716-652-9638

parts

Mail order only. For XK 120s, 140s, 150s and E-types. New E-type parts available, but mostly parting out complete cars. Restorable Jaguars for sale. Call 24 hours a day, seven days a week.

LA Machine
5960 Valentine Rd #9
Ventura, CA 93003
805-650-6644; FAX: 805-650-6633

convertible kits

See full listing in **Section One** under **Porsche**

Leatherique Leather Restoration Products
PO Box 2678
Orange Park, FL 32065
904-272-0992; FAX: 904-272-1534

leather cleaning
conditioning
products

See full listing in **Section One** under **Rolls-Royce/Bentley**

Lindley Restorations Ltd
Rt 422 RD 3
Pottstown, PA 19464
610-326-8484; FAX: 610-326-3845

parts
sales
service

Mail order and open shop. Monday thru Friday, 9 am-6 pm, 9 am-5 pm Saturdays. Jaguar, MG, Land Rover, Austin-Healey sales, service and parts. Jaguar: SS cars, XK 120, XK 140, XK 150, E-type, Series I, II and III, also Mark II, VII and IX, XJ6, XJS. Complete on-site facility. Body, paint, engine, transmission, suspension, upholstery and sub assemblies. Same ownership and location for 28 years. 7,500 sq feet located 30 miles west of Philadelphia via Expressway route.

Lister North America Ltd
6565 E 40
Tulsa, OK 74145
918-665-0021; FAX: 918-664-0804

performance parts

Mail order and open shop. Monday-Friday 8:30 to 5:30. Sells and installs restyling packages and performance components for Jaguar XJS, Jaguar XJ6 and 1984-1996 Corvettes.

LMARR Disk Ltd
PO Box 910
Glen Ellen, CA 95442-0910
707-938-9347; FAX: 707-938-3020

wheel discs

See full listing in **Section One** under **Rolls-Royce/Bentley**

John A Meering Jaguar Hoses — hoses
6743 Newcastle Ct
Port Tobacco, MD 20677
301-609-8557

Mail order only. Jaguar hoses. Correct size and shape. Heater, radiator and carburetor hoses for XK 120, 140, 150 and Mark 7, 8, 9. Complete sets only. Send SASE for details. Hoses are new, not NOS, and are of modern construction. Also can have made hoses for most post-war British cars.

Merely Motoring — automobilia / lapel badges / postcards
153 Danford Ln
Solihull
West Midlands B91 1QQ England
0121-733-2123
FAX: 0121-745-5256

See full listing in **Section Two** under **automobilia**

Mid-Jersey Motorama Inc — car dealer
1301 Asbury Ave
PO Box 1395
Asbury Park, NJ 07712
908-775-9885
Beeper: 908-840-6111
FAX: 908-775-9885

See full listing in **Section One** under **Cadillac/LaSalle**

Midwest Acorn Nut Company — fasteners / hardware
256 Minnesota Ave
Troy, MI 48083-4671
800-422-NUTS (6887)
FAX: 810-583-9130

See full listing in **Section Two** under **hardware**

Moss Motors Ltd — accessories / parts
PO Box 847
440 Rutherford St
Goleta, CA 93117
800-235-6954; FAX: 805-692-2525

See full listing in **Section One** under **MG**

Motorcars Ltd — parts
8101 Hempstead
Houston, TX 77008
713-863-9388; FAX: 713-863-8238
E-mail: mcltd@phoenix.net

Mail order and open shop. Monday to Friday 8 am-6 pm. Specializing in new and used parts for British automobiles such as Jaguar, MG, Triumph, Range Rover, BMW and Rolls-Royce. Repair for all of the above. 24 hour voice mail.

Mr Sport Car Inc — service
203 E Lincoln
Papillion, NE 68046
402-592-7559

Open shop, Monday-Saturday 8-6. Service for Jaguars, all years. We like XKs, XJs, all MGs, all TRs, Lotus, all 8-12 cylinder Ferraris. Have been working on these since 1960.

Muncie Imports & Classics — repair / restoration / upholstery
4401 St Rd 3 North
Muncie, IN 47303
800-462-4244; FAX: 317-287-9551

Mail order and open shop. Monday-Friday 7:30-5:30, Saturday 9-1. Specializing in Jaguar & Corvette restoration, service, repair, paint & body. Upholstery for XK 120, 140, 150, Marks & E-types. GW Bartlett Co factory authorized installer.

Nisonger Instrument S/S — gauges
570 Mamaroneck Ave
Mamaroneck, NY 10543
914-381-1952, FAX: 914-381-1953

See full listing in **Section Two** under **instruments**

Northwest Transmission Parts — transmission parts
13500 US 62
Winchester, OH 45697
800-327-1955 order line
513-442-2811 info
FAX: 513-442-6555

See full listing in **Section Two** under **transmissions**

NOS Locators — parts
587 Pawtucket Ave
Pawtucket, RI 02860
401-725-5000

See full listing in **Section One** under **MG**

Omni Specialties — parts / restoration / service
10418 Lorain Ave
Cleveland, OH 44111
800-791-9562; 216-251-2269
FAX: 216-251-6083

See full listing in **Section One** under **MG**

Pacific International Auto — parts / sales / service
1118 Garnet Ave
San Diego, CA 92109
619-274-1920; 619-454-1815

Mail order and open shop. British car specialists. Parts, sales, service, restorations. Hard-to-find parts for Jaguars, MGs, Triumphs. Jaguar XKEs, XK 120s, XK 140s, XK 150s, all sedans.

Peninsula Imports — accessories / parts / trim
3749 Harlem Rd
Buffalo, NY 14215
800-263-4538; FAX: 905-847-3021

See full listing in **Section One** under **BMW**

Philpenn Distributors Co — car dealer / parts / restoration / service
635 Lancaster Ave
Bryn Mawr, PA 19010
800-345-1023, 610-525-5900
FAX: 610-526-9841

Mail order and open shop. Monday-Friday 8 to 5. Jaguar distributor with full service and parts department. Also restoration and fabrication facilities for Jaguars, Aston Martins and Daimler.

Precision Autoworks — restorations
2202 Federal Street
E Camden, NJ 08105
609-966-0080, NJ
FAX: 610-649-3577, PA

See full listing in **Section One** under **Mercedes-Benz**

Precision Restoration Service Inc — restoration
1551 N Courtney Rd, Ste B-2
Independence, MO 64050
816-461-7500; FAX: 816-461-7504

See full listing in **Section Two** under **restoration shops**

Proper Jaguar   restoration
1806 S Alpine
Rockford, IL 61108
815-398-0303, 398-8664

Jaguar restoration, all years, by appointment. Also MGs and other sports and classic cars. Also restore and maintain vintage race cars. Have production and Formula 5000 experience.

Ragtops & Roadsters   race prep
203 S 4th St   repairs
Perkasie, PA 18944
215-257-1202; FAX: 215-257-2688

See full listing in **Section One** under **AC**

RAU Restoration   woodwork
2027 Pontius Ave
Los Angeles, CA 90025
PH/FAX: 310-445-1128

See full listing in **Section Two** under **woodwork**

Regal International Motor Cars Inc   car dealer
PO Box 6819
Hollywood, FL 33081
305-989-9777; FAX: 305-989-9778

See full listing in **Section One** under **Rolls-Royce/Bentley**

The Registry   periodical
Pine Grove
Stanley, VA 22851
540-778-3728; FAX: 540-778-2402
E-mail: britregstry@aol.com

See full listing in **Section Four** under **periodicals**

Restoration Services   restoration
16049 W 4th Ave
Golden, CO 80401
303-271-0356

See full listing in **Section One** under **Porsche**

Reward Service Inc   appraisals
172 Overhill Rd   restoration
Stormville, NY 12582   transportation
914-227-7647; FAX: 914-221-0293

Automotive restoration and mechanical rebuilding of Jaguars and other British sports cars for 25 years. Appraisals, personalized transportation and consultation on restoration projects, by appointment. References. International Society of Appraisers.

RM Auto Restoration Ltd   panel fabrication
825 Park Ave W   parts
Chatham, ON Canada N7M 5J6   restoration
519-352-4575; FAX: 519-351-1337

See full listing in **Section Two** under **restoration shops**

Scarborough Faire Inc   parts
1151 Main St
Pawtucket, RI 02860
800-556-6300; 401-724-4200
FAX: 401-724-5392

See full listing in **Section One** under **MG**

Shelton Dealerships   accessories
5740 N Federal Hwy   leasing
Ford Lauderdale, FL 33308   parts
954-493-5211; FAX: 954-772-2653   sales

See full listing in **Section One** under **Ferrari**

Special Interest Car Parts   parts
1340 Hartford Ave
Johnston, RI 02919
800-556-7496; FAX: 401-831-7760

Specializing in the distribution of British car parts worldwide for Jaguar 1948-on, MG and Midget, Triumph TR250, 6, 7, 8, Spitfire & GT6 models.

Sports & Classics   parts
PO Box 1787
512 Boston Post Rd, Dept H
Darien, CT 06820-1787

See full listing in **Section Two** under **body parts**

The Stable LTD   sales
217 Main St   service
Gladstone, NJ 07934
908-234-2055; FAX: 908-781-2599

Open shop Monday-Saturday 9 am-6 pm. Classic, special interest, sports and luxury cars, sales and service.

Straight Six Jaguar
24321 Hatteras St
Woodland Hills, CA 91367
PH/FAX: 818-716-1192

parts
service

Specializing in parts and service for Jaguars 1936-1987.

Terry's Jaguar Parts Inc
117 E Smith ST
Benton, IL 62812
800-851-9438; FAX: 618-438-2371

parts

Mail order and open shop. Monday thru Friday 8-5, Saturday 8-12. Specializing in Jaguar parts to present day.

See our ad on page 122

Thoroughbred Motors
3935 N Washington Blvd
Sarasota, FL 34234
941-359-2221, 941-359-2277
FAX: 941-359-2128

car dealer
parts

Mail order and open shop. Monday-Saturday 8:30 to 7. Buys and sells Jaguars, all years and models. Also parts for Jaguars, mainly vintage models. We ship only good, serviceable parts. Deal also in other exotic and vintage cars: Ferraris, Maseratis, Lamborghinis, Aston Martins, Austin-Healeys, Rolls-Royces, etc.

Tillack & Co Ltd
630 Mary Ann Dr
Redondo Beach, CA 90278
310-316-8760; FAX: 310-376-3392

parts
restoration

See full listing in **Section Two** under **restoration shops**

Van Nuys Motors
14422 Oxnard St
Van Nuys, CA 91403
818-988-5455

parts
restoration
sales
service

See full listing in **Section One** under **Mercedes-Benz**

Vantage Auto Interiors
11 Fahey St
Stamford, CT 06907
203-425-9533; FAX: 203-425-9535

upholstery

See full listing in **Section Two** under **interiors & interior parts**

Vicarage Jaguars
3952 Douglas Rd
Miami, FL 33133
305-444-8759; FAX: 305-443-6443

parts
restoration

Mail order and open shop. Monday-Friday 8 am-5 pm. Specializing in Jaguar restoration parts and upgrades for all postwar Jaguars.

Victory Autoservices
Box 5060, RR 1
W Baldwin, ME 04091
207-625-4581

parts
restoration

See full listing in **Section One** under **Austin-Healey**

Vintage Jaguar Spares
7804 Billington Ct
Fort Washington, MD 20744
301-248-6327; FAX: 301-248-5523

parts

Mail order only. "Mk IV", Mk V and SS-Jaguar. Price list free.

Welsh Jaguar Enterprises Inc
223 N 5th St, PO Box 4130
Steubenville, OH 43952
800-875-JAGS toll-free
614-282-8649; FAX: 614-282-1913

parts

Monday through Friday 9 am to 5 pm, Saturday 9 am to 1 pm. Welsh Enterprises Inc has over fifty thousand square feet of new, used and rebuilt Jaguar spares. With an expanding inventory, Welsh Enterprises continues to be the largest independent retailer of Jaguar spares for restoration and service. With a knowledge sales staff and worldwide shipping same day, Welsh Enterprises can offer all Jaguar enthusiasts fast and reliable service at a competitive price. We stock the largest inventory of new, used and rebuilt Jaguar spares found anywhere. Call today for your catalog and price guide.

See our ad on this page

Ed West CARS
1941 Jan Marie Pl
Tustin, CA 92680
714-832-2688

car dealer
parts

Mail order and open shop. Monday-Friday 9 to 5. For Jaguar XK 120s, 140s, 150s, Mk Is, IIs, VIIs, VIIIs and IXs. New, used and reproduction parts. Cars bought and sold. Twenty years' experience. Send 2 stamps for SASE with model and year of Jaguar for parts list.

Western Jaguar
Cordell R Newby
1625 North Western
Wenatchee, WA 98801
509-662-7748; FAX: 509-662-7748

parts

Mail order only. Specializing in 1949-51 Mark Vs with comprehensive inventory of new, NOS, reproduction and used parts for 1936-89 models. Catalog, $3.

World Upholstery & Trim | carpet kits
PO Box 4857 | **tops**
Thousand Oaks, CA 91359 | **upholstery kits**
800-222-9577; FAX: 818-707-2664
E-mail: worlduph@mail.vcnet.com

See full listing in **Section Two** under **interiors & interior parts**

British Car Care By Pearson's | car dealer
745 Orange Ave | **parts**
Winter Park, FL 32789 | **repairs**
407-647-0967 | **restoration**

See full listing in **Section One** under **MG**

Delta Motorsports Inc | accessories
2724 E Bell Rd | **catalog**
Phoenix, AZ 85032 | **parts**
602-265-8026; FAX: 602-971-8609

Mail order and open shop. Monday-Friday 8 to 5:30 MST. Factory authorized parts and accessories distributor for Jensen-Healey, Jensen Interceptor & Jensen GT.

Image Auto | apparel
31690 W 12 Mile #4 | **artwork**
Farmington Hills, MI 48334
800-414-2852; FAX: 810-553-0924

Mail order only. Jensen apparel, artwork, novelties, etc, all years.

JAE | parts
375 Pine #26 | **service**
Goleta, CA 93117 | **tech info**
805-967-5767; FAX: 805-967-6183

See full listing in **Section One** under **Lotus**

Jensen Cars Ltd | parts
140 Franklin Ave | **technical advice**
Wyckoff, NJ 07481-3465
201-847-8549, 8-10 pm EST
FAX: 201-342-4637 (24 hrs)

Jensen Interceptor parts for 1964-1976 Jensen CV8 and Interceptor.

Collector Car Buyers | car dealers
4046 11th St
Rockford, IL 61109
815-229-1258; FAX: 815-229-1238

See full listing in **Section Two** under **car dealers**

Dennis DuPont | automobilia
77 Island Pond Rd | **literature**
Derry, NH 03038 | **parts**
603-434-9290

See full listing in **Section One** under **Studebaker**

Eugene Gardner | license plates
10510 Rico Tatum Rd
Palmetto, GA 30268
770-463-4264

See full listing in **Section Two** under **license plates**

K-F-D Services Inc | parts
HC 65, Box 49 | **restoration**
Altonah, UT 84002
801-454-3098; FAX: 801-454-3099

Mail order and open shop. Monday-Saturday 9 am - 4 pm MST. Specializing in restoration parts and service & customized cars for Kaiser, Frazer, Darrin, Henry J, all years.

John E Parker | plastic repros
4860 N Desert Tortoise Pl | **rubber parts**
Tucson, AZ 85745-9213
520-743-3574

Mail order and open shop. Monday-Saturday 8 to 4. Large inventory of new reproduction rubber parts and plastic reproductions. For Kaiser-Frazers, Henry Js, Allstates and 1952-55 Willys Aeros. Kaiser-Frazer Owners' Club information available.

Waldron's Antique Exhaust Inc | exhaust systems
Box C 25872 M-86
Nottawa, MI 49075
616-467-7185; FAX: 616-467-9041

See full listing in **Section Two** under **exhaust systems**

Walker's Auto Pride Inc | parts
1425 E Hwy 105 | **restoration**
Monument, CO 80132
719-481-2730

Shop open Monday-Thursday 7:30 to 5:30; Saturday by appointment. Auto restoration, specializing in Kaiser-Frazer. Full line K-F parts. Body shop, general mechanics. Parts sales for Kaiser-Frazer cars including Henry J. Also K-E cars sold and repaired by appointment. 75 tons of parts available.

Zeug's K-F Parts | parts
1435 Moreno Dr
Simi Valley, CA 93063
818-718-7722 weekdays only

Mail order only. NOS and used Kaiser-Frazer, Henry J and Kaiser Darrin parts. Send $2 for parts list.

LMARR Disk Ltd | wheel discs
PO Box 910
Glen Ellen, CA 95442-0910
707-938-9347; FAX: 707-938-3020

See full listing in **Section One** under **Rolls-Royce/Bentley**

Rolls-Royce of Beverly Hills | parts
11401 West Pico Blvd
Los Angeles, CA 90064
310-477-4262, 800-321-9792
FAX: 310-473-7498

See full listing in **Section One** under **Rolls-Royce/Bentley**

Lamborghini

Aero Toy Store Gary Anzalone 1710 W Cypress Creek Rd Ft Lauderdale, FL 33309 800-404-2376; FAX: 954-771-3281	acquisitions sales

See full listing in **Section One** under **Ferrari**

Drummond Coach and Paint 531 Raleigh Ave El Cajon, CA 92020 619-579-7229; FAX: 619-579-2128	painting restoration

See full listing in **Section One** under **Ferrari**

Exoticars of Hunterdon 6 Washington St Frenchtown, NJ 08825 908-996-4889; FAX: 908-996-6938	machine work paint & bodywork restoration service welding/fabrication

See full listing in **Section One** under **Ferrari**

Kreimeyer Co 3211 N Wilburn Ave Bethany, OK 73008 405-789-9499; FAX: 405-789-7888	antennas/radios glass/parts/ wholesale repair/service

See full listing in **Section One** under **Mercedes-Benz**

London Stainless Steel Exhaust Centre 249-253 Queenstown Rd London SW8 3NP England 011-44-171622-2120 FAX: 011-44-171627-0991 E-mail: 101445.341@compuserv.com	exhaust systems

See full listing in **Section Two** under **exhaust systems**

Motorcar Gallery Inc 715 N Federal Hwy Fort Lauderdale, FL 33304 954-522-9900; FAX: 954-522-9966	car dealer

See full listing in **Section One** under **Ferrari**

Motorcars International 528 N Prince Ln Springfield, MO 65802 417-831-9999; FAX: 417-863-0777 E-mail: missy@motorcars-intl	accessories cars services tools

See full listing in **Section One** under **Ferrari**

Garry Roberts & Co 922 Sunset Dr Costa Mesa, CA 92627 888-FERRAR; FAX: 714-650-2730	cars parts service

See full listing in **Section One** under **Ferrari**

Rolls-Royce of Beverly Hills 11401 West Pico Blvd Los Angeles, CA 90064 310-477-4262, 800-321-9792 FAX: 310-473-7498	parts

See full listing in **Section One** under **Rolls-Royce/Bentley**

The Stable LTD 217 Main St Gladstone, NJ 07934 908-234-2055; FAX: 908-781-2599	sales service

See full listing in **Section One** under **Jaguar**

Tillack & Co Ltd 630 Mary Ann Dr Redondo Beach, CA 90278 310-316-8760; FAX: 310-376-3392	parts restoration

See full listing in **Section Two** under **restoration shops**

Bayless Inc 1111 Via Bayless Marietta, GA 30066-2770 770-928-1446; FAX: 770-928-1342 800-241-1446, order line (US & Canada)	accessories parts

See full listing in **Section One** under **Fiat**

Caribou Imports Inc 23151-A3 Alcalde Dr Laguna Hills, CA 92653 714-770-3136; FAX: 714-770-0815 E-mail: cariboulh@aol.com	parts

See full listing in **Section One** under **Fiat**

Celiberti Motors 615 Oak St Santa Rosa, CA 95404 800-872-3428; FAX: 707-523-1613	parts

See full listing in **Section One** under **Fiat**

Fiat Plus 318-A River St Santa Cruz, CA 95060 408-423-0218; 800-500-FIAT, orders FAX: 408-459-8128	parts repairs

See full listing in **Section One** under **Fiat**

International Auto Parts Inc Rt 29 N PO Box 9036 Charlottesville, VA 22906 800-726-0555, 804-973-0555 FAX: 804-973-2368	accessories parts

See full listing in **Section One** under **Alfa Romeo**

LINCOLN

Aabar's Cadillac & Lincoln Salvage & Parts
9700 NE 23rd
Oklahoma City, OK 73141
405-769-3318; FAX: 405-769-9542

parts

See full listing in **Section One** under **Cadillac/LaSalle**

Antique & Classic Cars
Rt 15, Box 454
Florence, AL 35633
205-760-0542

car locator

See full listing in **Section One** under **Cadillac/LaSalle**

Antique Auto Electric
9109 (rear) E Garvey Ave
Rosemead, CA 91770
818-572-0938

repro wiring

See full listing in **Section Two** under **electrical systems**

Auto Parts Exchange
PO Box 736
Reading, PA 19603
610-372-2813, 7-10 am, 7-12 pm,
7 days

NORS parts
NOS parts
rebuilt parts
used parts

7 days. Mail order and open shop. Open daily by appointment anytime. NOS, NORS and used parts for 1953-79 Lincolns and

1958-79 Thunderbirds. Parts tested before shipping if necessary. Rebuilding service for hydraulic top pumps, window motors. Brake and front end parts, etc. Remanufacturing parts for Lincolns. Worldwide shipping no problem.

Autowire Division
9109 (Rear) E. Garvey Avenue
Rosemead, CA 91770
818-572-0938; FAX: 818-288-3311

alternator
conversions/motors
relays
switches

See full listing in **Section One** under **Ford '54-up**

Ron Baker's Auto Inc
Rt 44
Putnam, CT 06260
860-928-7614, 800-962-9228
FAX: 860-928-0749

parts
service

Mail order and open shop. Specializing in 1961-1979 Lincoln parts & services. 61-66 Thunderbird convertible top electrical repairs. Over 1.5 million parts in 30,000 square foot warehouse. Four full time mechanics specializing in convertible tops, power windows, heat, a/c, etc.

Larry Blodget
Box 753
Rancho Mirage, CA 92270
619-862-1979

models

See full listing in **Section Two** under **models & toys**

Bob's Lincoln Zephyr Parts
27 Deacon Pl
Cresskill, NJ 07626
201-568-1915

chrome service
instruments
parts
water pumps

Mail order only. 1936-48 Continental and Zephyr parts. Rebuilt water pumps, coils, dist, carburetors, NOS rotors, points, dist caps, hubcaps, scripts, stoplight assy, chroming, show quality, dashboards, gauges, bumpers, aluminum door sills, stainless screw kits, restored medallions and thousands of other parts.

Bob Burgess 1955-56 Ford Parts Inc
793 Alpha-Bellbrook Rd
Bellbrook, OH 45305
513-426-8041

parts

See full listing in **Section One** under **Ford '54-up**

California Continental & T Bird Connection
PO Box 2281
Irwindale, CA 91706
818-962-6696 in CA

consultant
parts
repairs

Mail order only. Specialty company handling repairs, parts & consultation of Lincoln Continentals & Marks 1961-1979, especially tops, windows and tricky electrical problems. Lincoln & T-Bird parts & service 1961-1979. Electrical specialty repairs, vacuum controls for a/c, etc. Convertible parts & service.

Cape Cod Classic Cars
Pete Harvey
PO Box 280
Cataumet, MA 02534
508-548-0660; FAX: 508-457-0660

car dealer

See full listing in **Section One** under **Cadillac/LaSalle**

John Cashman
3460 Crews Lake Dr
Lakeland, FL 33813
813-876-0441, 813-870-1318

convertible
electrics
new & used parts
repairs

New and used parts for 1961-79 Lincolns. Specializing in 61-67 convertible electrical parts. Also, inquire about repair work on location at your home in central or south FL. Let my 15 years' experience solve your electrical and top problems.

Chrome Masters
1109 W Orange Ave, Unit D
Tallahassee, FL 32310
904-576-2100

chrome plating
pot metal
restoration

See full listing in **Section Two** under **plating & polishing**

Classic Auto Air Mfg Co
2020 W Kennedy Blvd
Tampa, FL 33606
813-251-4994, 813-251-2356

air conditioning
heating
parts

See full listing in **Section One** under **Mustang**

Classic Car Works Ltd
3050 Upper Bethany Rd
Jasper, GA 30143
770-735-3945

restoration

See full listing in **Section Two** under **restoration shops**

Classic Ford Sales
PO Box 60
E Dixfield, ME 04227
207-562-4443; FAX: 207-562-4576
E-mail: info@classicford.com

salvage yard

See full listing in **Section Five** under **Maine**

Classique Cars Unlimited
5 Turkey Bayou Rd, PO Box 249
Lakeshore, MS 39558
601-467-9633
FAX: 601-467-9207, MS
800-543-8691, USA

appraisals
parts
repairs
restorations

Mail order/phone order. Monday-Friday 9 to 6; some Saturdays 9 to 12 pm CST. 1958-88 Lincoln & Thunderbird new, used, reproduction parts. Three acres with three buildings full of parts for all your Lincoln & T-Bird needs. Shop work by appointment only. Appraisals for Antique, Classic, Milestone, Custom and Special Interest vehicles. Celebrating our 22nd year! Home of the Karen A Williams Collection featuring cars of famous personalities.

See our ad on page 126

Collector Cars & Route 66 Motors
Box 50715
Amarillo, TX 79159
806-358-2951; FAX: 806-358-2344

books
parts
photos
restoration

Mail order and open shop by appointment only. Buys, sells and restores collector Lincolns 1936-1948. The owner of the company, Marvin E Arnold, is a noted Lincoln authority. Distributors of the publication *Lincoln and Continental, Classic Motorcars, The Early Years* by Marvin E Arnold. Hardbound, 256 pages, 32 pages of color history of Lincoln and the Lincoln Motor Company. 1,000 illustrations. Beautifully embossed coffee table edition with a full color dust jacket, $39.95 postpaid; Canada add $5, foreign add $15.

Color-Ite Refinishing Co
Winning Colors
Rt 69
Bethany, CT 06524
203-393-0240; FAX: 203-393-0873

modern finishes
restoration service

See full listing in **Section Two** under **paints**

Bob Cook Classic Auto Parts Inc
2055 Van Cleave Rd, PO Box 600
Murray, KY 42071-0600
502-753-4000, 800-486-1137
FAX: 502-753-4600

new parts
NOS parts
reproduced parts

See full listing in **Section One** under **Ford '54-up**

Tony Copeland Ford Lincoln Mercury
1617 21st St
Lewiston, ID 83501
800-821-8174; FAX: 208-746-1543
E-mail: copeland@copelandford.com

parts
sales
service

See full listing in **Section One** under **Ford '54-up**

Buzz De Clerck
41760 Utica Rd
Sterling Heights, MI 48313
810-731-0765

parts

Mail order and open shop. All week 9 am to 9 pm. Specialize in 1969 to 1971 Lincoln Continental Mark III new and used parts. Can diagnose most problems with those cars over the phone or send to proper source for cure.

Don's Antique Auto Parts
37337 Niles Blvd
Fremont, CA 94536
415-792-4390

new parts
used parts

See full listing in **Section Two** under **comprehensive parts**

Edgerton Classics Ltd
RR 5 Box 199
Canastota, NY 13032
315-697-2722

restoration
woodworking

See full listing in **Section Two** under **restoration shops**

Mike Gerner, The Lincoln Factory
3636 Scheuneman Rd
Gemlake, MN 55110
612-426-8001

car dealer
parts
restoration

Mail order and open shop. Call first on shop hours. Buys and sells Lincolns, 1936-48 and has parts from over 100 Lincolns. Also does restoration and presently has twenty in personal collection.

R O Hommel
933 Osage Rd
Pittsburgh, PA 15243
412-279-8884

body tags
parts

Mail order only. For 1942-48 Lincoln Continentals. Used, NOS and reproduction parts. Manufactures reproduction body tags for 1942 to 1948 Lincolns and Continentals.

Horsepower Sales
100 New South Rd
Hicksville, NY 11801
516-937-3707; FAX: 516-937-3803

limousines

See full listing in **Section Two** under **limousine rentals**

Bill Horton
5804 Jones Valley Dr
Huntsville, AL 35802
205-881-6894

vacuum motors

See full listing in **Section One** under **Mercury**

Hot Rod & Custom Supply
1304 SE 10th St
Cape Coral, FL 33990
941-574-7744; FAX: 941-574-8820

custom parts
engine parts
speed parts

See full listing in **Section One** under **Ford '32-'53**

Kenroy Ford Parts
2 Folwell Ln
Mullica Hill, NJ 08062
609-848-4965; FAX: 608-468-2489

NOS parts

See full listing in **Section One** under **Ford '54-up**

Lake Orion Machine
1325 Heights Rd
Lake Orion, MI 48362
313-693-4636

exhaust systems

Mail order only. Exhaust systems for 1920 thru 1930 Lincolns. Also puchase any original parts for the above autos.

Lincoln Land
1928 Sherwood St
Clearwater, FL 34625
813-531-5351; FAX: 813-447-6179

cars
parts
service

Mail order and open shop. Monday-Friday 8 to 5. 1956-89 Lincoln Continental cars, parts and service. Daily parts shipments worldwide.

Lincoln Parts International
707 E 4th St, Bldg G
Perris, CA 92570
800-382-1656; 909-657-5588
FAX: 909-657-4758

parts

Mail order and open shop. Monday-Friday 8-5, Saturday 9-1. New, used and reproduction parts for 61-80s Lincolns, 72-79 Thunderbirds, 74-79 Cougars and 72-76 Montegos. Quality guaranteed parts. Shipments daily worldwide. VISA, MasterCard and American Express.

Lincoln-Rubber Reproductions
9109 E Garvey Ave
Rosemead, CA 91770
818-280-4546

parts

Mail order only. For 1940-48 Continentals. Catalog $4 USA.

Lincoln Services Ltd
Earle O Brown, Jr
229 Robinhood Ln
McMurray, PA 15317
412-941-4567 evenings

literature
parts

Mail order only. Parts bought, sold or traded for 1936-48 Lincoln Zephyrs and Continentals, emphasis on HV-12 engine parts. Also Lincoln literature. Free catalog. Also information on membership in the Lincoln Continental Owners Club and/or the Lincoln Zephyr Owners Club.

Maffucci Sales Company Inc
RD 1 Box 60, Rt 9 W
Athens, NY 12015-9707
518-943-0100; FAX: 518-943-4534

literature
parts

Shop open by appointment only, Monday-Friday 8 am to 5:30 pm. Specializing in obsolete Lincoln, Mercury auto parts for 1940s through early 1970s. Excellent inventory of new, reproduction and used auto parts and literature. Mostly mail order. Specialist in locating hard to find parts. Over 25 years' experience.

Mainly Convertibles
13805 W Hillsborough Ave
Tampa, FL 33635-9655
813-855-6869; FAX: 813-855-1376

parts
repair
restoration

Mail order and open shop. Monday-Friday 9 am to 5 pm. Parts, sales and restoration of 1950s-68 Lincoln convertibles, sedans and other luxury cars.

Mercury & Ford Molded Rubber
12 Plymouth Ave
Wilmington, MA 01887
508-658-8394

parts

See full listing in **Section One** under **Mercury**

Mid-Jersey Motorama Inc
1301 Asbury Ave, PO Box 1395
Asbury Park, NJ 07712
908-775-9885
Beeper: 908-840-6111
FAX: 908-775-9885

car dealer

See full listing in **Section One** under **Cadillac/LaSalle**

Midwest Acorn Nut Company
256 Minnesota Ave
Troy, MI 48083-4671
800-422-NUTS(6887)
FAX: 810-583-9130

fasteners
hardware

See full listing in **Section Two** under **hardware**

Miller Obsolete Parts
1329 Campus Dr
Vestal, NY 13850
607-722-5371; FAX: 607-729-7645
E-mail: fordpart@spectra.net

parts

See full listing in **Section One** under **Ford '32-'53**

Monument Motors Inc
PO Box 711
Great Barrington, MA 01230
413-637-1017

repair
restoration
used parts

See full listing in **Section One** under **Mustang**

Narragansett Reproductions
Ed & Miki Pease
107 Woodville Rd, PO Box 51
Wood River Junction, RI 02894
401-364-3839; FAX: 401-364-3830

wiring harnesses

See full listing in **Section Two** under **electrical systems**

NOS Only
414 Umbarger Rd, Unit E
San Jose, CA 95111
408-227-2353, 408-227-2354
FAX: 408-227-2355

NOS parts

See full listing in **Section Two** under **comprehensive parts**

Oak Bows
122 Ramsey Ave
Chambersburg, PA 17201
717-264-2602

top bows

See full listing in **Section Two** under **woodwork**

Regal International Motor Cars Inc
PO Box 6819
Hollywood, FL 33081
305-989-9777; FAX: 305-989-9778

car dealer

See full listing in **Section One** under **Rolls-Royce/Bentley**

Rocky Mountain V8 Ford Parts
1124 Clark Cir
Colorado Springs, CO 80915
719-597-8375

parts

See full listing in **Section One** under **Ford '32-'53**

Rowland's Antique Auto Parts
PO Box 387
Zillah, WA 98953
509-829-5026

cars
parts

Mail order and open shop. Tuesday-Saturday 9 to 5. 1939-69 Lincoln and Mercury parts. SASE absolutely required.

Southside Obsolete
6819 James Ave S
Minneapolis, MN 55423
612-866-1230

parts

See full listing in **Section One** under **Ford '32-'53**

Spark Plugs & Stuff
PO Box 33343
San Diego, CA 92163-3343
619-220-1745

tune-up kits

See full listing in **Section Two** under **ignition parts**

Tech-Art Publications
Jason Houston
Box 753
Ranchero Mirage, CA 92270
619-862-1979

books

See full listing in **Section Four** under **books & publications**

Gary Vorel
318 78th St
Niagara Falls, NY 14304
716-283-9716, 716-286-4996

parts
service

See full listing in **Section One** under **Ford '54-up**

Pat Walsh Restorations
Box Q
Wakefield, MA 01880
617-246-5565

literature
rubber parts

See full listing in **Section Two** under **rubber parts**

Bill Walter's Auto Service
315 Yale Ave
Morton, PA 19070
610-543-0626

service

See full listing in **Section Two** under **service shops**

The Wixom Connection
2204 Steffanie Ct
Kissimmee, FL 34746
407-933-4030

parts

Service by appointment only. References available. Specializing in 1969-71 Continental Mark III. 19 years' experience with Mark III. Limited selection of new & used parts available. Free consultation regarding your Mark III. Located near Walt Disney World.

LOCOMOBILE

Errol's Steam Works
3123 Baird Rd
North Vancouver, BC Canada
V7K 2G5
PH/FAX: 604-985-9494

castings
engines
parts

Mail order and open shop. Hours by appointment. Early steam carriage parts. Castings and finished machined parts, pumps, steam automatics, etc. Dry-Land steam automobile engines, casting kits, machined kits and finished, ready to run engines.

Barlow & Co
7 Maple Ave
Newton, NH 03858
603-382-3591; FAX: 603-382-4406

car dealer
restoration

See full listing in **Section Two** under **restoration shops**

Brammer Parts
Am Korreshof 5
D-40822 Mettmann Germany
02104-15777; FAX: 02104-15325

books
parts
shop manuals

Mail order only. Lotus shop manuals, parts lists, books, old racing magazines with Lotus articles, sports car & Lotus owner's magazine. Publisher of several Lotus reprints. Lotus parts, largest stock of Lotus parts outside the factory. Sunbeam Lotus, Jensen-Healey Lotus parts and many more. Please fax for information.

British Car Care By Pearson's
745 Orange Ave
Winter Park, FL 32789
407-647-0967

car dealer
parts
repairs
restoration

See full listing in **Section One** under **MG**

British Luxury Automotive Parts
257 Niagara St
Toronto, ON Canada M6J 2L7
416-693-8400; FAX: 416-694-3202
Beeper: 416-378-8182

new and used parts

See full listing in **Section One** under **Jaguar**

French Stuff
PO Box 39772
Glendale, CA 90039-0772
818-244-2498
FAX: 818-500-7628

accessories
engine rebuilding
parts
transaxle rebuilding

See full listing in **Section One** under **Renault**

JAE 375 Pine #26 Goleta, CA 93117 805-967-5767; FAX: 805-967-6183	**parts** **service** **tech info**

Mail order and open shop. Monday-Friday 7:30-5; Saturday by appointment. Parts, service and tech info for Lotus, English Ford and English specialist cars (TVR, Elva, Jensen, etc). Features *Unit 26*, a quarterly, information packed newsletter.

Kreimeyer Co 3211 N Wilburn Ave Bethany, OK 73008 405-789-9499; FAX: 405-789-7888	**antennas** **glass/parts** **wholesale** **radio service**

See full listing in **Section One** under **Mercedes-Benz**

Marcovicci-Wenz Engineering Inc 33 Comac Loop Ronkonkoma, NY 11779 516-467-9040; FAX: 516-467-9041	**engine parts** **services**

See full listing in **Section Two** under **racing**

Omni Specialties 10418 Lorain Ave Cleveland, OH 44111 800-791-9562; 216-251-2269 FAX: 216-251-6083	**parts** **restoration** **service**

See full listing in **Section One** under **MG**

Ragtops & Roadsters 203 S 4th St Perkasie, PA 18944 215-257-1202; FAX: 215-257-2688	**race prep** **repairs**

See full listing in **Section One** under **AC**

RD Enterprises Ltd 290 Raub Rd Quakertown, PA 18951 215-538-9323; FAX: 215-538-0158 E-mail: rdent@rdent.com	**parts**

Lotus owners: buy parts from RD Enterprises and you benefit from over 20 years' experience in Lotus cars. Expert assistance in choosing the right parts for your unique Lotus problem. Large inventory of original parts: engine, suspension, drivetrain, electrics, hydraulics, body seals, windscreens, badges; along with aftermarket parts: Spax adjustable shocks, Panasport light alloy wheels, stainless steel exhausts, Magard throttle linkages for Weber/Dell'orto carburetors, accessories, books, models. VISA, MC, AmEx. Same day shipping. Free flyer.

The Registry Pine Grove Stanley, VA 22851 540-778-3728; FAX: 540-778-2402 E-mail: britregstry@aol.com	**periodical**

See full listing in **Section Four** under **periodicals**

Replicarz 99 State St Rutland, VT 05701 802-747-7151 E-mail: replicarz@aol.com	**books** **kits** **models** **videos**

See full listing in **Section Two** under **racing**

Rolls-Royce of Beverly Hills 11401 West Pico Blvd Los Angeles, CA 90064 310-477-4262, 800-321-9792 FAX: 310-473-7498	**parts**

See full listing in **Section One** under **Rolls-Royce/Bentley**

Specialty Car Service Ltd 1330 Ritters Rd Reading, PA 19606 610-370-0410	**parts** **restoration** **service**

See full listing in **Section One** under **Morgan**

Sports & Classics PO Box 1787 512 Boston Post Rd, Dept H Darien, CT 06820-1787 203-655-8731; FAX: 203-656-1896	**interiors** **parts** **tops** **wire wheels**

See full listing in **Section Two** under **body parts**

Meridian Collision Center Inc 15724 E Meridian Puyallup, WA 98373-9510 206-848-2364, 800-523-1123 FAX: 206-840-1254	**restoration**

Specializes in Marmon 16 & Facel Vega. Full restoration and collision restoration of high value cars. We advertise in Hemmings. We are one of the largest restoration and collision shops on the West Coast. We guarantee all work in writing.

Bassett's Jaguar PO Box 245 Wyoming, RI 02898 401-539-3010; FAX: 401-539-7861	**parts** **restoration** **service** **upholstery**

See full listing in **Section One** under **Jaguar**

Caribou Imports Inc 23151-A3 Alcalde Dr Laguna Hills, CA 92653 714-770-3136; FAX: 714-770-0815 E-mail: cariboulh@aol.com	**parts**

See full listing in **Section One** under **Fiat**

Celiberti Motors 615 Oak St Santa Rosa, CA 95404 800-872-3428; FAX: 707-523-1613	**parts**

See full listing in **Section One** under **Fiat**

Drummond Coach and Paint 531 Raleigh Ave El Cajon, CA 92020 619-579-7229; FAX: 619-579-2128	**painting** **restoration**

See full listing in **Section One** under **Ferrari**

Exoticars of Hunterdon 6 Washington St Frenchtown, NJ 08825 908-996-4889; FAX: 908-996-6938	**machine work** **paint & bodywork** **restoration service** **welding/fabrication**

See full listing in **Section One** under **Ferrari**

The Fine Car Store 1105 Moana Dr San Diego, CA 92107 619-223-7766; FAX: 619-223-6838	car dealer

See full listing in **Section One** under **Ferrari**

HK Klassics Hy Kusnetz 16 Hausmann Ct Maplewood, NJ 07040 201-761-6642	appraisals

See full listing in **Section Two** under **appraisals**

International Auto Parts Inc Rt 29 N PO Box 9036 Charlottesville, VA 22906 800-726-0555, 804-973-0555 FAX: 804-973-2368	accessories parts

See full listing in **Section One** under **Alfa Romeo**

The Italian Car Registry 3305 Valley Vista Rd Walnut Creek, CA 94598-3943 510-458-1163	information source

See full listing in **Section Four** under **information sources**

Kreimeyer Co 3211 N Wilburn Ave Bethany, OK 73008 405-789-9499; FAX: 405-789-7888	antennas glass/parts wholesale radio service

See full listing in **Section One** under **Mercedes-Benz**

Langer Auto Museum Rudy Langer 4943 Ward Pkwy Kansas City, MO 64112 PH/FAX: 816-931-1188	vintage cars vintage motorcycles

See full listing in **Section Two** under **car dealers**

London Stainless Steel Exhaust Centre 249-253 Queenstown Rd London, SW8 3NP England 011-44-171622-2120 FAX: 011-44-171627-0991 E-mail:101445.341@compuserv.com	exhaust systems

See full listing in **Section Two** under **exhaust systems**

The McHugh Group 4602 Birch Ct Middletown, MD 21769 301-473-8333; FAX: 301-371-9447	appraisals

See full listing in **Section Two** under **appraisals**

MIE Corporation PO Box 1015 Mercer Island, WA 98040 206-455-4449; FAX: 206-646-5458	parts

Mail order and open shop. Maserati spare parts. $8,000,000 plus in new and used parts, over 30,000 line items in new parts alone. Knowledgeable personnel, computerized for easy ordering.

Motorcar Gallery Inc 715 N Federal Hwy Fort Lauderdale, FL 33304 954-522-9900; FAX: 954-522-9966	car dealer

See full listing in **Section One** under **Ferrari**

The Panel Shop Inc 1785 Barnum Ave Stratford, CT 06497 203-377-6208; FAX: 203-386-0486	Body parts for: **Aston Martin** **Bentley/Rolls-Royce** **Ferrari/Lotus**

See full listing in **Section Two** under **sheetmetal**

Garry Roberts & Co 922 Sunset Dr Costa Mesa, CA 92627 888-FERRAR; FAX: 714-650-2730	cars parts service

See full listing in **Section One** under **Ferrari**

Tillack & Co Ltd 630 Mary Ann Dr Redondo Beach, CA 90278 310-316-8760; FAX: 310-376-3392	parts restoration

See full listing in **Section Two** under **restoration shops**

Vintage Restorations The Old Bakery Windmill Street, Tunbridge Wells Kent TN2 4UU England UK 1892-525899 FAX: UK 1892-525499	accessories instruments

See full listing in **Section Two** under **instruments**

ABS Exotic Repair Inc 1561 N Federal Hwy Ft Lauderdale, FL 33304 954-566-7785; FAX: 954-566-7271	parts service

Open shop only. M-F 8:30 am-7 pm, Sat 8-12. Specialize in Mercedes-Benz, Jaguar and Rolls-Royce, all models, years. Mercedes-Benz and Jaguar service and parts. Classes for Mercedes-Benz and Jaguar owners. *Benz Smart* and *Jag Smart* are held monthly.

Aero Toy Store Gary Anzalone 1710 W Cypress Creek Rd Ft Lauderdale, FL 33309 800-404-2376; FAX: 954-771-3281	acquisitions sales

See full listing in **Section One** under **Ferrari**

ATVM 97 Mt Royal Ave Aberdeen, MD 21001 410-272-2252; FAX: 410-272-4940	literature parts

Mail order only. Mercedes-Benz parts and literature for 1934-1972 models.

Auto Craftsmen Restoration Inc	appraisals
27945 Elm Grove	restoration
San Antonio, TX 78261	
210-980-4027	

See full listing in **Section Two** under **restoration shops**

Auto Enthusiasts	seats
200 Everett Ave	
Chelsea, MA 02150	
617-889-0606; FAX: 617-889-0847	

Mail order and open shop. Monday-Friday 8-5. Manufacturer and distributer of Mercedes-Benz SL rear seats (72-96) and station wagon third seats (79-96).

Bassett's Jaguar	parts
PO Box 245	restoration
Wyoming, RI 02898	service
401-539-3010; FAX: 401-539-7861	upholstery

See full listing in **Section One** under **Jaguar**

BCP Sport & Classic Co	parts
10525 Airline Dr	service
Houston, TX 77037	
713-448-4739; FAX: 713-448-0189	

See full listing in **Section One** under **MG**

JJ Best & Co	financing
737 Main St	
PO Box 10	
Chatham, MA 02633	
508-945-6000; FAX: 508-945-6006	

See full listing in **Section Two** under **consultants**

Beverly Hills Motoring Accessories	accessories
205 S Robertson Blvd	
Beverly Hills, CA 90211	
310-657-4880; FAX: 310-659-4664	
E-mail: bhma@hollywood.cinenet.net	

Mail order and open shop. Monday-Saturday 9 am to 7 pm. Specializing in automotive accessories for Suburbans, Tahoes, Yukons, Mercedes-Benz, Hummers.

Blackhawk Collection	acquisitions
3600 Blackhawk Plaza Cir	sales
Danville, CA 94506-3600	
510-736-3444; FAX: 510-736-4375	

See full listing in **Section One** under **Duesenberg**

Blitzen Enterprises Inc	parts
8341 E Evans Rd, Suite 104	
Scottsdale, AZ 85260	
888-254-8936 toll-free	
FAX: 602-991-6301	

Mail order and open shop. Monday to Friday 8 to 5:30, Saturday 9 to 12. Mercedes-Benz parts for all 1950s on. Specializing in fast moving service items and difficult to find items. Wholesale to the public.

BMC Classics	parts
828 N Dixie Freeway	repair
New Smyrna Beach, FL 32168	restoration
904-426-6405; FAX: 904-427-4570	

See full listing in **Section One** under **Jaguar**

Boulevard Motoring Accessories	parts
7033 Topanga Canyon Blvd	repair
Canoga Park, CA 91303-1961	restoration
818-883-9696; FAX: 818-883-5530	

Mail order and open shop. Monday-Friday 8-6, Saturday 9-5, Sunday 11-4. Specializing in all cars and trucks for accessorizing and modifying. Car covers, floor mats, steering wheels, waxes, spoilers, dash covers, license frames, headlight covers, Recaro seats, tonneau covers, camper shells, sheepskin.

British Restorations	car dealer
4455 Paul St	restoration
Philadelphia, PA 19124	
215-533-6696	

See full listing in **Section One** under **Jaguar**

Brooklyn Motoren Werke Inc	parts
115 Market St	restoration
Brooklyn, WI 53521	service
608-455-7441; FAX: 608-455-7442	

Open shop. Monday-Friday. Restoration, service and parts for post-war Mercedes-Benz. Innovative engineering. Specializing in 300 series.

Bud's Parts for Classic Mercedes-Benz	parts
9130 Hwy 5	restoration
Douglasville, GA 30134	service
800-942-8444; FAX: 770-942-8400	

Mail order and open shop. M-F 8:30-6, Sat 9-2. Parts, service and complete restoration for 1955-1995 SL and sedan Mercedes at discounted prices.

Cabriolet Enterprises	consulting
2115 S Pontius Ave	parts
West Los Angeles, CA 90025	restoration services
310-472-2062; FAX: 310-478-3390	sales

Workshop open by appointment or by mail/FAX order please. Specializing in Mercedes-Benz cabriolets of the 1950s (in order of interest): 220, 300S, 170S and 300. Providing a full range of restoration services, sale of tops, headliners, boots and carpet sets, glass, NOS, used, rebuilt moldings, pot and sheetmetal and mechanical assemblies, luggage, 6/12 volt radios, original and reprinted literature, provenance research, inspections, movie studio rentals and sale of Type 187 original, complete and authentic coupes and cabriolets from my personal forty year collection. Robert H I Silver, proprietor.

CARS (Computer Aided Resale System)	car dealer
2724 Cove View Dr N	
Jacksonville, FL 32257	
904-448-0633; FAX: 904-448-0623	

See full listing in **Section Two** under **car dealers**

Celestial Mechanics	restoration
88 West 500 South	
Wellsville, UT 84339	
801-245-4987	

See full listing in **Section One** under **Volvo**

The Checkered Flag Collection Box 806 Millville, NJ 08332 609-327-1505	car dealer

See full listing in **Section One** under **Ferrari**

Classic Auto Concepts 1366 S Federal Hwy Pompano Beach, FL 33062 954-781-8440; FAX: 954-781-8449	car dealer

See full listing in **Section One** under **Porsche**

Classic Coachworks 735 Frenchtown Rd Milford, NJ 08848 908-996-3400	bodywork painting restoration

See full listing in **Section Two** under **restoration shops**

Dave's Auto Restoration 2285 Rt 307 E Jefferson, OH 44047 PH/FAX: 216-858-2227	upholstery

See full listing in **Section Two** under **interiors & interior parts**

EIS Engines Inc 215 SE Grand Ave Portland, OR 97214 503-232-5590; 800-547-0002 FAX: 503-232-5178	engines

Remanufacturing Mercedes-Benz passenger vehicle engines for both gas & diesel. Early & late models. Basically all types of the Mercedes-Benz engines.

European Connection 313-1/2 Main St Falmouth, KY 41040 800-395-8636; FAX: 606-654-3700	parts

Mail order only. New and used parts. Over 650 wrecked Mercedes for parts. Lots of NOS. UPS and trucking. VISA, MasterCard & Discover accepted.

European Parts Specialists Ltd PO Box 6783 Santa Barbara, CA 93160 805-683-4020; FAX: 805-683-3689	accessories parts

Specializes in parts & accessories for Mercedes, BMW, Porsche, Volvo, Saab, Volkswagen and Audi.

EuroTech Services International 108 Milarepa Rd Azalea, OR 97410 541-837-3636; FAX: 541-837-3737	parts

Mail order only. A German/American firm serving owners of Mercedes-Benz automobiles. Offers direct surface, air and 3 day courier procurement for "Germany-only" parts. Also uniquely specialized in sales, service and parts for exceptional Mercedes-Benz vehicles such as Unimog 4x4 trucks/tractors, off-road motorhomes and mobile workshops and auxiliary machinery in world-respected Unimog multi-implement technologies; 4x4 Gelaendewagen, 4x2 trucks, buses and motorhomes.

Exotic Wood Dash & Restorations 336 Cottonwood Ave Hartland, WI 53029 800-900-3274; FAX: 414-367-9474	restoration parts wood dash overlays

See full listing in **Section One** under **Jaguar**

Foreign Auto Tech Inc 12 Paul Gore St Boston, MA 02130 617-522-7863	race preparation restoration

A full service restoration facility for Mercedes-Benz of the 50s and 60s. Also maintains the most successful vintage racing program for Mercedes 300 SL and 190 SL models. Specializing in restoration and vintage race prep for Mercedes Benz 300 SL, 190 SL, 300 SEL 6.3.

Foreign Motors West 253 N Main St Natick, MA 01760 508-655-5350; FAX: 508-651-0178	car sales

See full listing in **Section One** under **Rolls-Royce/Bentley**

GAHH Inc 8116 Lankershim Blvd North Hollywood, CA 91605 818-767-6242; FAX: 818-767-2786	auto interiors convertible tops

Phone orders and installation shop. Monday-Friday 8 am to 5 pm. Manufacturers of deluxe auto interiors & convertible tops for Mercedes-Benz, Porsche, Jaguar, Rolls-Royce, BMW, Lexus and other exotic cars.

Grand Prix Classics Inc 7456 La Jolla Blvd La Jolla, CA 92037 619-459-3500; FAX: 619-459-3512	racing cars sports cars

See full listing in **Section Two** under **racing**

Griot's Garage 3500-A 20th St E Tacoma, WA 98424 800-345-5789; FAX: 206-922-7500 E-mail: griots@aol.com	car care products paint tools

See full listing in **Section Two** under **tools**

Gullwing Service Co Inc 106 Western Ave Essex, MA 01929 508-768-6919; FAX: 508-768-3523	car dealer mechanical service parts restoration

Shop open Monday-Thursday 8 to 6. Our restoration craftsmen offer mechanical, upholstery, parts, bodywork and paint, panel beating and coachbuilding services on classic Mercedes-Benz and other German cars of the 50s and 60s. Sales, consignment, purchasing of all classic automobiles.

Haz-Benz 174 Rogers St NE Atlanta, GA 30317 404-378-9911	brakes engine overhauls front end repair parts

Mail order and open shop. Monday-Friday 8 to 5 by appointment. Parts and service primarily for 300SL coupes and gullwings, 190SLs, 230s, 250s, 280SLs, 180, 190, 219 and 220 sedans. Post-1969 cars not accepted. Cars must have classic potential, emphasis on engine overhauls, mechanical and Hydrax transmission overhauls, major front end repair and all mechanical and hydraulic systems and brake booster rebuilding.

Hjeltness Restoration Inc 630 Alpine Way Escondido, CA 92029 619-746-9966; FAX: 619-746-7738	restoration service

See full listing in **Section Two** under **restoration shops**

Horst's Car Care 3160-1/2 N Woodford St Decatur, IL 62526 217-876-1112	engine rebuilding

Open shop only. Monday-Friday 8-5, Saturday 8-12. Mercedes-Benz engine rebuilding, 1950s-1990s.

House of Imports Inc 12203 W Colfax Ave Lakewood, CO 80215 303-232-2540; FAX: 303-232-3260	car dealer

Mail order and open shop. Monday-Saturday 9 to 6. Buys and sells used Mercedes-Benz.

International Restoration Specialist Inc PO Box 1303 Mt Airy, NC 27030 910-789-1548	parts restoration sales

See full listing in **Section One** under **Jaguar**

IPTC Automotive 300 SW 12th Ave Pompano Beach, FL 33069 800-277-3806	cars parts

See full listing in **Section One** under **BMW**

Italy's Famous Exhaust 2711 183rd St Redondo Beach, CA 90278 PH/FAX: 310-542-5432 E-mail: http://famous@earthlink.com	exhaust systems wheels

See full listing in **Section Two** under **exhaust systems**

JAM Engineering Corp PO Box 2570 Monterey, CA 93942 408-372-1787; 800-JAM-CORP	carburetors

See full listing in **Section Two** under **carburetors**

Georges B Karakolev 228 Rt 221 Napierville, QC Canada J0J 1L0 PH/FAX: 514-245-0028	car dealer parts restoration

See full listing in **Section Two** under **restoration aids**

King's Bumper Co Inc 1 Ontario Ave New Hartford, NY 13413 315-732-8988; FAX: 315-732-2602	chrome plating

See full listing in **Section Two** under **plating & polishing**

Kreimeyer Co 3211 N Wilburn Ave Bethany, OK 73008 405-789-9499; FAX: 405-789-7888	antennas parts/glass/ wholesale radios/repair

Specializing in auto glass for all vehicles: antique, classic, domestic, exotic and foreign at wholesale prices. Windshields and back glass for most models. Custom made glass and custom cutting available. Sales and repairs for Becker/Blaupunkt radios and Hirschmann antennas for BMW, Mercedes, Porsche, Ferrari, Lamborghini, etc. Specializing in new Mercedes parts, 1950-1995 at wholesale prices. Specializing in 190SL and 300SL parts. Engine, fuel system and transmission service available. Custom reproduction 300SLR and 300SL gullwing bodies.

LA Machine 5960 Valentine Rd #9 Ventura, CA 93003 805-650-6644; FAX: 805-650-6633	convertible kits

See full listing in **Section One** under **Porsche**

Langer Auto Museum Rudy Langer 4943 Ward Pkwy Kansas City, MO 64112 PH/FAX: 816-931-1188	vintage cars vintage motorcycles

See full listing in **Section Two** under **car dealers**

Leatherique Leather Restoration Products PO Box 2678 Orange Park, FL 32065 904-272-0992; FAX: 904-272-1534	leather cleaning conditioning products

See full listing in **Section One** under **Rolls-Royce/Bentley**

Lyco Engineering Inc 8645 N Territorial Rd Plymouth, MI 48170 313-459-7313; FAX: 313-459-2224	machine work parts

Mail order and open shop. Monday-Saturday 9 to 6. 30 years' experience with Mercedes-Benz 300SL cars, 1954-1964. Complete machine shop. Genuine and reproduction parts in stock. Engine, transmission, running gear, trim, tools, weather-strips/seals, glass, all brake parts, wheels chromed. Many remanufactured parts on exchange basis. Also extensive inventory of parts for 1952-1962 300 Series coupes and sedans (formerly supplied by Chuck Brahms).

Machina Locksmith 3 Porter St Watertown, MA 02172-4145 PH/FAX: 617-923-1683	car locks keys

See full listing in **Section Two** under **locks & keys**

McAdam Motorcars Ltd 215 Redoubt Rd Yorktown, VA 23692 757-898-7805; FAX: 757-898-9019	restoration

See full listing in **Section Two** under **restoration shops**

Mercedes Used Parts Bob Fatone 166 W Main St Niantic, CT 06357 860-739-1923; FAX: 860-691-0669	parts

Mail order and shop open by appointment only. Specializing in most all used replacement parts, engine, body, chrome, interior, etc, for Mercedes highline chassis #111 coupe & convertible Models 220SE, 250SE, 280SE and some 4-door cars for years 1960 thru 1971. 95% of orders are by mail.

Michael's Auto Parts 5875 NW Kaiser Rd Portland, OR 97229 503-690-7750; FAX: 503-690-7735	salvage yard

See full listing in **Section Five** under **Oregon**

Mid-Jersey Motorama Inc 1301 Asbury Ave, PO Box 1395 Asbury Park, NJ 07712 908-775-9885 Beeper: 908-840-6111 FAX: 908-775-9885	car dealer

See full listing in **Section One** under **Cadillac/LaSalle**

Midwestern Motors & Dismantlers 19785 W 12 Mi, Bldg 404 Southfield, MI 48076 810-559-8848	salvage yard

Mail order and open shop. Specializing in Mercedes-Benz.

Miller's Incorporated 7412 Count Cir Huntington Beach, CA 92647 714-375-6565; FAX: 714-847-6606 800-538-4222 order toll-free	parts

Mail order and open shop. Shop open Monday-Friday 8 am to 6 pm. Specializing in new parts for classic Mercedes-Benz with a major emphasis on SLs and the model years 1955 to 1980. We also stock routine maintenance parts for the 1980s models.

James J Montague West Rupert, VT 05776 802-394-2929	parts service

Mail order and open shop. Open by appointment only. Specializing in pre-1978 Mercedes-Benz gas and diesel cars. Selected pre-1968 foreign sports and exotic cars and pre-WW II US vehicles. Over 20 years' M-B repair & consultation.

Motorcars Ltd 8101 Hempstead Houston, TX 77008 713-863-9388; FAX: 713-863-8238 E-mail: mcltd@phoenix.net	parts

See full listing in **Section One** under **Jaguar**

Northern Motorsport Ltd PO Box 508, Rt 5 Wilder, VT 05088 802-296-2099; FAX: 802-295-6599	repair restoration sales service

See full listing in **Section Two** under **restoration shops**

Northwest Transmission Parts 13500 US 62 Winchester, OH 45697 800-327-1955 order line 513-442-2811 info FAX: 513-442-6555	transmission parts

See full listing in **Section Two** under **transmissions**

The Old Carb Doctor Rt 3, Box 338, Drucilla Church Rd Nebo, NC 28761 800-945-CARB (2272) 704-659-1428	carburetors fuel pumps

See full listing in **Section Two** under **carburetors**

Ottorich 619 Hammond St Chestnut Hill, MA 02167 617-738-5488	restoration

Open shop only. Monday to Friday 7:30 am to 5 pm. Performs complete restoration of Mercedes-Benz & BMW while also providing everyday technicals for these fine motor cars, both new & old.

Palo Alto Speedometer Inc 718 Emerson St Palo Alto, CA 94301 415-323-0243; FAX: 415-323-4632	instruments

Mail order and open shop. Monday through Friday 8 am to 5 pm. Instrument, gauge, clock repair, service and restoration of all makes and models.

Peninsula Imports 3749 Harlem Rd Buffalo, NY 14215 800-263-4538; FAX: 905-847-3021	accessories parts trim

See full listing in **Section One** under **BMW**

Performance Analysis Co 1345 Oak Ridge Turnpike, Suite 258 Oak Ridge, TN 37830 423-482-9175 E-mail: 7662.2133@compuserve.com	climate control cruise control

Mail order only. Specializing in climate control, cruise control, electronic modules and specialty parts for Mercedes-Benz automobiles.

Potomac, The Mercedes Experts 4305 Lime Kiln Rd Frederick, MD 21703 301-831-1111; FAX: 301-874-2450 E-mail: parts@erols.com	car dealer new parts used parts

Mail order. Monday-Friday 9 to 5. Closed from 12 to 1. Potomac sells only Mercedes-Benz parts. Over 2,000 dismantled 1950s to 1990s Mercedes. Emphasis is now on late models, but has a large stock of older cars. Specializing in: 1962-73 300SE, 300SEL, coupes, convertibles and sedans; 1962-72 W113 SL models: 230SL, 250SL, 280SL; 1972-88, W107 SLs: 280SL, 350SL, 450SL, SLC, 500SL, 380SL, 560SL and all other newer models. Car sales of classic restorable cars and late model rebuildable wrecks. Self service car owners, "pull your own parts" club. Full line of parts available at our factory outlet store.

John T Poulin Auto Sales/ **Star Service Center** 5th Ave & 111th St North Troy, NY 12182 518-235-8610	car dealer parts restoration service

Mail order and open shop. Monday-Saturday 9 am to 6 pm. Specializing in sales of Mercedes-Benz and has a repair shop for all service and restoration of Mercedes with many used and new parts. Been in business of Mercedes-Benz for 45 years (complete car care). 1950s-1990s Mercedes and BMW used cars.

Precious Metal Automotive **Restoration Co Inc** 1601 College Ave SE Grand Rapids, MI 49507 616-243-0220; FAX: 616-243-6646	broker restoration

Full service 6,500 square foot restoration shop devoted to 1950s and 1960s collectible Mercedes-Benz cars. More than 70 190SL restorations, plus 220, 220S/SE coupes and cabriolets, 230/250/280SL, 300 Series, etc. Cars bought, sold and brokered. Import/export experience. Very affordable rates, convenient midwest location. We subsidize your transport cost.

Precision Autoworks 2202 Federal Street E Camden, NJ 08105 609-966-0080, NJ FAX: 610-649-3577, PA	restorations

Full or partial cosmetic and/or mechanical restorations for Mercedes-Benz, all models after WW II, both for show or drive.

Proper Motor Cars Inc 1811 11th Ave N St. Petersburg, FL 33713-5794 813-821-8883; FAX: 813-895-4746	parts restoration

See full listing in **Section One** under **Rolls-Royce/Bentley**

RAU Restoration
2027 Pontius Ave
Los Angeles, CA 90025
PH/FAX: 310-445-1128

woodwork

See full listing in **Section Two** under **woodwork**

Regal International Motor Cars Inc
PO Box 6819
Hollywood, FL 33081
305-989-9777; FAX: 305-989-9778

car dealer

See full listing in **Section One** under **Rolls-Royce/Bentley**

Restoration Services
16049 W 4th Ave
Golden, CO 80401
303-271-0356

restoration

See full listing in **Section One** under **Porsche**

RM Auto Restoration Ltd
825 Park Ave W
Chatham, ON Canada N7M 5J6
519-352-4575; FAX: 519-351-1337

panel fabrication
parts
restoration

See full listing in **Section Two** under **restoration shops**

Ron's Restorations Inc
2968-B Ask Kay Dr
Smyrna, GA 30082
770-438-6102; FAX: 770-438-0037

interior trim
restoration

Specializing in interior trim replacement & repair & total restorations for all Mercedes-Benz automobiles.

Paul Russell & Company
106 Western Ave
Essex, MA 01929
508-768-6919; FAX: 508-768-3523

car dealer
coachbuilding
parts
restoration

See full listing in **Section Two** under **restoration shops**

Save-A-Star-Mike
55 Cliveden Ct
Lawrenceville, NJ 08648
609-987-8060; FAX: 609-987-1728

parts
salvage yard
service

Mail order and open shop. Mon-Fri. Specializing in Mercedes-Benz parts & service for dismantled parts for 1950s thru 1970s, new & rebuilt parts for all Mercedes.

Showroom Auto Sales
960 S Bascom Ave
San Jose, CA 95128
408-554-1550; FAX: 408-554-0550

car dealer

Open shop. Monday-Friday 10 am to 6 pm. Specializing in 1971 and older classic Mercede-Benz and older. Also more recent Porsche and Cadillac Allante vehicles.

Silver Star Restorations
116 Highway 19
Topton, NC 28781
704-321-4268; FAX: 704-321-6008

parts
restoration

Mail order and open shop. Monday-Friday 8 am to 5 pm. Restoration of, parts sales for Mercedes-Benz III chassis coupes and convertibles (220SE, 250SE, 280SE, 300SE coupes and convertibles).

**Southampton Auto &
Marine Upholstery**
471 N Hwy
Southampton, NY 11968
516-283-2616; FAX: 516-283-2617

carpets
interiors
tops

Shop open Monday-Friday 8 to 5; Saturday 9 to 2. Convertible tops, vinyl tops, custom convertibles, carpeting and complete interiors for antique and classic cars. Specializing in Mercedes. Thirty-five years' experience.

Sports Leicht Restorations
16 Maple Street
Topsfield, MA 01983
508-887-1900; FAX: 508-887-3889

restoration
sales
service

Restoration and service and sales. Specializing in Mercedes especially 190SL. Contact Alex Dearborn.

The Stable LTD
217 Main St
Gladstone, NJ 07934
908-234-2055; FAX: 908-781-2599

sales
service

See full listing in **Section One** under **Jaguar**

Star Classics Inc
7745 E Redfield #300
Scottsdale, AZ 85260
602-991-7495, 800-644-7827
FAX: 602-951-4096

parts
sales
service

Mail order and open shop. Monday-Friday 8-5. Parts, sales & service for Mercedes-Benz of the 50s. All the collectible models. Hood stars to tailpipe tip. anything made of rubber, chrome, etc. All lenses and trim items. Leather in all the original colors. Component restoration and exchange service available for same day shipping. All engine rebuild parts in stock for these models. Discount plan available. All credit cards accepted. Postwar to 1963. 170 sedan to the gullwing and the 300S/SC. Same day world wide shipping.

Star Quality
1 Alley Rd
La Grangeville, NY 12540
800-782-7199; FAX: 914-266-5394
E-mail: sq@mhv.net

parts

Mail order and open shop. Monday-Friday 8:30-5:30. Specializing in parts for Mercedes-Benz 190SL, 230/250/280SL, 350/450/380/560SL, 1955-1979.

Steve's Auto Restorations
4440 SE 174th Ave
Portland, OR 97236
503-665-2222; FAX: 503-665-2225

restoration

See full listing in **Section Two** under **restoration shops**

Stoddard Imported Cars Inc
38845 Mentor Ave
Willoughby, OH 44094-0908
216-951-1040 Ohio & overseas
800-342-1414; FAX: 216-946-9410
E-mail: sicars@ix.netcom.com

parts

See full listing in **One** under **Porsche**

Tri-Star Pete
1998-1/2 E 1st
Tempe, AZ 85281
602-829-7826; FAX: 602-968-6935

parts

Mail order and open shop. Monday-Friday 8-5. Specializing in 1950-1990 Mercedes used parts. Mercedes recycling with 500 cars to sell parts from.

United German Imports | brake parts
4556 Shetland Green | brakes
Alexandria, VA 22312
800-98-BRAKE; FAX: 703-916-1610
E-mail: ugibrakes2@aol.com

See full listing in **Section Two** under **brakes**

Van Nuys Motors | parts
14422 Oxnard St | restoration
Van Nuys, CA 91403 | sales
818-988-5455 | service

Mail order and open shop. Monday-Saturday 7 am to 6 pm. Specializing in Mercedes-Benz 50s, 60s, 70s parts, sales, service, restoration.

Vantage Auto Interiors | upholstery
11 Fahey St
Stamford, CT 06907
203-425-9533; FAX: 203-425-9535

See full listing in **Section Two** under **interiors & interior parts**

WTH-VMC (formerly Vintage Mercedes Cars Inc) | emblems
921 Sleeping Indian Rd | lenses
San Luis Rey, CA 92068 | manuals
800-WTH-5771 orders only | weatherstrips
619-941-8192, 9 to 4 PST
FAX: 619-941-6033
E-mail: wthvmc@fia.net

Mail order and shop open by appointment only. Specializes in 380, 500K, 540K, 770K, early 170, 220, 300, others through 1962. Sells lights, lenses, trumpet horns, new rubber, weatherstrip, brake cylinders and kits, exhaust covers, emblems, motor mounts, wiring harnesses, metric screws, wiper blades and motors, manuals. Send $5 for catalog. VISA/MasterCard accepted. Orders only: 800-WTH-5771.
Web site: http://home.fia.net/~wthvmc

Mercer Automobile Company | parts
210 Davis Rd | service
Magnolia, NJ 08049
609-784-4044

Shop open Monday-Friday 8 to 4:30. Parts and service for 1910-1922 Mercer automobiles.

AKH Wheels | Rallye wheels
1207 N A St | styled steel wheels
Ellensburg, WA 98926-2522 | vintage aluminum
509-962-3390

See full listing in **Section Two** under **wheels & wheelcovers**

AMK Products | parts
18600 E 96th St
Broken Arrow, OK 74012
918-455-2651; FAX: 918-455-7441

See full listing in **Section One** under **Mustang**

Antique Auto Electric | repro wiring
9109 (rear) E Garvey Ave
Rosemead, CA 91770
818-572-0938

See full listing in **Section Two** under **electrical systems**

Auto Krafters Inc | parts
PO Box 8
522 S Main St
Broadway, VA 22815
703-896-5910; FAX: 703-896-6412

See full listing in **Section One** under **Ford '54-up**

Autowire Division | alternator
9109 (Rear) E Garvey Avenue | conversions
Rosemead, CA 91770 | motors/relays
818-572-0938; FAX: 818-288-3311 | switches

See full listing in **Section One** under **Ford '54-up**

Bob Burgess 1955-56 Ford Parts Inc | parts
793 Alpha-Bellbrook Rd
Bellbrook, OH 45305
513-426-8041

See full listing in **Section One** under **Ford '54-up**

Dennis Carpenter Ford Reproductions | parts
PO Box 26398
Charlotte, NC 28221
704-786-8139; FAX: 704-786-8180

See full listing in **Section One** under **Ford '54-up**

Class-Tech Corp | wiring harnesses
62935 Layton Ave
Bend, OR 97701
800-874-9981

See full listing in **Section Two** under **electrical systems**

Classic Car Research | appraisals
29508 Southfield Rd | car locating
Southfield, MI 48076 | consultant
810-557-2880; FAX: 810-557-3511

See full listing in **Section Two** under **appraisals**

Classic Ford Sales | salvage yard
PO Box 60
E Dixfield, ME 04227
207-562-4443; FAX: 207-562-4576
E-mail: info@classicford.com

See full listing in **Section Five** under **Maine**

Classic Mercury Parts | parts
1393 Shippee Ln
Ojai, CA 93023
PH/FAX: 805-646-3345

Mail order only. Specializing in new, used, reproduction parts. Emblems, lenses, trunk liners, rubber parts, literature, manuals, stainless and chrome trim for 1949-1956 Mercury.

Bob Cook Classic Auto Parts Inc 2055 Van Cleave Rd, PO Box 600 Murray, KY 42071-0600 502-753-4000, 800-486-1137 FAX: 502-753-4600	**new parts** **NOS parts** **reproduced parts**

See full listing in **Section One** under **Ford '54-up**

Tony Copeland Ford Lincoln Mercury 1617 21st St Lewiston, ID 83501 800-821-8174; FAX: 208-746-1543 E-mail: copeland@copelandford.com	**parts** **sales** **service**

See full listing in **Section One** under **Ford '54-up**

Walt Dantzler 1567 Bertrand Dr Lafayette, LA 70560 318-234-1344, leave message FAX: 318-233-4113	**parts**

See full listing in **Section One** under **Ford '54-up**

Mike Dennis, Nebraska Mail Order 1845 S 48th St Lincoln, NE 68506 402-489-3036; FAX: 402-489-1148	**parts** **Trippe mounting** **brackets/hardware**

See full listing in **Section One** under **Ford '32-'53**

Engineering & Manufacturing Services Box 24362 Cleveland, OH 44124-0362 216-446-1620; FAX: 216-446-9590	**sheetmetal**

See full listing in **Section One** under **Ford '32-'53**

Gus R Garton 401 N 5th St Millville, NJ 08332 609-825-3618 evenings	**bicycles** **NOS parts** **sales literature**

See full listing in **Section One** under **Ford '32-'53**

Randy Goodling 2046 Mill Rd Elizabethtown, PA 17022-9401 717-367-6700	**parts** **parts locating**

Mail order and open shop. Shop open by appointment only. Specializing in parts and information on 1967-1973 Mercury Cougars.

Green Valentine Inc 5055 Covington Way Memphis, TN 38134 901-373-5555; FAX: 901-373-5568	**car dealer** **woodies**

See full listing in **Section Two** under **car dealers**

Highway Classics 949 N Cataract Ave, Unit J San Dimas, CA 91702 909-592-8819; FAX: 909-592-4239	**parts**

See full listing in **Section One** under **Ford '54-up**

Bill Horton 5804 Jones Valley Dr Huntsville, AL 35802 205-881-6894	**vacuum motors**

Mail order only. Rebuilder of headlight vacuum motors for 67-70 Mercury Cougar, 67-71 Thunderbird, 69-76 Lincoln, Lincoln Mk

III/IV and 70 Ford Torino. Mail order sales of 67-68 Cougar body parts including rechromed bumpers and restored grilles/taillight assemblies.

Hot Rod & Custom Supply 1304 SE 10th St Cape Coral, FL 33990 941-574-7744; FAX: 941-574-8820	**custom parts** **engine parts** **speed parts**

See full listing in **Section One** under **Ford '32-'53**

Joe's Auto Sales 5849-190th St E Hastings, MN 55033 612-437-6787	**parts**

See full listing in **Section One** under **Ford '54-up**

John's Classic Cougars 11522 E Lakewood Blvd Holland, MI 49424 616-396-0390; FAX: 616-396-0366	**accessories** **parts**

Mail order and open shop. Monday-Friday 9 to 5; Saturday by appointment. Specializing in new, good used and reproduction parts and accessories for 1967-73 Mercury Cougars only. Complete Cougar catalog available for $4. "Cougars are our only business...not a sideline!"

Kenroy Ford Parts 2 Folwell Ln Mullica Hill, NJ 08062 609-848-4965; FAX: 609-468-2489	**NOS parts**

See full listing in **Section One** under **Ford '54-up**

Ken's Cougars PO Box 5380 Edmond, OK 73013 405-340-1636; FAX: 405-340-5877	**parts**

Mail order and open shop. Monday-Friday 9-5 CST. Specializing in 1967-73 Mercury Cougar NOS, used and reproduction parts.

Lincoln Parts International 707 E 4th St, Bldg G Perris, CA 92570 800-382-1656; 909-657-5588 FAX: 909-657-4758	**parts**

See full listing in **Section One** under **Lincoln**

Ed Liukkonen 37 Cook Rd Templeton, MA 01468 508-939-8126	**accessories** **parts**

See full listing in **Section One** under **Ford '54-up**

Maffucci Sales Company Inc RD 1 Box 60, Rt 9 W Athens, NY 12015 518-943-0100; FAX: 518-943-4534	**literature** **parts**

See full listing in **Section One** under **Lincoln**

Mainly Convertibles 13805 W Hillsborough Ave Tampa, FL 33635 813-855-6869; FAX: 813-855-1376	**parts** **repair** **restoration**

See full listing in **Section One** under **Lincoln**

Mark's 1941-1948 Ford Parts | **parts**
97 Hoodlum Hill Rd
Binghamton, NY 13905
607-729-1693

See full listing in **Section One** under **Ford '32-'53**

Mercury & Ford Molded Rubber | **parts**
12 Plymouth Ave
Wilmington, MA 01887
508-658-8394

Mail order and open shop. Specialize in Mercury rubber parts. Sell 39-56 Mercury & Ford molded rubber parts. Also some 39-48 Mercury used parts and 39-41 reproduced metal parts. Can also supply Ford & Ford pickup rubber parts, many years.

Mercury Research Co | **new parts**
639 Glanker St | **shop manuals**
Memphis, TN 38112
PH/FAX: 901-323-2195, recorder

Mail order only. New parts for 1949-1959 Mercury cars. Largest selection of Mercury parts. 65 page catalog, $4. In business over 20 years. VISA, MasterCard, personal checks accepted.

Mercury Restorations | **NOS**
Larry Adams | **restoration**
40 Sunset Ridge | **used parts**
Clyde, NC 28721
PH/FAX: 704-452-2049

Mail order only. Restores 1941-48 Mercury dash plastic. Specializing in 1941-1948 Mercury and Ford and 1964-1965 Mercury Comet parts and restorations. Buys and sells 1941-48 & 1955-56 Mercury used parts and 1964-1965 Ranchero. Steering wheel restoration, Mercury and Ford. No new parts or catalog.

Miller Obsolete Parts | **parts**
1329 Campus Dr
Vestal, NY 13850
607-722-5371; FAX: 607-729-7645
E-mail: fordpart@spectra.net

See full listing in **Section One** under **Ford '32-'53**

Monument Motors Inc | **repair**
PO Box 711 | **restoration**
Great Barrington, MA 01230 | **used parts**
413-637-1017

See full listing in **Section One** under **Mustang**

C W Moss Ford Parts Inc | **NOS parts**
402 W Chapman Ave | **used parts**
Orange, CA 92666
714-639-3083, Orange; 909-629-5223, Pomona; FAX: 714-639-0329

See full listing in **Section One** under **Ford '03-'31**

Northeast Ford | **parts**
Box 66 | **restoration**
Rt 9
E Sullivan, NH 03445
603-847-9956, 800-562-FORD
FAX: 603-847-9691

See full listing in **Section One** under **Ford '54-up**

Northwest Classic Falcons Inc | **parts**
1964 NW Pettygrove St
Portland, OR 97209
503-241-9454; FAX: 503-241-1964

See full listing in **Section One** under **Ford '54-up**

NOS Only | **NOS parts**
414 Umbarger Rd, Unit E
San Jose, CA 95111
408-227-2353, 408-227-2354
FAX: 408-227-2355

See full listing in **Section Two** under **comprehensive parts**

Obsolete Ford Parts Co | **parts**
PO Box 787
Nashville, GA 31639
912-686-2470, 912-686-5101
FAX: 912-686-7125

See full listing in **Section One** under **Ford '54-up**

Old Dominion Mustang | **parts**
509 S Washington Hwy, Rt 1
Ashland, VA 23005
804-798-3348; FAX: 804-798-5105

See full listing in **Section One** under **Mustang**

Original Falcon, Comet, Ranchero, | **interiors**
Fairlane Interiors | **weatherstripping**
6343 Seaview Ave NW
Seattle, WA 98107-2664
206-781-5230; FAX: 206-781-5046
E-mail: falcons@ix.netcom.com

See full listing in **Section One** under **Ford '54-up**

Patrick's Antique Cars & Trucks | **parts**
PO Box 10648 | **speed equipment**
Casa Grande, AZ 85230
520-836-1117; FAX: 520-836-1104

See full listing in **Section One** under **Chevrolet**

Greg Purdy's Mustang Supply | **parts**
PO Box 784
Forest Hill, MD 21050
410-836-5991

See full listing in **Section One** under **Mustang**

Rapido Group | **accessories**
15930 SW 72nd Ave | **parts**
Portland, OR 97224
503-620-8400

Mail order and open shop. Monday-Thursday 8 am-5 pm, Friday 8 am-noon. Specializing in parts and accessories for Merkur XR4Ti, Merkur Scorpio, Mustang SVO, Turbo T-Bird and Turbo Cougar, all years and models.

Rock Valley Antique Auto Parts | **gas tanks**
Box 352
Rt 72 and Rothwell Rd
Stillman Valley, IL 61084
815-645-2271; FAX: 815-645-2740

See full listing in **Section One** under **Ford '32-'53**

Rocky Mountain V8 Ford Parts | **parts**
1124 Clark Cir
Colorado Springs, CO 80915
719-597-8375

See full listing in **Section One** under **Ford '32-'53**

Rowland's Antique Auto Parts
PO Box 387
Zillah, WA 98953
509-829-5026

cars
parts

See full listing in **Section One** under **Lincoln**

Sam's Vintage Ford Parts
5105 Washington
Denver, CO 80216
303-295-1709

parts

See full listing in **Section One** under **Ford '54-up**

Southside Obsolete
6819 James Ave S
Minneapolis, MN 55423
612-866-1230

parts

See full listing in **Section One** under **Ford '32-'53**

Special T's Unlimited Corp
PO Box 146
Prospect Heights, IL 60070
847-255-5494; FAX: 847-391-7082

general repair
parts
restoration
service

See full listing in **Section One** under **Ford '03-'31**

Pat Walsh Restorations
Box Q
Wakefield, MA 01880
617-246-5565

literature
rubber parts

See full listing in **Section Two** under **rubber parts**

Gene Winfield's Rod & Custom
7256 Eton Ave
Canoga Park, CA 91303
818-883-2611

fender skirts
metal repair panels
motor mount kits

We deal in fiberglass bodies for 41-48 Ford & 50-51 Mercury coupes or convertibles. Auto accessories: Mercury new and used stock parts, motor mount kits, fender skirts, metal repair panels, Winfield hat pins, T-shirts and posters, 8x10 black and white picture of old Winfield custom cars, drop sandals. Send $5 for new catalog (postage incl). We ship COD or VISA & MC.

Pete Groh
9957 Frederick Rd
Ellicott City, MD 21042-3647
410-750-2352

original British
keys
Wilmot Breeden

See full listing in **Section One** under **Jaguar**

Kip Motor Company Inc
13325 Denton Dr
Dallas, TX 75234
972-243-0440; FAX: 972-243-2387
E-mail: kipmotor@aol.com

literature
parts
restoration

See full listing in **Section One** under **Austin**

Metro Motors
Dale Cheney
1070 E Roland St
Carson City, NV 89701
702-883-7308

parts

Specializing in parts for Metropolitans. New, used and reconditioned. List available.

Metropolitan & British Triumph
9957 Frederick Rd
Ellicott City, MD 21042-3647
410-750-2352 evenings

NOS British parts
NOS British keys
Lucas & Girling
catalogs

Mail order only. Buys and sells NOS British parts. Keys cut by code, $5 single, $8 double sided cut, year, make of car. SASE with inquiry. Carlisle import flea market. Specializing in all British cars, Triumph, Metropolitan, MG, Jaguar, Morris, etc. British keys, FA, FP, FS (letter and number on side of key), $15.00 each.

Metropolitan Pit Stop
5324-26-28-30 Laurel Canyon Blvd
North Hollywood, CA 91607
800-PIT-STOP order toll-free
818-769-1515; FAX: 818-769-3500

literature
parts
restoration

Mail order and open shop with everything in Metropolitan parts. Monday-Friday 10 to 6. Repair shop for 22 years. Devoted exclusively to preservation, restoration and repair of Metropolitans. Will buy Metropolitan parts; and Metropolitan literature/memorabilia for permanent Metropolitan Historical Collection exhibition. Parts catalog free.

Treasure Chest Sales
413 Montgomery
Jackson, MI 49202
517-787-1475

parts

See full listing in **Section One** under **Nash**

Harold Wenner
5449 Tannery Rd
Schnecksville, PA 18078
610-799-5419

accessories
parts

See full listing in **Section One** under **AMC**

Wymer Classic AMC
Mark Wymer
340 N Justice St
Fremont, OH 43420
419-332-4291, 8 to 5 pm
419-334-6945 after 5 pm

NOS parts
repairs
used parts

See full listing in **Section One** under **AMC**

Abingdon Spares Ltd
PO Box 37
South St
Walpole, NH 03608
603-756-4768; FAX: 603-756-9614
800-225-0251 orders

parts

Mail order and open shop. Monday-Friday 9 to 5; Saturday 9 to 12 noon. Selling MGT series parts (TC, TD, TF models) only.

American-Foreign Auto Electric Inc — parts rebuilding
103 Main St
Souderton, PA 18964
215-723-4877

See full listing in **Section Two** under **electrical systems**

Antique & Classic Car Restoration — restoration
Hwy 107, Box 368
Magdalena, NM 87825

See full listing in **Section Two** under **restoration shops**

Automotive Artistry — restoration
679 W Streetboro St
Hudson, OH 44236
216-650-1503

See full listing in **Section One** under **Triumph**

Barlow & Co — car dealer restoration
7 Maple Ave
Newton, NH 03858
603-382-3591; FAX: 603-382-4406

See full listing in **Section Two** under **restoration shops**

BCP Sport & Classic Co — parts service
10525 Airline Dr
Houston, TX 77037
713-448-4739; FAX: 713-448-0189

Mail order and open shop. Specializing in British and German parts and service for MG, Triumph, Jaguar, BMW, Mercedes-Benz, Volvo, Porsche, Maserati from 1950 to 1996.

Bonnets Up — restoration
5736 Spring St
Clinton, MD 20735
301-297-4759

See full listing in **Section Two** under **coachbuilders & designers**

Boston MG Shop — MG specialist
40R Griggs St
Allston, MA 02134
617-731-2348

Open shop only. Weekdays 9 to 5. Specializing in MG TC, TD, TF, MGA.

Brit-Tek Ltd — MGB cars rustproofing systems
12 Parmenter Rd
Londonderry, NH 03053
800-255-5883

MGB performance & restoration parts & accessories. Free catalog. Distributor of Waxoyl rustproofing systems.

BritBooks — books
62 Main St
Otego, NY 13825
PH/FAX: 607-988-7956

See full listing in **Section Four** under **books & publications**

British Auto Parts Ltd — parts
93256 Holland Ln
Marcola, OR 97454
541-933-2880; FAX: 541-933-2302

See full listing in **Section One** under **Morris**

British Auto Shoppe Inc — parts service
1115 1st Ave
Silvis, IL 61282
309-796-2748; FAX: 309-796-2033

Mail order and open shop. Monday-Friday 8:30 am-5:30 pm, Saturday by appointment. Parts (new and used) and service for British cars. Engine rebuild, mechanical restoration and carb rebuilding for MG, Triumph, Austin-Healey, Jaguar, Mini, Morris & Austin.

British Car Care By Pearson's — car dealer parts repairs restoration
745 Orange Ave
Winter Park, FL 32789
407-647-0967

Open shop only. Monday-Friday 8 to 5. Repairs, restores, buys & sells British sports cars. Specializing in, but not limited to MGs. Large supply of new and used parts. Same owner and location for over 20 years.

British Car Magazine — periodical
PO Box 1683
Los Altos, CA 94023-1683
415-949-9680; FAX: 415-949-9685
E-mail: britcarmag@aol.com

See full listing in **Section Four** under **periodicals**

British Car Specialists — parts repairs restoration
2060 N Wilson Way
Stockton, CA 95205
209-948-8767; FAX: 209-948-1030
E-mail: healeydoc@aol.com

See full listing in **Section One** under **Austin-Healey**

British Miles — accessories literature parts restoration
9278 Old E Tyburn Rd
Morrisville, PA 19067
215-736-9300; FAX: 215-736-3089

Mail order and open shop. Open Monday-Friday 9 am to 6 pm. Specializing in new and used parts, restorations, repairs and bench rebuilding services for British sports cars, MG, Triumph, Austin-Healey and Jaguar. We also carry tech and workshop manuals, books and accessories. Deals in windshield wiper and lamp parts for kit cars.

See our ad on page 142

British Restorations — car dealer restoration
4455 Paul St
Philadelphia, PA 19124
215-533-6696

See full listing in **Section One** under **Jaguar**

British T Shop Inc — car dealer parts service
165 Rt 82
Oakdale, CT 06370
860-889-0178; FAX: 860-889-6096

Mail order and open shop. Open Monday, Tuesday, Thursday and Friday 8 to 5 pm; Wednesday 8 to noon and Saturday 9 to noon. For MG, Triumph, TVR featuring sales, service and parts. In addition to the British car line, we are authorized dealers for Belarus and Kioti tractors and equipped for sales, service and parts including all farm implements.

British Wiring Inc — wiring accessories wiring harnesses
20449 Ithaca Rd
Olympia Fields, IL 60461
PH/FAX: 708-481-9050

See full listing in **Section Two** under **electrical systems**

BritParts Midwest
603 Monroe St
LaPorte, IN 46350
219-324-5474
FAX: 219-324-7541

parts
restoration
service

See full listing in **Section One** under **Austin-Healey**

Brooklands Inc
503 Corporate Square
1500 NW 62nd St
Fort Lauderdale, FL 33309
954-776-2748
FAX: 954-772-8383
E-mail: rbiggs@lgc.net

accessories

See full listing in **Section Two** under **accessories**

Brooklands/MG Only
8235/8237 S Tacoma Way
Tacoma, WA 98499
206-584-2033

body shop
parts
restoration
service

Mail order and open shop. Monday-Friday 10 am to 6 pm. Full service facility for British cars. Parts, service, full or partial restorations, machine shop services. MGB, MGC specialists. Enthusiasts since 1969.

California Wire Wheel
6922 Turnbridge Way
San Diego, CA 92119
619-698-8255
FAX: 619-589-9032

rechroming
tires
tubes
wheels

See full listing in **Section Two** under **wheels & wheelcovers**

British Miles

9278 EAST TYBURN ROAD
MORRISVILLE, PA 19067
PH: 215-736-9300 • FAX 215-736-3089
VISA /MC

MG • TRIUMPH • A-H • JAGUAR

- • Extensive Inventory - New & Used Parts
- • Huge N.O.S. and Lucas Inventory
- • Performance and Restoration Items
- • Workshop and Parts Manuals
- • Over 200 MG's and Triumphs Dismantled
- • Knowledgeable Sales Staff with Hands on Experience
- • Hardcover MGB Parts Guide Available $5.00

Services Offered
- • *Restoration and Repairs on All British Cars*
- • *Component Rebuilding*
- • *Frame and Unitized Body Restructuring*
- • *Welding • Body Work*
- • *Expert Electrical and Mechanical Repairs*
- • *Interior and Upholstery Services*

COME SEE US AT OUR BOOTH
Spring & Fall Carlisle Spaces Nos. F102-105
Hershey Fall   WA-54-56

1-800-WE FIX MG *(for orders only)*
http://www.britishmiles.com

CARS (Computer Aided Resale System)
2724 Cove View Dr N
Jacksonville, FL 32257
904-448-0633; FAX: 904-448-0623

car dealer

See full listing in **Section Two** under **car dealers**

Classic Wood Mfg
1006 N Raleigh St
Greensboro, NC 27405
910-691-1344; FAX: 910-273-3074

wood kits
wood replacement

See full listing in **Section Two** under **woodwork**

Donovan Motorcar Service
4 Holmes Rd
Lenox, MA 01240
413-499-6000; FAX: 413-499-6699

restoration
service

See full listing in **Section One** under **Jaguar**

Doug's British Car Parts
2487 E Colorado Blvd
Pasadena, CA 91107
818-793-2494; FAX: 818-793-4339

accessories
parts

See full listing in **Section One** under **Jaguar**

Eberhardt Service
17710 Valley View Ave
Cleveland, OH 44135-1126

parts

Used parts only. An MG collector who buys, sells and trades used MG parts. Sells by mail and at British swap meets. Tons of modern MG Midget parts, lots of sales literature. Send SASE. Specializing in 1961-'79 MG Midgets and Austin-Healey Sprites, also purchasing prewar MG M-type parts, Land Rover parts and MG racing equipment.

Exotic Wood Dash & Restorations
336 Cottonwood Ave
Hartland, WI 53029
800-900-3274; FAX: 414-367-9474

restoration parts
wood dash overlays

See full listing in **Section One** under **Jaguar**

Don Flye
5 Doe Valley Rd
Petersham, MA 01366
508-724-3318

parts

See full listing in **Section One** under **Austin-Healey**

GF Embossed Notes
11 Caldwell Dr
Amherst, NH 03031
603-880-6217; FAX: 603-882-6590

note cards

See full listing in **Section Two** under **automobilia**

Pete Groh
9957 Frederick Rd
Ellicott City, MD 21042-3647
410-750-2352

original British
keys
Wilmot Breeden

See full listing in **Section One** under **Jaguar**

Lindley Restorations Ltd
Rt 422 RD 3
Pottstown, PA 19464
610-326-8484; FAX: 610-326-3845

parts
sales
service

See full listing in **Section One** under **Jaguar**

M & G Vintage Auto
265 Rt 17, Box 226
Tuxedo Park, NY 10987
914-753-5900, info
800-631-8990, orders
FAX: 914-753-5613

parts
restoration
service

"The Source" for all your MG needs. Largest supplier of new & used MG parts to the trade. We buy, sell, trade cars & parts, 13 car showroom and full shop on premises. We run a full stocked MG TC/TD/TF, MGA, MGB mail order house. We can expertly rebuild your engine, transmission, carbs and gauges. Fully illustrated catalogs available upon request.

Merely Motoring
153 Danford Ln
Solihull
West Midlands B91 1QQ England
0121-733-2123
FAX: 0121-745-5256

automobilia
lapel badges
postcards

See full listing in **Section Two** under **automobilia**

MG Automotive
3733-C Wilmington Pk
Kettering, OH 45429
513-294-7623

parts
restoration
service

Mail order and open shop. Monday-Friday 9 am-6 pm; Saturday 9 am-2 pm. Restoration, service and parts for British sports cars, MG, Triumph, Austin-Healey and Mini.

MG Parts Centre (Barry Walker)
Barley Leys Farm, Haselor Hill
Temple Grafton
NR Stratford-on-Avon B49 6NH UK
0044 1789-400181
FAX: 0044 1789-400230

parts

Mail order and open shop. Daily 10 to 7. For MGs only, 1929-53. M through TD parts. Many spares available.

MG Supermarket
#1 Rt 17
Tuxedo, NY 10987
917-753-5900; FAX: 917-753-5613

parts

Mail order and open shop. 6 days/week, no Sundays, 8 am-6 pm. Specializing in MG original new & used, all parts for rebuilding and new Lucas vacuum units, all English cars. New and rebuild distributor vacuum units for all English cars.

Mini Mania
31 Winsor St
Milpitas, CA 95035
408-942-5595; FAX: 408-942-5582
E-mail: minimania@aol.com

parts
service

See full listing in **Section One** under **Austin**

Mini Motors Classic Coachworks
2775 Cherry Ave NE
Salem, OR 97303
503-362-3187; FAX: 503-375-9609

parts
restoration
sales
service

See full listing in **Section One** under **Austin-Healey**

Moss Europe Ltd
Unit 15 Allington Way
Yarm Road Ind Estate, Darlington
Co Durham DLI 4QB England
01325-281343; FAX: 01325-485563

parts

Specializing in MG parts covering MGA, MGB, MGC and Midget/A-H Sprite, Mini, Land Rover.

Moss Motors Ltd
PO Box 847
440 Rutherford St
Goleta, CA 93117
800-235-6954; FAX: 805-692-2525

accessories
parts

Mail order and open shop. Monday-Saturday 6 am-5 pm PDT. We love British sports cars as much as you do! We're the oldest and largest supplier of quality parts and accessories for MG, Triumph, Austin-Healey and Jaguar. Free catalogs for MG TC-TD-TF, MGA, MGB, Sprite-Midget, Triumph TR2-4A, TR 250-6, TR7, Spitfire, Austin-Healey and Jaguar XK 120-150. Free quarterly newsletter with hundreds of sale items, tech articles and club news and events. Toll-free ordering with fast, dependable service and locations on both coasts. British Heritage approved supplier.

Motorcars Ltd
8101 Hempstead
Houston, TX 77008
713-863-9388; FAX: 713-863-8238
E-mail: mcltd@phoenix.net

parts

See full listing in **Section One** under **Jaguar**

Motorhead Ltd
2811-B Old Lee Highway
Fairfax, VA 22031
800-527-3140; FAX: 703-573-3165

parts
repairs

See full listing in **Section One** under **Austin-Healey**

Motormetrics
5500 Thomaston Rd
Macon, GA 31204
912-477-6771

used parts

See full listing in **Section One** under **Triumph**

Mr Sport Car Inc
203 E Lincoln
Papillion, NE 68046
402-592-7559

service

See full listing in **Section One** under **Jaguar**

Nisonger Instrument S/S
570 Mamaroneck Ave
Mamaroneck, NY 10543
914-381-1952, FAX: 914-381-1953

gauges

See full listing in **Section Two** under **instruments**

Northwest Import Parts
10042 SW Balmer
Portland, OR 97219
503-245-3806; FAX: 503-245-9617

parts

Mail order and open shop. Specializes in new parts for MG cars. Mechanical, interior, rubber, electrical and restoration parts for MGs 55-80.

NOS Locators
587 Pawtucket Ave
Pawtucket, RI 02860
401-725-5000

parts

Limited range of deeply discounted overstocks, closeouts, bulk buyouts, etc, primarily for British sports cars, late 50s on. Specific marques are: Austin-Healey, MG, Triumph, Jaguar

O'Connor Classic Autos
2569 Scott Blvd
Santa Clara, CA 95050
408-727-0430; FAX: 408-727-3987

car dealer
parts
restoration

Mail order and open shop. Tuesday through Friday 9 to 5.

Restored and unrestored MG cars, including TC, TD, TF, MGA, MGB. Full line of parts and restoration sevices.

Omni Specialties 10418 Lorain Ave Cleveland, OH 44111 800-791-9562; 216-251-2269 FAX: 216-251-6083	parts restoration service

Mail order and open shop. Open Monday-Friday 9:30 am to 6:30 pm. Specializing in repair, service, parts, restoration for MG, Jaguar, Triumph, Austin-Healey, Lotus and other European classics. Service and repair for a price that's fair. 30 years' experience.

Pacific International Auto 1118 Garnet Ave San Diego, CA 92109 619-274-1920; 619-454-1815	parts sales service

See full listing in **Section One** under **Jaguar**

Peninsula Imports 3749 Harlem Rd Buffalo, NY 14215 800-263-4538; FAX: 905-847-3021	accessories parts trim

See full listing in **Section One** under **BMW**

The Proper MG PO Box 201 97 Tenney St Georgetown, MA 01833 800-711-3368; FAX: 508-352-2751 E-mail: propermg@aol.com	parts

Mail order and open shop. Monday-Friday 9-5:30 by appointment only. New and reconditioned parts. Direct importers from England. Wholesale and retail, toll-free ordering. Fast, dependable service. Competitive prices, free MGB catalog. Specialist in MGB 1962-1980 and MG Midget 1961-1979.

Quality Coaches 20 W 38th St Minneapolis, MN 55409 612-824-4155	parts restoration service

Shop open Monday-Friday 8 to 6. Service and mechanical restorations for MGs and other British cars. Owned and operated by MG enthusiasts. Moss Motors distributor for new parts. Many used MGA and MGB parts in stock. Special order Moss parts 10% off list.

Ragtops & Roadsters 203 S 4th St Perkasie, PA 18944 215-257-1202; FAX: 215-257-2688	race prep repairs

See full listing in **Section One** under **AC**

The Registry Pine Grove Stanley, VA 22851 540-778-3728; FAX: 540-778-2402 E-mail: britregstry@aol.com	periodical

See full listing in **Section Four** under **periodicals**

The Roadster Factory PO Box 332 Armagh, PA 15920 800-234-1104; FAX: 814-446-6729 E-mail: trfmail@internetmci.com	accessories parts

See full listing in **Section One** under **Triumph**

Safety Fast Restoration Company 118 Park Ave E Rear Mansfield, OH 44901 419-525-0799; FAX: 419-289-6241 E-mail: mgmetcalf@aol.com	restoration

Shop open Monday-Friday 8:30 to 4:30 EST. Specializing in world class restoration of MGs, 1930-1955. Models covered include D, J, F, P, L, N, TA, TB, TC, TD, TF. High quality English built body tubs available, reasonable cost and lead time. Restored Best TC In The World voted in 1992.

Scarborough Faire Inc 1151 Main St Pawtucket, RI 02860 800-556-6300; 401-724-4200 FAX: 401-724-5392	parts

Manufacturers and wholesale distributor/exporter of high quality spares for post WW II MGs & Austin-Healeys.

Seven Enterprises Ltd 716 Bluecrab Rd Newport News, VA 23606 800-992-7007; FAX: 800-296-3327	accessories parts

See full listing in **Section One** under **Austin**

Shadetree Motors Ltd 3895 Mammoth Cave Ct Pleasanton, CA 94588-4919 PH/FAX: 510-846-1309	parts service

Mail order only. Monday-Friday 8 to 5. Established in 1979. Specializes in parts, services, component restoration for 1945-1980 MG sports cars. T series specialist. Registered with California State Bureau of Automotive Repair. Authorized Moss Motors parts distributor. Discount pricing/wholesale-retail.

Special Interest Car Parts — parts
1340 Hartford Ave
Johnston, RI 02919
800-556-7496; FAX: 401-831-7760

See full listing in **Section One** under **Jaguar**

Sports & Classics — parts
PO Box 1787
512 Boston Post Rd, Dept H
Darien, CT 06820-1787

See full listing in **Section Two** under **body parts**

Tiger Detailing — accessories / detailing / parts
PO Box 9875
North Hollywood, CA 91609-1875
PH/FAX: 818-982-1042
E-mail: tygrbeer7@aol.com

See full listing in **Section One** under **Sunbeam**

University Motors Ltd — events / line/bench service / restoration
6490 E Fulton
Ada, MI 49301
616-682-0800; FAX: 616-682-0801

Open shop Monday-Friday 9-6, Saturday 9-1, summers only. Specializing in MG restoration, parts, line & bench service and events, all years, all models. Now servicing other British autos.

V6 MGB — conversion plans / kits
Box 741992
Dallas, TX 75374

Mail order only. Conversion plans and kits for V6 MGBs only.

Victoria British Ltd — accessories / parts
Box 14991
Lenexa, KS 66285-4991
800-255-0088; 913-599-3299

Mail order catalog. Monday-Friday 7 to 9, Saturday-Sunday 9 to 5. One of the world's largest distributors of parts and accessories for British sports cars. Offering the most complete up-to-date information in our fully illustrated catalogs. Stocks over 20,000 line items for MG, Triumph, Austin-Healey and Sunbeam. Telephone orders are fast and easy with a reliable on-line computer entry system. As a distributor for British Motor Heritage in the US the company is able to provide original equipment and authentic reproduction parts. Great prices on high performance parts, accessories, upholstery, rubber and chrome trim.

See our ad on page 144

Victory Autoservices — parts / restoration
Box 5060, RR 1
W Baldwin, ME 04091
207-625-4581

See full listing in **Section One** under **Austin-Healey**

Web Accessories — fiberglass parts
PO Box 191
Old Bethpage, NY 11804
516-752-1710

See full listing in **Section Two** under **fiberglass parts**

Carl W Burst III — literature / parts / photographs
1600 N Woodlawn
St Louis, MO 63124
314-822-7807
314-822-8688, recorder

Mail order and open shop. Daily by appointment. Specializing in Moon, Hol-Tan, Diana, Windsor and Ruxton; all products of the Moon Motor Company, including factory photographs and technical specifications. Compiles addresses of owners of these marques. Will send free.

MoPar

AARcadia Parts Locating — parts
8294 Allport Ave
.Santa Fe Springs, CA 90670
310-698-8067; FAX: 310-696-6505

Mail order and open shop. Hours Mon-Fri 8 am-8 pm, Sat 9 am-5 pm. Specializing in new, used, reproduction parts. Sales and servicing of 1966-1974 Chrysler products. Componant rebuilding, all work done in house. If we don't have it, we'll find it free. We ship parts worldwide.

AKH Wheels — Rallye wheels / styled steel wheels / vintage aluminum
1207 N A St
Ellensburg, WA 98926-2522
509-962-3390

See full listing in **Section Two** under **wheels & wheelcovers**

Antique Auto Fasteners — fasteners / hardware / hose clamps / molding clips
Guy C Close, Jr & Son
13426 Valna Dr
Whittier, CA 90602
310-696-3307

See full listing in **Section Two** under **hardware**

Antique Automobile Radio Inc — radio accessories / radio parts / radio restoration
700 Tampa Rd
Palm Harbor, FL 34684
800-WE-FIX-AM; 813-785-8733
FAX: 813-789-0283

See full listing in **Section Two** under **radios**

Antique DeSoto-Plymouth — MoPar parts
4206 Burnett Dr
Murrysville, PA 15668
412-733-1818 eves
FAX: 412-243-4556 anytime

Mail order and open shop by appointment. Phone evenings. New old stock 1938 through 1960 Chrysler, Plymouth, Dodge, DeSoto parts. Hard-to-find MoPar parts: grilles, bumpers, chrome moldings, etc. Send SASE with list of wants. Satisfaction guaranteed on all we sell.

Arizona Parts
320 E Pebble Beach
Tempe, AZ 85282
602-966-6683
800-328-8766, code: 88602

accessories
literature
parts

Mail order only. For 1935-94 Chrysler Corporation vehicles. 39,000 item computer inventory using Chrysler part numbers with description and application available, (call for cost). New and used parts, accessories and literature stocked. Send SASE for current stock information.

Atlas Motor Parts
10621 Bloomfield St
Unit 32
Los Alamitos, CA 90720
310-594-5560; FAX: 310-936-1398

parts

Mail order, telephone and open shop sales Monday-Friday 9 to 5. NOS and reproduction parts for 1928-74 Chrysler Products: air filters, oil filters, shocks, motor mounts, molded radiator hoses, bearings, seals, gaskets, engine paint, fuel pumps, water pumps, power steering hoses and hardware. Brake, steering, suspension, engine, driveline, electrical, ignition and rubber parts. Send $5 for complete catalog or call or write with your needs. VISA/MasterCard and CODs welcome.

Auto Decals Unlimited Inc
11259 E Via Linda, Ste 100-201
Scottsdale, AZ 85259
602-860-9800; FAX: 602-860-8370

decals
stripe kits

See full listing in **Section Two** under **decals**

Barracuda Classic
1500 Adams Ave, #105-162
Costa Mesa, CA 92626
PH/FAX: 714-444-2507

accessories
parts

Mail order only. Specializing in parts and accessories for 1964-1974 MoPar parts for A, B and E-body.

Andy Bernbaum Auto Parts
315 Franklin St
Newton, MA 02158
617-244-1118

parts

Mail order and telephone order. New and NOS parts for 1930-62 Chrysler, Dodge, Plymouth and DeSoto cars and trucks. Comprehensive parts including mechanical, brake, suspension, weatherstripping, body, drivetrain, electric, trim, accessories and literature. 1930-62 catalog $4. For later years, call for availability. VISA, MasterCard and CODs accepted.

The Bumper Boyz
834 E Florence Ave
Los Angeles, CA 90001
213-587-8976, 800-995-1703
FAX: 213-587-2013

bumper repairs
reconditioning
sand blasting

See full listing in **Section One** under **Chevrolet**

Burchill Antique Auto Parts Inc
4150 24th Ave
Fort Gratiot, MI 48061
810-385-3838

parts
technical info

See full listing in **Section One** under **Chrysler**

Thomas Cavaliere
10 Marsha Terr
Parsippany, NJ 07054
201-334-8568

parts

Mail order and sales from home. Pre-1961 MoPar parts, including 4-cylinder (1928-32) Plymouth parts. Also parts for other cars, including sheetmetal.

Chrysler Power
PO Box 129
Mansfield, PA 16933
717-549-2282; FAX: 717-549-3366

performance parts

Founded 1980. 3,700 members. Mail order and open shop. Monday-Friday 8 to 5 pm. 15 years of enthusiast information and parts organization for MoPar enthusiasts, including National Hemi Owners Association, MoPar Muscle Club, Chrysler Performance Parts Association. Bimonthly publication: *Chrysler Power Magazine*, $19.75. Specializing in Chrysler and MoPar performance parts for 1962-78 Chrysler, Plymouth, Dodge. Do not need to be a MoPar enthusiast. Dues: $40/year.

The Classic Car Radio Co
2718 Koper Dr
Sterling Heights, MI 48310
810-977-7979; 810-268-2918 info
FAX: 810-977-0895

radios

See full listing in **Section Two** under **radios**

Clester's Auto Rubber Seals Inc
PO Box 459
Cleveland, NC 27013
704-637-9979; FAX: 704-636-7390

gloveboxes
headliners
molded rubber parts
weatherstripping

See full listing in **Section Two** under **rubber parts**

Coach Builders Muscle Car Parts & Services
PO Box 128
Baltimore, MD 21087-0128
410-426-5567

interiors
parts
rust remover

See full listing in **Section One** under **Chevrolet**

CSK Publishing Co Inc
299 Market St
Saddle Brook, NJ 07662
201-712-9300; FAX: 201-712-0990
E-mail: staff@cskpub.com

periodical

See full listing in **Section Four** under **periodicals**

Len Dawson
1557 Yokeko Dr
Anacortes, WA 98221
FAX: 360-293-1032

chrome & trim
items
electrical parts
mechanical parts

Mail order only. One of the world's largest inventories of NOS parts for 1935-83 Chrysler products. Full line of mechanical and electrical parts, plus thousands of chrome and trim items. Send SASE and Chrysler Corporation part numbers with inquiries.

Daniel N Dietrich
RD 1
Kempton, PA 19529
215-756-6078

restoration
trim parts

Mail order and open shop. Restores complete car bodies, 1941 to 1963 MoPar only, back to original factory finish. Also sells exterior chrome, stainless body moldings and trim.

Bruce Ebmeier
Obsolete Parts Depot
2905 N Osage Ave
Juniata, NE 68955-3002
FAX: 402-751-2566

parts

Mail order and open by appointment, so please call ahead for an appointment. Mostly new old stock MoPar parts, expanding inventory of mechanical, trim, lenses and some sheetmetal 1932-1982, but largely 1938-1962. Very little soft trim, accessories or muscle car parts. MoPar part numbers and group numbers are helpful, and be sure to include the application and an SASE for a reply. Foreign inquiries welcome. Primarily mail order, no regular hours. No catalog or list for a while yet, sorry.

Egge Machine Company | babbitting
11707 Slauson Ave | chassis
Santa Fe Springs, CA 90670 | motor mounts
310-945-3419 in CA | pistons/valves
800-866-EGGE; FAX: 310-693-1635 | wiring harnesses

See full listing in **Section Two** under **engine parts**

ETC Every Thing Cars | restoration
8727 Clarinda
Pico Rivera, CA 90660
310-949-6981

Shop open by phone appointment only. Deals in body, chassis, engine, trans, brakes, front ends, air conditioning, tune-ups, high-performance, carbs, ignition, detailing, frame-offs and partials. General auto restorations, '60s thru '75. References. R W Nash, owner, technician, craftsman. Reasonable rates. This business does not sell individual parts.

John Filiss | appraisals
45 Kingston Ave
Port Jervis, NY 12771
914-856-2942

See full listing in **Section Two** under **appraisals**

Giles Antique Auto Parts | parts
2505 W Blanchard
South Hutchinson, KS 67505
316-663-1664; FAX: 316-663-3710

Mail order and open shop. Specializing in MoPar parts. No SASE, if I haven't got the parts, I won't write back.

Goldfield Trim & Upholstery | top installation
1267 160th St | upholstery
Goldfield, IA 50542
515-254-3322

See full listing in **Section Two** under **interiors & interior parts**

Grand Touring | engine rebuilding
2785 E Regal Park Dr | machine shop
Anaheim, CA 92806 | restoration
714-630-0130; FAX: 714-630-6956 | suspension

See full listing in **Section Two** under **restoration shops**

Jim Harris | cars
16743 39th NE | parts
Seattle, WA 98155
206-364-6637

Mail order and open shop. Cars and parts, MoPar 1927-75. Specializes in sixties Imperials and MoPar muscle cars. In the hobby since 1974.

Mike Hershenfeld | parts
3011 Susan Rd
Bellmore, NY 11710
PH/FAX: 516-781-PART (7278)

Mail order only. Specializing in MoPar NOS 1932-70: engine, fuel, electrical, brakes, lenses, gauges, clutch, ignition, gaskets, cooling, suspension, chrome, literature.

Hidden Valley Auto Parts | parts
21046 N Rio Bravo
Maricopa, AZ 85239
602-252-2122, 602-252-6137
520-568-2945
FAX: 602-258-0951

See full listing in **Section One** under **Chevrolet**

Imperial Motors | parts
2165 Spencer Creek Rd
Campobello, SC 29322
864-895-3474

See full listing in **Section One** under **Chrysler**

Jeff Johnson Motorsports | accessories
4421 Aldrich Pl | literature
Columbus, OH 43214 | parts
614-268-1181; FAX: 614-268-1141

Mail order only. Specializing in parts, literature & accessories. NOS & repro for 1955 to current Chrysler product cars & trucks.

King & Queen Mufflers | exhaust systems
Box 423
Plumsteadville, PA 18949
PH/FAX: 215-766-8699

See full listing in **Section Two** under **exhaust systems**

Kramer Automotive Specialties | body parts
PO Box 5 | interiors
Herman, PA 16039 | sheetmetal
412-285-5566

Mail order only. Monday-Friday, noon to 6. A, B, C and E-body parts, race Hemi, St Hemi, max wedge, body and engine restoration items. 60s and early 70s Dodge, Plymouth, Chrysler, with emphasis on factory race cars and muscle cars. Sheetmetal, interiors and chrome in NOS, good used and reproduction.

The Last Precinct Police Museum | museum
Rt 6, Box 345B (62 Highway West)
Eureka Springs, AR 72632
501-253-4948; FAX: 501-253-4949

See full listing in **Section Six** under **Arkansas**

Leo R Lindquist | 1950s Hemi parts
Rt 2, Box 77 | NORS parts
Balaton, MN 56115-9215 | NOS parts
507-734-2051

Mail order and shop open by appointment. Specializing in 241 to 392 Hemi engines and parts (mainly used); many small pieces available. No high performance items. Also 1950s Chrysler Corporation vehicles and parts.

MikeCo Antique, Kustom & | lenses
Obsolete Auto Parts | parts
4053 Calle Tesoro, Unit C
Camarillo, CA 93012
805-482-1725; FAX: 805-987-8524

Mail order and open shop. Monday-Friday 3:30 pm to 7 pm, Saturday 10 am to 5 pm PDT, fax 24 hours. Specializing in lenses, stainless trim, tune-up and electrical, brake parts and weatherstrip for Chrysler product vehicles 1930s through 1975. Autolite & Delco electrical parts & weatherstrip for American made vehicles, 1915 through 1975. Heavy into Chrysler and General Motors with stock of parts for independent makes.

Mike's Auto Parts | bearings
Box 358 | engine parts
Ridgeland, MS 39158 | NOS parts
601-856-7214 | wall calendars

See full listing in **Section One** under **Chrysler**

Mitchell Motor Parts Inc | car dealer
1601 Thraikill Rd | parts
Grove City, OH 43123
614-875-4919; FAX: 614-875-9960

Mail order and open shop. Monday-Friday 9 am to 6 pm, Saturday 9 am to 1 pm. Original parts for Chrysler product vehicles, 1928-current. Supplying Chrysler product owners for over 20 years. The world's largest independent selection of MoPar brand parts with over 1,000,000 parts in stock at our 40,000 square foot warehouse. Also sells complete cars. Specializing in NOS, used and repro parts, complete and parts cars, for 1928-91 Chrysler, Plymouth, Dodge, DeSoto, Imperial and Dodge trucks. Billing address: PO Box 621, Fairmount, GA 30139.

MoPar Collector's Guide Magazine 10067 El Camino Ave Baton Rouge, LA 70815 504-926-6954; FAX: 504-924-5456	**magazine**

Mail order only. *MoPar Collector's Guide* magazine is the world's largest monthly MoPar only buy, sell, trade publication. Thousands of MoPar cars and parts listed for sale in each monthly issue. Buy on newsstand or subscribe. Subscribers always advertise free, which pays for subscription. Four to six four color feature car articles each month. Extensive price guide. New product section. Editorial column. Readers' letters. MasterCard and Visa accepted. Free current copy with your subscription when you mention this ad. Subscription rate: $25/year (12 issues).

Clayton T Nelson Box 259 Warrenville, IL 60555 708-369-6589	**NOS parts**

See full listing in **Section One** under **Oldsmobile**

NOS Reproductions 22425 Sefferlies Rd RR 3 Komoka, ON Canada N0L 1R0 519-471-2740; FAX: 519-471-7675	**parts**

Specializing in seat covers, headliners, door panels, weatherstripping and molded carpets for Ford, GM and Chrysler.

NS-One PO Box 2459, Dept VA Cedar Rapids, IA 52406 319-362-7717	**NOS parts**

See full listing in **Section One** under **Chrysler**

The Old Carb Doctor Rt 3, Box 338 Drucilla Church Rd Nebo, NC 28761 800-945-CARB (2272) 704-659-1428	**carburetors** **fuel pumps**

See full listing in **Section Two** under **carburetors**

Older Car Restoration Martin Lum, owner 304 S Main St, Box 428 Mont Alto, PA 17237 717-749-3383, 717-352-7701	**repro parts** **restoration**

Mail order and open shop. Monday-Friday 8 to 5. Partial or total restorations on all kinds of cars. Offers a line of 1928-31 MoPar reproduction parts. Chrysler, Dodge, DeSoto, Plymouth parts, service, mechanical and cosmetic restorations, chrome plating and appraisals also available. Also reproduction parts for 50s DeSotos.

Original Auto Interiors 7869 Trumble Rd Columbus, MI 48063-3915 810-727-2486; FAX: 810-727-4344 E-mail: knight@mich.com	**upholstery**

See full listing in **Section Two** under **upholstery**

Patterson Coachworks 8951 Henry Clay Blvd Clay, NY 13041 315-652-5794	**parts** **service**

See full listing in **Section One** under **Pontiac**

Performance Motor Parts Box 122 West Milton, OH 45383 PH/FAX: 513-698-4259	**parts**

Specializing in four-speed conversions on 1962 to 1976 MoPar muscle cars. Rebuilt Hurst shifters, A-833 rebuild kits, rebuilt transmissions, restored pistol grips, new torque shafts, clutch linkage, bellhousings, pedal assemblies, etc. From one small part to complete conversions. Call the 4-speed specialists!

Plymouth, Dodge, Chrysler, **DeSoto Parts** 935 Limecrest Rd Pittsburgh, PA 15668 412-733-1818 eves FAX: 412-243-4556 anytime	**NOS parts for** **DeSoto**

See full listing in **Section One** under **DeSoto**

Power Play, Bob Walker Rt 1 Box 95 Lowgap, NC 27024 910-352-4866; FAX: 910-789-8967	**parts**

See full listing in **Section One** under **Chrysler**

Sam Quinn Cadillac Parts Box 837 Estacada, OR 97023 503-637-3852	**parts**

See full listing in **Section One** under **Cadillac/LaSalle**

R & R Fiberglass & Specialties 4850 Wilson Dr NW Cleveland, TN 37312 423-476-2270	**body parts**

See full listing in **Section Two** under **fiberglass parts**

Reproduction Parts Marketing #3-1707 Sask Ave Saskatoon, SK Canada S7K 1P7 306-652-6668; FAX: 306-652-1123	**parts** **restoration** **service**

See full listing in **Section One** under **Chevrolet**

Riddle's/Mr Plymouth 452 Newton Seattle, WA 98109 206-285-6534 days	**decals** **overdrives** **parts & info** **repro parts**

Mail order only. Neil Riddle, proprietor. Parts 1940-1954. NOS, used and hard-to-find items a specialty. Send $2 for latest listing of products and reproductions. Technical advisor for Plymouth Owners Club, knowledgeable advice given. Also buy, sell, trade NOS parts. Old MoPar cars and parts locator service.

R/T Connection 1034 Dover St Warren, OH 44485 330-399-3959	**parts**

Mail order only. Sells NOS parts for 50s-60s-70s Chrysler product vehicles. Also some hard to find parts and some excellent used items. Also rebuilds 727 Torqueflite transmissions.

Spark Plugs & Stuff
PO Box 33343
San Diego, CA 92163-3343
619-220-1745

| | tune-up kits |

See full listing in **Section Two** under **ignition parts**

Special T's Unlimited Corp
PO Box 146
Prospect Heights, IL 60070
847-255-5494; FAX: 847-391-7082

| | general repair
parts
restoration
service |

See full listing in **Section One** under **Ford '03-'31**

Ed Spiegel
Box 402
Murrysville, PA 15668
412-733-1818 evenings

| | literature
parts |

See full listing in **Section One** under **Chrysler**

Ssnake-Oyl Products Inc
Rt 2, Box 269-6
Hawkins, TX 75765
903-769-4555; 903-769-4552

| | carpet underlay
firewall insulation
seatbelt restoration |

See full listing in **Section Two** under **interiors & interior parts**

Stainless Steel Brakes Corp
11470 Main Rd
Clarence, NY 14031
800-448-7722, 716-759-8666
FAX: 716-759-8688, 24 hr

| | brake accessories
disc brakes/rotors
parking brake kits
power steering
parts |

See full listing in **Section Two** under **brakes**

Stencils & Stripes Unlimited Inc
1108 S Crescent Ave #21
Park Ridge, IL 60068
708-692-6893; FAX: 708-692-6895

| | NOS decals
stripe kits |

See full listing in **Section Two** under **decals**

Stockton Wheel Service
648 W Fremont St
Stockton, CA 95203
209-464-7771, 800-395-9433
FAX: 209-464-4725

| | wheel repair |

See full listing in **Section Two** under **service shops**

Tags Backeast
PO Box 581
Plainville, CT 06062
860-747-2942

| | data plates
trim tags |

See full listing in **Section Two** under **special services**

Tiger Detailing
PO Box 9875
North Hollywood, CA 91609-1875
PH/FAX: 818-982-1042
E-mail: tygrbeer7@aol.com

| | accessories
detailing
parts |

See full listing in **Section One** under **Sunbeam**

Vintage Power Wagons Inc
302 S 7th St
Fairfield, IA 52556
515-472-4665; FAX: 515-472-4824

| | parts
trucks |

See full listing in **Section One** under **Dodge**

Pat Walsh Restorations
Box Q
Wakefield, MA 01880
617-246-5565

| | literature
rubber parts |

See full listing in **Section Two** under **rubber parts**

**Weimann's Literature &
Collectables**
16 Cottage Rd
Harwinton, CT 06791
860-485-0300
FAX: 860-485-1705, 24 hour

| | literature |

See full listing in **Section One** under **Plymouth**

Howard Whitelaw
6067 Richmond Rd
Cleveland (Solon), OH 44139
216-721-6755 days
216-439-2159 evenings & weekends
FAX: 216-721-6758

| | fenders |

Mail order and open shop. Open by appointment only.
Specializing in MoPar from 1933-74 (world's largest supply of
MoPar fenders), but some Nash, Buick and Rambler fenders
available. Send SASE with inquiry.

Wittenborn's Auto Service Inc
133 Woodside Ave
Briarcliff Manor, NY 10510
914-941-2744

| | MoPar |

Shop open Monday-Friday 8:30 to 5:45; evenings and Saturday
by appointment. Phone answering service. Repair and service on
cars from twenties to present. Alignments, wheel balancing,
steam cleaning. Emphasis on Plymouth Valiants and Dodge
Darts. Used parts for slant 6 Valiants and Darts 1961-80.
"Everything from oil changes and tune-ups to major mechanical
work. ASE certified mechanic."

Bonnets Up
5736 Spring St
Clinton, MD 20735
301-297-4759

| | restoration |

See full listing in **Section Two** under **coachbuilders & designers**

Cantab Motors Ltd
Valley Industrial Park
12 E Richardson Ln
Purcellville, VA 20132
540-338-2211; FAX: 540-338-2944

| | cars
parts
service |

Mail order and open shop. Monday to Friday, 9 to 5, weekends
by appointment. Specializing in new car and used car sales,
spare parts, restoration and service, vintage racing preparation
for Morgan sports cars (authorized US agent), Land and Range
Rovers.

Isis Imports Ltd
PO Box 2290
Gateway Station
San Francisco, CA 94126
415-433-1344; FAX: 415-788-1850

| | cars
parts
restoration |

Mail order and open shop everyday by appointment. Specializing
in Morgan cars, parts, service and restoration.

Morgan Motor Company Ltd
Pickersleigh Road
Malvern Link
Worcester WR14 2LL England
0168-4573104; FAX: 0168-4892295

| motors |
| parts |

Mail order and open shop. Monday-Friday 9 to 4. Motor manufacturer and parts supplier for Morgan. Annual catalog. Factory visits welcome by prior appointment.

Olde World Restorations
2727 Philmont Ave, Suite 350
Huntingdon Valley, PA 19006
215-947-8720; FAX: 215-947-8722

| parts |
| restoration |

Mail order and open shop. Monday-Friday 9 to 5:30 or by appointment. Morgan parts, repairs and restorations.

Specialty Car Service Ltd
1330 Ritters Rd
Reading, PA 19606
610-370-0410

| parts |
| restoration |
| service |

Open shop only. Shop open Monday-Friday by appointment only. 25 years' British specialty car experience. Custom fabricating, mig and tig welding, race preparation, restoration and routine maintenance. Specializing in service and parts for Morgan 3-wheeler to +8, AC, Lotus Elan, Seven, Cortina, and Aston Martin.

Sports & Classics
512 Boston Post Rd, Dept. H
Darien, CT 06820-1787
203-655-8731; FAX: 203-656-1896

| interiors |
| parts |
| tops |
| wire wheels |

See full listing in **Section Two** under **body parts**

British Auto Parts Ltd
93256 Holland Ln
Marcola, OR 97454
541-933-2880; FAX: 541-933-2302

| parts |

Mail order only. Specializing in providing new, used and rebuilt engine, transmission, brake, electrical and sheetmetal parts for Morris Minor, MG, Triumph and Jaguar.

British Auto Shoppe Inc
1115 1st Ave
Silvis, IL 61282
309-796-2748; FAX: 309-796-2033

| parts |
| service |

See full listing in **Section One** under **MG**

Pete Groh
9957 Frederick Rd
Ellicott City, MD 21042-3647
410-750-2352

| original British |
| keys |
| Wilmot Breeden |

See full listing in **Section One** under **Jaguar**

Manhattan Mini Inc
New York, NY 10036
212-921-8459
FAX: 212-719-5313

| sales |

See full listing in **Section One** under **Austin**

MG Automotive
3733-C Wilmington Pk
Kettering, OH 45429
513-294-7623

| parts |
| restoration |
| service |

See full listing in **Section One** under **MG**

Mini City Ltd
395 Summit Point Dr
Henrietta, NY 14467-9606
716-359-1400, FAX: 716-359-1428

| accessories |
| car dealer |
| literature/parts |
| tools |

See full listing in **Section One** under **Austin**

Mini Mania
31 Winsor St
Milpitas, CA 95035
408-942-5595; FAX: 408-942-5582
E-mail: minimania@aol.com

| parts |
| service |

See full listing in **Section One** under **Austin**

Mini Registry
395 Summit Point Dr
Henrietta, NY 14467
716-359-1400; FAX: 716-359-1428

See full listing in **Section Three** under **marque clubs**

Mini Store
PO Box 7973
Van Nuys, CA 91409-7973
818-893-1421

| cars |
| repairs |
| restorations |

See full listing in **Section One** under **Austin**

Motormetrics
5500 Thomaston Rd
Macon, GA 31204
912-477-6771

| used parts |

See full listing in **Section One** under **Triumph**

Patton Orphan Spares
28 Simon St
Babylon, NY 11702
516-669-2598

| parts |

See full listing in **Section One** under **Renault**

Seven Enterprises Ltd
716 Bluecrab Rd
Newport News, VA 23606
800-992-7007; FAX: 800-296-3327

| accessories |
| parts |

See full listing in **Section One** under **Austin**

All American Rambler
11661 Martens River Cir #M
Fountain Valley, CA 92708
714-662-7200

| manuals |
| parts |

See full listing in **Section One** under **AMC**

Blaser's Auto, Nash, Rambler, AMC
3200 48th Ave
Moline, IL 61265
309-764-3571; FAX: 309-764-1155

| NOS parts |

See full listing in **Section One** under **AMC**

Charles Chambers Parts
Box 60, HC 64
Goldthwaite, TX 76844

| parts |

Mail order only. Exclusively Nash parts. Good selection of items from ammeters to zerks. SASE required.

Doug Galvin Rambler Parts
7559 Passalis Ln
Sacramento, CA 95829
916-689-3356

| parts |

See full listing in **Section One** under **AMC**

Lucky Lee Lott (Author)
800 E Diana St
Tampa, FL 33604
813-238-5408 (24 hours)

| information
parts |

Mail order and open shop. Specializing in parts and information for Nash, Rambler, Ajax, Lafayette, 1902-1958. On I-275 North at Exit 31, just south of Sligh Ave in Tampa. There are Lucky Lee Lott Hell Drivers' cars of 1935-1955 on display from time to time with memorabilia of old time daredevils. Limited NOS stock from 1938 forward, plus source information. *Legend of Lucky Lee Lott Hell Drivers* autobiography now available with 150 pictures, turn-around, P/O, m/o, only $18.50 or send $2.90 book of stamps for autographed color photo only p/p.

Metropolitan Pit Stop
5324-26-28-30 Laurel Canyon Blvd
North Hollywood, CA 91607
818-769-1515; FAX: 818-769-3500

| parts
restoration
literature |

See full listing in **Section One** under **Metropolitan**

Garth B Peterson
122 N Conklin Rd
Veradale, WA 99037
509-926-4620 anytime

| accessories
parts
radios |

See full listing in **Section Two** under **comprehensive parts**

David Simon
19641 Victory Blvd
Reseda, CA 91335-6621
818-344-4639

| literature |

Mail order and open shop. Shop open by appointment only. Dealing in Nash, Rambler and AMC original unused and used shop manuals, owner's manuals, parts books and sales literature. Also owner's manuals (domestic) pre-1980 unused & used originals.

Treasure Chest Sales
413 Montgomery
Jackson, MI 49202
517-787-1475

| parts |

Mail order and open shop. Shop open by appointment only. Retail mail order parts source for Nash, Metropolitan and AMC made automobiles, all years, NOS and used.

Webb's Classic Auto Parts
5084 W State Rd 114
Huntington, IN 46750
PH/FAX: 219-344-1714

| NOS parts
used parts |

See full listing in **Section One** under **AMC**

Harold Wenner
5449 Tannery Rd
Schnecksville, PA 18078
610-799-5419

| accessories
parts |

See full listing in **Section One** under **AMC**

Howard Whitelaw
6067 Richmond Rd
Cleveland (Solon), OH 44139
216-721-6755 days
216-439-2159 evenings & weekends
FAX: 216-721-6758

| fenders |

See full listing in **Section One** under **MoPar**

Wymer Classic AMC
Mark Wymer
340 N Justice St
Fremont, OH 43420
419-332-4291, 8 to 5 pm
419-334-6945 after 5 pm

| NOS parts
repairs
used parts |

See full listing in **Section One** under **AMC**

James J Montague
West Rupert, VT 05776
802-394-2929

| parts |

See full listing in **Section One** under **Mercedes-Benz**

NSU/USA Jim Sykes
717 N 68th St
Seattle, WA 98103
206-784-5084

| literature
parts advice
restoration |

Mail order and open shop. Monday-Saturday 1 to 7 pm. Any type NSU including motorcycles and Wankels. Restoration and parts advice free with SASE. Over 25 years' experience.

4-Speeds by Darrell
PO Box 110, #3 Water St
Vermilion, IL 61955
217-275-3743; FAX: 217-275-3515

| transmissions |

See full listing in **Section Two** under **transmissions**

The 60 Oldsmobile Club
Dick Major
10895 E Hibma Rd
Tustin, MI 49688
616-825-2891; FAX: 616-825-8324

newsletter

Information for 1960 Oldsmobiles. We are a newsletter.

A & M SoffSeal Inc
104 May Dr
Harrison, OH 45030
800-426-0902
513-367-0028, service & info
FAX: 513-367-5506

rubber parts
weatherstripping

See full listing in **Section Two** under **rubber parts**

American Plastic Chrome
1398 Mar Ann Dr
Westland, MI 48185
313-721-1967 days
313-261-4454 eves

replating plastic

See full listing in **Section Two** under **plating & polishing**

Antique & Classic Cars Inc
326 S 2nd St
Hamilton, OH 45011
513-844-1146 in OH
800-798-3982 nationwide

bodywork
machine work
painting
parts
service

See full listing in **Section One** under **Buick/McLaughlin**

Art's Antique & Classic Auto Services
1985 E 5th St #15
Tempe, AZ 85281
602-899-6068

restoration

See full listing in **Section One** under **Buick/McLaughlin**

B & D Motors
1309 Kenwood
Cape Girardeau, MO 63701
573-334-3354

rubber parts
sheetmetal
trim

See full listing in **Section One** under **Chevrolet**

Be Happy Automatic Transmission Parts
414 Stivers Rd
Hillsboro, OH 45133
800-416-2862; FAX: 513-442-6133

trans rebuild kits

See full listing in **Section Two** under **transmissions**

Big Boy Accessories
581 Kenbridge Dr
Carson, CA 90746
310-324-4787

parts

See full listing in **Section One** under **Chevrolet**

Brothers Automotive Products
19715 County Rd 355
St Joseph, MO 64505
816-662-2060; FAX: 816-662-2084

parts
restoration

Mail order only. Specializing in parts & restorations for 1964-77 Oldsmobile Cutlass & 442 models. Convertibles are a specialty.

The Bumper Boyz
834 E Florence Ave
Los Angeles, CA 90001
213-587-8976, 800-995-1703
FAX: 213-587-2013

bumper repairs
reconditioning
sand blasting

See full listing in **Section One** under **Chevrolet**

Arthur Burrichter
24026 Highway 151
Monticello, IA 52310
319-465-3064; FAX: 319-465-6048

appraisals
car dealer

See full listing in **Section Two** under **car dealers**

Cars II
6747 Warren Sharon Rd
Brookfield, OH 44403
330-448-2074; FAX: 330-448-1908

parts

See full listing in **Section One** under **Cadillac/LaSalle**

Chevrolet Parts Obsolete
PO Box 0740
Murrieta, CA 92564-0740
909-279-2833; FAX: 909-279-4013

accessories
parts

See full listing in **Section One** under **Chevrolet**

Chewning's Auto Literature
2011 Elm Tree Terr
Buford, GA 30518
770-945-9795

literature
manuals

See full listing in **Section Two** under **literature dealers**

Coach Builders Muscle Car Parts & Services
PO Box 128
Baltimore, MD 21087-0128
410-426-5567

interiors
parts
rust remover

See full listing in **Section One** under **Chevrolet**

The Copper Cooling Works
2455 N 2550 E
Layton, UT 84040
801-544-9939

radiators

See full listing in **Section Two** under **radiators**

Don Cressman
495 Louise Ave N
Listowel, ON Canada N4W 3N5
519-291-1600; FAX: 519-291-1763

parts

See full listing in **Section One** under **Chevrolet**

JB Donaldson Co
2533 W Cypress
Phoenix, AZ 85009
602-278-4505; FAX: 602-278-1112

castings
steering wheels
wood parts

See full listing in **Section Two** under **steering wheels**

ECB, Ed Leek
13 Snipe Rd
Key Largo, FL 33037
PH/FAX: 305-451-0864

fiberglass parts

See full listing in **Section Two** under **fiberglass parts**

Egge Machine Company
11707 Slauson Ave
Santa Fe Springs, CA 90670
310-945-3419 in CA
800-866-EGGE
FAX: 310-693-1635

babbitting
chassis
motor mounts
pistons
valves
wiring harnesses

See full listing in **Section Two** under **engine parts**

Engineering & Manufacturing Services | sheetmetal
Box 24362
Cleveland, OH 44124-0362
216-446-1620; FAX: 216-446-9590

See full listing in **Section One** under **Ford '32-'53**

Extensions Plus Inc | body filler parts
3500 Park Central Blvd N
Pompano Beach, FL 33064
954-978-3362; FAX: 954-978-0630
E-mail: 4star@gate.net

See full listing in **Section Two** under **body parts**

John Filiss | appraisals
45 Kingston Ave
Port Jervis, NY 12771
914-856-2942

See full listing in **Section Two** under **appraisals**

Lectric Limited Inc | parts
7322 S Archer Road
Justice, IL 60458
708-563-0400; FAX: 708-458-2662

See full listing in **Section One** under **Corvette**

LES Auto Parts | parts
Box 81
Dayton, NJ 08810
908-329-6128

See full listing in **Section One** under **Chevrolet**

M & H Electric Fabricators Inc | wiring harnesses
13537 Alondra Blvd
Santa Fe Springs, CA 90670
310-926-9552; FAX: 310-926-9572

See full listing in **Section Two** under **electrical systems**

J Miller Restoration | parts
Rt 2, Box 281
Buchanan, TN 38222
901-642-5937

Mail order and open shop. Monday-Saturday 8 to 5. Oldsmobile specialist. Unrestored cars for sale. 1930-1960 parts. Other unrestored cars: Ford, Chrysler, GM. Listing available.

Clayton T Nelson | NOS parts
Box 259
Warrenville, IL 60555
708-369-6589

Mail order only. Specializing in NOS parts for Oldsmobile and MoPar, late 1940s to mid 1970s.

NOS Reproductions | parts
22425 Sefferlies Rd
RR 3
Komoka, ON Canada N0L 1R0
519-471-2740; FAX: 519-471-7675

See full listing in **Section One** under **MoPar**

The Paddock® Inc | accessories parts
PO Box 30
221 W Main
Knightstown, IN 46148
800-428-4319; FAX: 317-345-2264
E-mail: paddock@indy.net

See full listing in **Section One** under **Mustang**

Paddock West® Inc | accessories parts
1663 Plum Ln
PO Box 8547
Redlands, CA 92375
800-854-8532; FAX: 909-798-1482
E-mail: padwest@msn.com

See full listing in **Section One** under **Mustang**

M Parker Autoworks Inc | battery cables harnesses
150 Cooper Rd, Unit C-7
Dept HVAA
West Berlin, NJ 08091
609-753-0350; FAX: 609-753-0353

See full listing in **Section Two** under **electrical systems**

David Raine's Springcrafters | springs suspension parts
425 Harding Hwy
Carney's Point, NJ 08069
609-299-9141; FAX: 609-299-9157

See full listing in **Section Two** under **suspension parts**

REM Automotive Inc | interior parts
Box 241, Rt 1, Brandt Rd
Annville, PA 17003
717-838-4242; FAX: 717-838-5091

See full listing in **Section Two** under **restoration aids**

Ross' Automotive Machine Co Inc | racing engines rebuilding
1763 N Main St
Niles, OH 44446
330-544-4466

See full listing in **Section Two** under **engine rebuilding**

Harry Samuel | carpet fabrics interiors upholstery covers
65 Wisner St
Pontiac, MI 48342-1066
248-335-1900

See full listing in **Section Two** under **interiors & interior parts**

Spark Plugs & Stuff | tune-up kits
PO Box 33343
San Diego, CA 92163-3343
619-220-1745

See full listing in **Section Two** under **ignition parts**

Stencils & Stripes Unlimited Inc | NOS decals stripe kits
1108 S Crescent Ave #21
Park Ridge, IL 60068
708-692-6893; FAX: 708-692-6895

See full listing in **Section Two** under **decals**

Street-Wise Performance | differentials parts rebuild kits transmissions
Richie Mulligan
105 Creek Rd
Tranquility, NJ 07879
201-786-6668 day
201-786-7133 evenings

See full listing in **Section Two** under **transmissions**

NO PITCHING!

NO SIDE-SWAY!   NO ROLL!

Supercars Unlimited
8029 Unit A SW 17th
Portland, OR 97219-2857
503-244-8249; FAX: 503-244-9639

parts

Mail order only. Hours 9 am-4 pm PST. Replacement parts and restoration items, mechanical parts (no chrome or sheetmetal) for 1964 through 1977 Oldsmobile Cutlass, 4-4-2 and Hurst/ Olds. Cutlass/4-4-2 is all we do!

Tom's Classic Parts
5207 Sundew Terr
Tobyhanna, PA 18466
800-832-4073

parts

See full listing in **Section One** under **Chevrolet**

Triangle Automotive
PO Box 2293
Arcadia, CA 91077
818-357-2377
626-357-2377 (starting July 97)

parts

Mail order only. Specializing in original parts, body, interior, chrome and trim, options for 1965-77 Oldsmobile (Cutlass & 442). We can locate most choice used parts for other similar GM models as well.

Year One Inc
PO Box 129
Tucker, GA 30085
800-YEAR-ONE (932-7663)
770-493-6568 Atlanta & overseas
FAX: 800-680-6806
FAX: 770-496-1949 Atlanta/overseas

parts

See full listing in **Section Two** under **comprehensive parts**

Opel GT Source
8030 Remmet Ave, Unit 11
Canoga Park, CA 91304
818-992-7776; FAX: 818-712-9222

parts
technical info

Mail order and open shop. Monday-Friday 9 am-6 pm PST. Parts, technical information, restoration, high-performance, direct importer for German made Opels 1965-1975. Specializing in parts for 1968-1973 Opel GT. Largest inventory of new Opel parts in the US.

Opel Oldtimer Service Denmark
Mosede Kaervej 47
Greve DK-2670 Denmark
+45-42-901073, best 11 am-3 pm CST

literature
parts
parts locators

Mail order only. Specializing in parts, parts location, parts rebuilding, parts catalogues, shop manuals and other literature for rear wheel drive Opel automobiles.

Opel Parts & Service Inc
3961 S Military Hwy
Chesapeake, VA 23321
804-487-3851

parts
service

Mail order and open shop. M-F 10-5. Specializing in Opels since 1970. 57-75 Opel NOS, rebuilt, reproduction and used parts. Major components service. Specializing in Rekord, Kadette, Manta and GT.

Opels Unlimited
871 E Lambert Rd #C
La Habra, CA 90631
310-690-1051; FAX: 310-690-3352
E-mail: concept@primenet.com

parts
service

Mail order and open shop. Shop open Monday-Saturday 12 pm to 8 pm. Specializing in parts and service for all Opels made from 1960 to date. We have a club newsletter for free. We have a vast inventory of specialty parts and aftermarket power goodies for your car. We buy cars and parts all the time. Finder's fee paid. We stock many rust-free restorable California Opel bodies as cheap as $300 at all times. Remember our motto: If you bought it somewhere else you paid too much!

Antique & Classic Cars
Rt 15, Box 454
Florence, AL 35633
205-760-0542

car locator

See full listing in **Section One** under **Cadillac/LaSalle**

Antique & Classic Cars Inc
326 S 2nd St
Hamilton, OH 45011
513-844-1146 in OH
800-798-3982 nationwide

bodywork
machine work
painting
parts
service

See full listing in **Section One** under **Buick/McLaughlin**

**Be Happy Automatic
Transmission Parts**
414 Stivers Rd
Hillsboro, OH 45133
800-416-2862; FAX: 513-442-6133

trans rebuild kits

See full listing in **Section Two** under **transmissions**

Blackhawk Collection
3600 Blackhawk Plaza Cir
Danville, CA 94506-3600
510-736-3444; FAX: 510-736-4375

acquisitions
sales

See full listing in **Section One** under **Duesenberg**

**Bob's Radio & TV Service/
Vintage Electronics**
2300 Broad St
San Lius Obispo, CA 94401
805-543-2946; FAX: 805-782-0803

radios

See full listing in **Section Two** under **radios**

Bill Boudway
105 Deerfield Dr
Canandaigua, NY 14424
716-394-6172

restoration info

Mail order only. Copies of restoration information, advertising material and parts lists for Packard Twin Six automobiles, 1916 thru 1923.

Brasilia Press
PO Box 2023
Elkhart, IN 46515
FAX: 219-262-8799

models

See full listing in **Section Two** under **models & toys**

Brinton's Antique Auto Parts   parts
6826 SW McVey Ave
Redmond, OR 97756
541-548-3483; FAX: 541-548-8022

Mail order and open shop. Dismantles Packard cars and chassis
and sells the parts taken off them. Sixes, Eights and Super 8s.
Also 12-cylinders. Parts for 1920s-1958 Packards.

Arthur Burrichter   appraisals
24026 Highway 151   car dealer
Monticello, IA 52310
319-465-3064; FAX: 319-465-6048

See full listing in **Section Two** under **car dealers**

Cape Cod Classic Cars   car dealer
Pete Harvey
PO Box 280
Cataumet, MA 02534
508-548-0660; FAX: 508-457-0660

See full listing in **Section One** under **Cadillac/LaSalle**

Chrome Masters   chrome plating
1109 W Orange Ave, Unit D   pot metal restoration
Tallahassee, FL 32310
904-576-2100

See full listing in **Section Two** under **plating & polishing**

Classic Cars Inc   cars
1 Maple Terr   parts
Hibernia, NJ 07842
201-627-1975

Mail order only. Pre-WW II Packard parts and Packard cars for
1928-42. 4-page price sheet of new parts.

Classics 'n More Inc   repairs
1001 Ranck Mill Rd   restoration
Lancaster, PA 17602
717-392-0599; FAX 717-392-2371

See full listing in **Section Two** under **restoration shops**

Collector Car Appraisals   appraisals
L E Lazarus, Senior Appraiser
PO Box 6732
Rockford, IL 61125
815-229-1258; FAX: 815-229-1238

See full listing in **Section Two** under **appraisals**

Collector Cars-U-Can-Afford Ltd   car dealer
4046 11th St
Rockford, IL 61109
815-229-1258; FAX: 815-229-1238

See full listing in **Section One** under **Cadillac/LaSalle**

Collector's CARS Inc   restoration
150 E St Joseph St   service
Arcadia, CA 91006
818-447-2576; FAX: 818-447-1461

See full listing in **Section Two** under **restoration shops**

Tom Crook Classic Cars   car dealer
27611 42nd Ave S
Auburn, WA 98001
206-941-3454

See full listing in **Section Two** under **car dealers**

Dave's Auto Restoration   upholstery
2285 Rt 307 E
Jefferson, OH 44047
PH/FAX: 216-858-2227

See full listing in **Section Two** under **interiors & interior parts**

Deters Restorations   restoration
6205 Swiss Garden Rd
Temperance, MI 48182-1020
313-847-1820

See full listing in **Section Two** under **restoration shops**

Dexter Auto Inc   restoration
2096 W Shore Rd
Warwick, RI 02886
401-732-3575

See full listing in **Section Two** under **restoration shops**

JB Donaldson Co   castings
2533 W Cypress   steering wheels
Phoenix, AZ 85009   wood parts
602-278-4505; FAX: 602-278-1112

See full listing in **Section Two** under **steering wheels**

Dylan Bay Auto Museum   museum
1411 4th Ave, #1430   restoration
Seattle, WA 98101   storage
206-292-9874; FAX: 206-292-9876
E-mail: cbayley@dylanbay.com

See full listing in **Section Six** under **Washington**

Edgerton Classics Ltd   restoration
RR 5 Box 199   woodworking
Canastota, NY 13032
315-697-2722

See full listing in **Section Two** under **restoration shops**

Egge Machine Company   babbitting
11707 Slauson Ave   chassis
Santa Fe Springs, CA 90670   motor mounts
310-945-3419 in CA   pistons
800-866-EGGE   valves
FAX: 310-693-1635   wiring harnesses

See full listing in **Section Two** under **engine parts**

Jay M Fisher   radiator caps
Acken Dr 4-B   sidemount mirrors
Clark, NJ 07066
908-388-6442

See full listing in **Section Two** under **accessories**

From Rust To Riches   appraisals
14200 New Hampshire Ave   car dealer
Silver Spring, MD 20904   repairs
301-384-5856; FAX: 301-989-1866   restoration

See full listing in **Section Two** under **restoration shops**

Green Valentine Inc   car dealer
5055 Covington Way   woodies
Memphis, TN 38134
901-373-5555; FAX: 901-373-5568

See full listing in **Section Two** under **car dealers**

Guild of Automotive Restorers
18237 Woodbine Ave
Sharon, ON Canada L0G 1V0
905-895-0035; FAX: 905-895-0036
E-mail: theguild@interhop.com

restoration
sales
service

See full listing in **Section Two** under **restoration shops**

Hagerty Classic Insurance
PO Box 87
Traverse City, MI 49685
800-922-4050; FAX: 616-941-8227

insurance

See full listing in **Section Two** under **insurance**

James Hill
Box 547-V
Goodwell, OK 73939
405-349-2736 evenings/weekends

ignition parts
source list

Mail order and open shop located in home. Above address for school months; summers (June to mid-August): 1107 Washington, Emporia, KS 66801, PH: 316/343-6024 some evenings/weekends. Packard only: points for most 1935-56; mostly "Service" to Packard people in compiling and publishing my Source List. By the way, the next edition will be in 1998. Brass gasoline screen. He publishes *Sources of Packard Parts & Services* telling "who sells what" for $5 for the 33 page listing with value guaranteed! Current edition for 1996.

Interesting Parts Inc
Paul TerHorst
27526 N Owens Rd
Mundelein, IL 60060
PH/FAX: 847-949-1030

appraisals
gaskets
parts
storage
transport

See full listing in **Section Two** under **comprehensive parts**

Jesser's Classic Keys
26 West St, Dept HVA
Akron, OH 44303-2344
330-376-8181; FAX: 330-384-9129

automobilia
keys

See full listing in **Section Two** under **locks & keys**

L & L Antique Auto Trim
403 Spruce, Box 177
Pierce City, MO 65723
417-476-2871

runningboard
moldings

See full listing in **Section Two** under **special services**

Gerald J Lettieri
132 Old Main St
Rocky Hill, CT 06067
860-529-7177; FAX: 860-257-3621

gaskets
parts

See full listing in **Section Two** under **gaskets**

Lincoln Highway Packards
Main St, PO Box 94
Schellsburg, PA 15559
814-733-4356; FAX: 814-839-4276

engine rebuilding
restoration

Open shop Monday-Friday 8 to 4; other times by appointment. Specializing in restoration on Packards and Cords. We do auto restoration, engine, transmission, differential overhaul, carburetor rebuilding, starter, generator, regulator repair, rewiring.

Motor Car Restoration & Service
189-15 Devereese Rd
Chehalis, WA 98532
206-748-7977

painting
restoration

Engine, chassis and body restoration, lacquer painting and detailing. Specializing in Packards. Many used and reproduction Packard parts.

Oak Bows
122 Ramsey Ave
Chambersburg, PA 17201
717-264-2602

top bows

See full listing in **Section Two** under **woodwork**

Packard Archives
1876 English St
St Paul, MN 55109
612-484-1184; FAX: 612-771-1521

accessories
artwork
automobilia

Highest prices paid for Packard automobile dealership and factory memorabilia/collectibles. Cash for dealer giveaways, lapel pins, signs, NOS parts, literature, clocks, filmstrips & movies. Original artwork, accessories, Packard jewelry, rings, watches, awards, pin backs, buttons, advertising promotional items, master salesman awards, metal tin cans & bottles, etc, anything Packard.

Packard Farm
97 N 150 W
Greenfield, IN 46140
317-462-3124
800-922-1957 orders only
FAX: 317-462-8891

parts

Mail order and open shop. Monday-Friday 8:30 to 5. Saturday 8:30 to 12 noon by appointment. For Packards, Chevrolets and Studebakers.

Packard Friends Garage
1 Packard Pl
Welcome Center Exit 1 Rt 4
Fair Haven, VT 05743
802-265-3105, garage
802-265-7969; FAX: 802-265-8050

parts

Packard garage, repair and restoration. Packard only. Huge inventory of used, NOS and reproduction parts. All years but leaning heavily in the 1935 to 1942 Junior cars. Keeping about 200 parts cars. VISA, MasterCard and Discover. Offering a happiness guarantee with quick and friendly service. Currently shipping to 30 countries.

Packard Store
9 Hall Hill Rd
Sterling, CT 06377
860-564-5345

parts

Mail order or visit old barn full of Packard parts. A one stop place for 1940 Packards. We have a huge selection of sheetmetal, trim, interior and driveline parts for all models. Glass for gauges with letters and numbers. We have the paint for gauges and interior. Flock is available for all Packards, 30s-50s. Complete restorations.

Patrician Industries Inc
22644 Nona
Dearborn, MI 48124
313-565-3573

parts

Mail order and open shop. Shop open by appointment only. Handles a full line of new, used and reproduction Packard parts for Packards 1940-56.

Potomac Packard
3031 Hunt Rd
Oakton, VA 22124
800-859-9532 orders
FAX: 703-620-2626

wiring harnesses

Manufactures and supplies electrical wiring harnesses and equipment for Packards, 1916-1956. Our products are made to exacting standards, using Packard engineering drawings or original wiring harnesses as patterns. All harnesses are made using the correct gauge wire and color code then loomed or overbraided as original. Each wire is identified for easy installation. Our harnesses are 100 point in both appearance and service and satisfaction is assured or money refunded. Send $2 for 36-page catalog, includes a $5 coupon.

Restorations Unlimited II Inc
304 Jandus Rd
Cary, IL 60013
847-639-5818

restoration

See full listing in **Section Two** under **restoration shops**

RM Auto Restoration Ltd
825 Park Ave W
Chatham, ON Canada N7M 5J6
519-352-4575; FAX: 519-351-1337

panel fabrication
parts
restoration

See full listing in **Section Two** under **restoration shops**

R-Mac Publications Inc
Rt 3, Box 425
Jasper, FL 32052
904-792-2480; FAX: 904-792-3230

magazine

See full listing in **Section Four** under **books & publications**

Don Rook
184 Raspberry Ln
Mena, AR 71953
501-394-7555

parts

See full listing in **Section One** under **Chrysler**

Seattle Packard
PO Box 2262
Seattle, WA 98111
206-726-9625

repair
restoration

Specializing in repair, maintenance and restoration of collector cars 1897-1957, including Packard, Pierce, Franklin, Hudson, and Studebaker.

Steve's Studebaker-Packard
2287 Second St
Napa, CA 94559
707-255-8945

car dealer
parts
suspension repairs

Mail order and open shop. Evenings and weekends. Appointment suggested. Specialized Packard services, such as torsion-level suspension and tele-touch electric shift repairs and rebuilding. Specializing in parts for 1951-56 Packards and 1953-66 Studebakers. Packard and Studebaker vehicle sales.

John Ulrich
450 Silver Ave
San Francisco, CA 94112
510-223-9587 days

parts

Mail order and open shop by appointment only. Monday-Friday 9 to 5. Packard parts from 1928 to 1956. Approximately 20% of the inventory is NOS, the balance is from parted out cars. Strongest part of inventory is 38-41 Junior and Senior Series. I buy inventories. I have available sheetmetal, fenders, hoods, wheels, drums, trim, engines, transmissions, differentials, engine parts, switches, dash parts, gauges and 1,000s more parts. I also offer a no hassle guarantee, if not satisfied return within 60 days for refund or exchange.

Tom Vagnini
58 Anthony Rd
RR 3
Pittsfield, MA 01201
413-698-2526

used parts

Mail order and open shop Mon-Sat by appointment. 10 am-4 pm. Specializing in used parts for Packards 1923-1931, Chevrolet 1930-31.

Wallace Walmsley
4732 Bancroft St, #7
San Diego, CA 92116
619-283-3063

parts

Mail order and open shop. Shop open 6 days by appointment. Specializing in Packard parts, 1935-1942. Sunvisors for GM cars, 34-39 convertibles.

Woodgrain by Estes
7550 Richardson Rd
Sarasota, FL 34240
813-379-3669

woodgraining

See full listing in **Section Two** under **woodgraining**

ABS Exotic Repair Inc
1561 N Federal Hwy
Ft Lauderdale, FL 33304
954-566-7785; FAX: 954-566-7271

parts
service

See full listing in **Section One** under **Mercedes-Benz**

Tom Crook Classic Cars
27611 42nd Ave S
Auburn, WA 98001
206-941-3454

car dealer

See full listing in **Section Two** under **car dealers**

Foreign Motors West
253 N Main St
Natick, MA 01760
508-655-5350; FAX: 508-651-0178

car sales

See full listing in **Section One** under **Rolls-Royce/Bentley**

Wagner Automotive
1051 Schiff Ave
Cincinnati, OH 45205
513-244-6793

books
information
parts
parts locator

I am continuing the Peugeot hobby with some dealer NOS obsolete parts for Models 403, 404, 304, 504. Emphasis placed on Model 404 sedans, wagons, convertibles. Used 404 parts, too. Repair manuals and parts identification information, parts searching. Free advice and answering questions are all a part of the Peugeot fun. Presently looking for partners in parts collecting. Please write, SASE expected.

PIERCE-ARROW

The Brassworks   radiators
289 Prado Rd
San Louis Obispo, CA 93401
800-342-6759; FAX: 805-544-5615

See full listing in **Section Two** under **radiators**

Cobb's Antique Auto Restoration   restoration
717 Western Ave   service
Washington Court House, OH 43160
614-335-7489

See full listing in **Section Two** under **restoration shops**

L & L Antique Auto Trim   runningboard
403 Spruce, Box 177   moldings
Pierce City, MO 65723
417-476-2871

See full listing in **Section Two** under **special services**

Rank & Son Buick-GMC   car dealer
4200 N Green Bay Ave   parts
Milwaukee, WI 53209
414-372-4000

See full listing in **Section One** under **Buick/McLaughlin**

Eric Rosenau   restoration
16930 Handlebar Rd
Ramona, CA 92065
619-789-4597

Shop open by appointment only. Specializing in Pierce-Arrow.

Seattle Packard   repair
PO Box 2262   restoration
Seattle, WA 98111
206-726-9625

See full listing in **Section One** under **Packard**

AARcadia Parts Locating   parts
8294 Allport Ave
Santa Fe Springs, CA 90670
310-698-8067; FAX: 310-696-6505

See full listing in **Section One** under **MoPar**

AKH Wheels   Rallye wheels
1207 N A St   styled steel wheels
Ellensburg, WA 98926-2522   vintage aluminum
509-962-3390

See full listing in **Section Two** under **wheels & wheelcovers**

Antique DeSoto-Plymouth   MoPar parts
4206 Burnett Dr
Murrysville, PA 15668
412-733-1818 eves
FAX: 412-243-4556 anytime

See full listing in **Section One** under **MoPar**

Barracuda Classic   accessories
1500 Adams Ave, #105-162   parts
Costa Mesa, CA 92626
PH/FAX: 714-444-2507

See full listing in **Section One** under **MoPar**

Andy Bernbaum Auto Parts   parts
315 Franklin St
Newton, MA 02158
617-244-1118

See full listing in **Section One** under **MoPar**

Bill's Speed Shop   body parts
13951 Millersburg Rd
Navarre, OH 44662
330-832-9403; FAX: 330-832-2098

See full listing in **Section One** under **Chevrolet**

Burchill Antique Auto Parts Inc   parts
4150 24th Ave   technical info
Fort Gratiot, MI 48061
810-385-3838

See full listing in **Section One** under **Chrysler**

Thomas Cavaliere   parts
10 Marsha Terr
Parsippany, NJ 07054
201-334-8568

See full listing in **Section One** under **MoPar**

Convertible Service   convertible parts
5126-HA Walnut Grove Ave   top mechanism
San Gabriel, CA 91776   service
800-333-1140, 818-285-2255
FAX: 818-285-9004

See full listing in **Section Two** under **tops**

DeLorean Literature   collectibles
3116 Welsh Rd   literature
Philadelphia, PA 19136-1810
215-338-6142

See full listing in **Section One** under **DeLorean**

Lawrence DeSenville   mech & trim
Box 423   parts
1440 Kenilworth
Berwyn, IL 60402
708-788-6759

See full listing in **Section One** under **Chrysler**

Dynatech Engineering   motor mounts
PO Box 1446
Alta Loma, CA 91701-8446
805-492-6134

See full listing in **Section Two** under **suspension parts**

Bruce Ebmeier
Obsolete Parts Depot   parts
2905 N Osage Ave
Juniata, NE 68955-3002
FAX: 402-751-2566

See full listing in **Section One** under **MoPar**

ETC Every Thing Cars   restoration
8727 Clarinda
Pico Rivera, CA 90660
310-949-6981

See full listing in **Section One** under **MoPar**

Extensions Plus Inc   body filler parts
3500 Park Central Blvd N
Pompano Beach, FL 33064
954-978-3362; FAX: 954-978-0630
E-mail: 4star@gate.net

See full listing in **Section Two** under **body parts**

Historic Video Archives   videotapes
PO Box 189-VA
Cedar Knolls, NJ 07927-0189

See full listing in **Section Two** under **automobilia**

Imperial Motors   parts
2165 Spencer Creek Rd
Campobello, SC 29322
864-895-3474

See full listing in **Section One** under **Chrysler**

Jeff Johnson Motorsports   accessories
4421 Aldrich Pl   literature
Columbus, OH 43214   parts
614-268-1181; FAX: 614-268-1141

See full listing in **Section One** under **MoPar**

Koller Dodge   restoration parts
1565 W Ogden Ave
Naperville, IL 60540-3906
708-355-3411

See full listing in **Section One** under **Dodge**

Kramer Automotive Specialties   body parts
PO Box 5   interiors
Herman, PA 16039   sheetmetal
412-285-5566

See full listing in **Section One** under **MoPar**

Legendary Auto Interiors Ltd   soft trim
121 W Shore Blvd
Newark, NY 14513
800-363-8804; FAX: 800-732-8874

See full listing in **Section One** under **Chrysler**

Lloyd's Literature   literature
PO Box 491
Newbury, OH 44065
800-292-2665; 216-338-1527
FAX: 216-338-2222

See full listing in **Section Two** under **literature dealers**

MikeCo Antique, Kustom &   lenses
Obsolete Auto Parts   parts
4053 Calle Tesoro, Unit C
Camarillo, CA 93012
805-482-1725; FAX: 805-987-8524

See full listing in **Section One** under **MoPar**

Mitchell Motor Parts Inc   car dealer
1601 Thraikill Rd   parts
Grove City, OH 43123
614-875-4919; FAX: 614-875-9960

See full listing in **Section One** under **MoPar**

Clayton T Nelson   NOS parts
Box 259
Warrenville, IL 60555
708-369-6589

See full listing in **Section One** under **Oldsmobile**

NOS Reproductions   parts
22425 Sefferlies Rd
RR 3
Komoka, ON Canada N0L 1R0
519-471-2740; FAX: 519-471-7675

See full listing in **Section One** under **MoPar**

NS-One   NOS parts
PO Box 2459, Dept VA
Cedar Rapids, IA 52406
319-362-7717

See full listing in **Section One** under **Chrysler**

Performance Motor Parts   parts
Box 122
West Milton, OH 45383
PH/FAX: 513-698-4259

See full listing in **Section One** under **MoPar**

Plymouth, Dodge, Chrysler,   NOS parts for
DeSoto Parts   DeSoto
935 Limecrest Rd
Pittsburgh, PA 15668
412-733-1818 eves
FAX: 412-243-4556 anytime

See full listing in **Section One** under **DeSoto**

R & R Fiberglass & Specialties   body parts
4850 Wilson Dr NW
Cleveland, TN 37312
423-476-2270

See full listing in **Section Two** under **fiberglass parts**

Restorations By Julius   restoration
22434 Itasca St
Chatsworth, CA 91311
818-882-2866

Open shop only. Monday-Friday 8 am to 5 pm. Specializing in
66-71 Chrysler, Plymouth, Dodge.

Riddle's/Mr Plymouth   decals
452 Newton   overdrives
Seattle, WA 98109   parts & info
206-285-6534 days   repro parts

See full listing in **Section One** under **MoPar**

Roanoke Motor Co Inc   car dealer
422 N Main
Roanoke, IL 61561
309-923-7171; FAX: 309-923-7332

See full listing in **Section One** under **Chrysler**

R/T Connection   parts
1034 Dover St
Warren, OH 44485
330-399-3959

See full listing in **Section One** under **MoPar**

Paul Slater Auto Parts   parts
9496 85th St N
Stillwater, MN 55082
612-429-4235

See full listing in **Section One** under **Dodge**

Ed Spiegel   literature
Box 402   parts
Murrysville, PA 15668
412-733-1818 evenings

See full listing in **Section One** under **Chrysler**

Weimann's Literature &   literature
Collectables
16 Cottage Rd
Harwinton, CT 06791
860-485-0300
FAX: 860-485-1705, 24 hours

Mail order or appointment only. Plymouth, Dodge/Dodge truck, DeSoto, Chrysler, Imperial literature. We carry most 1928 to date showroom catalogs, folders, data/trim books, service/shop, parts listing books, plus tech service/sales records/filmstrips, etc. Owner's manuals, accessories, books. Almost anything paper. Color and b&w copying service for Plymouth. We buy, sell, trade. Please send stamped addressed envelope with inquiries.

Year One Inc   parts
PO Box 129
Tucker, GA 30085
800-YEAR-ONE (932-7663)
770-493-6568 Atlanta & overseas
FAX: 800-680-6806
FAX: 770-496-1949 Atlanta/overseas

See full listing in **Section Two** under **comprehensive parts**

PONTIAC®

4-Speeds by Darrell   transmissions
PO Box 110
#3 Water St
Vermilion, IL 61955
217-275-3743; FAX: 217-275-3515

See full listing in **Section Two** under **transmissions**

A & M SoffSeal Inc   rubber parts
104 May Dr   weatherstripping
Harrison, OH 45030
800-426-0902
513-367-0028, service & info
FAX: 513-367-5506

See full listing in **Section Two** under **rubber parts**

American Classics Unlimited Inc   automobilia
Frank Groll-Karen Groll   models & toys
PO Box 192   novelty license
Oak Lawn, IL 60454-0192   plates
PH/FAX: 708-424-9223   sales literature

See full listing in **Section Two** under **models & toys**

Art's Antique & Classic Auto   restoration
Services
1985 E 5th St #15
Tempe, AZ 85281
602-899-6068

See full listing in **Section One** under **Buick/McLaughlin**

Auto Decals Unlimited Inc   decals
11259 E Via Linda, Ste 100-201   stripe kits
Scottsdale, AZ 85259
602-860-9800; FAX: 602-860-8370

See full listing in **Section Two** under **decals**

B & D Motors   rubber parts
1309 Kenwood   sheetmetal
Cape Girardeau, MO 63701   trim
573-334-3354

See full listing in **Section One** under **Chevrolet**

Big Boy Accessories   parts
581 Kenbridge Dr
Carson, CA 90746
310-324-4787

See full listing in **Section One** under **Chevrolet**

Bill's Birds   new parts
1021 Commack Rd   repro parts
Dix Hills, NY 11746   used parts
516-243-6789, 516-667-3853

Mail order and open shop. Monday to Saturday, 8:30 am to 8 pm. Specializing in Pontiac Firebird parts new & used & 67 & up repro parts. We also have emblems for the 67-69 Firebird, GTO, LeMans and Tempest and also some big cars, Grand Prix & Bonneville. All emblems are top quality reproductions and some NOS.

Boneyard Stan   cars
218 N 69th Ave   parts
Phoenix, AZ 85043
602-936-8045

Mail order and open shop. Open 7 days a week. Call first. Specializing in 1950-80s Pontiac cars and parts. Also have many other types of cars and will locate cars and parts. Shipping anywhere, US, Canada, overseas.

The Bumper Boyz   bumper repairs
834 E Florence Ave   reconditioning
Los Angeles, CA 90001   sand blasting
213-587-8976, 800-995-1703
FAX: 213-587-2013

See full listing in **Section One** under **Chevrolet**

Camaro-Heaven
64 River Street
Rochester, NH 03867
800-CAMARO-1; FAX: 603-332-3299

cars
parts
salvage yard

See full listing in **Section One** under **Chevelle/Camaro**

Camaro Specialties
112 Elm St
East Aurora, NY 14052
716-652-7086; FAX: 716-652-2279

parts
restoration

See full listing in **Section One** under **Chevelle/Camaro**

Chevrolet Parts Obsolete
PO Box 0740
Murrieta, CA 92564-0740
909-279-2833; FAX: 909-279-4013

accessories
parts

See full listing in **Section One** under **Chevrolet**

Dick Choler Cars & Service Inc
640 E Jackson Blvd
Elkhart, IN 46516
219-522-8281; FAX: 219-522-8282

car dealer
literature
model cars

Mail order and open shop. Car dealer, literature, posters, car pictures and model cars of all years. Specializing in Pontiacs for 49 years, big, small or just Pontiacs. We counsel on all years to your satisfaction.

Classic Auto Literature
Box 53 Blueback, RR 2
Nanoose Bay, BC Canada V0R 2R0
250-468-9522

data books
literature/manuals
models/parts catalog
posters

See full listing in **Section two** under **literature dealers**

The Classic Car Radio Co
2718 Koper Dr
Sterling Heights, MI 48310
810-977-7979; info: 810-268-2918
FAX: 810-977-0895

radios

See full listing in **Section Two** under **radios**

Classic Industries Inc
Firebird Parts & Accessories Catalog
17832 Gothard St
Huntington Beach, CA 92647
800-854-1280 ext 210 toll-free in USA; FAX: 800-300-3081 toll-free

accessories
parts

Firebird/Trans Am parts and accessories catalog. Over 400 full color pages of the largest selection of original and reproduction products and accessories ever assembled. Easy to read format allows you to choose from literally thousands of different products, each containing a color photo and a brief description. Classic Industries is an official GM Restoration Parts licensee assuring the highest quality parts and accessories for 1967 through 1996 Firebirds and Trans Ams. Call or write for your personal copy today. Cost, $5.

See our ad inside the front cover

Clock Doc®
125 University Ave
Sewanee, TN 37375
800-256-5362; FAX: 615-598-5986

clock repairs
gauge repairs

See full listing in **Section Two** under **instruments**

Coach Builders Muscle Car Parts & Services
PO Box 128
Baltimore, MD 21087-0128
410-426-5567

interiors
parts
rust remover

See full listing in **Section One** under **Chevrolet**

Competitive Automotive Inc
2095 W Shore Rd (Rt 117)
Warwick, RI 02886
401-739-6262, 401-739-6288
FAX: 401-739-1497

parts
restoration

See full listing in **Section One** under **Chevelle/Camaro**

Don Cressman
495 Louise Ave N
Listowel, ON Canada N4W 3N5
519-291-1600; FAX: 519-291-1763

parts

See full listing in **Section One** under **Chevrolet**

CSK Publishing Co Inc
299 Market St
Saddle Brook, NJ 07662
201-712-9300; FAX: 201-712-0990
E-mail: staff@cskpub.com

periodical

See full listing in **Section Four** under **periodicals**

Custom Classic Cars
2046 E 12B Road
Bourbon, IN 46504
219-342-0399
E-mail: asmith7112@aol.com

parts
restoration

See full listing in **Section One** under **Chevrolet**

Dynatech Engineering
PO Box 1446
Alta Loma, CA 91701-8446
805-492-6134

motor mounts

See full listing in **Section Two** under **suspension parts**

Eagle Wire Products
3308 Valley Forge Dr
Knoxville, TN 37920
PH/FAX: 800-977-0030

wire harnesses

See full listing in **Section Two** under **electrical systems**

ECB, Ed Leek
13 Snipe Rd
Key Largo, FL 33037
PH/FAX: 305-451-0864

fiberglass parts

See full listing in **Section Two** under **fiberglass parts**

Egge Machine Company
11707 Slauson Ave
Santa Fe Springs, CA 90670
310-945-3419 in CA
800-866-EGGE
FAX: 310-693-1635

babbitting
chassis
motor mounts
pistons
valves
wiring harnesses

See full listing in **Section Two** under **engine parts**

Engineering & Manufacturing Services
Box 24362
Cleveland, OH 44124-0362
216-446-1620; FAX: 216-446-9590

sheetmetal

See full listing in **Section One** under **Ford '32-'53**

ETC Every Thing Cars — restoration
8727 Clarinda
Pico Rivera, CA 90660
310-949-6981

See full listing in **Section One** under **MoPar**

John Filiss — appraisals
45 Kingston Ave
Port Jervis, NY 12771
914-856-2942

See full listing in **Section Two** under **appraisals**

FireAro Restoration Parts Co — accessories / parts
935 Hedge Dr
Mississauga, ON Canada L4Y 1E9
PH/FAX: 905-277-3230

See full listing in **Section One** under **Chevelle/Camaro**

Fleetline Automotive — parts
PO Box 291
Highland, NY 12528
914-691-9228

See full listing in **Section Five** under **New York**

Fowlkes Realty & Auction — appraisals / auctions
500 Hale St
Newman Grove, NE 68758
800-275-5522; FAX: 402-447-6000

See full listing in **Section One** under **Chevrolet**

Green's Obsolete Parts — NOS parts / used parts
9 June St
Pepperell, MA 01463
508-433-9363; FAX: 508-433-8746

Mail order and open shop. Open Monday & Tuesday 9 to 9, Wednesday-Friday 9 to 6, Saturday 9 to 1 EST. Specializing in NOS and some used parts for all 1936-1986 Pontiacs. We have a large inventory of mostly NOS parts for most restorations. We can also answer most questions with our extensive library of Pontiac literature. Free computer parts lists available for specified years and models of Pontiacs.

Hjeltness Restoration Inc — restoration / service
630 Alpine Way
Escondido, CA 92029
619-746-9966; FAX: 619-746-7738

See full listing in **Section Two** under **restoration shops**

The Indian Artifacts Collection — jewelry
PO Box 350288
Brooklyn, NY 11235
718-332-4479

Mail order only. Specializing in sterling silver & 14kt gold jewelry (rings, pendants, earrings, tie tacks, cufflinks, etc) for Pontiac and Pontiac GTO automobile owners and enthusiasts. 1997 will see offerings for Grand Prix, Firebird/Trans Am and other Pontiac nameplates.

The Judge's Chambers — parts / automobilia
114 Prince George Dr
Hampton, VA 23669
757-838-2059 evenings

Mail order only. Parts for 1969-71 Pontiac GTO Judge, including stripe kits/decals, spoilers, glovebox emblems, hood tachometers, Ram Air systems, GTO & Judge memorabilia and videos. Also appraisals and services.

Dave Kauzlarich — literature / memorabilia
135 Kingston Dr
Slidell, LA 70458-1737
504-641-8543; FAX: 504-641-5001
E-mail: fierog97j@aol.com

See full listing in **Section Two** under **literature dealers**

Kurt Kelsey — parts dealer
Antique Pontiac Parts
14083 P Ave
Iowa Falls, IA 50126
515-648-9086

Mail order and open shop. Call ahead for directions. Also usually several Pontiacs for sale. Large stock of antique and obsolete Pontiac parts. Fast, personalized service.

King & Queen Mufflers — exhaust systems
Box 423
Plumsteadville, PA 18949
PH/FAX: 215-766-8699

See full listing in **Section Two** under **exhaust systems**

LA Machine — convertible kits
5960 Valentine Rd #9
Ventura, CA 93003
805-650-6644; FAX: 805-650-6633

See full listing in **Section One** under **Porsche**

Lectric Limited Inc — parts
7322 S Archer Road
Justice, IL 60458
708-563-0400; FAX: 708-458-2662

See full listing in **Section One** under **Corvette**

LES Auto Parts — parts
Box 81
Dayton, NJ 08810
908-329-6128

See full listing in **Section One** under **Chevrolet**

M & H Electric Fabricators Inc — wiring harnesses
13537 Alondra Blvd
Santa Fe Springs, CA 90670
310-926-9552; FAX: 310-926-9572

See full listing in **Section Two** under **electrical systems**

Original Auto Interiors — upholstery
7869 Trumble Rd
Columbus, MI 48063-3915
810-727-2486; FAX: 810-727-4344
E-mail: knight@mich.com

See full listing in **Section Two** under **upholstery**

Original Parts Group Inc — accessories / parts
17892 Gothard St
Huntington Beach, CA 92647
800-243-8355 US & Canada
714-841-5363; FAX: 714-847-8159

Mail order and open shop. Monday-Friday 7:30 am to 5 pm, Saturday 10 am to 3 pm PST. Manufacturer and distributor of original and reproduction 64-73 GTO, Tempest and LeMans parts and accessories: emblems, interior trim, moldings, sheetmetal, electrical, engine parts, dash pads, door panels, seat upholstery, chrome trim parts, weatherstripping, gaskets, body seals, underbody bushings and much more along with an extensive line of obsolete GM items.

See our ad on page 162

The Paddock® Inc | accessories parts
PO Box 30
221 W Main
Knightstown, IN 46148
800-428-4319; FAX: 317-345-2264
E-mail: paddock@indy.net

See full listing in **Section One** under **Mustang**

Paddock West® Inc | accessories parts
1663 Plum Ln
PO Box 8547
Redlands, CA 92375
800-854-8532; FAX: 909-798-1482
E-mail: padwest@msn.com

See full listing in **Section One** under **Mustang**

M Parker Autoworks Inc | battery cables harnesses
150 Cooper Rd, Unit C-7
Dept HVAA
West Berlin, NJ 08091
609-753-0350; FAX: 609-753-0353

See full listing in **Section Two** under **electrical systems**

Parts Unlimited Inc | interiors weatherstrips
Todd Bidwell
12101 Westport Rd
Louisville, KY 40245-1789
502-425-3766; FAX: 502-425-0055

See full listing in **Section One** under **Chevrolet**

Patterson Coachworks | parts service
8951 Henry Clay Blvd
Clay, NY 13041
315-652-5794

Mail order and open shop. Monday-Friday 8 am-6 pm. Specializing in Pontiac parts & services, both mechanical & auto body, for additional miscellaneous parts inventory - '40s, '50s, '60s, '70s.

Performance Years Pontiac | parts
320 Elm Ave
N Wale, PA 19454
215-699-3722; FAX: 215-699-3725
E-mail: perfyrs@aol.com

Mail order only. Pontiac parts for GTO, Tempest, LeMans, Firebird, Trans Am, Grand Prix, Catalina, Bonneville, 1955-1977.

Phoenix Graphix Inc | decals stripe kits
4025 E Chandler Blvd, Suite 70
Phoenix, AZ 85044
602-941-4550

See full listing in **Section Two** under **decals**

Pontiac Motor Division Specialties | appraisals car dealer parts restoration
20498 82nd Ave
Langley, BC Canada V2Y 2A9
604-888-4100

Specialized in 64-74 GTOs, 67-81 Firebirds, 62-77 Grand Prixs, 63-72 LeMans and all remaining Pontiacs, and now including Canadian Pontiacs 1960-70. Supply new, used, repro and restored parts. Large inventory of engine parts, research, verification, appraisals, restorations, project & parts cars, tri-power & Ram Air specialist. Supplying the Pontiac enthusiast continent wide since 1984.

Precision Pontiac | parts repairs
2719 Columbus Ave
Columbus, OH 43209
614-258-3500; FAX: 614-258-0060

Mail order only. Specializing in engine detail, shifters rebuilt and rechromed, 65-67 rally gauges, factory options, used small parts. Catalog $2.

David Raine's Springcrafters | springs suspension parts
425 Harding Hwy
Carney's Point, NJ 08069
609-299-9141; FAX: 609-299-9157

See full listing in **Section Two** under **suspension parts**

Ram Air Inc | engine balancing engine blueprinting performance products
17134 Wood
Melvindale, MI 48122
313-382-9036; FAX: 313-382-9480

Mail order and open shop. Saturday/Sunday 12 to 4. Offers performance engine blueprinting & balancing and engineering design of performance engine & driveline components, using the best available CAD/CAM/CAE technology. Also produces own line of performance products, ranging from our Pontiac V8 engine transporter to billet tool steel connecting rods. (We do build excitement!)

Redden's Relics | NOS parts
PO Box 300
Boiling Springs, PA 17007
717-245-2200; FAX: 717-258-4861
E-mail: reddeng@pa.net

Mail order only. For Pontiacs, NOS Firebirds, Tempests/GTOs, Grand Prixs and big Pontiacs. Send year, body style and $2 for computer list of NOS parts available.

Harry Samuel | carpet fabrics interiors upholstery covers
65 Wisner St
Pontiac, MI 48342-1066
248-335-1900

See full listing in **Section Two** under **interiors & interior parts**

Ssnake-Oyl Products Inc | carpet underlay firewall insulation seatbelt restoration
Rt 2, Box 269-6
Hawkins, TX 75765
903-769-4555; 903-769-4552

See full listing in **Section Two** under **interiors & interior parts**

Stencils & Stripes Unlimited Inc | NOS decals stripe kits
1108 S Crescent Ave #21
Park Ridge, IL 60068
708-692-6893; FAX: 708-692-6895

See full listing in **Section Two** under **decals**

Street-Wise Performance | differentials parts rebuild kits transmissions
Richie Mulligan
105 Creek Rd
Tranquility, NJ 07879
201-786-6668 days
201-786-7133 evenings

See full listing in **Section Two** under **transmissions**

Sutton Auto Sounds | radios
3463 Rolling Trail
Palm Harbor, FL 34684-3526
813-787-2717; FAX: 813-789-9215
E-mail: suttonauto@aol.com

See full listing in **Section Two** under **radios**

Tags Backeast
PO Box 581
Plainville, CT 06062
860-747-2942

data plates
trim tags

See full listing in **Section Two** under **special services**

Tom's Classic Parts
5207 Sundew Terr
Tobyhanna, PA 18466
800-832-4073

parts

See full listing in **Section One** under **Chevrolet**

Vintage Parts 411
PO Box 22893
San Diego, CA 92192
800-MOTORHEAD
FAX: 619-560-9900
E-mail: vp411@electriciti.com

books

See full listing in **Section Four** under **information sources**

Waldron's Antique Exhaust Parts Inc
PO Box C 25872 M-86
Nottawa, MI 49075
616-467-7185; FAX: 616-467-9041

exhaust systems

See full listing in **Section Two** under **exhaust systems**

Year One Inc
PO Box 129
Tucker, GA 30085
800-YEAR-ONE (932-7663)
770-493-6568 Atlanta & overseas
FAX: 800-680-6806
FAX: 770-496-1949 Atlanta/overseas

parts

See full listing in **Section Two** under **comprehensive parts**

356 Enterprises
Vic & Barbara Skirmants
27244 Ryan Rd
Warren, MI 48092
810-575-9544; FAX: 810-558-3616

parts

Mail order and open shop. Specializing in Porsche 356s made from 1948 through 1965. Offer goods or services for a variety of makes and models. Engines, transmissions, suspension, brakes, all mechanical parts and all racing and performance parts for these cars.

911 & Porsche World
PO Box 75
Tadworth
Surrey KT20 7XF England
01737 814311; FAX: 01737 814591

periodical

911 & Porsche World. Top quality magazine. Founded in 1990. Entirely independent of Dr Ing. h.c.F. Porsche AG and its dealers and any club or association. Full coverage of all things Porsche, technical advice, etc. Subscription: $59/yr (9 issues).

AM Racing Inc
PO Box 451
Danvers, MA 01923
PH/FAX: 508-774-4613

race prep
sales
vintage racing

See full listing in **Section Two** under **racing**

Automotion
193 Commercial St
Sunnyvale, CA 94068
800-777-8881; FAX: 408-736-9013
E-mail: automo@aol.com

parts

Mail order and open shop. Monday-Friday 8:30 am to 5 pm. Performances and restoration parts for all Porsches. We are America's favorite supplier of quality parts and accessories for Porsche owners. Select from over 12,800 products for speed, beauty and fun. All at extra value pricing.

Automotive Artistry
679 W Streetboro St
Hudson, OH 44236
216-650-1503

restoration

See full listing in **Section One** under **Triumph**

Bassett's Jaguar
PO Box 245
Wyoming, RI 02898
401-539-3010; FAX: 401-539-7861

parts
restoration
service
upholstery

See full listing in **Section One** under **Jaguar**

Best Deal
8171 Monroe St
Stanton, CA 90680
800-354-9202; FAX:714-995-5918

accessories
parts

Open shop. Monday-Friday 9 to 5; Saturday 9 to 3. Catalog of new and used Porsche parts and accessories available. 20 years in the business of selling new & used parts for 356, 911, 914, 924 and 944.

Beverly Hills Motoring Accessories
205 S Robertson Blvd
Beverly Hills, CA 90211
310-657-4880; FAX: 310-659-4664
E-mail: bhma@hollywood.cinenet.net

accessories

See full listing in **Section One** under **Mercedes-Benz**

Blitzen Enterprises Inc
8341 E Evans Rd, Suite 104
Scottsdale, AZ 85260
888-254-8936 toll-free
FAX: 602-991-6301

parts

See full listing in **Section One** under **Mercedes-Benz**

BMC Classics
828 N Dixie Freeway
New Smyrna Beach, FL 32168
904-426-6405; FAX: 904-427-4570

parts
repair
restoration

See full listing in **Section One** under **Jaguar**

Bud's Parts for
Classic Mercedes-Benz
9130 Hwy 5
Douglasville, GA 30134
800-942-8444; FAX: 770-942-8400

parts
restoration
service

See full listing in **Section One** under **Mercedes-Benz**

CARS | car dealer
(Computer Aided Resale System)
2724 Cove View Dr N
Jacksonville, FL 32257
904-448-0633; FAX: 904-448-0623

See full listing in **Section Two** under **car dealers**

Classic Auto Concepts | car dealer
1366 S Federal Hwy
Pompano Beach, FL 33062
954-781-8440; FAX: 954-781-8449

The purchase and sale of classic European and American vehicles. These vehicles include Mercedes, Porsche, Jaguar, Ferrari, DeLorean, Corvette, 55-57 T-Bird, Cadillac, Mustang and other similar classics.

Dave's Auto Restoration | upholstery
2285 Rt 307 E
Jefferson, OH 44047
PH/FAX: 216-858-2227

See full listing in **Section Two** under **interiors & interior parts**

Diablo Engineering | engines parts
8776 East Shea, #B3A-109
Scottsdale, AZ 85260
PH/FAX: 602-391-2569

Mail order only. Specializing in Porsche engines, used & new parts, engine rebuilding for Porsche 356, 912, 911, 930, 944.

Doc & Cy's Restoration Parts | parts
50 E Morris St
Indianapolis, IN 46225
800-950-0356; FAX: 317-634-5662

Mail order and open shop. Monday-Friday 9 am-5 pm. Specializing in restoration sheetmetal, rubber, trim, interior and mechanical parts for Porsche 356, 911/912, 914 and 924. New and used parts available.

Driven By Design | information products services
8440 Carmel Valley Rd
Carmel, CA 93923
408-625-1393, 800-366-1393
FAX: 408-625-9342

Mail order and open shop. Shop open Monday-Friday 9:30 to 6. Specializing in Porsche information products and services, videos/books for all years. Inspection videos for the 356, 911, 930, $39.95. Produces and distributes a video *How To Buy a Better Used Car*. Publishes *The Directory*, a resource book for Porsche parts suppliers (worldwide), for $24.95.

European Parts Specialists Ltd | accessories parts
PO Box 6783
Santa Barbara, CA 93160
805-683-4020; FAX: 805-683-3689

See full listing in **Section One** under **Mercedes-Benz**

GAHH Inc | auto interiors convertible tops
8116 Lankershim Blvd
North Hollywood, CA 91605
818-767-6242; FAX: 818-767-2786

See full listing in **Section One** under **Mercedes-Benz**

Grand Prix Classics Inc | racing cars sports cars
7456 La Jolla Blvd
La Jolla, CA 92037
619-459-3500; FAX: 619-459-3512

See full listing in **Section Two** under **racing**

Griot's Garage | car care products paint tools
3500-A 20th St E
Tacoma, WA 98424
800-345-5789; FAX: 206-922-7500
E-mail: griots@aol.com

See full listing in **Section Two** under **tools**

Hjeltness Restoration Inc | restoration service
630 Alpine Way
Escondido, CA 92029
619-746-9966; FAX: 619-746-7738

See full listing in **Section Two** under **restoration shops**

International Mercantile | rubber parts
PO Box 2818
Del Mar, CA 92014-2818
619-438-2205; 800-356-001
FAX: 619-438-1428

Mail order and open shop. Monday-Friday 9-3 PST. Specializes in molded and extruded rubber/plastic for 356A/B/C, 912/911 Porsche. Free brochure.

IPTC Automotive | cars parts
300 SW 12th Ave
Pompano Beach, FL 33069
800-277-3806

See full listing in **Section One** under **BMW**

Klasse 356 Inc | cars parts restoration
741 N New St
Allentown, PA 18102
800-634-7862; FAX: 610-432-8027
E-mail: parts@klasse356.com

Mail order and open shop. Monday-Friday, 8-5 EST. Cars and parts (new and used) as well as restoration for Porsche 356.

LA Machine | convertible kits
5960 Valentine Rd #9
Ventura, CA 93003
805-650-6644; FAX: 805-650-6633

Mail order and open shop. Monday-Saturday 9 am to 5 pm. Specializing in convertible conversions and kits for NSX, Porsche 911, SE Mercedes-Benz, XJ-S Jaguar, Fiero, Lexus SC. We convert hardtop cars to convertibles and sell do-it-yourself convertible conversion kits.

Machina Locksmith | car locks keys
3 Porter St
Watertown, MA 02172-4145
PH/FAX: 617-923-1683

See full listing in **Section Two** under **locks & keys**

The McHugh Group | appraisals
4602 Birch Ct
Middletown, MD 21769
301-473-8333; FAX: 301-371-9447

See full listing in **Section Two** under **appraisals**

Moonlight Ink | art
2736 Summerfield Rd
Winter Park, FL 32792-5112
407-628-8857; FAX: 407-671-5008

Mail order only. Specializing in fine art originals and graphic reproductions for Porsche and vintage racers. Licensed artist by Porsche AG. Art dealer inquiries invited; commissions.

Motorcars International
528 N Prince Ln
Springfield, MO 65802
417-831-9999; FAX: 417-863-0777
E-mail: missy@motorcars-intl

| accessories |
| cars |
| services |
| tools |

See full listing in **Section One** under **Ferrari**

Muncie Imports & Classics
4401 St Rd 3 North
Muncie, IN 47303
800-462-4244; FAX: 317-287-9551

| repair |
| restoration |
| upholstery |

See full listing in **Section One** under **Jaguar**

Palo Alto Speedometer Inc
718 Emerson St
Palo Alto, CA 94301
415-323-0243; FAX: 415-323-4632

| instruments |

See full listing in **Section One** under **Mercedes-Benz**

PAR Porsche Specialists
310 Main St
New Rochelle, NY 10801
914-637-8800, 800-367-7270
FAX: 914-637-6078

| accessories |
| car dealer |
| parts |

Mail order and open shop. Monday-Friday 8:30 to 5:30;
Saturday 9 to 1. Porsche specialist in both new and used parts
and accessories. 1965 to present Porsches, including 911, 930,
928, 944, 924 and 914. Also sells used and rebuildable cars.

Paul's Select (Porsche) ®
2280 Gail Dr
Riverside, CA 92509
PH/FAX: 909-685-9340

| parts |

Mail order. Monday-Friday 8 am to 4:30 pm PST. Closed
Wednesdays. Rare new and used parts and accessories for vintage air cooled Porsche® autos. Also many late 1970 911 high-
performance engine parts and technical usage available from
racer and mechanic. Used auto parts for vintage Porsche® autos
from 1954 through 1990, air cooled only. Access to many hi-performance & racing parts. Used engines available-V inventory,
356 and 911 Series autos and 914-6. Buying, selling and locating service available. 30+ years' experience.

Perfect Panels of America
1690 Thomas Paine Pkwy
Centerville, OH 45459
513-435-4548

| body panels |

Mail order and open shop. Monday-Friday 7:30 to 6; Saturday
9:30 to 12 noon. Manufacturer of replacement body panels for
Porsche 914 and 911. 914: hinge plate, hinge bolts, left and
right lower door patches, left and right roll panels, complete
right suspension consoles, left and right door steps, battery tray,
battery tray support, battery hold clamp, jack tubes, jack supports, left and right inner rockers. 911: left and right outer rockers, left and right inner rockers, jack tubes, jack plates.

Pony Parts of America
1690 Thomas Paine Pkwy
Centerville, OH 45459
513-435-4548

| 914/911 |
| body panels |

See full listing in **Section One** under **Mustang**

Precision Autoworks
2202 Federal Street
E Camden, NJ 08105
609-966-0080, NJ
FAX: 610-649-3577, PA

| restorations |

See full listing in **Section One** under **Mercedes-Benz**

Precision Restoration Service Inc
1551 N Courtney Rd, Ste B-2
Independence, MO 64050
816-461-7500; FAX: 816-461-7504

| restoration |

See full listing in **Section Two** under **restoration shops**

Replicarz
99 State St
Rutland, VT 05701
802-747-7151
E-mail: replicarz@aol.com

| books |
| kits |
| models |
| videos |

See full listing in **Section Two** under **racing**

Restoration Services
16049 W 4th Ave
Golden, CO 80401
303-271-0356

| restoration |

Mail order and open shop. Monday-Friday 8 am to 5 pm. An
automotive oriented shop, specializing since 1972 in Porsche,
Mercedes-Benz and vintage race cars and other exotics. Metal
replacement, fabrication, sandblasting, lead work, mig welding,
gas welding, complete paint, spot paint, detailing, upholstery
rebuilds, top rebuilds, trim repair, trim polishing, glass replacement, electrical repair, rewiring, mechanical overhauls, suspension overhauls, wheel refinishing, tire sales, auto locating services, appraisals, Porsche and Mercedes parts.

Paul Russell & Company
106 Western Ave
Essex, MA 01929
508-768-6919; FAX: 508-768-3523

| car dealer |
| coachbuilding parts |
| restoration |

See full listing in **Section Two** under **restoration shops**

Shelton Dealerships
5740 N Federal Hwy
Ford Lauderdale, FL 33308
954-493-5211; FAX: 954-772-2653

| accessories |
| leasing |
| parts |
| sales |

See full listing in **Section One** under **Ferrari**

Showroom Auto Sales
960 S Bascom Ave
San Jose, CA 95128
408-554-1550; FAX: 408-554-0550

| car dealer |

See full listing in **Section One** under **Mercedes-Benz**

Spyder Enterprises Inc
RFD 1682
Laurel Hollow, NY 11791-9644
516-367-3293 evenings
FAX: 516-367-3260

| accessories |
| books |
| parts |
| periodicals |

Mail order only. Vintage Porsche (356 & Spyder) cars, parts,
accessories, memorabilia, literature. Publishes for sale and/or
trade list. Publisher of fine quality automotive books and limited
edition artwork. Manufacturer of embroidered items and leather
accessories for the Porsche 356.

Stoddard Imported Cars Inc
38845 Mentor Ave
Willoughby, OH 44094-0908
216-951-1040 in Ohio & overseas
800-342-1414; FAX: 216-946-9410
E-mail: sicars@ix.netcom.com

| parts |

International Porsche and Mercedes parts mail order. Extensive
inventory for all model Porsches with emphasis on vintage
Porsche 356, 911, 914 and Mercedes 190SL, 230SL, 250SL,
280SL restoration. Catalogs available for 190SL-280SL Mercedes
and all model Porsches. Web site: http://www.stoddard.com

Stormin Norman's Bug Shop 201 Commerce Dr #3 Fort Collins, CO 80524 303-493-5873	repair restoration

See full listing in **Section One** under **Volkswagen**

Stuttgart Automotive Inc 1690 Thomas Paine Pkwy Centerville, OH 45459 513-435-4541	parts service

Mail order and open shop. For 1955-86 Porsches. Complete service. Many obsolete parts in stock for 356 Series.

Translog Motorsports 619-635 W Poplar St York, PA 17404 717-846-1885	car dealer parts restoration

Mail order and open shop. Monday-Saturday 9 to 6. Engine, transmission and body modifications to your specifications. Specializing in restoring Porsches. Large inventory of used and new Porsche parts. Custom-built Porsches. Specializing in 914-6 GT replicas, parts duplicated from the Sunoco 914-6 GT.

Tweeks Ltd 8148 Woodland Dr Indianapolis, IN 46278 317-875-0076; FAX: 317-875-0181 800-428-2200, IN warehouse 800-421-3776, CA warehouse	accessories parts restoration

Tweeks, your source for Porsche® parts and accessories since 1976. Tweeks offers the most complete line of reproduction and OEM parts including body, trim, interior, mechanical and performance parts. Tweeks also offers an exclusive line of clothing and

accessories. Don't miss your chance to receive Tweeks new Truck and Sport Utility Vehicle catalog with a wide range of parts and accessories to help you restore, maintain or customize your truck or SUV. And, Tweeks offers a complete line of parts and accessories for Datsun/Nissan Z-car owners. Call toll-free for the catalog of your choice: Porsche® catalog, $5; truck & SUV catalog, $3; Z-car catalog, $3. In Long Beach, CA: 3301 Hill St., Unit 408, Long Beach, CA 90804, PH: 310-494-4777.

See our ad on this page

United German Imports 4556 Shetland Green Alexandria, VA 22312 800-98-BRAKE; FAX: 703-916-1610 E-mail: ugibrakes2@aol.com	brake parts brakes

See full listing in **Section Two** under **brakes**

Visual Marketplace Online Inc 800 Silverado, Suite 324 La Jolla, CA 92037 619-459-3846; FAX: 619-459-3460 E-mail: pyoung@icreations.com	online auto ads

See full listing in **Section Four** under **information sources**

Willhoit Auto Restoration 1360 Gladys Ave Long Beach, CA 90804 310-439-3333; FAX: 310-439-3956	engine rebuilding restoration

Mail order and open shop. Shop open Monday-Friday 8 to 5. Complete in-house restoration services for all models of Porsche 356 (including 4 cam) as well as early 911. Including: show quality painting, metalwork and rust repair, engine and transaxle rebuilding, interior installation, car appraisals and pre-purchase inspections. Also a very large used parts inventory.

Zim's Autotechnik 1804 Reliance Pkwy Bedford, TX 76021 800-356-2964; FAX: 817-545-2002	parts service

Mail order and open shop. Monday-Friday 8-5:30, Saturday 9-1 CST. Porsche (only) service and parts. We specialize in the maintenance and repair of Porsche automobiles, Zim's has a large inventory of parts including hard to find parts for older vehicles. We have been in business for over 25 years.

RENAULT

4-CV Service 3301 Shetland Rd Beavercreek, OH 45434	accessories parts

Mail order only. NOS & used parts, accessories & information for restorers of Renault 4-CVs and related vehicles. Some Dauphine mechanical parts. Thirty-plus years' experience with all models of 1948-61 4-CVs. For information, contact Michael Self.

French Stuff PO Box 39772 Glendale, CA 90039-0772 818-244-2498; FAX: 818-500-7628	accessories engine rebuilding parts transaxle rebuilding

Direct importers, office in Paris. Established in 1958. Wholesale & mail order 24 hrs, phone & fax. Will call counter 4-8 PST for local pickups. Stock & high-performance parts & accessories for all models Renault, Peugeot, Alpine, Matra, Panhard, Deutsch-

Bonnet. Technical literature. Lotus Europas S1/S2: engines, transaxles, stock & hi-performance parts. V6 PRV engines & 5-speed transaxles for DeLorean & Peugeot. Engines & transaxle rebuilding all Renaults. Specialized R5 Turbo, Alpine, Gordini, V6.

Patton Orphan Spares 28 Simon St Babylon, NY 11702 516-669-2598	parts

Mail order only. Sells spare parts for orphan makes such as Renault Dauphines, Austin A40s and Morris Minor 1000s. Spares are mechanical parts primarily, new and used. Factory shop and parts manuals for same automobiles for sale.

ABS Exotic Repair Inc 1561 N Federal Hwy Ft Lauderdale, FL 33304 954-566-7785; FAX: 954-566-7271	parts service

See full listing in **Section One** under **Mercedes-Benz**.

Aero Toy Store Gary Anzalone 1710 W Cypress Creek Rd Ft Lauderdale, FL 33309 800-404-2376; FAX: 954-771-3281	acquisitions sales

See full listing in **Section One** under **Ferrari**.

Albers Rolls-Royce 190 W Sycamore Zionsville, IN 46077 317-873-2360; 317-873-2560 FAX: 317-873-6860	car dealer parts

America's oldest exclusive authorized Rolls-Royce/Bentley dealer. New and pre-owned motor cars available. Largest stock of parts in North America from pre-war to current series. We are now in our 4th decade of service "where total commitment to the product does make a difference." Please supply your chassis/identification number when ordering parts, Mon-Fri 8 am-5 pm.

Ashton Keynes Vintage Restorations Ltd A Keith Bowley Ashton Keynes, Swindon Wilshire England 01285/861-288 FAX: 01285/860-604	restoration coachbuilding

Coachbuilders and restorers of vintage and classic cars. Panel work, painting and electrical and mechanical restorations. Specializing in Rolls-Royce, Bentley, Jaguar and all classic marques. Engine reconditioning, white metaling and line boring, specialist machining.

Atlantic Enterprises 221 Strand Industrial Dr Little River, SC 29566 803-399-7565; FAX: 803-399-4600	steering assemblies

See full listing in **Section Two** under **chassis parts**.

Auto Craftsmen Restoration Inc 27945 Elm Grove San Antonio, TX 78261 210-980-4027	appraisals restoration

See full listing in **Section Two** under **restoration shops**.

Bassett Classic Restoration 2616 Sharon St, Suite D Kenner, LA 70062 PH/FAX: 504-469-2982 (have auto switching device)	parts plating restoration service

Mail order and open shop. Monday-Saturday 9 to 6. Upholstery, woodworking, reveneering and mechanical restorations. Parts, sales and service. Also paint, bodywork and cadmium plating. In business since 1973. We have restored RROC National First Place and Senior Award winning motor cars. We work on Rolls-Royce and Bentley motorcars exclusively.

Bassett's Jaguar PO Box 245 Wyoming, RI 02898 401-539-3010; FAX: 401-539-7861	parts restoration service upholstery

See full listing in **Section One** under **Jaguar**.

Be Happy Automatic Transmission Parts 414 Stivers Rd Hillsboro, OH 45133 800-416-2862; FAX: 513-442-6133	trans rebuild kits

See full listing in **Section Two** under **transmissions**.

Blackhawk Collection 3600 Blackhawk Plaza Cir Danville, CA 94506-3600 510-736-3444; FAX: 510-736-4375	acquisitions sales

See full listing in **Section One** under **Duesenberg**.

Borla East 600 A Lincoln Blvd Middlesex, NJ 08846 908-469-9666	exhaust systems

Mail order and open shop. Monday-Friday 9 to 5. Custom exhaust systems in 304 stainless steel or mild steel. For any car, but specializes in Rolls-Royce, Jaguar and Mercedes-Benz.

The Brassworks 289 Prado Rd San Louis Obispo, CA 93401 800-342-6759; FAX: 805-544-5615	radiators

See full listing in **Section Two** under **radiators**.

British Auto/USA 92 Londonderry Tpke Manchester, NH 03104 603-622-1050	restoration parts upholstery

See full listing in **Section One** under **Jaguar**.

British Luxury Automotive Parts 257 Niagara St Toronto, ON Canada M6J 2L7 416-693-8400; FAX: 416-694-3202 Beeper: 416-378-8182	new and used parts

See full listing in **Section One** under **Jaguar**.

British Restorations
4455 Paul St
Philadelphia, PA 19124
215-533-6696

car dealer
restoration

See full listing in **Section One** under **Jaguar**

British Things Inc
515 Ocean Ave
Santa Monica, CA 90402
310-394-4002; FAX: 310-394-3204

badges

Mail order only. Limited edition specialized car badges for Rolls-Royce & Bentley. Designed for special commemorative events, such as 90th commemorative for Rolls-Royce, plus solid stainless steel badge bars.

Michael Chapman
Priorsleigh, Mill Lane, Cleeve Prior
Worcestershire WR115JZ England
01789-773897; FAX: 01789-773588

automobilia

See full listing in **Section Two** under **automobilia**

Classic Coachworks
735 Frenchtown Rd
Milford, NJ 08848
908-996-3400

bodywork
painting
restoration

See full listing in **Section Two** under **restoration shops**

Coachbuilt Motors
907 E Hudson St
Columbus, OH 43211
614-261-1541

repairs

Mail order and open shop. Tuesday-Friday 8 to 5:30. Saturday by appointment. Rolls-Royce mail order and repair service shop.

Collectors Choice LTD
6400 Springfield, Lodi Rd
Dane, WI 53529
608-849-9878; FAX: 608-849-9879

parts
restoration
service

See full listing in **Section One** under **DeTomaso/Pantera**

Reg Collings
158 Lake Sylvan Close SE
Calgary, AB Canada T2J 3E6
403-271-1119; FAX: 403-278-3490

parts
service

Open shop. For pre and postwar Bentleys and Rolls-Royces. Pre-1916 brass car parts for sale, wanted and will help locating parts. Some repairs performed.

Dave's Auto Restoration
2285 Rt 307 E
Jefferson, OH 44047
PH/FAX: 216-858-2227

upholstery

See full listing in **Section Two** under **interiors & interior parts**

Deters Restorations
6205 Swiss Garden Rd
Temperance, MI 48182-1020
313-847-1820

restoration

See full listing in **Section Two** under **restoration shops**

Donovan Motorcar Service
4 Holmes Rd
Lenox, MA 01240
413-499-6000; FAX: 413-499-6699

restoration
service

See full listing in **Section One** under **Jaguar**

Enfield Auto Restoration Inc
4 Print Shop Rd
Enfield, CT 06082
860-749-7917; FAX: 860-749-2836

panel beating
restorations
Rolls-Royce parts
wood working

See full listing in **Section Two** under **restoration shops**

The Enthusiasts Shop
John Parnell
PO Box 80471
Baton Rouge, LA 70898
504-928-7456; FAX: 504-928-7665

cars
pre-war parts
transportation

Mail order only. Specializing in Rolls-Royce and Bentley cars and pre-war parts, transportation. Will purchase cars in any condition or location. Finder's fees.

Foreign Motors West
253 N Main St
Natick, MA 01760
508-655-5350; FAX: 508-651-0178

car sales

Mail order and open shop. Monday to Friday 8-6, Saturday 8 to noon. Specializing in Rolls-Royce/Bentley, Mercedes-Benz, BMW, Land Rover, Peugeot for all years and models.

From Rust To Riches
14200 New Hampshire Ave
Silver Spring, MD 20904
301-384-5856; FAX: 301-989-1866

appraisals
car dealer
repairs
restoration

See full listing in **Section Two** under **restoration shops**

GAHH Inc
8116 Lankershim Blvd
North Hollywood, CA 91605
818-767-6242; FAX: 818-767-2786

auto interiors
convertible tops

See full listing in **Section One** under **Mercedes-Benz**

Glazier Pattern & Coachworks
3720 Loramie-Washington Rd
Houston, OH 45333
513-492-7355; FAX: 513-492-9987

coachwork
interior woodwork
restoration

Mail order and open shop by appointment only. Structural and concours quality interior woodwork for coachbuilt classics. Rebuild, restore or remanufacture damaged or missing parts. Specialize in Rolls-Royces, Bentleys, etc. Award winning complete restorations.

Guild of Automotive Restorers
18237 Woodbine Ave
Sharon, ON Canada L0G 1V0
905-895-0035; FAX: 905-895-0036
E-mail: theguild@interhop.com

restoration
sales
service

See full listing in **Section Two** under **restoration shops**

Tony Handler's Inc
2028 Cotner Ave
Los Angeles, CA 90025
310-473-7773; FAX: 310-479-1197

parts

Mail order and open shop. Monday-Friday 8 to 6; Saturday and Sunday by appointment. World's largest stock of used parts for post-war Rolls-Royce and Bentley cars. Technical advice and personalized service. Turnkey and rebuildable Rolls-Royces, Bentleys and Tony at this location.

Peter Harper Stretton House, Northwich Road Lower Stretton Nr Warrington, WA4 4PF England 01925 730411; FAX: 01925 730224	**car dealer**

Call for appointment. Near M6 motorway. Car collector with 15-20 cars including some London to Brighton and brass age cars, prewar through 1965 Rolls-Royces and Bentleys. Usually a few prewar sports cars and open touring cars. Also pre-1930 motorcycles, usually around 15 flat tank machines, eg: Norton, AJS, Indian, FN (4), etc. No parts.

Hyannis Restoration 119 Thornton Dr Hyannis, MA 02601 508-775-8131; FAX: 508-790-2339	**restoration**

See full listing in **Section One** under **Ferrari**

Joe L Jordan 2615 Waugh Dr, #301 Houston, TX 77006-2799 713-680-3181; FAX: 713-680-3185	**car dealer** **limo service** **parts**

Mail order and open shop. Antique Rolls-Royce limo service. Rolls-Royce, 1956-1965 cars and parts bought/sold/traded. VW Karmann Ghia cars and parts bought/sold/traded. Car hauling service, 48 states.

David M King, Automotive Books 5 Brouwer Ln Rockville Centre, NY 11570 516-766-1561; FAX: 516-766-7502	**literature**

Mail order only. Automotive books, specializing in literature, books, catalogs, ads, manuals, etc for Rolls-Royces and Bentleys. Publishers of the Rolls-Royce Review, The Journal of Rolls-Royce and Bentley book and literature collecting.

Kreimeyer Co 3211 N Wilburn Ave Bethany, OK 73008 405-789-9499; FAX: 405-789-7888	**antennas** **glass/wholesale** **parts/wholesale** **radios/radio repair**

See full listing in **Section One** under **Mercedes-Benz**

Langer Auto Museum Rudy Langer 4943 Ward Pkwy Kansas City, MO 64112 PH/FAX: 816-931-1188	**vintage cars** **vintage motorcycles**

See full listing in **Section Two** under **car dealers**

Leatherique Leather Restoration Products PO Box 2678 Orange Park, FL 32065 904-272-0992; FAX: 904-272-1534	**leather cleaning** **conditioning** **products**

Mail order only. Leather restoration and preservation products for Rolls-Royce, Bentley, Jaguar (English Connolly leather), MG, Mercedes-Benz, Lincoln Continental, Lexus, BMW. Leather conditioning and cleaning. Named simply the best by Rolls-Royce car owners club since 1968. Also, custom color, matched leather dye, which is water based making it soft and natural, not brittle like lacquer dyes.

Lindley Restorations Ltd Rt 422 RD 3 Pottstown, PA 19464 610-326-8484; FAX: 610-326-3845	**parts** **sales** **service**

See full listing in **Section One** under **Jaguar**

LMARR Disk Ltd PO Box 910 Glen Ellen, CA 95442-0910 707-938-9347; FAX: 707-938-3020	**wheel discs**

Mail order only. Specializing in wheel discs for pre-war Rolls-Royce, PI, PII, PIII, 20/25, 25/30, Wraith, Bentley 3-1/2, 4-1/4, Speed 6, 8 litre, Bentley rear wheelcover, Alfa, Bugatti, Delage D8, Lagonda, Jaguar Mk IV, Hispano-Suiza, Lincoln, Voisin.

Marshall Antique & Classic Restorations 3714 Old Philadelphia Pike Bethlehem, PA 18015 610-868-7765; FAX: 610-868-7529	**coolant additives** **restoration services**

Specialize in restoration services for Rolls-Royce, Bentley, Mercedes-Benz. Distributor of No-Rosion™ products.

See our ad on this page

McLellan's Automotive History Robert McLellan 9111 Longstaff Dr Houston, TX 77031 713-772-3285; FAX: 713-772-3287	**books** **magazines** **programs** **sales literature**

See full listing in **Section Two** under **literature dealers**

Mid-Jersey Motorama Inc 1301 Asbury Ave PO Box 1395 Asbury Park, NJ 07712 908-775-9885 Beeper: 908-840-6111 FAX: 908-775-9885	**car dealer**

See full listing in **Section One** under **Cadillac/LaSalle**

Motorcar Gallery Inc   car dealer
715 N Federal Hwy
Fort Lauderdale, FL 33304
954-522-9900; FAX: 954-522-9966

See full listing in **Section One** under **Ferrari**

Mr Sport Car Inc   service
203 E Lincoln
Papillion, NE 68046
402-592-7559

See full listing in **Section One** under **Jaguar**

Northern Motorsport Ltd   repair
PO Box 508   restoration
Rt 5   sales
Wilder, VT 05088   service
802-296-2099; FAX: 802-295-6599

See full listing in **Section Two** under **restoration shops**

Northwest Transmission Parts   transmission parts
13500 US 62
Winchester, OH 45697
800-327-1955 order line
513-442-2811 info
FAX: 513-442-6555

See full listing in **Section Two** under **transmissions**

Omega Automobile Appraisals   appraisals
115 18 Ave SE
St Petersburg, FL 33705
PH/FAX: 813-894-5690

Open shop only. Monday-Saturday at customer's convenience.
Specializing in Rolls-Royce & Bentley. Appraises all makes, mod-
els and years of autos and trucks. Member of and schooled by
International Society of Appraisers.

Oregon Crewe Cutters Inc   parts
1665 Redwood Ave
Grants Pass, OR 97527
541-479-5663; FAX: 541-479-6339

Mail order and open shop. Shop open Monday-Friday 8 to 5.
World's largest stock of used parts for post-war Rolls-Royce and
Bentley cars. Technical advice and personalized service.

The Panel Shop Inc   body parts
1785 Barnum Ave
Stratford, CT 06497
203-377-6208; FAX: 203-386-0486

See full listing in **Section Two** under **sheetmetal**

John H Parnell   car dealer
PO Box 80471   literature
Baton Rouge, LA 70898   parts
504-928-7456; FAX: 504-928-7665

Buying, selling parts, literature for Rolls-Royce and Bentley cars,
pre 1966 specifically. Also I do inspections and transportation.
Finder's fees paid. References gladly furnished. Will buy any
condition cars.

Powers Parts Inc   literature
425 Pine Ave   parts
PO Box 796
Anna Maria, FL 34216
941-778-7270; FAX: 941-778-0289

Mail order and open shop. Monday-Friday 9 to 4. New and used
parts and literature for 1933-39 Bentleys, Rolls-Royces and WW II
small horsepower Rolls-Royces.

Precision Autoworks   restorations
2202 Federal Street
E Camden, NJ 08105
609-966-0080, NJ
FAX: 610-649-3577, PA

See full listing in **Section One** under **Mercedes-Benz**

Proper Motor Cars Inc   parts
1811 11th Ave N   restoration
St. Petersburg, FL 33713-5794
813-821-8883; FAX: 813-895-4746

Mail order only and open shop. Monday-Friday 8 to 4:30.
Restoration and maintenance of Rolls-Royces and Bentleys. Also
restoration and maintenance of vintage sports and racing cars.
All types of restoration. Mercedes-Benz, Ferrari, Citroen and
other European cars serviced and restored. Largest stock of
Rolls-Royce new and used parts in the Southeast. Bosch authorized service.

RAU Restoration   woodwork
2027 Pontius Ave
Los Angeles, CA 90025
PH/FAX: 310-445-1128

See full listing in **Section Two** under **woodwork**

Regal International Motor Cars Inc   car dealer
PO Box 6819
Hollywood, FL 33081
305-989-9777; FAX: 305-989-9778

Deals in Rolls-Royce, Mercedes, Jaguar, Avanti, special interest
cars.

RM Auto Restoration Ltd   panel fabrication
825 Park Ave W   parts
Chatham, ON Canada N7M 5J6   restoration
519-352-4575; FAX: 519-351-1337

See full listing in **Section Two** under **restoration shops**

Rolls-Royce of Beverly Hills   parts
11401 West Pico Blvd
Los Angeles, CA 90064
310-477-4262, 800-321-9792
FAX: 310-473-7498

Mail order and open shop. Monday through Friday 8 to 5:30 pm.
Specializing in Rolls-Royce and Bentley parts of all years. We
have recently started handling parts for pre-WW II models too.

The Stable LTD   sales
217 Main St   service
Gladstone, NJ 07934
908-234-2055; FAX: 908-781-2599

See full listing in **Section One** under **Jaguar**

Teddy's Garage   parts
8530 Louise Ave   restoration
Northridge, CA 91325   service
818-341-0505

Mail order and open shop. Monday-Friday 8 to 6. Restores, services and repairs Rolls-Royces, Bentleys, Jaguars, MGs and other fine British automobiles. We have a large stock of parts for pre-66 Rolls and Bentley cars. If we don't have it, we will get it. Finest workmanship for finest cars.

Turner Resources Inc	parts
623 E Main St, Ste 200	
Bridgewater, NJ 08807	
908-658-4000; FAX: 908-417-1500	

Mail order only. Specializing in OEM parts, both current production and obsolete, remanufactured parts, extensive range of proprietary alternatives to OEM parts for Rolls-Royce/Bentley cars 1946-1986. Our Turnerspares® Division delivers any parts still in production and stocked in America overnight. Our Turner-treasures® Division delivers additionally 6,000 items available nowhere else in the world overnight. Our Turnerworks® Division manufactures regularly economical alternatives to OEM parts. Our Turnerexchange® Division provides rebuilt exchange units for all operating assemblies fitted since 1946.

Van Nuys Motors	parts
14422 Oxnard St	restoration
Van Nuys, CA 91403	sales
818-988-5455	service

See full listing in **Section One** under **Mercedes-Benz**

Vantage Auto Interiors	upholstery
11 Fahey St	
Stamford, CT 06907	
203-425-9533; FAX: 203-425-9535	

See full listing in **Section Two** under **interiors & interior parts**

Vantage Motorworks Inc	restoration
1898 NE 151 St	sales
N Miami, FL 33162	service
305-940-1161; FAX: 305-949-7481	

Open shop only. Monday-Saturday 8 am-5 pm. Rolls-Royce/Bentley sales, service, restoration for postwar Rolls-Royce and Bentleys, particular emphasis on S/Cloud series, 1956-1967.

Vintage Restorations	accessories
The Old Bakery	instruments
Windmill Street, Tunbridge Wells	
Kent, TN2 4UU England	
UK 1892-525-899	
FAX: UK 1892-525499	

See full listing in **Section Two** under **instruments**

Atlantic British Ltd	accessories
PO Box 110	parts
Rover Ridge Dr	
Mechanicville, NY 12118	
800-533-2210; FAX: 518-664-6641	

Mail order only. I specialize in parts and accessories for Land Rover, Range Rover, Discovery and Sterlings.

Atlantic Enterprises	steering assemblies
221 Strand Industrial Dr	
Little River, SC 29566	
803-399-7565; FAX: 803-399-4600	

See full listing in **Section Two** under **chassis parts**

British Auto Parts Ltd	parts
93256 Holland Ln	
Marcola, OR 97454	
541-933-2880; FAX: 541-933-2302	

See full listing in **Section One** under **Morris**

British Luxury Automotive Parts	new & used parts
257 Niagara St	
Toronto, ON Canada M6J 2L7	
416-693-8400; FAX: 416-694-3202	
Beeper: 416-378-8182	

See full listing in **Section One** under **Jaguar**

British Motor Co	engine rebuilding
3825 W 11th Ave	
Eugene, OR 97402	
800-995-1895; FAX: 541-485-8544	

See full listing in **Section One** under **Jaguar**

British Pacific Ltd	parts
3317 Burton Ave	
Burbank, CA 91504	
818-841-8945; FAX: 818-841-3825	
E-mail: britpac@aol.com	

Mail order and retail counter. Shop open Monday-Friday 9 am to 6 pm. Exclusively Land Rover parts 1958-1997. Catalogs available for Series II, IIA, III; Defender, Discovery, Range Rover. Genuine, OEM & aftermarket parts and accessories.

Cantab Motors Ltd	cars
Valley Industrial Park	parts
12 E Richardson Ln	service
Purcellville, VA 20132	
540-338-2211; FAX: 540-338-2944	

See full listing in **Section One** under **Morgan**

Doug's British Car Parts	accessories
2487 E Colorado Blvd	parts
Pasadena, CA 91107	
818-793-2494; FAX: 818-793-4339	

See full listing in **Section One** under **Jaguar**

Foreign Motors West	car sales
253 N Main St	
Natick, MA 01760	
508-655-5350; FAX: 508-651-0178	

See full listing in **Section One** under **Rolls-Royce/Bentley**

Jaguar of Puerto Rico Inc	car dealer
PO Box 13055	parts
San Juan, PR 00908-3055	service
787-723-5177; FAX: 787-723-9488	

See full listing in **Section One** under **Jaguar**

Lindley Restorations Ltd	parts
Rt 422 RD 3	sales
Pottstown, PA 19464	service
610-326-8484; FAX: 610-326-3845	

See full listing in **Section One** under **Jaguar**

London Stainless Steel **Exhaust Centre** 249-253 Queenstown Rd London, SW8 3NP England 011-44-171622-2120 FAX: 011-44-171627-0991 E-mail: 101445.341@compuserv.com	exhaust systems

See full listing in **Section Two** under **exhaust systems**

Mid-Jersey Motorama Inc 1301 Asbury Ave PO Box 1395 Asbury Park, NJ 07712 908-775-9885; Beeper: 908-840-6111 FAX: 908-775-9885	car dealer

See full listing in **Section One** under **Cadillac/LaSalle**

Motorcars Ltd 8101 Hempstead Houston, TX 77008 713-863-9388; FAX: 713-863-8238 E-mail: mcltd@phoenix.net	parts

See full listing in **Section One** under **Jaguar**

Rovers West 940 S Warren Ave, Unit 143 Tucson, AZ 85719 520-670-9377; FAX: 520-670-9080 E-mail: rover@azstarnet.com	accessories parts

Mail/phone order hours: Monday-Friday 10 to 6; weekends by appointment. Specializing in new and used parts, high-performance parts, off-road accessories and optional equipment for Land Rover, Range Rovers, Rover 2000, 3500S, SD-1 Rovers.

Shelton Dealerships 5740 N Federal Hwy Ford Lauderdale, FL 33308 954-493-5211; FAX: 954-772-2653	accessories leasing parts sales

See full listing in **Section One** under **Ferrari**

Spectral Kinetics 17 Church St Garnerville, NY 10923 914-947-3126; FAX: 914-429-6041	parts restoration

Mail order and open shop by appointment. Specializes in the sale of new and used Rover sedan parts, particularly the 2000, 3500S and SD1 models. Also specializes in early Range Rovers. Rebuilding & restoration services. "We sell parts for what we drive."

European Parts Specialists Ltd PO Box 6783 Santa Barbara, CA 93160 805-683-4020; FAX: 805-683-3689	accessories parts

See full listing in **Section One** under **Mercedes-Benz**

Irving Galis 357 Atlantic Ave Marblehead, MA 01945	books dealer items literature

Mail order only. Out-of-print automobile books; Saab literature, books and dealer items list. Send SASE (each list).

Italy's Famous Exhaust 2711 183rd St Redondo Beach, CA 90278 PH/FAX: 310-542-5432 E-mail: http://famous@earthlink.com	exhaust systems wheels

See full listing in **Section Two** under **exhaust systems**

SIMCA Car Club 644 Lincoln St Amherst, OH 44001 216-988-9104 evenings (no return calls)	manuals/reprints parts inventory purchaser of cars/parts technical assistance

See full listing in **Section Three** under **Simca**

Miller Energy Inc 3200 South Clinton Ave S Plainfield, NJ 07080 908-755-6700; FAX: 908-755-0312 E-mail: allyon@aol.com	engine parts

Mail order only. Level gauge, sight glass for Stanley steam, engine.

Vintage Steam Products 396 North Rd Chester, NJ 07930-2327 201-584-3319	parts supplies

Mail order only. Specializing in reproduction parts and supplies for Stanleys and other early steam powered automobiles.

Stearns-Knight

Arthur W Aseltine 18215 Challenge Cut-Off Rd Forbestown, CA 95941 916-675-2773	parts research restoration

Mail order and open shop. Monday-Friday 8 to 5:30; Saturday and Sunday by appointment. Total or partial restoration of Stearns, Stearns-Knight, Daimler, Minerva and other sleeve-valve motorcars. 35 years' experience with sleeve-valve motors. All work guaranteed.

Autosport Specialty	decals
PO Box 9553	license plates
Knoxville, TN 37920	patches
615-573-2580	

See full listing in **Section Two** under **novelties**

The Bumper Boyz	bumper repairs
834 E Florence Ave	reconditioning
Los Angeles, CA 90001	sand blasting
213-587-8976, 800-995-1703	
FAX: 213-587-2013	

See full listing in **Section One** under **Chevrolet**

Classic Enterprises	sheetmetal
Box 92	
Barron, WI 54812	
715-537-5422	

Specializes in restoration reproductions (sheetmetal) for Studebakers and 46-68 Willys Jeeps. Floor pans for 57-58 Fords.

Dakota Studebaker Parts	parts
RR 1, Box 103A	
Armour, SD 57313	
605-724-2527	

Mail order only. Specializes in parts for Studebaker trucks, pickups and cars 1936-64.

Dennis DuPont	automobilia
77 Island Pond Rd	literature
Derry, NH 03038	parts
603-434-9290	

Mail order only. We sell NOS and used parts for Studebaker from mid 30s to 1966. We also have Studebaker literature, ads and automobilia. We buy Studebaker NOS parts, literature and automobilia. If it says Studebaker we're interested.

Eugene Gardner	license plates
10510 Rico Tatum Rd	
Palmetto, GA 30268	
770-463-4264	

See full listing in **Section Two** under **license plates**

Gus R Garton	bicycles
401 N 5th St	NOS parts
Millville, NJ 08332	sales literature
609-825-3618 evenings	

See full listing in **Section One** under **Ford '32-'53**

Kelley's Korner	parts
22 14th St	repair
Bristol, TN 37620	
423-968-5583	

Mail order and open shop. Monday-Saturday 9 to 5. Studebaker repair, parts for Studebaker cars and trucks 1925-1966. Engine rebuilds, brake overhauls, front end work, electrical work and wiring harnesses.

L & L Antique Auto Trim	runningboard
403 Spruce, Box 177	moldings
Pierce City, MO 65723	
417-476-2871	

See full listing in **Section Two** under **special services**

Loga Enterprises	convertible tops
5399 Old Town Hall Rd	interior parts
Eau Claire, WI 54701	
715-832-7302	

Mail order only. Specializing in Studebaker 1937-1966 for interior panels, firewall liners, headliners, kick pads, truck headliners, trunk mats, carpets, convertible tops, gloveboxes. Also door boards, firewall pads, hood pads, door clips, custom interior panels.

Packard Farm	parts
97 N 150 W	
Greenfield, IN 46140	
317-462-3124; FAX: 317-462-8891	
800-922-1957 orders only	

See full listing in **Section One** under **Packard**

Phil's Studebaker	NOS parts
11250 Harrison Rd	used parts
Osceola, IN 46561-9375	
219-674-0084	

Mail order. For 1947-66 Studebakers. NOS, reproduction and excellent used Studebaker parts and accessories.

Royal Gorge Studebaker	parts
109 W Front St	restoration
Florence, CO 81226	
719-784-4169 shop	
719-275-3289 home	

Mail order and open shop. Monday-Saturday 9 to 6. Specializing in restoration and parts for Studebakers, all years to 1966.

Charles Schnetlage	books
22136 Roscoe Blvd	engine paint
Canoga Park, CA 91304	rubber products
818-347-0334	

Mail order only. For Studebakers, books, rubber products, brake and mechanical parts, 1928 to 1957 engine paint.

Seattle Packard	repair
PO Box 2262	restoration
Seattle, WA 98111	
206-726-9625	

See full listing in **Section One** under **Packard**

Steve's Studebaker-Packard	car dealer
2287 Second St	parts
Napa, CA 94559	suspension repairs
707-255-8945	

See full listing in **Section One** under **Packard**

Studebaker of California	parts
1400 Santa Fe Ave	
Long Beach, CA 90813	
562-435-0157; FAX: 562-436-3074	

Open shop. Monday-Friday 8-4:30. Reproduction & NOS for postwar Studebaker and Avanti automobiles.

Studebaker Parts & Locations | **parts**
228 Marquiss Cir | **parts locator**
Clinton, TN 37716
615-457-3002

Mail order only. Specializing in parts, new and used, for 1939-1966 Studebakers, Avanti, Avanti II.

Studebakers West | **mechanical**
335A Convention Way | **rebuilding**
Redwood City, CA 94063 | **transmission parts**
415-366-8787 | **wiring harnesses**

Mail order and open shop. Monday-Friday 9 to 12 and 1 to 5; Saturday 9 to 12 noon. Mechanical, rebuilding of chassis and new wiring harnesses. Over 12,000 part numbers in stock. "Studebakers are our business, our only business."

Pat Walsh Restorations | **literature**
Box Q | **rubber parts**
Wakefield, MA 01880
617-246-5565

See full listing in **Section Two** under **rubber parts**

Grand Touring | **engine rebuilding**
2785 E Regal Park Dr | **machine shop**
Anaheim, CA 92806 | **restoration**
714-630-0130; FAX: 714-630-6956 | **suspension**

See full listing in **Section Two** under **restoration shops**

Stutz Specialty Inc | **parts**
522 Southview Ave | **restoration**
Fort Wayne, IN 46806
219-745-5168; FAX: 219-749-0297

Restoration and maintenance of all collector automobiles. Woodworking, mechanical, machine shop, sheetmetal and painting done in house.

Ernie Toth | **brake fluid**
8153 Cloveridge Rd | **literature**
Chagrin Falls, OH 44022 | **parts**
216-338-3565

Mail order only. Stutz 8-cyl cars 1926-1934 parts, literature, memorabilia. Dot S silicone brake fluid.

American-Foreign Auto Electric Inc | **parts**
103 Main St | **rebuilding**
Souderton, PA 18964
215-723-4877

See full listing in **Section Two** under **electrical systems**

Classic Sunbeam Auto Parts Inc | **body parts**
2 Tavano Rd | **carpets**
Ossining, NY 10562 | **electrical parts**
800-24-SUNBEAM | **upholstery**
E-mail: classicsun@aol.com

Mail order only. Phone hours: Monday through Saturday 10 to 10. New OEM quality reproductions of running parts, trim, upholstery, carpets, tops, electrical and body parts for all models of Sunbeams. 24 page catalog.

Doug's British Car Parts | **accessories**
2487 E Colorado Blvd | **parts**
Pasadena, CA 91107
818-793-2494; FAX: 818-793-4339

See full listing in **Section One** under **Jaguar**

Rootes Competition Associates | **parts**
21 N Rockburn St
York, PA 17402
717-755-5321

Mail order only. Refurbishing and reselling used parts. For Sunbeam Alpines. 26 years' experience in parts & service for Alpines.

Sunbeam Specialties | **parts**
PO Box 771 | **restoration supplies**
Los Gatos, CA 95031
408-371-1642; FAX: 408-371-8070

Mail order and open shop. Monday-Friday 8 to 5. Carries an extensive supply of mechanical, hydraulic and soft trim and restoration supplies for Sunbeam Alpine and Tiger cars. Will ship overseas. Fast service.

Tiger Detailing | **accessories**
PO Box 9875 | **detailing**
North Hollywood, CA 91609-1875 | **hat/lapel pins**
PH/FAX: 818-982-1042 | **literature**
E-mail: tygrbeer7@aol.com | **parts**

Mail order and detailing by appointment. Custom hat/lapel pins and stock for over 1,200 marques. Accessories for all makes, ie: car covers, custom floor mats, etc. We specialize in literature and recycled parts for 50s-60s Datsuns, 60s Sunbeams (Alpine & Tiger), Sabra, DeTomaso, and 68-70 MoPar with focus on 1970 Challenger, GTX and Super Bees.

Tiger Tom's | **parts**
15 Knight Rd | **service**
Harrisburg, PA 17111
PH/FAX: 717-566-6813
E-mail: tigertoms@aol.com

Mail order and shop. Monday-Friday 8 to 5. Restoration parts and service of all components for Sunbeam Alpine and Tiger.

Victoria British Ltd | **accessories**
Box 14991 | **parts**
Lenexa, KS 66285-4991
800-255-0088; 913-599-3299

See full listing in **Section One** under **MG**

TALBOT

Dragone Classic Motorcars 1797 Main St Bridgeport, CT 06604 203-335-4643; FAX: 203-335-9798	car dealer

See full listing in **Section Two** under **car dealers**

TERRAPLANE

Hudson Motor Car Co Memorabilia Ken Poynter 19638 Huntington Harper Woods, MI 48225 313-886-9292	literature memorabilia novelties signs

See full listing in **Section One** under **Hudson**

K-GAP Automotive Parts PO Box 3065 Santa Fe Springs, CA 90670 FAX: 714-523-0403	repro parts

See full listing in **Section One** under **Hudson**

Celestial Mechanics 88 West 500 South Wellsville, UT 84339 801-245-4987	restoration

See full listing in **Section One** under **Volvo**

CSI 1100 S Raymond Ave, Suite H Fullerton, CA 92831 714-879-7955; FAX: 714-879-7310 E-mail: 102263.1046@compuserve.com	accessories parts

See full listing in **Section One** under **BMW**

Keiser Motors 1169 Dell Ave #A Campbell, CA 95008 408-374-7303	Land Cruisers

Specializing in Toyota Land Cruisers, FJ40, FJ55, FJ60, FJ80.

Land Cruisers Solutions Inc 20 Thornell Rd Newton, NH 03858 508-462-5656, MA	accessories services

Mail order and open shop. Monday-Saturday 9-5 pm EST and by appointment. Land Cruisers Solutions specializes in OEM parts and aftermarket accessories, and provides services for the Toyota Land Cruiser, FJ40, FJ45, FJ60 and the new FJ80 models. LCS is the nation's original supplier of the revolutionary aluminum body tub for both the FJ40 & FJ45 Land Cruiser. LCS custom builds everyday driver, trail worthy or show quality FJ40 & FJ45 Land Cruisers. Contact LCS for friendly sound advice on all your Land Cruiser needs.

Maximliner Inc 150 E Race St Troy, OH 45373 513-339-0240; 800-624-2320 FAX: 513-335-5424	cargo mats floor mats

See full listing in **Section Two** under **carpets**

Spector Off-Road Inc 21600 Nordhoff St, Dept HM Chatsworth, CA 91311 818-882-1238, FAX: 818-882-7144 E-mail: specterlc@aol.com	accessories parts

Mail order and open shop. Monday-Friday 9 am-6 pm EST; 1st & 3rd Saturday 10 am-2 pm. Toyota Land Cruiser parts and accessories only. World's most complete line top quality new & used, unique & hard to find Land Cruiser items. 30,000 sq ft warehouse, largest collection of rare non-USA Land Cruisers on display in the world. We invite you to visit our showroom. We ship worldwide. Annual 500 page catalog with price list available, $5 USA, $15 foreign. Web site: http://www.sor.com

American-Foreign Auto Electric Inc 103 Main St Souderton, PA 18964 215-723-4877	parts rebuilding

See full listing in **Section Two** under **electrical systems**

Atlantic Enterprises 221 Strand Industrial Dr Little River, SC 29566 803-399-7565; FAX: 803-399-4600	steering assemblies

See full listing in **Section Two** under **chassis parts**

Automotive Artistry 679 W Streetboro St Hudson, OH 44236 216-650-1503	restoration

Open shop only. Monday-Friday 8 to 5. Restoration of sports cars, all years and makes. Partial or body-off. Complete services offered, mechanical, body, upholstery and painting.

BCP Sport & Classic Co 10525 Airline Dr Houston, TX 77037 713-448-4739; FAX: 713-448-0189	parts service

See full listing in **Section One** under **MG**

BritBooks 62 Main St Otego, NY 13825 PH/FAX: 607-988-7956	books

See full listing in **Section Four** under **books & publications**

British Auto Parts Ltd 93256 Holland Ln Marcola, OR 97454 541-933-2880; FAX: 541-933-2302	parts

See full listing in **Section One** under **Morris**

British Auto Shoppe Inc 1115 1st Ave Silvis, IL 61282 309-796-2748; FAX: 309-796-2033	parts service

See full listing in **Section One** under **MG**

British Car Care By Pearson's 745 Orange Ave Winter Park, FL 32789 407-647-0967	car dealer parts repairs restoration

See full listing in **Section One** under **MG**

British Car Magazine PO Box 1683 Los Altos, CA 94023-1683 415-949-9680; FAX: 415-949-9685 E-mail: britcarmag@aol.com	periodical

See full listing in **Section Four** under **periodicals**

British Car Specialists 2060 N Wilson Way Stockton, CA 95205 209-948-8767; FAX: 209-948-1030 E-mail: healeydoc@aol.com	parts repairs restoration

See full listing in **Section One** under **Austin-Healey**

British Miles 9278 Old E Tyburn Rd Morrisville, PA 19067 215-736-9300; FAX: 215-736-3089	accessories literature parts restoration

See full listing in **Section One** under **MG**

British Parts NW 4105 SE Lafayette Hwy Dayton, OR 97114 503-864-2001; FAX: 503-864-2081	parts

Mail/phone orders only. Monday-Friday 8 am to 5 pm. Direct importer for Triumph and Jaguar auto parts. Full line of poly bushings for Triumph. High-performance engine parts from TR3 to TR7.

British Restorations 4455 Paul St Philadelphia, PA 19124 215/533-6696	car dealer restoration

See full listing in **Section One** under **Jaguar**

British T Shop Inc 165 Rt 82 Oakdale, CT 06370 860-889-0178; FAX: 860-889-6096	car dealer parts service

See full listing in **Section One** under **MG**

British Wiring Inc 20449 Ithaca Rd Olympia Fields, IL 60461 PH/FAX: 708-481-9050	wiring accessories wiring harnesses

See full listing in **Section Two** under **electrical systems**

BritParts Midwest 603 Monroe St LaPorte, IN 46350 219-324-5474; FAX: 219-324-7541	parts restoration service

See full listing in **Section One** under **Austin-Healey**

Doug's British Car Parts 2487 E Colorado Blvd Pasadena, CA 91107 818-793-2494; FAX: 818-793-4339	accessories parts

See full listing in **Section One** under **Jaguar**

Eightparts 940 S Warren Ave, Unit #143 Tucson, AZ 85719 520-670-9377; FAX: 520-670-9080 E-mail: rover@azstarnet.com	accessories parts

Mail/phone order. Open Monday-Friday 10 to 6; weekends by appointment. Specializing in new and used parts, high-performance, accessories and optional equipment for TR8 and Stag. Also Triumph TR7 parts.

Don Flye 5 Doe Valley Rd Petersham, MA 01366 508-724-3318	parts

See full listing in **Section One** under **Austin-Healey**

Golden Gulf Classics Inc PO Box 490 22530 Hwy 49 Saucier, MS 39574 601-831-2650	repairs restorations

Mail order and open shop. Shop open Monday-Friday 7 am to 5 pm CDT and by appointment. Specializing in full or partial restorations, repairs and service for Triumph TR3s and TR4s and 1955, 56, 57 Chevys. In-house sheetmetal, paint, mechanical, electrical and rust repair.

John's Cars Inc 800 Jaguar Ln Dallas, TX 75226 214-426-4100; FAX: 214-426-3116	parts restoration service

See full listing in **Section One** under **Jaguar**

MG Automotive 3733-C Wilmington Pk Kettering, OH 45429 513-294-7623	parts restoration service

See full listing in **Section One** under **MG**

Mini Mania 31 Winsor St Milpitas, CA 95035 408-942-5595; FAX: 408-942-5582 E-mail: minimania@aol.com	parts service

See full listing in **Section One** under **Austin**

Moss Motors Ltd
PO Box 847
440 Rutherford St
Goleta, CA 93117
800-235-6954; FAX: 805-692-2525

accessories
parts

See full listing in **Section One** under **MG**

Motorcars Ltd
8101 Hempstead
Houston, TX 77008
713-863-9388; FAX: 713-863-8238
E-mail: mcltd@phoenix.net

parts

See full listing in **Section One** under **Jaguar**

Motorhead Ltd
2811-B Old Lee Highway
Fairfax, VA 22031
800-527-3140; FAX: 703-573-3165

parts
repairs

See full listing in **Section One** under **Austin-Healey**

Motormetrics
5500 Thomaston Rd
Macon, GA 31204
912-477-6771

used parts

Mail order. TR3, Morris Minor, MG Midget, MGA, Austin Seven, Alfa Romeo and Fiat X-19 used parts. Free price list with SASE.

Mr Sport Car Inc
203 E Lincoln
Papillion, NE 68046
402-592-7559

service

See full listing in **Section One** under **Jaguar**

Nisonger Instrument S/S
570 Mamaroneck Ave
Mamaroneck, NY 10543
914-381-1952; FAX: 914-381-1953

gauges

See full listing in **Section Two** under **instruments**

NOS Locators
587 Pawtucket Ave
Pawtucket, RI 02860
401-725-5000

parts

See full listing in **Section One** under **MG**

Omni Specialties
10418 Lorain Ave
Cleveland, OH 44111
800-791-9562; 216-251-2269
FAX: 216-251-6083

parts
restoration
service

See full listing in **Section One** under **MG**

Pacific International Auto
1118 Garnet Ave
San Diego, CA 92109
619-274-1920, 619-454-1815

parts
sales
service

See full listing in **Section One** under **Jaguar**

Peninsula Imports
3749 Harlem Rd
Buffalo, NY 14215
800-263-4538; FAX: 905-847-3021

accessories
parts
trim

See full listing in **Section One** under **BMW**

Ragtops & Roadsters
203 S 4th St
Perkasie, PA 18944
215-257-1202; FAX: 215-257-2688

race prep
repairs

See full listing in **Section One** under **AC**

The Roadster Factory
PO Box 332
Armagh, PA 15920
800-234-1104; FAX: 814-446-6729
E-mail: trfmail@internetmci.com

accessories
parts

Mail order Monday through Thursday, 7 am to 2 am; Friday and Saturday, 8 am to 6 pm; counter sales Monday through Saturday, 8 am to 6 pm. Mail order and counter sales of parts and accessories for Triumph TR2 through TR8, Spitfire, GT6 and MGB. Minor components to rebuilt units and body shells. Manufacturer of high quality replica parts. Company owned and operated by Triumph and MGB enthusiasts since 1978.

Special Interest Car Parts
1340 Hartford Ave
Johnston, RI 02919
800-556-7496; FAX: 401-831-7760

parts

See full listing in **Section One** under **Jaguar**

Sports & Classics
PO Box 1787
512 Boston Post Rd, Dept H
Darien, CT 06820-1787
203-655-8731; FAX: 203-656-1896

interiors
parts
tops
wire wheels

See full listing in **Section One** under **body parts**

The Registry
Pine Grove
Stanley, VA 22851
540-778-3728; FAX: 540-778-2402
E-mail: britregstry@aol.com

periodical

See full listing in **Section Four** under **periodicals**

Triumph World Magazine
PO Box 75
Tadworth
Surrey KT20 7XF England
01737 814311; FAX: 01737 814591

periodical

Triumph World magazine is a bi-monthly, top quality magazine devoted entirely to the ever-popular classic cars produced under the Triumph banner, such famous sports car models that carry the marque name to the four corners of the globe. The TR range, Spitfire and Stag plus those other unique models that epitomize the best of British styling and engineering. Subscription: $37/year (6 issues).

Victoria British Ltd
Box 14991
Lenexa, KS 66285-4991
800-255-0088; 913-599-3299

accessories
parts

See full listing in **Section One** under **MG**

Victory Autoservices
Box 5060
RR 1
W Baldwin, ME 04091
207-625-4581

parts
restoration

See full listing in **Section One** under **Austin-Healey**

Web Accessories   fiberglass parts
PO Box 191
Old Bethpage, NY 11804
516-752-1710

See full listing in **Section Two** under **fiberglass parts**

J Wood & Co Auctioneers   auctions
PO Box 852
Searsport, ME 04974
207-548-2113; FAX: 207-548-2888

See full listing in **Section Two** under **auctions & events**

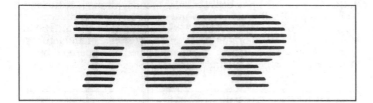

British T Shop Inc   car dealer
165 Rt 82   parts
Oakdale, CT 06370   service
860-889-0178; FAX: 860-889-6096

See full listing in **Section One** under **MG**

Classic Motor Works   parts
100 Station St
Johnstown, PA 15905
814-288-6911; FAX: 814-288-4455
E-mail: birdcmw@aol.com

Mail order only. New and used parts for TVR sports cars from Grantura to 280i.

JAE   parts
375 Pine #26   service
Goleta, CA 93117   tech info
805-967-5767; FAX: 805-967-6183

See full listing in **Section One** under **Lotus**

UK Spares/TVR Sports Cars   accessories
609 Highland St   car covers
Wethersfield, CT 06109-3979   convertible tops
203-563-1647; FAX: 203-529-3479   ignition parts

Mail order only. Specializing in TVR parts, service, restoration for all years/models TVR. Also supply parts for all other British cars. US importer. Lucas/Girling, Spax, Centerforce clutches, Lumenition ignition, MSD ignition, K&N filters, Bel-Ray synthetic lubricants, Hayden fans, Deves piston rings, Gunson's (UK) specialty tools including Colortune, cross-drilled/vented rotors, best custom-fit car covers/floor mats, convertible tops, replaceable bulb headlamps/aux lighting, OEM seatbelts, fire extinguishers, lug nuts, aluminum valve covers, door mirrors, books, manuals, accessories, giftware, authentic English picnic baskets.

Vanden Plas

From Rust To Riches   appraisals
14200 New Hampshire Ave   car dealer
Silver Spring, MD 20904   repairs
301-384-5856   restoration
FAX: 301-989-1866

See full listing in **Section Two** under **restoration shops**

4 ever 4   car dealer
Rt 10   parts
Marlow, NH 03456   service
603-446-7820

Mail order and open shop. Monday-Friday 9 to 6, Thursday 9 to 9, weekends by prior appointment only. Specializing in Volkswagen parts & services for air cooled vehicles. Purchases & sells vehicles, toys, parts & literature, full service shop, many NOS parts & thousands of tagged & tested used parts, UPS daily. Involved with VW since 1967. A friendly, one man business. No catalog.

Auto Engineering   parts
3661 Sacramento Dr, Unit D
San Luis Obispo, CA 93401
805-544-1041

See full listing in **Section One** under **Volvo**

Das Bulli Haus   parts
18 Ward Ln   sheetmetal
North Franklin, CT 06254
PH/FAX: 860-642-7242
E-mail: mcladm3@uconnvm.uconn.edu

Specializing in the largest selection of high quality metal repair parts for pre-67 Volkswagen buses and trucks. We also carry some parts for 68 and newer VW buses and trucks.
Web site: http://www2.calweb.com/%7ethom/dasbulli.html

Discount Auto Parts   505-877-6782
4703 Broadway SE
Albuquerque, NM 87105

See full listing in **Section Five** under **New Mexico**

European Parts Specialists Ltd   accessories
PO Box 6783   parts
Santa Barbara, CA 93160
805-683-4020
FAX: 805-683-3689

See full listing in **Section One** under **Mercedes-Benz**

JBUGS Car & Truck Depot 14222 Prairie Ave Hawthorne, CA 90250 310-978-0926, 800-445-2847 FAX: 310-978-3984	accessories parts

We stock over 3,000 new and used auto parts and accessories to keep your classic or newer water cooled Volkswagen running. We also carry a full line of interiors, door panels, seat covers, headliners, carpet kits to restore your car back to its original look. All interior items are manufactured by TMI Products Inc. Worldwide mail order service is available. Call toll-free and place your order.

John's Car Corner Rt 5, PO Box 85 Westminster, VT 05158 802-722-3180	body parts car dealer mechanical parts restoration service

Mail order and open shop. Monday-Friday 8 to 5; Saturday 9 to 12. Shop address: Rt 5, Westminster, VT 05158. Millions of new and used parts for Volkswagen, all years and all models.

Joe L Jordan 2615 Waugh Dr, #301 Houston, TX 77006-2799 713-680-3181; FAX: 713-680-3185	car dealer limo service parts

See full listing in **Section One** under **Rolls-Royce/Bentley**

People Kars 290 Third Ave Ext Rensselaer, NY 12144 PH/FAX: 518-465-0477	models/more VW toys

Mail order and shows. Specializing in toys, models and collectibles for all types and years of Volkswagens. People Kars feature VW models from Vitesse, Solido, Mini Champs, Shabak, Siku and more plus and extensive collection of older discontinued models, toys and promotional pieces, all with the VW enthusiast in mind. Please write for current catalog/list.

Stormin Norman's Bug Shop 201 Commerce Dr #3 Fort Collins, CO 80524 303-493-5873	repair restoration

Open shop. Summer hours: Monday-Friday 8 am-5:30 pm. Winter hours: Tuesday-Friday 8 am-5:30 pm. Repair and complete restoration services for Volkswagen Beetles.

Tabco Inc 11655 Chillicothe Rd Chesterland, OH 44026-1994 216-729-5151; FAX: 216-729-1251	body parts

See full listing in **Section Two** under **sheetmetal**

TMI Products Inc 191 Granite St Corona, CA 91719 909-272-1996; 800-624-7960 FAX: 909-272-1584 E-mail: tmiprods@aol.com	classic car interiors

The largest manufacturer of quality replacement upholstery trim products for classic cars. Specializing in Volkswagen models from 1949 to 1993 and Mustang from 1964-1/2 to 1973. TMI offers the finest trim products available today. Featuring all the correct colors, grains and patterns that are guaranteed to fit. Best of all the Mustang upholstery is MCA approved. Call or write today for your free catalog and local distributor. Please specify model of car.

United German Imports 4556 Shetland Green Alexandria, VA 22312 800-98-BRAKE; FAX: 703-916-1610 E-mail: ugibrakes2@aol.com	brake parts brakes

See full listing in **Section Two** under **brakes**

V-Dub's 'R' Us 5705 Gordon Dr Harrisburg, PA 17112 717-540-9972	literature parts toys

Mail order. Used, NOS and repro parts for air cooled Volkswagens. Sheetmetal, rubber parts, chrome trim, cabriolet parts, restored steering wheels. VW toys and literature. Restoration supplies and assistance. We use what we sell.

Volkswagen Collectors c/o Jerry Jess 3121 E Yucca St Phoenix, AZ 85028-2616 PH/FAX: 602-867-7672	literature memorabilia toys

Mail order only. Buys, sells and trades in anything for air cooled Volkswagens. We have a 17 page illustrated list, $1. Bug, bus, Ghia, type III, also VW tool kits, accessories, dealer memorabilia. Specializing in toys, literature, memorabilia for all air cooled Volkswagens including any Empi, Hazet, Herbie, The Love Bug material. Free VW locator service, we will find a buyer or sell your VW free!

West Coast Metric Inc 24002 Frampton Ave Harbor City, CA 90710 310-325-0005; FAX: 310-325-9733 E-mail: wcmi@earthlink.net	apparel carpets rubber parts

Mail order and open shop. Monday-Friday 7 am to 5 pm PST. Specializing in rubber & plastic restoration parts for 1946-1993 Volkswagen Bugs, Ghias, buses, Type IIIs, Things, Vanagons, Rabbit, Scirroco, Golf, Jetta, Cabriolet. VW apparel, car covers, carpets, decals, grille emblems, badges, hardware, upholstery, wiring harnesses.

VOLVO

Dick Ames Stainless Steel Exhaust 3963 Wilshire Cir Sarasota, FL 34238 813-923-8321; FAX: 813-923-9434	exhaust systems

See full listing in **Section One** under **Jaguar**

Auto Engineering 3661 Sacramento Dr, Unit D San Luis Obispo, CA 93401 805-544-1041	parts

Mail order only. Volvo, water-cooled VW parts. 20% to 30% off list. OEM brakes, air, fuel, oil filters, brake pads, shocks, Bosch electrical, factory parts. Free freight on orders over $300.

BCP Sport & Classic Co 10525 Airline Dr Houston, TX 77037 713-448-4739; FAX: 713-448-0189	parts service

See full listing in **Section One** under **MG**

Brasilia Press
PO Box 2023
Elkhart, IN 46515
FAX: 219-262-8799

models

See full listing in **Section Two** under **models & toys**

Celestial Mechanics
88 West 500 South
Wellsville, UT 84339
801-245-4987

restoration

Mail order and open shop. Weekends 7 am to 7 pm. Small shop where we average one loving restoration per year. No detail is too small. Projects begin in spring and are completed in the fall. Minor projects welcomed anytime. We are expensive but will barter. Specializing in Volvo 1800 models 1961-69, Mercedes-Benz 1960s and Toyota Land Cruiser.

Concours Cars of Colorado Ltd
2414 W Cucharras St
Colorado Springs, CO 80904
719-473-6288

accessories
parts
service

See full listing in **Section One** under **BMW**

Dan's Volvo Service
6615 S MacDill Ave
Tampa, FL 33611
813-831-1616

restoration

Shop open Monday-Friday 9 to 5. Complete repair and restoration service on all vintage PV544, 122-S, 1800-S Volvos, parts.

Ed Dennis
Rt 144, Box 9957
Ellicott City, MD 21042-3647
410-750-2352, 7-9 pm EST

American Car
Crest keys
Wilmot Breeden
keys

See full listing in **Section Two** under **locks & keys**

European Parts Specialists Ltd
PO Box 6783
Santa Barbara, CA 93160
805-683-4020; FAX: 805-683-3689

accessories
parts

See full listing in **Section One** under **Mercedes-Benz**

Foreign Autotech
3235 C Sunset Ln
Hatboro, PA 19040
215-441-4421; FAX: 215-441-4490

parts

Specializing in new, reproduction & used parts for Volvo P1800, P, S, E & ES Models 1961-1973.

Pete Groh
9957 Frederick Rd
Ellicott City, MD 21042-3647
410-750-2352

original British
keys
Wilmot Breeden

See full listing in **Section One** under **Jaguar**

David Hueppchen
N 6808 Hwy OJ
PO Box 540
Plymouth, WI 53073
414-893-2531; FAX: 414-893-6800

parts
service

Mail order and open shop. Monday-Friday, 9 am-noon, 2-6 pm. New and used parts, service by appointment for Volvo 122, 140, 1800, 240 and 262C Bertone coupe. Over 40 driver and parts cars on hand. Restoration, vintage race preparation also done.

Italy's Famous Exhaust
2711 183rd St
Redondo Beach, CA 90278
PH/FAX: 310-542-5432
E-mail: http://famous@earthlink.com

exhaust systems
wheels

See full listing in **Section Two** under **exhaust systems**

London Stainless Steel Exhaust Centre
249-253 Queenstown Rd
London, SW8 3NP England
011-44-171622-2120
FAX: 011-44-171627-0991
E-mail: 101445.341@compuserv.com

exhaust systems

See full listing in **Section Two** under **exhaust systems**

R E Pierce
47 Stone Rd
Wendell Depot, MA 01380
508-544-7442; FAX: 508-544-2978

parts
restoration

Tires to roof rack restorations on 122s, P-1800s and 140s. 18 years' of collecting and restoring classic Volvos. 78 parts cars and stock piles of used parts. Free estimates, reasonable prices. Located in north central MA, near Orange/Athol. Call for an appointment.

Michael A Stahl
PO Box 18036
Huntsville, AL 35804
205-882-6457

parts

See full listing in **Section One** under **Cadillac/LaSalle**

Swedish Classics Inc
PO Box 557
Oxford, MD 21654
800-258-4422; FAX: 410-226-5543

parts

Restoration and repair parts for vintage and new Volvos. Web site: swedishclassics.com

Van Nuys Motors
14422 Oxnard St
Van Nuys, CA 91403
818-988-5455

parts
restoration
sales
service

See full listing in **Section One** under **Mercedes-Benz**

Voluparts Inc
751 Trabert Ave NW
Atlanta, GA 30318
404-352-3402

parts

Mail order and open shop. Monday-Friday 9 to 6. 18,000 square foot warehouse. New, used and rebuilt Volvo parts.

Vovo Parts Inc
1801 W Evans
Denver, CO 80223
800-541-8686; FAX: 303-934-2099

parts

Specializes in Volvo parts. New, used, remanufactured. From 1968-1990 140, 160, 240, 260, 700 Series.

Gus R Garton	bicycles
401 N 5th St	NOS parts
Millville, NJ 08332	sales literature
609-825-3618 evenings	

See full listing in **Section One** under **Ford '32-'53**

Marky D's Bikes & Peddle Goods	bicycles
7047 Springridge Rd	mopeds
West Bloomfield, MI 48322	motorbikes
810-737-1657; FAX: 810-398-2581	peddle goods

See full listing in **Section Two** under **bicycles**

Michael J Welch	automobilia
3700 Rt 6, RR 2	pedal cars
Eastham, MA 02642	toy trucks
508-255-1437	

See full listing in **Section Two** under **models & toys**

Brian's 4WD Parts & Literature	literature
260 Tyler St	parts
East Haven, CT 06512	
PH/FAX: 203-469-4940	
E-mail: willysgp@aol.com	

Mail order only. Parts and literature for Jeep vehicles produced by Willys, Kaiser and AMC. New, used, rebuilt and NOS parts for 1945 to 1986 Jeeps. Active buyers of Jeep vehicles, parts, literature and collectibles. New Jeep enthusiasts always welcome.

Classic Enterprises	sheetmetal
Box 92	
Barron, WI 54812	
715-537-5422	

See full listing in **Section One** under **Studebaker**

Commonwealth Automotive	body rebuilding
Restorations	parts
1725 Hewins St	restoration
Ashley Falls, MA 01222	
413-229-3196	

See full listing in **Section Two** under **military vehicles**

JEBO Co Inc	accessories
24-49 28st, Ste 2	body parts
Astoria, NY 11102	
718-932-4866; FAX: 718-843-5866	

Mail order only. Specializing in body replacement, body parts, accessories, all in stainless steel for CJ Series Jeeps, Wranglers, Jeep Willys.

The Jeepster Man	literature
238 Ramtown Greenville Rd	parts
Howell, NJ 07731	
908-458-3966	

Mail order and open shop. Open Monday-Friday 9 to 5; Saturday 9 to 12. Large selection of Jeep and Jeepster parts. Send 75 cent SASE and model designation for free list. Shop manuals for all Willys vehicles. Contact The Jeepster Man for all hard to find parts. New items, horn rings, car covers, sunvisors, choke cables, o/s mirrors.

Mike's Auto Parts	bearings/engine parts
Box 358	NOS parts
Ridgeland, MS 39158	wall calendars
601-856-7214	windshield wipers

See full listing in **Section One** under **Chrysler**

John E Parker	plastic repros
4860 N Desert Tortoise Pl	rubber parts
Tucson, AZ 85745-9213	
602-743-3574	

See full listing in **Section One** under **Kaiser-Frazer**

Gary Saunders	collector
69 Braman Rd	
Waterford, CT 06385	
203-442-2933	

Buying for personal collection to eventually open museum for Willys Jeepsters, station wagons, forward control and pickups.

Tire Barn Inc	tires
255 Twinsburg Rd	
Northfield, OH 44067	
216-467-1284	
FAX: 216-467-1289, call first	

See full listing in **Section Two** under **tires**

The Willys Man	literature
Ron Ladley	parts
1850 Valley Forge Rd	vehicles
Lansdale, PA 19446	
610-584-1665; FAX: 610-584-8537	

Mail order and open shop. Weeknights & weekends. Supplier and adviser of 1933 thru 1942 Willys cars, trucks, parts and literature for over 25 years (no post-war Willys Jeep parts).

Willys Wood	wood parts
35336 Chauler Dr	
North Ridgeville, OH 44039	
216-327-2916	

Mail order only. Replacement body wood for 33/36, 40/41 Willys coupes, sedan deliveries and pickups, steel or fiberglass, stock or chopped. Kits or individual pieces available. Call or write for illustrated price list.

Willys Works Inc	car dealer
1933 W Gardner Ln	parts
Tucson, AZ 85705	restoration
520-888-5082	service

Mail order and open shop. Tuesday-Friday 10 to 6, Saturday 9 to 4. Primarily mechanical parts and Jeep universal, utility wagon and pickup, vintage and modern.

Tourguide:
Marque Specialists

Planning a trip? Or perhaps you would just like to know what old-car resources are in your home territory. In either case, the tourguide to Section One will help.

This tourguide offers you an alphabetical listing of marque specialists with open shops by state and foreign country. Simply turn to the page number indicated for complete information on the object of your visit, including hours of operation, complete address, and phone number.

176	Sunbeam Specialties, Los Gatos
18	Ed Swart Motors Inc, Torrance
111	T-Birds By Nick, Panorama City
172	Teddy's Garage, Northridge
111	Thunderbird Headquarters, Concord
106	TMC (Traction Master Co), Los Angeles
90	Truck 'N' Parts, Rosemead
53	True Connections, Riverside
137	Van Nuys Motors, Van Nuys
83	Vintage Speed Parts, Rosemead
123	Ed West CARS, Tustin
181	West Coast Metric Inc, Harbor City
168	Willhoit Auto Restoration, Long Beach
48	Wolf Automotive, Santa Ana

Colorado

9	Centerline Products, Boulder
18	Concours Cars of Colorado, Ltd, Colorado Springs
134	House of Imports, Inc, Lakewood
104	Mustang Classics, Denver
70	Pantera Performance Center, Castle Rock
167	Restoration Services, Golden
175	Royal Gorge Studebaker, Florence
99	Sam's Vintage Ford Parts, Denver
181	Stormin Norman's Bug Shop, Fort Collins
124	Walker's Auto Pride Inc, Monument

Connecticut

9	Alfas Unlimited Inc, Norfolk
84	Antique Ford V8 Parts, Union
141	British T Shop Inc, Oakdale
102	Classic Mustang Inc, Southington
81	Joe Lagana, Canterbury
104	Mostly Mustangs Inc, Hamden
104	Mustangs Unlimited, Manchester
104	New England Mustang Supply Inc, Bridgeport
44	PRO Antique Auto Parts, Windsor Locks
126	Ron Baker's Auto Inc, Putnam

Florida

131	ABS Exotic Repair Inc, Ft Lauderdale
10	American Performance Products, Cocoa
117	BMC Classics, New Smyrna Beach
141	British Car Care By Pearson's, Winter Park
102	Classic Auto Air Mfg Co, Tampa
35	Classic Chevy International, Orlando
53	Corvair Heaven, Ellenton
182	Dan's Volvo Service, Tampa
37	East Coast Chevy Inc, Doylestown
75	Euro Coachworks Inc, Fort Lauderdale
108	Hollywood Classic Motorcars Inc, Hallandale
128	Lincoln Land, Clearwater
151	Lucky Lee Lott (Author), Tampa
128	Mainly Convertibles, Tampa
77	Motorcar Gallery Inc, Fort Lauderdale
172	Omega Automobile Appraisals, St Petersburg
172	Powers Parts Inc, Anna Maria
172	Proper Motor Cars, Inc, St. Petersburg
77	Shelton Dealerships, Ford Lauderdale
123	Thoroughbred Motors, Sarasota
173	Vantage Motorworks Inc, N Miami
123	Vicarage Jaguars, Miami

Georgia

78	Bayless Inc, Marietta
55	Blue Ribbon Products, Atlanta
132	Bud's Parts for Classic Mercedes-Benz, Douglasville
65	Cobra Restorers Ltd, Kennesaw
81	Hancock's Engine Rebuilders and Balancing Service, Athens
133	Haz-Benz, Atlanta

96	Melvin's Classic Ford Parts Inc, Lithonia
104	Mustangs Unlimited, Norcross
43	Obsolete Chevrolet Parts Co, Nashville
97	Obsolete Ford Parts Co, Nashville
51	Rick's First Generation Camaro Parts, Bogart
90	Joe Smith Ford & Hot Rod Parts, Marietta
46	Super Sport Restoration Parts Inc, Lithonia
47	The Truck Shop, Nashville
182	Voluparts, Inc, Atlanta

Idaho

| 93 | Tony Copeland Ford Lincoln Mercury, Lewiston |

Illinois

79	Bob's Antique Auto Parts Inc, Rockford
141	British Auto Shoppe Inc, Silvis
114	Charleston Custom Cycle, Charleston
56	Chicago Corvette Supply, Justice
26	Collector Cars-U-Can-Afford Ltd, Rockford
53	Corvair Haven, Batavia
49	D & R Classic Automotive Inc, Warrenville
62	Lawrence DeSenville, Berwyn
134	Horst's Car Care, Decatur
40	Kessler's Antique Cars & Body Shop, Olney
104	Mustang of Chicago Ltd, Bensenville
46	Lyn Smith Nova Parts, Pontiac
83	Special T's Unlimited Corp, Prospect Heights
123	Terry's Jaguar Parts Inc, Benton

Indiana

16	BritParts Midwest, LaPorte
161	Dick Choler Cars & Service Inc, Elkhart
36	Custom Classic Cars, Bourbon
166	Doc & Cy's Restoration Parts, Indianapolis
80	Ed's Be-Bop Shop, Medora
121	Muncie Imports & Classics, Muncie
156	Packard Farm, Greenfield
104	The Paddock® Inc, Knightstown
60	Jack Podell Fuel Injection Spec, South Bend
115	TK Performance Inc, Evansville
12	Webb's Classic Auto Parts, Huntington

Iowa

87	Janssen's Repair Shop, Manson
163	Kurt Kelsey, Iowa Falls
42	Merv's Classic Chevy Parts, Iowa Falls
43	Old Car Parts, Clear Lake
72	Vintage Power Wagons, Inc, Fairfield
13	Weld-N-Fab Performance, Norwalk

Kansas

147	Giles Antique Auto Parts, South Hutchinson
108	Hein's Classic Cars, Durham
58	Kansas City Corvettes Inc, Overland Park
28	McVey's, Merriam

Kentucky

| 79 | Antique Auto Parts of Kentucky, Lexington |
| 84 | ARASCO, Newport |

Louisiana

| 169 | Bassett Classic Restoration, Kenner |

Maine

79	Bryant's Antique Auto Parts, Hampden
74	Kenneth Fogarty, New Vineyard
54	Maplewood Motors, Cape Neddick
17	Victory Autoservices, W Baldwin

Specialists

Maryland

55	Andover Automotive Inc, Laurel
68	Banzai Motorworks, Beltsville
56	Corvette Specialties of MD, Inc, Eldersburg
27	Driving Passion-1959, Clarksville
16	Healey Surgeons Inc, Takoma Park
82	Myers Model A Ford Parts & Mustang & Car Trailers, Williamsport

Massachusetts

132	Auto Enthusiasts, Chelsea
141	Boston MG Shop, Allston
119	Crow Engineering Jaguar Engines, Taunton
119	Donovan Motorcar Service, Lenox
80	Ezold's Model A Garage, Westfield
170	Foreign Motors West, Natick
80	Freeman's Garage, Norton
113	GMC Solutions, Franklin
163	Green's Obsolete Parts, Pepperell
133	Gullwing Service Co, Inc, Essex
39	Hampton Coach, Amesbury
76	Hyannis Restoration, Hyannis
40	J & K Old Chevy Stuff, Plymouth
81	Lang's Old Car Parts, Winchendon
87	LeBaron Bonney Co, Amesbury
139	Mercury & Ford Molded Rubber, Wilmington
104	Monument Motors, Inc, Great Barrington
135	Ottorich, Chestnut Hill
82	Pioneer Valley Model A Ford Inc, Easthampton
89	PV Antique & Classic Ford, Tewksbury
83	Mike Stein and Ed Stein, Southampton
61	Wild Bill's Corvette & Hi-Performance Center Inc, Norwood

Michigan

165	356 Enterprises, Warren
84	Keith Ashley, St Johns
20	Bob's Brickyard Inc, Brighton
62	Burchill Antique Auto Parts Inc, Port Huron
127	Buzz De Clerck, Sterling Heights
34	CARS Inc, Berkley
56	Corvette Central, Sawyer
56	Corvette Rubber Company, Cadillac
127	Buzz De Clerck, Sterling Heights
37	Experi-Metal Inc, Sterling Heights
86	Fairlane Automotive Specialties, St. Johns
138	John's Classic Cougars, Holland
54	Joseph A Kastelan, Ionia
134	Lyco Engineering, Inc, Plymouth
135	Midwestern Motors & Dismantlers, Southfield
18	Nostalgic Motor Cars, Wixom
156	Patrician Industries, Inc, Dearborn
111	Thunderbird Center, Hazel Park
145	University Motors Ltd, Ada

Minnesota

80	Classtique Upholstery & Top Co, Isanti
127	Mike Gerner, The Lincoln Factory, Gemlake
95	Joe's Auto Sales, Hastings
42	National Chevy Assoc, St Paul
144	Quality Coaches, Minneapolis
72	Paul Slater Auto Parts, Stillwater
90	Southside Obsolete, Minneapolis

Mississippi

178	Golden Gulf Classics, Inc, Saucier

Missouri

145	Carl W Burst III, St Louis
34	Jim Carter's Antique Truck Parts, Independence
34	Chevy Duty Pickup Parts, Kansas City
95	L B Repair, Savannah
77	Motorcars International, Springfield

Nebraska

121	Mr Sport Car Inc, Papillion

New Hampshire

180	4 ever 4, Marlow
140	Abingdon Spares, Ltd, Walpole
18	Bavarian Autosport, Portsmouth
118	British Auto/USA, Manchester
48	Camaro-Heaven, Rochester
85	Early Ford Parts and Service, Claremont
71	Fitzgerald Motorsports, Laconia
177	Land Cruisers Solutions Inc, Newton
97	Northeast Ford, E Sullivan
91	Yesteryear Restorations, Jaffrey

New Jersey

79	Antique Cars, Parts & Trains, Millville
169	Borla East, Middlesex
101	Central Jersey Mustang, Edison
56	Conte's Corvettes & Classics, Vineland
119	Eddie's Restorations, Elwood
37	Fifties Forever, Garfield
102	Garden State Mustang Inc, Fairfield
86	Gus R. Garton, Millville
86	Half Ton Fun, Jackson
183	The Jeepster Man, Howell
41	LES Auto Parts, Dayton
137	Mercer Automobile Company, Magnolia
44	Passenger Car Supply, Swedesboro
136	Save-A-Star-Mike, Lawrenceville
122	The Stable LTD, Gladstone
111	Sunyaks, Bound Brook

New Mexico

100	Valley Motor Supply, Roswell

New York

160	Bill's Birds, Dix Hills
108	Custom Autocraft Inc, St James
36	Dave's Auto Machine & Parts, Ischua
86	Early Ford V8 Sales Inc, Ballston Lake
57	Elmer's Auto Parts Inc, Webster
27	FEN Enterprises of New York Inc, Wappingers Falls
80	Ford Parts Specialists Div. of Joblot Automotive, Inc, Queens Village
87	Joblot Automotive Inc, Queens Village
58	Long Island Corvette Supply Inc, Copiague
81	Mac's Antique Auto Parts, Lockport
143	MG Supermarket, Tuxedo
14	Mini City Ltd, Henrietta
110	Muck Motor Ford Sales, Getzville
67	Norm's Custom Shop, Bath
164	Patterson Coachworks, Clay
19	Peninsula Imports, Buffalo
135	John T Poulin Auto Sales/Star Service Center, North Troy
90	S & S Antique Auto, Deposit
136	Southampton Auto & Marine Upholstery, Southampton
90	Dick Spadaro, Altamont
136	Star Quality, La Grangeville
20	Stephen's Auto Works, Kings Pk
112	Thunderbird Parts and Restoration, Clarence Center
149	Wittenborn's Auto Service Inc, Briarcliff Manor

North Carolina

92	Carolina Classics, Durham
108	Classic Sheetmetal Inc, Charlotte

36	Dixie Truck Works, Mount Pleasant
120	International Restoration Specialist Inc, Mt Airy
109	Jim's T-Bird Parts & Service, Winston-Salem
59	Morrison Motor Co, Concord
136	Silver Star Restorations, Topton
30	Southern US Car Export Inc, Raeford

Ohio

10	American Parts Depot, West Manchester
21	Antique & Classic Cars Inc, Hamilton
177	Automotive Artistry, Hudson
33	Bill's Speed Shop, Navarre
92	Bob Burgess 1955-56 Ford Parts Inc, Bellbrook
25	Cars II, Brookfield
108	Classic Auto Supply Company Inc, Coshocton
170	Coachbuilt Motors, Columbus
67	Edwards Crosley Parts, Mansfield
38	G & L Classics, West Chester
80	Gaslight Auto Parts Inc, Urbana
11	Kennedy American Inc, West Jefferson
143	MG Automotive, Kettering
147	Mitchell Motor Parts Inc, Grove City
144	Omni Specialties, Cleveland
167	Perfect Panels of America, Centerville
105	Pony Parts of America, Centerville
60	Proteam Corvette Sales Inc, Napoleon
105	Rode's Restoration, Galion
144	Safety Fast Restoration Company, Mansfield
83	Snyder's Antique Auto Parts Inc, New Springfield
168	Stuttgart Automotive Inc, Centerville
46	Trim Parts Inc, Milford
123	Welsh Jaguar Enterprises Inc, Steubenville
149	Howard Whitelaw, Cleveland (Solon)
47	Ted Williams Enterprises, Lisbon
12	Wymer Classic AMC, Fremont

Oklahoma

24	Aabar's Cadillac & Lincoln Salvage & Parts, Oklahoma City
156	James Hill, Goodwell
40	JR's Antique Auto, Claremore
138	Ken's Cougars, Edmond
120	Lister North America Ltd, Tulsa
97	Obsolete Ford Parts Inc, Oklahoma City
83	Varco Inc, Oklahoma City

Oregon

107	Bird Nest, Portland
155	Brinton's Antique Auto Parts, Redmond
118	British Motor Co, Eugene
36	Cliff's Classic Chevrolet Parts Co, Portland
85	Bob Drake Reproductions Inc, Grants Pass
37	The Filling Station, Lebanon
11	For Ramblers Only, Portland
17	Mini Motors Classic Coachworks, Salem
97	Northwest Classic Falcons Inc, Portland
143	Northwest Import Parts, Portland
43	Old Car Parts, Portland
172	Oregon Crewe Cutters Inc, Grants Pass
139	Rapido Group, Portland
111	T-Bird Sanctuary, Tualatin
90	Wescott's Auto Restyling, Boring

Pennsylvania

91	ABC Auto Upholstery & Top Company, Philadelphia
70	Avanti Auto Service, Glen Mills
55	Bairs Corvettes, Linesville
79	Bill's Model A Ford, Ferndale
107	Bob's Bird House, Chadds Ford
101	Tony D Branda Performance, Altoona
141	British Miles, Morrisville

118	British Restorations, Philadelphia
34	C & P Chevy Parts, Kulpsville
146	Chrysler Power, Mansfield
101	CJ Pony Parts Inc, Harrisburg
53	Corvair Ranch Inc, Gettysburg
57	Corvette World, Greensburg
57	County Corvette, Lionville
146	Daniel N Dietrich, Kempton
57	M F Dobbins, Inc, Hatboro
103	Glazier's Mustang Barn, Inc, Souderton
16	Healey Coop, Exeter
28	Holcombe Cadillac Parts, Bensalem
166	Klasse 356 Inc, Allentown
156	Lincoln Highway Packards, Schellsburg
120	Lindley Restorations Ltd, Pottstown
42	Martz Classic Chevy Parts, Thomasville
43	Ol' 55 Chevy Parts/East Coast Chevy Inc, Doylestown
150	Olde World Restorations, Huntingdon Valley
148	Older Car Restoration, Mont Alto
121	Philpenn Distributors Co, Bryn Mawr
9	Ragtops & Roadsters, Perkasie
179	The Roadster Factory, Armagh
60	Bob Sottile's Hobby Car Auto Sales, Inc, Martinsburg
150	Specialty Car Service, Ltd, Reading
64	Ed Spiegel, Murrysville
13	Steelwings, Ivyland
61	Stoudt Auto Sales, Reading
99	Tee-Bird Products Inc, Exton
112	Thunderbirds East, Chadds Ford
176	Tiger Tom's, Harrisburg
168	Translog Motorsports, York
183	The Willys Man, Lansdale

Puerto Rico

120	Jaguar of Puerto Rico Inc, San Juan

Rhode Island

117	Bassett's Jaguar, Wyoming

South Carolina

83	Smith & Jones Distributing Company Inc, West Columbia

Tennessee

85	Early Ford Parts, Memphis
175	Kelley's Korner, Bristol
153	J Miller Restoration, Buchanan
47	Volunteer State Chevy Parts, Greenbrier

Texas

141	BCP Sport & Classic Co, Houston
35	Classic Auto Restoration Services Inc, Rockwall
74	Edsel Associates, Fort Worth
28	Honest John's Caddy Corner, Justin
81	Howell's Sheetmetal Co, Nederland
120	John's Cars Inc, Dallas
171	Joe L Jordan, Houston
81	Kid Stuff, Porter
14	Kip Motor Company Inc, Dallas
41	Al Knoch Interiors, El Paso
59	Marcel's Corvette Parts, Humble
121	Motorcars Ltd, Houston
59	Old Air Products, Fort Worth

29   Selco Restoration, Richmond
111   T-Bird Nest, Southlake
106   Texas Mustang Parts Inc, Waco
168   Zim's Autotechnik, Bedford

Utah

182   Celestial Mechanics, Wellsville
124   K-F-D Services Inc, Altonah

Vermont

117   Best of Britain, South Ryegate
181   John's Car Corner, Westminster
54   Bill Cotrofeld Automotive Inc, East Arlington

Virginia

92   Auto Krafters Inc, Broadway
25   Cadillac Crazy, Boyce
149   Cantab Motors Ltd, Purcellville
104   Old Dominion Mustang, Ashland
154   Opel Parts & Service Inc, Chesapeake
54   Quality Customs, Richmond
15   Seven Enterprises Ltd, Newport News
61   Still Cruisin' Corvettes, Haymarket
106   Virginia Classic Mustang Inc, Broadway
61   Virginia Vettes Parts & Sales, Williamsburg

Washington

100   Andy's Classic Mustangs, Greenacres
142   Brooklands/MG Only, Tacoma
22   Buick Specialists, Kent
56   Corvette & High-Performance, Olympia
147   Jim Harris, Seattle
131   MIE Corporation, Mercer Island
151   NSU/USA Jim Sykes, Seattle
89   Old Ford Parts, Algona
98   Original Falcon, Comet, Ranchero, Fairlane Interiors, Seattle
44   Pick-ups Northwest, Snohomish
129   Rowland's Antique Auto Parts, Zillah
54   Safari O-Rings, Renton

Wisconsin

9   Alfa Heaven Inc, Aniwa
132   Brooklyn Motoren Werke Inc, Brooklyn
33   Butch's Trim, Big Bend
70   Collectors Choice LTD, Dane
16   Fourintune Garage Inc, Cedarburg
182   David Hueppchen, Plymouth
41   Lee's Classic Chevy Sales, Glenbeulah
96   Loyal Ford Mercury Inc, New Holstein
110   Regal Roadsters Ltd, Madison

Canada

32   All Chevy/Canadian Impala, Parksville, BC
170   Reg Collings, Calgary, AB
49   FireAro Restoration Parts Co, Mississauga, ON
82   McInnes Antique Auto, Niagara-on-the-Lake, ON
82   The Old Car Centre, Langley, BC
45   Reproduction Parts Marketing, Saskatoon, SK
14   Restorations Unlimited, Blenheim, ON
46   Scotts Super Trucks, Penhold, AB

England

143   MG Parts Centre (Barry Walker), NR Stratford-on-Avon
150   Morgan Motor Company Ltd, Worcester
83   Saturn Industries, Dorset
67   Barry Thorne, Surrey

Sweden

30   TA Motor AB, Lulea

Section Two:
Generalists

In this section, vendors who offer parts, literature, services or other items for a variety of makes and models are listed under general categories. As in Section One, if a vendor provides several services or products, an abbreviated subsidiary listing will appear in all of the appropriate sections with a cross reference to the main listing located in the category with the greatest concentration of the vendor's business.

The taglines located in the right-hand box of each listing provide a quick guide to what the vendor primarily offers.

This section of the Almanac is intended to serve owners of virtually every car make being collected. Restorers or collectors interested in parts or services for specific car marques should check Section One also, which presents vendor listings by marque specialty.

---

accessories

A-1 Street Rods — parts
631 E Las Vegas St
Colorado Springs, CO 80903
719-632-4920 or 719-577-4588
FAX: 719-634-6577

See full listing in **Section Two** under **street rods**

AAMP of America — audio accessories
13160 56th Ct, #502-508
Clearwater, FL 34620
813-572-9255; FAX: 813-573-9326
E-mail:
stinger.sales@stinger-aamp.com

Open shop to authorized dealers only. Hours vary according to dealer. Dealing in high end, high quality audio accessories of automotive application, power distribution and management, cellular, alarms.

Aardvark International — mirrors
PO Box 509
Whittier, CA 90601
310-699-8887; FAX: 310-699-2288
E-mail: gunth@ix.netcom.com

Mail order only. Specializing in Talbot™ sport mirrors for Alfa Romeo, Aston Martin, Austin-Healey, BMW, Cobra, Cooper, DeTomaso, Facel Vega, Ferrari, Fiat, Jaguar, Lamborghini, Lancia, Lotus, Maserati, Mercedes-Benz, MG, NSU, Opel, Porsche, Sunbeam, Triumph, TVR, Volkswagen, Iso, McLaren, Brabham & various race cars. Many models in chrome finish or aluminum. Housings are handspun to perfection. Three different mounting systems are available. Mirror elements are flat or convex "first surface" glass. Talbot™ mirrors are the finest money can buy and are stamped with the correct Talbot™ markings

---

AC Enterprises — gloveboxes
13387 Gladstone Ave
Sylmar, CA 91342
818-367-8337

Gloveboxes for most cars and trucks. Will work to sketch for custom application. SASE please.

Action Performance Inc — accessories
1619 Lakeland Ave
Bohemia, NY 11716
516-244-7100; FAX: 516-244-7172

Mail order and open shop. Mon-Fri 9:30-7:30, Sat 9-5:30, Sun 10-3. High-performance auto accessories for street, drag racing, oval track, pro-street.

Ad-Vance Promotions — accessories
Attn: Barbara Cicman
RR 5, Box 280
Pleasant Valley, NY 12569
PH/FAX: 914-635-3841

Ad specialty items. Anything imprinted with your logo, car club plates; key tags; belt buckles; mugs; jackets; shirts; caps (garments also embroidered). Our ROM is updated quarterly. It has 370,000 items. Other ideas: medallions, license plates and plate frames; patches; auto accessories. Anything with your logo. The above are for promotional purposes. Minimum quantities apply.

Al's Garage & Marine Repair Inc — accessories apparel tools
PO Box 156
Suquamish, WA 98392-0156
PH/FAX: 206-780-1223

Vintage good looks & quality with modern purpose & function best describes our eclectic line from early shop clothing to tool organizing systems, to transport & carry systems to the best coffee in the world. Great gift & holiday ideas as well.

American Autosecurity Equip Co — car alarms
236 East Star of India Ln
Carson, CA 90746
310-538-4670, 800-421-1096
FAX: 310-538-9932

See full listing in **Section Two** under **anti-theft**

American Performance Products — parts
675 S Industry Rd
Cocoa, FL 32926
407-632-8299; FAX: 407-632-5119

See full listing in **Section One** under **AMC**

Anacortes Brass Works Ltd — brass castings
PO Box 10
Anacortes, WA 98221
360-293-4515; FAX: 360-293-4516

See full listing in **Section Two** under **castings**

Anderson's
32700 Coastsite #102
Rancho Palos Verdes, CA 90275
310-377-1007; 800-881-9049
FAX: 310-377-0169

car door mono-
grams

Mail order only. Car door monograms, three initials pre-spaced for foolproof installation. Die cut from 3-M cast vinyl. Looks just like hand lettered enamel. Available in script, block, old English or in a circle.

Antique Auto Battery Mfg Co
2320 Old Mill Rd
Hudson, OH 44236
800-426-7580; FAX: 216-425-4642

batteries
battery cables

See full listing in **Section Two** under **batteries**

Antique Automobile Radio Inc
700 Tampa Rd
Palm Harbor, FL 34684
800-WE-FIX-AM; 813-785-8733
FAX: 813-789-0283

radio accessories
radio parts
radio restoration

See full listing in **Section Two** under **radios**

Antique Automotive Accessories
889 S Rainbow Blvd, Suite 642
Las Vegas, NV 89128
800-742-6777; FAX: 913-862-4646

accessories
tires

See full listing in **Section Two** under **tires**

Antique Radio Service
12 Shawmut Ave
Wayland, MA 01778
800-201-2635; FAX: 508-653-2418

radio service

See full listing in **Section Two** under **radios**

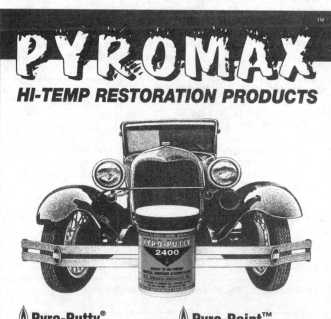

Aremco Products Inc
23 Snowden Ave
PO Box 429
Ossining, NY 10546
914-762-0685; FAX: 914-762-1663

compound

Mail order only. Aremco's new Pyromax line features high temperature sealers, adhesives and paints for repairing and coating pits, holes and cracks in engine blocks, cylinder heads, manifolds, headers and other exhaust components. Product trade names include Pyro-Putty, Pyro-Paint, Pyro-Weld and Pyro-Seal.

See our ad on this page

Atlantic British Ltd
PO Box 110
Rover Ridge Dr
Mechanicville, NY 12118
800-533-2210; FAX: 518-664-6641

accessories
parts

See full listing in **Section One** under **Rover/Land Rover**

Auto Accessories of America Inc
PO Box 427
Rt 322
Boalsburg, PA 16827
800-458-3475; FAX: 814-364-9615
Foreign: 814-364-2141

accessories
customizing
gifts & apparel
restoration

See full listing in **Section One** under **Corvette**

Auto Etc Neon
PO Box 531992
Harlingen, TX 78553
210-425-7487; FAX: 210-425-3025

signs
time pieces

See full listing in **Section One** under **Corvette**

Auto Lifters
3450 N Rock Rd, Bldg 500, Ste 507
Wichita, KS 67226
800-759-0703; FAX: 316-360-0015

lifts

See full listing in **Section Two** under **tools**

Auto-Mat Co
225A Park Ave
Hicksville, NY 11801
800-645-7258 orders
516-938-7373; FAX: 516-931-8438

accessories carpet
sets
interiors

See full listing in **Section Two** under **interiors & interior parts**

Automist Inc
PO Box 155
East Lansing, MI 48826
517-336-4443; FAX: 517-336-0178

waxes

See full listing in **Section Two** under **plating & polishing**

Automotive Specialty Accessory Parts Inc
PO Box 1907
Carson City, NV 89702
800-693-ASAP(2727)
FAX: 702-888-4545

parts

See full listing in **Section Two** under **tires**

Backyard Buddy Corp
1818 N Main St, PO Box 5104
Niles, OH 44446
330-544-9372; FAX: 330-544-9311

automotive lift

Mail order and open shop. We deal in automotive lifts. Factory direct results in least expensive lift on the market. Lift and all components are American made. Superior product produced and assembled by nuclear certified welders. Makes the most use of garage space. Perfect for storage and repairs on cars, trucks, etc. No expensive excavating inside/outside. Custom units built to specifications, Shipping worldwide, FOB Niles, Ohio. Talk to a technician, not a salesman. Web site: http://www.backyard-buddy.com

See our ad on this page

| **Bay Ridges Classic Chevy**
1362 Poprad Ave
Pickering, ON Canada L1W 1L1
905-839-6169; FAX: 905-420-6613 | **accessories**
parts |

See full listing in **Section One** under **Chevrolet**

| **Benkin & Co**
14 E Main St
Tipp City, OH 45371
513-667-5975; FAX: 513-667-5729 | **gas pumps**
neon clocks
neon signs |

See full listing in **Section Two** under **automobilia**

| **Billie Inc**
10519 Zion Dr
Fairfax, VA 22032
800-878-6328; FAX: 703-250-4586 | **garage diaper**
mats |

See full listing in **Section Two** under **car care products**

| **Bob Drake Reproductions Inc**
1819 NW Washington Blvd
Grants Pass, OR 97526
800-221-3673; FAX: 541-474-0099 | **repro parts** |

See full listing in **Section One** under **Ford '32-'53**

| **Bob's Classic Auto Glass**
21170 Hwy 36
Blachly, OR 97412
800-624-2130 | **glass** |

See full listing in **Section Two** under **glass**

| **Bonneville Sports Inc**
12461 Country Ln
Santa Ana, CA 92705
714-508-9724; FAX: 714-508-9725 | **accessories**
clothing |

See full listing in **Section Two** under **apparel**

| **Boulevard Motoring Accessories**
7033 Topanga Canyon Blvd
Canoga Park, CA 91303 91303-1961
818-883-9696; FAX: 818-883-5530 | **accessories**
car covers
floor mats |

See full listing in **Section One** under **Mercedes-Benz**

| **Brooklands Inc**
503 Corporate Square
1500 NW 62nd St
Fort Lauderdale, FL 33309
954-776-2748; FAX: 954-772-8383
E-mail: rbiggs@lgc.net | **accessories** |

Mail order and open shop. Open Monday-Friday 9 to 6. Specializing in Jaguar, MG, Triumph, Austin-Healey, Aston Martin, Morgan and AC cars, all years. Specializing in difficult to find parts and accessories, lighting, Smith's instruments, steering wheels, road wheels, gas caps, trim, mirrors, wiper systems, brightwork. Our 40 page color brochure is free and describes over 2,000 items.

| **Buick Bonery**
6970 Stamper Way
Sacramento, CA 95828
PH/FAX: 916-381-5271 | **parts** |

See full listing in **Section One** under **Buick/McLaughlin**

| **Canadian Mustang**
12844 78th Ave
Surrey, BC Canada V3W 8E7
604-594-2425; FAX: 604-594-9282 | **parts** |

See full listing in **Section One** under **Mustang**

| **Cardillo Classic Cadillac**
351 W 51st St
New York, NY 10019
212-247-1354 | **accessories**
top boots |

See full listing in **Section One** under **Cadillac/LaSalle**

| **Career Center**
1302 9th St
Wheatland, WY 82201
PH/FAX: 307-322-2063 | **license plates** |

See full listing in **Section Two** under **license plates**

| **Caribou Canvas**
23151-A3 Alcalde Dr
Laguna Hills, CA 92653
714-770-3136; FAX: 714-770-0815
E-mail: cariboulh@aol.com | **convertible tops** |

See full listing in **Section Two** under **tops**

7,000#
Heavy Duty Asymmetric Twin Post Lift

9,000#
Heavy Duty Asymmetric Twin Post Lift

BACKYARD BUDDY.®

Manufacturer of Automotive Lifts

The **#1** Choice of Homeowners
CALL NOW!
1-800-837-9353
Ask about our EZ payment plan

12,000#
4 Post Lift

9,000#
Ideal for Low Ceiling Height

Carpad Incorporated 400 Main St PO Box 204 Dayton, NV 89403-0204 702-246-0232; FAX: 702-246-0266	floor protector

Mail order and open shop. Shop open Monday-Friday 9 am to 5:30 pm. Carpad, the ultimate in garage floor protection, a year around answer to garage problems. Industrial vinyl floor cover, 1 inch raised sides, waterproof, non-flammable, 14 year life expectancy, available in silver or gold. Contains 60-120 gallons of water, snow, salt, sand, oils. Easy to clean. Helps eliminate slip/fall problems and tracking a mess around. Protects painted floors. Sizes to fit all vehicles, motorcycles, snowblowers, aircraft. Patented internationally. 30 day money back guarantee.

CBS Performance Automotive 2605-A W Colorado Ave Colorado Springs, CO 80904 800-685-1492; FAX: 719-578-9485	ignition systems performance products

See full listing in **Section Two** under **ignition parts**

Michael Chapman Priorsleigh, Mill Lane Cleeve Prior, Worcestershire, WR115JZ England 01789-773897; FAX: 01789-773588	automobilia

See full listing in **Section Two** under **automobilia**

Chev's of the 40's 2027 B St Washougal, WA 98671 360-835-9799; FAX: 360-835-7988	parts

See full listing in **Section One** under **Chevrolet**

Ed Cholakian Enterprises Inc dba All Cadillacs of the Forties 12811 Foothill Blvd Sylmar, CA 91342 818-361-1147; 800-808-1147 FAX: 818-361-9738	museum parts

See full listing in **Section One** under **Cadillac/LaSalle**

Classic Aire Car Coolers J & M Engineering Inc PO Box 739 Camas, WA 98607 PH/FAX: 360-834-5227	car cooler

Mail order only. Dealing in the modern version of the classic window mounted evaporative car cooler.

Classic Chevy International PO Box 607188 Orlando, FL 32860-7188 800-456-1956; FAX: 407-299-3341 E-mail: cciworld@aol.com	modified parts repro parts used parts

See full listing in **Section One** under **Chevrolet**

Classic Motors PO Box 1011 San Mateo, CA 94403 415-342-4117; FAX: 415-340-9473	appraiser locator service movie rentals parts/restoration

See full listing in **Section Two** under **restoration shops**

Cobra Restorers Ltd 3099 Carter Dr Kennesaw , GA 30144 770-427-0020; FAX: 770-427-8658	parts restoration service

See full listing in **Section One** under **Cobra**

Comet Products Cherry Parke 101-B Cherry Hill, NJ 08002 609-795-4810; FAX: 609-354-6313	emblems accessories

See full listing in **Section Two** under **grille emblem badges**

Comfy/Inter-American Sheepskins Inc 1346 Centinela Ave West Los Angeles, CA 90025-1901 800-521-4014; FAX: 310-442-6080 E-mial: 4858038@mcimail.com	floor mats seat covers

See full listing in **Section Two** under **interiors & interior parts**

Concours Cars of Colorado Ltd 2414 W Cucharras St Colorado Springs, CO 80904 719-473-6288	accessories parts service

See full listing in **Section One** under **BMW**

Convertible Service 5126-HA Walnut Grove Ave San Gabriel, CA 91776 800-333-1140, 818-285-2255 FAX: 818-285-9004	convertible parts top mechanism service

See full listing in **Section Two** under **tops**

Corvette & High-Performance Division of Classic & High Performance Inc 2840 Black Lake Blvd SW #D Olympia, WA 98512 360-754-7890	accessories parts

See full listing in **Section One** under **Corvette**

Corvette Central 5865 Sawyer Rd Dept HM Sawyer, MI 49125 616-426-3342; FAX: 616-426-4108	accessories parts

See full listing in **Section One** under **Corvette**

Corvette Specialties of MD Inc 1912 Liberty Rd Eldersburg, MD 21784 410-795-3180; FAX: 410-795-3247	parts restoration service

See full listing in **Section One** under **Corvette**

Creative Metal Products Inc 121 R N Douglas St Appleton, WI 54914 414-830-7975; FAX: 414-830-7976	storage system

See full listing in **Section Two** under **tools**

Crossfire 260 Hickory St, PO Box 263 Sharpsville, PA 16150 800-458-3478; FAX: 412-962-4639	accessories

See full listing in **Section Two** under **ignition parts**

Cruising International Inc 1000 N Beach St Daytona Beach, FL 32117 800-676-8961, 904-254-8753 FAX: 904-255-2460	automobilia decals license plates novelties porcelain signs

Manufacturer, wholesaler and exporter of license plates, hat pins, keychains, porcelain signs, belt buckles, decals and automotive novelties. Stock and custom orders. Please call for our catalog. Wir sprechen deutsch!

See our ad on page 320

Crutchfield Corp 1 Crutchfield Park Charlottesville, VA 22906 800-955-9009; FAX: 804-973-1862	car stereos

See full listing in **Section Two** under **radios**

Richard Culleton 4318 SW 19th Pl Cape Coral, FL 33914 800-931-7836 voice mail 315-685-7414 (home); 941-542-8640	accessories

Mail order and car shows only. Wholesale and retail. 50s nostalgic accessories. Moon products, shift knobs, specialty valve caps, door locks, etc.

Dare Carrying Case 9902 Mindy Ln Wilton, CA 95693 916-687-6018 home 916-947-5100 cellular	leather handles leather straps luggage trunks

Mail order only. Reproduces or designs custom luggage and trunks for antique and classic automobiles. Repairs and restores original luggage and trunks. Manufactures custom leather handles and straps per customer specifications.

Davies Corvette 5130 Main St New Port Richey, FL 34653 813-842-8000, 800-236-2383 FAX: 813-846-8216	customizing parts restoration

See full listing in **Section One** under **Corvette**

Buzz De Clerck 41760 Utica Rd Sterling Heights, MI 48313 810-731-0765	parts

See full listing in **Section One** under **Lincoln**

DeLorean One 20229 Nordhoff St Chatsworth, CA 91311 818-341-1796; FAX: 818-998-6381	body work parts service

See full listing in **Section One** under **DeLorean**

Development Associates 1520 S Lyon Santa Ana, CA 92705 714-835-9512; FAX: 714-835-9513 E-mail: 71460,1146@compuserve.com	electrical parts

See full listing in **Section Two** under **electrical systems**

Diamond Liners Inc 5430 Tweedy Blvd South Gate, CA 90280 213-567-1032 800-543-1212 CA only FAX: 213-566-2271	bedliners

Mail order and open shop. Specially formulated, sprayed-on polyurethane coating that provides a permanent textured surface. The coating protects against rust, corrosion and harsh chemicals. The liner is durable and resistant to impact or abrasions, EPA-safe and solvent-free. Diamond Liner fits every curve of your truck or equipment

Digital Design Inc PO Box 139 Merrick, NY 11566	sweatshirts T-shirts

See full listing in **Section Two** under **apparel**

Dr Cap (Brad Sullivan) 2550 Estero Blvd Ste 12 Ft Myers Beach, FL 33931 941-463-3741	custom license plates

See full listing in **Section Two** under **license plates**

Ed's Be-Bop Shop 10087 W Co Rd 300 S Medora, IN 47260 812-966-2203	accessories parts restoration

See full listing in **Section One** under **Ford '03-'31**

Enthusiast's Specialties 350 Old Connecticut Path Framingham, MA 01701 508-620-1942; FAX: 508-872-4914	automobilia tools

See full listing in **Section Two** under **automobilia**

The Enthusiasts Shop John Parnell PO Box 80471 Baton Rouge, LA 70898 504-928-7456; FAX: 504-928-7665	cars pre-war parts transportation

See full listing in **Section One** under **Rolls-Royce/Bentley**

Jim Estrup The Plateman Box 908 RR 3 Kennebunk, ME 04043 207-985-4800; FAX: 207-985-TAGS	license plates

See full listing in **Section Two** under **license plates**

Eurosport Daytona Inc 32 Oceanshore Blvd Ormond Beach, FL 32176 800-874-8044; 904-672-7199 FAX: 904-673-0821	license plates

See full listing in **Section Two** under **license plates**

Executive Boys Toys 200 S Jackson St Lima, OH 45804 419-227-9300	car dealer

See full listing in **Section Two** under **car dealers**

Jay M Fisher Acken Dr 4-B Clark, NJ 07066 908-388-6442	radiator caps sidemount mirrors

Mail order only. Mfg of sidemount mirrors, 1900 thru 1970, inside mirror restoration, windwing brackets, radiator caps, mascots, small parts fabrication, leather straps, restoration of any mirrors.

Fleetfoot Industries Inc
2680 Blake St
Denver, CO 80205
800-503-2727, 303-294-0647
FAX: 303-294-0333

accessories

Auto bras (front end covers), car covers, seat covers, tonneaus and other car accessories.

For Ramblers Only
2324 SE 34th Ave
Portland, OR 97214
503-232-0497
E-mail: ramblermac@aol.com

accessories
parts

See full listing in **Section One** under **AMC**

Ford Reproduction Parts Store
110 Ford Rd
PO Box 226
Bryan, OH 43506-0226
419-636-2475; FAX: 419-636-8449
E-mail: fordpart@bright.net

parts

See full listing in **Section One** under **Ford '54-up**

Ron Francis' Wire Works
167 Keystone Rd
Chester, PA 19013
610-485-1937

fuel injection
harnesses
wiring accessories
wiring kits

See full listing in **Section Two** under **electrical systems**

Gaslight Auto Parts Inc
PO Box 291
Urbana, OH 43078
513-652-2145; FAX: 513-652-2147

accessories
parts

See full listing in **Section One** under **Ford '03-'31**

Gasoline Alley LLC
PO Box 737, 1700E Iron Ave
Salina, KS 67402
913-822-1000; 800-326-8372
FAX: 913-827-9337

drip pans

Mail order only. Manufacture Perma-Pan drip pans which feature a DuPont Tedlar® top surface making the easiest cleaning pan on the market.

Griot's Garage
3500-A 20th St E
Tacoma, WA 98424
800-345-5789; FAX: 206-922-7500
E-mail: griots@aol.com

car care products
paint
tools

See full listing in **Section Two** under **tools**

Haneline Products Co
PO Box 430
Morongo Valley, CA 92256
619-363-6597
FAX: 619-363-7321

gauges
instrument panels
stainless parts
trim parts

See full listing in **Section Two** under **instruments**

Ned R Healy & Company Inc
17602 Griffin Ln
PO Box 2120
Huntington Beach, CA 92647
714-848-2251

accessories
parts

Sells parts, accessories supplies and die cast toy cars to new car dealers.

Hooker Headers
1024 W Brooks St
PO Box 4030
Ontario, CA 91761
909-983-5871

exhaust systems

See full listing in **Section Two** under **exhaust systems**

Hunters Custom Automotive
975 Main St
Nashville, TN 37206
615-227-6584; FAX: 615-227-4897

accessories
engine parts
fiberglass products

Mail order and open shop. Monday-Saturday 8 am to 5 pm. Dealing in street rod accessories, sport truck accessories, four wheel drive and off-road, hi-performance engine parts, fiberglass products, wheel and tire specialty store. All types speed/custom accessories for SUV's and Jeeps.

Image Auto
31690 W 12 Mile #4
Farmington Hills, MI 48334
800-414-2852; FAX: 810-553-0924

apparel
artwork

See full listing in **Section One** under **Jensen**

**Innovative Novelties/McGee
Enterprises**
PO Box 1375
Little Rock, AR 72203
501-835-8409; FAX: 501-835-7293
E-mail: kholland@cci.net

accessories

See full listing in **Section Two** under **novelties**

International AutoSport Inc
Rt 29 N
PO Box 9036
Charlottesville, VA 22906
800-726-1199; FAX: 804-973-2368
E-mail: iap1@international-auto.com

accessories

Mail order and open shop. Monday-Friday 9 am-6 pm, Saturday 9-3 pm. Accessories for life and leisure on the road: car covers, Zymol wax, luxurious floor mats, rubber mats and liners, leather lumbar cushions and visors, knives, Coleman coolers, car care products, cell phone and other travel products. Send or call for catalog.

International E-Z UP Inc
1601 Iowa Ave
Riverside, CA 92507
909-781-0843; FAX: 909-781-0586

awnings
canopies

E-Z UP instant shelters set up in less than 60 seconds with no ropes, poles or assembly required. The patented double-truss design is fully self-contained, perfect for race pits, car shows, sales booths and sun protection. Heavy duty fabric tops available in a variety of colors and custom silk-screening for high visibility. E-Z UPs range in sizes from 8x8 to 10x20 feet.

Jim's T-Bird Parts & Service
710 Barney Ave
Winston-Salem, NC 27107
910-784-9363

parts
restoration
service

See full listing in **Section One** under **Thunderbird**

Karl's Collectibles
28 Bates St
Lewiston, ME 04240
800-636-0457, 207-784-0098
FAX: 207-786-4576
E-mail: slalemand@aol.com

banks
collectibles
logo design

See full listing in **Section Two** under **models & toys**

KD Kanopy Inc
3755 W 69th Pl
Westminster, CO 80030
800-432-4435, 303-650-1310
FAX: 303-650-5093
E-mail: ocep02a@prodigy.com

canopies
tents

Quick set up canopies/tents that go up in a matter of minutes. Protection from sun and light showers. Side walls and accessories are available as well as customized graphics. Aluminum 10'x10' frame, weights 48 lbs. Sizes: 8'x8', 10'x10' and 10'x20'. Free carry bag and stakes.
Web site: http://www.kdkanopy.thomasregister.com

Klasse 356 Inc
741 N New St
Allentown, PA 18102
800-634-7862; FAX: 610-432-8027
E-mail: parts@klasse356.com

cars
parts
restoration

See full listing in **Section One** under **Porsche**

Kortesis Marketing Ent
PO Box 460543
Aurora, CO 80046
303-548-3995; FAX: 303-699-6660

radar jammers

See full listing in **Section Two** under **novelties**

Lee's Kustom Auto and Street Rods
RR 3, Box 3061A
Rome, PA 18837
717-247-2326

accessories
parts
restoration

See full listing in **Section Two** under **street rods**

Lord Byron Inc
420 Sackett Point Rd
North Haven, CT 06473
203-287-9881; FAX: 203-230-9633

fender covers

See full listing in **Section Two** under **car covers**

M & R Products
1940 SW Blvd
Vineland, NJ 08360
609-696-9450; FAX: 609-696-4999

hardware
tie-downs

Auto and motorcycle tie-downs, related hardware (driver restraints, window nets, arm restraints, collars for racing industry).

Mac Neil Automotive Products Ltd
2435 Wisconsin St
Downers Grove, IL 60515
800-441-6287; FAX: 630-769-0300

cargo liners
floor mats

See full listing in **Section Two** under **interiors & interior parts**

Larry Machacek
PO Box 515
Porter, TX 77365
713-429-2505

decals
license plates

See full listing in **Section Two** under **automobilia**

Madera Concepts
606 Olive St
Santa Barbara, CA 93101
800-800-1579, 805-962-1579
FAX: 805-962-7359

restoration
woodwork
woodwork repair

See full listing in **Section Two** under **woodwork**

Marc Miller Gallery
3 Railroad Ave
East Hampton, NY 11937
516-329-5299; FAX: 516-329-5319

furniture

See full listing in **Section Two** under **artwork**

Marcel's Corvette Parts
15100 Lee Rd #101
Humble, TX 77396
713-441-2111 info line; 800-546-2111 order line; FAX: 713-441-2111

parts

See full listing in **Section One** under **Corvette**

Max Neon Design Group
19807 Sussex Dr
St Clair Shores, MI 48081-3257
810-773-5000; FAX: 810-772-6224

custom face logos
neon clocks

See full listing in **Section Two** under **automobilia**

Meguiar's Inc
17991 Mitchell South
Irvine, CA 92714
714-752-8000; FAX: 714-752-5784

cleaners
polishes
waxes

Mail order only. Dealing in waxes, polishes and cleaners.

Millers Incorporated
7412 Count Circle
Huntington Beach, CA 92647
714-375-6565; FAX: 714-847-6603
E-mail: millermbz@aol.com

accessories
parts

See full listing in **Section One** under **Mercedes-Benz**

Mint Condition Auto Upholstery
PO Box 134
Silverdale New Zealand
PH/FAX: 64-9-424 2257

convertible tops
interiors
spring-gaiters
wheelcovers

See full listing in **Section Two** under **special services**

Mitchell Manufacturing
6 Acorn Ct
Novato, CA 94949-6603
800-238-5093

overdrives

See full listing in **Section One** under **Ford '03-'31**

Moroso Performance Products Inc
80 Carter Dr
Guilford, CT 06437
203-453-6571; FAX: 203-453-6906

accessories
parts

See full listing in **Section Two** under **racing**

Moss Motors Ltd
PO Box 847
440 Rutherford St
Goleta, CA 93117
800-235-6954; FAX: 805-692-2525

accessories
parts

See full listing in **Section One** under **MG**

Motorsport Auto
1139 W Collins Ave
Orange, CA 92667
714-639-2620; 800-633-6331
FAX: 714-639-7460

parts

See full listing in **Section One** under **Datsun**

Murphy's Motoring Accessories Inc
PO Box 618
Greendale, WI 53129-0618
800-529-8315; 414-529-8333

car covers

See full listing in **Section Two** under **car covers**

NMW Products
35 Orlando Dr
Raritan, NJ 08869
908-256-3800

dollies

Mail order and open shop. M-F 8-4:30. Manufacture of car dollies/engine shop dollies.

O'Brien Truckers
5 Perry Hill
North Grafton, MA 01536-1532
508-839-3033; FAX: 508-839-9490
E-mail: obrien_dennis@emc.com

accessories
belt buckles
plaques
valve covers

See full listing in **Section Two** under **plaques**

OJ Rallye Automotive
PO Box 540
N 6808 Hwy OJ
Plymouth, WI 53073
414-893-2531; FAX: 414-893-6800

accessories
car care products
lighting parts

See full listing in **Section Two** under **lighting equipment**

Olona Imaging
PO Box 92214
Albuquerque, NM 87199-2214
800-910-4237
E-mail: olonaimage@aol.com

mugs
t-shirts

See full listing in **Section Two** under **novelties**

Operations Plus
PO Box 26347
Santa Ana, CA 92799
PH/FAX: 714-962-2776

accessories
parts

See full listing in **Section One** under **Cobra**

Paul's Select (Porsche) ®
2280 Gail Dr
Riverside, CA 92509
PH/FAX: 909-685-9340

parts

See full listing in **Section One** under **Porsche**

PE Tie Down Straps
803 Petersburg Rd
Carlisle, PA 17013
800-TIE-DOWN; FAX: 717-258-1348

locks
tie-down straps
winches

See full listing in **Section Two** under **trailers**

People Kars
290 Third Ave Ext
Rensselaer, NY 12144
PH/FAX: 518-465-0477

models/more
VW toys

See full listing in **Section One** under **Volkswagen**

Performance Automotive Warehouse
8966 Mason Ave
Chatsworth, CA 91311
818-998-6000; FAX: 818-407-7204

accessories
engine parts

See full listing in **Section Two** under **engine parts**

J Pinto
2605 9th St
Long Island City, NY 11102
PH/FAX: 718-626-2403
E-mail: electritech@sprynet.com

windshield wiper
repair

See full listing in **Section Two** under **restoration aids**

Premier Designs Historic Costume
818 Selby St
Findlay, OH 45840
800-427-0907; FAX: 419-427-2239
E-mail: premier@bright.net

clothing

See full listing in **Section Two** under **apparel**

Prostripe
Div of Spartan International Inc
1845 Cedar St
Holt, MI 48842
800-248-7800; FAX: 517-694-7952

graphics
molding
pinstriping

See full listing in **Section Two** under **striping**

Protrim Inc
438 Calle San Pablo, Unit 1
Camarillo, CA 93012
805-987-2086; FAX: 805-389-5375

plating

See full listing in **Section Two** under **plating & polishing**

Pulfer & Williams
213 Forest Rd
PO Box 67
Hancock, NH 03449-0067
603-525-3532; FAX: 603-525-4293

mascots
nameplates
radiator emblems

See full listing in **Section Two** under **radiator emblems**

Quality Mfg & Dist
PO Box 20870
El Cajon, CA 92021
619-442-8686; FAX: 619-590-0123

tools

See full listing in **Section Two** under **tools**

Re-Flex Border Marker
138 Grant St
Lexington, MA 02173
617-862-1343

border markers
posts

See full listing in **Section Two** under **hardware**

Red Crown Valve Caps
PO Box 5301
Topeka, KS 66605
913-357-5007

automobilia

See full listing in **Section Two** under **automobilia**

Ron's Restorations Inc
2968-B Ask Kay Dr
Smyrna, GA 30082
770-438-6102; FAX: 770-438-0037

interior trim
restoration

See full listing in **Section One** under **Mercedes-Benz**

Jack Rosen, Mark II Parts
5225 Canyon Crest Dr
Suite 71-217H
Riverside, CA 92507
909-686-2752; FAX: 909-686-7245

parts

1956-57 Lincoln Mark II parts. Large inventory of NOS, NORS, used and rebuilt parts for Mark II and 1956-57 Lincoln autos. Car covers, custom made for any auto, 1900 to date, 4 fabrics, guaranteed lowest price.

RW & Able Inc
PO Box 2110
Chico, CA 95927
PH/FAX: 916-896-1513

door panels
interior accessories

See full listing in **Section Two** under **street rods**

Scotts Manufacturing
25520 Ave Stanford #304
Valencia, CA 91355
800-544-5596; FAX: 805-295-9342

electric fans

See full listing in **Section Two** under **electrical systems**

Scotts Super Trucks
Box 6772
1040 Emma St
Penhold, AB Canada T0M 1R0
403-886-5572; FAX: 403-886-5577

parts

See full listing in **Section One** under **Chevrolet**

Sea-Tac Specialties
Don Guilbault
6714-247 St Ct E
Graham, WA 98338
206-847-8545; FAX: 206-847-6455

hat pins
key chains

Wholesale stock pins for pin vendors. Custom orders for clubs, events, promoters, miscellaneous organizations. Catalog, $3, refunded with first order.

Silver State Restorations Inc
The Aday Collection
4655 Aircenter Cir
Reno, NV 89502
702-826-8886; FAX: 702-826-9191

restoration
service

See full listing in **Section Two** under **restoration shops**

Silverstate Cadillac Parts
PO Box 2161
Sparks, NV 89431
702-331-7252; FAX: 702-331-7887

parts

See full listing in **Section One** under **Cadillac/LaSalle**

Simpson
2415 Amsler St
Torrance, CA 90505
310-320-7231; FAX: 310-320-7179

driving suits
gloves
helmets
shoes

See full listing in **Section Two** under **apparel**

Smith & Jones Distributing Company Inc
1 Biloxi Square
West Columbia, SC 29170
803-822-8500; FAX: 803-822-8477

parts

See full listing in **Section One** under **Ford '03-'31**

So Cal Pickups Inc
6321 Manchester Blvd
Buena Park, CA 90621
714-994-1400; FAX: 714-994-2584

parts

See full listing in **Section One** under **Ford '54-up**

Specialty Custom Chrome Fasteners Inc
887 Grand Oaks Dr
Howell, MI 48843
800-588-2111; FAX: 517-548-5780

hardware

Mail order and open shop. Monday-Friday 9-5, Saturday 9-1. Stainless steel & chrome bolts, nuts, washers, engine kits, sheetmetal screws, machine screws and more.

Spector Off-Road Inc
21600 Nordhoff St, Dept HM
Chatsworth, CA 91311
818-882-1238, FAX: 818-882-7144
E-mail: specterlc@aol.com

accessories
parts

See full listing in **Section One** under **Toyota**

Spirit Enterprises
4325 Sunset Dr
Lockport, NY 14094
716-434-9938 showroom
716-434-0077 warehouse

stereo systems

See full listing in **Section Two** under **radios**

Stinger Inc
1375 17th Ave
McPherson, KS 67460
800-854-4850; 316-241-5580
FAX: 316-241-6000

lifts

See full listing in **Section Two** under **storage care products**

Street Player
73 40 Rio Linda Blvd H
Rio Linda, CA 95673
PH/FAX: 916-991-0464

accessories/tires
fender skirts
hydraulics/moldings
wire spoke rims

Accessories, fender skirts, hydraulics, moldings, tires, wire spoke rims, aircraft dumps. Catalog $7, cash/money order only.

Tavia Performance Products Inc
12851 Western Ave, Unit D
Garden Grove, CA 92841
714-892-4057; FAX: 714-892-5627

accessories
tools

See full listing in **Section Two** under **tools**

Tornado Air Management Systems
13360-H Firestone Blvd
Santa Fe Springs, CA 90670
310-926-5000; FAX: 310-926-1223
E-mail: j.k@ix.netcom.com

parts

Mail order and open shop. Monday-Friday 8:30 am to 4:30 pm. The Tornado is a non-moving stainless steel part that fits inside the air filter housing or air intake hose, depending on the engine. The air is re-directed to a swirling motion to better atomize the fuel for more power and better mileage. Improvements of 7 to 24% were confirmed by the Federal EPA and the California ARB licensed test lab. Most buyers are repeat or referred.

Tuxedo Turntables by Tuxedo Enterprises
4914 Gassner Rd
Brookshire, TX 77423
888-TUXEDO-T; FAX: 713-375-6630

display turntables

Mail order and open shop. By appointment only. Specializing in display turntables for show cars and other items (manufacture and sales), cars, motorcycles, etc.

UK Spares/TVR Sports Cars
609 Highland St
Wethersfield, CT 06109-3979
203-563-1647; FAX: 203-529-3479

	accessories
	car covers
	convertible tops
	ignition parts

See full listing in **Section One** under **TVR**

Ultimate Appearance Ltd
113 Arabian Trail
Smithfield, VA 23430
PH/FAX: 757-255-2620

	cleaners
	detailing products
	detailing services
	polish/wax

See full listing in **Section Two** under **car care products**

The V8 Store
3010 NE 49th St
Vancouver, WA 98663
360-693-7468, 360-694-7853
nights; FAX: 360-693-0982

	accessories
	parts
	service

See full listing in **Section Two** under **street rods**

Valco Cincinnati Consumer Products Inc
411 Circle Freeway Drive
Cincinnati, OH 45246
513-874-6550; FAX: 513-874-3612

	adhesives
	detailing products
	sealants
	tools

See full listing in **Section Two** under **tools**

Volkswagen Collectors
c/o Jerry Jess
3121 E Yucca St
Phoenix, AZ 85028-2616
PH/FAX: 602-867-7672

	literature
	memorabilia
	toys

See full listing in **Section One** under **Volkswagen**

Volunteer State Chevy Parts
Hwy 41 S
Greenbrier, TN 37073
615-643-4583; FAX: 615-643-5100

	accessories
	parts

See full listing in **Section One** under **Chevrolet**

Wallace Walmsley
4732 Bancroft St #7
San Diego, CA 92116
619-283-3063

	parts

See full listing in **Section One** under **Packard**

R L Williams Classic Corvette Parts
PO Box 3307
Palmer, PA 18043
610-258-2028; FAX: 610-253-6816

	literature
	parts

See full listing in **Section One** under **Corvette**

Wolf Automotive
201 N Sullivan
Santa Ana, CA 92703
800-444-9653, 714-835-2126
FAX: 714-835-9653

	car covers
	consoles
	steering wheels
	tire covers

See full listing in **Section One** under **Chevrolet**

York Petroleum Industries
dba YPI Inc
1011 Askham Dr
Cary, NC 27511-4703
919-319-5180; FAX: 919-319-7302

	floor protector

Mail order only. The Auto Tray garage/home floor protector and car wash reservoir.

air conditioning

Performance Analysis Co
1345 Oak Ridge Turnpike, Suite 258
Oak Ridge, TN 37830
423-482-9175
E-mail: 7662.2133@compuserve.com

	climate control
	cruise control

See full listing in **Section One** under **Mercedes-Benz**

Silverstate Cadillac Parts
PO Box 2161
Sparks, NV 89431
702-331-7252; FAX: 702-331-7887

	parts

See full listing in **Section One** under **Cadillac/LaSalle**

anti-theft

American Autosecurity Equip Co
236 East Star of India Ln
Carson, CA 90746
310-538-4670, 800-421-1096
FAX: 310-538-9932

	car alarms

Mail order only. We manufacture "Do-It-Yourself" car alarms for all cars. Call for brochure and/or nearest dealer.

Bathurst Inc
801 W 15 St
Tyrone, PA 16686
814-684-2603

	battery accessories

See full listing in **Section Two** under **electrical systems**

Ron Francis' Wire Works
167 Keystone Rd
Chester, PA 19013
610-485-1937

	wiring
	wiring kits

See full listing in **Section Two** under **electrical systems**

International AutoSport Inc
Rt 29 N
PO Box 9036
Charlottesville, VA 22906
800-726-1199; FAX: 804-973-2368
E-mail: iap1@international-auto.com

	accessories

See full listing in **Section Two** under **accessories**

ISG
21638 Lasser
Chatsworth, CA 91311
818-718-8816; FAX: 818-718-8832

	security devices

Mail order and open shop. Monday-Friday 10-4. State of the art security devices. Manufacturer of a satellite controlled vehicle immobilizer and various surveillance devices.

Miltronics Mfg Inc
95 Krif Rd
Keene, NH 03431
603-352-3333,
800-828-9089 order line
FAX: 603-352-4444

detection system

Driveway Alert, a wireless home monitoring and detection system, monitors areas such as driveways, walkways, garages, entryways and backyards. Also "Electric Art". We put realistic lights on prints of vintage autos and bikes, most makes and models, and put in handmade wood frame. Web site: www.miltronics.com

apparel

Al's Garage & Marine Repair Inc
PO Box 156
Suquamish, WA 98392-0156
PH/FAX: 206-780-1223

accessories
apparel
tools

See full listing in **Section Two** under **accessories**

Autosport Marketing
PO Box 29033
Christ Church 4 NZ New Zealand
PH/FAX: 00-64-3-3519476

apparel
automobilia

Mail order and open shop. Race days only. Dealing in motorsport merchandise.

Bonneville Sports Inc
12461 Country Ln
Santa Ana, CA 92705
714-508-9724; FAX: 714-508-9725

accessories
clothing

Mail order only. A complete line of clothing and accessories for men and women who enjoy performance pursuits. The 12 page color catalog has T-shirts, hats, leather jackets, dress shirts, shorts, belts, neon signs, books and lots more.

Business Forms Management Inc
PO Box 4390
Akron, OH 44321-0390
216-666-2980; FAX: 216-666-0844

photo transfers
silk screening

Mail order and open shop, 8:30 to 5:30 Monday-Friday. Photo transfers to T-shirts, sweatshirts, hats, mugs, tote bags, calendars, mouse pads, coasters. Also, silkscreening for club shirts & hats and printing of any kind.

California Car Cover Co
21125 Superior St
Chatsworth, CA 91311
800-423-5525; FAX: 818-998-2442

accessories
apparel
car covers
tools

See full listing in **Section Two** under **car covers**

Classic Motorcar Investments
3755 Terra Loma Dr
Bullhead City, AZ 86442
602-763-5869

apparel

Deals in 50s fashions, class jackets, poodle skirts, Elvis and Marilyn items and fabulous 50s fads.

Crazy About Cars
2727 Fairfield Commons, E137
Box 32095
Beavercreek, OH 45431
937-320-0969; FAX: 937-320-0970
E-mail: crazycarz@aol.com

art
models
nostalgia

See full listing in **Section Two** under **automobilia**

Digital Design Inc
PO Box 139
Merrick, NY 11566

sweatshirts
T-shirts

Wear the image of your automobile proudly on a T-shirt or sweatshirt. Custom made with computer assistance for you. Send us a clear (returnable) photo & $19.99 for Ts, $29.99 for sweats plus $4 shipping (NY residents add tax). 1st shirt full price, each additional shirt of same type & image save $5.

Ellingson Car Museum
20950 Rogers Dr
Rogers, MN 55374
612-428-7337; FAX: 612-428-4370

museum

See full listing in **Section Six** under **Minnesota**

Jerry Greer's Indian Engineering
8400 Monroe, #3
Stanton, CA 90680
714-826-9940

parts
restoration service

See full listing in **Section One** under **Indian.**

Hemmings Bookshelf
PO Box 76
Bennington, VT 05201
HMN Customer Service:
1-800-CAR-HERE ext 550
HMN Sunoco Filling Station:
802-447-3572

books, videos
HMN caps, t-shirts
HMN sweatshirts
HMN tote bags
HMN truck banks
Free Vintage
Vehicle Display

See full listing in **Section Four** under **books & publications**

Hooker Headers
1024 W Brooks St
PO Box 4030
Ontario, CA 91761
909-983-5871

exhaust systems

See full listing in **Section Two** under **exhaust systems**

Image Auto
31690 W 12 Mile #4
Farmington Hills, MI 48334
800-414-2852; FAX: 810-553-0924

apparel
artwork

See full listing in **Section One** under **Jensen**

Jan's Vintage Accessories
157 Maverick Rd
Woodstock, NY 12498
914-679-9601

clothing

Deals in reproduction antique period driving clothing. Free brochure on request.

Fay Knicely Antique Apparel
PO #1, Lynn Rd
Acworth, NH 03601
603-835-2295

vintage clothing

Shop open by appointment. General line of antique and vintage clothing, accessories, related goods. Same location since 1968. Call or write special needs. Retail outlet at Pleasant St Antiques Center, downtown Claremont, NH.

Motorcars International
528 N Prince Ln
Springfield, MO 65802
417-831-9999; FAX: 417-863-0777
E-mail: missy@motorcars-intl

accessories
cars
services
tools

See full listing in **Section One** under **Ferrari**

Motorsports Racing 914 S Santa Fe #101 Vista, CA 92084 619-630-0547; FAX: 619-630-3085	**accessories** **apparel** **art**

Mail order only. Your exclusive source for Mr Norm's Grand Spaulding Dodge genuine accessories, memorabilia and vehicle documentation, and Yenko Motorsports apparel and accessories, featuring The One and Only On The Planet 68 Yenko COPO Camaro. Also, a huge selection of automotive apparel for all enthusiasts, including the Match Race Madness line of nostalgia drag racing apparel, plus posters and more for street rods, customs, 50s cars, muscle cars, Camaros, Mustangs, Vettes, Harleys and race cars.

O'Brien Truckers 5 Perry Hill North Grafton, MA 01536-1532 508-839-3033; FAX: 508-839-9490 E-mail: obrien_dennis@emc.com	**accessories** **belt buckles** **plaques** **valve covers**

See full listing in **Section Two** under **plaques**

Olona Imaging PO Box 92214 Albuquerque, NM 87199-2214 800-910-4237 E-mail: olonaimage@aol.com	**mugs** **t-shirts**

See full listing in **Section Two** under **novelties**

People's Choice & Lost in the 50s 28170 Ave Crocker #209 Valencia, CA 91355 800-722-1965, 805-295-1965 FAX: 805-295-1931	**automobilia items** **celebrity items** **50s clothing** **50s memorabilia**

See full listing in **Section Two** under **automobilia**

Premier Designs Historic Costume 818 Selby St Findlay, OH 45840 800-427-0907; FAX: 419-427-2239 E-mail: premier@bright.net	**clothing**

Mail order only. Historic clothing for women and men. Victorian to 1930s. Products include dusters, motor caps, knickers, shirts, collars, ladies blouses, jackets & skirts, and many more items. Jodhpurs & helmets for motorcyclists.

Pronyne PO Box 1492 Pawtucket, RI 02862-1492 401-725-1118	**museum**

See full listing in **Section Six** under **Rhode Island**

Roadside Market 1000 Gordon M Buehrig Pl Auburn, IN 46706 219-925-9100; FAX: 219-925-4563	**automobilia**

See full listing in **Section Two** under **automobilia**

Simpson 2415 Amsler St Torrance, CA 90505 310-320-7231; FAX: 310-320-7179	**driving suits** **gloves** **helmets** **shoes**

Deals in Motorsport safety products including driving suits, gloves, shoes, helmets, crew uniforms and accessories.

Top Dead Center Apparel PO Box 753 18 Main Street Wells River, VT 05081 802-757-2553; FAX: 802-757-3312 E-mail: greenmtmonogram@connriver.net	**apparel**

Mail order and open shop. Open daily 9-5. Screen printed apparel for the automotive trade.

Transport-Nation Collectibles 24040 Camino Del Avion, Ste A-241 Monarch Beach, CA 92629 800-474-4404, 714-240-5126	**artwork** **collectibles**

See full listing in **Section Two** under **artwork**

West Coast Metric Inc 24002 Frampton Ave Harbor City, CA 90710 310-325-0005; FAX: 310-325-9733 E-mail: wcmi@earthlink.net	**apparel** **carpets** **rubber parts**

See full listing in **Section One** under **Volkswagen**

appraisals

A-One Auto Appraisals 19 Hope Ln Narragansett, RI 02882 401-783-7701, RI; 407-668-9610, FL	**appraisals**

Auto appraisals on all types antique, street rods, customs and special interest. License #472. New England area & Florida.

AAG-Auto Appraisal Group Inc PO Box 7034 Charlottesville, VA 22906 800-848-2886; FAX: 804-295-7918 E-mail: aag@autoappraisal.com	**appraisals**

Classic and collectible auto value specialists. Nationwide comprehensive professional service. Pre-purchase inspections, insurance documentation, estate tax matters, property settlements. IRS forms. Inspections by AAG certified examiners. Locations: California, Connecticut, Florida, Massachusetts, New Jersey, New York, North Carolina, Pennsylvania, Texas, Utah, Vermont, Virginia, Washington, Wisconsin. Extensive information gathering, originality and historical research, current market comparable analysis, factual reporting. Call: 804-295-1722; Web site: http://www.autoappraisal.com

Aero International Auto Appraisals Box 1955 Penhold, AB Canada T0M 1R0 403-886-5565	**appraiser** **consultant**

Open shop. Monday-Sunday 24 hours. We endeavor to have the best appraisal in western Canada with professional photography, 4 page detailed analysis, comprehensive current value research, in a quality portfolio done in triplicate. Can and will back up this appraisal in arbitration, long distance purchasing consultant. Recognized by GM Canada. Special interest automotive appraisals including motorcycles, boats, RVs, antique farm equipment and commercial equipment.

Allan's Automobile Appraisal Service 8997 River Crescent Suffolk, VA 23433 804-238-2984	**appraiser**

Antique and special interest vehicle appraisal with report provided. Photos and videos optional, flat rate report fee, pro-rata travel and expenses. Phone 8-6, recording on when not in.

Alt Auto Sales	car dealer

Alt Auto Sales
Box 364
Regina, SK Canada S4P 3A1
306-545-7119, 306-757-0369

See full listing in **Section Two** under **car dealers**

Antique & Classic Auto Appraisal	appraiser consultant

Antique & Classic Auto Appraisal
Robert F Keefe
18812 Monteverde Dr
Springhill, FL 34610
813-856-5168

Appraiser and consultant for antique, classic and special interest vehicles. 30 years' involvement in the old car field. Associate member of the International Society of Appraisers. Pre-purchase and travel available.

Antique & Special Interest Car Appraisals	appraiser

Antique & Special Interest Car Appraisals
22 Shipman Rd
Andover, MA 01810-1716
508-475-7707 evenings

Mail order and open shop. Antique and special interest cars only, full condition reports, history, narrative and candid report with actual value survey by comparisons. 25 years' experience.

Antique and Classic Auto Appraisal Service	appraiser

Antique and Classic Auto Appraisal Service
47 Dowlwood Dr
Wasaga Beach
ON Canada L0L 2P0
888-EVALUE8; 705-429-4556

Canada's largest and most respected professional appraisal firm. Founded in 1980. Now has franchised offices throughout Ontario. Recommended by both the CAA and APA. Extensive, successful court experience. Specializing in insurance documentation and pre-purchase assignments anywhere in North America.

Antique Autos of California	appraisals

Antique Autos of California
Carl Bergman
44133 10th St W
Lancaster, CA 93534-4245
805-948-9069; FAX: 805-948-9208

Mail order and open shop by appointment only. Appraising market value of all automobiles. Fax or phone for mail appraisals and prices.

Appraisal Express	appraiser

Appraisal Express
PO Box 925
Torrance, CA 90508-0925
310-782-2300; FAX: 310-782-2380

Value appraisals, damage repair estimates, total loss evaluations on collisions, recovered and unrecovered thefts. Value disputes and expert testimony. Licensed insurance adjusters. Founded by Bruce Summers in 1975. Heavy insurance carrier account base. Over 300 vehicles inspected each month. Servicing southern California. Six full time appraisers. 48 hour turnaround.

Appraisals R Us ET	appraisals

Appraisals R Us ET
Ed Thornton
15 Davis Dr
Alton, ON Canada L0N 1A0
519-942-0436

Appraiser and consultant of any type or vintage of automobile or truck which includes street rods and fire apparatus. Over thirty years in the old car hobby. A complete portfolio of quality typed reports supplemented with pictures.

Archer & Associates	appraiser consultant promotion sales & purchasing

Archer & Associates
1807 East Ave
Hayward, CA 94541
510-581-4911

Shop open Monday-Saturday 9 am to 10 pm.

Walt Armstrong	inspections

Walt Armstrong
RFD #3, Box 826
Woolwich, ME 04579
207-442-7450

Mail order and on-site visits. On-site inspections of cars in the Maine area for prospective buyers in other parts of the country. For antique and sports vehicles. Specializing in British cars. You can save time and money by having your prospective purchase inspected by me before you make your trip or I'll accompany you for advice.

Art's Appraisal Services Inc	appraisals consultant

Art's Appraisal Services Inc
PO Box 187
Manchester, CT 06045
860-646-4962

Professional appraising, 20 years' experience. For insurance, loan, donation, sale, purchase, divorce, business dissolution, estate settlement, taxation, bankruptcy, etc. Available at any time. 2nd location: 5904 Sandpipers Dr, Lakeland, FL 33809, PH: 941-815-0906.

Auto Consultants & Appraisal Service	appraisals

Auto Consultants & Appraisal Service
Charles J Kozelka
PO Box 111
Macedonia, OH 44056
216-467-0748

Professional appraisals for antique, classic, special interest and late model vehicles. Video appraisals at extra charge. Certified automobile accident and vehicle theft investigator. Expert witness and court testimony. Pre-purchase inspections or liquidation evaluations our specialty. Technical assistance on vehicle transactions, restorations or any auto related service. Consultant for commercial advertising, promotions, entertainment, special events, etc. Vehicle locator and broker service available.

Auto Evaluators	appraiser

Auto Evaluators
5062 S 108th St, Ste 225
Omaha, NE 68137
402-681-2968; FAX: 402-331-0638

Mail order and open shop by appointment. Appraisals of classic and late model cars for insurance, estates, bankruptcies, collateral and litigation of all types. Court tested, 20 years of automotive experience, appraisals by mail. Nationwide. Automotive legal consultant. Calls returned anywhere, phone 24 hrs.

Auto Nostalgia Enr	literature manuals

Auto Nostalgia Enr
332 St Joseph S
Mont St Gregoire, QC
Canada J0J 1K0
PH/FAX: 514-346-3644

See full listing in **Section Two** under **literature dealers**

Automotive Legal Service Inc
PO Box 626
Dresher, PA 19025
800-487-4947; 215-659-4947
FAX: 215-657-5843

appraisals

Open shop, Monday-Friday 9 am to 5 pm EST. State licensed automotive appraisal specialists. Antique, classic, exotic, kit, musclecar, pro street, street rod, cars, vans, trucks, original, restored, modified, incomplete, hard to value, insurance claims and restoration disputes, arbitration, litigation our specialty. Member Collector Car & Truck, NADA, OCPG Advisory Panels, National Muscle Car Association Regional director, qualified expert witness 87 times, also current model Accident Investigation/Reconstruction Lemon Law. Quality references, maximum credibility, reasonable rates, travel USA. Free consultation/consultation.

AVM Automotive Consulting
Box 338
Montvale, NJ 07645-0338
PH: 201-391-5194
FAX: 201-782-0663
E-mail: avmtony@aol.com

appraisals
consultant

Open shop, 9 am to 9 pm weekdays. Specializing in appraisals, pre-purchase inspections and consulting for antique, classic and custom vehicles and equipment. Will travel or by mail. Writing appraisals for over twenty years for legal and estate settlements. Automotive products and business consulting with 30 years of experience. Services are available for individuals, attorneys and corporations. Member of the International Automotive Appraisers Association makes prompt inspections possible worldwide.

Bill's Collector Cars
6478 County Rd #1
South Point, OH 45680
614-894-5175

appraiser
car dealer

See full listing in **Section Two** under **car dealers**

Blair Collectors & Consultants
2821 SW 167th Pl
Seattle, WA 98166
206-242-6745

appraiser
consultant
literature

Mail order and open shop. Monday through Friday, 9 am-10 pm PST. Collector car appraisals, cars and parts locating service, technical and restoration/customizing advice, car importing advice and assistance, data packages for all cars, buy/sell literature. Covers vintage, classic, muscle, street rods and imports. Professional engineer with over 40 years' experience.

Gerard Boucher
PO Box 171
Franklin, VT 05457
514-298-5438; FAX: 514-298-5698
Quebec, Canada

restoration

See full listing in **Section Two** under **restoration shops**

Bramhall Classic Autos
149 30th St
Toronto, ON Canada M8W 3C3
416-255-7201; FAX: 416-255-8446

appraisals
brokers
car & parts locator
consultants

See full listing in **Section Two** under **brokers**

Brandberry Antique Auto Appraisal
401 First Ave
Gallipolis, OH 45631
614-446-3225

appraiser

Appraisals by mail or in person. 25 years' experience.

Brookside Automotive Sales
363 E Main St
Rt 9, PO Box 312
East Brookfield, MA 01515
508-867-9266, 508-829-5366
508-885-2017 FAX: 508-867-2875

appraisals
car dealer
service

See full listing in **Section Two** under **car dealers**

David Brownell
PO Box 2183
Manchester Ctr, VT 05255
802-362-4719

appraiser
auctioneer

All makes and years. Will travel internationally. Collections a specialty. Serving individuals, banks, insurance companies, institutions for over 20 years. Experienced in cars and fine automobilia.

Bryant's Antique Auto Parts
851 Western Ave
Hampden, ME 04444
207-862-4019

appraisals
parts
sheetmetal service

See full listing in **Section One** under **Ford '03-'31**

Arthur Burrichter
24026 Highway 151
Monticello, IA 52310
319-465-3064; FAX: 319-465-6048

appraisals
car dealer

See full listing in **Section Two** under **car dealers**

CALSPECC Restorations
20818 E Weldon
Tivy Valley, CA 93657-9107
PH:/FAX: 209-787-2224

appraiser
car dealer

By appointment only. Specializing in all phases of restorations on British sports cars. Partial to body-off restorations. MG TC/TD/TF, MGA, Triumph, Austin-Healey, Morgan, Jaguars, etc.

CARS (Computer Aided Resale System)
2724 Cove View Dr N
Jacksonville, FL 32257
904-448-0633; FAX: 904-448-0623

car dealer

See full listing in **Section Two** under **car dealers**

Carters Auto Restorations
1433 Pawlings Rd
Phoenixville, PA 19460
215-666-5687

restoration

See full listing in **Section Two** under **bodywork**

Casey-Dyer Enterprises Inc
PO Box 7176
Alexandria, LA 71301
318-473-1802; FAX: 318-473-9578

appraiser
broker
car dealer

See full listing in **Section Two** under **car dealers**

Certified Auto Appraisal
PO Box 17609
Anaheim, CA 92817
714-966-1096; FAX: 714-498-7367

appraisals

Mail order and telephone. Expert automotive value appraisals for: insurance coverage, bank and credit union financing, disputed claims and settlement, estate probate, divorce settlement, charitable donation, IRS and DMV, buyers and sellers consultation, diminution of value reports. A member of Society of Automobile Historians.

Chicago Car Exchange
1 Collector Car Dr
Box 530
Lake Bluff, IL 60044
847-680-1950; FAX: 847-680-1961
E-mail: oldtoys@wwa.com

appraiser
car dealer
car locator
financing
storage

See full listing in **Section Two** under **car dealers**

Charles W Clarke Automotive Consultant/Appraiser
17 Saddle Ridge Dr
West Simsbury, CT 06092
203-658-2714

appraiser
consultant
car dealer

See full listing in **Section Two** under **consultants**

Classic Auto Appraisals
3497 Simpson Rd SE
Rochester, MN 55904
507-289-7111

appraisals

Appraisals for special interest, antique, milestones, muscle and classic cars. Our specialty: 50s, 60s rods and customs. For insurance coverage, estates, loan valuation, charitable contributions, marriage, business/settlements, pre-sale, pre-purchase inspections.

Classic Car Appraisal Service
Atlanta Office
1400 Lake Ridge Ct
Roswell, GA 30076
770-993-5622

appraiser

Open by appointment only. Donald R Peterson, president. Has appraised more than 11,000 collector cars since opening in 1974. Packard, Rolls-Royce and other CCCA Classics are our specialty. Member of CCCA, AACA, HCCA, VMCCA, MCS, RROC, PAC and SAH. A copy of our credentials will be mailed at your request. We also do diminished value appraisals, pre-purchase examinations and have served as an expert witness on dozens of occasions.

Classic Car Research
29508 Southfield Rd
Southfield, MI 48076
810-557-2880; FAX: 810-557-3511

appraisals
car locating
consultant

Appraisals, parts locating and consulting. Also Corvettes for sale under $10,000. Cougar, Mustang and Grand National parts and specialist. 10 years in business.

Classic Carriage House
5552 E Washington
Phoenix, AZ 85034
602-275-6825; FAX: 602-244-1538

restoration

See full listing in **Section Two** under **restoration shops**

Classic Datsun Motorsports
402 Olive Ave #A
Vista, CA 92083
PH/FAX: 619-940-6365
E-mail: lescan@cts.com

appraisals
literature
parts
restoration

See full listing in **Section One** under **Datsun**

Classic Motors
PO Box 1321
Shirley, MA 01464
508-425-4350

appraisals
car dealer
consulting

See full listing in **Section Two** under **car dealers**

Classic Motors Inc
Rich Adams
103 200th Ave
Union Grove, WI 53182
414-878-2525; FAX: 414-878-0400

car sales
trailer sales

See full listing in **Section Two** under **car dealers**

Classique Cars Unlimited
5 Turkey Bayou Rd
PO Box 249
Lakeshore, MS 39558
601-467-9633
FAX: 601-467-9207, MS
800-543-8691, USA

appraisals
parts
repairs
restorations

See full listing in **Section One** under **Lincoln**

Cochrane's Special Interest Brokers
Ed Cochrane
718 Livingston Ave
Shreveport, LA 71107
318-226-0458, 318-424-2861

appraisers
brokers
consultant
locator

See full listing in **Section Two** under **brokers**

Collector Car Appraisals
L E Lazarus, Senior Appraiser
PO Box 6732
Rockford, IL 61125
815-229-1258; FAX: 815-229-1238

appraisals

Mail order and open shop. Appraisals of antique, classic, special interest and specialty vehicles. Cited 3 times in *Guinness Book of World Records*. In business since 1964.

Collector Car & Truck Prices
41 N Main St
North Grafton, MA 01536
508-839-6707; FAX: 508-839-6266
E-mail: vmr@ultranet.com

price guide

See full listing in **Section Four** under **periodicals**

Collector Cars-U-Can-Afford Ltd
4046 11th St
Rockford, IL 61109
815-229-1258; FAX: 815-229-1238

car dealer

See full listing in **Section One** under **Cadillac/LaSalle**

Collector's Carousel
84 Warren Ave
Westbrook, ME 04092
207-854-0343; FAX: 207-856-6913

appraisals
sales
service

See full listing in **Section Two** under **car dealers**

Lance S Coren, CAA, CMA
20545 Eastwood Ave
Torrance, CA 90503-3611
310-370-4114; FAX: 310-371-4120

appraisals

Mail order and open by appointment only. The only FIA & ORDINEX Certified Automotive Appraiser in the western United States. Material damage appraisals, actual cash evaluations. Exotic, classic & race cars. American Bar Association & IRS qualified. Insurance, bank, charity, museum, court evaluations. Expert witness testimony. Arbitration & mediation. Auto manufacturer & Lloyds of London acknowledged expert. Celebrity clientele. 20 years' experience. Servicing the United States, Europe & Japan. Senior member: Society of Automotive Appraisers, International Automotive Appraisers Guild, Automotive Arbitration Council.

Generalists

Generalists

Corvette Enterprise Brokerage	appraiser
The Power Broker	broker
52 Van Houten Ave	car locator
Passaic Park, NJ 07055	investment
201-472-7021	planning

See full listing in **Section One** under **Corvette**

Creative Automotive Consultants	appraiser
PO Box 2221	car locator
San Rafael, CA 94912-2221	promotion
707-824-9004; FAX: 707-824-9002	

See full listing in **Section Two** under **consultants**

Dan's Classic Autos	appraiser
PO Box 1619	
New Caney, TX 77357	
713-354-2608; FAX: 713-689-5566	

Open shop only. Monday-Friday 8 am to 5 pm. Evaluations and damage appraisals on autos, trucks, buses, antique and classic cars, street rods and customs, motorcycles and salvage evaluations. Licensed insurance adjuster, state of Texas.

The Davis Registry	periodical
4073 Ruby	
Ypsilanti, MI 48197	
313-434-5581, 313-662-1001	

See full listing in **Section Four** under **books & publications**

Dearborn Automobile Co	car dealer
16 Maple St (at Rt 1)	appraisals
Topsfield, MA 01983	
508-887-6644; FAX: 508-887-3889	

Shop open Monday-Friday 9 to 5; Saturday 9 to 12 noon. All types of rare Mercedes bought, sold and brokered, appraisals. Specializing in fifties models. Appraiser for estates & insurance.

Robert DeMars Ltd	appraisers
222 Lakeview Ave, Ste 160-256	auto historians
West Palm Beach, FL 33401	car locator
561-832-0171	research library
FAX: 561-844-1493	resto consultants

Appraiser/Historians: telephone consultation worldwide for fast information and recommendations! Available in person by mail order & FAX. We're the 30 year pioneers of the field of collector car appraisal traveling the world. Low mileage, Antique, Classic, Sports, Muscle, Race, Pebble Beach Concours and prototype "Dream Cars" a specialty. Clients and inspectors thru US, Europe, Japan, South America. As historians and performance/race drivers with a large research library, we appreciate fine machinery and monitor the "Now Market" for trends and values. Pebble Beach, CA/Palm Beach, FL. Please note new main office and phone.

Doc's Jags	appraisals
125 Baker Rd	interiors
Lake Bluff, IL 60044	restoration
847-367-5247; FAX: 847-367-6363	

See full listing in **Section One** under **Jaguar**

Eckhaus Appraisal Service	appraiser
20818 E Weldon	
Tivy Valley, CA 93657-9107	
PH/FAX: 209-787-2224	

Established 1968. Inspection and appraisals for insurance coverage, lending institutions, estates, etc. Member International Society of Appraisers. Pre-purchase inspections anywhere in the world. One car or large collections.

Ellingson Car Museum	museum
20950 Rogers Dr	
Rogers, MN 55374	
612-428-7337; FAX: 612-428-4370	

See full listing in **Section Six** under **Minnesota**

Richard H Feibusch	appraisal
211 Dimmick Ave	
Venice, CA 90291	
310-392-6605; FAX: 310-396-1933	

Appraiser and automotive journalist. Recognized by the IRS, Probate Court and all major insurance companies. Antiques, classics, special interest, foreign, rods, customs and kit/home-built cars. Los Angeles area only.

FEN Enterprises of New York Inc	parts
PO Box 1559	restoration
Wappingers Falls, NY 12590	
914-462-5959; 914-462-5094	
FAX: 914-462-8450	

See full listing in **Section One** under **Cadillac/LaSalle**

Fiesta's Classic Car Center	appraisals
3901 N Kings Hwy	consignment sales
St Louis, MO 63115	storage
314-385-4567	

See full listing in **Section Two** under **storage**

John Filiss	appraisals
45 Kingston Ave	
Port Jervis, NY 12771	
914-856-2942	

Mail order and open shop by appointment. Specializes in low-cost, professional appraisals for insurance purposes, also divorces and estate settlements. Does business nationwide.

Freelance Appraisals Inc	appraisals
RR 1	consulting
Red Deer, AB Canada T4N 5E1	
403-347-4488; FAX: 403-347-4480	

Open shop Monday to Friday 9 am to 5 pm. Dealing in certified appraisals or consultation on anything of value: antiques, collectibles, classics, special interest automobiles, farm and commercial equipment and RVs. For buying or selling, insurance coverage, bank loans, estate values, legal disputes or arbitration. This professional carefully researched document with full color pictures is well accepted by major insurance companies, lending institutions and government agencies. Bill Woof CAGA owner.

From Rust To Riches	appraisals
14200 New Hampshire Ave	car dealer
Silver Spring, MD 20904	repairs
301-384-5856; FAX: 301-989-1866	restoration

See full listing in **Section Two** under **restoration shops**

The Generation Gap	broker
4989 Mercer University Dr	car dealer
Macon, GA 31210	
912-471-6325	

See full listing in **Section Two** under **car dealers**

The Gullwing Garage Ltd	appraisals
Bricklin SVI Specialists	literature
5 Cimorelli Dr	parts
New Windsor, NY 12553-6201	service
914-561-0019 anytime	

See full listing in **Section One** under **Bricklin**

Hand's Elderly Auto Care
2000 W Galveston St
Grand Prairie, TX 75051
214-642-4288

repair
restoration

See full listing in **Section Two** under **restoration shops**

Hawthorne Appraisals
Box 1332
Coaldale, AB Canada T1M 1N1
403-345-2101

appraisals
parts

Open shop only. Monday-Saturday, year round, 7 am-10 pm. Dealing in appraisals and some parts of the 1940, 50, 60 & 1970s cars & trucks.

Thos Hespenheide & Associates Ltd
410 Darby Rd
Havertown, PA 19083
610-446-7699, FAX: 610-446-7915

appraiser
rebuilding

Mail order and open shop. Monday-Friday 9 am to 6 pm. Been in the collector vehicle business for over 30 years. Appraises and evaluates most collectibles and refurbishes most mechanical components. Also magnetos, leather cone clutches, National repair manuals, rebuilding early carburetors, relining brake bands and shoes.

HK Klassics
Hy Kusnetz
16 Hausmann Ct
Maplewood, NJ 07040
201-761-6642

appraisals

Mail order and open shop. Monday to Friday 10 am-4 pm. Specializing in Italian, American, British, German autos of the 1950s, 1960s, 1970s. Import/export, autos, parts, tools.

Don Hoelscher, Auto Appraiser
52 Waynesboro Ct
St Charles, MO 63304
314-939-9667

appraiser

By appointment only. Appraisals of classic, antique, special interest/collector cars, trucks and other vehicles, all years and models.

Howe & Associates Appraisal Services
54 Marmora St
St Catharines, ON
Canada L2P 3C3
905-685-6473

appraiser

On-site and home service by appointment, mail order, open 7 days a week. To provide reasonable, affordable service to all types of vehicles. Registered tax appraiser for Ontario vehicle registration tax. Club discounts.

Hubbard and Associates
Appraisers of Collectible Autos
80 W Bellevue Dr #200
Pasadena, CA 91105
PH: 818-568-0122
FAX: 818-568-1510

appraiser

Office hours Monday-Friday 9 to 5, by appointment only. Appraisals for insurance, probate, marriage dissolution and pre-purchase inspections. Licensed, Board certified, Senior member American Society of Appraisers. Professional resume and references upon request. Twenty years' experience. Expert witness, arbitration & litigation.

International Automotive Appraisers Assoc
Box 338
Montvale, NJ 07645
201-391-3251; FAX: 201-782-0663
E-mail: avmtony@aol.com

appraisals

Open shop 8 am-5 pm weekdays. An association dedicated to appraisers and the automotive community. Open to qualified or licensed appraisers. Training programs for qualified applicants. The IAAA (International Automotive Appraisers Association) can be reached by writing or phoning.

Cy Kay Motors Ltd
1160 Waukegan Rd
Glenview, IL 60025
847-724-3100, 847-432-8793

appraiser
car dealer

See full listing in **Section Two** under **car dealers**

Ken's Cougars
PO Box 5380
Edmond, OK 73013
405-340-1636; FAX: 405-340-5877

parts

See full listing in **Section One** under **Mercury**

J A Kennedy Inc
1727 Hartford Tpke
North Haven, CT 06473
203-239-2227

appraiser

Specializing in appraisals of both damage and value for antique, classic and special interest cars.

Kruse International
PO Box 190
5540 County Rd 11-A
Auburn, IN 46706
800-968-4444; FAX: 219-925-5467

auction

See full listing in **Section Two** under **auctions & events**

Landry Classic MotorCars
34 Goodhue Ave
Chicopee, MA 01020
413-592-2746; FAX: 413-594-8378

appraiser

Open shop by appointment only 7 days. Specializing in all types of professional appraisals including stated value, pre-purchase inspections for all collector cars and trucks. Licensed and certified in several states. Member of 13 National clubs.

Bob Lichty
8211 E Wadora Circle NW
N Canton, OH 44720
330-966-0146

appraiser
consultant
promoter

Dealing in appraisals, inspections, consulting for insurance, legal, estates and purchasing. Also consultant to publishers for promotions, marketing, design and events promotion. Event producer. Event representative.

Lister Restorations
6565 E 40
Tulsa, OK 74145
918-663-6220; FAX: 918-664-0804

appraiser
restoration

See full listing in **Section Two** under **restoration shops**

M & L Automobile Appraisal
2662 Palm Terr
Deland, FL 32720
904-734-1761

appraiser

Open shop only. 7 days by appointment only. Florida state licensed to appraise antique, classic, special interest and custom/altered automobiles for insurance coverage, loan valuation, estate settlements or disputes.

M & M Automobile Appraisers Inc 4349 WN Peotone Rd Beecher, IL 60401-9757 708-258-6662, FAX: 708-258-9675	**appraiser** **broker**

Mail order and open shop. Open 7 days 1 pm to 8 pm. Appraises special interest, collectible and antique automobiles for insurance coverage, loan valuation, marriage or business dissolutions and value disputes. Also provides brokers and locators network.

Randall Marcus Vintage **Automobiles** 706 Hanshaw Rd Ithaca, NY 14850 607-257-5939; FAX: 607-272-8806	**broker** **car locator** **consultant**

See full listing in **Section Two** under **brokers**

Masterworks Auto Reconditioning 1127 Brush Run Rd Washington, PA 15301 412-267-3460	**restoration**

See full listing in **Section Two** under **restoration shops**

Mc Intyre Auctions PO Box 60 E Dixfield, ME 04227 207-562-4443; FAX: 207-562-4576 E-mail: info@classicford.com	**auctions** **automobilia** **literature** **petroliana**

See full listing in **Section Two** under **auctions & events**

Bill McCoskey 14200 New Hampshire Ave Silver Spring, MD 20904 301-384-5856; FAX: 301-989-1866	**appraisals** **repairs**

Certified value appraisals, diminution in value claims, insurance claim arbitration service and effective expert witness court testimony. Pre-claim value reconstruction and appraisal-by-mail service available. Over 25 years in the antique and classic car business and hobby, rare European cars a specialty. Well-equipped restoration shop on premises, offering top quality repairs to all antique and classic cars at below market prices. High quality repairs available worldwide, "have tools will travel".

The McHugh Group 4602 Birch Ct Middletown, MD 21769 301-473-8333; FAX: 301-371-9447	**appraisals**

Telephone orders only. Seven days 8 am to 10 pm. Appraisals: Maryland, Virginia, Delaware, District of Columbia and southern Pennsylvania. 35 years' experience. Expert witness, consultant, broker.

Memory Lane Motors Lindsay St S Fenelon Falls, ON Canada K0M 1N0 705-887-CARS	**car dealer** **restoration** **service**

See full listing in **Section Two** under **restoration shops**

Memory Lane Motors Inc 1231 Rt 176 Lake Bluff, IL 60044 847-362-4600	**appraisals** **car dealer** **storage**

See full listing in **Section Two** under **car dealers**

Dennis Mitosinka's Classic Cars **and Appraisals** 619 E Fourth St Santa Ana, CA 92701 714-953-5303; FAX: 714-953-1810	**appraisals** **books**

Appraisals of all types of autos. For the most professional service, for disputes in value, litigation, insurance, donations, diminished value purchases or sales. Call for cost estimates. Certified appraiser with over 26 years' experience. Also large selection of auto books, mostly out of print.

Omega Automobile Appraisals 115 18 Ave SE St Petersburg, FL 33705 PH/FAX: 813-894-5690	**appraisals**

See full listing in **Section One** under **Rolls-Royce/Bentley**

CT Peters Inc, Appraisers 2A W Front St Red Bank, NJ 07701 908-747-9450 Red Bank 908-528-9451 Brielle	**appraiser**

Mail order and open shop. Monday-Friday 9 am to 5 pm. Antique, classic and vintage motor cars appraised throughout the tri-state area since 1976. For insurance, fair market and estate values. Appointments at your premises available or send photographs for appraisal by mail. References available. We also offer fast, effective, discreet methods of selling investment quality automobiles through our exclusive tri-state area computer client mailing list.

Precision Autoworks 2202 Federal Street E Camden , NJ 08105 609-966-0080, NJ FAX: 610-649-3577, PA	**restorations**

See full listing in **Section One** under **Mercedes-Benz**

Prestige Thunderbird Inc 10215 Greenleaf Ave Santa Fe Springs, CA 90670 800-423-4751, 310-944-6237 FAX: 310-941-8677	**appraisals** **radios** **repairs** **restorations** **tires**

See full listing in **Section One** under **Thunderbird**

Professional **Specialties/Americana Coach** 513 S Woodlawn Ave, Ste 322 Wichita, KS 67218 316-684-1199; FAX: 316-684-6266	**appraisals** **literature**

Mail order only. Deal exclusively in ambulances, fire apparatus and some professional cars. Expert appraisals done on site or by mail. 31 years' experience. Also extensive dealer in ambulance, fire apparatus & professional car literature, manuals, etc.

Rader's Relics 2601 W Fairbanks Avenue Winter Park, FL 32789 407-647-1940; FAX: 407-647-1930	**appraiser** **car dealer**

See full listing in **Section Two** under **car dealers**

Reinholds Restorations c/o Rick Reinhold PO Box 178, 255 N Ridge Rd Reinholds, PA 17569-0178 717-336-5617	**appraisals** **repairs** **restoration**

See full listing in **Section Two** under **restoration shops**

Reward Service, Inc
172 Overhill Rd
Stormville, NY 12582
914-227-7647; FAX: 914-221-0293

appraisals
restoration
transportation

See full listing in **Section One** under **Jaguar**

Roy Rappa Appraisers
11 Virginia Rd
North White Plains , NY 10603
914-682-9030; FAX: 914-682-3127

appraisals

Appraisals for antique, classic & custom cars, motorcycles.

Richard C Ryder
828 Prow Ct
Sacramento, CA 95822
916-442-3424 anytime

appraiser

Collector car evaluations for individuals, insurance, lenders, legal or government agencies.

James T Sandoro
24 Myrtle Ave
Buffalo, NY 14204
716-855-1931

appraiser
consultant

Confidential automotive consultant, appraiser, expert witness, trial consultant. 33 years' full time experience. Unique qualifications. Retained by the largest collections, museums, government agencies, restoration shops. I can give you an overview and act as an expert in your behalf as well as a trial consultant regarding collector vehicles, motorcycles, memorabilia, etc. I only testify in cases I believe in. My referrals are from other appraisers, dealers and restorers. Available anywhere in the world.

Bernard A Siegal, ASA
Automotive Restoration Services
PO Box 140722
Dallas, TX 75214
214-827-2678; FAX: 214-826-0000

appraiser

Monday through Saturday 9 to 6 CST. Appraisals for all marques and all years. Valuation for insurance, pre-purchase inspection, physical damage appraisals, loss of value, divorces, estate settlements. One of ten Senior members of the American Society of Appraisers accredited and tested in this field. Eight areas of certification by Automotive Service Excellence. Licensed Texas adjuster. All valuation reports conform to USPAP standards.

Sotheby's
1334 York Avenue
New York, NY 10021
212-606-7920; FAX: 212-606-7886

auction company

See full listing in **Section Two** under **auctions & events**

Southern Classics
10301 Windtree Ln
Charlotte, NC 28215
704-532-9870

appraisals
photographs

Mail order only. Provides written appraisal of classic autos, and photographs of classic autos. Specializing in General Motors and big block Chevys.

Specialty Sales
4321 First St
Pleasanton, CA 94566
510-484-2262; FAX: 510-426-8535
E-mail: specialt@ix.netcom.com

appraiser
car dealer
locator
memorabilia

See full listing in **Section Two** under **car dealers**

Steele's Appraisal
Shore Dr, Box 276
Maynard, MA 01754
508-897-8984

appraiser

Mail order and open shop. Open 7 days 5 pm to 8 pm. Travels the New England area to view and appraise antique and special interest autos to prevent sight-unseen purchases by out-of-the-area buyers.

Still Cruisin' Corvettes
5759 Benford Dr
Haymarket, VA 20169
703-754-1960; FAX: 703-754-1222

appraisals
repairs
restoration

See full listing in **Section One** under **Corvette**

**Tamarack Automotive Appraisals
and Marine Surveys**
53 Sears Ln
Burlington, VT 05401
PH/FAX: 802-864-4003
E-mail: gtlittle@aol.com

appraiser
restoration

Established 1974. Appraisals to ASA and federal standards by Vermont licensed appraiser. Accredited member American Society of Appraisers. Member SAMS, ABYC.

Timeless Masterpieces
221 Freeport Dr
Bloomingdale, IL 60108
630-893-1058 evenings

appraiser
consultant

Appraisals, consulting, research, historian of pre-1975 antique, classic, vintage automobiles. Auction/agent representation. Write or call for information. Established 1976.

Top Hat John
PO Box 46024
Mt Clemens, MI 48046-6024
810-465-1933

appraisals

Appraisal service by Top Hat John, custom classic, special interest. Prior to purchase or sale, insurance coverage, settlement, investment portfolio, member Society of Automotive Historians. References. Local or travel. Able to identify, negotiate and close sale if necessary. Detail oriented.

Lou Trepanier, Appraiser #1
250 Highland St
Taunton, MA 02780
508-823-6512; FAX: 508-285-4841

appraiser
consultant

Stated value appraisals, antique, classic, customs and exotics. Consultant to hobbyists and businesses, licensed and appointed and sworn arbitrator for insurance, financial or legals. 40 years in automotive services. Guaranteed neutral umpire service for disputed claims.

USAppraisal
754 Walker
PO Box 472
Great Falls, VA 22066-0472
703-759-9100; FAX: 703-759-9099
E-mail: dhkinney@aol.com

appraisals

Shop open 7 days by appointment. Appraisals for all makes and models of automobiles and trucks of all years. Available nationwide. 25 years' collector car experience. All appraisals and record keeping conform to USPAP standards. David H Kinney, AM, accredited member American Society of Appraisers.

Generalists

Glenn Vaughn Restoration Services Inc
550 N Greenferry
Post Falls, ID 83854
208-773-3525; FAX: 208-773-3526

appraisals
restoration

See full listing in **Section Two** under **restoration shops**

Vehicle Appraisers Inc
59 Wheeler Ave
Milford, CT 06460
203-877-1066

appraisals

Open 7 days by appointment only. Fully licensed appraisal company specializing in collector vehicles. "Our only business is collector car appraising and it is a full-time endeavor." Private and commercial work.

Vintage Vehicles Co Inc
8190 20th Dr
Wautoma, WI 54982
414-787-2656

detail
restoration

See full listing in **Section Two** under **restoration shops**

Johnny Williams Services
2613 Copeland Rd
Tyler, TX 75701
903-597-3687
800-937-0900 voice mail #7225

appraiser
cars & parts locator
consultant
lighting systems
design

Mail order and open shop. Monday-Friday 4 pm to 10 pm CST. Active hobbyist who assists others on a one to one basis. Over 30 years' experience in most aspects of the old car field. Professional lighting consultant specializing in industrial and commercial installations. Special interest and street rod appraisals. Locates cars and parts. Offers sales consultation.

Yesterday's Auto Sales
2800 Lyndale Ave S
Minneapolis, MN 55408
612-872-9733; FAX: 612-872-1386

appraiser
car dealer

See full listing in **Section Two** under **car dealers**

Yesteryear Restorations
387 Nutting Rd
Jaffrey, NH 03452
603-532-7469

repair
restoration
sales
transportation

See full listing in **Section One** under **Ford '32-'53**

Chris M Zora ASA, ISA
PO Box 9939
Woodlands, TX 77386
713-362-8258

appraisals
consultant

Mail order and open shop. 7 days a week 8-6 CST. Appraisals, expert witness and consultant for purchase, sale or restoration supervision. All antique, classic, milestone, special interest, muscle cars, race cars, domestic and foreign motorcycles, trucks, trailers, RVs, automobilia, models and toys, street rod and street machines. Late model car-diminished value, lemon laws, deceptive trade litigation.

American Memory Prints
5935 N Belt W
Belleville, IL 62223
618-235-4788; FAX: 618-235-4899

artwork

Mail order only. Offering a variety of automotive artwork. Currently have the 55 and 57 Chevy, 53 and 63 Corvette, 65 Mustang, 57 T-Bird, 32 Ford roadster, 69 Camero and 34 Ford pickup. Beautifully framed in 8"x10", 11"x14" and 20"x24" sizes. The 11x14 and 20x24 sizes are framed with a history of the automobile.

Anderson's
32700 Coastsite #102
Rancho Palos Verdes, CA 90275
310-377-1007; 800-881-9049
FAX: 310-377-0169

car door mono-
grams

See full listing in **Section Two** under **accessories**

Antique Car Paintings
6889 Fairwood
Dearborn Heights, MI 48127
313-274-7774

color prints
ink drawings
original illustra-
tions

Mail order and open shop. Monday-Saturday 9-5. Retired Ford Motor Co artist with 45 years' experience. Has painted 1,184 original paintings of old cars. Also full color prints of 1932 Fords, 1936 Fords, Model As and 40 Fords, 1932 Duesenberg roadster, 1930 Cadillac roadster, 1934 Packard touring, 1930 Rolls-Royce touring.

Auto Art by Paul G McLaughlin
2720 Tennessee NE
Albuquerque, NM 87110
505-296-2554

artwork
toys

Mail order only. Automotive art in pen & ink, pencil, oil and watercolor. Photographs, toys and other auto memorabilia.

Auto Fashions & Creations
2209-B Hamlets Chapel Rd
Pittsboro, NC 27312
PH/FAX: 919-542-5566
press (*) for tone

auto sales
handcrafts
restoration
rubber ink stamps

See full listing in **Section Two** under **restoration shops**

Automobilia Shop
48 Belmont St
Melrose, MA 02176
617-665-1992; FAX: 617-665-8018

artwork
books
models

Mail order and open shop. Thursday & Friday 6 pm to 8 pm, Saturday 9 am to 5 pm. Auto related fine arts, books, miniature autos (diecast & kits).

Automotive Fine Art
37986 Tralee Trail
Northville, MI 48167
810-476-9529

artwork

Mail order and studio open by appointment only. Specializing in original, dramatic works of automotive art in permanent medium. Signed and numbered print editions of classic automobiles by artist Tom Hale.

Automotive Fine Art Society Quarterly
PO Box 325
Dept HMN
Lake Orion, MI 48361-0325
PH/FAX: 810-814-0627

periodical

See full listing in **Section Four** under **periodicals**

John E Boehm
T/A Boehm Design Ltd
PO Box 9096
Silver Spring, MD 20916
301-649-6449

artwork

Automotive art renderings of antique, classic, special interest and other historic and modern day automobiles. I also do artist drawings of buildings (both residential and commercial with or without cars). Also original automotive styling, designs, for individual need or for corporations. I also do art illustrations for publicity or promotional uses.

D LuAnn Brandt Photographic Art
Box 1092
Tempe, AZ 85280-1092
800-238-6830

artwork
Rt 66 memorabilia

Mail order only. Now available: color postcards featuring views from the Mother Road Route 66 (dealers, retailers wanted). Deals in photographic art featuring race, exotic and American classic cars. Also Route 66 related artwork. Business products include custom business cards, postcards and stationery. Any type of custom artwork.

Francois Bruere
8 Avenue Olivier Heuze
LeMans 72000 France
(33) 02-4377-1877
FAX: (33) 02-4324-2038

artwork

Specializing in artwork, hyperrealism paintings, limited editions for Harley-Davidson, Ferrari, Jaguar, American cars and ACO. 24 hours of LeMans races (exhibitions in Europe, USA, Japan, ask for dates and catalogues).

Business Forms Management Inc
PO Box 4390
Akron, OH 44321-0390
216-666-2980; FAX: 216-666-0844

photo transfers
silkscreening

See full listing in **Section Two** under **apparel**

BW Incorporated
PO Box 106
316 W Broadway
Browns Valley, MN 56219
800-950-2210; 612-695-2891 or
800-EAT-OILS/328-6457
FAX: 612-695-2893

artwork
car care products
dry enclosed covers
mice control
oil drip absorbent
storage care
products

See full listing in **Section Two** under **storage care products**

Car Collectables
32 White Birch Rd
Madison, CT 06443
PH/FAX: 203-245-7299

banks
Christmas cards
note cards

Mail order only. Company geared specifically to meet the interests of collectors, restorers and all those who appreciate vintage automobiles. Our company offers holiday greeting cards, beautifully illustrated in full color, as well as note cards, metal car coin banks and many other fine gift items, all with antique car motifs.

CARSoft
RD 1, BOX 3694
Rutland, VT 05701
802-773-3526

artwork
clip art

See full listing in **Section Two** under **automobilia**

Ceramicar
679 Lapla Rd
Kingston, NY 12401
PH/FAX: 914-338-2199

auto-related
ceramics

See full listing in **Section Two** under **novelties**

Classic Profiles Inc
5770 W Kinnickinnic River Pkwy
West Allis, WI 53219
414-328-9866; FAX: 414-328-1906

artwork

See full listing in **Section One** under **Corvette**

Classic Transportation
3667 Mahoning Ave
Youngstown, OH 44515
216-793-3026; FAX: 216-793-9729

automobilia

See full listing in **Section Two** under **automobilia**

Dash Graining by Mel Erikson
31 Meadow Rd
Kings Park, NY 11754
PH/FAX: 516-544-1102 days
360-7789 nights

dashboard
restoration

See full listing in **Section Two** under **woodgraining**

Chris Davis
3 Lower Howsell Rd
Malvern Link
Worcestershire, WR14 1ED England
01684-560410

bronzes

Foundry, bronze automotive sculptures including Bugatti, Ferrari, Invicta, Jaguar, Porsche and MG. See them at the Christopher Bell Collection, 200 Alvarado St, Monterey, California. Commissioned trophies a specialty.

Digital Design Inc
PO Box 139
Merrick, NY 11566

sweatshirts
T-shirts

See full listing in **Section Two** under **apparel**

Dr Cap (Brad Sullivan)
2550 Estero Blvd Ste 12
Ft Myers Beach, FL 33931
941-463-3741

custom license
plates

See full listing in **Section Two** under **license plates**

Driven By Desire
300 N Fraley St
Kane, PA 16735
814-837-7590; FAX: 814-837-0886

automobilia
car dealer
models

See full listing in **Section Two** under **car dealers**

Ferraris.com
52 Payn Ave
Chatham, NY 12037-1427
PH/FAX: 518-392-7234
E-mail: editor@ferraris.com

online guide

See full listing in **Section One** under **Ferrari**

**Gasoline Alley Publications,
a Division of Heritage Art
Editions Inc**
45 Parkview Cres
Strathroy, ON Canada N7G 4B1
888-365-5467, 519-245-5166
FAX: 519-245-5167

artwork

Mail order and open shop by appointment only. Specializing in automotive art, originals and limited edition prints.

Gasoline Classics
PO Box 1761
San Juan Capistrano, CA 92693
714-493-6690

artwork

Mail order only. Has 67 authentically detailed paintings of classic gas stations and cars from the 20s to the 60s by Jack Schmitt NWS. 23 are published as signed and numbered Limited Edition prints, 44 are published as signed prints. 8 page color catalog.

Gaylord Sales
Frank Ranghelli
125 Dugan Ln
Toms River, NJ 08753
908-349-9213; Fax: 908-341-5353

**automobilia
automotive art
mascots**

See full listing in **Section Two** under **radiator emblems & mascots**

Gee Gee Studios Inc
6636 S Apache Dr
Littleton, CO 80120
PH/FAX: 303-794-2788

drawings

Pen and ink and watercolor commission drawings of collector cars, homes, etc, plus numbered edition lithograph prints of over 75 cars and cycles. Catalog $2, refundable with purchase.

Rick Graves Photography
441 East Columbine, Suite H
Santa Ana, CA 92707
714-662-2623; FAX: 714-540-7843

photographic art

See full listing in **Section Two** under **racing**

Marc B Greenwald
c/o 6644 San Fernando Rd
Glendale, CA 91201
818-956-7933; FAX: 818-956-5160

parts

See full listing in **Section One** under **Alfa Romeo**

**Wayne Huffaker
Automobilia Artist**
925 S Mason Rd, Dept 168
Katy, TX 77450
713-579-8516

artwork

Mail order only. Automobilia art, limited edition prints and commission auto art. Specialize in period service station, diner, restaurant scenes highlighting cars and trucks of the 30s through 50s. Also have car-airplane art series.

**Edward L Hunt
Automotive Miniaturist**
1409 Yale Dr
Hollywood, FL 33021
954-966-0366

custom miniatures

Mail order and open shop. Monday-Friday 7-10 pm, Saturday 9-5 pm. Fine scale handbuilt automotive miniatures for collectors. Construction to commission. Classic open wheel and F-1 subjects a specialty.

Image Auto
31690 W 12 Mile #4
Farmington Hills, MI 48334
800-414-2852; FAX: 810-553-0924

**apparel
art work**

See full listing in **Section One** under **Jensen**

David Jones
The Pinstriper
19 Hope Ln
Narragansett, RI 02882
401-783-7701, RI; 407-668-9610, FL

striping

See full listing in **Section Two** under **striping**

Jack Juratovic
819 Absequami Trail
Lake Orion, MI 48362
PH/FAX: 810-814-0627

artwork

Mail order only. Automotive fine art, corporate and private commissions. Publish *Automotive Art* magazine. AFASQ

Karl's Collectibles
28 Bates St
Lewiston, ME 04240
800-636-0457, 207-784-0098
FAX: 207-786-4576
E-mail: slalemand@aol.com

**banks
collectibles
logo design**

See full listing in **Section Two** under **models & toys**

Dale Klee
25345 Eureka Ave
Wyoming, MN 55092
612-464-2200

fine art prints

Limited edition fine art prints with a rustic old car theme. Color brochures available. Prices range from $45 to $75 per print.

LA Ltd Design Graphics 822A S McDuffie St Anderson, SC 29624 PH/FAX: 864-231-7715	artwork design greeting cards

See full listing in **Section Two** under **automobilia**

David Lawrence Gallery PO Box 3702 Beverly Hills, CA 90212 310-278-0882; FAX: 310-278-0883	artwork drawings photography

Mail order and open shop by appointment only. Posters, photography, paintings, drawings and trophies. Mostly dealing in racing.

Legendary Motorcars 1 Wayside Village #350 Marmora, NJ 08223 800-926-3950; FAX: 609-399-2512	model cars

See full listing in **Section Two** under **models & toys**

Lost Highway Art Co PO Box 164 Bedford Hills, NY 10507-0164 914-234-6016	decals

See full listing in **Section Two** under **decals**

Max Neon Design Group 19807 Sussex Dr St Clair Shores, MI 48081-3257 810-773-5000; FAX: 810-772-6224	custom face logos neon clocks

See full listing in **Section Two** under **automobilia**

Mc Intyre Auctions PO Box 60 E Dixfield, ME 04227 207-562-4443; FAX: 207-562-4576; E-mail: info@classicford.com	auctions automobilia literature petroliana

See full listing in **Section Two** under **auctions & events**

Dan McCrary, Automotive Art Specialties PO Box 18795 Charlotte, NC 28218 704-372-2899; FAX: 704-375-8686	drawings paintings prints

Anyday by appointment. Original water color paintings, drawings and limited edition prints on a wide variety of automotive subjects.

Marc Miller Gallery 3 Railroad Ave East Hampton, NY 11937 516-329-5299; FAX: 516-329-5319	furniture

Mail order and open shop by appointment only. Furniture made from actual automobiles. 1959 Caddy couch, 1959 Caddy fin chair, 1950 DeSoto club chair, also complete auto environments for bars and clubs.

Moonlight Ink 2736 Summerfield Rd Winter Park, FL 32792-5112 407-628-8857; FAX: 407-671-5008	art

See full listing in **Section One** under **Porsche**

Moto Grafex 8603 Aztec NE Albuquerque, NM 87111 800-577-6686	portraits posters prints

Historic racing car art prints and posters. Automotive fine art portraits and accessories. Catalog only.

Motorhead Art & Collectibles 1917 Dumas Cir NE Tacoma, WA 98422 800-859-0164; FAX: 206-924-0788	art prints models

Deals in art prints, originals and sculptures, fine quality car models, collectibles and books.

Motorsports Racing 914 S Santa Fe #101 Vista, CA 92084 619-630-0547; FAX: 619-630-3085	accessories apparel art

See full listing in **Section Two** under **apparel**

Museum of Transportation 15 Newton St Brookline, MA 02146 617-522-6547; FAX: 617-524-0170	museum

See full listing in **Section Six** under **Massachusetts**

Neoclassic Neon 132 N Hanover St Carlisle, PA 17013 717-258-8088; FAX: 717-258-8288	neon logos neon wall art

Mail order and open shop. Monday-Saturday 9-5. Manufacturer of neon art (car & other). Designers and manufacturers of real neon auto wall pictorials, auto and oil company logos, custom neon logos and clocks, custom designs for commercial, home, garage and office applications. Call for tour appointment.

Packard Archives 1876 English St St Paul, MN 55109 612-484-1184; FAX: 612-771-1521	accessories artwork automobilia

See full listing in **Section One** under **Packard**

Paragon Models & Art 1431-B SE 10th St Cape Coral, FL 33990 941-458-0024; FAX: 941-574-4329	artwork models

See full listing in **Section Two** under **models & toys**

Pelham Prints 2819 N 3rd St Clinton, IA 52732-1717 319/242-0280	drawings note cards

Mail order only. Antique or classic autos illustrated for note cards. Also pen and ink and scratchboard drawings of antique and classic autos. Write for free information.

Photo Plaque Design 16508 McKinley St Belton, MO 64012 PH/FAX: 816-331-4073	car show plaques dash plaques

See full listing in **Section Two** under **plaques**

Hugo Prado Limited Edition Corvette Art Prints PO Box 18437 Chicago, IL 60618-0437 PH/FAX: 800-583-7627 E-mail: vetteart@aol.com	fine art prints

See full listing in **Section One** under **Corvette**

Reni Co - Twinks™
PO Box 186
Roselle Park, NJ 07204
PH/FAX: 908-245-1218

glass etching

Auto customizing art. Boat and truck "fancy" lettering. Vinyl lettering. Air brush. Auto portraiture. "Glass etching". Fine engraving: metal, wood, glass, stone, crystal, mirror. Custom design and traditional.

Ridgetop Studio
2433 N Nine Mile Rd
Sanford, MI 48657
517-687-5811

artwork

Mail order and open studio. Monday-Friday 9-6. Take your automobile out of the garage and park it on your wall. Enjoy it year round. Equipped to handle any medium: colored pencils, acrylics, watercolors, markers, gouache, pen and ink. Utmost creativity, specialized in satisfying the customer's request. Write or call for more information.

Frank Riley Automotive Art
PO Box 95
Hawthorne, NJ 07506
800-848-9459

automotive prints

Mail order only. Limited edition automotive prints by award winning artist. Museum quality printing on the best acid-free paper available. A beautiful investment, available framed or unframed. Brochure of all prints available upon request.

Scale Autoworks
Brady Ward
313 Bridge St #4
Manchester, NH 03104-5045
PH/FAX: 603-623-5925 ext 66

models

See full listing in **Section Two** under **models & toys**

Sparling Studios
Box 86B, RR 1
Quarry Rd
New Haven, VT 05472
PH/FAX: 802-453-4114

auto sculpture

Both mail order and open shop. Open daily 6 am-6 pm. Auto sculpture. Call for an appointment.

Top Dead Center Apparel
PO Box 753
18 Main Street
Wells River, VT 05081
802-757-2553; FAX: 802-757-3312
E-mail:
greenmtmonogram@connriver.net

apparel

See full listing in **Section Two** under **apparel**

Transport-Nation Collectibles
24040 Camino Del Avion, Ste A-241
Monarch Beach, CA 92629
800-474-4404, 714-240-5126

artwork
collectibles

Mail order and open shop. Tuesday-Sunday 11 to 7 pm. Specializing in Indy, NASCAR and Grand Prix, all fields of transportation including automotive, aviation, railroads, ships and motorcycle artwork and collectibles. Our artwork is enhanced by various authentic driver autographs and is framed, matted and ready to hang. We specialize in books, videos, autographed artwork, die cast and clothing. Our shop is located in the city of Orange, please call for specific directions

Peter Tytla Artist
PO Box 43
East Lyme, CT 06333-0043
860-739-7105

photographic
collages

Both mail order and open shop. Every day 9 am-9 pm.

Artwork/automotive art. Specializing in humorous photographic collages of rusty cars from the 20s and 30s. It takes 200 to 400 separate original photographs to create 1 image. 39 images available in 4 sizes, starting at $25. Framing (museum quality) approximately 25% below retail. I also specialize in personalization. I can put you, your family, car and dog, etc, in one of the images and it will appear that you are in it (only an additional $20).

Weber's Nostalgia Supermarket
6611 Anglin Dr
Fort Worth, TX 76119
817-534-6611; FAX: 817-534-3316
E-mail: webers@flash.net

collectibles
gas pump supplies
models
novelties & toys

See full listing in **Section Two** under **novelties**

Wheels of Time
PO Box 1218
Studio City, CA 91604
800-Wheels of Time

photography

See full listing in **Section Two** under **photography**

Danny Whitfield, Automotive Artist
11 North Plaza Blvd
Rochester Hills, MI 48307
810-299-3755

artwork

Mail order and open shop. Automotive fine art, auto design, graphic and technical illustrations, auto art commissions.

auctions & events

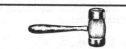

Amherst Antique Auto Show
157 Hollis Rd
Amherst, NH 03031
603-883-0605, NH
FAX: 617-641-0647, MA

swap meets

Antique swap & sell meets. Last Sunday of each month, April thru October (7 shows), open 6 am, since 1960. Largest in New Hampshire. 505 dealers, 150 show car spaces. Free admission, $5 site parking. Good food, beautiful grounds. Come have fun.

The Auction
3600 Blackhawk Plaza Cir
Danville, CA 94506-3600
510-736-0695; FAX: 510-736-7479

auctions

Annual antique and classic car auction of over 400 cars held at the Imperial Palace Hotel in Las Vegas.

"The Auction" Inc
3535 Las Vegas Blvd S, Bldg B
Las Vegas, NV 89109
702-794-3174; FAX: 702-369-7430

auction

Antique and classic car auction and exposition sale, held in Las Vegas, Nevada.

Auctioneer Phil Jacquier Inc
18 Klaus Anderson Rd
Southwick, MA 01077
413-569-6421; FAX: 413-569-6599

auctions

Open shop only. Hours vary. Has been in the auction business for 25 years and can handle auctions of any type. Offers a complete, efficient service and consultation costs you nothing.

Auto Transport Services 5367 Fargo Rd Avoca, MI 48006 810-324-2598	transport

See full listing in **Section Two** under **transport**

Barrett-Jackson Auction Co 5530 E Washington St Phoenix, AZ 85034 602-273-0791; FAX: 602-244-1538 E-mail: info@barrett-jackson.com	auctions

World's greatest classic car auction held annually in January. 1998 dates are 1/15/98 through 1/18/98. Featuring classic, collectible, sports, muscle, 50s & 60s automobiles.

Carlisle Productions 1000 Bryn Mawr Rd Carlisle, PA 17013-1588 717-243-7855; FAX: 717-243-0255 E-mail: cp@cpix.net	auctions car shows flea markets

Carlisle collector car events: Spring, April 17-20; Import, Kit Replicar, May 9-11; All Ford Nationals, June 6-8; All Truck Nationals, June 20-22; Chryslers, July 11-13; Summer, July 25-27; Rod & Custom Classic, August 8-10; Corvettes, August 22-24; Fall, October 2-5; Antiques & Collectibles, Spring Antiques, May 2-3; Autumn Antiques, September 12-13; Firefighters Jamboree & Fair, August 1-3; all events held at Carlisle PA fairgrounds. Contact Carlisle Productions at number listed to receive free events brochure.

See our ad on this page

Central Florida Auto Festival & Toy Expo 1420 N Galloway Rd Lakeland, FL 33810 941-686-8320	auto festival toy expo

Central Florida Auto Festival and Toy Expo, February 8th-9th, 1997, Polk City Fairgrounds, Auburndale Speedway, Auburndale, FL. 1,400 space swap meet, 900 table toy show, 600 show cars. 8 am-4 pm both days. Admission $5, free parking. Call for information.

Rick Cole Auction Co 7447 La Jolla Blvd La Jolla, CA 92037 619-350-0800; FAX: 619-350-0900 E-mail: auction96@gnn.com	auctions

Auction of antique, classic, sports & racing cars. Promoter of the annual Monterey and Newport Beach collector car auctions.

Chicago on Wheels PO Box 586 Cedar Lake, IN 46303 800-30-SHOWS; FAX: 219-374-5962	promotions

Auto shows, cruise nights, swap meets.

Collector Cars & Route 66 Motors Box 50715 Amarillo, TX 79159 806-358-2951; FAX: 806-358-2344	books parts photos restoration

See full listing in **Section One** under **Lincoln**

Coys of Kensington 2-4 Queen's Gate Mews London SW7 5QJ England 0171-584-7444 FAX: 0171-584-2733 E-mail: cars@coys.co.ur	auctions

We are an auction house. We are specialists in fine historic automobiles, values and auctioneers.

George Cross & Sons Inc PO Box 3923 Tustin, CA 92781 714-832-2041; FAX: 714-730-7710 E-mail: gotaswap@aol.com	car show swap meet

Mail order and open shop. Monday-Friday 9 am to 5 pm. George Cross & Sons Inc promotes The West Coast's largest antique auto, Corvette, Porsche, street rod and Volkswagen car show & swap meet, 8 times a year, at Fairplex in Pomona, California.

Cruise Consultants Group PO Box 338 Poynette, WI 53955 608-635-7751	book consultant

See full listing in **Section Two** under **consultants**

Ferraris.com 52 Payn Ave Chatham, NY 12037-1427 PH/FAX: 518-392-7234 E-mail: editor@ferraris.com	online guide

See full listing in **Section One** under **Ferrari**

Peter Ferraro Auto Transporters 186 S Prospect Ave Bergenfield, NJ 07621 800-624-6683; FAX: 201-387-7880	transport

See full listing in **Section Two** under **transport**

Generalists

| **Grapevine Convention & Visitors Bureau**
1 Liberty Park Plaza
Grapevine, TX 76051
800-457-6338; FAX: 817-488-1048 | **car shows**
conventions
meetings |

Grapevine, Texas, is located between Dallas and Fort Worth and offers the ideal location for car shows and car club conventions. The DFW Hilton and Hyatt Regency DFW have extensive experience in providing accommodations for car lovers. Ample parking, rural roads and a secure setting are just a few of the reasons why car clubs love Grapevine. Call for more information and a guide.

| **Hershey in the Spring**
PO Box 234
Annville, PA 17003
717-867-4810, 6-9 pm | **car corral**
car show
flea market |

Automotive flea market, car corral and car show, April 11, 12, 13, 1997. Located in Chocolatetown USA, Hershey, PA (White field). For more information, send SASE to HITS.

| **International Classic Auctions**
1265 S Gilbert Rd
Gilbert, AZ 85296
800-243-1957; FAX: 602-963-1277 | **auctions** |

| **Iowa Gas Swap Meet**
2417 Linda Dr
Urbandale, IA 50322
515-276-2099; 515-251-8811 | **auction**
swap meet |

Founded 1986. 500 members. Largest oil, gas and auto related advertising collectibles show, swap meet and auctions. Held annually in August in Des Moines. Annual publication mailed following each year's event. Registration fee: $18/year.

| **G Potter King Inc**
5 W Taunton Ave
Berlin, NJ 08009
609-768-6900 in NJ; 800-227-3868
FAX: 609-768-1383 | **auction**
show
flea market |

Atlantic City Classic Car Auction/Antique Show/Flea Market every Presidents' Day weekend, presented by G Potter King, Inc.

| **Klassic Kolor Auctions**
PO Box 1185
Venice, CA 90294-1185
818-985-3230; FAX: 818-980-1233 | **auction "color"**
broadcaster
master of
ceremonies |

Mail order only. Michael Ben-Edward is a broadcaster, actor and the voice of *Easyriders Video Tapes* (Gentle Ben). Specializing in auction ring "color" of vintage and classic motorcycles, automobiles and airplanes.

| **Kruse International**
PO Box 190
5540 County Rd 11-A
Auburn, IN 46706
800-968-4444; FAX: 219-925-5467 | **auctions** |

Open daily 8 am to 5 pm. Largest collector car auction company in the world. Also provide appraisals, private treaties. Conducts over 45 collector car events around the country. Call for free color brochure.

| **Lazarus Auto Collection**
PO Box 6732
Rockford, IL 61125
815-229-1258; FAX: 815-229-1238 | **arcade machines**
cars
jukeboxes |

See full listing in **Section Two** under **car dealers**

| **M & S Enterprises**
PO Box 2055
Valparaiso, IN 46384-2055
219-464-9918 | **auction** |

Held in August (2 weeks before Labor Day). Annual Midwest Corvette and Chevy show, swap and auction. Big swap meet, 42 class Chevy show, giant foodfest, beer garden and more. Free brochure, 219-464-9918.

| **Mc Intyre Auctions**
PO Box 60
E Dixfield, ME 04227
207-562-4443; FAX: 207-562-4576
E-mail: info@classicford.com | **auctions**
automobilia
literature
petroliana |

Mail order and open shop. Monday-Friday 9-5, closed Saturday. Established 1-15-1976, specializing in automobilia, toys, literature and petroliana. We host a large auto auction each Memorial Day in Maine. Call for details.

| **Dana Mecum Auctions Inc**
Box 422
Marengo, IL 60152
815-568-8888; FAX: 815-568-6615 | **auctions** |

Mail order and open shop. Monday-Friday 9 am-5 pm, Saturday by appointment.

| **Michigan Antique Festivals**
2156 Rudy Ct
Midland, MI 48642
517-687-9001 | **auto show**
swap meet |

Special interest auto show, sales lot and swap meet. Held at Midland, Michigan, fairgrounds, 1997 dates: May 31-June 1, July 26-27, September 27-28. Michigan Antique Festivals, the 29th year of shows. 1998 dates: May 30-31, July 25-26, September 26-27, the 30th year of shows. Featuring Michigan's largest special interest auto sales lot. For sale (and show) autos register at gate. Swap spaces by advance only. Write or call for information. Monday-Friday 7 pm to 9 pm.

| **Mid-America Auction Services**
2277 W Hwy 36, Ste 214
St Paul, MN 55113
612-633-9655; FAX: 612-633-3212
E-mail: midauction@aol.com | **auctions** |

Classic, collector and special interest automobile auctions. Motorcycle auctions, automobile and motorcycle appraisals. *Motorcycle Price Guide* is an antique, classic and special interest motorcycle price guide, for motorcycles 1905-1985. Includes special section devoted to auction results of 1,000 rare or low production makes and models. Cost: $20/year.

| **Museum of Transportation**
15 Newton St
Brookline, MA 02146
617-522-6547; FAX: 617-524-0170 | **museum** |

See full listing in **Section Six** under **Massachusetts**

| **Niagara CHT Productions Inc**
PO Box 112
Akron, NY 14001
716-542-2585 | **swap meets** |

"Niagara" auto swap meet and car shows, June 28, 29, 1997, Lockport, New York, Niagara County fairgrounds. Also produces other car-related events.

Pate Swap Meet | swap meet
Pate Museum of Transportation
PO Box 711
Fort Worth, TX 76101
817-332-1161

Third largest swap meet in US. Held in April of every year.

Red Baron's Antiques | auctions
6450 Roswell Rd
Atlanta, GA 30328
404-252-3770; FAX: 404-257-0268

Open shop. Monday-Friday 9-6, Saturday 9-4. Red Baron's Antiques is a retail store with exciting auctions thrice yearly. Each auction is no minimum, no reserve, featuring over 50 vintage automobiles, automobilia, as well as over 2,500 lots of important architectural antiques, decorative arts and collectibles, including chandeliers, fine furniture, sculpture, stained glass and much more. For a free color catalog, please call or write.

Riechmann Motorsport Promotions | racing events
38511 Frontier Ave
Palmdale, CA 93550
805-273-7089

See full listing in **Section Two** under **racing**

Garry Roberts & Co | cars
922 Sunset Dr | parts
Costa Mesa, CA 92627 | service
888-FERRAR; FAX: 714-650-2730

See full listing in **Section One** under **Ferrari**

Sotheby's | auctions
34-35 New Bond Street
London W1A 2AA England
44-171-314-4469
FAX: 44-171-408-5958

Regular international auctions of collector's motor vehicles, motorcycles and automobilia are held throughout the year. For advice on buying, selling or valuation please contact Sotheby's car department.

Sotheby's | auction sales
David Patridge
1334 York Ave
New York, NY 10021
212-606-7920; FAX: 212-606-7886

Inquiries: 603-786-2338; FAX: 603-786-2343, NH. International auction sales of vintage, classic, sports and racing automobiles. World auction records achieved for Duesenberg, Packard, Rolls-Royce, Bentley and Ferrari. All inquiries welcome.

Sparrow Auction Company | auction company
59 Wheeler Ave
Milford, CT 06460
PH/FAX: 203-877-1066

Both mail order and open shop by appointment. We are a full service auction company specializing in the auction of anything for and related to automobiles including automobiles, models, parts, literature and salvage. We will travel anywhere or you may consign items to our local auctions. We have experience in the auction of insurance salvage and the auction of salvage yards.

Springfield 97 Swap Meet & Car Show | swap meet
492 W Second St, Ste 204
Xenia, OH 45385
513-376-0111; FAX: 513-372-1171

Monday-Friday 8:30 am-5 pm. Swap meet, car show & cars for sale corral. Held at the Clark County Fairgrounds in Springfield,

OH, Exit 59 off I-70. Spring meet, Memorial Day weekend, May 23, 24, 25. Fall meet, Sept 5, 6, 7. To reserve spaces or for more information on either event call 513-376-0111.

Start/Finish Productions | swap meets
PO Box 2124
Vernon, CT 06066-5124
860-871-6376

Autoparts swap n' sell. 400 vendors, million parts. Antique, special interest, classic parts & accys. 12x15 ft space, Jan 18 & 19, 1997, Eastern States Expo, indoors, Springfield, MA, 30,000 attend.

Webster Auto Swap Meet | auction
6250 Tennessee Ave | car show
New Port Richey, FL 34653 | swap meet
800-438-8559; 813-848-7171
FAX: 813-846-8922

1st Sunday of each month. We have automotive, antique, swap meet, auction, car show, car corral, once a month except for July/August. Also a 3 day show 3rd weekend in February.

Tom Williams Auction Co | auctions
3311-C Lapeer Rd
Auburn Hills, MI 48326
810-373-8555; FAX: 810-373-9299

Our company has been producing car auctions across the country for 19 years. Some of these events have swap meets, car shows and other activities in conjunction with the auction.

J Wood & Co Auctioneers | auctions
PO Box 852
Searsport, ME 04974
207-548-2113; FAX: 207-548-2888

Special events. Office 8-12 weekdays. Vintage motorcycle auctions, antique and classic motorcycle auctions and events. March 8-11, Daytona; July 23, Ohio.

Zephyrhills Festivals and Auction Inc | auction
PO Box 848 | swap meet
Odessa, FL 33556
813-920-7206; FAX: 813-920-8512

Featuring huge automotive and antique swap meet, collector car auction, flywheel engines, antique auto exhibition racing and live music. Swap meet spaces are 10' wide x 30' deep. Held twice a year. Fall show held in November, weekend before Thanksgiving (1997 will be the 13th year) and winter show held weekend after President's Day in February (1997 will be 23rd year). Four day show, Thursday through Sunday. To consign a car, become a bidder or for more information call.

automobilia

Action Marketing | video
17 Verona Cr
Keswick, ON Canada L4P 3N7
800-494-4204; FAX: 905-476-9834

See full listing in **Section Two** under **videos**

American Classics Unlimited Inc | automobilia
Frank Groll-Karen Groll | models and toys
PO Box 192 | novelty license
Oak Lawn, IL 60454-0192 | plates
PH/FAX: 708-424-9223 | sales literature

See full listing in **Section Two** under **models & toys**

Generalists

American Memory Prints	artwork
5935 N Belt W	
Belleville, IL 62223	
618-235-4788; FAX: 618-235-4899	

See full listing in **Section Two** under **artwork**

Amherst Antique Auto Show	swap meets
157 Hollis Rd	
Amherst, NH 03031	
603-883-0605, NH	
FAX: 617-641-0647, MA	

See full listing in **Section Two** under **auctions & events**

Antiques Warehouse	automobilia
Michael J Welch	bikes
3700 Rt 6	toy trucks
Eastham, MA 02642	
508-255-1437	

See full listing in **Section Two** under **models & toys**

Aquarius Antiques	memorabilia
Jim & Nancy Schaut	toys
PO Box 10781	
Glendale, AZ 85318-0781	
602-878-4293;	
E-mail: nschaut@aztec.asu.edu	

Mail order only. Buys and sells antique toys, automobilia and advertising, especially auto and motorcycle racing memorabilia. Publishes a monthly catalog, available for $1.

Auto Art by Paul G McLaughlin	artwork
2720 Tennessee NE	toys
Albuquerque, NM 87110	
505-296-2554	

See full listing in **Section Two** under **artwork**

Auto Etc Neon	signs
PO Box 531992	time pieces
Harlingen, TX 78553	
210-425-7487; FAX: 210-425-3025	

See full listing in **Section One** under **Corvette**

Auto Nostalgia Enr	literature
332 St Joseph S	manuals
Mont St Gregoire, QC	
Canada J0J 1K0	
PH/FAX: 514-346-3644	

See full listing in **Section Two** under **literature dealers**

Auto Zone	books
1895 S Woodward Ave	magazines
Birmingham, MI 48009	models
800-647-7288; FAX: 810-852-4070	videos

See full listing in **Section Two** under **models & toys**

Automobilia	models
Division of Lustron Industries	
18 Windgate Dr	
New City, NY 10956	
PH/FAX: 914-639-6806	

See full listing in **Section Two** under **models & toys**

Automobilia International	automobilia
PO Box 606	
Peapack, NJ 07977	
908-469-9666	

By appointment only. Buying and selling automobilia of all kinds. Especially auto racing. Yearly auctions.

Autoquotes	price guide
2696 Brookmar	
York, PA 17404	
PH/FAX: 717-792-4936	

Mail order only. *Autoquotes* is a guide for annual dealer promotional model cars and features over 1,100 model cars made from 1934 to date. Values are given for three levels of collectible condition. Many photos every issue. $14.95/year.

Autosport Marketing	apparel
PO Box 29033	automobilia
Christ Church 4 NZ New Zealand	
PH/FAX: 00-64-3-3519476	

See full listing in **Section Two** under **apparel**

Be-Bops	Coke machines
1077 S Seguin	gas pumps
New Braunfels, TX 78130	
210-625-6056; 210-657-2135 home	

Mail order and open shop. 10-5 seven days. Second location: 7400 San Pedro, Suite 828, San Antonio, TX 78216, PH: 210-308-5983, 10-9. Gas pumps, Coke machines, jukeboxes, vintage advertising. Buy, sell, trade, restore.

Benkin & Co	gas pumps
14 E Main St	neon clocks
Tipp City, OH 45371	neon signs
513-667-5975; FAX: 513-667-5729	

Mail order and open shop, Monday-Saturday 10-5, Sun 1-5. Visi-Bowl gas pumps, drive-in theater speakers, globes, neon signs, neon clocks, parts, antiques, advertising, etc. Since 1985 over 1,200 pumps sold, over 1,700 drive-in speakers sold. Benkin & Co features 12,000 sq feet selling petroleum, collectibles, as well as general antiques of 40 dealers.

Berliner Classic Motorcars Inc	automobilia
1975 Stirling Rd	car dealer
Dania, FL 33004	motorcycles
954-923-7271; FAX: 954-926-3306	

See full listing in **Section Two** under **car dealers**

Bright Displays	neon signs
1314 Lakemont Dr	
Pittsburgh, PA 15243	
412-279-7037	

Mail order and open shop. Carlisle & Hershey flea markets. Antique auto & dealer's neon signs.

Brislawn/Morataya Castings	automobilia
7904 NE 6th Ave, B-138	castings
Vancouver, WA 98665	
360-699-5838; FAX: 360-576-0085	

See full listing in **Section Two** under **castings**

Brookside Automotive Sales	appraisals
363 E Main St	car dealer
Rt 9, PO Box 312	service
East Brookfield, MA 01515	
508-867-9266, 508-829-5366	
508-885-2017 FAX: 508-867-2875	

See full listing in **Section Two** under **car dealers**

C & N Reproductions Inc	pedal car parts
1341 Ashover Ct	pedal planes
Bloomfield Hills, MI 48455	
810-852-1998; FAX: 810-852-1999	
E-mail: ckcn@1x.netcom.com	

Mail order only. Pedal planes, plans, parts & kits (in steel or wood). Pedal car parts. http://aero.com/c-and-n

CalAutoArt
1520 S Lyon St
Santa Ana, CA 92705
714-835-9512; FAX: 714-835-9513
E-mail:
71460,1146@compuserve.com

**automobilia
photography**

Mail order. Monday-Friday 9 to 6 pm. World's largest supplier of automotive-theme jigsaw puzzles. Offers unique and exclusive line of exotic, collectible, vintage and racing car puzzles of Ferrari, Lamborghini, Jaguar, Mercedes, Porsche, Mustang, Shelby, Corvette and more. Truck, motorcycle and automobilia-theme puzzles also available. Offers museum-grade limited edition puzzle series for collectors. Will produce custom automotive-theme puzzles, posters and calendars on special order basis. Also specializing in automotive photography, both stock and commissioned. Free catalog available.

California Car Cover Co
21125 Superior St
Chatsworth, CA 91311
800-423-5525; FAX: 818-998-2442

**accessories
apparel
car covers
tools**

See full listing in **Section Two** under **car covers**

The Can Corner
PO Box VA 1173
Linwood, PA 19061
610-485-0824

audio tapes

Mail order only. Has been providing old car commercials on audio tape for the past 20 years. Now has 80+ 1 hour tapes (each different). Will research history of old time radio shows with car ads on them. Have list to send free with any order of old commercials upon request. Has over 1,000 different old time commercials from 1932 to 1975 and many modern such as DeSoto, Chrysler, Hudson, Nash, Studebaker, Willys, etc. Also has complete radio shows, prices upon request.

Career Center
1302 9th St
Wheatland, WY 82201
PH/FAX: 307-322-2063

license plates

See full listing in **Section Two** under **license plates**

Carpad Incorporated
400 Main St
PO Box 204
Dayton, NV 89403-0204
702-246-0232; FAX: 702-246-0266

floor protector

See full listing in **Section Two** under **accessories**

CARSoft
RD 1, BOX 3694
Rutland, VT 05701
802-773-3526

**artwork
clip art**

Mail order only. Classic, antique, muscle cars, street rods and old auto ad artwork. Terrific digitized clip art for your computer. Works with programs you probably already have to accent newsletters, notes, greeting cards, T-shirts and other print projects. 17 different sets of auto illustrations, many of which are 100% paint ready and may be easily customized or used to create full color scenes.

Castle Display Case Co
102 W Garfield Ave
New Castle, PA 16105-2544
412-654-6358

models

See full listing in **Section Two** under **models & toys**

**Central Florida Auto Festival &
Toy Expo**
1420 N Galloway Rd
Lakeland, FL 33810
941-686-8320

**auto festival
toy expo**

See full listing in **Section Two** under **auctions & events**

Ceramicar
679 Lapla Rd
Kingston, NY 12401
PH/FAX: 914-338-2199

**auto-related
ceramics**

See full listing in **Section Two** under **novelties**

Michael Chapman
Priorsleigh, Mill Lane
Cleeve Prior,
Worcestershire, WR115JZ England
01789-773897; FAX: 01789-773588

automobilia

Mail order only; shop open by prior appointment only. Specialize in RR/Bentley, Hispano and quality vehicle parts. Finest selection veteran, Edwardian, vintage lamps, horns, emblems, instruments, books, badges, tools, mascots, etc, all makes, 1890-1960. The finest selection in Europe. No inquiry is too large or too small.

"Check The Oil!" Magazine
PO Box 937
Powell, OH 43065-0937
614-848-5038; FAX: 614-436-4760

magazine

See full listing in **Section Two** under **petroliana**

Chewning's Auto Literature
2011 Elm Tree Terr
Buford, GA 30518
770-945-9795

**literature
manuals**

See full listing in **Section Two** under **literature dealers**

Class Glass and Performance Inc
101 Winston St
Cumberland, MD 21502
800-774-3456; FAX: 301-777-7044

**fiberglass bodies
parts**

See full listing in **Section Two** under **fiberglass parts**

Classic Auto Literature
Box 53 Blueback, RR 2
Nanoose Bay, BC Canada V0R 2R0
250-468-9522

**data books
literature
manuals
models/parts catalog**

See full listing in **Section Two** under **literature dealers**

Classic Mercury Parts
1393 Shippee Ln
Ojai, CA 93023
PH/FAX: 805-646-3345

parts

See full listing in **Section One** under **Mercury**

Classic Profiles Inc
5770 W Kinnickinnic River Pkwy
West Allis, WI 53219
414-328-9866; FAX: 414-328-1906

artwork

See full listing in **Section One** under **Corvette**

Classic Transportation	**automobilia**
3667 Mahoning Ave	
Youngstown, OH 44515	
216-793-3026; FAX: 216-793-9729	

Classic Transportation deals in automobilia and nostalgia including pedal car parts, gas pump restoration items, neon clocks, 50s clothing, repro signs and automotive art prints.

Classical Gas Antique Auto Museum & Sales	**car dealer**
245 E Collins	**museum**
Eaton, CO 80615	
800-453-7955, 970-454-1373	
FAX: 970-454-1368	

See full listing in **Section Two** under **car dealers**

Coker Tire	**tires**
1317 Chestnut St	
Chattanooga, TN 37402	
800-251-6336 toll-free	
423-265-6368, local & international	
FAX: 423-756-5607	

See full listing in **Section Two** under **tires**

Crazy About Cars	**art**
2727 Fairfield Commons, E137	**models**
Box 32095	**nostalgia**
Beavercreek, OH 45431	
937-320-0969; FAX: 937-320-0970	
E-mail: crazycarz@aol.com	

Mail order and open shop. Mon-Sat 10 am-9 pm, Sunday 12-6. I deal in the following: nostalgia, art, models, racing, muscle cars, clothing, books, videos. We have hard to find die cast and models of state and city police cars as well as fire dept apparatus. Web site: http://www.wspin.com/~crazy

Creative Products	**mailbox**
PO Box 27	
400 Seeley Ave	
Dunnell, MN 56127	
507-695-2301; FAX: 507-695-2302	

Mail order only. Fiberglass mailbox of a 30s style coupe car and 30s style coupe pickup.

Cruising International Inc	**automobilia**
1000 N Beach St	**decals**
Daytona Beach, FL 32117	**license plates**
800-676-8961, 904-254-8753	**novelties**
FAX: 904-255-2460	**porcelain signs**

See full listing in **Section Two** under **accessories**

Buzz De Clerck	**parts**
41760 Utica Rd	
Sterling Heights, MI 48313	
810-731-0765	

See full listing in **Section One** under **Lincoln**

DeLorean Literature	**collectibles**
3116 Welsh Rd	**literature**
Philadelphia, PA 19136-1810	
215-338-6142	

See full listing in **Section One** under **DeLorean**

Digital Design Inc	**sweatshirts**
PO Box 139	**T-shirts**
Merrick, NY 11566	

See full listing in **Section Two** under **apparel**

Driven By Desire	**automobilia**
300 N Fraley St	**car dealer**
Kane, PA 16735	**models**
814-837-7590; FAX: 814-837-0886	

See full listing in **Section Two** under **car dealers**

Eastwood Automobilia	**collectibles**
580 Lancaster Ave	**transportation**
Box 3014	
Malvern, PA 19355	
800-345-1178, M-F 8 am to 12 midnight, Saturday & Sunday 9 am to 5 pm EST; FAX: 610-644-0560	

Free transportation collectables catalog. You'll discover an interesting assortment of exclusive limited edition scale models, along with hard-to-find nostalgic items from many different areas of transportation history, cars & planes, tractors & trains. 30 day money back guarantee on all Eastwood products. Catalog free. web site: http://www.eastwoodco.com

The Eastwood Company-Tools	**paints**
580 Lancaster Ave	**plating & polishing**
Box 3014	**restoration aids**
Malvern, PA 19355	**rustproofing**
800-345-1178, M-F 8 am to 12 midnight, Saturday & Sunday 9 am to 5 pm EST; FAX: 610-644-0560	**stripping tools**
	sandblasters
	welders

See full listing in **Section Two** under **tools**

Eberhardt Service	**parts**
17710 Valley View Ave	
Cleveland, OH 44135-1126	

See full listing in **Section One** under **MG**

Eclectic Amusement Corporation	**juke boxes**
10 Smithfield St	**video games**
Pittsburgh, PA 15222	
412-434-0111; FAX: 412-434-0606	

See full listing in **Section Two** under **novelties**

Edward Tilley Automotive Collectibles	**automobilia**
PO Box 4233	**literature**
Cary, NC 27519-4233	**parts**
919-460-8262	
E-mail: edandsusan@aol.com	

Mail order only. Buys and sells automobiles, parts, books and literature, automobilia and vintage racing collectibles. All marques, USA and foreign, 1900-1993.

Ellingson Car Museum	**museum**
20950 Rogers Dr	
Rogers, MN 55374	
612-428-7337; FAX: 612-428-4370	

See full listing in **Section Six** under **Minnesota**

Enthusiast's Specialties	**automobilia**
350 Old Connecticut Path	**tools**
Framingham, MA 01701	
508-620-1942; FAX: 508-872-4914	

Mail order only. Import fine English hampers (picnic baskets). Also supply tire valve, logo caps, grille badges and "country of origin" magnetic plates. Specializing in European marques, European manufacturer inquiries invited. Also tool boxes & wall mounted air & water recoil hose reels.

Gaylord Sales
Frank Ranghelli
125 Dugan Ln
Toms River, NJ
908-349-9213;FAX: 908-341-5353

**automobilia
automotive art
mascots**

See full listing in **Section Two** under **radiator emblems & mascots**

Jim Estrup The Plateman
Box 908
RR 3
Kennebunk, ME 04043
207-985-4800; FAX: 207-985-TAGS

license plates

See full listing in **Section Two** under **license plates**

Eurosport Daytona Inc
32 Oceanshore Blvd
Ormond Beach, FL 32176
800-874-8044; 904-672-7199
FAX: 904-673-0821

license plates

See full listing in **Section Two** under **license plates**

EWA & Miniature Cars USA Inc
369 Springfield Ave
Box 188
Berkeley Heights, NJ 07922
908-665-7811; FAX: 908-665-7814

**books
models
subscriptions
videos**

See full listing in **Section Two** under **models & toys**

Executive Boys Toys
200 S Jackson St
Lima, OH 45804
419-227-9300

car dealer

See full listing in **Section Two** under **car dealers**

Frank Riley Automotive Art
PO Box 95
Hawthorne, NJ 07506
800-848-9459

automotive prints

See full listing in **Section Two** under **artwork**

Frontier Tank Center Inc
3800 Congress Pkwy
Richfield, OH 44286
216-659-3888; FAX: 216-659-9410

**automobilia
globes
pumps
signs**

See full listing in **Section Two** under **petroliana**

Galaxie Ltd
Box 655
Butler, WI 53007
414-790-0390; FAX: 414-783-7710

**kits
model trailers**

See full listing in **Section Two** under **models & toys**

GearBox Grannie's
492 W Second St, Ste 204
Xenia, OH 45385
513-372-1541; FAX: 513-372-1171

**collectibles
metal banks
tools**

See full listing in **Section Two** under **tools**

Georgia Marketing
PO Box 570
Winder, GA 30680
770-868-1042; FAX: 770-867-0786;
E-mail: peachgmp@mindsering.com

die cast replicas

See full listing in **Section Two** under **models & toys**

Get It On Paper
Gary Weickart, President
185 Maple St
Islip, NY 11751
516-581-3897

**automobilia
literature
toys**

Mail order and open shop. Every Saturday and Sunday 12 noon to 5 pm. Offers sales brochures, original ads, shop manuals and owner's manuals for your old cars and trucks. Also a nice selection of automotive books and magazines, models, toys, license plates, old advertising signs and the occasional old car. We need to acquire your model kit collection (either built or unbuilt). Call or send your list with prices for an immediate answer.

GF Embossed Notes
11 Caldwell Dr
Amherst, NH 03031
603-880-6217; FAX: 603-882-6590

note cards

Mail order only. Embossed note cards for auto enthusiasts. High quality, ecru stock, 4-1/2"x6" folded blank note cards, envelopes. Also 7-3/4"x16" calenders. Currently carrying MG T-types and 12 Fords, 1909 to 1960.

Jerry Goldsmith Promos
4634 Cleveland Heights
Lakeland, FL 33813
941-644-2437; FAX: 941-644-5013

models

Mail order and open shop. Tues-Sat 10-6. Corvette and Chevrolet promotional models from 1953 to present. Also other automobilia. Same day shipping. Price list available upon request. Visa/MC.

Grandpa's Attic
112 E Washington
Goshen, IN 46526
219-534-2778

toys

See full listing in **Section Two** under **models & toys**

Rick Graves Photography
441 East Columbine, Suite H
Santa Ana, CA 92707
714-662-2623; FAX: 714-540-7843

photographic art

See full listing in **Section Two** under **racing**

Marc B Greenwald
c/o 6644 San Fernando Rd
Glendale, CA 91201
818-956-7933; FAX: 818-956-5160

parts

See full listing in **Section One** under **Alfa Romeo**

Grey Motor Co
4982 Patterson Ave
Perris, CA 92571
909-943-5098; FAX: 909-943-5099

display cabinets

Mail order only. Display cabinets for collectibles, die cast models.

The Gullwing Garage Ltd
Bricklin SVI Specialists
5 Cimorelli Dr
New Windsor, NY 12553-6201
914-561-0019 anytime

**appraisals
literature
parts
service**

See full listing in **Section One** under **Bricklin**

Richard Hamilton
28 E 46th St
Indianapolis, IN 46205
317-283-1902

sales literature

See full listing in **Section Two** under **literature dealers**

Hanover Clocks Inc 5316 Hwy 421 N Wilmington, NC 28401 919-343-0400; FAX: 919-343-0101	**clock maker**

Mail order only. Custom clock maker for clubs, reproducing their logo on a variety of styles, many to choose from. Also, a beautiful custom pendulum clock printed in gold leaf with your favorite car or truck. Hundreds of models to choose from. Great gifts and awards. Free brochure.

Ken Hicks Promotionals 116 Bethea Rd, Suite 306 Fayetteville, GA 30214 770-460-1654; FAX: 770-460-8956	**collectibles** **price guide**

Mail order and open shop. Promotional Corvette collectibles and manufacturing of collectibles. Publication: *Promotional Press Release*, $12/year, price guide and product information on Corvette promotional models.

Historic Video Archives PO Box 189-VA Cedar Knolls, NJ 07927-0189	**videotapes**

Mail order only. The greatest (often the only) source of original TV commercials and promo films on video for antique and classic cars 1935-70. Tremendous selection, choose from over 1,000 titles! Auto racing, vintage TV shows, movies, documentaries, cartoons, newsreels, all kinds of rare footage. Tapes that cannot be found at local video stores, at prices the public can afford. Send $3 for our big illustrated catalog.

Wayne Huffaker, Automobilia Artist 925 S Mason Rd, Dept 168 Katy, TX 77450 713-579-8516	**artwork**

See full listing in **Section Two** under **artwork**

Edward L Hunt, Automotive Miniaturist 1409 Yale Dr Hollywood, FL 33021 954-966-0366	**custom miniatures**

See full listing in **Section Two** under **artwork**

Image Auto 31690 W 12 Mile #4 Farmington Hills, MI 48334 800-414-2852; FAX: 810-553-0924	**apparel** **artwork**

See full listing in **Section One** under **Jensen**

Steve Jelf-14 Box 200 Rt 5 Arkansas City, KS 67005 316-442-1626 after 2 pm CST	**signs**

Mail order and open shop by appointment. Large reproductions of antique auto, oil and other advertising signs, including several available nowhere else. Dozens available. Send SASE for details and free photos.

See our ad on this page

Jesser's Classic Keys 26 West St, Dept HVA Akron, OH 44303-2344 330-376-8181; FAX: 330-384-9129	**automobilia** **keys**

See full listing in **Section Two** under **locks & keys**

Jack Juratovic 819 Absequami Trail Lake Orion, MI 48362 PH/FAX: 810-814-0627	**artwork**

See full listing in **Section Two** under **artwork**

Karl's Collectibles 28 Bates St Lewiston, ME 04240 800-636-0457, 207-784-0098 FAX: 207-786-4576 E-mail: slalemand@aol.com	**banks** **collectibles** **logo design**

See full listing in **Section Two** under **models & toys**

The Klemantaski Collection 65 High Ridge Rd, Suite 219 Stamford, CT 06905 PH/FAX: 203-968-2970 E-mail: klemcoll@aol.com	**books** **photography**

See full listing in **Section Two** under **photography**

Harold Kloss PO Box 37 Humboldt, AZ 86329-0037 602-632-7684	**wood models**

See full listing in **Section Two** under **models & toys**

Kortesis Marketing Ent PO Box 460543 Aurora, CO 80046 303-548-3995; FAX: 303-699-6660	**radar jammers**

See full listing in **Section Two** under **novelties**

David Lawrence Gallery PO Box 3702 Beverly Hills, CA 90212 310-278-0882; FAX: 310-278-0883	**artwork** **drawings** **photography**

See full listing in **Section Two** under **artwork**

l'art et l'automobile
PO Box 1071
Amagansett, NY 11930-1071
516-267-3378; FAX: 516-267-3379

**artwork
memorabilia**

Mail order and open by appointment only. Specializing in automotive paintings, lithos, posters, models, toys, objects, sculpture, new and old books and memorabilia from the beginning of the automotive era to present. A unique place for the automotive enthusiast. Automobilia auction, mail order catalogs. Catalog subscriptions, $20/year.

LA Ltd Design Graphics
822A S McDuffie St
Anderson, SC 29624
PH/FAX: 864-231-7715

**artwork
design
greeting cards**

Christmas and all-occasion greeting cards featuring scenes with 1/43 scale die cast miniature cars & trucks, realistic detail. We also design old car event logos, produce newsletters and flyers, etc.

Legendary Motorcars
1 Wayside Village #350
Marmora, NJ 08223
800-926-3950; FAX: 609-399-2512

model cars

See full listing in **Section Two** under **models & toys**

Dave Lincoln
Box 331
Yorklyn, DE 19736
610-444-4144, PA

license plates

See full listing in **Section Two** under **license plates**

George & Denise Long
915 E Court St
Marion, NC 28752
704-652-9229 (24 hrs w/recorder)

automobilia

Mail order only. Broad range of automobilia, all makes, general to obscure. Emphasis in cars with promotional model cars, also other toy vehicle replicas, tin, rubber, die cast, plastic, ranging from Matchbox to pedal cars and large variety discontinued model kits. Vast assortment with majority old and very little new items. Huge stock of automobile dealership/service station premiums such as porcelain signs, jewelry, banks, key chains, ashtrays, rulers, literature, trinkets, giveaway novelties, etc.

Lost Highway Art Co
PO Box 164
Bedford Hills, NY 10507-0164
914-234-6016

decals

See full listing in **Section Two** under **decals**

Larry Machacek
PO Box 515
Porter, TX 77365
713-429-2505

**decals
license plates**

Mail order and open shop. Monday-Friday 9 to 4. Deals in vinyl decal reproductions of 1951-73 Texas safety inspection stickers ($20 each), plus original Texas license plates (1930-75) at various prices. Also sells reproduction WW II gasoline windshield ration stickers.

Main Attractions
PO Box 4923
Chatsworth, CA 91313
818-709-9855; FAX: 818-998-0906

**posters
videos**

See full listing in **Section Four** under **information sources**

Max Neon Design Group
19807 Sussex Dr
St Clair Shores, MI 48081-3257
810-773-5000; FAX: 810-772-6224

**custom face logos
neon clocks**

Mail order only. Designers, manufacturers, distributors of replica neon clocks depicting automotive, petro, motorcycle, etc, face logos. Custom face logos for individual or corporate clients.

Mc Intyre Auctions
PO Box 60
E Dixfield, ME 04227
207-562-4443; FAX: 207-562-4576
E-mail: info@classicford.com

**auctions
automobilia
literature
petroliana**

See full listing in **Section Two** under **auctions & events**

**Dan McCrary, Automotive Art
Specialties**
PO Box 18795
Charlotte, NC 28218
704-372-2899; FAX: 704-375-8686

**drawings
paintings
prints**

See full listing in **Section Two** under **artwork**

Merely Motoring
153 Danford Ln
Solihull
West Midlands, B91 1QQ England
0121-733-2123
FAX: 0121-745-5256

**automobilia
lapel badges
postcards**

Mail order only. Imaginative and unique range of modern memorabilia and gifts for the classic car enthusiast worldwide. Publishes a series of motoring postcards, greetings cards and writing paper, hand-printed tea towels featuring MG, Triumph, Mini, VW, Jaguar, etc. Design service offered. Select from over 500 designs of lapel badges and key rings. Trade inquiries more than welcome. Free catalog on request.

Mike's Auto Parts
Box 358
Ridgeland, MS 39158
601-856-7214

**bearings
engine parts
NOS parts
windshield wipers**

See full listing in **Section One** under **Chrysler**

Milestone Motorcars
Mark Tyra
12910 Sunnybrook Dr
Prospect, KY 40059
502-228-5945; FAX: 502-228-1856

**die cast cars
models**

Mail order only. Dealing in die cast cars and trucks along with dealer promotional models. We specialize in Corvettes and muscle cars in limited editions.

Marc Miller Gallery
3 Railroad Ave
East Hampton, NY 11937
516-329-5299; FAX: 516-329-5319

furniture

See full listing in **Section Two** under **artwork**

Miltronics Mfg Inc
95 Krif Rd
Keene, NH 03431
603-352-3333, 800-828-9089
order line
FAX: 603-352-4444

detection system

See full listing in **Section Two** under **anti-theft**

Mobilia PO Box 575 Middlebury, VT 05753 802-388-3071; FAX: 802-388-2215 E-mail: mobilia@aol.com	**periodical**

See full listing in **Section Four** under **periodicals**

Moonlight Ink 2736 Summerfield Rd Winter Park, FL 32792-5112 407-628-8857; FAX: 407-671-5008	**art**

See full listing in **Section One** under **Porsche**

Motorhead Art & Collectibles 1917 Dumas Cir NE Tacoma, WA 98422 800-859-0164; FAX: 206-924-0788	**art prints** **models**

See full listing in **Section Two** under **artwork**

Motorsports Racing 914 S Santa Fe #101 Vista, CA 92084 619-630-0547; FAX: 619-630-3085	**accessories** **apparel** **art**

See full listing in **Section Two** under **apparel**

Museum of Transportation 15 Newton St Brookline, MA 02146 617-522-6547; FAX: 617-524-0170	**museum**

See full listing in **Section Six** under **Massachusetts**

NEO Inc 631 Harrison St Defiance, OH 43512 419-784-1728; FAX: 419-782-9459	**clocks** **signs**

Reproduction metal car signs, automobile neon clocks, collectibles. Reproduction Coca-Cola, Pepsi & nostalgia products. Overseas shipments & USA.

Neoclassic Neon 132 N Hanover St Carlisle, PA 17013 717-258-8088; FAX: 717-258-8288	**neon logos** **neon wall art**

See full listing in **Section Two** under **artwork**

NJ Nostalgia Hobby 401 Park Ave Scotch Plains, NJ 07076 908-322-2676; FAX: 908-322-4079	**automobilia**

Both mail order and open shop Wednesday 10-6, Thursday-Friday 12-8, Saturday 10-6, Sunday 1-6. Automobilia: 1960's slot cars, H/O to 1/24, Aurora model motoring specialist, 1/18 die cast cars.

O'Brien Truckers 5 Perry Hill North Grafton, MA 01536-1532 508-839-3033; FAX: 508-839-9490 E-mail: obrien_dennis@emc.com	**accessories** **belt buckles** **plaques** **valve covers**

See full listing in **Section Two** under **plaques**

Oil Company Collectibles 411 Forest St LaGrange, OH 44050 216-355-6608; FAX: 216-355-4955	**books** **gasoline globes** **signs**

Mail order and open shop. Anytime 8 am-9 pm. Original gasoline globes, signs, etc. I buy and sell original gasoline globes, signs and related collectibles. We carry related books on same subject too.

Olona Imaging PO Box 92214 Albuquerque, NM 87199-2214 800-910-4237 E-mail: olonaimage@aol.com	**mugs** **t-shirts**

See full listing in **Section Two** under **novelties**

Packard Archives 1876 English St St Paul, MN 55109 612-484-1184; FAX: 612-771-1521	**accessories** **artwork** **automobilia**

See full listing in **Section One** under **Packard**

Park Drive Garage Antique Gas Pumps 5734 S 86th Cir Omaha, NE 68127 402-592-1710; FAX: 402-592-1882	**gas pumps**

Past Gas Company 308 Willard St Cocoa, FL 32922 407-636-0449; FAX: 407-636-1006	**automobilia** **gas pumps**

I sell restored gas pumps, Coke machines, neon clocks, etc. We offer a complete gas pump restoration catalog, $1.

People's Choice & Lost in the 50s 28170 Ave Crocker #209 Valencia, CA 91355 800-722-1965, 805-295-1965 FAX: 805-295-1931	**automobilia items** **celebrity items** **50s clothing** **50s memorabilia**

We have the world's largest variety of 50's stuff. Over 700 nostalgia products from bobbin head dogs to shrunken heads, poodle & 50s clothes, Kustom Kemp car stuff, car hop food, Elvis Presley, James Dean, Marilyn Monroe, Betty Boop, Felix the Cat, Coca Cola, Route 66 and much more. Send $2 for product list and flyers,

Peterson Automotive Museum 6060 Wilshire Blvd Los Angeles, CA 90036 213-930-CARS (2277)	**museum**

See full listing in **Section Six** under **California**

Hugo Prado Limited Edition Corvette Art Prints PO Box 18437 Chicago, IL 60618-0437 PH/FAX: 800-583-7627 E-mail: vetteart@aol.com	**fine art prints**

See full listing in **Section One** under **Corvette**

Premier Designs Historic Costume 818 Selby St Findlay, OH 45840 800-427-0907; FAX: 419-427-2239 E-mail: premier@bright.net	**clothing**

See full listing in **Section Two** under **apparel**

Pronyne PO Box 1492 Pawtucket, RI 02862-1492 401-725-1118	**museum**

See full listing in **Section Six** under **Rhode Island**

R-C Craft
PO Box 8220
Sylvania, OH 43560
419-474-6941

speed boat models

See full listing in **Section Two** under **models & toys**

Red Crown Auto Parts
1720 Rupert NE
Grand Rapids, MI 49505
616-361-9887

automobilia
literature
petroliana

See full listing in **Section Two** under **petroliana**

Red Crown Valve Caps
PO Box 5301
Topeka, KS 66605
913-357-5007

automobilia

Red and Gold Crown Valve Caps is a trade mark of Standard Oil Co. Red Crowns was a promotional item, produced in early 1940s thru the Golds from 1957 to 1959, which we have reproduced since 1980. From this same Crown style, we have reproduced eight (8) other colors for today's markets, blue, black, yellow, orange, white, green, lavender and pink. Dealer information available.

The Red House Collectible Toys
5961 Dry Ridge Rd
Cincinnati, OH 45252
PH/FAX: 513-385-5534

toys

See full listing in **Section Two** under **models & toys**

Rite Weld Co
10 Northfield Rd
Wallingford, CT 06492
203-265-5984; FAX: 203-284-5063

castings
engine repair

See full listing in **Section Two** under **automobilia**

Roadside Market
1000 Gordon M Buehrig Pl
Auburn, IN 46706
219-925-9100; FAX: 219-925-4563

automobilia

Mail order and open shop. Monday-Sunday 9-5. Books, models, toys, apparel, videos, publications, gifts, sculptures, etc, etc. General automobilia. Our shop is located at the National Automotive & Truck Museum of the United States (NATMUS).

San Remo Hobby and Toy
93 Beaver Dr
Kings Park, NY 11754-2209
516-724-5722

models
trading cards

See full listing in **Section Two** under **models & toys**

Scale Autoworks
Brady Ward
313 Bridge St #4
Manchester, NH 03104-5045
PH/FAX: 603-623-5925 ext 66

models

See full listing in **Section Two** under **models & toys**

Scale Collectors USA
8353 NW 54th St
Miami, FL 33166
305-592-9920; FAX: 305-592-9421

garage dioramas

Open Monday-Friday, 9-5. Handcrafted car garage dioramas suitable for 1:18 scale models. 3-D picture frames with real 1/2 a car 1:18 scale die cast models mounted onto the frame. Unique real size front end Austin Mini Cooper mounted onto a picture frame ready to be displayed on your wall. Excellent detail. Color catalog available at $5, black and white catalog at $2.

Ron Scobie Enterprises
7676 120th St N
Hugo, MN 55038
612-426-1023

gas pump parts

See full listing in **Section Two** under **petroliana**

Scott Signal Co
8368 W Farm Rd 84
Willard, MO 65781
417-742-5040

stoplights

Mail order and open shop. 7 days, 8 am to 8 pm. Stoplights, walk/don't walk, parking meters, sequencer kits, poles. $3 for 2 page color brochure.

Sea-Tac Specialties
Don Guilbault
6714-247 St Ct E
Graham, WA 98338
206-847-8545; FAX: 206-847-6455

hat pins
key chains

See full listing in **Section Two** under **accessories**

Silver Image Photographics
3102 Vestal Pkwy E
Vestal, NY 13850
607-797-8795

business cards
photo car cards
photofinishing

Mail order and open shop. Monday-Friday 9 to 6. Custom photo color lab. Makes custom photo car cards, color business cards with your car, your name & address, make & year of car. Enlargements and poster prints of your car.

Henri Simar J R
Rue du College, BP 172
B-4800 Verviers Belgium
PH/FAX: 3287335122

books
literature

See full listing in **Section Two** under **literature dealers**

Robert H Snyder
PO Drawer 821
Yonkers, NY 10702
914-476-8500
FAX: 914-476-8573, business hours

literature
parts

See full listing in **Section One** under **Cadillac**

Sparrow Auction Company
59 Wheeler Ave
Milford, CT 06460
PH/FAX: 203-877-1066

auction company

See full listing in **Section Two** under **auctions & events**

TCMB Models & Stuff
8207 Clinton Ave S
Bloomington, MN 55420-2315
612-884-3997; FAX: 612-473-0795

models

See full listing in **Section Two** under **models & toys**

Toy Sense Inc
257 North Amphlett Blvd
San Mateo, CA 94401-1805
415-579-7825; FAX: 415-579-7827
E-mail: toysense@netwizard.net

games
toys

Mail order only. Specializing in toys, games and novelties related to various cars. *Roadtrip*, the game for the miles.

Peter Tytla Artist
PO Box 43
East Lyme, CT 06333-0043
860-739-7105

photographic
collages

See full listing in **Section Two** under **artwork**

Volkswagen Collectors c/o Jerry Jess 3121 E Yucca St Phoenix, AZ 85028-2616 PH/FAX: 602-867-7672	**literature memorabilia toys**

See full listing in **Section One** under **Volkswagen**

Webster Auto Swap Meet 6250 Tennessee Ave New Port Richey, FL 34653 800-438-8559; 813-848-7171 FAX: 813-846-8922	**auction car show swap meet**

See full listing in **Section Two** under **auctions & events**

Michael J Welch 3700 Rt 6, RR 2 Eastham, MA 02642 508-255-1437	**automobilia pedal cars toy trucks**

See full listing in **Section Two** under **models & toys**

Wheels O' Time Museum PO Box 9636 Peoria, IL 61612-9636 309-243-9020	**museum**

See full listing in **Section Six** under **Illinois**

Wheels of Time PO Box 1218 Studio City, CA 91604 800-Wheels of Time	**photography**

See full listing in **Section Two** under **photography**

Kirk F White PO Box 999 New Smyrna Beach, FL 32170 904-427-6660; FAX: 904-427-7801	**models tin toys**

See full listing in **Section Two** under **models & toys**

R L Williams Classic Corvette Parts PO Box 3307 Palmer, PA 18043 610-258-2028; FAX: 610-253-6816	**literature parts**

See full listing in **Section One** under **Corvette**

Peter Woodend (Spares) PO Box 157 Takanini Auckland New Zealand PH/FAX: 64-9-298-3393	**automobilia engine parts gaskets pistons wiring harnesses**

See full listing in **Section One** under **Austin**

Zephyrhills Festivals and Auction Inc PO Box 848 Odessa, FL 33556 813-920-7206; FAX: 813-920-8512	**auction swap meet**

See full listing in **Section Two** under **auctions & events**

babbitting

S R Aldrich Engine Re-Building 352 River Rd Willington, CT 06279 203-429-3111	**engine rebuilding**

See full listing in **Section Two** under **engine rebuilding**

The Babbitt Pot Zigmont G Billus RD 1, E River Rd Fort Edward, NY 12828 518-747-4277	**bearing boring engine rebuilding rebabbitting**

Mail order and open shop. Monday-Friday 9 to 5; Saturday by appointment. Specializing in babbitt work and old engines for 20 years, using the best materials and best effort.

Car Collectables 32 White Birch Rd Madison, CT 06443 PH/FAX: 203-245-7299	**banks Christmas cards note cards**

See full listing in **Section Two** under **artwork**

Custom Friction Company 7366 Hillandale Rd Chesterland, OH 44026 216-729-4258	**babbitting line boring engine rebuilding & modifications**

See full listing in **Section Two** under **engine rebuilding**

Egge Machine Company 11707 Slauson Ave Santa Fe Springs, CA 90670 310-945-3419 in CA 800-866-EGGE FAX: 310-693-1635	**babbitting chassis motor mounts pistons valves wiring harnesses**

See full listing in **Section Two** under **engine parts**

Ezold's Model A Garage | **engine rebuilding**
1120 Southampton Rd | **restorations**
Westfield, MA 01805
413-562-0273

See full listing in **One** under **Section Ford '03-'31**

Harkin Machine Shop | **engine rebuilding**
903 43rd St NE | **rebabbitting**
Watertown, SD 57201
605-886-7880

See full listing in **Section Two** under **engine rebuilding**

Northwestern Auto Supply Inc | **parts**
1101 S Division
Grand Rapids, MI 49507
616-241-1714, 800-704-1078
FAX: 616-241-0924

See full listing in **Section Two** under **engine parts**

Paul's Rod & Bearing Ltd | **babbitting**
PO Box 29098
Parkville, MO 64152-0398
816-587-4747; FAX: 816-587-4312

Mail order and open shop. Monday-Friday, 7 am to 3:30 pm.
Babbitting of rods and main bearings for antique cars.

Precision Babbitt Service | **babbitting**
4681 Lincoln Ave | **engine rebuilding**
Beamsville, ON Canada L0R 1B3
905-563-4364

Mail order and open shop. Open evenings and Saturday.
Complete custom engine rebuilding. Babbitt bearings poured
and machined for any application, using certified tin-base alloy.
Specializes in, but not limited to, Model T, A, B and V8. All work
done in my shop.

Antique Auto Battery Mfg Co | **batteries**
2320 Old Mill Rd | **battery cables**
Hudson, OH 44236
800-426-7580; FAX: 216-425-4642

Batteries & battery cables. We have reproduction batteries to fit
all types of antique & classic cars and the reproduction cables.

Battery Ignition Co Inc | **parts**
91 Meadow St | **rebuilding**
Hartford, CT 06114 | **rebushing**
860-296-4215; FAX: 860-947-3259
E-mail: biscokid@aol.com

See full listing in **Section Two** under **carburetors**

Becker Sales | **battery master**
Rear 519 Wyoming Ave | **switches**
West Pittston, PA 18643
PH/FAX: 717-655-3869

Mail order. Battery, master switches, remote master switches &
sidemount battery masters. Battery master switch top mount,
$8.95; battery master switch sidemount, $11.95; battery master
switch remote, $17.95.

Collectors Auto Supply | **parts**
528 Appian Way
Coquitlam, BC Canada V3J 2A5
PH/FAX: 604-931-7278
E-mail:
jimcarpenter@bc.sympatico.cd

See full listing in **Section Two** under **comprehensive parts**

Deltran Corporation | **battery chargers**
801 US Hwy 92 E
Deland, FL 32724
904-736-7900; FAX: 904-736-9984

Mail order and open shop. Monday-Friday 7 am-5:30 pm.
Specialty battery chargers with the collector car enthusiast in
mind. Specifically, the Super Smart Battery Tender® designed
for batteries that are used infrequently. Temperature, voltage
and amperage controlled for safety and reliability.

See our ad on page 226

New Castle Battery Mfg Co | **batteries**
3601 Wilmington Rd
PO Box 5040
New Castle, PA 16105-0040
800-622-6733; 412-658-5501
FAX: 412-658-5559

Mail order and open shop. Monday-Friday 7:30 am-5 pm,
Saturday 8 am-12 pm. Antique and classic car reproduction batteries for Chevy, Chrysler, Ford and Mustang automobiles and
small pickups.

See our ad on this page

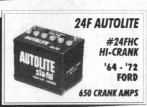

Silver State Restorations Inc, The Aday Collection
4655 Aircenter Cir
Reno, NV 89502
702-826-8886; FAX: 702-826-9191

restoration
service

See full listing in **Section Two** under **restoration shops**

Thunderbolt Traders Inc
6900 N Dixie Dr
Dayton, OH 45414-3297
513-890-3344; FAX: 513-890-9403

battery cables

See full listing in **Section One** under **Edsel**

R L Williams Classic Corvette Parts
PO Box 3307
Palmer, PA 18043
610-258-2028; FAX: 610-253-6816

literature
parts

See full listing in **Section One** under **Corvette**

bearings

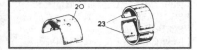

S R Aldrich Engine Re-Building
352 River Rd
Willington, CT 06279
203-429-3111

engine rebuilding

See full listing in **Section Two** under **engine rebuilding**

Allied Bearing Sales
8962 Ellis Ave
Los Angeles, CA 90034
310-837-0752; 800-421-3658
nationwide; FAX: 310-837-0755

bearings
seals

Mail order and open shop. Monday-Friday 8 to 4. Supplies all types of bearings for automotive applications. Ball, cylindrical roller and tapered roller bearings & seals. Many part numbers are for obsolete or classic cars. Foreign & domestic. Many obsolete seals also in stock.

Daytona Turbo Action Camshafts
1109 US #1
PO Box 5094
Ormond Beach, FL 32175
800-505-CAMS, 904-676-7478
FAX: 904-258-1582

camshafts
engine parts

Phone and mail order. Monday-Friday, 9 to 9. Specializing in obsolete engine parts and custom ground camshafts for postwar US cars and trucks. Visa, MC, Discover, AmEx.

Horst's Car Care
3160-1/2 N Woodford St
Decatur, IL 62526
217-876-1112

engine rebuilding

See full listing in **Section One** under **Mercedes-Benz**

National Drivetrain Inc
3125 S Ashland Ave #201
Chicago, IL 60608
800-507-4327; FAX: 312-376-9135

differential parts
transmission parts

See full listing in **Section Two** under **transmissions**

Northwestern Auto Supply Inc
1101 S Division
Grand Rapids, MI 49507
616-241-1714, 800-704-1078
FAX: 616-241-0924

parts

See full listing in **Section Two** under **engine parts**

OlCar Bearing Co
455 Lakes Edge Dr
Oxford, MI 48371
810-969-2628; FAX: 810-628-7879

bearings
seals

Mail order only. Bearings and seals for: axles, clutch, differential, pinion, transmission, steering knuckle and wheels. All years, most model cars and trucks.

Paul's Rod & Bearing Ltd
PO Box 29098
Parkville, MO 64152-0398
816-587-4747; FAX: 816-587-4312

babbitting

See full listing in **Section Two** under **babbitting**

Performance Transmissions
46 Walnut St
Shrewsbury, MA 01545
508-842-0672

restoration
trans parts, sales,
service
trans rebuilding

See full listing in **Section Two** under **transmissions**

Rochester Clutch & Brake Co
35 Niagara St
Rochester, NY 14605
716-232-2579; FAX: 716-232-3279

brakes
clutches

See full listing in **Section Two** under **brakes**

Total Seal Inc
11202 N 24th Ave, Suite 101
Phoenix, AZ 85029
602-678-4977, FAX: 602-678-4991

piston rings

See full listing in **Section Two** under **engine parts**

bicycles

Antiques Warehouse
Michael J Welch
3700 Rt 6
Eastham, MA 02642
508-255-1437

automobilia
bikes
toy trucks

See full listing in **Section Two** under **models & toys**

Coker Tire
1317 Chestnut St
Chattanooga, TN 37402
800-251-6336 toll-free
423-265-6368, local & international
FAX: 423-756-5607

tires

See full listing in **Section Two** under **tires**

Gaylord Sales
Frank Ranghelli
125 Dugan Ln
Toms River, NJ 08753
908-349-9213; Fax: 908-341-5353

automobilia
automotive art
mascots

See full listing in **Section Two** under **radiator emblems & mascots**

Marky D's Bikes & Peddle Goods
7047 Springridge Rd
West Bloomfield, MI 48322
810-737-1657; FAX: 810-398-2581

bicycles
mopeds
motorbikes
peddle goods

Buying and selling old/classic bicycles, mopeds, motorbikes and unusual peddle goods.

Premier Designs Historic Costume
818 Selby St
Findlay, OH 45840
800-427-0907; FAX: 419-427-2239
E-mail: premier@bright.net

clothing

See full listing in **Section Two** under **apparel**

Speed & Sport Chrome Plating Inc
404 Broadway
Houston, TX 77012
713-921-0235

chrome plating

See full listing in **Section Two** under **plating & polishing**

body parts

AAA Thunderbird Sales
35 Balsam Dr
Dix Hills, NY 11746
516-421-4473

parts

See full listing in **Section One** under **Thunderbird**

ADP Parts Services
14800 28th Ave N
Plymouth, MN 55447
800-825-0644; FAX: 612-553-0270

interchange info
manuals

See full listing in **Section Two** under **cars & parts locators**

Agape Auto
2825 Selzer Rd
Evansville, IN 47712
812-423-7332

fender skirts
wheelcovers

See full listing in **Section Two** under **wheels & wheelcovers.**

American Muscle
PO Box 270543
West Hartford, CT 06127
860-953-2575

parts

See full listing in **Section One** under **GMC**

American Performance Products
675 S Industry Rd
Cocoa, FL 32926
407-632-8299; FAX: 407-632-5119

parts

See full listing in **Section One** under **AMC**

Amherst Antique Auto Show
157 Hollis Rd
Amherst, NH 03031
603-883-0605, NH
FAX: 617-641-0647, MA

swap meets

See full listing in **Section Two** under **auctions & events**

Andy's Classic Mustangs
18502 E Sprague
Greenacres, WA 99016
509-924-9824

parts
service

See full listing in **Section One** under **Mustang**

Antique Auto Moldings
55 Paso Nogal Ct
Pleasant Hill, CA 94523
510-671-0862

moldings

Mail order and open shop. Monday-Saturday 8 to 8. Dealing in roof crown molding and drip molding for Fisher Bodied cars from 1926 through 1930. This molding may also fit other makes and years.

Keith Ashley
107 W Railroad St, Unit V
St Johns, MI 48879
517-224-6460; FAX: 517-224-9488

fiberglass parts

See full listing in **Section One** under **Ford '32-'53**

Auto Body Specialties Inc
Rt 66
Middlefield, CT 06455
860-346-4989; FAX: 860-346-4987

accessories
body parts

Mail order and open shop. Monday, Tuesday 9 to 5:30; Wednesday, Friday 9 to 5; Thursday 9 to 8; Saturday 9 to 3. Body parts and accessories, reproduction, original and used for GM, Ford, Chrysler 1950 to present cars, pickups and vans.

B & T Truck Parts
906 E Main St
PO Box 799
Siloam Springs, AR 72761
501-524-5959: FAX: 501-524-5559

pickup parts

See full listing in **Section Two** under **trucks & tractors**

Bay Ridges Classic Chevy
1362 Poprad Ave
Pickering, ON Canada L1W 1L1
905-839-6169; FAX: 905-420-6613

accessories
parts

See full listing in **Section One** under **Chevrolet**

Bill's Speed Shop
13951 Millersburg Rd
Navarre, OH 44662
330-832-9403; FAX: 330-832-2098

body parts

See full listing in **Section One** under **Chevrolet**

Bird Nest
PO Box 14865
Portland, OR 97293
800-232-6378; FAX: 503-234-2473

parts

See full listing in **Section One** under **Thunderbird**

Bob's Brickyard Inc
399 Washington St
Brighton, MI 48116
810-229-5302

parts

See full listing in **Section One** under **Bricklin**

Bob's Bird House
124 Watkin Ave
Chadds Ford, PA 19317
215-358-3420; FAX: 215-558-0729

parts

See full listing in **Section One** under **Thunderbird**

Boulevard Motoring Accessories 7033 Topanga Canyon Blvd Canoga Park, CA 91303-1961 818-883-9696; FAX: 818-883-5530	accessories car covers floor mats

See full listing in **Section One** under **Mercedes-Benz**

Class Glass and Performance Inc 101 Winston St Cumberland, MD 21502 800-774-3456; FAX: 301-777-7044	fiberglass bodies parts

See full listing in **Section Two** under **fiberglass parts**

The Buckle Man Douglas D. Drake 28 Monroe Ave Pittsford, NY 14534 716-381-4604	buckles

See full listing in **Section Two** under **hardware**

Classic Auto 251 SW 5th Ct Pompano Beach, FL 33060 954-786-1687	restoration

See full listing in **Section Two** under **restoration shops**

California Pony Cars 1906 Quaker Ridge Pl Ontario, CA 91761 909-923-2804; FAX: 909-947-8593 E-mail: 105232.3362@compuserv.com	parts

See full listing in **Section One** under **Mustang**

Classic Chevy International PO Box 607188 Orlando, FL 32860-7188 800-456-1956; FAX: 407-299-3341 E-mail: cciworld@aol.com	modified parts repro parts used parts

See full listing in **Section One** under **Chevrolet**

Canadian Mustang 12844 78th Ave Surrey, BC Canada V3W 8E7 604-594-2425; FAX: 604-594-9282	parts

See full listing in **Section One** under **Mustang**

Classic Ford Sales PO Box 60 E Dixfield, ME 04227 207-562-4443; FAX: 207-562-4576; E-mail: info@classicford.com	salvage yard

See full listing in **Section Five** under **Maine**

Cardillo Classic Cadillac 351 W 51st St New York, NY 10019 212-247-1354	accessories top boots

See full listing in **Section One** under **Cadillac**

Classic Sheetmetal Inc 4010 A Hartley St Charlotte, NC 28206 704-596-5186; FAX: 704-596-3895	body panels sheetmetal

See full listing in **Section One** under **Thunderbird**

Caribou Canvas 23151-A3 Alcalde Dr Laguna Hills, CA 92653 714-770-3136; FAX: 714-770-0815 E-mail: cariboulh@aol.com	convertible tops

See full listing in **Section Two** under **tops**

Collector Car Parts PO Box 6732 Rockford, IL 61125 815-229-1236; FAX: 815-229-1238	parts

See full listing in **Section Two** under **comprehensive parts**

Cars II 6747 Warren Sharon Rd Brookfield, OH 44403 330-448-2074; FAX: 330-448-1908	parts

See full listing in **Section One** under **Cadillac/LaSalle**

Custom Classic Cars 2046 E 12B Road Bourbon, IN 46504 219-342-0399 E-mail: asmith7112@aol.com	parts restoration

See full listing in **Section One** under **Chevrolet**

CARS Inc 1964 W 11 Mile Rd Berkley, MI 48072 810-398-7100; 810-398-7078	interior

See full listing in **Section One** under **Chevrolet**

D & R Classic Automotive Inc 30 W 255 Calumet Ave Warrenville, IL 60563 708-393-0009; FAX: 708-393-1397	parts

See full listing in **Section One** under **Chevelle/Camaro**

Jim Carter's Antique Truck Parts 1500 E Alton Independence, MO 64055 816-833-1913; FAX: 816-252-3749	truck parts

See full listing in **Section One** under **Chevrolet**

Dakota Studebaker Parts RR 1, Box 103A Armour, SD 57313 605-724-2527	parts

See full listing in **Section One** under **Studebaker**

Ed Cholakian Enterprises Inc dba All Cadillacs of the Forties 12811 Foothill Blvd Sylmar, CA 91342 818-361-1147; 800-808-1147; FAX: 818-361-9738	museum parts

See full listing in **Section One** under **Cadillac/LaSalle**

Das Bulli Haus 18 Ward Ln North Franklin, CT 06254 PH/FAX: 860-642-7242 E-mail: mcladm3@uconnvm.uconn.edu	parts sheetmetal

See full listing in **Section One** under **Volkswagen**

DeLorean One 20229 Nordhoff St Chatsworth, CA 91311 818-341-1796; FAX: 818-998-6381	body work parts service

See full listing in **Section One** under **DeLorean**

Dependable RV & Auto Service 2619 Rt 11 N Lafayette, NY 13084 315-677-5336	parts restoration service

See full listing in **Section Two** under **service shops**

Desert Valley Auto Parts 22500 N 21st Ave Phoenix, AZ 85027 602-780-8024; FAX: 602-582-9141	cars parts

See full listing in **Section Five** under **Arizona**

Design Fabrications **Pure Products Division** PO Box 40205 Santa Barbara, CA 93140-0205 805-965-6031	parts

See full listing in **Section Two** under **comprehensive parts**

Driving Passion-1959 7132 Chilton Ct Clarksville, MD 21029 PH/FAX: 301-596-9078	bumpers parts parts locating service

See full listing in **Section One** under **Cadillac/LaSalle**

Eckler's Quality Parts & **Accessories for Corvettes** PO Box 5637 Titusville, FL 32783 800-327-4868; FAX: 407-383-2059	accessories parts

See full listing in **Section One** under **Corvette**

Ehrenreich's Corvair Service 1728 Manor Pkwy Sheboygan, WI 53083-2827 414-458-1170	parts

See full listing in **Section One** under **Corvair**

Extensions Plus Inc 3500 Park Central Blvd N Pompano Beach, FL 33064 954-978-3362; FAX: 954-978-0630; E-mail: 4star@gate.net	body filler parts

Mail order and open shop. Cad, Buick, Olds body filler parts.

Fairlane Automotive Specialties 210 E Walker St St. Johns, MI 48879 517-224-6460	fiberglass bodies parts

See full listing in **Section One** under **Ford '32-'53**

For Ramblers Only 2324 SE 34th Ave Portland, OR 97214 503-232-0497 E-mail: ramblermac@aol.com	accessories parts

See full listing in **Section One** under **AMC**

John Giles Cars & Parts (ASV&S) 703 Morgan Ln Pascagoula, MS 39567 PH/FAX: 601-769-8904	car & parts locator exporter

See full listing in **Section Two** under **cars & parts locators**

Hawthorne Appraisals Box 1332 Coaldale, ALB Canada T1M 1N1 403-345-2101	appraisals parts

See full listing in **Section Two** under **appraisals**

Hoffman Automotive Distributor U.S. Hwy #1, Box 818 Hilliard, FL 32046 904-845-4421	parts

Mail order and open shop. Monday-Friday 9 to 5, Saturday 9 to 2. Started business in 1969. We sell NOS and reproduction parts, 1955 thru 1972 Chevy parts and are currently branching out to Mustang parts, 1968 thru 1972.

Holcombe Cadillac Parts 2933 Century Ln Bensalem, PA 19020 215-245-4560; FAX: 215-633-9916	parts

See full listing in **Section One** under **Cadillac/LaSalle**

Hollywood Classic Motorcars Inc 363 Ansin Blvd Hallandale, FL 33009 954-454-4641; FAX: 954-457-3801	cars parts

See full listing in **Section One** under **Thunderbird**

Bruce Horkey Cabinetry Rt 4, Box 188 Windom, MN 56101 507-831-5625; FAX: 507-831-0280	pickup parts

See full listing in **Section Two** under **woodwork**

Bill Horton 5804 Jones Valley Dr Huntsville, AL 35802 205-881-6894	vacuum motors

See full listing in **Section One** under **Mercury**

Howell's Sheetmetal Co PO Box 792 Nederland, TX 77627 409-727-1999	body panels sheetmetal

See full listing in **Section One** under **Ford '03-'31**

Impala Bob's Inc 9006 E Fannin, Dept HVAA12 Mesa, AZ 85207 602-986-0286; FAX: 602-986-3126 order line: 800-209-0678 toll-free FAX: 800-716-6237	parts restoration

See full listing in **Section One** under **Chevrolet**

Imperial Motors 2165 Spencer Creek Rd Campobello, SC 29322 864-895-3474	parts

See full listing in **Section One** under **Chrysler**

Generalists

Jefferis Hot Rod Autobody 4130-C Horizon Ln San Luis Obispo, CA 93401 800-807-1937; FAX: 805-543-4757	windshield glass kit

See full listing in **Section Two** under **glass**

K-F-D Services Inc HC 65, Box 49 Altonah, UT 84002 801-454-3098; FAX: 801-454-3099	parts restoration

See full listing in **Section One** under **Kaiser Frazer**

Klasse 356 Inc 741 N New St Allentown, PA 18102 800-634-7862; FAX: 610-432-8027 E-mail: parts@klasse356.com	cars parts restoration

See full listing in **Section One** under **Porsche**

KopyKatz Auto Body Parts 2536 N Sheridan Denver, CO 80214 303-458-5332; FAX: 303-477-1496	fenders hoods panels

Mail order and open shop. Monday-Friday 8 am-5 pm. Specializing in all new aft/mkt body parts: hoods, fenders, rust repair panels, quarter panels, etc for all makes & models, 1950 to 1997.

L & L Antique Auto Trim 403 Spruce, Box 177 Pierce City, MO 65723 417-476-2871	runningboard moldings

See full listing in **Section Two** under **special services**

Land Cruisers Solutions Inc 20 Thornell Rd Newton, NH 03858 508-462-5656, MA	accessories services

See full listing in **Section One** under **Toyota**

Lister North America Ltd 6565 E 40 Tulsa, OK 74145 918-665-0021; FAX: 918-664-0804	performance parts

See full listing in **Section One** under **Jaguar**

Marcel's Corvette Parts 15100 Lee Rd #101 Humble, TX 77396 713-441-2111 info line; 800-546-2111 order line; FAX: 713-441-2111	parts

See full listing in **Section One** under **Corvette**

David Martin Box 61 Roosevelt, TX 76874 915-446-4439	parts

See full listing in **Section One** under **Chrysler**

McDonald Obsolete Parts Company RR 3, Box 94 Rockport, IN 47635 812-359-4965; FAX: 812-359-5555	body parts chassis parts

See full listing in **Section One** under **Ford '32-'53**

Merv's Classic Chevy Parts 1330 Washington Iowa Falls, IA 50126 515-648-3168	parts

See full listing in **Section One** under **Chevrolet**

Michael's Auto Parts 5875 NW Kaiser Rd Portland, OR 97229 503-690-7750; FAX: 503-690-7735	cars parts salvage yard

See full listing in **Section Five** under **Oregon**

Mill Supply Inc 3241 Superior Ave Cleveland, OH 44114 800-888-5072; FAX: 216-241-0425 E-mail: info@millsupply.com	clips fasteners panels

See full listing in **Section Two** under **sheetmetal**

Motorsport Auto 1139 W Collins Ave Orange, CA 92667 714-639-2620; 800-633-6331 FAX: 714-639-7460	parts

See full listing in **Section One** under **Datsun**

Mustangs & More 2065 Sperry Ave #C Ventura , CA 93003 800-356-6573, 805-642-0887 FAX: 805-642-6468	accessories parts

See full listing in **Section One** under **Mustang**

Northwest Classic Falcons, Inc 1964 NW Pettygrove St Portland, OR 97209 503-241-9454; FAX: 503-241-1964	parts

See full listing in **Section One** under **Ford '54-up**

NOS Only 414 Umbarger Rd, Unit E San Jose, CA 95111 408-227-2353, 408-227-2354 FAX: 408-227-2355	NOS parts

See full listing in **Section Two** under **comprehensive parts**

The Panel Shop Inc 1785 Barnum Ave Stratford, CT 06497 203-377-6208; FAX: 203-386-0486	Body parts for: **Aston Martin** **Bentley/Rolls-Royce** **Ferrari**

See full listing in **Section Two** under **sheetmetal**

The Parts Scout® Bodo Repenn Diagonalstrasse 18A D-20537 Hamburg Germany *49-40-21980130 FAX: *49-40-21980132	parts parts locator

See full listing in **Section Two** under **comprehensive parts**

Paul's Select (Porsche) ® 2280 Gail Dr Riverside, CA 92509 PH/FAX: 909-685-9340	parts

See full listing in **Section One** under **Porsche**

Perfect Panels of America   body panels
1690 Thomas Paine Pkwy
Centerville, OH 45459
513-435-4548

See full listing in **Section One** under **Porsche**

Pony Parts of America   frame rails
1690 Thomas Paine Pkwy   floor boards
Centerville, OH 45459
513-435-4548

See full listing in **Section One** under **Mustang**

Precision Paint & Rust Removers   paint removal
Inc   rust removal
2415 W Industrial Blvd
Long Lake, MN 55356
PH/FAX: 612-476-4545

See full listing in **Section Two** under **rust removal & stripping**

R J & L Automotive Fasteners   fasteners
58 Bristol Ave
Rochester, NY 14617-2702
PH/FAX: 716-467-7421, phone 4-9
M-F, fax 24 hours

See full listing in **Section Two** under **hardware**

Raybuck Autobody Parts   body parts
RD 4, Box 170
Punxsutawney, PA 15767
814-938-5248; FAX: 814-938-4250

Mail order and open shop. Monday thru Friday 8-5. New high quality reproduction body parts for pickups, vans and jeeps.

Regal Roadsters, Ltd   replicars
301 W Beltline Hwy   restoration
Madison, WI 53713
PH/FAX: 608-273-4141

See full listing in **Section One** under **Thunderbird**

Renaissance Restorations   body parts
4588 Payne Dr   mechanical parts
Woodstock, GA 30188   restoration
770-591-9732

See full listing in **Section Two** under **restoration shops**

Replica Plastics   fiberglass parts
210 W Washington St
Box 1147
Dothan, AL 36301
800-873-5871; FAX: 334-792-1175

See full listing in **Section Two** under **fiberglass parts**

Roadster Restoration   parts
3730 Todrob Ln
Placerville, CA 95667
916-644-6777; FAX: 916-644-7252

See full listing in **Section One** under **Datsun**

Rocker King   body parts
804 Chicago Ave   sheetmetal parts
Waukesha, WI 53188-3511
414-549-9583
E-mail: sonoma@execpc.com

See full listing in **Section Two** under **sheetmetal**

S & S Antique Auto   parts
Pine St
Deposit, NY 13754
607-467-2929; FAX: 607-467-2109

See full listing in **Section One** under **Ford '32-'53**

Silverleaf Casting Co   casting
PO Box 662   mascots
116 S Grove St
Delton, MI 49046
616-623-6665

See full listing in **Section Two** under **castings**

Paul Slater Auto Parts   parts
9496 85th St N
Stillwater, MN 55082
612-429-4235

See full listing in **Section One** under **Dodge**

Smith & Jones Distributing   parts
Company Inc
1 Biloxi Square
West Columbia, SC 29170
803-822-8500; FAX: 803-822-8477

See full listing in **Section One** under **Ford '03-'31**

Sports & Classics   parts
PO Box 1787
512 Boston Post Rd, Dept H
Darien, CT 06820-1787

Mail order and open shop. Monday-Friday 9 to 6; Saturday 10 to 2. Fiberglass and steel body panels, wiring harnesses, convertible tops, leather upholstery, exhaust, trimmings, large stock of original factory parts, plus club discounts with proof of membership, etc. Manufactures replacement parts. Dealer inquiries invited. Parts for Austin-Healey, Lotus, MG, Morgan, Jaguar and Triumph. 350 page catalog, $10.

Star Quality   parts
1 Alley Rd
La Grangeville, NY 12540
800-782-7199; FAX: 914-266-5394
E-mail: sq@mhv.net

See full listing in **Section One** under **Mercedes-Benz**

Stilwell's Obsolete Car Parts   body parts
1617 Wedeking Ave   interiors
Evansville, IN 47711   parts
812-425-4794

See full listing in **Section One** under **Mustang**

Tabco Inc   body parts
11655 Chillicothe Rd
Chesterland, OH 44026-1994
216-729-5151; FAX: 216-729-1251

See full listing in **Section Two** under **sheetmetal**

Thompson Hill Metalcraft   metal forming
23 Thompson Hill Rd   panel beating
Berwick, ME 03901   welding
207-698-5756

See full listing in **Section Two** under **sheetmetal**

Bill Thomsen   salvage yard
Rt 4 Box 492
Moneta, VA 24121
540-297-1200

See full listing in **Section Five** under **Virginia**

Tri-Star Pete 1998-1/2 E 1st Tempe, AZ 85281 602-829-7826; FAX: 602-968-6935	**parts**

See full listing in **Section One** under **Mercedes-Benz**

Tug's Wholesale Auto Parts RR 3 Port Hope, ON Canada L1A 3V7 905-885-9191	**parts**

See full listing in **Section Two** under **fuel system parts**

John Ulrich 450 Silver Ave San Francisco, CA 94112 510-223-9587 days	**parts**

See full listing in **Section One** under **Packard**

Tom Vagnini 58 Anthony Rd RR 3 Pittsfield, MA 01201 413-698-2526	**used parts**

See full listing in **Section One** under **Packard**

Vintage Car Corral 1401 NW 53rd Ave PO Box 384 Gainesville, FL 32602 PH/FAX: 904-376-4513	**parts** **toys**

See full listing in **Section Two** under **comprehensive parts**

Wale's Antique Chevy Truck Parts 143 Center Carleton, MI 48117 313-654-8836	**parts**

See full listing in **Section One** under **Chevrolet**

Wallace Walmsley 4732 Bancroft St, #7 San Diego, CA 92116 619-283-3063	**parts**

See full listing in **Section One** under **Packard**

West Coast Sheetmetal Lawrence M Camuso 219 S 20th St San Jose, CA 95116 408-286-6537	**body parts**

Mail order only. Rust-free body parts for all late fifties to eighties American cars. Parts for all different body styles including doors, fenders, quarter panels, trunk lids, hoods, fuel tanks, etc. Specializing in Oldsmobiles.

Zephyrhills Festivals and Auction Inc PO Box 848 Odessa, FL 33556 813-920-7206; FAX: 813-920-8512	**auction** **swap meet**

See full listing in **Section Two** under **auctions & events**

bodywork

Ace Auto Body & Towing Ltd 65 S Service Rd Plainview, NY 11803 516-752-6065; FAX: 516-752-1484	**mechanical repairs** **restorations**

See full listing in **Section Two** under **restoration shops**

Adler's Antique Autos Inc 801 NY Route 43 Stephentown, NY 12168 518-733-5749 days 518-479-4103 nights	**auto preservation** **Chevrolet parts** **repair** **restoration**

See full listing in **Section Two** under **restoration shops**

Antique & Classic Cars Inc 326 S 2nd St Hamilton, OH 45011 513-844-1146 in OH 800-798-3982 nationwide	**bodywork** **machine work** **painting** **parts** **service**

See full listing in **Section One** under **Buick**

Auto Restoration by William R Hahn Palermo Auto Body 241 Church Rd (rear) Wexford, PA 15090 412-935-3790 days, 367-2538 eves	**restoration**

See full listing in **Section Two** under **restoration shops**

Auto Sport Restoration Alain Breton 110 Rue Du Couvent St Romain, QC Canada G0Y 1L0 PH/FAX: 418-486-7861	**restoration**

See full listing in **Section Two** under **restoration shops**

Bassett Classic Restoration 2616 Sharon St, Suite D Kenner, LA 70062 PH/FAX: 504-469-2982 (have auto switching device)	**parts** **plating** **restoration** **service**

See full listing in **Section One** under **Rolls-Royce/Bentley**

Bay Area Industrial Dry Stripping 151 11th St Richmond, CA 94801-3523 510-412-9890, 510-805-1887	**blasting** **paint removal**

See full listing in **Section Two** under **rust removal & stripping**

Beckley Auto Restorations Inc 4405 Capital Ave SW Battle Creek, MI 49015 616-979-3013	**restoration**

See full listing in **Section Two** under **restoration shops**

Berkshire Auto's Time Was Box 347, 10 Front Street Collinsville, CT 06022 860-693-2332	**restoration**

See full listing in **Section Two** under **restoration shops**

Generalists

Bob's Brickyard Inc
399 Washington St
Brighton, MI 48116
810-229-5302

parts

See full listing in **Section One** under **Bricklin**

Carters Auto Restorations
1433 Pawlings Rd
Phoenixville, PA 19460
610-666-5687

restoration

Open shop only. Monday-Friday 8:30 am to 6 pm. Full service restoration shop, 30 years' experience, body & mechanical work, certified welder.

Cedar Creek Coachworks Ltd
151 Conestoga Ln
Stephens City, VA 22655
540-869-0244; FAX: 540-869-9577

restoration
service

See full listing in **Section Two** under **restoration shops**

Classic Motors Unlimited
RD 1 Box 99C
Hooversville, PA 15936
814-479-7874

chemical stripping
metal work
restoration

See full listing in **Section Two** under **restoration shops**

Classic Sheetmetal Inc
4010 A Hartley St
Charlotte, NC 28206
704-596-5186; FAX: 704-596-3895

body panels
sheetmetal

See full listing in **Section One** under **Thunderbird**

Classics Plus LTD
N7306 Lakeshore Dr
N Fond du Lac, WI 54937
414-923-1007

restoration

See full listing in **Section Two** under **steering wheels**

Cobb's Antique Auto Restoration
717 Western Ave
Washington Court House, OH 43160
614-335-7489

restoration
service

See full listing in **Section Two** under **restoration shops**

Commonwealth Automotive Restorations
1725 Hewins St
Ashley Falls, MA 01222
413-229-3196

body rebuilding
parts
restoration

See full listing in **Section Two** under **military vehicles**

County Corvette
171 Eagleview Blvd
Lionville, PA 19353
610-363-0872; FAX: 610-363-5325

restoration
sales
service

See full listing in **Section One** under **Corvette**

Cover-It
17 Wood St
West Haven, CT 06516-3843
203-931-4747; FAX: 203-931-4754

all-weather shelters

See full listing in **Section Two** under **car covers**

Dan's Restorations
PO Box 144
Snake Hill Rd
Sand Lake, NY 12153
518-674-2061

restoration

Both mail order and open shop. Shop open Mon-Fri, most Sats 9-6. Special interest auto restorations. One stop restoration service for the working man's special interest car or 1/2 ton truck. Lifetime experience is applied to each project, one car at a time. Specializing in panel fabrication, hammer welding, gas, arc and mig welding. Woodgraining of dash and window frames, all PPG paints used including epoxy primers. Blocks bored, cyl head rebuilding, bead and sand blasting. Engine, frame, transmission and suspension repairs or swapping. Steel rod projects also welcome.

DeLorean One
20229 Nordhoff St
Chatsworth, CA 91311
818-341-1796; FAX: 818-998-6381

body work
parts
service

See full listing in **Section One** under **DeLorean**

East Coast Chevy Inc
Ol '55 Chevy Parts
4154A Skyron Dr
Doylestown, FL 18938
215-348-5568; FAX: 215-348-0560

parts
restoration

See full listing in **Section One** under **Chevrolet**

Foreign Autotech
3235 C Sunset Ln
Hatboro, PA 19040
215-441-4421; FAX: 215-441-4490

parts

See full listing in **Section One** under **Volvo**

Fuller's Restoration Inc
Old Airport Rd
Manchester Center, VT 05255
802-362-3643; FAX: 802-362-3360

repairs
restoration

See full listing in **Section Two** under **restoration shops**

GMS Restorations
20 Wilbraham St
Palmer, MA 01069
413-283-3800

restoration

See full listing in **Section Two** under **restoration shops**

Grey Hills Auto Restoration
PO Box 630
51 Vail Rd
Blairstown, NJ 07825
908-362-8232; FAX: 908-362-6796

restoration
service

See full listing in **Section Two** under **restoration shops**

Gullwing Service Co, Inc
106 Western Ave
Essex, MA 01929
508-768-6919; FAX: 508-768-3523

car dealer
mechanical service
parts
restoration

See full listing in **Section One** under **Mercedes-Benz**

Hatfield Restorations
PO Box 846
Canton, TX 75103
PH/FAX: 903-567-6742

restoration

See full listing in **Section Two** under **restoration shops**

Hein's Classic Cars 422 Douglas Durham, KS 67438 316-732-3335	restoration

See full listing in **Section One** under **Thunderbird**

Jefferis Hot Rod Autobody 4130-C Horizon Ln San Luis Obispo, CA 93401 800-807-1937; FAX: 805-543-4757	windshield glass kit

See full listing in **Section Two** under **glass**

Keilen's Auto Restoring 580 Kelley Blvd (R) North Attleboro, MA 02760 508-699-7768	restoration

See full listing in **Section Two** under **restoration shops**

Kwik Poly T Distributing Inc 24 St Henry Ct St Charles, MO 63301 314-724-1065	restoration aids

See full listing in **Section Two** under **restoration aids**

L & N Olde Car Co 9992 Kinsman Rd PO Box 378 Newbury, OH 44065 216-564-7204; FAX: 216-564-8187	restoration

See full listing in **Section Two** under **restoration shops**

Libbey's Classic Car Restoration Center 137 N Quinsigamond Ave Shrewsbury, MA 01545 PH/FAX: 508-792-1560	bodywork restoration service

See full listing in **Section Two** under **restoration shop**

Marchant Machine Corporation 11325 Maryland Ave Beltsville, MD 20705 301-937-4481; FAX: 301-937-1019 E-mail: dmarch4481@aol.com	metal forming machines

See full listing in **Section Two** under **sheetmetal**

Mastermind Inc 32155 Joshua Dr Wildomar, CA 92595 PH/FAX: 909-674-0509	parts restoration

See full listing in **Section One** under **Cadillac**

Masterworks Auto Reconditioning 1127 Brush Run Rd Washington, PA 15301 412-267-3460	restoration

See full listing in **Section Two** under **restoration shops**

McAdam Motorcars Ltd 215 Redoubt Rd Yorktown, VA 23692 757-898-7805; FAX: 757-898-9019	restoration

See full listing in **Section Two** under **restoration shops**

McCann Auto Restoration US Rt 1, PO Box 1025 Houlton, ME 04730 207-532-2206	custom work restoration sandblasting

See full listing in **Section Two** under **restoration shops**

Memory Lane Motors Lindsay St S Fenelon Falls, ON Canada K0M 1N0 705-887-CARS	car dealer restoration service

See full listing in **Section Two** under **restoration shops**

Mill Supply Inc 3241 Superior Ave Cleveland, OH 44114 800-888-5072; FAX: 216-241-0425 E-mail: info@millsupply.com	clips fasteners panels

See full listing in **Section Two** under **sheetmetal**

Motorguard Corporation 580 Carnegie St Manteca, CA 95337 209-239-9191; FAX: 209-239-5114	accessories tools

See full listing in **Section Two** under **tools**

Must For Rust Co PO Box 972 Cedar Ridge, CA 95924 888-297-9224 toll-free PH/FAX: 916-273-3576	rust remover

See full listing in **Section Two** under **rust removal & stripping**

Mustang Classics 3814 Walnut St Denver, CO 80205 303-295-3140	parts restoration sales service

See full listing in **Section One** under **Mustang**

New Era Motors 11611 NE 50th Ave, Unit 6 Vancouver, WA 98686 360-573-8788	restoration

See full listing in **Section Two** under **woodwork**

Guy R Palermo Auto Body 241 Church Rd (rear) Wexford, PA 15090 412-935-3790; FAX: 412-935-9121	bodywork restoration

Shop open M-F 8 to 5, some eves and Saturdays. Full or partial restoration, collision and custom work on foreign and domestic automobiles, trucks and motorcycles.

R E Pierce 47 Stone Rd Wendell Depot, MA 01380 508-544-7442; FAX: 508-544-2978	parts restoration

See full listing in **Section One** under **Volvo**

Pilgrim's Special Interest Autos 3888 Hill Rd Lakeport, CA 95453 PH/FAX: 707-262-1062	bodywork metal fabrication paint restoration

See full listing in **Section Two** under **restoration shops**

Pioneer Valley Model A Ford Inc | cars / parts / restoration
81 East St
Easthampton, MA 01027
413-584-8400; FAX: 413-584-7605
E-mail: pvma@aol.com

See full listing in **Section One** under **Ford '03-'31**

Renascence Restoration | body work / restoration
219 Park Ave
Beaver Dam, WI 53219
414-887-8285, 6-9 pm

See full listing in **Section Two** under **restoration shops**

Restorations Unlimited II Inc | restoration
304 Jandus Rd
Cary, IL 60013
847-639-5818

See full listing in **Section Two** under **restoration shops**

Rick's Relics | bodywork / painting / restoration
Wheeler Rd
Pittsburg, NH 03592
603-538-6612

See full listing in **Section Two** under **restoration shops**

RMR Restorations Inc | restoration
13 Columbia Dr, Unit 1
Amherst, NH 03031
PH/FAX: 603-880-6880 work
603-672-8335 home

See full listing in **Section Two** under **restoration shops**

Rocky's Advance Formula | wax hardener
40 Abbott Ave
Danbury, CT 06810
800-752-0245

See full listing in **Section Two** under **car care products**

Rod-1 Shop | street rods
210 Clinton Ave
Pitman, NJ 08071
609-228-7631; FAX: 609-582-5770

See full listing in **Section Two** under **street rods**

Ed Rouze | painting guide book
406 Sheila Blvd
Prattville, AL 36066
334-365-2381

See full listing in **Section Two** under **painting**

T Schmidt | rust removers
827 N Vernon
Dearborn, MI 48128-1542
313-562-7161

See full listing in **Section Two** under **rust removal & stripping**

Silver Star Restorations | parts / restoration
116 Highway 19
Topton, NC 28781
704-321-4268; FAX: 704-321-6008

See full listing in **Section One** under **Mercedes-Benz**

Stone Barn Inc | restoration
202 Rt 46, Box 117
Vienna, NJ 07880
908-637-4444; FAX: 908-637-4290

See full listing in **Section Two** under **restoration shops**

Stripping Technologies Inc | paint removal
2949 E Elvira Rd
Tucson, AZ 85706
800-999-0501; FAX: 520-741-9200
E-mail: sti@stripmaster.com

See full listing in **Section Two** under **rust removal & stripping**

Sunchaser Tools | metal-finishing kit / video
3202 E Foothill Blvd
Pasadena, CA 91107
818-795-1588; FAX: 818-795-6494

See full listing in **Section Two** under **restoration aids**

Techni Decapage | plastic media blasting
203 Rue Joseph-Carrier
Vaudreuil, QC Canada J7V 5V5
514-424-5696; FAX: 514-424-5667

See full listing in **Section Two** under **rust removal & stripping**

Vampire-Island Air Products | air dryers / filters
50 Four Coins Dr
Canonsburg, PA 15317
800-826-7473; FAX: 412-745-9024

See full listing in **Section Two** under **restoration shops**

Westwinds Motor Car Co | restoration
RD 2, Box 777, Cox Rd
Woodstock, VT 05091
802-457-4178; FAX: 802-457-3926

See full listing in **Section Two** under **restoration shops**

Willhoit Auto Restoration | engine rebuilding / restoration
1360 Gladys Ave
Long Beach, CA 90804
310-439-3333; FAX: 310-439-3956

See full listing in **Section One** under **Porsche**

Wilson's Rods and Classics, Gary R Wilson | restoration
Rt 1, Box 139
Holliday, MO 65258
816-327-5583

See full listing in **Section Two** under **restoration shops**

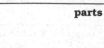

brakes

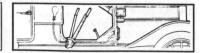

All British Car Parts, Inc
2847 Moores Rd
Baldwin, MD 21013
410-692-9572; FAX: 410-692-5654

parts

See full listing in **Section Two** under **electrical systems**

Allied Power Brake Co
8730 Michigan Ave
Detroit, MI 48210
313-584-8208

brakes

Mail order and open shop. Monday-Friday 8 to 5. Power brake specialists.

Antique Auto Parts Cellar
PO Box 3
6 Chauncy St
S Weymouth, MA 02190
617-335-1579; FAX: 617-335-1925

brake parts
chassis parts
engine parts
fuel pumps/kits
gaskets

See full listing in **Section Two** under **comprehensive parts**

Atlantic Antique Auto Parts
RR #6, PO Box 1388, Site 28
Armdale
Halifax, NS Canada B3L 4P4
902-479-0967

parts
service

See full listing in **Section Two** under **rubber parts**

Authentic Automotive
529 Buttercup Trail
Mesquite, TX 75149
972-289-6373

power brakes
power steering

See full listing in **Section One** under **Chevrolet**

Auto Engineering
3661 Sacramento Dr, Unit D
San Luis Obispo, CA 93401
805-544-1041

parts

See full listing in **Section One** under **Volvo**

Bairs Corvettes
316 Franklin St
Linesville, PA 16424
814-683-4223; FAX: 814-683-5200

parts
service

See full listing in **Section One** under **Corvette**

Bird Nest
PO Box 14865
Portland, OR 97293
800-232-6378; FAX: 503-234-2473

parts

See full listing in **Section One** under **Thunderbird**

Bronx Automotive
501 Tiffany St
Bronx, NY 10474
718-589-2979

parts

See full listing in **Section Two** under **ignition parts**

California Pony Cars
1906 Quaker Ridge Pl
Ontario, CA 91761
909-923-2804; FAX: 909-947-8593
E-mail:
105232.3362@compuserv.com

parts

See full listing in **Section One** under **Mustang**

Canadian Mustang
12844 78th Ave
Surrey, BC Canada V3W 8E7
604-594-2425; FAX: 604-594-9282

parts

See full listing in **Section One** under **Mustang**

Classic Tube
(Division of Classic & Performance
Spec Inc)
80 Rotech Dr
Lancaster, NY 14086
800-882-3711, 716-759-1800
FAX: 716-759-1014

brake lines
choke tubes
fuel lines
transmission lines
vacuum lines

Pre-bent brake, fuel, transmission, choke, vacuum lines manufactured in stainless or OE steel with stainless (an exclusive) or OE steel fittings. All lines are manufactured on CNC state-of-the-art tube benders for 100% accuracy. Applications for domestic or foreign cars and trucks, available from stock or made to your custom specifications. We lead the industry in the most accurate and largest selection of lines. Make your car or truck safer. Call 800-TUBES-1-1.

Collectors Auto Supply
528 Appian Way
Coquitlam, BC Canada V3J 2A5
PH/FAX: 604-931-7278
E-mail:
jimcarpenter@bc.sympatico.cd

parts

See full listing in **Section Two** under **comprehensive parts**

Dr vette
212 7th St SW
New Philadelphia, OH 44663
330-339-3370, 800-878-1022
orders; FAX: 330-339-6640

| | brakes |
| fuel system parts |
| repairs |

See full listing in **Section One** under **Corvettes**

East Spring Obsolete Auto Parts Inc
PO Box 3
Bethlehem, CT 06751
203-266-5488 evenings & weekends

parts

Mail order only. Deals in NOS. Brake boosters & kits (including Treadle-Vac and Hydro-Vac), hydraulics, drums and rotors, engine parts, fuel pumps, shocks, steering & suspension, motor mounts.

Eastern States Performance Outlet Inc
701 Pine Tree Rd
Danville, PA 17821
PH/FAX: 717-672-9413

suspension parts

See full listing in **Section Two** under **suspension parts**

Edwards Brothers Inc
14223 Hawthorn Ct
Fountain Hills, AZ 85268
602-837-9301

brake parts

Mail order only. Specialists in power brakes. Manufacturers of Moraine power brake kits exclusively, a "GM" power unit on early GM. Been in this business since 1963. All American cars 1955 through 1959.

See our ad on page 238

Egge Machine Company
11707 Slauson Ave
Santa Fe Springs, CA 90670
310-945-3419 in CA, 800-866-EGGE
FAX: 310-693-1635

| babbitting |
| chassis |
| motor mounts |
| pistons |
| valves |

See full listing in **Section Two** under **engine parts**

Ehrenreich's Corvair Service
1728 Manor Pkwy
Sheboygan, WI 53083-2827
414-458-1170

parts

See full listing in **Section One** under **Corvair**

George Frechette
14 Cedar Dr
Granby, MA 01033
800-528-5235

| brake cylinder |
| sleeving |

Sleeving of brake cylinders with stainless steel for most makes and models of older cars and motorcycles.

Thos Hespenheide & Associates Ltd
410 Darby Rd
Havertown, PA 19083
610-446-7699, FAX: 610-446-7915

| appraiser |
| rebuilding |

See full listing in **Section Two** under **appraisals**

Holcombe Cadillac Parts
2933 Century Ln
Bensalem, PA 19020
215-245-4560; FAX: 215-633-9916

parts

See full listing in **Section One** under **Cadillac/LaSalle**

Inline Tube
17540 14 Mile Rd
Fraser, MI 48026
810-294-4093; FAX: 810-294-7349
E-mail: inline@apk.net

| brake lines |
| choke tubes |
| fuel lines |
| transmission lines |
| vacuum lines |

Mail order and open shop. Monday-Friday 9 am-6 pm. Manufactures pre-bent brake lines, fuel lines, vacuum and transmission lines for any American auto. All lines are offered in original steel or stainless steel with a choice of OEM color coded or stainless fittings. All line kits come preformed with the correct factory bends and spring protectant or cloth wrap where used on the original. Straight length kits also available. Custom applications welcome.

Kanter Auto Products
76 Monroe St
Boonton, NJ 07005
800-526-1096; 201-334-9575
FAX: 201-334-5423

| car covers |
| carpets |
| parts |

See full listing in **Section Two** under **comprehensive parts**

Last Chance Repair & Restoration
PO Box 362A, Myers Rd
Shaftsbury, VT 05262

| repairs |
| restoration |

See full listing in **Section Two** under **restoration shops**

Glenn Malme
PO Box 1339
Downey, CA 90240
310-869-6491

rebuild kits

Mail order supplier of power brake and heater valve rebuilding kits for the owner/restorer. Deals in Bendix Treadle-Vac rebuild kits and Ranco heater valve rebuild kits for 1948 through 1975 vehicles.

Mike Hershenfeld
3011 Susan Rd
Bellmore, NY 11710
PH/FAX: 516-781-PART (7278)

parts

See full listing in **Section One** under **MoPar**

Muskegon Brake & Dist Co
848 E Broadway
Muskegon, MI 49444
616-733-0874; FAX: 616-733-0635

| brakes |
| springs |
| suspensions |

Mail order and open shop. Monday-Friday 7:30 to 5:30; Saturday 9 to 12. Retail/wholesale service. Brake, suspension and springs for most marques. Specializing in these parts and services for Corvettes. Sleeving of all brake cylinders. Have been in the same location since 1945. Manufactures leaf springs for all makes and models.

No Limit Engineering
1737 Production Circle
Riverside, CA 92509
FAX: 909-275-9232

| brakes |
| chassis parts |

See full listing in **Section Two** under **chassis parts**

Northwestern Auto Supply Inc
1101 S Division
Grand Rapids, MI 49507
616-241-1714, 800-704-1078
FAX: 616-241-0924

parts

See full listing in **Section Two** under **engine parts**

The Plasmeter Corporation | **brake drums**
173 Queen Ave SE
Albany, OR 97321
541-928-3233; FAX: 541-928-0596

See full listing in **Section One** under **Ford '03-'31**

Power Brake Booster Exchange Inc | **brake boosters**
4533 SE Division St
Portland, OR 97206
503-238-8882

Mail order and open shop. Monday-Friday 9-5. Power brake booster rebuilder, 1959-90. Plating available, 1 year warranty. Power brake booster only without master cylinder, call "Booster" Dewey.

Roadster Restoration | **parts**
3730 Todrob Ln
Placerville, CA 95667
916-644-6777; FAX: 916-644-7252

See full listing in **Section One** under **Datsun**

Rochester Clutch & Brake Co | **brakes**
35 Niagara St | **clutches**
Rochester, NY 14605
716-232-2579; FAX: 716-232-3279

Mail order and open shop. Monday-Friday 8:30-5:30. Specializing in clutch & brake remanufacturing, all vehicles & machines.

So Cal Pickups Inc | **parts**
6321 Manchester Blvd
Buena Park, CA 90621
714-994-1400; FAX: 714-994-2584

See full listing in **Section One** under **Ford '54 & up**

Stainless Steel Brakes Corp | **brake accessories**
11470 Main Road | **brake fluid/pads**
Clarence, NY 14031 | **disc brakes/rotors**
800-448-7722, 716-759-8666 | **parking brake kits**
FAX: 716-759-8688, 24 hr | **power steering parts**

Mail order, jobbers and w/ds welcome. Drum to disc brake "bolt-on", front or rear axle conversion kits for Ford, GM muscle cars, SUVs, pickups and Jeeps. New power steering control valves, cylinders and conversion kits for 1963-82 Corvettes. Stainless steel sleeved calipers, master cylinders and accessories for Mustang, Corvette, GM muscle cars, upscale imports, Mopars and AMC. New Corvette caliper housings, master cylinders and rear disc brake calipers with integral parking brakes. Stainless steel sleeves and pistons. Custom caliper rebuilding.

Straight Six Jaguar | **parts**
24321 Hatteras St | **service**
Woodland Hills, CA 91367
PH/FAX: 818-716-1192

See full listing in **Section One** under **Jaguar**

Ed Strain | **magnetos**
6555 44th St #2006 | **power brakes**
Pinellas Park, FL 33781
800-266-1623

Open shop. Monday-Friday 8 to 2. Rebuilder of power brake units for 1953-1960 Bendix, Treadle-Vac and Moraine, piston type only. Buy, sell and rebuild magnetos. We also wind coils.

Studebaker Parts & Locations | **parts**
228 Marquiss Cir | **parts locator**
Clinton, TN 37716
615-457-3002

See full listing in **Section One** under **Studebaker**

J F Sullivan | **brake drums**
14 Clarendon Rd
Auburn, NY 01501
508-792-9500

Mail order and open shop. Monday to Friday 10am to 6pm EST, Saturday by appointment. Brake system parts 1932-1976, wheel cylinders and master cylinders at wholesale. Machine work available with product design service. Consulting of all types along with parts locating service.

Ernie Toth | **brake fluid**
8153 Cloveridge Rd | **literature**
Chagrin Falls, OH 44022 | **parts**
216-338-3565

See full listing in **Section One** under **Stutz**

United German Imports | **brake parts**
4556 Shetland Green | **brakes**
Alexandria, VA 22312
800-98-BRAKE; FAX: 703-916-1610
E-mail: ugibrakes2@aol.com

Mail order only. United German Imports is dedicated to providing the full range of quality German brake components to the European auto enthusiast. You'll love our superb pricing on quality brake products including Ate, Zimmerman, Balo, FAG, Cohline, Pagid, Textar and Jurid. Give UGI the opportunity to meet your Porsche, Mercedes, BMW, VW or Audi brake component's needs, you won't be disappointed. UGI, where you can depend on German quality and exceptional prices.

Wallace Walmsley | **parts**
4732 Bancroft St, #7
San Diego, CA 92116
619-283-3063

See full listing in **Section One** under **Packard**

White Post Restorations | **brakes**
One Old Car Dr, PO Drawer D | **restoration**
White Post, VA 22663
540-837-1140; FAX: 540-837-2368

Brakes sleeved and completely rebuilt. Quick service. Lifetime written warranty. For the ultimate solution to your brake cylinder problems, call us now.

See our ad on page 384

brass cars/parts

Blaak Radiateurenbedryf | **radiators**
Blaaksedyk oost 19
Heinenoord 3274LA Netherlands
31-186-601732
FAX: 31-186-603044

See full listing in **Section Two** under **radiators**

Arthur Burrichter | **appraisals**
24026 Highway 151 | **car dealer**
Monticello, IA 52310
319-465-3064; FAX: 319-465-6048

See full listing in **Section Two** under **car dealers**

Colorado Car Collection Inc
3455 F St, Suite 3
Greeley, CO 80631
970-352-3915; FAX: 970-352-4172

| | car dealer |

See full listing in **Section Two** under **car dealers**

Custom Plating
3030 Alta Ridge Way
Snellville, GA 30278
770-736-1118

| | bumper specialist
chrome plating
parts |

See full listing in **Section Two** under **plating & polishing**

Peter Harper
Stretton House, Northwich Road
Lower Stretton
Nr Warrington, WA4 4PF England
01925 730411; FAX: 01925 730224

| | car dealer |

See full listing in **Section One** under **Rolls-Royce/Bentley**

Lang's Old Car Parts
202 School St
Winchendon, MA 01475
800-TPARTS-1; FAX: 508-297-2126

| | parts |

See full listing in **Section One** under **Ford '03-'31**

Ben McAdam
500 Clover Ln
Wheeling, WV 26003
304-242-3388

| | electrical parts |

See full listing in **Section Two** under **ignition parts**

Skills Unlimited Inc
7172 CR 33
Tiffin, OH 44883
PH/FAX: 419-992-4680
Shop: 419-448-4639

| | radiators |

See full listing in **Section Two** under **radiators**

Zephyrhills Festivals and Auction Inc
PO Box 848
Odessa, FL 33556
813-920-7206; FAX: 813-920-8512

| | auction
swap meet |

See full listing in **Section Two** under **auctions & events**

brokers

A AAuto Brokers Inc
13659 Victory Blvd, Suite #346
Van Nuys, CA 91401
800-770-7784; FAX: 818-904-0023

| | brokers
transport |

See full listing in **Section Two** under **transport**

AM Racing Inc
PO Box 451
Danvers, MA 01923
PH/FAX: 508-774-4613

| | race prep
sales
vintage racing |

See full listing in **Section Two** under **racing**

Associated Foreign Exchange Inc
201 Sansome St
San Francisco, CA 94104
800-752-2124; FAX: 415-391-3553
E-mail: 102172.261@compuserv.com

| | foreign currency
wires/drafts |

See full listing in **Section Two** under **special services**

Auto Consultants & Appraisal Service
Charles J Kozelka
PO Box 111
Macedonia, OH 44056
216-467-0748

| | appraisals |

See full listing in **Section Two** under **appraisals**

Bramhall Classic Autos
149 30th St
Toronto, ONT Canada M8W 3C3
416-255-7201; FAX: 416-255-8446

| | appraisals
brokers
car & parts locator
consultants |

Cars, parts and restorations. Specialists in Rolls-Royce, Bentley, Aston Martin, Jaguar, Ferrari and classic Mercedes-Benz and Porsche.

Cadillac Auto Display
PO Box 6732
Rockford, IL 61125
815-229-1258; FAX: 815-229-1238

| | museum |

See full listing in **Section Six** under **Illinois**

Certified Auto Appraisal
PO Box 17609
Anaheim, CA 92817
714-966-1096; FAX: 714-498-7367

| | appraisals |

See full listing in **Section Two** under **appraisals**

Charles W Clarke Automotive Consultant/Appraiser
17 Saddle Ridge Dr
West Simsbury, CT 06092
203-658-2714

| | appraiser
consultant
car dealer |

See full listing in **Section Two** under **consultants**

Classic Auto Brokers
18812 Monteverde Dr
Springhill, FL 34610
813-856-5168

| | broker |

Brokering only top quality vehicles. Specializes in Mustang, Shelby and Thunderbird.

Cochrane's Special Interest Brokers
Ed Cochrane
718 Livingston Ave
Shreveport, LA 71107
318-226-0458, 318-424-2861

| | appraisers
brokers
consultant
locator |

Mail order only. Will sell anything of special interest to the collector. Will locate special car, part, jukebox or anything collectible. We will do our best to find what you need. Complete services in one place. Also income tax, legal assistance, notary.

Collector Car & Truck Prices
41 N Main St
North Grafton, MA 01536
508-839-6707; FAX: 508-839-6266
E-mail: vmr@ultranet.com

| | price guide |

See full listing in **Section Four** under **periodicals**

Corvette Enterprise Brokerage
The Power Broker
52 Van Houten Ave
Passaic Park, NJ 07055
201-472-7021

> appraiser
> broker
> car locator
> investment planning

See full listing in **Section One** under **Corvette**

Freeman's Garage
19 Freeman St
Norton, MA 02766
508-285-6500

> parts
> restoration
> sales
> service

See full listing in **Section One** under **Ford '03-'31**

Mark Gillett
PO Box 9177
Dallas, TX 75209
PH/FAX: 214-902-9258; 011-525-
559-6240 Mexico City, Mexico
E-mail-autonet@onramp.net

> car locator
> sales

See full listing in **Section Two** under **car dealers**

The Gullwing Garage Ltd
Bricklin SVI Specialists
5 Cimorelli Dr
New Windsor, NY 12553-6201
914-561-0019 anytime

> appraisals
> literature
> parts
> service

See full listing in **Section One** under **Bricklin**

Hall of Fame & Classic Car Musem
DIRT
PO Box 240
1 Speedway Dr
Weedsport, NY 13166
315-834-6667; FAX: 315-834-9734

> museum

See full listing in **Section Six** under **New York**

HK Klassics
Hy Kusnetz
16 Hausmann Ct
Maplewood, NJ 07040
201-761-6642

> appraisals

See full listing in **Section Two** under **appraisals**

Kruse International
PO Box 190
5540 County Rd 11-A
Auburn, IN 46706
800-968-4444; FAX: 219-925-5467

> auction

See full listing in **Section Two** under **auctions & events**

Lazarus Auto Collection
PO Box 6732
Rockford, IL 61125
815-229-1258; FAX: 815-229-1238

> arcade machines
> cars
> jukeboxes

See full listing in **Section Two** under **car dealers**

M & M Automobile Appraisers Inc
4349 WN Peotone Rd
Beecher, IL 60401-9757
708-258-6662, FAX: 708-258-9675

> appraiser
> broker

See full listing in **Section Two** under **appraisals**

Randall Marcus Vintage
Automobiles
706 Hanshaw Rd
Ithaca, NY 14850
607-257-5939; FAX: 607-272-8806

> broker
> car locator
> consultant

Locator of fine vintage automobiles worldwide. Sales of high quality vintage cars also arranged. Consultation provided on

acquisition and liquidation of collections. Pre-purchase inspections and valuation gladly performed. Specializing in all pre-1940 automobiles as well as 1940s-1960s vintage British sports and touring cars.

Bill McCoskey
14200 New Hampshire Ave
Silver Spring, MD 20904
301-384-5856; FAX: 301-989-1866

> appraisals
> repairs

See full listing in **Section Two** under **appraisals**

Memory Lane Motors Inc
1231 Rt 176
Lake Bluff, IL 60044
847-362-4600

> appraisals
> car dealer
> storage

See full listing in **Section Two** under **car dealers**

Charlie Merrill
1041 Kenyon Rd
Twin Falls, ID 83301
208-736-0949

> broker
> car dealer
> car locator

Mail order and open shop, evenings & weekends. Sells good restorable cars and brokerage of cars for others. Also searches for particular cars of all makes.

Charles Noe
64 1/2 Greenwood Ave
Bethel, CT 06801
203-748-4222

> broker
> parts/
> auto purchases
> parts/auto sales

Sell automobiles for owners on commission. Specialize in 1932-33 Chevrolet and Hupmobiles, parts and cars. Listing service for all automobile makes. Always looking for quality cars and car parts. Also pedal car and pedal car parts.

Precious Metal Automotive
Restoration Co Inc
1601 College Ave SE
Grand Rapids, MI 49507
616-243-0220; FAX: 616-243-6646

> broker
> restoration

See full listing in **Section One** under **Mercedes-Benz**

Chris M Zora ASA, ISA
PO Box 9939
Woodlands, TX 77386
713-362-8258

> appraisals
> consultant

See full listing in **Section Two** under **appraisals**

camshafts

Air Flow Research
10490 Ilex Ave
Pacoima, CA 91331
818-890-0616; FAX: 818-890-0490

> cylinder heads

See full listing in **Section One** under **Chevrolet**

Atlas Engine Rebuilding Co Inc
8631 S. Avalon Blvd
Los Angeles, CA 90003
213-778-3497; FAX: 213-778-4556

> engine rebuilding
> machine work

See full listing in **Section Two** under **engine rebuilding**

**Automotive Specialty Accessory
Parts Inc**
PO Box 1907
Carson City, NV 89702
800-693-ASAP(2727)
FAX: 702-888-4545

parts

See full listing in **Section Two** under **tires**

British Parts NW
4105 SE Lafayette Hwy
Dayton, OR 97114
503-864-2001; FAX: 503-864-2081

parts

See full listing in **Section One** under **Triumph**

Cam-Pro
226 S Main
Choteau, MT 59422
406-466-5599

camshaft grinding

Mail order and open shop. Monday-Friday 10 to 3. Camshaft grinding and restoration.

Daytona Turbo Action Camshafts
1109 N US #1
PO Box 5094
Ormond Beach, FL 32175
800-505-CAMS, 904-676-7478
FAX: 904-258-1582

camshafts
engine parts

See full listing in **Section Two** under **bearings**

Egge Machine Company
11707 Slauson Ave
Santa Fe Springs, CA 90670
310-945-3419 in CA, 800-866-EGGE
FAX: 310-693-1635

babbitting
chassis
motor mounts
pistons
valves

See full listing in **Section Two** under **engine parts**

Gromm Racing Heads
666-J Stockton Ave
San Jose, CA 95126
408-287-1301

cylinder heads
racing parts

See full listing in **Section Two** under **racing**

Horst's Car Care
3160-1/2 N Woodford St
Decatur, IL 62526
217-876-1112

engine rebuilding

See full listing in **Section One** under **Mercedes-Benz**

**Performance Automotive
Warehouse**
8966 Mason Ave
Chatsworth, CA 91311
818-998-6000; FAX: 818-407-7204

accessories
engine parts

See full listing in **Section Two** under **engine parts**

**Tatom Custom Engines/Vintage
Vendors**
2718 Riverbend Rd
Mt Vernon, WA 98273
360-424-8314; FAX: 360-424-6717

engine rebuilding
machine shop

See full listing in **Section Two** under **engine rebuilding**

Tri-Star Pete
1998-1/2 E 1st
Tempe, AZ 85281
602-829-7826; FAX: 602-968-6935

parts

See full listing in **Section One** under **Mercedes-Benz**

car & parts locators

A AAuto Brokers Inc
13659 Victory Blvd, Suite #346
Van Nuys, CA 91401
800-770-7784; FAX: 818-904-0023

brokers
transport

See full listing in **Section Two** under **transport**

A-1 Street Rods
631 E Las Vegas St
Colorado Springs, CO 80903
719-632-4920 or 719-577-4588
FAX: 719-634-6577

parts

See full listing in **Section Two** under **street rods**

ADP Parts Services
14800 28th Ave N
Plymouth, MN 55447
800-825-0644; FAX: 612-553-0270

interchange info
manuals

Mail order only. *Hollander Manuals.* Interchange information for domestic vehicles from 1920s-1966 and domestic and foreign vehicles from 1965-1979.

All British Car Parts Inc
2847 Moores Rd
Baldwin, MD 21013
410-692-9572; FAX: 410-692-5654

parts

See full listing in **Section Two** under **electrical systems**

Amherst Antique Auto Show
157 Hollis Rd
Amherst, NH 03031
603-883-0605, NH
FAX: 617-641-0647, MA

swap meets

See full listing in **Section Two** under **auctions & events**

Auto Body Specialties Inc
Rt 66
Middlefield, CT 06455
860-346-4989; FAX: 860-346-4987

accessories
body parts

See full listing in **Section Two** under **body parts**

AVM Automotive Consulting
Box 338
Montvale, NJ 07645-0338
PH: 201-391-5194
FAX: 201-782-0663
E-mail: avmtony@aol.com

appraisals
consultant

See full listing in **Section Two** under **appraisals**

Bramhall Classic Autos
149 30th St
Toronto, ONT Canada M8W 3C3
416-255-7201; FAX: 416-255-8446

appraisals
brokers
car & parts locator
consultants

See full listing in **Section Two** under **brokers**

Cadillac Auto Display
PO Box 6732
Rockford, IL 61125
815-229-1258; FAX: 815-229-1238

museum

See full listing in **Section Six** under **Illinois**

Certified Auto Appraisal PO Box 17609 Anaheim, CA 92817 714-966-1096; FAX: 714-498-7367	**appraisals**

See full listing in **Section Two** under **appraisals**

Chev's of the 40's 2027 B St Washougal, WA 98671 360-835-9799; FAX: 360-835-7988	**parts**

See full listing in **Section One** under **Chevrolet**

Chicago Car Exchange 1 Collector Car Dr Box 530 Lake Bluff, IL 60044 847-680-1950; FAX: 847-680-1961 E-mail: oldtoys@wwa.com	**appraiser** **car dealer** **car locator** **financing** **storage**

See full listing in **Section Two** under **car dealers**

Classic Car Research 29508 Southfield Rd Southfield, MI 48076 810-557-2880; FAX: 810-557-3511	**appraisals** **car locating** **consultant**

See full listing in **Section Two** under **appraisals**

Cochrane's Special Interest Brokers Ed Cochrane 718 Livingston Ave Shreveport, LA 71107 318-226-0458, 318-424-2861	**appraisers** **brokers** **consultant** **locator**

See full listing in **Section Two** under **brokers**

Coffey's Classic Transmissions 2817 Hollis Ft Worth, TX 76111 817-834-8740; 817-439-1611	**transmissions**

See full listing in **Section Two** under **transmissions**

Collector Car Parts PO Box 6732 Rockford, IL 61125 815-229-1236; FAX: 815-229-1238	**parts**

See full listing in **Section Two** under **comprehensive parts**

Collector Car & Truck Prices 41 N Main St North Grafton, MA 01536 508-839-6707; FAX: 508-839-6266 E-mail: vmr@ultranet.com	**price guide**

See full listing in **Section Four** under **periodicals**

Collector's CARS Inc 150 E St Joseph St Arcadia, CA 91006 818-447-2576; FAX: 818-447-1461	**restoration** **service**

See full listing in **Section Two** under **restoration shops**

Corvette Enterprise Brokerage The Power Broker 52 Van Houten Ave Passaic Park, NJ 07055 201-472-7021	**appraiser** **broker** **consultant** **investment planning**

See full listing in **Section One** under **Corvette**

Buzz De Clerck 41760 Utica Rd Sterling Heights, MI 48313 810-731-0765	**parts**

See full listing in **Section One** under **Lincoln**

DeLorean One 20229 Nordhoff St Chatsworth, CA 91311 818-341-1796; FAX: 818-998-6381	**body work** **parts** **service**

See full listing in **Section One** under **DeLorean**

Robert DeMars Ltd 222 Lakeview Ave, Ste 160-256 West Palm Beach, FL 33401 561-832-0171; FAX: 561-844-1493	**appraisers** **auto historians** **car locator** **research library**

See full listing in **Section Two** under **appraisals**

Desert Valley Auto Parts 22500 N 21st Ave Phoenix, AZ 85027 602-780-8024; FAX: 602-582-9141	**salvage yard**

See full listing in **Section Five** under **Arizona**

Driving Passion-1959 7132 Chilton Ct Clarksville, MD 21029 PH/FAX: 301-596-9078	**bumpers** **parts** **parts locating service**

See full listing in **Section One** under **Cadillac/LaSalle**

Eastern Specialty Automotive Sales & Service Ltd 38 Yankeetown Rd Hammonds Plains, NS Canada B3Z 1K7 902-835-5912; FAX: 902-835-0310	**parts** **service** **transport**

Mail order and open shop. Every day 8 am to 8 pm. Parts and service for special interest cars. Specializing in engine restoration and rebuilding. Parts for all GM cars 1955-80; Mustangs 1964-73, carpet sets and interiors. 1947-80 Chev/GMC trucks. Hi-perf parts and accessories. Rust-free southern cars, trucks and sheetmetal.

Richard H Feibusch 211 Dimmick Ave Venice, CA 90291 310-392-6605; FAX: 310-396-1933	**appraiser**

See full listing in **Section Two** under **appraisals**

John Giles Cars & Parts (ASV&S) 703 Morgan Ln Pascagoula, MS 39567 PH/FAX: 601-769-8904	**car & parts locator** **exporter**

For foreign clients, locate and ship cars, trucks, day vans, limousines. Full spares support for all years, makes and models of American vehicles. Export only. Worldwide references.

Mark Gillett PO Box 9177 Dallas, TX 75209 PH/FAX: 214-902-9258 011-525-559-6240 Mexico City, Mexico; E-mail: autonet@onramp.net	**car locator** **sales**

See full listing in **Section Two** under **car dealers**

Glass Search/LOF 1975 Galaxie Ave Columbus, OH 43207 800-848-1351; FAX: 614-443-0709	**glass parts**

See full listing in **Section Two** under **glass**

Generalists

GMC Solutions
Robert English
PO Box 675
Franklin, MA 02038-0675
508-520-3900; FAX: 508-520-7861
E-mail: oldcarkook@aol.com

literature
parts

See full listing in **Section One** under **GMC**

The Gullwing Garage Ltd
Bricklin SVI Specialists
5 Cimorelli Dr
New Windsor, NY 12553-6201
914-561-0019 anytime

appraisals
literature
parts
service

See full listing in **Section One** under **Bricklin**

Happy Daze Classic Cars
257 Morris Ct
Fond du Lac, WI 54935
414-922-8450

car dealer

See full listing in **Section Two** under **car dealers**

Howe & Associates Appraisal Services
54 Marmora St
St Catharines, ONT Canada L2P 3C3
905-685-6473

appraiser

See full listing in **Section Two** under **appraisals**

Jim's T-Bird Parts & Service
710 Barney Ave
Winston-Salem, NC 27107
910-784-9363

parts
restoration
service

See full listing in **Section One** under **Thunderbird**

K-F-D Services Inc
HC 65, Box 49
Altonah, UT 84002
801-454-3098; FAX: 801-454-3099

parts
restoration

See full listing in **Section One** under **Kaiser-Frazer**

Land Yachts Automobile Restoration and Customizing
497 London Bridge Rd, Suite 101
Virginia Beach, VA 23454
757-431-0294; FAX: 757-431-4524

restoration

See full listing in **Section Two** under **restoration shops**

Landry Classic MotorCars
34 Goodhue Ave
Chicopee, MA 01020
413-592-2746; FAX: 413-594-8378

appraiser

See full listing in **Section Two** under **appraisals**

Dave Lincoln
Box 331
Yorklyn, DE 19736
610-444-4144, PA

license plates

See full listing in **Section Two** under **license plates**

Randall Marcus Vintage Automobiles
706 Hanshaw Rd
Ithaca, NY 14850
607-257-5939; FAX: 607-272-8806

broker
car locator
consultant

See full listing in **Section Two** under **brokers**

Memory Lane Motors Inc
1231 Rt 176
Lake Bluff, IL 60044
847-362-4600

appraisals
car dealer
storage

See full listing in **Section Two** under **car dealers**

Charlie Merrill
1041 Kenyon Rd
Twin Falls, ID 83301
208-736-0949

broker
car dealer
car locator

See full listing in **Section Two** under **brokers**

Muck Motor Ford Sales
10 Campbell Blvd
Getzville, NY 14068
800-228-6825; FAX: 716-688-5519

parts

See full listing in **Section One** under **Thunderbird**

National Parts Locator Service
636 East 6th St #81
Ogden, UT 84404-2415
801-392-9455

parts locator

Mail order only. Locates parts, accessories, literature, services, novelties, interior, upholstery, memorabilia for automobiles, trucks and motorcycles, foreign and domestic, from 1895-present. Also looking for an automobile, truck or a motorcycle? National and International Locator Directory. How to buy a used automobile? Auctions? Anything automotive, challenge us.

Old Tin Australia
PO Box 26
Wendouree, Victoria 3355 Australia
0353-36-1929; FAX: 0353-36-2930

salvage yard

See full listing in **Section Five** under **Australia**

Opel Oldtimer Service Denmark
Mosede Kaervej 47
Greve DK-2670 Denmark
+45-42-901073, best 11 am-3 pm
Central US time

literature
parts
parts locators

See full listing in **Section One** under **Opel**

The Parts Scout®
Bodo Repenn
Diagonalstrasse 18A
D-20537 Hamburg Germany
*49-40-21980130
FAX: *49-40-21980132

parts
parts locator

See full listing in **Section Two** under **comprehensive parts**

Paul's Select (Porsche) ®
2280 Gail Dr
Riverside, CA 92509
PH/FAX: 909-685-9340

parts

See full listing in **Section One** under **Porsche**

R E Pierce
47 Stone Rd
Wendell Depot, MA 01380
508-544-7442; FAX: 508-544-2978

parts
restoration

See full listing in **Section One** under **Volvo**

J Pinto
2605 9th St
Long Island City, NY 11102
PH/FAX: 718-626-2403
E-mail: electritech@sprynet.com

windshield wiper
repair

See full listing in **Section Two** under **restoration aids**

John T Poulin Auto Sales/Star Service Center
5th Avenue & 111th St
North Troy, NY 12182
518-235-8610

car dealer
parts
restoration service

See full listing in **Section One** under **Mercedes-Benz**

Precious Metal Automotive Restoration Co Inc
1601 College Ave SE
Grand Rapids, MI 49507
616-243-0220; FAX: 616-243-6646

broker
restoration

See full listing in **Section One** under **Mercedes-Benz**

RARE Corvettes
Joe Calcagno
Box 1080
Soquel, CA 95073
408-475-4442; FAX: 408-475-1115

cars
parts

See full listing in **Section One** under **Corvette**

REA Locating Services
3 Brower Ct
Marlton, NJ 08053
609-596-9235; FAX: 609-985-9870

car locator

Locating cars for export to overseas customers. Service includes locating, inspecting, photographing, purchasing & shipping.

Route 66 Classic Restorations
250 N 1st St
Wilmington, IL 60481
815-476-4290

restoration

See full listing in **Section Two** under **restoration shops**

Southern US Car Export Inc
135 Eulon Loop
Raeford, NC 28376
910-875-7534; FAX: 910-875-7731

repair
restoration
sales
transport

See full listing in **Section One** under **Cadillac/LaSalle**

Special Interest Car Parts
1340 Hartford Ave
Johnston, RI 02919
800-556-7496; FAX: 401-831-7760

parts

See full listing in **Section One** under **Jaguar**

Steve's Antiques & Restorations
Steve Verhoeven
5609 S 4300 W
Hooper, UT 84315
801-776-4835

parts
parts locator
POR-15 distributor

See full listing in **Section One** under **Ford '54-up**

Stone Barn Inc
202 Rt 46, Box 117
Vienna, NJ 07880
908-637-4444; FAX: 908-637-4290

restoration

See full listing in **Section Two** under **restoration shops**

J F Sullivan Co
14 Clarendon Rd
Auburn, MA 01501
508-792-9500

brake parts
consulting
machine work
parts locator

See full listing in **Section Two** under **brakes**

T-Bird Sanctuary
9997 SW Avery
Tualatin, OR 97062
503-692-9848, FAX: 503-692-9849

parts

See full listing in **Section One** under **Thunderbird**

Timeless Masterpieces
221 Freeport Dr
Bloomingdale, IL 60108
630-893-1058 evenings

appraiser
consultant

See full listing in **Section Two** under **appraisals**

US Oldies & Classics
Vunt 3
Holsbeek 3220 Belgium
3216446611; FAX: 3216446520

car dealer
parts

See full listing in **Section Two** under **car dealers**

Visual Marketplace Online Inc
800 Silverado, Suite 324
La Jolla, CA 92037
619-459-3846; FAX: 619-459-3460
E-mail: pyoung@icreations.com

online auto ads

See full listing in **Section Four** under **information sources**

Dale Wilch Sales/RPM Catalog
PO Box 12031
Kansas City, KS 66112
913-788-3219; FAX: 913-788-9682
E-mail: rpmcat@sound.net

speed equipment

See full listing in **Section Two** under **racing**

Johnny Williams Services
2613 Copeland Rd
Tyler, TX 75701
903-597-3687
800-937-0900, voice mail #7225

appraiser
car & parts locator
consultant
lighting systems design

See full listing in **Section Two** under **appraisals**

Chris M Zora ASA, ISA
PO Box 9939
Woodlands, TX 77386
713-362-8258

appraisals
consultant

See full listing in **Section Two** under **appraisals**

car care products

American Autosecurity Equip Co
236 East Star of India Ln
Carson, CA 90746
310-538-4670, 800-421-1096
FAX: 310-538-9932

car alarms

See full listing in **Section Two** under **anti-theft**

AmeriVap Systems
582 Armour Cir NE
Atlanta, GA 30324
404-876-2220; FAX: 404-876-3206

cleaning system

AmeriVap sanitizing systems. Low-pressure, high temperature, dry vapor, surface contact cleaning system, unlike any ever seen before. The ultimate manicuring tool, restores everything to its original condition.

Applied Chemical Specialties PO Box 241597 Omaha, NE 68124 800-845-8523; FAX: 402-390-9262	**corrosion protection**

See full listing in **Section Two** under **storage care products**

Autofresh International PO Box 54855 Oklahoma City, OK 73154-1855 405-752-0770; FAX: 405-752-5207	**deodorizing**

See full listing in **Section Two** under **interiors & interior parts**

Automotion 193 Commercial St Sunnyvale, CA 94068 800-777-8881; FAX: 408-736-9013 E-mail: automo@aol.com	**parts**

See full listing in **Section One** under **Porsche**

Backyard Buddy Corp 1818 N Main St, PO Box 5104 Niles, OH 44446 330-544-9372; FAX: 330-544-9311	**automotive lift**

See full listing in **Section Two** under **accessories**

Billie Inc 10519 Zion Dr Fairfax, VA 22032 800-878-6328; FAX: 703-250-4586	**garage diaper** **mats**

Mail and phone orders. 24 hours, 7 days a week. Super absorbent mats, garage diaper.

Leon Blackledge Sales Co 156 N School Ln Souderton, PA 18964-1153 215-734-4270; 800-525-7515 FAX: 215-723-7004	**polish**

Markets Wonder Tool, the only dual headed orbital polisher-sander. Complete line of Duragloss® and Wax Shop® polishes and cleaners. "Mr. Moly" (0.05 micron particle size molybdenum disulphide) engine treatment, "you will feel the difference," Kryptonite® steering wheel and brake to steering wheel security systems.

Boulevard Motoring Accessories 7033 Topanga Canyon Blvd Canoga Park, CA 91303-1961 818-883-9696; FAX: 818-883-5530	**accessories** **car covers** **floor mats**

See full listing in **Section One** under **Mercedes-Benz**

Brisson Enterprises PO Box 1595 Dearborn, MI 48121 313-584-3577	**lead**

Mail order only. Monday-Friday 10 am-6 pm EST. Tetraethyl lead for use in pre-1974 classic engines. Restores original horsepower, performance, protects upper cylinder valves and components. Sold by the gallon, mixes up to 100 gals of gasoline. $19.95/gal + UPS. Major credit cards accepted. Nothing is better than genuine lead.

Brit-Tek Ltd 12 Parmenter Rd Londonderry, NH 03053 800-255-5883	**MGB cars** **rustproofing systems**

See full listing in **Section One** under **MG**

Buenger Enterprises/GoldenRod **Dehumidifier** 3600 S Harbor Blvd Oxnard, CA 93035 800-451-6797; FAX: 805-985-1534	**dehumidifiers**

Mail order only. The GoldenRod dehumidifier protects your prized auto from dampness, rust and mildew. It is easy to install, maintenance free and operates for pennies a day. Our product is UL listed, made in the USA and guaranteed for ten years. You've spent so much time restoring your old car, why not protect it with the GoldenRod?

BW Incorporated PO Box 106 316 W Broadway Browns Valley, MN 56219 800-950-2210; 612-695-2891 or 800-EAT-OILS/328-6457 FAX: 612-695-2893	**artwork** **car care products** **dry enclosed covers** **mice control** **oil drip absorbent** **storage care products**

See full listing in **Section Two** under **storage care products**

Caladium Chemical Co 657 S Lakeview Rd Lake Placid, FL 33852 941-465-6345; FAX: 941-465-9734	**hand cleaner** **polishes** **waxes**

Mail order only. Formula 111 waterless hand cleaner, waxes and polishes, cleaners and protectants.

California Car Cover Co 21125 Superior St Chatsworth, CA 91311 800-423-5525; FAX: 818-998-2442	**accessories** **apparel** **car covers** **tools**

See full listing in **Section Two** under **car covers**

Capt Lee's Spra' Strip PO Box 203 Hermitage, TN 37076 800-421-9498; FAX: 615-889-1798	**paint remover**

See full listing in **Section Two** under **rust removal & stripping**

Car Care Group Box 338 Poynette, WI 53955 608-635-7751	**car care products**

Wax shop car care products.

Car Skates by P & J Products 988 Gordon Ct Birmingham, MI 48009 PH/FAX: 810-647-1879	**car skate**

See full listing in **Section Two** under **tools**

Color-Plus Leather Restoration **System** 2116 Morris Ave Union, NJ 07083 908-851-2811; FAX: 908-851-2910	**leather** **conditioning** **leather dye**

See full listing in **Section Two** under **leather restoration**

Comfy/Inter-American Sheepskins **Inc** 1346 Centinela Ave West Los Angeles, CA 90025-1901 800-521-4014; FAX: 310-442-6080 E-mail: 4858038@mcimail.com	**floor mats** **seat covers**

See full listing in **Section Two** under **interiors & interior parts**

Generalists

Cover-It 17 Wood St West Haven, CT 06516-3843 203-931-4747; FAX: 203-931-4754	**all-weather shelters**

See full listing in **Section Two** under **car covers**

Cover-Up Enterprises 1444 Manor Lane Blue Bell, PA 19422 800-268-3757; FAX: 215-654-0252	**car covers**

See full listing in **Section Two** under **car covers**

Creative Metal Products Inc 121 R N Douglas St Appleton, WI 54914 414-830-7975; FAX: 414-830-7976	**storage system**

See full listing in **Section Two** under **tools**

Cyclo Industries LLC 10190 Riverside Dr Palm Beach Gardens, FL 33410 800-843-7813; 561-775-9600 FAX: 561-622-1055	**cleaners lubricants**

Cyclo Industries LLC offers a complete line of professionally formulated, time tested cleaners, lubricants and additives in dynamic packages. Products designed for the complete maintenance and enhanced performance of motor vehicles, marine, home and industrial applications. Call or write for more information.

D-A Lubricant Co 1340 W 29th St Indianapolis, IN 46208 800-232-4503; FAX: 317-926-8132	**lubricants**

See full listing in **Section Two** under **lubricants**

Deltran Corporation 801 US Hwy 92 E Deland, FL 32724 904-736-7900; FAX: 904-736-9984	**battery chargers**

See full listing in **Section Two** under **batteries**

Dri-Wash & Guard Consulting Distributors Inc PO Box 1331 Palm Desert, CA 92261 619-346-1984; 800-428-1883 FAX: 619-568-6354	**automotive care products boat care products**

Cleans and protects virtually everything you own without using water; Enviro-tech International's waterless and water saving technologies make it simple, efficient and economical. Dri-Wash n' Guard cleans, seals, protects and polishes without scratching any non-porous surface, fine automobiles, RVs, boats, airplanes and equipment. A full line of carpet, fabric & upholstery, leather & vinyl, metal polish and home products are also available.

Emgee/Clean Tools 648 Blackhawk Dr Westmont, IL 60559 630-887-7707; FAX: 630-887-1347	**drying product**

The Absorber, an all purpose drying product that is compact and reusable. The Absorber dries faster and absorbs 50% more water than other drying products. A safe, non-abrasive, lintless material that is resistant to grease, oil and most chemicals. The Absorber is machine washable and will last for years.

Fast Lane Products PO Box 7000-50 Palos Verdes Peninsula, CA 90274 800-327-8669	**chamois drain tubs hand wringers**

Mail order only. Monday-Friday 9 am-5 pm PST. Commercial

quality hand wringers, drain tubs and premium synthetic chamois for easy maintenance of cars, trucks, airplanes and boats, with sparkling clean professional results.

Fleetfoot Industries Inc 2680 Blake St Denver, CO 80205 800-503-2727, 303-294-0647 FAX: 303-294-0333	**accessories**

See full listing in **Section Two** under **accessories**

Gasoline Alley LLC PO Box 737, 1700E Iron Ave Salina, KS 67402 913-822-1000; 800-326-8372 FAX: 913-827-9337	**drip pans**

See full listing in **Section Two** under **accessories**

Griot's Garage 3500-A 20th St E Tacoma, WA 98424 800-345-5789; FAX: 206-922-7500 E-mail: griots@aol.com	**car care products paint tools**

See full listing in **Section Two** under **tools**

Hunters Custom Automotive 975 Main St Nashville, TN 37206 615-227-6584; FAX: 615-227-4897	**accessories engine parts fiberglass products**

See full listing in **Section Two** under **accessories**

International AutoSport Inc Rt 29 N PO Box 9036 Charlottesville, VA 22906 800-726-1199; FAX: 804-973-2368 E-mail: iap1@international-auto.com	**accessories**

See full listing in **Section Two** under **accessories**

Kaleidoscope PO Box 86-H Mt Ephraim, NJ 08059 800-831-5163	**glass restoration scratch remover kit**

See full listing in **Section Two** under **restoration aids**

Koala International PO Box 255 Uwchland, PA 19480 610-458-8395; FAX: 610-458-8735	**convertible maintenance products**

Convertible top maintenance products. Used for cleaning, protecting and maintaining simulated and genuine convertible tops made vinyl. Also a plastic polish for removing scratches and haze from rear windows, lenses and bezels, permanently. Dealer inquiries are welcomed.

KozaK® Auto Drywash® Inc 6 S. Lyon St Batavia, NY 14020 716-343-8111, 800-237-9927 FAX: 716-343-3732 E-mail: erh01@aol.com	**cloths**

Mail order and open shop. Monday-Friday 8:30 to 4:30. Manufacturers of KozaK® Drywash® brand cleaning cloths for cars and furniture. Also, new printing services available with mailing services (i.e. Cheshire labeling and inserting). Call Ed Harding, President, for info.

Generalists

Leatherique Leather Restoration Products
PO Box 2678
Orange Park, FL 32065
904-272-0992; FAX: 904-272-1534

| leather cleaning conditioning products |

See full listing in **Section One** under **Rolls-Royce/Bentley**

Liquid Glass Enterprises Inc
PO Box 1170
Teaneck, NJ 07666
201-387-6755; FAX: 201-387-2168

| car care products |

Mail order only. Car care products.

M & R Products
1940 SW Blvd
Vineland, NJ 08360
609-696-9450; FAX: 609-696-4999

| hardware tie-downs |

See full listing in **Section Two** under **accessories**

Malm Chem Corp
PO Box 300, Dept HVA
Pound Ridge, NY 10576
914-764-5775; FAX: 914-764-5785
E-mail: jkolin@cloud9.net

| polish wax |

Dealing in auto wax, polishes and tools for their application. Web site: http://www.frazz.com/malm

Marshall Antique & Classic Restorations
3714 Old Philadelphia Pike
Bethlehem, PA 18015
610-868-7765; FAX: 610-868-7529

| coolant additives restoration services |

See full listing in **Section One** under **Rolls-Royce/Bentley**

Motorcar Valet Inc
PO Box 711777
Cottonwood, UT 84171
801-277-4596; FAX: 801-277-4680

| cleaners polishes waxes |

Mail order only. Autoglym Products, England's superior quality car care products, selected by Aston Martin, Jaguar, Rolls-Royce, McLaren, Penske racing and auto enthusiasts in 40 countries worldwide. Autoglym Products offers a full line of polishes, waxes, compounds, cleaners, dressings, specially woven cotton cloth and expert car care video.

Motorcars International
528 N Prince Ln
Springfield, MO 65802
417-831-9999; FAX: 417-863-0777
E-mail: missy@motorcars-intl

| accessories cars services tools |

See full listing in **Section One** under **Ferrari**

Murphy's Motoring Accessories Inc
PO Box 618
Greendale, WI 53129-0618
800-529-8315; 414-529-8333

| car covers |

See full listing in **Section Two** under **car covers**

OJ Rallye Automotive
PO Box 540
N 6808 Hwy OJ
Plymouth, WI 53073
414-893-2531; FAX: 414-893-6800

| accessories car care products lighting parts |

See full listing in **Section Two** under **lighting equipment**

PM Industries
442 Ridge Rd
West Milford, NJ 07480
800-833-8933; FAX: 201-728-2117

| chassis coatings permanent rust sealers |

See full listing in **Section Two** under **rustproofing**

Preserve Inc
1430 E 1800 N
Hamilton, IL 62341
217-746-2411; FAX: 217-746-2231

| storage containers |

See full listing in **Section Two** under **storage care products**

Protective Products Corp
Box 246
Johnston, IA 50131
800-666-0772; FAX: 515-999-2708

| chemical products |

See full listing in **Section Two** under **restoration aids**

Red Crown Valve Caps
PO Box 5301
Topeka, KS 66605
913-357-5007

| automobilia |

See full listing in **Section Two** under **automobilia**

Rhino Industries
14512 N Nebraska Ave
Tampa, FL 33613
813-977-7776; FAX: 813-977-5419

| cleaner |

Manufacturer of Black Again & Somthin Else interior and exterior cleaner and protectant.

Rocky's Advance Formula
40 Abbott Ave
Danbury, CT 06810
800-752-0245

| wax hardener |

Mail order only. Offering a hardener for car waxes. Makes car finishes hard as a rock. It's like putting two coats of wax on a car or truck.

T Schmidt
827 N Vernon
Dearborn, MI 48128-1542
313-562-7161

| rust removers |

See full listing in **Section Two** under **rust removal & stripping**

Showtime Auto Acc
899 N Market St
Selinsgrove, PA 17870
800-232-8861; FAX: 717-374-9525

| fasteners |

Mail order and open shop. Our shop is open Monday-Friday, 9 am to 5 pm. We specialize in car care products and stainless fasteners. Give us a call or stop in and visit our shop.

Silver Image Photographics
3102 Vestal Pkwy E
Vestal, NY 13850
607-797-8795

| business cards photo car cards photofinishing |

See full listing in **Section Two** under **automobilia**

Standard Abrasives Motor Sports
9351 Deering Ave
Chatsworth, CA 91311
800-383-6001
818-718-7070, ext 371
FAX: 800-546-6867

| abrasives |

See full listing in **Section Two** under **restoration aids**

Sterling Specialties | car care products
RR 4, Box 291
Lakes Rd
Monroe, NY 10950
914-782-7614

Mail order and open shop by appointment. Mon-Sat 8 am-5 pm.
Oil drain valves, Kozak cloths, Amsoil, Semichrome. Free
brochure.

Ultimate Appearance Ltd | cleaners / detailing products / detailing services / polish
113 Arabian Tr
Smithfield, VA 23430
PH/FAX: 757-255-2620

Stocking distributor for IBIZ world class detailing products (teflon
and silicone free), Novus plastic polishing line (cleaning and
restoring plastics as plastic windows on convertible tops) and
Stoner shine dressings and cleaners. Detailing seminars given by
appointment and auto detailing services. Catalog available.
MasterCard, VISA, Discover and American Express accepted.

Valco Cincinnati Consumer Products Inc | adhesives / detailing products / sealants / tools
411 Circle Freeway Drive
Cincinnati, OH 45246
513-874-6550; FAX: 513-874-3612

See full listing in **Section Two** under **tools**

The Wax Shop | cleaners / polishes / waxes
PO Box 10226
Bakersfield, CA 93389-0226
800-323-9192; FAX: 805-397-6817

Mail order and open shop. Monday-Friday 7 to 4 PST. The Wax
Shop specializes in premium quality car care products that are
the overwhelming choice among top restorers, detailers and collectors worldwide. Founded in 1980, The Wax Shop created and
manufactures its entire line of products. There are over 20 specialty products that range from waxes, polishes, cleaners and
dressings.

York Petroleum Industries | floor protector
dba YPI Inc
1011 Askham Dr
Cary, NC 27511-4703
919-319-5180; FAX: 919-319-7302

See full listing in **Section Two** under **accessories**

Ziebart/Tidy Car | accessories / detailing / rustproofing
803 Mount Royal Blvd
Pittsburgh, PA 15223
412-486-4711

See full listing in **Section Two** under **rustproofing**

car covers

Keeps Out Dust Damp and Light — THE GILBERT AUTO COVER

Auto-Mat Co | accessories / carpet sets / interiors
225A Park Ave
Hicksville, NY 11801
800-645-7258 orders
516-938-7373; FAX: 516-931-8438

See full listing in **Section Two** under **interiors & interior parts**

Automotive Interior Center | interior trim
1725A Bustleton Pike
Feasterville, PA 19053
PH/FAX: 215-953-7477

See full listing in **Section Two** under **interiors & interior parts**

Boulevard Motoring Accessories | accessories / car covers / floor mats
7033 Topanga Canyon Blvd
Canoga Park, CA 91303-1961
818-883-9696; FAX: 818-883-5530

See full listing in **Section One** under **Mercedes-Benz**

California Car Cover Co | accessories / apparel / car covers / tools
9525 DeSoto
Chatsworth, CA 91311
800-423-5525; FAX: 818-998-2442

Specializes in protecting your valuable automotive investments. We
offer covers made from six different materials to ensure your getting the best possible cover for your application and we have nearly
30,000 precision master patterns from which to build a custom fit
cover from. Other items in our line include specialty tools and
accessories for your garage, a wide assortment of car care products, novelty items and apparel. Catalog free for the asking.

Car Cover Company | car covers
146 W Pomona Ave
Monrovia, CA 91016
818-357-7718

Mail order and open shop. Monday-Friday 9 am to 5 pm.
Manufacturer of custom car covers for muscle cars and classics.
Specializing in selling wholesale to mail order houses. We can
make or get any car cover pattern for any car, provided our customers can use these patterns on an ongoing basis.

Carpad Incorporated | floor protector
400 Main St, PO Box 204
Dayton, NV 89403-0204
702-246-0232; FAX: 702-246-0266

See full listing in **Section Two** under **accessories**

Classic Motoring Accessories | accessories / car covers
146 W Pomona Ave
Monrovia, CA 91016
800-327-3045, 818-357-8264

Mail order and open shop. Monday-Friday 9 am to 5 pm. Manufactures own custom car covers for muscle cars and classics. Our
retail prices are lower than our competitors. Also has thousands of
chrome goodies, silver and gold jewelry with diamonds, fans, over-
heating equipment, Heartbeat of America jackets, valve covers and
much more. Please send for our free 64-page catalog.

Cover-It | all-weather shelters
17 Wood St
West Haven, CT 06516-3843
203-931-4747; FAX: 203-931-4754

Mail order and open shop. Mon-Fri 8-6, Sat 8-4. Our all-weather
shelters provide protection for cars, boats, trucks, RVs, motorcycles,
docks, pools, paint booths, sandblasting, workshops, industrial con-
tracts, greenhouses & more! Our shelters withstand wind, rain, snow,
sap & sun. From 4' to 60' wide, any length made with heavy duty galvanized steel frame with a waterproof UV treated "Rip-Stop" cover.
They are portable, assemble quickly & easily. The perfect solution for
covering anything & everything year-round, economically & securely.

Cover-Up Enterprises | car covers
1444 Manor Lane
Blue Bell, PA 19422
800-268-3757; FAX: 215-654-0252

Mail order and auto shows. High quality car covers, lowest prices
(from $49.95) for all cars, trucks, vans, cycles and limos (all years).

Fleetfoot Industries Inc | accessories
2680 Blake St
Denver, CO 80205
800-503-2727, 303-294-0647
FAX: 303-294-0333

See full listing in **Section Two** under **accessories**

International AutoSport Inc
Rt 29 N, PO Box 9036
Charlottesville, VA 22906
800-726-1199; FAX: 804-973-2368
E-mail: iap1@international-auto.com

accessories

See full listing in **Section Two** under **accessories**

Kanter Auto Products
76 Monroe St
Boonton, NJ 07005
800-526-1096; 201-334-9575
FAX: 201-334-5423

car covers
carpets
parts

See full listing in **Section Two** under **comprehensive parts**

Lord Byron Inc
420 Sackett Point Rd
North Haven, CT 06473
203-287-9881; FAX: 203-230-9633

fender covers

Specializing in official GM licensed auto fender covers. Lord Byron Inc manufactures custom printed auto fender covers. We can manufacture covers with custom logos for specialty car clubs and parts suppliers.

Motorcars International
528 N Prince Ln
Springfield, MO 65802
417-831-9999; FAX: 417-863-0777
E-mail: missy@motorcars-intl

accessories
cars
services
tools

See full listing in **Section One** under **Ferrari**

Murphy's Motoring Accessories Inc
PO Box 618
Greendale, WI 53129-0618
800-529-8315; 414-529-8333

car covers

Specialist in custom-fit car covers in six fabrics matched to application needs. Also have rail-system tonneau covers, dash savers, fender covers, front end masks and other car care and protection products. Car covers available in 33,000 custom-fit patterns for cars, trucks, vans and SUVs from 1900-97 models.

OJ Rallye Automotive
PO Box 540
N 6808 Hwy OJ
Plymouth, WI 53073
414-893-2531; FAX: 414-893-6800

accessories
car care products
lighting parts

See full listing in **Section Two** under **lighting equipment**

Pine Ridge Enterprise-CARJACKET
13165 Center Rd
Bath, MI 48808
800-5-CARBAG; FAX: 517-641-6444
E-mail: schoepk1@msualum.msu.edu

zippered car
storage bags

Mail/telephone order. Retail/wholesale. Sole manufacturer and distributor for CarJacket, MotoJacket and Omnibag. Send or call for the free brochure. We are automotive historians, enthusiasts and collectors. Needing to preserve our collection of Alfa Romeos and protect our investment, we researched and tested the bag storage concept. It works. Made of woven, nonbreathable polyethylene, the handsome CarJacket has a heavy duty zipper, double stitching and two brass locks. Nine sizes to fit most USA and import cars. OmniDry desiccant is used to remove moisture. See separate listing for the MotoJackets and Omnibags.

See our ad on this page

Pine Ridge Enterprise-MOTOJACKET
13165 Center Rd
Bath, MI 48808
800-5-CARBAG; FAX: 517-641-6444
E-mail: schoepk1@msualum.msu.edu

zippered motorcycle
storage bags

Mail/telephone order. Wholesale/retail. Sole manufacturer and distributor for MotoJacket, CarJacket and Omnibag. Send or call for the free brochure. While we are automotive historians, enthusiasts and collectors, we recognize the need to preserve collectable and special bikes. We researched and tested the bag storage concept nearly 15 years ago. It works. Made of woven, nonbreathable polyethylene, the handsome MotoJacket has a heavy duty zipper, double stitching and a brass lock. Three sizes to fit most USA and import bikes. OmniDry desiccant is used to remove moisture. See separate listing for the CarJackets and Omnibags.

See our ad on this page

Pine Ridge Enterprise-OMNIBAG
13165 Center Rd
Bath, MI 48808
800-5-CARBAG; FAX: 517-641-6444
E-mail: schoepk1@msualum.msu.edu

car storage bags

Mail/telephone order. Retail/wholesale. Sole manufacturer and distributor for Omnibag, CarJacket and MotoJacket. Send or call for the free brochure. Originators of the carbag concept with the introduction of Omnibag in 1983. We are automotive historians, enthusiasts and collectors. Needing to preserve our collection of Alfa Romeos and protect our investment, we researched and tested the bag storage concept. It works. And it does what we say. Omnibag is the original, economical bag for dry car storage. Three sizes to fit most vintage and special interest cars. OmniDry desiccant packets sent with each bag. See separate listing for the jackets.

See our ad on this page

Preserve Inc	storage containers
1430 E 1800 N	
Hamilton, IL 62341	
217-746-2411; FAX: 217-746-2231	

See full listing in **Section Two** under **storage care products**

Quik-Shelter	temporary garages
PO Box 1123	
Orange, CT 06477	
800-211-3730; FAX: 203-937-8990	

Both mail order and open shop. Monday-Friday 8-6 and Saturday 8-12. Manufacturing of all sizes of temporary/permanent garages for automobiles, boats, all types of storage. These structures are all pre-drilled and bolt together. They are extremely strong units & completely weatherproof.

Sailorette's Nautical Nook	covers
23005 W Kankakee River Dr	interiors
Wilmington, IL 60481	
815-476-2391; FAX: 815-476-2524	

See full listing in **Section Two** under **upholstery**

UK Spares/TVR Sports Cars	accessories
609 Highland St	car covers
Wethersfield, CT 06109-3979	convertible tops
PH/FAX: 203-563-1647	ignition parts

See full listing in **Section One** under **TVR**

West Coast Metric Inc	apparel
24002 Frampton Ave	carpets
Harbor City, CA 90710	rubber parts
310-325-0005; FAX: 310-325-9733	
E-mail: wcmi@earthlink.net	

See full listing in **Section One** under **Volkswagen**

Wolf Automotive	car covers
201 N Sullivan	consoles
Santa Ana, CA 92703	steering wheels
800-444-9653, 714-835-2126	tire covers
FAX: 714-835-9653	

See full listing in **Section One** under **Chevrolet**

York Petroleum Industries	floor protector
dba YPI Inc	
1011 Askham Dr	
Cary, NC 27511-4703	
919-319-5180; FAX: 919-319-7302	

See full listing in **Section Two** under **accessories**

car dealers

AC Motors	car dealer
534 N 1st St	
Grand Junction, CO 81501	
970-245-3344	

Mail order and open shop. Monday-Saturday 9:30 to 5. Collector car dealer specializing in sales of fifties and sixties special interest automobiles. Business started in 1983 by Gary Roberts.

Albers Rolls-Royce	car dealer
190 W Sycamore	parts
Zionsville, IN 46077	
317-873-2360; 317-873-2560	
FAX: 317-873-6860	

See full listing in **Section One** under **Rolls-Royce/Bentley**

Alfas Unlimited Inc	engine rebuilding
US Rt 44	parts
Norfolk, CT 06058	restoration
203-542-5351; FAX: 203-542-5993	service

See full listing in **Section One** under **Alfa Romeo**

Alt Auto Sales	car dealer
Box 364	
Regina, SAS Canada S4P 3A1	
306-545-7119, 306-757-0369	

Shop open by appointment only. Collector car dealership, listing service and appraisals. Specializes in luxury cars from 1954-76.

AM Racing Inc	race prep
PO Box 451	sales
Danvers, MA 01923	vintage racing
PH/FAX: 508-774-4613	

See full listing in **Section Two** under **racing**

Antique & Classic Automobiles	car dealer
Royce A Emerson	
Carlisle St, Ext D	
Hanover, PA 17331	
717-637-8344, 632-9182	

Shop open Monday-Friday 8 to 8. 30 years' dealing in fine, clean automobiles. Mostly Cadillac convertibles.

Antique & Classic Cars Inc	classic car sales
326 S 2nd St	
Hamilton, OH 45011	
513-844-1146 in OH	
800-798-3982 nationwide	

See full listing in **Section One** under **Buick/McLaughlin**

Appleton Garage	car dealer
PO Box B	parts
West Rockport, ME 04865	wheelcovers
207-594-2062	

See full listing in **Section Two** under **wheels & wheelcovers**

Auto Literature Outlet	car dealer
527 Hwy 431 S	literature
Boaz, AL 35957	parts
205-593-4111	

See full listing in **Section Two** under **literature dealers**

Auto Transport Services	transport
5367 Fargo Rd	
Avoca, MI 48006	
810-324-2598	

See full listing in **Section Two** under **transport**

Automatch International Inc	car dealer
CARS Division	locator services
2724 Cove View Dr N	
Jacksonville, FL 32257	
904-448-0736; FAX: 904-448-0623	

Mail order and open shop. Monday-Saturday. Computer aided sales, purchasing, liquidation, consignment, locator for all makes of special interest & other vehicles. Independent agents needed.

Jerry Bensinger	car dealer
191 Erskine Ave	
Youngstown, OH 44512	
330-788-1237; FAX: 330-788-1337	

Open shop only. Monday-Friday 9 to 5. Sales of very nice or

restorable Ferraris, Astons, Austin-Healeys, Jaguars, etc, and the more obscure: Stanguellini, McLaren, Royale, Crossle, etc. 20 years in business. International shipping. References. Some Porsches, Mercedes-Benz, motorcycles.

Berliner Classic Motorcars Inc 1975 Stirling Rd Dania, FL 33004 954-923-7271; FAX: 954-926-3306	automobilia car dealer motorcycles

Mail order and open shop. Monday thru Friday 9 am-5 pm, most Saturdays 10 am-1 pm. Licensed dealer that buys and sells classic and antique automobiles, classic motorcycles and a wide variety of memorabilia. 15,000 square foot showroom located in south Fort Lauderdale, Florida, minutes from the airport and interstate. We have it all, drivers to #1 judged show condition cars, American and European, jukeboxes, Coca-Cola items, gas pumps, music boxes, etc. We also accept items on consignment and for storage. Experienced in exporting.

Bill's Collector Cars 6478 County Rd #1 South Point, OH 45680 614-894-5175	appraiser car dealer

Shop open Mon-Sat 10-6, evenings and Sundays by appointment. Appraisals for estates, banks & individuals. Over 35 years' experience. Honesty & integrity in all our dealings with the old car hobby.

Gerard Boucher PO Box 171 Franklin, VT 05457 514-298-5438 FAX: 514-298-5698, QUE Canada	restoration

See full listing in **Section Two** under **restoration shops**

Bright Displays 1314 Lakemont Dr Pittsburgh, PA 15243 412-279-7037	neon signs

See full listing in **Section Two** under **automobilia**

Brookside Automotive Sales 363 E Main St Rt 9, PO Box 312 East Brookfield, MA 01515 508-867-9266; 508-829-5366 508-885-2017 FAX: 508-867-2875	appraisals car dealer service

Open shop only. Wed-Sun 10 am to 5 pm, appointments always welcome. Antique cars for sale, appraisals, some parts and automobilia.

Brothers Classic, Special Interest & Sports Cars 107 S Harper St, Box 134 Laurens, SC 29360 864-984-4211, 864-984-5520	car dealer

Open shop, 9:30 am to 4:00 pm, Monday-Saturday.

Bud's Chevrolets, Corvettes, ZR1s PO Box 128 St Marys, OH 45885 800-688-2837; FAX: 419-394-4781	car dealer

See full listing in **Section One** under **Corvette**

Arthur Burrichter 24026 Highway 151 Monticello, IA 52310 319-465-3064; FAX: 319-465-6048	appraisals car dealer

Antique brass cars, classic cars. Some 50s & 60s cars. 40 years of integrity. Appraisals, estate settlements. Buy/sell, consign.

Cadillac Auto Display PO Box 6732 Rockford, IL 61125 815-229-1258; FAX: 815-229-1238	museum

See full listing in **Section Six** under **Illinois**

CARS (Computer Aided Resale System) 2724 Cove View Dr N Jacksonville, FL 32257 904-448-0633; FAX: 904-448-0623	car dealer

Mail order and open shop. Specializing in Mercedes, Porsche, Ferrari, Lamborghini, Miata, Jaguar, Rolls-Royce, MG, Triumph, Austin-Healey, Morgan and other sports cars. Sports cars appraisals, locating and consulting. Independent agents needed.

Cars of Distinction 3358 F St San Diego, CA 92102 619-544-0063	antique cars classic cars

Buy and sell antique and classic cars.

Casey-Dyer Enterprises Inc PO Box 7176 Alexandria, LA 71301 318-473-1802; FAX: 318-473-9578	appraiser broker car dealer

Open shop only. Monday-Friday 9 am to 6 pm. Dealer/broker, insurance appraisals on all antique, classic and modern classic vehicles.

Chicago Car Exchange 1 Collector Car Dr Box 530 Lake Bluff, IL 60044 847-680-1950; FAX: 847-680-1961 E-mail: oldtoys@wwa.com	appraiser car dealer car locator financing storage worldwide shipping

Open shop. Monday through Friday 10 am-6 pm and Saturday 10-5. 20,000 square foot showroom with over 150 collectable cars. Buys, sells, consigns, appraises, locates, details and stores collector cars. Strives to give accurate representations of cars to long distance buyers. Establishes long-standing, working relationships with clients. Specialties are pre-war, vintage, muscle, Mercedes, Cadillac, Pontiac and Hudson. Financing available. Worldwide shipping. Phone/FAX for current inventory list.

Dick Choler Cars & Service Inc 640 E Jackson Blvd Elkhart, IN 46516 219-522-8281; FAX: 219-522-8282	car dealer literature model cars

See full listing in **Section One** under **Pontiac**

Charles W Clarke Automotive Consultant/Appraiser 17 Saddle Ridge Dr West Simsbury, CT 06092 203-658-2714	appraiser consultant car dealer

See full listing in **Section Two** under **consultants**

Classic Car Sales 760 Edison-Furlong Rd Furlong, PA 18925 215-794-7769; FAX: 215-794-2535 E-mail: mtaylor477@aol.com	car dealer

Open shop, Wednesday-Saturday, 12-5. Locating and selling classic cars. Consignment sales for people around the world.

See our ad on page 254

Classic Cars & Parts
Mike Chmilarski
PO Box 375
Lindenhurst, NY 11757
516-888-5717

car dealer
parts

Mail order and open shop. Shop open by appointment only. Buys, sells and trades General Motors cars and parts. Specializing in 1959-1972.

Classic Cars Inc
1 Maple Terr
Hibernia, NJ 07842
201-627-1975

cars
parts

See full listing in **Section One** under **Packard**

Classic Motors
PO Box 1321
Shirley, MA 01464
508-425-4350

appraisals
car dealer
consulting

Open by appointment only. Antique, classic and special interest vehicles. We specialize in brass era cars. Appraisals and pre-purchase inspection, all makes, models and years.

Classic Motors Inc
Rich Adams
103 200th Ave
Union Grove, WI 53182
414-878-2525; FAX: 414-878-0400

car sales
trailer sales

Mail order and open shop. Monday-Friday 9 am-7 pm, Saturday 9 am-1 pm. Antique, classic, collector car sales and Imperial car trailer sales.

Classical Gas Antique Auto Museum & Sales
245 E Collins
Eaton, CO 80615
800-453-7955, 970-454-1373
FAX: 970-454-1368

car dealer
museum

Mail order and open shop. Museum open 12 month/year round, M-F 9 am to 5:30 pm, Sat 9 am to 2 pm. 12,000 sq ft indoors of Antique, classic, special interest, street rods, cars and pickups from 1920 to 1970. Collectible signs and artwork, toys, pedal cars, rare aluminum intake manifolds & heads plus general automobilia and petroliana of all kinds. Previous movie cars & celebrity owned examples.

Coach Builders Limited Inc
PO Box 1978
High Springs, FL 32643
904-454-2060; FAX: 904-454-4080

car dealer
conv conversion

See full listing in **Section Two** under **restoration shops**

Coachworks Classic Cars Inc
1401 NW 53rd Ave
PO Box 1186
Gainesville, FL 32602
904-376-0660; FAX: 904-376-4513

car dealers

Mail order and open shop. Open Monday-Friday 11 to 5. Deals in collectable autos.

Collector Car & Truck Prices
41 N Main St
North Grafton, MA 01536
508-839-6707; FAX: 508-839-6266
E-mail: vmr@ultranet.com

price guide

See full listing in **Section Four** under **periodicals**

Collector Car Buyers
4046 11th St
Rockford, IL 61109
815-229-1258; FAX: 815-229-1238

car dealers

Mail order and open shop. Monday-Saturday 9-5, no Sunday hours. Buying pre-1975 autos in any condition junker to show car. Prefer midwestern vehicles or out of state when delivery available. Heavy in pre-1965 Cadillac, Buick, Packard, etc. We do not sell parts, but may be interested in your NOS parts inventory.

Collector Cars-U-Can-Afford Ltd
4046 11th St
Rockford, IL 61109
815-229-1258; FAX: 815-229-1238

car dealer

See full listing in **Section One** under **Cadillac/LaSalle**

Collector's Carousel
84 Warren Ave
Westbrook, ME 04092
207-854-0343; FAX: 207-856-6913

appraisals
sales
service

Antique auto sales, service and appraisals.

Collector's CARS Inc
150 E St Joseph St
Arcadia, CA 91006
818-447-2576; FAX: 818-447-1461

restoration
service

See full listing in **Section Two** under **restoration shops**

Colorado Car Collection Inc
3455 F St, Suite 3
Greeley, CO 80631
970-352-3915; FAX: 970-352-4172

car dealer

Mail order and open shop. Monday-Friday, Saturdays by

appointment, 8 am to 5 pm. Specializing in mostly pre-war (1942 and before) antique vehicles. We deal in most all makes & models that are available for this era. The vehicles are restored or good solid, complete original vehicles. We have a showroom for walk-in customers, even though most of our business is by phone and photos.

| Corvair Heaven
PO Box 13
Ellenton, FL 34222-0013
813-746-0478; FAX: 813-750-8167 | car dealer
literature
restoration |

See full listing in **Section One** under **Corvair**

| County Corvette
171 Eagleview Blvd
Lionville, PA 19353
610-363-0872; FAX: 610-363-5325 | restoration
sales
service |

See full listing in **Section One** under **Corvette**

| Tom Crook Classic Cars
27611 42nd Ave S
Auburn, WA 98001
206-941-3454 | car dealer |

Specializing in classic car sales for Packards, Cadillacs, Duesenberg, Jaguar, Ford and all classics 1925 to 1948.

| Davies Corvette
5130 Main St
New Port Richey, FL 34653
813-842-8000, 800-236-2383
FAX: 813-846-8216 | customizing
parts
restoration |

See full listing in **Section One** under **Corvette**

| Desert Valley Auto Parts
22500 N 21st Ave
Phoenix, AZ 85027
602-780-8024; FAX: 602-582-9141 | salvage yard |

See full listing in **Section Five** under **Arizona**

| Dragone Classic Motorcars
1797 Main St
Bridgeport, CT 06604
203-335-4643; FAX: 203-335-9798 | car dealer |

Open shop only. Monday-Friday 9 to 5. Saturday 9 to 3. High quality antique, classic and exotic cars such as Delahaye, Delage, Alfa Romeo, Bugatti, Hispano-Suiza, Isotta-Fraschini and quality early brass era cars. Always a fine selection.

| Driven By Desire
300 N Fraley St
Kane, PA 16735
814-837-7590; FAX: 814-837-0886 | automobilia
car dealer
models |

Mail order and open shop. Open Monday-Thursday 1 to 6, Friday 1 to 9, Saturday 12 to 5. Collector car sales, mostly 1960s. The area's largest selection of foreign and domestic model car and truck kits, paint, supplies, etc. Die cast metal models, specializing in 1/18 scale, books, posters, auto related T-shirts, marque jackets and general automobilia. Stock car racing items: jackets, T-shirts, fan flags and more.

| Driving Ambition
1026 SE Stark St
Portland, OR 97214
503-238-6011; FAX: 503-230-8838 | car dealer |

Showroom open 9-6 Monday-Friday. Buys and sells sports cars. British, German, Italian are specialties. Some domestic also. Lots of business in Europe and Japan.

| Duffy's Collectible Cars
250 Classic Car Ct SW
Cedar Rapids, IA 52404
319-364-7000 | car dealer |

Mail order and open shop. Monday-Saturday 8:30 to 5. Collector car sales and service. Specializing in cars from 1930-70. Fully restored hardtops and convertibles. 100 car showroom. Sales, finance, storage, delivery and appraisals. Celebrating our 56th year.

| Eckhaus Motor Company
20818 E Weldon
Tivy Valley, CA 93657-9107
PH/FAX: 209-787-2224 | car dealer
restoration shop |

By appointment only. Sales and restorations of British vehicles. Established 1968.

| Malcolm C Elder & Son
The Motor Shed, Middle Aston
Bicester
Oxfordshire OX6 3PX England
PH/FAX: 01869 340999 | car dealer
motorcycles |

Shop open Mon-Sat 9:30 to 5; other times by appointment. Home phone: Steeple Aston 01869 340606. Also deals in vintage and classic motorcycles, tires.

| Ellingson Car Museum
20950 Rogers Dr
Rogers, MN 55374
612-428-7337; FAX: 612-428-4370 | museum |

See full listing in **Section Six** under **Minnesota**

| Executive Boys Toys
200 S Jackson St
Lima, OH 45804
419-227-9300 | car dealer |

Dealing in classics, antiques and special interest cars. Customs, originals and lead sleds.

| The Fine Car Store
1105 Moana Dr
San Diego, CA 92107
619-223-7766; FAX: 619-223-6838 | cars |

See full listing in **Section One** under **Ferrari**

| Freeman's Garage
19 Freeman Street
Norton, MA 02766
508-285-6500 | parts
restoration
sales
service |

See full listing in **Section One** under **Ford '03-'31**

| Freman's Auto
138 Kountz Rd
Whitehall, MT 59759
406-287-5436; FAX: 406-287-9103 | car dealer
salvage yard |

Mail order only. We sell parts for all makes and models. 1950-1980, over 12,000 cars. Worldwide shipping. Some complete cars available.

| The Generation Gap
4989 Mercer University Dr
Macon, GA 31210
912-471-6325 | broker
car dealer |

Showroom hours 9-5 Monday-Friday, anytime by appointment. Specializing in collector type vehicle sales. Buy, sell, trade, broker. We offer a variety of cars for sale, maintaining an inventory of 30-40 cars.

Generalists

George's Auto & Tractor Sales Inc 1450 N Warren Rd North Jackson, OH 44451 330-538-3020; FAX: 330-538-3033	**Blue Dots; car dealer** **Dri-wash metal polish** **New Castle batteries** **upholstery cleaner**

Mail order and open shop. Monday-Friday 9 to 5. Also Blue Dots. New Castle batteries, Denman wide whitewall tires. Special interest autos. Dri-wash leather & vinyl treatment. Dri Wash-N-Guard waterless car wash & protective glaze. Fluid film rust & corrosion preventative.

Leo Gephart Classic Cars 7360 E Acoma Dr, Ste 14 Scottsdale, AZ 85260 602-948-2286, 602-998-8263 FAX: 602-948-2390	**car dealer** **parts**

Mail order and open shop. Monday-Friday 9 to 5; Saturday by appointment only. Antique and classic cars, exotic sports cars, historical race cars, Duesenbergs and early Ford V8s. Also Duesenberg parts: superchargers, bumpers, gas tanks, script sidemount mirrors and chassis parts. Over 40 years' experience dealing with high-performance cars of all eras. 1941 Cadillac parts. In the specialized car business over 45 years continuous service, 16 years at this same address.

Mark Gillett PO Box 9177 Dallas, TX 75209 PH/FAX: 214-902-9258 011-525-559-6240 Mexico City, Mexico; E-mail-autonet@onramp.net	**car locator** **sales**

Open by appointment only. Sales & locating of specialty cars & vintage race cars. Specializing in finding old, dead race cars. Extensive contacts in Latin America.

Green Valentine Inc 5055 Covington Way Memphis, TN 38134 901-373-5555; FAX: 901-373-5568	**car dealer** **woodies**

Specializing in wood station wagons, wood convertibles for any brand.

Gullwing Service Co Inc 106 Western Ave Essex, MA 01929 508-768-6919; FAX: 508-768-3523	**car dealer** **mechanical service** **parts** **restoration**

See full listing in **Section One** under **Mercedes-Benz**

Hall of Fame & Classic Car Musem DIRT PO Box 240, 1 Speedway Dr Weedsport, NY 13166 315-834-6667; FAX: 315-834-9734	**museum**

See full listing in **Section Six** under **New York**

Happy Daze Classic Cars 257 Morris Ct Fond Du Lac, WI 54935 414-922-8450	**car dealer**

Mail order and open shop. Cars shown by appointment only. Buys, sells and trades outstanding collectible cars from the 1930s through the early 1970s. All cars are displayed in our indoor, heated, sales facility. Specializing in rust-free, low mileage originals and cars which have undergone frame-off restorations.

Ken Hicks Promotionals 116 Bethea Rd, Suite 306 Fayetteville, GA 30214 770-460-1654; FAX: 770-460-8956	**collectibles** **price guide**

See full listing in **Section Two** under **automobilia**

Hollywood Classic Motorcars Inc 363 Ansin Blvd Hallandale, FL 33009 954-454-4641; FAX: 954-457-3801	**cars** **parts**

See full listing in **Section One** under **Thunderbird**

J & K Old Chevy Stuff Ship Pond Rd Plymouth, MA 02360 508-224-7616	**car dealer** **parts** **sheetmetal**

See full listing in **Section One** under **Chevrolet**

Cy Kay Motors Ltd 1160 Waukegan Rd Glenview, IL 60025 847-724-3100, 847-432-8793	**appraiser** **car dealer**

We buy, sell, trade, appraise, and locate cars. Restoration facilities. Consignments welcome, etc. Member International Society of Appraisers. Since 1955.

Langer Auto Museum Rudy Langer 4943 Ward Pkwy Kansas City, MO 64112 PH/FAX: 816-931-1188	**vintage cars** **vintage motorcycles**

Specializing in vintage cars and motorcycles such as Rolls-Royce, Maserati, Mercedes.

Lazarus Auto Collection PO Box 6732 Rockford, IL 61125 815-229-1258; FAX: 815-229-1238	**arcade machines** **cars** **jukeboxes**

Open shop only. Monday thru Saturday 9-5. No Sunday hours. Pre-1975 luxury cars, jukeboxes, arcade machines. Auto related signs, pumps, etc. Always buying quality items realistically priced. Car show and auction promoted.

W L Wally Mansfield Box 237, 526 E 2nd Blue Springs, NE 68318-0237 402-645-3546	**cars** **parts** **trucks**

See full listing in **Section Two** under **comprehensive parts**

Bill McCoskey 14200 New Hampshire Ave Silver Spring, MD 20904 301-384-5856; FAX: 301-989-1866	**appraisals** **repairs**

See full listing in **Section Two** under **appraisals**

Medicine Bow Motors Inc 343 One Horse Creek Rd Florence, MT 59833 406-273-0002	**car dealer**

Specializing in 46-51 Ford car parts. Handle 50s custom goodies. Builders of street rods, customs & quality restorations.

Memory Lane Motors Lindsay St S Fenelon Falls, ONT Canada K0M 1N0 705-887-CARS	**car dealer** **restoration** **service**

See full listing in **Section Two** under **restoration shops**

Memory Lane Motors Inc
1231 Rt 176
Lake Bluff, IL 60044
847-362-4600

appraisals
car dealer
storage

Open shop only, Monday thru Saturday, 9 am to 5 pm. Buys, sells, trades and consigns antique and classic cars. Also does vehicle appraisals and provides storage for automobiles.

Morrison Motor Co
1170 Old Charlotte Rd
Concord, NC 28025
704-782-7716; FAX: 704-788-9514

car dealer

See full listing in **Section One** under **Corvette**

Motorcar Gallery Inc
715 N Federal Hwy
Fort Lauderdale, FL 33304
954-522-9900; FAX: 954-522-9966

car dealer

See full listing in **Section One** under **Ferrari**

Mountain Fuel
Russell Van Aken
Gilboa, NY 12076

car dealer
machinery
parts

Mail order and open shop. Weekends during the day. 40 years as a car dealer. SASE required.

J C Nadeau
306 Notre Dame St N
Thetford Mines, QUE Canada G6G 2S4
418-338-1106

car dealer

Mail order only. Antique cars and parts bought and sold.

John T Poulin Auto Sales/Star Service Center
5th Ave & 111th St
North Troy, NY 12182
518-235-8610

car dealer
parts
restoration service

See full listing in **Section One** under **Mercedes-Benz**

Prestige Motors
120 N Bessie Rd
Spokane, WA 99212
PH/FAX: 509-926-3611

car dealer

Investment quality, special interest car retailer. We handle antiques, muscle cars, street rods, sports cars and classics.

Proteam Corvette Sales Inc
PO Box 606
Napoleon, OH 43545-0606
419-592-5086; FAX: 419-592-4242
E-mail: proteam@bright.net

car collection
car dealer

See full listing in **Section One** under **Corvette**

Rader's Relics
2601 W Fairbanks Ave
Winter Park, FL 32789
407-647-1940; FAX: 407-647-1930

appraiser
car dealer

Mail order and open shop. Monday-Friday 9 to 4:30, Saturday 9 to 12. 19 years in business at 1-4 and Fairbanks. Home of the two year buy-back warranty. We consider our greatest asset a good reputation locally and internationally. A 10% deposit holds any car for 30 days and is fully refundable if you come see the car and don't like it for any reason. Buying, selling and appraising antiques and classics. Keeping an inventory of about 40 cars at all times.

Rank & Son Buick-GMC
4200 N Green Bay Ave
Milwaukee, WI 53209
414-372-4000

car dealer
parts

See full listing in **Section One** under **Buick/McLaughlin**

RARE Corvettes
Joe Calcagno
Box 1080
Soquel, CA 95073
408-475-4442; FAX: 408-475-1115

cars
parts

See full listing in **Section One** under **Corvette**

Regal International Motor Cars Inc
PO Box 6819
Hollywood, FL 33081
305-989-9777; FAX: 305-989-9778

car dealer

See full listing in **Section One** under **Rolls-Royce/Bentley**

Retrospect Automotive
970-980 E Jericho Tpk
Huntington Station, NY 11746
516-421-0255; FAX: 516-421-0473

accessories
car sales
parts

Mail order and open shop. Monday-Saturday 8 am-6 pm. Parts and accessories, classic car sales of domestic cars, muscle cars of the 1950s thru 1972.

Sam's Auto Sales & Parts
PO Box 243
1800 S Greeley Hwy
Cheyenne, WY 82003
307-632-8648

car dealer
parts

Mail order and open shop. Monday-Friday 9 to 6. Deals in antique & classic cars and parts (plus storage).

Shelton Dealerships
5740 N Federal Hwy
Ford Lauderdale, FL 33308
954-493-5211; FAX: 954-772-2653

accessories
leasing
parts
sales

See full listing in **Section One** under **Ferrari**

Southern US Car Export Inc
135 Eulon Loop
Raeford, NC 28376
910-875-7534; FAX: 910-875-7731

repair
restoration
sales
transport

See full listing in **Section One** under **Cadillac/LaSalle**

Sparling Studios
Box 86B, RR 1
Quarry Rd
New Haven, VT 05472
PH/FAX: 802-453-4114

auto sculpture

See full listing in **Section Two** under **artwork**

Specialty Sales
4321 First St
Pleasanton, CA 94566
510-484-2262; FAX: 510-426-8535
E-mail: specialt@ix.netcom.com

appraiser
car dealer
locator
memorabilia

Open shop. 7 days a week 10 am-6 pm. All indoor showroom with over 150 privately owned cars on display and for sale. Collector, muscle, exotic and antique cars. Also gifts, memorabilia, books and magazines. Free full color brochure and car list available. Licensed, bonded dealer, est. 1978. See us on the internet: http://www.specialty-sales.com

Generalists

Thoroughbred Motors	**car dealer**
3935 N Washington Blvd	**parts**
Sarasota, FL 34234	
941-359-2221, 941-359-2277	
FAX: 941-359-2128	

See full listing in **Section One** under **Jaguar**

U S Oldies & Classics	**car dealer**
Vunt 3	**parts**
Holsbeek 3220 Belgium	
3216446611, FAX: 3216446520	

Mail order and open shop. Monday-Friday 1-7 pm Belgian time. Specializing in classic & vintage cars, American made automobiles 1930-1970, especially Cadillacs and Chrysler Products in good to perfect condition. We supply parts on order for the European market: Cadillac, T-Bird, Mustang, Corvette, Chrysler, etc.

Vintage Auto Parts	**car dealer**
PO Box 323	**new & used parts**
Temple, PA 19560-0323	
610-926-2485, 9 am-noon, 5-7 pm,	
answering machine	

See full listing in **Section One** under **BMW**

Volo Antique Auto Museum	**museum**
27582 Volo Village Rd	
Volo, IL 60073	
815-385-3644	
FAX: 815-385-0703	

See full listing in **Section Six** under **Illinois**

Westchester Vintage Coach Inc	**car dealer**
Box 252	
Yonkers, NY 10705	
914-693-1624	

Antique car sales. Appraisals only.

Willhoit Auto Restoration	**engine rebuilding**
1360 Gladys Ave	**restoration**
Long Beach, CA 90804	
310-439-3333; FAX: 310-439-3956	

See full listing in **Section One** under **Porsche**

Wiseman Motor Co Inc	**car dealer**
Bill Wiseman, Owner	
PO Box 848	
Marion, NC 28752	
704-724-9313	

Call for appointment. Shop located on Clear-Creek Rd (off Rt 70), five miles west of Marion. Buying and selling antique and classic cars from Model T to Mustang.

Yesterday's Auto Sales	**appraiser**
2800 Lyndale Ave S	**car dealer**
Minneapolis, MN 55408	
612-872-9733; FAX: 612-872-1386	

Open Monday-Thursday 10 to 6, Friday 10 to 4, Saturday 10 to 3. Since 1983, we have been a full time collector car dealer. Our inventory includes cars foreign and domestic, from the sixties back to the twenties. Located in an historic two story building near downtown Minneapolis.

carburetors

Andy's Classic Mustangs	**parts**
18502 E Sprague	**service**
Greenacres, WA 99016	
509-924-9824	

See full listing in **Section One** under **Mustang**

Apple Hydraulics Inc	**brake rebuilding**
1610 Middle Rd	**shock rebuilding**
Calverton, NY 11933-1419	
516-369-9515, 800-882-7753	
FAX: 516-369-9516	

See full listing in **Section Two** under **suspension parts**

Battery Ignition Co Inc	**parts**
91 Meadow St	**rebuilding**
Hartford, CT 06114	**rebushing**
860-296-4215; FAX: 860-947-3259	
E-mail: biscokid@aol.com	

Both mail order and open shop. Monday-Friday 8:30-5, Thursday until 8 pm. Since 1926 offering parts, rebuilding and rebushing services for most domestic carburetors, including automotive, marine, industrial and antique applications. Also available, search services for hard to find fuel system and electrical parts. Web site: http://www.neca.com/~biscokid

Brothers Automotive Products	**parts**
19715 County Rd 355	**restoration**
St Joseph, MO 64505	
816-662-2060; FAX: 816-662-2084	

See full listing in **Section One** under **Oldsmobile**

Carburetor Engineering	**carb rebuilding**
3324 E Colorado	**distributor rebuilding**
Pasadena, CA 91107	**fuel pump rebuilding**
818-795-3221	

Mail order and open shop. Monday-Friday 8:30 to 5. Carburetor Engineering was established in 1942. We custom rebuild antique and classic carburetors, fuel pumps and distributors, recolor carburetors and fuel pumps as original.

The Carburetor Refactory	**parts**
815 Harbour Way S #5	**rebuilding**
Richmond, CA 94804	**rebushing**
510-237-1277	

Mail order (UPS) and open shop. Monday-Thursday 7:30 to 5:30. Rebuild and rebush American and European carburetors. Also sells parts for those carburetors including throttle shafts, butterflies, rebuild kits, TPS, Varajet, pull-offs, etc.

The Carburetor Shop	**carburetors**
Rt 1, Box 230-A	**carburetor repair**
Eldon, MO 65026	**carb repair kits**
PH/FAX: 573-392-7378	

Open shop. Phone hours: Monday-Friday 8 am to 5 pm. Over 150,000 carburetors on hand 1900-1974. Rebuilding, restoration available. We guarantee our work. Manufacturer of rebuilding kits with following coverage: 1974-1925 99.9%; 1924-1912 80%; 1911-1904 25%. Other carburetors parts available with purchase of repair kit. Also huge library of original carburetor literature for sale. MasterCard and Visa accepted (no fee).

Carl's Ford Parts	**muscle parts**
23219 South ST	
Homeworth, OH 44634	
PH/FAX: 330-525-7291	

See full listing in **Section One** under **Mustang**

Generalists

Chicago Corvette Supply 7322 S Archer Rd Justice, IL 60458 708-458-2500; FAX: 708-458-2662	**parts**

See full listing in **Section One** under **Corvette**

The Classic Preservation Coalition PO Box 262 Taborton Rd Sand Lake, NY 12153-0262 518-674-2445	**restoration**

Mail order only. Deals in restoration/rebuilding of carburetors and fuel pumps. Many references. From driver's rebuild to show, all with tender love and care. Cars and boats.

Collector Car Parts PO Box 6732 Rockford, IL 61125 815-229-1236; FAX: 815-229-1238	**parts**

See full listing in **Section Two** under **comprehensive parts**

Corvair Underground PO Box 339 Dundee, OR 97115 503-434-1648, 800-825-8247 FAX: 503-434-1626	**parts**

See full listing in **Section One** under **Corvair**

Joe Curto Inc 22-09 126th St College Point, NY 11356 718-762-SUSU FAX: 718-762-6287 (h)	**English carbs** **English parts**

See full listing in **Section Two** under **comprehensive parts**

Ehrenreich's Corvair Service 1728 Manor Pkwy Sheboygan, WI 53083-2827 414-458-1170	**parts**

See full listing in **Section One** under **Corvair**

Ferris Auto Electric Ltd 106 Lakeshore Dr North Bay, ONT Canada P1A 2A6 705-474-4560; FAX: 705-474-9453	**parts** **service**

See full listing in **Section Two** under **electrical systems**

For Ramblers Only 2324 SE 34th Ave Portland, OR 97214 503-232-0497 E-mail: ramblermac@aol.com	**accessories** **parts**

See full listing in **Section One** under **AMC**

Thos Hespenheide & Associates Ltd 410 Darby Rd Havertown, PA 19083 610-446-7699, FAX: 610-446-7915	**appraiser** **rebuilding**

See full listing in **Section Two** under **appraisals**

J & C's Parts 7127 Ward Rd North Tonawanda, NY 14120 716-693-4090; FAX: 716-695-7144	**parts**

See full listing in **Section One** under **Buick/McLaughlin**

JAM Engineering Corp PO Box 2570 Monterey, CA 93942 408-372-1787; 800-JAM-CORP	**carburetors**

Mail order. Design and manufacture of 50 State Legal Weber and Holley carburetor replacement packages. Kits include linkage, air cleaner adapters, hardware and more. Specializing in BMW and Mercedes-Benz.

Ken's Carburetors 2301 Barnum Ave Stratford, CT 06497 203-375-9340	**carburetors** **distributors** **parts**

See full listing in **Section One** under **Ford '32-'53**

Midel Pty Ltd 4 Frazer Street Lakemba, NSW 2195 Australia 02-7595598; FAX: 02-7581155	**carburetor parts**

Mail order and open shop. Monday-Friday 9 to 5. Wholesale and retail spare parts sales of SU carburetors and fuel pumps and component parts for vehicles from the thirties to current models. Manufacturer of sand cast 2" SU carburetors and components. Restorer of carburetors and pumps. New carburetors for MG J, P, K3, L, TC, TD, TF.

Millers Incorporated 7412 Count Circle Huntington Beach, CA 92647 714-375-6565; FAX: 714-847-6603 E-mail: millermbz@aol.com	**accessories** **parts**

See full listing in **Section One** under **Mercedes-Benz**

The Old Carb Doctor Rt 3, Box 338, Drucilla Church Rd Nebo, NC 28761 800-945-CARB (2272) 704-659-1428	**carburetors** **fuel pumps**

Mail order and open shop. Open Monday-Saturday 8 am to 7 pm. Carburetors completely restored from core supplied by customer. Castings resurfaced and repaired, shafts rebushed and resealed, rust removal, steel and brass refinished, guaranteed full service restoration at reasonable rates, 1900-1980. Mechanical screw together fuel pumps of the same vintage also restored.

Ram Air Inc 17134 Wood Melvindale, MI 48122 313-382-9036; FAX: 313-382-9480	**engine balancing** **engine blueprinting** **performance** **products**

See full listing in **Section One** under **Pontiac**

Roadster Restoration 3730 Todrob Ln Placerville, CA 95667 916-644-6777; FAX: 916-644-7252	**parts**

See full listing in **Section One** under **Datsun**

Speed Service Inc 3049 W Irving Park Rd Chicago, IL 60618 312-478-1616	**distributors** **engine rebuilding** **magnetos**

See full listing in **Section Two** under **ignition parts**

Straight Six Jaguar 24321 Hatteras St Woodland Hills, CA 91367 PH/FAX: 818-716-1192	**parts** **service**

See full listing in **Section One** under **Jaguar**

Sugarbush Products Inc | carburetors
117 Bristol Rd
Chalfont, PA 18914
215-822-1495; FAX: 215-997-2519

Mail order and open shop. Monday-Friday 8 to 5. NOS and used carburetors bought and sold. Deals in vintage carburetors only.

Tornado Air Management Systems | parts
13360-H Firestone Blvd
Santa Fe Springs, CA 90670
310-926-5000; FAX: 310-926-1223
E-mail: j.k@ix.netcom.com

See full listing in **Section Two** under **accessories**

Tri-Star Pete | parts
1998-1/2 E 1st
Tempe, AZ 85281
602-829-7826; FAX: 602-968-6935

See full listing in **Section One** under **Mercedes-Benz**

Union Performance Co | parts
PO Box 324. 59 Mansfield St
Sharon, MA 02067
617-784-5367, voice mail
FAX: 617-784-5367

See full listing in **Section Two** under **electrical systems**

carpeting

Accurate Auto Tops & Upholstery Inc | tops upholstery
Miller Rd & W Chester Pike
Edgemont, PA 19028
610-356-1515; FAX: 610-353-8230

See full listing in **Section Two** under **upholstery**

Automotive Interior Center | interior trim
1725A Bustleton Pike
Feasterville, PA 19053
PH/FAX: 215-953-7477

See full listing in **Section Two** under **interiors & interior parts**

Bird Nest | parts
PO Box 14865
Portland, OR 97293
800-232-6378; FAX: 503-234-2473

See full listing in **Section One** under **Thunderbird**

Boulevard Motoring Accessories | accessories car covers floor mats
7033 Topanga Canyon Blvd
Canoga Park, CA 91303-1961
818-883-9696; FAX: 818-883-5530

See full listing in **Section One** under **Mercedes-Benz**

Custom Interiors | carpets headliners upholstery
PO Box 51174
Indian Orchard, MA 01151
800-423-6053; FAX: 413-589-9178

See full listing in **Section Two** under **upholstery**

D & R Classic Automotive Inc | parts
30 W 255 Calumet Ave
Warrenville, IL 60563
708-393-0009; FAX: 708-393-1397

See full listing in **Section One** under **Chevelle/Camaro**

Firewall Insulators & Quiet Ride Solutions | firewall insulators
6333 Pacific Ave, Ste 523
Stockton, CA 95207
209-477-4840; FAX: 209-477-0918

See full listing in **Section Two** under **upholstery**

Ford Reproduction Parts Store | parts
110 Ford Rd
PO Box 226
Bryan, OH 43506-0226
419-636-2475; FAX: 419-636-8449
E-mail: fordpart@bright.net

See full listing in **Section One** under **Ford '54-up**

International AutoSport Inc | accessories
Rt 29 N
PO Box 9036
Charlottesville, VA 22906
800-726-1199; FAX: 804-973-2368
E-mail: iap1@international-auto.com

See full listing in **Section Two** under **accessories**

Land Cruisers Solutions Inc | accessories services
20 Thornell Rd
Newton, NH 03858
508-462-5656, MA

See full listing in **Section One** under **Toyota**

Linearossa International Inc | parts
15281 Barranca Pkwy, #A
Irvine, CA 92618
714-727-1201; FAX: 714-727-0603

See full listing in **Section One** under **Fiat**

Maximliner Inc | cargo mats floor mats
150 E Race St
Troy, OH 45373
513-339-0240; 800-624-2320
FAX: 513-335-5424

Manufacturer of pickup and van cargo mats, tailgates and interior floor mats for all automotive vehicles. Maximliner Inc has been manufacturing pickup mats since 1972. We work with major mail order houses, our own distributors and automotive dealers throughout the United States.

Nanco Marketing Agency Inc | automotive carpeting
PO Box 97
Leominster, MA 01453
800-545-8547; FAX: 508-534-0677

Automotive carpeting, preformed automotive carpeting, most models, many colors. Also carpeting sold by the yard, Rt 66 apparel, tote bags, pocket books, pillows, etc.

Raybuck Autobody Parts | body parts
RD 4, Box 170
Punxsutawney, PA 15767
814-938-5248; FAX: 814-938-4250

See full listing in **Section Two** under **body parts**

Sailorette's Nautical Nook
23005 W Kankakee River Dr
Wilmington, IL 60481
815-476-2391; FAX: 815-476-2524

covers
interiors

See full listing in **Section Two** under **upholstery**

castings

Air Flow Research
10490 Ilex Ave
Pacoima, CA 91331
818-890-0616; FAX: 818-890-0490

cylinder heads

See full listing in **Section One** under **Chevrolet**

Alamillo Patterns
N McColl Rd, RR 4, Box 764
Edinburg, TX 78539
210-316-1527; FAX: 210-316-1439

machining
patterns

Both mail order and open shop. Monday thru Saturday 7 am-7 pm. Castings, patterns and machining. Alamillo Patterns has the manpower and technology necessary to meet your requirements on almost any kind of casting up to 500# on the following alloys. Cast iron, ductil iron, aluminum, bronze and steel. We also have complete support of our pattern shop insuring a high quality product.

Anacortes Brass Works Ltd
PO Box 10
Anacortes, WA 98221
360-293-4515; FAX: 360-293-4516

brass castings

Mail order and open shop. Monday-Friday 7 am to 3 pm. Dealing in custom brass castings, buckles, key fobs, emblems. Part reproduction (small).

ASC&P International
PO Box 255
Uwchland, PA 19480
610-458-8395; FAX: 610-458-8735

custom molding
fiberglass
plastic

See full listing in **Two** under **fiberglass parts**

Dwight H Bennett
PO Box 3173
Seal Beach, CA 90740-2173
PH/FAX: 310-498-6488

emblem repair
hardware repair
mascot repair
plaque repair

See full listing in **Section Two** under **radiator emblems & mascots**

Brislawn/Morataya Castings
7904 NE 6th Ave, B-138
Vancouver, WA 98665
360-699-5838; FAX: 360-576-0085

automobilia
castings

Mail order only. Dealing in castings and automobilia, cast Midgets, roadsters, coupes, Le-Sled mood lamp, rod vanes (hot rod weathervanes).

Chevy Shop
338 Main Ave, Box 75
Milledgeville, IL 61051
815-225-7565

custom castings
parts

See full listing in **Section One** under **Chevrolet**

Errol's Steam Works
3123 Baird Rd
North Vancouver, BC Canada V7K 2G5
PH/FAX: 604-985-9494

castings
engines
parts

See full listing in **Section One** under **Locomobile**

Fini-Finish Metal Finishing
24657 Mound Rd
Warren, MI 48091
810-758-0050; FAX: 810-758-0054

plating
polishing
pot metal repair

See full listing in **Section Two** under **plating & polishing**

Jay M Fisher
Acken Dr 4-B
Clark, NJ 07066
908-388-6442

radiator caps
sidemount mirrors

See full listing in **Section Two** under **accessories**

Harter Industries Inc
PO Box 502
Holmdel, NJ 07733
908-566-7055; FAX: 908-566-6977

parts
restoration

See full listing in **Section Two** under **comprehensive parts**

O'Brien Truckers
5 Perry Hill
North Grafton, MA 01536-1532
508-839-3033; FAX: 508-839-9490
E-mail: obrien_dennis@emc.com

accessories
belt buckles
plaques
valve covers

See full listing in **Section Two** under **plaques**

Richardson Restorations
1861 W Woodward Ave
Tulare, CA 93274
209-688-5002

repairs
restoration

See full listing in **Section Two** under **restoration shops**

Generalists

Rite Weld Co 10 Northfield Rd Wallingford, CT 06492 203-265-5984; FAX: 203-284-5063	**castings** **engine repair**

The repair of cracked engine blocks, cyl heads and industrial castings, all makes and models.

Silverleaf Casting Co PO Box 662 116 S Grove St Delton, MI 49046 616-623-6665	**casting** **mascots**

Mail order and open shop. Monday-Friday 9-5. We can reproduce any small part, be it broken, worn or just a sketch, in aluminum, brass, bronze, sterling silver or plastic. Highly detailed parts such as mascots a specialty. Complete pattern making, mold making and machine shop services. One part or a thousand. Investment (lost wax) Casting Co, in brass, bronze, silver and aluminum.

See our ad on page 261

chassis parts

Action Performance Inc 1619 Lakeland Ave Bohemia, NY 11716 516-244-7100; FAX: 516-244-7172	**accessories**

See full listing in **Section Two** under **accessories**

Alan's Axles 2300 Congress Ave Clearwater, FL 34623 800-741-0452; 813-784-0452	**axles**

Mail order and open shop, Monday-Friday 8-6, Saturday 9-5. Rear axle and carrier assembly rebuilding and custom rear axle work for all cars and light trucks. Gear changes, differential installation, axles resplined, housings narrowed, custom axle building is a specialty. Large stock of new and used gears, differentials, etc.

Antique Auto Parts Cellar PO Box 3 6 Chauncy St S Weymouth, MA 02190 617-335-1579; FAX: 617-335-1925	**brake parts** **chassis parts** **engine parts** **fuel pumps/kits** **gaskets/water pumps**

See full listing in **Section Two** under **comprehensive parts**

Atlantic Antique Auto Parts RR #6, PO Box 1388, Site 28 Armdale Halifax, NS Canada B3L 4P4 902-479-0967	**parts** **service**

See full listing in **Section Two** under **rubber parts**

Atlantic Enterprises 221 Strand Industrial Dr Little River, SC 29566 803-399-7565; FAX: 803-399-4600	**steering assemblies**

Mail and open shop. Monday-Friday 8 am-5 pm. Specializing in rebuilt rack and pinion steering assemblies for Jaguar, Aston Martin, Jensen, Triumph, Rover, Rolls-Royce, Bentley.

Authentic Automotive 529 Buttercup Trail Mesquite, TX 75149 972-289-6373	**power brakes** **power steering**

See full listing in **Section One** under **Chevrolet**

Bird Nest PO Box 14865 Portland, OR 97293 800-232-6378; FAX: 503-234-2473	**parts**

See full listing in **Section One** under **Thunderbird**

Bronx Automotive 501 Tiffany St Bronx, NY 10474 718-589-2979	**parts**

See full listing in **Section Two** under **ignition parts**

Bryant's Antique Auto Parts 851 Western Ave Hampden, ME 04444 207-862-4019	**appraisals** **parts** **sheetmetal service**

See full listing in **Section One** under **Ford '03-'31**

Bumpers by Briz 8002 NE Hwy 99, #260 Vancouver, WA 98665 360-573-8628	**bumpers**

Mail order only. Manufacture, retail, wholesale ribbed alloy bumpers for street rods, customs and trucks. Also bumper brackets, license plate guards, air scoops for brake backing plates and hubcaps for Kelsey-Hayes wheels.

Car-Line Manufacturing & **Distribution Inc** 1250 Gulf St PO Box 1192 Beaumont, TX 77701 409-833-9757; FAX: 409-835-2468	**chassis parts** **engine parts** **sheetmetal**

See full listing in **Section Two** under **sheetmetal**

Collector Car Parts PO Box 6732 Rockford, IL 61125 815-229-1236; FAX: 815-229-1238	**parts**

See full listing in **Section Two** under **comprehensive parts**

Collectors Auto Supply 528 Appian Way Coquitlam, BC Canada V3J 2A5 PH/FAX: 604-931-7278 E-mail: jimcarpenter@bc.sympatico.cd	**parts**

See full listing in **Section Two** under **comprehensive parts**

Dakota Studebaker Parts RR 1, Box 103A Armour, SD 57313 605-724-2527	**parts**

See full listing in **Section One** under **Studebaker**

Das Bulli Haus 18 Ward Ln North Franklin, CT 06254 PH/FAX: 860-642-7242 E-mail: mcladm3@uconnvm.uconn.edu	**parts** **sheetmetal**

See full listing in **Section One** under **Volkswagen**

Dependable RV & Auto Service 2619 Rt 11 N Lafayette, NY 13084 315-677-5336	**parts** **restoration** **service**

See full listing in **Section Two** under **service shops**

Generalists (side tab)

Early Ford V8 Sales Inc
9 Hills Rd
Ballston Lake, NY 12019
518-899-9974; FAX: 518-899-5303

parts

See full listing in **Section One** under **Ford '32-'53**

East Spring Obsolete Auto Parts Inc
PO Box 3
Bethlehem, CT 06751
203-266-5488 evenings & weekends

parts

See full listing in **Section Two** under **brakes**

Eastern States Performance Outlet Inc
701 Pine Tree Rd
Danville, PA 17821
PH/FAX: 717-672-9413

suspension parts

See full listing in **Section Two** under **suspension parts**

Eaton Detroit Spring Service Co
1555 Michigan Ave
Detroit, MI 48350
313-963-3839; FAX: 313-963-7047
E-mail: ken@eatonsprings.com

bushings
coil springs
leaf springs
shackles
U-bolts

See full listing in **Section Two** under **suspension parts**

Eckler's Quality Parts & Accessories for Corvettes
PO Box 5637
Titusville, FL 32783
800-327-4868; FAX: 407-383-2059

accessories
parts

See full listing in **Section One** under **Corvette**

Egge Machine Company
11707 Slauson Ave
Santa Fe Springs, CA 90670
310-945-3419 in CA, 800-866-EGGE
FAX: 310-693-1635

babbitting
chassis
motor mounts
pistons/valves
wiring harnesses

See full listing in **Section Two** under **engine parts**

Guldstrand Engineering Inc
11924 W Jefferson Blvd
Culver City, CA 90230
310-391-7108; FAX: 310-391-7424
E-mail: geiauto@aol.com

parts

See full listing in **Section One** under **Corvette**

Harter Industries Inc
PO Box 502
Holmdel, NJ 07733
908-566-7055; FAX: 908-566-6977

parts
restoration

See full listing in **Section Two** under **comprehensive parts**

Mike Hershenfeld
3011 Susan Rd
Bellmore, NY 11710
PH/FAX: 516-781-PART (7278)

parts

See full listing in **Section One** under **MoPar**

Highway Classics
949 N Cataract Ave, Unit J
San Dimas, CA 91702
909-592-8819; FAX: 909-592-4239

parts

See full listing in **Section One** under **Ford '54-up**

Hoffman Automotive Distributor
U.S. Hwy #1, Box 818
Hilliard, FL 32046
904-845-4421

parts

See full listing in **Section Two** under **body parts**

Holcombe Cadillac Parts
2933 Century Ln
Bensalem, PA 19020
215-245-4560; FAX: 215-633-9916

parts

See full listing in **Section One** under **Cadillac/LaSalle**

House of Powder Inc
Rt 71 & 1st St
PO Box 110
Standard, IL 61363
815-339-2648

powder coating
sandblasting

See full listing in **Section Two** under **service shops**

Inline Tube
17540 14 Mile Rd
Fraser, MI 48026
810-294-4093; FAX: 810-294-7349
E-mail: inline@apk.net

brake lines
choke tubes
fuel lines
transmission lines
vacuum lines

See full listing in **Section Two** under **brakes**

Jackson's Old Parts
4502 Grand Ave
Duluth, MN 55807
218-624-5791; 800-333-8059

parts

See full listing in **Section Two** under **engine parts**

Kenask Spring Co
307 Manhattan Ave
Jersey City, NJ 07307
201-653-4589

springs

See full listing in **Section Two** under **suspension parts**

Roger Kraus Racing
2896 Grove Way
Castro Valley, CA 94546
510-582-5031; FAX: 510-886-5605

shocks
tires
wheels

See full listing in **Section Two** under **tires**

Marcel's Corvette Parts
15100 Lee Rd #101
Humble, TX 77396
713-441-2111 info line
800-546-2111 order line
FAX: 713-441-2111

parts

See full listing in **Section One** under **Corvette**

David Martin
Box 61
Roosevelt, TX 76874
915-446-4439

parts

See full listing in **Section One** under **Chrysler**

McDonald Obsolete Parts Company
RR 3, Box 94
Rockport, IN 47635
812-359-4965; FAX: 812-359-5555

body parts
chassis parts

See full listing in **Section One** under **Ford '32-'53**

Michael's Auto Parts
5875 NW Kaiser Rd
Portland, OR 97229
503-690-7750; FAX: 503-690-7735

salvage yard

See full listing in **Section Five** under **Oregon**

Moroso Performance Products Inc
80 Carter Dr
Guilford, CT 06437
203-453-6571; FAX: 203-453-6906

accessories
parts

See full listing in **Section Two** under **racing**

No Limit Engineering
1737 Production Circle
Riverside, CA 92509
FAX: 909-275-9232

brakes
chassis parts

Mail order and open shop. Monday-Friday 9 to 6, Saturday 10 to 2 except race days. Specializing in custom chassis parts, brakes and steering for 48-56 Ford pickup and 47-59 Chevy pickup.

Northern Auto Parts Warehouse Inc
PO Box 3147
Sioux City, IA 51102
800-831-0884; FAX: 712-258-0088

parts

See full listing in **Section Two** under **engine parts**

Northwestern Auto Supply Inc
1101 S Division
Grand Rapids, MI 49507
616-241-1714, 800-704-1078
FAX: 616-241-0924

parts

See full listing in **Section Two** under **engine parts**

Jerrell Pickett
Box 218
Wessington, SD 57381
605-458-2344

literature
parts
sheet metal
wheels

See full listing in **Section Two** under **comprehensive parts**

PM Industries
442 Ridge Rd
West Milford, NJ 07480
800-833-8933; FAX: 201-728-2117

chassis coatings
permanent rust
sealers

See full listing in **Section Two** under **rustproofing**

Precision Paint & Rust Removers Inc
2415 W Industrial Blvd
Long Lake, MN 55356
PH/FAX: 612-476-4545

paint removal
rust removal

See full listing in **Section Two** under **rust removal & stripping**

Quanta Restoration and Preservation Products
45 Cissel Dr
North East, MD 21901
410-658-5700; FAX: 410-658-5758

fan belts
gas tanks

Mail order & retail store. Reproduction gas tanks, fan belts, paints for chassis and underhood, carburetor and driveshaft restoration services, hundreds of rebuilt carbs and one thousand fuel pumps in stock. Other location, retail address: 101 Ryan Dr, Rising Sun, MD 21911.

RARE Corvettes
Joe Calcagno
Box 1080
Soquel, CA 95073
408-475-4442; FAX: 408-475-1115

cars
parts

See full listing in **Section One** under **Corvette**

William H Robenolt
5121 S Bridget Point
Floral City, FL 34436
352-344-2007

front suspension
parts

See full listing in **Section Two** under **suspension parts**

Rochester Clutch & Brake Co
35 Niagara St
Rochester, NY 14605
716-232-2579; FAX: 716-232-3279

brakes
clutches

See full listing in **Section Two** under **brakes**

Smith & Jones Distributing Company Inc
1 Biloxi Square
West Columbia, SC 29170
803-822-8500; FAX: 803-822-8477

parts

See full listing in **Section One** under **Ford '03-'31**

Joe Smith Ford & Hot Rod Parts
2140 Canton Rd, Unit C
Marietta, GA 30066
800-235-4013; 770-426-9850
FAX: 770-426-9854

parts
service

See full listing in **Section One** under **Ford '32-'53**

Star Quality
1 Alley Rd
La Grangeville, NY 12540
800-782-7199; FAX: 914-266-5394
E-mail: sq@mhv.net

parts

See full listing in **Section One** under **Mercedes-Benz**

Bill Thomsen
Rt 4 Box 492
Moneta, VA 24121
540-297-1200

salvage yard

See full listing in **Section Five** under **Virginia**

Tri-Star Pete
1998-1/2 E 1st
Tempe, AZ 85281
602-829-7826; FAX: 602-968-6935

parts

See full listing in **Section One** under **Mercedes-Benz**

Union Performance Co
PO Box 324
59 Mansfield St
Sharon, MA 02067
617-784-5367, voice mail
FAX: 617-784-5367

parts

See full listing in **Section Two** under **electrical systems**

Tom Vagnini
58 Anthony Rd
RR 3
Pittsfield, MA 01201
413-698-2526

used parts

See full listing in **Section One** under **Packard**

Vintage Car Corral   parts
1401 NW 53rd Ave   toys
PO Box 384
Gainesville, FL 32602
PH/FAX: 904-376-4513

See full listing in **Section Two** under **comprehensive parts**

Wallace Walmsley   parts
4732 Bancroft St, #7
San Diego, CA 92116
619-283-3063

See full listing in **Section One** under **Packard**

Westbury Hot Rods   service
1130 Detroit Ave   sheetmetal
Concord, CA 94520   fabrication
510-682-9482; FAX: 510-682-9483

See full listing in **Section Two** under **street rods**

The Wheel Shoppe   performance parts
18011 Fourteen Mile Rd   welding
Fraser, MI 48026   wheel repair
810-415-7171; FAX: 810-415-7181
E-mail: jgs2nd@aol.com

See full listing in **Section Two** under **wheels & wheelcovers**

Wild Bill's Corvette & Hi-   parts
Performance Center Inc   rebuilding
451 Walpole St   service
Norwood, MA 02062
617-551-8858

See full listing in **Section One** under **Corvette**

clutches

Bob's Automotive Machine   engine parts
30 Harrison Ave   machine shop
Harrison, NJ 07029
201-483-0059; FAX: 201-483-6092

See full listing in **Section Two** under **machine work**

Orion Motors European Parts Inc   parts
10722 Jones Rd
Houston, TX 77065
800-736-6410; 713-894-1982
FAX: 713-849-1997

See full listing in **Section One** under **Alfa Romeo**

coachbuilders & designers

Ashton Keynes Vintage   restoration
Restorations Ltd   coachbuilding
A Keith Bowley
Ashton Keynes, Swindon
Wilshire England
01285/861-288
FAX: 01285/860-604

See full listing in **Section One** under **Rolls-Royce/Bentley**

Auto Fashions & Creations   auto sales
2209-B Hamlets Chapel Rd   handcrafts
Pittsboro, NC 27312   restoration
PH/FAX: 919-542-5566, press (*) for   rubber ink stamps
tone

See full listing in **Section Two** under **restoration shops**

Backyard Buddy Corp   automotive lift
1818 N Main St, PO Box 5104
Niles, OH 44446
330-544-9372; FAX: 330-544-9311

See full listing in **Section Two** under **accessories**

Bonnets Up   restoration
5736 Spring St
Clinton, MD 20735
301-297-4759

Mail order and open shop. By appointment only. Monday-Saturday 7 am to 3 pm. Ron Naida, owner, in business over 20 years. Provide numerous services, SU carb rebuilding to ground-up restorations on British, German and Italian marques. Our facilities consist of custom metal fabrication, wood working equipment, specialized assembly jigs. Full bodywork and paint facilities, and the latest in welding technology for accomplishing difficult jobs. We will handle any form of servicing to your specs.

Deters Restorations   restoration
6205 Swiss Garden Rd
Temperance, MI 48182-1020
313-847-1820

See full listing in **Section Two** under **restoration shops**

Euro Coachworks Inc   repair & fabrication
812 NW 57th St
Ft Lauderdale, FL 33309
954-772-8272; FAX: 954-772-8148

See full listing in **Section One** under **Ferrari**

Exotic Enterprises   fiberglass
459 Madeline Ave   manufacturing
Garfield, NJ 07026   fiberglass mold
201-523-2217, 201-956-7570   making

See full listing in **Section Two** under **fiberglass parts**

Fairlane Automotive Specialties   fiberglass bodies
210 E Walker St   parts
St. Johns, MI 48879
517-224-6460

See full listing in **Section One** under **Ford '32-'53**

Jack Juratovic   artwork
819 Absequami Trail
Lake Orion, MI 48362
PH/FAX: 810-814-0627

See full listing in **Section Two** under **artwork**

Georges B Karakolev   car dealer
228 Rt 221   parts
Napierville, QUE Canada J0J 1L0   restoration
PH/FAX: 514-245-0028

See full listing in **Section Two** under **restoration aids**

Land Yachts Automobile   restoration
Restoration and Customizing
497 London Bridge Rd, Suite 101
Virginia Beach, VA 23454
757-431-0294; FAX: 757-431-4524

See full listing in **Section Two** under **restoration shops**

Marshall Antique & Classic Restorations 3714 Old Philadelphia Pike Bethlehem, PA 18015 610-868-7765; FAX: 610-868-7529	**coolant additives** **restoration services**

See full listing in **Section One** under **Rolls-Royce/Bentley**

New Era Motors 11611 NE 50th Ave, Unit 6 Vancouver, WA 98686 360-573-8788	**restoration**

See full listing in **Section Two** under **woodwork**

Odyssey Restorations Inc 8080 Central Ave NE Spring Lake Park, MN 55432 612-786-1518; FAX: 612-786-1524	**parts** **restoration**

See full listing in **Section Two** under **restoration shops**

Pilgrim's Special Interest Autos 3888 Hill Rd Lakeport, CA 95453 PH/FAX: 707-262-1062	**bodywork** **metal fabrication** **paint** **restoration**

See full listing in **Section Two** under **restoration shops**

Precision Paint & Rust Removers Inc 2415 W Industrial Blvd Long Lake, MN 55356 PH/FAX: 612-476-4545	**paint removal** **rust removal**

See full listing in **Section Two** under **rust removal & stripping**

Ray's Upholstering 600 N St Frances Cabrini Ave Scranton, PA 18504 800-296-RAYS; FAX: 717-963-0415	**partial/total** **restoration**

See full listing in **Section Two** under **restoration shops**

Route 66 Classic Restorations 250 N 1st St Wilmington, IL 60481 815-476-4290	**restoration**

See full listing in **Section Two** under **restoration shops**

Thompson Hill Metalcraft 23 Thompson Hill Rd Berwick, ME 03901 207-698-5756	**metal forming** **panel beating** **welding**

See full listing in **Section Two** under **sheetmetal**

Vicarage Jaguars 3952 Douglas Rd Miami, FL 33133 305-444-8759; FAX: 305-443-6443	**parts** **restoration**

See full listing in **Section One** under **Jaguar**

The Woodie Works Box 346, RR 3 Arlington, VT 05250 802-375-9305	**woodworking**

See full listing in **Section Two** under **woodwork**

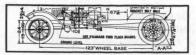

comprehensive parts

ADP Parts Services 14800 28th Ave N Plymouth, MN 55447 800-825-0644; FAX: 612-553-0270	**interchange info** **manuals**

See full listing in **Section Two** under **car & parts locators**

All British Car Parts Inc 2847 Moores Rd Baldwin, MD 21013 410-692-9572; FAX: 410-692-5654	**parts**

See full listing in **Section Two** under **electrical systems**

American Performance Products 675 S Industry Rd Cocoa, FL 32926 407-632-8299; FAX: 407-632-5119	**parts**

See full listing in **Section One** under **AMC**

Antique Auto Parts PO Box 64 60 View Dr Elkview, WV 25071 304-965-1821	**parts** **parts cars**

Mail order and open shop. Monday-Saturday 9 to dusk, except Wednesday closes at 5:30. Antique parts for all makes and models, plus 120 parts cars from 1935 to 1969. Parting out 100 cars and trucks from 1935-1972.

Antique Auto Parts Cellar PO Box 3 6 Chauncy St S Weymouth, MA 02190 617-335-1579; FAX: 617-335-1925	**brake parts** **chassis parts** **engine parts** **fuel pumps/kits** **gaskets/water pumps**

Mail order and open shop. Weekdays 9 am to 5 pm. Supplies new, new old stock and our own reproduction quality mechanical parts for US cars and trucks from 1910 to 1991. Revulcanizing motor mounts (100+ different ones, plus thousands of NOS), fuel pumps and kits, water pumps, motor parts: pistons, rings, valves, guides, tappets, timing components (more than 20 of our own manufacture), gaskets (more than 200 cut on our own dies); bearings and seals; brake and suspension parts; rebuilding services on starters, generators, tank senders, distributors, vacuum advances, clutches. Providing the hobby with guaranteed parts and services since 1975.

See our ad on page 267

Atlantic British Ltd PO Box 110 Rover Ridge Dr Mechanicville, NY 12118 800-533-2210; FAX: 518-664-6641	**accessories** **parts**

See full listing in **Section One** under **Rover/Land Rover**

Auto Parts Exchange PO Box 736 Reading, PA 19603 610-372-2813, 7-10 am, 7-12 pm, 7 days	**NORS parts** **NOS parts** **rebuilt parts** **used parts**

See full listing in **Section One** under **Lincoln**

Blaser's Auto, Nash, Rambler, AMC 3200 48th Ave Moline, IL 61265 309-764-3571; FAX: 309-764-1155	**NOS parts**

See full listing in **Section One** under **AMC**

Generalists

Chris' Parts Cars
1409 Rt 179
Lambertville, NJ 08530-3413
609-397-9045

cars
parts

Cars seen by appointment only. Complete cars from forties, fifties and sixties, many are restorable, and over 200 parts cars. Would rather sell complete cars, not parts, on most. Prices range from $75 to $475.

Classic Cars & Parts
Mike Chmilarski
PO Box 375
Lindenhurst, NY 11757
516-888-5717

car dealer
parts

See full listing in **Section Two** under **car dealers**

Classic Chevy International
PO Box 607188
Orlando, FL 32860-7188
800-456-1956; FAX: 407-299-3341
E-mail: cciworld@aol.com

modified parts
repro parts
used parts

See full listing in **Section One** under **Chevrolet**

Collector Car Parts
PO Box 6732
Rockford, IL 61125
815-229-1236; FAX: 815-229-1238

parts

Mail order only. Primarily Cadillac, GM, Buick, Duesenberg, Packard, Chrysler parts. Some Ford and Mercedes 1940-1969. We are a mail order parts depot for out of state orders. No COD and we buy pre-1975 luxury vehicles in any condition.

Collectors Auto Supply
528 Appian Way
Coquitlam, BC Canada V3J 2A5
PH/FAX: 604-931-7278
E-mail: jimcarpenter@bc.sympatico.cd

parts

Mechanical, braking, chassis, body and rubber parts for vehicles to 1909. Electrical and tune-up items a specialty. Free all makes illustrated tune-up parts catalogues for 1974 and earlier by mail or fax. Specify ignition system manufacturer: Asian (to 1960); Autolite (to mid 1920s); Delco-Remy (to mid 1920s); Bosch (to mid 1950s); Ducellier (to mid 1950s); Lucas (to mid 1930s); Marelli (to mid 1950s); SEV (to mid 1950s) and Ford (to 1909). No retail display. Second location: 1733 H St #330-793, Blaine, WA 98230-5107.

Corvette Specialties of MD Inc
1912 Liberty Rd
Eldersburg, MD 21784
410-795-3180; FAX: 410-795-3247

parts
restoration
service

See full listing in **Section One** under **Corvette**

Joe Curto Inc
22-09 126th St
College Point, NY 11356
718-762-SUSU
FAX: 718-762-6287 (h)

English carbs
English parts

Mail order and open shop. Monday-Friday 9 to 6:30 EST. Large stocks of SU and British Stromberg parts, new and used. Comprehensive rebuilding service, as well as a knowledgeable staff to serve you. We are also 24 years' in the British car trade, so we are well versed in the ins and outs of Lucas, Girling and Lockheed systems. We also offer full rebuilding of water pumps, starters, generators, wiper motors, calipers, servos.

FUEL PUMP KITS: 1928-70 9/92

| AC & AC-style | | Stewart Warner Mechanical Style | | | Carter |
| English AC | French AC | FISPA | Telecamit | SU Electrics | & Others... |

We make our own fresh new stock fuel pump kits for many of the above types of pumps. Kits contain diaphragms in reinforced nitrile rubber, good to 20% alcohol in your fuel, valves, gaskets, seals, & the other wearing parts required to rebuild a pump for reliable service.

Single-Action Kits: Repair pumps that pump fuel only at **$22.50** plus $5.00 shipping and handling in US.

Dual-Action Kits: Repair combination fuel and vacuum pumps at **$34.50** plus the same $5.00.

New Fuel Pumps: Can be custom assembled for many models. New arms, linkages, springs and mostly new castings produce a pump that is very close in appearance to the original. Rare script castings are sometimes available at additional cost. Single Action New Fuel Pumps range from $39.50 to $195.00, with most priced around $55.00. Dual-Action Pumps start at $65.00. New Electric Pumps are available in 6 & 12 volt for installation as backups. Rebuilt pumps, with used castings & new internals are available at times.

Rebuilding Services: While we encourage you to rebuild your own pump, and will help you over any rough spots by phone or by mail, we will rebuild your pump for you. Singles are $55.00 for labor and kit parts; Duals are $75.00 for labor and kit parts. Extra parts are, well, extra. We will rebuild some marine pumps. We will supply parts for aircraft pumps, but you must have these assembled by proper aircraft techs.

Fuel Pump Parts: Besides our kits we offer some repair parts. Pump actuating or rocker arms are not for sale. If an arm is worn out or damaged, it is time for a new pump. Certain castings are availabe. Glass and metal fuel bowls, and old-style add-on sediment bowls are available. Sets of screws for replacing damaged originals are available: single-action sets, $4.50; dual-action sets, $9.50.

Many Other Parts Too: Fuel pumps and kits are a small part of our inventory. We attempt to supply a wide range of new mechanical parts and gaskets for US cars and trucks from 1910 to 1992. Pistons, rings, valve-train parts, gaskets and seals, timing components, motor bearings, clutch and brake parts and services, electrical parts, transmission and driveline parts, bearings and grease seals, motor mounts, extensive suspension parts.

Many Services Available Too: Motor mount re-vulcanization for many rare applications, rebuilding of water pumps, starters and generators, distributors and vacuum advances, gas tank sending units, vacuum tanks, voltage regulators and solenoids, vacuum or electric wiper motors, temperature gauges, cam shaft regrinding and rebabbitting.

SASE With Inquiries Please!

We have served the restorer since 1975 with experienced parts people who try to be helpful. What we sell is intended to fit and to please or it may be returned intact and unused for replacement or refund. Thanks, and best of luck with your restoration.

Antique Auto Parts Cellar

VISA   MasterCard.

Tom Hannaford, Jr
PO Box 3
S Weymouth, MA 02190
617-335-1579

Davies Corvette
5130 Main St
New Port Richey, FL 34653
813-842-8000, 800-236-2383
FAX: 813-846-8216

customizing
parts
restoration

See full listing in **Section One** under **Corvette**

Daytona Turbo Action Camshafts
1109 N US #1, PO Box 5094
Ormond Beach, FL 32175
800-505-CAMS, 904-676-7478
FAX: 904-258-1582

camshafts
engine parts

See full listing in **Section Two** under **bearings**

**Design Fabrications, Pure
Products Division**
PO Box 40205
Santa Barbara, CA 93140-0205
805-965-6031

parts

Mail order and open shop. Monday through Friday 9 to 5 by appointment. Dealing in high quality reproduction parts: short run (one or more) molded plastic and rubber reproductions of unavailable automotive parts. Exact, high tolerance injection molded lenses (red, amber and clear), knobs, emblems, pads, gaskets and rubber parts. Process uses original part or machined aluminum model to fabricate mold set and parts for any make or model vehicle.

Don's Antique Auto Parts
37337 Niles Blvd
Fremont, CA 94536
415-792-4390

new parts
used parts

Mail order and open shop. Monday-Saturday 9:30 to 6. Deals in American parts up to 1954 for most cars and trucks. Specializes in 36-48 Lincoln Zephyrs and Continentals. New, used and rebuilt parts.

Bob Drake Reproductions Inc
1819 NW Washington Blvd
Grants Pass, OR 97526
800-221-3673; FAX: 541-474-0099

repro parts

See full listing in **Section One** under **Ford '32-'53**

East Spring Obsolete Auto Parts Inc
PO Box 3
Bethlehem, CT 06751
203-266-5488 evenings & weekends

parts

See full listing in **Section Two** under **brakes**

**Eckler's Quality Parts &
Accessories for Corvettes**
PO Box 5637
Titusville, FL 32783
800-327-4868; FAX: 407-383-2059

accessories
parts

See full listing in **Section One** under **Corvette**

Egge Machine Company
11707 Slauson Ave
Santa Fe Springs, CA 90670
310-945-3419 in CA, 800-866-EGGE
FAX: 310-693-1635

babbitting
chassis
motor mounts
pistons/valves
wiring harnesses

See full listing in **Section Two** under **engine parts**

FireAro Restoration Parts Co
935 Hedge Dr
Mississauga, ONT Canada L4Y 1E9
PH/FAX: 905-277-3230

accessories
parts

See full listing in **Section One** under **Chevelle/Camaro**

For Ramblers Only
2324 SE 34th Ave
Portland, OR 97214
503-232-0497
E-mail: ramblermac@aol.com

accessories
parts

See full listing in **Section One** under **AMC**

G & L Classics
8225 Taffy Dr
West Chester, OH 45069
513-779-1957

parts

See full listing in **Section One** under **Chevrolet**

John Giles Cars & Parts (ASV&S)
703 Morgan Ln
Pascagoula, MS 39567
PH/FAX: 601-769-8904

car & parts locator
exporter

See full listing in **Section Two** under **car & parts locators**

Gowen Auto Parts
Rt 2, PO Box 249
Coffeyville, KS 67337
316-251-4237

parts

Mail order and open shop. Antique and classic parts, 1910s-70s. Mostly engine, brake and suspension parts. Also classic rebuilt short blocks.

Haneline Products Co
PO Box 430
Morongo Valley, CA 92256
619-363-6597; FAX: 619-363-7321

gauges
instrument panels
stainless parts
trim parts

See full listing in **Section Two** under **instruments**

Harter Industries Inc
PO Box 502
Holmdel, NJ 07733
908-566-7055; FAX: 908-566-6977

parts
restoration

Mail order and shop open by appointment only. Restoration and replacement of almost any cast, machined, small formed sheet-metal or wood part for antique and classic cars. "We work from your old part, a borrowed part or a carefully dimensioned sketch or photograph." Service for car owners and restorers. Call or write to help solve hard-to-find parts problems.

HochKraeusen Racing
PO Box 716
18233 Madison Rd
Parkman, OH 44080-0716
216-548-2147

machine shop

See full listing in **Section Two** under **machine work**

Wayne Hood
228 Revell Rd
Grenada, MS 38901
601-227-8426

NORS parts
NOS parts

Mail order and open shop. Monday-Saturday 8 to 6. NOS, NORS parts for cars and trucks, 1930s-1960s. Specializes in fair prices and quick service. Have mostly mechanical parts and some lenses for all makes 1930s-1960s.

IMCADO Manufacturing Co
50 Winthrop Ave
PO Box 87
Umatilla, FL 32784-0087
352-669-3308

leather equipment

Mail order and open shop. Monday-Friday 9 to 5. Complete line of leather equipment for any motorcar ever built from 1896 on. Hood belts, top straps, crank holsters, fan belts, axle straps, gaiters, joint boots, etc. Original replacement authenticated and approved, prime grade cowhide with select hardware. 12-month warranty.

Indian Adventures Inc
121 South St, PO Box 206
Foxboro, MA 02035
508-359-4660; FAX: 508-359-5435

parts

Authorized retailers only. Specialty and reproduction parts for 60s and 70s cars including engine cradles, throttle shafts, license pockets, frame repair kits, rear end dollies, carburetor rebuild kits and other restoration helpers.

Interesting Parts Inc
Paul TerHorst
27526 N Owens Rd
Mundelein, IL 60060
PH/FAX: 847-949-1030

appraisals
gaskets
parts
storage
transport

Mail order and open shop. Open by appointment only. Local transportation and storage service. Classic parts especially for Packard, Cadillac, Auburn, etc. Also reproduction gaskets and appraisal services.

Jack's Auto Ranch
N6848 H Islandview Rd
Watertown, WI 53094
414-699-2521

used parts

Mail order and open shop. Monday-Friday 8 to 5; Saturday 8 to 12 noon. New and used auto parts, parts cars and complete line of NOS front end suspension parts and motors for all makes.

Jess Auto Supply Co
119 Market
Wilmington, DE 19801
302-654-6021

parts

Mail order and open shop. Monday-Friday 9 to 7; Saturday 9 to 3; Sunday 12 to 3. Auto parts store since 1919. Parts for cars covering 1940-1990. No body parts.

Kanter Auto Products
76 Monroe St
Boonton, NJ 07005
800-526-1096; or 201-334-9575
FAX: 201-334-5423

car cover
carpets
parts

Monday-Friday 8:30 to 6, Saturday 9 to 2. Helping you keep fun on the American road since 1960. New 76 page catalog, featuring front end kits, brakes, engine parts, interior/exterior trim, leather, exhaust, fuel and water pumps, suspension parts, weatherstripping, electrical parts, books and manuals, transmission parts, carburetors and more for 1930-1990 cars. Web site: http://www.kanter.com

Klasse 356 Inc
741 N New St
Allentown, PA 18102
800-634-7862; FAX: 610-432-8027
E-mail: parts@klasse356.com

cars
parts
restoration

See full listing in **Section One** under **Porsche**

Lee's Kustom Auto and Street Rods
RR 3, Box 3061A
Rome, PA 18837
717-247-2326

accessories
parts
restoration

See full listing in **Section Two** under **street rods**

Leo R Lindquist
Rt 2, Box 77
Balaton, MN 56115-9215
507-734-2051

1950s Hemi parts
NORS parts
NOS parts

See full listing in **Section One** under **MoPar**

M & T Manufacturing Co
Hopkins Lane Mill
PO Box 3730
Peace Dale, RI 02883
401-789-0472; FAX: 401-789-5650

parts
wooden bows

See full listing in **Section Two** under **woodwork**

Glenn Malme
PO Box 1339
Downey, CA 90240
310-869-6491

rebuild kits

See full listing in **Section Two** under **brakes**

W L Wally Mansfield
Box 237, 526 E 2nd
Blue Springs, NE 68318-0237
402-645-3546

cars
parts
trucks

Mail order and open shop. Shop open by appointment only. Prewar cars, trucks and parts. Specializing in Model T and A, NOS and good used parts. Also 1925-48 Chevrolet, 1914-48 Ford and 1920-26 Dodge, all makes to 1950.

Mark Auto Co Inc
Layton, NJ 07851
201-948-4157; FAX: 201-948-5458

parts
restoration supplies

See full listing in **Section One** under **Ford '03-'31**

The Maverick Connection
137 Valley Dr
Ripley, WV 25271
PH/FAX: 304-372-7825

literature
parts

See full listing in **Section One** under **Ford '54-up**

McVey's
5040 Antioch, Suite E
Merriam, KS 66203
913-722-0707; FAX: 913-722-1166

parts
trim

See full listing in **Section One** under **Cadillac/LaSalle**

Mooney's Antique Parts
HC 01, Box 645C
Goodrich, TX 77335
409-365-2899, 9 am to 6 pm
409-685-4577, 6-9 pm for orders only

engine parts
rubber parts

Mail order only. Monday-Friday 9 to 5:30; Saturday 9 to 12. Large line of parts for Chevrolets, 1916-54 passenger cars and 1947-54 pickups. Complete line of mechanical, transmission, engine, ignition, rubber parts, etc. Free catalog. Zoned for mail order only. Counter sales by chance or appointment.

Mustang Classics
3814 Walnut St
Denver, CO 80205
303-295-3140

parts
restoration
sales
service

See full listing in **Section One** under **Mustang**

Mustang of Chicago Ltd
1321 W Irving Park Rd
Bensenville, IL 60106
708-860-7077
FAX: 708-860-7120, 24 hrs

new & used parts

See full listing in **Section One** under **Mustang**

National Chevy Assoc
947 Arcade Street
St Paul, MN 55106
612-778-9522; FAX: 612-778-9686

parts

See full listing in **Section One** under **Chevrolet**

National Parts Locator Service
636 East 6th St #81
Ogden, UT 84404-2415
801-392-9455

parts locator

See full listing in **Section Two** under **car & parts locators**

NOS Only
414 Umbarger Rd, Unit E
San Jose, CA 95111
408-227-2353, 408-227-2354
FAX: 408-227-2355

NOS parts

Retail and mail order. Monday-Friday 9 am-6 pm PST. Specializing in new and obsolete Ford, Lincoln, Mercury parts from 1955 to current year. Car, truck and van parts. Authorized distributor of Dennis Carpenter repro.

Obsolete Auto Parts Co
PO Box 5, 143 Comleroy Rd
Kurrajong, NSW 2758 Australia
61-45-731424; FAX: 61-45-732106

parts

Mail order and open shop. Monday-Saturday 9 to 5. Shop address: 143 Comleroy Road. A.J. Noonan, owner. 1900 to 1960s new and used parts for English, Continental and American vehicles.

Old Ford Parts
35 4th Ave N
Algona, WA 98001
206-833-8494; FAX: 206-833-2190

parts

See full listing in **Section One** under **Ford '32-'53**

Original Parts Group Inc
17892 Gothard St
Huntington Beach, CA 92647
800-243-8355 US & Canada
714-841-5363; FAX: 714-847-8159

**accessories
parts**

See full listing in **Section One** under **Pontiac**

Parts House
2912 Hunter St
Fort Worth, TX 76112
817-451-2708; FAX: 817-496-8909

**accessories
parts**

Mail and telephone orders. Cars and light trucks: 1930-75 suspension/steering; engine valves, valve train, lifters, pistons, gaskets, bearings, starters, generators, fuel pumps, water pumps; brake parts, drivetrain bearings and seals, 1949-63 floor mats, trunk mats, car and truck seat covers; 1949-61 reproduction and NOS sheetmetal. Auto and truck parts, new and rebuilt.

The Parts Scout®
Bodo Repenn
Diagonalstrasse 18A
D-20537 Hamburg Germany
*49-40-21980130
FAX: *49-40-21980132

**parts
parts locator**

Mail order only. Parts locator, worldwide supply of quality spare parts and accessories. Specializing in luxury and sports cars of all makes from 1920 to 1975, fast international service, 24 hr FAX line.

Garth B Peterson
122 N Conklin Rd
Veradale, WA 99037
509-926-4620 anytime

**accessories
parts
radios**

Tremendous supply of NOS/used Hudson, Nash, AMC parts, accessories and sheetmetal. Also new/used parts and accessories for all 1930-1970 cars. Original car radios and hood ornaments for all cars. We try to do the impossible for you. SASE please.

Jerrell Pickett
Box 218
Wessington, SD 57381
605-458-2344

**literature
parts
sheet metal
wheels**

Shop open by chance. Sells used parts for cars to the fifties. Sheetmetal to the forties. Miscellaneous literature, some wire wheels, carbs, decklids, misc instrument clusters, hubcaps, window trim moldings, lights, radiator shells, horns, carburetors. Many miscellaneous chrome and die cast moldings to the fifties.

R E Pierce
47 Stone Rd
Wendell Depot, MA 01380
508-544-7442; FAX: 508-544-2978

**parts
restoration**

See full listing in **Section One** under **Volvo**

Pre-Sixties Cars and Parts Ltd
19234 Holland Landing Rd
Holland Landing, ONT
Canada L9N 1M8
PH/FAX: 905-836-6776 or
800-364-7710

parts

Mail order and open shop. Monday-Saturday 9 am-9 pm. Dealer in mechanical parts for North American cars 1920-1960. Have been established since 1979. Large and varied stock of parts. Buy and sell job lots.

Pro Motorcar Products Inc
22025 US 19 N
Clearwater, FL 34625
800-323-1090; 813-726-9225
FAX: 813-726-6587

**car care products
gauges
paint thickness
sanding block
screw saver**

Spot Rot® autobody gauge finds filler, hidden rust, collision damage, complete with used vehicle buying guide, $14.95. Pro Gauge® accurately measures paint thickness, avoid problems, $49. Multi-purpose Preppen Glass Fiber Brush cleans rust, electrical contacts, guns, etc, $6.95. ChipKit™ complete easy do-it-yourself fix for paint chips, scratches, includes PrepPen, $16.95. Liquid Torque® removes stripped screws, $5.95. Microbrush lint free minibrush for quick touch up in hard to reach areas, $6.95. Pro Block professional final finish sanding block, $11.95.

Sam Quinn Cadillac Parts
Box 837
Estacada, OR 97023
503-637-3852

parts

See full listing in **Section One** under **Cadillac/LaSalle**

RB's Obsolete Automotive
18421 Hwy 99
Lynnwood, WA 98037
206-670-6739; FAX: 206-670-9151

parts

Mail order and open shop. Shop open Tues-Thurs 10 to 5:30, Friday 10-5, Saturday 10 to 3. Deals in aftermarket products for

street rods, classics, antiques and special interest vehicles. Specializing in Chevrolet and Ford cars and trucks.

R-D-T Plans and Parts PO Box 2272 Merced, CA 95344 209-383-4441	car parts trailer plans

See full listing in **Section Two** under **trailers**

Reproduction Parts Marketing #3-1707 Sask Ave Saskatoon, SAS Canada S7K 1P7 306-652-6668; FAX: 306-652-1123	parts restoration service

See full listing in **Section One** under **Chevrolet**

Restoration Specialties and Supply Inc PO Box 328, 148 Minnow Creek Ln Windber, PA 15963 814-467-9842; FAX: 814-467-5323	parts

Mail order and open shop. Monday-Friday 9 to 5. Weatherstripping, clips, fasteners, mattings, screws and bolts. Family-owned corporation with each order receiving the prompt attention it deserves. 95% of all orders are shipped the same day as received. Illustrated catalog available, $3.50 USA; $5 Canada & overseas.

Restoration Supply Company 2060 Palisade Dr Reno, NV 89509 702-825-5663; FAX: 702-825-9330 E-mail: restoration@rsc.reno.nv.us	accessories restoration supplies

See full listing in **Section Two** under **restoration aids**

Roaring Twenties Antiques Rt 1 Box 104-D Madison, VA 22727 703-948-3744, 703-948-6290 FAX: 703-948-3744	parts/ automobilia signs gasoline collectibles

Open Thursday-Monday 10-5, Sunday 12-5. Automobilia, car parts, signs, service station and gasoline collectibles, collectible toy cars and trucks, interesting and unique memorabilia for sale. Rt 29N, 2 miles south of scenic Madison, Virginia. In the foothills of the Blue Ridge, 26 miles north of Charlottesville, 90 miles south of Washington, DC.

Scarborough Faire Inc 1151 Main St Pawtucket, RI 02860 800-556-6300; 401-724-4200 FAX: 401-724-5392	parts

See full listing in **Section One** under **MG**

Donald E Schneider Marinette & Menominee RR 1, N7340 Miles Rd Porterfield, WI 54159 715-732-4958	parts

Mail order and open shop. Open by appointment only. NOS parts for 1930-69 cars and trucks. No body parts. Club parts being sold to finance club projects.

Selco Restoration 9315 FM 359 Richmond, TX 77469 713-342-9751	parts restoration service

See full listing in **Section One** under **Cadillac/LaSalle**

Joe Smith Ford & Hot Rod Parts 2140 Canton Rd, Unit C Marietta, GA 30066 800-235-4013; 770-426-9850 FAX: 770-426-9854	parts service

See full listing in **Section One** under **Ford '32-'53**

Special Interest Cars 451 Woody Rd Oakville, ONT Canada L6K 2Y2 905-844-8063; FAX: 905-338-8063	parts

Mail order and open shop. Monday-Friday 8-5:30, Saturday 9-5. Canada's largest obsolete automotive warehouse specializing in hard to find steering and brake parts. Currently supply 50-60 dealers. Also large stock of import brake, ignition, water pumps, clutches, suspension, etc by Lucas, Quinton Hazel and other makes for sale enbloc or will break up for quantity sales wholesale. Also an obsolete Ford warehouse, inquire for all your needs.

Speed & Spares America (IPM Group) 16123 Runnymede St, Unit H Van Nuys, CA 91406-2952 818-781-1711; FAX: 818-781-8842	parts racing equipment

Mail order and open shop. Monday-Friday 8 to 4. Supplies parts and racing equipment to businesses overseas. NOS and replacement parts and racing equipment for 1950 to present GMCs, Fords, Chryslers and AMC/Jeeps. Also warehouse in England: Speed & Spares America, Unit 4, Epsom Business Park, Kiln Ln, Epsom, Surrey KT17 1JF, England. PH: 01372-745-747; FAX: 01372-728-485.

Speedway Motors Inc 300 Speedway Cir Lincoln, NE 68502 402-474-4411; FAX: 402-477-7476	parts

Mail order and open shop. Monday-Friday 7 am-7 pm February through July (8 am-6 pm all other months); Saturday 9-1. Over 22,000 unique parts for the restorer and street rodder are available through our 325 page annual catalog. Specializes in hard to find parts including an extensive selection of flathead Ford parts. Offers 100s of fiberglass replacement body parts from our own factory. Affordable street rod kits and so much more.

Star Classics Inc 7745 E Redfield #300 Scottsdale, AZ 85260 602-991-7495, 800-644-7827 FAX: 602-951-4096	parts sales service

See full listing in **Section One** under **Mercedes-Benz**

Straight Six Jaguar 24321 Hatteras St Woodland Hills, CA 91367 PH/FAX: 818-716-1192	parts service

See full listing in **Section One** under **Jaguar**

Super Sport Restoration Parts Inc 7138 Maddox Rd Lithonia, GA 30058 770-482-9219	NOS parts used parts

See full listing in **Section One** under **Chevrolet**

Thunderbird Headquarters 1080 Detroit Ave Concord, CA 94518 800-227-2174, US FAX: 510-689-1771	accessories literature parts upholstery

See full listing in **Section One** under **Thunderbird**

Generalists

TMC Publications
5817 Park Heights Ave
Baltimore, MD 21215
410-367-4490; FAX: 410-466-3566

| literature |
| Mercedes parts |

See full listing in **Section Two** under **literature dealers**

Jim Tucker
29597 Paso Robles Rd
Valley Center, CA 92082
619-749-3488

| carburetors |
| heater valves |
| trans gears |
| U-joints |

Mail order and open shop. Shop open by appointment. Specializing in new Ranco & Harrison thermostatically controlled heater control valves. Also rebuild your original heater valve, 1949-1963, all makes. Vacuum & mechanical valves for cars 1963-1975 also on hand. Carburetors for all makes 1946-1970 (rebuilt) in stock. Transmission gears and U-joints also on hand, for 1948-1963 cars. In business full time for 15 years. Advertising in *Hemmings Motor News*.

Vintage Acquisition
PO Box 907
Palm Harbor, FL 34682
813-787-5643 inquiries/orders
FAX: 813-787-8210

| cars |
| parts |
| speed equipment |

Buy, sell, trade vintage, performance cars, parts, speed equipment, domestic & export.

Vintage Auto Parts
PO Box 323
Temple, PA 19560-0323
610-926-2485, 9 am-noon, 5-7 pm,
answering machine

| car dealer |
| new & used parts |

See full listing in **Section One** under **BMW**

Vintage Auto Parts Inc
24300 Woodinville-Snohomish Hwy
Woodinville, WA 98072
800-426-5911; 206-486-0777
FAX: 206-486-0778

| cars |
| parts |

Mail order and open shop. Monday-Saturday 8 to 5 PST. 10,000 square foot warehouse full of new old stock parts for 1916-70 American cars and trucks, plus 10 acres of wrecked 1935-70 American cars and trucks for parts. "Since 1959, we have had one of the most complete stocks on earth."

Vintage Car Corral
1401 NW 53rd Ave, PO Box 384
Gainesville, FL 32602
PH/FAX: 904-376-4513

| parts |
| toys |

Mail order and open shop. Open Monday-Friday 11 am to 5 pm. Specializing in parts and toys, Ertl, spec cast for 30s thru 70s.

Gary Vorel
318 78th St
Niagara Falls, NY 14304
716-283-9716, 716-286-4996

| parts |
| service |

See full listing in **Section One** under **Ford '54-up**

Wild Bill's Corvette &
Hi-Performance Center Inc
451 Walpole St
Norwood, MA 02062
617-551-8858

| parts |
| rebuilding |
| service |

See full listing in **Section One** under **Corvette**

R Donald Williams
RD 1, Box 111
Brotherton Rd
Berlin, PA 15530
814-267-3250

| parts |

Mail order and open shop. Monday-Saturday. Phone after 3 pm. Miscellaneous antique auto parts, gaskets, ignition and engines.

BS Wisniewski Inc/Wizzy's
1801 S 2nd St
Milwaukee, WI 53204
800-328-6554; FAX: 414-645-5457

| engine/ignition |
| mechanical |
| suspension |
| transmission |

Mail order and open shop. Monday-Friday 8-5. Collector car parts since 1914. Ignition, suspension and engine parts for cars and trucks 1920s to date. NOS pistons, cast iron rings, valves, gaskets, transmission gears, wheel bearings, seals, hydraulics, spark plugs and much more. For over 80 years, we've always guaranteed the fit. Call us for your mechanical parts or free brochure. Club buying tours and other vendors are welcome.

Ed Wright
16 Carnavon Cir
Springfield, MA 01109
413-782-3032

| accessories |
| literature |
| parts |

Mail order only. Above address April - Nov. Assortment of lights, mirrors, gas & radiator caps, hubcaps, Bosch 6v wiper and accessories primarily from the twenties and thirties. Taillight lenses & rims, teens, 1920s-30s. Some early 12 volt wipers. Some owner's manuals. A few NOS 1928-40 Ford parts. SASE required with accurate description or sketch of item desired. "A hobby." In Florida, 4118 Palmtree Blvd, Cape Coral, FL 33904, PH: 813-549-2759, no collect calls.

Year One Inc
PO Box 129
Tucker, GA 30085
800-YEAR-ONE (932-7663)
770-493-6568 Atlanta & overseas
FAX: 800-680-6806
FAX: 770-496-1949 Atlanta & overseas

| parts |

Specializing in new factory and high quality reproduction parts, tools & accessories. 64-72 Chevelle, El Camino & Monte Carlo, 500+ page catalog (with 132 pages in color); 64-72 GTO/LeMans, 325+ page catalog; 67-81 Camaro, 525+ page catalog; 66-74 A, B and E-body Dodge/Plymouth, 600+ page catalog; 62-74 Chevy II/Nova, 350+ page catalog; 67-81 Firebird, 400+ page catalog; 58-72 Impala (and other fullsize Chevrolets), 400+ page catalog; 64-72 Skylark/ Gran Sport, 325+ page catalog; and 64-72 Cutlass/442, 375+ page catalog. Knowledgeable salesman, free technical support, same day shipping and more. Catalogs $5 each ($7.50 refunded with first order).

Zim's Autotechnik
1804 Reliance Pkwy
Bedford, TX 76021
800-356-2964; FAX: 817-545-2002

| parts |
| service |

See full listing in **Section One** under **Porsche**

consultants

AAG-Auto Appraisal Group Inc
PO Box 7034
Charlottesville, VA 22906
800-848-2886; FAX: 804-295-7918
E-mail: aag@autoappraisal.com

| appraisals |

See full listing in **Section Two** under **appraisals**

Aero International Auto Appraisals
Box 1955
Penhold, ALB Canada T0M 1R0
403-886-5565

appraiser
consultant

See full listing in **Section Two** under **appraisals**

AM Racing Inc
PO Box 451
Danvers, MA 01923
PH/FAX: 508-774-4613

race prep
sales
vintage racing

See full listing in **Section Two** under **racing**

Auto Consultants & Appraisal Service
Charles J Kozelka
PO Box 111
Macedonia, OH 44056
216-467-0748

appraisals

See full listing in **Section Two** under **appraisals**

Automotive Legal Service Inc
PO Box 626
Dresher, PA 19025
PH/FAX: 800-487-4947

appraisals

See full listing in **Section Two** under **appraisals**

AVM Automotive Consulting
Box 338
Montvale, NJ 07645-0338
PH: 201-391-5194
FAX: 201-782-0663
E-mail: avmtony@aol.com

appraisals
consultant

See full listing in **Section Two** under **appraisals**

JJ Best & Co
737 Main St, PO Box 10
Chatham, MA 02633
508-945-6000; FAX: 508-945-6006

financing

Open Monday to Friday 8 to 9, Saturday 10 to 3 EST. Specializing in financing antique, collectible, sports, exotic and fine automobiles. Great rates and long terms, 5-12 years. We will take an application on the phone and usually let a customer know within 1 hour of approval or denial. We are very familiar with most cars from 190185 and we offer financing up to 80% of market value.

Blair Collectors & Consultants
2821 SW 167th Pl
Seattle, WA 98166
206-242-6745

appraiser
consultant
literature

See full listing in **Section Two** under **appraisals**

Bramhall Classic Autos
149 30th St
Toronto, ONT Canada M8W 3C3
416-255-7201; FAX: 416-255-8446

appraisals
brokers
cars & parts locator
consultants

See full listing in **Section Two** under **brokers**

Arthur Burrichter
24026 Highway 151
Monticello, IA 52310
319-465-3064; FAX: 319-465-6048

appraisals
car dealer

See full listing in **Section Two** under **car dealers**

CalAutoArt
1520 S Lyon St
Santa Ana, CA 92705
714-835-9512; FAX: 714-835-9513
E-mail: 71460,1146@compuserve.com

automobilia
photography

See full listing in **Section Two** under **automobilia**

The Can Corner
PO Box VA 1173
Linwood, PA 19061
215-485-0824

audio tapes

See full listing in **Section Two** under **automobilia**

Car Care Group
Box 338
Poynette, WI 53955
608-635-7751

car care products

See full listing in **Section Two** under **car care products**

Carters Auto Restorations
1433 Pawlings Rd
Phoenixville, PA 19460
215-666-5687

restoration

See full listing in **Section Two** under **bodywork**

Casey-Dyer Enterprises Inc
PO Box 7176
Alexandria, LA 71301
318-473-1802; FAX: 318-473-9578

appraiser
broker
car dealer

See full listing in **Section Two** under **car dealers**

Certified Auto Appraisal
PO Box 17609
Anaheim, CA 92817
714-966-1096; FAX: 714-498-7367

appraisals

See full listing in **Section Two** under **appraisals**

Charles W Clarke Automotive Consultant/Appraiser
17 Saddle Ridge Dr
West Simsbury, CT 06092
203-658-2714

appraiser
consultant
car dealer

Classic Car Research
29508 Southfield Rd
Southfield, MI 48076
810-557-2880; FAX: 810-557-3511

appraisals
car locating
consultant

See full listing in **Section Two** under **appraisals**

Cochrane's Special Interest Brokers
Ed Cochrane
718 Livingston Ave
Shreveport, LA 71107
318-226-0458, 318-424-2861

appraisers
brokers
consultant
locator

See full listing in **Section Two** under **brokers**

Collector Car Appraisals
L E Lazarus, Senior Appraiser
PO Box 6732
Rockford, IL 61125
815-229-1258; FAX: 815-229-1238

appraisals

See full listing in **Section Two** under **appraisals**

Collector Cars-U-Can-Afford Ltd
4046 11th St
Rockford, IL 61109
815-229-1258; FAX: 815-229-1238

car dealer

See full listing in **Section One** under **Cadillac/LaSalle**

| Lance S Coren, CAA, CMA
20545 Eastwood Ave
Torrance, CA 90503-3611
310-370-4114; FAX: 310-371-4120 | appraisals |

See full listing in **Section Two** under **appraisals**

| Corvette Enterprise Brokerage
The Power Broker
52 Van Houten Ave
Passaic Park, NJ 07055
201-472-7021 | appraiser
broker
consultant
investment planning |

See full listing in **Section One** under **Corvette**

| Creative Automotive Consultants
PO Box 2221
San Rafael, CA 94912-2221
707-824-9004; FAX: 707-824-9002 | appraiser
car locator
promotion |

Appraisals for all collector vehicles. Auto location service, worldwide. Period vehicles for the visual arts industry and special events. We need listings of all age and type vehicles. All periods (1900's-1990's). Auction coordination and support. Vehicle investment/purchase consultation. All hours by appointment.

| Cruise Consultants Group
PO Box 338
Poynette, WI 53955
608-635-7751 | book
consultant |

Mail order only. Consults on car clubs and club events. Shows, cruises and fund raising. Publish *Car Club Handbook*.

| Robert DeMars Ltd
222 Lakeview Ave, Ste 160-256
West Palm Beach, FL 33401
561-832-0171; FAX: 561-844-1493 | appraisers
auto historians
car locator
research library |

See full listing in **Section Two** under **appraisals**

| Development Associates
1520 S Lyon
Santa Ana, CA 92705
714-835-9512; FAX: 714-835-9513
E-mail: 71460,1146@compuserve.com | electrical parts |

See full listing in **Section Two** under **electrical systems**

| Driving Passion-1959
7132 Chilton Ct
Clarksville, MD 21029
PH/FAX: 301-596-9078 | bumpers
parts
parts locating service |

See full listing in **Section One** under **Cadillac/LaSalle**

| Freelance Appraisals Inc
RR 1
Red Deer, ALB Canada T4N 5E1
403-347-4488; FAX: 403-347-4480 | appraisals
consulting |

See full listing in **Section Two** under **appraisals**

| Freeman's Garage
19 Freeman St
Norton, MA 02766
508-285-6500 | parts
restoration
sales/service |

See full listing in **Section One** under **Ford '03-'31**

| Mark Gillett
PO Box 9177
Dallas, TX 75209
PH/FAX: 214-902-9258
011-525-559-6240 Mexico City,
Mexico; E-mail-autonet@onramp.net | car locator
sales |

See full listing in **Section Two** under **car dealers**

| Thos Hespenheide & Associates Ltd
410 Darby Rd
Havertown, PA 19083
610-446-7699, FAX: 610-446-7915 | appraiser
rebuilding |

See full listing in **Section Two** under **appraisals**

| HK Klassics
Hy Kusnetz
16 Hausmann Ct
Maplewood, NJ 07040
201-761-6642 | appraisals |

See full listing in **Section Two** under **appraisals**

| HochKraeusen Racing
PO Box 716
18233 Madison Rd
Parkman, OH 44080-0716
216-548-2147 | machine shop |

See full listing in **Section Two** under **machine work**

| Hank Hoiler Olde Car Shoppe
431 Portzer Rd
Quakertown, PA 18951
215-536-1334 | consultant
light maintenance |

Shop open by appointment only. Light maintenance and problem solving. Consulting. Actively in the automotive restoration business 55 years. Now continue with consulting. Only American manufactured vehicles.

| IPTC Publishing
300 SW 12th Ave
Pompano Beach, FL 33069
800-653-4198 | manuals |

See full listing in **Section Four** under **books & publications**

| ISG
21638 Lasser
Chatsworth, CA 91311
818-718-8816; FAX: 818-718-8832 | security devices |

See full listing in **Section Two** under **anti-theft**

| Eliot James Enterprises Inc
PO Box 3986
Dana Point, CA 92629-8986
714-661-0889; FAX: 714-661-1901 | development info |

See full listing in **Section Four** under **books & publications**

| LA Ltd Design Graphics
822A S McDuffie St
Anderson, SC 29624
PH/FAX: 864-231-7715 | artwork
design
greeting cards |

See full listing in **Section Two** under **automobilia**

| Landry Classic MotorCars
34 Goodhue Ave
Chicopee, MA 01020
413-592-2746; FAX: 413-594-8378 | appraiser |

See full listing in **Section Two** under **appraisals**

Lazarus Auto Collection
PO Box 6732
Rockford, IL 61125
815-229-1258; FAX: 815-229-1238

arcade machines
cars
jukeboxes

See full listing in **Section Two** under **car dealers**

M & L Automobile Appraisal
2662 Palm Terr
Deland, FL 32720
904-734-1761

appraiser

See full listing in **Section Two** under **appraisals**

Randall Marcus Vintage Automobiles
706 Hanshaw Rd
Ithaca, NY 14850
607-257-5939; FAX: 607-272-8806

broker
car locator
consultant

See full listing in **Section Two** under **brokers**

Bill McCoskey
14200 New Hampshire Ave
Silver Spring, MD 20904
301-384-5856; FAX: 301-989-1866

appraisals
repairs

See full listing in **Section Two** under **appraisals**

Memory Lane Motors Inc
1231 Rt 176
Lake Bluff, IL 60044
847-362-4600

appraisals
car dealer
storage

See full listing in **Section Two** under **car dealers**

Patterson Coachworks
8951 Henry Clay Blvd
Clay, NY 13041
315-652-5794

parts
service

See full listing in **Section One** under **Pontiac**

Performance Analysis Co
1345 Oak Ridge Turnpike, Suite 258
Oak Ridge, TN 37830
423-482-9175
E-mail: 7662.2133@compuserve.com

climate control
cruise control

See full listing in **Section One** under **Mercedes-Benz**

Reward Service Inc
172 Overhill Rd
Stormville, NY 12582
914-227-7647; FAX: 914-221-0293

appraisals
restoration
transportation

See full listing in **Section One** under **Jaguar**

Route 66 Classic Restorations
250 N 1st St
Wilmington, IL 60481
815-476-4290

restoration

See full listing in **Section Two** under **restoration shops**

Still Cruisin' Corvettes
5759 Benford Dr
Haymarket, VA 20169
703-754-1960; FAX: 703-754-1222

appraisals
repairs
restoration

See full listing in **Section One** under **Corvette**

Stone Barn Inc
202 Rt 46, Box 117
Vienna, NJ 07880
908-637-4444; FAX: 908-637-4290

restoration

See full listing in **Section Two** under **restoration shops**

J F Sullivan Co
14 Clarendon Rd
Auburn, MA 01501
508-792-9500

brake parts
consulting
machine work
parts locator

See full listing in **Section Two** under **brakes**

Tamarack Automotive Appraisals and Marine Surveys
53 Sears Ln
Burlington, VT 05401
PH/FAX: 802-864-4003
E-mail: gtlittle@aol.com

appraiser
restoration

See full listing in **Section Two** under **appraisals**

JC Taylor Antique Automobile Insurance Agency
320 S 69th St
Upper Darby, PA 19082
800-345-8290

insurance

See full listing in **Section Two** under **insurance**

Thermax Inc
5385 Alpha Ave
Reno, NV 89506
800-247-7177; FAX: 702-972-4809

cleaning process

Since 1971, Thermax has pioneered the cleaning industry as it is known today. The Therminator models are manufactured for fast, easy cleaning of vehicle interiors. Improve the quality of your interior, save time by using Thermax and make more money in the process. The Thermax distributor can show you the advantage of the Therminator line. Call today and receive a free demonstration which allows you to see the latest in cleaning technology.

Timeless Masterpieces
221 Freeport Dr
Bloomingdale, IL 60108
630-893-1058 evenings

appraiser
consultant

See full listing in **Section Two** under **appraisals**

USAppraisal
754 Walker, PO Box 472
Great Falls, VA 22066-0472
703-759-9100; FAX: 703-759-9099
E-mail: dhkinney@aol.com

appraisals

See full listing in **Section Two** under **appraisals**

Valco Cincinnati Consumer Products Inc
411 Circle Freeway Drive
Cincinnati, OH 45246
513-874-6550; FAX: 513-874-3612

adhesives
detailing products
sealants
tools

See full listing in **Section Two** under **tools**

Johnny Williams Services
2613 Copeland Road
Tyler, TX 75701
903-597-3687
800-937-0900 voice mail #7225

appraiser
cars & parts locator
consultant
lighting systems
design

See full listing in **Section Two** under **appraisals**

Generalists

Wolfson Engineering
512 Parkway W
Las Vegas, NV 89106
PH/FAX: 702-384-4196

mech engineering

See full listing in **Section Two** under **special services**

Chris M Zora ASA, ISA
PO Box 9939
Woodlands, TX 77386
713-362-8258

appraisals
consultant

See full listing in **Section Two** under **appraisals**

custom cars

American Autowire Systems Inc
150 Cooper Rd, Unit C-8
Dept HVAA
West Berlin, NJ 08091
800-482-WIRE; FAX: 609-753-0353

battery cables
electrical systems
switches/
components

See full listing in **Section Two** under **street rods**

Amherst Antique Auto Show
157 Hollis Rd
Amherst, NH 03031
603-883-0605, NH
FAX: 617-641-0647, MA

swap meets

See full listing in **Section Two** under **auctions & events**

Bob's Classic Auto Glass
21170 Hwy 36
Blachly, OR 97412
800-624-2130

glass

See full listing in **Section Two** under **glass**

Boop Photography
2347 Derry St
Harrisburg, PA 17104-2728
717-564-8533
E-mail: msboop@paonline.com

photography

See full listing in **Section Two** under **photography**

Bumpers by Briz
8002 NE Hwy 99, #260
Vancouver, WA 98665
360-573-8628

bumpers

See full listing in **Section Two** under **chassis parts**

F J Cabrera Enterprises
15507 Normandie Ave, #103
Gardena, CA 90247
310-532-8894; FAX: 310-515-0928

accessories
lights

See full listing in **Section Two** under **restoration aids**

Cadillac Auto Display
PO Box 6732
Rockford, IL 61125
815-229-1258; FAX: 815-229-1238

museum

See full listing in **Section Six** under **Illinois**

Central Florida Auto Festival & Toy Expo
1420 N Galloway Rd
Lakeland, FL 33810
941-686-8320

auto festival
toy expo

See full listing in **Section Two** under **auctions & events**

Classic Motors Unlimited
RD 1 Box 99C
Hooversville, PA 15936
814-479-7874

chemical stripping
metal work
restoration

See full listing in **Section Two** under **restoration shops**

Coffey's Classic Transmissions
2817 Hollis
Ft Worth, TX 76111
817-834-8740; 817-439-1611

transmissions

See full listing in **Section Two** under **transmissions**

Crossfire
260 Hickory St, PO Box 263
Sharpsville, PA 16150
800-458-3478; FAX: 412-962-4639

accessories

See full listing in **Section Two** under **ignition parts**

Custom Auto Radiator
495 Hyson Rd
Jackson, NJ 08527
908-928-3700/ FAX: 908-364-7474

radiators

See full listing in **Section Two** under **radiators**

Custom Plating
3030 Alta Ridge Way
Snellville, GA 30278
770-736-1118

bumper specialist
chrome plating
parts

See full listing in **Section Two** under **plating & polishing**

Early Wheel Co Inc
Box 1438
Santa Ynez, CA 93460
805-688-1187; FAX: 805-688-0257

steel wheels

See full listing in **Section Two** under **wheels & wheelcovers**

Ed's Be-Bop Shop
10087 W Co Rd 300 S
Medora, IN 47260
812-966-2203

accessories
parts
restoration

See full listing in **Section One** under **Ford '03-'31**

Executive Boys Toys
200 S Jackson St
Lima, OH 45804
419-227-9300

car dealer

See full listing in **Section Two** under **car dealers**

Exotic Enterprises
459 Madeline Ave
Garfield, NJ 07026
201-523-2217, 201-956-7570

fiberglass
manufacturing
fiberglass mold
making

See full listing in **Section Two** under **fiberglass parts**

Guldstrand Engineering Inc
11924 W Jefferson Blvd
Culver City, CA 90230
310-391-7108; FAX: 310-391-7424
E-mail: geiauto@aol.com

parts

See full listing in **Section One** under **Corvette**

Hunters Custom Automotive
975 Main St
Nashville, TN 37206
615-227-6584; FAX: 615-227-4897

accessories
engine parts
fiberglass products

See full listing in **Section Two** under **accessories**

Inland Empire Driveline Service Inc
4035 E Guasti Rd, #301
Ontario, CA 91761
800-800-0109; FAX: 909-390-3038

drive shafts
pinion yokes

See full listing in **Section Two** under **machine work**

K & K Insurance Group Inc
PO Box 2338
Fort Wayne, IN 46801-2338
800-548-0858; FAX: 219-459-5511

insurance

See full listing in **Section Two** under **insurance**

K-F-D Services Inc
HC 65, Box 49
Altonah, UT 84002
801-454-3098; FAX: 801-454-3099

parts
restoration

See full listing in **Section One** under **Kaiser-Frazer**

LA Machine
5960 Valentine Rd #9
Ventura, CA 93003
805-650-6644; FAX: 805-650-6633

convertible kits

See full listing in **Section One** under **Porsche**

Land Cruisers Solutions Inc
20 Thornell Rd
Newton, NH 03858
508-462-5656, MA

accessories
services

See full listing in **Section One** under **Toyota**

**Land Yachts Automobile
Restoration and Customizing**
497 London Bridge Rd, Suite 101
Virginia Beach, VA 23454
757-431-0294; FAX: 757-431-4524

restoration

See full listing in **Section Two** under **restoration shops**

Lazarus Auto Collection
PO Box 6732
Rockford, IL 61125
815-229-1258; FAX: 815-229-1238

arcade machines
cars
jukeboxes

See full listing in **Section Two** under **car dealers**

Lokar Inc
10924 Murdock Dr
Knoxville, TN 37922
423-966-2269; FAX: 423-671-1999

performance parts

See full listing in **Section Two** under **street rods**

Memoryville USA Inc
1008 W 12th St
Rolla, MO 65401
573-364-1810

restoration

See full listing in **Section Two** under **restoration shops**

Marc Miller Gallery
3 Railroad Ave
East Hampton, NY 11937
516-329-5299; FAX: 516-329-5319

furniture

See full listing in **Section Two** under **artwork**

No Limit Engineering
1737 Production Circle
Riverside, CA 92509
FAX: 909-275-9232

brakes
chassis parts

See full listing in **Section Two** under **chassis parts**

Pilgrim's Special Interest Autos
3888 Hill Rd
Lakeport, CA 95453
PH/FAX: 707-262-1062

bodywork
metal fabrication
paint
restoration

See full listing in **Section Two** under **restoration shops**

Power Effects
1800H Industrial Park Dr
Grand Haven, MI 49417
616-847-4200; FAX: 616-847-4210

exhaust systems

See full listing in **Section Two** under **exhaust systems**

Prestige Motors
120 N Bessie Rd
Spokane, WA 99212
PH/FAX: 509-926-3611

car dealer

See full listing in **Section Two** under **car dealers**

Ray's Upholstering
600 N St Frances Cabrini Ave
Scranton, PA 18504
800-296-RAYS; FAX: 717-963-0415

partial/total
restoration

See full listing in **Section Two** under **restoration shops**

RB's Prototype Model & Machine Co
44 Marva Ln
Stamford, CT 06903
PH/FAX: 203-329-2715

machine work

See full listing in **Section Two** under **service shops**

Ridgefield Auto Upholstery
34 Bailey Ave
Ridgefield, CT 06877
203-438-7583

interiors
tops

See full listing in **Section Two** under **interiors & interior parts**

RMR Restorations Inc | restoration
13 Columbia Dr, Unit 1
Amherst, NH 03031
PH/FAX: 603-880-6880 work
603-672-8335 home

See full listing in **Section Two** under **restoration shops**

Rod-1 Shop | street rods
210 Clinton Ave
Pitman, NJ 08071
609-228-7631; FAX: 609-582-5770

See full listing in **Section Two** under **street rods**

RW & Able Inc | door panels
PO Box 2110 | interior accessories
Chico, CA 95927
PH/FAX: 916-896-1513

See full listing in **Section Two** under **street rods**

decals

GA$OLINE

Anderson's | car door
32700 Coastsite #102 | monograms
Rancho Palos Verdes, CA 90275
310-377-1007; 800-881-9049
FAX: 310-377-0169

See full listing in **Section Two** under **accessories**

Auto Decals Unlimited Inc | decals
11259 E Via Linda, Ste 100-201 | stripe kits
Scottsdale, AZ 85259
602-860-9800; FAX: 602-860-8370

Mail order only. Automotive decals & stripe kits for all muscle cars, all years, makes and models.

Auto Nostalgia Enr | literature
332 St Joseph S | manuals
Mont St Gregoire, QC Canada J0J 1K0
PH/FAX: 514-346-3644

See full listing in **Section Two** under **literature dealers**

Benkin & Co | gas pumps
14 E Main St | neon clocks
Tipp City, OH 45371 | neon signs
513-667-5975; FAX: 513-667-5729

See full listing in **Section Two** under **automobilia**

Bright Displays | neon signs
1314 Lakemont Dr
Pittsburgh, PA 15243
412-279-7037

See full listing in **Section Two** under **automobilia**

The Buick Nut-Joe Krepps | repro parts
2486 Pacer Ln S
Cocoa, FL 32926-2606
PH/FAX: 407-636-8777

See full listing in **Section One** under **Buick/McLaughlin**

Cruising International Inc | automobilia
1000 N Beach St | decals
Daytona Beach, FL 32117 | license plates
800-676-8961, 904-254-8753 | novelties
FAX: 904-255-2460 | porcelain signs

See full listing in **Section Two** under **accessories**

Del's Decals | decals
6150 Baldwin St
Hudsonville, MI 49426

Mail order only. Engine compartment decals for the air cleaner, oil filter, valve cover, etc. SASE for free list. Please state make.

Eurosport Daytona Inc | license plates
32 Oceanshore Blvd
Ormond Beach, FL 32176
800-874-8044; 904-672-7199
FAX: 904-673-0821

See full listing in **Section Two** under **license plates**

Ford Reproduction Parts Store | parts
110 Ford Rd
PO Box 226
Bryan, OH 43506-0226
419-636-2475; FAX: 419-636-8449
E-mail: fordpart@bright.net

See full listing in **Section One** under **Ford '54-up**

Hemmings Motor News | free HMN
Free Decal Request | windshield decal
PO Box 256
Bennington, VT 05201

Free, full-color window decal for *Hemmings Motor News* readers who want to share their enthusiasm for old cars. Please send self-addressed stamped envelope and specify the quantity (one-five), that you can use.

Lost Highway Art Co
PO Box 164
Bedford Hills, NY 10507-0164
914-234-6016

decals

Mail order only. Original, new old stock water-dip souvenir/travel decals. Decals were a feature of Highway Touring in the 1940s, 50s and 60s. A wide variety lets you choose to show where your car is from, where its been or where you'd like to drive it someday. Also collectible just as they are: state maps and symbols, national parks, tourist attractions and major cities and roadside attractions of all kinds.

See our ad on page 278

Larry Machacek
PO Box 515
Porter, TX 77365
713-429-2505

decals
license plates

See full listing in **Section Two** under **automobilia**.

Operations Plus
PO Box 26347
Santa Ana, CA 92799
PH/FAX: 714-962-2776

accessories
parts

See full listing in **Section One** under **Cobra**.

Osborn Reproductions Inc
101 Ridgecrest Dr
Lawrenceville, GA 30245
770-962-7556; FAX: 770-962-5881

decals
manuals

Mail order and open shop. Monday-Friday 8 am to 5 pm. Largest selection of restoration decals, owner's and shop manuals. All new catalog $5, refundable.
Web site: http://www.osborn-reproduction.com

People Kars
290 Third Ave Ext
Rensselaer, NY 12144
PH/FAX: 518-465-0477

models/more
VW toys

See full listing in **Section One** under **Volkswagen**.

Phoenix Graphix Inc
4025 E Chandler Blvd, Suite 70
Phoenix, AZ 85044
602-941-4550

decals
stripe kits

Mail order only. "Any decal, any car, any year!" Specialists in 1964-1991 Trans-Am, Z-28, Mustang, Plymouth and Dodge decals. Carries all lines, including Turbo and Special Edition packages. Affordable. High quality and original appearance. We are a GM licensed manufacturer. Established 1985.

Prostripe
Div of Spartan International Inc
1845 Cedar St
Holt, MI 48842
800-248-7800; FAX: 517-694-7952

graphics
molding
pinstriping

See full listing in **Section Two** under **striping**.

Star Classics Inc
7745 E Redfield #300
Scottsdale, AZ 85260
602-991-7495, 800-644-7827
FAX: 602-951-4096

parts
sales
service

See full listing in **Section One** under **Mercedes-Benz**.

Stencils & Stripes Unlimited Inc
1108 S Crescent Ave #21
Park Ridge, IL 60068
708-692-6893; FAX: 708-692-6895

NOS decals
stripe kits

Mail order only. Offers reproduction paint and stripe kits along with NOS decals and stripes. Kits are available for Camaro,

Chevelle, El Camino, Corvette, Nova, Olds 442, Dodge, Plymouth, Pontiac T/A, GTO and H/O models, plus Ford. All reproduction kits use special high performance vinyls. Specializing in reproduction paint stencil, decals and stripes for 1967 and up GM, Ford, Chrysler and GMC. Licensed by GM.

Stick-Em-Up Inc
PO Box 3111
Livermore, CA 94551-3111
415-426-1040; FAX: 415-426-1085
E-mail: stickemup@trivalley.com

decals
fasteners

Mail order. Monday-Friday 7 to 6. Custom stickers for rod runs, events, souvenirs, etc. Also bumper stickers, windshield stickers, etc. Also titanium nuts & bolts. 19 years serving the public and wholesale.

electrical systems

AAMP of America
13160 56th Ct, #502-508
Clearwater, FL 34620
813-572-9255
FAX: 813-573-9326
E-mail: stinger.sales@stinger-aamp.com

audio accessories

See full listing in **Section Two** under **accessories**.

Ace Auto Body & Towing Ltd
65 S Service Rd
Plainview, NY 11803
516-752-6065; FAX: 516-752-1484

mechanical repairs
restorations

See full listing in **Section Two** under **restoration shops**.

All British Car Parts Inc
2847 Moores Rd
Baldwin, MD 21013
410-692-9572; FAX: 410-692-5654

parts

Buys, sells, researches new and new old stock Lucas, Girling, Lockheed. Current, discontinued, NLA, supersessions, hard to find items. Lamps, lenses, switches, ignition, starters, alternators, brake hydraulics & components, virtually anything Lucas, Girling, Lockheed, post 1950 to today. FAX your obsolete Lucas/Girling list for offer.

American Autosecurity Equip Co
236 East Star of India Ln
Carson, CA 90746
310-538-4670, 800-421-1096
FAX: 310-538-9932

car alarms

See full listing in **Section Two** under **anti-theft**.

American Autowire Systems Inc
150 Cooper Rd, Unit C-8
Dept HVAA
West Berlin, NJ 08091
800-482-WIRE; FAX: 609-753-0353

battery cables
electrical systems
switches/
components

See full listing in **Section Two** under **street rods**.

American-Foreign Auto Electric Inc
103 Main Street
Souderton, PA 18964
215-723-4877

parts
rebuilding

Monday-Friday 8:30 to 5. We are a discount foreign car parts jobber. Specializing in parts for British cars, MG, Triumph, Austin-Healey. Our shop rebuilds alternators, generators and starters. For all cars, American and foreign.

Generalists

Antique Auto Battery Mfg Co 2320 Old Mill Rd Hudson, OH 44236 800-426-7580; FAX: 216-425-4642	**batteries** **battery cables**

See full listing in **Section Two** under **batteries**

Antique Auto Electric 9109 (Rear) E Garvey Ave Rosemead, CA 91770 818-572-0938	**repro wiring**

Shop open Monday-Friday 9 to 5. For all years and models. Specializing in 1908-48 Fords, Mercurys and Lincolns, SASE required for catalog and information. New alternator conversion catalogs for As and V8s, $6. Specify catalog desired.

Antique Radio Service 12 Shawmut Ave Wayland, MA 01778 800-201-2635; FAX: 508-653-2418	**radio service**

See full listing in **Section Two** under **radios**

Barnett & Small Inc 151E Industry Ct Deer Park, NY 11729 516-242-2100; FAX: 516-242-2101	**electrical parts**

Antique auto parts, all NOS. Also generators, voltage regulators, starters, speedometers, carburetors and electric wiper motors. 47 years in business. Auto parts dealers.

Bathurst Inc 801 W 15 St Tyrone, PA 16686 814-684-2603	**battery accessories**

Mail and phone orders. Battery disconnect switches for protection of car and mechanics.

Robert D Bliss 2 Delmar Pl Edison, NJ 08837 908-549-0977	**ignition parts** **electrical parts**

Mail order and open shop. Monday-Friday after 6 pm; Saturday and Sunday all day. New distributor caps, rotors, points, condensers, voltage regulators, headlight, ignition, starter, stoplight switches; horn relays; generator and starter parts from 1920-70.

British Wiring Inc 20449 Ithaca Rd Olympia Fields, IL 60461 PH/FAX: 708-481-9050	**wiring accessories** **wiring harnesses**

Specializing in wiring harnesses and wiring accessories for British classic cars and motorcycles. British Wiring Inc is the US distributor for the largest British harness manufacturer. We stock a large selection of harnesses, terminals, grommets, connectors, etc. Along with bulk wire. Harness price lists are available free of charge (specify marque) and our accessory catalog is $2, refundable with purchase. Harnesses for prewar models are available.

Bryant's Antique Auto Parts 851 Western Ave Hampden, ME 04444 207-862-4019	**appraisals** **parts** **sheetmetal service**

See full listing in **Section One** under **Ford '03-'31**

Chicago Corvette Supply 7322 S Archer Rd Justice, IL 60458 708-458-2500; FAX: 708-458-2662	**parts**

See full listing in **Section One** under **Corvette**

Class-Tech Corp 62935 Layton Ave Bend, OR 97701 800-874-9981	**wiring harnesses**

Mail order only. Authentic reproduction Ford wiring harnesses through the 50s, this includes Mercury, pickups, and 1955-57 T-Birds. Dealer inquiries welcome.

Classic Car Club of Southern California PO Box 3742 Orange, CA 92857	**generators** **starters**

Mail order only. Deals in tags, decals for use on starters, generators and oil filters, plus special items for certain makes, 1925-1948. SASE for free illustrated list.

Dakota Studebaker Parts RR 1, Box 103A Armour, SD 57313 605-724-2527	**parts**

See full listing in **Section One** under **Studebaker**

Development Associates 1520 S Lyon Santa Ana, CA 92705 714-835-9512; FAX: 714-835-9513 E-mail: 71460,1146@compuserve.com	**electrical parts**

Mail order and open shop. Monday-Friday 9 am to 6 pm. Retails and wholesales advanced electronic sequencers for 1965-68 Thunderbirds and 1967-68 Cougars. These units replace the original electro-mechanical motor and cam switch assembly no longer available from Ford. These improved units are compatible in form and fit and offer substantial ownership benefits in terms of performance, reliability and installation ease. This company, with over 25 years of hardware/software and systems experience, also offers its services for development of custom automotive electronics.

Eagle Wire Products — wire harnesses
3308 Valley Forge Dr
Knoxville, TN 37920
PH/FAX: 800-977-0030

Specializing in automotive wiring/wire harnesses for 1953-82 Corvettes and GM cars and trucks 1947-72. Provides the finest quality reproduction harnesses on the market. Our harnesses are made using the original GM specs and gives you that factory fit look. Wire harnesses, battery cables, switches and other electrical components at the best prices. Call anytime, available evenings and weekends for your convenience, plus a toll-free number.

Early Ford V8 Sales Inc — parts
9 Hills Rd
Ballston Lake, NY 12019
518-899-9974; FAX: 518-899-5303

See full listing in **Section One** under **Ford '32-'53**

Ferris Auto Electric Ltd — parts / service
106 Lakeshore Dr
North Bay, ONT Canada P1A 2A6
705-474-4560; FAX: 705-474-9453

Mail order and open shop. Monday-Friday 8 to 5:30. For your antique vehicle requirements, specializing in custom wiring harness, either braided or plastic wire, rebuilding of generators, starters, alternators, carburetors, distributors or magnetos and speedometers. Speedometer cables and casings made to order.

Ron Foertch — rewiring
Box 952
Cortland, NY 13045
607-753-3383 ext 210

Shop open by appointment only. Rewires trucks, buses and fire engines. Fleet rates available.

Ron Francis' Wire Works — fuel injection / harnesses / wiring accessories / wiring kits
167 Keystone Rd
Chester, PA 19013
610-485-1937; 800-292-1940, orders

Mail order only. Custom wiring kits for cars, trucks and kit cars. Fuel injection harnesses, wiring accessories. 72-page catalog filled with trick wiring and switches for $2.

Fun Projects Inc — electrical parts / mechanical parts
2723 Curtiss St
Downers Grove, IL 60515
630-584-1471; FAX: 630-971-3246
E-mail: piewagon@mcs.com

Mail order only. Design and manufacture of electrical parts for vintage cars. Makes voltage regulators for Ford cars, 1919-39 and other cars on special order. Voltage regulators for Ford tractors also. Early Model T Ford mechanical parts.

GMS Restorations — restoration
20 Wilbraham St
Palmer, MA 01069
413-283-3800

See full listing in **Section Two** under **restoration shops**

Harnesses Unlimited — wiring harnesses / wiring supplies
PO Box 435
Wayne, PA 19087
610-688-3998

Mail order only. USA manufacturer of wiring harness systems that use cloth braided and lacquered wire. Each system comes with installation instructions and wiring schematics. All makes except Ford, Lincoln and Mercury. Also offering wiring supplies and harness braiding service. Catalog or information, $5. If calling by phone, leave message, all calls are returned.

Mike Hershenfeld — parts
3011 Susan Rd
Bellmore, NY 11710
PH/FAX: 516-781-PART (7278)

See full listing in **Section One** under **MoPar**

Innovative Novelties/McGee Enterprises — accessories
PO Box 1375
Little Rock, AR 72203
501-835-8409; FAX: 501-835-7293
E-mail: kholland@cci.net

See full listing in **Section Two** under **novelties**

Jim's T-Bird Parts & Service — parts / restoration / service
710 Barney Ave
Winston-Salem, NC 27107
910-784-9363

See full listing in **Section One** under **Thunderbird**

Keilen's Auto Restoring — restoration
580 Kelley Blvd (R)
North Attleboro, MA 02760
508-699-7768

See full listing in **Section Two** under **restoration shops**

L & N Olde Car Co — restoration
9992 Kinsman Rd
PO Box 378
Newbury, OH 44065
216-564-7204; FAX: 216-564-8187

See full listing in **Section Two** under **restoration shops**

Last Chance Repair & Restoration — repairs / restoration
PO Box 362A, Myers Rd
Shaftsbury, VT 05262

See full listing in **Section Two** under **restoration shops**

Lincoln Highway Packards — engine rebuilding / restoration
Main St, PO Box 94
Schellsburg, PA 15559
814-733-4356; FAX: 814-839-4276

See full listing in **Section One** under **Packard**

M & H Electric Fabricators Inc — wiring harnesses
13537 Alondra Blvd
Santa Fe Springs, CA 90670
310-926-9552; FAX: 310-926-9572

Mail order and open shop. Mon-Fri 8-4:30. We deal in the manufacturing of exact reproduction wiring harnesses for most GM vehicles from 1955 to 1976. Call for applications and pricing.

See our ad on page 280

Ben McAdam — electrical parts
500 Clover Ln
Wheeling, WV 26003
304-242-3388

See full listing in **Section Two** under **ignition parts**

Michael's Auto Parts — salvage yard
5875 NW Kaiser Rd
Portland, OR 97229
503-690-7750; FAX: 503-690-7735

See full listing in **Section Five** under **Oregon**

Motorsport Auto
1139 W Collins Ave
Orange, CA 92667
714-639-2620; 800-633-6331
FAX: 714-639-7460

parts

See full listing in **Section One** under **Datsun**

Narragansett Reproductions
Ed & Miki Pease
107 Woodville Rd, PO Box 51
Wood River Junction, RI 02894
401-364-3839; FAX: 401-364-3830

wiring harnesses

Mail order only. Phone hours 10 to 5 EST. Lincoln parts 1936-1957, Ford parts 1932-1960. Wiring harnesses for all makes and models from 1900 to 1980. Authentic, reproduction wiring harnesses manufactured in our plant. Send $2 for catalog, stating year and model of vehicle.

Painless Wiring
9505 Santa Paula Dr
Fort Worth, TX 76116
817-292-9315; FAX: 817-292-4024
E-mail: painlesswiring@airmail.net

accessories parts

See full listing in **Section Two** under **wiring harnesses**

M Parker Autoworks Inc
150 Cooper Rd, Unit C-7
Dept HVAA
West Berlin, NJ 08091
609-753-0350; FAX: 609-753-0353

battery cables/ harnesses

Mail order and open shop. Mon-Fri 8 am-5 pm. We are the largest manufacturer of replacement wiring harnesses, battery cables, etc for 1955-75 GM cars and trucks. All factory-fit harnesses are built to original GM specifications with emphasis on

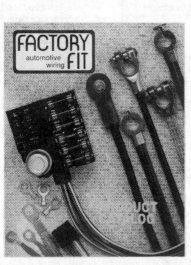
quality and originality using original GM components and specs. High-performance alternator and HEI modifications are available. Factory-fit harnesses are supported by a knowledgeable technical support staff and backed by a money back guarantee. VISA, MC, COD accepted. Catalog $4. Dealer inquiries welcome.

See our ad on this page

Bruce Paul
508 Balsam Rd
Cherry Hill, NJ 08003
609-428-8559

repair service

Mail order only. Over 30 years' experience repairing and rebuilding the various electric motors, clocks, generators and alternators used on 1940 through present day autos, (clocks only through 1975). Repair and servicing of starters, window motors, a/c-heater motors, wiper motors, power seat motors.

Performance Analysis Co
1345 Oak Ridge Turnpike, Suite 258
Oak Ridge, TN 37830
423-482-9175
E-mail: 7662.2133@compuserve.com

climate control cruise control

See full listing in **Section One** under **Mercedes-Benz**

PerTronix Inc
1268 E Edna Pl
Covina, CA 91724
818-331-4801; FAX: 818-967-1054

ignition systems

See full listing in **Section Two** under **ignition parts**

J Pinto
2605 9th St
Long Island City, NY 11102
PH/FAX: 718-626-2403
E-mail: electritech@sprynet.com

windshield wiper repair

See full listing in **Section Two** under **restoration aids**

Dennis Portka
4326 Beetow Dr
Hamburg, NY 14075
716-649-0921

horns

See full listing in **Section One** under **Corvette**

Potomac Packard
3031 Hunt Rd
Oakton, VA 22124
800-859-9532 orders
FAX: 703-620-2626

wiring harnesses

See full listing in **Section One** under **Packard**

Rhode Island Wiring Services Inc
567 Liberty Ln, Box 434
W Kingston, RI 02892
401-789-1955; FAX: 401-783-0091

wiring harnesses

Mail order and open shop. Monday-Friday 9 to 5. Exact reproduction wiring harnesses using braided or plastic wire, depending on original.

Rockland Auto Electric
88 S Main St
Pearl River, NY 10965
914-735-3362, 914-735-3372

electrical parts

Mail order and open shop. Monday-Friday 8 to 5:30; Saturday 8 to 5. Rebuilds starters, generators and alternators for all years and makes of automobiles and other motor vehicles.

Scotts Manufacturing
25520 Ave Stanford #304
Valencia, CA 91355
800-544-5596; FAX: 805-295-9342

electric fans

Deals in custom built electric cooling fans, 8" to 18" radiator
fans in 6-, 12- and 24-volt. Also transmission and engine oil
coolers with electric fans.
Web site: http://websitexeartlink.net/~scottsfans

Silicone Wire Systems
3462 Kirkwood Dr
San Jose, CA 95117-1549

ignition wire sets

See full listing in **Section One** under **Corvair**

Silver State Restorations Inc
The Aday Collection
4655 Aircenter Cir
Reno, NV 89502
702-826-8886; FAX: 702-826-9191

restoration
service

See full listing in **Section Two** under **restoration shops**

Sunburst Technology
PO Box 598
Lithia Springs, GA 30057
770-949-2979; FAX: 770-942-6091
E-mail: 10274592422@compuserv.com

electronic
technical consultant

See full listing in **Section Four** under **information sources**

Thunderbolt Traders Inc
6900 N Dixie Dr
Dayton, OH 45414-3297
513-890-3344; FAX: 513-890-9403

battery cables

See full listing in **Section One** under **Edsel**

Union Performance Co
PO Box 324, 59 Mansfield St
Sharon, MA 02067
617-784-5367, voice mail
FAX: 617-784-5367

parts

Mail order and open shop. Shop open by appointment only.
Specializing in bulbs and sealed beams, carburetors, fuel
pumps, spotlights, fog lamps, ignition and tune-up parts, generators, starters and voltage regulators, switches and vacuum controls, suspension components, brake systems and engine parts
for both cars and trucks.

Yankee Peddler Motorsports
11300 Fortune Circle
Wellington, FL 33414
561-798-6606; FAX: 561-798-6706

electrical
components
hardware

Mail order only. Electrical and hardware components.

YnZ's Yesterdays Parts
333 E Stuart Ave A
Redlands, CA 92374
909-798-1498; FAX: 909-335-6237

wiring harnesses

Mail order only. For over 1,850 different makes and models.
Copies of original wiring harnesses using lacquer coated, braided
wire. Catalog $2.

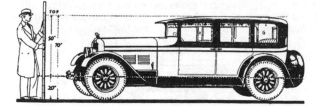

engine parts

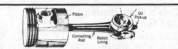

Action Performance Inc
1619 Lakeland Ave
Bohemia, NY 11716
516-244-7100; FAX: 516-244-7172

accessories

See full listing in **Section Two** under **accessories**

Advanced Results Company Inc
3042 Scott Blvd
Santa Clara, CA 95054
800-272-9898, 408-986-0123
FAX: 408-986-0125

oil drain system

Mail order and open shop. Shop open Monday-Friday 8 am to 5
pm. Deals in power drain oil change systems. A redesigned drain
plug with a bayonette connector on the outside and a spring-
loaded valve (check valve) on the inside. Attach to an ordinary
suction pump and it evacuates more oil and sediment than the
old gravity drain in just 90 seconds, eliminates need to remove
and reinstall the drain plug. Reduces wear, cleaner too.

S R Aldrich Engine Re-Building
352 River Rd
Willington, CT 06279
203-429-3111

engine rebuilding

See full listing in **Section Two** under **engine rebuilding**

Atlantic Antique Auto Parts
RR #6, PO Box 1388, Site 28
Armdale
Halifax, NS Canada B3L 4P4
902-479-0967

parts
service

See full listing in **Section Two** under **rubber parts**

Atlas Engine Rebuilding Co Inc
8631 S. Avalon Blvd
Los Angeles, CA 90003
213-778-3497; FAX: 213-778-4556

engine rebuilding
machine work

See full listing in **Section Two** under **engine rebuilding**

B & B Cylinder Head
320 Washington St
West Warwick, RI 02893
401-828-4900, 800-800-4143

cylinder heads

Mail order and open shop. Monday to Saturday 8 to 4:30. Cylinder
heads, restoration, fabrication, high-performance, no-lead conversions. Antique, obsolete to late model high tech. Custom engines
built completely. Motorcycles, tractors, trucks, etc.

Bayless Inc
1111 Via Bayless
Marietta, GA 30066-2770
770-928-1446; FAX: 770-928-1342
800-241-1446, order line
(US & Canada)

accessories
parts

See full listing in **Section One** under **Fiat**

Bob's Automotive Machine
30 Harrison Ave
Harrison, NJ 07029
201-483-0059; FAX: 201-483-6092

engine parts
machine shop

See full listing in **Section Two** under **machine work**

Bob's Bird House   parts
124 Watkin Ave
Chadds Ford, PA 19317
215-358-3420; FAX: 215-558-0729

See full listing in **Section One** under **Thunderbird**

Brisson Enterprises   lead
PO Box 1595
Dearborn, MI 48121
313-584-3577

See full listing in **Section Two** under **car care products**

British Parts NW   parts
4105 SE Lafayette Hwy
Dayton, OR 97114
503-864-2001; FAX: 503-864-2081

See full listing in **Section One** under **Triumph**

Bronx Automotive   parts
501 Tiffany St
Bronx, NY 10474
718-589-2979

See full listing in **Section Two** under **ignition parts**

Brothers Automotive Products   parts
19715 County Rd 355   restoration
St Joseph, MO 64505
816-662-2060; FAX: 816-662-2084

See full listing in **Section One** under **Oldsmobile**

Bryant's Antique Auto Parts   appraisals
851 Western Ave   parts
Hampden, ME 04444   sheetmetal service
207-862-4019

See full listing in **Section One** under **Ford '03-'31**

Cam-Pro   camshaft grinding
226 S Main
Choteau, MT 59422
406-466-5599

See full listing in **Section Two** under **camshafts**

Carl's Ford Parts   muscle parts
23219 South ST
Homeworth, OH 44634
PH/FAX: 330-525-7291

See full listing in **Section One** under **Mustang**

Car-Line Manufacturing &   chassis parts
Distribution Inc   engine parts
1250 Gulf St   sheetmetal
PO Box 1192
Beaumont, TX 77701
409-833-9757; FAX: 409-835-2468

See full listing in **Section Two** under **sheetmetal**

Cars II   parts
6747 Warren Sharon Rd
Brookfield, OH 44403
330-448-2074; FAX: 330-448-1908

See full listing in **Section One** under **Cadillac/LaSalle**

Stan Chernoff   mechanical parts
1215 Greenwood Ave   restoration parts
Torrance, CA 90503   technical info
310-320-4554; FAX: 310-328-7867   trim parts
E-mail: az589@lafn.org

See full listing in **Section One** under **Datsun**

Chicago Corvette Supply   parts
7322 S Archer Rd
Justice, IL 60458
708-458-2500; FAX: 708-458-2662

See full listing in **Section One** under **Corvette**

Ed Cholakian Enterprises Inc   museum
dba All Cadillacs of the Forties   parts
12811 Foothill Blvd
Sylmar, CA 91342
818-361-1147; 800-808-1147
FAX: 818-361-9738

See full listing in **Section One** under **Cadillac/LaSalle**

Collectors Auto Supply   parts
528 Appian Way
Coquitlam, BC Canada V3J 2A5
PH/FAX: 604-931-7278
E-mail: jimcarpenter@bc.sympatico.cd

See full listing in **Section Two** under **comprehensive parts**

Corvair Underground   parts
PO Box 339
Dundee, OR 97115
503-434-1648, 800-825-8247
FAX: 503-434-1626

See full listing in **Section One** under **Corvair**

Creative Metal Products Inc   storage system
121 R N Douglas St
Appleton, WI 54914
414-830-7975; FAX: 414-830-7976

See full listing in **Section Two** under **tools**

Crossfire   accessories
260 Hickory St, PO Box 263
Sharpsville, PA 16150
800-458-3478; FAX: 412-962-4639

See full listing in **Section Two** under **ignition parts**

Custom Plating   bumper specialist
3030 Alta Ridge Way   chrome plating
Snellville, GA 30278   parts
770-736-1118

See full listing in **Section Two** under **plating & polishing**

Dakota Studebaker Parts   parts
RR 1, Box 103A
Armour, SD 57313
605-724-2527

See full listing in **Section One** under **Studebaker**

Dale Manufacturing   harmonic balancers
3425 Fairhaven St NE
Salem, OR 97303
503-364-8685

Specializing in harmonic balancer rebuilding (for those cars where the factory no longer offers replacement/new balancers for sale). Seventeen years' experience and over 4,000 rebuilt. Lifetime guarantee on rubber bond. Your balancer rebuilt and returned in your shipping carton. Visa/MC welcome.

Daytona Turbo Action Camshafts
1109 US #1
PO Box 5094
Ormond Beach, FL 32175
800-505-CAMS, 904-676-7478
FAX: 904-258-1582

**camshafts
engine parts**

See full listing in **Section Two** under **bearings**

Early Ford V8 Sales Inc
9 Hills Rd
Ballston Lake, NY 12019
518-899-9974; FAX: 518-899-5303

parts

See full listing in **Section One** under **Ford '32-'53**

East Spring Obsolete Auto Parts Inc
PO Box 3
Bethlehem, CT 06751
203-266-5488 evenings & weekends

parts

See full listing in **Section Two** under **brakes**

**Eastern States Performance
Outlet Inc**
701 Pine Tree Rd
Danville, PA 17821
PH/FAX: 717-672-9413

suspension parts

See full listing in **Section Two** under **suspension parts**

**Eckler's Quality Parts &
Accessories for Corvettes**
PO Box 5637
Titusville, FL 32783
800-327-4868; FAX: 407-383-2059

**accessories
parts**

See full listing in **Section One** under **Corvette**

Egge Machine Company
11707 Slauson Ave
Santa Fe Springs, CA 90670
310-945-3419 in CA
800-866-EGGE; FAX: 310-693-1635

**babbitting
chassis
motor mounts
pistons/valves
wiring harnesses**

Mail order and walk-ins. Monday-Friday 8 to 5 PST. "The Parts House for Old Cars." Manufactures pistons, valves and guides for antique and classic cars, trucks, motorcycles, tractors and marine engines. Engine bearings and kits, stainless valves, gaskets, seals, motor mounts, carburetor and fuel pump kits, chassis parts and wiring harnesses. Full rebuild services for oil, water and fuel pumps, clutches and pressure plates, starters and generators. Nickel babbitt service, 136-page catalog, free.

See our ad inside the back cover

Ehrenreich's Corvair Service
1728 Manor Pkwy
Sheboygan, WI 53083-2827
414-458-1170

parts

See full listing in **Section One** under **Corvair**

EIS Engines Inc
215 SE Grand Ave
Portland, OR 97214
503-232-5590; 800-547-0002
FAX: 503-232-5178

engines

See full listing in **Section One** under **Mercedes-Benz**

Errol's Steam Works
3123 Baird Rd
North Vancouver, BC Canada V7K 2G5
PH/FAX: 604-985-9494

**castings
engines
parts**

See full listing in **Section One** under **Locomobile**

Ezold's Model A Garage
1120 Southampton Rd
Westfield, MA 01805
413-562-0273

**engine rebuilding
restorations**

See full listing in **Section One** under **Ford '03-'31**

Foreign Autotech
3235 C Sunset Ln
Hatboro, PA 19040
215-441-4421; FAX: 215-441-4490

parts

See full listing in **Section One** under **Volvo**

Gaslight Auto Parts Inc
PO Box 291
Urbana, OH 43078
513-652-2145; FAX: 513-652-2147

**accessories
parts**

See full listing in **Section One** under **Ford '03-'31**

John Giles Cars & Parts (ASV&S)
703 Morgan Ln
Pascagoula, MS 39567
PH/FAX: 601-769-8904

**car & parts locator
exporter**

See full listing in **Section Two** under **car & parts locators**

Good Old Days Garage Inc
2340 Farley Pl
Birmingham, AL 35226
205-822-4569

**engine building
parts
service**

See full listing in **Section One** under **Ford '03-'31**

Gromm Racing Heads
666-J Stockton Ave
San Jose, CA 95126
408-287-1301

**cylinder heads
racing parts**

See full listing in **Section Two** under **racing**

Mike Hershenfeld
3011 Susan Rd
Bellmore, NY 11710
PH/FAX: 516-781-PART (7278)

parts

See full listing in **Section One** under **MoPar**

Clinton Hickey Antique Auto
158 Bissonnette St
Valleyfield, QUE Canada J6T 3P7
514-371-1340

parts

See full listing in **Section Two** under **suspension parts**

James Hill
Box 547-V
Goodwell, OK 73939
405-349-2736 evenings/weekends

**ignition parts
source list**

See full listing in **Section One** under **Packard**

Hollywood Classic Motorcars Inc
363 Ansin Blvd
Hallandale, FL 33009
954-454-4641; FAX: 954-457-3801

**cars
parts**

See full listing in **Section One** under **Thunderbird**

Horst's Car Care
3160-1/2 N Woodford St
Decatur, IL 62526
217-876-1112

engine rebuilding

See full listing in **Section One** under **Mercedes-Benz**

Jackson's Old Parts
4502 Grand Ave
Duluth, MN 55807
218-624-5791; 800-333-8059

| parts |

Mail order and open shop. Mon-Fri 8 to 5:30; Sat 8 to 1. Large automotive parts store which purchases the older automotive parts from other automotive parts stores, warehouse distributors and aftermarket manufacturers. We sell the parts that an automotive parts store considers obsolete as it is no longer listed in current catalogs. Sell NOS engine, chassis, brake and drivetrain parts which are old, obsolete or no longer in production from 1930-69.

Jahns Quality Pistons
1360 N Jefferson St
Anaheim, CA 92807
714-579-3795, 800-225-0277
FAX: 714-524-6607

| piston rings
pistons |

Specializing in pistons, pins and piston rings for all applications and years from 1-3/4 to 10 inch bores. Antiques, imports, industrial, tractors, trucks and experimental.

Kanter Auto Products
76 Monroe St
Boonton, NJ 07005
800-526-1096 or 201-334-9575
FAX: 201-334-5423

| car covers
carpets
parts |

See full listing in **Section Two** under **comprehensive parts**

Ken's Carburetors
2301 Barnum Ave
Stratford, CT 06497
203-375-9340

| carburetors
distributors
parts |

See full listing in **Section One** under **Ford '32-'53**

Lindskog Balancing
1170 Massachusetts Ave
Boxborough, MA 01719-1415
508-263-2040; FAX: 508-263-4035

| engine balancing |

See full listing in **Section Two** under **engine rebuilding**

Linearossa International Inc
15281 Barranca Pkwy #A
Irvine, CA 92618
714-727-1201; FAX: 714-727-0603

| parts |

See full listing in **Section One** under **Fiat**

David Martin
Box 61
Roosevelt, TX 76874
915-446-4439

| parts |

See full listing in **Section One** under **Chrysler**

Midwestern Motors & Dismantlers
19785 W 12 Mi, Bldg 404
Southfield, MI 48076
810-559-8848

| salvage yard |

See full listing in **Section One** under **Mercedes-Benz**

Miller Energy Inc
3200 South Clinton Ave
S Plainfield, NJ 07080
908-755-6700; FAX: 908-755-0312
E-mail allyon@aol.com

| engine parts |

See full listing in **Section One** under **Stanley**

Millers Incorporated
7412 Count Circle
Huntington Beach, CA 92647
714-375-6565; FAX: 714-847-6603
E-mail: millermbz@aol.com

| accessories
parts |

See full listing in **Section One** under **Mercedes-Benz**

Moline Engine Service Inc
3227 23rd Ave
Moline, IL 61265
309-764-9735

| parts
rebuilding |

Shop open Monday-Friday 7 to 4:30. Complete auto machine shop stocking crankshafts, cylinder heads, connecting rods, etc, for cars from 1950 to date. Engine rebuilding, balancing, crankshaft exchange. Internal engine parts all US made. 45 years in business.

Mooney's Antique Parts
HC 01, Box 645C
Goodrich, TX 77335
409-365-2899, 9 am to 6 pm
409-685-4577, 6-9 pm, orders only

| engine parts
rubber parts |

See full listing in **Section Two** under **comprehensive parts**

Moroso Performance Products Inc
80 Carter Dr
Guilford, CT 06437
203-453-6571; FAX: 203-453-6906

| accessories
parts |

See full listing in **Section Two** under **racing**

Motor Bay Co
PO Box 460828
San Antonio, TX 78246
800-456-6642

| tools |

See full listing in **Section Two** under **tools**

Northern Auto Parts Warehouse Inc
PO Box 3147
Sioux City, IA 51102
800-831-0884; FAX: 712-258-0088

| parts |

Hundreds of engine rebuild kits available. Plus carbs, manifolds, oil pumps, etc from stock to performance. We have the part you're looking for.

Northwestern Auto Supply Inc
1101 S Division
Grand Rapids, MI 49507
616-241-1714, 800-704-1078
FAX: 616-241-0924

| parts |

Mail order and open shop. Monday-Saturday 8 am to 5:30 pm. An old time parts store that services the old car enthusiast along with current inventory. Deals with all mechanical parts for the engine, brakes, suspension, drivetrain and ignition. When ordering, call and ask for Sam.

NOS Only
414 Umbarger Rd, Unit E
San Jose, CA 95111
408-227-2353, 408-227-2354
FAX: 408-227-2355

| NOS parts |

See full listing in **Section Two** under **comprehensive parts**

O'Brien High Tech Auto
33 Pheasant Ln
Aliso Viejo, CA 92656
714-583-1780, 800-227-8290
FAX: 714-583-1889
E-mail: ohtind@aol.com

| cellular phone exts
& access
parts |

See full listing in **Section One** under **Cadillac/LaSalle**

Opel Oldtimer Service Denmark
Mosede Kaervej 47
Greve DK-2670 Denmark
+45-42-901073, best 11 am-3 pm
Central US time

literature
parts
parts locators

See full listing in **Section One** under **Opel**

Operations Plus
PO Box 26347
Santa Ana, CA 92799
PH/FAX: 714-962-2776

accessories
parts

See full listing in **Section One** under **Cobra**

Parts House
2912 Hunter St
Fort Worth, TX 76112
817-451-2708; FAX: 817-496-8909

accessories
parts

See full listing in **Section Two** under **comprehensive parts**

The Parts Scout®
Bodo Repenn
Diagonalstrasse 18A
D-20537 Hamburg Germany
*49-40-21980130
FAX: *49-40-21980132

parts
parts locator

See full listing in **Section Two** under **comprehensive parts**

Paul's Select (Porsche) ®
2280 Gail Dr
Riverside, CA 92509
PH/FAX: 909-685-9340

parts

See full listing in **Section One** under **Porsche**

Performance Automotive Warehouse
8966 Mason Ave
Chatsworth, CA 91311
818-998-6000; FAX: 818-407-7204

accessories
engine parts

Mail order only. Phone order and tech line available 7 days a week. Deals in stock and high-performance engine parts and accessories for domestic 6- and 8-cylinder engines, 1955 and later. Complete 630+ page catalog available.

PerTronix Inc
1268 E Edna Pl
Covina, CA 91724
818-331-4801; FAX: 818-967-1054

ignition systems

See full listing in **Section Two** under **ignition parts**

Jerrell Pickett
Box 218
Wessington, SD 57381
605-458-2344

literature
parts
sheetmetal
wheels

See full listing in **Section Two** under **comprehensive parts**

Power Play, Bob Walker
Rt 1 Box 95
Lowgap, NC 27024
910-352-4866; FAX: 910-789-8967

parts

See full listing in **Section One** under **Chrysler**

Ram Air Inc
17134 Wood
Melvindale, MI 48122
313-382-9036; FAX: 313-382-9480

engine balancing
engine blueprinting
performance
products

See full listing in **Section One** under **Pontiac**

Red Bird Racing
5621 NE Issler St
Vancouver, WA 98661
360-694-9929

parts

See full listing in **Section One** under **Chevrolet**

Red's Headers
22950 Bednar Ln
Fort Bragg, CA 95437-8411
707-964-7733

headers
mechanical parts

See full listing in **Section One** under **Ford '32-'53**

Renaissance Restorations
4588 Payne Dr
Woodstock, GA 30188
770-591-9732

body parts
mechanical parts
restoration

See full listing in **Section Two** under **restoration shops**

Rite Weld Co
10 Northfield Rd
Wallingford, CT 06492
203-265-5984; FAX: 203-284-5063

castings
engine repair

See full listing in **Section Two** under **automobilia**

Roadster Restoration
3730 Todrob Ln
Placerville, CA 95667
916-644-6777; FAX: 916-644-7252

parts

See full listing in **Section One** under **Datsun**

Rochester Clutch & Brake Co
35 Niagara St
Rochester, NY 14605
716-232-2579; FAX: 716-232-3279

brakes
clutches

See full listing in **Section Two** under **brakes**

SC Automotive
Rt 3 Box 9
New Ulm, MN 56073
507-354-1958; FAX: 800-6477-FAXS

parts
restoration

See full listing in **Section One** under **Chevrolet**

Scotts Manufacturing
25520 Ave Stanford #304
Valencia, CA 91355
800-544-5596; FAX: 805-295-9342

electric fans

See full listing in **Section Two** under **electrical systems**

Smith & Jones Distributing Company Inc
1 Biloxi Square
West Columbia, SC 29170
803-822-8500; FAX: 803-822-8477

parts

See full listing in **Section One** under **Ford '03-'31**

Joe Smith Ford & Hot Rod Parts
2140 Canton Rd, Unit C
Marietta, GA 30066
800-235-4013; 770-426-9850
FAX: 770-426-9854

parts
service

See full listing in **Section One** under **Ford '32-'53**

Special Interest Car Parts
1340 Hartford Ave
Johnston, RI 02919
800-556-7496; FAX: 401-831-7760

parts

See full listing in **Section One** under **Jaguar**

Speed Service Inc
3049 W Irving Park Rd
Chicago, IL 60618
312-478-1616

distributors
engine rebuilding
magnetos

See full listing in **Section Two** under **ignition parts**

Star Quality
1 Alley Rd
La Grangeville, NY 12540
800-782-7199; FAX: 914-266-5394
E-mail: sq@mhv.net

parts

See full listing in **Section One** under **Mercedes-Benz**

Straight Six Jaguar
24321 Hatteras St
Woodland Hills, CA 91367
PH/FAX: 818-716-1192

parts
service

See full listing in **Section One** under **Jaguar**

Studebaker Parts & Locations
228 Marquiss Cir
Clinton, TN 37716
615-457-3002

parts
parts locator

See full listing in **Section One** under **Studebaker**

J F Sullivan Co
14 Clarendon Rd
Auburn, MA 01501
508-792-9500

brake parts
consulting
machine work
parts locator

See full listing in **Section Two** under **brakes**

Swedish Classics Inc
PO Box 557
Oxford, MD 21654
800-258-4422; FAX: 410-226-5543

parts

See full listing in **Section One** under **Volvo**

TA Motor AB
Torpslingan 21
Lulea S 97347 Sweden
+46-920-18888
FAX: +46-920-18821

accessories
parts

See full listing in **Section One** under **Cadillac/LaSalle**

Tatom Custom Engines/
Vintage Vendors
2718 Riverbend Rd
Mt Vernon, WA 98273
360-424-8314; FAX: 360-424-6717

engine rebuilding
machine shop

See full listing in **Section Two** under **engine rebuilding**

Tavia Performance Products Inc
12851 Western Ave, Unit D
Garden Grove, CA 92841
714-892-4057; FAX: 714-892-5627

accessories
tools

See full listing in **Section Two** under **tools**

T-Bird Sanctuary
9997 SW Avery
Tualatin, OR 97062
503-692-9848, FAX: 503-692-9849

parts

See full listing in **Section One** under **Thunderbird**

Total Seal Inc
11202 N 24th Ave, Suite 101
Phoenix, AZ 85029
602-678-4977, FAX: 602-678-4991

piston rings

Total Seal, in its 29th year, is the manufacturer of Total Seal gapless piston rings that are currently used extensively in the performance market. Using gapless technology, Total Seal offers a more efficient ring that will cut engine leakdown to 2% or less. By cutting the blow-by, your engine will have cleaner oil, improved bearing life, more power and run more efficiently. Total Seal stocks many hard to find applications.

Tri-Star Pete
1998-1/2 E 1st
Tempe, AZ 85281
602-829-7826; FAX: 602-968-6935

parts

See full listing in **Section One** under **Mercedes-Benz**

Vibratech Inc (Fluidampr)
11980 Walden Ave
Alden, NY 14004
716-937-3603; FAX: 716-937-4692

performance parts

We manufacture Fluidamprs-performance harmonic dampers, used in high-performance street and race applications.

Paul Weaver's Garage
680 Sylvan Way
Bremerton, WA 98310
360-373-7870

rings

NOS piston rings one through ten inch, by size. For all engines to 1980. Please specify oversize, standard.

Dave Wilton
1344 Manhattan Dr
Paradise, CA 95969
916-872-0122

engine parts

See full listing in **Section One** under **Ford '03-'31**

Winslow Mfg Co
5700 Dean Ave
Raleigh, NC 27604
919-790-9713

parts rebuilding

Mail order only. Proprietorship specializing in the rebuilding and reconstruction of worn machinery and automobile parts with original rubber bushings. New material is high strength silicone. Harmonic balancer and flexible coupling rebuilding.

engine rebuilding

356 Enterprises
Vic & Barbara Skirmants
27244 Ryan Rd
Warren, MI 48092
810-575-9544; FAX: 810-558-3616

parts

See full listing in **Section One** under **Porsche**

Action Performance Inc
1619 Lakeland Ave
Bohemia, NY 11716
516-244-7100; FAX: 516-244-7172

accessories

See full listing in **Section Two** under **accessories**

Aldrich Auto Supply Inc
95 Prospect St
Hatfield, MA 01038
413-247-0230, 800-533-2306

engine rebuilding

Mail order and open shop. Mon-Fri 8 to 5:30, Sat 8 to 1. Auto engine rebuilding shop specializing in unleaded gas conversions and complete overhauls of classic, vintage and hi-performance engines. Also repair of cracked aluminum & cast iron engine components.

S R Aldrich Engine Re-Building
352 River Rd
Willington, CT 06279
203-429-3111

engine rebuilding

Mail order and open shop by appointment. Monday-Friday. Engine rebuilding and babbitting, babbitt bearings, align boring, piston and crankshaft grinding. A growing engine shop expanding services to better serve the antique vehicle owner. Also looking for good used/repairable equipment and tooling.

Andy's Classic Mustangs
18502 E Sprague
Greenacres, WA 99016
509-924-9824

*parts
service*

See full listing in **Section One** under **Mustang**

Antique Automotive Engineering Inc
3560 Chestnut Pl
Denver, CO 80216
303-296-7332; 800-846-7332

*babbitt service
engine restoration*

Open Monday-Friday 8 to 4:30; weekends by appointment. Babbitt pouring, align boring and complete engine restoration, balanced Model A Ford engines, counterbalanced crankshafts, drilled cranks for full pressure oil systems, cut-down flywheels with V8 clutches and pressure plates; hot rod Model Bs and V8s; high compression heads.

Atlas Engine Rebuilding Co Inc
8631 S. Avalon Blvd
Los Angeles, CA 90003
213-778-3497; FAX: 213-778-4556

*engine rebuilding
machine work*

Open shop only. Monday-Friday 8 to 5. In business for over 30 years. Complete engine rebuilding and machine shop. Crankshaft grinding and camshaft grinding. All internal engine parts.

B & B Cylinder Head
320 Washington St
West Warwick, RI 02893
401-828-4900, 800-800-4143

cylinder heads

See full listing in **Section Two** under **engine parts**

Bicknell Engine Company
7055 Dayton Rd
Enon, OH 45323
513-864-5224

*repair
restoration*

See full listing in **Section One** under **Buick/McLaughlin**

Bob's Automotive Machine
30 Harrison Ave
Harrison, NJ 07029
201-483-0059

*engine parts
machine shop*

See full listing in **Section Two** under **machine work**

BPE Racing Heads
702 Dunn Way
Placentia, CA 92870
714-572-6072; FAX: 714-572-6073

cylinder heads

See full listing in **Section Two** under **machine work**

Cam-Pro
226 S Main
Choteau, MT 59422
406-466-5599

camshaft grinding

See full listing in **Section Two** under **camshafts**

Carters Auto Restorations
1433 Pawlings Rd
Phoenixville, PA 19460
215-666-5687

restoration

See full listing in **Section Two** under **bodywork**

Cedar Creek Coachworks Ltd
151 Conestoga Ln
Stephens City, VA 22655
540-869-0244; FAX: 540-869-9577

*restoration
service*

See full listing in **Section Two** under **restoration shops**

Cobb's Antique Auto Restoration
717 Western Ave
Washington Court House, OH 43160
614-335-7489

*restoration
service*

See full listing in **Section Two** under **restoration shops**

Collector's CARS Inc
150 E St Joseph St
Arcadia, CA 91006
818-447-2576; FAX: 818-447-1461

*restoration
service*

See full listing in **Section Two** under **restoration shops**

County Corvette
171 Eagleview Blvd
Lionville, PA 19353
610-363-0872; FAX: 610-363-5325

*restoration
sales
service*

See full listing in **Section One** under **Corvette**

Crow Engineering
433 Tremont St
Taunton, MA 02780
800-537-4146

engine rebuilding

See full listing in **Section One** under **Jaguar**

Custom Friction Company
7366 Hillandale Rd
Chesterland, OH 44026
216-729-4258

*babbitting
line boring
engine rebuilding
modifications*

Complete rebuilding of early brass age car engines. Babbitting, boring, modifications, seals installed. Thirty-six years' experience. Special friction material for cone clutches and planetary bands. New one and two cylinder crankshafts made.

Dale Manufacturing
3425 Fairhaven St NE
Salem, OR 97303
503-364-8685

harmonic balancers

See full listing in **Section Two** under **engine parts**

Diablo Engineering
8776 East Shea, #B3A-109
Scottsdale, AZ 85260
PH/FAX: 602-391-2569

*engines
parts*

See full listing in **Section One** under **Porsche**

**Eastern Specialty Automotive
Sales & Service Ltd**
38 Yankeetown Rd
Hammonds Plains
NS Canada B3Z 1K7
902-835-5912; FAX: 902-835-0310

	parts
	service
	transport

See full listing in **Section Two** under **car & parts locators**

EIS Engines Inc
215 SE Grand Ave
Portland, OR 97214
503-232-5590; 800-547-0002
FAX: 503-232-5178

| | engines |

See full listing in **Section One** under **Mercedes-Benz**

Errol's Steam Works
3123 Baird Rd
North Vancouver
BC Canada V7K 2G5
PH/FAX: 604-985-9494

	castings
	engines
	parts

See full listing in **Section One** under **Locomobile**

Ezold's Model A Garage
1120 Southampton Rd
Westfield, MA 01805
413-562-0273

| | engine rebuilding |
| | restorations |

See full listing in **Section One** under **Ford '03-'31**

Grand Touring
2785 E Regal Park Dr
Anaheim, CA 92806
714-630-0130; FAX: 714-630-6956

	engine rebuilding
	machine shop
	restoration
	suspension

See full listing in **Section Two** under **restoration shops**

Grey Hills Auto Restoration
PO Box 630, 51 Vail Rd
Blairstown, NJ 07825
908-362-8232; FAX: 908-362-6796

| | restoration |
| | service |

See full listing in **Section Two** under **restoration shops**

Gullwing Service Co Inc
106 Western Ave
Essex, MA 01929
508-768-6919; FAX: 508-768-3523

	car dealer
	mechanical service
	parts
	restoration

See full listing in **Section One** under **Mercedes-Benz**

Harkin Machine Shop
903 43rd St NE
Watertown, SD 57201
605-886-7880

| | engine rebuilding |
| | rebabbitting |

Mail order and open shop. Rebabbitting engine bearings and complete rebuilding of antique car engines.

Hein's Classic Cars
422 Douglas
Durham, KS 67438
316-732-3335

| | restoration |

See full listing in **Section One** under **Thunderbird**

Thos Hespenheide & Associates Ltd
410 Darby Rd
Havertown, PA 19083
610-446-7699, FAX: 610-446-7915

| | appraiser |
| | rebuilding |

See full listing in **Section Two** under **appraisals**

Hollywood Classic Motorcars Inc
363 Ansin Blvd
Hallandale, FL 33009
954-454-4641; FAX: 954-457-3801

| | cars |
| | parts |

See full listing in **Section One** under **Thunderbird**

Horst's Car Care
3160-1/2 N Woodford St
Decatur, IL 62526
217-876-1112

| | engine rebuilding |

See full listing in **Section One** under **Mercedes-Benz**

Klasse 356 Inc
741 N New St
Allentown, PA 18102
800-634-7862; FAX: 610-432-8027
E-mail: parts@klasse356.com

	cars
	parts
	restoration

See full listing in **Section One** under **Porsche**

Knight Automotive Engineering Inc
Kettle Cove Industrial Park
743 Western Ave, Rt 127
Gloucester, MA 01930
508-525-3491

| | engine rebuilding |

Mail order and open shop. Monday-Friday 8 to 5, Saturday by appointment. Complete automotive machine shop including babbitting and align boring. Custom rebuilding of all makes of engines. Specializing in rebuilding Ford engines from Model Ts to present. Providing the automotive hobby with quality engine rebuilding for over 20 years. Visitors always welcome. Stop by or call.

Koffel's Place
4300 Haggerty Rd
Walled Lake, MI 48390
810-363-5239; FAX: 810-363-0023

| | engine rebuilding |
| | machine shop |

Mail order and open shop. Mon-Fri 8 am-6 pm, Wed 8 am-9 pm. Two locations providing quality service and parts. Engine building for racing, collector cars, street rods, antique cars and boats. Complete in-house machine shop services and dyno testing.

Koffel's Place II 740 River Rd Huron, OH 44839 419-433-4410; FAX: 419-433-2166	**engine rebuilding** **machine shop**

Two locations providing quality service and parts. Mail order and open shop. Mon-Fri 8 am-6 pm, Wed 8 am-9 pm. Engine building for racing, collector cars, street rods, antique cars and boats. Complete in-house machine shop services and dyno testing.

Krem Engineering 10204 Perry Hwy Meadville, PA 16335 814-724-4806	**engine rebuilding** **repairs** **restoration**

See full listing in **Section Two** under **restoration shops**

L & N Olde Car Co 9992 Kinsman Rd PO Box 378 Newbury, OH 44065 216-564-7204; FAX: 216-564-8187	**restoration**

See full listing in **Section Two** under **restoration shops**

Last Chance Repair & Restoration PO Box 362A, Myers Rd Shaftsbury, VT 05262	**repairs** **restoration**

See full listing in **Section Two** under **restoration shops**

Libbey's Classic Car Restoration Center 137 N Quinsigamond Ave Shrewsbury, MA 01545 PH/FAX: 508-792-1560	**bodywork** **restoration** **service**

See full listing in **Section Two** under **restoration shops**

Lincoln Highway Packards Main St, PO Box 94 Schellsburg, PA 15559 814-733-4356; FAX: 814-839-4276	**engine rebuilding** **restoration**

See full listing in **Section One** under **Packard**

Lindskog Balancing 1170 Massachusetts Ave Boxborough, MA 01719-1415 508-263-2040; FAX: 508-263-4035	**engine balancing**

Complete engine balancing and individual engine component balancing. Antique work is our specialty.

Masterworks Auto Reconditioning 1127 Brush Run Rd Washington, PA 15301 412-267-3460	**restoration**

See full listing in **Section Two** under **restoration shops**

McAdam Motorcars Ltd 215 Redoubt Rd Yorktown, VA 23692 757-898-7805; FAX: 757-898-9019	**restoration**

See full listing in **Section Two** under **restoration shops**

Moline Engine Service Inc 3227 23rd Ave Moline, IL 61265 309-764-9735	**parts** **rebuilding**

See full listing in **Section Two** under **engine parts**

Northern Auto Parts Warehouse Inc PO Box 3147 Sioux City, IA 51102 800-831-0884; FAX: 712-258-0088	**parts**

See full listing in **Section Two** under **engine parts**

Odyssey Restorations Inc 8080 Central Ave NE Spring Lake Park, MN 55432 612-786-1518; FAX: 612-786-1524	**parts** **restoration**

See full listing in **Section Two** under **restoration shops**

PerTronix Inc 1268 E Edna Pl Covina, CA 91724 818-331-4801; FAX: 818-967-1054	**ignition systems**

See full listing in **Section Two** under **ignition parts**

Pioneer Valley Model A Ford Inc 81 East St Easthampton, MA 01027 413-584-8400; FAX: 413-584-7605 E-mail: pvma@aol.com	**cars** **parts** **restoration**

See full listing in **Section One** under **Ford '03-'31**

Pitcher's Auto Restoration 54 Metaterraine Ave Perryville, RI 02879 401-783-4392	**engine repair** **parts** **restoration**

See full listing in **Section Two** under **restoration shops**

Power Play, Bob Walker Rt 1 Box 95 Lowgap, NC 27024 910-352-4866; FAX: 910-789-8967	**parts**

See full listing in **Section One** under **Chrysler**

Ram Air Inc 17134 Wood Melvindale, MI 48122 313-382-9036; FAX: 313-382-9480	**engine balancing** **engine blueprinting** **performance** **products**

See full listing in **Section One** under **Pontiac**

Roadrunner Tire & Auto 4850 Hwy 377 S Fort Worth, TX 76116 817-244-4924	**restoration** **speedometer repair**

See full listing in **Section Two** under **restoration shops**

Ross' Automotive Machine Co Inc 1763 N Main St Niles, OH 44446 330-544-4466	**racing engines** **rebuilding**

Mail order and open shop. Specializing in 1949-64 Olds motors. Deals in 1949-70 Chev, Olds, Buick, Pontiac. Stock rebuilds, unleaded conversions, racing engines, balancing, dyno testing, etc. We are a six man racing engine shop with the most modern equipment including dyno and ultrasonic testing. We are capable of very close tolerance machining as we build NASCAR motors and are especially interested in 1949-64 Olds motors.

Scotts Manufacturing 25520 Ave Stanford #304 Valencia, CA 91355 800-544-5596; FAX: 805-295-9342	**electric fans**

See full listing in **Section Two** under **electrical systems**

Generalists

Shepard's Automotive	appraisals
Division of Fine Ride Industries	**engine**
4131 S Main St	**remanufacturing**
Akron, OH 44319	
330-644-2000; FAX: 330-644-6522	

Specialist in remanufacturing antique motors. Custom rebuilding of standard or performance motors, cracked/damaged blocks no longer a problem. Internationally known for our Cadillac, Wedge, Hemi motors. Specializing in 1930 to 70s power plants. Light manufacturing of parts. Large stock. All work in our "in-house" hi-tech machine shops. Show quality motors. Engine, prerun 4 hrs, our custom built run stands to assure your guarantee. 45 years of engine building. "Best on the block."

Silver Star Restorations	parts
116 Highway 19	restoration
Topton, NC 28781	
704-321-4268; FAX: 704-321-6008	

See full listing in **Section One** under **Mercedes-Benz**

Silver State Restorations Inc	restoration
The Aday Collection	service
4655 Aircenter Cir	
Reno, NV 89502	
702-826-8886; FAX: 702-826-9191	

See full listing in **Section Two** under **restoration shops**

Joe Smith Ford & Hot Rod Parts	parts
2140 Canton Rd, Unit C	service
Marietta, GA 30066	
800-235-4013; 770-426-9850	
FAX: 770-426-9854	

See full listing in **Section One** under **Ford '32-'53**

Speed Service Inc	distributors
3049 W Irving Park Rd	engine rebuilding
Chicago, IL 60618	magnetos
312-478-1616	

See full listing in **Section Two** under **ignition parts**

Stone Barn Inc	restoration
202 Rt 46, Box 117	
Vienna, NJ 07880	
908-637-4444; FAX: 908-637-4290	

See full listing in **Section Two** under **restoration shops**

Straight Six Jaguar	parts
24321 Hatteras St	service
Woodland Hills, CA 91367	
PH/FAX: 818-716-1192	

See full listing in **Section One** under **Jaguar**

Tamarack Automotive Appraisals	appraiser
and Marine Surveys	restoration
53 Sears Ln	
Burlington, VT 05401	
PH/FAX: 802-864-4003	
E-mail: gtlittle@aol.com	

See full listing in **Section Two** under **appraisals**

Tatom Custom Engines/	engine rebuilding
Vintage Vendors	machine shop
2718 Riverbend Rd	
Mt Vernon, WA 98273	
360-424-8314; FAX: 360-424-6717	

In business for over 10 years. Engine restoration and the construction of vintage, specialty, hi-performance and race engines.

I have a full service machine shop including cast iron repair. I also have a substantial number of major brand speed equipment parts available.

Teddy's Garage	parts
8530 Louise Ave	restoration
Northridge, CA 91325	service
818-341-0505	

See full listing in **Section One** under **Rolls-Royce/Bentley**

Thul Auto Parts Inc	boring
225 Roosevelt Ave	machine work
Plainfield, NJ 07060	rebabbitting
908-754-3333 FAX: 908-756-0239	vintage auto parts

Shop open Mon-Fri, 8 to 5:30. Rebabbitting, crankshaft grinding and build up, align boring, resleeving, reboring, large general machine shop. Some old engines and parts, cracked blocks and heads repaired. Resleeving, reboring, crack repairs, large general machine shop.

Total Seal Inc	piston rings
11202 N 24th Ave, Suite 101	
Phoenix, AZ 85029	
602-678-4977, FAX: 602-678-4991	

See full listing in **Section Two** under **engine parts**

Wild Bill's Corvette &	parts
Hi-Performance Center Inc	rebuilding
451 Walpole St	service
Norwood, MA 02062	
617-551-8858	

See full listing in **Section One** under **Corvette**

Wilson's Rods and Classics	restoration
Gary R Wilson	
Rt 1, Box 139	
Holliday, MO 65258	
816-327-5583	

See full listing in **Section Two** under **restoration shops**

Peter Woodend (Spares)	automobilia
PO Box 157	engine parts
Takanini	gaskets
Auckland New Zealand	pistons
PH/FAX: 64-9-298-3393	wiring harnesses

See full listing in **Section One** under **Austin**

Yesteryear Restorations	repair
387 Nutting Rd	restoration
Jaffrey, NH 03452	sales
603-532-7469	transportation

See full listing in **Section One** under **Ford '32-'53**

Zim's Autotechnik	parts
1804 Reliance Pkwy	service
Bedford, TX 76021	
800-356-2964; FAX: 817-545-2002	

See full listing in **Section One** under **Porsche**

exhaust systems

Aremco Products Inc | compound
23 Snowden Ave
PO Box 429
Ossining, NY 10546
914-762-0685; FAX: 914-762-1663

See full listing in **Section Two** under **accessories**

Automotive Specialty Accessory Parts Inc | parts
PO Box 1907
Carson City, NV 89702
800-693-ASAP(2727)
FAX: 702-888-4545

See full listing in **Section Two** under **tires**

Borla East | exhaust systems
600 A Lincoln Blvd
Middlesex, NJ 08846
908-469-9666

See full listing in **Section One** under **Rolls-Royce/Bentley**

Borla Performance Ind Inc | exhaust systems
5901 Edison Dr, Dept HMN
Oxnard, CA 93033
805-986-8600; FAX: 805-986-8999

Mail order only. Manufacturers of the most comprehensive line of performance exhaust systems in the industry. Products are made in the USA of T-304 aircraft quality stainless steel. Patented, award and race winning technology. Web site: www.borla.com

Tony D Branda Performance | accessories / decals / emblems / sheetmetal / wheels
Shelby and Mustang Parts
1434 E Pleasant Valley Blvd
Altoona, PA 16602
814-942-1869; FAX: 814-944-0801

See full listing in **Section One** under **Mustang**

Cars of the Past | restoration
11180 Kinsman Rd
Newbury, OH 44065
216-564-2277

See full listing in **Section Two** under **restoration shops**

Chev's of the 40's | parts
2027 B St
Washougal, WA 98671
360-835-9799; FAX: 360-835-7988

See full listing in **Section One** under **Chevrolet**

Corvette Central | accessories / parts
5865 Sawyer Rd
Dept HM
Sawyer, MI 49125
616-426-3342; FAX: 616-426-4108

See full listing in **Section One** under **Corvette**

D & R Classic Automotive Inc | parts
30 W 255 Calumet Ave
Warrenville, IL 60563
708-393-0009; FAX: 708-393-1397

See full listing in **Section One** under **Chevelle/Camaro**

Double S Exhausts LP | exhausts
Station Rd
Cullompton, Devon Ex15 1BW
Great Britain

Mail order and open shop. Monday-Friday 9-5. Specializing in stainless steel exhaust & later pipes.

Jim Fortin | exhaust systems
95 Weston St
Brockton, MA 02401-3334
508-586-4855

Mail order and open shop by appointment only. Phone hours: Monday-Friday 11 am to 9 pm; weekends by chance. Exhaust systems manufactured for most cars and light trucks from 1909 to muscle car era. Pipes manufactured in heavy steel, inquire for aluminized or stainless steel. Most mufflers aluminized. Have large amount of NORS mufflers available from mid 50s to late 60s. We also have carburetor heat tubes for 20s, 30s Buicks. Lower radiator water connector tubes available for MoPar, GM, Ford, Hudson, Packard. Guaranteed satisfaction on all parts I sell. Established 1967. At 50, I've been exhausting myself for almost 30 years. SASE for letter reply, prefer calls.

Headers by "Ed" Inc | headers
2710-NV 16th Ave S
Minneapolis, MN 55407
612-729-2802

Mail order and open shop. Mon-Fri, 8:30-5. Pre-1975 V8 car headers. V8/Allison V12 vertical exit pull/Mudbog headers. Header kits, header parts for over one hundred different 4, 6, V6, V8, V12 engines. Very informative header catalog, $5.50. Informative header parts catalog (learn how to build headers better than any you can buy), $3.95. 90-minute header design audio cassette (with reference charts), will make you a header design expert, $10.95. Since 1962.

See our ad on this page

Generalists

High Performance Coatings 550 W 3615 S Salt Lake City, UT 84115 801-262-6807; FAX: 801-262-6307 E-mail: hpcsales@hpcoatings.com	**coatings**

Mail order and open shop. Mon-Fri 8 am to 5 pm. Specializing in all cars and motorcycles exhaust system coatings, thermal barrier coatings, dry film lubricative coatings, corrosion resistant coatings.

Hooker Headers 1024 W Brooks St, PO Box 4030 Ontario, CA 91761 909-983-5871	**exhaust systems**

Mail order only. Dealing in automotive exhaust systems including headers, mufflers. Cat-back exhaust systems and dual exhaust systems. We also manufacture a line of off-road accessories like nerf bars and push bars.

Italy's Famous Exhaust 2711 183rd St Redondo Beach, CA 90278 PH/FAX: 310-542-5432 E-mail: http://famous@earthlink.com	**exhaust systems** **wheels**

Mail order only. 24 hours. Dealing in Daytona free flow exhaust systems and Campagnolo wheels. We are the exclusive global distributor for FAZA.

King & Queen Mufflers Box 423 Plumsteadville, PA 18949 PH/FAX: 215-766-8699	**exhaust systems**

Mail order and shows only. Specializing in exhaust systems for "domestic" vintage autos & trucks.

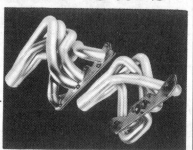

Lister North America Ltd 6565 E 40 Tulsa, OK 74145 918-665-0021; FAX: 918-664-0804	**performance parts**

See full listing in **Section One** under **Jaguar**

London Stainless Steel Exhaust Centre 249-253 Queenstown Rd London, SW8 3NP England 011-44-171622-2120 FAX: 011-44-171627-0991 E-mail: 101445.341@compuserv.com	**exhaust systems**

Mail order and open shop. Mon-Sat 8:30 to 5:30. The widest range of stainless steel exhausts anywhere, fast UPS delivery.

Marcel's Corvette Parts 15100 Lee Rd #101 Humble, TX 77396 713-441-2111 info line 800-546-2111 order line FAX: 713-441-2111	**parts**

See full listing in **Section One** under **Corvette**

Porcelain Patch & Glaze Co Inc 966 86th Ave Oakland, CA 94621 510-635-2188	**porcelain enameling**

Open shop. Monday-Friday 8 to 4. Specializes in porcelain enameling of intake and exhaust manifolds. Welding and repairs available. UPS orders.

Power Effects 1800H Industrial Park Dr Grand Haven, MI 49417 616-847-4200; FAX: 616-847-4210	**exhaust systems**

Power Effects® performance components and engineered systems are designed for cars, sport trucks, sport utility vehicles and street rods. Flange mounted cast aluminum exhaust components and mandrel bent tubing provide maximum flexibility and ease of installation. Aluminum tuneable Power Capsules™ replace conventional mufflers offering superior air flow and a deep, rich-sounding exhaust. Aluminum Power Tips™ finish off the tailpipe end and are available to fit 2-1/4, 2-1/2, 2-3/4 and 3-inch tubing.

Protrim Inc 438 Calle San Pablo, Unit 1 Camarillo, CA 93012 805-987-2086; FAX: 805-389-5375	**plating**

See full listing in **Section Two** under **plating & polishing**

RD Enterprises Ltd 290 Raub Rd Quakertown, PA 18951 215-538-9323; FAX: 215-538-0158 E-mail: rdent@rdent.com	**parts**

See full listing in **Section One** under **Lotus**

Red Bird Racing 5621 NE Issler St Vancouver, WA 98661 360-694-9929	**parts**

See full listing in **Section One** under **Chevrolet**

Red's Headers 22950 Bednar Ln Fort Bragg, CA 95437-8411 707-964-7733	**headers** **mechanical parts**

See full listing in **Section One** under **Ford '32-'53**

SC Automotive | parts
Rt 3 Box 9 | restoration
New Ulm, MN 56073 |
507-354-1958; FAX: 800-6477-FAXS |

See full listing in **Section One** under **Chevrolet**

Stahl Headers Inc | exhaust systems
1515 Mount Rose Ave |
York, PA 17403 |
717-846-1632; FAX: 717-854-9486 |

Mail order only. Manufacturers of high performance exhaust systems (headers). Exhaust parts and accessories.

See our ad on page 294

Waldron's Antique Exhaust Inc | exhaust systems
PO Box C, 25872 M-86 |
Nottawa, MI 49075 |
800-503-9428, 616-467-7185 |
FAX: 616-467-9041 |

Mail order and open shop. Monday-Friday 9 to 5. New exhaust systems for 1925-65 cars. Oldest and most complete old car exhaust system supplier in the USA.

fans

Flex-a-lite
4540 S Adams
Tacoma, WA 98409
206-475-5772; FAX: 206-474-6013
E-mail: flex@flex-a-lite.com

Dealing in high-performance cooling fans, both electric and belt-driven. Transmission and engine oil coolers.

fiberglass parts

American Performance Products | parts
675 S Industry Rd |
Cocoa, FL 32926 |
407-632-8299; FAX: 407-632-5119 |

See full listing in **Section One** under **AMC**

ASC&P International | custom molding
PO Box 255 | fiberglass
Uwchland, PA 19480 | plastic
610-458-8395; FAX: 610-458-8735 |

Injection molded plastic reproduction. Also compression molded fiberglass from original parts. Short run production is our specialty. In-house mold making to insure quality. Casting services of plastics also available. Hardness ranges from floppy (rubber) to rigid. Will repair original bakelite parts as well as other old styles of plastic.

Keith Ashley | fiberglass parts
107 W Railroad St, Unit V |
St Johns, MI 48879 |
517-224-6460; FAX: 517-224-9488 |

See full listing in **Section One** under **Ford '32-'53**

Auto Accessories of America Inc | accessories
PO Box 427, Rt 322 | customizing
Boalsburg, PA 16827 | gifts & apparel
800-458-3475; FAX: 814-364-9615 | restoration
Foreign: 814-364-2141 |

See full listing in **Section One** under **Corvette**

Auto Body Specialties Inc | accessories
Rt 66 | body parts
Middlefield, CT 06455 |
860-346-4989; FAX: 860-346-4987 |

See full listing in **Section Two** under **body parts**

Bairs Corvettes | parts
316 Franklin St | service
Linesville, PA 16424 |
814-683-4223; FAX: 814-683-5200 |

See full listing in **Section One** under **Corvette**

Bob's Brickyard Inc | parts
399 Washington St |
Brighton, MI 48116 |
810-229-5302 |

See full listing in **Section One** under **Bricklin**

Tony D Branda Performance | accessories
Shelby and Mustang Parts | decals
1434 E Pleasant Valley Blvd | emblems
Altoona, PA 16602 | sheetmetal
814-942-1869; FAX: 814-944-0801 | wheels

See full listing in **Section One** under **Mustang**

Cardillo Classic Cadillac | accessories
351 W 51st St | top boots
New York, NY 10019 |
212-247-1354 |

See full listing in **Section One** under **Cadillac/LaSalle**

Class Glass and Performance Inc | fiberglass bodies
101 Winston St | parts
Cumberland, MD 21502 |
800-774-3456; FAX: 301-777-7044 |

Mail order and open shop. Monday through Saturday, 7:30 am to 5 pm. Fiberglass bodies and parts for street rod, racing and antique cars. Specializing in complete 32 Chevy roadster 3-window coupe, 5 passenger coupe and 53 Studebaker. Many parts for 28 to 34 Fords, 39 to 85 Dodge pickups, Camaros, Chevelles, Mustangs and Chevy pickups from 1939 to 1988. We also make racing fiberglass as well as racing go-cart bodies and antique gas pump parts.

Corvette Central | accessories
5865 Sawyer Rd, Dept HM | parts
Sawyer, MI 49125 |
616-426-3342; FAX: 616-426-4108 |

See full listing in **Section One** under **Corvette**

D & D Plastic Chrome Plating | chroming
Jim & Marty Price | plating
4534 S Detroit Ave |
Toledo, OH 43614 |
419-389-1748 |

See full listing in **Section Two** under **plating & polishing**

ECB, Ed Leek | fiberglass parts
13 Snipe Rd |
Key Largo, FL 33037 |
PH/FAX: 305-451-0864 |

Specializing in Fiberglas extensions and fillers for replacement of rotted Butyl rubber OEMs on GM autos. Cadillac, Buick, Oldsmobile, Chevrolet, 1973-91, most models and some Pontiacs.

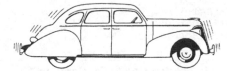

Exotic Enterprises 459 Madeline Ave Garfield, NJ 07026 201-523-2217, 201-956-7570	**fiberglass manufacturing fiberglass mold making**

Mail order and open shop. Monday-Saturday 9:30 am to 5 pm. 32 years' experience. Specializing in fiberglass mold making and manufacturing any type of automotive parts or complete cars. We can copy or design anything you need. One part or one thousand. Quick service, low cost. We manufacture the Preston Tucker car in fiberglass and supply all parts needed. We make custom hoods, scopes, ground FX Countach, F4T, 308, 512, Diablo replica cars, and custom fiberglass. We sell fiberglass material resins, gelcoat, tools. We offer free advice on kits and fiberglass repair & parts. Please call for your needs.

Fairlane Automotive Specialties 210 E Walker St St. Johns, MI 48879 517-224-6460	**fiberglass bodies parts**

See full listing in **Section One** under **Ford '32-'53**

Fibre Glast Developments Corp 1944 Neva Dr Dayton, OH 45414 800-821-3283; FAX: 513-274-7267 E-mail: fibreglast@aol.com	**supplies tools**

See full listing in **Section Two** under **restorations aids**

HochKraeusen Racing PO Box 716 18233 Madison Rd Parkman, OH 44080-0716 216-548-2147	**machine shop**

See full listing in **Section Two** under **machine work**

Bruce Horkey Cabinetry Rt 4, Box 188 Windom, MN 56101 507-831-5625; FAX: 507-831-0280	**pickup parts**

See full listing in **Section Two** under **woodwork**

Kwik Poly T Distributing Inc 24 St Henry Ct St Charles, MO 63301 314-724-1065	**restoration aids**

See full listing in **Section Two** under **restoration aids**

Langley Paint & Body 3560 E Bethel Ln Bloomington, IN 47408 812-336-2244	**fiberglass parts painting restoration**

Mail order and open shop. Monday-Friday 8 to 5:30. For all American and foreign cars. Fiberglass parts made to customer's designs. Trick and custom painting. We refinished the 1981 Indy 500 car for sponsor Sergio Valente, which won the PPG award for best color and design. Also complete body restoration, lead work and refinishing. Member Society of Automotive Engineers.

Lister North America Ltd 6565 E 40 Tulsa, OK 74145 918-665-0021; FAX: 918-664-0804	**performance parts**

See full listing in **Section One** under **Jaguar**

Marcel's Corvette Parts 15100 Lee Rd #101 Humble, TX 77396 713-441-2111 info line 800-546-2111 order line FAX: 713-441-2111	**parts**

See full listing in **Section One** under **Corvette**

The Maverick Connection 137 Valley Dr Ripley, WV 25271 PH/FAX: 304-372-7825	**literature parts**

See full listing in **Section One** under **Ford '54-up**

McMillan Fender Sales/ Truckin' Plus Fibreglass Rt 1 Owen Sound ONT Canada N4K 5N3 519-371-0579	**fiberglass parts**

Mail order and open shop. Seven days a week, 8 am-11 pm. Manufactures thick fiberglass antique truck and some car parts. Each fender is made up and stays in the mold for 24 hours to assure straightness. Specializes in 1935 to 1979 pickups, Fords, Chevys, Dodges, Internationals, impact resistant, black gelcoat. Also runningboards, visors and tilt fronts for 1/2 ton trucks. Catalog, $3.

R & R Fiberglass & Specialties 4850 Wilson Dr NW Cleveland, TN 37312 423-476-2270	**body parts**

Dealing in fiberglass, fenders, runningboards, grille shells and misc fiberglass body parts for Ford, Chevy, Plymouth, Dodge, Ford 1923-40 car/truck, Chevy 1932-41 car/32-54 truck, Plymouth 1931-36 car/1933-38 truck, Dodge 1931-36 car/1933-38 truck. Also aluminum grille insert for Plymouth and Dodge 1932-36 car and 1933-38 Dodge truck.

Regal Roadsters Ltd 301 W Beltline Hwy Madison, WI 53713 PH/FAX: 608-273-4141	**replicars restoration**

See full listing in **Section One** under **Thunderbird**

Replica Plastics 210 W Washington St Box 1147 Dothan, AL 36301 800-873-5871; FAX: 334-792-1175	**fiberglass parts**

Mail order and open shop. Monday-Friday 7 am to 6 pm. Dealing in fiberglass quarter panel extensions. Replica Plastics furnishes over 300 fiberglass replacement panels for all GM cars. We ship worldwide, same day.

Speedway Motors Inc 300 Speedway Cir Lincoln, NE 68502 402-474-4411; FAX: 402-477-7476	**parts**

See full listing in **Section Two** under **comprehensive parts**

Web Accessories PO Box 191 Old Bethpage, NY 11804 516-752-1710	**fiberglass parts**

Triumph transmission and tunnel covers, MGA front apron and fenders, MGB front air dam.

Wescott's Auto Restyling 19701 SE Hwy 212 Boring, OR 97009 800-523-6279; FAX: 503-658-2938	**body parts**

See full listing in **Section One** under **Ford '32-'53**

Gene Winfield's Rod & Custom 7256 Eton Ave Canoga Park, CA 91303 818-883-2611	**fender skirts metal repair panels motor mount kits**

See full listing in **Section One** under **Mercury**

filters

fire engines

Pipercross USA | air filter
31 Winsor St
Milpitas, CA 95035
408-942-5595; FAX: 408-942-5582
E-mail: piperxusa@aol.com

Mail order and open shop. Monday-Saturday 8 to 6. High performance foam air filters for vintage cars.

financing

Associated Foreign Exchange Inc | foreign currency wires/drafts
201 Sansome St
San Francisco, CA 94104
800-752-2124; FAX: 415-391-3553
E-mail: 102172.261@compuserv.com

See full listing in **Section Two** under **special services**

Blueprint Auto Insurance Agency | insurance
100 Corporate Pl
Peabody, MA 01960
800-530-5305; FAX: 508-535-3759
E-mail: blueprint@gnn.com

See full listing in **Section Two** under **insurance**

First National Bank of Sumner | financing
PO Box 145
Sumner, IL 62466
618-936-2396; FAX: 618-936-2240

Offering simple interest loan financing for the purchase of antique and collector automobiles.

IPTC Automotive | cars parts
300 SW 12th Ave
Pompano Beach, FL 33069
800-277-3806

See full listing in **Section One** under **BMW**

IPTC Publishing | manuals
300 SW 12th Ave
Pompano Beach, FL 33069
800-653-4198

See full listing in **Section Four** under **books & publications**

Land Yachts Automobile Restoration and Customizing | restoration
497 London Bridge Rd, Suite 101
Virginia Beach, VA 23454
757-431-0294; FAX: 757-431-4524

See full listing in **Section Two** under **restoration shops**

JC Taylor Antique Automobile Insurance Agency | insurance
320 S 69th St
Upper Darby, PA 19082
800-345-8290

See full listing in **Section Two** under **insurance**

Carburetor Engineering | carburetor rebuilding distributor rebuilding fuel pump rebuilding
3324 E Colorado
Pasadena, CA 91107
818-795-3221

See full listing in **Section Two** under **carburetors**

Ceramicar | auto-related ceramics
679 Lapla Rd
Kingston, NY 12401
PH/FAX: 914-338-2199

See full listing in **Section Two** under **novelties**

Darrell's Automotive and Restorations | repairs restorations
2639 N Tripp Ave
Odessa, TX 79763
915-381-7713

Mail order and open shop. Mon-Fri 9-5. Automotive repairs and restorations. Specializes in all Fords and fire apparatus. Buys, sells and restores fire apparatus. Also buys and sells antique cars, trucks and parts. Front end alignment & tire balance.

Ben McAdam | electrical parts
500 Clover Ln
Wheeling, WV 26003
304-242-3388

See full listing in **Section Two** under **ignition parts**

Professional Specialties/ Americana Coach | appraisals literature
513 S Woodlawn Ave, Ste 322
Wichita, KS 67218
316-684-1199; FAX: 316-684-6266

See full listing in **Section Two** under **appraisals**

Reinholds Restorations | appraisals repairs restoration
c/o Rick Reinhold
PO Box 178, 255 N Ridge Rd
Reinholds, PA 17569-0178
717-336-5617

See full listing in **Section Two** under **restoration shops**

R-Mac Publications Inc | magazine
Rt 3, Box 425
Jasper, FL 32052
904-792-2480; FAX: 904-792-3230

See full listing in **Section Four** under **books & publications**

Westwinds Motor Car Co | restoration
RD 2, Box 777, Cox Rd
Woodstock, VT 05091
802-457-4178; FAX: 802-457-3926

See full listing in **Section Two** under **restoration shops**

Wheels O' Time Museum | museum
PO Box 9636
Peoria, IL 61612-9636
309-243-9020

See full listing in **Section Six** under **Illinois**

fuel system parts

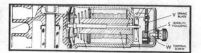

Antique Auto Parts Cellar
PO Box 3
6 Chauncy St
S Weymouth, MA 02190
617-335-1579; FAX: 617-335-1925

| | brake parts |
| chassis parts |
| engine parts |
| fuel pumps/kits |
| gaskets/water pumps |

See full listing in **Section Two** under **comprehensive parts**

Atlantic Antique Auto Parts
RR #6, PO Box 1388, Site 28
Armdale
Halifax, NS Canada B3L 4P4
902-479-0967

parts
service

See full listing in **Section Two** under **rubber parts**

Automotive Specialty Accessory Parts Inc
PO Box 1907
Carson City, NV 89702
800-693-ASAP(2727)
FAX: 702-888-4545

parts

See full listing in **Section Two** under **tires**

Brisson Enterprises
PO Box 1595
Dearborn, MI 48121
313-584-3577

lead

See full listing in **Section Two** under **car care products**

Bronx Automotive
501 Tiffany St
Bronx, NY 10474
718-589-2979

parts

See full listing in **Section Two** under **ignition parts**

Chicago Corvette Supply
7322 S Archer Rd
Justice, IL 60458
708-458-2500; FAX: 708-458-2662

parts

See full listing in **Section One** under **Corvette**

The Classic Preservation Coalition
PO Box 262
Taborton Rd
Sand Lake, NY 12153-0262
518-674-2445

restoration

See full listing in **Section Two** under **carburetors**

Classic Tube
(Division of Classic & Performance Spec Inc)
80 Rotech Dr
Lancaster, NY 14086
800-882-3711, 716-759-1800
FAX: 716-759-1014

brake lines
choke tubes
fuel lines
transmission lines
vacuum lines

See full listing in **Section Two** under **brakes**

Dr Vette
212 7th St SW
New Philadelphia, OH 44663
330-339-3370, 800-878-1022 orders; FAX: 330-339-6640

brakes
fuel system parts
repairs

See full listing in **Section One** under **Corvettes**

East Spring Obsolete Auto Parts Inc
PO Box 3
Bethlehem, CT 06751
203-266-5488 evenings & weekends

parts

See full listing in **Section Two** under **brakes**

Ferris Auto Electric Ltd
106 Lakeshore Dr
North Bay, ONT Canada P1A 2A6
705-474-4560; FAX: 705-474-9453

parts
service

See full listing in **Section Two** under **electrical systems**

Ron Francis' Wire Works
167 Keystone Rd
Chester, PA 19013
610-485-1937

fuel injection
harnesses
wiring accessories
wiring kits

See full listing in **Section Two** under **electrical systems**

Gas Tank Renu USA
12727 Greenfield
Detroit, MI 48227
800-932-2766; FAX: 313-273-4759

fuel tank repair

Repair of fuel tanks for automotive & marine industries. Lifetime warranty on any vehicle less than 3/4 ton.

Arthur Gould
6 Dolores Ln
Fort Salonga, NY 11768
516-754-5010; FAX: 516-754-0212

fuel pumps
water pumps

Largest stock of fuel pumps and water pumps in the US. Fastest turnaround on rebuilding. One year guarantee on all work.

Hotchkiss Vacuum Tank Service
2102 S Brentwood Pl
Essexville, MI 48732-1489
517-894-2073

repair kits
restoration

Mail order only. Restoration of the vacuum fuel feed system tank, repair kits, gaskets and parts.

Inline Tube
17540 14 Mile Rd
Fraser, MI 48026
810-294-4093; FAX: 810-294-7349
E-mail: inline@apk.net

brake lines
choke tubes
fuel lines
transmission lines
vacuum lines

See full listing in **Section Two** under **brakes**

Kanter Auto Products
76 Monroe St
Boonton, NJ 07005
800-526-1096; 201-334-9575
FAX: 201-334-5423

car covers
carpets
parts

See full listing in **Section Two** under **comprehensive parts**

Ken's Carburetors
2301 Barnum Ave
Stratford, CT 06497
203-375-9340

carburetors
distributors
parts

See full listing in **Section One** under **Ford '32-'53**

Montclair Radiator Service
10598 Rose Ave
Montclair, CA 91763
714-621-9531

fuel tanks
radiators

See full listing in **Section Two** under **radiators**

Motor Bay Co
PO Box 460828
San Antonio, TX 78246
800-456-6642

tools

See full listing in **Section Two** under **tools**

O'Brien High Tech Auto
33 Pheasant Ln
Aliso Viejo, CA 92656
714-583-1780, 800-227-8290
FAX: 714-583-1889
E-mail: ohtind@aol.com

cellular phone exts
& access
parts

See full listing in **Section One** under **Cadillac/LaSalle**

Paul's Select (Porsche) ®
2280 Gail Dr
Riverside, CA 92509
PH/FAX: 909-685-9340

parts

See full listing in **Section One** under **Porsche**

Performance Automotive Warehouse
8966 Mason Ave
Chatsworth, CA 91311
818-998-6000; FAX: 818-407-7204

accessories
engine parts

See full listing in **Section Two** under **engine parts**

Jack Podell Fuel Injection Spec
106 Wakewa Ave
South Bend, IN 46617
219-232-6430; FAX: 219-234-8632

fuel system parts
fuel system
rebuilding

See full listing in **Section One** under **Corvette**

John T Poulin Auto Sales/Star Service Center
5th Avenue & 111th St
North Troy, NY 12182
518-235-8610

car dealer
parts
restoration service

See full listing in **Section One** under **Mercedes-Benz**

Quality Mfg & Dist
PO Box 20870
El Cajon, CA 92021
619-442-8686; FAX: 619-590-0123

tools

See full listing in **Section Two** under **tools**

Quanta Restoration and Preservation Products
45 Cissel Dr
North East, MD 21901
410-658-5700; FAX: 410-658-5758

fan belts
gas tanks

See full listing in **Section Two** under **chassis parts**

Renner's Corner
10320 E Austin
Manchester, MI 48158
313-428-8424; FAX: 313-428-1090

engine snubber kits
fuel pipes
fuel pump kits
gauge rebuild kits

See full listing in **Section One** under **Ford '32-'53**

Tornado Air Management Systems
13360-H Firestone Blvd
Santa Fe Springs, CA 90670
310-926-5000; FAX: 310-926-1223
E-mail: j.k@ix.netcom.com

parts

See full listing in **Section Two** under **accessories**

Tug's Wholesale Auto Parts
RR 3
Port Hope, ONT Canada L1A 3V7
905-885-9191

parts

Imports clean used gas tanks and assorted body parts and bumpers from the southern US into Canada. Also sells a large amount of new aftermarket tanks.

Union Performance Co
PO Box 324, 59 Mansfield St
Sharon, MA 02067
617-784-5367, voice mail
FAX: 617-784-5367

parts

See full listing in **Section Two** under **electrical systems**

Zim's Autotechnik
1804 Reliance Pkwy
Bedford, TX 76021
800-356-2964; FAX: 817-545-2002

parts
service

See full listing in **Section One** under **Porsche**

gaskets

Antique Auto Parts Cellar
PO Box 3
6 Chauncy St
S Weymouth, MA 02190
617-335-1579; FAX: 617-335-1925

brake parts
chassis parts
engine parts
fuel pumps/kits
gaskets/water pumps

See full listing in **Section Two** under **comprehensive parts**

Aremco Products Inc
23 Snowden Ave, PO Box 429
Ossining, NY 10546
914-762-0685; FAX: 914-762-1663

compound

See full listing in **Section Two** under **accessories**

Be Happy Automatic Transmission Parts
414 Stivers Rd
Hillsboro, OH 45133
800-416-2862; FAX: 513-442-6133

trans rebuild kits

See full listing in **Section Two** under **transmissions**

Jim Carter's Antique Truck Parts
1500 E Alton
Independence, MO 64055
816-833-1913; FAX: 816-252-3749

truck parts

See full listing in **Section One** under **Chevrolet**

Clester's Auto Rubber Seals Inc
PO Box 459
Cleveland, NC 27013
704-637-9979; FAX: 704-636-7390

gloveboxes/headliners
molded rubber
parts
weatherstripping

See full listing in **Section Two** under **rubber parts**

Corvair Underground
PO Box 339
Dundee, OR 97115
503-434-1648, 800-825-8247
FAX: 503-434-1626

parts

See full listing in **Section One** under **Corvair**

Egge Machine Company
11707 Slauson Ave
Santa Fe Springs, CA 90670
310-945-3419 in CA, 800-866-EGGE
FAX: 310-693-1635

> babbitting
> chassis
> motor mounts
> pistons/valves
> wiring harnesses

See full listing in **Section Two** under **engine parts**

Gerald J Lettieri
132 Old Main St
Rocky Hill, CT 06067
860-529-7177; FAX: 860-257-3621

> gaskets
> parts

Gaskets, head, manifold, oil pan, full engine sets, copper O-rings. Over 25 years of satisfied service.

Molina Gaskets
23126 Mariposa Ave
Torrance, CA 90502
310-539-1883; FAX: 310-539-3886

> head gaskets

Specializing in copper and asbestos headgaskets, custom made for any car, tractor or marine engine.

National Drivetrain Inc
3125 S Ashland Ave #201
Chicago, IL 60608
800-507-4327; FAX: 312-376-9135

> differential parts
> transmission parts

See full listing in **Section Two** under **transmissions**

Northern Auto Parts Warehouse Inc
PO Box 3147
Sioux City, IA 51102
800-831-0884; FAX: 712-258-0088

> parts

See full listing in **Section Two** under **engine parts**

Olson's Gaskets
3059 Opdal Rd E
Port Orchard, WA 98366
360-871-1207, 24 hr machine

> gaskets

Mail and phone orders. Monday-Saturday. Engine gaskets, NOS, new production, handmaking service. Full sets, head gaskets, manifolds, etc, for cars, trucks, tractors, etc. 24 hour answering machine. Visa/MC.

Orion Motors European Parts Inc
10722 Jones Rd
Houston, TX 77065
800-736-6410; 713-894-1982
FAX: 713-849-1997

> parts

See full listing in **Section One** under **Alfa Romeo**

Performance Automotive Warehouse
8966 Mason Ave
Chatsworth, CA 91311
818-998-6000; FAX: 818-407-7204

> accessories
> engine parts

See full listing in **Section Two** under **engine parts**

Powers Parts Co
Roy F Powers
1354 Ridge Rd
Fabius, NY 13063
315-683-5376

> gaskets

Mail order and open shop. Open 6 days by chance, call first. NOS gaskets, car, truck, tractor, industrial. Light on classics.

Standard Abrasives Motor Sports
9351 Deering Ave
Chatsworth, CA 91311
800-383-6001
818-718-7070, ext 371
FAX: 800-546-6867

> abrasives

See full listing in **Section Two** under **restoration aids**

Studebaker Parts & Locations
228 Marquiss Cir
Clinton, TN 37716
615-457-3002

> parts
> parts locator

See full listing in **Section One** under **Studebaker**

Total Seal Inc
11202 N 24th Ave, Suite 101
Phoenix, AZ 85029
602-678-4977, FAX: 602-678-4991

> piston rings

See full listing in **Section Two** under **engine parts**

John Ulrich
450 Silver Ave
San Francisco, CA 94112
510-223-9587 days

> parts

See full listing in **Section One** under **Packard**

R Donald Williams
RD 1, Box 111, Brotherton Rd
Berlin, PA 15530
814-267-3250

> parts

See full listing in **Section Two** under **comprehensive parts**

Peter Woodend (Spares)
PO Box 157
Takanini Auckland New Zealand
PH/FAX: 64-9-298-3393

> automobilia
> engine parts
> gaskets/pistons
> wiring harnesses

See full listing in **Section One** under **Austin**

glass

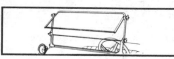

Muneef Alwan
7400 Crosa Countre Rd
Oroville, CA 95966
916-534-6683

> glass
> steering wheels

See full listing in **Section One** under **Ford '32-'53**

American Restorations Unlimited TA
14 Meakin Ave, PO Box 34
Rochelle Park, NJ 07662
201-843-3567; FAX: 201-843-3238
E-mail: amerrest@aol.com

> restoration parts

Mail order and open shop. Mon-Sat 8 am-8 pm. A complete service company. We represent 120 manufacturers of restoration parts from 1950-1979. Glass, trans kits, weatherstripping, Chevy interiors, sheetmetal, clock restoration, trim parts, engines, suspensions, literature, etc. Transmission parts & kits, manual & automatic, 1930-70s. Major supplier of flat glass, 1920-60s. Hard to find Camaro & Corvette parts. Muscle cars, Vettes, Mustangs, T-Birds and GM. Rebuilding service of your engine or transmissions. If it's American, we can supply the customer.

Bartelstone Glass
2184 Jerome Ave
Bronx, NY 10453-1089
800-288-6452; FAX: 800-288-6395
E-mail: edfennell@aol.com

> glass

Auto glass, curved parts for all domestic and foreign cars.

Bob's Classic Auto Glass   **glass**
21170 Hwy 36
Blachly, OR 97412
800-624-2130

Mail order only. Phone hours: 7 days a week, 9 to 9. Antique auto glass for all makes and models, 1920-60. No foreign. Reproduced in clear, green, grey and bronze.

Fox Lite Inc   **plastic glazings**
Airplane Plastics Co
8300 Dayton Rd
Fairborn, OH 45324
513-864-1966; FAX: 513-864-7010

Open shop Monday-Friday 8 am-5 pm EST/EDT. Dealing in custom plastic glazings on all makes. Windshields, backlights, headlamp shields, aircraft canopies and glazings. Restorations: customs, street rods, aircrafts and boats.

Glass Search/LOF   **glass parts**
1975 Galaxie Ave
Columbus, OH 43207
800-848-1351; FAX: 614-443-0709

Mail order and open shop. Monday-Friday 8 am-6 pm EST. Glass Search carries an inventory of over 70,000 glass parts. We have the auto glass you need. Original classic parts per original specifications. Corvettes, Buick, Chevy, Olds, just to name a few. We also can supply original glass parts for Ferrari, Jaguar, Rolls-Royce and a number of exotic vehicles. Need a part cut to pattern? We can supply that also. LOF's Glass Search team is always ready to serve you.

See our ad on page 302

Jefferis Hot Rod Autobody   **windshield glass kit**
4130-C Horizon Ln
San Luis Obispo, CA 93401
800-807-1937; FAX: 805-543-4757

Mail order and open shop. Mon-Fri 8 am-5:30 pm, Sat 10 am-3 pm. Replace your leaky, rusty original windshield, without any modifications, with an easy installation of a new flush mount V butt fixed glass for 37 to 53 Ford, Chevy cars and trucks and others. Kit includes: complete instructions, (aluminum base frames for 37-39 Fords); clear, green, gray or bronze tinted glass; clear silicone, urethane sealer, heavy drip check caulking, interior finish bonding strip and exterior rubber finish beading or weather strip as needed. Shipping UPS, ground or next day air. Visa, M/C, Discover, American Express or money order.

JLM   **power window lifts**
PO Box 1348, Maud Rd
Palmer, AK 99645
907-745-4670; FAX: 907-745-5510

Mail order only. Power window lifts for all cars with flat glass. 12v conversion units.

Kaleidoscope   **glass restoration**
PO Box 86-H   **scratch remover kit**
Mt Ephraim, NJ 08059
800-831-5163

See full listing in **Section Two** under **restoration aids**

Mercedes Used Parts   **parts**
Bob Fatone
166 W Main St
Niantic, CT 06357
860-739-1923; FAX: 860-691-0669

See full listing in **Section One** under **Mercedes-Benz**

N/C Ind Antique Auto Parts   **windshield frames**
301 S Thomas Ave, PO Box 254
Sayre, PA 18840
717-888-6216; FAX: 717-888-1821

Mail order and open shop. Shop open Monday-Friday 8 am to 5 pm. Specializing in windshield frames for almost all makes and models cars and trucks. 1933-34 Plymouth and Dodge parts.

NOS Locators   **parts**
587 Pawtucket Ave
Pawtucket, RI 02860
401-725-5000

See full listing in **Section One** under **MG**

OEM Glass Inc   **auto glass**
PO Box 362, Rt 9 E
Bloomington, IL 61702
309-662-2122; FAX: 309-663-7474

Mail order only. Auto and truck glass for 1920-1976 cars and trucks. Specializing in original logos and date codes for show cars.

Redden's Auto Glass Engraving   **engraving**
7219 W 75 S
Lafayette, IN 47905-9263
317-572-2293

Open by appointment only. We engrave any automobile, boat, truck, RV glass (excluding windshields) using a high speed drill. Equipment is portable so work can be done at customer's residence. We can engrave any design that can be photocopied.

Rick's Relics   **bodywork**
Wheeler Rd   **painting**
Pittsburg, NH 03592   **restoration**
603-538-6612

See full listing in **Section Two** under **restoration shops**

Riverhill Glass & Truck Co   **glass**
570 Mifflin Rd   **paint**
Jackson, TN 38301
901-422-4218

See full listing in **Section Two** under **painting**

Sanders Reproduction Glass   **glass**
PO Box 522
Hillsboro, OR 97123
503-648-9184 weekdays 8 to noon

Mail order only. Specializing in superior quality flat laminated safety glass for 30s, 40s, 50s cars. Cut to original patterns, authentically detailed with sandblasted script, dated month and year, rounded polished edges and inlaid black edging. Meticulous craftsmanship is evident on every piece. Specializing in Fords, Lincolns and Mercs. Official licensed product Ford Motor Co.

So Cal Pickups Inc   **parts**
6321 Manchester Blvd
Buena Park, CA 90621
714-994-1400; FAX: 714-994-2584

See full listing in **Section One** under **Ford '54-up**

Bill Thomsen   **salvage yard**
Rt 4 Box 492
Moneta, VA 24121
540-297-1200

See full listing in **Section Five** under **Virginia**

Missing A Glass Part?

Put Us On The Case!

LOF GlassSearch®

1-800-848-1351

We're able to meet logo & brand name requirements and we accept Visa & Mastercard.

© 1996 Libbey-Owens-Ford Co.

Scott Young
332 Devon Dr
San Rafael, CA 94903
415-472-5126

glass reproductions

Mail order only. Furnishing dash glass and metal instrument dial restoration for over 13 years. Dash glass silkscreened (numbers on glass) for speedometers, clocks and radios. In-stock dash glass for over 200 cars in the 30s, 40s and early 50s. Authentic metal dial restoration (numbers on metal). Our process is appropriate for show cars or cars of value.

grille emblem badges

British Things Inc
515 Ocean Ave
Santa Monica, CA 90402
310-394-4002; FAX: 310-394-3204

badges

See full listing in **Section One** under **Rolls-Royce/Bentley**

Comet Products
Cherry Parke 101-B
Cherry Hill, NJ 08002
609-795-4810; FAX: 609-354-6313

emblems
accessories

Mail order only. Manufactures car emblem badges for the front car grille. Over 500 types are available: countries, states, autos, auto clubs, military, fraternal organizations, etc. Also makes lapel pins, belt buckles, key chains, key fobs, decals, patches, magnetic country of origin ovals. Catalog $3. Dept HV.

Enthusiast's Specialties
350 Old Connecticut Path
Framingham, MA 01701
508-620-1942; FAX: 508-872-4914

automobilia
tools

See full listing in **Section Two** under **automobilia**

Eurosport Daytona Inc
32 Oceanshore Blvd
Ormond Beach, FL 32176
800-874-8044; 904-672-7199
FAX: 904-673-0821

license plates

See full listing in **Section Two** under **license plates**

Protrim Inc
438 Calle San Pablo, Unit 1
Camarillo, CA 93012
805-987-2086; FAX: 805-389-5375

plating

See full listing in **Section Two** under **plating & polishing**

So Cal Pickups Inc
6321 Manchester Blvd
Buena Park, CA 90621
714-994-1400; FAX: 714-994-2584

parts

See full listing in **Section One** under **Ford '54-up**

Swedish Classics Inc
PO Box 557
Oxford, MD 21654
800-258-4422; FAX: 410-226-5543

parts

See full listing in **Section One** under **Volvo**

West Coast Metric Inc
24002 Frampton Ave
Harbor City, CA 90710
310-325-0005; FAX: 310-325-9733
E-mail: wcmi@earthlink.net

apparel
carpets
rubber parts

See full listing in **Section One** under **Volkswagen**

hardware

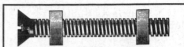

Antique Auto Fasteners
Guy C Close, Jr & Son
13426 Valna Dr
Whittier, CA 90602
310-696-3307

fasteners
hardware
hose clamps
molding clips

Mail order and open shop. Fasteners for upholstery and cloth tops. Molding trim clips and bolts. (We match samples for most cars thru 1965.) Stainless capped bumper bolts. Brass Sherman hose clamps. NOS Swiss & Ferro lock mechanisms for 1935-36 MoPar, 1935-49 Ford closed cars; miscellaneous springs; 34-55 inside door handles; 39-47 GM trunk handles. Striker plates, special screws and bolts, trim hardware, speed nuts, hinge pins, door checkstraps, pedal pads, assist straps and robe ropes. Illustrated catalog $4. SASE.

See our ad on page 304

Auto Hardware Specialties
3123 McKinley Ave
Sheldon, IA 51201
712-324-2091; FAX: 712-324-2480

hardware fasteners

See full listing in **Section One** under **Chevrolet**

Dwight H Bennett
PO Box 3173
Seal Beach, CA 90740-2173
PH/FAX: 310-498-6488

emblem repair
hardware repair
mascot repair
plaque repair

See full listing in **Section Two** under **radiator emblems & mascots**

Big Flats Rivet Co
35 Sunny Dell Cir
Horseheads, NY 14845
607-562-3501; FAX: 607-562-3711

rivets
tools

Mail order only. Rivets and installation tools for all makes of antique autos.

The Buckle Man
Douglas D Drake
28 Monroe Ave
Pittsford, NY 14534
716-381-4604

buckles

Strap buckles for all types of needs (I do not sell leather straps, only the buckles for your straps). These are NOS buckles, brass, nickel and black for all your restoration needs: sidemount and mirror tie downs, top and windshield strap buckles, trunk strap buckles, spring cover buckles, trunk and luggage strap buckles, etc. Whether it is for a brass era car or a classic, try The Buckle Man. Over 125 buckle styles, 10,000 in stock. Send photocopy of your needs and I will match to my stock.

Creative Metal Products Inc
121 R N Douglas St
Appleton, WI 54914
414-830-7975; FAX: 414-830-7976

storage system

See full listing in **Section Two** under **tools**

East Coast Chevy Inc
Ol '55 Chevy Parts
4154A Skyron Dr
Doylestown, FL 18938
215-348-5568; FAX: 215-348-0560

parts
restoration

See full listing in **Section One** under **Chevrolet**

The Enthusiasts Shop | **cars**
John Parnell | **pre-war parts**
PO Box 80471 | **transportation**
Baton Rouge, LA 70898
504-928-7456; FAX: 504-928-7665

See full listing in **Section One** under **Rolls-Royce/Bentley**

Fast Lane Products | **chamois**
PO Box 7000-50 | **drain tubs**
Palos Verdes Peninsula, CA 90274 | **hand wringers**
800-327-8669

See full listing in **Section Two** under **car care products**

Harter Industries Inc | **parts**
PO Box 502 | **restoration**
Holmdel, NJ 07733
908-566-7055; FAX: 908-566-6977

See full listing in **Section Two** under **comprehensive parts**

JLM | **power window lifts**
PO Box 1348, Maud Rd
Palmer, AK 99645
907-745-4670; FAX: 907-745-5510

See full listing in **Section Two** under **glass**

M & R Products | **hardware**
1940 SW Blvd | **tie-downs**
Vineland, NJ 08360
609-696-9450; FAX: 609-696-4999

See full listing in **Section Two** under **accessories**

Midwest Acorn Nut Company | **fasteners**
256 Minnesota Ave | **hardware**
Troy, MI 48083-4671
800-422-NUTS (6887)
FAX: 810-583-9130

We manufacture chrome and high lustre stainless steel fasteners & related hardware for many of the old classic cars as well as street rods, cars & trucks.

Mr G's Enterprises | **fasteners**
5613 Elliott Reeder Rd | **screw kits**
Fort Worth, TX 76117
817-831-3501; FAX: 817-831-0638
E-mail: mrgs@flash.net

Mail order and open shop. Monday-Friday 9-5. Specializing in fasteners, screw kits and rechrome plastic for all makes and models.

Old Ford Parts | **parts**
35 4th Ave N
Algona, WA 98001
206-833-8494; FAX: 206-833-2190

See full listing in **Section One** under **Ford '32-'53**

Pennsylvania Metal Cleaning | **derusting**
200 17th St | **stainless fasteners**
Monaca, PA 15061-1969 | **stripping**
412-728-5535

See full listing in **Section Two** under **rust removal & stripping**

Quality Mfg & Dist | **tools**
PO Box 20870
El Cajon, CA 92021
619-442-8686; FAX: 619-590-0123

See full listing in **Section Two** under **tools**

R J & L Automotive Fasteners
58 Bristol Ave
Rochester, NY 14617-2702
PH/FAX: 716-467-7421
phone 4-9 M-F, fax 24 hours

fasteners

Specializing in manufacturing obsolete or those "hard to find" fasteners. Also carries 1,000s of original style clips & fasteners. Samples are required for a proper match. Dealers inquire.

RB's Prototype Model & Machine Co
44 Marva Ln
Stamford, CT 06903
PH/FAX: 203-329-2715

machine work

See full listing in **Section Two** under **service shops**

Re-Flex Border Marker
138 Grant St
Lexington, MA 02173
617-862-1343

border markers
posts

Mail order only. Flexible border markers and posts for marking driveways, parking areas, work areas or anywhere that must be made more visible.

Restoration Supply Company
2060 Palisade Dr
Reno, NV 89509
702-825-5663; FAX: 702-825-9330
E-mail: restoration@rsc.reno.nv.us

accessories
restoration supplies

See full listing in **Section Two** under **restoration aids**

Shobolts
1161 Harrison St
Windsor, ONT Canada N9C 3J4
PH/FAX: 519-256-2292

fasteners

Sales of chrome, stainless steel and polished stainless steel fasteners, nuts, bolts, screws, washers, etc. Standard and metric automotive hardware.

Tavia Performance Products Inc
12851 Western Ave, Unit D
Garden Grove, CA 92841
714-892-4057; FAX: 714-892-5627

accessories
tools

See full listing in **Section Two** under **tools**

Totally Stainless
1709 Old Harrisburg Rd
Gettysburg, PA 17325
717-337-2151; FAX: 717-337-1663

stainless hardware

Mail order only. Stainless steel bolts, screws, nuts, washers, clamps and more. Offers the largest selection of US and metric fasteners available. Over 5,000 ready to install assembly kits are available.

Tom Vagnini
58 Anthony Rd, RR 3
Pittsfield, MA 01201
413-698-2526

used parts

See full listing in **Section One** under **Packard**

Yankee Peddler Motorsports
11300 Fortune Circle
Wellington, FL 33414
561-798-6606; FAX: 561-798-6706

electrical
components
hardware

See full listing in **Section Two** under **electrical systems**

heaters

Blaak Radiateurenbedryf
Blaaksedyk oost 19
Heinenoord 3274LA Netherlands
31-186-601732
FAX: 31-186-603044

radiators

See full listing in **Section Two** under **radiators**

Performance Analysis Co
1345 Oak Ridge Turnpike, Suite 258
Oak Ridge, TN 37830
423-482-9175
E-mail: 7662.2133@compuserve.com

climate control
cruise control

See full listing in **Section One** under **Mercedes-Benz**

hubcaps

Burr Nyberg Screw-on Hubcaps
200 Union Blvd #425
Denver, CO 80228
FAX: 303-988-7145

hubcaps

Original Screw-on Hubcaps Reproduced: many cars of the teens, 20s and early 30s had screw-on hubcaps that through the ages became dented or lost. We are now able to reproduce exact copies of original hubcaps made by a craftsman to the highest quality standard. Any screw-on hubcap can be made following your original sample or pattern. Current prices are given upon request. Delivery time is usually 12-16 weeks.

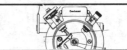

ignition parts

Atlantic Antique Auto Parts
RR #6, PO Box 1388, Site 28
Armdale
Halifax, NS Canada B3L 4P4
902-479-0967

parts
service

See full listing in **Section Two** under **rubber parts**

Automotive Specialty Accessory Parts Inc
PO Box 1907
Carson City, NV 89702
800-693-ASAP(2727)
FAX: 702-888-4545

parts

See full listing in **Section Two** under **tires**

Battery Ignition Co Inc
91 Meadow St
Hartford, CT 06114
860-296-4215; FAX: 860-947-3259
E-mail: biscokid@aol.com

parts
rebuilding
rebushing

See full listing in **Section Two** under **carburetors**

Robert D Bliss
2 Delmar Pl
Edison, NJ 08837
908-549-0977

ignition parts
electrical parts

See full listing in **Section Two** under **electrical systems**

Bronx Automotive
501 Tiffany St
Bronx, NY 10474
718-589-2979

parts

Mail order only. Mostly parts for 1930-70. Taillight lenses, ignition parts, fuel pumps, brakes, suspension parts, engine parts, other assorted parts. Carb kits, brake wheel cylinders & kits. Early high performance manifolds, cams, carbs, valve covers, etc.

CBS Performance Automotive
2605-A W Colorado Ave
Colorado Springs, CO 80904
800-685-1492; FAX: 719-578-9485

ignition systems
performance
products

Mail order and open shop. Monday-Saturday 8-6. Never change points again! CBS Performance is your supplier for the Ignitor by Pertronix. The Ignitor replaces your points and condenser with an electronic ignition system that fits neatly inside your stock distributor cap. The Ignitor is available for most vehicles between 1956 and 1974 and is only $79. Call for more information.

See our ad on this page

Collectors Auto Supply
528 Appian Way
Coquitlam, BC Canada V3J 2A5
PH/FAX: 604-931-7278;
E-mail: jimcarpenter@bc.sympatico.cd

parts

See full listing in **Section Two** under **comprehensive parts**

Crossfire
260 Hickory St, PO Box 263
Sharpsville, PA 16150
800-458-3478; FAX: 412-962-4639

accessories

Manufacturer of specialty ignition components and custom car parts. Call our toll-free number for our latest brochure.

NEVER CHANGE POINTS AGAIN!

IGNITOR
PERTRONIX INC

Solid-State Electronic Breakerless Ignition System

$79

• Performance - Fast starts, every time.
• Protection - Unaffected by dirt, oil, moisture.
• Convenience - Entire system fits in distributor.
• Economy - Improves fuel mileage, eliminates minor tuneups.
• Easy installation - One-piece installation in minutes.
• Dependability - 30 month factory warranty.

60-72 Chrysler
57-74 GM • 57-74 Ford
Foreign applications
available

Now available for
49-56 Ford 8 cyl.
12v negative ground
$109

Give Us A Call
800-685-1492

2605-A W. Colorado Ave.
Colo. Spgs., CO 80904

FREE SHIPPING
SATISFACTION GUARANTEED

Egge Machine Company
11707 Slauson Ave
Santa Fe Springs, CA 90670
310-945-3419 in CA, 800-866-EGGE
FAX: 310-693-1635

babbitting/chassis
motor mounts
pistons
valves
wiring harnesses

See full listing in **Section Two** under **engine parts**

Ferris Auto Electric Ltd
106 Lakeshore Dr
North Bay, ONT Canada P1A 2A6
705-474-4560; FAX: 705-474-9453

parts
service

See full listing in **Section Two** under **electrical systems**

Ficken Auto Parts
Box 11
132 Calvert Ave
Babylon, NY 11702
516-587-3332; FAX: 516-661-9125

ignition parts
wiper parts

See full listing in **Section Two** under **windshield wipers**

Gaslight Auto Parts Inc
PO Box 291
Urbana, OH 43078
513-652-2145; FAX: 513-652-2147

accessories
parts

See full listing in **Section One** under **Ford '03-'31**

H-E Ignition Parts Co
Furnace Ln
Cambridge, NY 12816
518-677-5971, 518-677-3253
FAX: 518-677-5972

ignition parts

Manufacturer of distributor caps and rotors for passenger cars from 1910 to date.

Ignition Distributor Service
19042 SE 161st
Renton, WA 98058
206-255-8052

rebuilding

Mail order only. Complete rebuilding of standard and electronic distributors, bushings, ball bearing advance plates, vacuum advances, small parts, core distributors available. Also rebuilding Q-Jet carburetors. Repairing throttle shaft air leaks, calibration of idle circuit, repair fuel leaks.

J & C's Parts
7127 Ward Rd
North Tonawanda, NY 14120
716-693-4090; FAX: 716-695-7144

parts

See full listing in **Section One** under **Buick/McLaughlin**

Ken's Carburetors
2301 Barnum Ave
Stratford, CT 06497
203-375-9340

carburetors
distributors
parts

See full listing in **Section One** under **Ford '32-'53**

Tom Lamano
478 N Country Rd
St James, NY 11780
516-862-7193

distributor
rebuilding

Mail order only. Distributor rebuilding, restoration, fabrication and dual point or electronic conversion of any year, make or type distributor. Strobing and curving done on Sun, Allen and Rotunda machines. Over 30 years of distributor rebuilding experience. All work guaranteed. Also sell complete distributors, points, rotors, condensers, distributor caps, vacuum advances and other small electrical parts.

See our ad on page 307

Ben McAdam 500 Clover Ln Wheeling, WV 26003 304-242-3388	**electrical parts**

Mail and phone order anytime. Open shop by appointment. Ignition parts 1913-65. Electrical parts & points, distributor caps, rotors, condensers, generator & starter brushes. Abbot thru Wolsey.

MikeCo Antique, Kustom & Obsolete Auto Parts 4053 Calle Tesoro, Unit C Camarillo, CA 93012 805-482-1725; FAX: 805-987-8524	**lenses parts**

See full listing in **Section One** under **Mopar**

Moroso Performance Products Inc 80 Carter Dr Guilford, CT 06437 203-453-6571; FAX: 203-453-6906	**accessories parts**

See full listing in **Section Two** under **racing**

MSD Ignition 1490 Henry Brennan Dr El Paso, TX 79936 915-857-5200; FAX: 915-857-3344 E-mail: msdign@msdignition.com	**ignition parts**

Manufacturer of high-performance ignition systems and accessories.

PerTronix Inc 1268 E Edna Pl Covina, CA 91724 818-331-4801; FAX: 818-967-1054	**ignition systems**

PerTronix is a leading manufacturer of solid-state electronic igni-tion systems. The ignitor is a retro-fit replacement for breaker points and fits entirely inside the distributor. The kit can be installed as quickly as a set of points. Never change points again! This may sound too good to be true, but an ignitor has no moving parts and never wears out. PerTronix has ignitors to fit most mid-60s to mid-70 cars.

Restoration Supply Co 2060 Palisade Dr Reno, NV 89509 702-825-5663; FAX: 702-825-9330 E-mail: restoration@rsc.reno.nv.us	**accessories restoration supplies**

See full listing in **Section Two** under **restoration aids**

Silicone Wire Systems 3462 Kirkwood Dr San Jose, CA 95117-1549	**ignition wire sets**

See full listing in **Section One** under **Corvair**

Spark Plugs & Stuff PO Box 33343 San Diego, CA 92163-3343 619-220-1745	**tune-up kits**

Mail order only. Dealing in tune-up kits (includes points, con-denser, rotor, caps and plugs) for 30s, 40s, 50s and 60s, some 20s American cars. Also rebuilt and cores. Distributors for 20s, 30s, 40s, 50s and 60s American cars only.

Special Interest Autos 602 A St NE Ardmore, OK 73401 405-226-0270; FAX: 405-226-0233	**restoration parts**

See full listing in **Section Two** under **restoration shops**

Speed Service Inc 3049 W Irving Park Rd Chicago, IL 60618 312-478-1616	**distributors engine rebuilding magnetos**

Mail order and open shop. Monday thru Saturday, 9 am-7 pm. Distributor and Vertex magneto specialists. Distributors rebuilt, no matter how old. We can also custom make magnetos and dis-tributors. Complete competition engine rebuilding.

Ed Strain 6555 44th St #2006 Pinellas Park, FL 33781 800-266-1623	**magnetos power brakes**

See full listing in **Section Two** under **brakes**

Sunburst Technology PO Box 598 Lithia Springs, GA 30057 770-949-2979; FAX: 770-942-6091 E-mail: 10274592422@compuserv.com	**electronic/ technical consultant**

See full listing in **Section Four** under **information sources**

UK Spares/TVR Sports Cars 609 Highland St Wethersfield, CT 06109-3979 203-563-1647; FAX: 203-529-3479	**accessories car covers convertible tops ignition parts**

See full listing in **Section One** under **TVR**

John Ulrich 450 Silver Ave San Francisco, CA 94112 510-223-9587 days	**parts**

See full listing in **Section One** under **Packard**

Generalists

BS Wisniewski Inc/Wizzy's
1801 S 2nd St
Milwaukee, WI 53204
800-328-6554; FAX: 414-645-5457

engine/ignition
mechanical
suspension
transmission

See full listing in **Section Two** under **comprehensive parts**

Yankee Peddler Motorsports
11300 Fortune Circle
Wellington, FL 33414
561-798-6606; FAX: 561-798-6706

electrical
components
hardware

See full listing in **Section Two** under **electrical systems**

Zim's Autotechnik
1804 Reliance Pkwy
Bedford, TX 76021
800-356-2964; FAX: 817-545-2002

parts
service

See full listing in **Section One** under **Porsche**

instruments

AAMP of America
13160 56th Ct, #502-508
Clearwater, FL 34620
813-572-9255; FAX: 813-573-9326
E-mail: stinger.sales@stinger-aamp.com

audio accessories

See full listing in **Section Two** under **accessories**

Albrico Auto & Truck Parts
PO Box 3179
Camarillo, CA 93010
805-482-9792; FAX: 805-383-1013

lamp assemblies
lenses

See full listing in **Section Two** under **lighting equipment**

Bill's Speedometer Shop
109 Twinbrook Pl
Sidney, OH 45365
513-492-7800

repairs
restoration

Mail order only. Restoration and repair of speedometers, clocks, gauges and speedometer cables.

Clock Doc®
125 University Ave
Sewanee, TN 37375
800-256-5362; FAX: 615-598-5986

clock repairs
gauge repairs

Mail order and open shop. Monday-Friday 7:30 am to 6 pm CST, Saturdays vary. Dealing in quartz conversions, clock, radio, switch, electric motor, tachometer, speedometer, fuel sender, gauge repair, sales and restoration.

Corvette Clocks by Roger
24 Leisure Ln
Jackson, TN 38305
901-664-6120; FAX: 901-664-1627

repair
restoration

Mail order and open shop. Monday-Friday 8 am to 5 pm. Specializing in the repair/restoration of 53-82 Corvette speedometers, tachometers, small gauges, complete instrument clusters, glovebox doors, clocks both mechanical and quartz conversions, wiper motors, headlight motors and radios. Corvette Clocks by Roger has an established reputation in the Corvette world for excellence in this field. We are also a dealer for Custom Autosound who specializes in manufacturing quality upgraded radios that specifically fit the old Corvettes. Should you have questions, our staff is ready to assist you.

Corvette Specialties of MD Inc
1912 Liberty Rd
Eldersburg, MD 21784
410-795-3180; FAX: 410-795-3247

parts
restoration
service

See full listing in **Section One** under **Corvette**

Development Associates
1520 S Lyon
Santa Ana, CA 92705
714-835-9512; FAX: 714-835-9513
E-mail: 71460,1146@compuserve.com

electrical parts

See full listing in **Section Two** under **electrical systems**

Ferris Auto Electric Ltd
106 Lakeshore Dr
North Bay, ONT Canada P1A 2A6
705-474-4560; FAX: 705-474-9453

parts
service

See full listing in **Section Two** under **electrical systems**

Haneline Products Co
PO Box 430
Morongo Valley, CA 92256
619-363-6597; FAX: 619-363-7321

gauges
instrument panels
stainless parts
trim parts

Mail order only. Manufactures "bolt-in" retro instrument panel kits complete with gauges, engine turned stainless steel accessories, instrument and dash fascias, door sills, firewalls, trim parts for cars and trucks 1920s to 1980s. Complete dash assemblies. Custom parts and decorative items made to order. Distributors for: Faria, Westach (dual and quad accessory gauges), Cyberdyne, Classic and Stewart Warner gauges. "Painless" wiring. Wescott, Poli Form, Brookville, Fairlane and other dashes. Large pattern inventory.

Harter Industries Inc
PO Box 502
Holmdel, NJ 07733
908-566-7055; FAX: 908-566-6977

parts
restoration

See full listing in **Section Two** under **comprehensive parts**

Instrument Services Inc
11765 Main St
Roscoe, IL 61073
800-558-2674; FAX: 800-623-6416

clocks

Mail order and open shop. Monday-Friday 8-4:30. All makes and models of 1920-1988 clocks restored and quartz converted. Do-it-yourself original electric and quartz conversion kits available for most 1961-1987 Borg clocks. Thousands of NOS clocks in stock.

International Speedometer
9540 W Ogden Ave
Brookfield, IL 60513
708-387-0606; FAX: 708-387-0240

sales
service

Mail order and open shop. Monday-Saturday 8 to 5. Service for all years and makes speedometers, tachometers and clocks.

Charles Ivey Speedometer Service
2144 Wallace Dr
Wichita, KS 67218
316-683-6765

instruments
repair

Mail order and open shop. Monday-Saturday 9 to 3. Speedometer restoration and repair for Model A and early V8 (plus other 4 cylinder) 1928-31 and 32-37 Fords. Dials and odometers renewed, only those on the market and furnished by the customer. Inquire on other than Ford products.

Kortesis Marketing Ent
PO Box 460543
Aurora, CO 80046
303-548-3995; FAX: 303-699-6660

radar jammers

See full listing in **Section Two** under **novelties**

LaPina-Monaco Inc | **speedometers**
616 Classon Ave | **windshield wipers**
Brooklyn, NY 11238
718-789-8400

Mail order and open shop. Mon-Fri 8 to 5; Sat 8 to 12 noon.

David Lindquist, Automobile Clock | **clock repair**
Repair
12427 Penn St
Whittier, CA 90602
310-698-4445

Mail order and open shop. Monday-Friday 1 to 7 PST. Automobile clock repair services and automobile clock sales. Quartz conversions on most 1956-up domestic automobile clocks.

Carlton Marsden Co | **car clocks**
403 High St
Wild Rose, WI 54984
414-622-3473

Repair and restoration of all car clocks up to 1975.

Nisonger Instrument S/S | **gauges**
570 Mamaroneck Ave
Mamaroneck, NY 10543
914-381-1952, FAX: 914-381-1953

Open shop Monday to Friday 8 to 4:30 pm. Specializing in rebuilding and sales of British automobile gauges and related Smith's items. Gearboxes, cables, ammeters, clocks, fuel, oil and water gauges, chronometric tachs and speedos. British motorcycles also, WW II and up. Also VDO mechanical speedometers for VW, BMW, Porsche, Mercedes-Benz, Audi.

O'Brien High Tech Auto | **cellular phone exts**
33 Pheasant Ln | **& access**
Aliso Viejo, CA 92656 | **parts**
714-583-1780, 800-227-8290
FAX: 714-583-1889
E-mail: ohtind@aol.com

See full listing in **Section One** under **Cadillac/LaSalle**

Old Car Woodgraining | **dashboard**
27902 45th Ave S | **restoration**
Auburn, WA 98001 | **woodgraining**
206-854-5247

See full listing in **Section Two** under **woodgraining**

Palo Alto Speedometer Inc | **instruments**
718 Emerson St
Palo Alto, CA 94301
415-323-0243; FAX: 415-323-4632

See full listing in **Section One** under **Mercedes-Benz**

Reynolds Speedometer Repair | **repair**
4 Lobao Dr | **restoration**
Danvers, MA 01923 | **sales**
508-774-6848

Mail order and open shop. Quality repair and restoration of American and European speedometers, tachometers, cables, gauges, dial and glass refinishing, plating. NOS and restored units for sale.

Roadrunner Tire & Auto | **restoration**
4850 Hwy 377 S | **speedometer repair**
Fort Worth, TX 76116
817-244-4924

See full listing in **Section Two** under **restoration shops**

Speed-o-Tac | **repairs**
3328 Silver Spur Ct | **restoration**
Thousand Oaks, CA 91360
805-492-6600

Mail order and open shop. Shop open 6 days 9 to 5. Dealing in repair, service and restoration of vintage and classic mechanical speedometers and tachometers, including the following: Stewart-Warner, SS White, Waltham, AC Delco, GM, King Seeley, Ford, Chrysler, Motometer US, Motometer European, all VDO instruments: Porsche, M-B, BMW, VW, etc. Cables and ratio boxes made to order (to correct cable input to the speedometer). SASE for free data sheet to determine ratio needs. Call before shipping instrument for repair.

The Temperature Gauge Guy | **gauges repaired**
45 Prospect St
Essex Junction, VT 05452
802-878-2811, VT
813-733-6716, FL

Mail order. Winter address: 521 Wood St, Dunedin, FL 34698; phone: 813-733-6716. Repair of temperature gauges and of some King-Seeley gas gauges. No electric instrument or radiator cap motometer repair.

Tom Vagnini | **used parts**
58 Anthony Rd, RR 3
Pittsfield, MA 01201
413-698-2526

See full listing in **Section One** under **Packard**

Vintage Restorations | **accessories**
The Old Bakery | **instruments**
Windmill Street, Tunbridge Wells
Kent TN2 4UU England
UK 1892-525899
FAX: UK 1892-525499

Mail order and open shop. Open by appointment only. Specializing in the complete restoration, supply and fabrication of instruments and dashboard accessories, mostly for European sports and exotic cars such as Alfa Romeo, Alvis, Aston Martin, Bentley, Bugatti, Ferrari, Maserati, MG, Rolls-Royce, and Riley. MasterCard and VISA accepted. Send for leaflet.

Westberg Manufacturing Inc | **gauges**
3400 Westach Way | **tachometers**
Sonoma, CA 95476
707-938-2121; FAX: 707-938-4968

Mail order and open shop. Dual 2-1/16 gauges available. In business 50 years.

insurance

American Collectors Insurance Inc | **insurance**
385 N Kings Hwy, PO Box 8343
Cherry Hill, NJ 08002
800-360-2277; FAX: 609-779-7289

Protect your classic car or truck (15 years old or older) with an "agreed value" policy by American Collectors Insurance. We insure all types of collector vehicles, from the stately sedans of 60 years ago to the muscle cars of the 1970s. Call or write for your free rate quote. Ask about our programs for antique/classic boats (25+ years old) and collectibles (auto memorabilia, model cars/trucks, toys, etc).

Automotive Legal Service Inc | **appraisals**
PO Box 626
Dresher, PA 19025
PH/FAX: 800-487-4947

See full listing in **Section Two** under **appraisals**

	insurance
Robert T Barbero CPCU c/o Commerce Ins Group 23200 Chagrin Blvd, Bldg 3 Suite 95D Beachwood, OH 44122 800-284-5867; 216-595-3504 FAX: 216-765-7101	

Mail order and open shop. 8:30 am to 5 pm EST, 24 hour fax. Classic auto insurances including vintage motorcycles, street rods. Based on availability, certain states may be excluded. Agency also offers all lines of insurance. In business for over 50 years.

	insurance
Blueprint Auto Insurance Agency 100 Corporate Pl Peabody, MA 01960 800-530-5305; FAX: 508-535-3759 E-mail: blueprint@gnn.com	

Mail order only. Antique and collector car insurance available in most states. True agreed value for autos 15 years old & older.

	appraisals
Certified Auto Appraisal PO Box 17609 Anaheim, CA 92817 714-966-1096; FAX: 714-498-7367	

See full listing in **Section Two** under **appraisals**

	insurance
Classic Car Lobby Henri Simar Jr Rue Des Combattants, 81 4800 Verviers Belgium PH/FAX: 3287335122	

Mail order and open shop. 9-12, 2-6, closed Sunday only. Specialist for classic cars insurance and insurance broker.

	insurance
Collector Car Insurance Inc PO Box 414 Leo, IN 46765 219-627-7637, 800-787-7637 FAX: 219-627-6317	

Insurance for street rods, customs, antiques, exotics, collectible Corvettes, automobiles.

	insurance
Condon & Skelly Collectible Vehicle Insurance 121 E Kings Hwy, Ste 203 Maple Shade, NJ 08052 800-257-9496	

Collector vehicle insurance for authentic antiques, classics, special interest, muscle and sports cars, motorcycles and trucks. We also offer insurance for street rods, customs, modifieds, kit & replicars. Underwritten by A+ rated St Paul Mercury Insurance. We've been providing special protection for more than 20 years. We meet our insured's coverage needs with a price that makes sense. Call 800-257-9496 for a personal estimate and free brochure.

	insurance
Hagerty Classic Insurance PO Box 87 Traverse City, MI 49685 800-922-4050; FAX: 616-941-8227	

Mail order only. Provides agreed value coverage, superior service and exceptionally competitive rates for antique, classic, limited edition and special interest vehicles. Offers flexible mileage, usage and underwriting guidelines and a variety of appropriate liability packages to meet your needs. The program is underwritten by Greenwich Insurance Company which is rated A (excellent) by A M Best. Trust your classic to nothing less than Hagerty Classic Insurance. Call or write for a no-obligation quote.

	insurance
K & K Insurance Group Inc PO Box 2338 Fort Wayne, IN 46801-2338 800-548-0858; FAX: 219-459-5511	

Mail order and open shop. Monday-Friday 8 am-5 pm EST. Affordable specialty auto insurance for antique cars, street rods, custom cars and kit cars which are at least 20 years old or older. Rates, coverage limits and availability vary per state. Call 800-548-0858 for a free quote and more information.

	auction company
Sparrow Auction Co 59 Wheeler Ave Milford, CT 06460 PH/FAX: 203-877-1066	

See full listing in **Section Two** under **auctions & events**

	insurance
State Farm Mike Moses, Agent 605 E Irving Park Rd Roselle, IL 60172 630-980-9510; FAX: 630-980-9499 E-mail: mike.moses.b8th@statefarm.com	

Largest auto insurer of antiques and classics. Serving the metro Chicago and suburbs only.

	insurance
JC Taylor Antique Automobile Insurance Agency 320 S 69th St Upper Darby, PA 19082 800-345-8290	

Classic and antique automobile insurance.

	insurance
Zehr Insurance Brokers Ltd 65 Huron St New Hamburg, ONT Canada N0B 2G0 519-662-1710; FAX: 519-662-2025	

Mail order and open shop. Monday-Friday 9 to 5. Special rated auto insurance for antique, classic, special interest automobiles plus all lines of general insurance in Ontario.

interiors & interior parts

	upholstery
ABC Auto Upholstery & Top Co 1634 Church St Philadelphia, PA 19124 215-289-0555	

See full listing in **Section One** under **Ford '54-up**

	tops upholstery
Accurate Auto Tops & Upholstery Inc Miller Rd & W Chester Pike Edgemont, PA 19028 610-356-1515; FAX: 610-353-8230	

See full listing in **Section Two** under **upholstery**

	interiors upholstery
Al's Auto Interiors Rt 2, S12626 Donald Rd Spring Green, WI 53588 608-588-7146	

Open shop only. Monday-Friday 8 to 6; Saturday 8 to 1. Complete handcrafting of interiors specializing in antique, classic and custom. One man shop guarantees complete attention to quality. No mail orders!

	parts
American Muscle PO Box 270543 West Hartford, CT 06127 860-953-2575	

See full listing in **Section One** under **GMC**

Generalists

Andover Automotive Inc
PO Box 3143
Laurel, MD 20709
410-381-6700; FAX: 410-381-6703

parts
seat belts

See full listing in **Section One** under **Corvette**

Aromas Muscle Cars
424 Rose Ave, PO Box 385
Aromas, CA 95004

interiors
trim parts

Mail order and open shop. Monday-Friday 8-5. Specializing in restorations of GM, Ford, Chrysler muscle cars. Dealing in soft trim parts and major parts. Also installations for same and full restorations.

Auto Accessories of America Inc
PO Box 427, Rt 322
Boalsburg, PA 16827
800-458-3475; FAX: 814-364-9615
Foreign: 814-364-2141

accessories
customizing
gifts & apparel
restoration

See full listing in **Section One** under **Corvette**

Auto Custom Carpet
Jeff Moses
PO Box 1350, 1429 Noble St
Anniston, AL 36202
800-633-2358; 205-236-1118
FAX: 800-516-8274

carpets
floor coverings

See full listing in **Section One** under **Chevrolet**

Auto-Mat Co
225A Park Ave
Hicksville, NY 11801
800-645-7258 orders
516-938-7373; FAX: 516-931-8438

accessories
carpet sets
interiors

Mail order and open shop. Shop open Monday-Friday 8 to 5; Saturday 8 to 1. Auto interiors and accessories. Custom fit, ready to install carpet sets, upholstery, tops, headliners, trunk mats. Also Recaro seats, carpet logo mats, steering wheels, sheepskins, car covers and much more. Showroom and installations. Send $3 for new catalog. Covers all foreign and domestic cars and trucks. Also included is a 24 page overstock clearance list with savings of 50-90% off carpet sets and other products.

Auto Upholstery Unlimited
36 Glenmoor Dr
East Haven, CT 06512
203-467-6433

upholstery supplies
convertible tops

Mail order only. Supplying original equipment NOS fabrics and vinyls, snaps and fasteners. Send sample of material needed and SASE for free match. Yardage available. Carpeting and convertible tops.

Autofresh International
PO Box 54855
Oklahoma City, OK 73154-1855
405-752-0770; FAX: 405-752-5207

deodorizing

Dealerships available USA only. Complete deodorizing and refreshening system. Dealership packages $5,500. Complete training, equipment and supplies since 1990.

Automotive Interior Center
1725A Bustleton Pike
Feasterville, PA 19053
PH/FAX: 215-953-7477

interior trim

Automotive interior trim including leather, vinyl and cloth seats, door panels, headliners, carpeting and more. Repair and installation of convertible tops and vinyl roofs. Seat frame and convertible top (hydraulic and electric) repairs.

B & T Truck Parts
906 E Main St, PO Box 799
Siloam Springs, AR 72761
501-524-5959: FAX: 501-524-5559

pickup parts

See full listing in **Section Two** under **trucks & tractors**

G W Bartlett Co Inc
1912 N Granville Ave
Muncie, IN 47303
800-338-8034, US & Canada
FAX: 317-289-1251

convertible tops
interiors
rubber seals

See full listing in **Section One** under **Jaguar**

BAS Ltd Jaguar Trim Specialist
250 H St, Unit 8110
Blaine, WA 98231
800-998-9956; FAX: 206-332-0984

interior parts

See full listing in **Section One** under **Jaguar**

Bob's Bird House
124 Watkin Ave
Chadds Ford, PA 19317
215-358-3420; FAX: 215-558-0729

parts

See full listing in **Section One** under **Thunderbird**

Brothers Automotive Products
19715 County Rd 355
St Joseph, MO 64505
816-662-2060; FAX: 816-662-2084

parts
restoration

See full listing in **Section One** under **Oldsmobile**

Buenger Enterprises/
GoldenRod Dehumidifier
3600 S Harbor Blvd
Oxnard, CA 93035
800-451-6797; FAX: 805-985-1534

dehumidifiers

See full listing in **Section Two** under **car care products**

F J Cabrera Enterprises
15507 Normandie Ave, #103
Gardena, CA 90247
310-532-8894; FAX: 310-515-0928

accessories
lights

See full listing in **Section Two** under **restoration aids**

Canadian Mustang
12844 78th Ave
Surrey, BC Canada V3W 8E7
604-594-2425; FAX: 604-594-9282

parts

See full listing in **Section One** under **Mustang**

CARS Inc
1964 W 11 Mile Rd
Berkley, MI 48072
810-398-7100; 810-398-7078

interior

See full listing in **Section One** under **Chevrolet**

Central Jersey Mustang
36 Craig St
Edison, NJ 08817
908-572-3939; FAX: 908-985-8653

parts
restoration
service

See full listing in **Section One** under **Mustang**

Stan Chernoff
1215 Greenwood Ave
Torrance, CA 90503
310-320-4554; FAX: 310-328-7867
E-mail: az589@lafn.org

mechanical parts
restoration parts
technical info
trim parts

See full listing in **Section One** under **Datsun**

Chicago Corvette Supply
7322 S Archer Rd
Justice, IL 60458
708-458-2500; FAX: 708-458-2662

parts

See full listing in **Section One** under **Corvette**

Classic Chevy International
PO Box 607188
Orlando, FL 32860-7188
800-456-1956; FAX: 407-299-3341
E-mail: cciworld@aol.com

modified parts
repro parts
used parts

See full listing in **Section One** under **Chevrolet**

Classic Mustang Inc
24A Robert Porter Rd
Southington, CT 06489
800-243-2742; FAX: 203-276-9986

accessories
parts

See full listing in **Section One** under **Mustang**

Classic Trim Inc
Mick Stamm
3401 S 1st St
Abilene, TX 79605-1708
915-676-8788

collectibles
trim
upholstery

See full listing in **Section Two** under **motorcycles**

Classtique Auto Products
PO Box 278-HMN
Isanti, MN 55040
612-444-4025; FAX: 612-444-9980

carpet sets
headliners

Mail order and open shop. Dealing in ready to install carpet sets, headliners, convertible tops and many related parts for most American cars 1950s-1970s. All GM, Ford, Chrysler, etc cars. $1 requested for samples, advise year & body style of car, send samples if possible for match. Established 1959.

Classtique Upholstery & Top Co
PO Box 278 HK
Isanti, MN 55040
612-444-4025; FAX: 612-444-9980

top kits
upholstery kits

See full listing in **Section One** under **Ford '03-'31**

Color-Plus Leather Restoration System
2116 Morris Ave
Union, NJ 07083
908-851-2811; FAX: 908-851-2910

leather conditioning
leather dye

See full listing in **Section Two** under **leather restoration**

Comfy/Inter-American Sheepskins Inc
1346 Centinela Ave
West Los Angeles, CA 90025-1901
800-521-4014; FAX: 310-442-6080
E-mial: 4858038@mcimail.com

floor mats
seat covers

Mail order and open shop. Monday-Friday 7:30-5, Saturday 10-4. Specializing in sheepskin seat covers and sheepskin floor mats for most all automobiles & airplanes. I also offer sheepskin accessories: heel pads, seat belts covers, steering wheel covers, wash mitts. Web site: http://www.comfysheep.com

Corbeau Seats
9503 South 560 West
Sandy, UT 84070
801-255-3737; FAX: 801-255-3222
E-mail: info@corbeau.com

bucket seats

Custom bucket seats.

Dom Corey Upholstery & Antique Auto
Fairhaven Business Park
1 Arsene Way
Fairhaven, MA 02719
508-997-6555

carpets/conv tops
dash covers
door panels
headliners
seats
upholstery

Mail order and open shop. Monday-Friday 8:30 to 5 EST. Specializing in vehicle interiors, both new and old (1902-1994). Custom design interiors and redo originals as needed. Mostly car show and muscle cars as well as 20s through 50s. Does seats, carpets, door panels, headliners, convertible tops, dash covers, tonneau covers, motorcycles, trucks, Land Rovers, boat tops, etc.

Corvair Ranch Inc
1079 Bon-Ox Rd
Gettysburg, PA 17325
PH/FAX: 717-624-2805

parts
restoration
service

See full listing in **Section One** under **Corvair**

Corvair Underground
PO Box 339
Dundee, OR 97115
503-434-1648, 800-825-8247
FAX: 503-434-1626

parts

See full listing in **Section One** under **Corvair**

Corvette Central
5865 Sawyer Rd, Dept HM
Sawyer, MI 49125
616-426-3342; FAX: 616-426-4108

accessories
parts

See full listing in **Section One** under **Corvette**

Corvette Specialties of MD Inc
1912 Liberty Rd
Eldersburg, MD 21784
410-795-3180; FAX: 410-795-3247

parts
restoration
service

See full listing in **Section One** under **Corvette**

Timothy Cox Firewall Insulators
6333 Pacific Ave, Suite 523
Stockton, CA 95207
PH/FAX: 209-477-4840

firewall insulators
gloveboxes
quiet ride solutions

Mail order only. Manufactures firewall insulator panels (upholstery) just like OEMs did originally. Currently have patterns for nearly 300 cars and trucks, 1928-1972, including "Bitchin" firewalls for street rods. Also makes specialty items including gloveboxes, heater plenum, air/defroster ducts, etc. If the pattern for your car is not available, send your old original for reproduction. Each insulator comes ready to install with insulation, all holes punched and detailed to look and fit just like the original. Standards are exacting and work is guaranteed.

See our ad on page 313

Custom Interiors
PO Box 51174
Indian Orchard, MA 01151
800-423-6053; FAX: 413-589-9178

carpets
headliners
upholstery

See full listing in **Section Two** under **upholstery**

D & R Classic Automotive Inc 30 W 255 Calumet Ave Warrenville, IL 60563 708-393-0009; FAX: 708-393-1397	**parts**

See full listing in **Section One** under **Chevelle/Camaro**

Dash Graining by Mel Erikson 31 Meadow Rd Kings Park, NY 11754 PH/FAX: 516-544-1102 days 516-360-7789 nights	**dashboard** **restoration**

See full listing in **Section Two** under **woodgraining**

Dave's Auto Restoration 2285 Rt 307 E Jefferson, OH 44047 PH/FAX: 216-858-2227	**upholstery**

Mail order and open shop. Open Monday-Friday 8:30 to 5:30, Saturday 8:30 to 12 noon. Specializing in automotive upholstery for all makes and models, Porsche, Jaguar, Mercedes, Rolls-Royce, Bentley, Packard, Ferrari, Pierce-Arrow, Duesenberg and Auburn Cord, from 1900 to present.

Doc's Jags 125 Baker Rd Lake Bluff, IL 60044 847-367-5247; FAX: 847-367-6363	**appraisals** **interiors** **restoration**

See full listing in **Section One** under **Jaguar**

Douglass Interior Products 2000 124th Ave NE Bellevue, WA 98005 206-455-2120; FAX: 206-451-4779	**leather hides** **vinyl**

Deals in genuine leather hides, wide selection of colors in stock. All top selection European cowhide. Average size 55 sq ft. Also carries trim weight leather in selected colors. Vinyl, carpet and sheepskin, all in stock.

See our ad on page 314

Doyle's Upholstery & Canvas 3195 Hwy 441 Fruitland Park, FL 34731 352-787-2460	**upholstery** **materials**

Mail order and open shop. Shop open Monday-Friday 9 to 5; other times by appointment. Shop located on Hwy 441. Closing out all fabrics and vinyls 54-72 inches. One yard or total lot. We have approximately 4,000 yards on hand. Please call or write if interested for super prices.

East Coast Chevy Inc Ol '55 Chevy Parts 4154A Skyron Dr Doylestown, FL 18938 215-348-5568; FAX: 215-348-0560	**parts** **restoration**

See full listing in **Section One** under **Chevrolet**

Eastern Specialty Automotive **Sales & Service Ltd** 38 Yankeetown Rd Hammonds Plains, NS Canada B3Z 1K7 902-835-5912; FAX: 902-835-0310	**parts** **service** **transport**

See full listing in **Section Two** under **car & parts locators**

Ed's Be-Bop Shop 10087 W Co Rd 300 S Medora, IN 47260 812-966-2203	**accessories** **parts** **restoration**

See full listing in **Section One** under **Ford '03-'31**

The Enthusiasts Shop John Parnell PO Box 80471 Baton Rouge, LA 70898 504-928-7456; FAX: 504-928-7665	**cars** **pre-war parts** **transportation**

See full listing in **Section One** under **Rolls-Royce/Bentley**

Firewall Insulators & Quiet Ride **Solutions** 6333 Pacific Ave, Ste 523 Stockton, CA 95207 209-477-4840; FAX: 209-477-0918	**firewall insulators**

See full listing in **Section Two** under **upholstery**

Foreign Autotech 3235 C Sunset Ln Hatboro, PA 19040 215-441-4421; FAX: 215-441-4490	**parts**

See full listing in **Section One** under **Volvo**

GAHH Inc 8116 Lankershim Blvd North Hollywood, CA 91605 818-767-6242; FAX: 818-767-2786	**auto interiors** **convertible tops**

See full listing in **Section One** under **Mercedes-Benz**

FINE SCOTTISH LEATHER, FROM ANDREW MUIRHEAD & SON LTD., IS NOW AVAILABLE FOR THE DISCRIMINATING AUTO ENTHUSIAST. EXCLUSIVELY FROM DOUGLASS INTERIOR PRODUCTS.

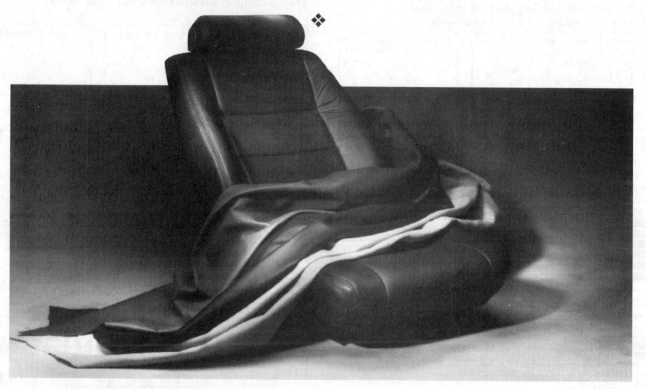

Selected from the top 5% of all European hides, Douglass Fine Scottish Leather is renowned for its stunning beauty and durability. Chosen, for example, more than any other leather by the world's leading airlines and aircraft manufacturers.

Renowned, too, for exceptional value. Large, clean hides provide superior cutting yields, at competitive square foot costs.

Finished at Scotland's famous centuries' old Andrew Muirhead & Son tannery, our leather is full top grain, and aniline dyed for a deep, rich finish.

Douglass also carries a new TRIM-WEIGHT leather, whose thin profile is ideal for hard-to-fit areas like glareshields and arm caps. Ask us about it!

We have over 3500 hides in stock and available for immediate shipment.

For pricing, and a complete set of complimentary samples, call us at 206-455-2120. Or toll-free at 800-722-7272.

DOUGLASS
INTERIOR PRODUCTS

206-455-2120. Or toll-free at 800-722-7272.

Corporate Offices • 2000 124th Avenue N.E. • Bellevue, Washington 98005 • Telephone 800-722-7272 or 206-455-2120 • Fax 206-451-4779

Goldfield Trim & Upholstery 1267 160th St Goldfield, IA 50542 515-254-3322	top installation **upholstery**

Open shop by appointment only. Trained restoration specialist with emphasis on reupholstering of pre-1950 vehicles to original style. Do not stock materials.

Hampton Coach Inc 6 Chestnut St, PO Box 6 Amesbury, MA 01950 508-388-8047, 888-388-8726 FAX: 508-388-1113	fabrics **top kits**

See full listing in **Section One** under **Chevrolet**

Harmon's Inc Hwy 27 N, PO Box 6C Geneva, IN 46740 219-368-7221; FAX: 219-368-9396	interiors **parts**

See full listing in **Section One** under **Chevrolet**

Highway Classics 949 N Cataract Ave, Unit J San Dimas, CA 91702 909-592-8819; FAX: 909-592-4239	**parts**

See full listing in **Section One** under **Ford '54-up**

Bill Hirsch Auto Parts 396 Littleton Ave Newark, NJ 07103 201-642-2404; FAX: 201-642-6161	enamel lacquer hubcaps **top material**

See full listing in **Section Two** under **paints**

Hoffman Automotive Distributor US Hwy #1, Box 818 Hilliard, FL 32046 904-845-4421	**parts**

See full listing in **Section Two** under **body parts**

Impala Bob's Inc 9006 E Fannin, Dept HVAA12 Mesa, AZ 85207 602-986-0286; FAX: 602-986-3126 order line: 800-209-0678 toll-free FAX: 800-716-6237	parts **restoration**

See full listing in **Section One** under **Chevrolet**

Infinite Rainbows Auto Upholstery PO Box 408 North San Juan, CA 95960 916-292-3106	interiors **tops**

Shop open by appointment only, call days or evenings. Specialist in the upholstering of award winning original interiors & tops. Close to Sacramento, CA and Reno, NV. Complete handcrafted interiors by fifth generation craftsman, one man shop provides absolute attention to detail. Thomas Bridwell, owner/upholsterer.

Just Dashes Inc 5941 Lemona Ave Van Nuys, CA 91411 818-780-9005; FAX: 818-780-9014 800-247-DASH	armrests dash pads door panels **headrests**

Worldwide mail order and open shop. Monday-Friday 8:30 to 5:30. Manufactures and restores dash pads, door panels, armrests and consoles using OEM materials and an exclusive thermo-forming process. Also available: reproduction, OEM, NOS and used dash pads. Specializing in vehicles 1954 and up. All work guaranteed.

Klasse 356 Inc 741 N New St Allentown, PA 18102 800-634-7862; FAX: 610-432-8027 E-mail: parts@klasse356.com	cars parts **restoration**

See full listing in **Section One** under **Porsche**

Al Knoch Interiors 130 Montoya Rd El Paso, TX 79932 800-880-8080; FAX: 915-581-1545	carpets interiors tooling services **tops**

See full listing in **Section One** under **Chevrolet**

Koolmat PO Box 207, 1922 Coventry Brunswick, OH 44212 330-273-6011; FAX: 330-273-9858	**insulators**

See full listing in **Section Two** under **restoration aids**

Kwik Poly T Distributing Inc 24 St Henry Ct St Charles, MO 63301 314-724-1065	**restoration aids**

See full listing in **Section Two** under **restoration aids**

LeBaron Bonney Co PO Box 6, 6 Chestnut St Amesbury, MA 01913 508-388-3811; 800-221-5408 FAX: 508-388-1113	fabrics interior kits **tops**

See full listing in **Section One** under **Ford '32-'53**

Legendary Auto Interiors Ltd 121 W Shore Blvd Newark, NY 14513 800-363-8804; FAX: 800-732-8874	**soft trim**

See full listing in **Section One** under **Chrysler**

Loga Enterprises 5399 Old Town Hall Rd Eau Claire, WI 54701 715-832-7302	convertible tops **interior parts**

See full listing in **Section One** under **Studebaker**

Lokar Inc 10924 Murdock Dr Knoxville, TN 37922 423-966-2269; FAX: 423-671-1999	**performance parts**

See full listing in **Section Two** under **street rods**

Mac Neil Automotive Products Ltd 2435 Wisconsin St Downers Grove, IL 60515 800-441-6287; FAX: 630-769-0300	cargo liners **floor mats**

Mail order and open shop. Monday-Friday 9 am-5 pm with exceptions. Floor mats and cargo liners. All vehicles, 80+ applications.

Madera Concepts 606 Olive St Santa Barbara, CA 93101 800-800-1579, 805-962-1579 FAX: 805-962-7359	restoration woodwork **woodwork repair**

See full listing in **Section Two** under **woodwork**

Generalists

Majestic Truck Parts   parts
17726 Dickerson
Dallas, TX 75252
214-248-6245

See full listing in **Section One** under **Chevrolet**

Mercedes Used Parts   parts
Bob Fatone
166 W Main St
Niantic, CT 06357
860-739-1923; FAX: 860-691-0669

See full listing in **Section One** under **Mercedes-Benz**

Merv's Classic Chevy Parts   parts
1330 Washington
Iowa Falls, IA 50126
515-648-3168

See full listing in **Section One** under **Chevrolet**

Mint Condition Auto Upholstery   convertible tops
PO Box 134   interiors
Silverdale New Zealand   spring-gaiters
PH/FAX: 64-9-424 2257   wheelcovers

See full listing in **Section Two** under **special services**

Motorsport Auto   parts
1139 W Collins Ave
Orange, CA 92667
714-639-2620; 800-633-6331
FAX: 714-639-7460

See full listing in **Section One** under **Datsun**

Muncie Imports & Classics   repair
4401 St Rd 3 North   restoration
Muncie, IN 47303   upholstery
800-462-4244; FAX: 317-287-9551

See full listing in **Section One** under **Jaguar**

Norm's Custom Shop   interiors
6897 E William St Ext   tops
Bath, NY 14810
607-776-2357; FAX: 607-776-4541

See full listing in **Section One** under **Cord**

Old Car Woodgraining   dashboard
27902 45th Ave S   restoration
Auburn, WA 98001   woodgraining
206-854-5247

See full listing in **Section Two** under **woodgraining**

Original Auto Interiors   upholstery fabrics
7869 Trumble Rd
Columbus, MI 48063
810-727-2486; FAX: 810-727-4344
E-mail: knight@mich.com

NOS 1950s-1980s automotive upholstery, seat cloth and vinyl
yardage. Original molded carpet sets, 1955-1994. 1958-1966
Thunderbird interior trim including seat covers, carpets, headliners, trunk mats.

Original Parts Group Inc   accessories
17892 Gothard St   parts
Huntington Beach, CA 92647
800-243-8355, US & Canada
714-841-5363; FAX: 714-847-8159

See full listing in **Section One** under **Pontiac**

Parts House   accessories
2912 Hunter St   parts
Fort Worth, TX 76112
817-451-2708; FAX: 817-496-8909

See full listing in **Section Two** under **comprehensive parts**

Parts Unlimited Inc   interiors
Todd Bidwell   weatherstrips
12101 Westport Rd
Louisville, KY 40245-1789
502-425-3766; FAX: 502-425-0055

See full listing in **Section One** under **Chevrolet**

Passenger Car Supply   parts
102 Cloverdale Rd
Swedesboro, NJ 08085
609-467-7966

See full listing in **Section One** under **Chevrolet**

RARE Corvettes   cars
Joe Calcagno   parts
Box 1080
Soquel, CA 95073
408-475-4442; FAX: 408-475-1115

See full listing in **Section One** under **Corvette**

RAU Restoration   woodwork
2027 Pontius Ave
Los Angeles, CA 90025
PH/FAX: 310-445-1128

See full listing in **Section Two** under **woodwork**

Ray's Upholstering   partial/total
600 N St Francis Cabrini Ave   restoration
Scranton, PA 18504
717-346-4661; FAX: 717-963-0415

See full listing in **Section Two** under **restoration shops**

REM Automotive Inc   interior parts
Box 241, Rt 1, Brandt Rd
Annville, PA 17003
717-838-4242; FAX: 717-838-5091

See full listing in **Section Two** under **restoration aids**

Restoration Specialties   interiors
John Sarena   restoration
124 North F St
Lompoc, CA 93436
805-736-2627

See full listing in **Section One** under **Chevrolet**

Ridgefield Auto Upholstery   interiors
34 Bailey Ave   tops
Ridgefield, CT 06877
203-438-7583

Both mail order and open shop Monday-Friday 8 am-6 pm,
Saturday 8 am-noon. Foreign & domestic, antique to present,
complete or partial interior replacement or restoration, convert-
ible top, repair & replacement, custom made and ready made.
One man shop assures strict attention to quality & detail.
Custom work a speciality.

Ron's Restorations Inc   interior trim
2968-B Ask Kay Dr   restoration
Smyrna, GA 30082
770-438-6102; FAX: 770-438-0037

See full listing in **Section One** under **Mercedes-Benz**

RW & Able Inc
PO Box 2110
Chico, CA 95927
PH/FAX: 916-896-1513

door panels
interior accessories

See full listing in **Section Two** under **street rods**

Sailorette's Nautical Nook
23005 W Kankakee River Dr
Wilmington, IL 60481
815-476-2391; FAX: 815-476-2524

covers
interiors

See full listing in **Section Two** under **upholstery**

Harry Samuel
65 Wisner St
Pontiac, MI 48342-1066
810-335-1900
248-335-1900 (effective 5-10-97)

carpet
fabrics
interiors
upholstery covers

Mail and phone orders. Soft trim for 1950-77 Buick, Cadillac, Chevrolet, Ford, Lincoln, Mercury, Mopar, Oldsmobile and (specializing in) Pontiac. Cut and sewn and molded carpets for above cars plus NOS factory original carpets for 1961-64 Buicks, Oldsmobiles and Pontiacs. Original seat upholstery covers for 1960-67 Bonnevilles and Venturas, some 2+2. Headliners, package trays, hood pads, trunk kits, vinyl and cloth yardage and more for all GM cars, some Chrysler and Ford cars.

Scarborough Faire Inc
1151 Main St
Pawtucket, RI 02860
800-556-6300; 401-724-4200
FAX: 401-724-5392

parts

See full listing in **Section One** under **MG**

Scholz Specialty Products Co
61 Endicott St, Building 32
Norwood, MA 02062
617-762-8321, 800-762-8006
FAX: 617-762-1792

dashboard covers
supplies
upholstery repair

Mail order and open shop. Monday-Friday 8:30 to 5:30. Distributor of products to the specialized repair and reconditioning industries. Dashboard covers, door panels, armrests. Vinyl, leather and hard plastic paints, dyes, repair and reconditioning tools and chemicals, velour repair products.

Silver Star Restorations
116 Highway 19
Topton, NC 28781
704-321-4268; FAX: 704-321-6008

parts
restoration

See full listing in **Section One** under **Mercedes-Benz**

Silverleaf Casting Co
PO Box 662, 116 S Grove St
Delton, MI 49046
616-623-6665

casting
mascots

See full listing in **Section Two** under **castings**

Paul Slater Auto Parts
9496 85th St N
Stillwater, MN 55082
612-429-4235

parts

See full listing in **Section One** under **Dodge**

Smith & Jones Distributing Co Inc
1 Biloxi Square
West Columbia, SC 29170
803-822-8500; FAX: 803-822-8477

parts

See full listing in **Section One** under **Ford '03-'31**

Robert H Snyder
PO Drawer 821
Yonkers, NY 10702
914-476-8500
FAX: 914-476-8573, business hours

literature
parts

See full listing in **Section One** under **Cadillac/LaSalle**

So Cal Pickups Inc
6321 Manchester Blvd
Buena Park, CA 90621
714-994-1400; FAX: 714-994-2584

parts

See full listing in **Section One** under **Ford '54-up**

Southampton Auto & Marine Upholstery
471 N Hwy
Southampton, NY 11968
516-283-2616

carpets
interiors
tops

See full listing in **Section One** under **Mercedes-Benz**

Ssnake-Oyl Products Inc
Rt 2, Box 269-6
Hawkins, TX 75765
903-769-4555; FAX: 903-769-4552

carpet underlay
firewall insulation
seatbelt restoration

Mail order only. Seat belts restored to show quality condition. NOS seatbelts, automotive insulation systems underlayment, water shields and firewall insulation. Specializing in seatbelt restoration for 50s, 60s and 70s American made automobiles.

Star Quality
1 Alley Rd
La Grangeville, NY 12540
800-782-7199; FAX: 914-266-5394
E-mail: sq@mhv.net

parts

See full listing in **Section One** under **Mercedes-Benz**

Stilwell's Obsolete Car Parts
1617 Wedeking Ave
Evansville, IN 47711
812-425-4794

body parts
interiors
parts

See full listing in **Section One** under **Mustang**

Swedish Classics Inc
PO Box 557
Oxford, MD 21654
800-258-4422; FAX: 410-226-5543

parts

See full listing in **Section One** under **Volvo**

T-Bird Sanctuary
9997 SW Avery
Tualatin, OR 97062
503-692-9848, FAX: 503-692-9849

parts

See full listing in **Section One** under **Thunderbird**

Bill Thomsen
Rt 4 Box 492
Moneta, VA 24121
540-297-1200

salvage yard

See full listing in **Section Five** under **Virginia**

Thunderbird Headquarters
1080 Detroit Ave
Concord, CA 94518
800-227-2174, US
FAX: 510-689-1771

accessories
literature
parts
upholstery

See full listing in **Section One** under **Thunderbird**

TMI Products Inc 191 Granite St Corona, CA 91719 909-272-1996; 800-624-7960 FAX: 909-272-1584 E-mail: tmiprods@aol.com	**classic car interiors**

See full listing in **Section One** under **Volkswagen**

Town Auto Top and Restoration Co 78 Bloomfield Ave, PO Box 167 Pine Brook, NJ 07058 201-575-9333; FAX: 201-808-8366	**convertible repairs interiors**

See full listing in **Section Two** under **tops**

Ultimate Upholstery 13384 Fallen Leaf Rd Poway, CA 92064 619-451-3340	**interiors top restoration upholstery**

See full listing in **Section Two** under **restoration shops**

Vantage Auto Interiors 11 Fahey St Stamford, CT 06907 203-425-9533; FAX: 203-425-9535	**upholstery**

Open shop only. Monday thru Friday 8 am-6 pm. A full service upholstery shop specializing in handmade coachbuilt interiors and convertible tops. Have extensive experience with European sports cars of the 50s and 60s; however, we also restore many domestic and foreign automobiles of distinction dating back to the 1920s, including fabric bodied. Shop has created many custom interiors for show cars, hot rods and prototypes. Currently the exclusive interior shop for Callaway cars.

Victoria British Ltd Box 14991 Lenexa, KS 66285-4991 800-255-0088; 913-599-3299	**accessories parts**

See full listing in **Section One** under **MG**

Volunteer State Chevy Parts Hwy 41 S Greenbrier, TN 37073 615-643-4583; FAX: 615-643-5100	**accessories parts**

See full listing in **Section One** under **Chevrolet**

Wale's Antique Chevy Truck Parts 143 Center Carleton, MI 48117 313-654-8836	**parts**

See full listing in **Section One** under **Chevrolet**

Westwinds Motor Car Co RD 2, Box 777, Cox Rd Woodstock, VT 05091 802-457-4178; FAX: 802-457-3926	**restoration**

See full listing in **Section Two** under **restoration shops**

Willow Grove Auto Top 43 N York Rd Willow Grove, PA 19090 215-659-3276	**interiors tops upholstery**

Open shop only. Monday-Friday 8:30-5:30. Auto interiors, auto tops & custom upholstery.

Woolies (I&C Woolstenholmes Ltd) Off Blenheim Way, Northfields Ind Est Market Deeping Nr Peterborough, PE6 8LD England 0044-1778-347347 FAX: 0044-1778-341847	**accessories trim upholstery**

Mail order and open shop. Monday-Friday 8:30 to 5; other times by appointment. Woolies trim, wing pipings, window channels, headlinings, leather/cloth & vinyls, duck & mohair hoodings, moquettes, carpets, felt and Hardura off-the-roll, Bedford cords, rubber & sponge extrusions, fasteners and draught excluders. Also extruded aluminum sections, leather renovation kits and black/polished pressed aluminum number plates, 3-1/2 inch & 3-1/8 inch digit size and goggles. Catalog $3 (in bills).

World Upholstery & Trim PO Box 4857 Thousand Oaks, CA 91359 800-222-9577; FAX: 818-707-2664 E-mail: worlduph@mail.vcnet.com	**carpet kits tops upholstery kits**

Mail order and open shop. Shop open Monday-Friday 8:30 to 5. Specializing in seat upholstery kits, carpet kits, headliners, convertible tops and related items for Mercedes-Benz, Porsche, BMW, Jaguar, Alfa Romeo, Fiat, Volkswagen and Miata.

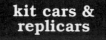 

kit cars & replicars

Keith Ashley 107 W Railroad St, Unit V St Johns, MI 48879 517-224-6460; FAX: 517-224-9488	**fiberglass parts**

See full listing in **Section One** under **Ford '32-'53**

Automotive Legal Service Inc PO Box 626 Dresher, PA 19025 PH/FAX: 800-487-4947	**appraisals**

See full listing in **Section Two** under **appraisals**

Backyard Buddy Corp 1818 N Main St, PO Box 5104 Niles, OH 44446 330-544-9372; FAX: 330-544-9311	**automotive lift**

See full listing in **Section Two** under **accessories**

Certified Auto Appraisal PO Box 17609 Anaheim, CA 92817 714-966-1096; FAX: 714-498-7367	**appraisals**

See full listing in **Section Two** under **appraisals**

Class Glass and Performance Inc 101 Winston St Cumberland, MD 21502 800-774-3456; FAX: 301-777-7044	**fiberglass bodies parts**

See full listing in **Section Two** under **fiberglass parts**

Custom Auto Radiator 495 Hyson Rd Jackson, NJ 08527 908-928-3700; FAX: 908-364-7474	**radiators**

See full listing in **Section Two** under **radiators**

EVA Sports Cars RR 1 Vankleek Hill, ONT Canada K0B 1R0 613-678-3377; FAX: 613-678-6110	kit cars

Shop open five days a week, Saturday by appointment. The Diva, 50s style roadster, fiberglass body and tube steel space frame. In-house A-arm top and lower front suspension, 5-link rear, uses Chevy 350 cu in small block motor and vintage style model with Aero screens now available.

Exotic Enterprises 459 Madeline Ave Garfield, NJ 07026 201-523-2217, 201-956-7570	fiberglass manufacturing fiberglass mold making

See full listing in **Section Two** under **fiberglass parts**

Fairlane Automotive Specialties 210 E Walker St St. Johns, MI 48879 517-224-6460	fiberglass bodies parts

See full listing in **Section One** under **Ford '32-'53**

K & K Insurance Group Inc PO Box 2338 Fort Wayne, IN 46801-2338 800-548-0858; FAX: 219-459-5511	insurance

See full listing in **Section Two** under **insurance**

Koolmat PO Box 207, 1922 Coventry Brunswick, OH 44212 330-273-6011; FAX: 330-273-9858	insulators

See full listing in **Section Two** under **restoration aids**

Lee's Kustom Auto and Street Rods RR 3, Box 3061A Rome, PA 18837 717-247-2326	accessories parts restoration

See full listing in **Section Two** under **street rods**

Little Old Cars 3410 Fulton Dr NW Canton, OH 44718 216-455-4685	model cars

See full listing in **Section Two** under **models & toys**

Lokar Inc 10924 Murdock Dr Knoxville, TN 37922 423-966-2269; FAX: 423-671-1999	performance parts

See full listing in **Section Two** under **street rods**

Memory Lane Motors Lindsay St S Fenelon Falls, ONT Canada K0M 1N0 705-887-CARS	car dealer restoration service

See full listing in **Section Two** under **restoration shops**

Marc Miller Gallery 3 Railroad Ave East Hampton, NY 11937 516-329-5299; FAX: 516-329-5319	furniture

See full listing in **Section Two** under **artwork**

Norm's Custom Shop 6897 E William St Ext Bath, NY 14810 607-776-2357; FAX: 607-776-4541	interiors tops

See full listing in **Section One** under **Cord**

Operations Plus PO Box 26347 Santa Ana, CA 92799 PH/FAX: 714-962-2776	accessories parts

See full listing in **Section One** under **Cobra**

Power Effects 1800H Industrial Park Dr Grand Haven, MI 49417 616-847-4200; FAX: 616-847-4210	exhaust systems

See full listing in **Section Two** under **exhaust systems**

Regal Roadsters Ltd 301 W Beltline Hwy Madison, WI 53713 PH/FAX: 608-273-4141	replicars restoration

See full listing in **Section One** under **Thunderbird**

RW & Able Inc PO Box 2110 Chico, CA 95927 PH/FAX: 916-896-1513	door panels interior accessories

See full listing in **Section Two** under **street rods**

Saturn Industries 143 Wimborne Rd Poole, Dorset BH15 2BCR England 01202-674982; FAX: 01202-668274	axles instruments literature repro parts

See full listing in **Section One** under **Ford '03-'31**

Visual Marketplace Online Inc 800 Silverado, Suite 324 La Jolla, CA 92037 619-459-3846; FAX: 619-459-3460 E-mail: pyoung@icreations.com	online auto ads

See full listing in **Section Four** under **information sources**

Wheel-A-Dapters 9103 E Garvey Ave Rosemead, CA 91770 818-288-2290	replicar kits

Mail order and open shop. Monday-Friday 12 to 5; Saturday 9 to 3. For replicar kits using wire Ford wheels. Also Ford, Pinto, Chevrolet and Volkswagen. Most 4/5/6 lug combinations. Adapter catalog $4. Refundable.

leather restoration

Color-Plus Leather Restoration System 2116 Morris Ave Union, NJ 07083 908-851-2811; FAX: 908-851-2910	leather conditioning leather dye

Mail order only. Leather & vinyl restoration products & colorants. Our leather dye, Surflex, is a water-base colorant. Our leather conditioning oil, Softener, is the best leather treatment on the market (customers told me so).

Generalists

**Leatherique Leather Restoration
Products**
PO Box 2678
Orange Park, FL 32065
904-272-0992
FAX: 904-272-1534

**leather cleaning
conditioning
products**

See full listing in **Section One** under **Rolls-Royce/Bentley**

license plates

American Classics Unlimited Inc
Frank Groll-Karen Groll
PO Box 192
Oak Lawn, IL 60454-0192
PH/FAX: 708-424-9223

**automobilia
models & toys
novelty license
plates
sales literature**

See full listing in **Section Two** under **models & toys**

Autosport Specialty
PO Box 9553
Knoxville, TN 37920
615-573-2580

**decals
license plates
patches**

See full listing in **Section Two** under **novelties**

Be-Bops
1077 S Seguin
New Braunfels, TX 78130
210-625-6056
210-657-2135

**Coke machines
gas pumps**

See full listing in **Section Two** under **automobilia**

Career Center
1302 9th St
Wheatland, WY 82201
PH/FAX: 307-322-2063
E-mail: phale@wyoming.com

license plates

Mail order only. Specializing in 1960s Wyoming license plates
(car & truck). Cars: 1967 red/white, 1968 brown/gold & extras.
"Real cowboy plates," plain $7. Mounted with barbwire, $16.

Corvair Heaven
PO Box 13
Ellenton, FL 34222-0013
813-746-0478; FAX: 813-750-8167

**car dealer
literature
restoration**

See full listing in **Section One** under **Corvair**

Cruising International Inc
1000 N Beach St
Daytona Beach, FL 32117
800-676-8961, 904-254-8753
FAX: 904-255-2460

**automobilia
decals
license plates
novelties
porcelain signs**

See full listing in **Section Two** under **accessories**

Norman D'Amico
44 Middle Rd
Clarksburg, MA 01247
413-663-6886

license plates

Mail order and open shop. License plates of all states, years, types
and countries. Also driving licenses, registrations, plate color and
data information charts, etc. Miscellaneous license plate frames.

Darryl's
266 Main St
Duryea, PA 18642
717-451-1600

restoration

Mail order only. Show quality license plate restoration with all
damage, dents, tears, holes, rust, etc, repaired to new condition
and painted in original colors, numbers will duplicate originals
not brush painted or taped off. This is the finest restoration
available. We do car, truck, motorcycle, bicycle, reflective number, reflective background plates and duplications. Our plates
have an automotive quality hand polished and waxed finish. Call
or write for more information.

Richard Diehl
5965 W Colgate Pl
Denver, CO 80227
303-985-7481

license plates

Mail order only. License plates, buy, sell, trade.

Dr Cap (Brad Sullivan)
2550 Estero Blvd Ste 12
Ft Myers Beach, FL 33931
941-463-3741

**custom license
plates**

Hand-made, customized, embossed, personalized automobile
plates (tags). Hundreds of styles, colors, logos and designs to
enhance the vehicle. Vehicle lettering, magnetic signs.

Jim Estrup The Plateman
Box 908, RR 3
Kennebunk, ME 04043
207-985-4800; FAX: 207-985-TAGS

license plates

Mail order only. Hundreds of license plates available to display
on your vintage vehicle or on your garage wall. Most states available. Car, motorcycle, commercial, low numbers, foreign and
various other desirable types. Singles and pairs. Many years
available up to the 1990's. Receive a free genuine license plate
when you request my license plate sales list. Want lists and special requests cheerfully accepted. Fast and friendly service.
Plates also bought and traded.

Eurosign Metalwerke Inc
PO Box 93-6331
Margate, FL 33093
954-979-1448; FAX: 954-970-0430

license plates

Mail order only. Eurosign Metalwerke Inc is the leading manufacturer of antique license plates from the United States and around the world. Our antique replica plates are stamped in metal and look so good that thousands of Hemmings' readers have been satisfied customers. Our plates are also used in Hollywood movies, TV shows and commercials.

See our ad on this page

Eurosport Daytona Inc
32 Oceanshore Blvd
Ormond Beach, FL 32176
800-874-8044; 904-672-7199
FAX: 904-673-0821

license plates

The manufacturer of classic and vanity license plates, frames and accessories. Specializing in laser cut Lazer-Tags™, stainless steel and authentic Euro plates. The largest selection of license plates available in the USA.

Eugene Gardner
10510 Rico Tatum Rd
Palmetto, GA 30268
770-463-4264

license plates

Mail order and open shop. Open by appointment only. Phone hours: 7 am to 8 pm. License plates bought, sold and traded. Discounts on large orders. Send SASE for The License Plate Club information.

Get It On Paper
Gary Weickart, President
185 Maple St
Islip, NY 11751
516-581-3897

automobilia
literature
toys

See full listing in **Section Two** under **automobilia**

Richard Hurlburt
27 West St
Greenfield, MA 01301
413-773-3235

license plates
parts
toys

Mail order and open shop. Auto related collectibles and toys. New and used parts for 1972-79 Datsun model 620 pickup trucks. Also antique, classic, aircraft-related items, advertising signs, vehicle literature. Large stock of 1903-80 USA, Canada, and foreign license plates. Send wants with SASE.

International AutoSport Inc
Rt 29 N, PO Box 9036
Charlottesville, VA 22906
800-726-1199; FAX: 804-973-2368
E-mail: iap1@international-auto.com

accessories

See full listing in **Section Two** under **accessories**

Dave Lincoln
Box 331
Yorklyn, DE 19736
610-444-4144, PA

license plates

Mail order and open shop by appointment. License plates, USA/foreign. All years and types. Buy, sell, swap. Thousands

available. Porcelains a specialty. Recent plates sold in bulk. YOM, birth year, etc. SASE with specific requests. Collections, accumulations wanted. Will travel.

George & Denise Long
915 E Court St
Marion, NC 28752
704-652-9229 (24 hrs w/recorder)

automobilia

See full listing in **Section Two** under **automobilia**

Larry Machacek
PO Box 515
Porter, TX 77365
713-429-2505

decals
license plates

See full listing in **Section Two** under **automobilia**

O'Brien Truckers
5 Perry Hill
North Grafton, MA 01536-1532
508-839-3033; FAX: 508-839-9490
E-mail: obrien_dennis@emc.com

accessories
belt buckles
plaques
valve covers

See full listing in **Section Two** under **plaques**

Anthony V Polio
746 N Greenbrier Dr
Orange, CT 06477
203-795-6434

license plates

Mail order only. License plates professionally repainted, including city and political tags. Twenty-seven years servicing the hobby with fast, efficient, professional service. Three week turn-around time. Durable custom mixed enamel used as original. We duplicate single plates into pairs, call for pricing. Thousands of plates for sale. Plates restored at $35 ea. Add $5 p&h.

Protrim Inc
438 Calle San Pablo, Unit 1
Camarillo, CA 93012
805-987-2086; FAX: 805-389-5375

| | plating |

See full listing in **Section Two** under **plating & polishing**

Toy Sense Inc
257 North Amphlett Blvd
San Mateo, CA 94401-1805
415-579-7825; FAX: 415-579-7827
E-mail: toysense@netwizard.net

| | games
toys |

See full listing in **Section Two** under **automobilia**

Al Trommers Rare Auto Literature
59 West Front Street, Mailbox #1
Keyport Mini Mall
Keyport, NJ 07735

| | hubcaps
license plates
literature/records
wheelcovers |

See full listing in **Section Two** under **literature dealers**

lighting equipment

Albrico Auto & Truck Parts
PO Box 3179
Camarillo, CA 93010
805-482-9792; FAX: 805-383-1013

| | lamp assemblies
lenses |

Mail order only. Dealing in lenses, lamp assemblies, lamp bezels and housings, speedometers and dash instruments.

All British Car Parts Inc
2847 Moores Rd
Baldwin, MD 21013
410-692-9572; FAX: 410-692-5654

| | parts |

See full listing in **Section Two** under **electrical systems**

Robert D Bliss
2 Delmar Pl
Edison, NJ 08837
908-549-0977

| | ignition parts
electrical parts |

See full listing in **Section Two** under **electrical systems**

F J Cabrera Enterprises
15507 Normandie Ave, #103
Gardena, CA 90247
310-532-8894; FAX: 310-515-0928

| | accessories
lights |

See full listing in **Section Two** under **restoration aids**

Collins Metal Spinning
6371 W 100 S
New Palestine, IN 46163
317-894-3008

| | headlight rims |

Mail order and open shop. Monday-Saturday 8:30 to 4:30; other times by appointment. Anything round in brass, copper, aluminum and steel.

Mike Dennis, Nebraska Mail Order
1845 S 48th St
Lincoln, NE 68506
402-489-3036; FAX: 402-489-1148

| | parts
Trippe mounting
brackets/hardware |

See full listing in **Section One** under **Ford '32-'53**

Design Fabrications
Pure Products Division
PO Box 40205
Santa Barbara, CA 93140-0205
805-965-6031

| | parts |

See full listing in **Section Two** under **comprehensive parts**

Development Associates
1520 S Lyon
Santa Ana, CA 92705
714-835-9512; FAX: 714-835-9513
E-mail: 71460,1146@compuserve.com

| | electrical parts |

See full listing in **Section Two** under **electrical systems**

The Enthusiasts Shop
John Parnell
PO Box 80471
Baton Rouge, LA 70898
504-928-7456; FAX: 504-928-7665

| | cars
pre-war parts
transportation |

See full listing in **Section One** under **Rolls-Royce/Bentley**

George's Auto & Tractor Sales Inc
1450 N Warren Rd
North Jackson, OH 44451
330-538-3020; FAX: 330-538-3033

| | Blue Dots/car dealer
carpet cleaner
Dri-wash metal polish
New Castle batteries |

See full listing in **Section Two** under **car dealers**

W F Harris Lighting
PO Box 5023
Monroe, NC 28111-5023
704-283-7477; FAX: 704-283-6880

| | work lights |

Mail order only. Automotive work lights. Underhood and underdash task lights, larger work lights with accessories including rolling light/tool tray and rolling light cart that can be propped up for work on sides of vehicles.

Headlight Headquarters
Donald I Axelrod
35 Timson St
Lynn, MA 01902
617-598-0523

| | lights
parts |

Mail order and open shop. Open by appointment only. Headlights and headlight parts for 1914-39 automobiles. No Ford. SASE required.

Leigh & Sharon Knudson Truck Light Sales
719 Ohms Way
Costa Mesa, CA 92627
714-645-5938; FAX: 714-646-8031

| | stoplights
truck lights
turn signals |

Restoration and re-marketing of glass era truck lights. Amber arrow turn signals, stoplights and glass-lensed marker lights a specialty. No electric headlights available from us.

MikeCo Antique, Kustom & Obsolete Auto Parts
4053 Calle Tesoro, Unit C
Camarillo, CA 93012
805-482-1725; FAX: 805-987-8524

| | lenses
parts |

See full listing in **Section One** under **Mopar**

OJ Rallye Automotive
PO Box 540, N 6808 Hwy OJ
Plymouth, WI 53073
414-893-2531; FAX: 414-893-6800

| | accessories
lighting parts |

Mail order and open shop. Monday-Friday, 9 am-noon, 2-6 pm. World's largest assortment of European lighting part numbers in stock. Carello, Cibie, Hella, Lucas, Marchal, PIAA and other prewar to current high tech fog, driving and headlight parts, bulbs and kits available in 6-, 12- and 24-volt. Restoration of lamps is also offered. Other quality accessories and car care products sold, retail and wholesale.

Tail Light Emporium | lenses
PO Box 1716
Litchfield Park, AZ 85340
602-853-0405

Mail order only. Specializing in tail lamp, parking lamp and back-up lamp lenses and assemblies, common to very rare. New, used and reproduction from 1937-77. Over 30,000 pieces in stock.

UK Spares/TVR Sports Cars | accessories / car covers / convertible tops / ignition parts
609 Highland St
Wethersfield, CT 06109-3979
PH/FAX: 203-563-1647

See full listing in **Section One** under **TVR**

Union Performance Co | parts
PO Box 324, 59 Mansfield St
Sharon, MA 02067
617-784-5367, voice mail
FAX: 617-784-5367

See full listing in **Section Two** under **electrical systems**

Vintage Lamp Repair | resilvering
PO Box 1122, 290 Haines Ln
Merlin, OR 97532
541-474-5664; FAX: 541-476-9096

Mail order and open shop. Mon-Fri 9 am-5 pm. Headlight reflectorization for all 1939 or earlier automobiles and trucks, plus many postwar European cars. Our high-tech process is the only one to use if you drive your car. Sole licensee of Uvira Laser Optics Inc process.

Johnny Williams Services | appraiser / car & parts locator / consultant / lighting systems / design
2613 Copeland Road
Tyler, TX 75701
903-597-3687
800-937-0900, voice mail #7225

See full listing in **Section Two** under **appraisals**

limousine rentals

Horsepower Sales | limousines
100 New South Rd
Hicksville, NY 11801
516-937-3707; FAX: 516-937-3803

Specializing in limousine sales.

Land Yachts Automobile Restoration and Customizing | restoration
497 London Bridge Rd, Suite 101
Virginia Beach, VA 23454
757-431-0294; FAX: 757-431-4524

See full listing in **Section Two** under **restoration shops**

literature dealers

1893 THE COMPLETE MOTORIST *1914*
If air in it, a four-inch tire eighty, a five-inch tire 100 pounds, and so on through
the various sizes. It is a proven fact that under-inflation paves the way for about
5 per cent of all tire troubled, hence the importance of proper inflation. The

All-American Auto Mags | literature
The Old Co-Op
114 Middlewich Rd
Clive, Winsford, Cheshire
CW7 3NT England
01606-558252; FAX: 01606-559211

Mail order and open shop. Monday-Saturday 10 am-5 pm. American auto mags, books, videos, manuals, handbooks, sales

literature, posters and prints. Large selection of mag back-issue. Worldwide mail order.

American Classics Unlimited Inc | automobilia / models & toys / novelty license plates / sales literature
Frank Groll-Karen Groll
PO Box 192
Oak Lawn, IL 60454-0192
PH/FAX: 708-424-9223

See full listing in **Section Two** under **models & toys**

Antique Auto Literature & Keys | keys / literature
1100 Shady Oaks
Ann Arbor, MI 48103
313-761-2490; FAX: 313-761-3235

Mail order only. Keys and locks for 1900-60 cars, or keys cut from code or from original lock. Auto literature includes thousands of shop manuals and sales catalogs.

Applegate & Applegate | literature / manuals / paint charts / photos
Box 260
Annville, PA 17003
717-964-2350

Mail order only. American and foreign automotive car and truck literature, accessory catalogs, owner's manuals, paint charts, tune-up charts, factory issued photographs, automotive stock certificates and corporate annual reports. Over 4,000 different reproductions of factory issued 8x10 black and white photographs of American cars and trucks. 10,000 other American and foreign photographs available for personal research, reference or publication for a nominal charge or one-time publication fee. Wholesale and retail sales.

Armchair Motorist | back issues
RR #2, Box B11
Kettleby, ONT Canada L0G 1J0
905-939-8902

Mail order only. Out of print automotive books and materials. MG specialist. Road and Track back issues. List of current items on request.

The Auto Buff | books / literature / manuals
Books & Collectibles
13809 Ventura Blvd
Sherman Oaks, CA 91423
E-mail: alan.h.simon@support.com

Mail order only. Automotive literature including out-of-print books, owner's manuals, shop manuals and sales literature covering antique and modern cars from racing to restoration.

Auto/Link | books
PO Box 460723
Houston, TX 77056-8723
713-973-1008
713-973-1133 on-line service
E-mail: alink@accesscom.net

See full listing in **Section Four** under **books & publications**

Auto Literature Outlet | car dealer / literature / parts
527 Hwy 431 S
Boaz, AL 35957
205-593-4111

Mail order and open shop by chance or appointment. Phone days 9 to 5. Specializing in shop manuals, owner's manuals, sales literature, automotive art, magazines and advertisements. 40 years in the car business. SASE with all inquiries please.

Generalists

The Auto Literature Store | literature
PO Box 935 | manuals
Annandale, MN 55302-0935
612-274-3005; FAX: 612-274-2380

Mail order and open shop by appointment. Sells service manuals, technical bulletins, parts books, sales literature, paint chips, owner's manuals, showroom items, all domestic makes.

Auto Nostalgia Enr | literature
332 St Joseph S | manuals
Mont St Gregoire, QC Canada J0J 1K0
PH/FAX: 514-346-3644

Mail order and open shop. Monday-Saturday 9 am-9 pm, closed Sundays. Automotive literature, shop manuals, parts lists, car books, tractor manuals, new & used. Also models, plastic, die cast, all makes, white metal.

Auto-West Advertising | sales literature
Gary Hinkle
PO Box 3875
Modesto, CA 95352
209-524-9541, 209-522-4777

Mail order and open shop. Open by appointment only. Specializes in all US and foreign postwar literature, postcards and owner's manuals.

Auto World Books | literature
Box 562 | magazines
Camarillo, CA 93011 | research service
805-987-5570

Mail order only. Car and truck literature, manuals and magazines, US and foreign. Free research service.

Automobilia Shop | artwork
48 Belmont St | books
Melrose, MA 02176 | models
617-665-1992; FAX: 617-665-8018

See full listing in **Section Two** under **artwork**

Automotive Bookstore | books
1830 12th Ave | manuals
Seattle, WA 98122
206-323-6719

Mail order and open shop. Monday through Friday, 10 am-4 pm. Out of print bookstore specializing in original factory shop manuals for domestic, Asian and European cars, trucks and motorcycles. Thousands of auto related magazines, too. We also stock a large selection of aftermarket manuals of all kinds. The store also has books on the building trades, antique electronics, woodworking, metalworking and boats. Located on Seattle's Capitol Hill at the corner of Twelfth Ave and E Denny Way.

Alex Barton-Hibbs | press kits
Suite #4, Grosvenor Mansions | sales literature
2/3 Claremont, Hastings
East Sussex, TN341HA England
PH/FAX: UK +441424 440100

Mail order only. Sales brochures and press kits available from all the European and Detroit auto shows. Also carry large stock of postwar brochures from most makes. Worldwide mail order service, prompt, friendly attention given. Especially enjoy dealing with Americans.

Irv Bishko Literature | literature
14550 Watt Rd
Novelty, OH 44072
216-338-4811

Authentic original shop manuals, parts books, sales brochures, owner's manuals, dealer albums, color/upholstery and data books, etc. Wide selection of domestic and foreign literature for cars and trucks, 1900 to present. SASE or phone.

Blair Collectors & Consultants | appraiser
2821 SW 167th Pl | consultant
Seattle, WA 98166 | literature
206-242-6745

See full listing in **Section Two** under **appraisals**

M K Boatright | books
629 Santa Monica | literature
Corpus Christi, TX 78411 | models
512-852-6639; FAX: 512-853-7168

Mail order only. For US and foreign cars and trucks from the fifties to the eighties. Sales albums, model cars, library books and other miscellaneous literature.

BritBooks | books
62 Main St
Otego, NY 13825
PH/FAX: 607-988-7956

See full listing in **Section Four** under **books & publications**

Rodney Brockman | literature
24862 Ridge Rd | shop manuals
Elwood, IL 60421 | signs
815-478-3633

See full listing in **Section One** under **Chevrolet**

Broken Kettle Books | literature
Eldon J Bryant
702 E Madison St
Fairfield, IA 52556
515-472-8643

Mail order or by appointment. Large selection of older car literature.

The Can Corner | audio tapes
PO Box VA 1173
Linwood, PA 19061
215-485-0824

See full listing in **Section Two** under **automobilia**

Cardillo Classic Cadillac | accessories
351 W 51st St | top boots
New York, NY 10019
212-247-1354

See full listing in **Section One** under **Cadillac/LaSalle**

Ken Case | gas globes
5706 E 5th Pl | literature
Tulsa, OK 74112 | signs
918-835-5872

Mail order only. Literature for all types of cars and trucks. Also gas and oil related items including signs, globes, cans, road maps, etc.

Chewning's Auto Literature | literature
2011 Elm Tree Terr | manuals
Buford, GA 30518
770-945-9795

Mail order only. Specializing in literature for all makes and models. Shop manuals, owner's manuals, sales catalogs, parts books, etc. Also buy automotive literature. Send list or call for a prompt, courteous reply.

Dick Choler Cars & Service Inc | car dealer
640 E Jackson Blvd | literature
Elkhart, IN 46516 | model cars
219-522-8281; FAX: 219-522-8282

See full listing in **Section One** under **Pontiac**

Classic Auto Literature
Box 53 Blueback, RR 2
Nanoose Bay, BC Canada V0R 2R0
250-468-9522

data books
literature/manuals
models/parts catalog
posters

Mail orders our specialty. Dealing in all types of automotive literature. Shop, owner's and body manuals; parts catalogs; sales brochures; magazine ads; posters; wiring diagrams; dealer albums and facts books. Also, die casts, plastic models and some memorabilia. Canadian requests, please include SASE.

Classic Data
1240 SE Gideon St
Portland, OR 97202
503-234-8617; FAX: 503-234-8618
E-mail: hfreedman@aol.com

shop manual

See full listing in **Section One** under **Chevrolet**

Collector Cars & Route 66 Motors
Box 50715
Amarillo, TX 79159
806-358-2951; FAX: 806-358-2344

books
parts
photos
restoration

See full listing in **Section One** under **Lincoln**

Colonel Bill White
Auto Literature Sales
PO Box 7-AA
Hudson, KY 40145-0007
502-257-8642; FAX: 502-257-8643

literature

Automobile and truck sales literature, owner's manuals.

The Davis Registry
4073 Ruby
Ypsilanti, MI 48197
313-434-5581, 313-662-1001

periodical

See full listing in **Section Four** under **publications**

Buzz De Clerck
41760 Utica Rd
Sterling Heights, MI 48313
810-731-0765

parts

See full listing in **Section One** under **Lincoln**

DeLorean Literature
3116 Welsh Rd
Philadelphia, PA 19136-1810
215-338-6142

collectibles
literature

See full listing in **Section One** under **DeLorean**

Driven By Desire
300 N Fraley St
Kane, PA 16735
814-837-7590; FAX: 814-837-0886

automobilia
car dealer
models

See full listing in **Section Two** under **car dealers**

Elliott Motorbooks
3023-142 Ave
Edmonton, AB Canada T5Y 1J1
403-475-1548
E-mail: 102670.233@compuserve.com

books

Mail order only. New and original books, literature and manuals for antique cars, trucks and tractors. Inquiries welcome.

Executive Boys Toys
200 S Jackson St
Lima, OH 45804
419-227-9300

car dealer

See full listing in **Section Two** under **car dealers**

Faxon Auto Literature
3901 Carter Ave
Riverside, CA 92501
800-458-2734; FAX: 909-786-4166

literature
manuals

Open Monday-Friday 6 am-6 pm. Find all of your manuals and literature with one free call, 800-458-2734. You can own the best manuals and literature for your vehicle. We are familiar with every manual and most of the literature that exists. We will match the correct book to your needs from the most complete inventory in the world. Money back guarantee. Inquiries use 909-786-4177. Visa, MasterCard, American Express and Discover welcome; also CODs or money order.

Fibre Glast Developments Corp
1944 Neva Dr
Dayton, OH 45414
800-821-3283; FAX: 513-274-7267
E-mail: fibreglast@aol.com

supplies
tools

See full listing in **Section Two** under **restorations aids**

Kenneth Fogarty
Anson Valley Rd
New Vineyard, ME 04956
207-652-2210; FAX: 207-652-2255

literature
parts

See full listing in **Section One** under **Essex**

Get It On Paper
Gary Weickart, President
185 Maple St
Islip, NY 11751
516-581-3897

automobilia
literature
toys

See full listing in **Section Two** under **automobilia**

GMC Solutions
Robert English
PO Box 675
Franklin, MA 02038-0675
508-520-3900; FAX: 508-520-7861
E-mail: oldcarkook@aol.com

literature
parts

See full listing in **Section One** under **GMC**

Marc B Greenwald
c/o 6644 San Fernando Rd
Glendale, CA 91201
818-956-7933; FAX: 818-956-5160

parts

See full listing in **Section One** under **Alfa Romeo**

Richard Hamilton
28 E 46th St
Indianapolis, IN 46205
317-283-1902

sales literature

Mail order only. Dealing in sales literature for Australian, British, Canadian, French, Indian, Mexican, Japanese & US cars. Also offer books, press kits, ads, models and magazines. Have Ferrari and other exotic literature (Bitter, Excalibur, etc).

Justin Hartley
17 Fox Meadow Ln
West Hartford, CT 06107-1216
860-523-0056, 860-604-9950 cellular; FAX: 860-233-8840

reprinted literature

See full listing in **Section One** under **Cadillac/LaSalle**

James Hill
Box 547-V
Goodwell, OK 73939
405-349-2736 evenings/weekends

ignition parts
source list

See full listing in **Section One** under **Packard**

Generalists

Historic Video Archives	videotapes
PO Box 189-VA	
Cedar Knolls, NJ 07927-0189	

See full listing in **Section Two** under **automobilia**

Homer's Mechanical Books	farm tractors
409 Hampton Creek Ct	marine
Columbia, SC 29209	motorcycles
888-5HOMERS toll-free	repair manuals
803-783-8873 nights	

We are a mail order company featuring repair manuals for farm tractors (antique and modern). We also have manuals for motorcycles, marine engines, ATVs, jet skis, outdoor power equipment, snowmobiles, cars and trucks. We sell How To videos, restoration guides and histories for farm tractors. Call for a free list. We buy all of repair manuals of all types. We are especially interested in buying farm tractor repair manuals, parts catalogues and sales literature.

Hosking Cycle Works	books
136 Hosking Ln	manuals
Accord, NY 12404	motorcycle parts
914-626-4231; FAX: 914-626-3245	reprints

Mail order only. Shop manuals, parts books, marque histories, reprints and new computer back issue magazine service; now have world's largest collection of enamel lapel pins (hat pins) for all motorcycles in addition to our books. Catalog listing over 1,000 motorcycle books, free via third class; $1 first class mail. ROKON RT and MX 340 motorcycle parts. Service and parts books. Anything for vintage racing or show restorations of ROKON motorcycles.

Import Car Parts Marketing	books
Steve Fields	
7944 Clover Hill Ln	
Fair Oaks, CA 95628	
916-863-5513; FAX: 916-863-5519	
E-mail: jsfields@earthlink.net	

Mail order only. Shop open by appointment. Specializing in out-of-print automotive and motorcycle history books. Racing, sports cars, import and American cars. Also race programs and race magazines. Free catalog.

International Automobile Archives	sales literature
Kai Jacobsen	
Wiesenweg 3b	
85757 Karlsfeld Germany	
011-49-8131-93158	
FAX: 011-49-8131-93015	

Mail order and open shop. Automotive sales literature of the postwar period from all countries of the world. Also technical data available for nearly every car from 1947 until today. Specializes in sports and exotic cars. List: $2 airmail.

Jeff Johnson Motorsports	accessories
4421 Aldrich Pl	literature
Columbus, OH 43214	parts
614-268-1181; FAX: 614-268-1141	

See full listing in **Section One** under **MoPar**

Bob Johnson's Auto Literature	literature
21 Blandin Ave	manuals
Framingham, MA 01701	
508-872-9173; FAX: 508-626-0991	

Mail order vnd open shop. Monday-Friday 10 am to 6 pm. Deals in factory auto literature such as shop manuals, parts books, owner's manuals, sales catalogs, dealer albums, etc.

Dave Kauzlarich	literature
135 Kingston Dr	memorabilia
Slidell, LA 70458-1737	
504-641-8543; FAX: 504-641-5001	
E-mail: fierog97j@aol.com	

Mail order only. Buying, selling and trading 1984-88 Pontiac and Fiero literature and memorabilia.

David M King, Automotive Books	literature
5 Brouwer Ln	
Rockville Centre, NY 11570	
516-766-1561; FAX: 516-766-7502	

See full listing in **Section One** under **Rolls-Royce/Bentley**

Shepard Kinsman	sales literature
909 Eastridge	
Miami, FL 33157	
305-255-7067; E-mail:	
autolitk@dcfreenet.seflin.lib.fl.us	

Large 1931-1980. Domestic and foreign collection being sold. Marque lists available.

Dan Kirchner	owner's manuals
404 N Franklin	sales literature
Dearborn, MI 48128	shop manuals
313-277-7187	

Mail order only. Automotive literature, shop manuals, owner's manuals, sales literature, dealer books, 1900 to present. SASE with wants.

Kosters Motorboghandel	owner's manuals
Ostergade 9	shop manuals
8900 Randers, Denmark	
45-86-42-6613; FAX: 45-86-42-0813	

Mail order and open shop. Specializes in European shop manuals and owner's manuals for cars and motorcycles, from turn-of-the-century onwards.

David Lawrence Gallery	artwork
PO Box 3702	drawings
Beverly Hills, CA 90212	photography
310-278-0882; FAX: 310-278-0883	

See full listing in **Section Two** under **artwork**

Lloyd's Literature	literature
PO Box 491	
Newbury, OH 44065	
800-292-2665; 216-338-1527	
FAX: 216-338-2222	

Mail order only. Shop manuals, owner's manuals, sales literature, parts books, dealer albums. Specialize in automobile literature for all US & foreign cars & trucks 1915-95. SASE with all inquiries. Fast dependable service.

George & Denise Long	automobilia
915 E Court St	
Marion, NC 28752	
704-652-9229 (24 hrs w/recorder)	

See full listing in **Section Two** under **automobilia**

Ron Magnuson	owner's manuals
PO Box 448	sales literature
North Plains, OR 97133	shop manuals
503-647-2353	

Mail order only. Original auto literature for most makes and years; shop and owner's manuals, sales brochures and more. Prewar a specialty.

The Maverick Connection 137 Valley Dr Ripley, WV 25271 PH/FAX: 304-372-7825	**literature parts**

See full listing in **Section One** under **Ford '54-up**

McBride Auto Ads 585-V Prospect Ave West Hartford, CT 06105 860-523-1622	**magazine ads**

Mail order only. Supplies vintage magazine ads for US and foreign vehicles, 1899-present. Stock of over 175,000 ads, thousands added monthly. No lists provided. "Please send us specific wants and we will send you a selection on approval; buy what you need, return what you don't." Send $3.20 in stamps with first order for postage. VISA/MasterCard.

McCoy's Memorabilia 35583 N 1830 E Rossville, IL 60963-7175 217-748-6513	**memorabilia racing literature**

Mail order. Buying and selling Indy 500 literature, memorabilia and vintage auto magazines, computer search for information on auto races, race cars, race car drivers, vintage autos, tech info.

Ken McGee Holdings Inc 232 Britannia Rd W Goderich, ON Canada N7A 2B9 519-524-5821; FAX: 519-524-4134	**literature**

Largest stock of original North American car and truck literature in Canada. "Specializing in pre-war." Car and truck original literature from 1897-1990. Sales brochures, parts and shop manuals, owner's manuals, data books, dealer albums, etc. Major credit cards accepted. Next day shipping. If selling your collection, please write us, thank you.

Mc Intyre Auctions PO Box 60 E Dixfield, ME 04227 207-562-4443; FAX: 207-562-4576 E-mail: info@classicford.com	**auctions automobilia literature petroliana**

See full listing in **Section Two** under **auctions & events**

McLellan's Automotive History Robert McLellan 9111 Longstaff Dr Houston, TX 77031 713-772-3285; FAX: 713-772-3287	**books magazines programs sales literature**

Mail order only. High quality rare books, sales literature, press kits, magazines, programs, posters and automobilia bought and sold. Domestic and foreign. 1900 to present. Racing, classics, antiques and sports cars. Free 40 page catalog, published 6 times a year. Over 1,000,000 items. Source of information for over 40 years.

R J Miller 7823 Woodville Rd Naples, NY 14512 716-374-8197	**literature manuals memorabilia**

Mail order and selected car shows in the Northeast. Store open by appointment. Original sales literature, shop and owner's manuals, parts catalogs, auto related books, paper goods and collectibles.

Walter Miller 6710 Brooklawn Pkwy Syracuse, NY 13211 315-432-8282; FAX: 315-432-8256	**literature**

Mail order only. 1900-present US and foreign automobile literature. World's largest selection. Over 2,000,000 pieces of original sales brochures and manuals, automobiles and trucks.

Mobey's 318 Burkhart Ln, PO Box 535 Gallipolis, OH 45631 614-446-9700	**literature memorabilia**

Mail order only. Also buys HET memorabilia and literature.

MotoMedia PO Box 489 Landsdowne, PA 19050 PH/FAX: 610-623-6930	**books magazines**

Mail order and flea market sales. More than 20,000 carefully selected issues and 300 books in stock. General interest and racing a specialty. VISA and MasterCard accepted. $2.50 for current lists.

Opel Oldtimer Service Denmark Mosede Kaervej 47 Greve DK-2670 Denmark +45-42-901073, best 11 am-3 pm Central US time	**literature parts parts locators**

See full listing in **Section One** under **Opel**

Original Ford Motor Co Literature PO Box 7-AA Hudson, KY 40145-0007 502-257-8642; FAX: 502-257-8643	**collectibles literature**

See full listing in **Section One** under **Ford '32-'53**

Osborn Reproductions Inc 101 Ridgecrest Dr Lawrenceville, GA 30245 770-962-7556; FAX: 770-962-5881	**decals manuals**

See full listing in **Section Two** under **decals**

Packard Archives 1876 English St St Paul, MN 55109 612-484-1184; FAX: 612-771-1521	**accessories artwork automobilia**

See full listing in **Section One** under **Packard**

Glen Pancoma 1205 Melrose Way Vista, CA 92083 619-724-1779	**manuals sales literature**

Ads, sales brochures, owner's & shop manuals & misc 1899 to present. All are originals only, mostly all in excellent to mint condition. Back issues of Hemmings, Cars & Parts and many others, all exc to mint cond. My choice month & year, only 25¢ each plus shipping & handling. Your satisfaction guaranteed or full refund.

Parts of the Past PO Box 602 Waukesha, WI 53187 414-679-4212	**literature**

Shop manuals, owner's manuals, sales literature for most 1930s-1990s American cars, trucks. Call or send SASE with needs for quote. VISA/MasterCard accepted.

Peerless Co-Operator Newsletter 1094 Brookdale Dr Crestline, OH 44827 419-683-3174	**ads literature manuals**

See full listing in **Section Four** under **newsletters**

Jerrell Pickett
Box 218
Wessington, SD 57381
605-458-2344

literature
parts
sheet metal
wheels

See full listing in **Section Two** under **comprehensive parts**

Paul Politis
Box 335, HC 75
McConnellsburg, PA 17233
717-987-3702; FAX: 717-987-4284

manuals
sales literature

Mail order only. Over 100,000 reasonably priced shop manuals, owner manuals, sales literature, paint chip sets for US & import cars and trucks, 1910-present. Serving the hobby since 1974.

J Preikschat
PO Box 310
White City, SK Canada S0G 5B0

literature

Mail order only. Canadian automotive literature and aftermarket parts manuals. GM parts from the fifties and sixties and AMC parts from the sixties.

**Professional
Specialties/Americana Coach**
513 S Woodlawn Ave, Ste 322
Wichita, KS 67218
316-684-1199; FAX: 316-684-6266

appraisals
literature

See full listing in **Section Two** under **appraisals**

Bert Provisor
930 S Holt Ave
Los Angeles, CA 90035
310-652-0518

data/facts books
owners manuals
shop manuals
showroom albums

Shop, body, parts and owner's manuals, showroom albums, data/facts books, wiring diagrams, service bulletins, color chips, accessories, warranties. *National Service Data, Motors*, and some sales literature. SASE only. Largest selection of original manuals west of the Mississippi.

Samlerborsen
Jacobys Alle 2-4
DK 1806 Frederiksberg C Denmark
+45-33254022; FAX: +45-33250622

books
toys

Open shop only. Shop open Monday-Friday 12 to 5:30. Deals in motorbooks, models and toys, new and second-hand, Tekno, Dinky, Corgi, Solido, etc. Publisher of the book Tekno Made in Denmark by Dorte Johansen.

**Schiff European Automotive
Literature Inc**
373 Richmond St
Providence, RI 02903-4739
401-453-5370; FAX: 401-453-5372

literature

Mail order, phone and FAX orders, in store 8 am-4 pm Monday-Friday; 8 am-12 pm Saturday. Barry Schiff, owner. Sales literature, owner's manuals, parts catalogs and workshop manuals for all European and Japanese cars.

Henri Simar J R
Rue du College, BP 172
B-4800 Verviers Belgium
PH/FAX: 3287335122

books
literature

Mail order and open shop by appointment. Dealing in sales literature, handbooks, workshop manuals, books, posters, magazines. I am collecting all MG, Mini, Lotus, John Player Special, James Bond items.

Robert H Snyder
PO Drawer 821
Yonkers, NY 10702
914-476-8500; FAX: 914-476-8573,
business hours

literature
parts

See full listing in **Section One** under **Cadillac/LaSalle**

Sparling Studios
Box 86B, RR 1, Quarry Rd
New Haven, VT 05472
PH/FAX: 802-453-4114

auto sculpture

See full listing in **Section Two** under **artwork**

Sparrow Auction Company
59 Wheeler Ave
Milford, CT 06460
PH/FAX: 203-877-1066

auction company

See full listing in **Section Two** under **auctions & events**

Thunderbird Headquarters
1080 Detroit Ave
Concord, CA 94518
800-227-2174, US
FAX: 510-689-1771

accessories
literature
parts
upholstery

See full listing in **Section One** under **Thunderbird**

**Edward Tilley Automotive
Collectibles**
PO Box 4233
Cary, NC 27519-4233
919-460-8262
E-mail: edandsusan@aol.com

automobilia
literature
parts

See full listing in **Section Two** under **automobilia**

TMC Publications
5817 Park Heights Ave
Baltimore, MD 21215
410-367-4490; FAX: 410-466-3566

literature
manuals

Mail order and open shop. Open Monday-Saturday 9 to 5. Specializing in workshop manuals for Mercedes-Benz cars produced from 1946-1993. Also owner's manuals, wiring diagrams, parts books, literature, etc. We also carry BMW, Jaguar, Audi, Porsche, Peugeot, Subaru, Mitsubishi, Saab, Volvo and Lexus.

Al Trommers Rare Auto Literature
59 West Front Street, Mailbox #1
Keyport Mini Mall
Keyport, NJ 07735

hubcaps
license plates
literature/records
wheelcovers

Mail order only. Shop open by written request only, include SASE. Specializing in thousands of hard & soft cover auto books, tons of old auto magazines and club publications. Lots of Chilton Motors' repair manuals, lots of NOS original literature, brochures, shop manuals, owner's manuals, postcards, license plates, hubcaps, wheelcovers, music, records and tapes from when your car was new, doo whops, rock & roll, jazz, etc. Originals and reissues, plus much more.

Richard Veen
PO Box 6282
Amsterdam 1005 EG Netherlands
020-6821533

sales catalogs

Mail order. Mainly dealing in hard-to-get new sales catalogs, especially exotics.

Vintage Books   books
6613 E Mill Plain   literature
Vancouver, WA 98661
360-694-9519; FAX: 360-694-7644
E-mail: vintageb@teleport.com

Mail order and open shop. Monday-Friday 10 to 8, Saturday 10
to 6, Sunday 12 to 5. General stock bookstore specializing in
automotive literature. We have a large selection of books (general
and marque history, restoration, etc), plus shop manuals,
owner's manuals, sales literature, ads and magazines.

Vintage Motorbooks   books
42 NW Wallula
Gresham, OR 97030-6814
PH/FAX: 503-661-1482

Mail order only. Large selection of out-of-print, rare and collectible
automotive/motoring history books. Marques, personalities, racing, travel. Send $5 for catalog US, $10 overseas. VISA, MC.

Ted Weems   books/catalogs
PO Box 810665   manuals
Dallas, TX 75381-0665   promotional models
214-247-8169

Mail order only. Sales catalogs, owner's and shop manuals, parts
catalogs, hard and soft cover books, magazines and dealer promotional model cars. Buys, sells and trades. A leading dealer in
the Southwest in literature and promotional items for 25 years.

Weimann's Literature & Collectables   literature
16 Cottage Rd
Harwinton, CT 06791
860-485-0300
FAX: 860-485-1705, 24 hour

See full listing in **Section One** under **Plymouth**

White Auto Literature Mart   literature
PO Box 7-AA
Hudson, KY 40145-0007
502-257-8642; FAX: 502-257-8643

Original sales literature for most cars and trucks. Quarter-mil-
lion piece inventory, SASE with your needs.

John W Wimble   sales literature
1407 Stoneycreek Dr
Richmond, VA 23233

Mail order only. Postwar sales literature. Extensive list available,
$5 appreciated but not necessary. Prompt, professional service,
low prices, satisfaction guaranteed. Also buying.

Zephyrhills Festivals   auction
& Auction Inc   swap meet
PO Box 848
Odessa, FL 33556
813-920-7206; FAX: 813-920-8512

See full listing in **Section Two** under **auctions & events**

locks & keys

Autotec   lock work
12915 Eastbrook Pl
Brookfield, WI 53005-6520
414-797-9988, 8 am to 10 pm CST

Mail order and open shop by appointment. We do foreign &
domestic vehicle lock work exclusively. Repairs, recoding, making keys. This is a full-time occupation. In business since 1982.
Large inventory.

Ed Dennis   American Car
Rt 144, Box 9957   Crest keys
Ellicott City, MD 21042-3647   Wilmot Breeden
410-750-2352, 7-9 pm EST   keys

Mail order only. Key cut by code for American and British cars
and Triumph motorcycles. Need number and SASE, cost is $8
each. Also have Wilmot Breeden keys, FA, FP, FS and FT, cost is
$15 each. American Car Crest keys, example: Ford, DeSoto, etc,
$15 each. All inquiries should include year, make of car, your
daytime/weekend telephone number and a SASE.

Highway Classics   parts
949 N Cataract Ave, Unit J
San Dimas, CA 91702
909-592-8819; FAX: 909-592-4239

See full listing in **Section One** under **Ford '54-up**

Jesser's Classic Keys   automobilia
26 West St, Dept HVA   keys
Akron, OH 44303-2344
330-376-8181; FAX: 330-384-9129

Mail order, car shows and open shop, shop open 10 to 4 five
days, mail order 9 to 9 EST seven days. Complete line of NOS
keys and gold plated keys for all American cars and trucks from
1900 to date. Keys stamped and cut by code. We have many of
those hard to find keys and lock cylinders, please inquire and
include year, make and model. We also carry automobilia, key
rings, grille badges, belt buckles, pins, money clips and more;
VISA, M/C, AmEx, Discover.

Machina Locksmith   car locks
3 Porter St   keys
Watertown, MA 02172-4145
PH/FAX: 617-923-1683

All vehicle lockwork, car locks in stock.

McGard Inc   lug nuts
3875 California Rd   wheel locks
Orchard Park, NY 14127
716-662-8980; FAX: 716-662-8985

Deals in wheel locks and lug nuts.

Metropolitan & British Triumph   NOS British parts
9957 Frederick Rd   NOS British keys
Ellicott City, MD 21042-3647   Lucas & Girling
410-750-2352 evenings   catalogs

See full listing in **Section One** under **Metropolitan**

Performance Years Classic Locks   keys
320 Elm Ave   locks
N Wale, PA 19454
215-699-6681; FAX: 215-699-3725
E-mail: perfyrs@aol.com

Mail order only. Automotive locks and keys. Specializing in
1950s thru 1970s ignitions, door, glove, console and trunk locks
and lock sets.

William Slavik   keys
906 Broadway   locks
Bedford, OH 44146
216-232-8132

Model A locks, keys and ignition switch rebuilding.

U-Con Corporation   door lock kits
15323 Proctor Ave
Industry, CA 91745
818-855-0944; FAX: 818-855-0934

Dealing in power door lock kits, power window kits, remote entry
kits and power trunk kits, "Universal."

Uhlenhopp Lock
29983 Superior Rd
Clarksville, IA 50619
319-278-4355

	lock restoration
	NOS locks
	rebuilding
	rekeying

Mail order and open shop.

lubricants

Billie Inc
10519 Zion Dr
Fairfax, VA 22032
800-878-6328; FAX: 703-250-4586

| | garage diapers |
| | mats |

See full listing in **Section Two** under **car care products**

Brisson Enterprises
PO Box 1595
Dearborn, MI 48121
313-584-3577

| | lead |

See full listing in **Section Two** under **car care products**

D-A Lubricant Co
1340 W 29th St
Indianapolis, IN 46208
800-232-4503; FAX: 317-926-8132

| | lubricants |

Mail order and through distributors. Manufacturer of premium lubricant products for more than 75 years. Products are formulated to protect classic, vintage and special interest autos. Dealer inquiries welcome.

High Performance Coatings
550 W 3615 S
Salt Lake City, UT 84115
801-262-6807; FAX: 801-262-6307
E-mail: hpcsales@hpcoatings.com

| | coatings |

See full listing in **Section Two** under **exhaust systems**

Motor Bay Co
PO Box 460828
San Antonio, TX 78246
800-456-6642

| | tools |

See full listing in **Section Two** under **tools**

O'Brien High Tech Auto
33 Pheasant Ln
Aliso Viejo, CA 92656
714-583-1780, 800-227-8290
FAX: 714-583-1889
E-mail: ohtind@aol.com

	cellular phone exts
	& access
	parts

See full listing in **Section One** under **Cadillac/LaSalle**

Pacific Moly Lubricants
5165 G St
Chino, CA 91710
909-591-1480; FAX: 909-591-8916

| | lubricants |

Mail order and will call (call anytime). Distributors and dealers welcome. Manufacturing and market for Automoly additives to crankcase, trans, differential, plus moly all purpose grease. VISA and MasterCard accepted.

Rocky's Advance Formula
40 Abbott Ave
Danbury, CT 06810
800-752-0245

| | wax hardener |

See full listing in **Section Two** under **car care products**

VACO Inc
PO Box 6
Florence, MA 01060
413-586-0978

| | lubricators |

Mail order only. Upper cylinder lubricators.

Valco Cincinnati Consumer Products Inc
411 Circle Freeway Drive
Cincinnati, OH 45246
513-874-6550; FAX: 513-874-3612

	adhesives
	detailing products
	sealants
	tools

See full listing in **Section Two** under **tools**

machine work

Alan's Axles
2300 Congress Ave
Clearwater, FL 34623
800-741-0452; 813-784-0452

| | axles |

See full listing in **Section Two** under **chassis parts**

S R Aldrich Engine Re-Building
352 River Rd
Willington, CT 06279
203-429-3111

| | engine rebuilding |

See full listing in **Section Two** under **engine rebuilding**

Antique & Classic Cars Inc
326 S 2nd St
Hamilton, OH 45011
513-844-1146 in OH
800-798-3982 nationwide

	bodywork
	machine work
	painting
	parts
	service

See full listing in **Section One** under **Buick/McLaughlin**

Atlas Engine Rebuilding Co Inc
8631 S Avalon Blvd
Los Angeles, CA 90003
213-778-3497; FAX: 213-778-4556

| | engine rebuilding |
| | machine work |

See full listing in **Section Two** under **engine rebuilding**

B & B Cylinder Head
320 Washington St
West Warwick, RI 02893
401-828-4900, 800-800-4143

| | cylinder heads |

See full listing in **Section Two** under **engine parts**

Bob's Automotive Machine
30 Harrison Ave
Harrison, NJ 07029
201-483-0059; FAX: 201-483-6092

| | engine parts |
| | machine shop |

Mail order and open shop. Mon-Fri 9-6, Sat 9-12. Specializing in early 60s Ford engine parts. Area's most complete machine shop service from boring to balancing, to complete engine dynamometer analysis.

BPE Racing Heads 702 Dunn Way Placentia, CA 92870 714-572-6072; FAX: 714-572-6073	**cylinder heads**

Mail order and open shop. Monday-Friday 8-6. Cylinder head restoration, repair and modification. Cast iron and aluminum head welding. Seat and guide installation.

EIS Engines Inc 215 SE Grand Ave Portland, OR 97214 503-232-5590; 800-547-0002 FAX: 503-232-5178	**engines**

See full listing in **Section One** under **Mercedes-Benz**

Errol's Steam Works 3123 Baird Rd North Vancouver, BC Canada V7K 2G5 PH/FAX: 604-985-9494	**castings engines parts**

See full listing in **Section One** under **Locomobile**

George Frechette 14 Cedar Dr Granby, MA 01033 800-528-5235	**brake cylinder sleeving**

See full listing in **Section Two** under **brakes**

George's Speed Shop 716 Brantly Ave Dayton, OH 45404 513-233-0353; FAX: 513-236-3501	**machine shop race engine parts race engine building**

See full listing in **Section Two** under **racing**

Gromm Racing Heads 666-J Stockton Ave San Jose, CA 95126 408-287-1301	**cylinder heads racing parts**

See full listing in **Section Two** under **racing**

Harter Industries Inc PO Box 502 Holmdel, NJ 07733 908-566-7055; FAX: 908-566-6977	**parts restoration**

See full listing in **Section Two** under **comprehensive parts**

HochKraeusen Racing PO Box 716 18233 Madison Rd Parkman, OH 44080-0716 216-548-2147	**machine shop**

Mail order and open shop by appointment. HochKraeusen Racing: complete machine shop services for rare machines and exotics. Magnafluxing, flowbench, heat treating, porting, gear undercutting, prototype parts, rebuild service. Old World aesthetic and attention to detail, three generations of machine tooling. Paul Lynn PHD, Mark Lynn MS Eng.

Horst's Car Care 3160-1/2 N Woodford St Decatur, IL 62526 217-876-1112	**engine rebuilding**

See full listing in **Section One** under **Mercedes-Benz**

Inland Empire Driveline Service Inc 4035 E Guasti Rd, #301 Ontario, CA 91761 800-800-0109; FAX: 909-390-3038	**drive shafts pinion yokes**

We repair and modify OEM driveshafts. We produce custom, higher capacity, driveshafts using steel, aluminum and carbon fiber tubing. We produce higher capacity pinion yokes for many Ford, GM and Mopar third members. Prize winning quality concours to pro-stock.

Koffel's Place II 740 River Rd Huron, OH 44839 419-433-4410; FAX: 419-433-2166	**engine rebuilding machine shop**

See full listing in **Section Two** under **engine rebuilding**

Krem Engineering 10204 Perry Hwy Meadville, PA 16335 814-724-4806	**engine rebuilding repairs restoration**

See full listing in **Section Two** under **restoration shops**

Lindskog Balancing 1170 Massachusetts Ave Boxborough, MA 01719-1415 508-263-2040; FAX: 508-263-4035	**engine balancing**

See full listing in **Section Two** under **engine rebuilding**

Marchant Machine Corporation 11325 Maryland Ave Beltsville, MD 20705 301-937-4481; FAX: 301-937-1019 E-mail: dmarch4481@aol.com	**metal forming machines**

See full listing in **Section Two** under **sheetmetal**

McGee Motorsports Group 29121 Arnold Dr Sonoma, CA 95476 707-996-1112; FAX: 707-996-9148	**race prep restoration**

See full listing in **Section Two** under **racing**

Mid Valley Engineering 16637 N 21st St Phoenix, AZ 85022 602-482-1251; FAX: 602-788-0812	**machine work parts restoration**

See full listing in **Section Two** under **transmissions**

Performance Transmissions 46 Walnut St Shrewsbury, MA 01545 508-842-0672	**restoration trans parts, sales, service trans rebuilding**

See full listing in **Section Two** under **transmissions**

RB's Prototype Model & Machine Co 44 Marva Ln Stamford, CT 06903 PH/FAX: 203-329-2715	**machine work**

See full listing in **Section Two** under **service shops**

Red's Headers 22950 Bednar Ln Fort Bragg, CA 95437-8411 707-964-7733	**headers mechanical parts**

See full listing in **Section One** under **Ford '32-'53**

Rochester Clutch & Brake Co
35 Niagara St
Rochester, NY 14605
716-232-2579; FAX: 716-232-3279

brakes
clutches

See full listing in **Section Two** under **brakes**

Simons Balancing & Machine
1987 Ashley River Rd
Charleston, SC 29407
803-766-3911; FAX: 803-766-9003

machine work

Balancing, boring, crank grinding, flywheel work, line boring, rod work, valve work.

Start Your Engine
110 Third St
Fair Haven, NJ 07704
908-530-1190

machine work

Both mail order and open shop. Start Your Engine. By mail professional diversified machining facility. Automotive experience since 1969. Parts manufacturing in plastic, aluminum, brass, steel, antiques, hot rods, street rods, race cars, boats, motorcycles and imports. Specializing in but not limited to brackets, clamps, hangers, bushings, grommets, flanges, spacers, hose seperators, mounting brackets. Small or large runs from your print or sample. Ask for Mike, 908-530-1190 Monday-Friday 9-6 EST.

J F Sullivan Co
14 Clarendon Rd
Auburn, MA 01501
508-792-9500

brake parts
consulting
machine work
parts locator

See full listing in **Section Two** under **brakes**

Tatom Custom Engines/Vintage Vendors
2718 Riverbend Rd
Mt Vernon, WA 98273
360-424-8314; FAX: 360-424-6717

engine rebuilding
machine shop

See full listing in **Section Two** under **engine rebuilding**

Thul Auto Parts Inc
PO Box 446
Plainfield, NJ 07060
908-754-3333 FAX: 908-756-0239

boring
machine work
rebabbitting
vintage auto parts

See full listing in **Section Two** under **engine rebuilding**

manufacturing

Clark & Clark Specialty Products Inc
568 Central Ave
Holland, MI 49423
616-396-4157; FAX: 616-396-0983
E-mail: obertro@macatawa.org

manufacturing

Specializing in the development and manufacturing of short-run (100-5,000 annual volume) products. We supply about 50 automotive parts and accessories to catalog sellers and retail shops. From polyethylene transmission covers to brass logo tire valve caps. Plastics, metals, composites, wood, upholstered goods. Rotational molding, injection molding, thermoforming, casting, stamping, laser cutting, weldments, CNC routing and machining, screw machine turnings, etc. Wholesale only. Always looking for product ideas, automotive or otherwise. 9 am-5 pm Eastern Standard Time.

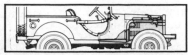

military vehicles

Ace Auto Body & Towing Ltd
65 S Service Rd
Plainview, NY 11803
516-752-6065; FAX: 516-752-1484

mechanical repairs
restorations

See full listing in **Section Two** under **restoration shops**

Automobilia
Division of Lustron Industries
18 Windgate Dr
New City, NY 10956
PH/FAX: 914-639-6806

models

See full listing in **Section Two** under **models & toys**

The Beachwood Canvas Works
PO Box 137
Island Heights, NJ 08732
908-929-3168; FAX: 908-929-3479

canvas covers
parts
tops
upholstery

Research and reproduction of canvas tops, seat cushions, enclosures, decals, wiring harnesses, top bows and other antique four-wheel drive products to original manufacturers' specifications. Supply antique military & civilian Jeep and truck parts & canvas.

Commonwealth Automotive Restorations
1725 Hewins St
Ashley Falls, MA 01222
413-229-3196

body rebuilding
parts
restoration

Mail order and open shop. Open Monday-Saturday 8 am to 8 pm, Sunday by appointment. Specializing in complete body, mechanical work, turnkey vehicles built to order, civilian, military, parts and supplies. Jeep body rebuilding service one of many specialties.

The Davis Registry
4073 Ruby
Ypsilanti, MI 48197
313-434-5581, 313-662-1001

periodical

See full listing in **Section Four** under **books & publications**

Dusty Memories Ltd
118 Oxford Hgts Rd
Somerset, PA 15501-1134
814-443-2393; FAX: 814-443-6468

rentals

Rental of military vehicles, trucks and tractors for veterans' organizations, movies, commercials and shows.

Kick-Start Motorcycle Parts Inc
PO Box 9347
Wyoming, MI 49509
616-245-8991

parts

See full listing in **Section One** under **Harley-Davidson**

Koolmat
PO Box 207
1922 Coventry
Brunswick, OH 44212
330-273-6011; FAX: 330-273-9858

insulators

See full listing in **Section Two** under **restoration aids**

Nelson's Surplus Jeeps and Parts
1024 E Park Ave
Columbiana, OH 44408
330-482-5191 weekdays 9 to 12 noon

| car dealer |
| parts |
| tires |

Mail order and open shop. Saturday 10:30-5 other times by appointment. Specializing in military Jeeps, parts and all sizes of US military tread tires.

Paragon Models & Art
1431-B SE 10th St
Cape Coral, FL 33990
941-458-0024; FAX: 941-574-4329

| artwork |
| models |

See full listing in **Section Two** under **models & toys**

Redi-Strip Company
100 West Central Ave
Roselle, IL 60172
630-529-2442; FAX: 630-529-3626

| abrasive media |
| paint removal |
| plastic media |
| rust removal |

See full listing in **Section Two** under **rust removal & stripping**

Reider Racing Enterprises Inc
12351 Universal Dr
Taylor, MI 48180
800-522-2707, 313-946-1330
FAX: 313-946-8672

| axle components |

See full listing in **Section Two** under **racing**

Richardson Restorations
1861 W Woodward Ave
Tulare, CA 93274
209-688-5002

| repairs |
| restoration |

See full listing in **Section Two** under **restoration shops**

This Old Truck Magazine
PO Box 562
Yellow Springs, OH 45387
800-767-5828; 937-767-1433
FAX: 937 767-2726
E-Mail: antique@antiquepower.com

| magazine |

See full listing in **Section Four** under **periodicals**

Wallace W Wade Specialty Tires
530 Regal Row, PO Box 560906
Dallas, TX 75356
800-666-TYRE; 214-688-0091
FAX: 214-634-8465

| tires |

See full listing in **Section Two** under **tires**

models & toys

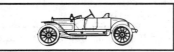

American Classics Unlimited Inc
Frank Groll-Karen Groll
PO Box 192
Oak Lawn, IL 60454-0192
PH/FAX: 708-424-9223

| automobilia |
| models and toys |
| novelty license |
| plates |
| sales literature |

Mail order, car shows and showroom. Collectible transportation models include all makes of current and older dealer promotional model cars, promotional model trucks/banks, die cast model cars, model kits and accessories. 1/87th thru 1/12th scales are carried along with current boxed Matchbox #1-75 issues. SASE for free listing. Also, in our showroom, we have sales literature, books, magazines, 6x12 novelty license plates and other automobilia. Open Monday thru Thursday. Call for details and hours.

Antiques Warehouse
Michael J Welch
3700 Rt 6
Eastham, MA 02642
508-255-1437

| automobilia |
| bikes |
| toy trucks |

Mail order and open shop. Daily, winters by appointment. Antique toys, buy, sell, trade, pressed steel, pedal cars, balloon tire bikes, automobilia, petroliana, nostalgia and much, much more. Now open at Atlantic Oaks Camp, Michael Welch, 3700 Rt 6, Eastham, MA 02642, PH: 508-255-1437.

Aquarius Antiques
Jim & Nancy Schaut
PO Box 10781
Glendale, AZ 85318-0781
602-878-4293
E-mail: nschaut@aztec.asu.edu

| memorabilia |
| toys |

See full listing in **Section Two** under **automobilia**

Asheville DieCast
1412 Brevard Rd
Asheville, NC 28806-9560
800-343-4685; 704-667-9690
FAX: 704-667-1110
E-mail: asheville-diecast@worldnet.att.net

| banks |
| models |

Mail order and open shop. Monday-Friday 9-5:30, Saturday 9-5. Die cast replicas & banks of cars, trucks, buses, planes.

Astro Models
13856 Roxanne Rd
Sterling Heights, MI 48312-5673
810-268-3479

| accessories |
| parts |

Mail order only. Deals in model car parts and accessories, model car wired distributors, model car license plates, drag truck support decals and model car storage bags. 1/24, 1/25 scale only.

Auto Nostalgia Enr
332 St Joseph S
Mont St Gregoire, QC Canada
J0J 1K0
PH/FAX: 514-346-3644

| literature |
| manuals |

See full listing in **Section Two** under **literature dealers**

Auto Zone
1895 S Woodward Ave
Birmingham, MI 48009
800-647-7288; FAX: 810-852-4070

| books |
| magazines |
| models |
| videos |

Mail order and open shop. Monday-Friday 10 am-9 pm, Sat 10 am-7 pm, Sun noon-5 pm. Large selection of automotive books covering all makes and topics. Scale models from Bang, Brooklin, PMA and Jouef, as well as plastic kits and promos. Magazines, both new and old, from around the world. Videos, posters & much more. The store for the auto enthusiast.

Automobilia
Division of Lustron Industries
18 Windgate Dr
New City, NY 10956
PH/FAX: 914-639-6806

| models |

Mail order only. 1/43 scale die-cast auto models of classic, historic and racing cars by Brumm, Best, Bang, Rio, Norev, PMA, Replicars, etc. Also, military pieces, micro racers, car badges, military armor, display cases and more. Also offers convenience of automatic shipments and extra savings to club members.

Automobilia Shop
48 Belmont St
Melrose, MA 02176
617-665-1992; FAX: 617-665-8018

| artwork |
| books |
| models |

See full listing in **Section Two** under **artwork**

Autophile Car Books 1685 Bayview Ave Toronto, ON Canada M4G 3C1 PH/FAX: 416-483-8898	**books** **models**

See full listing in **Section Four** under **books & publications**

Autoquotes 2696 Brookmar York, PA 17404 PH/FAX: 717-792-4936	**price guide**

See full listing in **Section Two** under **automobilia**

Autosport Marketing PO Box 29033 Christ Church 4 NZ New Zealand PH/FAX: 00-64-3-3519476	**apparel** **automobilia**

See full listing in **Section Two** under **apparel**

Berliner Classic Motorcars Inc 1975 Stirling Rd Dania, FL 33004 954-923-7271; FAX: 954-926-3306	**automobilia** **car dealer** **motorcycles**

See full listing in **Section Two** under **car dealers**

Larry Blodget Box 753 Rancho Mirage, CA 92270 619-862-1979	**models**

We specialize in F&F/Post cereal models and auto dealer promo models from the 50s and 60s. Ford products our specialty, but we always have GM, Chrysler and others for sale.

Bonneville Sports Inc 12461 Country Ln Santa Ana, CA 92705 714-508-9724; FAX: 714-508-9725	**accessories** **clothing**

See full listing in **Section Two** under **apparel**

Brasilia Press PO Box 2023 Elkhart, IN 46515 FAX: 219-262-8799	**models**

Dealing in Brooklin, US Model Mint, Goldvarg, Robeddie, Lansdowne and Somerville handmade miniature automobiles. As importers we will furnish dealer listing.

Brown & Associates PO Box 54 Washington Crossing, PA 18977 PH/FAX: 215-493-6393	**model cars**

Specializing in Doepke models for MT and Jaguar mfg in the 50s.

C & N Reproductions Inc 1341 Ashover Ct Bloomfield Hills, MI 48455 810-852-1998; FAX: 810-852-1999 E-mail: ckcn@1x.netcom.com	**pedal car parts** **pedal planes**

See full listing in **Section Two** under **automobilia**

CalAutoArt 1520 S Lyon St Santa Ana, CA 92705 714-835-9512; FAX: 714-835-9513 E-mail: 71460,1146@compuserve.com	**automobilia** **photography**

See full listing in **Section Two** under **automobilia**

Car Collectables 32 White Birch Rd Madison, CT 06443 PH/FAX: 203-245-7299	**banks** **Christmas cards** **note cards**

See full listing in **Section Two** under **artwork**

Castle Display Case Co 102 W Garfield Ave New Castle, PA 16105-2544 412-654-6358	**models**

Mail order only. Handmade oak display cases made for model cars, trucks, trains, farm tractors, etc. Large selection of vertical and horizontal sizes available.

Central Florida Auto Festival **& Toy Expo** 1420 N Galloway Rd Lakeland, FL 33810 941-686-8320	**auto festival** **toy expo**

See full listing in **Section Two** under **auctions & events**

Ceramicar 679 Lapla Rd Kingston, NY 12401 PH/FAX: 914-338-2199	**auto-related** **ceramics**

See full listing in **Section Two** under **novelties**

Classic Construction Models 6590 SW Fallbrook Pl Beaverton, OR 97008 503-626-6395; FAX: 503-646-1996	**models**

Toy and model versions of race cars and hot rods.

Classic Transportation 3667 Mahoning Ave Youngstown, OH 44515 216-793-3026; FAX: 216-793-9729	**automobilia**

See full listing in **Section Two** under **automobilia**

Crazy About Cars 2727 Fairfield Commons, E137 Box 32095 Beavercreek, OH 45431 937-320-0969; FAX: 937-320-0970 E-mail: crazycarz@aol.com	**art** **models** **nostalgia**

See full listing in **Section Two** under **automobilia**

DeLorean Literature 3116 Welsh Rd Philadelphia, PA 19136-1810 215-338-6142	**collectibles** **literature**

See full listing in **Section One** under **DeLorean**

Dominion Models PO Box 515 Salem, VA 24153 PH/FAX: 540-375-3750	**models**

Mail order only. We specialize in 1/43rd scale diecast & white metal models of American cars. Free illustrated brochure available.

Driven By Desire 300 N Fraley St Kane, PA 16735 814-837-7590; FAX: 814-837-0886	**automobilia** **car dealer** **models**

See full listing in **Section Two** under **car dealers**

Eastwood Automobilia
580 Lancaster Ave
Box 3014
Malvern, PA 19355
800-345-1178, M-F 8 am to midnight
Sat & Sun 9 am to 5 pm EST
FAX: 610-644-056

collectibles
transportation

See full listing in **Section Two** under **automobilia**

Eclectic Amusement Corporation
10 Smithfield St
Pittsburgh, PA 15222
412-434-0111; FAX: 412-434-0606

juke boxes
video games

See full listing in **Section Two** under **novelties**

EWA & Miniature Cars USA Inc
369 Springfield Ave
Box 188
Berkeley Heights, NJ 07922
908-665-7811; FAX: 908-665-7814

books
models
subscriptions
videos

Mail order and showroom. Publishes *Classic & Sportscar*. Subscription rate: $59/year. Monthly publication filled with timely news, previews of upcoming events, auction news & event information. Includes huge classified section. Published in England. Featuring 8,000 different scale models from 400 manufacturers. Also available are subscriptions for 36 foreign automobile magazines, including back issues and 2,500 different auto books. Also 600 auto videos. Almost 10,000 different products. Huge 100-page color catalog $4.

Dick Faulkner
3760 Meier St
Los Angeles, CA 90066
310-397-6118

hot wheels

Mail order only. Specializing in all Hot Wheels.

Frontier Tank Center Inc
3800 Congress Pkwy
Richfield, OH 44286
216-659-3888; FAX: 216-659-9410

automobilia
globes
pumps
signs

See full listing in **Section Two** under **petroliana**

Galaxie Ltd
Box 655
Butler, WI 53007
414-790-0390; FAX: 414-783-7710

kits
model trailers

Mail order only. 1/25 scale model trailer kits and vintage dragster model kits.

GearBox Grannie's
492 W Second St, Ste 204
Xenia, OH 45385
513-372-1541; FAX: 513-372-1171

collectibles
metal banks
tools

See full listing in **Section Two** under **tools**

Georgia Marketing
PO Box 570
Winder, GA 30680
770-868-1042; FAX: 770-867-0786
E-mail: peachgmp@mindspring.com

die cast replicas

Georgia Marketing and Peachstate Motorsports are manufacturers and distributors of exclusive, limited quantity, high quality die cast replicas. GMP models include current and vintage stock car and spring car replicas. Peachstate offers limited runs of serialized 1:64 scale die cast racing transporters. GMP also offers custom production for individuals and companies utilizing these same collector grade quality molds. Products are marketed directly to the collector and distributed through an exclusive dealer network. Call or fax 8 to 5 EST for more details.

Get It On Paper
Gary Weickart, President
185 Maple St
Islip, NY 11751
516-581-3897

automobilia
literature
toys

See full listing in **Section Two** under **automobilia**

Jerry Goldsmith Promos
4634 Cleveland Heights
Lakeland, FL 33813
941-644-2437; FAX: 941-644-5013

models

See full listing in **Section Two** under **automobilia**

Grandpa's Attic
112 E Washington
Goshen, IN 46526
219-534-2778

toys

Mail order and open shop. Monday-Friday 9:30 to 5, Saturday until 3. Specializing in diecast collector toys.

Grey Motor Co
4982 Patterson Ave
Perris, CA 92571
909-943-5098; FAX: 909-943-5099

display cabinets

See full listing in **Section Two** under **automobilia**

H D Garage
Barry Brown
18 Dumas St
Hull, QUE Canada J8Y 2M6
819-771-8504; FAX: 819-771-2502
E-mail: cc708@freenet.carleton.ca

art work
literature
motorcycles

See full listing in **Section Two** under **motorcycles**

Richard Hamilton
28 E 46th St
Indianapolis, IN 46205
317-283-1902

sales literature

See full listing in **Section Two** under **literature dealers**

Ken Hicks Promotionals
116 Bethea Rd, Suite 306
Fayetteville, GA 30214
770-460-1654; FAX: 770-460-8956

collectibles
price guide

See full listing in **Section Two** under **automobilia**

Edward L Hunt, Automotive Miniaturist
1409 Yale Dr
Hollywood, FL 33021
954-966-0366

custom miniatures

See full listing in **Section Two** under **artwork**

International House of Toys
16582 Jamesville Rd
Muskego, WI 53150
414-422-9505; FAX: 414-422-9507

toys

Mail order and open shop. 7 days a week, 10-4. Specializing in die cast toys.

Investment Toys for Big Boys 1510 Pennsylvania Ave York, PA 17404 717-848-1180	**model kits**

Mail order and open shop. Monday-Saturday 10 am-4 pm. Model kits, especially automobiles, military, figures, airplanes & monster kits, boats & Lionel trains, old automobile toys.

Jack Juratovic 819 Absequami Trail Lake Orion, MI 48362 PH/FAX: 810-814-0627	**artwork**

See full listing in **Section Two** under **artwork**

Karl's Collectibles 28 Bates St Lewiston, ME 04240 800-636-0457, 207-784-0098 FAX: 207-786-4576 E-mail: slalemand@aol.com	**banks collectibles logo design**

Mail order and open shop. Monday-Friday 9-5. Die cast banks & collectibles, as well as custom logo & printing needs. We design, market and broker collectibles, specializing in the motorcycle trade but not exclusive. We design logos for new companies as well as companies looking for that new look.

Harold Kloss PO Box 37 Humboldt, AZ 86329-0037 520-632-7684	**wood models**

Mail order only. Builds one of a kind wood models for any make or model. Custom orders. All handcrafted.

LA Ltd Design Graphics 822A S McDuffie St Anderson, SC 29624 PH/FAX: 864-231-7715	**artwork design greeting cards**

See full listing in **Section Two** under **automobilia**

The Last Precinct Police Museum Rt 6, Box 345B (62 Highway West) Eureka Springs, AR 72632 501-253-4948; FAX: 501-253-4949	**museum**

See full listing in **Section Six** under **Arkansas**

Legendary Motorcars 1 Wayside Village #350 Marmora, NJ 08223 800-926-3950; FAX: 609-399-2512	**model cars**

Producer of handbuilt model cars for the connoisseur collector. Very limited production. 1/43rd scale, resin cast, retail price $325 and up. First issue is a 1960 Lincoln Continental Mark V coupe and convertible. Second issue is a 1956 Continental Mark II coupe and convertible. Call, write or FAX for more information.

Limited Editions PO Box 11011 Springfield, IL 62791 217-525-0413; FAX: 217-525-7047	**models**

Mail order only. Produces the official Bloomington Gold promotional models, Special Collection XIII, Corvette models and the Bloomington Gold Road Tour Corvette promotional models. The promo models are numbered and titled and produced in very limited quantities. The promos were produced in 1991-1995 and the 1996s are presently in production. We have a few of the new 1996 B/G promos left, available on a first come, first served

basis. Please order immediately. The models are available by mail. The models are also available at the annual Bloomington Gold Show at Springfield, IL in the Exposition Building.

Little Old Cars 3410 Fulton Dr NW Canton, OH 44718 216-455-4685	**model cars**

Mail order and open shop. Monday-Friday 4 pm to 10 pm; Saturday and Sunday 8 am to 10 pm. Specializing in promotional model cars from 1950s and up. Also unbuilt kits. Buy, sell and trade. All correspondences welcome. No catalog available. Please include SASE for immediate response.

George & Denise Long 915 E Court St Marion, NC 28752 704-652-9229 (24 hrs w/recorder)	**automobilia**

See full listing in **Section Two** under **automobilia**

Marky D's Bikes & Peddle Goods 7047 Springridge Rd West Bloomfield, MI 48322 810-737-1657; FAX: 810-398-2581	**bicycles mopeds motorbikes peddle goods**

See full listing in **Section Two** under **bicycles**

Milestone Motorcars Mark Tyra 12910 Sunnybrook Dr Prospect, KY 40059 502-228-5945; FAX: 502-228-1856	**die cast cars models**

See full listing in **Section Two** under **automobilia**

Marc Miller Gallery 3 Railroad Ave East Hampton, NY 11937 516-329-5299; FAX: 516-329-5319	**furniture**

See full listing in **Section Two** under **artwork**

The Model Shop W7982 County Z PO Box 68, Dept HF Onalaska, WI 54650 608-781-1864; FAX: 608-781-7143 E-mail: dkulas@centuryinter.net	**model kits**

Mail order only. Over 3,000 different kits of model car and truck (current and discontinued). Plus paints, decals, showcases and other modeling supplies. Send $3 for 104 page catalog. PH/FAX orders 24 hours a day, 7 days a week.

Moto-Mini Rte. 4, Box 516A-H McKinney, TX 75070-9642 800-890-2686; FAX: 214-837-2356	**models toy motorcycles**

Mail order only. Moto-Mini is dedicated to the collector of toy and model motorcycles. MIniature motorcycles from around the world are available. All types from plastic and metal to all metal limited editions, even custom handcarved wood models are available. Send $1 for current catalog of models and other gift items.

Motorhead Art & Collectibles 1917 Dumas Cir NE Tacoma, WA 98422 800-859-0164; FAX: 206-924-0788	**art prints models**

See full listing in **Section Two** under **artwork**

New Era Toys	toy restoration
PO Box 10	
68 Delaware Ave	
Lambertville, NJ 08530	
609-397-2113	

Mail order and open shop. Workshop open weekdays, retail shop 7 days 9-5. Specializing in pressed steel toy vehicle restorations, 1920s to 1950s for our customers. We also do vintage pedal cars and sell collectable toy vehicles such as Dinky, Corgi, cast iron, plastic, etc, etc!

Paragon Models & Art	artwork models
1431-B SE 10th St	
Cape Coral, FL 33990	
941-458-0024; FAX: 941-574-4329	

Mail order and open shop. Mon-Fri 9-5. Die cast models and automotive artwork.

People Kars	models/more VW toys
290 Third Ave Ext	
Rensselaer, NY 12144	
PH/FAX: 518-465-0477	

See full listing in **Section One** under **Volkswagen**

PM Research Inc	books models
4110 Niles Hill Rd	
Wellsville, NY 14895	
716-593-3169; FAX: 716-593-5637	

Mail order only. Model steam engines, model pipe and miniature pipe fittings. We offer two model boilers and four model machine shop tools that really work. We also have a line of Stirling hot air engines and accessories and carry a large selection of books relating to the above subjects. Catalogs are available for $2.

Hugo Prado Limited Edition Corvette Art Prints	fine art prints
PO Box 18437	
Chicago, IL 60618-0437	
PH/FAX: 800-583-7627	
E-mail: vetteart@aol.com	

See full listing in **Section One** under **Corvette**

Pronyne	museum
PO Box 1492	
Pawtucket, RI 02862-1492	
401-725-1118	

See full listing in **Section Six** under **Rhode Island**

R-C Craft	speed boat models
PO Box 8220	
Sylvania, OH 43560	
419-474-6941	

Mail order only. 16" mahogany speed boat models, battery operated, working lights, electric motor. Varnished mahogany models of Chris-Craft, Garwood, Hacker Craft. 6 models to choose from, $335 each. Visa, MC accepted.

The Red House Collectible Toys	toys
5961 Dry Ridge Rd	
Cincinnati, OH 45252	
PH/FAX: 513-385-5534	

Dealing in collectible toys, primarily auto related toys, but am interested in many kinds of vintage toys and related collectibles. Have some for sale and will also buy.

Rentalex Toy Department	models toys
1022 Skipper Rd	
Tampa, FL 33613	
888-971-9990 toll-free	
813-971-3940	

Mail order and open shop. Mon-Sat 8 am-4 pm. Die cast model toys. Trucks and construction equipment for First Gear, Conrad, N2G, Ertl.

Rideable Antique Bicycle Replicas	bicycles tires
2329 Eagle Ave	
Alameda, CA 94501	
510-769-0980; FAX: 510-521-7145	
E-mail: mbarron@barrongroup.com	

See full listing in **Section Two** under **motorcycles**

Roadside Market	automobilia
1000 Gordon M Buehrig Pl	
Auburn, IN 46706	
219-925-9100; FAX: 219-925-4563	

See full listing in **Section Two** under **automobilia**

Samlerborsen	books toys
Jacobys Alle 2-4	
DK 1806 Frederiksberg C Denmark	
+45-33254022; FAX: +45-33250622	

See full listing in **Section Two** under **literature dealers**

San Remo Hobby and Toy	models trading cards
93 Beaver Dr	
Kings Park, NY 11754-2209	
516-724-5722	

Model car kits: Johnny Lightning Collector Edition/Hobby Editions.

Scale Autoworks	models
Brady Ward	
313 Bridge St #4	
Manchester, NH 03104-5045	
PH/FAX: 603-623-5925 ext 66	

Mail order only. A professional builder of Pocher Classic 1/8 scale models, specializing in Bugatti and Alfa Romeo. All models are built to the customers specifications, and include real leather and wood interiors, automotive quality paint and added engine details, wiring and linkages. Custom paint and coachwork are available, including mahogany skiff bodied cars. Each model also includes a custom hardwood and glass display case.

Scott Signal Co	stoplights
8368 W Farm Rd 84	
Willard, MO 65781	
417-742-5040	

See full listing in **Section Two** under **automobilia**

Sinclair's Auto Miniatures Inc	miniature cars
PO Box 8403	
Dept HVA	
Erie, PA 16505	
PH/FAX: 814-838-2274, 24 hrs/day	

Collectors' items in 1:43 and other scales. Die cast and handmade from $16 to $500. American cars of the 50s; European exotics; "cars of the movie stars and the famous and infamous;" Indy 500 pace cars. The "original" cars by mail company, established 1964. Major credit cards honored. Big colorful catalogue, $2 cash, check or m/o ($4 catalogue rebate).

Sparling Studios	**auto sculpture**
Box 86B, RR 1, Quarry Rd	
New Haven, VT 05472	
PH/FAX: 802-453-4114	

See full listing in **Section Two** under **artwork**

Sparrow Auction Company	**auction company**
59 Wheeler Ave	
Milford, CT 06460	
PH/FAX: 203-877-1066	

See full listing in **Section Two** under **auctions & events**

Spec Cast	**models**
428 6th Ave NW, Box 368	
Dyersville, IA 52040-0368	
319-875-8706; FAX: 319-875-8056	

Spec Cast is a leading manufacturer of quality diecast and pewter collectibles. Including vehicles and airplane books, 1/16 tractors, belt buckles and pewter replicas. Spec Cast will also be introducing diecast model kits in Fall 1997.

TCMB Models & Stuff	**models**
8207 Clinton Ave S	
Bloomington, MN 55420-2315	
612-884-3997; FAX: 612-473-0795	

Mail order only. Metal model kits, 1/25 scale vehicle banks and 1/43rd scale vehicles.

Tech-Art Publications	**books**
Jason Houston	
Box 753	
Ranchero Mirage, CA 92270	
619-862-1979	

See full listing in **Section Four** under **books & publications**

Edward Tilley Automotive Collectibles	**automobilia** **literature** **parts**
PO Box 4233	
Cary, NC 27519-4233	
919-460-8262	
E-mail: edandsusan@aol.com	

See full listing in **Section Two** under **automobilia**

Toy Sense Inc	**games** **toys**
257 North Amphlett Blvd	
San Mateo, CA 94401-1805	
415-579-7825; FAX: 415-579-7827	
E-mail: toysense@netwizard.net	

See full listing in **Section Two** under **automobilia**

Toys For Collectors	**models**
PO Box 1406	
Attleboro Falls, MA 02763	
508-695-0588; FAX: 508-699-8649	

Mail order and showroom open by appointment. Scale models of automobiles, fire trucks, construction equipment, military, etc in various scales. We carry one of the largest selections of metal models, factory and handbuilt, ready to display, no kits, color catalog available for $6.

Vintage Car Corral	**parts** **toys**
1401 NW 53rd Ave	
PO Box 384	
Gainesville, FL 32602	
PH/FAX: 904-376-4513	

See full listing in **Section Two** under **comprehensive parts**

Volkswagen Collectors	**literature** **memorabilia** **toys**
c/o Jerry Jess	
3121 E Yucca St	
Phoenix, AZ 85028-2616	
PH/FAX: 602-867-7672	

See full listing in **Section One** under **Volkswagen**

Michael J Welch	**automobilia** **pedal cars** **toy trucks**
3700 Rt 6, RR 2	
Eastham, MA 02642	
508-255-1437	

Open daily or winters by appointment. Now open at Atlantic Oaks Camp. Antique toys, buy, sell, trade, pressed steel, pedal cars, balloon tire bikes, automobilia, petroliana, nostalgia and much, much more.

Wheels O' Time Museum	**museum**
PO Box 9636	
Peoria, IL 61612-9636	
309-243-9020	

See full listing in **Section Six** under **Illinois**

Kirk F White	**models** **tin toys**
PO Box 999	
New Smyrna Beach, FL 32170	
904-427-6660; FAX: 904-427-7801	

Mail order and open shop by appointment only. Early gas engined racing cars of all types. Early historied hot rods, racing memorabilia, fine large scale racing models. All types of early European transportation tin toys.

Yankee Candle Car Museum	**museum**
5 North St	
South Deerfield, MA 01373	
413-665-2020; FAX: 413-665-2399	

See full listing in **Section Six** under **Massachusetts**

Clarence Young Autohobby	**dealer promos** **promo price guide** **resin cars/toys/kits** **slush-metal banks**
302 Reems Creek	
Weaverville, NC 28787	
PH/FAX: 704-645-5243	

Mail order and open shop by appointment. Dealer promotionals, kits, toy cars, trucks and tractors. Manufacturer of 1/25th scale metal car banks. Publisher of *Autoquotes*, an annual dealer promo information and value guide.

George R Zaninovich	**models** **toys**
28562 S Montereina Dr	
Rancho Palos Verdes, CA 90275	
310-832-2282	

Mail order only. Deals in toy model cars & trucks. Cast iron, stamped steel, tin, plastic, die cast and promotional models. Buy-sell-trade. Since 1966.

motorcycles

Automotive Interior Center	**interior trim**
1725A Bustleton Pike	
Feasterville, PA 19053	
PH/FAX: 215-953-7477	

See full listing in **Section Two** under **interiors & interior parts**

Barlow & Co	**car dealer** **restoration**
7 Maple Ave	
Newton, NH 03858	
603-382-3591; FAX: 603-382-4406	

See full listing in **Section Two** under **restoration shops**

Berliner Classic Motorcars Inc 1975 Stirling Rd Dania, FL 33004 954-923-7271; FAX: 954-926-3306	**automobilia** **car dealer** **motorcycles**

See full listing in **Section Two** under **car dealers**

BPE Racing Heads 702 Dunn Way Placentia, CA 92870 714-572-6072; FAX: 714-572-6073	**cylinder heads**

See full listing in **Section Two** under **machine work**

Francois Bruere 8 Avenue Olivier Heuze LeMans 72000 France (33) 02-4377-1877 FAX: (33) 02-4324-2038	**artwork**

See full listing in **Section Two** under **artwork**

BW Incorporated PO Box 106 316 W Broadway Browns Valley, MN 56219 800-950-2210; 612-695-2891 or 800-EAT-OILS/328-6457 FAX: 612-695-2893	**artwork** **car care products** **dry enclosed covers** **mice control** **oil drip absorbent** **storage care** **products**

See full listing in **Section Two** under **storage care products**

Classic Trim Inc Mick Stamm 3401 S 1st St Abilene, TX 79605-1708 915-676-8788	**collectibles** **trim** **upholstery**

Mail order and open shop. Monday-Friday 8 am-5 pm CST. Automotive upholstery, tops and interior restoration/customization and leather interiors for all models as well as antique and vintage motorcycle parts and restoration service. Buy/sell hard to find parts, bikes, quality motorcycle collectibles, license plates, oil cans, posters, clothing, signs, obsolete inventories, retired dealerships. Harley-Davidson specialists. Items or collections purchased.

Coker Tire 1317 Chestnut St Chattanooga, TN 37402 800-251-6336 toll-free 423-265-6368, local & international FAX: 423-756-5607	**tires**

See full listing in **Section Two** under **tires**

Ed Dennis Rt 144, Box 9957 Ellicott City, MD 21042-3647 410-750-2352, 7-9 pm EST	**American Car** **Crest keys** **Wilmot Breeden** **keys**

See full listing in **Section Two** under **locks & keys**

Malcolm C Elder & Son The Motor Shed, Middle Aston Bicester Oxfordshire OX6 3PX England PH/FAX: 01869 340999	**car dealer** **motorcycles**

See full listing in **Section Two** under **car dealers**

Jim Estrup The Plateman Box 908, RR 3 Kennebunk, ME 04043 207-985-4800; FAX: 207-985-TAGS	**license plates**

See full listing in **Section Two** under **license plates**

George Frechette 14 Cedar Dr Granby, MA 01033 800-528-5235	**brake cylinder** **sleeving**

See full listing in **Section Two** under **brakes**

John Giles Cars & Parts (ASV&S) 703 Morgan Ln Pascagoula, MS 39567 PH/FAX: 601-769-8904	**car & parts locator** **exporter**

See full listing in **Section Two** under **car & parts locators**

H D Garage Barry Brown 18 Dumas St Hull, QUE Canada J8Y 2M6 819-771-8504; FAX: 819-771-2502 E-mail: cc708@freenet.carleton.ca	**art work** **literature** **motorcycles**

Rare pre WW II motorcycles and related literature and art works (bronzes, paintings, miniatures, etc), Brough-Superior, Crocker, early Harley (especially racers) and American 4-cylinder specialist. Parts information and restoration and location services for these and others.

Harper's Moto Guzzi 32401 Stringtown Rd Greenwood, MO 64034 800-752-9735; 816-697-3411 FAX: 816-566-3413	**accessories** **bikes** **parts**

Mail order and open shop. Monday-Friday 9-5, Saturday 9-1, closed Sundays and all holidays. We are exploding with lots of stock. New, used and hard to find Moto Guzzi bikes and parts. Lots of NOS too. Aftermarket accessories for the Moto Guzzi motorcycle, only $3 for aftermarket catalog, USA. Foreign air mail $5 US. Bike flyer available, listing most of the bikes we have for sale. We ship bikes and parts worldwide. Visa, MasterCard, American Express or cash.
Web site: http://www.harpermotoguzzi.com

Hooker Headers 1024 W Brooks St PO Box 4030 Ontario, CA 91761 909-983-5871	**exhaust systems**

See full listing in **Section Two** under **exhaust systems**

Hosking Cycle Works 136 Hosking Ln Accord, NY 12404 914-626-4231; FAX: 914-626-3245	**books** **manuals** **motorcycle parts** **reprints**

See full listing in **Section Two** under **literature dealers**

House of Powder Inc Rt 71 & 1st St PO Box 110 Standard, IL 61363 815-339-2648	**powder coating** **sandblasting**

See full listing in **Section Two** under **service shops**

Indian Joe Martin's Antique Motorcycle Parts PO Box 3156 Chattanooga, TN 37404 615-698-1787	**parts**

Mail order only. Indian and Harley-Davidson motorcycle business offering NOS, military surplus and quality reproduction parts for Indian and pre-1973 Harley-Davidson motorcycles, shipped worldwide. Parts catalog available for $3 USA and Canada or $5 for foreign air mail.

J & P Custom Plating Inc
807 N Meridian St
PO Box 16
Portland, IN 47371
219-726-9696; FAX: 219-726-9346

electro-plating

See full listing in **Section Two** under **plating & polishing**

Karl's Collectibles
28 Bates St
Lewiston, ME 04240
800-636-0457, 207-784-0098
FAX: 207-786-4576
E-mail: slalemand@aol.com

banks
collectibles
logo design

See full listing in **Section Two** under **models & toys**

Kick-Start Motorcycle Parts Inc
PO Box 9347
Wyoming, MI 49509
616-245-8991

parts

See full listing in **Section One** under **Harley-Davidson**

Lindskog Balancing
1170 Massachusetts Ave
Boxborough, MA 01719-1415
508-263-2040; FAX: 508-263-4035

engine balancing

See full listing in **Section Two** under **engine rebuilding**

M & R Products
1940 SW Blvd
Vineland, NJ 08360
609-696-9450; FAX: 609-696-4999

hardware
tie-downs

See full listing in **Section Two** under **accessories**

Main Attractions
PO Box 4923
Chatsworth, CA 91313
818-709-9855; FAX: 818-998-0906

posters
videos

See full listing in **Section Four** under **information sources**

Marky D's Bikes & Peddle Goods
7047 Springridge Rd
West Bloomfield, MI 48322
810-737-1657; FAX: 810-398-2581

bicycles
mopeds
motorbikes
peddle goods

See full listing in **Section Two** under **bicycles**

Mid-America Auction Services
2277 W Hwy 36, Ste 214
St Paul, MN 55113
612-633-9655; FAX: 612-633-3212
E-mail: midauction@aol.com

auctions

See full listing in **Section Two** under **auctions & events**

Moores Cycle Supply
49 Custer St
West Hartford, CT 06110
860-953-1689; FAX: 860-953-4366

motorcycles
parts

Mail order and open shop. Monday thru Friday 12-8, Saturday 2-5. Deals in motorcycles, parts for Triumphs, BSA, Norton motorcycles.

Moto-Mini
Rte. 4, Box 516A-H
McKinney, TX 75070-9642
800-890-2686; FAX: 214-837-2356

models
toy motorcycles

See full listing in **Section Two** under **models and toys**

Motorsports Racing
914 S Santa Fe #101
Vista, CA 92084
619-630-0547; FAX: 619-630-3085

accessories
apparel
art

See full listing in **Section Two** under **apparel**

National Parts Locator Service
636 East 6th St #81
Ogden, UT 84404-2415
801-392-9455

parts locator

See full listing in **Section Two** under **car & parts locators**

Paragon Models & Art
1431-B SE 10th St
Cape Coral, FL 33990
941-458-0024; FAX: 941-574-4329

artwork
models

See full listing in **Section Two** under **models & toys**

Premier Designs Historic Costume
818 Selby St
Findlay, OH 45840
800-427-0907; FAX: 419-427-2239
E-mail: premier@bright.net

clothing

See full listing in **Section Two** under **apparel**

Redi-Strip Company
100 West Central Ave
Roselle, IL 60172
630-529-2442; FAX: 630-529-3626

abrasive media
paint removal
plastic media
rust removal

See full listing in **Section Two** under **rust removal & stripping**

Reinholds Restorations
c/o Rick Reinhold
PO Box 178, 255 N Ridge Rd
Reinholds, PA 17569-0178
717-336-5617

appraisals
repairs
restoration

See full listing in **Section Two** under **restoration shops**

Rideable Antique Bicycle Replicas
2329 Eagle Ave
Alameda, CA 94501
510-769-0980; FAX: 510-521-7145
E-mail: mbarron@barrongroup.com

bicycles
tires

Mail order only. Specializing in 1880 full size antique high wheel bicycles, 15 different models from 1870 to 1895. Solid rubber tires for pedal cars, tea carts, buggy wheel, gasoline cart. 1880 replica catalogs. Bicycle oil lamps; 1950s replica bicycles, parts, wheels, whitewall tires. Schwinn Stingray replica parts, spring forks, frames, etc.

Rocky Mountain Motorcycle Museum & Hall of Fame
308 E Arvada St
Colorado Springs, CO 80906
PH/FAX: 719-633-6329

museum

See full listing in **Section Six** under **Colorado**

Sanders Antique Auto Restoration 1120 22nd St Rockford, IL 61108 815-226-0535	restoration

See full listing in **Section Two** under **restoration shops**

Speed & Sport Chrome Plating Inc 404 Broadway Houston, TX 77012 713-921-0235	chrome plating

See full listing in **Section Two** under **plating & polishing**

Standard Abrasives Motor Sports 9351 Deering Ave Chatsworth, CA 91311 800-383-6001, 818-718-7070, ext 371 FAX: 800-546-6867	abrasives

See full listing in **Section Two** under **restoration aids**

TK Performance Inc 1508 N Harlan Ave Evansville, IN 47711 812-422-6820; FAX: 812-422-5282	engine building machine work restoration

See full listing in **Section One** under **Harley-Davidson**

Toys n' Such 437 Dawson St Sault Sainte Marie, MI 49783 906-635-0356	parts

Mail order only. For English cycles, 40s to 60s, some German and Italian parts from same years, along with dealer brochures. Also buying toy motorcycles and race cars. Mopar parts for sale, NOS, 40s to 60s; also dealer brochures for sale. US & European, including Canadian.

Vehicles In Motion 1000 W Crosby #100 Carrollton, TX 75006 214-242-2453; FAX: 214-446-1919	directory purchasing guide

See full listing in **Section One** under **Harley-Davidson**

Walneck's Classic Cycle Trader 7923 Janes Ave Woodridge, IL 60517 630-985-4995; FAX: 630-985-2750	magazine

See full listing in **Section Four** under **periodicals**

Xanders' Britbikes 1280 Stringtown Rd Grove City, OH 43123 614-871-9001 E-mail: axanders@computrek.org	motorcycle parts

Specialists in parts, accessories, service and machine work for Norton Twins and unit construction Triumph & BSA. Mail order service. Bikes & parts bought & sold.

novelties

Action Marketing 17 Verona Cr Keswick, ON Canada L4P 3N7 800-494-4204; FAX: 905-476-9834	video

See full listing in **Section Two** under **videos**

American Arrow Corp 105 Kinross Clawson, MI 48017 313-588-0425; FAX: 313-435-4670	chroming mascots wire wheel rebuilding

Mail order and open shop. Open by appointment only. Stainless steel mascots, plastic lenses, spotlights, Pilot Ray lights and tonneau windshields. Also wire wheel rebuilding and chroming. Also automotive art. Art quality trophies, catalog $3.

Anacortes Brass Works Ltd PO Box 10 Anacortes, WA 98221 360-293-4515; FAX: 360-293-4516	brass castings

See full listing in **Section Two** under **castings**

Anderson's 32700 Coastsite #102 Rancho Palos Verdes, CA 90275 310-377-1007; 800-881-9049 FAX: 310-377-0169	car door monograms

See full listing in **Section Two** under **accessories**

Auto Etc Neon PO Box 531992 Harlingen, TX 78553 210-425-7487; FAX: 210-425-3025	signs time pieces

See full listing in **Section One** under **Corvette**

Autosport Specialty PO Box 9553 Knoxville, TN 37920 615-573-2580	decals license plates patches

Mail order only. Custom made patches, decals, key fobs, license plates and frames for most special interest car clubs & dealers.

Be-Bops 1077 S Seguin New Braunfels, TX 78130 210-625-6056; 210-657-2135	Coke machines gas pumps

See full listing in **Section Two** under **automobilia**

Benkin & Co 14 E Main St Tipp City, OH 45371 513-667-5975; FAX: 513-667-5729	gas pumps neon clocks neon signs

See full listing in **Section Two** under **automobilia**

Bonneville Sports Inc 12461 Country Ln Santa Ana, CA 92705 714-508-9724; FAX: 714-508-9725	accessories clothing

See full listing in **Section Two** under **apparel**

F J Cabrera Enterprises 15507 Normandie Ave, #103 Gardena, CA 90247 310-532-8894; FAX: 310-515-0928	accessories lights

See full listing in **Section Two** under **restoration aids**

CalAutoArt 1520 S Lyon St Santa Ana, CA 92705 714-835-9512; FAX: 714-835-9513 E-mail: 71460,1146@compuserve.com	automobilia photography

See full listing in **Section Two** under **automobilia**

Generalists

Generalists

Career Center
1302 9th St
Wheatland, WY 82201
PH/FAX: 307-322-2063

license plates

See full listing in **Section Two** under **license plates**

Castle Display Case Co
102 W Garfield Ave
New Castle, PA 16105-2544
412-654-6358

models

See full listing in **Section Two** under **models & toys**

Ceramicar
679 Lapla Rd
Kingston, NY 12401
PH/FAX: 914-338-2199

auto-related
ceramics

Mail order only. We manufacture non-model specific, non-year specific fantasy ceramic automobile cookie jars, lamp bases, coin banks. Big, 14"x9"x9", colorful and chromy. Please send for price list and dazzling photo.

Classic Motorcar Investments
3755 Terra Loma Dr
Bullhead City, AZ 86442
602-763-5869

apparel

See full listing in **Section Two** under **apparel**

Classic Transportation
3667 Mahoning Ave
Youngstown, OH 44515
216-793-3026; FAX: 216-793-9729

automobilia

See full listing in **Section Two** under **automobilia**

Collectibles "R" Us
6001 Canyon Rd
Harrisburg, PA 17111
717-558-2653

memorabilia

Mail order only. Porcelain reproduction auto signs, copper automotive printers' blocks, auto pins and jewelry. Coca-Cola & 50s collectibles.

Cruising International Inc
1000 N Beach St
Daytona Beach, FL 32117
800-676-8961, 904-254-8753
FAX: 904-255-2460

automobilia
decals
license plates
novelties
porcelain signs

See full listing in **Section Two** under **accessories**

Crutchfield Corp
1 Crutchfield Park
Charlottesville, VA 22906
800-955-9009; FAX: 804-973-1862

car stereos

See full listing in **Section Two** under **radios**

Richard Culleton
4318 SW 19th Pl
Cape Coral, FL 33914
800-931-7836 voice mail
315-685-7414 (home); 941-542-8640

accessories

See full listing in **Section Two** under **accessories**

Dr Cap (Brad Sullivan)
2550 Estero Blvd Ste 12
Ft Myers Beach, FL 33931
941-463-3741

custom license
plates

See full listing in **Section Two** under **license plates**

Driven By Desire
300 N Fraley St
Kane, PA 16735
814-837-7590; FAX: 814-837-0886

automobilia
car dealer
models

See full listing in **Section Two** under **car dealers**

Eclectic Amusement Corporation
10 Smithfield St
Pittsburgh, PA 15222
412-434-0111; FAX: 412-434-0606

juke boxes
video games

Mail order and open shop. Monday-Friday 10 am-5 pm. Classic jukeboxes, classic video games and driving games, classic pinball machines and other amusement games.

Ed's Be-Bop Shop
10087 W Co Rd 300 S
Medora, IN 47260
812-966-2203

accessories
parts
restoration

See full listing in **Section One** under **Ford '03-'31**

Eurosport Daytona Inc
32 Oceanshore Blvd
Ormond Beach, FL 32176
800-874-8044; 904-672-7199
FAX: 904-673-0821

license plates

See full listing in **Section Two** under **license plates**

Galaxie Ltd
Box 655
Butler, WI 53007
414-790-0390; FAX: 414-783-7710

kits
model trailers

See full listing in **Section Two** under **models & toys**

Grey Motor Co
4982 Patterson Ave
Perris, CA 92571
909-943-5098; FAX: 909-943-5099

display cabinets

See full listing in **Section Two** under **automobilia**

Historic Video Archives
PO Box 189-VA
Cedar Knolls, NJ 07927-0189

videotapes

See full listing in **Section Two** under **automobilia**

Image Auto
31690 W 12 Mile #4
Farmington Hills, MI 48334
800-414-2852; FAX: 810-553-0924

apparel
artwork

See full listing in **Section One** under **Jensen**

Innovative Novelties/McGee Enterprises
PO Box 1375
Little Rock, AR 72203
501-835-8409; FAX: 501-835-7293
E-mail: kholland@cci.net

accessories

Mail order only. Micro-Jet electronic ignition torch. Nevr-Spill balancing drink holder for car, boat, etc. MagicEyes hands-free adjustable flashlight. Tire Alert hassle-free tire pressure monitors and other innovative products not readily available at retail outlets.

Steve Jelf-14
Box 200 Rt 5
Arkansas City, KS 67005
316-442-1626 after 2 pm CST

signs

See full listing in **Section Two** under **automobilia**

Karl's Collectibles	banks
28 Bates St	collectibles
Lewiston, ME 04240	logo design
800-636-0457, 207-784-0098	
FAX: 207-786-4576	
E-mail: slalemand@aol.com	

See full listing in **Section Two** under **models & toys**

Kortesis Marketing Ent	radar jammers
PO Box 460543	
Aurora, CO 80046	
303-548-3995; FAX: 303-699-6660	

Mail order only. Laser and radar jammers. Also detector/jammer combos, 100% FCC legal. No more tickets or manufacturer pays them. 3 yr warranty, 30 day money back guarantee. Units starting at $65. Free shipping and handling. Call or write for free brochures. Guaranteed lowest prices.

LA Ltd Design Graphics	artwork
822A S McDuffie St	design
Anderson, SC 29624	greeting cards
PH/FAX: 864-231-7715	

See full listing in **Section Two** under **automobilia**

George & Denise Long	automobilia
915 E Court St	
Marion, NC 28752	
704-652-9229 (24 hrs w/recorder)	

See full listing in **Section Two** under **automobilia**

Lost Highway Art Co	decals
PO Box 164	
Bedford Hills, NY 10507-0164	
914-234-6016	

See full listing in **Section Two** under **decals**

Larry Machacek	decals
PO Box 515	license plates
Porter, TX 77365	
713-429-2505	

See full listing in **Section Two** under **automobilia**

Merely Motoring	automobilia
153 Danford Ln	lapel badges
Solihull	postcards
West Midlands B91 1QQ England	
0121-733-2123	
FAX: 0121-745-5256	

See full listing in **Section Two** under **automobilia**

Moonlight Ink	art
2736 Summerfield Rd	
Winter Park, FL 32792-5112	
407-628-8857; FAX: 407-671-5008	

See full listing in **Section One** under **Porsche**

S K Narwid	badges
5 Tsataga Ct	
Brevard, NC 28712-9258	
704-884-6679	

Mail order only. Limited amount of car shows' international car badges, badge bars, clips and badge mounts.

Olona Imaging	mugs
PO Box 92214	t-shirts
Albuquerque, NM 87199-2214	
800-910-4237	
E-mail: olonaimage@aol.com	

Mail order only. Specializing in personalized/custom promotional, novelty items such as photo/logo ceramic mugs, ceramic steins, computer mouse pads, T-shirts, sweatshirts and coasters. Can be customized with your photo and custom caption (make, model, your name, etc). Group/club and wholesale discounts available.

Original Ford Motor Co Literature	collectibles
PO Box 7-AA	literature
Hudson, KY 40145-0007	
502-257-8642; FAX: 502-257-8643	

See full listing in **Section One** under **Ford '32-'53**

Park Avenue China Inc	ceramic mugs
428 Park Ave	glassware
East Palestine, OH 44413	plates
PH/FAX: 330-426-3328	

Mail order and open shop. Monday thru Friday 9-5, Saturday until noon. Dealing in coffee mugs and tankards, glazed ivory porcelain with color decal, 7 oz and 9 oz. Several designs available. All US made. No set-up charge for custom decal work. No minimum order. Custom auto design logo on 8-1/2" porcelain plates available. Custom glassware also available. Satisfaction assured. Quantity discounts. All prices plus UPS. Also optional gold band at rim. Call for details.

Past Patterns	clothing
PO Box 2446	patterns
Richmond, IN 47375-2446	
317-962-3333; FAX: 317-962-3773	
E-mail: pastpat@thepoint.net	

Mail order only. Each multi-sized pattern is a fascinating view into the past. Victorian and Edwardian catalog covering the years 1830-1939, $4.

People Kars	models/more
290 Third Ave Ext	VW toys
Rensselaer, NY 12144	
PH/FAX: 518-465-0477	

See full listing in **Section One** under **Volkswagen**

People's Choice & Lost in the 50s	automobilia items
28170 Ave Crocker #209	celebrity items
Valencia, CA 91355	50s clothing
800-722-1965, 805-295-1965	50s memorabilia
FAX: 805-295-1931	

See full listing in **Section Two** under **automobilia**

Prestige Products	belt buckles
PO Box 994462	plaques
Redding, CA 96099-4462	

Mail order only. Featuring solid bronze plaques to customer's design and club logo belt buckles. No minimum order and competitive prices.

R-C Craft	speed boat models
PO Box 8220	
Sylvania, OH 43560	
419-474-6941	

See full listing in **Section Two** under **models & toys**

Generalists

The Red House Collectible Toys
5961 Dry Ridge Rd
Cincinnati, OH 45252
PH/FAX: 513-385-5534

toys

See full listing in **Section Two** under **models & toys**

Re-Flex Border Marker
138 Grant St
Lexington, MA 02173
617-862-1343

border markers
posts

See full listing in **Section Two** under **hardware**

Rideable Antique Bicycle Replicas
2329 Eagle Ave
Alameda, CA 94501
510-769-0980; FAX: 510-521-7145
E-mail: mbarron@barrongroup.com

bicycles
tires

See full listing in **Section Two** under **motorcycles**

Joseph Russell
455 Ollie
Cottage Grove, WI 53527
608-839-4736

accessories
collectibles
memorabilia

Auto memorabilia, unusual old spark plugs, collectibles, motometers, glass swirl gearshift knobs, Ford plant badges, license plate attachments. Model T keys, watch fobs and accessories bought and sold.

Scott Signal Co
8368 W Farm Rd 84
Willard, MO 65781
417-742-5040

stoplights

See full listing in **Section Two** under **automobilia**

Silver Image Photographics
3102 Vestal Pkwy E
Vestal, NY 13850
607-797-8795

business cards
photo car cards
photofinishing

See full listing in **Section Two** under **automobilia**

Sky Signs Balloons Ltd
Box 887
Valley Forge, PA 19481
215-933-6952; 800-582-4095
FAX: 215-935-7808

balloons

Mail order and open shop. Monday-Friday 9 to 5. Builds and sells giant cold air and helium balloons used for both indoor and outdoor advertising. Also giant cold air product replicas and special shapes, banners and flags.

Sparling Studios
Box 86B, RR 1
Quarry Rd
New Haven, VT 05472
PH/FAX: 802-453-4114

auto sculpture

See full listing in **Section Two** under **artwork**

Toy Sense Inc
257 North Amphlett Blvd
San Mateo, CA 94401-1805
415-579-7825; FAX: 415-579-7827
E-mail: toysense@netwizard.net

games
toys

See full listing in **Section Two** under **automobilia**

Peter Tytla Artist
PO Box 43
East Lyme, CT 06333-0043
860-739-7105

photographic
collages

See full listing in **Section Two** under **artwork**

Weber's Nostalgia Supermarket
6611 Anglin Dr
Fort Worth, TX 76119
817-534-6611; FAX: 817-534-3316
E-mail: webers@flash.net

collectibles
gas pump supplies
models
novelties & toys

Mail order and open shop. Monday-Friday 9 to 5. Specializing in gas pump restoration, supplies, ie: globes, signs, decals, hoses, nozzles, glass, rubber, etc. Also large selection of gameroom decor and old photos. Catalog free with order or $4, refundable.

Wheels of Time
PO Box 1218
Studio City, CA 91604
800-Wheels of Time

photography

See full listing in **Section Two** under **photography**

Yankee Candle Car Museum
5 North St
South Deerfield, MA 01373
413-665-2020; FAX: 413-665-2399

museum

See full listing in **Section Six** under **Massachusetts**

painting

Ace Auto Body & Towing Ltd
65 S Service Rd
Plainview, NY 11803
516-752-6065; FAX: 516-752-1484

mechanical repairs
restorations

See full listing in **Section Two** under **restoration shops**

Auto Restoration by
William R Hahn
Palermo Auto Body
241 Church Rd (rear)
Wexford, PA 15090
412-935-3790 days, 367-2538 eves

restoration

See full listing in **Section Two** under **restoration shops**

Auto Sport Restoration
Alain Breton
110 Rue Du Couvent
St Romain, QC Canada G0Y 1L0
PH/FAX: 418-486-7861

restoration

See full listing in **Section Two** under **restoration shops**

Bay Area Industrial Dry Stripping
151 11th St
Richmond, CA 94801-3523
510-412-9890, 510-805-1887

blasting
paint removal

See full listing in **Section Two** under **rust removal & stripping**

Beckley Auto Restorations Inc
4405 Capital Ave SW
Battle Creek, MI 49015
616-979-3013

restoration

See full listing in **Section Two** under **restoration shops**

Generalists

Benfield's Auto Body 213 Trent St Kernersville, NC 27284 PH/FAX: 910-993-5772	body repair paint

Open shop only. Specialize in paint and body repair.

Cars of the Past 11180 Kinsman Rd Newbury, OH 44065 216-564-2277	restoration

See full listing in **Section Two** under **restoration shops**

Classic Auto 251 SW 5th Ct Pompano Beach, FL 33060 954-786-1687	restoration

See full listing in **Section Two** under **restoration shops**

Classic Auto Rebuilders/CAR Box 9796 Fargo, ND 58106	painting restoration woodwork

See full listing in **Section Two** under **restoration shops**

Classics Plus LTD N7306 Lakeshore Dr N Fond du Lac, WI 54937 414-923-1007	restoration

See full listing in **Section Two** under **steering wheels**

County Auto Restoration 6 Gavin Rd Mont Vernon, NH 03057 603-673-4840	body work brakes restoration woodwork

See full listing in **Section Two** under **restoration shops**

Dan's Restorations PO Box 144, Snake Hill Rd Sand Lake, NY 12153 518-674-2061	restoration

See full listing in **Section Two** under **bodywork**

Davies Corvette 5130 Main St New Port Richey, FL 34653 813-842-8000, 800-236-2383 FAX: 813-846-8216	customizing parts restoration

See full listing in **Section One** under **Corvette**

The Eastwood Company-Tools 580 Lancaster Ave Box 3014 Malvern, PA 19355 800-345-1178, M-F 8 am-midnight Sat & Sun 9 am-5 pm EST FAX: 610-644-0560	paints plating & polishing restoration aids rustproofing stripping tools sandblasters welders

See full listing in **Section Two** under **tools**

Fastech Inc 24 Center Dr Gilberts, IL 60136 708-836-1633; FAX: 708-836-1530	breathing systems

Mail order and open shop. Shop open Monday-Friday 9 to 5.
Specializing in fresh air breathing systems for the painter.

GMS Restorations 20 Wilbraham St Palmer, MA 01069 413-283-3800	restoration

See full listing in **Section Two** under **restoration shops**

Grey Hills Auto Restoration PO Box 630 51 Vail Rd Blairstown, NJ 07825 908-362-8232; FAX: 908-362-6796	restoration service

See full listing in **Section Two** under **restoration shops**

Hatfield Restorations PO Box 846 Canton, TX 75103 PH/FAX: 903-567-6742	restoration

See full listing in **Section Two** under **restoration shops**

High Performance Coatings 550 W 3615 S Salt Lake City, UT 84115 801-262-6807; FAX: 801-262-6307 E-mail: hpcsales@hpcoatings.com	coatings

See full listing in **Section Two** under **exhaust systems**

Hjeltness Restoration Inc 630 Alpine Way Escondido, CA 92029 619-746-9966; FAX: 619-746-7738	restoration service

See full listing in **Section Two** under **restoration shops**

Keilen's Auto Restoring 580 Kelley Blvd (R) North Attleboro, MA 02760 508-699-7768	restoration

See full listing in **Section Two** under **restoration shops**

L & N Olde Car Co 9992 Kinsman Rd PO Box 378 Newbury, OH 44065 216-564-7204; FAX: 216-564-8187	restoration

See full listing in **Section Two** under **restoration shops**

Langley Paint & Body 3560 E Bethel Ln Bloomington, IN 47408 812-336-2244	fiberglass parts painting restoration

See full listing in **Section Two** under **fiberglass parts**

Libbey's Classic Car Restoration Center 137 N Quinsigamond Ave Shrewsbury, MA 01545 PH/FAX: 508-792-1560	bodywork restoration service

See full listing in **Section Two** under **restoration shop**

Masterworks Auto Reconditioning 1127 Brush Run Rd Washington, PA 15301 412-267-3460	restoration

See full listing in **Section Two** under **restoration shops**

McAdam Motorcars Ltd
215 Redoubt Rd
Yorktown, VA 23692
757-898-7805; FAX: 757-898-9019

restoration

See full listing in **Section Two** under **restoration shops**

Must For Rust Co
PO Box 972
Cedar Ridge, CA 95924
888-297-9224 toll-free
PH/FAX: 916-273-3576

rust remover

See full listing in **Section Two** under **rust removal & stripping**

Pilgrim's Special Interest Autos
3888 Hill Rd
Lakeport, CA 95453
PH/FAX: 707-262-1062

bodywork
metal fabrication
paint
restoration

See full listing in **Section Two** under **restoration shops**

Pioneer Valley Model A Ford Inc
81 East St
Easthampton, MA 01027
413-584-8400; FAX: 413-584-7605
E-mail: pvma@aol.com

cars
parts
restoration

See full listing in **Section One** under **Ford '03-'31**

Pro-Strip
2415 W State Blvd
Fort Wayne, IN 46808
219-436-2828; FAX: 219-432-1941

rust removal

See full listing in **Section Two** under **rust removal & stripping**

Products Finishing Corp of CT
523 West Ave
Norwalk, CT 06850
203-853-0444; FAX: 203-853-0445
E-mail: werden@prodfin.com

painting
plating

Both mail order and open shop Monday-Friday 6:45 am-10:30 pm. Powder & spray painting, anodizing and zinc plating.

Redi-Strip Company
100 West Central Ave
Roselle, IL 60172
630-529-2442; FAX: 630-529-3626

abrasive media
paint removal
plastic media
rust removal

See full listing in **Section Two** under **rust removal & stripping**

Restorations Unlimited II Inc
304 Jandus Rd
Cary, IL 60013
847-639-5818

restoration

See full listing in **Section Two** under **restoration shops**

Rick's Relics
Wheeler Rd
Pittsburg, NH 03592
603-538-6612

bodywork
painting
restoration

See full listing in **Section Two** under **restoration shops**

Riverbend Abrasive Blasting
44308 St Rt 36 W
Coshocton, OH 43812-9741
614-622-0867

blasting
painting
polishing
restoration

See full listing in **Section Two** under **rust removal & stripping**

Riverhill Glass & Truck Co
570 Mifflin Rd
Jackson, TN 38301
901-422-4218

glass
paint

Custom, antique auto, truck glass. 67-72 GM truck parts. Buy, sell, trade. "Joshua 24:15." Joey Blackmon, owner.

RMR Restorations Inc
13 Columbia Dr, Unit 1
Amherst, NH 03031
PH/FAX: 603-880-6880 work
603-672-8335 home

restoration

See full listing in **Section Two** under **restoration shops**

Ed Rouze
406 Sheila Blvd
Prattville, AL 36066
334-365-2381

painting guide book

Mail order only. Author of comprehensive how-to automobile painting guide. Details every step from start to finish. Written in easy-to-understand language. Title: *Paint Your Car Like A Pro.* Also author of *555 Restoration, Performance & Appearance Tips,* a compilation of 555 restoration tips in a 120-page book using the same easy-to-read format. Covers everything from air compressors to welding.

T Schmidt
827 N Vernon
Dearborn, MI 48128-1542
313-562-7161

rust removers

See full listing in **Section Two** under **rust removal & stripping**

Stone Barn Inc
202 Rt 46, Box 117
Vienna, NJ 07880
908-637-4444; FAX: 908-637-4290

restoration

See full listing in **Section Two** under **restoration shops**

Stripping Technologies Inc
2949 E Elvira Rd
Tucson, AZ 85706
800-999-0501; FAX: 520-741-9200
E-mail: sti@stripmaster.com

paint removal

See full listing in **Section Two** under **rust removal & stripping**

Vampire-Island Air Products
50 Four Coins Dr
Canonsburg, PA 15317
800-826-7473; FAX: 412-745-9024

air dryers
filters

See full listing in **Section Two** under **restoration shops**

Verne's Chrome Plating Inc
1559 W El Segundo Blvd
Gardena, CA 90249
PH/FAX: 213-754-4126

chrome plating
polishing
powder coating

See full listing in **Section Two** under **plating & polishing**

Willhoit Auto Restoration
1360 Gladys Ave
Long Beach, CA 90804
310-439-3333; FAX: 310-439-3956

engine rebuilding
restoration

See full listing in **Section One** under **Porsche**

paints

Automotive Paints Unlimited
4585 Semora Rd
Roxboro, NC 27573
910-599-5155
E-mail: rayapultd@roxboro.net

acrylic enamels
acrylic lacquers
paints
polyurethanes

Mail order and open shop. Mon-Fri 9 to 5. Supplier of paints for vehicles 1904-present. In business since 1976. The Paint Place.

Benfield's Auto Body
213 Trent St
Kernersville, NC 27284
PH/FAX: 910-993-5772

body repair
paint

See full listing in **Section Two** under **painting**

Color-Ite Refinishing Co
Winning Colors
Rt 69
Bethany, CT 06524
203-393-0240; FAX: 203-393-0873

modern finishes
restoration service

Mail order and open shop. Monday-Friday 9 to 5; Saturday 9 to 2. Original paint colors in modern finishes. Restorations and sales of original 1940 through 48 Lincoln Continentals, full or partial restorations, specializing in early Lincolns.

Fastech Inc
24 Center Dr
Gilberts, IL 60136
708-836-1633; FAX: 708-836-1530

breathing systems

See full listing in **Section Two** under **painting**

Hibernia Auto Restorations Inc
One Maple Terr
Hibernia, NJ 07842
201-627-1882; FAX: 201-627-3503

lacquer
restoration

See full listing in **Section Two** under **restoration shops**

Bill Hirsch Auto Parts
396 Littleton Ave
Newark, NJ 07103
201-642-2404; FAX: 201-642-6161

enamel lacquer
hubcaps
top material

Mail order and open shop. Monday-Friday 8 to 4. Manufacturer of hubcaps for Cadillac, Chevrolet, Buick, Packard, Ford, Pierce-Arrow. Engine enamels for most American cars, exhaust and manifold paints, gas tank sealer, gas preservative, miracle rust-proof paint, leather, broadcloth, Bedford cloth, top material, carpet, carpet sets, car covers, convertible tops, much more.

Imperial Restoration Inc
308 Lockport St
Lemont, IL 60439
630-257-5822; FAX: 630-257-5892

engine enamels
gas tank sealer
paint/rust remover
rust preventives

See full listing in **Section Two** under **restoration aids**

Metro Authentic Finishes
2576B West Point Ave
College Park, GA 30337
404-767-3378

paint

See full listing in **Section One** under **Corvette**

Must For Rust Co
PO Box 972
Cedar Ridge, CA 95924
888-297-9224 toll-free
PH/FAX: 916-273-3576

rust remover

See full listing in **Section Two** under **rust removal & stripping**

Plasti-Kote Co Inc
1000 Lake Rd
Medina, OH 44256
800-431-5928; 330-725-4511, ext 320
FAX: 330-723-3674

engine enamels
trunk paints

Engine enamels, hi-heat (1200 degrees) paint. Trunk paints, sandable (lacquer) primer. Exact match exterior paint (1975-present). Nitrocellulose lacquers. Metal flake & candy apple colors. Web site: http://www.plasti~kote.com

PM Industries
442 Ridge Rd
West Milford, NJ 07480
800-833-8933; FAX: 201-728-2117

chassis coatings
permanent rust sealers

See full listing in **Section Two** under **rustproofing**

Quanta Restoration & Preservation Products
45 Cissel Dr
North East, MD 21901
410-658-5700; FAX: 410-658-5758

fan belts
gas tanks

See full listing in **Section Two** under **chassis parts**

Rocky's Advance Formula
40 Abbott Ave
Danbury, CT 06810
800-752-0245

wax hardener

See full listing in **Section Two** under **car care products**

Ed Rouze
406 Sheila Blvd
Prattville, AL 36066
334-365-2381

painting guide book

See full listing in **Section Two** under **painting**

Tar Heel Parts Inc
PO Box 2604
Matthews, NC 28106-2604
800-322-1957; 704-845-1847 (local)
FAX: 704-845-5447

buffing supplies

See full listing in **Section Two** under **plating & polishing**

petroliana

GA$OLINE

Al's Garage & Marine Repair Inc
PO Box 156
Suquamish, WA 98392-0156
PH/FAX: 206-780-1223

accessories
apparel
tools

See full listing in **Section Two** under **accessories**

Antiques Warehouse
Michael J Welch
3700 Rt 6
Eastham, MA 02642
508-255-1437

automobilia
bikes
toy trucks

See full listing in **Section Two** under **models & toys**

Asheville DieCast 1412 Brevard Rd Asheville, NC 28806-9560 800-343-4685; 704-667-9690 FAX: 704-667-1110 E-mail: asheville-diecast@worldnet.att.net	**banks** **models**

See full listing in **Section Two** under **models & toys**

Benkin & Co 14 E Main St Tipp City, OH 45371 513-667-5975; FAX: 513-667-5729	**gas pumps** **neon clocks** **neon signs**

See full listing in **Section Two** under **automobilia**

Berliner Classic Motorcars Inc 1975 Stirling Rd Dania, FL 33004 954-923-7271; FAX: 954-926-3306	**automobilia** **car dealer** **motorcycles**

See full listing in **Section Two** under **car dealers**

Brisson Enterprises PO Box 1595 Dearborn, MI 48121 313-584-3577	**lead**

See full listing in **Section Two** under **car care products**

Central Florida Auto Festival **& Toy Expo** 1420 N Galloway Rd Lakeland, FL 33810 941-686-8320	**auto festival** **toy expo**

See full listing in **Section Two** under **auctions & events**

"Check The Oil!" Magazine PO Box 937 Powell, OH 43065-0937 614-848-5038; FAX: 614-436-4760	**magazine**

"Check The Oil!" magazine is a bi-monthly publication for enthusiasts and collectors of the memorabilia and history of the petroleum industry. Anything associated with the oil and gas business of days gone by, eg: gas pumps, globes, signs, maps, oil bottles, etc. Subscription rate: $20 US; $30 Canada; $37 overseas.

Classic Transportation 3667 Mahoning Ave Youngstown, OH 44515 216-793-3026; FAX: 216-793-9729	**automobilia**

See full listing in **Section Two** under **automobilia**

Classical Gas Antique Auto **Museum & Sales** 245 E Collins Eaton, CO 80615 800-453-7955, 970-454-1373 FAX: 970-454-1368	**car dealer** **museum**

See full listing in **Section Two** under **car dealers**

Jim Estrup The Plateman Box 908, RR 3 Kennebunk, ME 04043 207-985-4800; FAX: 207-985-TAGS	**license plates**

See full listing in **Section Two** under **license plates**

Frontier Tank Center Inc 3800 Congress Pkwy Richfield, OH 44286 216-659-3888; FAX: 216-659-9410	**automobilia** **globes** **pumps** **signs**

Mail order and open shop. Petroliana signs, globes, pumps, service station advertising.

Steve Jelf-14 Box 200, Rt 5 Arkansas City, KS 67005 316-442-1626 after 2 pm, CST	**signs**

See full listing in **Section Two** under **automobilia**

Dave Lincoln Box 331 Yorklyn, DE 19736 610-444-4144, PA	**license plates**

See full listing in **Section Two** under **license plates**

George & Denise Long 915 E Court St Marion, NC 28752 704-652-9229 (24 hrs w/recorder)	**automobilia**

See full listing in **Section Two** under **automobilia**

Max Neon Design Group 19807 Sussex Dr St Clair Shores, MI 48081-3257 810-773-5000; FAX: 810-772-6224	**custom face logos** **neon clocks**

See full listing in **Section Two** under **automobilia**

Mc Intyre Auctions PO Box 60 E Dixfield, ME 04227 207-562-4443; FAX: 207-562-4576 E-mail: info@classicford.com	**auctions** **automobilia** **literature** **petroliana**

See full listing in **Section Two** under **auctions & events**

Red Crown Auto Parts 1720 Rupert NE Grand Rapids, MI 49505 616-361-9887	**automobilia** **petroliana**

Mail order, swap meets. Specializing in petroliana, automotive memorabilia, auto promotional items, dealer giveaways and oil company collectibles.

The Red House Collectible Toys 5961 Dry Ridge Rd Cincinnati, OH 45252 PH/FAX: 513-385-5534	**toys**

See full listing in **Section Two** under **models & toys**

Ron Scobie Enterprises 7676 120th St N Hugo, MN 55038 612-426-1023	**gas pump parts**

Mail order only. Manufacturing parts for antique gasoline pumps and air meters. I also make "Master" oil bottle spouts from the original machines.

Scott Signal Co 8368 W Farm Rd 84 Willard, MO 65781 417-742-5040	**stoplights**

See full listing in **Section Two** under **automobilia**

Generalists

Michael J Welch 3700 Rt 6, RR 2 Eastham, MA 02642 508-255-1437	automobilia **pedal cars** **toy trucks**

See full listing in **Section Two** under **models & toys**

Zephyrhills Festivals & Auction Inc PO Box 848 Odessa, FL 33556 813-920-7206; FAX: 813-920-8512	**auction** **swap meet**

See full listing in **Section Two** under **auctions & events**

Automobilia Shop 48 Belmont St Melrose, MA 02176 617-665-1992; FAX: 617-665-8018	artwork **books** **models**

See full listing in **Section Two** under **artwork**

Boop Photography 2347 Derry St Harrisburg, PA 17104-2728 717-564-8533 E-mail: msboop@paonline.com	**photography**

Mail order and open shop. Sunday-Saturday, 9 am-9 pm EST. Automotive photography: drag racing, classics, street rods. Former car club photographer. Nikon equipment. 5 years' experience. Degree in photography.

CalAutoArt 1520 S Lyon St Santa Ana, CA 92705 714-835-9512; FAX: 714-835-9513 E-mail: 71460,1146@compuserve.com	automobilia **photography**

See full listing in **Section Two** under **automobilia**

Larry Couzens Photography 16 East 17th St New York City, NY 10003 212-620-9790; FAX: 212-620-9791	**photography**

Specializing in custom photography of your car. This service is for individual owners, car clubs or businesses. Color, black & white or antique toned prints, all sizes. Areas covered: NY, NJ, CT, plus other states by special arrangement. 20 years' professional experience. Special photographic packages for car clubs. Free brochure available.

Rick Graves Photography 441 East Columbine, Suite H Santa Ana, CA 92707 714-662-2623; FAX: 714-540-7843	**photographic art**

See full listing in **Section Two** under **racing**

Richard Hamilton 28 E 46th St Indianapolis, IN 46205 317-283-1902	**sales literature**

See full listing in **Section Two** under **literature dealers**

The Klemantaski Collection 65 High Ridge Rd, Suite 219 Stamford, CT 06905 PH/FAX: 203-968-2970 E-mail: klemcoll@aol.com	books **photography**

Mail order only. Motor racing photography by Louis Klemantaski, Nigel Snowdon and Edward Eves. We also publish books of our photographs. We supply enthusiasts, collectors, authors and publishers worldwide.

LA Ltd Design Graphics 822A S McDuffie St Anderson, SC 29624 PH/FAX: 864-231-7715	artwork **design** **greeting cards**

See full listing in **Section Two** under **automobilia**

The Last Precinct Police Museum Rt 6, Box 345B (62 Highway West) Eureka Springs, AR 72632 501-253-4948; FAX: 501-253-4949	**museum**

See full listing in **Section Six** under **Arkansas**

David Lawrence Gallery PO Box 3702 Beverly Hills, CA 90212 310-278-0882; FAX: 310-278-0883	artwork **drawings** **photography**

See full listing in **Section Two** under **artwork**

Moonlight Ink 2736 Summerfield Rd Winter Park, FL 32792-5112 407-628-8857; FAX: 407-671-5008	**art**

See full listing in **Section One** under **Porsche**

Practical Images PO Box 245 Haddam, CT 06438-0245 860-704-0525 E-mail: leswho@iconn.net	photo scanning **video conversions**

Mail order only. Digital photo scanning, photos, slides, negatives, artwork, International VHS video conversions, freelance 35mm photography and digital photography (for Internet, advertisments, desk top publishing, personal usage, etc). Please write for more information.

Silver Image Photographics 3102 Vestal Pkwy E Vestal, NY 13850 607-797-8795	business cards **photo car cards** **photofinishing**

See full listing in **Section Two** under **automobilia**

Southern Classics 10301 Windtree Ln Charlotte, NC 28215 704-532-9870	appraisals **photographs**

See full listing in **Section Two** under **appraisals**

Richard Spiegelman Productions Inc 19 Guild Hall Dr Scarborough, ONT Canada M1R 3Z7 416-759-1644	**photography** **slides**

See full listing in **Section Four** under **information sources**

Sunflower Studios
8 Scottsdale Rd
South Burlington, VT 05403
802-862-3768

photography

Fine art automobile photography on location. Specialists in car show photography.

Peter Tytla Artist
PO Box 43
East Lyme, CT 06333-0043
860-739-7105

photographic
collages

See full listing in **Section Two** under **artwork**.

Wheels of Time
PO Box 1218
Studio City, CA 91604
800-Wheels of Time

photography

Mail order only. Put yourself into one of our authentic photographic scenes, driving a period classic. Put yourself behind Wheels of Time. We offer an expanding line of products, specializing in sales to car clubs and museums. We also produce truly memorable and powerful commemorative items for your special events. Free color brochure.

 plaques   Sterling.

Anacortes Brass Works Ltd
PO Box 10
Anacortes, WA 98221
360-293-4515; FAX: 360-293-4516

brass castings

See full listing in **Section Two** under **castings**.

ISG AUTOMOTIVE
General Motors
Plastic Automotive Reproductions
(NOSR)

Initial Product Offering of Buick Parts

Part# 1171771 1956 Hubcap Center
Medallion
Part# 1171771 1957 Hubcap Center
Medallion

- ISG Automotive manufactures NOSR products under GM Reproduction Division License.
- ISG Automotive is dedicated to bringing you concourse quality at affordable prices.
- All parts are made in America using GM dies when possible, if not available, ISG Automotive has dies made by American craftsmen.
- We want your "want list" for Buick products from 1936-1970.
- Our products are distributed through authorized GM Resellers and GM New Car Parts Departments. Call for our authorized distributor or to submit your want list.

ISG Automotive, 1-800-266-4744, 5075

Shoreham Place, Suite 280, San Diego, CA 92122
Fax: 452-8500; E-Mail: isgauto@cnsii.com

GM **Restoration Parts**

Bright Displays
1314 Lakemont Dr
Pittsburgh, PA 15243
412-279-7037

neon signs

See full listing in **Section Two** under **automobilia**.

Cruising International Inc
1000 N Beach St
Daytona Beach, FL 32117
800-676-8961, 904-254-8753
FAX: 904-255-2460

automobilia
decals
license plates
novelties
porcelain signs

See full listing in **Section Two** under **accessories**.

Nostalgic Reflections
PO Box 350
Veradale, WA 99037
PH/FAX: 509-226-3522

dash glass
decals
porcelain radiator
medallions

Mail order and open shop. Shop open Monday-Saturday from 8 to 6. Reproduction serial plates, decals, door sill plates, porcelain medallions, instrument faces, dash glass and special castings and plating.

O'Brien Truckers
5 Perry Hill
North Grafton, MA 01536-1532
508-839-3033; FAX: 508-839-9490
E-mail: obrien_dennis@emc.com

accessories
belt buckles
plaques
valve covers

Mail order only. Cast aluminum car club plaques, belt buckles & key chains. Air cleaners & nostalgic engine accessories. Complete line of No Club Lone Wolf items, license plate toppers, valley covers, Hemi valve covers, lakepipe caps and many other nostalgic accessories.

Photo Plaque Design
16508 McKinley St
Belton, MO 64012
PH/FAX: 816-331-4073

car show plaques
dash plaques

Specializing in custom engraved car event awards and participant dash plaques. Your cars and ideas can be captured on a one of a kind photo engraved plaque to commemorate your event. Our photo engraving has the highest resolution available today for remarkable, finely detailed, engraved images. Send SASE for catalogue and sample.

Toy Sense Inc
257 North Amphlett Blvd
San Mateo, CA 94401-1805
415-579-7825; FAX: 415-579-7827
E-mail: toysense@netwizard.net

games
toys

See full listing in **Section Two** under **automobilia**.

plastic parts

The Bumper Doctor
9414 E San Salvador #167
Scottsdale, AZ 85258
602-314-1349
E-mail: bumperdoc@aol.com

bumpers
parts

We train individuals to repair all automotive plastic parts. Bumpers are our main business. We recycle all urethane and plastic bumpers to as-new condition.

ISG Automotive Co | repro parts
5075 Shoreham Pl, #280
San Diego, CA 92122
619-452-2100; FAX: 619-452-8500

Dealing in General Motors external plastic reproduction parts for all GM autos 1935-1975, Cadillac, Chevrolet, LaSalle, Oldsmobile and Pontiac. All parts licensed and approved by General Motors. All parts made in USA.

See our ad on page 350

plating & polishing

A & A Plating Inc | plating
9400 E Wilson Rd | polishing
Independence, MO 64053
816-833-0045; FAX: 816-254-1517

Mail order and open shop. Monday-Friday 7 am to 6 pm, Sat 8 am to 12 pm. Chrome, nickel and copper plating for steel, aluminum, die cast and brass, cast iron, potmetal. Polishing of stainless steel, brass, aluminum, copper, nickel and silver.

Advanced Plating & Powder Coating | plating
955 E Trinity Ln | powder coating
Nashville, TN 37207
800-588-6686; FAX: 615-262-7935

Dealing in chrome, 24 kt gold, black chrome, nickel, acid copper and copper plating and powder coating. Complete restoration service, all work guaranteed.

American Plastic Chrome | replating plastic
1398 Mar Ann Dr
Westland, MI 48185
313-721-1967 days
313-261-4454 eves

Specializing in replating plastic interior parts for most cars from late 50s to early 70s using the original vacuum metalizing process. This multi-step process will restore your plastic parts to their original shine & brilliance. Replating instrument gauge cluster bezels, armrest bases, domelight bezels, etc, for most cars from late 50s to early 70s.

Automist Inc | waxes
PO Box 155
East Lansing, MI 48826
517-336-4443; FAX: 517-336-0178

Mail order and open shop. Premium car care products including Automist™ automotive detailing mist. Mirage™ Premium Carnauba microwax. Condition™ rubber/vinyl treatment. Alloy™ Premium wheel cleaner and other accessory items.

Bassett Classic Restoration | parts
2616 Sharon St, Suite D | plating
Kenner, LA 70062 | restoration
PH/FAX: 504-469-2982 (have auto | service
switching device)

See full listing in **Section One** under **Rolls-Royce/Bentley**

Castle Metal Finishing | chrome restoration
15 Broad St | metal polishing
Hudson, MA 01749 | plating
508-562-7294

Chrome restorations, zinc & cadmium plating, metal polishing & buffing.

Caswell Electroplating in Miniature | plating kits
4336 Rt 31
Palmyra, NY 14522
315-597-5140; FAX: 315-597-1457
E-mail: caswell@vivanet.com

Mail order only. Professional quality plating kits for chrome, nickel, black oxide, anodizing, zinc and chromating, silver and gold, copper. Tanks, heaters, chemicals and manuals. Complete line of professional buffing and polishing tools and supplies.

Chevy Shop | custom castings
338 Main Ave | parts
Box 75
Milledgeville, IL 61051
815-225-7565

See full listing in **Section One** under **Chevrolet**

Chrome Masters | chrome plating
1109 W Orange Ave, Unit D | pot metal
Tallahassee, FL 32310 | restoration
904-576-2100

Mail order and open shop. Monday-Saturday 8 am-6 pm. Restoration of pitted pot metal and chrome plating for all vintage, antique car buffs.

Classic Auto Rebuilders/CAR | painting
Box 9796 | restoration
Fargo, ND 58106 | woodwork

See full listing in **Section Two** under **restoration shops**

Classic Auto Restoration | plating
437 Greene St | polishing
Buffalo, NY 14212 | restoration
716-896-6663

See full listing in **Section Two** under **restoration shops**

Classics Plus LTD | restoration
N7306 Lakeshore Dr
N Fond du Lac, WI 54937
414-923-1007

See full listing in **Section Two** under **steering wheels**

County Auto Restoration | body work
6 Gavin Rd | brakes
Mont Vernon, NH 03057 | restoration
603-673-4840 | woodwork

See full listing in **Section Two** under **restoration shops**

Custom Chrome Plating Inc | electroplating
963 Mechanic St | plating
PO Box 125 | polishing
Grafton, OH 44044
216-926-3116

Mail order and open shop. Monday-Thursday 8-5, Friday 8-4. Polishing, buffing and electroplating. Chrome, nickel, copper plating on customer's parts.

Custom Plating | bumper specialist
3030 Alta Ridge Way | chrome plating
Snellville, GA 30278 | parts
770-736-1118

Chrome plating 34 years. Antique bumper specialist, straightening included. Engine, suspension, interior, exterior parts. Polishing and straightening of aluminum and stainless trim.

D & D Plastic Chrome Plating Jim & Marty Price 4534 S Detroit Ave Toledo, OH 43614 419-389-1748	**chroming** **plating**

Mon-Sat. We rechrome your plastic or fiberglass parts such as dash bezels, arm rests, etc. Put the interior of your collector car back to the original finish. We have a 3 week turnaround.

Dalmar 11759 S Cleveland Ave, Suite 28 Ft Myers, FL 33907 941-275-6540; FAX: 941-275-1731 E-mail: dalmar@peganet.com	**electroplating** **plating supplies**

Electroplating and electroforming equipment, chemicals, supplies and kits. Featuring chrome, nickel, gold, copper, silver, brass, bronze and cadmium plating. Our kits will plate on metallic and non-metallic surfaces. We manufacture both brush and tank plating kits. Free catalog.

Fini-Finish Metal Finishing 24657 Mound Rd Warren, MI 48091 810-758-0050; FAX: 810-758-0054	**plating** **polishing** **pot metal repair**

Polishing and buffing on all metals. Copper, nickel, chrome & cadmium plating on all metals. Repair work on pot metal (zinc die cast) our specialty.

Jay M Fisher Acken Dr 4-B Clark, NJ 07066 908-388-6442	**radiator caps** **sidemount mirrors**

See full listing in **Section Two** under **accessories**.

Haneline Products Co PO Box 430 Morongo Valley, CA 92256 619-363-6597; FAX: 619-363-7321	**gauges** **instrument panels** **stainless parts** **trim parts**

See full listing in **Section Two** under **instruments**.

Impala Bob's Inc 9006 E Fannin, Dept HVAA12 Mesa, AZ 85207 602-986-0286; FAX: 602-986-3126 order line: 800-209-0678 toll-free FAX: 800-716-6237	**parts** **restoration**

See full listing in **Section One** under **Chevrolet**.

J & L Industries 6 Gem Ave Los Gatos, CA 95032 408-356-3943	**polishing**

Mail order only. Dealing in stainless trim straightening and polishing. Also aluminum castings polished.

King's Bumper Co Inc 1 Ontario Ave New Hartford, NY 13413 315-732-8988; FAX: 315-732-2602	**chrome plating**

Mail order and open shop. Monday-Friday, 8 am-5 pm. Chrome plating.

Martin's of Philadelphia 7327 State Rd Philadelphia, PA 19136 215-331-5565; FAX: 215-331-7113	**buffing** **copper plating** **metal grinding**

I specialize in copper plating, nickel and chrome, metal grinding

buffing of antique, classic auto parts, also boats, barber chairs, etc. Any collectible for refinishing of all auto parts for all years, makes and models.

Paul's Chrome Plating Inc 341 Mars-Valencia Rd Mars, PA 16046 800-245-8679; 412-625-3135 FAX: 412-625-3060	**repair** **restoration**

Mail order and open shop. Monday-Friday 8 to 5; Wednesday evening 7-8:30 pm; Saturday by appointment only. Triple plate rechroming, repair and restoration of all metal parts, including pot metal (zinc die cast).

Pot Metal Restorations 4794 C Woodlane Cir Tallahassee, FL 32303 904-562-3847	**pot metal restoring** **rechroming**

Mail order only. Pitted pot metal restoration and rechroming.

Precision Pot Metal/ **Bussie Restoration Inc** 1008 Loring Ave #28 Orange Park, FL 32073 904-269-8788	**pot metal** **restoration**

Mail order and open shop. Mon-Fri 8-4:30. Restoration of pitted or broken pot metal parts. Our exclusive process fills all pits without grinding.

Products Finishing Corp of CT 523 West Ave Norwalk, CT 06850 203-853-0444; FAX: 203-853-0445 E-mail: werden@prodfin.com	**painting** **plating**

See full listing in **Section Two** under **painting**.

Protrim Inc 438 Calle San Pablo, Unit 1 Camarillo, CA 93012 805-987-2086; FAX: 805-389-5375	**plating**

Dealing in plastic metalizing, we metalize raw plastic parts in chrome for exterior use on cars.

Qual Krom-Great Lakes Plant 4725-A Iroquois Ave Erie, PA 16511 800-673-2427; FAX: 814-899-8632	**plating** **repairs** **restoration**

Mail order and open shop. Monday-Friday 8-5, Saturday by appointment. Custom restoration plating of your parts, guaranteed show quality only. We do all repairs necessary to restore your steel, zinc die castings & stainless steel parts.

Riverbend Abrasive Blasting 44308 St Rt 36 W Coshocton, OH 43812-9741 614-622-0867	**blasting** **painting** **polishing** **restoration**

See full listing in **Section Two** under **rust removal & stripping**.

Speed & Sport Chrome Plating Inc 404 Broadway Houston, TX 77012 713-921-0235	**chrome plating**

Mail order and open shop. Monday-Friday 8-5:30 CST. Antique cars & trucks, muscle cars, race cars, show cars, street cars. Specializing in chrome plating on all the above. 15 day service, all work guaranteed. Triple show chrome.

Standard Abrasives Motor Sports
9351 Deering Ave
Chatsworth, CA 91311
800-383-6001, 818-718-7070, ext 371
FAX: 800-546-6867

abrasives

See full listing in **Section Two** under **restoration aids**

Star Chrome
4009 Ogden Ave
Chicago, IL 60623
312-521-9000

plating
polishing

Mail order and open shop. Monday-Saturday 6 to 12 noon. Chrome, gold, and nickel plating and polishing for antique and classic cars, street rods and motorcycles. Specializing in pot metal repair and restoration of the highest quality. Work taken only in the am. All work show quality and guaranteed. In business since 1970.

Tar Heel Parts Inc
PO Box 2604
Matthews, NC 28106-2604
800-322-1957; 704-845-1847 (local)
FAX: 704-845-5447

buffing supplies

Mail order only. Tar Heel Parts Inc is a buffing specialty and auto restoration supply company. We offer Baldor buffers, buffing supplies, arbors and mandrels, abrasives, Clecos (wedge lock), flanging pliers, Seymour paints, sandblasters, bead blast cabinets, Rotabroach spot weld cutters and more. Please call for more information and a complimentary catalog.

The Wheel Shoppe
18011 Fourteen Mile Rd
Fraser, MI 48026
810-415-7171; FAX: 810-415-7181
E-mail: jgs2nd@aol.com

performance parts
welding
wheel repair

See full listing in **Section Two** under **wheels & wheelcovers**

Verne's Chrome Plating Inc
1559 W El Segundo Blvd
Gardena, CA 90249
PH/FAX: 213-754-4126

chrome plating
polishing
powder coating

Specializing in restoration quality chrome plating. Also polishing and powder coating.

racing

356 Enterprises
Vic & Barbara Skirmants
27244 Ryan Rd
Warren, MI 48092
810-575-9544; FAX: 810-558-3616

parts

See full listing in **Section One** under **Porsche**

Action Performance Inc
1619 Lakeland Ave
Bohemia, NY 11716
516-244-7100; FAX: 516-244-7172

accessories

See full listing in **Section Two** under **accessories**

Air Flow Research
10490 Ilex Ave
Pacoima, CA 91331
818-890-0616; FAX: 818-890-0490

cylinder heads

See full listing in **Section One** under **Chevrolet**

Alan's Axles
2300 Congress Ave
Clearwater, FL 34623
800-741-0452; 813-784-0452

axles

See full listing in **Section Two** under **chassis parts**

AM Racing Inc
PO Box 451
Danvers, MA 01923
PH/FAX: 508-774-4613

race prep
sales
vintage racing

Mail order and open shop. Open Monday-Friday 8 am to 5 pm. Sales, search, preparation and showing of vintage, historic, classic and special interest cars, especially racing from the 1940s through 1960s.

American Autowire Systems Inc
150 Cooper Rd, Unit C-8
Dept HVAA
West Berlin, NJ 08091
800-482-WIRE; FAX: 609-753-0353

battery cables
electrical systems
switches/
components

See full listing in **Section Two** under **street rods**

Andy's Classic Mustangs
18502 E Sprague
Greenacres, WA 99016
509-924-9824

parts
service

See full listing in **Section One** under **Mustang**

Skip Barber Racing School
29 Brook St
Lakeville, CT 06039
860-435-1300; FAX: 860-435-1321
E-mail: speed@skipbarber.com

racing school

The Skip Barber Racing School, the world's largest, offers on-track racing programs for experienced vintage competitors and aspiring racers alike, ranging from the 3 hour *Introduction to Racing (sm)* to the industry standard *Three Day Competition Course (sm)*. Classes are taught in open-wheel Formula Dodge race cars and are available nationwide. Skip Barber Racing also offers advanced street driving schools, teaching street-based defensive driving techniques. Call for details.

Bonneville Sports Inc
12461 Country Ln
Santa Ana, CA 92705
714-508-9724; FAX: 714-508-9725

accessories
clothing

See full listing in **Section Two** under **apparel**

Boop Photography
2347 Derry St
Harrisburg, PA 17104-2728
717-564-8533
E-mail: msboop@paonline.com

photography

See full listing in **Section Two** under **photography**

BPE Racing Heads
702 Dunn Way
Placentia, CA 92870
714-572-6072; FAX: 714-572-6073

cylinder heads

See full listing in **Section Two** under **machine work**

Class Glass and Performance Inc
101 Winston St
Cumberland, MD 21502
800-774-3456; FAX: 301-777-7044

fiberglass bodies
parts

See full listing in **Section Two** under **fiberglass parts**

Cobra Restorers Ltd 3099 Carter Dr Kennesaw, GA 30144 770-427-0020; FAX: 770-427-8658	parts restoration service

See full listing in **Section One** under **Cobra**

Coffey's Classic Transmissions 2817 Hollis Ft Worth, TX 76111 817-834-8740; 817-439-1611	transmissions

See full listing in **Section Two** under **transmissions**

Custom Auto Radiator 495 Hyson Rd Jackson, NJ 08527 908-928-3700; FAX: 908-364-7474	radiators

See full listing in **Section Two** under **radiators**

Diablo Engineering 8776 East Shea, #B3A-109 Scottsdale, AZ 85260 PH/FAX: 602-391-2569	engines parts

See full listing in **Section One** under **Porsche**

Doug's Corvette Service 11634 Vanowen St North Hollywood, CA 91605 818-765-9117	race prep repairs

See full listing in **Section One** under **Corvette**

George's Speed Shop 716 Brantly Ave Dayton, OH 45404 513-233-0353; FAX: 513-236-3501	machine shop race engine parts race engine building

Open shop only. Stock to full race engine parts and building. Full machine shop service. Two in-house dyno cells.

Georgia Marketing PO Box 570 Winder, GA 30680 770-868-1042; FAX: 770-867-0786 E-mail: peachgmp@mindsering.com	die cast replicas

See full listing in **Section Two** under **models & toys**

Grand Prix Classics Inc 7456 La Jolla Blvd La Jolla, CA 92037 619-459-3500; FAX: 619-459-3512	racing cars sports cars

Open shop only. Mon-Fri 9 am to 5 pm, weekends by appointment only. The purchase and sale of historic sports and racing cars for 50s-60s Porsche, Mercedes-Benz (pre-80s), Jaguar (pre-80s), pre-80 Alfa Romeo, race cars, American makes pre-80.

Rick Graves Photography 441 East Columbine, Suite H Santa Ana, CA 92707 714-662-2623; FAX: 714-540-7843	photographic art

Mail order only. Limited edition photographic art for vintage Indy type race cars. Example: Parnelli Jones 1st rear engine Lotus Ford.

Gromm Racing Heads 666-J Stockton Ave San Jose, CA 95126 408-287-1301	cylinder heads racing parts

Open shop Mon-Fri 8:30-5:30. Specializing in hi-performance (racing, RV & vintage) cylinder heads and racing parts sales.

Historic Video Archives PO Box 189-VA Cedar Knolls, NJ 07927-0189	videotapes

See full listing in **Section Two** under **automobilia**

Hooker Headers 1024 W Brooks St PO Box 4030 Ontario, CA 91761 909-983-5871	exhaust systems

See full listing in **Section Two** under **exhaust systems**

Edward L Hunt, Automotive Miniaturist 1409 Yale Dr Hollywood, FL 33021 954-966-0366	custom miniatures

See full listing in **Section Two** under **artwork**

Hunters Custom Automotive 975 Main St Nashville, TN 37206 615-227-6584; FAX: 615-227-4897	accessories engine parts fiberglass products

See full listing in **Section Two** under **accessories**

Inland Empire Driveline Service Inc 4035 E Guasti Rd, #301 Ontario, CA 91761 800-800-0109; FAX: 909-390-3038	drive shafts pinion yokes

See full listing in **Section Two** under **machine work**

Koffel's Place II 740 River Rd Huron, OH 44839 419-433-4410; FAX: 419-433-2166	engine rebuilding machine shop

See full listing in **Section Two** under **engine rebuilding**

Krem Engineering 10204 Perry Hwy Meadville, PA 16335 814-724-4806	engine rebuilding repairs restoration

See full listing in **Section Two** under **restoration shops**

Lindskog Balancing 1170 Massachusetts Ave Boxborough, MA 01719-1415 508-263-2040; FAX: 508-263-4035	engine balancing

See full listing in **Section Two** under **engine rebuilding**

M & R Products 1940 SW Blvd Vineland, NJ 08360 609-696-9450; FAX: 609-696-4999	hardware tie-downs

See full listing in **Section Two** under **accessories**

Main Attractions PO Box 4923 Chatsworth, CA 91313 818-709-9855; FAX: 818-998-0906	posters videos

See full listing in **Section Four** under **information sources**

Generalists

Marcovicci-Wenz Engineering Inc 33 Comac Loop Ronkonkoma, NY 11779 516-467-9040; FAX: 516-467-9041	**Cosworth engines**

Mail order and open shop. Open Monday-Saturday 8 am to 6 pm. Specializing in engine parts and services for road racing motors of the 60s, 70s and 80s. Also Cosworth and Ferrari.

McGee Motorsports Group 29121 Arnold Dr Sonoma, CA 95476 707-996-1112; FAX: 707-996-9148	**race prep** **restoration**

Open Mon-Fri 8:30-6, often weekends. Located at Sears Point International Raceway. Modern and vintage race car preparation, fabrication, restoration. Car and driver on-track development and training. Custom modifications or authentic restorations. Modification, fabrication and development for current race cars.

Mid Valley Engineering 16637 N 21st St Phoenix, AZ 85022 602-482-1251; FAX: 602-788-0812	**machine work** **parts** **restoration**

See full listing in **Section Two** under **transmissions**

Mitchell Manufacturing 6 Acorn Ct Novato, CA 94949-6603 800-238-5093	**overdrives**

See full listing in **Section One** under **Ford '03-'31**

Moonlight Ink 2736 Summerfield Rd Winter Park, FL 32792-5112 407-628-8857; FAX: 407-671-5008	**art**

See full listing in **Section One** under **Porsche**

Moroso Performance Products Inc 80 Carter Dr Guilford, CT 06437 203-453-6571; FAX: 203-453-6906	**accessories** **parts**

Manufacturer of quality performance parts and accessories.

Motorsports Racing 914 S Santa Fe #101 Vista, CA 92084 619-630-0547; FAX: 619-630-3085	**accessories** **apparel** **art**

See full listing in **Section Two** under **apparel**

National Drivetrain Inc 3125 S Ashland Ave #201 Chicago, IL 60608 800-507-4327; FAX: 312-376-9135	**differential parts** **transmission parts**

See full listing in **Section Two** under **transmissions**

OJ Rallye Automotive PO Box 540 N 6808 Hwy OJ Plymouth, WI 53073 414-893-2531; FAX: 414-893-6800	**accessories** **car care products** **lighting parts**

See full listing in **Section Two** under **lighting equipment**

Orlandi Trailer 3120 Moorpark Ave San Jose, CA 95117 408-296-5748; FAX: 408-247-1219	**trailers**

See full listing in **Section Two** under **trailers**

Power Effects 1800H Industrial Park Dr Grand Haven, MI 49417 616-847-4200; FAX: 616-847-4210	**exhaust systems**

See full listing in **Section Two** under **exhaust systems**

Pronyne PO Box 1492 Pawtucket, RI 02862-1492 401-725-1118	**museum**

See full listing in **Section Six** under **Rhode Island**

Ram Air Inc 17134 Wood Melvindale, MI 48122 313-382-9036; FAX: 313-382-9480	**engine balancing** **engine blueprinting** **performance** **products**

See full listing in **Section One** under **Pontiac**

RD Enterprises Ltd 290 Raub Rd Quakertown, PA 18951 215-538-9323; FAX: 215-538-0158 E-mail: rdent@rdent.com	**parts**

See full listing in **Section One** under **Lotus**

Reider Racing Enterprises Inc 12351 Universal Dr Taylor, MI 48180 800-522-2707, 313-946-1330 FAX: 313-946-8672	**axle components**

Mail order and open shop. Monday-Friday 8:30-7, Saturday 9-2. Carrying a full line of high-performance axle components for most domestic and many import cars and light trucks. Stocking a wide variety of axle components and promising same day shipping, we can help to keep your project on track. Whether your plans include a rebuild of your classic car or modifying a Jeep for aggressive off-roading, we can supply all your gearing needs.

Replicarz 99 State St Rutland, VT 05701 802-747-7151 E-mail: replicarz@aol.com	**books** **kits** **models** **videos**

Mail order only. Die cast miniature models, plastic model kits, books, videos. We specialize in racing, current and Vintage Formula 1, Indy, DTM, WSC, LeMans and more.

Riechmann Motorsport Promotions 38511 Frontier Ave Palmdale, CA 93550 805-273-7089	**racing events**

Organizing motorsport racing events featuring stock cars, vintage sprint cars, as well as other forms of oval and road racing for cars and motorcycles. Also, set-up of car displays. Promoters of the Walt James Vintage Sprint and Midget gathering every Thanksgiving weekend at Willow Springs Motorsports Park.

Garry Roberts & Co 922 Sunset Dr Costa Mesa, CA 92627 888-FERRAR; FAX: 714-650-2730	**cars** **parts** **service**

See full listing in **Section One** under **Ferrari**

Ross' Automotive Machine Co Inc 1763 N Main St Niles, OH 44446 330-544-4466	**racing engines** **rebuilding**

See full listing in **Section Two** under **engine rebuilding**

Simons Balancing & Machine 1987 Ashley River Rd Charleston, SC 29407 803-766-3911; FAX: 803-766-9003	machine work

See full listing in **Section Two** under **machine work**

Speed & Spares America (IPM Group) 16123 Runnymede St, Unit H Van Nuys, CA 91406-2952 818-781-1711; FAX: 818-781-8842	parts racing equipment

See full listing in **Section Two** under **comprehensive parts**

Speed Service Inc 3049 W Irving Park Rd Chicago, IL 60618 312-478-1616	distributors engine rebuilding magnetos

See full listing in **Section Two** under **ignition parts**

Ed Swart Motors Inc 2675 Skypark Dr Unit 103 Torrance, CA 90505 310-530-9715; FAX: 310-530-9786	cars parts restoration

See full listing in **Section One** under **Bitter**

Tatom Custom Engines/ **Vintage Vendors** 2718 Riverbend Rd Mt Vernon, WA 98273 360-424-8314; FAX: 360-424-6717	engine rebuilding machine shop

See full listing in **Section Two** under **engine rebuilding**

Tavia Performance Products Inc 12851 Western Ave, Unit D Garden Grove, CA 92841 714-892-4057; FAX: 714-892-5627	accessories tools

See full listing in **Section Two** under **tools**

Edward Tilley Automotive **Collectibles** PO Box 4233 Cary, NC 27519-4233 919-460-8262 E-mail: edandsusan@aol.com	automobilia literature parts

See full listing in **Section Two** under **automobilia**

Thompson Hill Metalcraft 23 Thompson Hill Rd Berwick, ME 03901 207-698-5756	metal forming panel beating welding

See full listing in **Section Two** under **sheetmetal**

Tornado Air Management Systems 13360-H Firestone Blvd Santa Fe Springs, CA 90670 310-926-5000; FAX: 310-926-1223 E-mail: j.k@ix.netcom.com	parts

See full listing in **Section Two** under **accessories**

Total Seal Inc 11202 N 24th Ave, Suite 101 Phoenix, AZ 85029 602-678-4977, FAX: 602-678-4991	piston rings

See full listing in **Section Two** under **engine parts**

Transport-Nation Collectibles 24040 Camino Del Avion, Ste A-241 Monarch Beach, CA 92629 800-474-4404, 714-240-5126	artwork collectibles

See full listing in **Section Two** under **artwork**

Valco Cincinnati Consumer **Products Inc** 411 Circle Freeway Drive Cincinnati, OH 45246 513-874-6550; FAX: 513-874-3612	adhesives detailing products sealants tools

See full listing in **Section Two** under **tools**

Vintage Acquisition PO Box 907 Palm Harbor, FL 34682 813-787-5643 inquiries/orders FAX: 813-787-8210	cars parts speed equipment

See full listing in **Section Two** under **comprehensive parts**

Jon Ward Motorsports 3100 FM 1703 PO Box 238 Alpine, TX 79831 915-837-3250; FAX: 915-837-5878	engines race cars

Mail order and open shop. Monday-Saturday 7:30-5:30 CST. Deals in vintage race cars, fabrication, engine, chassis. Cars for the Carrera Pan Americana and Mille Miglia. Proven winners.

The Wheel Shoppe 18011 Fourteen Mile Rd Fraser, MI 48026 810-415-7171; FAX: 810-415-7181 E-mail: jgs2nd@aol.com	performance parts welding wheel repair

See full listing in **Section Two** under **wheels & wheelcovers**

Kirk F White PO Box 999 New Smyrna Beach, FL 32170 904-427-6660; FAX: 904-427-7801	models tin toys

See full listing in **Section Two** under **models & toys**

Dale Wilch Sales (RPM Magazine) 2217 N 99th Kansas City, KS 66109 913-788-3219; FAX: 913-788-9682 E-mail: rpmcat@sound.net	speed equipment

Used speed equipment catalog listing parts and equipment published bimonthly. Restoration of muscle cars. Subscription: $20/2 years.

Yankee Peddler Motorsports 11300 Fortune Circle Wellington, FL 33414 561-798-6606; FAX: 561-798-6706	electrical components hardware

See full listing in **Section Two** under **electrical systems**

radiator emblems & mascots

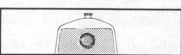

Dwight H Bennett PO Box 3173 Seal Beach, CA 90740-2173 PH/FAX: 310-498-6488	emblem repair hardware repair mascot repair plaque repair

Mail order and open shop by arrangement, 7 days. Deals in

repair, restoration and reproduction of metal cast and/or fabricated objects that other people say are irreparable such as: emblems, enameled emblems, chrome strips, trim, mascots, hardware, photoetched plaques, silkscreen plaques, white metal repair, door handles, knobs, etc. I also do prototyping and custom one-off pieces.

Brass Script Arthur Evans 32 Richmond-Belvidere Rd Bangor, PA 18013-9544 610-588-7541	**brass script**

Brass script for antique car radiators. Over 800 original scripts. SASE required for pencil rub and price.

British Things Inc 515 Ocean Ave Santa Monica, CA 90402 310-394-4002; FAX: 310-394-3204	**badges**

See full listing in **Section One** under **Rolls-Royce/Bentley**

Jay M Fisher Acken Dr 4-B Clark, NJ 07066 908-388-6442	**radiator caps sidemount mirrors**

See full listing in **Section Two** under **accessories**

Gaylord Sales Frank Ranghelli 125 Dugan Ln Toms River, NJ 08753 908-349-9213; FAX: 908-341-5353	**automobilia automotive art mascots**

Mascots, automotive art: paintings, bronzes, collector posters, all forms of automobilial. I have mail order, do car shows (mostly the big ones, Carlisle, Hershey, Auburn, Scottsdale, etc). I have done the above for 23 yrs. Always interested in purchasing items.

Mike Z Kleba PO Box 70 Mallorytown, ON Canada K0E 1R0 613-923-5934	**hood ornaments radiator caps**

Radiator caps and hood ornaments. Mascots, collector, repair-restore, buy, swap, sell.

Pulfer & Williams 213 Forest Rd, PO Box 67 Hancock, NH 03449-0067 603-525-3532; FAX: 603-525-4293	**mascots nameplates radiator emblems**

Mail order only. Manufactures emblems, nameplates, handles reproduction mascots.

Silverleaf Casting Co PO Box 662, 116 S Grove St Delton, MI 49046 616-623-6665	**casting mascots**

See full listing in **Section Two** under **castings**

radiators	

American Honeycomb Radiator Mfg Neil Thomas 171 Hwy 34 Holmdel, NJ 07733 718-948-7772 days 908-946-8743 eves	**manufacturing repairs**

Mail order and open shop. Monday-Friday 9 to 4 EST. Manu-

facturer of cartridge type cartridge and cellular antique radiators. Also manufactures odd one-of-a-kind radiators and refurbishes antique radiators. Exhibited in national and private airplane and automobile museums. Send for free color brochure.

See our ad on this page

Applied Chemical Specialties PO Box 241597 Omaha, NE 68124 800-845-8523; FAX: 402-390-9262	**corrosion protection**

See full listing in **Section Two** under **storage care products**

Blaak Radiateurenbedryf Blaaksedyk oost 19 Heinenoord 3274LA Netherlands 31-186-601732 FAX: 31-186-603044	**radiators**

Mail order and open shop. Monday-Friday 8:30 am-5:30 pm. Specializing in pre-1940 radiators.

The Brassworks 289 Prado Rd San Louis Obispo, CA 93401 800-342-6759; FAX: 805-544-5615	**radiators**

Mail order and open shop. Monday-Friday 8-5. Manufactures all foreign and domestic radiators, 1890s-up. Model T to Rolls-Royce and everything in between. All work guaranteed. Ship worldwide.

Cal West Auto Air & Radiators Inc 24309 Creekside Rd #119 Valencia, CA 91355 800-535-2034; FAX: 805-254-6120	**a/c condensers heaters radiators**

Mail order and open shop. Monday-Saturday. Radiators (new, recored & custom), air conditioning condensers and heaters. 55-

57 Chevy, Camaro, Corvette, Mustang & T-Bird radiators. Antique radiators available. Open 24 hrs/7 days for emergencies. Call, fax or point your browser for your free custom catalog. Web site: http://www.calwest~radiators.com

| **Carters Auto Restorations**
1433 Pawlings Rd
Phoenixville, PA 19460
215-666-5687 | restoration |

See full listing in **Section Two** under **bodywork**

| **The Copper Cooling Works**
2455 N 2550 E
Layton, UT 84040
801-544-9939 | radiators |

Mail order only. Builds new, exact copies of the disc and tube radiators used on the early chain drive cars. Started in 1966 and has had many new radiators on top winning cars throughout the world. Specializing in Cadillac and Oldsmobile.

| **Custom Auto Radiator**
495 Hyson Rd
Jackson, NJ 08527
908-928-3700; FAX: 908-364-7474 | radiators |

Mail order and open shop. Monday-Friday 9-5, Saturday 9-1. Custom Auto Radiator manfactures high performance radiators for a complete line of street rods, cars & trucks, customs, kit cars, lead sleds, race, etc. Radiators are made from copper & brass and/or aluminum. Send SASE to above address for free brochure. We specialize in customs.

| **Gano Filter**
1205 Sandalwood Ln
Los Altos, CA 94024
415-968-7017 | coolant filters |

Mail order only. In-line coolant filter. Prevents radiator clogging. Permanent, easily cleaned accessory. Available in brass or transparent, durable thermoplastic. Satisfaction guaranteed or money back. Free information on request.

| **Glen Ray Radiators Inc**
2105 Sixth St
Wausau, WI 54401
800-537-3775 | rebuilding
recoring |

Mail order and open shop. Monday-Friday 7 to 5:30. Radiator rebuilding and recoring.

| **Highland Radiator Inc**
Rt 9 W
Highland, NY 12528
914-691-7020; FAX: 914-691-2489 | parts
service |

Mail order and open shop. Monday-Friday 8 am to 5 pm. Complete auto radiator repair and services facility. Specializing in antique, classic, special interest and all types of automotive radiators. Expertly repaired, restored, rebuilt or recored, quality craftsmanship. Honeycomb cores available. 34 years' experience.

| **Kassa's Parts & Accessories**
3277 Staunton Rd
Edwardsville, IL 62025
PH/FAX: 618-656-8359 | accessories
parts |

Mail order and open shop. Open 8 am to 10 pm daily. Radiators, highest quality reproductions for all makes and models from 55 to 92. New brass and copper, tanks stamped to original look. 1 year warranty, money back guarantee. VISA and M/C. Also, 63 to 74 OEM radiator core supports, like orig.

| **Marshall Antique & Classic Restorations**
3714 Old Philadelphia Pike
Bethlehem, PA 18015
610-868-7765; FAX: 610-868-7529 | coolant additives
restoration services |

See full listing in **Section One** under **Rolls-Royce/Bentley**

| **Mattson's Radiator**
10529 Beach Blvd
Stanton, CA 90680
714-826-0357, 800-814-4238
FAX: 714-826-1126
E-mail: cam13@1x.netcom.com | electric fans
radiators |

Mail order and open shop. Monday-Friday 7-5:30 and Saturday 7-12. Custom and stock radiators, electric fans, new gas tanks and gas tank refurbishing.

| **Montclair Radiator Service**
10598 Rose Ave
Montclair, CA 91763
714-621-9531 | fuel tanks
radiators |

Shop open Monday-Friday 7 to 5; Saturday 7 to 12 noon. Modification of radiators. Works on all types of cars including desert cool, cellular, heavy duty and CL cores. Specializing in antique car radiators. Also restored fuel tanks. Twenty-three years' experience.

| **Obsolete Chevrolet Parts Co**
524 Hazel Ave
PO Box 68
Nashville, GA 31639
912-686-5812 | engine parts
radiators
rubber parts
transmissions |

See full listing in **Section One** under **Chevrolet**

| **Powell Radiator Service**
PO Box 427
Wilmington, OH 45177
513-382-2096 | restoration |

Mail order and open shop. Monday-Friday, 8-5 EST. Show quality restorations on any type or year of radiator (except aluminum). Some old radiators in stock needing restoration but available for sale or restoration.

| **Raybuck Autobody Parts**
RD 4, Box 170
Punxsutawney, PA 15767
814-938-5248; FAX: 814-938-4250 | body parts |

See full listing in **Section Two** under **body parts**

| **RB's Obsolete Automotive**
18421 Hwy 99
Lynnwood, WA 98037
206-670-6739; FAX: 206-670-9151 | parts |

See full listing in **Section Two** under **comprehensive parts**

| **S & S Antique Auto**
Pine St
Deposit, NY 13754
607-467-2929; FAX: 607-467-2109 | parts |

See full listing in **Section One** under **Ford '32-'53**

| **Skills Unlimited Inc**
7172 CR 33
Tiffin, OH 44883
PH/FAX: 419-992-4680
Shop: 419-448-4639 | radiators |

Mail order and open shop. Open Monday-Saturday 8 am to 8

pm. Deals in replacement of authentic vintage radiator cores and complete radiators.

Vintage Radiators Main Street, Abthorpe Nr. Towcester, Northants NN12 8QN England 44 1327 857726 FAX: 44 1327 858294	**radiator cores**

Supplies radiator cores for antique automobiles, especially the brass era, gilled tubes and dummy honeycomb.

AAMP of America 13160 56th Ct, #502-508 Clearwater, FL 34620 813-572-9255; FAX: 813-573-9326 E-mail: stinger.sales@stinger-aamp.com	**audio accessories**

See full listing in **Section Two** under **accessories**

Antique Auto Radio 6601 W 35th St S Wichita, KS 67215 316-522-5750	**parts** **radios** **repair**

Mail order and open shop. Auto radio repair, radios for sale and tubes and repair parts.

Antique Automobile Radio Inc 700 Tampa Rd Palm Harbor, FL 34683 800-WE-FIX-AM; 813-785-8733 FAX: 813-789-0283	**radio accessories** **radio parts** **radio restoration**

Mail order and open shop. Monday-Friday 8 to 4:30 EST. Automobile radio restoration and FM conversions, 1932-62 US cars only. Manufactures over 60 types of radio vibrators, power inverters (to operate 12 volt accessories on 6 volt systems) and FM conversion kits. Stocks speakers, tubes, transformers, antennas, dial glass. 3,500+ radios in inventory. VISA, MasterCard, Discover. Free catalog. Dealer inquiries invited.

See our ad on this page

Antique Radio Service 12 Shawmut Ave Wayland, MA 01778 800-201-2635; FAX: 508-653-2418	**radio service**

Mail order and open shop. Monday-Friday 8:30-5:30 by appointment. Radios bought, sold, traded, restored, rebuilt, speaker repair, vibrators. FM conversions, power inverters and boosters.

Bob's Radio & TV Service/ **Vintage Electronics** 2300 Broad St San Lius Obispo, CA 94401 805-543-2946; FAX: 805-782-0803	**radios**

Mail order and open shop with museum. Monday through Fridays and most Saturdays, 8 am to 5:30 pm. Vintage car restoration and FM additions. Years 1932-1966, most models, American only. Radio stays original looking. Vintage home radios also welcome. Flat rates on car radios. Visa and MasterCard accepted. Restorations only, no parts for sale. Pre 1950 service literature for home and car radios for sale.

The Classic Car Radio Co 2718 Koper Dr Sterling Heights, MI 48310 810-977-7979; info: 810-268-2918 FAX: 810-977-0895	**radios**

Mail order and open shop. Monday-Friday 9-6 EST; Saturday by appointment. World's largest stock of factory original radios. Specializing in Corvette & Chevrolet. Buy, sell, trade, restore & convert to AM-FM. Factory original radios with state of the art Kenwood internals. Web site: http://www.car~trek.com/ccr

Classic Car Radio Service 25 Maple Rd PO Box 764 Woodacre, CA 94973 415-488-4596; FAX: 415-488-1512 E-mail: healy@classicradio.com	**radio repair** **radio restoration**

Mail order and open shop. Shop open seven days a week 9 to 6. Deals in radio repair and restoration, all makes from the 1920s up. Highest quality repair and restoration. Ultrasonically cleaned tuning mechanism. Old parts completely replaced using USA mil spec parts and scope sweep alignment. We guarantee complete customer satisfaction for five (5) years parts and labor. Be true to your car. Inquire for free brochure. Family owned since 1955. Web site: http://www.classicradio.com

Corvette Clocks by Roger 24 Leisure Ln Jackson, TN 38305 901-664-6120; FAX: 901-664-1627	**repair** **restoration**

See full listing in **Section Two** under **instruments**

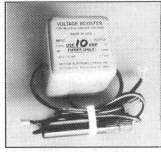
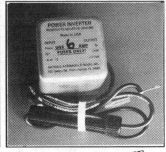

Crutchfield Corp
1 Crutchfield Park
Charlottesville, VA 22906
800-955-9009; FAX: 804-973-1862

car stereos

Car stereo components and systems, home theater & home audio, video, car security products, telephones, extensive technical support available on 800 line for customers.

Custom Autosound Mfg
808 W Vermont Ave
Anaheim, CA 92805
800-888-8637; FAX: 714-533-0361
E-mail: carl@globalmark.com

accessories
custom radios
speakers

See full listing in **Section One** under **Chevrolet**

Elliott's Car Radio
313 Linfield Rd
Parkerford, PA 19457
610-495-6360; FAX: 610-495-7723

radio repairs
speaker kits

Mail order and open shop. Monday to Friday 9 am to 5 pm, work on vehicles by appointment. Specializing in the repair of car radios & tape decks. Repair & sales of car radios 1958 to 1994. Speaker kits for Chevelle 1965 to 1972, speaker kits for GM cars 1965 to 1980.

Jim Gensch
1810 Juliet
St Paul, MN 55105
612-690-2029

radios
repair
vibrators

Mail order and open shop. Open by appointment only. Vintage car and home radio repair, 1920s to 1960. Hundreds of restored car radios in stock through the 1970s.

Grandpa's Radio Shop
26 Queenston Crescent
Kitchener, ONT Canada N2B 2V5
519-576-2570

radio restoration

See full listing in **Section One** under **Ford '54-up**

William Hulbert Jr
PO Box 151
13683 Rt 11
Adams Center, NY 13606
315-583-5765

radios

Radios, pre 1959. Restored sets for sale or restore yours. Dead sets taken on trade. One year guarantee after you've installed it in your car and are using it. Will also trade for parts for my own cars and trucks.

Jackson Speaker Service
217 Crestbrook Dr
Jackson, MI 49203
517-789-6400

radio repairs
speakers

Mail order and open shop. Monday-Saturday 9 am-5 pm. Repair and reconing of car and truck loud speakers for all cars, 1934 thru present. Provides original speakers and grilles and some radios.

Jukebox Friday Night
1114 Robert Dr
Cochran, GA 31014
912-934-8866

parts
repairs
restoration

Mail order only. Repair, restore, parts for car radios. Repair, parts for juke boxes. Electronic parts: tubes, vibrators, transformers.

Marquette Radio
7852 W Sycamore Dr
Orland Park, IL 60462
708-633-0545

radios
tape players

Mail order and open shop. Original 1963-85 factory AM-FM radios and tape players.

Norman's Classic Auto Radio
7651 Park Blvd
Pinellas Park, FL 33781
813-546-1788

custom sales
radio repairs

National mail order and open shop. Shop open every day, appointments requested. Specializing in 2 week turn-around for radio repairs, restorations and sales. Repairs/restorations for 1930 to 1968 US automobiles. Sales of custom radios that "fit to full" original radio space for most years and makes. Quality work with reasonable prices.

Passenger Car Supply
102 Cloverdale Rd
Swedesboro, NJ 08085
609-467-7966

parts

See full listing in **Section One** under **Chevrolet**

Prestige Thunderbird Inc
10215 Greenleaf Ave
Santa Fe Springs, CA 90670
800-423-4751, 310-944-6237
FAX: 310-941-8677

appraisals
radios
repairs
restorations
tires

See full listing in **Section One** under **Thunderbird**

Spirit Enterprises
4325 Sunset Dr
Lockport, NY 14094
716-434-9938 showroom
716-434-0077 warehouse

stereo systems

Mail order and open shop. Shop open daily, 8 to 8. Hard-to-find car kits from fifties through seventies, plus new releases. Specializing in stereo systems for high-performance, American made cars. Some rare options and aftermarket accessories.

Sutton Auto Sounds
3463 Rolling Trail
Palm Harbor, FL 34684-3526
813-787-2717; FAX: 813-789-9215
E-mail: suttonauto@aol.com

radios

Mail order only. Dealing in US factory car radios and tape players 1963-1979. I restore these radios and also do FM conversions. FM conversions cannot be detected from either side of the dash. I also manufacture reverberation units.

Vintage Radio Restorations
900 Crestview Dr
Newberg, OR 97132
503-538-2392;
E-mail:cerasin9@northwest.com

radio repair

Mail order and open shop. Automobile radio restoration and repair, speaker reconing. Specializing in all American OEM makes. Web site: http://www.northwest.com/rcemasin9

Vintage Radio Shop
Wilford Wilkes Sr
101 Swoope St, Box 103
Brisbin, PA 16620
814-378-8526; FAX: 814-378-6149

parts
radios
repairs

Mail order or open by appointment. Exclusively European auto radios 1940s to 1970. Tube or transistor. Blaupunkt, Becker, Telefunken, Radiomobile, etc. The only shop catering to these specialized auto radios exclusively. Repairs, restoration. Stocking new dial faces, knobs, push-buttons, etc. Visa/MC. All work done by myself personally.

Vintique Electronics	repair
Jack Shaymow	
52 "C" Tilford	
Deerfield Beach, FL 33442	
954-427-1222	

Mail order and open shop. Monday-Friday 10 am to 7 pm. A one man service organization specializing in repair and overhaul of vacuum tube equipped radios. Shop contains all instrumentation with documents and parts required to perform and accomplish all phases of repairs and services on vintage radios to manufacturer's specifications. 45 years' experience. Delco, Mopar, FoMoCo, Motorola, Philco, etc. 6 volt radios converted to 12 volts, including British, Italian and German radios.

George Zaha	FM conversions
615 Elizabeth	radios
Rochester, MI 48307	speakers
810-651-0959 evenings	

Radios repaired, sold and purchased since 1934. Over 50 years of service guarantees you the best quality at the best prices. FM conversions, vibrators, speaker reconing, massive stock of radios and NOS parts inventory. Complete sales and service facility. All work fully guaranteed one year.

restoration aids

AARcadia Parts Locating	parts
8294 Allport Ave	
Santa Fe Springs, CA 90670	
310-698-8067; FAX: 310-696-6505	

See full listing in **Section One** under **MoPar**

Accessible Systems Inc	auto rotisserie
440 Matson Rd	
Jonesborough, TN 37659	
423-975-8907; FAX: 423-975-8908	
E-mail: access@tricon.net	

We have manufactured the Bottoms-Up Lift line of auto rotisseries for 8 years. They allow the body, frame or both together to be lifted and rotated at any angle for easy access. Do a better quality restoration job and do it quicker and easier. We also now have a tilter for turning a whole vehicle on its side for the less than frame-off repair needs. Call or write for free catalog.

ADP Parts Services	interchange info
14800 28th Ave N	manuals
Plymouth, MN 55447	
800-825-0644; FAX: 612-553-0270	

See full listing in **Section Two** under **car & parts locators**

Albrico Auto & Truck Parts	lamp assemblies
PO Box 3179	lenses
Camarillo, CA 93010	
805-482-9792; FAX: 805-383-1013	

See full listing in **Section Two** under **lighting equipment**

AmeriVap Systems	cleaning system
582 Armour Cir NE	
Atlanta, GA 30324	
404-876-2220; FAX: 404-876-3206	

See full listing in **Section Two** under **car care products**

Amherst Antique Auto Show	swap meets
157 Hollis Rd	
Amherst, NH 03031	
603-883-0605, NH	
FAX: 617-641-0647, MA	

See full listing in **Section Two** under **auctions & events**

Antique Automotive Accessories	accessories
889 S Rainbow Blvd, Suite 642	tires
Las Vegas, NV 89128	
800-742-6777; FAX: 913-862-4646	

See full listing in **Section Two** under **tires**

Antique Radio Service	radio service
12 Shawmut Ave	
Wayland, MA 01778	
800-201-2635; FAX: 508-653-2418	

See full listing in **Section Two** under **radios**

Aremco Products Inc	compound
23 Snowden Ave	
PO Box 429	
Ossining, NY 10546	
914-762-0685; FAX: 914-762-1663	

See full listing in **Section Two** under **accessories**

Atlantic British Ltd	accessories
PO Box 110	parts
Rover Ridge Dr	
Mechanicville, NY 12118	
800-533-2210; FAX: 518-664-6641	

See full listing in **Section One** under **Rover/Land Rover**

Autofresh International	deodorizing
PO Box 54855	
Oklahoma City, OK 73154-1855	
405-752-0770; FAX: 405-752-5207	

See full listing in **Section Two** under **interiors & interior parts**

Automotion	parts
193 Commercial St	
Sunnyvale, CA 94068	
800-777-8881; FAX: 408-736-9013	
E-mail: automo@aol.com	

See full listing in **Section One** under **Porsche**

Bay Area Industrial Dry Stripping	blasting
151 11th St	paint removal
Richmond, CA 94801-3523	
510-412-9890, 510-805-1887	

See full listing in **Section Two** under **rust removal & stripping**

Bob's Brickyard Inc	parts
399 Washington St	
Brighton, MI 48116	
810-229-5302	

See full listing in **Section One** under **Bricklin**

Bob's Classic Auto Glass	glass
21170 Hwy 36	
Blachly, OR 97412	
800-624-2130	

See full listing in **Section Two** under **glass**

Generalists

Bob's Bird House
124 Watkin Ave
Chadds Ford, PA 19317
215-358-3420; FAX: 215-558-0729

parts

See full listing in **Section One** under **Thunderbird**

Brisson Enterprises
PO Box 1595
Dearborn, MI 48121
313-584-3577

lead

See full listing in **Section Two** under **car care products**

The Buckle Man
Douglas D Drake
28 Monroe Ave
Pittsford, NY 14534
716-381-4604

buckles

See full listing in **Section Two** under **hardware**

Buenger Enterprises/GoldenRod Dehumidifier
3600 S Harbor Blvd
Oxnard, CA 93035
800-451-6797; FAX: 805-985-1534

dehumidifiers

See full listing in **Section Two** under **car care products**

C & P Chevy Parts
50 Schoolhouse Rd
PO Box 348VA
Kulpsville, PA 19443
215-721-4300, 800-235-2475
FAX: 215-721-4539

parts
restoration
supplies

See full listing in **Section One** under **Chevrolet**

F J Cabrera Enterprises
15507 Normandie Ave, #103
Gardena, CA 90247
310-532-8894; FAX: 310-515-0928

accessories
lights

Mail order only. Nostalgia items, Blue Dots, dummy spotlights, skirts, early Ford, Chevy, reproduction items also for Mustang & Corvette. Rod lights, headlights, exhaust tips.

Capt Lee's Spra' Strip
PO Box 203
Hermitage, TN 37076
800-421-9498; FAX: 615-889-1798

paint remover

See full listing in **Section Two** under **rust removal & stripping**

CARS Inc
1964 W 11 Mile Rd
Berkley, MI 48072
810-398-7100; 810-398-7078

interior

See full listing in **Section One** under **Chevrolet**

Caswell Electroplating in Miniature
4336 Rt 31
Palmyra, NY 14522
315-597-5140; FAX: 315-597-1457
E-mail: caswell@vivanet.com

plating kits

See full listing in **Section Two** under **plating & polishing**

Stan Chernoff
1215 Greenwood Ave
Torrance, CA 90503
310-320-4554; FAX: 310-328-7867
E-mail: az589@lafn.org

mechanical parts
restoration parts
technical info
trim parts

See full listing in **Section One** under **Datsun**

Ciadella Enterprises Inc
3116 S 52nd St
Tempe, AZ 85282-3212
602-968-4179; FAX: 602-438-6585

truck interiors
upholstery

See full listing in **Section One** under **Chevrolet**

Classic Data
1240 SE Gideon St
Portland, OR 97202
503-234-8617; FAX: 503-234-8618
E-mail: hfreedman@aol.com

shop manual

See full listing in **Section One** under **Chevrolet**

Classic Mercury Parts
1393 Shippee Ln
Ojai, CA 93023
PH/FAX: 805-646-3345

parts

See full listing in **Section One** under **Mercury**

Color-Plus Leather Restoration System
2116 Morris Ave
Union, NJ 07083
908-851-2811; FAX: 908-851-2910

leather conditioning
leather dye

See full listing in **Section Two** under **leather restoration**

Composition Materials Co Inc
1375 Kings Hwy E
Fairfield, CT 06430
800-262-7763; FAX: 203-335-9728

plastic media

Mail order only. Plastic media blasting. Composition Materials manufactures five grades of Plasti-Grit plastic media. Plasti-Grit can quickly remove primers and top coats without harming sensitive surfaces. It is custom designed for stripping fiberglass, plastic, sheetmetal in preparation for professional restoring and repainting. Technical assistance and reference to local restoration facilities is available. The media is safe, economical, recyclable and environmentally preferred.

Cover-It
17 Wood St
West Haven, CT 06516-3843
203-931-4747; FAX: 203-931-4754

all-weather shelters

See full listing in **Section Two** under **car covers**

Dalmar
11759 S Cleveland Ave, Suite 28
Ft Myers, FL 33907
941-275-6540; FAX: 941-275-1731
E-mail: dalmar@peganet.com

electroplating
plating supplies

See full listing in **Section Two** under **plating & polishing**

Daytona MIG
1821 Holsonback Dr
Daytona Beach, FL 32117
800-331-9353; FAX: 904-274-1237

plasma cutters
welders

See full listing in **Section Two** under **tools**

Dearborn Classics
PO Box 1248
Sunset Beach, CA 90742
714-372-3175; FAX: 714-372-3801

accessories
restoration parts

See full listing in **Section One** under **Ford '54-Up**

**Design Fabrications,
Pure Products Division**
PO Box 40205
Santa Barbara, CA 93140-0205
805-965-6031

parts

See full listing in **Section Two** under **comprehensive parts**

Development Associates
1520 S Lyon
Santa Ana, CA 92705
714-835-9512; FAX: 714-835-9513
E-mail: 71460,1146@compuserve.com

electrical parts

See full listing in **Section Two** under **electrical systems**

Dr vette
212 7th St SW
New Philadelphia, OH 44663
330-339-3370, 800-878-1022 orders
FAX: 330-339-6640

**brakes
fuel system parts
repairs**

See full listing in **Section One** under **Corvettes**

Bob Drake Reproductions Inc
1819 NW Washington Blvd
Grants Pass, OR 97526
800-221-3673; FAX: 541-474-0099

repro parts

See full listing in **Section One** under **Ford '32-'53**

**Dri-Wash & Guard
Consulting Distributors Inc**
PO Box 1331
Palm Desert, CA 92261
619-346-1984; 800-428-1883
FAX: 619-568-6354

**automotive care
products
boat care products**

See full listing in **Section Two** under **car care products**

Early Wheel Co Inc
Box 1438
Santa Ynez, CA 93460
805-688-1187; FAX: 805-688-0257

steel wheels

See full listing in **Section Two** under **wheels & wheelcovers**

**Eastern Specialty Automotive
Sales & Service Ltd**
38 Yankeetown Rd
Hammonds Plains, NS Canada
B3Z 1K7
902-835-5912; FAX: 902-835-0680

**parts
service
transport**

See full listing in **Section Two** under **car & parts locators**

The Eastwood Company-Tools
580 Lancaster Ave
Box 3014
Malvern, PA 19355
800-345-1178, M-F 8 am to 12 midnight, Saturday & Sunday 9 am to 5
pm EST; FAX: 610-644-0560

**paints
plating & polishing
restoration aids
rustproofing
stripping tools
sandblasters
welders**

See full listing in **Section Two** under **tools**

The Enthusiasts Shop
John Parnell
PO Box 80471
Baton Rouge, LA 70898
504-928-7456; FAX: 504-928-7665

**cars
pre-war parts
transportation**

See full listing in **Section One** under **Rolls-Royce/Bentley**

Extensions Plus Inc
3500 Park Central Blvd N
Pompano Beach, FL 33064
954-978-3362; FAX: 954-978-0630
E-mail: 4star@gate.net

body filler parts

See full listing in **Section Two** under **body parts**

Fibre Glast Developments Corp
1944 Neva Dr
Dayton, OH 45414
800-821-3283; FAX: 513-274-7267
E-mail: fibreglast@aol.com

**supplies
tools**

Mail order and open shop. Monday-Friday 8:30-4:30. Raw materials for all types of fiberglass work including Kevlar, graphite,
resins. All tools needed to complete the job. Retail distributor.

**Firewall Insulators & Quiet Ride
Solutions**
6333 Pacific Ave, Ste 523
Stockton, CA 95207
209-477-4840; FAX: 209-477-0918

firewall insulators

See full listing in **Section Two** under **upholstery**

Ron Francis' Wire Works
167 Keystone Rd
Chester, PA 19013
610-485-1937

**wiring
wiring kits**

See full listing in **Section Two** under **electrical systems**

Gasoline Alley LLC
PO Box 737, 1700 E Iron Ave
Salina, KS 67402
913-822-1000; 800-326-8372
FAX: 913-827-9337

drip pans

See full listing in **Section Two** under **accessories**

Hoffman Automotive Distributor
U.S. Hwy #1, Box 818
Hilliard, FL 32046
904-845-4421

parts

See full listing in **Section Two** under **body parts**

House of Powder Inc
Rt 71 & 1st St
PO Box 110
Standard, IL 61363
815-339-2648

**powder coating
sandblasting**

See full listing in **Section Two** under **service shops**

Imperial Restoration Inc
308 Lockport St
Lemont, IL 60439
630-257-5822; FAX: 630-257-5892

**engine enamels
gas tank sealer
paint/rust remover
rust preventives**

Mail order only. POR-15 restoration products which include
POR-15 rust preventive paint (applied directly over rust to seal it
permanently), gas tank sealer, high temp coatings, engine enamels (matching factory colors), paint remover/stripper, metal
ready rust remover, epoxy putty and more.

Inline Tube
17540 14 Mile Rd
Fraser, MI 48026
810-294-4093; FAX: 810-294-7349
E-mail: inline@apk.net

**brake lines
choke tubes
fuel lines
transmission lines
vacuum lines**

See full listing in **Section Two** under **brakes**

Generalists

J & K Old Chevy Stuff
Ship Pond Rd
Plymouth, MA 02360
508-224-7616

| car dealer |
| parts |
| sheetmetal |

See full listing in **Section One** under **Chevrolet**

Kaleidoscope
PO Box 86-H
Mt Ephraim, NJ 08059
800-831-5163

| glass restoration |
| scratch remover kit |

Specializing in automotive glass restoration for the past 25 years. Sell the original windshield scratch remover kit through mail order and local car shows. Check or money order only please.

Georges B Karakolev
228 Rt 221
Napierville, QUE Canada J0J 1L0
PH/FAX: 514-245-0028

| car dealer |
| parts |
| restoration |

Restoration of luxury and classic cars. Buying and selling of antique vehicles. Vintage auto and parts specialist. Specializing in Jaguar and Mercedes for all early models. Chrome, stainless bare steel nipples & spokes. Die cast model cars, British & European models. MGBs bought and sold.

Ken's Cougars
PO Box 5380
Edmond, OK 73013
405-340-1636; FAX: 405-340-5877

| parts |

See full listing in **Section One** under **Mercury**

Kenask Spring Co
307 Manhattan Ave
Jersey City, NJ 07307
201-653-4589

| springs |

See full listing in **Section Two** under **suspension parts**

Al Knoch Interiors
130 Montoya Rd
El Paso, TX 79932
800-880-8080; FAX: 915-581-1545

| carpets |
| interiors |
| tooling services |
| tops |

See full listing in **Section One** under **Chevrolet**

Koolmat
PO Box 207
1922 Coventry
Brunswick, OH 44212
330-273-6011; FAX: 330-273-9858

| insulators |

Insulation products for all models and makes of vehicles on land and aircraft. We make insulation for floors, firewall, spark plug boot insulators and sleeving for spark plug wires, also Bulsa (air pockets) for floors with extreme heat because of exhaust systems.

Kwik Poly T Distributing Inc
24 St Henry Ct
St Charles, MO 63301
314-724-1065

| restoration aids |

Mail order only. Kwik Poly is used in all types of wood problems and reconstructuring, plus dozens of other restoration repairs, including fuel tanks, oil tanks, steering wheels, fiberglass, rusted sheetmetal, electrical, engine, pitted surface repairs, molding.

Leatherique Leather Restoration Products
PO Box 2678
Orange Park, FL 32065
904-272-0992; FAX: 904-272-1534

| leather cleaning/ |
| conditioning |
| products |

See full listing in **Section One** under **Rolls-Royce/Bentley**

Loga Enterprises
5399 Old Town Hall Rd
Eau Claire, WI 54701
715-832-7302

| convertible tops |
| interior parts |

See full listing in **Section One** under **Studebaker**

Madera Concepts
606 Olive St
Santa Barbara, CA 93101
800-800-1579, 805-962-1579
FAX: 805-962-7359

| restoration |
| woodwork |
| woodwork repair |

See full listing in **Section Two** under **woodwork**

Malm Chem Corp
PO Box 300, Dept HVA
Pound Ridge, NY 10576
914-764-5775; FAX: 914-764-5785
E-mail: jkolin@cloud9.net

| polish |
| wax |

See full listing in **Section Two** under **car care products**

Marchant Machine Corporation
11325 Maryland Ave
Beltsville, MD 20705
301-937-4481; FAX: 301-937-1019
E-mail: dmarch4481@aol.com

| metal forming |
| machines |

See full listing in **Section Two** under **sheetmetal**

Mint Condition Auto Upholstery
PO Box 134
Silverdale New Zealand
PH/FAX: 64-9-424 2257

| convertible tops |
| interiors |
| spring-gaiters |
| wheelcovers |

See full listing in **Section Two** under **special services**

Mitchell Manufacturing
6 Acorn Ct
Novato, CA 94949-6603
800-238-5093

| overdrives |

See full listing in **Section One** under **Ford '03-'31**

Motorcar Valet Inc
PO Box 711777
Cottonwood, UT 84171
801-277-4596; FAX: 801-277-4680

| cleaners |
| polishes |
| waxes |

See full listing in **Section Two** under **car care products**

Motorguard Corporation
580 Carnegie St
Manteca, CA 95337
209-239-9191; FAX: 209-239-5114

| accessories |
| tools |

See full listing in **Section Two** under **tools**

Muscle Express
509 Commerce Way W #3
Jupiter, FL 33458
800-323-3043 order line
561-744-3043 tech line

| parts |

See full listing in **Section One** under **Chevelle/Camaro**

OEM Glass Inc
PO Box 362, Rt 9 E
Bloomington, IL 61702
309-662-2122; FAX: 309-663-7474

| auto glass |

See full listing in **Section Two** under **glass**

Original Parts Group Inc
17892 Gothard St
Huntington Beach, CA 92647
800-243-8355 US & Canada
714-841-5363; FAX: 714-847-8159

| accessories |
| parts |

See full listing in **Section One** under **Pontiac**

Pennsylvania Metal Cleaning
200 17th St
Monaca, PA 15061-1969
412-728-5535

| derusting |
| stainless fasteners |
| stripping |

See full listing in **Section Two** under **rust removal & stripping**

People's Choice & Lost in the 50s
28170 Ave Crocker #209
Valencia, CA 91355
800-722-1965, 805-295-1965
FAX: 805-295-1931

| automobilia items |
| celebrity items |
| 50s clothing |
| 50s memorabilia |

See full listing in **Section Two** under **automobilia**

J Pinto
2605 9th St
Long Island City, NY 11102
PH/FAX: 718-626-2403
E-mail: electritech@sprynet.com

| windshield wiper |
| repair |

Electric motors and all switches, relays, solenoids (including overdrive) restored, 6 and 12 volt. Stay original. OEM specs or better. "We can when others can't™". 50+ years' experience: w/wiper, w/washer, headlight, fan, blower, conv top, horns, power window, locks, seat, antenna, most $50-$75. No charge if unrestorable. Free 3 day shipping West, Midwest. Send to: J Pinto, 26-05 Ninth St, Long Island City, NY 11102.
Web site: http://home.sprynet.com/sprynet/electritech/

PM Industries
442 Ridge Rd
West Milford, NJ 07480
800-833-8933; FAX: 201-728-2117

| chassis coatings |
| permanent rust |
| sealers |

See full listing in **Section Two** under **rustproofing**

Pollard Co
Joe Pollard
9331 Johnell Rd
Chatsworth, CA 91311
PH/FAX: 818-999-1485

| parts |

See full listing in **Section One** under **Checker**

Precision Paint & Rust Removers Inc
2415 W Industrial Blvd
Long Lake, MN 55356
PH/FAX: 612-476-4545

| paint removal |
| rust removal |

See full listing in **Section Two** under **rust removal & stripping**

Preserve Inc
1430 E 1800 N
Hamilton, IL 62341
217-746-2411; FAX: 217-746-2231

| storage containers |

See full listing in **Section Two** under **storage care products**

Protective Products Corp
Box 246
Johnston, IA 50131
800-666-0772; FAX: 515-999-2708

| chemical products |

Unique chemical products which greatly reduce the labor time in restoration and surface care products which produce prize winning results.

Quanta Restoration and Preservation Products
45 Cissel Dr
North East, MD 21901
410-658-5700; FAX: 410-658-5758

| fan belts |
| gas tanks |

See full listing in **Section Two** under **chassis parts**

RB's Obsolete Automotive
18421 Hwy 99
Lynnwood, WA 98037
206-670-6739; FAX: 206-670-9151

| parts |

See full listing in **Section Two** under **comprehensive parts**

R J & L Automotive Fasteners
58 Bristol Ave
Rochester, NY 14617-2702
PH/FAX: 716-467-7421, phone 4-9
M-F, fax 24 hours

| fasteners |

See full listing in **Section Two** under **hardware**

Red Crown Valve Caps
PO Box 5301
Topeka, KS 66605
913-357-5007

| automobilia |

See full listing in **Section Two** under **automobilia**

REM Automotive Inc
Box 241, Rt 1, Brandt Rd
Annville, PA 17003
717-838-4242; FAX: 717-838-5091

| interior parts |

REM supplies manufactured soft good parts throughout the United States. Parts are die-cut for precision fit for most all domestic cars. Production, warehousing and shipping is done in our facility. Renowned for our ability to fabricate, in-house, nearly everything we sell, as well as to develop customer generated special projects. At REM, the emphasis is on quality and delivery to the customer.

Restoration Supply Company
2060 Palisade Dr
Reno, NV 89509
702-825-5663; FAX: 702-825-9330
E-mail: restoration@rsc.reno.nv.us

| accessories |
| restoration |
| supplies |

Mail order only. Deals in authentic hard to find restoration supplies and accessories for the automobile and marine enthusiast.

Restorations Unlimited
Box 1118
Blenheim, ONT Canada N0P 1A0
519-676-8455

| metal fabrication |
| restoration |

See full listing in **Section One** under **Auburn**

Rocky's Advance Formula
40 Abbott Ave
Danbury, CT 06810
800-752-0245

| wax hardener |

See full listing in **Section Two** under **car care products**

RW & Able Inc
PO Box 2110
Chico, CA 95927
PH/FAX: 916-896-1513

| door panels |
| interior accessories |

See full listing in **Section Two** under **street rods**

T Schmidt
827 N Vernon
Dearborn, MI 48128-1542
313-562-7161

rust removers

See full listing in **Section Two** under **rust removal & stripping**

Ron Scobie Enterprises
7676 120th St N
Hugo, MN 55038
612-426-1023

gas pump parts

See full listing in **Section Two** under **petroliana**

Paul Slater Auto Parts
9496 85th St N
Stillwater, MN 55082
612-429-4235

parts

See full listing in **Section One** under **Dodge**

Standard Abrasives Motor Sports
9351 Deering Ave
Chatsworth, CA 91311
800-383-6001, 818-718-7070, ext
371; FAX: 800-546-6867

abrasives

Mail order only. Monday-Friday 8 am to 5 pm PST. Specialty abrasives and surface conditioning products to make work easier, cleaner and more productive on a variety of restoration and customization applications including: frame work, body work, wheels and trim. Product kits available. Call for free catalog.

Sunchaser Tools
3202 E Foothill Blvd
Pasadena, CA 91107
818-795-1588; FAX: 818-795-6494

metal-finishing kit
video

Mail order and open shop. Monday-Friday 9-6 pm. Autobody tools, hand, air and electric tools. This tool company has been written about in over 35 magazine articles because of their unique new method of dent repair where no bondo is needed. It's called the "Friction System", by using their 9" stainless amazing shrinking disc, it accurately heat shrinks the stretched part in dents so it will return to its original shape. This system will work on all sheetmetal whether on a Honda hood or a Model A fender. This system actually anneals the once damaged panel so it will return to the same workability as if never hit. There is a 100% guarantee to work for anyone who gets properly trained through their complete 3.5 hour training video course and must purchase the "Friction System" kit.

Tar Heel Parts Inc
PO Box 2604
Matthews, NC 28106-2604
800-322-1957; 704-845-1847 (local)
FAX: 704-845-5447

buffing supplies

See full listing in **Section Two** under **plating & polishing**

This Old Truck Magazine
PO Box 562
Yellow Springs, OH 45387
800-767-5828; 937-767-1433
FAX: 767-2726
E-Mail: antique@antiquepower.com

magazine

See full listing in **Section Four** under **periodicals**

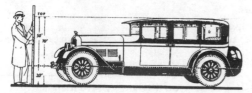

TMI Products Inc
191 Granite St
Corona, CA 91719
909-272-1996; 800-624-7960
FAX: 909-272-1584
E-mail: tmiprods@aol.com

classic car
interiors

See full listing in **Section One** under **Volkswagen**

Ultimate Appearance Ltd
113 Arabian Trail
Smithfield, VA 23430
PH/FAX: 757-255-2620

cleaners
detailing products
detailing services
polish/wax

See full listing in **Section Two** under **car care products**

Vampire-Island Air Products
50 Four Coins Dr
Canonsburg, PA 15317
800-826-7473; FAX: 412-745-9024

air dryers
filters

See full listing in **Section Two** under **restoration shops**

Vintage Parts 411
PO Box 22893
San Diego, CA 92192
800-MOTORHEAD
FAX: 619-560-9900
E-mail: vp411@electriciti.com

books

See full listing in **Section Four** under **information sources**

Williams Lowbuck Tools Inc
4175 California Ave
Norco, CA 91760
909-735-7848; FAX: 909-735-1210
E-mail: wlowbuck@aol.com

tools

See full listing in **Section Two** under **tools**

World Upholstery & Trim
PO Box 4857
Thousand Oaks, CA 91359
800-222-9577; FAX: 818-707-2664
E-mail: worlduph@mail.vcnet.com

carpet kits
tops
upholstery kits

See full listing in **Section Two** under **interiors & interior parts**

Wymer Classic AMC
Mark Wymer
340 N Justice St
Fremont, OH 43420
419-332-4291, 8 to 5 pm
419-334-6945 after 5 pm

NOS parts
repairs
used parts

See full listing in **Section One** under **AMC**

restoration shops

Absolutely British II
1720 S Grove Ave, Unit A
Ontario, CA 91761
PH/FAX: 909-947-0200

restoration
service

Shop open Monday-Friday 7 am to 4:30 pm. Restoration, service and parts for Austin-Healey, MG and Triumph TR2-6 sports cars.

AC Motors
534 N 1st St
Grand Junction, CO 81501
970-245-3344

car dealer

See full listing in **Section Two** under **car dealers**

Ace Auto Body & Towing Ltd 65 S Service Rd Plainview, NY 11803 516-752-6065; FAX: 516-752-1484	**mechanical repairs** **restorations**

Open shop Mon-Fri 8 am to 5 pm. Partial and complete restorations, mechanical repairs, rewiring services, powdercoating, oven-baked polyurethane painting, plastic media paint stripping.

See our ad on this page

Adams Custom Engines Inc 1115 Nixon Ave Reno, NV 89509 702-358-8070; FAX: 702-358-8040	**restorations**

Mail order and open shop. Shop open Monday-Friday 8 am to 5 pm. Full and partial restorations of antique and classic automobiles. 30 years' experience. Specializing in woodgraining. Quality work for the most discriminating, National award winning work. 334 body-off restorations since 1965.

Adler's Antique Autos Inc 801 NY Route 43 Stephentown, NY 12168 518-733-5749 days 518-479-4103 nights	**auto preservation** **Chevrolet parts** **repair** **restoration**

Shop open Monday - Friday 9 to 5. Specialty shop capable of mig welding, panel fabrication and repairs, sandblasting and painting to the customer's specifications. Chevrolet parts available for salvage. Also mechanical work done on old Chevrolets. 600 vintage Chevys in inventory. Expert on Chevrolet Advance Design trucks 1947-55. We keep 'em running! See work we've done 24 years ago still going strong!

Alfas Unlimited Inc US Rt 44 Norfolk, CT 06058 203-542-5351; FAX: 203-542-5993	**engine rebuilding** **parts** **restoration** **service**

See full listing in **Section One** under **Alfa Romeo**

American Dream Machines 28058 Old Valley Pike Toms Brook, VA 22660 540-436-3429; FAX: 540-465-4989	**restoration**

Mail order only. Used parts for 60s and 70s. Chrysler A, B and E-bodies. Chrysler products are also restored.

Antique & Classic Car Restoration Hwy 107, Box 368 Magdalena, NM 87825	**restoration**

Shop open by appointment only. Specializing in complete frame-up restorations for MG, Paige, Reo and Jaguar.

Antique Auto Restoration 1975 Del Monte Blvd Seaside, CA 93955 408-393-9411; FAX: 408-393-1041	**restoration**

The Antique Auto Shop 603 Lytle Ave Elsmere, KY 41018 606-342-8363; FAX: 606-342-9076	**mechanical service** **restoration**

Shop open Monday-Friday 6 to 4:30. Restoration on antique, classic and sport cars from body off the frame show cars to partial and component restoration. Same location 20 years. Appraisals by appointment. Custom car covers.

See our ad on this page

Antique Vehicle Maintenance 57 Cannonball Rd Pompton Lakes, NJ 07442 201-616-6300	restoration

Shop open Monday-Saturday 7:30 to 4. Body and mechanical restoration, metal fabrication, show paint, upholstery and electrical, machine shop on premises, problem solvers. In-house babbitt work & horseless carriage repair. Steam spoken here. Auto locator & pre-purchase appraisals, you really should call.

Aromas Muscle Cars 424 Rose Ave PO Box 385 Aromas, CA 95004	interiors trim parts

See full listing in **Section Two** under **interiors & interior parts**

Art's Antique & Classic Auto Services 1985 E 5th St #15 Tempe, AZ 85281 602-899-6068	restoration

See full listing in **Section One** under **Buick/McLaughlin**

Auto Craftsmen Restoration Inc 27945 Elm Grove San Antonio, TX 78261 210-980-4027	appraisals restoration

Mail order and open shop. Monday-Friday 8 to 5. Specializing in Mercedes-Benz and Rolls-Royce, Mustang convertibles, others considered. Top winning show cars have been restored by this shop.

THE ANTIQUE AUTO SHOP

Let us transform that special car in your garage to its original Elegance!

◇ Pride in Workmanship
◇ Complete Mechanical Service
◇ Metal finishing & Lead Work
◇ Show Winning Paint

THE ANTIQUE AUTO SHOP
603 Lytle Ave., Elsmere, KY 41018
(606) 342-8363

Full or Partial Restoration of your Classic, Special Interest or Sports Car

(20 minutes south of Cincinnati, OH)

Auto Fashions & Creations 2209-B Hamlets Chapel Rd Pittsboro, NC 27312 PH/FAX: 919-542-5566, press (*) for tone	auto sales handcrafts restoration rubber ink stamps

First come first served list. Call anytime, 919-542-5566. Press (*) for fax; press (4) for rubber ink stamp information and auto restoration services; press (3) for an updated in shop progress report; press (2) for classic auto sales. If you have further questions, leave a message or write to all the above address. Danny will return all inquiries. Thank you for reading this ad.

Auto Restoration by William R Hahn Palermo Auto Body 241 Church Rd (rear) Wexford, PA 15090 412-935-3790 days, 367-2538 eves	restoration

Open shop only. Auto Restoration by William R Hahn is a department of Palermo Auto Body specializing in investment grade restoration of investment grade collectable automobiles. Providing show quality with exceptional road going durability.

Auto Sport Restoration Alain Breton 110 Rue Du Couvent St Romain, QC Canada G0Y 1L0 PH/FAX: 418-486-7861	restoration

Mail order and open shop. Monday-Saturday 8 am-9 pm. Restoration for classic, antique and special interest vehicles. Specializing in body work, painting and rust repair, wiring. High quality work.

B & L Body Shop 104 Brookside Waynesville, NC 28786-4524 704-456-8277	restoration

Complete restoration of antique autos. Call first for confirmation. Established in 1968.

Banzai Motorworks 6735 Midcities Ave Beltsville, MD 20705 301-937-5746	pre-purchase insp/consultation repairs/restoration service

See full listing in **Section One** under **Datsun**

Barlow & Co 7 Maple Ave Newton, NH 03858 603-382-3591; FAX: 603-382-4406	car dealer restoration

Mail order and open shop. Daily 8 to 5. Specializing in restoration, service, import and export for classic British autos & motorcycles. MG, Autsin-Healey, Jaguar, Lotus.

See our ad on page 369

Barr's Antique Auto Restoration 1934 W 33rd St Erie, PA 16508 814-864-9085	restoration

Open Monday-Friday 8 to 5, other times by appointment. Full service antique auto restoration shop. Minor repairs to complete restorations.

Bassett Classic Restoration 2616 Sharon St, Suite D Kenner, LA 70062 PH/FAX: 504-469-2982 (have auto switching device)	parts plating restoration service

See full listing in **Section One** under **Rolls-Royce/Bentley**

Bay Area Industrial Dry Stripping 151 11th St Richmond, CA 94801-3523 510-412-9890, 510-805-1887	blasting paint removal

See full listing in **Section Two** under **rust removal & stripping**

Bayliss Automobile Restorations 2/15 Bon Mace Close, Berkeley Vale Via Gosford, NSW 2261 Australia 043-885253; FAX: 043-893152	repainting repairs sheetmetal work

Repairing, rebodying and repainting of vintage, thoroughbred and classic cars. Body panels and sheetmetal work fabricated to your specifications. All mechanical and upholstery work can also be undertaken. Locating service for that hard to find vintage, classic or sports cars.

Beckley Auto Restorations Inc 4405 Capital Ave SW Battle Creek, MI 49015 616-979-3013	restoration

Open shop only. Monday-Friday 8-4:30; Saturday by appointment. Restoration of antique, classic and special interest cars and trucks.

See our ad on page 370

Berkshire Auto's Time Was Box 347, 10 Front Street Collinsville, CT 06022 860-693-2332	restoration

Specializing in repair of street rods, custom or classic cars including insurance claim work. Our frame-work is second to none. We can custom mix any color in urethane paint. Motto: "Repair, not total, your old car". Also, full body-off or partial restorations with impeccable detail for competition or personal pleasure.

Bicknell Engine Company 7055 Dayton Rd Enon, OH 45323 513-864-5224	repair restoration

See full listing in **Section One** under **Buick/McLaughlin**

Bill's Model A Ford PO Box 220, Rt 611 Ferndale, PA 18921 610-847-8030	parts restoration

See full listing in **Section One** under **Ford '03-'31**

Billie Inc 10519 Zion Dr Fairfax, VA 22032 800-878-6328; FAX: 703-250-4586	garage diaper mats

See full listing in **Section Two** under **car care products**

Blackheart Enterprises Ltd 65 S Service Rd Plainview, NY 11803 516-752-6065; FAX: 516-694-1078	parts restoration

See full listing in **Section One** under **Checker**

Bob's F-100 Parts Co 9372 Mission Blvd Riverside, CA 92509 909-681-1956; FAX: 909-681-1960	parts

See full listing in **Section One** under **Ford '54-up**

Bonnet to Boot 7217 Geyser Ave Reseda, CA 91335 818-704-7770; FAX: 818-340-8674	restoration

Mail order and open shop. Restoration shop. Service and parts for Bentley, Jaguar and Rolls-Royce. Original British license plates. Colortone. Tool dealer.

Bonnets Up 5736 Spring St Clinton, MD 20735 301-297-4759	restoration

See full listing in **Section Two** under **coachbuilders & designers**

J D Booth Ltd RR 2 Box 2390 Spring Grove, PA 17362-9644 717-229-0805	restoration

Open shop only. Monday-Friday 8 am to 5:30 pm EST, Saturday by appointment. Restoration and maintenance of classic cars. Specializing in British and Italian.

A H Boucher Associates 9 Spruce St Cornwall on Hudson, NY 12520 914-534-9092; FAX: 914-735-9032	painting restoration

Shop open by appointment only. Restoration includes structural woodwork, rusty unit body repair, hand fabrication of panels, aluminum bodies, painting and mechanical work. Specializing in Mercedes-Benz 1930-69, plus Porsches and Lancias, "but will tackle anything."

Gerard Boucher PO Box 171 Franklin, VT 05457 514-298-5438; FAX: 514-298-5698, Quebec, Canada	**restoration**

Shop open Monday-Sunday 8 to 5 pm. Open for visit "by appointment." Selling my restoration shop; have a large inventory of antique cars for sale.

Bright Displays 1314 Lakemont Dr Pittsburgh, PA 15243 412-279-7037	**neon signs**

See full listing in **Section Two** under **automobilia**.

British Auto/USA 92 Londonderry Tpke Manchester, NH 03104 603-622-1050	**restoration** **parts** **upholstery**

See full listing in **Section One** under **Jaguar**.

British Car Specialists 2060 N Wilson Way Stockton, CA 95205 209-948-8767; FAX: 209-948-1030 E-mail: healeydoc@aol.com	**parts** **repairs** **restoration**

See full listing in **Section One** under **Austin-Healey**.

British Miles 9278 Old E Tyburn Rd Morrisville, PA 19067 215-736-9300; FAX: 215-736-3089	**accessories** **literature** **parts** **restoration**

See full listing in **Section One** under **MG**.

Brooklands/MG Only 8235/8237 S Tacoma Way Tacoma, WA 98499 206-584-2033	**body shop** **parts** **restoration** **service**

See full listing in **Section One** under **MG**.

Brothers Automotive Products 19715 County Rd 355 St Joseph, MO 64505 816-662-2060; FAX: 816-662-2084	**parts** **restoration**

See full listing in **Section One** under **Oldsmobile**.

Bryant's Antique Auto Parts 851 Western Ave Hampden, ME 04444 207-862-4019	**appraisals** **parts** **sheetmetal service**

See full listing in **Section One** under **Ford '03-'31**.

Cars of the Past 11180 Kinsman Rd Newbury, OH 44065 216-564-2277	**restoration**

Shop open. Monday-Friday 8 to 5:30, Saturday 8:30 to 12. Complete or partial restorations on antiques, classics, special interest, exotics and trucks. We do custom painting and graphics, custom pipe bending on all types of exhaust, including stainless steel. 1955-57 Chevys, Corvettes, 1955-57 T-Birds and trucks are our specialties.

Carters Auto Restorations 1433 Pawlings Rd Phoenixville, PA 19460 215-666-5687	**restoration**

See full listing in **Section Two** under **bodywork**.

Cedar Creek Coachworks Ltd 151 Conestoga Ln Stephens City, VA 22655 540-869-0244; FAX: 540-869-9577	**restoration** **service**

Open shop only. Mon thru Fri 8 am-5 pm, Sat by appointment. Restoration and service on collectible vehicles for domestic and some import makes. Full service facility.

Celestial Mechanics 88 West 500 South Wellsville, UT 84339 801-245-4987	**restoration**

See full listing in **Section One** under **Volvo**.

Central Alabama Restorations Ed Rouze, Owner 1665 McQueen Smith Rd S Prattville, AL 36066 334-361-7433	**appraisals** **restoration**

Complete restoration work. Full-time, 5-man shop. New, modern building. Partials or complete restorations. Rust fabrication, welding, painting, blasting, bodywork, interiors, appraisals. Reliable and honest. Quality workmanship, fair rates. Many National winners. Restorations are our only business.

Central Jersey Mustang 36 Craig St Edison, NJ 08817 908-572-3939; FAX: 908-985-8653	**parts** **restoration** **service**

See full listing in **Section One** under **Mustang**.

Clapper Restorations 9420 E Lake Shore Rd Clinton, WI 53525 608-676-5475	restoration

Open shop. Monday-Saturday 8 to 5. Complete shop restoration service, National trophy winning work. Specializing in 50s and 60s and muscle cars.

Classic Auto 251 SW 5th Ct Pompano Beach, FL 33060 954-786-1687	restoration

We are involved in the restoration of autos. Specializing in Ford products, Mustangs and T-Birds. Also street rods, custom cars, custom painting.

Classic Auto Rebuilders/CAR Box 9796 Fargo, ND 58106	painting/woodwork restoration

Mail order and open shop. Shop open by appointment only. Complete and partial restorations, plating, castings, welding, painting, convertible conversions, trim work, woodwork, customizing and metal work and parts fabrication. Complete coach and limousine building.

Classic Auto Restoration 437 Greene St Buffalo, NY 14212 716-896-6663	plating polishing restoration

Mail order. Chrome plating, pot metal repair, stainless steel repair & polishing, aluminum polishing, top show quality for over 25 years by United Custom Plating Ltd, 905-791-0990.

Classic Auto Restoration Service Inc 113 National Dr Rockwall, TX 75087 214-722-9663	restoration

See full listing in **Section One** under **Chevrolet**

Classic Car Radio Service 25 Maple Rd PO Box 764 Woodacre, CA 94973 415-488-4596; FAX: 415-488-1512 E-mail: healy@classicradio.com	radio repair radio restoration

See full listing in **Section Two** under **radios**

Classic Car Works Ltd 3050 Upper Bethany Rd Jasper, GA 30143 770-735-3945	restoration

Monday-Saturday 8 am to 6 pm. Service and restoration of all antique, classic & sports cars, American and foreign. Specialize in Jaguars and all English cars for all years & models. Electrical and mechanical problems solved. Expert paint, body and interior work. All convertible tops repaired and replaced.

Classic Carriage House 5552 E Washington Phoenix, AZ 85034 602-275-6825; FAX: 602-244-1538	restoration

Restoration, sales and appraisals by Craig Jackson, certified by Internal Society of Appraisers.

Classic Cartoons Auto Restoration 10860 SW 74th Ave Portland, OR 97223 503-246-1287	gauge repairs

Specializing in gauge repairs and complete cosmetic restorations. All types of instruments, speedometers, tachs, fuel, fuel senders, rebuilt, electric & mechanical, temperature gauges, ammeters, clocks, etc, voltage conversions. Custom work for street rodders, mechanical temperature gauges lenghtened. Some obsolete senders in stock. 20 years of professional service and experience. Guaranteed quality craftmanship, concours or custom.

Classic Coachworks 735 Frenchtown Rd Milford, NJ 08848 908-996-3400	bodywork painting restoration

Shop open Monday-Saturday by appointment only. Restoration and restyling facility specializing in cars from 1950 to the present. All work performed by certified craftsmen and supervised by a certified master craftsman. Bodywork, painting and restorations for 50s to present Corvette, Mustang, T-Bird, Mercedes, Rolls-Royce and Porsche. Collision work to all years, makes and models.

Classic Coachworks 4209 Misty Ridge Dr Haymarket, VA 20169 703-754-9366; FAX: 703-754-4933	dealer

Complete body and frame restoration. If it's metal, we can install it or make it. Dedication to detail always. Reasonable prices. Porsche, Jaguar, Shelby, Mustangs, Fords, MG, TR, plus all other classics.

Classic Datsun Motorsports 402 Olive Ave #A Vista, CA 92083 PH/FAX: 619-940-6365 E-mail: lescan@cts.com	appraisals literature parts restoration

See full listing in **Section One** under **Datsun**

Classic Motors PO Box 1011 San Mateo, CA 94403 415-342-4117; FAX: 415-340-9473	appraiser locator service movie rentals parts/restoration

Mail order and open shop. Monday-Friday 9 to 6. Automotive restoration. Specializing in convertibles and collector cars. Appraisals, service and parts for convertibles and collector cars. Corvette parts locator service. Collectable car & truck locator service. Movie car & prop rental service specializing in convertibles, sports cars & Corvettes.

Classic Motors Unlimited RD 1 Box 99C Hooversville, PA 15936 814-479-7874	chemical stripping metal work restoration

Open daily 8 to 5, Saturday by appointment only. Specializing in all aspects of auto and truck restorations, complete or partial. Techniques, blasting (sand, glass bead, plastic media), chemical stripping, collision repair, customs, fiberglass repair, mechanical repair, metal refinishing, plastic repair, painting, street rods & woodworking. All work performed to utmost perfection.

Classics and Customs 6414 123rd Ave N Largo, FL 33771 888-221-1847 toll-free 813-536-8372	**appraisals** **painting** **restoration** **rust repairs**

Business open Monday-Friday 8 am to 6 pm; Sat by appointment. Partial and complete frame-up restorations. Specializing in 50s-60s GM products including traditional sheetmetal fabricating, metal finishing and welding. Award winning body and finish work. Show quality detailing. All of this and superior service too. Our customers' tastes are simple, they prefer the very best, they prefer Classics and Customs. How can we help you?

Classics 'n More Inc 1001 Ranck Mill Rd Lancaster, PA 17602 717-392-0599; FAX 717-392-2371	**repairs** **restoration**

Shop open Monday to Friday 8:00 to 4:30. Restoration shop, classics, antiques, Corvettes, T-Birds, Mustangs, Triumphs, VWs and others. Specializes in automotive restoration for cars of the twenties to cars and trucks of the nineties. Deals in all phases of automotive repair, frame-up restoration to everyday driver cars.

Classics Plus LTD N7306 Lakeshore Dr N Fond du Lac, WI 54937 414-923-1007	**restoration**

See full listing in **Section Two** under **steering wheels**

Coach Builders Limited Inc PO Box 1978 High Springs, FL 32643 904-454-2060; FAX: 904-454-4080	**car dealer** **conv conversion**

Monday-Friday 8 to 5. Convertible conversions of Cadillac Eldorado, Buick Riviera.

Cobb's Antique Auto Restoration 717 Western Ave Washington Court House, OH 43160 614-335-7489	**restoration** **service**

Shop open Monday-Friday 8 to 5 or by appointment. Complete restoration, service or maintenance of pre -1942 antique and classic cars. Specializing in Pierce-Arrow, Franklin, L-29 Cord and other early antique and classic cars.

Cobra Restorers Ltd 3099 Carter Dr Kennesaw, GA 30144 770-427-0020; FAX: 770-427-8658	**parts** **restoration** **service**

See full listing in **Section One** under **Cobra**

Collector Cars & Route 66 Motors Box 50715 Amarillo, TX 79159 806-358-2951; FAX: 806-358-2344	**books** **parts** **photos** **restoration**

See full listing in **Section One** under **Lincoln**

Collector's Carousel 84 Warren Ave Westbrook, ME 04092 207-854-0343; FAX: 207-856-6913	**appraisals** **sales** **service**

See full listing in **Section Two** under **car dealers**

Collector's CARS Inc 150 E St Joseph St Arcadia, CA 91006 818-447-2576; FAX: 818-447-1461	**restoration** **service**

Mail order and open shop. Tues-Sat 8-5, closed noon hour.

Routine service repairs & complete restorations, full time parts sourcing for all Packard, foreign & domestic brands made between 1896-1975.

Collectors Choice LTD 6400 Springfield, Lodi Rd Dane, WI 53529 608-849-9878; FAX: 608-849-9879	**parts** **restoration** **service**

See full listing in **Section One** under **DeTomaso/Pantera**

Color-Ite Refinishing Co Winning Colors Rt 69 Bethany, CT 06524 203-393-0240; FAX: 203-393-0873	**modern finishes** **restoration service**

See full listing in **Section Two** under **paints**

Commonwealth Automotive Restorations 1725 Hewins St Ashley Falls, MA 01222 413-229-3196	**body rebuilding** **parts** **restoration**

See full listing in **Section Two** under **military vehicles**

Concours Quality Auto Restoration 32535 Pipeline Rd Gresham, OR 97080 503-663-4335	**auto restoration** **potmetal restoration** **repro gloveboxes**

Mail order and open shop. Monday-Saturday 8 to 6 or leave message. Ground-up restoration to 100 point, highest quality standard of all cars, all years. Specializing in pot metal welding & repair and restoration. Also glovebox reproduction, all cars with original style and color interior flocking.

Corvair Heaven PO Box 13 Ellenton, FL 34222-0013 813-746-0478; FAX: 813-750-8167	**car dealer** **literature** **restoration**

See full listing in **Section One** under **Corvair**

Corvette Specialties of MD Inc 1912 Liberty Rd Eldersburg, MD 21784 410-795-3180; FAX: 410-795-3247	**parts** **restoration** **service**

See full listing in **Section One** under **Corvette**

County Auto Restoration 6 Gavin Rd Mont Vernon, NH 03057 603-673-4840	**body work** **brakes** **restoration** **woodwork**

Open shop. Monday-Friday 8 to 5, Saturday by appointment. A small shop that specializes in total frame-up or partial restoration on antique cars and trucks - foreign or domestic. Sheetmetal panel and part fabrication, painting, woodwork, woodgraining, and upholstering. We also service antique vehicles. Over 40 years' experience. References upon request.

Custom Classic Cars 2046 E 12B Road Bourbon, IN 46504 219-342-0399 E-mail: asmith7112@aol.com	**parts** **restoration**

See full listing in **Section One** under **Chevrolet**

Generalists

Dan's Restorations
PO Box 144
Snake Hill Rd
Sand Lake, NY 12153
518-674-2061

restoration

See full listing in **Section Two** under **bodywork**

Dan's Volvo Service
6615 S MacDill Ave
Tampa, FL 33611
813-831-1616

restoration

See full listing in **Section One** under **Volvo**

Dash Graining by Mel Erikson
31 Meadow Rd
Kings Park, NY 11754
PH/FAX: 516-544-1102 days
360-7789 nights

dashboard
restoration

See full listing in **Section Two** under **woodgraining**

Davies Corvette
5130 Main St
New Port Richey, FL 34653
813-842-8000, 800-236-2383
FAX: 813-846-8216

customizing
parts
restoration

See full listing in **Section One** under **Corvette**

DeLorean One
20229 Nordhoff St
Chatsworth, CA 91311
818-341-1796; FAX: 818-998-6381

body work
parts
service

See full listing in **Section One** under **DeLorean**

Dependable RV & Auto Service
2619 Rt 11 N
Lafayette, NY 13084
315-677-5336

parts
restoration
service

See full listing in **Section Two** under **service shops**

Deters Restorations
6205 Swiss Garden Rd
Temperance, MI 48182-1020
313-847-1820

restoration

Mail order and open shop. Monday-Friday 7-5, Saturday 9-2. Antique, special interest & street rod restorations complete & partial. Sheetmetal fabrication.

Dexter Auto Inc
2096 W Shore Rd
Warwick, RI 02886
401-732-3575

restoration

Ask for George Simone when inquiring about our services and about your restoration needs. Over thirty years of affordable and detailed restorations offered. We can fully restore or do partial restorations. Remember Packards are our specialty. Many First Places and references. Our shop rate is $35 per hour.

Diablo Engineering
8776 East Shea, #B3A-109
Scottsdale, AZ 85260
PH/FAX: 602-391-2569

engines
parts

See full listing in **Section One** under **Porsche**

DiSchiavi Enterprises Inc
1248 Yardville Allentown Rd
Allentown, NJ 08501
609-259-0787

restoration

Complete & partial restoration of antique automobiles. Specializing in 1953-1996 Chevrolet Corvettes. We restore to NCRS standards.

M F Dobbins Inc
16 E Montgomery Avenue
Hatboro, PA 19040
215-443-0779

literature
parts
restoration

See full listing in **Section One** under **Corvette**

Doc's Jags
125 Baker Rd
Lake Bluff, IL 60044
847-367-5247; FAX: 847-367-6363

appraisals
interiors
restoration

See full listing in **Section One** under **Jaguar**

Doctor Jaguar Inc
740 W 16th St
Costa Mesa, CA 92627
714-646-2816; FAX: 714-574-8097

restoration
service

See full listing in **Section One** under **Jaguar**

Greg Donahue Collector Car Restorations Inc
12900 S Betty Pt
Floral City, FL 34436
352-344-4329; FAX: 352-344-0015

parts
restoration

See full listing in **Section One** under **Ford '54-up**

Dylan Bay Auto Museum
1411 4th Ave, #1430
Seattle, WA 98101
206-292-9874; FAX: 206-292-9876
E-mail: cbayley@dylanbay.com

museum
restoration
storage

See full listing in **Section Six** under **Washington**

East Coast Chevy Inc
Ol '55 Chevy Parts
4154A Skyron Dr
Doylestown, FL 18938
215-348-5568; FAX: 215-348-0560

parts
restoration

See full listing in **Section One** under **Chevrolet**

Eckhaus Motor Company
20818 E Weldon
Tivy Valley, CA 93657-9107
PH/FAX: 209-787-2224

car dealer
restoration shop

See full listing in **Section Two** under **car dealers**

Eddie's Restorations
4725 Rt 30
Elwood, NJ 08217
609-965-2211

restoration

See full listing in **Section One** under **Jaguar**

Edgerton Classics Ltd
RR 5 Box 199
Canastota, NY 13032
315-697-2722

restoration
woodworking

Open weekdays 9 to 5 or by appointment. Classic auto restoration. Twenty years' experience utilizing the most technologically advanced materials combined with old fashioned craftsmanship to produce high point, show-winning restorations of full classics. The finest metal working, fabrication, woodworking and mechanical work available. Absolutely the highest attention to detail and originality. Full or partial projects considered. Investment quality autos available.

Enfield Auto Restoration Inc	**panel beating**
4 Print Shop Rd	**restorations**
Enfield, CT 06082	**Rolls-Royce parts**
860-749-7917; FAX: 860-749-2836	**wood working**

Mail order and open shop. Monday-Friday 8 to 5:30. Full service. Restoration, panel beating, fabrication services, wood working, body work and paint, maintenance sales and services, wire-on leather service and coach building. Springfield Rolls-Royce parts.

Ezold's Model A Garage	**engine rebuilding**
1120 Southampton Rd	**restorations**
Westfield, MA 01805	
413-562-0273	

See full listing in **Section One** under **Ford '03-'31**

FEN Enterprises of New York Inc	**parts**
PO Box 1559	**restoration**
Wappingers Falls, NY 12590	
914-462-5959; 914-462-5094	
FAX: 914-462-8450	

See full listing in **Section One** under **Cadillac/LaSalle**

Flatlander's Hot Rod	**parts**
1005 W 45th St	**restoration**
Norfolk, VA 23508	**street rods**
804-440-1932; FAX: 804-423-8601	

See full listing in **Section Two** under **street rods**

Fore's Restoration	**restoration**
211 Sutton Rd	
Big Cove, AL 35763-9782	
205-518-9782	

M-F 8:30 to 6. Restoration of Ts to classics. We have built many show cars since 1973. Small business with personalized service.

Fourintune Garage Inc	**restoration**
W63 N147 Washington Ave	
Cedarburg, WI 53012	
414-375-0876	

See full listing in **Section One** under **Austin-Healey**

Franklin Buggy Werkes	**engine rebuilding**
510 Main St	**restoration**
Florence, KS 66851	**sheetmetal**
316-878-4684	**woodgraining**

Shop open Monday-Saturday 8:30 to 5:30. Restoration for classic, antique and special interest automobiles. Specializing in metal work, steel, aluminum. No plastics used. Woodgraining, mechanicals, wiring, wooden body restructuring and customizing. If you want it done right, we welcome your calls.

George Frechette	**brake cylinder**
14 Cedar Dr	**sleeving**
Granby, MA 01033	
800-528-5235	

See full listing in **Section Two** under **brakes**

Freeman's Garage	**parts**
19 Freeman St	**restoration**
Norton, MA 02766	**sales**
508-285-6500	**service**

See full listing in **Section One** under **Ford '03-'31**

Freman's Auto	**car dealer**
138 Kountz Rd	**salvage yard**
Whitehall, MT 59759	
406-287-5436; FAX: 406-287-9103	

See full listing in **Section Two** under **car dealers**

From Rust To Riches	**appraisals**
14200 New Hampshire Ave	**car dealer**
Silver Spring, MD 20904	**repairs**
301-384-5856; FAX: 301-989-1866	**restoration**

Mail order and open shop (by appointment only, please). Largest old car shop in the Washington, DC & Baltimore areas. Full service repair & award-winning restoration of all cars, 1900-1970. Specialists in Packards, Cadillac, Rolls-Royce, Bentley, Vanden Plas Princess & other American or British cars. Worldwide export of parts and cars, expert appraisals, broker service and consignments. 7,000 sq ft facility on 12 acres with over 25 years in the old car business & hobby.

Frontier Tank Center Inc	**automobilia**
3800 Congress Pkwy	**globes**
Richfield, OH 44286	**pumps**
216-659-3888; FAX: 216-659-9410	**signs**

See full listing in **Section Two** under **petroliana**

Fuller's Restoration Inc	**repairs**
Old Airport Rd	**restoration**
Manchester Center, VT 05255	
802-362-3643; FAX: 802-362-3360	

Open shop only. Monday thru Friday 8 am to 5 pm. Rust, collision and restoration, all makes and models, free estimates.

G & J Shore Weld Unlimited	**fabrication**
200-21 E 2nd St	**rust removal**
Huntington Station, NY 11746	**sheetmetal**
516-549-4503	**welding**

See full listing in **Section Two** under **rust removal & stripping**

Gaslite Garage	**engine rebuilding**
137 Lakeland Ave	**repairs**
Sayville, NY 11782	
PH/FAX: 516-589-7831	

Mail order and open shop. Mon-Fri 8-6, Sat 9-2. Antique, classic auto repairs & rebuilding. Everything from complete engine rebuilding, transmission rebuilding, rears, clutches, brakes, rewiring, complete parts fabrications, 57-59 Ford retractable top repairs, 61-67 Lincoln convertible repair, Hydro-Electric power top and window rebuilding. Rebuilding & repairs on all semi-automatics, fluid-drive, Hudson Electric-hand and Drivemaster, Cord Preselector transmissions, overdrives, vacuum tank rebuilding. Vintage Jaguar rebuilding. Some parts sales. Early brass car rebuilding & repairing.

G E Antique Creations	**renovation**
10721 Forest St	
Santa Fe Springs, CA 90670	
310-946-2660	

Mail order and open shop. Tuesday-Friday 9 to 5; Saturday 9 to 3. Renovation in stainless steel, brass, aluminum, pot metal welding and straightening. Repairs auto side moldings. Specialties are moldings, hubcaps and ornaments.

Mike Gerner, The Lincoln Factory	**car dealer**
3636 Scheuneman Rd	**parts**
Gemlake, MN 55110	**restoration**
612-426-8001	

See full listing in **Section One** under **Lincoln**

Glazier's Mustang Barn Inc 531 Wambold Rd Souderton, PA 18964 215-723-9674; FAX: 215-723-6277	accessories parts restoration service

See full listing in **Section One** under **Mustang**

GMS Restorations 20 Wilbraham St Palmer, MA 01069 413-283-3800	restoration

Mail order and open shop. Monday to Saturday 8 am to 5:30 pm EST. Dealing in full restoration services for all domestic classic and antique cars.

Golden Gulf Classics Inc PO Box 490 22530 Hwy 49 Saucier, MS 39574 601-831-2650	repairs restorations

See full listing in **Section One** under **Triumph**

Grand Touring 2785 E Regal Park Dr Anaheim, CA 92806 714-630-0130; FAX: 714-630-6956	engine rebuilding machine shop restoration suspension

Parts mail order and open shop. Monday-Saturday 8 to 5. Complete in-house restoration facilities offering paint, interior, plating, machine shop, engine building/dyno services. Custom design & fabrication of body panels, suspension, interior and engine parts. Specializing in 1900-1970 automobiles and motorcycles, including GM, Ford, Duesenberg, Mopar, Packard, Stutz, vintage race cars, plus British, Japanese and European bikes. From body-off restorations to simple repairs, we provide the best craftsmanship available. Our restorations have been featured in every major auto and motorcycle publication and have won every major concours event including Pebble Beach.

Grey Hills Auto Restoration PO Box 630, 51 Vail Rd Blairstown, NJ 07825 908-362-8232; FAX: 908-362-6796	restoration service

Offering services for all makes & models, antique, classic, collector, muscle cars & street rods.

Guild of Automotive Restorers 18237 Woodbine Ave Sharon, ON Canada L0G 1V0 905-895-0035; FAX: 905-895-0036 E-mail: theguild@interhop.com	restoration sales service

The Guild is dedicated to the restoration and sale of the world's great cars. With a true commitment to the highest standards, we restore and service all worthwhile automobiles with an emphasis on the full classics of the 20s and 30s. From complete frame-off restorations to small repairs and service. The Guild offers fine quality workmanship. We service a variety of cars including Rolls-Royce, Bugatti, Bentley, Packard, Pierce-Arrow, and many more.

Hand's Elderly Auto Care 2000 W Galveston St Grand Prairie, TX 75051 214-642-4288	repair restoration

Mail order and open shop. Monday-Friday 8 am to 5 pm. Maintaining, repairing and restoring antique automobiles, turn of the century to the 50s.

Haneline Products Co PO Box 430 Morongo Valley, CA 92256 619-363-6597; FAX: 619-363-7321	gauges instrument panels stainless parts trim parts

See full listing in **Section Two** under **instruments**

Harbor Auto Restoration 1504 SW 3rd St Pompano Beach, FL 33069 954-785-7887; FAX: 954-785-7388	restoration

Open shop only. Monday-Friday 8 am-4 pm, Saturday by appointment. Auto restoration for all makes and years.

See our ad on this page

Hatfield Restorations PO Box 846 Canton, TX 75103 PH/FAX: 903-567-6742	restoration

Open shop only. Monday-Friday 8-5. Complete or partial restorations. Street rod design and construction. Woodwork and metal fabrication. Quality workmanship and attention to detail. We invite you to come by and visit the shop.

Hein's Classic Cars 422 Douglas Durham, KS 67438 316-732-3335	restoration

See full listing in **Section One** under **Thunderbird**

Hibernia Auto Restorations Inc One Maple Terr Hibernia, NJ 07842 201-627-1882; FAX: 201-627-3503	lacquer restoration

Shop open Monday-Friday 7 to 5. Restoration of any collectible car, full or partial restoration. Nitrocellulose and acrylic lacquer for sale.

Hjeltness Restoration Inc
630 Alpine Way
Escondido, CA 92029
619-746-9966; FAX: 619-746-7738

restoration
service

Specializes in the restoration, service and repair of Mercedes 300SL and other classic automobiles. Internationally recognized for our attention to authenticity and detail.

Hollywood Classic Motorcars Inc
363 Ansin Blvd
Hallandale, FL 33009
954-454-4641; FAX: 954-457-3801

cars
parts

See full listing in **Section One** under **Thunderbird**

The Horn Shop
7129 Oriskany Rd
Rome, NY 13440

horn restoration

Mail order only. Rebuilds the motor section of your antique auto, motorcycle or boat horn. Mechanical and electrical repairs, includes the rewinding of the field coils and armature. If your horn is damaged beyond repair or missing completely, we will try to locate the correct horn for your marque's year and model. For inspection and written estimate of repairs, send the horn motor section, $7.50 and a SASE.

Hyannis Restoration
119 Thornton Dr
Hyannis, MA 02601
508-775-8131; FAX: 508-790-2339

restoration

See full listing in **Section One** under **Ferrari**

Impala Bob's Inc
9006 E Fannin, Dept HVAA12
Mesa, AZ 85207
602-986-0286; FAX: 602-986-3126,
order line: 800-209-0678; toll-free
FAX: 800-716-6237

parts
restoration

See full listing in **Section One** under **Chevrolet**

Jim's T-Bird Parts & Service
710 Barney Ave
Winston-Salem, NC 27107
910-784-9363

parts
restoration
service

See full listing in **Section One** under **Thunderbird**

John's Car Corner
Rt 5, PO Box 85
Westminster, VT 05158
802-722-3180

body parts
car dealer
mechanical parts
restoration service

See full listing in **Section One** under **Volkswagen**

JWF Restorations Inc
11955 SW Faircrest St
Portland, OR 97225-4615
503-643-3225; FAX: 503-646-4009

restoration

See full listing in **Section One** under **AC**

Georges B Karakolev
228 Rt 221
Napierville, QUE Canada J0J 1L0
PH/FAX: 514-245-0028

car dealer
parts
restoration

See full listing in **Section Two** under **restoration aids**

K-F-D Services Inc
HC 65, Box 49
Altonah, UT 84002
801-454-3098; FAX: 801-454-3099

parts
restoration

See full listing in **Section One** under **Kaiser-Frazer**

Keilen's Auto Restoring
580 Kelley Blvd (R)
North Attleboro, MA 02760
508-699-7768

restoration

Open shop only. Monday to Friday 8 am to 5 pm, Saturday 8 to 12. Restoring all years and makes of cars and trucks, all types of painting and customizing, street rods and mechanical repairs.

Kelley's Korner
22 14th St
Bristol, TN 37620
423-968-5583

parts
repair

See full listing in **Section One** under **Studebaker**

Ken's Cougars
PO Box 5380
Edmond, OK 73013
405-340-1636; FAX: 405-340-5877

parts

See full listing in **Section One** under **Mercury**

Ken's Klassics
20803 State Hwy 60
Muscoda, WI 53573-9602
FAX: 608-739-4241

car sales
restoration

Shop open Monday-Friday 8 to 5; Saturday by appointment. Established in 1981. A complement of seven experienced craftsmen specializing in complete and partial restorations of classic, collectible and special interest vehicles. Meticulous workmanship performed at reasonable rates and honest billings. Certified PPG show quality paint and refinishing services. National show and pleasure car restorations. References gladly given. Please visit our beautiful facility anytime.

Kip Motor Company Inc
13325 Denton Dr
Dallas, TX 75234
972-243-0440; FAX: 972-243-2387
E-mail: kipmotor@aol.com

literature
parts
restoration

See full listing in **Section One** under **Austin**

Krem Engineering
10204 Perry Hwy
Meadville, PA 16335
814-724-4806

engine rebuilding
repairs
restoration

Mail order and open shop. Monday thru Friday 8 am-5 pm. Restoration problems are what we do best. We do the stuff no one else can or wants to do. We can make or repair the uncommon, non-existent or difficult components. We also do problem engine and driveline rebuilds. We will use original manufacturing practices and procedures whenever possible. Twenty-three years' experience. Automobile, airplane, train, boat or machine.

L & N Olde Car Co
9992 Kinsman Rd, PO Box 378
Newbury, OH 44065
216-564-7204; FAX: 216-564-8187

restoration

Complete or partial restoration. Specializing in collector and show automobiles. Concours or to custom specifications, show quality paint and finish, sheetmetal and aluminum fabrication. Wood fabrication and coachwork, mechanical, electrical, lead work. Machine work and parts fabrication. Maintenance work and repairs. Serving our customers since 1976.

See our ad on page 377

Generalists

Land Yachts Automobile Restoration and Customizing
497 London Bridge Rd, Suite 101
Virginia Beach, VA 23454
757-431-0294; FAX: 757-431-4524

restoration

Open shop only. Monday through Friday 7 am to 5 pm. Restoration to original or custom, driver or show of all makes and models. Specialize in antique and custom limousine coachwork. Clients are encouraged to become intimately involved in the process and participation is invited.

Langley Paint & Body
3560 E Bethel Ln
Bloomington, IN 47408
812-336-2244

fiberglass parts
painting
restoration

See full listing in **Section Two** under **fiberglass parts**

Last Chance Repair & Restoration
PO Box 362A, Myers Rd
Shaftsbury, VT 05262

repairs
restoration

Mail order and open shop. Monday to Friday 7 am to 3:30 pm. Chassis preparations and restoration. Original Model A Ford parts and bodies available. Five years' Great American Race experience. Emphasis on reliability.

LaVine Restorations Inc
1349 Beech Rd
Nappanee, IN 46550
219-773-7561; FAX: 219-773-7595

restoration

Shop open Monday-Friday 8 to 5; Saturday by appointment. Specializing in professional National show restorations and pleasure car restorations.

L B Repair
1308 W Benten
Savannah, MO 64485-1549
816-324-3913

restoration

See full listing in **Section One** under **Ford '54-up**

Lee's Kustom Auto and Street Rods
RR 3, Box 3061A
Rome, PA 18837
717-247-2326

accessories
parts
restoration

See full listing in **Section Two** under **street rods**

Libbey's Classic Car Restoration Center
137 N Quinsigamond Ave
Shrewsbury, MA 01545
PH/FAX: 508-792-1560

bodywork
restoration
service

Open shop. Mon-Fri 9 am-6 pm, some Sat 9 am-12 noon. Complete & partial restoration, service, problem solving, mechanical, electrical & bodywork for all types of classic & special interest cars and antiques. Have done restorations on several Duesenbergs (two CCAC 100 pt cars), as well as Stanley Steamers, Packards, T-Birds, Mustangs and Cadillacs.

Jeff Lilly Restoration Inc
11125 FM 1560
San Antonio, TX 78254
PH/FAX: 210-695-5151

classic car
restoration
street rod building

Classic cars and custom street rods built on an hourly basis. Separate buildings for mechanical, body, painting, upholstery, assembly, creates organization, efficiency and a cleaner finished product of highest quality. Computerized disassembly process to find all the parts needed for your classic. 3/16 gaps on body

panels with wave free paint will complement your cars physique. Our work appears monthly in national magazines for your review in choosing us as your restoration company.

Lincoln Highway Packards
Main St, PO Box 94
Schellsburg, PA 15559
814-733-4356; FAX: 814-839-4276

engine rebuilding
restoration

See full listing in **Section One** under **Packard**

Lindskog Balancing
1170 Massachusetts Ave
Boxborough, MA 01719-1415
508-263-2040; FAX: 508-263-4035

engine balancing

See full listing in **Section Two** under **engine rebuilding**

Lister Restorations
6565 E 40
Tulsa, OK 74145
918-663-6220; FAX: 918-664-0804

appraiser
restoration

Mail order and open shop. Monday-Friday 8:30 to 5:30. Complete and partial restorations of US and European special interest cars with emphasis on Shelby-Cobras.

Madera Concepts
606 Olive St
Santa Barbara, CA 93101
800-800-1579, 805-962-1579
FAX: 805-962-7359

restoration
woodwork
woodwork repair

See full listing in **Section Two** under **woodwork**

Marchant Machine Corporation | metal forming machines
11325 Maryland Ave
Beltsville, MD 20705
301-937-4481; FAX: 301-937-1019
E-mail: dmarch4481@aol.com

See full listing in **Section Two** under **sheetmetal**

Marshall Antique & Classic Restorations | coolant additives restoration services
3714 Old Philadelphia Pike
Bethlehem, PA 18015
610-868-7765; FAX: 610-868-7529

See full listing in **Section One** under **Rolls-Royce/Bentley**

Mastermind Inc | parts restoration
32155 Joshua Dr
Wildomar, CA 92595
PH/FAX: 909-674-0509

See full listing in **Section One** under **Cadillac/LaSalle**

Masterworks Auto Reconditioning | restoration
1127 Brush Run Rd
Washington, PA 15301
412-267-3460

Open shop only. Shop open Monday-Friday 8:30 to 6. Performs 100 point restorations on all makes and models, foreign and domestic, old or new. Auto body repair, fabrication, customizing and reconditioning, also complete mechanical repair.

McAdam Motorcars Ltd | restoration
215 Redoubt Rd
Yorktown, VA 23692
757-898-7805; FAX: 757-898-9019

Shop open Monday-Friday 8 am to 5 pm or by appointment. Specializing in restoring vintage and other special interest motor cars, full or partial restorations to the owner's wishes. Complete engine rebuilding and painting facilities are available. For special interest motor cars, Ferrari, Mercedes-Benz and Mustangs.

McCann Auto Restoration | custom work restoration sandblasting
US Rt 1, PO Box 1025
Houlton, ME 04730
207-532-2206

Open shop only. Monday-Friday 8 to 5. Complete or partial restoration of classic, antique or special interest cars & trucks. Also sandblasting & custom work.

McGee Motorsports Group | race prep restoration
29121 Arnold Dr
Sonoma, CA 95476
707-996-1112; FAX: 707-996-9148

See full listing in **Section Two** under **racing**

Memory Lane Motors | car dealer restoration service
Lindsay St S
Fenelon Falls, ONT Canada
K0M 1N0
705-887-CARS

Mail order and open shop. Monday-Friday 8 to 5, Saturday 8:30 to noon usually. Interesting older autos, talked about enthusiastically. Bought, sold, serviced, recreated. We restore antique and classic vehicles, mechanical and body repair, Krown rust control center, float vehicles on a ramp truck. Used motor vehicles for sale.

Memoryville USA Inc | restoration
1008 W 12th St
Rolla, MO 65401
573-364-1810

Mail order and open shop. Monday-Friday 8 am-4:30 pm. We can restore any automobile, partial or complete, either for driving or to show quality, in one of the largest established restoration shops in the United States. Restoration is done in our shop by highly skilled craftsmen, with over 25 years' experience, who specialize in all phases of restoration work including mechanical, woodworking, painting, upholstering, pinstripping, woodgraining and parts fabrication. For more information, write or call us for our free brochure.

Alan Mest Early Model Auto Repair | mechanical repair restoration
17212 Gramercy Pl
Gardena, CA 90247
310-532-8657, 372-1039
FAX: 310-376-6009

Shop open six days 9 to 6. Repair and restoration of all pre-1955 American made autos.

Mid Valley Engineering | machine work parts restoration
16637 N 21st St
Phoenix, AZ 85022
602-482-1251; FAX: 602-788-0812

See full listing in **Section Two** under **transmissions**

Midwestern Motors & Dismantlers | salvage yard
19785 W 12 Mi, Bldg 404
Southfield, MI 48076
810-559-8848

See full listing in **Section One** under **Mercedes-Benz**

Muncie Imports & Classics | repair restoration upholstery
4401 St Rd 3 North
Muncie, IN 47303
800-462-4244; FAX: 317-287-9551

See full listing in **Section One** under **Jaguar**

Muscle Express | parts
509 Commerce Way W #3
Jupiter, FL 33458
800-323-3043 order line
561-744-3043 tech line

See full listing in **Section One** under **Chevelle/Camaro**

Must For Rust Co | rust remover
PO Box 972
Cedar Ridge, CA 95924
888-297-9224 toll-free
PH/FAX: 916-273-3576

See full listing in **Section Two** under **rust removal & stripping**

Mustang Classics | parts restoration sales service
3814 Walnut St
Denver, CO 80205
303-295-3140

See full listing in **Section One** under **Mustang**

Mustangs & More | parts restoration
2065 Sperry Ave #C
Ventura, CA 93003
800-356-6573; FAX: 805-642-6468

See full listing in **Section One** under **Mustang**

Tony Nancy Enterprises
4363 Woodman Ave
Sherman Oaks, CA 91423
PH/FAX: 818-789-6926

restoration

Mail order and open shop. Monday-Friday 9:30 to 6:30. Complete restoration and fabrication of classic and special interest cars. Over 30 years, same location. Quality for the most discriminating.

NCA Automotive
4235 W Lewis Ave
Phoenix, AZ 85009
602-272-9009

restoration

Stainless steel restoration, straightening and polishing. Also aluminum.

New Era Motors
11611 NE 50th Ave, Unit 6
Vancouver, WA 98686
360-573-8788

restoration

See full listing in **Section Two** under **woodwork**

Norm's Custom Shop
6897 E William St Ext
Bath, NY 14810
607-776-2357; FAX: 607-776-4541

interiors
tops

See full listing in **Section One** under **Cord**

Northern Motorsport Ltd
PO Box 508, Rt 5
Wilder, VT 05088
802-296-2099; FAX: 802-295-6599

repair
restoration
sales
service

Open shop. Monday-Friday 8 to 6. We specialize in service, repair and mechanical restoration of pre-70s Rolls-Royces, Bentleys, Mercedes, Bugattis and Packards. We are a full service shop providing service and repairs to current model year European automobiles as well as our beloved antiques. With machine tools on premises, we can fabricate some parts. We can provide references and pictures upon request. Contact: Mike Zack. We also sell European and antique automobiles.

Oak Bows
122 Ramsey Ave
Chambersburg, PA 17201
717-264-2602

convertible tops
restoration

Mail order and open shop. Monday-Friday 8 to 5. Complete top restoration. Specializing in early Ford. Oak steam bent bows, irons and sockets.

Odyssey Restorations Inc
8080 Central Ave NE
Spring Lake Park, MN 55432
612-786-1518; FAX: 612-786-1524

parts
restoration

Mail order and open shop. Monday-Friday 8 to 5. Full or partial restoration of brass and classic cars only to concours standards. Complete engine and chassis restoration and rebuilding for show and tour. Body restoration including coachbuilding in aluminum and steel, wood, fabric and paint. Specialists in CCCA Classics and parts for Franklins.

Old Car Woodgraining
27902 45th Ave S
Auburn, WA 98001
206-854-5247

dashboard
restoration
woodgraining

See full listing in **Section Two** under **woodgraining**

Old Coach Works Restoration Inc
1206 Badger St
Yorkville, IL 60560
630-553-0414; FAX: 630-553-1053

appraisals
body repairs
restoration

Open shop only, Monday-Friday 7 am to 5 pm, Saturday by appointment. Specializing in complete restoration service on all classic, antique and special interest automobiles. Maintenance program available for all cars. Will do minor body repairs and paint work. Nationwide pickup and delivery. Appraisal service also available.

Older Car Restoration
Martin Lum, Owner
304 S Main St, Box 428
Mont Alto, PA 17237
717-749-3383, 352-7701

repro parts
restoration

See full listing in **Section One** under **MoPar**

Bob Ore Restorations
4725 Iroquois Ave
Erie, PA 16511
814-898-3933; FAX: 814-899-8632

chemical stripping
chrome plating
restoration

Open Monday-Friday, 8 am to 5 pm, Saturday 8 am to 11:30 am. Specializing in complete or partial restoration, service and maintenance of all automobiles. In house chemical stripping and show quality chrome plating. Enclosed transport, references available. 25 years' experience.

Ottorich
619 Hammond St
Chestnut Hill, MA 02167
617-738-5488

restoration

See full listing in **Section One** under **Mercedes-Benz**

Guy R Palermo Auto Body
241 Church Rd (rear)
Wexford, PA 15090
412-935-3790; FAX: 412-935-9121

bodywork
restoration

See full listing in **Section Two** under **bodywork**

Patterson Coachworks
8951 Henry Clay Blvd
Clay, NY 13041
315-652-5794

parts
service

See full listing in **Section One** under **Pontiac**

A Petrik
504 Edmonds Ave NE
Renton, WA 98056
206-255-4852

heater control
valve rebuilding

Mail order only. Rebuilding service for all Ranco and Harrison heater control valves, 1930s thru 1960s. Established 1972.

R E Pierce
47 Stone Rd
Wendell Depot, MA 01380
508-544-7442; FAX: 508-544-2978

parts
restoration

See full listing in **Section One** under **Volvo**

Pilgrim's Special Interest Autos
3888 Hill Rd
Lakeport, CA 95453
PH/FAX: 707-262-1062

bodywork
metal fabrication
paint
restoration

Shop open Monday-Friday 8 am-5 pm, Saturday 8 to noon. Offers restoration, metal fabrication, body and paint.

Pioneer Valley Model A Ford Inc 81 East St Easthampton, MA 01027 413-584-8400; FAX: 413-584-7605 E-mail: pvma@aol.com	cars parts restoration

See full listing in **Section One** under **Ford '03-'31**

Pitcher's Auto Restoration 54 Metaterraine Ave Perryville, RI 02879 401-783-4392	engine repair parts restoration

Mail order and open shop. Monday-Friday 8 to 5; Saturday by appointment. Complete or partial restorations for all vehicles. Also babbitt bearing service and complete engine service for early cars including gas and steam powered. Mechanical repairs and fabrications for hard-to-find parts.

Precious Metal Automotive Restoration Co Inc 1601 College Ave SE Grand Rapids, MI 49507 616-243-0220; FAX: 616-243-6646	broker restoration

See full listing in **Section One** under **Mercedes-Benz**

Precision Pot Metal/ Bussie Restoration Inc 1008 Loring Ave #28 Orange Park, FL 32073 904-269-8788	pot metal restoration

See full listing in **Section Two** under **plating & polishing**

Precision Restoration Service Inc 1551 N Courtney Rd, Ste B-2 Independence, MO 64050 816-461-7500; FAX: 816-461-7504	restoration

Mail order and open shop. Monday-Friday 8-5. Restoration, body, paint and metal fabrication for Porsche (all years), Austin-Healey (big cars, 100-X and 3000), Jaguar (E-types), T-Birds (55-57).

Proper Jaguar 1806 S Alpine Rockford, IL 61108 815-398-0303, 398-8664	restoration

See full listing in **Section One** under **Jaguar**

Al Prueitt & Sons Inc 8 Winter Ave, PO Box 158 Glen Rock, PA 17327 717-428-1305; 800-766-0035 FAX: 717-235-4428	restoration upholstery woodwork

Shop open Monday-Friday 8 to 4:30. Complete restorations, upholstery, wood refinishing for antique and classic cars. Expert paint & bodywork, all types of mechanical work. Rolls-Royce service. We are a family run business with over thirty years' experience restoring cars of all makes. Please visit our shop anytime.

Quality Coaches 20 W 38th St Minneapolis, MN 55409 612-824-4155	parts restoration service

See full listing in **Section One** under **MG**

Ray's Upholstering 600 N St Frances Cabrini Ave Scranton, PA 18504 800-296-RAYS; FAX: 717-963-0415	partial/total restoration

Open Monday thru Friday 8-5. We restore antique, classic and specialized automobiles. Partial or total restorations.

RB's Prototype Model & Machine Co 44 Marva Ln Stamford, CT 06903 PH/FAX: 203-329-2715	machine work

See full listing in **Section Two** under **service shops**

Realistic Auto Restorations Inc 2519 6th Ave S St Petersburg, FL 33712 813-327-5162; FAX: 813-327-1877	restoration

Complete or partial restorations on antique, special interest, foreign & domestic autos. Specialists in sheetmetal fabrication, paint & body, mechanics, upholstery, woodwork, wiring and stainless steel repair, etc. Family owned & operated since 1978. Many Concours and National trophy winners. No job too small.

Redding Corp Box 477 George's Mills, NH 03751 603-763-2566; FAX: 603-763-5682	restoration

Open shop Monday-Friday 8-4 EST. We offer general restoration services tailored to the customer's needs and desires.

Regal Roadsters Ltd 301 W Beltline Hwy Madison, WI 53713 PH/FAX: 608-273-4141	replicars restoration

See full listing in **Section One** under **Thunderbird**

Reinholds Restorations c/o Rick Reinhold PO Box 178, 255 N Ridge Rd Reinholds, PA 17569-0178 717-336-5617	appraisals repairs restoration

Open shop only. Monday thru Friday 8 am to 5 pm, Saturdays & evenings by appointment. Complete quality restorations, repairs, service, appraisals, cars, trucks, fire engines, motorcycles. Anything, wood working, engine rebuilding, gas tank tumble cleaning, woodgraining.

Renaissance Restorations 4588 Payne Dr Woodstock, GA 30188 770-591-9732	body parts mechanical parts restoration

Restoration, repair and maintenance of British vehicles. Specializing in Jaguar cars.

Renascence Restoration 219 Park Ave Beaver Dam, WI 53219 414-887-8285, 6-9 pm	body work restoration

Shop open Monday-Saturday by appointment only. Restoration of pre-WW II cars preferred. Quality wood framework, panel fabrication and paint work at working man prices.

Reproduction Parts Marketing #3-1707 Sask Ave Saskatoon, SAS Canada S7K 1P7 306-652-6668; FAX: 306-652-1123	parts restoration service

See full listing in **Section One** under **Chevrolet**

Restoration Specialties John Sarena 124 North F St Lompoc, CA 93436 805-736-2627	interiors restoration

See full listing in **Section One** under **Chevrolet**

Restorations Unlimited II Inc 304 Jandus Rd Cary, IL 60013 847-639-5818	restoration

Open shop only. Monday-Friday 7 am to 5 pm, Saturday by appointment. A full service restoration center performing all phases in-house. Paint, upholstery, panel forming. Concours preparation. Restorations of foreign & domestic, aluminum, steel & glass. We have a history of winning cars at Pebble Beach, Meadowbrook, LCOC, AACA. Call us for that special project. Celebrating our 26th year in the restoration business. Web site: http://www.dwinc.com/ruii

Richard's Auto Restoration RD 3, Box 83A Wyoming, PA 18644 717-333-4191	restoration

Mail order and open shop. Monday-Friday 7:30 to 3:30. Sandblasting and glass bead work done.

Richardson Restorations 1861 W Woodward Ave Tulare, CA 93274 209-688-5002	repairs restoration

Shop open by appointment only. Repair and restoration of antique autos, tractors and farm machinery. Sand casting of small parts. Complete or partial restorations.

Rick's Relics Wheeler Rd Pittsburg, NH 03592 603-538-6612	bodywork painting restoration

Shop open Monday-Saturday 8 to 5. Complete and partial restorations for antique, classic and special interest cars. Painting, glasswork, wiring, body work with lead. All makes, foreign and domestic. 36 years' experience in the trade.

Riverbend Abrasive Blasting 44308 St Rt 36 W Coshocton, OH 43812-9741 614-622-0867	blasting painting polishing restoration

See full listing in **Section Two** under **rust removal & stripping**

RM Auto Restoration Ltd 825 Park Ave W Chatham, ONT Canada N7M 5J6 519-352-4575; FAX: 519-351-1337	panel fabrication parts restoration

Complete award-winning or partial restorations of Cadillac, Packard, Jaguar, Rolls-Royce, Stutz, Ferrari and Mercedes-Benz. All work done in-house to the highest quality. We are located 45 minutes east of Detroit. Shop hours are Monday thru Friday 9-5 and Saturday by appointment.

RMR Restorations Inc 13 Columbia Dr, Unit 1 Amherst, NH 03031 PH/FAX: 603-880-6880 work 603-672-8335 home	restoration

Mail order and open shop. Call anytime (home or work). Specializing in restoring your classic. Over 26 years' experience. Complete or partial restorations, metal fabrication including frame repair or modifications, metal work and lead work. Nothing is impossible. If you can imagine it, we can do it. If you are restoring your own classic and have any questions, please contact Bob Ryan, 603-880-6880.

Road Scholar 51 Floyd's Run Bohemia, NY 11716 516-673-8318, 9-10:30 am EST 516-369-4296, 7:30-10 pm EST	restoration

Shop open Monday-Saturday 10 am to 6 pm by appointment. A full service, 8,000 sq ft restoration facility dedicated to quality. We cater to British, German and Italian marques, but do not limit our services to such. All marques are welcomed. Vintage race car preparation and trackside services are available. Motorcycle restoration too. Good access to project vehicles & enclosed transport available.

Roadrunner Tire & Auto 4850 Hwy 377 S Fort Worth, TX 76116 817-244-4924	restoration speedometer repair

Mail order and open shop. Monday-Friday 7:30-5:30 CST. Mechanical restoration, engine rebuilding, suspension, brakes. Also mail order speedometer repair. Have had 12 Great Race entries, all finished.

Rod-1 Shop 210 Clinton Ave Pitman, NJ 08071 609-228-7631; FAX: 609-582-5770	street rods

See full listing in **Section Two** under **street rods**

Rode's Restoration 1406 Lohr Rd Galion, OH 44833 419-468-5182; FAX: 419-462-1753	parts restoration

See full listing in **Section One** under **Mustang**

Ron's Restorations Inc 2968-B Ask Kay Dr Smyrna, GA 30082 770-438-6102; FAX: 770-438-0037	interior trim restoration

See full listing in **Section One** under **Mercedes-Benz**

Route 66 Classic Restorations 250 N 1st St Wilmington, IL 60481 815-476-4290	restoration

Mail order and open shop. Monday-Thursday 9-8 pm, Friday-Sunday 9-10 pm. Climate controlled storage, customer work areas, full restoration services. In-house canvas and upholstery, major body and paint, machine shop and custom metal fabrication and welding. Retail parts. We restore and preserve any vehicle requiring exacting detail and professional researched restoration.

Paul Russell & Company 106 Western Ave Essex, MA 01929 508-768-6919; FAX: 508-768-3523	car dealer coachbuilding parts restoration

Shop open Monday-Thursday 8 to 6. Our restoration craftsmen offer mechanical, upholstery, parts, bodywork and paint, panel beating and coachbuilding services on all 50s and pre-war European classics such as Mercedes-Benz, Bugatti, Porsche, BMW, Hispano-Suiza, Alfa Romeo, etc. Sales, consignment, purchasing of all classic automobiles.

Safety Fast Restoration Company 118 Park Ave E Rear Mansfield, OH 44901 419-525-0799; FAX: 419-289-6241 E-mail: mgmetcalf@aol.com	restoration

See full listing in **Section One** under **MG**

Sanders Antique Auto Restoration	**restoration**
1120 22nd St	
Rockford, IL 61108	
815-226-0535	

Shop open Monday-Friday 8 to 4:30. Partial and complete restorations plus some repair. "Most of our work is antique and classic cars, but we enjoy special interest and sports cars, street rods and motorcycles, and an occasional boat."

SC Automotive	**parts**
Rt 3 Box 9	**restoration**
New Ulm, MN 56073	
507-354-1958; FAX: 800-6477-FAXS	

See full listing in **Section One** under **Chevrolet**

Schaeffer & Long	**restoration**
210 Davis Rd	
Magnolia, NJ 08049	
609-784-4044	

Shop open Monday-Friday 8 to 4:30. Restorations, complete or partial.

Selco Restoration	**parts**
9315 FM 359	**restoration**
Richmond, TX 77469	**service**
713-342-9751	

See full listing in **Section One** under **Cadillac/LaSalle**

Sheldon Classic Auto Restoration Inc	**restoration**
1245 N 3rd, Space G	
Lawrence, KS 66044	
913-843-6776	

A one man shop with a solid track record. Over twenty years' experience. Ten years in business. Full restorations only please. Vintage American and European.

Shelton Dealerships	**accessories**
5740 N Federal Hwy	**leasing**
Ford Lauderdale, FL 33308	**parts**
954-493-5211; FAX: 954-772-2653	**sales**

See full listing in **Section One** under **Ferrari**

Silver Star Restorations	**parts**
116 Highway 19	**restoration**
Topton, NC 28781	
704-321-4268; FAX: 704-321-6008	

See full listing in **Section One** under **Mercedes-Benz**

Silver State Restorations Inc **The Aday Collection**	**restoration**
4655 Aircenter Cir	**service**
Reno, NV 89502	
702-826-8886; FAX: 702-826-9191	

Shop open Monday-Friday 8-5. We have over 80 years of combined experience in restoring high quality antique, classic & special interest automobiles. Our complete 20,000 sq ft "In-House" restoration facility specializes in complete "frame-up" show quality restorations as well as partial restorations to the personal level you are seeking. Services include: paint, body work, metal fabrication, mechanical, electrical, upholstery, appraisals & consignments. We also have maintenance and service programs for all pre 1973 makes and models.

Chris Smith's Creative	**parts**
Workshop Motorcar Restoration	**restoration**
118 NW Park St	**service**
Dania, FL 33004	
305-920-3303; FAX: 305-920-9950	

Mail order and open shop. Monday-Friday 9 to 5. First quality ground-up, frame-off restorations. Parts, wood, steel and aluminum fabrication. Upholstery and trim. Complete in-house service specializing in Mercedes, Ferrari, Porsche, Lamborghini, antiques & special interest autos. Immersion paint and rust removal. Sandblasting parts, fabrication, detail, race car prep. Also large reference library.

Southern US Car Export Inc	**repair**
135 Eulon Loop	**restoration**
Raeford, NC 28376	**sales**
910-875-7534; FAX: 910-875-7731	**transport**

See full listing in **Section One** under **Cadillac/LaSalle**

Special Interest Autos	**restoration**
602 A St NE	**parts**
Ardmore, OK 73401	
405-226-0270; FAX: 405-226-0233	

Mail order and open shop. Monday-Friday 9 to 5. Small, family-operated business with fast, courteous and dependable service. Also specializes in high quality restoration for distributors, starters and generators. Electrical parts and restoration for all 1910-1970s makes and models.

Speed & Sport Chrome Plating Inc	**chrome plating**
404 Broadway	
Houston, TX 77012	
713-921-0235	

See full listing in **Section Two** under **plating & polishing**

STAR II	**parts**
PO Box 923	**restoration**
332 S Washington St	
Goliad, TX 77963	
512-645-2301; FAX: 512-645-8990	

Shop open Monday-Friday 8:30 to 5:30. Restorations, complete or partial for antique, classic or special interest vehicles. Custom work on bodies, frames or kit cars. Can custom paint, sandblast, bead blast, metal & lead work, frame repairs or modifications. Over 30 years' experience in automotive repair. Parts sources available for most years and makes. Contact owner operators, Don or Alice.

Steve's Auto Restorations	**restoration**
4440 SE 174th Ave	
Portland, OR 97236	
503-665-2222; FAX: 503-665-2225	

Mail order and open shop. Monday-Friday 7 to 4:30. Complete "ground-up" show quality restorations on antiques and classics, specializing in 300SL Mercedes, pre-war Mercedes, one-off and production run classics. Street rod design and construction. Mechanical, body work, paint, wiring, upholstery, metal fabrication. Resilvering of headlight reflectors. Complete light restoration, Halogen conversions, headlight lens, bulb and gasket sales.

Still Cruisin' Corvettes	**appraisals**
5759 Benford Dr	**repairs**
Haymarket, VA 20169	**restoration**
703-754-1960; FAX: 703-754-1222	

See full listing in **Section One** under **Corvette**

Stone Barn Inc   restoration
202 Rt 46, Box 117
Vienna, NJ 07880
908-637-4444; FAX: 908-637-4290

Restores antique, classic, exotic & special interest automobiles.

Stormin Norman's Bug Shop   repair
201 Commerce Dr #3   restoration
Fort Collins, CO 80524
303-493-5873

See full listing in **Section One** under **Volkswagen**

Stripping Technologies Inc   paint removal
2949 E Elvira Rd
Tucson, AZ 85706
800-999-0501; FAX: 520-741-9200
E-mail: sti@stripmaster.com

See full listing in **Section Two** under **rust removal & stripping**

Stutz Specialty Inc   parts
522 Southview Ave   restoration
Fort Wayne, IN 46806
219-745-5168; FAX: 219-749-0297

See full listing in **Section One** under **Stutz**

Tamarack Automotive Appraisals   appraiser
& Marine Surveys   restoration
53 Sears Ln
Burlington, VT 05401
PH/FAX: 802-864-4003
E-mail: gtlittle@aol.com

See full listing in **Section Two** under **appraisals**

T-Bird Nest   parts
2550 E Southlake Blvd   repairs
Southlake, TX 76092   restoration
817-481-1776

See full listing in **Section One** under **Thunderbird**

Techni Decapage   plastic media
203 Rue Joseph-Carrier   blasting
Vaudreuil, QC Canada J7V 5V5
514-424-5696; FAX: 514-424-5667

See full listing in **Section Two** under **rust removal & stripping**

Teddy's Garage   parts
8530 Louise Ave   restoration
Northridge, CA 91325   service
818-341-0505

See full listing in **Section One** under **Rolls-Royce/Bentley**

Thunderbirds East   parts
Andy Lovelace   restoration
140 Wilmington W Chester Pike
Chadds Ford, PA 19317
610-358-1021; FAX: 610-558-9615

See full listing in **Section One** under **Thunderbird**

Tillack & Co Ltd   parts
630 Mary Ann Dr   restoration
Redondo Beach, CA 90278
310-316-8760; FAX: 310-376-3392

Est. 1979 as full service restoration shop. Specializing in Italian & English exotics, Ferrari, Jaguar, Porsche, 356, Cisitalia,

Lamborghini, Maserati. Fully licensed auto dealership. Full restoration, parts, custom welding, machining and fabrication, race prep. Tax deferred exchanges & collection management.

Ultimate Upholstery   interiors
13384 Fallen Leaf Rd   top restoration
Poway, CA 92064   upholstery
619-451-3340

Shop open by appointment only. Emphasis on finely crafted interior and top restoration. Exclusively for antique and classic cars from 1900-1948 and exotic cars. Bill Podsedly, owner.

Vampire-Island Air Products   air dryers
50 Four Coins Dr   filters
Canonsburg, PA 15317
800-826-7473; FAX: 412-745-9024

Manufacturer of compressed air dryers, filters, auto drains.

Glenn Vaughn Restoration   appraisals
Services Inc   restoration
550 N Greenferry
Post Falls, ID 83854
208-773-3525; FAX: 208-773-3526

Automobile restoration: complete or partial, show car or driver restorations. Located in a low overhead area, so our labor rates are very competitive, while our focus is on efficiency, quality and integrity.

Veley's Restoration   paint
35161 SE Bluff   restoration
Boring, OR 97009   woodwork
503-663-7682

Shop open by appointment only. Concours winning restorations, complete or partial metal finishing, leadwork, paint, woodwork, mechanical and street rods, customs. We pay attention to details (car storage also).

Vicarage Jaguars   parts
3952 Douglas Rd   restoration
Miami, FL 33133
305-444-8759; FAX: 305-443-6443

See full listing in **Section One** under **Jaguar**

Vintage Radiators   radiator cores
Main Street, Abthorpe,
Nr. Towcester,
Northants, NN12 8QN England
44 1327 857726
FAX: 44 1327 858294

See full listing in **Section Two** under **radiators**

Vintage Vehicles Co Inc   detail
8190 20th Dr   restoration
Wautoma, WI 54982
414-787-2656

Open shop, Monday-Friday, 8:30-5:30. Many years' experience restoring classic, antique, sports and special interest cars. Also weld, remove dents and polish to factory finish: aluminum and stainless moldings, grilles, shells, hubcaps and beauty rings. Nationally recognized, complete or partial restorations. Complete facilities for all aspects of restoration. Strong on classics and foreigns.

Pete Watson Enterprises   car dealer
PO Box 488   restoration
Epworth, GA 30541
706-632-7675

Shop open by appointment only. Specializing in Fords.

West Coast Classics Inc 795 W San Jose Ave Claremont, CA 91711 909-624-7156	car sales

Shop open by appointment only. Car sales and antique and collector car toys for sale. Parts cars available. Also fender skirts, hubcaps, parts & motors.

Westwinds Motor Car Co RD 2, Box 777, Cox Rd Woodstock, VT 05091 802-457-4178; FAX: 802-457-3926	restoration

Open shop only. Monday-Friday 8 am to 5 pm. A small shop offering complete restoration services, mechanical, bodywork, upholstery. Rust repairs our specialty. All makes and models of automobiles, trucks and motorcycles.

The Wheel Shoppe 18011 Fourteen Mile Rd Fraser, MI 48026 810-415-7171; FAX: 810-415-7181 E-mail: jgs2nd@aol.com	performance parts welding wheel repair

See full listing in **Section Two** under **wheels & wheelcovers**

White Post Restorations One Old Car Dr, PO Drawer D White Post, VA 22663 540-837-1140; FAX: 540-837-2368	restoration

Complete or partial for all automobiles older than 25 years. One of the largest, modern, fully equipped with the best and most experienced employees in the world. Call us if you want a good driver or national show winner.

See our ad on this page

Dale Wilch Sales (RPM Magazine) 2217 N. 99th Kansas City, KS 66109 913-788-3219; FAX: 913-788-9682 E-mail: rpmcat@sound.net	speed equipment

See full listing in **Section Two** under **racing**

Wild Bill's Corvette & Hi-Performance Center Inc 451 Walpole St Norwood, MA 02062 617-551-8858	parts rebuilding service

See full listing in **Section One** under **Corvette**

Willhoit Auto Restoration 1360 Gladys Ave Long Beach, CA 90804 310-439-3333; FAX: 310-439-3956	engine rebuilding restoration

See full listing in **Section One** under **Porsche**

Wilson's Classic Auto 417 Kaufman, Rt 150 PO Box 58 Congerville, IL 61729 309-448-2408; FAX: 309-448-2409	restoration

Open shop only. Monday-Friday 8-5; Saturday 8-12. Award winning restorations, total or partial. We care more about quality than low price. Give us a call.

Wilson's Rods and Classics **Gary R Wilson** Rt 1, Box 139 Holliday, MO 65258 816-327-5583	restoration

Open shop. Monday through Friday, 8 am-5 pm. Specializing in restoring classic cars and building street rods. I have tools for fabricating sheetmetal parts; lathe and milling machine for light machine work. With 20 years' experience, I can complete entire vehicles with exception of upholstery. Customers speak directly with owner who also does all the work. Can supply references.

WTH Service and Restorations Inc 6561 Commerce Ct Warrenton, VA 20187-2300 540-349-3034; FAX: 540-349-9652 E-mail: wthauto@wthrestorations.com	restorations

Open shop only. Monday-Thursday 7-5, other times by appointment. High quality restoration 20 years or older automobiles, tractors, motorcycles and some toys.

WW Motor Cars & Parts Inc 132 N. Main Street PO Box 667 Broadway, VA 22815 540-896-8243; FAX: 540-896-8244	restoration

Open Monday-Thursday 7 to 5:30; Friday and Saturday by appointment. Complete or partial restorations of antique and classic automobiles and trucks. Our goal is to perform restoration work of national award winning caliber, whether it be for a trailer only show car, or just a "good driver". Quality, economical work, guaranteed. Special services include steering wheel restoration. We also offer consignment sales.

Yesteryear Restorations 387 Nutting Rd Jaffrey, NH 03452 603-532-7469	repair restoration sales transportation

See full listing in **Section One** under **Ford '32-'53**

rubber parts

A & M SoffSeal Inc
104 May Dr
Harrison, OH 45030
800-426-0902; 513-367-0028,
service & info; FAX: 513-367-5506

rubber parts
weatherstripping

Manufactures the highest quality weatherstripping and rubber detail parts for GM cars and trucks, Chrysler performance A, B and E body cars, customs and street rods. SoffSeal's USA made weatherstripping, rubber details, pedal pads, extrusions and gasket materials are engineered with sun and ozone resistant materials and "Attention to Detail™". These parts can be purchased directly from SoffSeal or from any one of our many worldwide dealer/distributors.

A-1 Street Rods
631 E Las Vegas St
Colorado Springs, CO 80903
719-632-4920 or 719-577-4588
FAX: 719-634-6577

parts

See full listing in **Section Two** under **street rods**

American Performance Products
675 S Industry Rd
Cocoa, FL 32926
407-632-8299; FAX: 407-632-5119

parts

See full listing in **Section One** under **AMC**

Antique Automotive Accessories
889 S Rainbow Blvd, Suite 642
Las Vegas, NV 89128
800-742-6777; FAX: 913-862-4646

accessories
tires

See full listing in **Section Two** under **tires**

Atlantic Antique Auto Parts
RR #6, PO Box 1388, Site 28
Armdale
Halifax, NS Canada B3L 4P4
902-479-0967

parts
service

Mail order and open shop. Monday-Saturday 9 to 8. Deals in repro, NOS, new stock parts, ie: chassis, body, rubber, electrical & mechanical & trim for all North American makes, 1909-90 cars & trucks. Also restores autos & has licensed mechanic on staff. Locator of many parts.

Bay Ridges Classic Chevy
1362 Poprad Ave
Pickering, ONT Canada L1W 1L1
905-839-6169; FAX: 905-420-6613

accessories
parts

See full listing in **Section One** under **Chevrolet**

Brothers Truck Parts
5670 Schaefer Ave, Unit G
Chino, CA 91710
800-977-2767, FAX: 909-517-3142
E-mail: brothers96@aol.com

accessories
parts

See full listing in **Section Two** under **trucks & tractors**

Stan Chernoff
1215 Greenwood Ave
Torrance, CA 90503
310-320-4554; FAX: 310-328-7867
E-mail: az589@lafn.org

mechanical parts
restoration parts
technical info
trim parts

See full listing in **Section One** under **Datsun**

Chev's of the 40's
2027 B St
Washougal, WA 98671
360-835-9799; FAX: 360-835-7988

parts

See full listing in **Section One** under **Chevrolet**

Classic Mercury Parts
1393 Shippee Ln
Ojai, CA 93023
PH/FAX: 805-646-3345

parts

See full listing in **Section One** under **Mercury**

Clester's Auto Rubber Seals Inc
PO Box 459
Cleveland, NC 27013
704-637-9979; FAX: 704-636-7390

gloveboxes
headliners/parts
molded rubber
weatherstripping

Mail order and open shop. Monday-Friday 8:30-5. We manufacture rubber weatherstripping (ie: windshield seals, door seals, trunk seals), molded rubber parts and other products including gloveboxes and headliners for Chevrolet, Ford and MoPar cars and trucks. Also International Harvester pickups and travelalls.

Convertible Service
5126-HA Walnut Grove Ave
San Gabriel, CA 91776
800-333-1140, 818-285-2255
FAX: 818-285-9004

convertible parts
top mechanism
service

See full listing in **Section Two** under **tops**

Corvette Rubber Company
10640 W Cadillac Rd
Cadillac, MI 49601
616-779-2888; FAX: 616-779-9833

rubber products
weatherstripping

See full listing in **Section One** under **Corvette**

Design Fabrications, Pure Products Division
PO Box 40205
Santa Barbara, CA 93140-0205
805-965-6031

parts

See full listing in **Section Two** under **comprehensive parts**

Don's Obsolete Auto Parts
2315-10 N Pearl St #207
Tacoma, WA 98406
206-759-4407;
E-mail: dkleask@nwrain.com

door seals
restoration
supplies
trunk seals

Open Monday- Friday 9-5 PST. Specializing in American made quality trunk & door seals, also carry a complete line of restoration supplies. Catalog available, $4.

Extensions Plus Inc
3500 Park Central Blvd N
Pompano Beach, FL 33064
954-978-3362; FAX: 954-978-0630
E-mail: 4star@gate.net

body filler parts

See full listing in **Section Two** under **body parts**

Ford Reproduction Parts Store
110 Ford Rd
PO Box 226
Bryan, OH 43506-0226
419-636-2475; FAX: 419-636-8449
E-mail: fordpart@bright.net

parts

See full listing in **Section One** under **Ford '54-up**

Foreign Autotech — parts
3235 C Sunset Ln
Hatboro, PA 19040
215-441-4421; FAX: 215-441-4490

See full listing in **Section One** under **Volvo**

Hoffman Automotive Distributor — parts
U.S. Hwy #1, Box 818
Hilliard, FL 32046
904-845-4421

See full listing in **Section Two** under **body parts**

Impala Bob's Inc — parts / restoration
9006 E Fannin, Dept HVAA12
Mesa, AZ 85207
602-986-0286; FAX: 602-986-3126,
order line: 800-209-0678; toll-free
FAX: 800-716-6237

See full listing in **Section One** under **Chevrolet**

International Mercantile — rubber parts
PO Box 2818
Del Mar, CA 92014-2818
619-438-2205; 800-356-0012
FAX: 619-438-1428

See full listing in **Section One** under **Porsche**

Karr Rubber Manufacturing — rubber parts
133 Lomita St
El Segundo, CA 90245
310-322-1993; 800-955-5277

Mail order and open shop. Mon-Fri 9 to 5. Manufactures custom made and production rubber extrusions and moldings. Send us your old extruded or molded rubber and we will reproduce it, with very few exceptions. Some tooling costs may be necessary.

KopyKatz Auto Body Parts — fenders / hoods / panels
2536 N Sheridan
Denver, CO 80214
303-458-5332; FAX: 303-477-1496

See full listing in **Section Two** under **body parts**

Legendary Auto Interiors Ltd — soft trim
121 W Shore Blvd
Newark, NY 14513
800-363-8804; FAX: 800-732-8874

See full listing in **Section One** under **Chrysler**

The Maverick Connection — literature / parts
137 Valley Dr
Ripley, WV 25271
PH/FAX: 304-372-7825

See full listing in **Section One** under **Ford '54-Up**

Mercury & Ford Molded Rubber — parts
12 Plymouth Ave
Wilmington, MA 01887
508-658-8394

See full listing in **Section One** under **Mercury**

Merv's Classic Chevy Parts — parts
1330 Washington
Iowa Falls, IA 50126
515-648-3168

See full listing in **Section One** under **Chevrolet**

MikeCo Antique, Kustom & Obsolete Auto Parts — lenses / parts
4053 Calle Tesoro, Unit C
Camarillo, CA 93012
805-482-1725; FAX: 805-987-8524

See full listing in **Section One** under **MoPar**

Millers Incorporated — accessories / parts
7412 Count Circle
Huntington Beach, CA 92647
714-375-6565; FAX: 714-847-6603
E-mail: millermbz@aol.com

See full listing in **Section One** under **Mercedes-Benz**

Mooney's Antique Parts — engine parts / rubber parts
HC 01, Box 645C
Goodrich, TX 77335
409-365-2899, 9 am to 6 pm
409-685-4577, 6-9 pm nights
for orders only

See full listing in **Section Two** under **comprehensive parts**

Motorsport Auto — parts
1139 W Collins Ave
Orange, CA 92667
714-639-2620; 800-633-6331
FAX: 714-639-7460

See full listing in **Section One** under **Datsun**

Northwest Classic Falcons Inc — parts
1964 NW Pettygrove St
Portland, OR 97209
503-241-9454; FAX: 503-241-1964

See full listing in **Section One** under **Ford '54-Up**

Obsolete Chevrolet Parts Co — engine parts / radiators / rubber parts / transmissions
524 Hazel Ave
PO Box 68
Nashville, GA 31639
912-686-5812

See full listing in **Section One** under **Chevrolet**

Old Auto Rubber Company — parts
4/4 Appin Place
PO Box 328, St. Mary's 2760
Dunheved, Sydney Australia
61 (2) 9623-5333
FAX: 61 (2) 9833-1041, 24 hrs

Mail order and open shop. Monday-Friday 8:30 to 5 pm. Specializing in mail order. Extrusions, molded rubber parts, door & screen seals, body hardware, engine & suspension mounts. Also sheetmetal body panels & rust repair sections. Inhouse rubber moldings, small run specialists. Post samples, Fax drawings. Prompt quotations. Vintage to mid-80s for all Australian Holden & Ford. Major British, many Japanese & American models. When in Sydney, come & visit. Catalog #19, $20/ US airmail.

Original Parts Group Inc — accessories / parts
17892 Gothard St
Huntington Beach, CA 92647
800-243-8355 US & Canada
714-841-5363; FAX: 714-847-8159

See full listing in **Section One** under **Pontiac**

Pollard Co
Joe Pollard
9331 Johnell Rd
Chatsworth, CA 91311
PH/FAX: 818-999-1485

| | parts |

See full listing in **Section One** under **Checker**

**Quanta Restoration
& Preservation Products**
45 Cissel Dr
North East, MD 21901
410-658-5700; FAX: 410-658-5758

| | fan belts
gas tanks |

See full listing in **Section Two** under **chassis parts**

Raybuck Autobody Parts
RD 4, Box 170
Punxsutawney, PA 15767
814-938-5248; FAX: 814-938-4250

| | body parts |

See full listing in **Section Two** under **body parts**

RB's Obsolete Automotive
18421 Hwy 99
Lynnwood, WA 98037
206-670-6739; FAX: 206-670-9151

| | parts |

See full listing in **Section Two** under **comprehensive parts**

Rhino Industries
14512 N Nebraska Ave
Tampa, FL 33613
813-977-7776; FAX: 813-977-5419

| | cleaner |

See full listing in **Section Two** under **car care products**

Silverstate Cadillac Parts
PO Box 2161
Sparks, NV 89431
702-331-7252; FAX: 702-331-7887

| | parts |

See full listing in **Section One** under **Cadillac/LaSalle**

Star Quality
1 Alley Rd
La Grangeville, NY 12540
800-782-7199; FAX: 914-266-5394
E-mail: sq@mhv.net

| | parts |

See full listing in **Section One** under **Mercedes-Benz**

Steele Rubber Products Inc
6180 Hwy 150 E
Denver, NC 28037
800-544-8665; 704-483-9343
FAX: 704-483-6650

| | repro rubber parts |

Mail order and open shop. Monday-Friday 8 to 5; orders accepted 24 hours. "Top quality US rubber, first in detailed and faithful to original." For 1925-mid 70s American cars except Ford.

See our ad on this page

Swedish Classics Inc
PO Box 557
Oxford, MD 21654
800-258-4422; FAX: 410-226-5543

| | parts |

See full listing in **Section One** under **Volvo**

Thunderbird Headquarters
1080 Detroit Ave
Concord, CA 94518
800-227-2174, US
FAX: 510-689-1771

accessories
literature
parts
upholstery

See full listing in **Section One** under **Thunderbird**

Wale's Antique Chevy Truck Parts
143 Center
Carleton, MI 48117
313-654-8836

parts

See full listing in **Section One** under **Chevrolet**

Pat Walsh Restorations
Box Q
Wakefield, MA 01880
617-246-5565

literature
rubber parts

Mail order only. Mon-Fri 8 am to 5 pm. Specializing in weatherseals, floor mats, NOS, rubber, service manuals, parts books, trunk mats, interiors, carpets, trunk interiors, window seals, glass runs and settings, other restoration items 1900s-1980s.

Wefco Rubber Manufacturing Company Inc
21000 Osborne St Ste 2
Canoga Park, CA 91304-1758
818-886-8872; FAX: 818-886-8875

rubber extrusions

Mail order and open shop. Monday-Friday 7 to 4. Extrusions: rubber and soft sponge, die cuts, windshield rubber splicing. Send sample or drawing of molded parts needed and 1/2-inch sample or drawing of extrusion needed. "No job too big or too small." Catalog $10.

West Coast Metric Inc
24002 Frampton Ave
Harbor City, CA 90710
310-325-0005; FAX: 310-325-9733
E-mail: wcmi@earthlink.net

apparel
carpets
rubber parts

See full listing in **Section One** under **Volkswagen**

The Wixom Connection
2204 Steffanie Ct
Kissimmee, FL 34746
407-933-4030

parts

See full listing in **Section One** under **Lincoln**

World Upholstery & Trim
PO Box 4857
Thousand Oaks, CA 91359
800-222-9577; FAX: 818-707-2664
E-mail: worlduph@mail.vcnet.com

carpet kits
tops
upholstery kits

See full listing in **Section Two** under **interiors & interior parts**

rust removal & stripping

Ace Auto Body & Towing Ltd
65 S Service Rd
Plainview, NY 11803
516-752-6065; FAX: 516-752-1484

mechanical repairs
restorations

See full listing in **Section Two** under **restoration shops**

AmeriVap Systems
582 Armour Cir NE
Atlanta, GA 30324
404-876-2220; FAX: 404-876-3206

cleaning system

See full listing in **Section Two** under **car care products**

Antique Sandblasting
A David Allen
370 S Fifth E
Rexburg, ID 83440
208-356-8640

metal parts
sandblasting

Shop open variable hours during the summer. Specializing in metal parts for antique cars. Pickup and delivery at no cost. Free estimates.

B & L Body Shop
104 Brookside
Waynesville, NC 28786-4524
704-456-8277

restoration

See full listing in **Section Two** under **restoration shops**

Bay Area Industrial Dry Stripping
151 11th St
Richmond, CA 94801-3523
510-412-9890, 510-805-1887

blasting
paint removal

Shop open Monday-Friday 9:30 to 6:30, Saturday and Sunday by appointment. Specializing in the stripping of Corvettes. Plastic media blasting specializing in automotive sheetmetal, mechanical parts and fiberglass coating and paint removal. Superior to conventional stripping methods, no chemicals, no residue, far less abrasive than sandblasting. No pitting or warping. Safe and reliable service.

F J Cabrera Enterprises
15507 Normandie Ave, #103
Gardena, CA 90247
310-532-8894; FAX: 310-515-0928

accessories
lights

See full listing in **Section Two** under **restoration aids**

Capt Lee's Spra' Strip
PO Box 203
Hermitage, TN 37076
800-421-9498; FAX: 615-889-1798

paint remover

Mail order and open shop. Monday-Friday 12 pm to 4:30 pm CST. Dealing in auto Spra' Strip Paint Remover. Capt Lee's Rust-Away and Metal Prep & Conditioner.

Castle Metal Finishing
15 Broad St
Hudson, MA 01749
508-562-7294

chrome restoration
metal polishing
plating

See full listing in **Section Two** under **plating & polishing**

Classic Motors Inc
Rich Adams
103 200th Ave
Union Grove, WI 53182
414-878-2525; FAX: 414-878-0400

car sales
trailer sales

See full listing in **Section Two** under **car dealers**

Composition Materials Co Inc
1375 Kings Hwy E
Fairfield, CT 06430
800-262-7763; FAX: 203-335-9728

plastic media

See full listing in **Section Two** under **restoration aids**

| County Auto Restoration
6 Gavin Rd
Mont Vernon, NH 03057
603-673-4840 | **body work**
brakes
restoration
woodwork |

See full listing in **Section Two** under **restoration shops**

| Dry Stripping Facilities Network
220 7th St SE
Canton, OH 44702
330-455-1181; FAX: 330-455-1191 | **paint removal**
stripping |

Network of coating removal & surface preparation specialists
employing the new technology of plastic media blasting. As of
April 1994, over 120 shops located throughout the US & Canada.

| Fini-Finish Metal Finishing
24657 Mound Rd
Warren, MI 48091
810-758-0050; FAX: 810-758-0054 | **plating**
polishing
pot metal repair |

See full listing in **Section Two** under **plating & polishing**

| G & J Shore Weld Unlimited
200-21 E 2nd St
Huntington Station, NY 11746
516-549-4503 | **fabrication**
rust removal
sheetmetal
welding |

Open shop only. Monday-Friday 9 to 5, Saturday 9 to noon.
Specializing in rust removal and custom sheetmetal fabrication
(aftermarket parts on availability). Offers other welding services
including aluminum, cast aluminum, cast iron, stainless steel,
steel and custom pipe bending (roll bars, bumpers and cages).
We are able to meet your needs.

| Guyson Corp of USA
W J Grande Industrial Park
Saratoga Springs, NY 12866-9044
518-587-7894; FAX: 518-587-7840 | **restoration aids** |

Manufacturers of blast cleaning and surface finishing cabinets,
both manually operated and automatic.

| Imperial Restoration Inc
308 Lockport St
Lemont, IL 60439
630-257-5822; FAX: 630-257-5892 | **engine enamels**
gas tank sealer
paint/rust remover
rust preventives |

See full listing in **Section Two** under **restoration aids**

| Must For Rust Co
PO Box 972
Cedar Ridge, CA 95924
888-297-9224 toll-free
PH/FAX: 916-273-3576 | **rust remover** |

We are the manufacturers of an environmentally friendly rust
remover/inhibitor, MP-7.

| Nor-Cal Metal Stripping
10010 Old Redwood Hwy
Windsor, CA 95492
800-698-9470 | **rust removal** |

Shop open Monday-Friday 9 to 5; Saturday 9 to 12. Paint and
rust removal by chemical immersion process. Eighteen foot
tanks with car body and frame capacity.

| Paul's Chrome Plating Inc
341 Mars-Valencia Rd
Mars, PA 16046
800-245-8679; 412-625-3135
FAX: 412-625-3060 | **repair**
restoration |

See full listing in **Section Two** under **plating & polishing**

| Pennsylvania Metal Cleaning
200 17th St
Monaca, PA 15061-1969
412-728-5535 | **derusting**
stainless fasteners
stripping |

Mail order and open shop. Monday-Friday 8 am to 5 pm,
Saturday 8 am to noon. Opened in 1978. Can strip and derust
anything from a bolt to a body, using non-destructive alkaline
system. Tanks are 20 feet in length. Individuals, commercial or
industrial. Extensive selection of stainless steel nuts, bolts,
washers, screws, cotter pins, wood screws and nails. Specialty
items include exhaust system clamps. Model A bumper end bolts
and door hinge screws in stainless steel.

| Precision Paint &
Rust Removers Inc
2415 W Industrial Blvd
Long Lake, MN 55356
PH/FAX: 612-476-4545 | **paint removal**
rust removal |

Open shop only. Monday-Friday 8-5, Saturday 9-12. Paint and
rust removal, plastic media & alkaline immersion. Large
20'x8'x6' tank. Complete bodies & frames depainted and derust-
ed. On site professional metal fabrication services. State of the
art facilities.

| Pro-Strip
2415 W State Blvd
Fort Wayne, IN 46808
219-436-2828; FAX: 219-432-1941 | **rust removal** |

Mail order and open shop. Monday-Friday 7-5; Saturday 8-12.
Pro-Strip offers complete rust and paint removal from individual
parts to complete automobiles. Pro-Strip can custom powder
coat your part in a wide variety of colors, also buffing and polishing on metal.

| Raybuck Autobody Parts
RD 4, Box 170
Punxsutawney, PA 15767
814-938-5248; FAX: 814-938-4250 | **body parts** |

See full listing in **Section Two** under **body parts**

| Redi-Strip Company
100 West Central Ave
Roselle, IL 60172
630-529-2442; FAX: 630-529-3626 | **abrasive media**
paint removal
plastic media
rust removal |

Open shop or mail order. Monday thru Friday 8 am to 5 pm,
Saturday 8:30 am-11:30 am. Chemical paint and alkaline elec-
trolytic immersion process rust removal. Also non-abrasive
blasting removes paint and coatings from delicate substrates.
Abrasive blasting removes rust and etch and texturize surfaces.

| Richard's Auto Restoration
RD 3, Box 83A
Wyoming, PA 18644
717-333-4191 | **restoration** |

See full listing in **Section Two** under **restoration shops**

| Riverbend Abrasive Blasting
44308 St Rt 36 W
Coshocton, OH 43812-9741
614-622-0867 | **blasting**
painting
polishing
restoration |

Mail order and open shop. Shop open Monday-Friday 9 am-5
pm, Saturday by appointment. Multi-media abrasive blasting,
stainless steel trim restoration, metal buffing and polishing,
vehicle restoration and painting. Emphasis on fine unhurried
workmanship.

Generalists

T Schmidt
827 N Vernon
Dearborn, MI 48128-1542
313-562-7161

rust removers

Mail order only. Deals in Oxisolv rust removers, metal preps, degreasers, wire wheel cleaners and parts washers.

StripMasters of Nashville Inc
206B Cole Ave
Nashville, TN 37210
615-255-4850, 800-356-8205

paint stripping

Monday-Friday 7:30 am to 4:30 pm. Family owned and operated paint stripping service. Paint is removed by plastic media blasting. The low pressure blasting of plastic chips completely strips paint, leaving the metal or fiberglass as new. No pits or panel warpage. Dry paint stripping for metal or fiberglass cars, trucks, boats, airplanes and parts.

Stripping Technologies Inc
2949 E Elvira Rd
Tucson, AZ 85706
800-999-0501; FAX: 520-741-9200
E-mail: sti@stripmaster.com

paint removal

Mail order and open shop. Monday-Friday 7 am to 5 pm MST, Saturdays by appointment. Plastic media blasting equipment & services. For rapid, economic, safe & environmentally considerate removal of paint from metal, plastic, fiberglass and other services. Stripping Technologies Inc was incorporated in 1987.

Tar Heel Parts Inc
PO Box 2604
Matthews, NC 28106-2604
800-322-1957; 704-845-1847 (local)
FAX: 704-845-5447

buffing supplies

See full listing in **Section Two** under **plating & polishing**

Techni Decapage
203 Rue Joseph-Carrier
Vaudreuil, QC Canada J7V 5V5
514-424-5696; FAX: 514-424-5667

plastic media blasting

Open shop only. Monday-Saturday. Plastic media blasting, specialists in the precision removal of paint and surface coatings and rust.

Tri-State Metal Cleaning
4725 Iroquois Ave
Erie, PA 16511
814-898-3933
FAX: 814-899-8632 after 3:30 pm

cleaning
rust removal
stripping

Mail order and open shop. Monday-Friday 8 am-5 pm. Large capacity tanks, 18' long x 8' wide x 6' deep, to remove many years of accumulated grime, paint & rust from bodies, engines & frames. When we do the dirty work, hundreds of labor hours of hand cleaning & stripping are eliminated.

Ziebart/Tidy Car
803 Mount Royal Blvd
Pittsburgh, PA 15223
412-486-4711

accessories
detailing
rustproofing

See full listing in **Section Two** under **rustproofing**

rustproofing

Applied Chemical Specialties
PO Box 241597
Omaha, NE 68124
800-845-8523; FAX: 402-390-9262

corrosion protection

See full listing in **Section Two** under **storage care products**

Graf International
4336 Willick Rd
Niagara Falls, ON Canada L2E 6S6
905-295-3118; FAX: 905-295-6610

rust preventative

Instead of rust, Noverox. Noverox Formula anti-rust does not contain pollutants such as lead, zinc, chromates, mineral acids. It is non-flammable. Noverox does not damage painted surfaces. Rust preventative and neutralizer. Paint right over rust.

See our ad on page 391

High Performance Coatings
550 W 3615 S
Salt Lake City, UT 84115
801-262-6807; FAX: 801-262-6307
E-mail: hpcsales@hpcoatings.com

coatings

See full listing in **Section Two** under **exhaust systems**

Imperial Restoration Inc
308 Lockport St
Lemont, IL 60439
630-257-5822; FAX: 630-257-5892

engine enamels
gas tank sealer
paint/rust remover
rust preventives

See full listing in **Section Two** under **restoration aids**

Memory Lane Motors
Lindsay St S
Fenelon Falls, ON Canada K0M 1N0
705-887-CARS

car dealer
restoration
service

See full listing in **Section Two** under **restoration shops**

PM Industries
442 Ridge Rd
West Milford, NJ 07480
800-833-8933; FAX: 201-728-2117

chassis coatings
permanent rust
sealers

Mail order and open shop. Monday thru Friday 8 am-9 pm EST. Permanent type rust preventative sealer/surfacers, chassis & firewall coatings, rust removers. Coatings in exact colors for quality restorations. High heat jet turbine coatings.

Preserve Inc
1430 E 1800 N
Hamilton, IL 62341
217-746-2411; FAX: 217-746-2231

storage containers

See full listing in **Section Two** under **storage care products**

Rust Never Sleeps
420 3rd Ave S
Lakeworth, FL 33460
800-820-6203

rust proofing

Mail order only. Electronic rust proofing.

Ziebart/Tidy Car
803 Mount Royal Blvd
Pittsburgh, PA 15223
412-486-4711

accessories
detailing
rustproofing

Shop open Monday-Friday 8 to 5, Saturday 9 to 12. We treat rusted metal with rust inhibitors then rust protect the entire vehicle. We also detail restored and unrestored cars and trucks along with custom accessories.

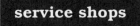 **service shops**

American Plastic Chrome 1398 Mar Ann Dr Westland, MI 48185 313-721-1967 days 313-261-4454 eves	**replating plastic**

See full listing in **Section Two** under **plating & polishing**

Antique Radio Service 12 Shawmut Ave Wayland, MA 01778 800-201-2635; FAX: 508-653-2418	**radio service**

See full listing in **Section Two** under **radios**

Auto Sport Restoration Alain Breton 110 Rue Du Couvent St Romain, QC Canada G0Y 1L0 PH/FAX: 418-486-7861	**restoration**

See full listing in **Section Two** under **restoration shops**

Autofresh International PO Box 54855 Oklahoma City, OK 73154-1855 405-752-0770; FAX: 405-752-5207	**deodorizing**

See full listing in **Section Two** under **interiors & interior parts**

Banzai Motorworks 6735 Midcities Ave Beltsville, MD 20705 301-937-5746	**pre-purchase insp/consultation repairs/service restoration**

See full listing in **Section One** under **Datsun**

Bicknell Engine Company 7055 Dayton Rd Enon, OH 45323 513-864-5224	**repair restoration**

See full listing in **Section One** under **Buick/McLaughlin**

Billie Inc 10519 Zion Dr Fairfax, VA 22032 800-878-6328; FAX: 703-250-4586	**garage diaper mats**

See full listing in **Section Two** under **car care products**

Bob's Bird House 124 Watkin Ave Chadds Ford, PA 19317 215-358-3420; FAX: 215-558-0729	**parts**

See full listing in **Section One** under **Thunderbird**

Bright Displays 1314 Lakemont Dr Pittsburgh, PA 15243 412-279-7037	**neon signs**

See full listing in **Section Two** under **automobilia**

British Car Specialists 2060 N Wilson Way Stockton, CA 95205 209-948-8767; FAX: 209-948-1030 E-mail: healeydoc@aol.com	**parts repairs restoration**

See full listing in **Section One** under **Austin-Healey**

Brookside Automotive Sales 363 E Main St, Rt 9, PO Box 312 East Brookfield, MA 01515 508-867-9266, 508-829-5366 508-885-2017 FAX: 508-867-2875	**appraisals car dealer service**

See full listing in **Section Two** under **car dealers**

Cedar Creek Coachworks Ltd 151 Conestoga Ln Stephens City, VA 22655 540-869-0244; FAX: 540-869-9577	**restoration service**

See full listing in **Section Two** under **restoration shops**

Central Jersey Mustang 36 Craig St Edison, NJ 08817 908-572-3939; FAX: 908-985-8653	**parts restoration service**

See full listing in **Section One** under **Mustang**

Classic Car Works Ltd 3050 Upper Bethany Rd Jasper, GA 30143 770-735-3945	**restoration**

See full listing in **Section Two** under **restoration shops**

Generalists

Cobb's Antique Auto Restoration
717 Western Ave
Washington Court House, OH 43160
614-335-7489

restoration
service

See full listing in **Section Two** under **restoration shops**

Coffey's Classic Transmissions
2817 Hollis
Ft Worth, TX 76111
817-834-8740; 817-439-1611

transmissions

See full listing in **Section Two** under **transmissions**

Collector's CARS Inc
150 E St Joseph St
Arcadia, CA 91006
818-447-2576; FAX: 818-447-1461

restoration
service

See full listing in **Section Two** under **restoration shops**

Dependable RV & Auto Service
2619 Rt 11 N
Lafayette, NY 13084
315-677-5336

parts
restoration
service

Mail order and open shop. Open Monday-Friday 9 to 6 or by appointment. Deals in recreational vehicle and general auto/truck repair, but have acquired a large and diverse collection of early Ford V8 and sixties musclecar parts, also engages in restoration and street rod fabrication.

Doc's Jags
125 Baker Rd
Lake Bluff, IL 60044
847-367-5247; FAX: 847-367-6363

appraisals
interiors
restoration

See full listing in **Section One** under **Jaguar**

Exotic Enterprises
459 Madeline Ave
Garfield, NJ 07026
201-523-2217, 201-956-7570

fiberglass
manufacturing
fiberglass mold
making

See full listing in **Section Two** under **fiberglass parts**

Freeman's Garage
19 Freeman St
Norton, MA 02766
508-285-6500

parts
restoration
sales
service

See full listing in **Section One** under **Ford '03-'31**

Golden Gulf Classics Inc
PO Box 490, 22530 Hwy 49
Saucier, MS 39574
601-831-2650

repairs
restorations

See full listing in **Section One** under **Triumph**

Gullwing Service Co Inc
106 Western Ave
Essex, MA 01929
508-768-6919; FAX: 508-768-3523

car dealer
mechanical service
parts
restoration

See full listing in **Section One** under **Mercedes-Benz**

House of Powder Inc
Rt 71 & 1st St, PO Box 110
Standard, IL 61363
815-339-2648

powder coating
sandblasting

Mail order and open shop. Monday-Friday 8-5; Saturday 8-12. Services which include powder coating, aluma-coating and sandblasting for all makes of cars, trucks, motorcycles, etc.

Ignition Distributor Service
19042 SE 161st
Renton, WA 98058
206-255-8052

rebuilding

See full listing in **Section Two** under **ignition parts**

Kelley's Korner
22 14th St
Bristol, TN 37620
423-968-5583

parts
repair

See full listing in **Section One** under **Studebaker**

Kenask Spring Co
307 Manhattan Ave
Jersey City, NJ 07307
201-653-4589

springs

See full listing in **Section Two** under **suspension parts**

Memoryville USA Inc
1008 W 12th St
Rolla, MO 65401
573-364-1810

restoration

See full listing in **Section Two** under **restoration shops**

Midwestern Motors & Dismantlers
19785 W 12 Mi, Bldg 404
Southfield, MI 48076
810-559-8848

salvage yard

See full listing in **Section One** under **Mercedes-Benz**

Mustang Classics
3814 Walnut St
Denver, CO 80205
303-295-3140

parts
restoration
sales
service

See full listing in **Section One** under **Mustang**

Northern Motorsport Ltd
PO Box 508, Rt 5
Wilder, VT 05088
802-296-2099; FAX: 802-295-6599

repair
restoration
sales
service

See full listing in **Section Two** under **restoration shops**

The Old Carb Doctor
Rt 3, Box 338, Drucilla Church Rd
Nebo, NC 28761
800-945-CARB (2272)
704-659-1428

carburetors
fuel pumps

See full listing in **Section Two** under **carburetors**

Opel Oldtimer Service Denmark
Mosede Kaervej 47
Greve DK-2670 Denmark
+45-42-901073, best 11 am-3 pm CST

literature
parts
parts locators

See full listing in **Section One** under **Opel**

Performance Transmissions
46 Walnut St
Shrewsbury, MA 01545
508-842-0672

restoration
trans parts/sales/
service
trans rebuilding

See full listing in **Section Two** under **transmissions**

Pioneer Valley Model A Ford Inc 81 East St Easthampton, MA 01027 413-584-8400; FAX: 413-584-7605 E-mail: pvma@aol.com	cars parts restoration

See full listing in **Section One** under **Ford '03-'31**

John T Poulin Auto Sales/ **Star Service Center** 5th Avenue & 111th St North Troy, NY 12182 518-235-8610	car dealer parts restoration service

See full listing in **Section One** under **Mercedes-Benz**

Quality Coaches 20 W 38th St Minneapolis, MN 55409 612-872-4155	parts restoration service

See full listing in **Section One** under **MG**

RB's Prototype Model & Machine Co 44 Marva Ln Stamford, CT 06903 PH/FAX: 203-329-2715	machine work

Both mail order and open shop Monday-Friday 8-6 EST.
Fabricating or machining parts to rebuild parts for automobiles.
Custom machine work (no engine internals). Duplicating small
parts for cars (radio knobs, handles, springs, bushings, plastic
parts, etc). No job too small.
Web site: http://www.alcasoft.com/rbsprototype

Reinholds Restorations c/o Rick Reinhold PO Box 178, 255 N Ridge Rd Reinholds, PA 17569-0178 717-336-5617	appraisals repairs restoration

See full listing in **Section Two** under **restoration shops**

Rochester Clutch & Brake Co 35 Niagara St Rochester, NY 14605 716-232-2579; FAX: 716-232-3279	brakes clutches

See full listing in **Section Two** under **brakes**

Ron's Restorations Inc 2968-B Ask Kay Dr Smyrna, GA 30082 770-438-6102; FAX: 770-438-0037	interior trim restoration

See full listing in **Section One** under **Mercedes-Benz**

Selco Restoration 9315 FM 359 Richmond, TX 77469 713-342-9751	parts restoration service

See full listing in **Section One** under **Cadillac/LaSalle**

Simons Balancing & Machine 1987 Ashley River Rd Charleston, SC 29407 803-766-3911; FAX: 803-766-9003	machine work

See full listing in **Section Two** under **machine work**

Speed & Sport Chrome Plating Inc 404 Broadway Houston, TX 77012 713-921-0235	chrome plating

See full listing in **Section Two** under **plating & polishing**

Star Classics Inc 7745 E Redfield #300 Scottsdale, AZ 85260 602-991-7495, 800-644-7827 FAX: 602-951-4096	parts sales service

See full listing in **Section One** under **Mercedes-Benz**

Still Cruisin' Corvettes 5759 Benford Dr Haymarket, VA 20169 703-754-1960; FAX: 703-754-1222	appraisals repairs restoration

See full listing in **Section One** under **Corvette**

Stockton Wheel Service 648 W Fremont St Stockton, CA 95203 209-464-7771, 800-395-9433 FAX: 209-464-4725	wheel repair

Mail order and open shop. Shop open Monday-Friday 8 to 5.
Specializing in wheel straightening and fabrication of GM and
MoPar Rallye wheels in various offsets and widths. Straightens
and repairs all steel and aluminum wheels.

Tamarack Automotive Appraisals **& Marine Surveys** 53 Sears Ln Burlington, VT 05401 PH/FAX: 802-864-4003 E-mail: gtlittle@aol.com	appraiser restoration

See full listing in **Section Two** under **appraisals**

Teddy's Garage 8530 Louise Ave Northridge, CA 91325 818-341-0505	parts restoration service

See full listing in **Section One** under **Rolls-Royce/Bentley**

Vampire-Island Air Products 50 Four Coins Dr Canonsburg, PA 15317 800-826-7473; FAX: 412-745-9024	air dryers filters

See full listing in **Section Two** under **restoration shops**

Bill Walter's Auto Service 315 Yale Ave Morton, PA 19070 610-543-0626	service

Open shop only. Monday-Friday 8:30-5. Quaint, very clean,
country style garage. Owner with 38 years of experience.
Specializes in Lincoln (all models) service for 1960-79, mechanical repairs to cars of the fifties, sixties and seventies.

White Post Restorations One Old Car Dr, PO Drawer D White Post, VA 22663 540-837-1140; FAX: 540-837-2368	brakes restoration

See full listing in **Section Two** under **brakes**

Wild Bill's Corvette & **Hi-Performance Center Inc** 451 Walpole St Norwood, MA 02062 617-551-8858	parts rebuilding service

See full listing in **Section One** under **Corvette**

Wittenborn's Auto Service Inc
133 Woodside Ave
Briarcliff Manor, NY 10510
914-941-2744

MoPar

See full listing in **Section One** under **MoPar**

Wymer Classic AMC
Mark Wymer
340 N Justice St
Fremont, OH 43420
419-332-4291, 8 to 5 pm
419-334-6945 after 5 pm

NOS parts
repairs
used parts

See full listing in **Section One** under **AMC**

sheetmetal

**American Restorations
Unlimited TA**
14 Meakin Ave, PO Box 34
Rochelle Park, NJ 07662
201-843-3567; FAX: 201-843-3238
E-mail: amerrest@aol.com

restoration parts

See full listing in **Section Two** under **glass**

Auto Body Specialties Inc
Rt 66
Middlefield, CT 06455
860-346-4989; FAX: 860-346-4987

accessories
body parts

See full listing in **Section Two** under **body parts**

Automotion
193 Commercial St
Sunnyvale, CA 94068
800-777-8881; FAX: 408-736-9013
E-mail: automo@aol.com

parts

See full listing in **Section One** under **Porsche**

B & T Truck Parts
906 E Main St, PO Box 799
Siloam Springs, AR 72761
501-524-5959: FAX: 501-524-5559

pickup parts

See full listing in **Section Two** under **trucks & tractors**

Bay Ridges Classic Chevy
1362 Poprad Ave
Pickering, ON Canada L1W 1L1
905-839-6169; FAX: 905-420-6613

accessories
parts

See full listing in **Section One** under **Chevrolet**

Bonnets Up
5736 Spring St
Clinton, MD 20735
301-297-4759

restoration

See full listing in **Section Two** under **coachbuilders & designers**

Tony D Branda Performance
Shelby & Mustang Parts
1434 E Pleasant Valley Blvd
Altoona, PA 16602
814-942-1869; FAX: 814-944-0801

accessories
decals
emblems
sheetmetal
wheels

See full listing in **Section One** under **Mustang**

Brothers Truck Parts
5670 Schaefer Ave, Unit G
Chino, CA 91710
800-977-2767, FAX: 909-517-3142
E-mail: brothers96@aol.com

accessories
parts

See full listing in **Section Two** under **trucks & tractors**

**Car-Line Manufacturing &
Distribution Inc**
1250 Gulf St, PO Box 1192
Beaumont, TX 77701
409-833-9757; FAX: 409-835-2468

chassis parts
engine parts
sheetmetal

Mail order and open shop. Monday-Friday 8 am to 5 pm. Manufacturing USA sheetmetal, wood and seat springs for Model T and A Fords, 1909-31. We also carry a full line of engine and chassis parts. Some V8 parts (metal, seat springs). Catalog available.

CARS Inc
1964 W 11 Mile Rd
Berkley, MI 48072
810-398-7100; 810-398-7078

interior

See full listing in **Section One** under **Chevrolet**

Jim Carter's Antique Truck Parts
1500 E Alton
Independence, MO 64055
816-833-1913; FAX: 816-252-3749

truck parts

See full listing in **Section One** under **Chevrolet**

Classic Enterprises
Box 92
Barron, WI 54812
715-537-5422

sheetmetal

See full listing in **Section One** under **Studebaker**

Classic Mustang Inc
24A Robert Porter Rd
Southington, CT 06489
800-243-2742; FAX: 203-276-9986

accessories
parts

See full listing in **Section One** under **Mustang**

Classic Sheetmetal Inc
4010 A Hartley St
Charlotte, NC 28206
704-596-5186; FAX: 704-596-3895

body panels
sheetmetal

See full listing in **Section One** under **Thunderbird**

County Auto Restoration
6 Gavin Rd
Mont Vernon, NH 03057
603-673-4840

body work
brakes
restoration
woodwork

See full listing in **Section Two** under **restoration shops**

Das Bulli Haus
18 Ward Ln
North Franklin, CT 06254
PH/FAX: 860-642-7242
E-mail: mcladm3@uconnvm.uconn.edu

parts
sheetmetal

See full listing in **Section One** under **Volkswagen**

Desert Valley Auto Parts
22500 N 21st Ave
Phoenix, AZ 85027
602-780-8024; FAX: 602-582-9141

salvage yard

See full listing in **Section Five** under **Arizona**

Driving Passion-1959 7132 Chilton Ct Clarksville, MD 21029 PH/FAX: 301-596-9078	bumpers parts parts locating service

See full listing in **Section One** under **Cadillac/LaSalle**

Early Ford V8 Sales Inc 9 Hills Rd Ballston Lake, NY 12019 518-899-9974; FAX: 518-899-5303	parts

See full listing in **Section One** under **Ford '32-'53**

Engineering & Manufacturing Services Box 24362 Cleveland, OH 44124-0362 216-446-1620; FAX: 216-446-9590	sheetmetal

See full listing in **Section One** under **Ford '32-'53**

FEN Enterprises of New York Inc PO Box 1559 Wappingers Falls, NY 12590 914-462-5959; 914-462-5094 FAX: 914-462-8450	parts restoration

See full listing in **Section One** under **Cadillac/LaSalle**

Foreign Autotech 3235 C Sunset Ln Hatboro, PA 19040 215-441-4421; FAX: 215-441-4490	parts

See full listing in **Section One** under **Volvo**

Franklin Buggy Werkes 510 Main St Florence, KS 66851 316-878-4684	engine rebuilding restoration sheetmetal woodgraining

See full listing in **Section Two** under **restoration shops**

G & J Shore Weld Unlimited 200-21 E 2nd St Huntington Station, NY 11746 516-549-4503	fabrication rust removal sheetmetal welding

See full listing in **Section Two** under **rust removal & stripping**

Gaslight Auto Parts Inc PO Box 291 Urbana, OH 43078 513-652-2145; FAX: 513-652-2147	accessories parts

See full listing in **Section One** under **Ford '03-'31**

Howell's Sheetmetal Co PO Box 792 Nederland, TX 77627 409-727-1999	body panels sheetmetal

See full listing in **Section One** under **Ford '03-'31**

Imperial Motors 2165 Spencer Creek Rd Campobello, SC 29322 864-895-3474	parts

See full listing in **Section One** under **Chrysler**

J & K Old Chevy Stuff Ship Pond Rd Plymouth, MA 02360 508-224-7616	car dealer parts sheetmetal

See full listing in **Section One** under **Chevrolet**

KopyKatz Auto Body Parts 2536 N Sheridan Denver, CO 80214 303-458-5332; FAX: 303-477-1496	fenders hoods panels

See full listing in **Section Two** under **body parts**

Kwik Poly T Distributing Inc 24 St Henry Ct St Charles, MO 63301 314-724-1065	restoration aids

See full listing in **Section Two** under **restoration aids**

L & N Olde Car Co 9992 Kinsman Rd, PO Box 378 Newbury, OH 44065 216-564-7204; FAX: 216-564-8187	restoration

See full listing in **Section Two** under **restoration shops**

Linearossa International Inc 15281 Barranca Pkwy, #A Irvine, CA 92618 714-727-1201; FAX: 714-727-0603	parts

See full listing in **Section One** under **Fiat**

Marchant Machine Corporation 11325 Maryland Ave Beltsville, MD 20705 301-937-4481; FAX: 301-937-1019 E-mail: dmarch4481@aol.com	metal forming machines

Mail order only. Manufacturer of metal forming machines for car restoration.

Bob Marriott 497 Delaware Ave Delmar, NY 12054	sheetmetal parts shop manuals

See full listing in **Section One** under **Thunderbird**

The Maverick Connection 137 Valley Dr Ripley, WV 25271 PH/FAX: 304-372-7825	literature parts

See full listing in **Section One** under **Ford '54-up**

McCann Auto Restoration US Rt 1, PO Box 1025 Houlton, ME 04730 207-532-2206	custom work restoration sandblasting

See full listing in **Section Two** under **restoration shops**

Merv's Classic Chevy Parts 1330 Washington Iowa Falls, IA 50126 515-648-3168	parts

See full listing in **Section One** under **Chevrolet**

Mill Supply Inc
3241 Superior Ave
Cleveland, OH 44114
800-888-5072; FAX: 216-241-0425
E-mail: info@millsupply.com

*clips
fasteners
panels*

Replacement panels and supplies for collision and rust repair.
Mill Supply carries the widest selection of replacement panels for
your car, truck or van. Plus a variety of fasteners, clips and body
shop supplies. Call or write for specific information. Complete
192-page catalog, $4.

Millers Incorporated
7412 Count Circle
Huntington Beach, CA 92647
714-375-6565; FAX: 714-847-6603
E-mail: millermbz@aol.com

*accessories
parts*

See full listing in **Section One** under **Mercedes-Benz**

Must For Rust Co
PO Box 972
Cedar Ridge, CA 95924
888-297-9224 toll-free
PH/FAX: 916-273-3576

rust remover

See full listing in **Section Two** under **rust removal & stripping**

No Limit Engineering
1737 Production Circle
Riverside, CA 92509
FAX: 909-275-9232

*brakes
chassis parts*

See full listing in **Section Two** under **chassis parts**

The Panel Shop Inc
1785 Barnum Ave
Stratford, CT 06497
203-377-6208; FAX: 203-386-0486

*body parts for
Aston Martin
Bentley/Rolls-Royce
Ferrari/Lotus*

Complete fabrication of partial or complete bodies. All cars and
makes. Custom work also done on motorbikes in aluminum or
steel. No job too big or too small. Work from drawings, blueprints or imagination. Rolls-Royce, Aston Martin trained hands
workman. You deal with the people that do the work.

Parts House
2912 Hunter St
Fort Worth, TX 76112
817-451-2708; FAX: 817-496-8909

*accessories
parts*

See full listing in **Section Two** under **comprehensive parts**

Passenger Car Supply
102 Cloverdale Rd
Swedesboro, NJ 08085
609-467-7966

parts

See full listing in **Section One** under **Chevrolet**

Jerrell Pickett
Box 218
Wessington, SD 57381
605-458-2344

*literature
parts
sheetmetal
wheels*

See full listing in **Section Two** under **comprehensive parts**

**Precision Paint & Rust
Removers Inc**
2415 W Industrial Blvd
Long Lake, MN 55356
PH/FAX: 612-476-4545

*paint removal
rust removal*

See full listing in **Section Two** under **rust removal & stripping**

Precision Restoration Service Inc
1551 N Courtney Rd, Ste B-2
Independence, MO 64050
816-461-7500; FAX: 816-461-7504

restoration

See full listing in **Section Two** under **restoration shops**

Raybuck Autobody Parts
RD 4, Box 170
Punxsutawney, PA 15767
814-938-5248; FAX: 814-938-4250

body parts

See full listing in **Section Two** under **body parts**

Rocker King
804 Chicago Ave
Waukesha, WI 53188-3511
414-549-9583
E-mail: sonoma@execpc.com

*body parts
sheetmetal*

Mail order only. Sells reproduction rocker panels, dog legs, door
skins, quarter panel and fender sections for cars made from
1935-64. Phone sales evenings and weekends. Mail order replies,
include SASE.

S & S Antique Auto
Pine St
Deposit, NY 13754
607-467-2929; FAX: 607-467-2109

parts

See full listing in **Section One** under **Ford '32-'53**

Sherman & Associates Inc
28460 Groesbeck Hwy
Roseville, MI 48066
810-774-8297; FAX: 810-774-7361

sheetmetal

Dealing in automotive and light truck sheetmetal. Rust repair
panels, radiators, condensers, header panels, etc, and hard to
find parts used by automotive body shops. Hundreds of reproduction parts and patch panels for vintage restorations with
emphasis on the muscle car era.

Silverstate Cadillac Parts
PO Box 2161
Sparks, NV 89431
702-331-7252; FAX: 702-331-7887

parts

See full listing in **Section One** under **Cadillac/LaSalle**

Tabco Inc
11655 Chillicothe Rd
Chesterland, OH 44026-1994
216-729-5151; FAX: 216-729-1251

body parts

Mail order and open shop. Monday thru Friday 8:30 am-5 pm.
We manufacture and distribute steel rust repair parts for cars,
trucks and vans, both domestic and foreign.

Thompson Hill Metalcraft
23 Thompson Hill Rd
Berwick, ME 03901
207-698-5756

*metal forming
panel beating
welding*

Open shop only. Monday-Friday 9 to 5. Panel beating, metal
forming, metal finishing and welding. Aluminum and steel.
Hand-builts, customs and antiques.

John Ulrich
450 Silver Ave
San Francisco, CA 94112
510-223-9587 days

parts

See full listing in **Section One** under **Packard**

USATCO/US AirTool Int'l
60 Fleetwood Ct
Ronkonkoma, NY 11779-6951
516-471-3300; FAX: 516-471-3308

| wheel machines shrinkers/stretchers bench/floor models tools |

See full listing in **Section Two** under **tools**

Jon Ward Motorsports
3100 FM 1703, PO Box 238
Alpine, TX 79831
915-837-3250; FAX: 915-837-5878

| engines race cars |

See full listing in **Section Two** under **racing**

Westbury Hot Rods
1130 Detroit Ave
Concord, CA 94520
510-682-9482; FAX: 510-682-9483

| service sheetmetal fabrication |

See full listing in **Section Two** under **street rods**

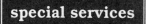 special services

A AAuto Brokers Inc
13659 Victory Blvd, Suite #346
Van Nuys, CA 91401
800-770-7784; FAX: 818-904-0023

| brokers transport |

See full listing in **Section Two** under **transport**

Aero International Auto Appraisals
Box 1955
Penhold, AB Canada T0M 1R0
403-886-5565

| appraiser consultant |

See full listing in **Section Two** under **appraisals**

Alan's Axles
2300 Congress Ave
Clearwater, FL 34623
800-741-0452; 813-784-0452

| axles |

See full listing in **Section Two** under **chassis parts**

American Automotive Heritage Foundation (AAHF)
PO Box 482
Carlisle, PA 17013-0482
717-240-0976; FAX: 717-240-0931

| legislative watch organization |

See full listing in **Section Three** under **legislative watch organizations**

Antique Automotive Accessories
889 S Rainbow Blvd, Suite 642
Las Vegas, NV 89128
800-742-6777; FAX: 913-862-4646

| accessories tires |

See full listing in **Section Two** under **tires**

Antique Radio Service
12 Shawmut Ave
Wayland, MA 01778
800-201-2635; FAX: 508-653-2418

| radio service |

See full listing in **Section Two** under **radios**

Associated Foreign Exchange Inc
201 Sansome St
San Francisco, CA 94104
800-752-2124; FAX: 415-391-3553
E-mail: 102172.261@compuserv.com

| foreign currency wires/drafts |

Open Monday-Friday 7:15 am to 5 pm PST. Provides wires and

drafts denominated in foreign currencies at discount rates for companies and individuals who need to make international payments. Free exchange rate quotes are available.

Authentic Automotive
529 Buttercup Trail
Mesquite, TX 75149
972-289-6373

| power brakes power steering |

See full listing in **Section One** under **Chevrolet**

Auto Transport Services
5367 Fargo Rd
Avoca, MI 48006
810-324-2598

| transport |

See full listing in **Section Two** under **transport**

Autofresh International
PO Box 54855
Oklahoma City, OK 73154-1855
405-752-0770; FAX: 405-752-5207

| deodorizing |

See full listing in **Section Two** under **interiors & interior parts**

Automotive Legal Service Inc
PO Box 626
Dresher, PA 19025
PH/FAX: 800-487-4947

| appraisals |

See full listing in **Section Two** under **appraisals**

Automotive Ventures Inc
4989 Mercer University Blvd
Macon, GA 31210
912-471-1645

| sales |

Automotive promotions. Also buying and selling automobiles. Normal inventory of 20-30 cars. Exit #2 off I-475; showroom and offices.

Bairs Corvettes
316 Franklin St
Linesville, PA 16424
814-683-4223; FAX: 814-683-5200

| parts service |

See full listing in **Section One** under **Corvette**

Skip Barber Racing School
29 Brook St
Lakeville, CT 06039
860-435-1300; FAX: 860-435-1321
E-mail: speed@skipbarber.com

| racing school |

See full listing in **Section Two** under **racing**

Blueprint Auto Insurance Agency
100 Corporate Pl
Peabody, MA 01960
800-530-5305; FAX: 508-535-3759
E-mail: blueprint@gnn.com

| insurance |

See full listing in **Section Two** under **insurance**

Bob's Classic Auto Glass
21170 Hwy 36
Blachly, OR 97412
800-624-2130

| glass |

See full listing in **Section Two** under **glass**

Generalists

CalAutoArt 1520 S Lyon St Santa Ana, CA 92705 714-835-9512; FAX: 714-835-9513 E-mail: 71460,1146@compuserve.com	**automobilia photography**

See full listing in **Section Two** under **automobilia**

Carburetor Engineering 3324 E Colorado Pasadena, CA 91107 818-795-3221	**carburetor rebuilding distributor rebuilding fuel pump rebuilding**

See full listing in **Section Two** under **carburetors**

Cochrane's Special Interest Brokers Ed Cochrane 718 Livingston Ave Shreveport, LA 71107 318-226-0458, 318-424-2861	**appraisers brokers consultant locator**

See full listing in **Section Two** under **brokers**

Larry Couzens Photography 16 East 17th St New York City, NY 10003 212-620-9790; FAX: 212-620-9791	**photography**

See full listing in **Section Two** under **photography**

Timothy Cox Firewall Insulators 6333 Pacific Ave, Suite 523 Stockton, CA 95207 PH/FAX: 209-477-4840	**firewall insulators gloveboxes quiet ride solutions**

See full listing in **Section Two** under **interiors & interior parts**

Dan's Restorations PO Box 144, Snake Hill Rd Sand Lake, NY 12153 518-674-2061	**restoration**

See full listing in **Section Two** under **bodywork**

Dash Graining by Mel Erikson 31 Meadow Rd Kings Park, NY 11754 PH/FAX: 516-544-1102 days 516-360-7789 nights	**dashboard restoration**

See full listing in **Section Two** under **woodgraining**

Robert DeMars Ltd 222 Lakeview Ave, Ste 160-256 West Palm Beach, FL 33401 561-832-0171; FAX: 561-844-1493	**appraisers auto historians car locator research library**

See full listing in **Section Two** under **appraisals**

Harold Doebel PO Box 321, Dept HVAA Ocean Gate, NJ 08740 908-269-1206	**videotapes**

A specialty video organization dealing in vintage automotive promos, commercials and racing subjects from 1886 to the present. Also general nostalgia and railroad subjects. We do mail order and some car shows. Send $4 for complete list.

Dusty Memories Ltd 118 Oxford Hgts Rd Somerset, PA 15501-1134 814-443-2393; FAX: 814-443-6468	**rentals**

See full listing in **Section Two** under **military vehicles**

Exotic Car Transport Inc PO Box 91 Ocoee, FL 34761 407-293-9524; FAX: 407-293-4783	**transport**

See full listing in **Section Two** under **transport**

Ferris Auto Electric Ltd 106 Lakeshore Dr North Bay, ON Canada P1A 2A6 705-474-4560; FAX: 705-474-9453	**parts service**

See full listing in **Section Two** under **electrical systems**

First National Bank of Sumner PO Box 145 Sumner, IL 62466 618-936-2396; FAX: 618-936-2240	**financing**

See full listing in **Section Two** under **financing**

Glass Search/LOF 1975 Galaxie Ave Columbus, OH 43207 800-848-1351; FAX: 614-443-0709	**glass parts**

See full listing in **Section Two** under **glass**

GMS Restorations 20 Wilbraham St Palmer, MA 01069 413-596-9936; FAX: 413-596-8115	**restoration**

See full listing in **Section Two** under **restoration shops**

Guldstrand Engineering Inc 11924 W Jefferson Blvd Culver City, CA 90230 310-391-7108; FAX: 310-391-7424 E-mail: geiauto@aol.com	**parts**

See full listing in **Section One** under **Corvette**

HochKraeusen Racing PO Box 716, 18233 Madison Rd Parkman, OH 44080-0716 216-548-2147	**machine shop**

See full listing in **Section Two** under **machine work**

Hodges Custom Haulers 9076 Scale Rd Benton, KY 42025 PH/FAX: 502-898-2356	**truck beds**

See full listing in **Section Two** under **trailers**

Ed Howell PO Box 73 Folly Beach, SC 29439	**printing**

Custom printing: business cards, raffle tickets, club membership cards, sales-books, letterheads, flyers, computer software, mailing lists.

Incredible England Tours 14200 New Hampshire Ave Silver Spring, MD 20904 301-384-5856; FAX: 301-989-1866	**tours**

Puts together small groups to tour automotive, steam, castles and palaces in England. Very reasonable rates. Also planning 1997 tours for Beaulieu Autojumble and Essen old car show/flea market in Germany. Planning 1997 tour of castles, car museums, car factories in Rhine Valley, Germany.

Generalists

The Infinite Garage
211 Dimmick Ave
Venice, CA 90291
310-392-6605; FAX: 310-396-1933

rentals

Supplies and modifies antique, sports and special interest cars and trucks for film, video and fashion photography. British vehicles are our speciality.

Inland Empire Driveline Service Inc
4035 E Guasti Rd, #301
Ontario, CA 91761
800-800-0109; FAX: 909-390-3038

drive shafts
pinion yokes

See full listing in **Section Two** under **machine work**

IPTC Publishing
300 SW 12th Ave
Pompano Beach, FL 33069
800-653-4198

manuals

See full listing in **Section Four** under **books & publications**

Jackson Speaker Service
217 Crestbrook Dr
Jackson, MI 49203
517-789-6400

radio repairs
speakers

See full listing in **Section Two** under **radios**

Kaleidoscope
PO Box 86-H
Mt Ephraim, NJ 08059
800-831-5163

glass restoration
scratch remover kit

See full listing in **Section Two** under **restoration aids**

Kenask Spring Co
307 Manhattan Ave
Jersey City, NJ 07307
201-653-4589

springs

See full listing in **Section Two** under **suspension parts**

Klassic Kolor Auctions
PO Box 1185
Venice, CA 90294-1185
818-985-3230; FAX: 818-980-1233

auction "color"
broadcaster
master of ceremonies

See full listing in **Section Two** under **auctions & events**

Krem Engineering
10204 Perry Hwy
Meadville, PA 16335
814-724-4806

engine rebuilding
repairs
restoration

See full listing in **Section Two** under **restoration shops**

L & L Antique Auto Trim
403 Spruce, Box 177
Pierce City, MO 65723
417-476-2871

runningboard
moldings

Mail order only. Dealing in runningboard moldings.

Lee's Kustom Auto & Street Rods
RR 3, Box 3061A
Rome, PA 18837
717-247-2326

accessories
parts
restoration

See full listing in **Section Two** under **street rods**

M & L Automobile Appraisal
2662 Palm Terr
Deland, FL 32720
904-734-1761

appraiser

See full listing in **Section Two** under **appraisals**

Mar-Ke Woodgraining
1102 Hilltop Dr
Loveland, CO 80537
970-663-7803; FAX: 970-663-1138

woodgraining

See full listing in **Section Two** under **woodgraining**

Bill McCoskey
14200 New Hampshire Ave
Silver Spring, MD 20904
301-384-5856; FAX: 301-989-1866

appraisals
repairs

See full listing in **Section Two** under **appraisals**

Dan McCrary
Automotive Art Specialties
PO Box 18795
Charlotte, NC 28218
704-372-2899; FAX: 704-375-8686

drawings
paintings
prints

See full listing in **Section Two** under **artwork**

Memoryville USA Inc
1008 W 12th St
Rolla, MO 65401
573-364-1810

restoration

See full listing in **Section Two** under **restoration shops**

Mint Condition Auto Upholstery
PO Box 134
Silverdale, New Zealand
PH/FAX: 64-9-424 2257

convertible tops
interiors
spring-gaiters
wheelcovers

Mail order and open shop. Shop open Monday-Friday 8 to 5. Deals in coach-trimming classic and vintage cars. manufactures spring-gaiters (handmade leather-gaiters), interiors, convertible tops, wheelcovers, etc.

Mohonk Children's Services Inc
66 Weston Rd
Westport, CT 06880
203-226-6665; FAX: 203-227-6467

contributions

The Mohonk Boys Home and Children's Services provides tax deductible contributions for donations of automobiles, especially antique or classic. We do some restoration and can haul as necessary. We also accept some antique boats and much memorabilia. We keep some cars and those we eventually sell go exclusively to the direct support of educational and recreational programs.

Northern Digital Classics
Suite 96
L'Anse, MI 49946
888-632-6678; FAX: 906-353-8282
E-mail: ndcdezin@up.net

website design

Mail order and open shop. Monday-Friday 4 pm-11 pm. Northern Digital Classics provides services for publications and printing. Have won many awards for our designs in publications. Internet services include the advertising of your business or service through a classified ad or can design you a web site and place it on the internet for $99 for one year. You can also find classic cars and Mustang parts 1964-73 for sale, free advertised car shows and events, automobilia/memorabilia and custom designed posters. Web site: http://wwwndcnorth.com

Old Car Woodgraining 27902 45th Ave S Auburn, WA 98001 206-854-5247	dashboard restoration woodgraining

See full listing in **Section Two** under **woodgraining**

The Parts Scout® Bodo Repenn Diagonalstrasse 18A D-20537 Hamburg Germany *49-40-21980130 FAX: *49-40-21980132	parts parts locator

See full listing in **Section Two** under **comprehensive parts**

Bruce Paul 508 Balsam Rd Cherry Hill, NJ 08003 609-428-8559	repair service

See full listing in **Section Two** under **electrical systems**

PC Automotive Calendars PO Box 2002 Madison, WI 53701 608-829-1234	calendars

Corvette calendars, postcards, posters and photos. Call for information.

Performance Analysis Co 1345 Oak Ridge Turnpike, Suite 258 Oak Ridge, TN 37830 423-482-9175 E-mail: 7662.2133@compuserve.com	climate control cruise control

See full listing in **Section One** under **Mercedes-Benz**

J Pinto 2605 9th St Long Island City, NY 11102 PH/FAX: 718-626-2403 E-mail: electritech@sprynet.com	windshield wiper repair

See full listing in **Section Two** under **restoration aids**

Dennis Portka 4326 Beetow Dr Hamburg, NY 14075 716-649-0921	horns

See full listing in **Section One** under **Corvette**

Practical Images PO Box 245 Haddam, CT 06438-0245 860-704-0525 E-mail: leswho@iconn.net	photo scanning video conversions

See full listing in **Section Two** under **photography**

Precision Pot Metal/ Bussie Restoration Inc 1008 Loring Ave #28 Orange Park, FL 32073 904-269-8788	pot metal restoration

See full listing in **Section Two** under **plating & polishing**

Premier Designs Historic Costume 818 Selby St Findlay, OH 45840 800-427-0907; FAX: 419-427-2239 E-mail: premier@bright.net	clothing

See full listing in **Section Two** under **apparel**

R&S Canopies 10823 East G Ave Richland, MI 49083 616-665-4004	canopy kits

Mail order only. Canopy kits, A-frame and cabana. Sell all canopy accessories. Silver tarps are all UV-treated, waterproof and heat reflective. We also carry a complete line of E-Z Up canopies.

RB's Prototype Model & Machine Co 44 Marva Ln Stamford, CT 06903 PH/FAX: 203-329-2715	machine work

See full listing in **Section Two** under **service shops**

Redi-Strip Company 100 West Central Ave Roselle, IL 60172 630-529-2442; FAX: 630-529-3626	abrasive media paint/rust removal plastic media

See full listing in **Section Two** under **rust removal & stripping**

Riechmann Motorsport Promotions 38511 Frontier Ave Palmdale, CA 93550 805-273-7089	racing events

See full listing in **Section Two** under **racing**

Rite Weld Co 10 Northfield Rd Wallingford, CT 06492 203-265-5984; FAX: 203-284-5063	castings engine repair

See full listing in **Section Two** under **automobilia**

Albert A Rogers II 29A Young Rd Charlton, MA 01507 508-248-3555	parts storage

See full listing in **Section One** under **Ford '32-'53**

T Schmidt 827 N Vernon Dearborn, MI 48128-1542 313-562-7161	rust removers

See full listing in **Section Two** under **rust removal & stripping**

Silver Image Photographics 3102 Vestal Pkwy E Vestal, NY 13850 607-797-8795	business cards photo car cards photofinishing

See full listing in **Section Two** under **automobilia**

Silverstate Cadillac Parts PO Box 2161 Sparks, NV 89431 702-331-7252; FAX: 702-331-7887	parts

See full listing in **Section One** under **Cadillac/LaSalle**

Sparling Studios Box 86B, RR 1, Quarry Rd New Haven, VT 05472 PH/FAX: 802-453-4114	auto sculpture

See full listing in **Section Two** under **artwork**

Generalists

Special T's Unlimited Corp PO Box 146 Prospect Heights, IL 60070 847-255-5494; FAX: 847-391-7082	general repair parts restoration service

See full listing in **Section One** under **Ford '03-'31**

Speed & Sport Chrome Plating Inc 404 Broadway Houston, TX 77012 713-921-0235	chrome plating

See full listing in **Section Two** under **plating & polishing**

Ed Strain 6555 44th St #2006 Pinellas Park, FL 33781 800-266-1623	magnetos power brakes

See full listing in **Section Two** under **brakes**

Stripping Technologies Inc 2949 E Elvira Rd Tucson, AZ 85706 800-999-0501; FAX: 520-741-9200 E-mail: sti@stripmaster.com	paint removal

See full listing in **Section Two** under **rust removal & stripping**

J F Sullivan Co 14 Clarendon Rd Auburn, MA 01501 508-792-9500	brake parts consulting machine work parts locator

See full listing in **Section Two** under **brakes**

Tags Backeast PO Box 581 Plainville, CT 06062 860-747-2942	data plates trim tags

Mail order restoration of data plates, trim tags for 1952-69 Ford family; 1960-74 MoPars; 1930s-70s GM family. Legitimate authentic cars only.

Tamarack Automotive Appraisals **& Marine Surveys** 53 Sears Ln Burlington, VT 05401 PH/FAX: 802-864-4003 E-mail: gtlittle@aol.com	appraiser restoration

See full listing in **Section Two** under **appraisals**

Techni Decapage 203 Rue Joseph-Carrier Vaudreuil, QC Canada J7V 5V5 514-424-5696; FAX: 514-424-5667	plastic media blasting

See full listing in **Section Two** under **rust removal & stripping**

Toronto Vintage Vehicles Eric S Lynd 10 Alderton Ct Islington, Toronto, ON Canada M9A 3X8 416-239-3693; 705-762-5794	vehicles for movies

Shop open anytime 9:30 am to 10 pm EST. Picture vehicle coordinator supplying antique and collector vehicles for movies, TV commercials, video in Toronto. I own 10 vehicles and I am a broker for over 500 picture vehicles.

Valley Wire Wheel Service 7306 Coldwater Canyon #16 North Hollywood, CA 91605 818-765-3258; FAX: 818-765-8358	wheel restoration wheels

See full listing in **Section Two** under **wheels & wheelcovers**

Vintage Lamp Repair PO Box 1122, 290 Haines Ln Merlin, OR 97532 541-474-5664; FAX: 541-476-9096	resilvering

See full listing in **Section Two** under **lighting equipment**

Vod Varka Springs US Rt 30, PO Box 170 Clinton, PA 15026 412-859-6897 home PH/FAX: 412-695-3268 work	anything of wire wire forms wire springs

Mail order only. Manufacturer of custom wire springs and wire forms and anything made of wire. No job too big or too small. Clubs and dealers welcome.

Jon Ward Motorsports 3100 FM 1703, PO Box 238 Alpine, TX 79831 915-837-3250; FAX: 915-837-5878	engines race cars

See full listing in **Section Two** under **racing**

Welshfield Studios 17767 Rapids Rd Hiram, OH 44234 PH/FAX: 216-834-0233	design editing printing

Custom editing, design, printing, publication and mailing of newsletters, club magazines, advertisements, fliers. Over 25 years' experience in automotive journalism. Our unique photo enhancement and printing techniques provide a high-quality, low-cost alternative for your club newsletter, magazine or advertising brochures. Call or write for quotes and samples.

The Wheel Shoppe 18011 Fourteen Mile Rd Fraser, MI 48026 810-415-7171; FAX: 810-415-7181 E-mail: jgs2nd@aol.com	performance parts welding wheel repair

See full listing in **Section Two** under **wheels & wheelcovers**

White Post Restorations One Old Car Dr, PO Drawer D White Post, VA 22663 540-837-1140; FAX: 540-837-2368	brakes restoration

See full listing in **Section Two** under **brakes**

Dale Wilch Sales/RPM Catalog PO Box 12031 Kansas City, KS 66112 913-788-3219; FAX: 913-788-9682 E-mail: rpmcat@sound.net	speed equipment

See full listing in **Section Two** under **racing**

Wild About Wheels 274 Great Rd Acton, MA 01720-4702 508-264-9921; 800-538-0539 (orders) FAX: 508-264-9547	videotapes

Mail order only. Specializing in automotive videotapes; event and specialty videos on all makes and models.

Winslow Mfg Co 5700 Dean Ave Raleigh, NC 27604 919-790-9713	parts rebuilding

See full listing in **Section Two** under **engine parts**

Wolfson Engineering 512 Parkway W Las Vegas, NV 89106 PH/FAX: 702-384-4196	mech engineering

Mail order and open shop. Open by appointment. Major and minor mechanical engineering projects, modifications, research and development, designs, welding, fabrication. Difficult new and used parts secured. Specialist in Rolls-Royce and American muscle cars. Member SAE, Society of Automotive Engineers and 30 year member RROC. Not accepting assignments with Asian cars or computer related electronics.

steering wheels

Muneef Alwan 7400 Crosa Countre Rd Oroville, CA 95966 916-534-6683	glass steering wheels

See full listing in **Section One** under **Ford '32-'53**

Backwards Unlimited Attn: Jim or Ingrid Ellis 4143 Gunderson Rd NE Poulsbo, WA 98370 360-697-1471; FAX: 360-697-4871	restoration

Most steering wheels restored, from 1932-57. All work completed in durable butyrate plastic (not painted). Three year guarantee. Full time business since 1975.

Classics Plus LTD N7306 Lakeshore Dr N Fond du Lac, WI 54937 414-923-1007	restoration

Specializing in the restoration of stock, modified or street rod automobiles. Also complete restoration of steering wheels, plus a variety of woodgrainings.

Comfy/Inter-American Sheepskins Inc 1346 Centinela Ave West Los Angeles, CA 90025-1901 800-521-4014; FAX: 310-442-6080 E-mial: 4858038@mcimail.com	floor mats seat covers

See full listing in **Section Two** under **interiors & interior parts**

JB Donaldson Co 2533 W Cypress Phoenix, AZ 85009 602-278-4505; FAX: 602-278-1112	castings steering wheels wood parts

Mail order only. Show quality plastic steering wheel castings for Cadillac, Buick, Oldsmobile and Packard steering wheels. Also

steering wheel recasting. Galaxie parts. Woody parts, complete kits and complete restorations for GM, Buicks and Packards 1937-53.

Gary's Steering Wheel Restoration 2677 Ritner Hwy Carlisle, PA 17013 717-243-5646	repairs

Mail order and open shop. Open Monday-Friday 5 pm to 9 pm, Saturday 8 am to 5 pm. We repair all types of plastic steering wheels, solid colors, two-tone and plastic woodgrain. We repair cracks using an acrylic plastic and repaint using five coats of primers and sealers and four coats of flex acrylic urethane and then color sand and buff the wheels. Since 1981. Free estimates. Your satisfaction guaranteed. See us at the Carlisle Spring, Summer and Fall meets at Space K189, and at Corvettes at Carlisle at space D129.

Grant Products Inc 700 Allen Ave Glendale, CA 91201 213-849-3171; FAX: 818-241-4683	steering wheels

Manufacturers of a complete line of custom steering wheels. Sell wholesale only.

Wolf Automotive 201 N Sullivan Santa Ana, CA 92703 800-444-9653, 714-835-2126 FAX: 714-835-9653	car covers consoles steering wheels tire covers

See full listing in **Section One** under **Chevrolet**

storage

Berliner Classic Motorcars Inc 1975 Stirling Rd Dania, FL 33004 954-923-7271; FAX: 954-926-3306	automobilia car dealer motorcycles

See full listing in **Section Two** under **car dealers**

BW Incorporated PO Box 106 316 W Broadway Browns Valley, MN 56219 800-950-2210; 612-695-2891 or 800-EAT-OILS (328-6457) FAX: 612-695-2893	artwork car care products dry enclosed covers mice control oil drip absorbent storage care products

See full listing in **Section Two** under **storage care products**

Car Skates by P & J Products 988 Gordon Ct Birmingham, MI 48009 PH/FAX: 810-647-1879	car skate

See full listing in **Section Two** under **tools**

Chicago Car Exchange 1 Collector Car Dr, Box 530 Lake Bluff, IL 60044 847-680-1950; FAX: 847-680-1961 E-mail: oldtoys@wwa.com	appraiser car dealer car locator financing storage

See full listing in **Section Two** under **car dealer**

| Collector's Carousel
84 Warren Ave
Westbrook, ME 04092
207-854-0343; FAX: 207-856-6913 | **appraisals**
sales
service |

See full listing in **Section Two** under **car dealers**

| Deltran Corporation
801 US Hwy 92 E
Deland, FL 32724
904-736-7900; FAX: 904-736-9984 | **battery chargers** |

See full listing in **Section Two** under **batteries**

| Exotic Car Transport Inc
PO Box 91
Ocoee, FL 34761
407-293-9524; FAX: 407-293-4783 | **transport** |

See full listing in **Section Two** under **transport**

| Family Sports Storage Inc
4400 Killarney Park Dr
Burton, MI 48529
313-743-5670 | **storage** |

Shop open by appointment only. Either heated inside storage or outside storage.

| Fiesta's Classic Car Center
3901 N Kings Hwy
St Louis, MO 63115
314-385-4567 | **appraisals**
consignment sales
storage |

Open shop. Open every day, except holidays. Specializing in clean, secure storage. Your classic is protected by a 24-hour state-of-the-art security system. Conveniently located in the center of the USA. Can assist in preparation and transportation to car shows and auctions. Consignment sales showroom available. Will build-to-suit multi-car garages per your specifications. Base rate for 1997 is $40 per month per vehicle.

| Interesting Parts Inc
Paul TerHorst
27526 N Owens Rd
Mundelein, IL 60060
PH/FAX: 847-949-1030 | **appraisals**
gaskets/parts
storage
transport |

See full listing in **Section Two** under **comprehensive parts**

| Memory Lane Motors Inc
1231 Rt 176
Lake Bluff, IL 60044
847-362-4600 | **appraisals**
car dealer
storage |

See full listing in **Section Two** under **car dealers**

| Preserve Inc
1430 E 1800 N
Hamilton, IL 62341
217-746-2411; FAX: 217-746-2231 | **storage containers** |

See full listing in **Section Two** under **storage care products**

| Albert A Rogers II
29A Young Rd
Charlton, MA 01507
508-248-3555 | **parts**
storage |

See full listing in **Section One** under **Ford '32-'53**

| Route 66 Classic Restorations
250 N 1st St
Wilmington, IL 60481
815-476-4290 | **restoration** |

See full listing in **Section Two** under **restoration shops**

| Steelmaster Building Corp
2500 Military Trail N, Suite 400
Boca Raton, FL 33431
800-527-4044; FAX: 561-994-1708 | **garages**
workshops |

Mail order only. Steel buildings for garages/workshops.

| York Petroleum Industries
dba YPI Inc
1011 Askham Dr
Cary, NC 27511-4703
919-319-5180; FAX: 919-319-7302 | **floor protector** |

See full listing in **Section Two** under **accessories**

storage care products

| Applied Chemical Specialties
PO Box 241597
Omaha, NE 68124
800-845-8523; FAX: 402-390-9262 | **corrosion**
protection |

Mail order only. No-Rosion, a powerful new cooling system additive which can be used with or without antifreeze to prevent corrosion/rusting of radiators, heater cores and water pumps. Also prevents pitting and electrolysis of aluminum cooling components and erosion of wet-sleeve cylinder liners. Industrial-grade, ASTM tested and approved corrosion protection for all six metals commonly found in cooling systems. Extends the life of antifreeze so flushing is necessary only once every five years.

| Archway Press Inc
19 W 44th St
New York, NY 10036
800-374-4766 | **garage blueprints** |

See full listing in **Section Four** under **books & publications**

| Billie Inc
10519 Zion Dr
Fairfax, VA 22032
800-878-6328; FAX: 703-250-4586 | **garage diaper**
mats |

See full listing in **Section Two** under **car care products**

| Buenger Enterprises/
GoldenRod Dehumidifier
3600 S Harbor Blvd
Oxnard, CA 93035
800-451-6797; FAX: 805-985-1534 | **dehumidifiers** |

See full listing in **Section Two** under **car care products**

| BW Incorporated
PO Box 106
316 W Broadway
Browns Valley, MN 56219
800-950-2210; 612-695-2891 or
800-EAT-OILS (328-6457)
FAX: 612-695-2893 | **artwork**
car care products
dry enclosed covers
mice control
oil drip absorbent
storage care
products |

Mail order and open shop. Mfg and design special products needed for all aspects of storage and care. Specializing in products that protect cars, trucks and motorcycles from mice, moisture and other related damages. Also carry a line of fine art prints. Mfg: DRYPAC (protects interiors from moisture buildup). Auto-Shield/Cycle-Shield (airtight enclosed dehumidified covers). PEST-AWAY (commercial device that stops mice damages). *Classic Car Storage* VHS (500 storage tips). PetroPal (all-natural oil absorbent mat). Free catalog available.

Car Care Group
Box 338
Poynette, WI 53955
608-635-7751

car care products

See full listing in **Section Two** under **car care products**

Carpad Incorporated
400 Main St, PO Box 204
Dayton, NV 89403-0204
702-246-0232; FAX: 702-246-0266

floor protector

See full listing in **Section Two** under **accessories**

Cover-Up Enterprises
1444 Manor Lane
Blue Bell, PA 19422
800-268-3757; FAX: 215-654-0252

car covers

See full listing in **Section Two** under **car covers**

D-A Lubricant Co
1340 W 29th St
Indianapolis, IN 46208
800-232-4503; FAX: 317-926-8132

lubricants

See full listing in **Section Two** under **lubricants**

Deltran Corporation
801 US Hwy 92 E
Deland, FL 32724
904-736-7900; FAX: 904-736-9984

battery chargers

See full listing in **Section Two** under **batteries**

**Dri-Wash & Guard
Consulting Distributors Inc**
PO Box 1331
Palm Desert, CA 92261
619-346-1984; 800-428-1883
FAX: 619-568-6354

automotive care
products
boat care products

See full listing in **Section Two** under **car care products**

Murphy's Motoring Accessories Inc
PO Box 618
Greendale, WI 53129-0618
800-529-8315; 414-529-8333

car covers

See full listing in **Section Two** under **car covers**

Preserve Inc
1430 E 1800 N
Hamilton, IL 62341
217-746-2411; FAX: 217-746-2231

storage containers

Mail order and open shop. Monday-Sunday 24 hours.
Manufacture environmentally controlled storage containers for collector cars and motorcycles. First storage system that preserves cars or motorcycles in dust-free atmosphere, and stops corrosion.

Albert A Rogers II
29A Young Rd
Charlton, MA 01507
508-248-3555

parts
storage

See full listing in **Section One** under **Ford '32-'53**

Stinger Inc
1375 17th Ave
McPherson, KS 67460
800-854-4850; 316-241-5580
FAX: 316-241-6000

lifts

Mail order only. Home and commercial storage, cleaning, chang-

ing oil, double-stacking or multiple storage. Portable, 115- or 230-volt, powder-coated. Residential, commercial storage, hobby and boat lifts.

York Petroleum Industries
dba YPI Inc
1011 Askham Dr
Cary, NC 27511-4703
919-319-5180; FAX: 919-319-7302

floor protector

See full listing in **Section Two** under **accessories**

street rods

A-1 Street Rods
631 E Las Vegas St
Colorado Springs, CO 80903
719-632-4920 or 719-577-4588
FAX: 719-634-6577

parts

Mail order and open shop. Monday-Saturday 10 to 5. Specialize in Chevrolet 1937-57 and Ford 1928-48 parts. Sell antique and classic car parts, street rod parts, accessories, rubber parts, chassis parts and cars.

American Autowire Systems Inc
150 Cooper Rd, Unit C-8, Dept HVAA
West Berlin, NJ 08091
800-482-WIRE; FAX: 609-753-0353

battery cables
electrical systems
switches/
components

The premier manufacturer of cutting edge automotive electrical systems covering street rods, street machines, race cars, custom cars and original equipment segments of the car market. Primary emphasis is on technically superior complete panel systems incorporating late model innovations in the easiest to install system on the market. Full line of accessory wiring kits and related components. Technical support and money back guarantee. VISA/MC accepted. Dealer inquiries welcome.

A-One Auto Appraisals
19 Hope Ln
Narragansett, RI 02882
401-783-7701, RI; 407-668-9610, FL

appraisals

See full listing in **Section Two** under **appraisals**

Keith Ashley
107 W Railroad St, Unit V
St Johns, MI 48879
517-224-6460; FAX: 517-224-9488

fiberglass parts

See full listing in **Section One** under **Ford '32-'53**

Auto Transport Services
5367 Fargo Rd
Avoca, MI 48006
810-324-2598

transport

See full listing in **Section Two** under **transport**

Automotive Legal Service Inc
PO Box 626
Dresher, PA 19025
PH/FAX: 800-487-4947

appraisals

See full listing in **Section Two** under **appraisals**

Bob's Classic Auto Glass
21170 Hwy 36
Blachly, OR 97412
800-624-2130

glass

See full listing in **Section Two** under **glass**

Bob's F-100 Parts Co
9372 Mission Blvd
Riverside, CA 92509
909-681-1956; FAX: 909-681-1960

parts

See full listing in **Section One** under **Ford '54-up**

Bonneville Sports Inc
12461 Country Ln
Santa Ana, CA 92705
714-508-9724; FAX: 714-508-9725

accessories
clothing

See full listing in **Section Two** under **apparel**

Boop Photography
2347 Derry St
Harrisburg, PA 17104-2728
717-564-8533
E-mail: msboop@paonline.com

photography

See full listing in **Section Two** under **photography**

BPE Racing Heads
702 Dunn Way
Placentia, CA 92870
714-572-6072; FAX: 714-572-6073

cylinder heads

See full listing in **Section Two** under **machine work**

Bumpers by Briz
8002 NE Hwy 99, #260
Vancouver, WA 98665
360-573-8628

bumpers

See full listing in **Section Two** under **chassis parts**

CAR Street Rod Parts Inc
495 Hyson Rd
Jackson, NJ 08527
908-928-3701; FAX: 908-364-7474

parts

Mail order and open shop. Monday-Friday 9-5, Saturday 9-1.
CAR offers a complete line of street rod parts: rims, frames,
chassis, fiberglass bodies, gas tanks, seats, gauges, air conditioning units and components, radiators, electric and mechanical fans, brakes, shifters, steering wheels, power windows,
hoods, grilles, dashes, etc. For the best price in town call CAR.

CBS Performance Automotive
2605-A W Colorado Ave
Colorado Springs, CO 80904
800-685-1492; FAX: 719-578-9485

ignition systems
performance
products

See full listing in **Section Two** under **ignition parts**

Cedar Creek Coachworks Ltd
151 Conestoga Ln
Stephens City, VA 22655
540-869-0244; FAX: 540-869-9577

restoration
service

See full listing in **Section Two** under **restoration shops**

**Central Florida Auto Festival
& Toy Expo**
1420 N Galloway Rd
Lakeland, FL 33810
941-686-8320

auto festival
toy expo

See full listing in **Section Two** under **auctions & events**

Class Glass & Performance Inc
101 Winston St
Cumberland, MD 21502
800-774-3456; FAX: 301-777-7044

fiberglass bodies
parts

See full listing in **Section Two** under **fiberglass parts**

The Classic Car Radio Company
2718 Koper Dr
Sterling Heights, MI 48310
810-977-7979

radios
services
wheelcovers

See full listing in **Section Two** under **radios**

Classic Motors Unlimited
RD 1 Box 99C
Hooversville, PA 15936
814-479-7874

chemical stripping
metal work
restoration

See full listing in **Section Two** under **restoration shops**

**Classical Gas Antique Auto
Museum & Sales**
245 E Collins
Eaton, CO 80615
800-453-7955; 970-454-1373
FAX: 970-454-1368

car dealer
museum

See full listing in **Section Two** under **car dealers**

**Cochrane's Special Interest
Brokers**
Ed Cochrane
718 Livingston Ave
Shreveport, LA 71107
318-226-0458, 318-424-2861

appraisers
brokers
consultant
locator

See full listing in **Section Two** under **brokers**

Coffey's Classic Transmissions
2817 Hollis
Ft Worth, TX 76111
817-834-8740; 817-439-1611

transmissions

See full listing in **Section Two** under **transmissions**

Collector's Carousel
84 Warren Ave
Westbrook, ME 04092
207-854-0343; FAX: 207-856-6913

appraisals
sales
service

See full listing in **Section Two** under **car dealers**

Timothy Cox Firewall Insulators
6333 Pacific Ave, Suite 523
Stockton, CA 95207
PH/FAX: 209-477-4840

firewall insulators
gloveboxes
quiet ride solutions

See full listing in **Section Two** under **interiors & interior parts**

Crossfire
260 Hickory St, PO Box 263
Sharpsville, PA 16150
800-458-3478; FAX: 412-962-4639

accessories

See full listing in **Section Two** under **ignition parts**

Richard Culleton
4318 SW 19th Pl
Cape Coral, FL 33914
800-931-7836 voice mail
315-685-7414 (home); 941-542-8640

accessories

See full listing in **Section Two** under **accessories**

Custom Auto Radiator
495 Hyson Rd
Jackson, NJ 08527
908-928-3700; FAX: 908-364-7474

accessories

See full listing in **Section Two** under **radiators**

Custom Plating
3030 Alta Ridge Way
Snellville, GA 30278
770-736-1118

| bumper specialist chrome plating **parts** |

See full listing in **Section Two** under **plating & polishing**

Dan's Restorations
PO Box 144, Snake Hill Rd
Sand Lake, NY 12153
518-674-2061

| **restoration** |

See full listing in **Section Two** under **bodywork**

Dependable RV & Auto Service
2619 Rt 11 N
Lafayette, NY 13084
315-677-5336

| **parts restoration service** |

See full listing in **Section Two** under **service shops**

Deters Restorations
6205 Swiss Garden Rd
Temperance, MI 48182-1020
313-847-1820

| **restoration** |

See full listing in **Section Two** under **restoration shops**

Bob Drake Reproductions Inc
1819 NW Washington Blvd
Grants Pass, OR 97526
800-221-3673; FAX: 541-474-0099

| **repro parts** |

See full listing in **Section One** under **Ford '32-'53**

Early Wheel Co Inc
Box 1438
Santa Ynez, CA 93460
805-688-1187; FAX: 805-688-0257

| **steel wheels** |

See full listing in **Section Two** under **wheels & wheelcovers**

Eastern Specialty Automotive Sales & Service Ltd
38 Yankeetown Rd
Hammonds Plains, NS Canada
B3Z 1K7
902-835-5912; FAX: 902-835-0680

| **parts service transport** |

See full listing in **Section Two** under **car & parts locators**

Ed's Be-Bop Shop
10087 W Co Rd 300 S
Medora, IN 47260
812-966-2203

| **accessories parts restoration** |

See full listing in **Section One** under **Ford '03-'31**

Executive Boys Toys
200 S Jackson St
Lima, OH 45804
419-227-9300

| **car dealer** |

See full listing in **Section Two** under **car dealers**

Fairlane Automotive Specialties
210 E Walker St
St Johns, MI 48879
517-224-6460

| **fiberglass bodies parts** |

See full listing in **Section One** under **Ford '32-'53**

Flatlander's Hot Rods
1005 W 45th St
Norfolk, VA 23508
804-440-1932; FAX: 804-423-8601

| **chassis manufacturing parts street rods** |

Open daily. Traditional and nostalgic hot rod parts. Manufacturer of 1932 Ford 5-w coupe and roadster bodies as well as complete chassis for 1928-1934 Ford cars and trucks. Also manufacture hot rod tubular axles and many related components for street rods 1928-48. MC/Visa, worldwide shipping. Catalog $3.

Ron Francis' Wire Works
167 Keystone Rd
Chester, PA 19013
610-485-1937

| **wiring wiring kits** |

See full listing in **Section Two** under **electrical systems**

The Generation Gap
4989 Mercer University Dr
Macon, GA 31210
912-471-6325

| **broker car dealer** |

See full listing in **Section Two** under **car dealers**

Grey Hills Auto Restoration
PO Box 630
51 Vail Rd
Blairstown, NJ 07825
908-362-8232; FAX: 908-362-6796

| **restoration service** |

See full listing in **Section Two** under **restoration shops**

Gromm Racing Heads
666-J Stockton Ave
San Jose, CA 95126
408-287-1301

| **cylinder heads racing parts** |

See full listing in **Section Two** under **racing**

Hatfield Restorations
PO Box 846
Canton, TX 75103
PH/FAX: 903-567-6742

| **restoration** |

See full listing in **Section Two** under **restoration shops**

High Performance Coatings
550 W 3615 S
Salt Lake City, UT 84115
801-262-6807; FAX: 801-262-6307
E-mail: hpcsales@hpcoatings.com

| **coatings** |

See full listing in **Section Two** under **exhaust systems**

The Hot Rod Shop
16741 State Rd 1
Spencerville, IN 46788
219-627-5474; FAX: 219-627-6317

| **car dealer collectible autos & street rods** |

Mail order and open shop. Monday-Saturday 10 am to 6 pm. Street rod and collector car dealer. Specializing in 1941-48 Ford parts. Street rod and GM chassis conversion.

House of Powder Inc Rt 71 & 1st St PO Box 110 Standard, IL 61363 815-339-2648	**powder coating sandblasting**

See full listing in **Section Two** under **service shops**

Howell's Sheetmetal Co PO Box 792 Nederland, TX 77627 409-727-1999	**body panels sheetmetal**

See full listing in **Section One** under **Ford '03-'31**

Hunters Custom Automotive 975 Main St Nashville, TN 37206 615-227-6584; FAX: 615-227-4897	**accessories engine parts fiberglass products**

See full listing in **Section Two** under **accessories**

Inland Empire Driveline Service Inc 4035 E Guasti Rd, #301 Ontario, CA 91761 800-800-0109; FAX: 909-390-3038	**drive shafts pinion yokes**

See full listing in **Section Two** under **machine work**

Jefferis Hot Rod Autobody 4130-C Horizon Ln San Luis Obispo, CA 93401 800-807-1937; FAX: 805-543-4757	**windshield glass kit**

See full listing in **Section Two** under **glass**

K & K Insurance Group Inc PO Box 2338 Fort Wayne, IN 46801-2338 800-548-0858; FAX: 219-459-5511	**insurance**

See full listing in **Section Two** under **insurance**

Keilen's Auto Restoring 580 Kelley Blvd (R) North Attleboro, MA 02760 508-699-7768	**restoration**

See full listing in **Section Two** under **restoration shops**

Koffel's Place II 740 River Rd Huron, OH 44839 419-433-4410; FAX: 419-433-2166	**engine rebuilding machine shop**

See full listing in **Section Two** under **engine rebuilding**

Koolmat PO Box 207, 1922 Coventry Brunswick, OH 44212 330-273-6011; FAX: 330-273-9858	**insulators**

See full listing in **Section Two** under **restoration aids**

Lee's Kustom Auto & Street Rods RR 3, Box 3061A Rome, PA 18837 717-247-2326	**accessories parts restoration**

Mail order and open shop. Monday-Friday 8 to 5, Saturday 8 to 12. Complete shop for street rods, kit cars, race cars & total restorations on antique & classic autos. A one stop shop for parts, upholstery, engine, speed equipment, etc & accessories. Autos bought and sold.

Lokar Inc 10924 Murdock Dr Knoxville, TN 37922 423-966-2269; FAX: 423-671-1999	**performance parts**

Mail order only. Manufacturer of US quality made performance products. Shifters, emergency hand brakes and brake cables. Throttle cables, kick-down kits, component mounting brackets and flexible transmission dipsticks. Other products include flexible engine dipstick, throttle pedal assemblies, hood and trunk release kits, back-up light switch/neutral safety switch kits, cut-to-fit speedometer cables, etc. Applications available for all transmission applications, including new LT-1 engines.

M & R Products 1940 SW Blvd Vineland, NJ 08360 609-696-9450; FAX: 609-696-4999	**hardware tie-downs**

See full listing in **Section Two** under **accessories**

Main Attractions PO Box 4923 Chatsworth, CA 91313 818-709-9855; FAX: 818-998-0906	**posters videos**

See full listing in **Section Four** under **information sources**

Masterworks Auto Reconditioning 1127 Brush Run Rd Washington, PA 15301 412-267-3460	**restoration**

See full listing in **Section Two** under **restoration shops**

Charlie Merrill 1041 Kenyon Rd Twin Falls, ID 83301 208-736-0949	**broker car dealer car locator**

See full listing in **Section Two** under **brokers**

Motorsports Racing 914 S Santa Fe #101 Vista, CA 92084 619-630-0547; FAX: 619-630-3085	**accessories apparel art**

See full listing in **Section Two** under **apparel**

Murphy's Motoring Accessories Inc PO Box 618 Greendale, WI 53129-0618 800-529-8315; 414-529-8333	**car covers**

See full listing in **Section Two** under **car covers**

No Limit Engineering 1737 Production Circle Riverside, CA 92509 FAX: 909-275-9232	**brakes chassis parts**

See full listing in **Section Two** under **chassis parts**

Norm's Custom Shop 6897 E William St Ext Bath, NY 14810 607-776-2357; FAX: 607-776-4541	**interiors tops**

See full listing in **Section One** under **Cord**

Obsolete Ford Parts Inc 8701 S I-35 Oklahoma City, OK 73149 405-631-3933; FAX: 405-634-6815	**parts**

See full listing in **Section One** under **Ford '54-up**

Generalists

Painless Wiring	accessories
9505 Santa Paula Dr	parts
Fort Worth, TX 76116	
817-292-9315; FAX: 817-292-4024	
E-mail: painlesswiring@airmail.net	

See full listing in **Section Two** under **wiring harnesses**

Paintwerks by Jeff Tischler	pinstriping
PO Box 376	
Hibernia, NJ 07842	
201-627-9208	

See full listing in **Section Two** under **striping**

People's Choice & Lost in the 50s	automobilia items
28170 Ave Crocker #209	celebrity items
Valencia, CA 91355	50s clothing
800-722-1965, 805-295-1965	50s memorabilia
FAX: 805-295-1931	

See full listing in **Section Two** under **automobilia**

Performance Automotive Warehouse	accessories
8966 Mason Ave	engine parts
Chatsworth, CA 91311	
818-998-6000; FAX: 818-407-7204	

See full listing in **Section Two** under **engine parts**

Pick-ups Northwest	parts
7130 Bickford Ave	trim
Snohomish, WA 98290	
360-568-9166; FAX: 360-568-1233	

See full listing in **Section One** under **Chevrolet**

Pilgrim's Special Interest Autos	bodywork
3888 Hill Rd	metal fabrication
Lakeport, CA 95453	paint
PH/FAX: 707-262-1062	restoration

See full listing in **Section Two** under **restoration shops**

Jack Podell Fuel Injection Spec	fuel system parts
106 Wakewa Ave	fuel system
South Bend, IN 46617	rebuilding
219-232-6430; FAX: 219-234-8632	

See full listing in **Section One** under **Corvette**

Power Effects	exhaust systems
1800H Industrial Park Dr	
Grand Haven, MI 49417	
616-847-4200; FAX: 616-847-4210	

See full listing in **Section Two** under **exhaust systems**

Prestige Motors	car dealer
120 N Bessie Rd	
Spokane, WA 99212	
PH/FAX: 509-926-3611	

See full listing in **Section Two** under **car dealers**

RB's Obsolete Automotive	parts
18421 Hwy 99	
Lynnwood, WA 98037	
206-670-6739; FAX: 206-670-9151	

See full listing in **Section Two** under **comprehensive parts**

Red Crown Valve Caps	automobilia
PO Box 5301	
Topeka, KS 66605	
913-357-5007	

See full listing in **Section Two** under **automobilia**

Red's Headers	headers
22950 Bednar Ln	mechanical parts
Fort Bragg, CA 95437-8411	
707-964-7733	

See full listing in **Section One** under **Ford '32-'53**

Reider Racing Enterprises Inc	axle components
12351 Universal Dr	
Taylor, MI 48180	
800-522-2707, 313-946-1330	
FAX: 313-946-8672	

See full listing in **Section Two** under **racing**

Restorations Unlimited II Inc	restoration
304 Jandus Rd	
Cary, IL 60013	
847-639-5818	

See full listing in **Section Two** under **restoration shops**

RMR Restorations Inc	restoration
13 Columbia Dr, Unit 1	
Amherst, NH 03031	
PH/FAX: 603-880-6880 work	
603-672-8335 home	

See full listing in **Section Two** under **restoration shops**

Rock Valley Antique Auto Parts	gas tanks
Box 352, Rt 72 and Rothwell Rd	
Stillman Valley, IL 61084	
815-645-2271; FAX: 815-645-2740	

See full listing in **Section One** under **Ford '32-'53**

Rod-1 Shop	street rods
210 Clinton Ave	
Pitman, NJ 08071	
609-228-7631; FAX: 609-582-5770	

Open shop only. Monday thru Friday 7 am-5 pm, weekends by appointment. Street rods, restorations of 30, 40, 50 & 60 cars, original or customs and muscle cars, turnkey or partial. Welding, wiring, performance, chassis modifications, front end installations, sheetmetal work and bodywork.

RW & Able Inc	door panels
PO Box 2110	interior accessories
Chico, CA 95927	
PH/FAX: 916-896-1513	

Mail order only. Designer of door panels and interior accessories that allow the street rodder/restorer to do much of the upholstery work themselves, without sewing, drilling or the use of screws or clips. Thom Taylor, Taylor Designs and other designers have produced a series of thirteen custom designs. In addition to door panels, a complete line of cowl panels, quarter panels, package trays, trunk kits, door pulls, armrests and speaker templates are available.

Sanders Antique Auto Restoration	restoration
1120 22nd St	
Rockford, IL 61108	
815-226-0535	

See full listing in **Section Two** under **restoration shops**

Saturn Industries 143 Wimborne Rd Poole, Dorset BH15 2BCR England 01202-674982; FAX: 01202-668274	axles instruments literature repro parts

See full listing in **Section One** under **Ford '03-'31**

Joe Smith Ford & Hot Rod Parts 2140 Canton Rd, Unit C Marietta, GA 30066 800-235-4013; 770-426-9850 FAX: 770-426-9854	parts service

See full listing in **Section One** under **Ford '32-'53**

Sparrow Auction Company 59 Wheeler Ave Milford, CT 06460 PH/FAX: 203-877-1066	auction company

See full listing in **Section Two** under **auctions & events**

Speedway Motors Inc 300 Speedway Cir Lincoln, NE 68502 402-474-4411; FAX: 402-477-7476	parts

See full listing in **Section Two** under **comprehensive parts**

Steve's Auto Restorations 4440 SE 174th Ave Portland, OR 97236 503-665-2222; FAX: 503-665-2225	restoration

See full listing in **Section Two** under **restoration shops**

Tatom Custom Engines/ Vintage Vendors 2718 Riverbend Rd Mt Vernon, WA 98273 360-424-8314; FAX: 360-424-6717	engine rebuilding machine shop

See full listing in **Section Two** under **engine rebuilding**

Thompson Hill Metalcraft 23 Thompson Hill Rd Berwick, ME 03901 207-698-5756	metal forming panel beating welding

See full listing in **Section Two** under **sheetmetal**

Tornado Air Management Systems 13360-H Firestone Blvd Santa Fe Springs, CA 90670 310-926-5000; FAX: 310-926-1223 E-mail: j.k@ix.netcom.com	parts

See full listing in **Section Two** under **accessories**

Transport-Nation Collectibles 24040 Camino Del Avion, Ste A-241 Monarch Beach, CA 92629 800-474-4404, 714-240-5126	artwork collectibles

See full listing in **Section Two** under **artwork**

The V8 Store 3010 NE 49th St Vancouver, WA 98663 360-693-7468, 360-694-7853 nights FAX: 360-693-0982	accessories parts service

Mail order and open shop. Monday-Friday 7:30 to 5 nights and Saturday by appointment. Rod and custom supply store special-

izing in authentic fifties accessories. Also have both used and NOS engine, drivetrain, body parts, flathead speed equipment.

Jon Ward Motorsports 3100 FM 1703, PO Box 238 Alpine, TX 79831 915-837-3250; FAX: 915-837-5878	engines race cars

See full listing in **Section Two** under **racing**

Wescott's Auto Restyling 19701 SE Hwy 212 Boring, OR 97009 800-523-6279; FAX: 503-658-2938	body parts

See full listing in **Section One** under **Ford '32-'53**

Westbury Hot Rods 1130 Detroit Ave Concord, CA 94520 510-682-9482; FAX: 510-682-9483	service sheetmetal fabrication

Shop open Monday-Friday 8 to 5:30 pm. Full service hot rod and custom facilities. Handcrafted metal fabrication, including custom chassis from 28-present, sheetmetal forming, wiring.

Kirk F White PO Box 999 New Smyrna Beach, FL 32170 904-427-6660; FAX: 904-427-7801	models tin toys

See full listing in **Section Two** under **models & toys**

Johnny Williams Services 2613 Copeland Road Tyler, TX 75701 903-597-3687 800-937-0900 voice mail #7225	appraiser car & parts locator consultant lighting systems design

See full listing in **Section Two** under **appraisals**

Wilson's Rods and Classics Gary R Wilson Rt 1, Box 139 Holliday, MO 65258 816-327-5583	restoration

See full listing in **Section Two** under **restoration shops**

Yankee Peddler Motorsports 11300 Fortune Circle Wellington, FL 33414 561-798-6606; FAX: 561-798-6706	electrical components hardware

See full listing in **Section Two** under **electrical systems**

striping

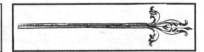

Auto Decals Unlimited Inc 11259 E Via Linda, Ste 100-201 Scottsdale, AZ 85259 602-860-9800; FAX: 602-860-8370	decals stripe kits

See full listing in **Section Two** under **decals**

David Jones The Pinstriper 19 Hope Ln Narragansett, RI 02882 401-783-7701, RI; 407-668-9610, FL	striping

Open shop only. Variable hours. Also travels to jobs. Over 30 years' experience applying handpainted pinstripe and scrolls on all automobile and related objects.

Paintwerks by Jeff Tischler PO Box 376 Hibernia, NJ 07842 201-627-9208	**pinstriping**

Shop open by appointment only. Custom hand-painted pinstriping and monogramming. Specializing in street rods, kustoms, classic automobiles and motorcycles. Some traveling possible. Located in Rockaway, NJ, area. 27 years' experience.

Prostripe Div of Spartan International Inc 1845 Cedar St Holt, MI 48842 800-248-7800; FAX: 517-694-7952	**graphics** **molding** **pinstriping**

Pinstriping, graphics, molding, window tint. We are manufacturers of the above items. Our customer service department will refer callers to our installer shops.

suspension parts

356 Enterprises Vic & Barbara Skirmants 27244 Ryan Rd Warren, MI 48092 810-575-9544; FAX: 810-558-3616	**parts**

See full listing in **Section One** under **Porsche**

A-1 Shock Absorber Co Shockfinders Division 2225 W Wabansia Ave Chicago, IL 60647 312-395-0700; 800-344-1966 FAX: 312-395-0739	**shocks** **sway bars**

Both mail order and open shop. Monday-Friday 8-5. Hard-to-find shock specialists. Tube type shocks for cars & trucks 1928-79 in stock. Gas or hydraulic, 1-3/16" or 1-3/8" piston size. Also spring assist and air shocks. Lever shocks rebuilt for domestic and foreign applications. No struts, hydraulics or low riders. Want the best shocks available? Our gas-charged extra heavy duty shocks have a 50% larger piston, twice the oil capacity and heavier gauge metal compared to a heavy duty.

See our ad on page 608

Action Performance Inc 1619 Lakeland Ave Bohemia, NY 11716 516-244-7100; FAX: 516-244-7172	**accessories**

See full listing in **Section Two** under **accessories**

Alan's Axles 2300 Congress Ave Clearwater, FL 34623 800-741-0452; 813-784-0452	**axles**

See full listing in **Section Two** under **chassis parts**

Antique Auto Parts Cellar PO Box 3 6 Chauncy St S Weymouth, MA 02190 617-335-1579; FAX: 617-335-1925	**brake/chassis parts** **engine parts** **fuel pumps/kits** **gaskets** **water pumps**

See full listing in **Section Two** under **comprehensive parts**

Apple Hydraulics Inc 1610 Middle Rd Calverton, NY 11933-1419 516-369-9515; 800-882-7753 FAX: 516-369-9516	**brake rebuilding** **shock rebuilding**

Mail order and open shop. Monday-Friday 9 to 5. Shock absorbers rebuilt, knee action and lever type. Largest USA rebuilder of Delco, Armstrong, Girling, Houdaille, American, British and other vintage shocks 1915-74. Brake cylinders sleeved and completely rebuilt, service includes brake masters, boosters, servos, wheel cylinders, calipers and rebuild kits. Fast service. Fast service, VISA/MC, COD orders welcome. Free catalog.

Atlantic Enterprises 221 Strand Industrial Dr Little River, SC 29566 803-399-7565; FAX: 803-399-4600	**steering assemblies**

See full listing in **Section Two** under **chassis parts**

Authentic Automotive 529 Buttercup Trail Mesquite, TX 75149 972-289-6373	**power brakes** **power steering**

See full listing in **Section One** under **Chevrolet**

Auto Accessories of America Inc PO Box 427, Rt 322 Boalsburg, PA 16827 800-458-3475; FAX: 814-364-9615 Foreign: 814-364-2141	**accessories** **customizing** **gifts & apparel** **restoration**

See full listing in **Section One** under **Corvette**

Automotion 193 Commercial St Sunnyvale, CA 94068 800-777-8881; FAX: 408-736-9013 E-mail: automo@aol.com	**parts**

See full listing in **Section One** under **Porsche**

Bairs Corvettes 316 Franklin St Linesville, PA 16424 814-683-4223; FAX: 814-683-5200	**parts** **service**

See full listing in **Section One** under **Corvette**

British Parts NW 4105 SE Lafayette Hwy Dayton, OR 97114 503-864-2001; FAX: 503-864-2081	**parts**

See full listing in **Section One** under **Triumph**

California Pony Cars 1906 Quaker Ridge Pl Ontario, CA 91761 909-923-2804; FAX: 909-947-8593 E-mail: 105232.3362@compuserv.com	**parts**

See full listing in **Section One** under **Mustang**

Canadian Mustang 12844 78th Ave Surrey, BC Canada V3W 8E7 604-594-2425; FAX: 604-594-9282	**parts**

See full listing in **Section One** under **Mustang**

Central Jersey Mustang 36 Craig St Edison, NJ 08817 908-572-3939; FAX: 908-985-8653	**parts** **restoration** **service**

See full listing in **Section One** under **Mustang**

Stan Chernoff 1215 Greenwood Ave Torrance, CA 90503 310-320-4554; FAX: 310-328-7867 E-mail: az589@lafn.org	**mechanical parts** **restoration parts** **technical info** **trim parts**

See full listing in **Section One** under **Datsun**

Chicago Corvette Supply 7322 S Archer Rd Justice, IL 60458 708-458-2500; FAX: 708-458-2662	**parts**

See full listing in **Section One** under **Corvette**

Classic Chevy International PO Box 607188 Orlando, FL 32860-7188 800-456-1956; FAX: 407-299-3341 E-mail: cciworld@aol.com	**modified parts** **repro parts** **used parts**

See full listing in **Section One** under **Chevrolet**

Classic Mustang Inc 24A Robert Porter Rd Southington, CT 06489 800-243-2742; FAX: 203-276-9986	**accessories** **parts**

See full listing in **Section One** under **Mustang**

Coil Spring Specialties 632 W Bertrand St Mary's, KS 66536 913-437-2025; FAX: 913-437-2266	**custom coil springs**

Mail order only. We deal in custom coil springs for all makes and models. Specializing in classic and muscle car applications. We 100% calibrate to factory specifications so you get the right spring the first time. We can also custom make springs for any special application you may require.

See our ad on this page

Corvair Underground PO Box 339 Dundee, OR 97115 503-434-1648, 800-825-8247 FAX: 503-434-1626	**parts**

See full listing in **Section One** under **Corvair**

Custom Plating 3030 Alta Ridge Way Snellville, GA 30278 770-736-1118	**bumper specialist** **chrome plating** **parts**

See full listing in **Section Two** under **plating & polishing**

Dr vette 212 7th St SW New Philadelphia, OH 44663 330-339-3370, 800-878-1022 orders; FAX: 330-339-6640	**brakes** **fuel system parts** **repairs**

See full listing in **Section One** under **Corvettes**

Dynatech Engineering PO Box 1446 Alta Loma, CA 91701-8446 805-492-6134	**motor mounts**

Mail order only. Leading provider of muscle car motor mounts. Dynatechs patented "lock up" design. Allows the engine to float on the insulators during normal driving then lock-up during hard acceleration. These mounts improve launch characteristics and eliminate the need for harsh solid mounts. When installed they look like standard OEM mounts. Call or write for a free *Mitymounts* catalog.

East Spring Obsolete Auto Parts Inc PO Box 3 Bethlehem, CT 06751 203-266-5488 evenings & weekends	**parts**

See full listing in **Section Two** under **brakes**

Eastern States Performance Outlet Inc 701 Pine Tree Rd Danville, PA 17821 PH/FAX: 717-672-9413	**suspension parts**

Mail order and open shop. Monday-Friday 9 am- 8 pm, Saturday & Sunday by appointment. Suspension parts. New leaf springs, coil springs, shackle kits, bushings, U-bolts, front end parts. Most makes, models and years, generally 1950s to present with an expanding inventory of leaves/accessories for 1930s and 1940s. Leaves start at $90 pr, coils start at $40 pr. Also available, brake drums & rotors. VISA, MasterCard, Discover or COD accepted. Shipped UPS.

Eaton Detroit Spring Service Co	coil springs
1555 Michigan Ave	leaf springs
Detroit, MI 48216	
313-963-3839; FAX: 313-963-7047	
E-mail: ken@eatonsprings.com	

Mail order and open shop. Monday-Friday 8 to 5:30, Supplies any leaf or coil spring for American cars and trucks from the 1902 curved dash Oldsmobile to present. With a library of over 17,000 OEM blueprints, we can manufacture to OEM specs or custom make to your specs. Complete line of shackles, bushings and U-bolts. We are licensed by both Ford Motor and GM restoration parts programs which guarantees the quality and authenticity of our springs and components.
Web Site: http://www.eatonsprings.com/eds.html

Egge Machine Company	babbitting
11707 Slauson Ave	chassis
Santa Fe Springs, CA 90670	motor mounts
310-945-3419 in CA, 800-866-EGGE	pistons/valves
FAX: 310-693-1635	wiring harnesses

See full listing in **Section Two** under **engine parts**

FEN Enterprises of New York Inc	parts
PO Box 1559	restoration
Wappingers Falls, NY 12590	
914-462-5959; 914-462-5094	
FAX: 914-462-8450	

See full listing in **Section One** under **Cadillac/LaSalle**

Five Points Classic Auto Shocks	shock absorbers
2911 A S Main	
Santa Ana, CA 92707	
714-979-0451	

Mail order and open shop. Monday-Friday 9-5. Deals in shock absorbers. Rebuilds lever type shocks for all makes and models. Rebuilds certain tubular shocks.

For Ramblers Only	accessories
2324 SE 34th Ave	parts
Portland, OR 97214	
503-232-0497	
E-mail: ramblermac@aol.com	

See full listing in **Section One** under **AMC**

Guldstrand Engineering Inc	parts
11924 W Jefferson Blvd	
Culver City, CA 90230	
310-391-7108; FAX: 310-391-7424	
E-mail: geiauto@aol.com	

See full listing in **Section One** under **Corvette**

Mike Hershenfeld	parts
3011 Susan Rd	
Bellmore, NY 11710	
PH/FAX: 516-781-PART (7278)	

See full listing in **Section One** under **MoPar**

Clinton Hickey Antique Auto	parts
158 Bissonnette St	
Valleyfield, QC Canada J6T 3P7	
514-371-1340	

Mail order only. Monday-Saturday 9 to 9. Antique auto parts and accessories, NOS only, all makes.

Holcombe Cadillac Parts	parts
2933 Century Ln	
Bensalem, PA 19020	
215-245-4560; FAX: 215-633-9916	

See full listing in **Section One** under **Cadillac/LaSalle**

Hunters Custom Automotive	accessories
975 Main St	engine parts
Nashville, TN 37206	fiberglass products
615-227-6584; FAX: 615-227-4897	

See full listing in **Section Two** under **accessories**

Jack's Auto Ranch	used parts
N6848 H Islandview Rd	
Watertown, WI 53094	
414-699-2521	

See full listing in **Section Two** under **comprehensive parts**

Kanter Auto Products	car covers
76 Monroe St	carpets
Boonton, NJ 07005	parts
800-526-1096; or 201-334-9575	
FAX: 201-334-5423	

See full listing in **Section Two** under **comprehensive parts**

Kenask Spring Co	springs
307 Manhattan Ave	
Jersey City, NJ 07307	
201-653-4589	

Mail order and open shop. Monday thru Saturday 9 am-4 pm. Dealing in auto and truck leaf springs and coil springs, also all parts related to springs. Rubbers, bushings, U-bolts, shackles, hangers, pins, bolts, insulators, etc. We also install what we sell.

Roger Kraus Racing	shocks
2896 Grove Way	tires
Castro Valley, CA 94546	wheels
510-582-5031; FAX: 510-886-5605	

See full listing in **Section Two** under **tires**

L B Repair	restoration
1308 W Benten	
Savannah, MO 64485-1549	
816-324-3913	

See full listing in **Section One** under **Ford '54-up**

Linearossa International Inc	parts
15281 Barranca Pkwy, #A	
Irvine, CA 92618	
714-727-1201; FAX: 714-727-0603	

See full listing in **Section One** under **Fiat**

Lister North America Ltd	performance parts
6565 E 40	
Tulsa, OK 74145	
918-665-0021; FAX: 918-664-0804	

See full listing in **Section One** under **Jaguar**

Mint Condition Auto Upholstery	convertible tops
PO Box 134	interiors
Silverdale New Zealand	spring-gaiters
PH/FAX: 64-9-424 2257	wheelcovers

See full listing in **Section Two** under **special services**

| Muskegon Brake & Dist Co
848 E Broadway
Muskegon, MI 49444
616-733-0874; FAX: 616-733-0635 | **brakes**
springs
suspensions |

See full listing in **Section Two** under **brakes**

| No Limit Engineering
1737 Production Circle
Riverside, CA 92509
FAX: 909-275-9232 | **brakes**
chassis parts |

See full listing in **Section Two** under **chassis parts**

| Northern Auto Parts Warehouse Inc
PO Box 3147
Sioux City, IA 51102
800-831-0884; FAX: 712-258-0088 | **parts** |

See full listing in **Section Two** under **engine parts**

| Northwest Classic Falcons Inc
1964 NW Pettygrove St
Portland, OR 97209
503-241-9454; FAX: 503-241-1964 | **parts** |

See full listing in **Section One** under **Ford '54-up**

| Northwestern Auto Supply Inc
1101 S Division
Grand Rapids, MI 49507
616-241-1714, 800-704-1078
FAX: 616-241-0924 | **parts** |

See full listing in **Section Two** under **engine parts**

| The Parts Scout®
Bodo Repenn
Diagonalstrasse 18A
D-20537 Hamburg Germany
*49-40-21980130
FAX: *49-40-21980132 | **parts**
parts locator |

See full listing in **Section Two** under **comprehensive parts**

| Pollard Co
Joe Pollard
9331 Johnell Rd
Chatsworth, CA 91311
PH/FAX: 818-999-1485 | **parts** |

See full listing in **Section One** under **Checker**

| David Raine's Springcrafters
425 Harding Hwy
Carney's Point, NJ 08069
609-299-9141; FAX: 609-299-9157 | **springs**
suspension parts |

Mail order only. New replacement coil springs, 1934-84; also leaf springs and suspension parts. Specialty custom raised or lowered coil springs.

| RARE Corvettes
Joe Calcagno
Box 1080
Soquel, CA 95073
408-475-4442; FAX: 408-475-1115 | **cars**
parts |

See full listing in **Section One** under **Corvette**

| Rare Parts Inc
621 Wilshire Ave
Stockton, CA 95203
209-948-6005; FAX: 209-948-2851 | **suspension parts** |

Mail order and open shop. Open five days a week 8 to 5.

Purchases and manufactures suspension parts for vehicles from 1930-94. We distribute through all W/D, jobbers and auto repair/restoration businesses.

| RB's Obsolete Automotive
18421 Hwy 99
Lynnwood, WA 98037
206-670-6739; FAX: 206-670-9151 | **parts** |

See full listing in **Section Two** under **comprehensive parts**

| RD Enterprises Ltd
290 Raub Rd
Quakertown, PA 18951
215-538-9323; FAX: 215-538-0158
E-mail: rdent@rdent.com | **parts** |

See full listing in **Section One** under **Lotus**

| Red Bird Racing
5621 NE Issler St
Vancouver, WA 98661
360-694-9929 | **parts** |

See full listing in **Section One** under **Chevrolet**

| Roadster Restoration
3730 Todrob Ln
Placerville, CA 95667
916-644-6777; FAX: 916-644-7252 | **parts** |

See full listing in **Section One** under **Datsun**

| William H Robenolt
5121 S Bridget Point
Floral City, FL 34436
352-344-2007 | **front suspension**
parts |

Mail order and open shop by appointment only. Obsolete NOS/NORS front suspension parts. Mid thirties thru seventies. Write for availability and quote, fair prices and prompt service.

| Shockfinders
Division of A-1 Shock Absorber Co
2225 W Wabansia Ave
Chicago, IL 60647
312-395-0700; 800-344-1966
FAX: 312-395-0739 | **shocks**
sway bars |

Both mail order and open shop. Monday-Friday 8-5. Hard to find shock specialists. Tube type shocks for cars and trucks 1928-79 in stock. Gas or hydraulic, 1-3/16" or 1-3/8" piston size. Also spring assist and air shocks. Lever shocks rebuilt for domestic and foreign applications. No struts, hydraulics or low riders. Want the best shocks available? Our gas charged extra heavy duty shocks have a 50% larger piston, twice the oil capacity and heavier gauge metal compared to a heavy duty.

See our ad on page 608

| Spax USA
31 Winsor St
Milpitas, CA 95035
408-942-5595; FAX: 408-942-5582
E-mail: usaspax@aol.com | **shocks**
springs
struts |

Mail order and open shop. Monday-Saturday 8 to 6. Specializing in shocks, struts, springs and conversion kits for all vintage European cars.

| Star Classics Inc
7745 E Redfield #300
Scottsdale, AZ 85260
602-991-7495, 800-644-7827
FAX: 602-951-4096 | **parts**
sales
service |

See full listing in **Section One** under **Mercedes-Benz**

Studebaker Parts & Locations 228 Marquiss Cir Clinton, TN 37716 615-457-3002	**parts** **parts locator**

See full listing in **Section One** under **Studebaker**

Swedish Classics Inc PO Box 557 Oxford, MD 21654 800-258-4422; FAX: 410-226-5543	**parts**

See full listing in **Section One** under **Volvo**

TA Motor AB Torpslingan 21 Lulea S 97347 Sweden +46-920-18888 FAX: +46-920-18821	**accessories** **parts**

See full listing in **Section One** under **Cadillac/LaSalle**

T-Bird Sanctuary 9997 SW Avery Tualatin, OR 97062 503-692-9848, FAX: 503-692-9849	**parts**

See full listing in **Section One** under **Thunderbird**

Thunderbird Headquarters 1080 Detroit Ave Concord, CA 94518 800-227-2174, US FAX: 510-689-1771	**accessories** **literature** **parts** **upholstery**

See full listing in **Section One** under **Thunderbird**

TMC (Traction Master Co) 2917 W Olympic Blvd Los Angeles, CA 90006 213-382-1131	**suspensions**

See full listing in **Section One** under **Mustang**

Jon Ward Motorsports 3100 FM 1703 PO Box 238 Alpine, TX 79831 915-837-3250; FAX: 915-837-5878	**engines** **race cars**

See full listing in **Section Two** under **racing**

Westbury Hot Rods 1130 Detroit Ave Concord, CA 94520 510-682-9482; FAX: 510-682-9483	**service** **sheetmetal** **fabrication**

See full listing in **Section Two** under **street rods**

tires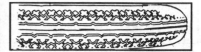

Antique Automotive Accessories 889 S Rainbow Blvd, Suite 642 Las Vegas, NV 89128 800-742-6777; FAX: 913-862-4646	**accessories** **tires**

Specializing in wide whitewall radials, redline radials and original type bias ply tires.

Automotive Specialty Accessory Parts Inc PO Box 1907 Carson City, NV 89702 800-693-ASAP(2727) FAX: 702-888-4545	**parts**

Mail order only. Open 7 days a week, 24 hours a day. Dealing in mail order performance auto parts.

Coker Tire 1317 Chestnut St Chattanooga, TN 37402 800-251-6336 toll-free 423-265-6368, local & int'l FAX: 423-756-5607	**tires**

Call for a free catalog featuring authentic, original equipment tires, tubes and flaps for Model Ts to muscle cars. Vintage brands such as Firestone, Firestone Wide Oval, BF Goodrich Silvertowns, Vintage Michelin and US Royal. Also available, the world's first true wide whitewall radial tire and muscle car wheels. Helpful sales staff, toll-free number and major credit cards accepted. Web site: http://www.coker.com

See our ad on this page

Innovative Novelties/ McGee Enterprises PO Box 1375 Little Rock, AR 72203 501-835-8409; FAX: 501-835-7293 E-mail: kholland@cci.net	**accessories**

See full listing in **Section Two** under **novelties**

Roger Kraus Racing 2896 Grove Way Castro Valley, CA 94546 510-582-5031; FAX: 510-886-5605	**shocks** **tires** **wheels**

Mail order and open shop. Monday-Friday 8:30 am-5:30 pm. Dealing in vintage race and street tires, specializing in Goodyear,

Generalists

Avon and Dunlop. Wheels: American Racing, Dayton wire wheels, Panasport wheels, Halibrand wheels, Monocoque wheels and Jongbloed wheels. Koni shocks. Hand tire mounting systems and balancers.

Orlandi Trailer 3120 Moorpark Ave San Jose, CA 95117 408-296-5748; FAX: 408-247-1219	**trailers**

See full listing in **Section Two** under **trailers**

Prestige Thunderbird Inc 10215 Greenleaf Ave Santa Fe Springs, CA 90670 800-423-4751, 310-944-6237 FAX: 310-941-8677	**appraisals** **radios** **repairs** **restorations** **tires**

See full listing in **Section One** under **Thunderbird**

Rhino Industries 14512 N Nebraska Ave Tampa, FL 33613 813-977-7776; FAX: 813-977-5419	**cleaner**

See full listing in **Section Two** under **car care products**

Rideable Antique Bicycle Replicas 2329 Eagle Ave Alameda, CA 94501 510-769-0980; FAX: 510-521-7145 E-mail: mbarron@barrongroup.com	**bicycles** **tires**

See full listing in **Section Two** under **motorcycles**

O B Smith Chevy Parts PO Box 11703 990 New Circle Rd NW Lexington, KY 40577 606-253-1957; FAX: 606-233-3129	**parts** **tires**

See full listing in **Section One** under **Chevrolet**

Tavia Performance Products Inc 12851 Western Ave, Unit D Garden Grove, CA 92841 714-892-4057; FAX: 714-892-5627	**accessories** **tools**

See full listing in **Section Two** under **tools**

Tire Barn Inc 255 Twinsburg Rd Northfield, OH 44067 216-467-1284 FAX: 216-467-1289, call first	**tires**

Specializing in hard to get antique tires from 1926-60, 30 Sayors and Schoville 4-door vans, 30 Jordan 4-door, 29 Chrysler 4-door and 31 Hupmobile.

The Tire Source Inc 2828 30th St Boulder, CO 80301 303-443-3021; 800-422-8473 FAX: 303-449-9842	**race tires**

Mail order and open shop. Monday-Friday 8-5:30, Saturday 8-2. Dealing in Goodyear vintage race tires.

Universal Tire Co 987 Stony Battery Rd Lancaster, PA 17601 800-233-3827; 800-321-1934 FAX: 717-898-0949	**tires**

Mail order and open shop. Monday-Friday, 8-5. Established 1968. Knowledgeable sales staff. Tires for vintage and classic

automobiles. Also tubes with metal valve stems, authentic hardware and brass runningboard trim.

Wallace W Wade Specialty Tires PO Box 560906 530 Regal Row Dallas, TX 75356 800-666-TYRE, 214-688-0091 FAX: 214-634-8465	**tires**

Mail order and open shop. Monday-Friday 8:30 to 5:30; Saturday 9 to noon. Antique auto tires in many brands, plus obsolete Michelin tires, military ND tires. Tire chains, repair materials for tires, patches, boots. Antique truck tires, vintage tractor tires, tires for cannons, pedal car tires, turf and lawn tires. Checker flags and pennants, race track flags, car club pennants. Flags for all countries.

Willies Antique Tires 5257 W Diversey Ave Chicago, IL 60639 773-622-4037, 800-742-622 FAX: 773-622-0623	**tires** **wire wheels**

Open shop. Monday-Friday 8:30 to 5:30; Saturday 9 to 2. New tires for antique, classic and muscle cars. BF Goodrich, Firestone, US Royals, Cadillac and Thunderbird chrome wire wheels and more. Mounting and balancing available. Fast service.

tools

A & I Supply 401 Radio City Dr N Pekin, IL 61554 800-260-2647; FAX: 309-382-1420	**tools**

Mail order and open shop. Monday-Friday 8 to 5; Saturday 9 to 1. Stock your shop with 15,000 different tools and equipment. Name brand hand tools, body shop tools, air tools, power tools, air compressors, abrasives specialty tools, sheetmetal equipment and all type of shop equipment.

S R Aldrich Engine Re-Building 352 River Rd Willington, CT 06279 203-429-3111	**engine rebuilding**

See full listing in **Section Two** under **engine rebuilding**

American International Tool **Industries Inc** 1140 Reservoir Ave, Ste LO1 Cranston, RI 02920 401-942-7855, 800-932-5872 FAX: 401-942-6120	**tools**

Mail order only. Offering a socket called the Multi-Socket which can fit all metric and standard nuts/bolts, stripped nuts/bolts, square nuts, wing nuts, eye bolts and thumb screws.

Auto Lifters 3450 N Rock Rd, Bldg 500, Ste 507 Wichita, KS 67226 800-759-0703; FAX: 316-360-0015	**lifts**

Automotion 193 Commercial St Sunnyvale, CA 94068 800-777-8881; FAX: 408-736-9013 E-mail: automo@aol.com	**parts**

See full listing in **Section One** under **Porsche**

Backyard Buddy Corp
1818 N Main St, PO Box 5104
Niles, OH 44446
330-544-9372; FAX: 330-544-9311

automotive lift

See full listing in **Section Two** under **accessories**

California Car Cover Co
21125 Superior St
Chatsworth, CA 91311
800-423-5525; FAX: 818-998-2442

accessories
apparel
car covers
tools

See full listing in **Section Two** under **car covers**

Car Skates by P & J Products
988 Gordon Ct
Birmingham, MI 48009
PH/FAX: 810-647-1879

car skate

Mail order only. Car Skate, for moving cars and trailers in any direction.

Creative Metal Products Inc
121 R N Douglas St
Appleton, WI 54914
414-830-7975; FAX: 414-830-7976

storage system

Mail order only. Stack and tote tool, part and fastener storage system. All galvanized steel tray is ideal for restorations or general repair. Individual compartments provide organized storage. Trays stack to save space.

Custom Bandsaw Blades
103 N High St
Muncie, IN 47308-0543
800-378-0761; FAX: 317-289-2889

bandsaw blades

Mail order and open shop. Monday-Friday, 8 am-4 pm EST. Bandsaw blades made to custom lengths to fit any machine. Large selection of blade material in stock.

Daytona MIG
1821 Holsonback Dr
Daytona Beach, FL 32117
800-331-9353; FAX: 904-274-1237

plasma cutters
welders

Mail order and open shop. Monday-Friday 9 to 5, Saturday 9 to 12. Specializing in providing welding and plasma arc cutting equipment to the hobbyist and professionals. From portable machines to industrial heavy duty equipment and all consumables and accessories.

Deltran Corporation
801 US Hwy 92 E
Deland, FL 32724
904-736-7900; FAX: 904-736-9984

battery chargers

See full listing in **Section Two** under **batteries**

The Eastwood Company-Tools
580 Lancaster Ave
Box 3014
Malvern, PA 19355
800-345-1178, M-F 8 am to 12 midnight, Sat & Sun 9 am to 5 pm EST;
FAX: 610-644-0560

paints
plating & polishing
restoration aids
rustproofing
stripping tools
sandblasters
welders

See tools you never knew existed! In our full color catalog featuring welders, sandblast cabinets, buffing supplies, detail paints and plating kits, paint and pinstriping supplies, metal working tools, engine and electric tools, books, videos and more! Call or write to above address and phone. Catalog free!
Web site: http://www.eastwoodco.com

Enthusiast's Specialties
350 Old Connecticut Path
Framingham, MA 01701
508-620-1942; FAX: 508-872-4914

automobilia
tools

See full listing in **Section Two** under **automobilia**

Fast Lane Products
PO Box 7000-50
Palos Verdes Peninsula, CA 90274
800-327-8669

chamois
drain tubs
hand wringers

See full listing in **Section Two** under **car care products**

W L Fuller Inc
PO Box 8767, 7A Cypress St
Warwick, RI 02888-0767
401-467-2900; FAX: 401-467-2905

woodworking tools

Mail order and open shop. Monday-Friday 8 to 5. Countersinks, counterbores, and drills. "Immediate postpaid shipment on all stock sizes." Woodworking tools and sharpening service.

GearBox Grannie's
492 W Second St, Ste 204
Xenia, OH 45385
513-372-1541; FAX: 513-372-1171

collectibles
metal banks
tools

Mail order only. Offers a wide variety of rare, dealership type tools for the automobile enthusiast. Also available are many books on decoding and identifying VIN numbers, body codes and casting numbers, and more. Also carry gifts and collectibles such as the highly desirable die cast metal banks. Call or write today for a free catalog.

Griot's Garage
3500-A 20th St E
Tacoma, WA 98424
800-345-5789; FAX: 206-922-7500
E-mail: griots@aol.com

car care products
paint
tools

Direct mail catalog. Offers quality US and European tools, premium car care products, garage organizers, automotive paints, non-lifting concrete floor paint, the finest tool boxes, automotive accessories and collectibles, over 2,500 products for your garage. Call today for a free 64-page catalog.

Harbor Freight Tools
3491 Mission Oaks Blvd
Camarillo, CA 93011
800-423-2567

tools

Mail order only. Harbor Freight tools offers the finest professional quality tools and equipment at the lowest prices, guaranteed. Let our catalog be your source for thousands of brand name tools. Call to receive your free catalog.

HTP America Inc
261 Woodwork Ln
Palatine, IL 60067-4930
800-USA-WELD toll-free
FAX: 847-934-7389

welding tools

Mail order and open shop. Monday-Friday 9 to 5:30. Selling mig welders, plasma cutters, metalworking tools, welding supplies and related equipment to body shops, garages, home restorers, street rodders and hobbyists.

Hydraulic Jack Inc
PO Box 18
Accord, NY 12404
914-626-2510; FAX: 914-626-5258

parts
tools

Mail order and open shop. Monday-Friday 8:30-4. Parts and tools for repairing hydraulic jacks and cylinders. Catalog $3.

**Innovative Novelties/
McGee Enterprises**
PO Box 1375
Little Rock, AR 72203
501-835-8409; FAX: 501-835-7293
E-mail: kholland@cci.net

accessories

See full listing in **Section Two** under **novelties**

Kingsbury Dolly Co Inc
128 Kingsbury Rd
Walpole, NH 03608
800-413-6559
E-mail: kingdoly@sover.net

dollies

Manufacture and sales of Kingsbury Shop Auto Dollies™. Dollies move whole cars, parts of cars, motors, equipment and more. The dollies work with jack stands, under tires, or under chassis. Easy rolling 4" casters. Satisfaction guaranteed. Please call for fax number.

Malm Chem Corp
PO Box 300, Dept HVA
Pound Ridge, NY 10576
914-764-5775; FAX: 914-764-5785
E-mail: jkolin@cloud9.net

polish
wax

See full listing in **Section Two** under **car care products**

Mill Supply Inc
3241 Superior Ave
Cleveland, OH 44114
800-888-5072; FAX: 216-241-0425
E-mail: info@millsupply.com

clips
fasteners
panels

See full listing in **Section Two** under **sheetmetal**

Moroso Performance Products Inc
80 Carter Dr
Guilford, CT 06437
203-453-6571; FAX: 203-453-6906

accessories
parts

See full listing in **Section Two** under **racing**

Motor Bay Co
PO Box 460828
San Antonio, TX 78246
800-456-6642

tools

Mail order only. I manufacture oil filter discharge control tools, we offer our tool in two sizes. 80mm and 100mm (please see our ad in *Hemmings*). Our Filter Cup captures oil discharged when an oil filter, or when a fuel/water seperator, is released from a motor.

Motorguard Corporation
580 Carnegie St
Manteca, CA 95337
209-239-9191; FAX: 209-239-5114

accessories
tools

Deals in collision repair and refinishing tools and accessories. Studwelders for dent removal. Specialty sanding and cutting tools. Compressed air filters for spray painting. Products available through Parts Supply Jobbers (PBE).

Motorsport Tools
7561-A Orr Rd
Charlotte, NC 28213
704-596-0350; FAX: 704-596-0707

English wheels
metalworking tools

Mail order and open shop. Monday thru Friday 9 to 5 pm. English wheels and metalworking equipment. Largest selection of English wheels. Fully assembled floor model machines from $1,045. Also English wheel kits, parts, accessories and plans. Full line of metalworking tools and equipment including glass

bead cabinets, sandblasters, bead rollers, shrinker/stretchers, tubing notchers, tubing benders, sheetmetal breaks, sheers, videos, books and more. Catalog available.

Northern Auto Parts Warehouse Inc
PO Box 3147
Sioux City, IA 51102
800-831-0884; FAX: 712-258-0088

parts

See full listing in **Section Two** under **engine parts**

PE Tie Down Straps
803 Petersburg Rd
Carlisle, PA 17013
800-TIE-DOWN; FAX: 717-258-1348

locks
tie-down straps
winches

See full listing in **Section Two** under **trailers**

Production Tool Supply of Ohio
10801 Brookpark Rd
Cleveland, OH 44130
216-265-0000 local
FAX: 216-265-0094
800-362-0142, nationwide

compressors
cutting tools
hand tools
shop supplies

Mail order and open shop. Monday-Friday 8 to 5, Saturday 8 to 12 noon. Full stocking distributor of over 100,000 tools of all kinds, available at discounts of up to 70% off list prices. VISA, MasterCard and COD shipments daily. 800-plus page catalog available free. Deals in tools, abrasives, machine tools, compressors, cutting tools, woodworking tools, hand tools, shop supplies.

Quality Mfg & Dist
PO Box 20870
El Cajon, CA 92021
619-442-8686; FAX: 619-590-0123

tools

Mail order only. Dealing in tools, ("Trick Fill" fueling clips).

Re-Flex Border Marker	border markers
138 Grant St	posts
Lexington, MA 02173	
617-862-1343	

See full listing in **Section Two** under **hardware**

Sunchaser Tools	metal-finishing kit
3202 E Foothill Blvd	video
Pasadena, CA 91107	
818-795-1588; FAX: 818-795-6494	

See full listing in **Section Two** under **restoration aids**

Tavia Performance Products Inc	accessories
12851 Western Ave, Unit D	tools
Garden Grove, CA 92841	
714-892-4057; FAX: 714-892-5627	

Manufactures engine building tools, testing equipment, fasteners, tire gauges and accessories.

TiP Tools & Equipment	abrasive blasters
7075 Route 446, PO Box 649	air compressors
Canfield, OH 44406	tools
330-533-3384 local	
800-321-9260 US/Canada	
FAX: 330-533-2876	

Mail order and open shop. Mon-Fri 9 to 6, Sat 9 to 1. Manufacturer/supplier of abrasive blasters, glassbead cabinets, parts and supplies. Plus air compressors, HVLP paint systems, buffing, welding and other related restoration equipment. Free 72-page catalog. Over 26 years' experience.

See our ad on page 417

USATCO/US AirTool Int'l	bench/floor models
60 Fleetwood Ct	shrinkers/stretchers
Ronkonkoma, NY 11779-6951	tools
516-471-3300; FAX: 516-471-3308	wheel machines

Mail order and open shop. Riveting and sheetmetal tools, impact wrenches, temporary fasteners, air sanders, air drills, air grinders and accessories. Offices in Gardena, CA, Miami, FL.

Valco Cincinnati Consumer Products Inc	adhesives
411 Circle Freeway Drive	detailing products
Cincinnati, OH 45246	sealants
513-874-6550; FAX: 513-874-3612	tools

Valco Cincinnati is the sole manufacturer of the Tube-Grip™, a patented 14-gauge steel tool which applies 10 times more pressure to a flexible tube than squeezing by hand. It allows you to squeeze 96% of the material out of the tube. In addition, Valco offers a complete line of high quality sealants, adhesives, detailers, lubricants and thread lockers for automotive applications.

Weld USA	metal working tools
862 Farmington Ave	welders
Bristol, CT 06010	
860-826-6662	
800-WELD-USA, orders	
800-MIG-WELD, customer service	
FAX: 860-826-5500	

Mail order only. 24-hour ordering. Customer service Monday to Friday 8 am to 4:30 pm. The fabricator's source for affordable welders, plasma arc cutting systems, torch outfits, welding accessories, consumables, metal working tools. Free catalog.

Williams Lowbuck Tools Inc	tools
4175 California Ave	
Norco, CA 91760	
909-735-7848; FAX: 909-735-1210	
E-mail: wlowbuck@aol.com	

Mail order and open shop. Shop open Monday-Friday 9 am to 4 pm. Deals in metal fabricating tools for tubing and sheetmetal.

tops

AAA Thunderbird Sales	parts
35 Balsam Dr	
Dix Hills, NY 11746	
516-421-4473	

See full listing in **Section One** under **Thunderbird**

Accurate Auto Tops & Upholstery Inc	tops
Miller Rd & W Chester Pike	upholstery
Edgemont, PA 19028	
610-356-1515; FAX: 610-353-8230	

See full listing in **Section Two** under **upholstery**

British Parts NW	parts
4105 SE Lafayette Hwy	
Dayton, OR 97114	
503-864-2001; FAX: 503-864-2081	

See full listing in **Section One** under **Triumph**

Brothers Automotive Products	parts
19715 County Rd 355	restoration
St Joseph, MO 64505	
816-662-2060; FAX: 816-662-2084	

See full listing in **Section One** under **Oldsmobile**

California Convertible Co	top parts
1950 Lindsley Park Dr	
San Marcos, CA 92069-3337	
619-746-8211	

Mail order and open shop. Monday-Friday 8 to 5:30. For American convertibles only. Top parts.

Caribou Canvas	convertible tops
23151-A3 Alcalde Dr	
Laguna Hills, CA 92653	
714-770-3136; FAX: 714-770-0815	
E-mail: cariboulh@aol.com	

Mail order and open shop. Shop open Monday-Friday 9:30 am to 5 pm PST. Manufactures canvas convertible tops for all sport, import and domestic automobiles. We are specialists in Italian, British and German vehicle applications. Our products are available for worldwide shipping.

Classic Trim Inc	collectibles
Mick Stamm	trim
3401 S 1st St	upholstery
Abilene, TX 79605-1708	
915-676-8788	

See full listing in **Section Two** under **motorcycles**

Classtique Auto Products	carpet sets
PO Box 278-HMN	headliners
Isanti, MN 55040	
612-444-4025; FAX: 612-444-9980	

See full listing in **Section Two** under **interiors & interior parts**

Classtique Upholstery & Top Co
PO Box 278 HK
Isanti, MN 55040
612-444-4025; FAX: 612-444-9980

top kits
upholstery kits

See full listing in **Section One** under **Ford '03-'31**

Convertible Service
5126-HA Walnut Grove Ave
San Gabriel, CA 91776
800-333-1140, 818-285-2255
FAX: 818-285-9004

convertible parts
top mechanism
service

For domestic cars from 1946 to present. Manufactures and sells convertible top mechanism replacement parts. 6- and 12-volt electric and hydraulic top motors, hydraulic top lift cylinders and window lift cylinders, hose assemblies, top latches, relays, top switches, folding top frames. Distributor for Metro Molded Parts. Convertible top weatherstripping sets and weatherstripping and rubber parts in general. Most parts shipped same day. Overnight delivery available. Send $1 (to cover postage) and we'll send you our catalog of convertible parts.

Dom Corey Upholstery &
Antique Auto
1 Arsene Way
Fairhaven Business Park
Fairhaven, MA 02719
508-997-6555

carpets/conv tops
dash covers
door panels
headliners
seats
upholstery

See full listing in **Section Two** under **interiors & interior parts**

Goldfield Trim & Upholstery
1267 160th St
Goldfield, IA 50542
515-254-3322

top installation
upholstery

See full listing in **Section Two** under **interiors & interior parts**

Hydro-E-Lectric
48 Appleton Rd
Auburn, MA 01501
508-832-3081; FAX: 508-832-7929

convertible top
parts
power window parts

Convertible top and power window parts and repair. All parts are new. 1939-97 available. Phone for information today.

Al Knoch Interiors
130 Montoya Rd
El Paso, TX 79932
800-880-8080; FAX: 915-581-1545

carpets
interiors
tooling services
tops

See full listing in **Section One** under **Chevrolet**

Loga Enterprises
5399 Old Town Hall Rd
Eau Claire, WI 54701
715-832-7302

convertible tops
interior parts

See full listing in **Section One** under **Studebaker**

Norm's Custom Shop
6897 E William St Ext
Bath, NY 14810
607-776-2357; FAX: 607-776-4541

interiors
tops

See full listing in **Section One** under **Cord**

NOS Locators
587 Pawtucket Ave
Pawtucket, RI 02860
401-725-5000

parts

See full listing in **Section One** under **MG**

Ray's Upholstering
600 N St Frances Cabrini Ave
Scranton, PA 18504
800-296-RAYS; FAX: 717-963-0415

partial/total
restoration

See full listing in **Section Two** under **restoration shops**

Rhino Industries
14512 N Nebraska Ave
Tampa, FL 33613
813-977-7776; FAX: 813-977-5419

cleaner

See full listing in **Section Two** under **car care products**

Ridgefield Auto Upholstery
34 Bailey Ave
Ridgefield, CT 06877
203-438-7583

interiors
tops

See full listing in **Section Two** under **interiors & interior parts**

Ron's Restorations Inc
2968-B Ask Kay Dr
Smyrna, GA 30082
770-438-6102; FAX: 770-438-0037

interior trim
restoration

See full listing in **Section One** under **Mercedes-Benz**

The Bill Stevenson Company
PO Box 5037
Kent, WA 98064-5368
206-852-0584; FAX: 206-854-7520

hood insulation

Mail order and open shop. 1941-86 hood insulation.

TMI Products Inc
191 Granite St
Corona, CA 91719
909-272-1996; 800-624-7960
FAX: 909-272-1584
E-mail: tmiprods@aol.com

classic car
interiors

See full listing in **Section One** under **Volkswagen**

Town Auto Top and Restoration Co
78 Bloomfield Ave
PO Box 167
Pine Brook, NJ 07058
201-575-9333; FAX: 201-808-8366

convertible repairs
interiors

Shop open Monday-Friday 8:30 to 5:30. All types of hands-on custom work. Interior restorations of all types, especially leather restoring. Some scissor frame convertible parts. Also 1971-76 GM available. Interior parts and engines for these cars also available. Convertibles our specialties. Complete restoration of classic autos, quality oriented support network of shops and mechanics, upholstery, engine, chrome and body. You always get what you pay for, plus special attention to the details for over 30 years.

Ultimate Appearance Ltd
113 Arabian Trail
Smithfield, VA 23430
PH/FAX: 757-255-2620

cleaners
detailing products
detailing services
polish/wax

See full listing in **Section Two** under **car care products**

Ultimate Upholstery
13384 Fallen Leaf Rd
Poway, CA 92064
619-451-3340

interiors
top restoration
upholstery

See full listing in **Section Two** under **restoration shops**

Victoria British Ltd Box 14991 Lenexa, KS 66285-4991 800-255-0088; 913-599-3299	**accessories** **parts**

See full listing in **Section One** under **MG**

Willow Grove Auto Top 43 N York Rd Willow Grove, PA 19090 215-659-3276	**interiors** **tops** **upholstery**

See full listing in **Section Two** under **interiors & interior parts**

World Upholstery & Trim PO Box 4857 Thousand Oaks, CA 91359 800-222-9577; FAX: 818-707-2664 E-mail: worlduph@mail.vcnet.com	**carpet kits** **tops** **upholstery kits**

See full listing in **Section Two** under **interiors & interior parts**

trailers

Beam Distributors PO Box 524, 231 South St Davidson, NC 28036 704-892-9853	**trailers**

Dealer United Express Line enclosed trailers. Large stock of enclosed trailers for all your automotive needs. Serving the old car hobby since 1968.

C & C Manufacturing Co 300 S Church St Hazleton, PA 18201 717-454-0819; FAX: 717-454-5131	**trailers**

Mail order and open shop. Specializing in the manufacturing of custom car carriers to transport antique automobiles for the past 30 years.

Captain Trailer Sales 1931 N Appleton St Appleton, WI 54911 414-735-0273	**d-rings/hitches** **new tires** **wheels** **winches**

Open Monday-Friday 8 am to 6 pm, weekends by appointment. Authorized dealer for Haulmark & United Expressline enclosed trailers. Specialize in race and collector car haulers, custom orders always welcome. All sizes available, tag, fifth wheel or gooseneck. We also carry a full line of open car carriers, utility, tilt, skidsteer haulers, etc. For all your trailer needs, call David for more information and a price quote. Nationwide delivery always available. Lot location: Hwy 41, Kaukauna, WI.

Chernock Motorcars PO Box 134, Airport Rd Hazleton, PA 18201 717-455-1752; FAX: 717-455-7585	**trailers**

Enclosed & open car trailers, cargo and concession trailers custom built. International orders welcome.

Classic Motors Inc Rich Adams 103 200th Ave Union Grove, WI 53182 414-878-2525; FAX: 414-878-0400	**car sales** **trailer sales**

See full listing in **Section Two** under **car dealers**

Classic Trailers 21900 US 12 Sturgis, MI 49091 616-651-9319; 800-826-1960	**trailers/** **open & enclosed**

Monday-Friday 8 to 5. Manufacturer of open and enclosed auto trailers to meet the needs of your classic car. Call for dealer nearest you. Web site: http://classicmfg.com

D & D Trailers Inc 100 Lexington Ave Trenton, NJ 08618 609-771-0001; 800-533-0442 FAX: 609-771-4479	**trailers** **accessories**

Mail order and open shop. Monday-Saturday 8 to 4:30; other times by appointment. Custom built car carriers and utility trailers. Distributor of Wells Cargo enclosed trailers. Also carries tie downs, winches and trailer parts.

Eliminator Trailers 1427 Valley Dr Syracuse, NY 13207 800-469-5885; FAX: 315-469-1377	**trailers**

Shop open Monday-Friday 8 to 4. Manufactures trailers.

Galaxie Ltd Box 655 Butler, WI 53007 414-790-0390; FAX: 414-783-7710	**kits** **model trailers**

See full listing in **Section Two** under **models & toys**

Tommy Gale Trailer Sales **& Service** Glassport-Elizabeth Rd Elizabeth, PA 15037 412-464-0119; FAX: 412-384-8532	**trailers**

Open shop only. Monday-Friday 8:30-5 pm, Saturday 8:30-2 pm. I specialize in enclosed race, classic car, gooseneck and custom trailers.

Golden West Trailer Sales 1686 W Sierra Hwy Acton, CA 93510 805-269-5012; FAX: 805-269-0763	**trailers**

Open 7 days a week. Monday-Saturday 9-6; Sunday 10-6. Deals in Featherlite, Topline and Texas Bragg trailers. Open and enclosed trailers in steel or aluminum. Has in stock standard models as well as custom design trailers.

Haulmark Industries Inc PO Box 281, 14054 CR #4 Bristol, IN 46507 219-825-5867; FAX: 219-825-9816	**trailers**

Manufacturer of enclosed trailers for vintage automobiles.

Hodges Custom Haulers 9076 Scale Rd Benton, KY 42025 PH/FAX: 502-898-2356	**truck beds**

Mail order and open shop. Monday-Friday 8 am to 5 pm. Specializing in truck beds for hauling antique cars.

Mobile Structures Inc/MSI Trailers 2405 Cassopolis St Elkhart, IN 46514 800-348-8541; FAX: 219-264-4399	**trailers**

Specializing in car and cargo trailers.

Nyles Haulmark Trailer Sales 352 Macedon Center Rd Fairport, NY 14450 716-223-6433	car carriers

Open shop. Monday-Friday 9-5, Saturday 9-12. Enclosed and open car carriers for vintage autos, race cars, snowmobiles. Three major lines: Haulmark, Interstate I, Car Mate.

Orlandi Trailer 3120 Moorpark Ave San Jose, CA 95117 408-296-5748; FAX: 408-247-1219	trailers

Dealers in trailers, open and enclosed, 10' to 48', new and used. Full stock of parts and accessories, service and repair. Trailer hitches and wiring. We deliver nationwide. Custom interiors, double or triple car haulers, living quarters. 17 years of service. Distributor for Pace American and Rally.

PE Tie Down Straps 803 Petersburg Rd Carlisle, PA 17013 800-TIE-DOWN; FAX: 717-258-1348	locks tie-down straps winches

Mail order only. Tie-down straps, D-rings, wheel clocks, trailer and receiver locks, electric winches. We specialize in antique and classic car tie-downs. Over 12 years serving the hobby. Call us for fast, friendly service.

R-D-T Plans and Parts PO Box 2272 Merced, CA 95344 209-383-4441	car parts trailer plans

Mail order and open shop. Monday-Friday 8 to 5. Trailer plans designed and sold. Also miscellaneous car parts for Packards, Cadillacs, Fords, Chevrolet and American underslung cars, along with Ferrari.

Timber Wolf Trailers Inc 57974 CR 3 S Elkhart, IN 46517 219-522-3777; FAX: 219-522-7141	trailers

Custom and stock enclosed car trailers. All sizes and gvw ratings, all types of options.

Trailer World Inc 800 Three Springs Rd Bowling Green, KY 42104 502-843-4587, 800-872-2833 FAX: 502-781-8221	trailers

Mail order and open shop. Monday-Friday 7:30 to 5:30, Saturday 8-12. Open and enclosed, United Expressline, Storm, Classic and US Cargo enclosed trailers. Various type steel, all aluminum, fifth wheel and tag models.

Trailers Ltd 308 W Washington Morton, TX 79346 806-266-5646; FAX: 806-266-5846	trailers

Mail order and open shop. Monday-Saturday 9-7 pm. Builds custom-built enclosed trailers for transporting race cars, antique cars, show cars, etc.

Trailers of New England Inc Boston Rd, Rt 20 Palmer, MA 01069 413-289-1211; FAX: 413-289-1292	trailers

Mail order and open shop. Mon-Fri 8:30-5, Sat 8:30 to noon. Specializing in Wells Cargo enclosed trailers, open trailers, trailer design and customizing, trailer parts, hitches and tie-down products.

Trailersource 117 Barber Rd SE Marietta, GA 30060 800-241-4275; FAX: 404-426-8850	trailers

Open Monday-Friday 8:30 to 5:30, Saturday 10 to 2. Sells car haulers, cargo, concession, living quarters and horse trailers. Pace American, Avenger and others in steel and aluminum. Full service shop. In business since 1974. Delivery nationwide. Cars hauled, rental trailers. Custom designs a specialty.

Trailex Inc 60 Industrial Park Dr, PO Box 553 Canfield, OH 44406 330-533-6814; 800-282-5042 toll-free FAX: 330-533-9118	aluminum trailers tow dollys

Shop open Monday-Friday 8 to 5; Saturday 8 to 12 noon. "Trailers made from heat treated aluminum extrusions, anodized for lasting beauty." Also aluminum auto tow dollys.

Transport Designs Inc 240 Streibeigh Ln Montoursville, PA 17754 717-368-1403; FAX: 717-368-2398	trailers

Mail order and open shop. Open Monday-Friday 8 to 5, weekends by appointment. Specializing in the manufacturing of enclosed car trailers for any year, any style car. Custom work is our specialty.

Wells Cargo Inc PO Box 728-134 Elkhart, IN 46515 800-348-7553, Tues-Fri FAX: 219-264-5938	trailers

Wells Cargo manufactures a full line of enclosed, steel-structured trailers for hauling all types of collector automobiles. 24 models from which to choose. Ball hitch trailers: 18 to 32 feet. 5th wheel, inverted 5th wheel and A-frame 5th wheel trailers: 24 to 48 feet. Payloads, 4,200 to 11,880 lbs. GVWR: 7,700 to 16,000 lbs. Choose from an impressive list of customizing options. Free "no obligation" quotes available. 3-year warranty program. Nationwide dealer network.

transmissions

356 Enterprises Vic & Barbara Skirmants 27244 Ryan Rd Warren, MI 48092 810-575-9544; FAX: 810-558-3616	parts

See full listing in **Section One** under **Porsche**

4-Speeds by Darrell PO Box 110, #3 Water St Vermilion, IL 61955 217-275-3743; FAX: 217-275-3515	transmissions

Mail order and open shop. Monday-Friday 8-5; Saturday 8-12 CST. Rebuilt transmissions. Show quality Borg-Warner T-10, M-21 and M-22, including all related parts. Specializes in build date transmissions for Corvette, Chevy 1958-up, Chevelle, Camaro, Buick, Pontiac and Oldsmobile.

Alan's Axles 2300 Congress Ave Clearwater, FL 34623 800-741-0452; 813-784-0452	axles

See full listing in **Section Two** under **chassis parts**

American Muscle | **parts**
PO Box 270543
West Hartford, CT 06127
860-953-2575

See full listing in **Section One** under **GMC**

American Restorations | **restoration parts**
Unlimited, TA
14 Meakin Ave, PO Box 34
Rochelle Park, NJ 07662
201-843-3567; FAX: 201-843-3238
E-mail: amerrest@aol.com

See full listing in **Section Two** under **glass**

Be Happy Automatic | **trans rebuild kits**
Transmission Parts
414 Stivers Rd
Hillsboro, OH 45133
800-416-2862; FAX: 513-442-6133

Mail order only. Owner operated by David and Mona Crone.
Dealing in automatic transmission rebuild kits, external dry-up
kits and hard parts, 1940-65. NOS, NORS, good used, Dynaflow,
Dual path, Flightpitch, Hydramatic, Jetaway, Slim Jim, Roto 5,
Powerglide, Turboglide, Powerflite, Torqueflite, 3-band,
Ultramatic, etc. Technical assistance, exploded views, trou-
bleshooting and repair literature. Orders for individual gaskets,
seals, etc welcome. Free wholesale price list. We're open late for
our West Coast customers. MC/VISA/Discover, CODs accepted.

Bicknell Engine Company | **repair**
7055 Dayton Rd | **restoration**
Enon, OH 45323
513-864-5224

See full listing in **Section One** under **Buick/McLaughlin**

British Parts NW | **parts**
4105 SE Lafayette Hwy
Dayton, OR 97114
503-864-2001; FAX: 503-864-2081

See full listing in **Section One** under **Triumph**

California Pony Cars | **parts**
1906 Quaker Ridge Pl
Ontario, CA 91761
909-923-2804; FAX: 909-947-8593
E-mail: 105232.3362@compuserv.com

See full listing in **Section One** under **Mustang**

Carl's Ford Parts | **muscle parts**
23219 South ST
Homeworth, OH 44634
PH/FAX: 330-525-7291

See full listing in **Section One** under **Mustang**

Classic Tube | **brake lines**
(Division of Classic & Performance | **choke tubes**
Spec Inc) | **fuel lines**
80 Rotech Dr | **transmission lines**
Lancaster, NY 14086 | **vacuum lines**
800-882-3711, 716-759-1800
FAX: 716-759-1014

See full listing in **Section Two** under **brakes**

Coffey's Classic Transmissions | **transmissions**
2817 Hollis
Ft Worth, TX 76111
817-834-8740; 817-439-1611

Mail order and open shop. Monday-Friday 8 am-5:30 pm

Central. Specializing in transmission parts and service for early
model classic standard and automatic transmissions. Classic,
vintage and racing transmissions, parts and service.

David Edwards-Transmission Parts | **automatic**
56 Dale St, PO Box 245 | **transmission**
Needham Heights, MA 02194-0245 | **kits/parts**
PH/FAX: 617-449-2065

Mail order only. SASE not required. Phone hours: Monday-
Friday 6 pm to 11:30 pm; Saturday and Sunday by chance. For
all automatic transmissions from 1946 to the present except
Flightpitch and Ultramatics. Kits, bands, pumps, bushings,
washers, drums and other miscellaneous parts in stock. Daily
UPS shipments.

FATSCO Transmission Parts | **parts**
112 Lehigh Dr | **transmissions**
Fairfield, NJ 07004
800-524-0485; FAX: 201-227-5414

Mail order and open shop. Monday-Friday 8 to 5. Transmission
parts. US automatic and manual transmission parts from 1946
to present. Some parts for older manual transmissions.

HochKraeusen Racing | **machine shop**
PO Box 716, 18233 Madison Rd
Parkman, OH 44080-0716
216-548-2147

See full listing in **Section Two** under **machine work**

Inline Tube | **brake lines**
17540 14 Mile Rd | **choke tubes**
Fraser, MI 48026 | **fuel lines**
810-294-4093; FAX: 810-294-7349 | **transmission lines**
E-mail: inline@apk.net | **vacuum lines**

See full listing in **Section Two** under **brakes**

IPTC Automotive | **cars**
300 SW 12th Ave | **parts**
Pompano Beach, FL 33069
800-277-3806

See full listing in **Section One** under **BMW**

Last Chance Repair & Restoration | **repairs**
PO Box 362A, Myers Rd | **restoration**
Shaftsbury, VT 05262

See full listing in **Section Two** under **restoration shops**

Lister North America Ltd | **performance parts**
6565 E 40
Tulsa, OK 74145
918-665-0021; FAX: 918-664-0804

See full listing in **Section One** under **Jaguar**

Lokar Inc | **performance parts**
10924 Murdock Dr
Knoxville, TN 37922
423-966-2269; FAX: 423-671-1999

See full listing in **Section Two** under **street rods**

MFR Enterprises | **differentials**
PO Box 216 | **transmissions**
118 E Main
Wales, WI 53183
414-968-4222; FAX: 414-968-9616

Mail order and open shop. Shop open Monday-Saturday 8 am to
4:30 pm. Manual transmissions and differentials for GM, Ford

Generalists

and Chrysler cars. We have many old parts and can adapt new parts in old cases.

Michael's Auto Parts	**salvage yard**
5875 NW Kaiser Rd	
Portland, OR 97229	
503-690-7750; FAX: 503-690-7735	

See full listing in **Section Five** under **Oregon**

Mid Valley Engineering	**machine work**
16637 N 21st St	**parts**
Phoenix, AZ 85022	**restoration**
602-482-1251; FAX: 602-788-0812	

Mail order and open shop. Monday thru Friday 8-5:30, Saturday by appointment. Large inventory of antique Hewland parts. Complete fabrication and machine shop facilities for race car restoration. MVE Shur shifter side door pat pen for T-10 transmissions.

Midwestern Motors & Dismantlers	**salvage yard**
19785 W 12 Mi, Bldg 404	
Southfield, MI 48076	
810-559-8848	

See full listing in **Section One** under **Mercedes-Benz**

Mitchell Manufacturing	**overdrives**
6 Acorn Ct	
Novato, CA 94949-6603	
800-238-5093	

See full listing in **Section One** under **Ford '03-'31**

National Drivetrain Inc	**differential parts**
3125 S Ashland Ave #201	**transmission parts**
Chicago, IL 60608	
800-507-4327; FAX: 312-376-9135	

Specializes in transmission, transfer case and differential parts for all models, foreign and domestic. All gearing and assemblies related to manual transmission transfer case and differential.

Northwest Transmission Parts	**transmission parts**
13500 US 62	
Winchester, OH 45697	
800-327-1955 order line	
513-442-2811 info	
FAX: 513-442-6555	

Automatic and standard shift parts back to 1933. Gears, shafts, bearings, kits for automatics, bands, pumps, drums, bushings, etc. Also parts for Mercedes, Rolls-Royce and Jaguar automatics in stock. Automatic transmission flywheels. Motor and transmission mounts back to 1933.

Obsolete Chevrolet Parts Co	**engine parts**
524 Hazel Ave	**radiators**
PO Box 68	**rubber parts**
Nashville, GA 31639	**transmissions**
912-686-5812	

See full listing in **Section One** under **Chevrolet**

Orion Motors European Parts Inc	**parts**
10722 Jones Rd	
Houston, TX 77065	
800-736-6410; 713-894-1982	
FAX: 713-849-1997	

See full listing in **Section One** under **Alfa Romeo**

Performance Transmissions 46 Walnut St Shrewsbury, MA 01545 508-842-0672	**restoration** **trans parts/sales/** **service** **trans rebuilding**

Mail order and open shop. Monday-Saturday 9 to 6 pm.
Standard transmission rebuilding only since 1968. Rebuilt
3/4/5-speeds in stock. Muncie, Borg-Warner, Ford Toploader,
GM Saginaw specialists. Complete units in stock. Worldwide
sales, service. Customer cores accepted. RPS daily. AMC to Z-28.

Street-Wise Performance Richie Mulligan 105 Creek Rd Tranquility, NJ 07879 201-786-6668 days, 201-786-7133 evenings; FAX: 201-786-7899	**differentials** **parts** **rebuild kits** **transmissions**

Mail order and open shop. Monday-Saturday 9 am-6 pm. Used
or rebuilt GM standard and performance 3, 4 & 5-speed gear
boxes. Guaranteed, special dated units and parts. New/used
gears, rebuilder's kits & directions. Factory/Hurst shifters, related parts. Rebuilt 1955-1980s GM 10/12-bolt positrac rear ends,
r & p sets, carriers, axles. Over 25 years' individual experience.
20 years family operated. Huge inventory, same day shipping on
most orders. Free consulting advice & referrals. Spring/Fall
Englishtown swap meet spaces RK 58-60. Dealer/restorer
inquiries welcomed.

Teddy's Garage 8530 Louise Ave Northridge, CA 91325 818-341-0505	**parts** **restoration** **service**

See full listing in **Section One** under **Rolls-Royce/Bentley**

John Ulrich 450 Silver Ave San Francisco, CA 94112 510-223-9587 days	**parts**

See full listing in **Section One** under **Packard**

Universal Transmission Co 23361 Dequindre Rd Hazel Park, MI 48030 800-882-4327; FAX: 810-398-2581	**transmission parts**

Dealing in standard transmission parts for American cars from
Model A till tomorrow. A family owned business since 1948.
Wholesale/retail.

See our ad on page 423

Vicarage Jaguars 3952 Douglas Rd Miami, FL 33133 305-444-8759; FAX: 305-443-6443	**parts** **restoration**

See full listing in **Section One** under **Jaguar**

Dale Wilch Sales/RPM Catalog PO Box 12031 Kansas City, KS 66112 913-788-3219; FAX: 913-788-9682 E-mail: rpmcat@sound.net	**speed equipment**

See full listing in **Section Two** under **racing**

Dan Williams Toploader **Transmissions** 206 E Dogwood Dr Franklin, NC 28734 704-524-9085 noon-midnight FAX: 704-524-4848	**transmissions**

See full listing in **Section One** under **Ford '54-up**

Dave Wilton 1344 Manhattan Dr Paradise, CA 95969 916-872-0122	**engine parts**

See full listing in **Section One** under **Ford '03-'31**

Zim's Autotechnik 1804 Reliance Pkwy Bedford, TX 76021 800-356-2964; FAX: 817-545-2002	**parts** **service**

See full listing in **Section One** under **Porsche**

A AAuto Brokers Inc 13659 Victory Blvd, Suite #346 Van Nuys, CA 91401 800-770-7784; FAX: 818-904-0023	**brokers** **transport**

Mail order and open shop. Monday-Saturday 7 am to 6 pm PST.

Auto Transport Services 5367 Fargo Rd Avoca, MI 48006 810-324-2598	**transport**

Transporting automobiles.

Cedar Creek Coachworks Ltd 151 Conestoga Ln Stephens City, VA 22655 540-869-0244; FAX: 540-869-9577	**restoration** **service**

See full listing in **Section Two** under **restoration shops**

Classic Express 221 E Washington Houston, MS 38851 800-722-7377; FAX: 601-456-3730	**transport**

Classic Express specializes in the transportation of antique,
classic and exotic automobiles throughout the 48 United States.
In specially enclosed transporters, door to door and fully
insured.

Collector's Carousel 84 Warren Ave Westbrook, ME 04092 207-854-0343; FAX: 207-856-6913	**appraisals** **sales** **service**

See full listing in **Section Two** under **car dealers**

Eastern Specialty Automotive **Sales & Service Ltd** 38 Yankeetown Rd Hammonds Plains, NS Canada B3Z 1K7 902-835-5912; FAX: 902-835-0310	**parts** **service** **transport**

See full listing in **Section Two** under **car & parts locators**

Exotic Car Transport Inc PO Box 91 Ocoee, FL 34761 407-293-9524; FAX: 407-293-4783	**transport**

Nationwide transportation of exotic, vintage and luxury automobiles on open carrier and enclosed vans.

See our ad on page 425

Peter Ferraro Auto Transporters 186 S Prospect Ave Bergenfield, NJ 07621 800-624-6683; FAX: 201-387-7880	transport

Tommy Gale Trailer Sales & **Service** Glassport-Elizabeth Rd Elizabeth, PA 15037 412-464-0119; FAX: 412-384-8532	trailers

See full listing in **Section Two** under **trailers**

Hodges Custom Haulers 9076 Scale Rd Benton, KY 42025 PH/FAX: 502-898-2356	truck beds

See full listing in **Section Two** under **trailers**

Intercity Lines Inc River Rd, Box 1299 Warren, MA 01083 800-221-3936; FAX: 413-436-9422	transport

Open Monday-Friday 9 to 6 and Saturday, 9 to 12 noon. Specializing in enclosed transportation of collector cars throughout all 48 states and Canada.

Interconti Forwarding Ltd PO Box 1, Landmark, MainRoad Salcombe Devon, TQ8 8LB England 0154884 3191; FAX: 0154884 3414	car locator transport

Shop open Monday-Friday 9 to 12 and 2 to 5. International vehicle forwarding and shipping specialists. Free vintage, classic car location service for England.

Interesting Parts Inc Paul TerHorst 27526 N Owens Rd Mundelein, IL 60060 PH/FAX: 847-949-1030	appraisals gaskets parts storage transport

See full listing in **Section Two** under **comprehensive parts**

K & J Carriers Inc 4403 Westgrove Dr Dallas, TX 75248 800-280-4285; 214-735-0900 FAX: 214-735-0434	transportation

Open shop. Monday-Saturday 9-6. Enclosed transportation of antique, classic and exotic automobiles.

Libbey's Classic Car **Restoration Center** 137 N Quinsigamond Ave Shrewsbury, MA 01545 PH/FAX: 508-792-1560	bodywork restoration service

See full listing in **Section Two** under **restoration shops**

Passport Transport Ltd 37 Progess Pkwy St Louis, MO 63043 800-325-4267; FAX: 314-878-7295	transport

Enclosed transportation of antique, classic and special interest cars. Over 100,000 vehicles transported nationwide since we "invented" this business in 1970. To provide the best service possible, we custom design and build our air-ride trailers

specifically to handle the unique requirements of these vehicles. Passport Transport, the first and still the finest in enclosed auto transportation.

Reliable Carriers Inc 3324 E Atlanta Ave Phoenix, AZ 85040 800-528-5030; FAX: 602-243-3620	automotive transportation

Specializing in automotive transportation of prototypes and collectibles. Several added features on trucks prevent damage. Insured for full value of vehicles, up to $1,000,000 per load. Not the cheapest, but the best.

See our ad on page 426

Reward Service Inc 172 Overhill Rd Stormville, NY 12582 914-227-7647; FAX: 914-221-0293	appraisals restoration transportation

See full listing in **Section One** under **Jaguar**

Southern US Car Export Inc 135 Eulon Loop Raeford, NC 28376 910-875-7534; FAX: 910-875-7731	repair restoration sales transport

See full listing in **Section One** under **Cadillac/LaSalle**

Special Projects 27520 117th Ave SE Kent, WA 98031 800-CAR-HAUL (227-4285) FAX: 206-630-2506	transport

10 years experience moving vintage, classic and special interest autos and trucks. Uses small trucks and trailers, moving 2 vehi-

cles per truck. Your vehicle is moved direct, no reloading. Specializes in pre-1930 vehicles, racing cars, large cars (Packard, Cadillac, Pierce, etc), round-trip racing meets and car shows, basket cases with spare parts. Insured, honest and reliable.

Trailers Ltd	**trailers**
308 W Washington	
Morton, TX 79346	
806-266-5646	
FAX: 806-266-5846	

See full listing in **Section Two** under **trailers**

Trailersource	**trailers**
117 Barber Rd SE	
Marietta, GA 30060	
800-241-4275	
FAX: 404-426-8850	

See full listing in **Section Two** under **trailers**

Treasure Coast Auto Transport	**transport**
5883 Glen Eagle Way	
Stuart, FL 34997	
800-862-5468	

Enclosed and open auto transportation on East Coast.

Yesteryear Restorations	**repair**
387 Nutting Rd	**restoration**
Jaffrey, NH 03452	**sales**
603-532-7469	**transportation**

See full listing in **Section One** under **Ford '32-'53**

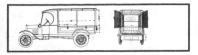

trucks & tractors

Auto Transport Services	**transport**
5367 Fargo Rd	
Avoca, MI 48006	
810-324-2598	

See full listing in **Section Two** under **transport**

B & T Truck Parts	**pickup parts**
906 E Main St	
PO Box 799	
Siloam Springs, AR 72761	
501-524-5959: FAX: 501-524-5559	

Specializing in 1960 to 1966 Chevrolet and GMC pickup truck parts for body restoration.

Phillip S Baumgarten	**emblems**
277 SW 33rd Ct	**ID plates**
Fort Lauderdale, FL 33315-3305	
954-764-1306; FAX: 954-764-1701	

Mail order only. Vehicle identification plates, instruction plates, make and model plates and emblem repros for Mack trucks and Mack fire trucks for 1920 through 1966. Cummins diesel emblems. New item: Hall-Scott hood side emblem.

Bob's F-100 Parts Co	**parts**
9372 Mission Blvd	
Riverside, CA 92509	
909-681-1956; FAX: 909-681-1960	

See full listing in **Section One** under **Ford '54-up**

Brothers Truck Parts
5670 Schaefer Ave, Unit G
Chino, CA 91710
800-977-2767, FAX: 909-517-3142
E-mail: brothers96@aol.com

accessories
parts

Mail order and open shop. Monday -Friday 8 to 5 pm PST.
Specializing in 1947-1972 Chevy and GMC trucks restoration
parts and custom accessories.

See our ad on this page

Carburetor Engineering
3324 E Colorado
Pasadena, CA 91107
818-795-3221

carburetor rebuilding
distributor rebuilding
fuel pump rebuilding

See full listing in **Section Two** under **carburetors**

Jim Carter's Antique Truck Parts
1500 E Alton
Independence, MO 64055
816-833-1913; FAX: 816-252-3749

truck parts

See full listing in **Section One** under **Chevrolet**

Chevy Duty Pickup Parts
4319 NW Gateway
Kansas City, MO 64150
816-741-8029; FAX: 816-741-5255
E-mail: chevyduty@aol.com

pickup parts

See full listing in **Section One** under **Chevrolet**

Classic Motors Unlimited
RD 1 Box 99C
Hooversville, PA 15936
814-479-7874

chemical stripping
metal work
restoration

See full listing in **Section Two** under **restoration shops**

Clester's Auto Rubber Seals Inc
PO Box 459
Cleveland, NC 27013
704-637-9979; FAX: 704-636-7390

gloveboxes
headliners/parts
molded rubber
weatherstripping

See full listing in **Section Two** under **rubber parts**

Coker Tire
1317 Chestnut St
Chattanooga, TN 37402
800-251-6336 toll-free
423-265-6368, local & international
FAX: 423-756-5607

tires

See full listing in **Section Two** under **tires**

Dearborn Classics
PO Box 1248
Sunset Beach, CA 90742
714-372-3175; FAX: 714-372-3801

accessories
restoration parts

See full listing in **Section One** under **Ford '54-up**

Desert Valley Auto Parts
22500 N 21st Ave
Phoenix, AZ 85027
602-780-8024; FAX: 602-582-9141

salvage yard

See full listing in **Section Five** under **Arizona**

Dixie Truck Works
10495 Hwy 73 E
Mount Pleasant, NC 28124
704-436-2407

parts

See full listing in **Section One** under **Chevrolet**

Dusty Memories Ltd
118 Oxford Hgts Rd
Somerset, PA 15501-1134
814-443-2393; FAX: 814-443-6468

rentals

See full listing in **Section Two** under **military vehicles**

Early Wheel Co Inc
Box 1438
Santa Ynez, CA 93460
805-688-1187; FAX: 805-688-0257

steel wheels

See full listing in **Section Two** under **wheels & wheelcovers**

Egge Machine Company
11707 Slauson Ave
Santa Fe Springs, CA 90670
310-945-3419 in CA; 800-866-EGGE
FAX: 310-693-1635

babbitting
chassis
motor mounts
pistons/valves
wiring harnesses

See full listing in **Section Two** under **engine parts**

Jim Estrup The Plateman
Box 908
RR 3
Kennebunk, ME 04043
207-985-4800; FAX: 207-985-TAGS

license plates

See full listing in **Section Two** under **license plates**

Fuller's Restoration Inc
Old Airport Rd
Manchester Center, VT 05255
802-362-3643; FAX: 802-362-3360

repairs
restoration

See full listing in **Section Two** under **restoration shops**

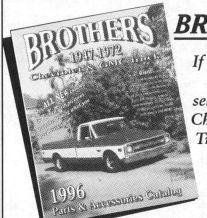

Gilbert's Early Chevy Pickup Parts | pickup parts
PO Box 1316
470 Rd 1 NW
Chino Valley, AZ 86323
PH/FAX: 602-636-5337
E-mail: gilb@goodnet.com

Specializes in reproduction and new parts for 47-66 Chevrolet & GMC pickups. Fast, friendly service.

Great Lakes Auto "N" Truck Restoration | parts
PO Box 251
Mayville, MI 48744
517-683-2614

See full listing in **Section One** under **Chevrolet**

Heavy Chevy Truck Parts | parts
PO Box 650
17445 Heavy Chevy Rd
Siloam Springs, AR 72761
501-524-9575; FAX: 501-524-4873
or 800-317-2277

See full listing in **Section One** under **Chevrolet**

Hodges Custom Haulers | truck beds
9076 Scale Rd
Benton, KY 42025
PH/FAX: 502-898-2356

See full listing in **Section Two** under **trailers**

Inland Empire Driveline Service Inc | drive shafts, pinion yokes
4035 E Guasti Rd, #301
Ontario, CA 91761
800-800-0109; FAX: 909-390-3038

See full listing in **Section Two** under **machine work**

Keilen's Auto Restoring | restoration
580 Kelley Blvd (R)
North Attleboro, MA 02760
508-699-7768

See full listing in **Section Two** under **restoration shops**

Kenask Spring Co | springs
307 Manhattan Ave
Jersey City, NJ 07307
201-653-4589

See full listing in **Section Two** under **suspension parts**

Leigh & Sharon Knudson Truck Light Sales | stoplights, truck lights, turn signals
719 Ohms Way
Costa Mesa, CA 92627
714-645-5938; FAX: 714-646-8031

See full listing in **Section Two** under **lighting equipment**

LMC Truck | accessories, parts
PO Box 14991
Lenexa, KS 66285
800-222-5664; FAX: 913-599-0323

See full listing in **Section One** under **Chevrolet**

Lokar Inc | performance parts
10924 Murdock Dr
Knoxville, TN 37922
423-966-2269; FAX: 423-671-1999

See full listing in **Section Two** under **street rods**

Majestic Truck Parts | parts
17726 Dickerson
Dallas, TX 75252
214-248-6245

See full listing in **Section One** under **Chevrolet**

MAR-K Quality Parts | bed parts, customizing parts, trim parts
6625 W Wilshire
Oklahoma City, OK 73132
405-721-7945; FAX: 405-721-8906

Mail order and retail. Manufacturer and supplier of pickup truck parts for restoration and for custom pickups. Includes bed parts, battery trays, custom rolled pans and tailgate covers.

Maximliner Inc | cargo mats, floor mats
150 E Race St
Troy, OH 45373
513-339-0240; 800-624-2320
FAX: 513-335-5424

See full listing in **Section Two** under **carpets**

National Parts Locator Service | parts locator
636 East 6th St #81
Ogden, UT 84404-2415
801-392-9455

See full listing in **Section Two** under **car & parts locators**

New Era Motors | restoration
11611 NE 50th Ave, Unit 6
Vancouver, WA 98686
360-573-8788

See full listing in **Section Two** under **woodwork**

Obsolete Ford Parts Inc | parts
8701 S I-35
Oklahoma City, OK 73149
405-631-3933; FAX: 405-634-6815

See full listing in **Section One** under **Ford '54-up**

Orlandi Trailer | trailers
3120 Moorpark Ave
San Jose, CA 95117
408-296-5748; FAX: 408-247-1219

See full listing in **Section Two** under **trailers**

Paragon Models & Art | artwork, models
1431-B SE 10th St
Cape Coral, FL 33990
941-458-0024; FAX: 941-574-4329

See full listing in **Section Two** under **models & toys**

Pick-ups Northwest | parts, trim
7130 Bickford Ave
Snohomish, WA 98290
360-568-9166; FAX: 360-568-1233

See full listing in **Section One** under **Chevrolet**

Power Effects | exhaust systems
1800H Industrial Park Dr
Grand Haven, MI 49417
616-847-4200; FAX: 616-847-4210

See full listing in **Section Two** under **exhaust systems**

R-Mac Publications Inc
Rt 3, Box 425
Jasper, FL 32052
904-792-2480; FAX: 904-792-3230

magazine

See full listing in **Section Four** under **books & publications**

Redi-Strip Company
100 West Central Ave
Roselle, IL 60172
630-529-2442; FAX: 630-529-3626

abrasive media
paintremoval
plastic media
rust removal

See full listing in **Section Two** under **rust removal & stripping**

Reider Racing Enterprises Inc
12351 Universal Dr
Taylor, MI 48180
800-522-2707, 313-946-1330
FAX: 313-946-8672

axle components

See full listing in **Section Two** under **racing**

Rentalex Toy Department
1022 Skipper Rd
Tampa, FL 33613
888-971-9990 toll-free
813-971-3940

models
toys

See full listing in **Section Two** under **models & toys**

Richardson Restorations
1861 W Woodward Ave
Tulare, CA 93274
209-688-5002

repairs
restoration

See full listing in **Section Two** under **restoration shops**

Rock Valley Antique Auto Parts
Box 352
Rt 72 and Rothwell Rd
Stillman Valley, IL 61084
815-645-2271; FAX: 815-645-2740

gas tanks

See full listing in **Section One** under **Ford '32-'53**

Scotts Super Trucks
Box 6772
1040 Emma St
Penhold, AB Canada T0M 1R0
403-886-5572; FAX: 403-886-5577

parts

See full listing in **Section One** under **Chevrolet**

Silver State Restorations Inc
The Aday Collection
4655 Aircenter Cir
Reno, NV 89502
702-826-8886; FAX: 702-826-9191

restoration
service

See full listing in **Section Two** under **restoration shops**

Simons Balancing & Machine
1987 Ashley River Rd
Charleston, SC 29407
803-766-3911; FAX: 803-766-9003

machine work

See full listing in **Section Two** under **machine work**

Slim's Garage
PO Box 49
Seminary, MS 39479-0049
PH/FAX: 601-722-9861

garden tractors

Mail order and open shop. Weekdays 9 to 5. Specializing in garden tractors.

Tabco Inc
11655 Chillicothe Rd
Chesterland, OH 44026-1994
216-729-5151; FAX: 216-729-1251

body parts

See full listing in **Section Two** under **sheetmetal**

This Old Truck Magazine
PO Box 562
Yellow Springs, OH 45387
800-767-5828; 937-767-1433
FAX: 767-2726
E-Mail: antique@antiquepower.com

magazine

See full listing in **Section Four** under **periodicals**

Union Performance Co
PO Box 324
59 Mansfield St
Sharon, MA 02067
617-784-5367, voice mail
FAX: 617-784-5367

parts

See full listing in **Section Two** under **electrical systems**

Valley Motor Supply
1402 E Second St
Roswell, NM 88201
505-622-7450

accessories
parts

See full listing in **Section One** under **Ford '54-up**

Wallace W Wade Specialty Tires
530 Regal Row
PO Box 56096
Dallas, TX 75356
800-666-TYRE; 214-688-0091
FAX: 214-634-8465

tires

See full listing in **Section Two** under **tires**

Wale's Antique Chevy Truck Parts
143 Center
Carleton, MI 48117
313-654-8836

parts

See full listing in **Section One** under **Chevrolet**

Michael J Welch
3700 Rt 6, RR 2
Eastham, MA 02642
508-255-1437

automobilia
pedal cars
toy trucks

See full listing in **Section Two** under **models & toys**

Weld-N-Fab Performance
PO Box 356
Norwalk, IA 50211
515-981-4928

gas pumps
machine work
tractors

See full listing in **Section One** under **Anglia**

Westwinds Motor Car Co
RD 2, Box 777, Cox Rd
Woodstock, VT 05091
802-457-4178; FAX: 802-457-3926

restoration

See full listing in **Section Two** under **restoration shops**

Wheels O' Time Museum
PO Box 9636
Peoria, IL 61612-9636
309-243-9020

museum

See full listing in **Section Six** under **Illinois**

trunks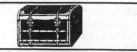

 **upholstery**

Auto Body Specialties Inc Rt 66 Middlefield, CT 06455 860-346-4989; FAX: 860-346-4987	accessories body parts

See full listing in **Section Two** under **body parts**

Automotive Interior Center 1725A Bustleton Pike Feasterville, PA 19053 PH/FAX: 215-953-7477	interior trim

See full listing in **Section Two** under **interiors & interior parts**

Benkin & Co 14 E Main St Tipp City, OH 45371 513-667-5975; FAX: 513-667-5729	gas pumps neon clocks neon signs

See full listing in **Section Two** under **automobilia**

Hooker Headers 1024 W Brooks St PO Box 4030 Ontario, CA 91761 909-983-5871	exhaust systems

See full listing in **Section Two** under **exhaust systems**

Mac Neil Automotive Products Ltd 2435 Wisconsin St Downers Grove, IL 60515 800-441-6287; FAX: 630-769-0300	cargo liners floor mats

See full listing in **Section Two** under **interiors & interior parts**

T-Bird Sanctuary 9997 SW Avery Tualatin, OR 97062 503-692-9848, FAX: 503-692-9849	parts

See full listing in **Section One** under **Thunderbird**

Varco Inc 8200 S Anderson Rd Oklahoma City, OK 73150 405-732-1637	fitted luggage trunks

See full listing in **Section One** under **Ford '03-'31**

Vintage Trunks 5 Brownstone Rd East Granby, CT 06026-9705 860-658-0353 E-mail: jhdeso@ccmail.monsanto.com	trunks

Mail order only. Plans and hardware for authentic wood construction of luggage trunks for Model As and other vintage autos. Drawing package contains prints, hardware listing and prices, history, instructions and fabric samples. Send SASE for information and price list. Have full line of trunk hardware on hand for your trunk restoration.

Accurate Auto Tops & Upholstery Inc Miller Rd & W Chester Pike Edgemont, PA 19028 610-356-1515; FAX: 610-353-8230	tops upholstery

Accurate Auto Tops is a full service top and upholstery shop specializing in classic and antique restorations and street rod interiors.

Automotive Interior Center 1725A Bustleton Pike Feasterville, PA 19053 PH/FAX: 215-953-7477	interior trim

See full listing in **Section Two** under **interiors & interior parts**

Bird Nest PO Box 14865 Portland, OR 97293 800-232-6378; FAX: 503-234-2473	parts

See full listing in **Section One** under **Thunderbird**

Ciadella Enterprises Inc 3116 S 52nd St Tempe, AZ 85282-3212 602-968-4179; FAX: 602-438-6585	truck interiors upholstery

See full listing in **Section One** under **Chevrolet**

Classic Trim Inc Mick Stamm 3401 S 1st St Abilene, TX 79605-1708 915-676-8788	collectibles trim upholstery

See full listing in **Section Two** under **motorcycles**

Color-Plus Leather Restoration System 2116 Morris Ave Union, NJ 07083 908-851-2811; FAX: 908-851-2910	leather conditioning leather dye

See full listing in **Section Two** under **leather restoration**

Comfy/Inter-American Sheepskins Inc 1346 Centinela Ave West Los Angeles, CA 90025-1901 800-521-4014; FAX: 310-442-6080 E-mial: 4858038@mcimail.com	floor mats seat covers

See full listing in **Section Two** under **interiors & interior parts**

Custom Interiors PO Box 51174 Indian Orchard, MA 01151 800-423-6053; FAX: 413-589-9178	carpets headliners upholstery

Mail order only. Interior parts. We manufacture seat upholstery for all makes domestic and foreign from 1928-1996. We also offer carpets, molded or cut and sewn and headliners too, to customize your project.

Doc's Jags 125 Baker Rd Lake Bluff, IL 60044 847-367-5247; FAX: 847-367-6363	appraisals interiors restoration

See full listing in **Section One** under **Jaguar**

East Coast Chevy Inc
Ol '55 Chevy Parts
4154A Skyron Dr
Doylestown, FL 18938
215-348-5568; FAX: 215-348-0560

**parts
restoration**

See full listing in **Section One** under **Chevrolet**

FEN Enterprises of New York Inc
PO Box 1559
Wappingers Falls, NY 12590
914-462-5959; 914-462-5094
FAX: 914-462-8450

**parts
restoration**

See full listing in **Section One** under **Cadillac/LaSalle**

**Firewall Insulators
& Quiet Ride Solutions**
6333 Pacific Ave, Ste 523
Stockton, CA 95207
209-477-4840; FAX: 209-477-0918

firewall insulators

Mail order only. Manufactures firewall insulator panels (upholstery) just like OEMs did originally. Currently have patterns for nearly 300 cars and trucks, 1928-1972, including Bitchin' firewalls for street rods. Also makes specialty items including gloveboxes, heater plenum, air/defroster ducts, etc. If the pattern for your car is not available, send your old original for reproduction. Each insulator comes ready to install with insulation, all holes punched and detailed to look and fit just like the original. Standards are exacting and work is guaranteed. Also specializes in automotive insulation and sound deadening materials.

See our ad on page 313

Ken's Cougars
PO Box 5380
Edmond, OK 73013
405-340-1636; FAX: 405-340-5877

parts

See full listing in **Section One** under **Mercury**

Koolmat
PO Box 207
1922 Coventry
Brunswick, OH 44212
330-273-6011; FAX: 330-273-9858

insulators

See full listing in **Section Two** under **restoration aids**

Land Cruisers Solutions Inc
20 Thornell Rd
Newton, NH 03858
508-462-5656, MA

**accessories
services**

See full listing in **Section One** under **Toyota**

Linearossa International Inc
15281 Barranca Pkwy, #A
Irvine, CA 92618
714-727-1201; FAX: 714-727-0603

parts

See full listing in **Section One** under **Fiat**

Memoryville USA Inc
1008 W 12th St
Rolla, MO 65401
573-364-1810

restoration

See full listing in **Section Two** under **restoration shops**

Original Auto Interiors
7869 Trumble Rd
Columbus, MI 48063-3915
810-727-2486; FAX: 810-727-4344
E-mail: knight@mich.com

upholstery

Mail order and open shop. Monday-Friday 9 am-5 pm Eastern. Upholstery materials for vehicles from the 1950s-1980s. All American made cars. Thunderbird seat covers 1961-1966, the most original available. NOS seat covers for selected MoPars 1957-1964, and MoPar reproductions 1963-1976. OEM carpet sets for most vehicles mid-50s to present. Also available: headliners, floor mats, trunk mats, convertible tops and boots and windlace.

Route 66 Classic Restorations
250 N 1st St
Wilmington, IL 60481
815-476-4290

restoration

See full listing in **Section Two** under **restoration shops**

Sailorette's Nautical Nook
23005 W Kankakee River Dr
Wilmington, IL 60481
815-476-2391; FAX: 815-476-2524

**covers
interiors**

Monday-Friday 9 am-5 pm, other times by appointment. Custom handcrafted vehicle interiors which includes seat reupholstering, door panels and carpets for old and new vehicles. Also specializing in custom covers for cars, trucks, motorcycles, marine covers, marine convertible tops.

Thunderbird Headquarters
1080 Detroit Ave
Concord, CA 94518
800-227-2174; FAX: 510-689-1771

parts

See full listing in **Section One** under **Thunderbird**

West Coast Metric Inc
24002 Frampton Ave
Harbor City, CA 90710
310-325-0005; FAX: 310-325-9733
E-mail: wcmi@earthlink.net

**apparel
carpets
rubber parts**

See full listing in **Section One** under **Volkswagen**

videos

Action Marketing
17 Verona Cr
Keswick, ON Canada L4P 3N7
800-494-4204; FAX: 905-476-9834

video

Mail order only. 24 hours. *Presidential Limousines*, VHS video tape (approx 50 min), featuring the more prominent White House presidential limousines used from Franklin D Roosevelt to Bill Clinton, 11 in all. The only video of its kind ever produced, acknowledged by the US Secret Service and all the surviving former US presidents. $19.95 + $3.95 s&h.

Dalmar
11759 S Cleveland Ave, Suite 28
Ft Myers, FL 33907
941-275-6540; FAX: 941-275-1731
E-mail: dalmar@peganet.com

**electroplating
plating supplies**

See full listing in **Section Two** under **plating & polishing**

Eclectic Amusement Corporation
10 Smithfield St
Pittsburgh, PA 15222
412-434-0111; FAX: 412-434-0606

juke boxes
video games

See full listing in **Section Two** under **novelties**

Fibre Glast Developments Corp
1944 Neva Dr
Dayton, OH 45414
800-821-3283; FAX: 513-274-7267
E-mail: fibreglast@aol.com

supplies
tools

See full listing in **Section Two** under **restorations aids**

GMC Solutions
Robert English
PO Box 675
Franklin, MA 02038-0675
508-520-3900; FAX: 508-520-7861
E-mail: oldcarkook@aol.com

literature
parts

See full listing in **Section One** under **GMC**

The Gullwing Garage Ltd
Bricklin SVI Specialists
5 Cimorelli Dr
New Windsor, NY 12553-6201
914-561-0019 anytime

appraisals
literature
parts
service

See full listing in **Section One** under **Bricklin**

Richard Hamilton
28 E 46th St
Indianapolis, IN 46205
317-283-1902

sales literature

See full listing in **Section Two** under **literature dealers**

Motorsport Tools
7561-A Orr Rd
Charlotte, NC 28213
704-596-0350; FAX: 704-596-0707

English wheels
metalworking tools

See full listing in **Section Two** under **tools**

Practical Images
PO Box 245
Haddam, CT 06438-0245
860-704-0525
E-mail: leswho@iconn.net

photo scanning
video conversions

See full listing in **Section Two** under **photography**

Roadside Market
1000 Gordon M Buehrig Pl
Auburn, IN 46706
219-925-9100; FAX: 219-925-4563

automobilia

See full listing in **Section Two** under **automobilia**

Video Resources NY Inc
220 W 71 St
New York, NY 11229
212-724-7055; FAX: 212-595-0189

videos

Mail order only. We have a rare collection of automobile videos and TV shows, commercials from the 1950s and 1960s. Each tape is 60 minutes, SP speed. Send for free newsletter or $6 for our complete catalog.

Yankee Candle Car Museum
5 North St
South Deerfield, MA 01373
413-665-2020; FAX: 413-665-2399

museum

See full listing in **Section Six** under **Massachusetts**

wheels & wheelcovers

Agape Auto
2825 Selzer Rd
Evansville, IN 47712
812-423-7332

fender skirts
wheelcovers

Mail order only. Specializing in fender skirts, sunvisors and hubcaps. Reproduction and original fender skirts for most 1935-69 US cars. Also wheelcovers for 1949-80 US cars. Wheelcovers are mostly used, some NOS.

AKH Wheels
1207 N A St
Ellensburg, WA 98926-2522
509-962-3390

Rallye wheels
styled steel wheels
vintage aluminum

Mail order. Sales of vintage wheels, American Racing Torque Thrusts, 200S (Coke bottles), CP-200s, slots, etc. Aluminum wheels by Ansen, Mickey Thompson, Parnelli Jones, Appliance, Superior, Forsythe, ET, Fenton, Halibrand, Hurst and Radar Corp. I also have most factory styled steel and Rallye wheels from Ford, GM, Mercury, Dodge, Buick, Olds, Plymouth, Pontiac and AMC. 600 wheels in stock. Access to 1,000s. For one rare wheel or a set, I can help.

American Arrow Corp
105 Kinross
Clawson, MI 48017
313-588-0425; FAX: 313-435-4670

chroming
mascots
wire wheel
rebuilding

See full listing in **Section Two** under **novelties**

Antique Wheels
1805 SW Pattulo Way
West Linn, OR 97068
503-638-5275

respoking

Respoking of wood and steel felloed wheels of all shapes and sizes of spokes. Only straight grain, FAS hickory wood used. Tracer lathing for uniformity and machine sandings for smoothness. Shipped with wood ready for paint or varnish.

Appleton Garage
PO Box B
West Rockport, ME 04865
207-594-2062

car dealer
parts
wheelcovers

Mail order and open shop. Monday-Friday 9 to 4. We have over 10,000 used/new wheelcovers and hubcaps for sale. Also sells GM cars, trucks and parts from 1960 to 1987. Specializing in 1962-66 full size Chevrolets, 1969-72 Chevy/GMC pickups.

Tony D Branda Performance
Shelby and Mustang Parts
1434 E Pleasant Valley Blvd
Altoona, PA 16602
814-942-1869; FAX: 814-944-0801

accessories
decals
emblems
sheetmetal
wheels

See full listing in **Section One** under **Mustang**

Burr Nyberg Screw-on Hubcaps
200 Union Blvd #425
Denver, CO 80228
FAX: 303-988-7145

hubcaps

See full listing in **Section Two** under **hubcaps**

Generalists

California Pony Cars	parts
1906 Quaker Ridge Pl	
Ontario, CA 91761	
909-923-2804; FAX: 909-947-8593	
E-mail: 105232.3362@compuserv.com	

See full listing in **Section One** under **Mustang**

California Wire Wheel	rechroming
6922 Turnbridge Way	tires
San Diego, CA 92119	tubes
619-698-8255; FAX: 619-589-9032	wheels

Mail order or appointment only. Specializing in wire wheel restoration of American, British, and Italian wire wheels, (eg Franklin, Duesenberg, Ferrari, MG, etc.). Chrome, stainless, painted spokes and custom colors. New wire wheels for British cars tires, tubes, knock-off wheel hubs. MGs bought, sold, and refurbished. Die-cast model car stockist specializing in British and European models.

Calimer's Wheel Shop	wooden wheels
30 E North St	
Waynesboro, PA 17268	
717-762-5056; FAX: 717-762-5021	

Mail order and open shop. Monday-Friday, 8 am until 5 pm. Rebuilding of wooden wheels using the customer's metal parts. Wheels made of hickory for years. Late 1890s to 1930.

Sam Clark	wheel rims
PO Box 1817	
Lucerne Valley, CA 92356	
PH/FAX: 619-248-9025	

Mail order only. Manufacturer of ultra-quality wheel rim assemblies for the finest large early automobiles. Specializing in 27 inch Firestone style. Producing rims since 1981, for Alco, Chadwick, Delauney-Belleville, Hispano-Suiza, Isotta-Fraschini, Locomobile, Lozier, Mercedes, Oldsmobile, Packard, Pierce-Arrow, Pope-Hartford, Thomas Flyer and others.

The Classic Car Radio Co	radios
2718 Koper Dr	
Sterling Heights, MI 48310	
810-977-7979; 810-268-2918, info	
FAX: 810-977-0895	

See full listing in **Section Two** under **radios**

Coker Tire	tires
1317 Chestnut St	
Chattanooga, TN 37402	
800-251-6336 toll-free	
423-265-6368, local & international	
FAX: 423-756-5607	

See full listing in **Section Two** under **tires**

Donald Davenport	rim clamps
PO Box 6144	
Metairie, LA 70009	

Mail order only. Demountable rim clamps, bolts and nuts.

Dayton Wheel Products	parts
1147 S Broadway St	restoration
Dayton, OH 45408	service
800-862-6000; 513-461-1707	
FAX: 513-461-1615	

Office open Monday-Friday 8:30 to 4:30. Wire wheel restoration for Dayton, Borrani, Kelsey-Hayes, Motor Wheel, Dunlop, etc. Also, manufacturer of replacement spline-drive wire wheels and quality knock-off and bolt-on wire wheels.

Buzz De Clerck	parts
41760 Utica Rd	
Sterling Heights, MI 48313	
810-731-0765	

See full listing in **Section One** under **Lincoln**

Early Wheel Co Inc	steel wheels
Box 1438	
Santa Ynez, CA 93460	
805-688-1187; FAX: 805-688-0257	

Mail order only. Manufactures steel wheels for the street rod, pickup and restoration market. Wheel widths from 5" to 14" wide. Hubcaps and trim rings available for our wheels.

Enthusiast's Specialties	automobilia
350 Old Connecticut Path	tools
Framingham, MA 01701	
508-620-1942; FAX: 508-872-4914	

See full listing in **Section Two** under **automobilia**

George's Auto & Tractor Sales Inc	batteries/Blue Dots
1450 N Warren Rd	car dealer
North Jackson, OH 44451	metal polish
330-538-3020; FAX: 330-538-3033	upholstery cleaner

See full listing in **Section Two** under **car dealers**

Giant Auto Wreckers Inc	dismantling
23944 Pine St	hubcaps
Newhall, CA 91321	wheelcovers
805-259-4678; FAX: 805-259-7008	

Mail order and open shop. Monday-Friday 8 to 5. Auto dismantling and auto accessories. Over 100,000 used original hubcaps and wheelcovers in stock, 1940 to present. Specializing in dismantling Fiat 124 and X19 only, small parts our specialty.

HRE Performance Wheels	aluminum wheels
2540 Pioneer Ave	
Vista, CA 92083	
619-941-2008; FAX: 619-598-5885	

Mail order and open shop. Monday-Friday 8 am to 5 pm. Custom built to order, 3-piece modular aluminum wheels, numerous styles in a wide variety of sizes and finishes, for all makes and models of automobiles.

Hubcap Jack Inc	hubcaps
1330 Market St	wheelcovers
Linwood, PA 19061	
610-485-1155; FAX: 610-494-2989	

Mail order and open shop. Open Monday-Friday 9 to 5, Saturday 9 to 4. Specializing in hubcaps and wheelcovers for cars, trucks, imports and classics.

Hubcap Mike	hubcaps
26242 Dimension, Ste 150	wheelcovers
Lake Forest, CA 92630	
714-597-8120; FAX: 714-597-8123	

Wheelcovers, hubcaps and trim rings, 1946 to 1996. Specializing in reproduction hubcaps for Chevy Rallye and 68-69 Ford GT wheels. Also baby moons, crossbars and much more. Same day shipping available on all orders. Money back satisfaction guarantee.

Generalists

| The Hubcap Store
Rt 22 & 4th St
Easton, PA 18042
800-HUBCAPS
FAX: 610-252-9883 | hubcaps
wheelcovers
wheels |

Mail order and open shop. Open Monday-Saturday 8:30 to 6:30. Wheels, wheelcovers from 1946-1995. Over 100,000 in stock, 28,000 square foot building. UPS daily. 18 years in business. VISA, MasterCard, American Express, Discover accepted. Buy, sell, trade-ins accepted.

See our ad on this page

| Italy's Famous Exhaust
2711 183rd St
Redondo Beach, CA 90278
PH/FAX: 310-542-5432
E-mail: http://famous@earthlink.com | exhaust systems
wheels |

See full listing in **Section Two** under **exhaust systems**

| Roger Kraus Racing
2896 Grove Way
Castro Valley, CA 94546
510-582-5031
FAX: 510-886-5605 | shocks
tires
wheels |

See full listing in **Section Two** under **tires**

| LMARR Disk Ltd
PO Box 910
Glen Ellen, CA 95442-0910
707-938-9347
FAX: 707-938-3020 | wheel discs |

See full listing in **Section One** under **Rolls-Royce/Bentley**

| James McConville Vintage
Chevy Parts
4205 W 129th St, #22
Hawthorne, CA 90250
310-675-8877 9 am to noon PST | front mats
runningboard mats |

See full listing in **Section One** under **Chevrolet**

| McGard Inc
3875 California Rd
Orchard Park, NY 14127
716-662-8980; FAX: 716-662-8985 | lug nuts
wheel locks |

See full listing in **Section Two** under **locks & keys**

| OJ Rallye Automotive
PO Box 540
N 6808 Hwy OJ
Plymouth, WI 53073
414-893-2531; FAX: 414-893-6800 | accessories
car care products
lighting parts |

See full listing in **Section Two** under **lighting equipment**

| Operations Plus
PO Box 26347
Santa Ana, CA 92799
PH/FAX: 714-962-2776 | accessories
parts |

See full listing in **Section One** under **Cobra**

| Jerrell Pickett
Box 218
Wessington, SD 57381
605-458-2344 | literature
parts
sheetmetal
wheels |

See full listing in **Section Two** under **comprehensive parts**

| RD Enterprises Ltd
290 Raub Rd
Quakertown, PA 18951
215-538-9323; FAX: 215-538-0158
E-mail: rdent@rdent.com | parts |

See full listing in **Section One** under **Lotus**

| Red Crown Valve Caps
PO Box 5301
Topeka, KS 66605
913-357-5007 | automobilia |

See full listing in **Section Two** under **automobilia**

| Sports & Classics Wire Wheels
512 Boston Post Rd
Darien, CT 06820 | wire wheels |

Painted and chrome wire wheels, warehouse distributors for Dayton wire wheels, Panasport Rallye wheels and original Minilite bolt-on and splined wheels. Specializing in all makes, dealer and export inquiries invited. Free brochures.

| Stockton Wheel Service
648 W Fremont St
Stockton, CA 95203
209-464-7771; 800-395-9433
FAX: 209-464-4725 | wheel repair |

See full listing in **Section Two** under **service shops**

| Al Trommers Rare Auto Literature
59 West Front Street, Mailbox #1
Keyport Mini Mall
Keyport, NJ 07735 | hubcaps
license plates
literature/records
wheelcovers |

See full listing in **Section Two** under **literature dealers**

Ultra Wheel Co
6300 Valley View Ave
Buena Park, CA 90620
714-994-1444; FAX: 714-994-0723

custom wheels

Manufacturer only of custom wheels, one-piece, two-piece, composite and wire wheels.

Valley Wire Wheel Service
7306 Coldwater Canyon #16
North Hollywood, CA 91605
818-765-3258; FAX: 818-765-8358

wheel restoration
wheels

Mail order and open shop. Monday-Friday 8:30 to 5:30. Restoration of all styles of wire, steel, aluminum and mag. Straightening, truing, polishing, painting, powdercoating, chrome. Since 1969 we have been restoring wheels from daily drivers to concours. References upon request. We sell new and used wheels and tires, custom jobs are no problem. Some antique wheels in stock, we also buy old wheels. Helping to keep them on the road, call us, we're here to help.

The Vintage Wheel Shop
19842 Via Redonda
Sonora, CA 95370
209-533-0468

wooden wheels

Mail order and open shop. Monday-Saturday 8 am to 5 pm. Rebuilding wooden wheels.

Westbury Hot Rods
1130 Detroit Ave
Concord, CA 94520
510-682-9482; FAX: 510-682-9483

service
sheetmetal
fabrication

See full listing in **Section Two** under **street rods**

Wheel Repair Service of New England
317 Southbridge St, Rt 12
Auburn, MA 01501
508-832-4949; FAX: 508-832-3969

new wire wheels
wire wheel
restoration

Mail order and open shop. Wire wheel restoration specialists since 1962. Replacement spokes available in bare, chrome or polished stainless finishes. New Dayton wire wheels available to fit most cars. Save up to 35% off factory prices.

The Wheel Shoppe
18011 Fourteen Mile Rd
Fraser, MI 48026
810-415-7171; FAX: 810-415-7181
E-mail: jgs2nd@aol.com

performance parts
welding
wheel repair

Wheels our specialty. We repair those gouges, bends and chips and polish aluminum wheels to a beautiful high-lustre finish (also cycle, auto parts). Replacement wheels? We have new and used, OEM, aluminum and steel. Special heavy duty performance parts for Mustangs include solid motor mounts and frame connectors. Welding and fabricating jobs? We're equipped. We ship UPS, even Hawaii and Alaska. Become one of our happy and satisfied customers, call today!

Willies Antique Tires
5257 W Diversey Ave
Chicago, IL 60639
773-622-4037; 800-742-6226
FAX: 773-622-0623

tires
wire wheels

See full listing in **Section Two** under **tires**

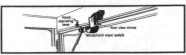

windshield wipers

Antique Automotive Accessories
889 S Rainbow Blvd, Suite 642
Las Vegas, NV 89128
800-742-6777; FAX: 913-862-4646

accessories
tires

See full listing in **Section Two** under **tires**

Bill's Speedometer Shop
109 Twinbrook Pl
Sidney, OH 45365
513-492-7800

repairs
restoration

See full listing in **Section Two** under **instruments**

Clean Sweep
Kent Jaquith
760 Knight Hill Rd
Zillah, WA 98953
509-865-2481

motors
repairs
wiper parts

Mail order and open shop. Rebuilding of all vacuum type wiper motors. Quick turnaround time. New and rebuilt vacuum wiper motors, some arms, blades and transmissions. Also rebuilding Hydro-wipe wiper motors.

Ezold's Model A Garage
1120 Southampton Rd
Westfield, MA 01805
413-562-0273

engine rebuilding
restorations

See full listing in **Section One** under **Ford '03-'31**

Ficken Auto Parts
Box 11
132 Calvert Ave
Babylon, NY 11702
516-587-3332; FAX: 516-661-9125

ignition parts
wiper parts

Mail order only. Phone hours: Monday-Friday 9 to 5. Trico windshield wiper motors (vacuum), NOS or we can also rebuild your vacuum motor. Arms, blades, linkages and repair kits. Ignition tune-up parts. In business for 30 years. Money back guarantee. Has booth at Hershey and Carlisle auto shows.

LaPina-Monaco Inc
616 Classon Ave
Brooklyn, NY 11238
718-789-8400

speedometers
windshield wipers

See full listing in **Section Two** under **instruments**

Mike's Auto Parts
Box 358
Ridgeland, MS 39158
601-856-7214

NOS parts/bearings
engine parts
wall calendars
windshield wipers

See full listing in **Section One** under **Chrysler**

J Pinto
2605 9th St
Long Island City, NY 11102
PH/FAX: 718-626-2403
E-mail: electritech@sprynet.com

windshield wiper
repair

See full listing in **Section Two** under **restoration aids**

Star Classics Inc
7745 E Redfield #300
Scottsdale, AZ 85260
602-991-7495; 800-644-7827
FAX: 602-951-4096

parts
sales
service

See full listing in **Section One** under **Mercedes-Benz**

Windshield Wiper Service
9109 (rear) E Garvey Ave
Rosemead, CA 91770
818-280-4546

parts
service

Mail order and open shop. Monday-Friday 9 to 5. Arms, blades and miscellaneous parts. Repair and rebuilding of vacuum and electric windshield wiper motors. Five day service.

wiring harnesses

AAMP of America
13160 56th Ct, #502-508
Clearwater, FL 34620
813-572-9255; FAX: 813-573-9326
E-mail: stinger.sales@stinger-aamp.com

audio accessories

See full listing in **Section Two** under **accessories**

Chev's of the 40's
2027 B St
Washougal, WA 98671
360-835-9799; FAX: 360-835-7988

parts

See full listing in **Section One** under **Chevrolet**

D & R Classic Automotive Inc
30 W 255 Calumet Ave
Warrenville, IL 60563
708-393-0009; FAX: 708-393-1397

parts

See full listing in **Section One** under **Chevelle/Camaro**

Ron Francis' Wire Works
167 Keystone Rd
Chester, PA 19013
610-485-1937

wiring
wiring kits

See full listing in **Section Two** under **electrical systems**

Painless Wiring
9505 Santa Paula Dr
Fort Worth, TX 76116
817-292-9315; FAX: 817-292-4024
E-mail: painlesswiring@airmail.net

accessories
parts

We sell through dealers nationwide. Wiring harnesses and electrical accessories. Our universal style harnesses are designed for easy installation and fit most street rods, restorations, customs, classics, pickups or jeeps.

Passenger Car Supply
102 Cloverdale Rd
Swedesboro, NJ 08085
609-467-7966

parts

See full listing in **Section One** under **Chevrolet**

Protrim Inc
438 Calle San Pablo, Unit 1
Camarillo, CA 93012
805-987-2086; FAX: 805-389-5375

plating

See full listing in **Section Two** under **plating & polishing**

woodgraining

Adams Custom Engines Inc
1115 Nixon Ave
Reno, NV 89509
702-358-8070; FAX: 702-358-8040

restorations

See full listing in **Section Two** under **restoration shops**

Beckley Auto Restorations Inc
4405 Capital Ave SW
Battle Creek, MI 49015
616-979-3013

restoration

See full listing in **Section Two** under **restoration shops**

Benfield's Auto Body
213 Trent St
Kernersville, NC 27284
PH/FAX: 910-993-5772

body repair
paint

See full listing in **Section Two** under **painting**

Classics Plus LTD
N7306 Lakeshore Dr
N Fond du Lac, WI 54937
414-923-1007

restoration

See full listing in **Section Two** under **steering wheels**

Dan's Restorations
PO Box 144
Snake Hill Rd
Sand Lake, NY 12153
518-674-2061

restoration

See full listing in **Section Two** under **restoration shops**

Dash Graining by Mel Erikson
31 Meadow Rd
Kings Park, NY 11754
PH/FAX: 516-544-1102 days
360-7789 nights

dashboard
restoration

Mail order and open shop. 5 days a week, 9 to 6. Active service in dashboard restoration for 15 years. Most business conducted by phone & UPS delivery. Phone estimates given. A hand process, matching original patterns as close to original as possible. Also restoration of some clock & speedometer faces. I can also restore exterior simulated wood for station wagons. Restoration of simulated wood finish on metal dashboards & interior trim for autos from the 1920s-1950s.

Walter A Finner
11131 Etiwanda Ave
Northridge, CA 91326
818-363-6076

woodgraining

Mail order and open shop. Many years' experience. Many show car winners. Send SASE for information.

Bill Gratkowski
515 N Petroleum St
Titusville, PA 16354
814-827-1782 eves
814-827-6111 days

woodgraining

Mail order and open shop. Has been doing woodgraining for 20 years, national show winning quality, low prices, quick turnaround, with references.

C D Hall
1217 Newport Ave
Long Beach, CA 90804
PH/FAX: 310-494-5048

woodgraining

Mail order and professional open work shop, 9 am to 6 pm PST. Serving the West Coast and nationwide. Specializing in old time woodgraining faux finishes. Quality craftsmanship for your classics, woodies, hot rods, sports, antique interiors and exteriors. All work is done by hand with only fine artwork in mind. Most work completed in 3 to 4 weeks or less.

Jay Products
PO Box 21095
Cleveland, OH 44121
216-382-1447

woodgraining

Mail order only. For the do-it-yourselfer. Kit contains one pint basecoat, 1/2 pint finish, two brushes, graining tool, and instructions. Walnut or mahogany. Price: $39 mailed.

Bob Kennedy
Woodgraining Service
8609 Ocean View
Whittier, CA 90605
310-693-8739

woodgraining

Mail order and open shop. Monday-Friday 8 to 5. Duplication of original grain.

Mar-Ke Woodgraining
1102 Hilltop Dr
Loveland, CO 80537
970-663-7803; FAX: 970-663-1138

woodgraining

Woodgraining dashes & moldings for autos, trucks. Metal or plastic trim pieces, original & custom. Specializing in burling.

Old Car Woodgraining
27902 45th Ave S
Auburn, WA 98001
206-854-5247

dashboard
restoration
woodgraining

Mail order and open shop. All days, all hours. Small shop specializing in dashboard restoration and woodgraining on steel. Have experience with many marques including Packard, Cadillac, Chevrolet, Ford, Hudson, Jaguar, etc. Also specialize in collector car detailing. Top quality, low prices.

Woodgrain by Estes
7550 Richardson Rd
Sarasota, FL 34240
813-379-3669

woodgraining

Mail order only. 28 years' experience serving major restorers, museums and individuals utilizing the original process factory graining, which incorporates photo etched plates to apply the graining. We are not part-timers. This is all we do.

woodwork

Bassett Classic Restoration
2616 Sharon St, Suite D
Kenner, LA 70062
PH/FAX: 504-469-2982 (have auto switching device)

parts
plating
restoration
service

See full listing in **Section One** under **Rolls-Royce/Bentley**

Beckley Auto Restorations Inc
4405 Capital Ave SW
Battle Creek, MI 49015
616-979-3013

restoration

See full listing in **Section Two** under **restoration shops**

Bicknell Engine Company
7055 Dayton Rd
Enon, OH 45323
513-864-5224

repair
restoration

See full listing in **Section One** under **Buick/McLaughlin**

Bonnets Up
5736 Spring St
Clinton, MD 20735
301-297-4759

restoration

See full listing in **Section Two** under **coachbuilders & designers**

Calimer's Wheel Shop
30 E North St
Waynesboro, PA 17268
717-762-5056; FAX: 717-762-5021

wooden wheels

See full listing in **Section Two** under **wheels & wheelcovers**

Classic Wood Mfg
1006 N Raleigh St
Greensboro, NC 27405
910-691-1344; FAX: 910-273-3074

wood kits
wood replacement

Mail order and open shop. Monday-Friday 7:30 to 5 EST. Appointment advised. Ford Model T and A, Chevrolet 1927-1936, MG T Series and MGA wood kits from stock. Dealer program available to qualifying full-line new parts dealers. Custom made wood for other cars from your old pattern.

County Auto Restoration
6 Gavin Rd
Mont Vernon, NH 03057
603-673-4840

body work
brakes
restoration
woodwork

See full listing in **Section Two** under **restoration shops**

Chuck & Judy Cubel
PO Box 278
Superior, AZ 85273
PH/FAX: 520-689-2734 eves

wood parts

See full listing in **Section One** under **Ford '03-'31**

JB Donaldson Co
2533 W Cypress
Phoenix, AZ 85009
602-278-4505; FAX: 602-278-1112

castings
steering wheels
wood parts

See full listing in **Section Two** under **steering wheels**

Enfield Auto Restoration Inc
4 Print Shop Rd
Enfield, CT 06082
860-749-7917; FAX: 860-749-2836

panel beating
restorations
Rolls-Royce parts
wood working

See full listing in **Section Two** under **restoration shops**

David J Entler Restorations
RD 2, Box 479C
Glen Rock, PA 17327
717-235-2112, 8 am to 5 pm
Monday thru Friday EST

woodwork

Structural woodwork restoration for 1933 thru 1936 Chevrolet and GM bodies. Rewooding of all other bodies.

Exotic Wood Dash & Restorations
336 Cottonwood Ave
Hartland, WI 53029
800-900-3274; FAX: 414-367-9474

restoration parts
wood dash overlays

See full listing in **Section One** under **Jaguar**

Franklin Buggy Werkes
510 Main St
Florence, KS 66851
316-878-4684

restoration
sheetmetal
woodgraining
engine rebuilding

See full listing in **Section Two** under **restoration shops**

Glazier Pattern & Coachworks
3720 Loramie-Washington Rd
Houston, OH 45333
513-492-7355; FAX: 513-492-9987

coachwork
interior woodwork
restoration

See full listing in **Section One** under **Rolls-Royce/Bentley**

Grey Hills Auto Restoration
PO Box 630
51 Vail Rd
Blairstown, NJ 07825
908-362-8232; FAX: 908-362-6796

restoration
service

See full listing in **Section Two** under **restoration shops**

Hanover Clocks Inc
5316 Hwy 421 N
Wilmington, NC 28401
919-343-0400; FAX: 919-343-0101

clock maker

See full listing in **Section Two** under **automobilia**

Harbor Freight Tools
3491 Mission Oaks Blvd
Camarillo, CA 93011
800-423-2567

tools

See full listing in **Section Two** under **tools**

Hatfield Restorations
PO Box 846
Canton, TX 75103
PH/FAX: 903-567-6742

restoration

See full listing in **Section Two** under **restoration shops**

Bruce Horkey Cabinetry
Rt 4, Box 188
Windom, MN 56101
507-831-5625; FAX: 507-831-0280

pickup parts

Mail order and open shop. Monday-Friday 8 to 5, Saturday by appointment. Replacement wood, metal & fiberglass pickup parts for 1928-95 Ford, 1932-95 Chevy/GMC, and 1933-95 Dodge pickups.

See our ad on this page

KC Wood Mfg
412 Hillside Dr
Greensboro, NC 27401
910-274-5496

wood kits
wood replacement

Mail order. Monday-Saturday 7:30-5:30. Chevrolet wood kits from stock. Structural wood replacement for any marque, car or truck from your patterns.

Kwik Poly T Distributing Inc
24 St Henry Ct
St Charles, MO 63301
314-724-1065

restoration aids

See full listing in **Section Two** under **restoration aids**

M & T Manufacturing Co
Hopkins Lane Mill
PO Box 3730
Peace Dale, RI 02883
401-789-0472; FAX: 401-789-5650

parts
wooden bows

Mail order only. Monday-Friday 9 to 5. Manufactures wood top bows for classic convertible cars. Stocks bows for VW, Jaguar and Mercedes-Benz, Rolls-Royce, Lincoln, Ford and others.

Madera Concepts
606 Olive St
Santa Barbara, CA 93101
800-800-1579; 805-962-1579
FAX: 805-962-7359

restoration
woodwork
woodwork repair

Woodwork restoration, reveneering and repair specialists. From chips and scratches to total basket cases, we've got you covered. Unsurpassed service, fastest "turn-around" time, 100 point "concours" quality and expert color and veneer matching. OEM replacements for many European vehicles. Call to discuss any repairs you may need. Free phone estimates available on commonly repaired components. Over 1,200 exotic wooden dashboard and interior trim packages for late model cars and trucks. Automotive woodwork is all we do!

Martin Carriage House
350 N Park Ave
Warren, OH 44481
330-395-8442

wood bodies

New all wood bodies for most pre-1912 automobiles. Repair work to save a good original body.

Generalists

Memoryville USA Inc
1008 W 12th St
Rolla, MO 65401
573-364-1810

restoration

See full listing in **Section Two** under **restoration shops**

New Era Motors
11611 NE 50th Ave, Unit 6
Vancouver, WA 98686
360-573-8788

restoration

Mail order and open shop. Monday-Friday 8 am to 5 pm. We offer complete or partial restoration of any wood framed composite antique or classic automobile body, complete frame-off restorations also available. Seat spring duplicating services performed.

Oak Bows
122 Ramsey Ave
Chambersburg, PA 17201
717-264-2602

top bows

Steam bent top bows duplicating your original bow. All bows steam bent like the original, not glued. No danger of separation. Send patterns, sockets or old bows for duplication. All SASEs will be answered.

Old Car Woodgraining
27902 45th Ave S
Auburn, WA 98001
206-854-5247

dashboard
restoration
woodgraining

See full listing in **Section Two** under **woodgraining**

Prestige Autowood
140 N Harrison Ave
Campbell, CA 95008
408-370-3705; FAX: 408-370-3792

dashboards

Mail order and open shop. Monday-Saturday 9 to 6. Manufactures both show quality and OEM replacement hardwood dashboards for Austin-Healey, Lotus, Jaguar, Morgan, MG, Sunbeam, Triumph and other British marques. We are America's most respected dashboard maker for the past 20 years. Our dashboards will exceed the wildest expectations of the most discriminating customer.

Al Prueitt & Sons Inc
8 Winter Ave
PO Box 158
Glen Rock, PA 17327
717-428-1305; 800-766-003
 FAX: 717-235-4428

restoration
upholstery
woodworking

See full listing in **Section Two** under **restoration shops**

RAU Restoration
2027 Pontius Ave
Los Angeles, CA 90025
PH/FAX: 310-445-1128

woodwork

Mail order and open shop. Monday-Friday 8 to 6; Saturday and Sunday by appointment. Decorative and structural wood for contemporary and historical automobiles. We specialize in exquisite finishing, rebuilding, coachwork and custom steering wheels, all with unsurpassed results. From elegant driver to concours champion, we offer the complete solution for your woodwork needs.

See our ad on this page

Reinholds Restorations
c/o Rick Reinhold
PO Box 178, 255 N Ridge Rd
Reinholds, PA 17569-0178
717-336-5617

appraisals
repairs
restoration

See full listing in **Section Two** under **restoration shops**

Silver Star Restorations
116 Highway 19
Topton, NC 28781
704-321-4268; FAX: 704-321-6008

parts
restoration

See full listing in **Section One** under **Mercedes-Benz**

Vintage Woodworks
PO Box 49
Iola, WI 54945
715-445-3791

upholstery
woodwork

Shop address: Depot St, Iola, WI 54945. Complete woodworking and upholstery including Chrysler Town & Country cars.

Willys Wood
35336 Chauler Dr
North Ridgeville, OH 44039
216-327-2916

wood parts

See full listing in **Section One** under **Willys**

Wood Excel Ltd
1545 Green Hill Rd
Collegeville, PA 19426
610-584-1725

woodwork

Mail order and open shop. Monday-Friday 10 to 6. Repairs veneer and refinishes wood in automobiles including Rolls-

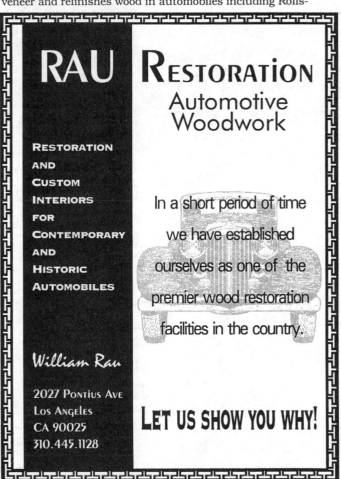

Royce, Jaguar, Mercedes-Benz, Packard, Cadillac, Lincoln, etc. If possible, one piece is given free before any business is done.

The Wood N'Carr 3231 E 19th St Signal Hill, CA 90804 310-498-8730; FAX: 310-985-3360	**woodwork** **wood parts**

Mail order and open shop. Mon-Fri 8 to 4:30. Automotive woodworking, specializing in woodies from stock to hot rod. Also replacement wood parts for 1932-36 Ford V8 other than station wagon. In business for over 20 years. We work on all makes and models. Has expanded into a newer, bigger facility at a new location. We do garnish wood trims for Jag, Bentley, Rolls, and Mercedes too.

The Woodie Works Box 346, RR 3 Arlington, VT 05250 802-375-9305	**woodworking**

Mail order and open shop. Monday to Saturday 9 to 6. We are a complete woodworking shop dedicated to the preservation of the wooden vehicle. We provide a complete range of services including research and design, repair, reproduction, replacement and refinishing. New work or custom work is welcome, as are unusual marques, trucks and commercial vehicles. Complete patterns for 33-36 Ford wagons, 1949-51 Ford wagons and 41-54 Chevrolet Cantrells in house. If your vehicle has wooden parts, you should be talking to us.

Generalists

Tourguide:
Generalists

Planning a trip? Or perhaps you would just like to know what old-car resources are in your home territory. In either case, the tourguide to Section Two will help.

This tourguide offers you an alphabetical listing of old car generalists with open shops by state and foreign country. Simply turn to the page number indicated for complete information on the object of your visit, including hours of operation, complete address, and phone number.

Generalists

250	Cover-It, West Haven
255	Dragone Classic Motorcars, Bridgeport
374	Enfield Auto Restoration Inc, Enfield
340	Moores Cycle Supply, West Hartford
346	Products Finishing Corp of CT, Norwalk
252	Quik-Shelter, Orange
393	RB's Prototype Model & Machine Co, Stamford
316	Ridgefield Auto Upholstery, Ridgefield
233	Sports & Classics, Darien
214	Peter Tytla Artist, East Lyme
318	Vantage Auto Interiors, Stamford

Delaware

269	Jess Auto Supply Co, Wilmington

Florida

262	Alan's Axles, Clearwater
359	Antique Automobile Radio Inc, Palm Harbor
252	Automatch International Inc, Jacksonville
253	Berliner Classic Motorcars Inc, Dania
193	Brooklands Inc, Fort Lauderdale
253	CARS (Computer Aided Resale System), Jacksonville
351	Chrome Masters, Tallahassee
372	Classics and Customs, Largo
254	Coachworks Classic Cars Inc, Gainesville
416	Daytona MIG, Daytona Beach
227	Deltran Corporation, Deland
313	Doyle's Upholstery & Canvas, Fruitland Park
231	Extensions Plus Inc, Pompano Beach
221	Jerry Goldsmith Promos, Lakeland
375	Harbor Auto Restoration, Pompano Beach
231	Hoffman Automotive Distributor, Hilliard
212	Edward L Hunt, Automotive Miniaturist, Hollywood
268	IMCADO Manufacturing Co, Umatilla
337	Paragon Models & Art, Cape Coral
352	Precision Pot Metal/Bussie Restoration Inc, Orange Park
257	Rader's Relics, Winter Park
337	Rentalex Toy Department, Tampa
225	Scale Collectors USA, Miami
382	Chris Smith's Creative, Dania
240	Ed Strain, Pinellas Park
272	Vintage Car Corral, Gainesville
361	Vintique Electronics, Deerfield Beach

Georgia

371	Classic Car Works Ltd, Jasper
222	Ken Hicks Promotionals, Fayetteville
279	Osborn Reproductions Inc, Lawrenceville
217	Red Baron's Antiques, Atlanta
421	Trailersource, Marietta

Idaho

242	Charlie Merrill, Twin Falls

Illinois

421	4-Speeds by Darrell, Vermilion
415	A & I Supply, N Pekin
410	A-1 Shock Absorber Co, Chicago
253	Chicago Car Exchange, Lake Bluff
205	Collector Car Appraisals, Rockford
254	Collector Car Buyers, Rockford
345	Fastech Inc, Gilberts
392	House of Powder Inc, Standard
416	HTP America Inc, Palatine
308	Instrument Services Inc, Roscoe
308	International Speedometer, Brookfield
358	Kassa's Parts & Accessories, Edwardsville
256	Lazarus Auto Collection, Rockford
208	M & M Automobile Appraisers Inc, Beecher
315	Mac Neil Automotive Products Ltd, Downers Grove

360	Marquette Radio, Orland Park
216	Dana Mecum Auctions Inc, Marengo
257	Memory Lane Motors Inc, Lake Bluff
379	Old Coach Works Restoration Inc, Yorkville
404	Preserve Inc, Hamilton
389	Redi-Strip Company, Roselle
381	Restorations Unlimited II Inc, Cary
381	Route 66 Classic Restorations, Wilmington
431	Sailorette's Nautical Nook, Wilmington
382	Sanders Antique Auto Restoration, Rockford
413	Shockfinders, Chicago
307	Speed Service Inc, Chicago
353	Star Chrome, Chicago
415	Willies Antique Tires, Chicago
384	Wilson's Classic Auto, Congerville

Indiana

322	Collins Metal Spinning, New Palestine
416	Custom Bandsaw Blades, Muncie
335	Grandpa's Attic, Goshen
406	The Hot Rod Shop, Spencerville
310	K & K Insurance Group Inc, Fort Wayne
216	Kruse International, Auburn
296	Langley Paint & Body, Bloomington
377	LaVine Restorations Inc, Nappanee
389	Pro-Strip, Fort Wayne
225	Roadside Market, Auburn

Iowa

255	Duffy's Collectible Cars, Cedar Rapids
330	Uhlenhopp Lock, Clarksville

Kansas

359	Antique Auto Radio, Wichita
374	Franklin Buggy Werkes, Florence
268	Gowen Auto Parts, Coffeyville
308	Charles Ivey Speedometer Service, Wichita

Kentucky

367	The Antique Auto Shop, Elsmere
420	Hodges Custom Haulers, Benton
421	Trailer World Inc, Bowling Green

Louisiana

253	Casey-Dyer Enterprises Inc, Alexandria

Maine

432	Appleton Garage, West Rockport
336	Karl's Collectibles, Lewiston
216	Mc Intyre Auctions, E Dixfield
378	McCann Auto Restoration, Houlton
396	Thompson Hill Metalcraft, Berwick

Maryland

295	Class Glass and Performance Inc, Cumberland
328	TMC Publications, Baltimore

Massachusetts

289	Aldrich Auto Supply Inc, Hatfield
353	AM Racing Inc, Danvers
203	Antique & Special Interest Car Appraisals, Andover
266	Antique Auto Parts Cellar, S Weymouth
214	Auctioneer Phil Jacquier Inc, Southwick
210	Automobilia Shop, Melrose
273	JJ Best & Co, Chatham
332	Commonwealth Automotive Restorations, Ashley Falls
312	Dom Corey Upholstery & Antique Auto, Fairhaven
320	Norman D'Amico, Clarksburg
206	Dearborn Automobile Co, Topsfield
375	GMS Restorations, Palmer

Generalists

321	Richard Hurlburt, Greenfield
425	Intercity Lines Inc, Warren
326	Bob Johnson's Auto Literature, Framingham
376	Keilen's Auto Restoring, North Attleboro
290	Knight Automotive Engineering Inc, Gloucester
377	Libbey's Classic Car Restoration Center, Shrewsbury
424	Performance Transmissions, Shrewsbury
309	Reynolds Speedometer Repair, Danvers
381	Paul Russell & Company, Essex
317	Scholz Specialty Products Company, Norwood
209	Steele's Appraisal, Maynard
421	Trailers of New England Inc, Palmer
435	Wheel Repair Service of New England, Auburn

Michigan

238	Allied Power Brake Co, Detroit
210	Antique Car Paintings, Dearborn Heights
333	Auto Zone, Birmingham
351	Automist Inc, East Lansing
369	Beckley Auto Restorations Inc, Battle Creek
359	The Classic Car Radio Co, Sterling Heights
373	Deters Restorations, Temperance
412	Eaton Detroit Spring Service Co, Detroit
239	Inline Tube, Fraser
360	Jackson Speaker Service, Jackson
290	Koffel's Place, Walled Lake
239	Muskegon Brake & Dist Co, Muskegon
399	Northern Digital Classics, L'Anse
286	Northwestern Auto Supply Inc, Grand Rapids
431	Original Auto Interiors, Columbus
355	Reider Racing Enterprises Inc, Taylor
214	Ridgetop Studio, Sanford
262	Silverleaf Casting Co, Delton
199	Specialty Custom Chrome Fasteners Inc, Howell
295	Waldron's Antique Exhaust Inc, Nottawa
214	Danny Whitfield, Automotive Artist, Rochester Hills

Minnesota

403	BW Incorporated, Browns Valley
312	Classtique Auto Products, Isanti
293	Headers by "Ed" Inc, Minneapolis
438	Bruce Horkey Cabinetry, Windom
286	Jackson's Old Parts, Duluth
379	Odyssey Restorations Inc, Spring Lake Park
389	Precision Paint & Rust Removers Inc, Long Lake
258	Yesterday's Auto Sales, Minneapolis

Mississippi

268	Wayne Hood, Grenada
429	Slim's Garage, Seminary

Missouri

351	A & A Plating Inc, Independence
258	The Carburetor Shop, Eldon
403	Fiesta's Classic Car Center, St Louis
339	Harper's Moto Guzzi, Greenwood
378	Memoryville USA Inc, Rolla
227	Paul's Rod & Bearing Ltd, Parkville
380	Precision Restoration Service Inc, Independence
225	Scott Signal Co, Willard
384	Wilson's Rods and Classics, Gary R Wilson, Holliday

Montana

243	Cam-Pro, Choteau

Nebraska

271	Speedway Motors Inc, Lincoln

Nevada

367	Adams Custom Engines Inc, Reno
194	Carpad Incorporated, Dayton
382	Silver State Restorations Inc, The Aday Collection, Reno

New Hampshire

368	Barlow & Co, Newton
372	County Auto Restoration, Mont Vernon
380	Redding Corp, George's Mills
381	Rick's Relics, Pittsburg
381	RMR Restorations Inc, Amherst

New Jersey

357	American Honeycomb Radiator Mfg, Holmdel
300	American Restorations Unlimited, TA, Rochelle Park
368	Antique Vehicle Maintenance, Pompton Lakes
204	AVM Automotive Consulting, Montvale
280	Robert D Bliss, Edison
330	Bob's Automotive Machine, Harrison
405	CAR Street Rod Parts Inc, Jackson
358	Custom Auto Radiator, Jackson
420	D & D Trailers Inc, Trenton
335	EWA & Miniature Cars USA Inc, Berkeley Heights
296	Exotic Enterprises, Garfield
422	FATSCO Transmission Parts, Fairfield
375	Hibernia Auto Restorations Inc, Hibernia
347	Bill Hirsch Auto Parts, Newark
207	HK Klassics, Maplewood
207	International Automotive Appraisers Assoc, Montvale
269	Kanter Auto Products, Boonton
412	Kenask Spring Co, Jersey City
337	New Era Toys, Lambertville
224	NJ Nostalgia Hobby, Scotch Plains
198	NMW Products, Raritan
282	M Parker Autoworks Inc, West Berlin
208	CT Peters Inc, Appraisers, Red Bank
390	PM Industries, West Milford
408	Rod-1 Shop, Pitman
382	Schaeffer & Long, Magnolia
332	Start Your Engine, Fair Haven
424	Street-Wise Performance, Tranquility
292	Thul Auto Parts Inc, Plainfield
419	Town Auto Top and Restoration Co, Pine Brook

New York

367	Ace Auto Body & Towing Ltd, Plainview
191	Action Performance Inc, Bohemia
367	Adler's Antique Autos Inc, Stephentown
410	Apple Hydraulics Inc, Calverton
311	Auto-Mat Co, Hicksville
226	The Babbitt Pot, Fort Edward
267	Joe Curto Inc, College Point
235	Dan's Restorations, Sand Lake
436	Dash Graining by Mel Erikson, Kings Park
392	Dependable RV & Auto Service, Lafayette
373	Edgerton Classics Ltd, Canastota
420	Eliminator Trailers, Syracuse
389	G & J Shore Weld Unlimited, Huntington Station
374	Gaslite Garage, Sayville
221	Get It On Paper, Islip
358	Highland Radiator Inc, Highland
416	Hydraulic Jack Inc, Accord
352	King's Bumper Co Inc, New Hartford
248	KozaK® Auto Drywash® Inc, Batavia
309	LaPina-Monaco Inc, Brooklyn
355	Marcovicci-Wenz Engineering Inc, Ronkonkoma
257	Mountain Fuel, Gilboa
309	Nisonger Instrument S/S, Mamaroneck
421	Nyles Haulmark Trailer Sales, Fairport
300	Powers Parts Co, Fabius
257	Retrospect Automotive, Huntington Station
240	Rochester Clutch & Brake Co, Rochester

282 Rockland Auto Electric, Pearl River
225 Silver Image Photographics, Vestal
360 Spirit Enterprises, Lockport
240 JF Sullivan, Auburn
418 USATCO/US AirTool Int'l, Ronkonkoma

North Carolina

333 Asheville DieCast, Asheville
347 Automotive Paints Unlimited, Roxboro
345 Benfield's Auto Body, Kernersville
385 Clester's Auto Rubber Seals Inc, Cleveland
417 Motorsport Tools, Charlotte
259 The Old Carb Doctor, Nebo
387 Steele Rubber Products Inc, Denver

Ohio

192 Backyard Buddy Corp, Niles
310 Robert T Barbero, CPCU, Beachwood
218 Benkin & Co, Tipp City
252 Jerry Bensinger, Youngstown
201 Business Forms Management Inc, Akron
370 Cars of the Past, Newbury
372 Cobb's Antique Auto Restoration, Washington Court House
220 Crazy About Cars, Beavercreek
351 Custom Chrome Plating Inc, Grafton
313 Dave's Auto Restoration, Jefferson
433 Dayton Wheel Products, Dayton
363 Fibre Glast Developments Corp, Dayton
301 Fox Lite Inc, Fairborn
348 Frontier Tank Center Inc, Richfield
256 George's Auto & Tractor Sales Inc, North Jackson
354 George's Speed Shop, Dayton
301 Glass Search/LOF, Columbus
329 Jesser's Classic Keys, Akron
291 Koffel's Place II, Huron
336 Little Old Cars, Canton
333 Nelson's Surplus Jeeps and Parts, Columbiana
224 Oil Company Collectibles, LaGrange
343 Park Avenue China Inc, East Palestine
358 Powell Radiator Service, Wilmington
417 Production Tool Supply of Ohio, Cleveland
389 Riverbend Abrasive Blasting, Coshocton
291 Ross' Automotive Machine Co Inc, Niles
358 Skills Unlimited Inc, Tiffin
396 Tabco Inc, Chesterland
418 TiP Tools & Equipment, Canfield
421 Trailex Inc, Canfield

Oklahoma

377 Lister Restorations, Tulsa
382 Special Interest Autos, Ardmore

Oregon

372 Concours Quality Auto Restoration, Gresham
255 Driving Ambition, Portland
240 Power Brake Booster Exchange Inc, Portland
382 Steve's Auto Restorations, Portland
323 Vintage Lamp Repair, Merlin
360 Vintage Radio Restorations, Newberg

Pennsylvania

252 Antique & Classic Automobiles, Hanover
368 Auto Restoration by William R Hahn, Wexford
204 Automotive Legal Service Inc, Dresher
368 Barr's Antique Auto Restoration, Erie
349 Boop Photography, Harrisburg
369 J D Booth Ltd, Spring Grove
218 Bright Displays, Pittsburgh
420 C & C Manufacturing Co, Hazleton,
433 Calimer's Wheel Shop, Waynesboro

235 Carters Auto Restorations, Phoenixville
253 Classic Car Sales, Furlong
371 Classic Motors Unlimited, Hooversville
372 Classics 'n More Inc, Lancaster
255 Driven By Desire, Kane
411 Eastern States Performance Outlet Inc, Danville
342 Eclectic Amusement Corporation, Pittsburgh
360 Elliott's Car Radio, Parkerford
420 Tommy Gale Trailer Sales & Service, Elizabeth
402 Gary's Steering Wheel Restoration, Carlisle
436 Bill Gratkowski, Titusville
207 Thos Hespenheide & Associates Ltd, Havertown
433 Hubcap Jack Inc, Linwood
434 The Hubcap Store, Easton
336 Investment Toys for Big Boys, York
376 Krem Engineering, Meadville
407 Lee's Kustom Auto and Street Rods, Rome
378 Masterworks Auto Reconditioning, Washington
301 N/C Ind Antique Auto Parts, Sayre
213 Neoclassic Neon, Carlisle
227 New Castle Battery Mfg Co, New Castle
379 Oak Bows, Chambersburg
379 Bob Ore Restorations, Erie
236 Guy R Palermo Auto Body, Wexford
352 Paul's Chrome Plating Inc, Mars
389 Pennsylvania Metal Cleaning, Monaca
380 Al Prueitt & Sons Inc, Glen Rock
352 Qual Krom-Great Lakes Plant, Erie
380 Ray's Upholstering, Scranton
233 Raybuck Autobody Parts, Punxsutawney
380 Reinholds Restorations, Reinholds
271 Restoration Specialties and Supply Inc, Windber
381 Richard's Auto Restoration, Wyoming
249 Showtime Auto Acc, Selinsgrove
344 Sky Signs Balloons, Ltd, Valley Forge
260 Sugarbush Products Inc, Chalfont
421 Transport Designs Inc, Montoursville
390 Tri-State Metal Cleaning, Erie
415 Universal Tire Co, Lancaster
393 Bill Walter's Auto Service, Morton
272 R Donald Williams, Berlin
318 Willow Grove Auto Top, Willow Grove
439 Wood Excel Ltd, Collegeville
390 Ziebart/Tidy Car, Pittsburgh

Rhode Island

283 B & B Cylinder Head, West Warwick
416 W L Fuller Inc, Warwick
409 David Jones, Narragansett
380 Pitcher's Auto Restoration, Perryville
282 Rhode Island Wiring Services Inc, W Kingston

South Carolina

262 Atlantic Enterprises, Little River
253 Brothers Classic, Special Interest & Sports Cars, Laurens

South Dakota

290 Harkin Machine Shop, Watertown

Tennessee

388 Capt Lee's Spra' Strip, Hermitage
308 Clock Doc®, Sewanee
308 Corvette Clocks by Roger, Jackson
196 Hunters Custom Automotive, Nashville
390 StripMasters of Nashville Inc, Nashville

Texas

261 Alamillo Patterns, Edinburg
368 Auto Craftsmen Restoration Inc, San Antonio
218 Be-Bops, New Braunfels

394	Car-Line Manufacturing & Distribution Inc, Beaumont
339	Classic Trim Inc, Abilene
422	Coffey's Classic Transmissions, Ft Worth
206	Dan's Classic Autos, New Caney
297	Darrell's Automotive and Restorations, Odessa
375	Hand's Elderly Auto Care, Grand Prairie
375	Hatfield Restorations, Canton
425	K & J Carriers Inc, Dallas
223	Larry Machacek, Porter
304	Mr G's Enterprises, Fort Worth
381	Roadrunner Tire & Auto, Fort Worth
352	Speed & Sport Chrome Plating Inc, Houston
382	STAR II, Goliad
421	Trailers Ltd, Morton
415	Wallace W Wade Specialty Tires, Dallas
356	Jon Ward Motorsports, Alpine
344	Weber's Nostalgia Supermarket, Fort Worth
210	Johnny Williams Services, Tyler
210	Chris M Zora ASA, ISA, Woodlands

Utah

294	High Performance Coatings, Salt Lake City

Vermont

374	Fuller's Restoration Inc, Manchester Center
377	Last Chance Repair & Restoration, Shaftsbury
379	Northern Motorsport Ltd, Wilder
202	Top Dead Center Apparel, Wells River
384	Westwinds Motor Car Co, Woodstock
440	The Woodie Works, Arlington

Virginia

370	Cedar Creek Coachworks Ltd, Stephens City
406	Flatlander's Hot Rods, Norfolk
196	International AutoSport Inc, Charlottesville
377	Land Yachts Automobile Restoration and Customizing, Virginia Beach
378	McAdam Motorcars Ltd, Yorktown
271	Roaring Twenties Antiques, Madison
384	WTH Service and Restorations Inc, Warrenton

Washington

261	Anacortes Brass Works Ltd, Anacortes
324	Automotive Bookstore, Seattle
204	Blair Collectors & Consultants, Seattle
435	Clean Sweep, Zillah
385	Don's Obsolete Auto Parts, Tacoma
439	New Era Motors, Vancouver
350	Nostalgic Reflections, Veradale
437	Old Car Woodgraining, Auburn
270	RB's Obsolete Automotive, Lynnwood
385	Don's Obsolete Auto Parts, Tacoma
419	The Bill Stevenson Company, Kent
409	The V8 Store, Vancouver
272	Vintage Auto Parts Inc, Woodinville
329	Vintage Books, Vancouver

West Virginia

266	Antique Auto Parts, Elkview

Wisconsin

310	Al's Auto Interiors, Spring Green
420	Captain Trailer Sales, Appleton
371	Clapper Restorations, Clinton
254	Classic Motors Inc, Union Grove
358	Glen Ray Radiators Inc, Wausau
335	International House of Toys, Muskego
269	Jack's Auto Ranch, Watertown
376	Ken's Klassics, Muscoda
422	MFR Enterprises, Wales

322	OJ Rallye Automotive, Plymouth
272	Vintage Vehicles Co Inc, Wautoma
272	BS Wisniewski Inc/Wizzy's, Milwaukee

Wyoming

257	Sam's Auto Sales & Parts, Cheyenne

Australia

259	Midel Pty Ltd, Lakemba
270	Obsolete Auto Parts Co, Kurrajong
386	Old Auto Rubber Company, Dunheved, Sydney

Belgium

310	Classic Car Lobby, 4800 Verviers
258	U S Oldies & Classics, Holsbeek

Canada

202	Aero International Auto Appraisals, Penhold, ALB
385	Atlantic Antique Auto Parts, Halifax, NS
324	Auto Nostalgia Enr, Mont St Gregoire, QC
368	Auto Sport Restoration, St Romain, QC
244	Eastern Specialty Automotive Sales & Service Ltd, Hammonds Plains, NS
319	EVA Sports Cars, Vankleek Hill, ONT
281	Ferris Auto Electric Ltd, North Bay, ONT
206	Freelance Appraisals Inc, Red Deer, ALB
207	Hawthorne Appraisals, Coaldale, ALB
296	McMillan Fender Sales/Truckin' Plus Fibreglass, Owen Sound, ONT
378	Memory Lane Motors, Fenelon Falls, ONT
227	Precision Babbitt Service, Beamsville, ONT
270	Pre-Sixties Cars and Parts Ltd, Holland Landing, ONT
271	Special Interest Cars, Oakville, ONT
390	Techni Decapage, Vaudreuil, QC
401	Toronto Vintage Vehicles, Islington, Toronto, ONT
310	Zehr Insurance Brokers Ltd, New Hamburg, ONT

Denmark

326	Kosters Motorboghandel, 8900 Randers
328	Samlerborsen, DK 1806 Frederiksberg C

England

323	All-American Auto Mags, Clive, Winsford, Cheshire
293	Double S Exhausts LP, Cullompton, Devon
255	Malcolm C Elder & Son, Oxfordshire
425	Interconti Forwarding Ltd, Devon
294	London Stainless Steel Exhaust Centre, London
318	Woolies (I&C Woolstenholmes Ltd), NR Peterborough

Germany

326	International Automobile Archives, 85757 Karlsfeld

Netherlands

357	Blaak Radiateurenbedryf, Heinenoord

New Zealand

201	Autosport Marketing, Christ Church
399	Mint Condition Auto Upholstery, Silverdale

Generalists

Section Three:
Clubs & Organizations

Since it began, the *Hemmings' Vintage Auto Almanac* has sought to present the most comprehensive list of old car hobby clubs and related organizations ever published. Here, with expanded listings and entries, the hobbyist will find six main categories:

Multi-marque clubs. Generally, these organizations welcome anyone with a sincere interest in the old car hobby. They are listed alphabetically by club name.

Marque clubs. These clubs specialize in serving enthusiasts of certain car makes. Some require ownership of the particular marque for membership. They are listed alphabetically by marque.

Registries. These are associations primarily interested in maintaining rosters of owners of particular marques, although some are also structured as actual clubs with activities, dues, events, etc. They are listed alphabetically by marque.

Specialty clubs. These are clubs with a specialized focus such as license plates, racing and other unique car subjects. They are listed alphabetically by club name.

Statewide and local clubs. These are organizations serving hobbyists within specific geographical area. They are listed alphabetically by state.

Legislative watch organizations. This is a listing of groups devoted to promoting and protecting the collector car hobby's interests in legislative matters. National organizations are listed first, followed by state/local groups. National and state/local groups are each listed alphabetically by organization name.

Multi-marque Clubs

356 Registry Inc
Barbara Skirmants
27244 Ryan Rd
Warren, MI 48092
810-558-3692; FAX: 810-558-3616

Founded 1974. 5,300 members. No restrictions to join, ownership is not required. Local and national events and a complete listing of local clubs, free classified ads to members. The most complete source of parts and suppliers for the Porsche 356 model car. Bi-monthly publication (on every odd numbered month), *356 Registry*, 50 page color cover magazine with 5-8 full feature color articles every year. Technical, mechanical and restoration articles. Historical information and book reviews. Literature and model collecting, vintage racing coverage. Dues: $25/year US, $35/year Canada/Mexico, $45/year International.

48 'N Under Inc
708 Water St
Sauk City, WI 53583
608-643-8146

For membership information, contact at the above address: George Koehler. Founded 1966. 27 members. Must want to own an old car or be in the process of buying or restoring one before membership is accepted. Dues: $7.50/year individual, $15/year couple.

A Merry Car Club
Resp Nieuwlandt Peter
116 Langestraat
9300 Aalst, Belgium
011-32-702861; FAX: 011-32-710653

Founded 1985. 300 members. Dedicated to the preservation, restoration and maintenance of American cars over 25 years old. Bimonthly publication, Dutch/French, 40 pages. Lots of stories, technical and humorous. 10 plus or minus meetings year. Spare parts service and others. Dues: 2.000 BEF.

50s & 60s Cruisin' Car Club
PO Box 22001
St Petersburg, FL 33742-2001

See full listing **on page 501**

The Alberta Post-War Car Society
PO Box 1221
Edmonton, AB Canada T5J 2M4
403-467-0074

Founded 1976. 110 members. The society is dedicated to the preservation, restoration and enjoyment of cars built in the post-war era. We recognize cars manufactured from 1945 to 15 years of age. Ownership of a vehicle is not necessary, just the enjoyment of them. We are an active club with many day trips and outings throughout the year. We do not stop activities in the winter months. Dues: $30/year.

American Motors Club Olympic Peninsula
5851 NE Lincoln Rd E
Poulsbo, WA 98370
360-598-4449

Founded 1996. 10+ members. AMC OP is a new and growing Olympic Peninsula based chapter of AMC World Clubs. Serves the Olympic Peninsula region of Washington state. Membership is open to all enthusiasts of AMC, Nash, Hudson, AM General and Jeep vehicles manufactured by American Motors Corporation from 1954 to 1987. Meets monthly and has newsletter, free ads, local parts sources and network, participates in local and regional shows and racing events, plus much more. Dues: $10/year.

American Motorsport International
7963 Depew St
Arvada, CO 80003-2527
303-428-8760; FAX: 303-428-1070

Founded 1987. International club for owners and enthusiasts of American Motors cars, 1955 to 1988. Large bimonthly club publication. Dues: $25/year. Parent organization is AMC World Clubs, Inc. Telephone-tech and restoration help six days a week for members.

American Station Wagon Owners Association
6110 Bethesda Way
Indianapolis, IN 46254-5060
317-291-0321

Founded 1996. 80+ members. The American Station Wagon Owners Association is dedicted to the preservation of this great vehicle and is open to anyone with a sincere interest in wagons. Members receive a quarterly, full color newsletter, *The Wagon Roundup*. Benefits of membership include a window decal and free advertisement in the newsletter. The first annual ASWOA convention will be held in Indianapolis, Indiana in July of 1997. Call or write for more information. Dues: $20/year.

American Truck Historical Society
300 Office Park Dr
Birmingham, AL 35223
205-870-0566; FAX: 205-870-3069

For membership information, contact at the above address: Larry L Scheef, Managing Director. Founded 1971. 15,300 members. Maintains library and archives containing history, photos and films of the truck industry. Bimonthly magazine: Wheels of Time. Membership has increased to $25/year US, $35/year Canada (US) and we now have over 19,000 members. Annual *ATHS Show Time* color album, $20.

Antique Automobile Club of America
501 W Governor Road
PO Box 417
Hershey, PA 17033
717-534-1910 AACA; 534-2082 library

Founded 1935. 55,000 members. Dedicated to the preservation, restoration and maintenance of automobiles and automotive history. Bi-monthly publication: *Antique Automobile*. Prospective membership sponsor not mandatory. Library and research center services available. Dues: $24/year individual, $26/year couple.

regions:

Alabama *Boll Weevil Region, Allen Kahl, 6 Palomino Rd, Phenix City, AL 36867*

Central Alabama Region, David A Fletcher, 3507 Vaughn Rd, Montgomery, AL 36106

Deep South Region, John L Reid, 2601 Mountbrook Dr, Mobile, AL 36693

Dixie Region, Janice L Hyche, 3294 Hillard Dr, Birmingham, AL 35243

Muscle Shoals Region, Donald K Helton, Rt 10 Box 8B, Florence, AL 35633

Northeast Alabama Region, Kitta Vanpelt, 108 Tabor Ct, Gadsden, AL 35901

South Alabama Region, Minnie P Casey, 122 Casey St, Brewton, AL 36427

Tennessee Valley Region, Lloyd W Culp, 1819 Corrine Ave, SW, Decatur, AL 35601

Alaska *Antique Auto Mushers of Alaska Region, George B Chase, 7341 Clairborne Dr, Anchorage, AK 99502*

Vernon L. Nash Antique Auto Club of Fairbanks Region, Mebble Hansen, 502 McKinley Dr, Fairbanks, AK 99712

Arizona *A.A.C.M.E. Region, Karen Rodgers, 2901 N 80th Ln, Phoenix, AZ 85033*

Metro Phoenix Region, Edwin T Cain Jr, 19616 N 37th Way, Phoenix, AZ 85024

Sedona Car Club Region, George Brush, 530 Concho Dr, Sedona, AZ 86351

Southern Arizona Vintage Motorcycle Enthusiasts Region, Karen A Barnett, 5561 W Louisiana St, Tucson, AZ 85746

Tucson Region, Bill Schoening, 542 N Country Club Rd, Tucson, AZ 85716

California *Antelope Valley Region, David Floyd, 3235 East Ave, H-6, Lancaster, CA 93535*

Cabrillo Region, Jack Passey Jr, 425 Hecker Pass Rd, Watsonville, CA 95076

California Region, Patricia Thibos, 4081 Tulare Ct, Concord, CA 94521

El Camino Region, Sandy Fiehmann, 1676 McGregor Way, San Jose, CA 95129

Foothills Region, Richard E Eckert, 1623 Ben Roe Dr, Los Altos, CA 94024

Golden Gate Region, John H Marshall, 100 Meriam Dr, San Rafael, CA 94903

Kern County Region, George Blackledge, 229 Montalvo Dr, Bakersfield, CA 93309

Monterey Bay Classic European Motorcycle Club Region, Mario Saviano, 450-A Hilby Ave, Seaside, CA 93955

Mother Lode Region, Duane C Bennett, PO Box 424, Sonora, CA 95370

Northern California Antique Motorcycle Region, Lloyd Riggs, 880 Hawthorne Dr, Walnut Creek, CA 94546

Orange County Region, Kenneth A Brody, 19303 Barroso St, Rowland Heights, CA 91748

Palm Springs Region, Bill Rothenbuhler, 4972 Hilton Head Dr, Banning, CA 92220

Redwood Empire Region, Allan C St Marie, 838 Lightwood Ct, Rohnert Park, CA 94928

Salinas Valley Region, Edward A McGlochin, East Garzas Rd, Carmel Valley, CA 93924

San Diego Region, Dan W Conner, 16514 Casero Rd, San Diego, CA 92128

San Diego Region, Fallbrook Vintage Car Chapter, Jack Splitstone, 1647 Via Vista, Fallbrook, CA 92028

San Luis Obispo Region, John Osborne, Rt 1, Box 65A, Templeton, CA 93465

Santa Barbara Region, Michael McLaughlin, 3718 Essex St, Santa Barbara, CA 93105

Santa Clarita Valley Region, Warren C Russell, 23649 Mill Valley Rd, Valencia, CA 91355

Southern California Region, Duane Kjellin, 519 Paseo De Los Reyes, Redondo Beach, CA 90277

Southern California Region, Valley Chapter, John H Avans, 23614 Neargate Dr, Newhall, CA 91321

Southwestern Two Wheelers Region, Harry McGill, 1261 Emory St, Imperial Beach, CA 91932

Sun and Sand Region, C Erik Baltzar, 44750 San Pascual, PO Box 1331, Palm Desert, CA 92261

Valle Del Sur Region, Robert H Vonkonsky, 5543 Drysdale Dr, San Jose, CA 95124

Valley of the Flowers Region, Robert McCarthy, 425 South C St, Lompoc, CA 93436

Colorado *Poudre Valley Region, Dan Henderson, 3824 Nite Ct, Ft Collins, CO 80525*

Rocky Mountain Region, Denver Chapter, Ted G Rossi, 1325 W 148th Ave, Westminster, CO 80020

Rocky Mountain Region, Ted G Rossi, 1325 W 148th Ave, Westminster, CO 80020

Ye Olde Auto Club Chapter, J D Bernard, 14706 E 134th Pl, Brighton, CO 80601

Connecticut *Central Connecticut Region, George Scheyd, 97 Fleetwood Rd, Newington, CT 06111*

Connecticut Valley Region, Edward F Lafleur, 24 Ames Ave, West Springfield, MA 01089

Fairfield County Connecticut Region, Ralph DeAngelis, 1321 Hope St, Stamford, CT 06907

Gateway Antique Auto Club Region, Peter A Cavanna, 636 Hope St, Stamford, CT 06907

Housatonic Valley Region, Clifford B Pomeroy Jr, 115 Upland Rd, New Milford, CT 06776

Shoreline Antique Auto Club Region, Mrs Marlis Jacobowitz, 341 Fitch Hill Rd, Uncasville, CT 06382

Delaware *Brandywine Region*, Mel Chase, 242 Cheltenham Rd, Newark, DE 19711

District of Columbia *National Capital Region/* W E Peugh, 4405 Dittmar, Alexandria, VA 22207

Florida *Ancient City Region*, A Frank Phillips, 20 Contera Dr, St. Augustine, FL 32084

Azalea Region, Frank A Frohlich, 7677 Oak Forest Rd, PO Box 405, Lake Geneva, FL 32160

Cape Canaveral Region, Philip S Levine, 1501 Orange St, Melbourne Beach, FL 32951

Edison Region, Wanda Hodge, 218 SE 20th Ct, Cape Coral, FL 33990

Florida Region, Steven C Cooley Sr, 33550 CR 44B, Eustis, FL 32726

Florida West Coast Region, John Blackard, 14968 Imperial Point Dr N, Largo, FL 34644

Fort Lauderdale Region, Nancy J Brandt, 2933 NW 17th Terr, Fort Lauderdale, FL 33311

Highland Lakes Region, David H Root, 210 Bay Blossom Dr, Sebring, FL 33870

Hillsborough Region, Mario Acosta III, 3404 Tampa Bay Blvd, Tampa, FL 33607

Imperial Polk Region, Jack K Highnan, 3224 Carlton Cir W, Lakeland, FL 33803

Indian River Region, George Button II, 239 Spinnaker Dr, Vero Beach, FL 32963

Kingdom of the Sun Region, Carol A Scoglio, 2506 NE 19th Ct, Ocala, FL 34470

Kissimmee-St. Cloud Region, Patricia G Wilson, 2334 St Croix St, Kissimmee, FL 34741

Lemon Bay Region, Paul E Webb, 418 Cypress Forest Dr, Englewood, FL 34223

Lemon Bay Region, Royal Palm Chapter, Richard F Ellsworth, PO Box 381151, Murdock, FL 33938

Lemon Bay Region, Venice Chapter, Peter A Chapman, 1817 Flametree Ln, Venice, FL 34293

Miracle Strip Region, Joseph A Lynn, 4504 Baywood Dr, Lynn Haven, FL 32444

Naples-Marco Island Region, Robert E Vik, 2209 Regal Way, Naples, FL 33942

North Central Florida Region, Don McCullen, 9325 NW 59th Ln, Gainesville, FL 32606

Northeast Florida Region, Gail L Gaynor, 2284 Constitution Dr, Orange Park, FL 32073

Peace River Region, Jim Kantor, 410 Medici Ct, Punta Gorda, FL 33950

Richey Region, Jack E Helmig, 5231 Manor Dr, New Port Richey, FL 34652

South Florida Region, Bob B Mayer, 10285 SW 135th St, Miami, FL 33176

Space Coast Region, Floyd L Dodd, 1785 Cowan Dr, Titusville, FL 32796

Sunshine Region, Ardis B Thorpe, 4979 Hubner Cir, Sarasota, FL 34241

Sunshine Region, Rare Birds of Florida Chapter, W Arnold Slight, 1197 Larchmont Dr, Englewood, FL 34223

Suwannee River Region, Tommie W Richardson, Rt 3, Box 387-H, Ft White, FL 32038

Tallahassee Region, Dan E Rainey Sr, 910 San Luis Rd, Tallahassee, FL 32304

Treasure Coast Region, Edward D Levy, 4380 NE Joe's Point Rd, Stuart, FL 34996

Vintage Auto Club Palm Beach Region, Leonard Symons, PO Box 4051, Lantana, FL 33465

Vintage Wheels of Manatee County Region, Arthur W Engelhard, 5306 7th Ave Dr W/ Bradenton, FL 34209

Volusia Region, Nick Uhl, PO Box 439, Oak Hills, FL 32759

,est Florida Region, Todd F Chappell, 30 Wilkes Dr, Pensacola FL 32503

Wheels in Motion Flagler County Chapter, Norman A Walker, 18 S Claymont Ct, Palm Coast, FL 32137

Georgia *Apple Country of North Georgia Region*, Roy W Smith, 22 Logan St, Ellijay, GA 30540

Artesian City Region, Lillian Law, 3205 Sylvester Rd, Lot 14, Albany, GA 31705

Athens, Georgia Region, Harold Stephenson, Rt 1, Box 225, Winterville, GA 30683

Brunswick-Golden Isles Region, James F Simpson, 1322 E Oak St, St Simons Island, GA 31522

Cherokee Region, Norman C Layton, PO Box 922, Cartersville, GA 30120

Clocktower Region, Terry Maloney, 9 Meadow Lake Cir, Rome, GA 30161

Coastal Georgia of Savannah Region, Raymond Daiss, Rt 3, Box 449, Savannah, GA 31406

Georgia-Alabama Region, Brannon D Williams, 127 Pine Terr, Pine Mountain, GA 31822

Griffin Piedmont Region, Howell A Fowler Jr, 2435 Fayetteville Rd, Griffin, GA 30223

Middle Georgia Region, Charles H Johnson, PO Box 1689, Byron, GA 31008

Northeast Georgia Antique Auto Region, James H Kinney, Rt 2, Box 303, Mt Airy, GA 30563

Northwest Georgia Region, H Francis Brantley, 2500 Ravine Way N, Dalton, GA 30720

Pecan Region, Benjamin Parker, 7649 Summerhill Rd, Boston, GA 31626

Pecan Region, Taylor County Old Car Chapter, Tom Williams, Rt 2, Box 38-A, Perry, FL 32347

Southeastern Region, James E Cain, 163 Big Canoe, Jasper, GA 30143

Sowega Region, Bill Flowers, PO Box 751, Cairo, GA 31728

Tiftarea Region, Stephen L Millette, 2214 Meadowbrook Dr, Tifton, GA 31794

West Georgia Region, Robert Myers, 109 Golfview Ct, Carrollton, GA 30117

Hawaii   *Aloha Region, H Cecil Fasick, 44-615 Kaneohe Bay Dr, Kaneohe, HI 96744*

Idaho   *North Idaho-Phans Region, Ernie Booth, PO Box 246, Athol, ID 83801*

Illinois   *Illinois Brass Touring Region, Howard Deyoung, 2929 Danne Rd, Crete, IL 60417*

Illinois Region, Charles J Kuhn, 2206 Catherine St, Northbrook, IL 60062

Illinois Region, Des Plaines Valley Chapter, Lee E Nelson, 522 S Washington St, Lockport, IL 60441

Illinois Region, Fox Valley Chapter, Arthur H Swanson, 14N330 French Rd, Hampshire, IL 60140

Illinois Region, Gas & Brass Chapter, Donald H Sonichsen, 308 W Kentucky Rd, Beecher, IL 60401

Illinois Region, Momence Chapter, Eldon M Fraser, 615 Jonette Ave, Bradley, IL 60915

Illinois Region, North Shore Chapter, James M Rubenstein, 2880 Idelwood Ln, Highland Park, IL 60035

Illinois Region, Silver Springs Chapter, Norman Olson, 615 N Lafayette, Sandwich, IL 60548

Illinois Region, Waukegan Chapter, George Schurrer, 5502 Chasefield Cir, McHenry, IL 60050

Illinois Valley Region, David Moss, 2355 Ridgefield Rd, Princeton, IL 61356

Mississippi Valley Region, Don Mitchell, 717 N Main St, Port Byron, IL 61275

Muddy T Region, Howard DeYoung, 2929 E Danne Rd, Crete, IL 60417

Southern Illinois Region, William L Morse, 396 May Apple Ln, Carbondale, IL 62901

Indiana   *St Joe Valley Region, Richard W Chandler, 68244 Cassopolis Rd, Cassopolis, MI 49031*

White River Valley Region, Anna D Cousins, 7355 Mikesell Dr, Indianapolis, IN 46260

Iowa   *Cedar Rapids Region/ Fredric G Templer, 139 Heath St NW, Cedar Rapids, IA 52405*

Cedar Valley Region, Ronald L Adams, 2777 Larrabee Ave, Denver, IA 50622

Des Moines Region, Richard Hardie, 6840 Panorama Dr, Panora, IA 50216

Iowa Great Lakes Region, Jay E Prather, 421 W 11th St, Spencer, IA 51301

Iowa Valley Region, James J Conrey, 205 W 6th St, West Liberty, IA 52776

Marshalltown Area Restorers Region, Dale E Benskin, 1201 S 3rd Ave, Marshalltown, IA 50158

Niapra Region, Floyd Burton, 11987 Co Hwy D25, Alden, IA 50006

Niva Region, H W Montgomery, 780 W 6th St, Garner, IA 50438

Siouxland Region, Robert Sweeney, 4120 Stone Ave, Sioux City, IA 51106

Tall Corn Region, Raymond D Elsberry, PO Box 565, Ogden, IA 50212

Kansas   *Cherokee Strip Region, Stephen W Smith, 1705 West Estates, Arkansas City, KS 67005*

Lawrence Region, George M Lauppe, 1309 N 1056 Rd, Lawrence, KS 66046

Topeka Region, Earl A Goheen Jr, 3234 SW 11th St, Topeka, KS 66604

Kentucky   *Blue Grass, David C Estes, 2242 Sulphur Well Rd, Nicholasville, KY 40356*

Kyana Region, Jim Hicks, 112 W Flaget St, Bardstown, KY 40004

Lincoln Trail Region, Jerry T Mills, 6495 Bardstown Rd, Elizabethtown, KY 42701

Northern Kentucky Region, James T Schrimpf, 1231 Anderson Ferry Rd, Cincinnati, OH 45238

Southern Kentucky Region, Frank J Fox, 10461 US Hwy 431 S, Dunmor, KY 42339

Twin Lakes Region, Howard Brandon, Hazel Hwy, Rt 4, Murray, KY 42071

Louisiana   *Louisiana Region, Baton Rouge Chapter, Charlie Matthews, 901 Sharp Rd, Baton Rouge, LA 70815*

Louisiana Region, Central Louisiana Chapter, Rodger Peters, 2710 Patty Dr, Pineville, LA 71360

Louisiana Region, Contraband Chapter, Lee Roy Meaux, 225 Hazel St, Sulphur, LA 70663

Louisiana Region, Crescent City Chapter, August S Lorio, 120 Cameron, Gretna, IA 70056

Louisiana Region, Evangeline Chapter, Glenn Noto, 316 St Pierre Blvd, Carencro, LA 70520

Louisiana Region, Patrick J Lehrmann, 3408 Lyndell Dr, Chalmette, LA 70043

Louisiana Region, Slidell Antique Car Chapter, George D Huntington, 61439 N Military Rd, Slidell, LA 70461

Louisiana Region, St Bernard Chapter, Joseph Lebeau Jr, 3633 Charles Dr, Chalmette, LA 70043

Maine   *Maine Region, Jeffrey C Orwig, 123 Paris Hill Rd #21, South Paris, ME 04281*

Maryland   *Bay Country Region, Paul Connolly, 28372 Oaklands Rd, Easton, MD 21601*

Chesapeake Region, Harry E Wilhelm Jr, 7220 Kennebunk Rd, Baltimore, MD 21244

Eastern Shore Region, George C Rubenson Jr, 717 Burning Tree Cir, Salisbury, MD 21801

Harford Region, Larry L Leedy, 2903 Grier Nursery Rd, Forest Hill, MD 21050

Mason-Dixon Region, J Stanley Stratton, 2390 Woodstock Rd, Chambersburg, PA 17201

Model A Ford Foundation Region, Howard A Minners, 4700 Locust Hill Ct, Bethesda, MD 20814

Queen City Region, Jeanne E Eaton, 10103 Town Creek Rd NE, Flinstone, MD 21530

Sugarloaf Mountain Region, Hunter L Mauck, PO Box 251, Clarksburg, MD 20871

Massachusetts   *Massachusetts Region, Lawrence A Grassie, 301 King St, Raynham, MA 02767*

Michigan   *Blue Water Region, Gary L Minnie, 7700 State Rd, Burtchville, MI 48059*

Boyne Country Region, Patrick J Kubesh, 632 State St, Boyne City, MI 49712

Flint Region, Dougal Brow, 4224 Leith St, Burton, MI 48509

Inland Lakes Region, Janet Lockwood, 178 Michelson Rd, Houghton Lake, MI 48629

Irish Hills Region, Beth McGowen, 418 Glenwood St, Delta, OH 43515

Northwestern Michigan Region, Clarence V Smith, 1086 Rasho Rd, Traverse City, MI 49684

Saginaw Valley Region, Richard Humphreys, 666 Belair Dr, Saginaw, MI 48603

Sanilac Region, Michael Forton, 4407 French Line Rd, Applegate, MI 48401

West Michigan Region, Stanley Windemuller, A-11664 Graafschap Rd, Holland, MI 49423

Wolverine State Region, Robert A Gilstorff, 16751 Merriman, Romulus, MI 48174

Minnesota Minnesota Region, 412 Lakes Chapter, Duane P Wething, 1241 Summit, Detroit Lakes, MN 56501

Minnesota Region, Arrowhead Chapter, Raymond H Rodenwald, 4110 E Superior St, Duluth, MN 55804

Minnesota Region, Capitol City Chapter, Dale E Ives, 1884 N Adolphus St, St Paul, MN 55117

Minnesota Region, Central Chapter, Duane C Shuck, 9304 Nicollet Ave, Bloomington, MN 55420

Minnesota Region, Dairyland Chapter, Willis H Selle, 1440 US Hwy 63, Turtle Lake, WI 54889

Minnesota Region, Hiawatha Chapter, Robert J Ronningen, 5617 Villa Rd NW, Rochester, MN 55901

Minnesota Region, Little Crow Chapter, Russell N Johnson, 7230 159th St NE, Atwater, MN 56209

Minnesota Region, Mille Lacs Lake Chapter, Harold O Thorsbakken, 12723 St Hwy 23, Milaca, MN 56353

Minnesota Region, Old Abe Chapter, Paul E Rydning, 3528 London Rd, Eau Claire, WI 54701

Minnesota Region, Pioneer Chapter, Thomas F Rasmussen, 4365 Virginia Ave, Shoreview, MN 55126

Minnesota Region, Prairieland Chapter, Arlo L Raatz, 711 9th St N, New Ulm, MN 56073

Minnesota Region, River Bend Chapter, Wayne Mediger, 221 Nash, Belle Plaine, MN 56011

Minnesota Region, Thomas H Leafgren, 5630 Omar Ave N, Stillwater, MN 55082

Minnesota Region, Viking Chapter, A Peter Johnson, Rt 1, Box 3, Houston, MN 55943

Mississippi Catahoula Junque Collectors Association Region, Paula Gould, 97 Model T Cir, Monroeville, AL 36460

Missouri Gateway City Region, Paul Meyer, 11694 Mark Twain, Bridgeton, MO 63044

KC Metro Region, James H Clyde, 3756 N 83rd St, Kansas City, KS 66109

Show Me Region, Raymond H Metzler, 10429 Gregory Ct, St Louis, MO 63128

Nebraska Omaha Region, Larry Rader, 8933 N 56th Ave Cir, Omaha, NE 68152

Trailblazers Region, Leon Kriesel, HC 77 Box 2, Gurley, NE 69141

Nevada Northern Nevada Region, Charles D Wells, 936 Copperwood Dr, Fallon, NV 89406

New Jersey Ankokas Region, Robert A Petters, 382 Thurman Ave, West Berlin, NJ 08091

Curved Dash Olds Owners Club Region, Robert Giuliani, 72 Northwood Ave, Demarest, NJ 07627

Garden State Half Century Region, John Memmelaar Jr, 305 Forsythia Ct, Franklin Lakes, NJ 07417

Garden State Model A Region, Charles B Epley, 870 Rambler Ave, Runnemede, NJ 08078

Jersey Cape Region, David A Gross, 441 Eighth Ave, Absecon Highlands, NJ 08201

Mid-Jersey Region, Raymond Bouchard, 2 W Laurelwood Dr, Lawrenceville, NJ 08648

New Jersey Region, David L Zimmerman, 6 Tainter St, PO Box 213, Peapack, NJ 07977

New Jersey Region, Depression Vehicles Chapter, Doris M Werndly, 164 Bowden Rd, Cedar Grove, NJ 07009

New Jersey Region, Watchung Mountain Chapter, John Bedner, 82 Ravine Dr, Colonia, NJ 07067

South Jersey Region, Ronald W Scott, 1714 Herbert Blvd, Williamstown, NJ 08094

New Mexico Eastern New Mexico Region, Mary Ellen Cater, 226 New Mexico 88, Portales, NM 88130

Southeastern New Mexico Region, Belva J Martin, 501 W Gold, Hobbs, NM 88240

Valley Vintage Motorcar Region, Ron Wagoner, 1110 San Juan Dr, Roswell, NM 88201

New York Algonquin Region, Rich Stenman, 8 Cortland St, Norwich, NY 13815

Batavia Region, Thomas J Kuter Sr, 563 Riga Mumford Rd, Churchville, NY 14428

Black River Valley Region, Frederick J Killian III, 241 Charles St, Watertown, NY 13601

Catskill Region, Lou Kiefer, 47 Cooper Rd, Monticello, NY 12701

Chatauqua Lake Region, Margaret V Naetzker, 2130 S Maple, Ashville, NY 14710

Chemung Valley Region, Robert E Tripp, 26 William St, Hornell, NY 14843

F.R. Porter Region, Andrew Netusil, 586 Rt 25A, Rocky Point, NY 11778

Fingerlakes Region, Brian D Parker, 2377 W Genessee Turnpike, Camillus, NY 13031

Genesee Valley Antique Car Society Region, Carolyn A Pulver, 24 Blandford Ln, Fairport, NY 14450

Greater New York Region, Richard J Carrano, 581 Gaynor Pl, West Hempstead, NY 11552

Greenwood Lake Region, Ronald Proscia, 265 Buckshollow Road, Mahopac, NY 10541

Iroquois Region, Gary Muehlbauer, 102 Martin Ave, Johnson City, NY 13790

Kinzua Valley Region, David A Metcalf, 607 West St, Warren, PA 16365

Lake Erie Region, Edward Ferber, 431 Lake Breeze, Angola, NY 14006

Livingston Region, Mark Rowland, PO Box 142, Livonia, NY 14487

Mid-Hudson Region, Helmuth F Bihn, 673 South Rd, Poughkeepsie, NY 12601

Clubs & Organizations

Clubs & Organizations

New York State Allegheny Valley Region, Joe Oliver, 3298 Maple Ave, Allegany, NY 14706

Onaquaga Region, Stanley A Lovelace, 3537 NY Rt 79, Harpursville, NY 13787

Oneida Lake Region, Howard J Miller, 137 Northwood Way, Camillus, NY 13031

Peconic Bay Region, Margaret M Vitale, 951 Hawkins Ave, PO Box 1254, Lake Grove, NY 11755

Ramapo Valley Region, Dr Stephen Lazar, 7 Arcadian Dr, Spring Valley, NY 10977

Rolling Antiquers Old Car Club Norwich Region, Raymond C Hart /PO Box 168, Norwich, NY 13815

Schoharie Valley Region, Ronald Davis, RD 2, Box 935, Cobleskill, NY 12043

St Lawrence-Adirondack Region, Keitha J MacIntire, Riverside Heights, Box 218, Raymondville, NY 13678

Staten Island Region, Philip Boffa, 4 Merrick Ct, Middletown, NJ 07748

Tioga Antique Auto Club Region, Howard Seymour, 25 Stratton Rd, Newark Valley, NY 13811

Vanderbilt Cup Region, Arthur Gould, 6 Dolores Ln, Ft Salonga, NY 11768

Wayne Drumlins Antique Auto Region, Beverly J Good, 712 Waterloo Geneva Rd, Waterloo, NY 13165

Westchester NY Region, Richard E Marks, 2 Sudbury Dr, Yonkers, NY 10710

Whiteface Mountain Region, Spencer A Egglefield, High St, Elizabethtown, NY 12932

Wyoming Valley Region, James Fox, 18 High St, Attica, NY 14011

North Carolina Foothills Region, Calvin C Moore Sr, 5000 Forest Ridge Dr, Hickory, NC 28602

Hornets Nest Region, Robert M Moore, 4807 Pioneer Ln, Matthews, NC 28105

Land of the Sky Region, John A Marotta, 2 Sedgefield Dr, Candler, NC 28715

Mountaineer Region, Robert J Schiess, PO Box 477, Balsam, NC 28707

North Carolina Region, Alamance Chapter, Sylvia B Smith, 407 Boggs Ranch Rd, Graham, NC 27253

North Carolina Region, Cape Fear Chapter, William Johnson, 617 Porters Neck Rd, Wilmington, NC 28405

North Carolina Region, Coastal Plains Chapter, Linwood Lewis, Rt 4, Box 285, Washington, NC 27889

North Carolina Region, East Carolina Chapter, Denise Breton, Rt 2 , Box 143M, Angier, NC 27501

North Carolina Region, First Capital Antique Car Club Chapter, Bruce H Ashley, 104 Plantation Dr, New Bern, NC 28562

North Carolina Region, Fresh Water Chapter, Walter R Linhardt, 105 Waterlilly Loop, Edenton, NC 27932

North Carolina Region, Furniture Land Chapter, Lawrence Ridge, 1705 Sexton Rd, Denton, NC 27239

North Carolina Region, General Greene Chapter, Jerry Bodden, 1442 Town Creek Rd, Eden, NC 27288

North Carolina Region, Hillbilly Chapter, Don Lewis Sprinkle, 9 Eller Ford Rd, Weaverville, NC 28787

North Carolina Region, Morehead City Chapter, Carl L Tilghman, 269 Copeland Rd, Beaufort, NC 28516

North Carolina Region, New River Chapter, Herb Oakes, 102 Converse Dr, Jacksonville, NC 28546

North Carolina Region, North Central Chapter, Jimmy C Lawson, 127 Martindale Dr, Danville, VA 24541

North Carolina Region, Old Salem Chapter, Larry C Shore, 751 Hallmark Dr, Rural Hall, NC 27045

North Carolina Region, San-Lee Chapter, David Jones, 2009 Hamilton Dr, Sanford, NC 27330

North Carolina Region, Sherman M Carey, 110 Terrace Pl, Lincolnton, NC 28092

North Carolina Region, Triangle Chapter, Ted Brooks, 5005 Fielding Dr, Raleigh, NC 27606

North Carolina Region, Uwharrie Chapter, Howard Smith, 8215 Castor Rd, Salisbury, NC 28146

North Carolina Region, Zooland Chapter, Jerry Rook, 5081 Burton Rd, Thomasville, NC 27360

Transylvania Region, Jerry M Arnold, PO Box 268, Brevard, NC 28712

North Dakota Magic City Region, Allen Larson, 516 23rd St NW, Minot, ND 58701

North Dakota Region, Devils Lake Chapter, Glenn Lannoye, Woodland Pl, Devils Lake, ND 58301

North Dakota Region, Gary G Keller, 507 Schroeder Dr, Grand Forks, ND 58201

North Dakota Region, Red River Chapter, Geneva Olstad, 5012 Co Rd 31, Fargo, ND 58102

Ohio Ohio Region, Canton Chapter, Glenn D Tschantz, 312 E Chestnut St, Orrville, OH 44667

Ohio Region, Central Chapter, Dick L Marsh, 149 Fairfield Ave, Newark, OH 43055

Ohio Region, Commodore Perry Chapter, Earl R Conrad, 350 Beebe Ave, Elyria, OH 44035

Ohio Region, Evelyn M Rush, 3895 Clotts Rd, Gahanna, OH 43230

Ohio Region, Meander Chapter, Ben R McMullin, 45 Forest Hill Dr, Hubbard, OH 44425

Ohio Region, Northern Chapter, Robert J McAnlis, 8359 Eaton Dr, Chagrin Falls, OH 44023

Ohio Region, Southern Chapter, Nora J Schreel, 3104 Catalpa Dr, Dayton, OH 45405

Ohio Region, Western Reserve Chapter, Shirley M Payne, 3518 Austinburg Rd, Ashtabula, OH 44004

Oklahoma Cimmaron Region, John Pollock, 19500 NE Meador Ln, Harrah, OK 73045

Enid, Oklahoma Region, Mark A Jones, 302 E Cedar Ave, Enid, OK 73701

Okie Region, Nancy J English, R4 Box 19B, Lindsay, OK 73052

Tulsa Region, Joe D Smith, 5400 E Princeton St, Broken Arrow, OK 74014

Pennsylvania *Allegheny Mountain Region,* Governors' Chapter, Mervin S Lucas, 531 E Beaver St, Bellefonte, PA 16823

Allegheny Mountain Region, Russell G Bambarger, 205 E Seycamore St, Snow Shoe, PA 16874

Anthracite Region, Joseph S Forish, 607 E Blaine St, McAdoo, PA 18237

Butler-Old Stone House Region, John W Maharg /146 Valencia Rd, Renfrew, PA 16053

Central Mountains Region, Charles J Ross, 110 S Third St, PO Box 247, Clearfield, PA 16830

Coke Center Region, Bruce W Sleasman, 233 S 5th St, Youngwood, PA 15697

Covered Bridge Region, Ronald L Wilson, 12 Grove St, Washington, PA 15301

Delaware Valley Region, Fred Schempp, 1301 Snyder Rd, Lansdale, PA 19446

Endless Mountains Region, Howard Crain, RD 2, Box 223, Towanda, PA 18848

Flood City Region, David A Mihalko Jr, 2507 Park Ave, Windber, PA 15963

Fort Bedford Region, George A Greenawalt, RR 1, Box 97, Manns Choice, PA 15550

Gettysburg Region, Gerald D Black, 125 Hunterstown Rd, Gettysburg, PA 17325

Hershey Region, James R Nowak, 5912 Jacobs Ave, Harrisburg, PA 17112

Keystone Region, Adam W Anderson, 30 S Madison Ave, Upper Darby, PA 19082

Kiski Valley Region, James Vigna, 324 Harrison Ave, Leechburg, PA 15656

Kit-Han-Ne Region, William E Clepper, RD 1, Box 13, Cowansville, PA 16218

Lakelands Region, Daryl R Timko, 5947 Everett Hull Rd, Fowler, OH 44418

Lanchester Region, Albert E Storrs Jr, 105 Main Line Dr, Coatesville, PA 19320

Laurel Highlands Region, Howard J Finney, 267 Lancewood Pl, Greensburg, PA 15601

Lehigh Valley Region, Roland W Hoffman, Box 2082, Fox Gap Rd, Bangor, PA 18013

Mon Valley Region, Myron L Shoaf, RD 1, Box 1015, Ruffsdale, PA 15679

Northeastern Pennsylvania Region, Donna Martin, 172 Old East End Blvd, Wilkes-Barre, PA 18702

Northwestern Pennsylvania Region /Leroy E Lindsey, 11871 Rt 6 W, Corry, PA 16407

Ontelaunee Region, Burton A Johnson, 3627 Sunrise Ave, Allentown, PA 18103

Pennsylvania Dutch Region, George W Ulrich, 1040 E Cherry St, Palmyra, PA 17078

Pennsylvania Oil Region, Donald N Hull, PO Box 65, Cranberry, PA 16319

Pittsburgh Golden Triangle Region, William H Salvatora Jr, 251 Fassinger Rd, Evans City, PA 16033

Pocono Region, Jake Matthenius, 516 Victory Ave, Phillipsburg, NJ 08865

Pottstown Region, Stephen R Stastney, 1131 Graber Rd, Red Hill, PA 18076

Presque Isle Region, Daryl Waldinger, 3650 Hartman Rd, Erie, PA 16510

Presque Isle Region, French Creek Valley Chapter, Everett L Hites, RD 2, Box 373, Albion, PA 16401

Punxsutawney Region, Shannock Valley Car Club Chapter, David Powers, 815 Main St, Rural Valley, PA 16249

Punxsutawney Region, William C Bertres, RD 1, Box 552, Marion Center, PA 15759

Scranton Region, Mary Volz, 1921 E Elm St, Scranton, PA 18505

Shenango Valley Region, James B Kistler, 5055 Hoagland-Blackstub Rd, Cortland, OH 44410

Shikellamy Region, George O Campbell, Rt 1, Box 1118, Hughsville, PA 17737

Snapper's Brass and Gas Touring Region, Randall F Hall Jr, 8061 Rowan Rd, Cranberry Twp, PA 16066

Sugar Bush Region, Merle W Weyand, Rt 3, Box 77, Rockwood, PA 15557

Susquehanna Valley Region, Alvin C Rex, RR 4, Box 4019, Berwick, PA 18603

Susquehannock Region, Larry A Keller, 1021 Washington Blvd, Williamsport, PA 17701

Valley Forge Region, William Neth Jr, 3000 Tower Rd, Huntington Valley, PA 19006

Wayne-Pike Region, Robert Compton, 614 John St, Hawley, PA 18428

Western Pennsylvania Region, Thomas V Milligan, RD 2, Box 449-S, Greensburg, PA 15601

Wolf Creek Region, Robert Buchanan, 46 Irishtown Rd, Grove City, PA 16127

Rhode Island *Westerly-Pawcatuck Region,* Robert Burdick, 70 Sunrise Ave, Pawcatuck, CT 06379

South America *Colombia South America Region,* Victor Valencia, PO Box 49477, Medellin, Colombia, South America

South Carolina *Charleston-Low Country Region,* Roy B McLean, 1936 Varner St, Summerville, SC 29483

Chicora Region, Gus H Hardee, 106 W Coker Ln, Conway, SC 29526

Coastal Carolina Region, Sharon Monheit, 407 Temple Rd, Ladson, SC 29456

Emerald City Region, Don Taylor, 105 Chatham Dr, Greenwood, SC 29649

Gascar Region, Richard T Long Jr, 4626 Stiletto Ct, Martinez, GA 30907

Peach Blossom Region, Lewis Painter, 563 Houston St, Spartanburg, SC 29303

Piedmont Carolina Region, Terry DeVore, 133 Brook Dr, Gaffney, SC 29340

Sandlapper Region, Jim Hartin, 121 Varnadore Rd, Blythwood, SC 29016

Single Cylinder Cadillac Registry Region, Paul A Ianuario, 311 Nature Trail Dr, Greer, SC 29651

South Carolina Region, Patricia A Buis, 118 Quail Run Ct, Greenwood, SC 29646

Sparkle City Region, Ruffner Campbell, 196 Ellington Dr, Spartanburg, SC 29301

Swamp Fox Region, Kelly T Key, 3311 TV Rd, Florence, SC 29501

Upstate Classic Memories Region, Gordon R McCall, 108 McCall Cir, Seneca, SC 29678

Clubs & Organizations

South Dakota *South Dakota Region,* Harry Tuttle, 103 8th St W, Brookings, SD 57006

Tennessee *Appalachian Region,* Ronald A Freeman, 260 Earhart Rd, Bluff City, TN 37618

Battlefield Region, Todd McNeilage, 1386 Buckingham Cir, Franklin, TN 37064

Celebration City Region, Dr John Derryberry, 2322 Hwy 231 N, Shelbyville, TN 37160

Cherokee Valley Region, Faye Rice, 2575 Hensley Rd NW, Cleveland, TN 37312

Chickamauga Region, W Hunter Byington, 1217 Peter Pan Rd, Lookout Mountain, GA 30750

Clinton Region, William N Arnold Jr, 8004 Harmon Rd, Powell, TN 37849

Dan'l Boone Region, David E Berry, 1717 Ft Henry Dr, Kingsport, TN 37664

Davy Crockett Region, Robert Laxton, 1404 Woodmont Dr, Greeneville, TN 37743

East Tennessee Region, Jimmy H Hammett, 336 Oran Rd, Knoxville, TN 37922

Mid-South Region, Joyce S Gray, 2842 Darolyn, Bartlett, TN 38134

Middle Tennessee Region, Ronald Bice, 203 Deerfield Ln, Franklin, TN 37064

North Alabama Region, Robert Hill, 4003 Belle Orchard Dr, Fayetteville, TN 37334

Stones River Region, Lanny McGowan, 2453 Rocky Fork Rd, Nolensville, TN 37153

Sumner County, Tennessee Region, Wendell J Marshall, 166 Evergreen Cir, Hendersonville, TN 37075

Tims Ford Region, Robert Morris, 944 Maxwell Rd, Belvidere, TN 37306

Tobacco Belt Region, Rudolph M Reddic, 2505 Hickory Dr, Springfield, TN 37172

Walden Ridge Region, Jim Loukes, PO Box 464, Kingston, TN 37763

Texas *Amarillo Region,* Jerry R Harris, 505 West Central, Amarillo, TX 79108

Big Bend Region, David F Durant, 900 N Bird, Alpine, TN 79830

Big Spring Region, Steve Barrington, RR 2, Box 28, Lamesa, TX 79331

Central Texas Region, Cheryl Tatro, 2606 Double Tree St, Round Rock, TX 78681

Golden Crescent Region, Gordon O Smith, 266 Padre Ln, Victoria, TX 77905

Gulf Coast Region, Golden Triangle Chapter, John J Gontarek, 5227 Grant, Groves, TX 77619

Gulf Coast Region, Peter S Reinthaler, 4918 Bellview, Bellaire, TX 77401

Hill Country Region, Julius Neuhoffer, 2505 Lower Turtle Creek Rd, Kerrville, TX 78028

Northeast Texas Region, David Gish Jr, 2303 Webb St, Greenville, TX 75402

Rio Grande Valley Region, Tom Hellums, 3020 Hummingbird, McAllen, TX 78504

Snyder Wheels Region, Gale E Titus, 1228 CR 241, Snyder, TX 79549

South Texas Region, John C Mosley, 9370 Teakwood Ln, Garden Ridge, TX 78266

Texas Region, Colin E Hiley, 4706 El Salvadore Ct, Arlington, TX 76017

Texas Region, Red River Valley Honkers Chapter, John W Scharle, Rt 3, Box 266-5, Paris, TX 75462

West Texas Region, Ralph J Webb, 3401 W Gold Course Rd, Midland, TX 79703

Wichita Falls Region, Tim Donovan, 1526 Celia Dr, Wichita Falls, TX 76302

WildflowerRegion, John R Flanagan, 2904 Pecan Valley Dr, Temple, TX 76502

Wool Capital Region, Merlin Hurt, 3109 Tanglewood Dr, San Angelo, TX 76904

Virginia *Accomack-Northampton Region,* Emmett H Bailey, 433 Mason Ave, Cape Charles, VA 23310

Bluestone Region, Benny Buckner, 1807 Honaker Ave, Princeton, WV 24740

Bull Run Region, Gene E Welch, 1773 Macedonia Church Rd, White Post, VA 22663

Crater Antique Auto Club Region, Frederick J Fann, 15628 Rowlett Rd, Chesterfield, VA 23838

Historic Fredericksburg Region, Frank W Vanable, 806 Glazebrook Dr, Fredericksburg, VA 22407

Historic Virginia Peninsula Region, Lloyd W Williams, 1411 Laurens Rd, Gloucester Point, VA 23062

Lynchburg Region, Lennis P Wade, 1515 Langhorne Rd, Lynchburg, VA 24503

Martinsville-Danville Region, Lillard O Shelton, 232 Lansbury Dr, Danville, VA 24540

Mountain Empire Region, Elmer D Mottesheard, Box 82, Abby Ct, Dublin, VA 24084

Northern Neck Region, Earl D Beauchamp Jr, Rt 1, Box 1830, PO Box 999, Montross, VA 22520

Piedmont Region, James F Conley, 12 S Keswick Dr, Troy, VA 22974

Richmond Region, Richard D Ivey, 10473 Old Telegraph Rd, Ashland, VA 23005

Roanoke Valley Region, Jake M Gilmore, 212 Overlook Rd, Vinton, VA 24179

Shenandoah Region, Jeffrey W Feltner, 109 Julee Dr, Winchester, VA 22602

Tidewater Region, Ivan L Joslin, 3160 Lynnhaven Dr, Virginia Beach, VA 23451

Tri-County Region, Larry R Huffman, Rt 1, Box 91, Linville, VA 22834

Waynesboro-Staunton Region, Paul W Wampler, PO Box 7, New Hope, VA 24469

Washington *Evergreen Region,* Betty Jo King, 15424 SE 240th St, Kent, WA 98042

Tacoma Region, Robert H Brooks, 21520 SE 346th St, Auburn, WA 98092

West Virginia *Greenbrier Valley Region,* Raleigh L Sanford, Rt 1, Box 697, Rainelle, WV 25962

Huntington Region, Dana K Watts, 7 Valley Lake Estates, Kenova, WV 25530

Kanawha Valley Region, John A McCoy, 980 Greendale Dr, Charleston, WV 25302

Mid-Ohio Valley Region, John B Barnard, 954 Maple Ln, Sistersville, WV 26175

Northern Panhandle Region, James E Bowery, 260 Park Addition, Wellsburg, WV 26070

West Virginia Region, Robert H Squires, Rt 1, Box 249, Mount Clare, WV 26408

Wisconsin *Blackhawk Region*, Mark J McClenathan, 5671 Rural Edge Dr, Roscoe, IL 61073

Northern Lakes Region, James J Meyers, E5890 County Rd K, Algoma, WI 54201

Wisconsin Region, Fred Olsen, W194N13589 Fond du Lac Ave, Richfield, WI 53076

Wyoming *Big Horn Mountain Region*, Jacqualyn L Dygert, 1730 W Loucks St, Sheridan, WY 82801

Buzzard's Breath Touring Region, Daniel Binger, 3578 Essex Rd, Cheyenne, WY 82001

High Plains Region, Laramie Hi Wheelers Chapter, Robert Young, 2442 Mountain Shadow Ln, Laramie, WY 82070

High Plains Region, Oak Spokes Chapter, Curtis Wright, 3520 Capitol Ave, Cheyenne, WY 82001

High Plains Region, Peter M Lindahl, 715 Mitchell St, Laramie, WY 82070

Canada *Lord Selkirk Region*, T R Turner, 11 Woodgreen Pl, Winnipeg, MB Canada R3J 1H4

Maple Leaf Region, David J Gurney, PO Box 809, Richmont, ON Canada K0A 2X0

Ontario Region, Mervin A Wadsworth, 759 Skyline Rd, Ennismore, ON Canada K0L 1T0

St. Lawrence Valley Region, Steven W Polite, RR 2, Spencerville, ON Canada K0E 1X0

Central America *Club de Autos Antiquos de Costa Rica Region*, Gaspar Ortuno Sr, PO Box 3641-1000, San Jose, Costa Rica, Central America

Antique Motorcycle Club of America Inc
Box 300
Sweetser, IN 46987

For membership information, contact at the above address: Dick Winger, 317-384-5421. Founded 1954. Over 6,000 members. A non-profit organization devoted to the hobby of seeking out, preserving, restoring and exhibiting antique motorcycles, and to the exchange of fellowship and information. For owners and those interested in old motorcycles. Considered antique: 35 years old. Quarterly publication: *The Antique Motorcycle*. Dues: $20/year US, $28/year Canada, $40/year foreign.

Antique Truck Club of America Inc
PO Box 291
Hershey, PA 17033
717-533-9032

Founded 1971. 1,800 members. Open to owners of commercial vehicles or those who have an interest in the history, preservation, restoration and operation of antique commercial vehicles. Dues: $25/year US; $30/year Canada.

Atlantic Coast Old Timers
Auto Racing Club
4 Elm Dr
Newtown, CT 06470
203-426-0813

For information, contact at the above address: Boyd P Hanauer, 203-426-0813. Should be an antique race car enthusiast. Running exhibition races and appearing at Still Shows for the purpose of preserving the history of auto racing.

Bakersfield Car Club Council
Lynn Hubbard, Chairperson
1908 Belle Terr
Bakersfield, CA 93304-4352
805-397-7786

Founded 1985. We are a council of car clubs numbering 40+ clubs in the Kern County area. We try to coordinate a calendar of events and disseminate information amongst us. We have a monthly newsletter. We accept automotive ads.

British Car Club ASBL
Rue du College, BP 153
B-4800 Verviers Belgium
PH/FAX: 3287335122

Founded 1988. 2,500 members. Open to all British car lovers. Monthly magazine Gentleman Driver, $30 US, all you must know about British cars. Insurance scheme, spare parts and technical service, club shop, clubhouse for members. Dues: $30 US/year.

Butterfield Trail Antique Auto Club
Roger Lohrmeyer
2509 Henry Dr
Hays, KS 67601
913-628-8712 work, 628-2386 evenings
FAX: 913-628-2050

Founded 1973. 50 members. Open to anyone who has an interest in the promotion of the automobile special interest hobby. Ownership not required. Annual car show and swap meet. Monthly meetings and newsletter. Dues: $15/year.

CC Riders
6900 N Dixie Dr
Dayton, OH 45414-3297
513-890-3344; FAX: 513-890-9403

Founded 1990. 85 members. Anyone can join. Sponsor a spring break-out, summer cruise and picnic and a car show for charity. Dues: none.

Classic Car Club of America
1645 Des Plaines River Rd, Suite 7
Des Plaines, IL 60018
847-390-0443; FAX: 847-390-7118

Founded 1952. 5,500 members. Open to select makes and models of cars dating from 1925 through 1948. Dedicated to the collection, preservation and enjoyment of fine cars. Dues: $30/year.

Contemporary Historical Vehicle Assoc Inc
PO Box 98
Tecumseh, KS 66542-0098
913-233-6715

Founded 1967. 2,000 members. Recognizes all vehicles built since 1928, up to 20 years old. Activities are open to all cars, commercial vehicles, motorcycles and military land vehicles. Dues: $25/year domestic; $35 year foreign; $300/life membership.

regions:

Arizona *Southern Arizona Region (SARCHVA)*, Robert Shirley, Director, 2050 Calle De Vida, Tucson, AZ 85715

California *Coastal Valleys Region*, Bob Boynton, Director, PO Box 2194, Winnetka, CA 91386-2194

Klassic Uniques Car Club, Jerry Gorley, Director, c/o Box 813, Vacaville, CA 95696-0813

Mt Shasta Region, Bill Jasper, Director, PO Box 91645, Redding, CA 96049-1645

Redwood Region, Jerry Washburn, Director, 2732 Limerick Rd, San Pablo, CA 94806

Sacramento-Sierra Region, Charlene Arora, Director, 52 Calle Linda, Elk Grove, CA 95624

Santa Clara Valley Region, Howard Stanke, Director, 33708 Desert Rd, Acton, CA 93501

Siskiyou Region, Barbara Freeman, Director, PO Box 1172, Yreka, CA 96097

So-Cal Region, Darwyn Lumley, Director, c/o PO Box 254, Fullerton, CA 92632

Temecula Valley Car Club, Norb Dean, Director, Box 891811, Murietta, CA 92564-1811

Valley Cruisers, Mark Loudermilk, Director, 1552 Washington, San Jacinto, CA 92583

Verdugo Vintage Vehicles, Randy Huebner, Director, c/o PO Box 8036, La Crescenta, CA 91214-8036

Florida   *Sunshine Region,* John W Cushing, Director, 12002 Lillian Ave N, Largo, FL 34648

Georgia   *Etowah-Bartow Region,* Thomas Evans, Director, PO Box 34, Cartersville, GA 30120

Ocmulgee Region, Steve Lyles, Director, PO Box 3085, Macon, GA 31205

Kansas   *Sunflower Region,* John Flory, Director, 714 SE Croco Rd, Topeka, KS 66607-2610

Michigan   *Heritage Region,* Ted Cram, Director, 311 Elmhill, Rochester, MI 48063

Montana   *Giant Springs Region,* Gary J Lane, Director, 1320 2nd Ave N, Great Falls, MT 59404

Nevada   *Comstock Reno Region,* Laura Lee Evans, Director, PO Box 18512, Reno, NV 89511

New Mexico   *Roadrunners Region of Southern New Mexico,* Don "Doc" Stoops, Director, 925 Spruce, Truth or Consequences, NM 87901

New York   *Big Apple Region,* Carol Widdows, Director, 78-02 87th St, Glendale, NY 11385

Ohio   *Buckeye Region,* Kathy Hines, Director, 111 Vine St, Bluffton, OH 45817

Ohio River Region, Janet Sell, Director, 1577 Cleveland Ave, East Liverpool, OH 43920

Oregon   *Contemporary Autos of Southern Oregon (CASO),* Art Bigelow, Director, PO Box 41, Shady Cove, OR 97539

Mt Hood Region, Neil Cohen, Director, Box 86, Dundee, OR 97115

Convertible Owners Club of Greater Baltimore
208 Brightside Ave
Pikesville, MD 21208-4806
410-484-1715, 410-337-0697

Founded 1985. 100 members. Convertible owners (both antique & modern) enjoying their cars by participating in parades, exhibits, promotions, movies, etc. Newsletter, "Top Down News". Dues: $12/year.

Deutscher Automobil Veteranen Club
Dachsstr 52
Wiesbaden D-65207 Germany
06122-12180; FAX: 06150-52243

Founded 1965. 1,250 members. 14 sections all over Germany. Monthly meetings, quarterly club news, open to all marques. Dues: 100 DM/year.

Garden State Chapter: Pontiac Oakland Club International
118 Starr Pl
Wyckoff, NJ 07481
201-652-5651

Established 1973. Steve Kiellar pres/Bill Wolf editor. Dedicated to all Pontiacs & Oaklands, bi-monthly newsletter, spring all GM show, fall Pontiac show. Jackets, T-shirts, cruise nights, junk-yard tours. Dues: $10 per year, National Club membership required.

Goodguys Rod & Custom Association
PO Box 424
Alamo, CA 94507
510-838-9876; FAX: 510-820-8241

Founded 1980, 30,000+ members. 25 events throughout the USA. Publisher of the giant sized *Goodtimes Gazette*. Dues: $25/year.

The HO7 Registry
PO Box 2653
Mission Viejo, CA 92690
E-mail: ho7@earthlink.net

Founded 1995. For owners of 1975-80 Chevrolet Monza 2+2, Oldsmobile Starfire, Buick Skyhawk and Pontiac Sunbird sport hatch. Participants directory. No annual dues.

Horseless Carriage Club of America
128 S Cypress St
Orange, CA 92866-1357
714-538-HCCA; FAX: 714-538-5764

Founded 1937. 10,000 members. Membership offered to collectors, historians, anyone interested in early cars. Pioneer motor vehicles are the major interest of the HCCA and its members. Basically a touring club. *Horseless Carriage Gazette* published 6 times a year. Annual national tours are limited to vehicles of 1915 or older vintage. Annual dues are $35 per family membership which include 6 yearly issues of the Gazette.

International Bus Collectors Club
1518 "C" Trailee Dr
Charleston, SC 29407-4144
803-571-2489

For information, contact at the above address: Robert B Redden. Founded 1979. 973 members. Open to all motor bus enthusiasts. Offers various scale model buses and all types of bus memorabilia for sale. Publishes books about the motor bus industry along with frequent club newsletters. Hosts meets of vintage as well as present day coaches. Holds two meetings yearly in different locations called Bus Bash, drawing 2,000 people. Magazine: International Bus Collector. Large historic bus video library.

The International King Midget Car Club
9409 W St Rt 571
Laura, OH 45337
937-698-5144

Founded 1992. 166 members. No restrictions to join. Benefits are meeting other King Midget owners and to preserve the history of the King Midget car. Publish 3 newsletters plus additional information throughout the year. There is an International King Midget Car Club Jamboree in August every year. Also, mini events such as parades or tours starting spring through fall. Dues: $15.

International Peugeot 604 Club
10 Rue De Paris
78460 Chevreuse France
1-30-52-49-64

Founded 1996. 75 members. Dues: 300 Francs/year.

Clubs & Organizations

International Society for Vehicle Preservation
PO Box 50046
Tucson, AZ 85703-1046
520-622-2201; E-mail: isup@aztexcorp.com

Founded 1983. A non-profit organization dedicated to gathering and disseminating information for the restorer, preservationist and auto historian. Actively encourages preservation and restoration of vehicles and artifacts and acts as "government watchdog," alerting of governmental actions, which may infringe our right to continued enjoyment of such vehicles. Biannual magazine: *Restoration*, and quarterly news bulletin. Dues: $15/year. Sponsor and organizing body of the International Automotive Awards, Banquet & Conference held each December. http://www.aztexcorp.com

Kustom Kemps of America
Rt 1 Box 1521A
Bill Hailey Dr
Cassville, MO 65625
417-847-2940; FAX: 417-847-3647

Founded 1980. 10,000 members. 1935-64 (Lead Sled Division) and 1965-present (Late Model Division). Publication: *Trendsetter* magazine. Dues: $25/yr.

Lambda Car Club International
Delaware Valley Region
515 W Chelten Ave, Suite 1009
Philadelphia, PA 19144
610-692-4399

Founded 1987. 50 members. A non-profit organization promoting fellowship among all peoples especially lesbians and gays interested in old and special interest motor vehicles. Annual international convention. Annual regional car show. Bi-monthly international newsletter. Monthly regional newsletter. Monthly socials and summer cruise-ins. Technical and social advisories. Dues: $27.50/year.

Lambda Car Club International (LCCI)
PO Box 2501
Columbus, OH 43216

Founded 1981. 1,500+ members. Open to anyone aged 18 and above. Serving gay & lesbian community. Interest in cars and automobilia is all that's required for membership. Recognizes all cars foreign and domestic. Networking with members all over the country re cars & parts sources, technical know-how. Dues $17.50 (plus $5 for an associate)/yearly.

Massillon Area Car Club
7981 Windward Trace Cir NW
Massillon, OH 44646
330-837-5069

Founded 1974. 80 members. Monthly meetings, yearly car shows. Monthly newsletter, *Gas Line*. Dues: $10/year.

The Microcar and Minicar Club
PO Box 43137
Upper Montclair, NJ 07043
201-366-1410

Founded 1991. 800+ members. Successor to the Heinkel-Messerschmitt-Isetta Club. We are dedicated to the enjoyment and preservation of all small and unusual cars. Our quarterly magazine, *Minutia*, features news, technical information, parts sources and classified advertisements. Nationwide events and club representatives. Monthly meetings in Hackensack, NJ. Annual National Meet held in conjunction with the TVR Club's "Out of the Woodwork" show, Round Valley Reservoir, Lebanon, NJ, the Sunday preceding Columbus Day. Dues: $20/yr Canada & US, $30/yr overseas.

The Mid-America Old Time Automobile Association
8 Jones Ln
Morrilton, AR 72110
PH/FAX: 501-727-5427

For membership information, contact: MOTAA. Founded 1959. 1,000 members in 29 affiliated clubs. The club recognizes automobiles 25 years old or older. Publication: *Antique Car Times*, published six times/year. Dues: $15/year. Annual auto show and swap meet held the third weekend in June at the Museum of Automobiles on Petit Jean Mountain, Morrilton, Arkansas.

Midwestern Council of Sports Car Clubs
147 S Winston Dr
Palatine, IL 60067
847-359-0204

Founded 1958. 980 members. Sports car racing for vintage and current era cars. On-track driver schools (3/yr). Open track autocross/time trials. Wheel to wheel racing. Free introductory series in Rolling Meadows, IL. SASE for free info packet. Publications: *Klaxon* monthly newsletter, picture annual, annual rule book. Dues: $40/year.

The Milestone Car Society, Land of Lakes Chapter
PO Box 27348
Golden Valley, MN 55427-0348
612-377-1234

Founded 1975. 65 members. No restrictions to join. Annual Concours d'Elegance in July. Very active chapter of National Milestone Car Society. Dues: $15/year.

Milestone Car Society of California Inc
1255 La Brea Dr
Thousand Oaks, CA 91362
805-497-1955; FAX: 805-496-5056

Founded 1974. 100 members. MCS of California is club dedicated to the preservation of stock cars built after the Second World War to 1976. Involved in providing our members with information on their marque interest and involved in car shows, parades, clinics and excursions. Our activities have an emphasis on the entire family enjoying their vintage automobiles. Bimonthly publication: *Milestone Memo*. Offers information on monthly meets and events, yearly calendar, automobile legislation, restoration tips. Dues: $20/year.

National Chevy/GMC Truck Association
PO Box 607458
Orlando, FL 32860
407-889-5549; FAX: 407-886-7571

Founded 1989. Mail order and open shop, Monday-Friday 9-5. Association dedicated to the preservation and restoration of all 1918-1972 Chevy/GMC trucks. In our official publication, Pickups 'n Panels In Print magazine, subscribers have access to classified ads, event notices and it also features subscribers' trucks in this quality four color, 16-20 page publication. Free classified ads, tech advice. Dues: $30/year.

North American MGA Register
Don Holle, Registrar
PO Box 11746
Albuquerque, NM 87192
505-293-9085

A volunteer, non-profit, national register, founded 1975, with 2,000 members. Serving the MGAs, Magnettes and period variants 1954-1963. Annual event "Get Together" and bi-monthly newsletter *MGA!* Local chapters in many areas. A register of the MGCC, England. Annual membership $25.

North American MGB Register
Gene Cooper
15625 Woodland Cir
Prior Lake, MN 55372
800-NAMGBR-1

Founded 1990. 2,000 members. A volunteer, non-profit, national register serving the MGB, MGB/GT, Midget, Midget 1500 and MG 1100/1300, 1961-1980. Annual event convention and an annual general meeting. Bi-monthly magazine, *MGB Driver*. Local chapters in many areas. A register of the MGCC, England. Dues: $25/year.

Northern Mopars Auto Club
4416 16A St SW
Calgary, AB Canada T2T 4L5
403-287-0765; E-mail: hemibob@cia.com or markl@sa-cgy.valmet.com

Founded 1986. 175 members. For all Mopar enthusiasts (Dodge, Plymouth, Chrysler, DeSoto, etc). Bi-monthly newsletter containing a buy/sell, wanted section, free to members. Yearly show and swap (7th annual this year). Dues: $25/year Canadian.

Northwoods Region Shelby American Automobile Club
2945 N 70th St
Milwaukee, WI 53210-1226
414-257-2402

Founded 1975. 260 members. Open to all Ford powered vehicles. Publication: *Frost Bits*, bi-monthly newsletter. Events include: (Feb) Daytona 500 brunch; (August) All-Ford show in Wisconsin Dells; (Sept) open track/Midwest Invitational at Road America; (Oct) Fall Colorama road tour. Dues: $15/year.

Pioneer Automobile Touring Club
220 Jefferson St
Lehighton, PA 18235
610-377-2375

For membership information, contact at the above address: Carol Myers. Founded 1967. 200 members. Tours limited to cars of 1915 or earlier.

Pittsburgh CARS
1008 Wren Dr
Kennedy Twp, PA 15136
412-331-7153

Founded 1991. 150 members. To have an interest in classics, antiques, rods and specialty CARS. Monthly newsletter, numerous cruises or car show, picnic, Christmas party, etc. Dues: $20/year.

Plymouth County Auto Club
PO Box 88
Carver, MA 02330
508-866-4633, Pete; 508-866-2709, Chuck

Founded 1981. 40 members. Monthly meetings. Summer get togethers & cruises. Family oriented. All makes & car lovers. Dues: $35/year family membership.

Police Car Owners of America
Rt 6, Box 345B
Eureka Springs, AR 72632
501-253-4948; FAX: 501-253-4949

Founded 1991. 700 members. Open to all makes police cars. Also to model builders. Members receive shoulder patch, decal, key ring, ID card and subscription to quarterly newsletter which features free advertising to members. We have state and regional chapters. Dues: $25/year US.

Shenandoah Region Antique Automobile Club of America
PO Box 3326
Winchester, VA 22601-3326

Founded 1958. 200 members. No restrictions to join, just the interest in preservation and restoration of antique vehicles. Monthly membership meeting 1st Thursday of each month. 37th annual car show & flea market. 1997 event, May 10. Over 600 vehicles displayed. Some monthly events are dinner meetings, we attend local meets and have a yearly tour and Sunday outings. Monthly publication, *Splitrim*, presents the President's message to the members, lists up-coming events, birthdays, deaths, get well wishes, vehicles for sale, items wanted, dinner meal info, automotive articles, etc. Dues: $10/year.

The tii Register
Bob Murphy
6790 Monarda Ct
Houston, TX 77069
PH/FAX: 713-583-2676

Founded 1981. 100 members. A special interest group for the BMW 2002tii. Quarterly newsletter, technical data and assistance. Past newsletters and manuals available. Group is dedicated to keeping the tii enjoyable and available. Dues: $10/year.

Valley Forge Region AACA
539 N Trooper Rd
Norristown, PA 19403
215-539-4775

Founded 1976. 210 members. Must be recommended by another member to join. Antique automobile club interested in the preservation of antique, classic and historic automobiles and memorabilia. Dues: $15/year.

Veteran Motor Car Club of America
PO Box 360788
Strongsville, OH 44136
216-238-2771

For information contact at the above address: Wm E Donze, MD. Founded 1938. 5,700 members. Dues $35/year.

chapters:

Arizona *Southwest Region*, Central Arizona, Ladd Maize, President, PO Box 1568, Camp Verde, AZ 86322

Southwest Region, Coyote, Dave Green, President, 2113 Avenida Planeta, Tucson, AZ 85710

Southwest Region, Dorothy Houdek, Vice Director, 4041 W Monte Cristo, Phoenix, AZ 87001

Southwest Region, Harold Hawes, Secretary/Treasurer, 5154 Calle Virda, Sierra Vista, AZ 85635

Southwest Region, Hummingbird, Bud Derr, President, 3447 E Willow Dr, Sierra Vista, AZ 85635

Southwest Region, Phoenix, Linda J Butch, President, 4040 S Taylor, Tempe, AZ 85282

Southwest Region, Route 66 Car Club of Flagstaff, Oriol Lozano, President, 2401 N US Hwy 66, Lot 102, Flagstaff, AZ 86001

Southwest Region, Valley Roadrunners, George Sanders, President, 2815 E Orion St, Gilbert, AZ 85234

California *California Region*, Carol Williams, Director, 12201 Gasten Rd, Madera, CA 93638

California Region, Los Angeles, Ray Williams, President, 6141 N Loma, Temple City, CA 91780

California Region, Nickel Age Touring Club, Mike Giddens, President, 45 Woodland Ave #10, Rafael, CA 94901

California Region, Southern California, David Shaffer, President, 3534 Via Ventada, Escondido, CA 92029

Colorado *Mountain and Plains Region,* Colorado West, George A Nicholas, President, 618 Stonegate Dr, Grand Junction, CO 81504

Mountain and Plains Region, Denver Mile High, Sandi Lappin, President, 14283 W 44th Dr, Golden, CO 80403

Mountain and Plains Region, Jenny Thrailkill, Secretary, 766-24 Rd, Grand Junction, CO 81505

Mountain and Plains Region, John Koll, Treasurer, 7613 Thunderbird Ln, Colorado Springs, CO 80919

Mountain and Plains Region, Loveland, Tom Sas, President, 4935 W 9th St, Greely, CO 80634

Mountain and Plains Region, Montrose, Ralph W Merwin Sr, President, 9009 60.75 Rd, Montrose, CO 81401

Mountain and Plains Region, Pikes Peak, Harold Naber, President, 11125 E Hwy 24, Peyton, CO 80831

Mountain and Plains Region, Pueblo-Arkansas Valley, Barney Gaffney, President, 375 S Pin High Dr, Pueblo West, CO 81007

Mountain and Plains Region, Richard Jenkins, Director, 1513 W 29th, Loveland, CO 80538

Mountain and Plains Region, Royal Gorge, Roger Zinke, President, 103 Canyon in Los Pinos, Florence, CO 81226

Mountain and Plains Region, San Luis Valley, Roland Ford, President, 587 Pine, Monte Vista, CO 81144

Florida *Florida Region,* Lowell Cooper, Vice Director, 1245 N Greenway Dr, Coral Gables, FL 33134

Florida Region, Roadrunners, Bruce Farnell, President, 4006 San Juan St, Tampa, FL 33629

Florida Region, Steve Wolf, Director, 6720 SW 104 St, Pinecrest, FL 33156

Florida Region, Sun Coast, George Harvey, President, 9301 SW 92 Ave, Apt 207C, Miami, FL 33176

Idaho *Bonneville Region,* Bettry Born, Secretary, 3980 Georgia Ln, Ammon, ID 83406

Bonneville Region, Eastern Idaho, Lynn Erickson, President, 712 S 35th W, Idaho Falls, ID 83402

Bonneville Region, Magic Valley, Loren Holloway, President, 4333 N 2100 E, Filer, ID 83328

Bonneville Region, Raymond R Born, Director, 3980 Georgia Ln, Ammon, ID 83406

Bonneville Region, Tri-City, Paul Bennett, President, 1070 W Walker Creek Rd, McCammen, ID 83250

Indiana *NARHS Region,* Ernie Holden, Director, 349 Arbor Dr, Carmel, IN 46032

Ohio Valley Region, Dolores Orlando, Secretary, 5444 Dutch Hollow Rd, Aurora, IN 47001

Kansas *Midwest Region,* Missouri Valley, Walter Mitschke, President, 9117 Roe, Prairie Village, KS 66207

Mountain and Plains Region, Bob Bethell, Vice Director, PO Box 186, Alden, KS 67512

Mountain and Plains Region, Kanza, Richard Schrock, President, 8 Hazel Ln, South Hutchinson, KS 67505

Kentucky *Kentucky Region,* Bluegrass, Bill Bates, President, 3309 Grasmare Dr, Lexington, KY 40503

Kentucky Region, James Poe, Vice Director, 3466 Mt Horeb Pike, Lexington, KY 40511

Kentucky Region, Jerry Baker, Director, 216 Northland Dr, Paris, KY 40361

Kentucky Region, John B Stinger, Treasurer, 6209 Two Springs Ln, Louisville, KY 40207

Kentucky Region, Louisville, John H Caperton, President, 3112 Boxhill Ct, Louisville, KY 40222

Kentucky Region, Martha Baker, Secretary, 216 Northland Dr, Paris, KY 40361

Massachusetts *Connecticut Valley Region,* Edward LaFleur, Director, 24 Ames Ave, West Springfield, MA 01089

New England Region, Colonial, Edmund F LeLand III, President, 254 Great Pond Rd, North Andover, MA 01845

New England Region, Edmund F LeLand III, Director, 254 Great Pond Rd, North Andover, MA 01845

New England Region, Joseph Antanavich, Secretary, 8 Oak St, Ballardvale, MA 01810

New England Region, Richard Viau, Vice Director, 81 Glenwood St, Lowell, MA 01852

Michigan *Great Lakes Region,* Battle Creek, Asa Jenney, President, 172 E Gull Lake Dr, Augusta, MI 49012

Great Lakes Region, Blue Water, Robert C Burchill, President, 2316 17th Ave, Port Huron, MI 48060

Great Lakes Region, Brass & Gas, Mike Nash, President, 11980 S 26th St, Vicksburg, MI 49097

Great Lakes Region, Brighton, Neil Fisher, President, 3155 Hunter Rd, Brighton, MI 48116

Great Lakes Region, Carl Dawes, Director, 3209 Erie Dr, Orchard Lake, MI 48324

Great Lakes Region, Detroit, Gary Rimer, President, 22315 Tredwell, Farmington Hills, MI 48336

Great Lakes Region, Henry W Hartson, Vice Director, 16840 Mayfield, Livonia, MI 48154

Great Lakes Region, Huron Valley, Wilfred Ross, President, 9117 Sioux, Redford, MI 48239

Great Lakes Region, Jackson Cascades, Leo Warren, President, 3500 Hoyer Rd, Jackson, MI 49201

Great Lakes Region, Lakeshore, Ken Carver, President, 23500 Brookdale, St Clair Shores, MI 48082

Great Lakes Region, Lansing, Thomas Wellman, President, 721 Wolverine Rd, Mason, MI 48854

Great Lakes Region, Lloyd Leach, Treasurer, 43558 Six Mile Rd, Northville, MI 48167

Missouri *Midwest Region,* Jim Clock, Secretary/Treasurer, 708 NW Eagle Ridge, Lee's Summit, MO 64081

Midwest Region, Kansas City, Larry Neaves, President, 431 Hardesty, Kansas City, MO 64123

Midwest Region, Michael Welsh, Director, 7501 Manchester, Kansas City, MO 64138

Nevada *Western Region,* Art Foote, Director, 3535 Freedom Ave, Las Vegas, NV 89121

Western Region, Clyde Baker, Vice Director, 3193 Nottingham Dr, Las Vegas, NV 89121

Western Region, Grace Smith, Secretary, 2825 Golf Links Dr, Las Vegas, NV 89128

Western Region, High Rollers, Stephen Barsuk, President, 5743 Ladybank Ct, Las Vegas, NV 89110

Western Region, Sandy Ferreira, Treasurer, 3913 San Joaquin, Las Vegas, NV 89114

New Jersey *New York Region,* Donald Meyer, Vice Director, 2010 Oamington Rd, Bedminster, NJ 07921

New York Region, Edward Rowan, Director, 160 Van Houton Ave, Chatham, NJ 07928

New York Region, Garden State, Robert Giuliani, President, 72 Northwood Ave, Demarest, NJ 07627

New York Region, John Hovey, Treasurer, 400 Pathway Manor, Wyckoff, NJ 07481

New York Region, Robert Losco, Secretary, 20 Spencer Ln, Warren, NJ 07060

New Mexico *Southwest Region,* Albuquerque, William W Sullivan, President, 324 Hermosa SE, Albuquerque, NM 87108

New York *New York Region,* Long Island Old Car Club, William Ryrrel, President, 24 Bellecrest Ave, East Northport, NY 11731

New York Region, Niagara-Frontier, Paul H Will Jr, President, S-5063 Lakeshore Rd, Hamburg, NY 14075

North Carolina *Kentucky Region,* Smoky Mountain, Lee Molineaux, President, 59 Laurel Lake Rd, Franklin, NC 28734

Ohio *Buckeye-Keystone Region,* Anne Glenn, Secretary, 540 Moody St, Akron, OH 44305

Buckeye-Keystone Region, Canton, Walter Stockert, President, 985 Weber Ave SW, Strasburg, OH 44680

Buckeye-Keystone Region, Delbert Mohler, Vice Director, 6040 Firestone Rd, North Canton, OH 44721

Buckeye-Keystone Region, Emerald Necklace, George Kanaan, President, 9 N Rocky River Dr, Berea, OH 44017

Buckeye-Keystone Region, Robert Ebert, Treasurer, 3300 Thomson Cir, Rocky River, OH 44116

Buckeye-Keystone Region, Walter Stockert, Director, 985 Weber Ave SW, Strasburg, OH 44680

Great Lakes Region, Black Swamp, Ed Davis, President, 24893 Rocky Road, Perrysburg, OH 43551

Great Lakes Region, Defiance, Don Meyers, President, 23480 St Rt 613, Rt 2, Continental, OH 45831

Great Lakes Region, Toledo, Tom Stibbe, President, 5848 Jeffrey Ln, Sylvania, OH 43560

NARHS Region, George Kanaan, Secretary, 9 N Rocky River Dr, Berea, OH 44017

NARHS Region, Serge Krauss, Treasurer, 3114 Edgehill Rd, Cleveland Heights, OH 44118

NARHS Region, Tom Saal, Vice Director, 1488 W Clifton, Lakewood, OH 44107

Ohio Valley Region, Ed Kraemer, Vice Director, 3174 Lake Pointe Ct, Cincinnati, OH 45248

Ohio Valley Region, Eileen Deller, Treasurer, 4581 Foley Rd, Cincinnati, OH 45238

Ohio Valley Region, Rick Donahue, Director, 3552 Neihesel, Cincinnati, OH 45248

Tri-State Region, Albert Pavlik Jr, Director, 1803 Norton Pl, Steubenville, OH 43952

Tri-State Region, Steel Valley, Robert H Kaine, President, 159 Gumps Ln, Wintersville, OH 43952

Rhode Island *New England Region,* Joseph Kent, Treasurer, 70 Lantern Ln, Exeter, RI 02822

New England Region, Viking, Roger and Susan Paul, Presidents, 43 Heritage Rd, North Kingstown, RI 02852

South Dakota *Mountain and Plains Region,* Gold Dust, William Kuhl, President, 306 S 13th St, Hot Springs, SD 57747

Texas *Southwest Region,* Bexar Touring, John Jones, President, PO Box 1705, Boerne, TX 78006

Southwest Region, Cowtown Touring, Platt Allen, President, PO Box 470713, Fort Worth, TX 76147

Southwest Region, Fredericksburg, Alan Parker, President, 1030 Cedarhill Dr, Fredericksburg, TX 78624

Southwest Region, Key to the Hills, James George, President, 25615 Dull Knife Tr, San Antonio, TX 78255

Southwest Region, Permian Basin Oil Burners, Wes Read, President, PO Box 728, Odessa, TX 79760

Southwest Region, Platt Allen, Director, PO Box 470713, Fort Worth, TX 76147

Utah *Bonneville Region,* Amy Wernz, Treasurer, 545 W 2nd S, Provo, UT 84601

Bonneville Region, Cache Valley, Otto Derr, President, 238 S 400 E, Logan, UT 84321

Bonneville Region, Copper Classics, Edward M Curry, President, PO Box 25, Hanna, UT 84031

Bonneville Region, Duane L Leek, Vice Director, 1611 E Spyglass Cir, Sandy, UT 84092

Bonneville Region, Utah, Terry L Anderson, President, 8126 S 2225 E, South Weber, UT 84405

Washington *Northwest Region,* Capitol City, Vern Hummel, President, 816 NE Roosevelt, Olympia, WA 98506

Northwest Region, Cliff Seat, Vice Director, 9634 Cse Rd SW, Olympia, WA 98502

Northwest Region, Fred Gilchrist, Director, 1734 Woodcock Rd, Sequim, WA 98382

Northwest Region, Jeanette Friis, Secretary, 6518 32nd Ave NW, Olympia, WA 98502

Northwest Region, Sequim Valley, Nick Dante, President, 223 Hudon Rd, Sequim, WA 98382

Northwest Region, Sue Hulse, Treasurer, 2223 O'Brien Rd, Port Angeles, WA 98362

Wisconsin *Kentucky Region,* Nickel Age Touring Club, Donna Wall, President, 7658 Pine Harbor Dr, Chippewa Falls, WI 54729

Wyoming *Mountain and Plains Region,* Oil Country, Don M Carr, President, 1235 S Wilson, Casper, WY 82601

The Vintage Car Club of New Zealand Inc
PO Box 2546
Christchurch New Zealand
03-366-4461; FAX: 03-366-0273

Founded 1946. 5,200 members. Dedicated to the preservation of historic vehicles and New Zealand's motoring history. Members benefit from access to research material, parts, etc. Approximately 150 events and meets annually, 36 branches throughout the country and a National magazine, Beaded Wheels, New Zealand's only veteran and vintage motoring magazine containing restoration and rally articles, technical tips and swap meet information. Subscription rate: $27.00 (o/s rates on application), 6 times/year. Dues: $50-$70/year, varies by region.

Vintage Wheels Antique Car Club
Rt 4, Box 165
Great Bend, KS 67530
316-793-7162

Founded 1975. 50 members. Dedicated to the preservation of and interest in antique and special interest vehicles. Dues: $50/year.

Viper Club of America
31690 W 12 Mile Rd
Farmington Hills, MI 48334
810-998-1110; FAX: 810-553-2138

Founded 1996. 875 members. Must own a Viper and be a member of Regional club (optional). Subscription to *Viper Quarterly,* member card and badge, liability insurance. Dues: $25/year.

White Owners Register
1624 Perkins Dr
Arcadia, CA 91006
818-355-7679 evenings

Founded 1970. 300 members. Caters to owners of White, Indiana, Cletrac, Rollin, Templar, Rubay vehicles. Technical data shared. We cooperate with VWTA. Dues: none.

Winchester Speedway Old Timers' Club Inc
PO Box 291
Urbana, OH 43078
513-652-2145; FAX: 513-652-2147

Founded 1972. 500 members. Hold annual Winchester Speedway Old Timers' convention in July at the Winchester Speedway, Winchester, IN. Vintage race car drivers, owners, mechanics and fans encouraged to join. Membership includes newsletter 4 times/year. Dues: $20/year.

Winged Warriors
216 12th St
Boone, IA 50036
515-432-3001

Founded 1975. 500 members. Open to all 1962-74 B-body performance MoPars, specializing in Daytonas, Superbirds and

1969 Charger 500s. Ownership is not required for membership. Monthly newsletter. Free classified ad section for members. Dues: $25/year US, $30/year outside US.

WPC Club Pacific Wonderland Region
PO Box 762
Clackamas, OR 97015

Founded 1995. 50 members. Membership in National WPC Club required. Pacific Wonderland Region covers Oregon and southwest Washington state. Monthly meetings and newsletter. For owners/admirers of Chrysler Corp and related vehicles. Dues: $10/year.

Marque Clubs

The Abarth Register, USA Inc
1298 Birch St
Uniondale
Long Island, NY 11553-2008
516-481-2092; FAX: 516-538-7118

For membership information, contact at the above address: Gerald Rothman, Director. Founded 1973. 200 members. For Abarth and Cisitalia owners and enthusiasts. Do not have to own one to belong. Organized for the restoration, preservation and enjoyment of the Abarth and Cisitalia marques. Affiliated with Abarth Club of United Kingdom, Abarth Corsa Deutschland of Germany, Club Abarth, France, Club Abarth, Japan, Svenska Abarth Registret, Sweden, RIA, Registro Italiano Abarth, Italy. Quarterly newsletter. Dues: $30/year USA; $35/year foreign. Club maintains excellent data base network of Abarth information and parts sources.

AC Owner's Club Ltd
11955 SW Faircrest St
Portland, OR 97225-4615
503-643-3225; FAX: 503-646-4009

The world's largest organization of AC owners and enthusiasts. AC ownership not required. Monthly magazine. US registrar: Jim Feldman, 11955 SW Faircrest St, Portland, OR 97225-4615.

AJS/Matchless Owners Club of England
North American Section
PO Box 317
Yardley, PA 19067
609-658-0552, NJ

AJS
MATCHLESS

Editor: John Diederich, 7401 South Blvd, Charlotte, NC 28217. 300 plus members in US and Canada, 1,800 plus worldwide. Sample newsletter is $1. Dues: $10/year.

Alfa Romeo Owners Club
2468 Gum Tree Ln
Fallbrook, CA 92028
619-728-4875, 800-399-AROC

Founded 1958. Over 4,500 members. Dedicated to history and traditions of Alfa Romeo. Provides technical information for efficient and safe operation of Alfas. Many chapters provide social and driving events and teach safe and skillful driving. Monthly publication: *Alfa Owner.* Dues: $45/year.

Texas Hill Country Alfa Romeo Owners Club
PO Box 523
Alpine, TX 79831-0523
915-837-1717

Founded 1982. 50 members. Club events and benefits include Hill Country tours, autocrosses, local and National monthly newsletters, technical info, AROC tech hotlines, tech sessions. Meetings in Austin or San Antonio. Dues: $45/year.

The Allard Owners Club
1 Dalmeny Avenue
London,
N7 OLD   England

For membership information contact at the above address: Miss P Hulse. Founded 1951. 175 members. Monthly newsletter. Dues: £25 per year.

The Allard Register
8 Paget Close
Horsham
West Sussex, RH13 6HD   England

For membership information contact at the above address: R W May. Phone: Horsham 61372. Founded 1966. 148 members. Free bulletins with technical and spare parts information. Membership meets in both the US and the UK.

Alvis Owner Club of North America
140 Race St
PO Box 46
Bainbridge, PA 17502
PH/FAX: 717-426-3842

150 members. Dues: $10/year.

AMC Pacer Club
2628 Queenston Rd
Cleveland Heights, OH 44118
216-371-0226

Founded 1993. 300 members. Exclusively for lovers of 1975-1980 AMC Pacers. Quarterly publication, national meets, free ads, window decal. Dues $12/year.

AMC Rambler Club
2645 Ashton Rd
Cleveland Heights, OH 44118
216-371-5946

Founded 1980. 1,300 members. Quarterly publications, parts source guide, production handbook, window decal, free ads. Local chapters, National and Regional meets for 1958-1969 AMCs. Dues: $18/year.

AMC World Clubs
7963 Depew St
Arvada, CO 80003-2527
303-428-8760; FAX: 303-428-1070

Founded 1974. 1,500 members. Comprised of the union of the Classic AMX Club, International and American Motorsport, Int. AMC World Clubs is for those interested in AMC/AMX/Rambler/AMC-Jeep vehicles 1954 to 1987. Telephone technical and restoration assistance six days a week. Large 28-32 page bimonthly magazine. Dues: $25/year.

American Motors Club Northwest
PO Box 66672
Burien, WA 98166
206-878-1757

Founded circa 1980. 50+ members. AMC NW is the Seattle-Tacoma based chapter of AMC World Clubs. Serves Seattle, Tacoma and Everett areas of Washington state. Open to all enthusiasts of AMC, Nash, Hudson, AM General and Jeep vehicles manufactured by American Motors Corporation from 1954 to 1987. Meets monthly and has newsletter, free ads, local parts sources and network, participates in local and regional shows and racing events, plus much more. Dues: $20/year.

National American Motors Drivers & Racers Association
PO Box 987
Twin Lake, WI 53181-0987
414-396-9552

Founded 1977. 1,224 members. No restrictions. NAMDRA is

dedicated to all facets of AMC ownership including racing, car shows, restoration, competition, performance and all modern day automobilia. Publishes *Tough Americans*, 12 newsletters per year. 40+ pages w/free ads for members and paid commerical ads. Articles on member's vehicles, restoration and repair tips, performance tips, upcoming events listings, contests, etc. National & regional meets yearly. Chapters. Dues: $24/year.

Total Performance AMC Club
1511 19th Ave W
Bradenton, FL 34205

Founded 1983. Currently has over 500 members. No restrictions to join. Main purpose is to provide technical, repair and performance information on the marque. Free ads. Monthly newsletter. Dues: $19/year.

American Austin-Bantam Club
351 Wilson Rd
Willshire, OH 45898-9551
419-495-2569

Founded 1962. 600 members. Annual meet with judging. Club newsletters 6 times a year. Roster updates, technical assistance, leads of parts & vehicles for sale. Dues: $12/year single, $15/year husband & wife, $18/year foreign.

Pacific Bantam Austin Club
1589 N Grand Oaks Ave
Pasadena, CA 91104
818-791-2617

For membership information, contact at the above address: Norm Booth. Founded 1969. 200 members. Club is open to American Austin, American Bantam and all pre-World War II British Austin Seven enthusiasts. Dues: $15/year US, $20/year other countries.

Amilcar Register
Cleeve Cottage
Cobham Way
East Horsley, Surrey, KT24 5BH
England
PH/FAX: +44-483-282466

For membership information, contact at the above address: Len Battyll. Founded 1955. 110 members. Full membership for owners of Amilcars and Salmsons. Catering also for all light French sports cars, Senechal, BNC, Vernon-Derby, etc. Dues: £13/ Europe, £15/ US and Australia

Amphicar Car Club
Rue du College, BP-153
B-4800 Verviers Belgium
PH/FAX: 3287335122

Founded 1988. 20 members. No restriction to join. The club is open to all Amphicar lovers. Free newsletter. Dues: none.

Classic AMX Club International
7963 Depew St
Arvada, CO 80003
303-428-8760; FAX: 303-428-1070

Founded 1973. 1,235 members. Open to owners and enthusiasts of the 1968, 1969, 1970 two passenger sport coupe. Large 28 page all AMC bi-monthly magazine. Telephone assistance on restoration, questions of originality, etc. Largest collection of AMX historical artifacts in the world. Dues: $25/year.

Austin Works East
71 Boardley Rd
Sandwich, MA 02563
PH/FAX: 508-420-9472
E-mail: austnworks@aol.com

Founded 1977. 400+ members. Should own or be interested in pre-1954 English Austins. Dues: none. Club supplies, parts and technical assistance.

Austin-Healey Club of America Inc
603 E Euclid Ave
Arlington Heights, IL 60004-5707
847-255-4069; FAX: 847-590-7907

For membership information, contact at the above address: Edie Anderson, Founded 1961. Over 3,300 members. Club offers services for all Austin-Healeys and Austin-Healey Sprites. Monthly newsletter: *Chatter*. Dues: $35/Jan-July, $25/Aug-Dec plus local club dues. $56 surface; $76 air/foreign.

chapters:

Albama	*Rodney Martin*, 85 Rifle Range Ridge, Wetumpka, AL 36092-4120
Colorado	*Rocky Mountain*, Marty VanScoyk, 8334 W Nevada Pl, Lakewood, CO 80226
DC (MD-VA)	*Capital Area*, Dave Doyle, 12503 Two Farm Dr, Silver Spring, MD 20904
Florida	*Orlando*, Richard Smith, 4203 Lake Lockhart Dr, Orlando, FL 32810-3515
	Pensacola, Don Haugen, 9183 S Ponderosa, Mobile, AL 36575-7251
	St Johns, Porter Ramsey, 1241 Grove Park Blvd, Jacksonville, FL 32216
	Tampa Bay, Marion Brantley, 2696 66th Terr S, St Petersburg, FL 33712
Georgia	*Central GA*, Len Thomas, 2140 Mountain Ln, Stone Mountain, GA 30087-1034
Illinois	*Illini*, Dave Young, 3816 W Bluff Rd, Springfield, IL 62707-9279
	Midwest, Bill Naretta, 404 Peach Tree Cir, Loves Park, IL 61111
Indiana	*Indianapolis*, Jim Richmond, 13088 Tarkington Common, Carmel, IN 46033
	Northern Indiana, Jon Needler, 8308 S Anthony Blvd, Ft Wayne, IN 46816
Iowa	*Heartland Healey*, Mark Long, 830 22nd St, Rock Island, IL 61201-2616
Kansas	*Kansas City*, Steven Dupus, 13016 Cardiff, Olathe, KS 66062
Kentucky	*Bluegrass*, Mike Schneider, 110 N Rastetter, Louisville, KY 40206
Michigan	*SE Michigan*, Brian Thornton, 4618 Mandalay, Royal Oak, MI 48073-1624
Minnesota	*Geoff Rossi*, 3641 DuPont S, Minneapolis, MN 55409
Missouri	*Gateway*, John Thousand, 9008 Crest Oak, Crestwood, MO 61326
Nebraska	*Flatwater*, Jim Danielson, 1310 Idylwild Dr, Lincoln, NE 68503
New England/ Eastern NY	*Northeast*, Paul Dunnell, 299 River Rd, Chesterfield, NH 03466
New Mexico	*Roadrunner*, Bill Lawrence, 5521 Sabrosa Dr NE, Albuquerque, NM 87111-1750
New York	*Niagara Frontier*, Rick Margo, 210 W Hazeltine Ave, Kenmore, NY 14217
North Carolina	*Carolinas*, Carl Brown, 7 Pickett Ave, Spencer, NC 28159
	Triad, Gary Brierton, 271 Dalewood Dr #W, Winston Salem, NC 27104
Ohio	*Miami Valley*, Gregg Sipe, 2058 S Belleview Dr, Bellbrook, OH 45305
	Mid-Ohio, Nancy Cole, 822 Mohawk St, Columbus, OH 43206

	NE Ohio, Bill Ebersole, 10609 Cedar Rd, Chesterland, OH 44026
	Ohio Valley, Don Klein, 1370 Karahill Dr, Cincinnati, OH 45240
Oklahoma	*Oklahoma AH Owners*, Don Ethridge, 816 Bell Dr, Midwest City, OK 73110
Pennsylvania	*Three Rivers*, Tom Felts, 5114 Scenic Dr, Murraysville, PA 15668
Tennessee	*Middle TN Region*, Robbie Cook, 311 Winston Dr, Whitehouse, TN 37188
	Smoky Mountain, Rick Hayes, 9024 Tall Timber Dr, Knoxville, TN 37931
Texas	*Gulf Coast*, Roger Williams, 911 Sycamore, Richmond, TX 77469
	North Texas, Rob Brown, 7720 LaAvenida, Dallas, TX 75248
	South Texas, George Crombie, 10204 Shavano Cove, Austin, TX 78749-6900
Utah	*Bonneville*, Dave Maxwell, 1752 Paulista Way, Sandy, UT 84093
Virginia	*,apital Area* (See DC)
	Tidewater, Bill Parks, 25 Museum Dr, Newport News, VA 23601
Washington	*Cascade*, Chuck Breckenridge, 7015 Olympic View Dr, Edmonds, WA 98026
Wisconsin	*LeRoy & Sue Joppa*, PO Box 131, Laona, WI 54541-0131
Canada	*Bluewater*, Murray Schreder, 772 Ross Ave, Sarnia, ON Canada N7T 1K5
	Quebec, Roger Hamel, 317 Julie, St Eustache, QB Canada J7P 3R8
	Southern Ontario, Les Vass, 511 Guelph Line, Ste 702, Burlington, ON Canada L7R 3M3

Austin-Healey Club, Pacific Centre
PO Box 6197
San Jose, CA 95150
415-494-3343

Founded 1970. 2,500 members. All Healey enthusiasts. Award winning, colorful, glossy monthly magazine, regional activities, technical assistance, annual West Coast Meet and Healey advertising. Members domestic and worldwide. Dues: $35/year; $55/year outside US.

Mini Registry
395 Summit Point Dr
Henrietta, NY 14467
716-359-1400; FAX: 716-359-1428

For membership information, contact at the above address: Clark Holden, Registrar. Founded 1967. 9,000 members. Must own an Austin or Morris Mini or Mini variant. Dues: none. The Mini Registry was founded to sustain, universalize and generally contribute to enthusiasm for Minis in ways which are not for profit.

DKW Club of America
260 Santa Margarita Ave
Menlo Park, CA 94025
415-321-6640; FAX: 415-329-0129
E-mail: jowett@best.com

See full listing in **Section Three** under **DKW**

Clubs & Organizations

Avanti Owners Association Int'l
PO Box 28788
Dallas, TX 75228
800-527-3452 US
214-709-6185 foreign

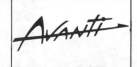

For membership contact: Mr Sheldon Harrison, Membership Secretary, at the above address. Founded 1963. 1,500 members. Open to all Avanti owners. Supports the Avanti marque from the 1963 Studebaker Avanti to the 1989 Avanti produced today. Ownership of an Avanti is not necessary to be a member. Publishes *Avanti Quarterly* magazine. Contains information on meets, member experiences, repairs, parts and cars for sale. Dues: $22/year.

Total Performance Avanti Club
1511 19th Ave W
Bradenton, FL 34205

Founded 1973. 400 members. No restrictions to join. All Avanti and Studebaker owners are welcome. Main purpose is to provide technical, parts, repair and performance information on the marque. Monthly newsletter. Dues: $19.

Bentley Drivers Club Ltd
16 Chearsley Rd, Long Crendon
Aylesbury
Bucks, HP18 9AW   England
01844-208233; FAX: 01844-208923

For membership information, contact at the above address: Secretary. Founded 1936. 2,800 members. Open to present and past owners of Bentleys and enthusiasts. International club. Dues: £50/year UK and overseas members.

The Berkeley Exchange & Register
46 Elm St
N Andover, MA 01845

Founded 1980. For information, contact at the above address: Nat Stevens, 508-687-3421. Organized for the exchange of information and parts for restoring the British Berkeley car produced between 1956 and 1961. Monthly publication: *British Berkeley Enthusiast Club Newsletter*. Dues: $10 one time membership charge and $24/year.

Berkeley Newsletter
PO Box 162282
Austin, TX 78716-2282
512-327-6231; E-mail:
gerronsh@aol.com

Founded 1990. 50 members. The only newsletter in North America devoted exclusively to Berkeley automobiles. Free ads to subscribers. Dues: $12/year.

North American Bitter SC Registry
PO Box 9638
Richmond, VA 23228
804-262-3511; E-mail:
opelprez@earthlink.net

Founded 1995. 5 members. The registry is a part of the North American Opel Association. Membership includes all the NAOA benefits. Being that the Bitter is largely an Opel under the skin, the NAOA decided to create the registry to help owners of our sister marque. Dues: $15/year.

BMW Car Club of America
2130 Massachusetts Ave
Cambridge, MA 02140
800-878-9292; FAX: 617-876-3424

Founded 1969. 30,000 members. Open to BMW enthusiasts and owners. Benefits include monthly *Roundel*, our colorful, informative 100-plus page magazine featuring maintenance tips, test results of new products and exciting articles with tips on

enhancing your BMW and ensuring its lasting value. Many of 60+ local chapters offer driving schools, tech sessions, rallies, autocrosses, social events and more. Dues: $35/year.

Vintage BMW Motorcycle Owners Ltd
PO Box 67
Exeter, NH 03833

For information, contact at the above address: Roland M. Slabon, Editor, 603/772-9799. Founded 1972. 5,100 members. Devoted solely to the preservation, restoration, enjoyment and use of pre-1970 (vintage, antique and classic) BMW motorcycles. Extensive worldwide parts and publication service. Bimonthly illustrated publication: *Vintage BMW Bulletin*. Dues $12/year.

Bricklin International Owners Club
Norm Canfield, President
213 Southwoods Drive
Fredericksburg, TX 78624
210-997-6134

Founded 1975. 500 members. A non-profit club dedicated to the preservation and enjoyment of the Bricklin SV1. Providing parts and service information. Two National meets per year and numerous regional functions. Quarterly magazine. Technical manuals. Dues: $35/year.

Organization of Bricklin Owners
Joseph F DeLorenzo, President
PO Box 24775
Rochester, NY 14624
716-247-1575

Founded 1975. 680 members. Created to serve owners of the Bricklin SV1 in the maintenance and preservation of their gull-wing motorcars. Owners only. National organization.

Bristol Owners Club (BOC)
PO Box 60
Brooklandville, MD 21022
410-484-1834

Founded 1971. 850 members. For membership information contact Lee Raskin, US Secretary at the above address. Recognizes the Bristol marque and Bristol-powered automobiles. Formed to further interests in Bristol cars from 1946 to present. Quarterly publication and newsletters. Social and technical events. Dues: $40/year US or £25.00 sterling.

American Bugatti Club
4484 Howe Hill Rd
Camden, ME 04843
207-236-8288; FAX: 207-236-0869

For membership, register or other general information, contact the club secretary, Andy Rheault, 4484 Howe Hill Rd, Camden, ME 04843. Founded 1960. 350 members worldwide. Club promotes interest in, preservation and use of Bugattis as well as serving as an information network for those interested in the marque. The Register keeps track of Bugattis in North America. Quarterly publication; *Pur Sang,*. Subscriptions available to non members. Members' dues: $50/year.

1929 Buick Silver Anniversary Club
75 Oriole Parkway
Toronto, ON M4V 2E3 Canada
416-322-7475
E-mail: 75317.3253@compuserve.com

Founded 1987. 250 members. International newsletter and directory devoted to the restoration and preservation of 1929 Buicks, McLaughlin Buicks (Canadian) and Holden-bodied Buicks (Australian). Open to owners of 1929 Buicks. Newsletter published 4 times/year. dues $15 US/year.

1937-38 Buick Club
1005 Rilma Ln
Los Altos, CA 94022
PH/FAX: 415-941-4587
E-mail: harrylogan@earthlink.net

Founded 1980. 500 members. International club devoted to restoration, preservation and enjoyment of 1937 and 1938 Buick automobiles. Open to those seriously interested in 1937-38 Buicks, is not necessary to own one. Magazine published 6 times/year: *The Torque Tube*. Dues: $34/year.

Austin Buick Turbo Club
2219 Klattenhoff Dr
Austin, TX 78728
512-251-5948

Founded 1989. 30 members. Specializing in 1984 to 1987 Grand National and Buick Regal Turbo vehicles. Monthly meeting and frequent club trips and race events. Dues: $20/year.

Buick Club of America
PO Box 401927
Hesperia, CA 92340-1927
619-947-2485; FAX: 619-947-2465

Founded 1966. 10,000 members. Founded for the preservation and restoration of those vehicles built by the Buick Motor Division of General Motors Corporation. Dues: $30/year US; $48/year foreign.

chapters:

Arizona *Valley of the Sun #8898*, Raul Gaitan, PO Box 985, Phoenix, AZ 85001

California *California Capitol #14501*, Cecil Don, PO Box 162346, Sacramento, CA 95816

Central Valley #2553, Garry Scott, 7101 N Monte, Fresno, CA 93711

Inland Empire #15637, Eugene Terres, 599 Westmont, Hemet, CA 92543

Los Angeles #10675, Russ Drosendahl, PO Box 10073, Canoga Park, CA 91309-1073

Northern California #16747, Bob Hamro, 3241 Williams Rd, San Jose, CA 95117

Orange County #26776, Baron Night, PO Box 3531, Tustin, CA 92681-3531

San Gabriel Valley #8377, Lou Baiocco, PO Box 2355, Pasadena, CA 91102-2355

Colorado *Mile High #5806*, Lou Scott, 4735 S Galapago, Englewood, CO 80110

Rocky Mountain #11728, Ed Bunker, PO Box 1286, Berthoud, CO 80513

Connecticut *Yankee*, Tony Vespoli, Nancy B Thompson #25425, 630 Middlebury Rd, Watertown, CT 06795

Delaware *Delmarva #18454*, Don Addor, 721 E State St, Millsboro, DE 19966

Florida *Space Coast #20720*, Richard Gauchat, 737 Galloway Ct, Winter Springs, FL 32708, 407-695-4412

Sunshine State #6396, Ken Liska, 1424 Dogwood Ct, Kissimmee, FL 34744

Georgia *Dixie #21011*, Roddy Pearce, 432 E Pharr Rd, Decatur, GA 30030

Illinois *Chicagoland #23714*, Roy Wager, PO Box 863, Arlington Heights, IL 60006-0863, 815-895-9474

Indiana *Central Indiana #22547*, Dean Kyle, 2005 N Glenridge Dr, Indianapolis, IN 46218

Iowa *Hawkeye #15140*, Alan Oldfield, 1610 Douglas Ct, Marion, IA 52302

Kansas *Mid America #3194*, Steve Hartwich, 8240 Summit, Kansas City, MO 64114-2244

Wheatland #26747, Rod Taylor, PO Box 780999, Wichita, KS 67207

Maryland *B. O. O. M. #18163*, Craig Bober, 100 S Ritter Ln, Owings Mills, MD 21117

Massachusetts *Central New England #11420*, Patrick Hayes, 33 W Parsons Ln, North Hampton, MA 01060

Minute Man #20839, Lee Johansson, 22 Russell Trufant Rd, Carver, MA 02330

Michigan *Buicktown #9025*, Del Cutter, 5259 Durwood Dr, Swartz Creek, MI 48473

Central Michigan #7899, Harold Messenger, 5801 Hughes Rd, Lansing, MI 48911-4717

Southeast Michigan #6969, Elizabeth L Lawson, 251 Nottingham Dr, Troy, MI 48098-3278

West Michigan #2280, Del Carpenter, 458 Maethy SE, Grand Rapids, MI 49548

Minnesota *Fireball #12595*, Jim Jaeger, PO Box 24776, Edina, MN 55424

Gopher State #20339, Kevin Kinney, 976 W Minnehaha, St Paul, MN 55104

Missouri *St Louis Gateway #25580*, Russ Miller, 230 Birmingham Dr, O'Fallon, MO 63366

Nebraska *Crossroads #6892*, Larry D Robb, 9346 Monroe St, Omaha, NE 68127

Nevada *Southern Nevada #1234*, Richard King, 4261 E Rochelle Ave, Las Vegas, NV 89121

New Jersey *Jersey Shore*, Sharon Erven #24587, Dave Hart #8166, 526 Park Ave, Union Beach, NJ 07735

North Jersey #9503, Joseph D Bell, 33 Inwood Rd, Essex Fells, NJ 07021

New York *Central New York #18810*, Charles Paddock, 4352 Vinegar Hill Rd, Skaneateles, NY 13152

Empire State #11644, Nicolas Pagani, 825 Main St, New Rochelle, NY 10801

Finger Lakes #12872, Dorothy Wallace, 37 Little Briggins Cir, Fairport, NY 14450

Long Island #20626, David B Millard, 91 Claridge Ln, East Islip, NY 11730

Niagara Frontier #12937, Joe Territo, 7264 Townline Rd, North Tonawanda, NY 14120

Ohio *Akron-Canton #20440*, Doug Santee, 4433 Foresthill Rd, Stow, OH 44224-2010

Central Ohio #20185, John Westfall, 10360 State Rt 559, North Lewisburg, OH 43060

Glass City #2549, Dan Myers, 2209 N Reiman Rd, Genoa, OH 43430-9752, 419-855-3223

Northeast Ohio #1818, Bill Horak, 18337 Fairville Ave, Cleveland, OH 44135-3909

River Towne Road Masters #12839, Ronald D Goldstone, 4034 Catherine Ave, Norwood, OH 45212

Youngstown Buicks of Yesteryear #9948, Steve Goricki, 529 E Judson Ave, Youngstown, OH 44502

Oregon *Portland Area #19618*, Bruce Ankarberg, PO Box 14224, Portland, OR 97293-0224

Pennsylvania *Appalachian #18899*, Gene Cunningham, PO Box 409, Hastings, PA 16642

Free Spirit #25766, Bob Teel, 4351 Dumpling Dr, Orefield, PA 18069

National Pike #7347, Leon Moyer, RD 2, Box 565, Ruffsdale, PA 15679

Northwest PA #20137, Frederick Blass Jr, 2238 Elk St, Lake City, PA 10423

Philadelphia '76 #11459, Joe Walker, 8116 Burholme Ave, Philadelphia, PA 19111

South Carolina *Carolina #13701*, John Huffman, PO Box 614, Clemson, SC 27633

Tennessee *Music City #17816*, John Morgan, c/o L G Arrowood, 6300 Murray Ln, Brentwood, TN 37027

Texas *Lone Star #1962*, Cecil Miles, 14021 Stoneshire, Houston, TX 77060

North Texas #25603, Roy Fairies, 129 Oriole Dr, Arlington, TX 76010

Virginia *Northern Virginia #23520*, Phillip Strassner, 433 Cavalier Rd, Rileyville, VA 22650

Old Dominion #4169, Charles Gills, 8311 Trabue Rd, Richmond, VA 23235-2540

Washington *Inland Northwest #20958*, John Salancy, 2301 W 36th Ave, Kennewick, WA 99337

North Cascade #23473, Dean Eldridge, 11820 127th Ave NE, Lake Steves, WA 98258

Puget Sound #30384, Lee Davis, 10801 Woodley Ave S, Seattle, WA 98178

Washington DC *Metro #17058*, John Nordin, 11511 Fairfax Station Rd, Fairfax Station, VA 22039

Wisconsin *Cream City #14606*, Bud Armstrong, 1926 Surrey Ln, Grafton, WI 53024, 414-377-7258

Dairyland #8385, Fred Pennings, N603 Kavanaugh Rd, Kaukauna, WI 54130, 414-766-1333

Rock Valley #1390, Eugene Ziells, 9006 N Evansville-Brooklyn Rd, Evansville, WI 53536

Buick GS Club of America
1213 Gornto Rd
Valdosta, GA 31602
912-244-0577

Founded 1982. 5,000 members. Dedicated to Buick owners who enjoy the performance of their cars. Emphasis is on racing as well as showing. Open to all Buick performance enthusiasts. Members receive the *GS X-tra* magazine containing performance build-ups, feature stories, tech tips, free classifieds and much more. GS Nationals held the first weekend of May. Dues: $30/year.

Buick Reatta Division
Buick Club of America
c/o Bob Peterson
17 Dundee Ct
Mahwah, NJ 07430-1509
201-529-2556

Founded 1993. 400 members. Reatta Division is a branch of the Buick Club of America. Membership open to both owners & non-owners. Members have all the privileges of the Buick Club of America. Reatta Annual Meet is in conjunction with National BCA Meet. Dues: $10/year in addition to BCA dues of $30/year.

New Zealand Buick Enthusiasts
26 Dunraven Place
Torbay, Auckland 1310
New Zealand
09-473-6856

Founded 1988. 180 members. Open to anyone interested in the preservation and restoration of Buick cars in New Zealand.

Quarterly magazine published. Restoration tips, cars and parts for sale and wanted. Dues: $10/year New Zealand, $15/year overseas.

Riviera Owners Association
PO Box 26344
Lakewood, CO 80226
303-987-3712
E-mail: roa@ixnetcom.com

Founded 1984. 2,900 members. For information, contact at the above address: Ray Knott, 303-987-3712. International membership. Open to owners and enthusiasts of the Riviera by Buick (1963-96). Bimonthly 36-page magazine: *RIVIEW*. Technical tips, parts and service locator, free classifieds and more. Dues: $20/year (USA), $30/year Canada and foreign, US funds only.

1958 Cadillac Owners Association
PO Box 850029
Braintree, MA 02185
617-843-4485

Founded March 1991. 170 members. Organized for the common good, mutual benefit and cooperative assistance of the 1958 Cadillac owner. Must own or be interested in 1958 Cadillacs. Please send a large self-addressed stamped envelope to club address for membership application and brochure. Publishes bi-monthly Newsletter of Motordom's Masterpiece. Dues: one time donation of $22 to sponsor a Newsletter.

Allante Appreciation Group
313 E Jewett St
Dodgeville, WI 53533
800-664-5224; FAX: 770-662-5178
E-mail: allante@pointers.com

Founded 1994. 1,550+ members. Ten newsletters per year. Internet homepage. Fax back service. Member library, national and local group meets and shows. Dues: $30/year.

Allante Owner's Association
140 Vintage Way, #454
Novato, CA 94945
415-382-1973; FAX: 415-883-0203
E-mail: allantefan@aol.com

Founded 1991. 2,500+ members. *Allante Avenues* is a high quality, award winning quarterly magazine with many photos, technical information, regional events, accessory information and sales and resale Allantes and parts exchange. Toll-free number 1-888-ALLANTE, Visa, M/C and AmEx. Subscription rate: $25/year without membership. Dues: $40/year.

Brougham Owners Association
PO Box 254
Berea, OH 44017
216-243-0726

Founded in 1988. 175 members. Devoted to the preservation, restoration and maintenance of the 1957-1960 Eldorado Brougham. Quarterly *B.O.A. Newsletter*, 15-25 pages of historical data, restoration tips, parts and maintenance. Dues: $25/year.

Cadillac Club of North Jersey
76 Phillip Dr
Rockaway, NJ 07866
201-328-1991

Founded 1991. 275 members. An active, local club dedicated to the preservation, restoration and enjoyment of Cadillacs over 15 years old. Parades, shows, monthly newsletter, weekly outdoor meetings during warm weather months. Dues: $20.

Cadillac Convertible Owners of America
PO Box 269
Ossining, NY 10562

For membership information, contact at the above address: Roberta Lynne, membership secretary. Founded 1977. 450 members. Open only to Cadillac convertible owners or owners-to-be. Dues $50/year.

Classic Cadillac Club Deutschland eV
Windmuehlenstr 49
50129 Bergheim Germany
FAX: +49-2234-801217
E-mail: Michael_Thiele@msn.com

Founded 1991. 180 members. Open to all Cadillac owners or owners to be. Bi-monthly newsletter, *The Standard*, some regional meetings and a national meeting every May. Dues: 120 DM Europe, 150 DM worldwide/year.

California Checker Club
1080 N Holliston Ave
Pasadena, CA 91104-3014
818-794-7973

Founded 1990, 50+ members. Open to people interested in Checker auto, ownership not required. We have a newsletter, data base of parts, cross reference numbers, annual show and periodic get-togethers. Dues: $5/year outside southern Calif; $10 for southern Calif residents.

Checker Car Club of America
15536 Sky Hawk Dr
Sun City West, AZ 85375-6512
602-546-9052

For membership information, contact at the above address: Steven D Wilson, President. Founded 1982. Over 900 members. Open to anyone interested in Checkers. Publish quarterly newsletter, *Checkerboard News*. Dues: $10/year North America; $15/year foreign. Members contribute articles. Send for application.

Canadian Classic Chevys
14 E 39th St
Hamilton, ONT Canada L8V 4H1
905-389-6361

Founded 1985. 80 members. Interest in 1955, 56, 57 Chevys. Preservation, restoration and enjoyment of all 1955-57 Chevy cars and trucks from original unrestored to full custom. Dues: $20/year (Canadian).

Chevrolet Nomad Association
8653 W Hwy 2
Cairo, NE 68824
402-393-7281

Founded 1988. 900 members. Preservation of 1955, 1956 and 1957 Chevy Nomads. 10 mailings a year, one annual convention. Dues: $25/year US, $30/year Canada, $35/year foreign.

Classic Chevy Club International Inc
PO Box 607188
Orlando, FL 32860
800-456-1957; FAX: 407-299-3341

World's largest organization devoted to 55-56-57 Chevrolets. New, used, NOS, modified parts. We now stock a full line of reproduction and modified parts for 1955 thru 1966 passenger cars. We publish a monthly magazine, 32 page, color with classifieds, feature cars, tech help and more. $35/year. Call: 800-456-1957.

See our ad on page 35

Cosworth Vega Owners Association
147 Hiram St
Pittsburgh, PA 15209-2133
412-821-8429

For information, contact at the above address: Susan Rupert, membership director. Founded 1978. 16 regional chapters. Annual National Roundup. Quarterly magazine: *Cosworth Vega News*. Dues: $30/year.

Fifty 5 6 7 Club
2021 Wiggins Ave
Saskatoon, SAS Canada S7J 1W2
306-343-0567; FAX: 306-343-5670

For membership information, contact at the above address: National Club Office. Founded 1974. 1,000 to 1,200 members. An organization for the support, promotion, restoration and preservation of the 1955-56-57 Chevrolets, including Chevrolet and GM trucks, Corvettes and Pontiacs. (Owner or enthusiast.) Dues: $45/year (G/S tax included).

Houston Classic Chevy Club
127 Bellaire Ct
Bellaire, TX 77401
713-667-4085

Founded 1989. 100 members. The only restriction is the love of the classic Chevy. Strives to keep the mystique of the 55-56-57 classic Chevy alive through restoration and preservation. An active club who meets once a month, takes cruises and picnics monthly. Benefits are discounted parts, expert advice and help from members, great cruises, picnics, parade and the autorama. Monthly newsletter, *Classic Chevy Chatter*, includes the previous meeting's minutes, tech articles, event calendar, swap sheet and feature cars, etc, included with membership. Dues: $25/year.

Lake Erie (Ohio) Region Vintage Chevrolet Club of America Inc
8439 Celianna Dr
Strongsville, OH 44136
216-238-6579

Founded 1966. 120 members. Must be a member of National organization, The Vintage Chevrolet Club of America, Inc (dues: $25/year). Monthly newsletter, *The Chevroletter*. Swap meet, car shows, tours, social events. Dues: $10/year.

Late Great Chevys
PO Box 607824
Orlando, FL 32860
407-886-1963; FAX: 407-886-7571

Founded 1980. 10,500 members. Open to those interested in 1958-64 Chevys. Monthly publication: *Late Great Chevys*. Restoration parts, free advertising. Subscription rates: $30/year 2nd class, $40/year 1st class. Dues: $30/year.

Lone Star Chevy Club
101 Morning Cloud
Austin, TX 78734
512-261-3459

Founded 1988. 24 members. Local chapter of Late Great Chevy National Club, 1958-1964 Chevys. Dues: $12/year.

Mid-Atlantic Nomad Association
337 Springdale Ave
York, PA 17403

Founded 1970. 200 members. Dedicated to the preservation, restoration and enjoyment of 1955-57 Chevy Nomad wagons and Pontiac Safaris. Dues: $10/year.

National Impala Association
PO Box 968
2928 4th Ave
Spearfish, SD 57783
605-642-5864; FAX: 605-642-5868

Founded 1980. 3,000 members worldwide. Bi-monthly publication. 1958-1969 full size Chevrolets. Dues: $30 second class, $40 first class, $60 overseas.

North-East Chevy/GMC Truck Club
Bryant J Stewart
PO Box 155
Millers Falls, MA 01349
Mike DeWick, 508-371-7477; Bryant Stewart, 508-544-7714

Founded 1983. 500 members. Open to owners and enthusiasts of pre-1973 Chevy/GMC trucks. Main objective is to promote the restoration and preservation of pre-1973 Chevy/GMC trucks and gather early GM truck owners with the same kindred pursuits and spirit. Quarterly publication: *Stove-Bolt News*. Dues: $20/year.

Steel City Classics
701 Prestley Ave
Carnegie, PA 15106
412-276-0384

Founded 1976. 220 members. Monthly newsletter. 2 swap meets, spring and fall; all Chevy show in September; 2 bus trips to Spring and Fall Carlisle; 2 membership parties/meetings, spring and fall; picnic, family oriented club, try to include everyone (kids model show at car show, kids judge cars at picnic). Began as 55-57 Chevy club, but in recent years expanded to include all Chevys. Dues: $10/year.

Treasure State Classics
817 Edith St
Missoula, MT 59801-3905
406-549-5798

Founded 1979. Our concern is for the preservation and restoration of 1955-56-57 Chevrolet cars, pickups and Corvettes. Welcomes members from across Montana. Must have a sincere interest in 1955-56-57 Chevrolets. Summer-fall meetings in various parts of Montana. Newsletter, classic fellowship and fun. 100% chapter of Classic Chevy International. Chapter of Bow Tie Chevys. Dues: $15/year.

Tri-Chevy Association
24862 Ridge Rd
Elwood, IL 60421
815-478-3633

Founded 1972. 97 members. Open to all 1955-57 Chevy owners and enthusiasts. Annual swap meet and car show second Sunday in June. Dues: $15/year.

Vintage Chevrolet Club of America
PO Box 5387
Orange, CA 92613-5387
818-963-CHEV

Founded 1961. 8,000 members. Monthly magazine *Generator & Distributor*. We meet through the year. Our express purpose is the restoring, preserving and enjoying of older Chevrolets.

Connecticut Chevelle Connection
PO Box 6094
Wolcott, CT 06716-0094
203-879-4016, 203-879-4067

Founded 1991. Over 200 members and growing. Our purpose is to encourage restoration and/or preservation and promote general interest in the 1964-1987 Chevrolet Chevelle, Malibu and El

Camino. Monthly meetings, tech talks by guest speakers, parts swaps, newsletter, cruises, car shows, picnic and Christmas party. Dues: $20/year.

International Camaro Club Inc
National Headquarters
2001 Pittston Ave
Scranton, PA 18505
717-585-4082

3,500 plus members. Dedicated to serving the needs of the Camaro owner and enthusiast. Helps fellow members locate parts and supply ID, body tag info, etc. Open to owners and enthusiasts of 1967 to present Camaros. Local/Regional events, Annual Camaro Nationals, Pace Car Registry, 1967-69 Registry for L78/L89 Camaros, we have a 1981 Yenko Turbo Z Registry. Recognizes Z10 coupes. Bi-monthly publication: *In the Fast Lane*. Dues: $20/year US, $25/year Canada, $35/year overseas (US funds please).

National Chevelle Owners Association
7343-J W Friendly Ave
Greensboro, NC 27410
910-854-8935

Founded 1982. 7,000 members. Monthly color magazine: *The Chevelle Report*, which contains information covering 1964-87 Chevelles and El Caminos. Dues: $30/yearUS, $40/year Canada, $55/year all other countries. US funds only.

New England Chevelle & El Camino Association
Jim Goodwin
4 State St
Shrewsbury, MA 01545
PH/FAX: 508-845-9752

Founded 1990. 85 members. Open to those who own or have an interest in the real Heartbeat of America/Chevelles/El Caminos. Monthly newsletter. Friendly exchange of ideas, club meets and get togethers. Member discounts from parts suppliers. Dues: $20/yr.

United States Camaro Club
PO Box 608167
Orlando, FL 32860
407-880-1967; FAX: 407-880-1972

Founded in 1984. 15,000 members. No restrictions to join. Publishes a beautiful full-color bi-monthly 72+ page magazine, Camaro Enthusiast. Local chapters, annual convention(s). Calling 800-CAMAROS gets our tech experts who will answer with tech, decode & numbers help on all Chevys, $1.95/minute w/credit card. Dues: $30 anywhere.

Central Pennsylvania Corvair Club
1751 Chesley Rd
York, PA 17403-4001
717-845-9347

Founded 1975. 80 members. Monthly meetings, tours, parades, shows and annual Mini-Convention. Monthly newsletter: Action. Dues: $10/year.

Circle City Corvair Club
PO Box 17325
Indianapolis, IN 46217
317-271-4504

Founded 1974. 50 members. Purpose is to promote admiration, ownership, care and maintenance of the Corvair. Monthly meetings are held, third Saturday of month, 10 am at Hubler Chevrolet. Open to anyone interested in the Corvair. Newsletter: Valveclatter. Co-host: Hoosier Auto Show, etc. Dues: $9/year.

City Car Club (Corvairs) Inc
30 Camel St
Fairhaven, MA 02719-2102
508-993-2861

Founded 1956. 27 members. Group of Corvair enthusiasts meeting every month to work on club members' cars and further Corvair interest. Monthly publication: Vairgram, free to members. Dues $8/year.

Colonial Corvair Club
27 Phillips Dr
Westford, MA 01886-3404
508-692-9849; FAX: 603-645-5731,
NH, attn: K. Rolt
E-mail: kdrolt@sanders.com

Founded 1980. 25-30 members. Monthly business meetings, tech sessions, car shows, picnics and tours. A chapter of CORSA. Monthly publication, *Vair Waves*. Dues: $12/year.

Corvair Society of America (CORSA)
PO Box 607
Lemont, IL 60439-0607
630-257-6530; FAX: 630-257-5540

Founded 1969. 6,000 members. Dedicated to the operation, preservation, restoration and enjoyment of the Corvair automobile and its derivatives. Monthly publication: *CORSA Communique*. Dues: $27/year US, $30/year Canadian, $40/year overseas. US funds please.

First State Corvair Club Inc
1306 Friar Rd
Newark, DE 19713
302-737-3577

Founded 1982. 48 members. Annual show & banquet, monthly meetings & newsletters, various activities throughout the year. Dues: $12/year.

Aquia Creek Corvette Club
PO Box 986
Stafford, VA 22554
703-659-5234; FAX: 703-659-9112

Founded 1987. 25 members. Annual Carlisle tour, monthly newsletter. Dues: $15/year.

Blue Ridge Corvette Club Inc
PO Box 1
Stuarts Draft, VA 24477
703-828-2418 after 6 pm

Founded 1972. 90 members. Must attend 2 club events and must be elected into club. Benefits, club car shows, club picnic, cruise-ins and road tours in the Blue Ridge Mountains (money raised goes to Ronald McDonald House). Monthly newsletter. Dues: $20/year.

British Columbia Corvette Club
PO Box 80508
Burnaby, BC Canada V5H 3X9
604-738-VETT

Founded 1965. 75 Members. Meets 1st Wed of month, 7 pm at Dueck GM, 86 SE Marine Dr, Vancouver, BC, Canada, V5X 4P8. Call for event information. Dues: $40/year.

Brookville Corvette Club
PO Box 221
Brookville, OH 45309
513-833-5533

Founded 1982. 62 members. Must own or lease a Corvette. Members receive a 20% discount on Vette parts from our sponsor Boose Chevrolet. Monthly newsletter, *The Flags*. We meet on the 2nd Thursday of the month at 7 pm at Brookville Library. We host Cruise Into Summer each year, 400+ free car show, each year, 400+. Dues: $20/year.

Candlewood Valley Corvettes Inc
PO Box 2205
Danbury, CT 06813-2205
203-355-3878

Founded 1979. 125 members. Must own or be the principal driver of a Corvette. Meets the third Thursday of every month at the Stony Hill firehouse, Bethel, CT. Holds an annual all Corvette car show in August at which time a new Corvette is raffled off. All proceeds go to local charities. For more information call Jim Volinski at 203-355-3878. Annual dues: $20 single, $25 family.

Cascade Corvette Club
PO Box 363
Eugene, OR 97440
541-683-2538

Open to all Corvette owners. Our activities include tours, auto crosses, car shows, rallies, picnics, technical sessions and many social events throughout the year. Meets on the second Friday of every month at Joe Romina Chevrolet, located at 2020 Franklin Blvd, Eugene, Oregon. "Guests are always welcome!"

Central Kentucky Corvettes
PO Box 12931
Lexington, KY 40583
606-223-1626

Founded 1973. 50 members. Interest in Corvette or Chevrolet in general. We hold an annual car show for charity, raising $2,500. Publish monthly newsletter, have monthly club meeting and hold events such as CS rallies, mall shows, picnics and seminars. Meet in Lexington, KY 2nd Tuesday at 7. Dues $25-$30/year.

Circle City Corvette Club Inc
7111 E Hiner Ln
Indianapolis, IN 46219
317-359-1221

Founded 1977. 46 members. Must own Corvette. Meetings 1st & 3rd Thursday at Blossom Chevrolet, 1800 N Shadeland Ave. Sponsor Heavy Chevy Showdown and Corvette Cruise at Corvette Nationals. Rally in June. Other events for charity. Area parades and high school homecomings. Dues: $65/year.

Classic Corvette Club UK
Alan Warwick
45 Old Stoke Rd
Aylesbury, Bucks HP21 8DE UK
1296-432928

Founded 1979. 700 Members. Ownership of Corvette not necessary. Holds monthly meetings, Corvette Nationals in July annually. Dues: £25/year.

Classic Glass Corvette Club
PO Box 4936
Marietta, GA 30061
770-662-4320

Founded 1958. 100+ members. Must attend 3 meetings prior to joining. Primarily a social club, some car shows, Corvette restorations. *Vette Set*, monthly club newsletter. Dues: $35/member.

Club Corvette Sweden
Box 2093
14102 Huddinge Sweden
046-11-59030; FAX: 046-11-58005

Founded 1974. 900 Members. Must be owner of a Corvette. Cheaper insurance available. *Corvette Magazine* is published quarterly, contains 60 pages; 10 big Corvette events a year. Dues: 600sek/year.

Coal Country Corvette Club
RD 2, Box 348
Eighty Four, PA 15330
412-228-8663; FAX: 412-225-9838

Founded 1981. 53 members. Must have a Corvette. Meets monthly, puts out a monthly newsletter, has rallies & car shows during the year. Dues: $20/year.

Corvette Club Norway
Boks 55 Bryn
0611 Oslo Norway
+47-222-61290; FAX: +47-222-60321

Founded 1992. 180 members. Club for Corvette owners, meeting 10 times a year, quarterly publication. Dues: 350 NOK/year.

Corvette Club of Delaware Valley
PO Box 397
Willow Grove, PA 19090
215-938-7722; FAX: 215-663-9685

Founded 1958. 270+ members. Must be a Corvette owner to join this club. Benefits include club discounts at various vendors (including goods and services), technical seminars and problem solving assistance, publication to members monthly called the *Gas Cap*, annual judged show since 1970 (1995 is 25th consecu-

tive year), called *The Calvacade of Corvettes*, other activities include charitable fundraising and shows, rallies, picnics, etc. Dues: $30/year.

Corvette Club of Rhode Island
Jerry Walsh, President
PO Box 3622
Cranston, RI 02910-0622
401-294-4927

Founded 1964. 102 members. Must be 18 years or older and own a Corvette. You receive membership card and monthly newsletter. Business meeting first Wednesday of the month. Social meeting monthly. From rallies, car shows to dine-outs. Dues: $36/year.

Corvette Marque Club of Seattle
6002 52nd Ave NE
Seattle, WA 98115-7712
206-525-5109

Founded 1963. 130+ members. Must own a Corvette. Dues: $30/year.

Corvette Memphis
6971 Heathside Cv
Memphis, TN 38119

Founded 1974. 100 members. Meets 2nd Tuesday of each month at 7 pm at Serra Chevrolet. Dues: $60/year.

Corvettes Limited of Los Angeles
PO Box 661281
Arcadia, CA 91066
213-257-4346

Founded 1957. 65 members. Dues: $30/year single, $40/year couple.

Corvettes of Sonoma County
PO Box 1318
Rohnert Park, CA 94927-1318
707-585-1488

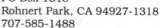

Founded 1979. 64 members. Must own or enjoy Corvettes. Dues: $20/year.

Corvettes of Southern California
PO Box 3603
Anaheim, CA 92803
714-776-6416

Founded 1956. 225 members. Must be registered owner of Corvette and 21 years old. Dues: $30/year.

Corvettes Unlimited
PO Box 33433
Granada Hills, CA 91394-0059
818-366-3687

Founded 1966. 39 members. Must own a Corvette. Members compete in cars shows, races, rallies and attend various Corvette functions. WSCC membership is included with insurance coverage for events. Members receive a discount at our sponsor's dealership.

Corvettes Unlimited Corvette Club
1120 Fairmount Ave
Vineland, NJ 08360

Founded 1977. 250 members. Must own a Corvette, and membership is limited to the southern New Jersey area. Dues $20/year single membership, $25/year couple. South Jersey's largest Corvette club. Benjamin F Notaro, Jr.-President.

Cyclone Corvettes Inc
3028 Northridge Pkwy
Ames, IA 50014-4581
515-292-0017

Founded 1978. 106 members. Only need interest in CorvettesMonthly club newsletter *Vettelines*. Meetings, social events and parties, road trips and cruises, car shows and competitive events. Funkhanas, road rallies. Receive membership packet, jacket patch, club parts discounts, camaraderie. Sponsor of annual All Iowa Corvette Fest. Dues: $20/year, active; $10/year, associate.

Eastern Mass Corvette Club Inc
PO Box 531
Dover, MA 02030-0531
508-668-7229

Founded 1983. 60 members. Must own a Chevrolet Corvette. Social club with owner network, monthly newsletter, car shows, rallies, cruise nights, racing, weekend getaways, monthly meetings. Dues: $25/year.

First State Corvette Club
PO Box 275
Camden, DE 19934
302-697-6971

Founded 1970. A fun loving group dedicated to Corvette enthusiasm. Monthly meetings are held the first Wednesday of each month. At least one club event is planned each month consisting of rallies, shows, community services and just plain fun.

Fort Lauderdale Corvette Club Inc
PO Box 491332
Fort Lauderdale, FL 33349

Founded 1991. 90 members. Must attend 3 meetings & 3 socials before being voted on. Belong to NCCC. Publishes monthly newsletter, attends some major shows in force, local shows, rallies, drags and holds at least one social a month. Dues: $60/year.

The Heartbeat of America Corvette Club
4647 Ardmore
Sterling Heights, MI 48310
810-979-5968

Founded 1992. 55 members. Must own or have interest in the Corvette. Willing to work on charitable fundraisers. Dues: $50/year.

Mid Maine Vettes
PO Box 265
Auburn, ME 04212-0265
207-782-8952

Founded 1979. 16 members. Must own Corvette. Publishes monthly newletter, schedules various Corvette related activities during the year. Dues: $20/year.

National Corvette Owners Association
900 S Washington St G13
Falls Church, VA 22046
703-533-7222; FAX: 703-533-1153

Founded 1975. 12,000 members. For Corvette owners. Discounts on interior products, Chevy dealers, automotive outlets, Corvette auto insurance and more. Monthly publication, *For Vettes Only*. Dues: $35/year.

See our ad on pages 470 & 608

National Corvette Restorers Society
6291 Day Rd
Cincinnati, OH 45252
513-385-8526; FAX: 513-385-8554

Founded 1974. 13,000 members. Membership is open to persons interested in the restoration, preservation and history of 1953-82 Corvettes. 30 chapters in the US. Dues: $30/year US; $35/year Canada; $45/year foreign.

National Council of Corvette Clubs Inc
PO Box 5032
Lafayette, IN 47903
800-245-VETT

Founded 1960. 13,000 members. A non-profit club dedicated to the enhancement, promotion and enjoyment of the Corvette. A service organization that provides communication and exchange of ideas between members and promotes activities on a national scale. Must own a Corvette to join. Quarterly publication: *Blue Bars*. Dues: $30/new membership, $20/renewal.

Natural Glass Corvette Assoc
33 Malapardis Rd
Morris Plains, NJ 07950
201-538-1991

Founded 1970. 50 members. Interest in Corvettes necessary. Annual show to benefit a local charity, parts discount from club sponsor, monthly newsletter, annual tech session. Meet every second Wednesday. Call for details. Dues: $25/year.

North Shore Corvettes of Mass
61 Russell St
Peabody, MA 01960
508-535-3587

Founded 1965. 88 members. Meetings are 3rd Thursday of month at Uno's Restaurant, Lynnfield, MA; Tuesday night cruise night at Uno's, starts May 9th until Oct. Call for information. Dues: $25/year.

Ozaukee Corvette Club
PO Box 371
Cedarburg, WI 53012

Founded 1979. For enthusiasts to get together and participate in activities with America's only true sports car, the Chevrolet Corvette. A social organization rather than a strict competitive group with activities that are geared toward individual and family enjoyment. Club activities include monthly meetings, car shows, picnics, road rallies, cruises and holiday get togethers. Annual dues: $15 individual, $20 family.

River Cities Corvette Club
9113 Stonecrest Dr
Louisville, KY 40272
502-935-2598; FAX: 502-935-2074

Founded 1986. 55 members. Must own Corvette. Publish local monthly newsletter. Events: volunteer car club for National Corvette museum events and for Louisville Auto museum events. Dues $25/year.

SLO Vettes
PO Box 14134
San Louis Obispo, CA 93401
805-549-9022

Founded 1975. 50 members. For Corvette owners in the San Luis Obispo County in California. Monthly newsletter, meetings and fun event. Dues: $45/year.

Solid Axle Corvette Club (SACC)
Box 2288
North Highlands, CA 95660-8288
916-729-1165

Founded 1986. 800 members. SACC is a National club dedicated to enjoying the 1953 through 1962 Corvettes. Founder Noland Adams. Membership is a family membership. Ownership is not required and dues include a subscription to quarterly magazine. Provides technical panel assistance with annual National convention and Regional meets. Show locations are selected to provide activities for the whole family and suitable facilities for the Corvette. Dues: $24/year.

Steeltown Corvette Club
1707 Jancey St
Pittsburgh, PA 15206
412-361-3750

Founded 1972. 210 members. Open to all Corvette enthusiasts. Monthly meetings and newsletter. Annual car show, Christmas party and picnic. Other events include cruises, drag racing, auto cross and road rallies. Numerous parties and fun driving events including weekend road trips. Dues: $20/year.

United Council of Corvette Clubs (UCCC)
33 Shiawassee Ave, Ste C
Akron, OH 44333
330-867-0215; FAX: 330-867-0216

Founded 1978. 250 members. Must be at least 18 years old, own a Corvette and have good standing in the community. There are quarterly meetings, quarterly newsletter called *The Corvette Chronicle*, annual convention in July and regional events. Dues $25/year.

Valley Vettes Corvette Club
PO Box 2373
Yakima, WA 98907
509-452-6646 days, 509-248-1931 nights

Founded 1967. 90 members. Monthly events, big annual event the 2nd weekend in June called Vette-A-Bration. Over 100 Corvettes for car show and shine, BBQ, road rally, picnic, breakfast, 2 day event, cars all over the Northwest attend. Sponsored by Sunfair Chevrolet & Pepsi. Monthly newsletter on upcoming events, *Valley Vettes*, includes listing of officers. Newsletter is sent also to 10 Corvettes in the Northwest. Dues: $45/year couple.

Ventura County Corvette Club
PO Box 24106
Ventura, CA 93002
805-485-5536

Founded 1958. 50 members. Membership limited to Corvette owners and enthusiasts. Non-profit organization raising monies for local charities. Fun loving group that gathers to enjoy and enhance Corvette ownership. Monthly newsletter, bimonthly meetings, monthly run or event, yearly car show. All cars welcome to compete in many categories. Dues: $50/year.

Vettes of Coastal Maine
PO Box 650
Bath, ME 04530
207-882-9617; FAX: 207-882-9086

Founded in 1977. 35 members. Corvette ownership not required. Annual weekend event held in resort area on coast draws Corvette owners from US & Canada; other activities weekends during Vette season, at least twice a month in winter. Dues: $20/year.

Vintage Corvettes of Southern California
PO Box 4873
Thousand Oaks, CA 91359

Founded 1971. 100+ members. Need to have an interest in early Corvettes. Monthly newsletter, *Vintage Notes*. Monthly meetings, 1st Saturday of the month. Dues: $35/year.

Wabash Valley Corvette Club Inc
PO Box 265
Terre Haute, IN 47808-0265
812-234-3039

Founded 1982. 40 Members. Must own a Corvette. Monthly newsletter, cruise & car show, Bash on the Bash, late July. Proceeds go to Ronald McDonald's children's charity. Dues: $25/year.

ZR-1 Owners Registry
Attn: Larry Merow
29 Lucille Dr
Sayville, NY 11782
PH/FAX: 516-563-9242

Founded Aug 1991. 1,700 members. Membership open to any person, business or company with a special interest in the ZR-1 Corvette. *ZR-1 Registry Newsletter,* published 9 times a year, with articles of interest to ZR-1 enthusiasts, technical & human interest is included in dues. Dues: $60/year.

Airflow Club of America
796 Santree Cir
Las Vegas, NV 89110
702-438-4362

For membership information, contact at the above address: Bill Gordon, 702/468-4362. Founded 1962. 600 members. Should be Chrysler or DeSoto Airflow owner or enthusiast. Monthly newsletters including membership roster. National meets annually. Dues $20/year US; $27/year outside North America.

California Chrysler Products Club
PO Box 2660
Castro Valley, CA 94546
510-889-0533

Founded 1967. 400 members. Dedicated to the preservation, restoration and enjoyment of Chrysler product cars and literature. Open to all years and models of Chrysler products. Publication: *Silver Dome Gazette*. Dues: $15/year.

Chrysler 300 Club Inc
PO Box 570309
Miami, FL 33257-0309
800-416-3443; FAX: 305-253-5978

Founded 1969. 650 members. No restrictions to join. Bi-monthly newsletter, *Brute Force*, technical advice, buy and sell ads for Chrysler, parts and cars, articles submitted by members, historical articles on Chrysler 300. Reporting of National 300 meets, Regional club events and show calendar. Dues: $25 USA, $30 Canada (US funds only), $35 foreign/year.

Chrysler 300 Club International Inc
4900 Jonesville Rd
Jonesville, MI 49250
517-849-2783; FAX: 517-849-7445

For membership information, contact at the above address: Eleanor Riehl. Founded 1969. 850 members. Ownership of a 1955-65 letter series 300 or a 1970 Hurst 300 preferred, but any interested person may join. Eight publications per year offering technical assistance, cars and parts locating assistance, classifieds as well as announcements of national and international meets. Dues: $17/year third class US only, $20/year first class US and foreign.

Chrysler 300 Club, Lone Star Chapter
Ken Doyle, Events Coordinator
27 Gay Dr
Kerrville, TX 78028-9009
817-865-2278

For membership information, contact: RC Woltersdorf, VP Membership, 210-655-3877. Founded 1979. 38 member families. Interested in the restoration, preservation and enjoyment of Chrysler 300 Series automobiles, 1955-1971 and 1979. Publication: *Lone Star Chapter News*, bimonthly. Dues: $12/year.

Chrysler Product Owners Club Inc
Ray Montgomery
806 Winhall Way
Silver Spring, MD 20904
301-622-2962

Founded 1979. 350 members. Dedicated to the preservation, restoration and enjoyment of all Chrysler product automobiles including Chrysler, Imperial, Dodge, DeSoto, Plymouth, Maxwell and Chalmers. Technical advisors available to provide info on maintenance, restoration and parts location. Monthly technical seminar provides forum for problem solving and hands-on technical experience. Monthly newsletter lists events, club activities, technical advice and sources for parts. Free want/for sale ads to members. Dues $12.

Chrysler Restorers Club of New Zealand Inc
PO Box 673
Manurewa, Auckland New Zealand

Founded 1976. 150 members. Nationwide New Zealand club dedicated to the restoration and preservation of North American vehicles. Magazine published approximately every 6 weeks. Dues: $20/new joining fee; $35/year, New Zealand dollars.

Chrysler Town & Country Owners Registry
c/o Peter Gariepy
3420 N Dodge Blvd, Ste F
Tucson, AZ 85716-1469
602-881-8101

Founded 1973. 350 members. Promotes interest in and preservation of the Chrysler wooden bodied 1941-50 Town & Country, the 1949-50 Royal station wagon and the 1983-86 LeBaron Town & Country convertible. Quarterly newsletter, *Timber Tales* (32 pages) and membership registry. Joint meets with National Woody Club. Dues: $25/year.

National Chrysler Products Club
c/o Edward W Botchie, President
160 Joyce Dr
Fayetteville, PA 17222
717-352-7673

Founded 1979. 707 members. Purpose of the club: preservation, restoration and exhibition of Chrysler products cars and trucks with emphasis on friendship and family fun. Newsletter 7 times a year, national meet and regional meets. Dues: $20/year.

National Hemi Owners Association
1693 S Reese Rd
Reese, MI 48757
517-868-4921

Founded 1975. Open to owners & enthusiasts of Chrysler hemispherical combustion-chambered engines. Dues: $35/yr US, $40/yr Canada & Mexico, $45/yr overseas. (All funds US$).

Northeast Hemi Owners Association
2022 Cherri Dr
Falls Church, VA 22043-1314
703-893-9370

For information, contact: Mike McGuire, 2022 Cherri Dr, Falls Church, VA 22043-1314; PH: 703-893-9370. 200 members. Dedicated to preserving, restoring and enjoying Chrysler hi-performance vehicles, not strictly the Hemi. Two meets per year in the northeast US. A people-oriented club for all ages and backgrounds. Bimonthly newsletter. Dues: $25/year or $30/year married couple.

Slant 6 Club of America
PO Box 4414
Salem, OR 97302
503-581-2230

Founded 1980. 2,000 members. Open to all slant 6 Chrysler products, especially Darts and Valiants. Ownership not required for membership. 20 regional chapters with meets and other events. Quarterly magazine: *Slant 6 News*. Dues: $22/year.

Citroen Car Club, Auckland Inc
PO Box 74393, Market Road
Auckland New Zealand
0061-9-2777614; FAX: 0061-9-2784301

Founded 1964. 90 members. Caters to owners and people interested in all models of Citroens. Monthly meet and event. Monthly newsletter and quarterly New Zealand magazine. Dues: $30/year.

Cooper Car Club
14 Biscayne Dr
Ramsey, NJ 07446
FAX: 201-825-8285

COOPER

Founded 1987. 185 members. Worldwide organization to promote the use and restoration of Cooper cars. Also to recognize a place in motor racing history for Charles and John Cooper. Quarterly newsletter. Dues: $20/year.

Mini Cooper Car Club of New Zealand (Inc)
Tony Maulder, President
PO Box 9069
Auckland New Zealand
09-5284581

COOPER

Founded 1981. 100 members. To get Cooper owners together for social, technical, racing, touring, information purposes and to help promote the marque. Generally Mini Cooper owners or those who wish to own one. Club night first Tuesday each month, 156 Kepa Road, Orakei, Auckland, 7:30 pm. We also have a Mini Cooper Register of as many Coopers as we can find in New Zealand. Monthly (11 per year) magazine: Cooper Mag. Club events, technical advice on Mini Coopers, articles from other mags, etc on Mini Coopers. Dues: $30 NZ plus postage.

Crosley Automobile Club Inc
Attn: Jim Friday
217 N Gilbert
Iowa City, IA 52245

For membership information, contact at the above address: J. Friday. Founded 1969. 1,200 members, should be a Crosley enthusiast. Dues: $12/year.

Clubs & Organizations

DAF Club-America
293 Hudson St
Hackensack, NJ 07601
201-343-1252, 201-342-3684; FAX:
201-342-3568

Founded 1980. 10 members. West Coast address: 706 Monroe St, Santa Rosa, CA 95405. Club consists of owners of DAF cars and others with an interest in DAFs. Dedicated to the presesrvation of DAFs and promotion of the CVT transmission pioneered by DAF. Publication: *DAF Bulletin.* Dues: $10/year.

Daimler & Lanchester Owners Club Ltd
 The Manor House
Trewyn, Abergavenny
Gwent, NP7 7PG, England
PH/FAX: 01873-890737

For membership information, contact at the above address: John Ridley. Founded 1964. Over 2,500 members. Dues: $50/year airmail, plus $16 initiation fee.

Datsun Roadster Association
11520 Seahurst Rd
Richmond, BC Canada V7A 3P2

A National Datsun Roadster Club with 400+members inUS-Canada-Japan-Australia. Several annual events. 4 newsletters a year. Dues $25/year.

Datsun "Z" Club Inc
PO Box 24-176
Royal Oak, Auckland 1030 New Zealand
PH/FAX: 64-9-636-5443

Founded 1981. 168 members. Possessors of Nissan/Datsun Fairlady, Fairlady Z, 260Z, 240Z, 280Z/ZX, 300ZX. Quarterly magazine. Motorsport, social, technical assist, parts supply. Dues: $60/year.

Z Club of Georgia
333 England Pl
Marietta, GA 30066
770-926-2390; FAX: 770-475-2802

Founded 1992. 225 members. Must own a Z or ZX. Discounts, rallies, autocross, road racing, monthly newsletter. Monthly meeting 1st Tuesday at Hooter's, Jimmy Carter Blvd, Norcross, GA. Dues: $25/single, $30/family.

Club Delahaye
B P 15
59640 Dunkerque
France
3 28 29 68 68; FAX: 3 28 61 07 32

Two road meets in different towns in France each year as well as club-sponsored dinners in Paris. Bulletin published four times a year. Dues 500 Francs/year.

DeLorean Mid-Atlantic
515 W Chelten Ave, Suite 1009
Philadelphia, PA 19144
215-849-5160

Founded 1985. 125 members. All DeLorean enthusiasts welcome. Annual regional meet. Quarterly newsletter. Monthly tech-socials, including free door adjustment social. Parts interchange list. Technical advisories. Dues: $12/years.

DeLorean Owners Association
879 Randolph Rd
Santa Barbara, CA 93111
PH/FAX: 805-964-5296; E-mail:
www.delorean@impulse.net

Founded 1983. 2,000 members. Conducts National and Regional events. Publishes a full color, 40 page, quarterly magazine. Non-profit. Dues: $60/year. E-mail to: www.delorean@impulse.net

DeSoto Club of America
403 S Thornton St
Richmond, MO 64085
816-421-6006; 816-470-3048

For membership information, contact at the above address: Walter O'Kelly. Founded 1972. Dedicated to preserving and restoring the DeSoto automobile. Publishes newsletter: *DeSoto Days*, bimonthly. Dues: $15/year.

Pantera International
18586 Main St, Suite 100
Huntington Beach, CA 92648
714-848-6674; FAX: 714-843-5851

Founded 1973. Members worldwide. DeTomaso factory authorized. Ownership not required. Publishing quarterly color magazine and authoritative book. Your leading source for technical, collecting, restoration, vintage racing, historical, personality and feature car information. Many cars for sale. Annual convention in Monterey each August where we are the sole sponsoring club for the DeTomaso marque at the Concours Italiano. Club store has many DeTomaso theme items. Dues $50 US, $60 foreign per year. Visit our web site: http://www.panteracars.com

Divco Club of America
PO Box 1142
Kingston, WA 98346-1142
360-598-3938

Divco

Founded 1991. Over 300 members. Dedicated to the preservation and restoration of Divco vehicles. Open to all Divco enthusiasts. Newsletter provides information, parts sources, history, help and encouragement, free classifieds for members. For information contact: Les Bagley, newsletter editor. Dues: $18/year. Other classes available.

DKW Club of America
260 Santa Margarita Ave
Menlo Park, CA 94025
415-321-6640; FAX: 415-329-0129
E-mail: jowett@best.com

Serving Auto Union and DKW owners and enthusiasts worldwide. Fun, informative newsletter, parts and information sources and healthy doses of encouragement. Annual membership is just $15 in North America, $20 elsewhere. Contact Byron Brill at the address listed for more information.

D.A.R.T.S.
PO Box 9
Wethersfield, CT 06129-0009
860-257-8434 evenings 8-10 pm
E-mail: dart340@gnn.com

Founded 1986. 375 members. A service club for high performance 1967-1972 Dodge Darts and Demons. Quarterly newsletters provide events, technical information and restoration information. Free ads to buy and sell are encouraged to be used. Dues: $10/year.

Dodge Brothers Club
PO Box 151
North Salem, NY 10560

Founded 1983. 1,100 members. Open to anyone interested in Dodge Brothers or Graham Brothers vehicles 1914-1938. Ownership of vehicle is not required for membership.

Membership includes subscription to bi-monthly 32 page magazine, annual meets at locations across the US and Canada. The purpose of the club is to enjoy and exchange information on D-B & G-B vehicles, the brothers and their company. Members receive discounts on publications, video tapes and other items related to D-B or G-B produced by the club's historical research committee. Technical advisors are available to assist with questions related to the restoration or maintenance of vehicles. Worldwide membership. Dues: $18 US & Canadian, $26 (US funds) foreign.

FWD Performance Club
PO Box 90
Vanlue, OH 45890-0090
419-387-7003

Founded 1991. 240 members. Committed to preserving the history and creating a future for Shelby built and inspired Dodge powered automobiles. Ownership not mandatory, enthusiasm is. Membership includes a monthly publication, *The Puller*, and other benefits. An annual convention is held in different parts of the county each year. *The Puller* provides historical, technical and general interest information about Shelby built and inspired Dodge powered automobiles. Dues: $18/year.

Midwest Shelby-Dodge Auto Club Inc
14620 W 93rd St
Lenexa, KS 66215-3076
913-541-0532; 314-831-4412 or
913-721-2032 evenings; E-mail:
sdacmw@aol.com

Open to enthusiasts of Shelby-Dodge and/or related MoPar vehicles. The Midwest Region of the Shelby-Dodge Auto Club is dedicated to preserving and enjoying "Carroll Shelby influenced" Dodge vehicles manufactured since 1983. We meet once per month, issue a monthly newsletter and sponsor events all year. Dues: $15/year, payable to Shelby-Dodge Auto Club, Midwest. (A not-for-profit club).

Shelby Dodge Automobile Club
PO Box 4631
Lutherville, MD 21094-4631
215-721-8656; E-mail: sdac@gdb.org

The Shelby Dodge Automobile Club (SDAC) is an automotive enthusiast club whose aim is to preserve the spirit of power by Dodge, unleashed by Shelby. The SDAC newsletter, *Up Front*, features articles and information on Shelby Dodge and Dodge Shelby vehicles (Omni GLH, Shelby Charger, GLHS, CSX, Lancer and Shelby Dakota, Daytonas, Shadow, Spirit R/T, Shelby Can Am and Viper and more). Annual national convention. Many local chapters and events.

Durant Family Registry
2700 Timber Ln
Green Bay, WI 54313-5899

For information, contact at the above address: Jeff Gillis. Founded 1976. 425 members. Club covers Durant, Star, Flint, Rugby (commercial and export), DeVaux and the Canadian Frontenac. Club library includes parts and service manuals, owner's manuals as well as sales literature and other items relating to these marques. Some reproduction parts available. Also Durant product information. Quarterly publication. Dues: $20/year US and Canada, $25/year foreign.

Edsel Owners Club of America Inc
816 Richard Ln
Danville, CA 94526
510-837-6410; FAX: 510-837-1602

For membership information, contact Harold Kleckner, Membership Vice President, at the address shown. Club founded 1967, 1,000+ members world-wide. Edsel ownership not necessary. Dues: $25/year US and Canada, $30/year foreign, US dollars.

International Edsel Club
PO Box 371
Sully, IA 50251
515/594-4284

Founded 1969. 1,025 members. A family club dedicated to owning and restoring Edsels. Annual meeting the second week of August. Monthly newsletter: Edseletter. Dues: $15/year.

Elva Owners of America
318 Adrian
Berea, OH 44017
216-243-2894

Founded 1990. 150+ members. Open to anyone interested in Elva cars. We publish a newsletter five to six times a year and offer listings of cars and parts for sale. We are involved with reproducing parts for early Elvas. We hold a reunion every five years (the next is at Road America with all Elva models represented). We have a registry of serial numbers and information on all models. Dues: $25/year.

Ferrari Club of America Inc
3186 Alton Rd
Atlanta, GA 30341
PH/FAX: 800-328-0444

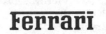

Founded 1962. Approximately 4,000 members. Monthly and quarterly publications, meets in all parts of country and at major US race tracks. Technical advice available. Call above number for more information or to join by credit card.

Fiat Club Belgio-Abarth Corse
PO Box 10
2018 Antwerpen-11
Philippe Bacquaert Belgium
PH/FAX: 03-232-13-32

Founded 1986. 400 members. All classic Fiats & Abarths, club magazine and mailing, Classic Club Race Assoc, October, F1 circuit Zolder. Dues: 1,100bf/year.

Fiat-Lancia Unlimited (FLU)
PO Box 193, Dept HVA
Shillington, PA 19607

Founded 1986. 600 members. Must have interest in Fiat group cars. Ownership not required. Enthusiast group dedicated to keeping the Fiat marque alive in North America. Many activities including annual meet. Bi-monthly newsletter: Fiat Ricambi. Ties with other American and foreign clubs. Not just Spyders and X1/9s. Strong Lancia Beta membership. Dues: $18/year US; $24/year Canada; $36 international.

Rear Engine Fiat Club
PO Box 682
Sun Valley, CA 91353
818-768-3552

Founded 1988 by Jonathan Thompson of *Road & Track* for lovers of rear engine Fiats and derivative cars. Four driving events per year plus Fiat swap meet, car show. Quarterly newsletter. Dues: $15/year.

The 54 Ford Club of America
1517 N Wilmot #144
Tucson, AZ 85712
PH/FAX: 520-886-1184
E-mail: wmvc06a@prodigy.com

Founded 1986. 520 members. Open to 54 Ford owners and those interested in 54 Fords. Quarterly newsletter. Dues: $15/year.

The Club of American Ford
Taljo 18492
Akersberga Sweden
854022975; FAX: 854023976
E-mail: jab@algonet.se

Founded 1976. 1,000 members. Must own an American Ford to join. http://www.algonet.se/~jab/ford.html

Consul-Zephyr-Zodiac Car Club Inc Auckland
PO Box 99257
Newmarket, Auckland New Zealand
09-5768330, president

Founded 1981. 85 members. The objects for which the ACZZCC (Inc) are established is to promote a good image and name of the car and the recreation of its members by the encouragement and participation in all activities incorporating the car. Monthly meet & run, yearly national or international meet. Monthly magazine, runs include displays, shows, fun runs, etc. Dues: $30 (NZ) full, $15 (NZ) associate, $10 (NZ) joining fee.

Crown Victoria Association
PO Box 6
Bryan, OH 43506
419-636-2475

For membership information, contact the above address. Founded 1978. 1,500 members. Club recognizes all 1954-56 Fords. Ownership of a car is not essential. Dues: $29/year US and Canada, $45/year foreign, US funds please.

The Early Ford V8 Club of America
PO Box 2122
San Leandro, CA 94577
510-606-1925
E-mail: fordv8club@aol.com

Founded 1963. 8,500 members. Must be interested in Fords, 1932 to 1953. A national historical society dedicated to the restoration and preservation of Ford Motor Company vehicles from 1932 through 1953. Bimonthly publication: *V8 Times*, all about flathead Fords. Dues: $30/year.

Fabulous Fifties Ford Club of America
PO Box 286
Riverside, CA 92502
909-591-2168

350 members. Dedicated to the preservation and restoration of all Ford Motor Company products built from 1949 to 1960. Ford ownership not required. Quarterly publication. Dues: $25/year US and Canada, $40/year foreign (US funds).

Fairlane Club of America
1334 Lakeview Ave, RR 1
East Peoria, IL 61611-9754
309-822-8602

1,600 members. Dedicated to the preservation and restoration of the mid-size 1962-70 Fairlanes, 1968-71 Torinos and 1962-63 Mercury Meteors. Bimonthly newsletter. Please include SASE with inquiry. Dues: $24/year US, $28/year Canada, $32/year overseas. (In US funds).

FoMoCo Owners Club
PO Box 19665
Denver, CO 80219
303-784-5505

A national, family oriented, social club devoted to the acquisition, restoration, maintenance and exhibition of all Ford Motor Co. 4-wheeled vehicles from 1903 thru 15 years old.

Ford-Freak Club of Finland
PO Box 351
00531 Helsinki Finland
+358-0-534915

Founded 1987. 200 members. For all US Ford fans. Keep up good Ford humor, Ford-Freak magazine 4 times year. Meets: Ford Nationals, Ford Konference, swap & meet, Henry Ford Memorial Run. Dues: 100 FIM/year.

Great Lakes Roadster Club
PO Box 302
Bath, OH 44210

For membership infromation, contact: Jerry A. Barker.

International Ford Retractable Club
PO Box 389
Marlboro, MA 01752
508-359-5857; FAX: 508-481-9536

Founded 1971. 1,200 members. Promotes the restoration, preservation and further interest in the 1957, 1958, 1959 Skyliner retractable hardtop produced by Ford Motor Co. Car ownership not required. Dues: $30 US, $32 Canadian, $41 foreign/yr.

Model A Drivers
PO Box 83
Shawano, WI 54166
715-524-3180

Founded 1985. 120 members. Promotes fun and friendship in the operating of Model A Fords, 1928-31. Dues: $10/year.

Model A Ford Cabriolet Club
PO Box 515
Porter, TX 77365
713-429-2505

Founded 1980, currently 400 members. The club is a special interest group of the Model A Ford Club of America (MAFCA) and the Model A Restorers Club (MARC). Formed to provide a way to exchange information and parts among owners and enthusiasts of the cabriolet (a rare body style of the Model A Fords manufactured from 1929-31). Quarterly publication, *The Cabrioletter*, included in dues. Contains club announcements, technical articles and classified ads. Dues: $12/year (USA & Canada), $15/year overseas.

Model A Ford Club of America
250 S Cypress
La Habra, CA 90631
310-697-2712, 310-697-2737
FAX: 310-690-7452

Founded 1957. 32,000 members. Interest in the Model A Ford. Technical information in the *Restore the Club* publication, national meets on the even year. Dedicated to the restoration and preservation of the Model A Ford. Over 300 chapters, 22 international chapters, 14 special interest and body style groups. The club is the largest car club in the world devoted to a single model. Dues: $30/year, $34 foreign/year, $36 foreign 1st class/year.

See our ad on page 477

chapters:

Alabama	*Heart of Dixie A's*, 26561 Martin Branch Rd, Madison, AL 35758
Alaska	*Alaskan A's*, 3612 Delores Dr, Eagle River, AK 99577
	MAFC of the North, 4128 Parsons, Anchorage, AK 99504
Arizona	*Ah-ooo-gah A's of Arizona*, 8315 E Vernon Ave, Scottsdale, AZ 85257

Arizona Traveling A's, 1212 E Alameda Dr, Tempe, AZ 85282

Hi-Country A's, 1601 Quail Run, Prescott, AZ 86303

Model A Restorers Club of Arizona, PO Box 5255, Mesa, AZ 85201

Patagonia T & A, PO Box 2175, Nogales, AZ 85628

Phoenix Model A Club, PO Box 35702, Phoenix, AZ 85069

Tucson, 2003 S 4th, Tucson, AZ 85713

Arkansas 50th Anniversary A's, 16921 Crystal Valley Rd, Little Rock, AR 72210

Natural State A's, 17644 Fox Hollow, Garfield, AR 72732

Texarkana A's, 4902 Fernwood, Texarkana, AR 75502

California A-400 Group, 2222 Loma Vista, Pasadena, CA 91104

Acorn A's, Box 2321, Castro Valley, CA 94546

Adobe A's, 1250 Orange St, Red Bluff, CA 96080

Amador A's, PO Box 967, Pine Grove, CA 95665

Angel City, 4528 2nd Ave, Los Angeles, CA 90043

Auburn A's, Box 4345, Auburn, CA 95604

Bakersfield, Box 1616, Bakersfield, CA 93302

Bay Area, 181 Alpine Way, San Bruno, CA 94066

Blossom Trail A's, PO Box 26, Reedley, CA 93654

Brake Away A's, 5121 Vernon Ave, Fremont, CA 94536

Butte-View A's, PO Box 3591, Yuba City, CA 95992

Capistrano Valley A's, Box 614, San Juan Capistrano, CA 92693

Capitol A's, Box 1416, Carmichael, CA 95609 -1416

Central California Regional Group of MAFCA, 4326 E Lane Ave, Fresno, CA 93702

Charter Oak A's, Box 3696, Visalia, CA 93278-3696

Chico A's, 2674 Ceres Ave, Chico, CA 95926

Conejo Valley, PO Box 332, Newbury Park, CA 91319

Cruisin' A's, 42221 Harmony Dr, Hemet, CA 92544

Cuesta Crankers, Box 714, San Luis Obispo, CA 93406

Delta A's, Box 7328, Stockton, CA 95267

Diablo A's, Box 6125, Concord, CA 94524

Diamond Tread, Box 4563, Downey, CA 90241

Eastern Sierra Model A Ford Club, 777 Rome Dr, Bishop, CA 93514

Eel River Valley A's, Box 688, Fortuna, CA 95540

El Camino A's, PO Box 1754, San Mateo, CA 94401

Exclusive A's, 1549 Poppy Peak, Pasadena, CA 91105

Feather River A's, PO Box 1833, Quincy, CA 95971

Flying Quail, PO Box 1994, Salinas, CA 93901

Four Bangers, 20207 Stagg St, Canoga Park, CA 91306

Four Ever Four Cylinder A's, 39480 Colleen Way, Temecula, CA 92592-8438

Gateway A's, Box 1429, Merced, CA 95340

Golden Feather, 2016 W Lincoln St, Oroville, CA 95965

Gra-Neva, Box 2415, Grass Valley, CA 95945

GRAMPA, Box 2201, Monterey, CA 93940

Hangtown A's, Box 2296, Placerville, CA 95667

Happy Honkers, PO Box 1912, Porterville, Ca 93258-1912

Heartland A's, PO Box 3665, Ontario, CA 91761

Henry's A's, Box 46, Livermore, CA 94550

Henry's Originals, 8821 La Entrada, Whittier, CA 90605

Humboldt Bay A's, PO Box 6664, Eureka, CA 95501

Jewel City, Box 1833, Glendale, CA 91209

Lake County A's, PO Box 634, Clearlake, CA 95422

Linden A's, 16956 E Hwy 26, Linden, CA 95236

Main Bearings, 2870 Brandt, La Verne, CA 91750

Marin A's, Box 2864, San Rafael, CA 94901

Mariposa Four Bangers, 5840 Evergreen Ln, Mariposa, CA 95338

Modesto Area A's, Box 6073, Modesto, CA 95355

Mother Lode A's, Box 1500, Murphys, CA 95247

Mountain Quail, Box 539, Loyalton, CA 96118

Napa Valley A's, Box 2656, Napa, CA 94558

Northern California Regional Group, 2674 Ceres, Chico, CA 95926

Oakdale A's, PO Box 60, Oakdale, CA 95361

Orange County, PO Box 10595, Santa Ana, CA 92711

Palomar, Box 821, Carlsbad, CA 92018

Paradise Valley, 124 S "E" St, San Bernardino, CA 92401

Phaeton Club (35-A, B), 1049 Don Pablo Dr, Arcadia, CA 91006

Pomona Valley, Box 2302, Pomona, CA 91769

Queen Mary, 34378 Olive Grove Rd, Lake Elsinore, CA 92330

Redding Rambling A's, Box 3872, Redding, CA 96049

Reliable A's, Box 160322, Sacramento, CA 95816

San Diego, Box 15053, San Diego, CA 92175

San Fernando Valley, Box 2713, Van Nuys, CA 91404

Santa Anita A's, Box 904, Arcadia, CA 91006

Santa Barbara, PO Box 60358, Santa Barbara, CA 93160

Santa Clara Valley, PO Box 6072, San Jose, CA 95150

Sierra, Box 2065, Fresno, CA 93718-2065

Sis-Q-A's, 523 N Oregon St, Yreka, CA 96097

Sonoma A's, Box 4052, Santa Rosa, CA 95402

Sonora A's, Box 382, Sonora, CA 95370-0382

Southern California Region, 5528 N Lenore, Arcadia, CA 91006

Spark'n A's, 2640 Rustic Oak Ct, Rocklin, CA 95677

Tokay A's, Box 861, Lodi, CA 95241

Touring A's, 1777 Rosswood Dr, San Jose, CA 95124

Towe Ford Museum of California, 2200 Front St, Sacramento, CA 95818

Ukulele A's Plus, PO Box 2922, Carmichael, CA 95609-2922

US A's, PO Box 805, Cedar Ridge, CA 95924

Ventura, PO Box 5584, Ventura, CA 93005

Whittier, Box 1908, Whittier, CA 90609

Colorado   *Animas A's*, 6842 County Rd 203, Durango, CO 81301

Ford Model AA Truck Club, 1365 Cherryvale Rd, Boulder, CO 80303

Mile-Hi, PO Box 5554, Terminal Annex, Denver, CO 80217

Pike's Peak, PO Box 1929, Colorado Springs, CO 80901

Southern Colorado A's, Box 5221, Pueblo, CO 81002

Connecticut   *Connecticut*, 5 Brownstone Rd, East Granby, CT 06026

Fairfield County A's, 5 Ridge Dr, Westport, CT 06880

Northwestern Connecticut A's, 65 Woodbridge Ln, Thomaston, CT 06787

Florida   *Columbia A's*, RR 3, Box 4641, Ft White, FL 32038

First Coast, 4938 Glade Hill St, Jacksonville, FL 32207

Model A's of Greater Orlando, 120 Parsons Rd, Longwood, FL 32779

Moonport, PO Box 1611, Cocoa, FL 32922

Northwest Florida, 728 Rodney Ave, Ft Walton Beach, FL 32548

Palm Beach, 1340 Scottsdale Rd E, West Palm Beach, FL 33417

Panhandle A's, PO Box 411, Panama City, FL 32402

Georgia   *Georgia*, PO Box 5, Lilburn, GA 30247

Georgia Shade Tree A's, 1110 Terrace Circle Dr, North Augusta, GA 29841-4349

Hawaii   *Aloha*, 301 Lunalilo Home Rd, Honolulu, HI 96825

Idaho   *Magic Valley Model A Ford Club*, 2339 Forest Vale Dr, Twin Falls, ID 83301

Snake River A's, PO Box 882, Fruitland, ID 83619

Treasure Valley, c/o Fred Gooding, 20441 Fargo Rd, Wilder, ID 83676

Illinois   *Chain O'Lakes*, Box 420, Antioch, IL 60002

Chicagoland A's, 1201 W Glenn Ln, Mount Prospect, IL 60056

Fourever Fours, PO Box 6407, Peoria, IL 61601

Naper A's, Box 245, Naperville, IL 60566

North Shore Model A's, 1764 Bowling Green, Lake Forest, IL 60045

Prairie A's, 309 Carrie Ave, Urbana, IL 61801

Salt Creek A's, 611 E Harding Ave, LaGrange Park, IL 60525

Sangamon Valley, PO Box 4462, Springfield, IL 62708

Secrets of Speed Society, 723 W Randolph, Chicago, IL 60661

Indiana   *Sycamore A's*, RR 22, Box 410, Terre Haute, IN 47802

Iowa   *Central Iowa MAFC*, PO Box 259, Des Moines, IA 50301

Humbolt, 312 2nd St N, Humbolt, IA 50548

Kansas   *Henry Leavenworth*, 3909 Shrine Park, Leavenworth, KS 66048

Plain Ol' A's, 24250 W 83rd, Lenexa, KS 66227

Wichita A's, PO Box 25, Wichita, KS 67201-0025

Kentucky   *Falls City*, 6495 Bardstown Rd, Elizabethtown, KY 42701

Louisiana   *Acadiana*, Box 12401, New Iberia, LA 70562

Ark-La-Tex A's, 503 E Kings Hwy, Shreveport, LA 71105

New Orleans, PO Box 1674, Metairie, LA 70001

North Lake A's, PO Box 701, Covington, LA 70434

Clubs & Organizations

Red Stick, 2527 Broussard St, Baton Rouge, LA 70808

Maryland MAFC of Greater Baltimore, 5930 Old Washington Rd, Sykesville, MD 21784

Model A Ad Collectors, 4700 Locust Hill Ct, Bethesda, MD 20814

Massachusetts Cape Cod, 115 Windjammer Ln, Eastham, MA 02642

Massachusetts Bay, 183 Worcester St, Taunton, MA 02780

Minuteman, PO Box 545, Sudbury, MA 01776

Postal A's, 22 Burlington Rd, Bedford, MA 01730

Town Car Society, 197 Amity St, Amherst, MA 01002

Western MA Model A Ford Restorers, 96 Craiwell Ave, West Springfield, MA 01089

Worcester County, PO Box 36, North Oxford, MA 01537

Michigan Authentic A's, 1205 S Ridge, Canton, MA 48188

Minnesota Lady Slipper A's, 110 6th St NE, Stewartville, MN 55976

Town Sedan Club, 9325 31st Ave N, New Hope, MN 55427

Twin Cities, 6041 Morgan Ave S, Minneapolis, MN 55419

Missouri Heart of America, 2100 Walnut St, Kansas City, MO 64108

Mid-Missouri Model A Restorers Club, 1407 Colonial Dr, Fulton, MO 65251

Show Me Model A Club, Rt 3, Box 292D, Cole Camp, MO 65325

Southwest Missouri, PO Box 9735, Springfield, MO 65801

Nebraska Cornhusker, 7801 E Avon Ln, Lincoln, NE 68505

Golden Rod, 1605 Ave C, Cozad, NE 69130

Meadowlark, Box 6011, Omaha, NE 68106

Nevada Battle Born A's, 5880 Sun Valley Blvd, Sun Valley, NV 89433

Las Vegas Valley, 5425 N Durango Dr, Las Vegas, NV 89129

Sagebrush, Box 1034, Carson City, NV 89702

Silver State A's, PO Box 2012, Elko, NV 89801

New Hampshire White Mountain, 16 Martin Rd, Weare, NH 03281

New Jersey Cohanzick Region, PO Box 1446, Millville, NJ 08332

New Jersey, 518 Warren St, Scotch Plains, NJ 07076

Watchung Valley, 116 Ashland Rd, Summit, NJ 07901

New Mexico Poco Quatros, 3435 Vassar Dr NE, Albuquerque, NM 87107

New York Adirondack A's, PO Box 1246, Clifton Park, NY 12065

Lakeshore, 776 Stony Point Rd, Spencerport, NY 14559-9721

Long Island, PO Box 1204, Smithtown, NY 11787-0959

Model A Ford Club of Westchester, 23 Main St, Mt Kisco, NY 10549

Model A's of Rockland, 3 Barbara Rd, New City, NY 10956

Mohican, Rt 1, Mason Rd, Mohawk, NY 13407

New York City, 17 Midland Rd, Staten Island, NY 10308

NY-PA Twin Tiers, PO Box 2, Elmira, NY 14902

Onondaga Model A Buffs, Canal Rd, Memphis, NY 13112

Queen City A's, 3883 Walden Ave, Lancaster, NY 14086

Southern Tier, RR #1. Box 53A, Mannsville, NY 13661

Spark & Throttle, 38-01 Little Neck Pkwy, Little Neck, NY 11363

North Carolina Eastern Carolina, Rt 13, Box 363, Greenville, NC 27858

Queen City, PO Box 31783, Charlotte, NC 28231

Thermal Belt, Rt 1, Box 220-B, Ellenboro, NC 28040

Winston-Salem, 1821 Fannwood, Winston-Salem, NC 27107

Ohio Cincinnati, 4239 School Section, Cincinnati, OH 45211

Dayton-Buckeye, PO Box 271, Englewood, OH 45322

Northern Ohio, 410 North St, Chardon, OH 44024

Ohio Valley Region, PO Box 62303, Sharonville, OH 45241

Oklahoma Okie A's, 401 S Owen Dr, Mustang, OK 73064

Ouachita, PO Box 463, Broken Bow. OK 74728

Sooner, PO Box 83192, Oklahoma City, OK 73148

Territorial, 216 E Edwards St, Edmond, OK 73034

Tulsa, Box 580581, Tulsa, OK 74158

Oregon Azalea A's, 2350 Quines Creek Rd, Azalea, OR 97410

Beaver, 14655 NW Bonneville Loop, Beaverton, OR 97006

Blue Mountain A's, Box 1724, Pendleton, OR 97801

DeLuxe Tudor Sedan Owner's Group, 5595 Pioneer Rd, Medford, OR 97501

Enduring A's, PO Box 1428, Albany, OR 97321

Henry's Lady, 1990 Midway Ave, Grants Pass, OR 97527

High Desert A's, PO Box 5602, Bend, OR 97708

McKenzie A's, Box 7271, Eugene, OR 97401

Myrtlewood A's, Box 996, Coos Bay, OR 97420

Northwest Region, 17470 SE Tickle Creek Rd, Boring, OR 97009

Willamette Valley, PO Box 3031, Salem, OR 97302

Pennsylvania Beaver Valley, 3763 37th St, Beaver Falls, PA 15010

Delaware Valley, 5821 Ditman St, Philadelphia, PA 19135

Lehigh Valley, Box 9031, Bethlehem, PA 18018-9031

Mercer A's, 1865 S Easton Rd, Doylestown, PA 18901

North Penn A's, 1651 N Wales Rd, Norristown, PA 19403

Steamtown A's, 1251 Gravel Pond Rd, Clarks Summit, PA 18411

Rhode Island *Little Rhody,* 622 Hatchery Rd, North Kingstown, RI 02852

South Carolina *Low Country Chapter, MAFCA,* 1675 Wappoo Rd, Charleston, SC 29407

Palmetto, 1720 Pisgah Church Rd, Lexington, SC 29072

Western Carolina Model A Ford Club, 6 Crestline Dr, Greenville, SC 29609

Tennessee *Lookout A's,* 5410 Sky Valley Dr, Hixson, TN 37343

Memphis, 691 Stratford Rd, Memphis, TN 38122

Middle Tennessee, Box 110424, Nashville, TN 37222-0424

Smoky Mountain, PO Box 3816, Knoxville, TN 37917

Texas *31 Fordor Slant Windshield Group,* 6919 Cornelia Ln, Dallas, TX 75214

Abilene, PO Box 2962, Abilene, TX 79604

Alabama, 7708 Briaridge Rd, Dallas, TX 75248

Alamo A's, Box 700156, San Antonio, TX 78270

Autumn Trails, Rt 5, Box 52635, Winnsboro, TX 75494

Bluebonnet, PO Box 1, Copperas Cove, TX 76522

Cabriolet Club (68-A, B, C), PO Box 515, Porter, TX 77365

Capitol City A's, 8002 Baywood Dr, Austin, TX 78759

Cross Timbers Model A Ford Club, PO Box 407, Hico, TX 76457

Dallas, Box 1028, Addison, TX 75001-1028

Devil's River A's, 124 E Garfield Ave, Del Rio, TX 78840

Fort Worth, 6611 Anglin Dr, Fort Worth, TX 76119

Four States A's, 11 Azalea, Texarkana, TX 75503

Golden Triangle A's, 795 Belvedere, Beaumont, TX 77706

Greater Houston Model A Restorers Club, 220 Ilfrey, Baytown, TX 77520

International Victoria Association, 11084 Windjammer, Frisco, TX 75034

Lone Star Model A Ford Club, 420 Oak Crest Ln, Georgetown, TX 78628

Model A Ford Foundation Inc, PO Box 310293, New Braunfels, TX 78132-0293

Oil City A's, Rt 2, Box 26H, Luling, TX 78648

Piney Wood A's, Box 7855, The Woodlands, TX 77387

Plainview A's, PO Box 772, Plainview, TX 79072

Rio Grande A's, Box 2371, McAllen, TX 78501

Texas Panhandle, PO Box 9602, Amarillo, TX 79105

Texas Region of MAFCA (Tex A's), 12230 Madrigal, San Antonio, TX 78233

Texas Road A O's, 4606 Cashell-Spring Dr, Houston, TX 77069

Texoma A's, 75 Sara Sue Ln, Wichita Falls, TX 76302

Tyler, PO Box 130953, Tyler, TX 75713-0953

Victoria A's, Box 441, Victoria, TX 77902

Woody Wagons, PO Box 341, McAllen, TX 78501

Utah *Beehive A's,* 3310 Taylor Ave, Ogden, UT 84403

Vermont *Green Mountain,* Box 127, Essex Junction, VT 05453

Virginia *Colonial Virginia,* 400 Pagan Rd, Smithfield, VA 23430

George Washington, 3903 Old Lee Hwy (Rt 237), Fairfax, VA 22030

Old Dominion, 7207 Hermitage Rd, Richmond, VA 23228

Skyline, N Flora, Rt 1, Box 162, Gottoes, VA 24441

Washington *Apple Valley,* Box 1205, Yakima, WA 98907

Columbia Basin, Box 6904, Kennewick, WA 99336

Cowlitz Valley A's, PO Box 2343, Longview, WA 98632

Evergreen, Box 15133, Wedgewood Station, Seattle, WA 98115

Gallopin' Gertie, Box 14, Tacoma, WA 98401

Inland Empire, Box 4220, Station B, Spokane, WA 99202

Moonona, Box 408, Lake Stevens, WA 98258

Southwest Washington Volcano A's, Box 84633, Vancouver, WA 96684

Walla Walla Sweet A's, PO Box 1511, Walla Walla, WA 99362

Wisconsin *Central Wisconsin,* Box 492, Wisconsin Rapids, WI 54494

Nickle A's, 3323 W Justin St, Appleton, WI 54910

Wisconsin, 11728 North Ave, Wauwatosa, WI 53226

Argentina *Club Ford de la Argentina,* Santa Fe 1394 (1059), Buenos Aires, Argentina

Australia *Model A Ford Club of South Australia,* PO Box 202, Adelaide, South Australia 5006

Model A Ford Club of Victoria, 79 Kathryn Rd, Knoxfield, Victoria, Australia 3180

Model A Restorers of Australia, PO Box 320, Dickson ACT, 2602 Australia

New South Wales & Down Under, PO Box 162, Panania, NSW, Australia

Western Model A's, PO Box 42, Palmyra, Western Australia 6157

Belgium *Ancient Ford Club of Belgium,* 350 Micksebaan, B2930, Brasschaat, Belgium

Brazil *Clube do Fordinho,* Rua Almirante Mariath, 144-CEP-0418, Sao Paulo, Brazil

Canada *Canada Capital A's,* 54 Perrin Ave, Nepean, ON Canada K2J 2X5

Golden Boy A's, 1158 Redwood, Winnepeg, MB Canada R2X 0Y6

Model A Owners of Canada, Box 31, Station A, Scarborough, ON Canada M1K 5B9

Pacific Model A Club, 14363 28th Ave, Surrey, BC Canada V4P 2H2

Scotia A's, Southern Ohio, RR 2, Yarmouth, NS Canada B0W 3E0

Stampede City, Box 57069, Sunridge PO, Calgary, AB Canada T1Y 5T4

Totem A & T, Box 82181, North Burnaby, BC Canada

Van Isle A & B, 1939 Meadowbank Rd, Saanichton, BC Canada V8M 1X9

Japan Model A Club of Japan, 2-15-13 Taira-Cho, Meguro-Ku, Tokyo, Japan

New Zealand Canterbury, Box 4212, Christchurch, New Zealand

Hawkes Bay Model A Club, 42 Gemini Ave, Palmerston N, New Zealand

North Island Model A Ford Club, Box 57017, Owairaka, Auckland, New Zealand

Rebel A's, 492 Main Rd Hope, RR 1, Richmond, Nelson, New Zealand

Top of the South A's, PO Box 3260, Richmond, Nelson, New Zealand

Norway Eiker A Ford Club Norway, c/o Leif Rust, 3300 Hokksund, Norway

Puerto Rico Puerto Rico, Rafael Lamar 517, Hato Rey, Puerto Rico 00918

San Juan, Escarlata #84, Urb Mumnoz Rivera, Guaynabo, San Juan, Puerto Rico 00657

South Africa South Africa, 84 Provident S, Parow 7500, Cape Province, South Africa

Sweden Sweden, Svenska A-Fordarna, Hogabergsgatan 43, 331 41 Varnamo, Sweden

Uruguay Club Ford A del Uruguay, Box 181, Montevideo, Uruguay

The Model A Ford Club of Great Britain
Lone Pine Cottage, Main Rd
Nutbourne
West Sussex PO18 8RT England
01243-5722222

Founded in 1988. 159 members. For owners and devotees of the Ford Model A and derivatives. For information contact membership registrar Mr S Sheppard at the above address.

Model A Restorer's Club
24800 Michigan Ave
Dearborn, MI 48124-1713
313-278-1455; FAX: 313-278-2624

Founded 1952. 9,800+ members. No restrictions to join. Must be a member to attend meets. Model A Ford owners, 1928-1931. Publishes Model A News, bi-monthly, which includes restoration and era fashions, club related items. Parts, service, supplier's ads. Dues: $20/year (subscription included).

The Model T Ford Club of America
PO Box 743936
Dallas, TX 75374-3936
214-783-7531

Founded 1965. 7,500 members. Dues: $22/year US, $27/year Canada and $28/year foreign (US funds please).

chapters:

Arizona Canyon Country Model T Club, c/o Russ Furstnow, 4030 N Lugano Way, Flagstaff, AZ 86004

Model T Ford Club of Southern Arizona, c/o Larry Price, 5876 E South Wilshire Dr, Tucson, AZ 85711

Sun Country Model T Club, Box 56634, Phoenix, AZ 85079

Tucson Touring T's, c/o Frank Ramsower, 2726 N Mountain View, Tucson, AZ 85712

Arkansas Arkansas Model T Ford Club, c/o M.B. Cia, 4200 "A" St, Little Rock, AR 72205

California Antelope Valley Chapter, c/o T V Gorden, PO Box 2058, California City, CA 93504

Bay Area T's, c/o Rick Silvera, 2949 Los Altos Way, Antioch, CA 94509

Central Coast Model T Club, PO Box 1117, Templeton, CA 93465

Central Sierra Chapter, c/o Alex Lehman, 15715 Ave 13, Madera, CA 93637

Don Pedro Model T Club, c/o Jim W Ashby, 212 Crawford Rd, Modesto, CA 95356

Fiddletown Flivvers, c/o David "Oluf" Olufson, 24750 Shake Ridge Rd, Volcano, CA 95689-9613

Long Beach Model T Club, PO Box 15841, Long Beach, CA 90841

Model T Ford Club of Kern County, Box 885, Bakersfield, CA 93302-0885

Model T Ford Club of San Diego, c/o Heather Bowker, 15838 Oak Valley Rd, Ramona, CA 92065

Mother Lode Model T Ford Club, Box 4901, Auburn, CA 95603-0901

Northern California Model T Club, c/o Ron Delucchi, 1028 Seascape Cir, Rodeo, CA 94572

Orange County Model T Ford Club, 1919 Valencia, Santa Ana, CA 92706

Redwood Empire Model T Club, PO Box 6452, Santa Rosa, CA 95406

Riverside-Corona Chapter, PO Box 51177, Riverside, CA 92517

Sacramento Valley Model T Ford Club, Box 492, Carmichael, CA 95608-0492

San Fernando Valley Chapter, c/o Clara Jo Ostergren, 8656 Balcom Ave, Northridge, CA 91325

Santa Clara Valley Model T Ford Club, PO Box 2081, Saratoga, CA 95070

South Bay Model T Ford Club, PO Box 797, Manhattan Beach, CA 90267-0797

Colorado Centennial Model T Club of Northern Colorado, c/o Geary Baese, 610 W Mountain Ave, Fort Collins, CO 80521

High Plains Model T Club, Box 366, Akron, CO 80720

Mile High Chapter, c/o Rick Holdaway, 6237 W 78th Ave, Arvada, CO 80003

Northeast Colorado Model T Club, c/o Deb Fritzler, 13945 Corene Rd, Sterling, CO 80751

Southern Colorado Model T Club, Box 5626, Pueblo, CO 81003

Connecticut Connecticut Crankin' Yanks, c/o Byron Smith, 97 Old County Rd, Higganum, CT 06441

Florida Northeast Florida Chapter, 844 River Rd, Orange Park, FL 32073

Sunny T's of South Florida, c/o Matthew B Sellers, 3030 NE 40th Ct, Fort Lauderdale, FL 33308

Idaho *Western Idaho Model T Ford Club,* c/o Don Borchers, 3590 Jullion, Boise, ID 83704

Illinois *Ill-IA-MO Chapter,* c/o Elvin Townsend, Rt 5, 1 Sunview, Quincy, IL 62301

Prairie State Model T Ford Club, Box 17, Latham, IL 62543

Indiana *Indy 500 Chapter,* c/o Jack Daron, 10462 N Co Rd 950E, Brownsburg, IN 46112-9639

Iowa *Early Chariots of Council Bluffs,* c/o Herbert H Wiepert, 3014 Ave E, Council Bluffs, IA 51501

Heart of Iowas Ts, c/o Thomas Gray, 3923 52nd St, Des Moines, IA 50310

Kansas *East Central Kansas Ts,* c/o Bud Redding, 1938 Reaper Rd NE, Waverly, KS 66871

Flatland Ts Model T Club, c/o Ray Zehr, 437 S Main, Hesston, KS 67062

Sunflower State Crankers, Box 531, Hays, KS 67601

Kentucky *Burley Belt Chapter,* c/o Jack Lemley, 3191 Vince Rd, Nicholasville, KY 40356

Golden Crossroads Chapter, c/o Ted Aschman, 214 Morningside Dr, Elizabethtown, KY 42701

River City Chapter, c/o Jim Hicks, 112 W Flaget St, Bardstown, KY 40004

Somerset Chapter, c/o Andy Mounce, Box 1, Somerset, KY 42502

Louisiana *Red River Valley Chapter,* c/o Claude Corbett, 625 Pierremont, Shreveport, LA 71106

Maryland *Blue and Gray Chapter,* c/o Dottie Keeler, 841 Francis Scott Key Hwy, Box 56, Keymar, MD 21757

Massachusetts *Central Mass Model T Club,* PO Box 371, Upton, MA 01568

Old Colony Model T Club, 130 Old Oaken Bucket Rd, Scituate, MA 02066

Western Massachusetts Model T Club, c/o Dan Krug, 5 South Rd, Easthampton, MA 01027

Yankee Ingenui Ts, c/o George Livermore, 92 Mill St S, Lancaster, MA 01561

Minnesota *Model T Club of Lake Minnetonka,* c/o Neil Blesi, 2064 Shadywood Rd, Wayzata, MN 55391

North Star State Chapter, c/o Herman Brihn, 11200 Washburn Ave S, Bloomington, MN 55431

Mississippi *Magnolia State Model T Ford Club,* c/o Dean Spencer, 13516 Wilfred Seymour Rd, Ocean Springs, MS 39564

Missouri *Greater St. Louis Chapter,* c/o Pat Itterly, 12858 Crab Thicket, St Louis, MO 63131

Heart of the Ozarks Chapter, c/o Betty Ringgenberg, Rt 2, Box 212, Everton, MO 65646

Kingdom of Callaway Chapter, c/o Vicki McDaniel, 5 Bartley Ln, Fulton, MO 65251

Montana *Rocky Mountain Model T Club,* c/o Ralph Starr, 2108 Rattlesnake Rd, Missoula, MT 59802

Nebraska *Centennial T Club of Omaha,* c/o Robert Pounds, Rt 1, Box 64, Blair, NE 68008

Nevada *Silver State Model T Ford Club,* c/o Jim Huntington, PO Box 21814, Carson City, NV 89702

Southern Nevada Model T Club, 5617 Alfred Dr, Las Vegas, NV 89108

New Hampshire *Central New Hampshire Model T Club,* c/o David Simmering, 121 South Rd, Hopkinton, NH 03229

New Jersey *North Jersey Tinker Ts,* c/o Gary Paulsen, 790 Franklin Tpke, Allendale, NJ 07401

T-Bones Chapter, c/o Jim Dowgin, Box 216, Dayton, NJ 08810

Tri-State Tin Lizzie Tourists, c/o Chris Paulsen, 790 Franklin Tpke, Allendale, NJ 07401

New Mexico *Tin Lizzies of Albuquerque,* PO Box 30473, Albuquerque, NM 87190-0473

New York *Capitol District Chapter,* c/o William Clough, Box 27, Knox, NY 12107-0027

Central New York Chapter, c/o Steve Davis, RD 2, Box 842, West Winfield, NY 13491

Flivver Drivers Inc, c/o Douglas H Lockwood, 347 S Clinton St, Albion, NY 14411

NY-PA Twin Ters Vintage Ford Club, c/o Bruce Bruckner, 5065 Co Rd 14, Odessa, NY 14869-9730

North Dakota *Viking Country Chapter,* c/o Reginald Urness, 3510 Belmont Rd, Grand Forks, ND 58201

Ohio *Model T Ford Club of Northwest Ohio,* c/o Jack A Putnam, 1215 Hancock Rd 28, Bluffton, OH 45817-9656

North Coast Bumps and Grinds Chapter, c/o Jerry Javorek, 27805 Sherwood Dr, Westlake, OH 44145

Ohio River Valley Ts, c/o Lola Wells, 7359 Fallen Timber Rd, Lucasville, OH 45648

Southwest Ohio Model T Club, c/o Dessie Ann Armstrong, 4094 Chico Ct, Springfield, OH 45502

Oklahoma *Model T Ford Club of Tulsa,* PO Box 691874, Tulsa, OK 74169-1874

Oregon *Northwest Vintage Speedster Club,* c/o Chuck Kroll, 630 SW 126th Ave, Beaverton, OR 97005

Rose City Model T Ford Club, Box 3901, Portland, OR 97208

Willamette Valley Chapter, Box 13313, Salem, OR 97309

Pennsylvania *Quaker City Chapter,* c/o Al Irvine, 5821 Ditman Ave, Philadelphia, PA 19135

Valley Forge Chapter, c/o Robert Arters, Box 65, Phoenixville, PA 19460-0065

Rhode Island *Model T Ford Owners of Southern New England,* c/o George Pakuris, 41 Reeland Ave, Warwick, RI 02886

South Dakota *Black Hills Model T Club,* c/o Les Schuchardt, Box 136, Spearfish, SD 57783

South Dakota *Dakota Hills Climbers Chapter,* c/o David Drew, 13120 Mountain Park Rd, Rapid City, SD 57702

Texas *Centex Tin Lizzies,* PO Box 70, Manchaca, TX 78652

Cowtown Model T Ford Club, 4424 Idledell Dr, Fort Worth, TX 76116-7611

Dallas-Fort Worth Chapter, c/o Shirley Cain, 1307 Apache, Richardson, TX 75080

Paso Del Norte Model T Ford Club, c/o Dick Lemon, 4834 Olmos, El Paso, TX 79922

Space City Ts Chapter, c/o Dan McDonald, 6430 Neff St, Houston, TX 77074

Texas Model T Speedster Club, c/o Gerald Cain, 1307 Apache Dr, Richardson, TX 75080

Utah Bonneville Chapter, c/o Rex Zollinger, 1126 S 2183 E, Bountiful, UT 84010

Washington Inland Empire Chapter, PO Box 11708, Spokane, WA 99211-1708

Puget Sound Chapter, c/o Randy Murray, 2312 NE 91st St, Seattle, WA 98115

Three Rivers Chapter, Box 7083, Kennewick, WA 99336-7083

Wisconsin Kettle Moraine Model T Ford Club, c/o Burdella Miller, W211 N6876 Pheasant St, Menomonee Falls, WI 53051

Marshfield Model T Ford Club, c/o Dennis Rose, W5351 County Rd N, Owen, WI 54460

Wisconsin Capitol Model T Ford Club, 2123 Jovina St, Cross Plains, WI 53528

Australia Ford "T" Register of Australia, PO Box 380, Hindmarsh, SA 5007, Australia

Model T Ford Club of Australia, PO Box 2658, Parramatta NSW 2151, Australia

Model T Ford Club of Victoria, c/o Secretary, PO Box 383, Chadstone Centre PO, VIC 3128, Australia

Austria Model T Ford Club of Austria, c/o Wolfgang Posch, Hochsatzeng 17, A-1140 Wien (Vienna), Austria

Belgium Ancient Ford Club of Belgium, c/o Roger de Decker, 350 Micksebaan, B-2930 Brasschaat, Belgium

Canada Foothills Model T Ford Club, c/o Reg Kober, 6119 Norfolk Dr NW, Calgary, AB Canada T2K 5J8

Klondike Chapter, c/o M. Walkemeyer, 10629 150th St, Edmonton, AB Canada T5P 1R1

Running Board Bandits, c/o Ralph Anderson, Rt 5, Box 11, Prince Albert, SK Canada S6V 5R3

Saskatchewan Dus't Spokes Chapter, c/o Allen Clow, 16 Acadia Bay, Regina, SK Canada S4S 4T6

The 2-4-Ts Club, c/o Allen Clark, 723 Demel Pl, Victoria, BC Canada V9C 3L6

Great Britain Model T Ford Register of Great Britain, c/o Les Croft, 2 Loupfell Dr, Morecambe, Lancashire LA4 4SB, Great Britain

Holland Ford T Register of Holland, c/o A Martini, Postbus 2146, 1180 EC Amstelveen, Holland

New Zealand Model T Ford Club of New Zealand, c/o Rod McKenzie, 39 Francis Drake St, Waipukurau 4176, New Zealand

Nifty Fifties Ford Club of Northern Ohio
PO Box 142
Macedonia, OH 44056
216-556-0099

Founded 1976. 100 members. Limited to northeast Ohio. Publication: Nifty Fifties News. Club events, local car shows, general club news. Dues: $20/year.

The Ranchero Club
1339 Beverly Rd
Port Vue, PA 15133

Founded 1982. No restrictions to join. Bimonthly publication: The Ranchero Courier, featuring technical information. Dues: $25/July 1st to July 1st.

Ranchero-Torino Club of Arizona
8037 E Tuliptree St
Tucson, AZ 85730-4621
520-886-6420

Founded 1986. 30-50 members. We specialize in Ranchero-Torino and any Ford-powered vehicles. Newsletter, monthly meetings. Two annual shows: All Ford Spring Classic in April and a Celebration of the Automobile, The Outpost Classic, in November, proceeds to Kids at Risk in southern Arizona. Dues: $20 for voting members; $15 for associates (non-voting); $30 US currency international rate.

Shelby American Automobile Club
PO Box 788
Sharon, CT 06069
FAX: 860-364-0769

For information, contact at the above address: Rick Kopec 860-364-0449. Founded 1975. 6,200 members. Ownership not essential. Open to all enthusiasts of high performance Fords, Bosses, Panteras, Griffiths, Mustangs, etc. The club's magazine, The Shelby American. Dues $36.50/year.

Special Interest Fords of the 50s Club
17723 Shadow Valley
Spring, TX 77379
713-376-4274

Alberta Mustangs Auto Club
PO Box 36092
Lakeview PO
Calgary, ALB Canada T3E 7C6
403-932-6645

Founded 1979. 80 members. A non-profit organization made up of individuals and families who share a common interest in Mustangs, Cougars and special interest Fords. Membership entitles holder to bimonthly newsletter, membership roster and discount on admission to club events. Major event is the Presidential Show and Shine held in June. Dues: $30/year.

Badgerland Mustang Club
PO Box 338
Poynette, WI 53955
608-635-7751

100 member families. Family oriented club. A Mustang Club of America Regional group. We serve south central Wisconsin for all owners and fans of Mustangs from 1964 to the present. Our activities include tours, cruises, rallies, tech seminars and shows. We work with the Big Brothers and Sisters of Dane and Columbia counties to help them raise funds and to provide support for their programs. Dues: $15/year.

Club Mustang Quebec
180 St Antoine
Levis, QUE Canada G6V 5Y8
418-837-5709

Founded 1989. 150+ members. Open to everyone, owner or not. Many activities, monthly meeting. Dues: $40/year Canadian.

Clubs & Organizations

Diablo Valley Mustang Association
3613 Hammond Pl
Concord, CA 94519-1505
510-827-9197

Founded 1979. 85 members. Open to all Mustangers. Dedicated to the restoration, preservation and enjoyment of all Ford Mustangs. A Mustang is not required for membership, enthusiasm is. Meetings 2nd Wednesday of month, 7 pm at Fuddruckers, Concord, CA. Dues: $15/single, $20/family. $20 initiation fee.

Greater Rochester Mustangs & Fords
PO Box 90536
Rochester, NY 14609
716-342-2926

Founded 1991. 80 members. Rochester's only car club for the Mustang and Ford enthusiast . Picnics, shows, wine tour and other events. Send postage stamp for copy of our newsletter called Horsepower. Dues: $5/year.

Greater Vancouver Mustang Association
PO Box 44526
2405 E Broadway
Vancouver, BC Canada V5M 1Y0
604-438-9373

Founded 1981. 320 members. Ownership is not mandatory but enthusiasm is. Non profit car club dedicated to the restoration and appreciation of the Mustang automobile. Monthly publication, meets 3rd Sunday each month at the Canada Games Pool Community Center, New Westminster, BC. Dues: $30 year, spouse/$5 extra; $25/year, renewals.

Lubbock Mustang Club
PO Box 6154
Lubbock, TX 79493-6154
806-794-6135

Founded 1983. 85 members (families). Family-oriented club designed for its membership to enjoy and preserve the Mustang. Monthly meeting and newsletter. Annual show and swap meet. Dues: $15/year.

Mid-Ohio Valley Mustang Club
908 George St
Belpre, OH 45714
614-423-9464

Founded 1983. 38 families/members. Ford owners of Ford Motor Co vehicles (Mustangs, other Fords, Mercury, Lincoln, Edsel). Monthly 4-page newsletter called Pony Tales. One monthly meeting, one all-Ford auto show in August, tours. Dues: $5 to $10/year.

Mustang & Classic Ford Club of New England
PO Box 963
North Attleboro, MA 02761
508-699-4717

Founded 1980. 350 members. Membership is open to owners of any year Ford vehicle. Sponsors auto shows, swap meets and automotive clinic programs and drag racing. Also offers a parts locating service. Bimonthly magazine: Classic Comments. Dues: $15/year.

Mustang Club of America
800 Progress Industrial Blvd
Lawrenceville, GA 30243
PH/FAX: 770-682-9955, hours 9-4
M-F, EST

For membership information, contact at the above address: National Headquarters. Founded 1976. Over 8,500 members and 110 regional groups. Should be an enthusiast of Ford Mustangs, Bosses and Shelbys. "Largest Mustang club in the world." Dues: $30/US, $40/Canadian, $65/foreign. Visa/MasterCard accepted.

See our ad on this page

regions:

Alabama   *Heart of Dixie Mustang Club,* David Cowless (22676), President, 3111 Pelzer Ave, Montgomery, AL 36109, 334-271-1943

Ken Garrett, National Director, 4448 White Acres Rd, Montgomery, AL 36106, 334-277-5822

Mobile Bay Mustang Club, John Kaeser (30053), President, 7688 Cornwallis St, Saraland, AL 36571, 334-675-7391Raymond Cochran (22523), National Director, 10225 Rebel Rd, Daphne, AL 36526, 334-626-5744

Model City Mustang Club, Dale Garrett (18842), President, 774 Garrett Ave, Oxford, AL 36203, 205-831-1559Charlie Ping (25255), National Director, 580 Kingsway Dr, Anniston, AL 36201, 205-237-5535

Rocket City Mustang Club, Vickie Denton (21001), President, 1204 Oakwood St NW, Hartselle, AL 35640, 205-751-0542Mike Denton (21001), National Director, 1204 Oakwood St NW, Hartselle, AL 35640, 205-751-0542

Arizona   *Old Pueblo Mustang Club,* Laurie Slawson (32451), President and National Director, 7561 E Dos Mujeres, Tucson, AZ 85715, 520-296-4933

Arkansas *Central Arkansas Mustangers,* Fred Foster (29221), President, 8 Arcadia Cir, Bryant, AR 72022, 501-847-0672Jerry Oldridge (24117), National Director, 616 Sherwood Ave, Sherwood, AR 72116, 501-835-5398

NW Arkansas Mustang Club, Steve Sanders (25835), President, PO Box 254, Springdale, AR 72764Donna Sanders (25835), National Director, 2049 Reed Ave, Springdale, AR 72764, 501-750-6327

Ozarks Regional Mustang Club, Gene Call (28023), President, PO Box 891, Harrison, AR 72602, 501-741-1237Gary Richart (24939), National Director, 8 Crestview Rd, Harrison, AR 73423, 501-741-6854

California *Golden Hills Mustang Club,* Tim Leathers (33718), President, PO Box 497, Fairfield, CA 94533, 916-662-5342Robert Rand (28457), National Director, 2006 Goodman Ct, Fairfield, CA 94533-2726, 707-426-3103

Mustangs Owner's Club of CA, Rex White, President, 6846 Louise Ave, Van Nuys, CA 91406, 818-991-6937Craig Cunningham (20704), National Director, 6845 Aldea Ave, Van Nuys, CA 91406, 818-758-1826

Sacramento Area Mustang Club, Gary Bergeron (31872), President, PO Box 188455, Sacramento, CA 95818, 916-395-9920Allen Krasich (26310), National Director, 7432 Creekridge Ln, Citrus Heights, CA 95610, 916-729-0453

Vintage Mustang Owners Association, Kevin Patten (34297), President, PO Box 5772, San Jose, CA 95150-5772, 408-377-2626Barbara McNair, National Director, 1559 Alta Glenn Dr #4, San Jose, CA 95125-4419

Canada *Golden Horseshoe Mustang Association,* Jim King (31666), President and National Director, 7199 Windrush Ct, Mississauga, ON Canada L5N 6K1, 905-824-4464

Southwestern Ontario Mustang, Bob Proulx (23459), President, 105 Meleod Cres, London, ON Canada N5X 1S9, 519-438-6291Daniel Bell (36009), National Director, Box 2, 123 Tiner Ave, Dorchester, ON Canada N0J 1E0

Colorado *Front Range Mustang Club,* Tom Kay (31187), President, 1167 W 133rd Way, Westminister, CO 80234, 303-451-9296Leon Cooley (3035), National Director, 1248 S Raritan, Denver, CO 80223, 303-934-3525

Delaware *First State Mustangs,* Richard Langshaw (21981), President, 3 Malvern Rd, Newark, DE 19713, 302-737-5196Robert Jankowski (19415), National Director, 203 N Ruth Ellen Ct, Newark, DE 19711

Lower Delaware Mustang Club, Kenneth Cannon (30870), President, 1960 Milford-Harrington Hwy, Milford, DE 19960, 302-422-2179Sherri Baynum (33400), National Director, PO Box 255, Felton, DE 19943, 302-284-8199

Florida *Classic Mustang of Tampa,* Mike Scott (33069), President, PO Box 290493, Tampa, FL 33617, 813-985-5795Mike Scott (33069), National Director, 12012 52 St, Temple Terrace, FL 33617, 813-985-5795

Emerald Coast Mustang Club, Ron Savoie (31263), President, PO Box 4431, Ft Walton Beach, FL 32549, 904-678-1978Ron Savoie (31263), National Director, 1110 Rita Ln, Niceville, FL 32578, 904-678-1978

First Generation Mustang Club, Paul Licalsi (23384), President, 8058 Marcella Dr, Orlando, FL 32836, 407-352-7309Wayne Johnson (17774), National Director, 1133 Ocean Shore Blvd #105, Ormond Beach, FL 32176, 904-441-1443

Gold Coast Mustang Club, Sam Pampenalla (18365), President and National Director, 10975 NW 5th Ct, Coral Springs, FL 33065, 305-752-4146

Gulf Coast Region Mustang Club, Jim Avery (34471), President and National Director, 1344 Dog Track Rd, Pensacola, FL 32506, 904-453-8637

Hernando County Mustang Association, Tony Lagone (6612), President and National Director, 25256 Plum St, Brooksville, FL 34601, 904-796-0854

Imperial Mustangs of Polk Co, John Lindsey (29435), President and National Director, 5098 Varty Rd, Winter Haven, FL 33884, 813-324-9282

Magic City Mustangs Inc, George Barber, President, 10981 SW 44th St, Miami, FL 33165, 305-221-6777Maritza Guerra, National Director, 7707 Camino Real #B-210, Miami, FL 33143, 304-858-4541

Mid-Florida Mustang Club, Larry Goebel (33062), President, PO Box 2426, Orlando, FL 32802, 407-889-0799Bob DeCardenas (22031), National Director, 102 N Indian Cir, Cocoa, FL 32922, 407-631-2891

Mustang Club of W Central Florida, Raymond Baker (32086), President, 3215 49th St, Sarasota, FL 34235, 941-351-3789John Watjen (20391), National Director, 1761 Valencia Dr, Venice, FL 34292, 941-497-1509

Space Coast Mustang Club, Art Griffin (25745), President, 2556 Sellers Ln, Melbourne, FL 32935, 407-254-7087Stewart Jones (28349), National Director, 880 Hawaii Ave NW, Palm Bay, FL 32907, 407-984-1125

Suncoast Mustang Club, John T Moody (4204), President, PO Box 4622, Clearwater, FL 34618, 813-786-3048William Zulas (22645), National Director, PO Box 7235, Clearwater, FL 34618, 813-726-7033

Surf Mustang Club of South Florida, Marc Schultz (24566), President and National Director, 582 Ranchero Rd, Ste 1, Belle Glade, FL 33230, 407-996-5520

SW Florida Mustang Club, Steve Keppen (30480), President, 3101 Terrace Ave, Naples, FL 33942, 813-939-7245Steve Kepper, National Director, 1722 SE 2nd St, Cape Coral, FL 33990, 813-939-7245

Georgia *Central Savannah River Area,* Steve Prewitt (33803), President, PO Box 211726, Augusta, GA 30917, 706-860-4535Rick Lawless (14274), National Director, 4303 Roswell Dr, Martinez, GA 30907, 706-855-5783

Cherokee Regional Mustang Club, Jason Sloan (26487), President, 179 New Zion Rd, Calhoun, GA 30701Jonathon Parker (25226), National Director, 2685 McDaniel Station Rd SW, Calhoun, GA 30701

Flag City Mustang Club, George Davis (31504), President, 2374 Lancelot Pl, Macon, GA 31206, 912-788-3731Bob Nix (31502), National Director, 107 Camellia Cr, Warner Robbins, GA 31093, 912-923-8013

Georgia Regional Mustang Club, Tony Garcia (28769), President, 613 Dahlia Way, Acworth, GA 30102, 770-928-3662Norman Lawrence, National Director, 1331 Yates Ave SW, Austell, GA 30001, 770-435-1766

Heart of Georgia, James Dickey (32224), President and National Director, 365 Old Perry Rd, Bonaire, GA 31005-9551, 912-923-4842

Northeast Georgia Mustang Club, Mike Fussell (22515), President, 5120 Shadow Path Ln, Lilburn, GA 30247, 770-469-5452Ricky Simmons (17874), National Director, PO Box 387, Demorest, GA 30535, 706-778-6329

Savannah Mustang Club, Johnny Moore (26368), President, PO Box 13204, Savannah, GA 31416, 912-352-4643Johnny Moore (26368), National Director, 3717 Eastgate Dr, Savannah, GA 31416, 912-352-4643

Tara Mustang Club, Donny Brown (21006), President, 2130 Eastwood Dr, Snellville, GA 30278, 770-979-1029Nathaniel Keys (30284), National Director, 4602 High Grate Ln, Lithonia, GA 30038, 404-981-2208

Illinois *Central Illinois Mustangers,* Jim Fannin (18064), President, RR #3, Box 109, Bloomington, IL 61704, 309-829-3359Floyd Scranton, National Director, 61 Ronald Dr, Decatur, IL 62526, 217-877-0604

Northern Mustang Corral, Terry Hebert (25447), President and National Director, 1200 King Arthur Ln, Bourbonnais, IL 60914, 815-932-5285

Rock Valley Mustang Club, Scott Fleming (23954), President and National Director, 6079 Wild Rose Ln, Roscoe, IL 61073, 815-389-8828

Shiloh Valley Mustang Association, Scott Courtney (29219), President, 1705 N 16th St, Belleville, IL 62223, 618-476-3370Ray Boisemenue (8673), National Director, 16 Brittany Ln, Belleville, IL 62223, 618-235-4634

Southern Illinois Mustang Association, Tony Goodrich (30415), President, 211 Everest, Glen Carbon, IL 60234, 217-839-2404Tom Sherman (18841), National Director, 510 Fulton St, Gillespie, IL 62033, 217-838-2484

Indiana *Michiana Mustangs,* Brad Milliken (28353), President, 53308 Old Farm Rd, Elkhart, IN 46514, 219-674-4321Tom & Carol Podemski (17084), National Directors, 1526 W Calvert, South Bend, IN 46613

Mustang Club of Indianapolis, Steve Perrine (31482), President and National Director, 1270 Orchard Park N Dr, Indianapolis, IN 46280, 317-846-4506

Old Fort Mustangers Club Inc, Cord Lewton, President, PO Box 5082, Fort Wayne, IN 46895Cord Lewis, National Director, 5808 Fontana Dr, Fort Wayne, IN 46815

Pony Express Mustang Club, Greg Stillwell (30182), President, 1617 Wedeking, Evansville, IN 47708Robert Scrivner (20411), National Director, 2235 S Eastern Pkwy, Owensboro, KY 42303

Kansas *SC Kansas Mustang Club,* Rick Richardson (33899), President, PO Box 49365, Wichita, KS 67201-9365, 316-522-7682Mark & Delores Hughes (32955), National Directors, 14616 E 47th St, Derby, KS 67037, 316-733-1310

Vintage Mustang Club of Kansas City, Charlotte Leach (20079), President, PO Box 40082, Overland Park, KS 66202, 913-782-0704Rick Lage (21025), National Director, 7601 W 66th Terr, Overland Park, KS 66202, 913-432-6913

Kentucky *Bluegrass Mustang Club,* Steve Ulmer (36568), President, PO Box 11732, Lexington, KY 40577-1732, 606-259-9732Steve Ulmer (36568), National Director, 326 S Broadway Park, Lexington, KY 40504-2809, 606-259-9732

Derby City Mustangs, Gene Smith (25544), President and National Director, 2510 Regal Rd, LaGrange, KY 40031, 502-241-8170

Louisiana *Baton Rouge Mustangers Inc,* Duane Vince (36781), President, PO Box 686, Brusly, LA 70719-0686, 504-749-1994Gene Millspaugh (3799), National Director, 2225 Woodthrush Dr, Baton Rouge, LA 70819, 504-275-6460

Cajun Mustangers, Rodney Breaux (20178), President and National Director, 1216 Post Oak Rd #9, Sulphur, LA 70663

Classic Mustang Association of N.O., Jack Rouse (37665), PresidentJoe Sensebe, National Director, 2401 Jean Lafitte Pkwy, Chalmette, LA 70043

Michigan *Mustang Owners of Southeast Michigan,* Francis Lundgren (24622), President, PO Box 39088, Redford, MI 48239, 313-283-1849Francis Lundgren (24622), National Director, 13593 Windemere, Southgate, MI 48194-24, 313-283-1849

Mississippi *Mid-Mississippi Mustangs,* Bobby Schumpert (33529), President, 4363 Redwood Cir, Jackson, MS 39212, 601-371-0255David Braband (24462), National Director, 429 Lee St, Jackson, MS 39212, 601-373-0677

Mississippi Coast Mustang Club, John Wester (33523), President and National Director, 350 Stone Cir, Biloxi, MS 39531, 601-388-5256

Missouri *Greater Ozarks Mustang Club,* Robert Snook, Presdent, PO Box 4725, Springfield, MO 65808, 417-581-4552Robert Snook, National Director, 1418 E Walnut Lawn, Springfield, MO 65804, 417-883-5812

Mid-America Mustangers, Keith Marquis (36463), President and National Director, 9746 E 27th Terr, Independence, MO 64052, 816-836-5987, 816-373-0231

Show-Me Mustang Club, Mitch Mitchell (24522), President, 253 Savoy, Lake St Louis, MO 63367John Palmer (27694), National Director, 16213 Berry View Ct, Wildwood, MO 63011, 314-458-0809

New Jersey *Garden State Region Mustangs,* Sue Danner (29075), President, 14 Hayward St, Bound Brook, NJ 08805, 201-469-4169Dave Zimmerman (7993), National Director, 6 Tainter St, Peapack, NJ 07977, 908-234-0535

South Jersey Mustang Club, Herb Sharp (27775), President, 1013 Chateau Ct, Atoc, NJ 08004, 609-768-8428Ken Moore (22413), National Director, 208 Oakshade Rd, Tabernacle, NJ 08088, 609-268-8079

New Mexico *Rio Grande Mustang Club,* Richard Jockisch (25438), President, 12825 Cedarbrook Ave NE, Albuquerque, NM 87111, 505-299-4573Janice Short (10576), National Director, 12825 Cedarbrook Ave NE, Albuquerque, NM 87111, 505-299-4573

New York *Adirondack Shelby-Mustang Club,* Scott Mercer (26617), President and National Director, 567 Victory Cir, Ballston Spa, NY 12020, 518-885-2680

Classic Mustang Long Island, Trudy Kent (11896), President and National Director, PO Box 1011, N Massapequa, NY 11758, 516-798-6223

Greater Rochester Mustang Club, Al Sampson (30350), President, PO Box 18734, Rochester, NY 14618-0734, 716-581-0239Mary Beth Mros (29252), National Director, 14 Orchid Dr, Rochester, NY 14616-1046, 716-581-0239

Twin Tiers Regional Group, Blaine Overacker (8998), President and National Director, 241 Middle Rd, Horseheads, NY 13845, 607-739-1975

North Carolina *Carolina Regional Mustang Club,* Dave Goff (25511), President, 4655 Hwy 73 E, Concord, NC 28025, 704-788-1345Norman Demers (33108), National Director, 3306 Rillett Ct, Charlotte, NC 28269, 704-599-0324

Eastern NC Regional Mustang, Leslie Joyner, President and National Director, 301 S Caswell St, La Grange, NC 25551, 919-566-3826

Gate City Triad Mustang Club, Randy Stone (36040), President, 151 Wolfetrail Rd, Greensboro, NC 27406, 910-275-5590Max Wicker (04836), National Director, 1225 Shamrock Dr, Burlington, NC 27215, 910-226-1777

Heart of Carolina Mustang Club, Edward "Chip" Hill (27272), President, PO Box 2593, Chapel Hill, NC 27515, 919-542-1318Al Dulaney (22207), National Director, 54 Creekside Cir, Pittsboro, NC 27312-1318, 919-542-1318

S.E.N.C. Regional Mustang Club, Robert O Smith (28545), President and National Director, 495 Rivenbarktown Rd, Wallace, NC 28466, 910-285-4895

Sandhills Regional Mustang Club, Laurin Cooper (19552), President, 5736 Sagamore Re, Hope Mills, NC 28348, 910-425-9282Archie Outland (21187), National Director, 1915 Lyon Rd, Fayetteville, NC 28303, 910-484-3749

Tar Heel Mustang Club, Bill Weaver (19098), President, 304 Fosterri Dr, Rocky Mount, NC 27801, 919-446-6639Don C Phillips (10730), National Director, 410 Holly Hill Rd, Murfreesboro, NC 27855, 919-398-4405

Ohio *Classic Mustang Club of Ohio,* Mark Morley (37182), President and National Director, 1233 Colston Dr, Westerville, OH 43081, 614-895-7059

Mahoning Valley Mustangs, Mike Quinn (31054), President, 2002 Woodgate, Austintown, OH 44515, 330-270-1415Bob Miller (34116), National Director, 648 Wyndclift Cir, Austintown, OH 44515, 330-793-4942

Mid-Ohio Valley Mustang Club, Connie Weiss (05451), President, 908 George St, Belpre, OH 45714, 614-423-9464Russ Alton (05435), National Director, 2306 Prunty Ct, Parkersburg, WV 26101

Northeastern Ohio Regional, Norm Clark (30769), President, 5489 Young Rd, Stow, OH

44224, 216-650-4277Angelia Miller (34116), National Director, 648 Wyndclift Cir, Austintown, OH 44515, 216-793-4942

Tri-State Mustang Club, Gene Kennedy, President, 8810 Eagle Creek Ct, West Chester, OH 45069, 513-874-7441Al Friedel, National Director, 10423 Lochcrest, Cincinnati, OH 45231, 513-771-4558

Oklahoma *Arkansas Valley Mustang Club,* Larry Hall (25809), President and National Director, Rt 5 Box 796, Muldrow, OK 74948, 918-427-5346

Green Country Classic Mustangs, Carolyn Figert (32709), President, PO Box 471361, Tulsa, OK 74147-1361Carl Henderson (16890), National Director, 1633 E Thompson, Sapulpa, OK 74066

Oklahoma Mustang Club, Bob Mollohan (20498), President, 1602 Ridgecrest, El Reno, OK 73036, 405-262-6650Steve Hendrix (13076), National Director, 415 Greenwood Dr, Mustang, OK 73064, 405-376-4103

Pennsylvania *Centre Region Mustang Club,* Dan Workman (20756), President, PO Box 91, Lemont, PA 16851, 814-238-7792Matthew Mostoller (22855), National Director, 102 Oak Glen Rd, PA Furnace, PA 16865

First Pennsylvania Mustang, Steve Eitner (26716), President, 3924 Main St, Slatedale, PA 18079, 610-767-0576Jerry Yarbrough (31829), National Director, 1823 Creek Rd, Hatfield, PA 19440, 215-368-4893

Lake Erie Mustang Owners Club, Jerry Trocki (16505), President, PO Box 8602, Erie, PA 16505, 814-833-5042David L Turner (27707), National Director, 19039 Hillcrest Dr, Corry, PA 16407, 814-663-1131

North Central Mustang Club, Rod Dieffenbacher (21406), President, 315 Klump Rd, Cogan Station, PA 17728Bob Neitz (23702), National Director, 490 Prince St, Northumberland, PA 17857, 717-473-7085

Valley Forge Mustang Club, Mike Yoder (24223), President, 440 Hause Ave, Sanatoga, PA 19464, 610-326-0741Frank Trevisan, National Director, 2898 Eastburn Ave, Broomall, PA 19008

Puerto Rico *Puerto Rico Mustang Club,* Luis F Lugo (17524), President and National Director, GPO Box 3397, Aguadilla, PR 00605

Rhode Island *Mustang Club of New England,* Vincent Letourmeau (2374), President, PO Box 1554, Woonsocket, RI 02895Jim Silverman (27762), National Director, 72 Westhaven Dr, Brockton, MA 02401, 508-674-5462

South Carolina *Central South Carolina Regional Group,* David Phillips (34793), President and National Director, PO Box 232, Springfield, SC 29146, 803-258-3839

Foothills Regional Group, Marvin Brown, President and National Director, 308 Pisah Dr, Greenville, SC 29609, 864-292-0629

SC Coastal Region Mustang Club, Charles F Hall, President and National Director, 616 S Laurel St, Summerville, SC 29483, 803-538-8066

South Dakota *Rapid Mustang Club,* Mark Weishaar (26373), President and National Director, 125 Macarthur, Rapid City, SD 57701, 605-341-8877

Tennessee *First Tennessee Regional,* Bob Davis (7053), President, 5031 Dublin Rd, Kingsport, TN 37664, 423-323-2212Delphia Cox (335), National Director, 407 Claymore Dr, Kingsport, TN 37663, 423-239-5418

Golden Circle Mustang Club, Francis Williams, President, PO Box 1091, Jackson, TN 38302Gene Privett (3100), National Director, 1112 N 30th St, Humboldt, TN 38343, 901-784-4594

Lakeway Mustang Club, Pamela Jo Trent (28212), President and National Director, 3040 Cherokee Dr, Morristown, TN 37814, 423-585-8453

Music City Regional Group, William Sanford (26979), President, 3916 Bradley Ct, Antioch, TN 37013, 615-834-7150Jim Chism (28864), National Director, 100 Park Circle Dr, Dickson, TN 37055, 615-446-0520

Mustangs of Memphis, Mike Cunningham (30286), President, 9445 Pleasant Ridge Rd, Arlington, TN 38002, 901-829-2175George Johnson, National Director, 397 Ashley Ln, Brighton, TN 38001, 901-829-2175

Tennessee Valley Mustang Club, Gerry Vermillion (23406), President, PO Box 5294, Oak Ridge, TN 37831-5294, 615-376-4225Georgia Knazovich (24894), National Director, 9528 Continental Dr, Knoxville, TN 37922, 423-691-2012

Thunder Valley Mustang Club, Ken Hall (33544), President and National Director, 6922 Glover Rd, Chattanooga, TN 37416, 615-344-5763

Texas *Mustang Club of Houston,* Les Blankenship (28427), President, 15034 Margison, Houston, TX 77084, 713-463-4245Mark Amen (33104), National Director, 22318 Smokey Hill, Katy, TX 77450, 713-392-1347

San Antonio Mustang Club, Mike Frazier (28458), President, 3238 Lasses, San Antonio, TX 78223, 210-930-2943Jack Klug (28590), National Director, 4226 Mabuni, San Antonio, TX 78218, 210-653-6046

Southeast Texas Mustang Club, Rodney Breaux (20178), President, PO Box 8848, Lumberton, TX 77657, 409-755-1470Rodney Breaux (20178), National Director, Rt 2 Box 130, Lumberton, TX 77657, 409-755-1470

Texas Panhandle Mustang Club, Elmer Thornton (33981), President, Rt 8 Box 35-11, Amarillo, TX 79102, 806-373-3104Bill Howell (28621), National Director, 7918 Fenley, Amarillo, TX 70105, 806-353-0164

Texoma Mustang Club, Bob Brown (21259), President and National Director, 1908 Laurel Rd, Gainesville, TX 76240

Virginia *Central Virginia Mustang Club,* Kenny Fischer (5766), President, 6506 Lothaire Ct, Richmond, VA 23234, 804-743-1490 Paul Oliver (30905), National Director, 13505 W Poplar Grove, Midlothian, VA 23113, 804-744-8016

Lynchburg Area Mustang Club, Peggy Tomlinson (16333), President, 300 Westburg Dr, Lynchburg, VA 24502, 804-239-1594Doug Cooper (13257), National Director, Rt 2 Box 390, Huddleston, VA 24104, 540-297-7614

Mustang Club of Tidewater, Robert J Colston (33875), President, 103 Seabreeze Ln, Suffolk,

VA 23435, 804-484-3792Doug Sample (24843), National Director, 705 Eskine St, Hampton, VA 23666-1956, 804-825-9295

Shenandoah Valley Mustang Club, Bob Snyder (12463), President, PO Box 2015, Winchester, VA 22601, 304-876-6830Bob Snyder (12463), National Director, Rt 3 Box 422, Harpers Ferry, WV 25425, 304-876-6830

Southeastern Virginia Mustang Club, Fred Prickett (29914), President, 2516 Adventure Tr, Virginia Beach, VA 23454, 804-340-8993Jim Pletl (21943), National Director, 1055 Brandon Ave, Norfolk, VA 23507, 804-622-3575

Washington *Mustangs Northwest,* Scott Robinson, President and National Director, PO Box 53145, Bellevue, WA 98015-3145, 206-298-3604

Mustangs West Car Club, Mark Folden, President and National Director, PO Box 5876, Lacey, WA 98503, 360-736-5722

Pierce County Mustang Club, Bill Ochs (24957), President and National Director, 306 Main St, Steilacoom, WA 98388-2104, 206-588-5912

Wisconsin *Badgerland Mustang Club,* Dean Hillestad (20951), President, PO Box 338, Poynette, WI 53955, 608-635-7751Dennis & Kelley Fields, National Directors, 206 S Warren, South Wayne, WI 53587, 608-439-4648

Western Wisconsin Regional, Herb Long, President, 755 W US Hwy 16, West Salem, WI 54669John Heim (28033), National Director, 3005 Farnam, La Cross, WI 54601

Wisconsin Early Mustangers, Scott Moen (18161), President and National Director, 2511 W Carrington Ave, Oak Creek, WI 53154, 414-567-2622

Mustang Owners Club International
Paul McLaughlin
2720 Tennessee NE
Albuquerque, NM 87110
505-296-2554

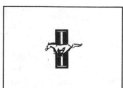

Founded 1975. 500 members. Open to all Mustangs and Mustang enthusiasts from the earliest to the latest. Stock, restored, modified, race, etc., all welcomed. Large reference library available to answer questions pertaining to Mustangs. Newsletter: The Pony Express. Dues: $15/year US, $18/year foreign.

Mustang SVO Owners Association Inc
4222 I-75 Business Spur
Sault Ste Marie, MI 49783-3620
705-525-7861 (SVO1); FAX: 705-525-5178, Ontario, Canada

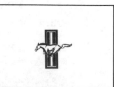

Founded 1989. 400+ members. Dedicated to locating and documenting the SVO Mustang and serving the needs of SVO Mustang owners. Newsletter three times yearly. Collectible insurance appraisal service. National convention, technical support and modification support. Dues: $30/year.

Pacific Cascade Mustang Club
PO Box 58582
Renton, WA 98058

Founded 1965. Open to owners of Ford powered vehicles with a valid license and insurance. Discounts to members at area businesses. Believed to be the oldest club in existence today. All

years of Mustangs (and Cougars) are welcome. Monthly newsletter, *The Pegasus*. Annual car show, tech sessions, family oriented. Dues: $25/year.

Show-Me Mustang Club
Attn: Don Orbin
PO Box 147
Hazelwood, MO 63042
314-831-3673

Founded 1986. 92 members. Founded to perpetuate enjoyment of Mustang automobiles. Ownership not necessary. Family oriented organization. Monthly meetings, annual show, monthly club social functions, including picnics, displays, cruises and how to. Dues: $12/year.

Sierra Mustang Club of Sacramento
PO Box 1793
Fair Oaks, CA 95628

Founded 1981. 298 members. Open to all Mustang enthusiasts, ownership not necessary. Primary purpose is to promote the enjoyment and preservation of the 1964-1/2 to 1973 classic Mustang. Meetings held fourth Wednesday of each month at the Smud Building, 6201 S Street, Sacramento, CA, at 7 pm. Benefits include monthly SMC newsletter and discounts at various Ford dealerships and participating vendors. Fred Asbury, president. Dues: $25/year for primary member, $5 each associate member.

Sonoma County Mustang Club
PO Box 8716
Santa Rosa, CA 95407
707-765-1653

Founded 1990. 36 members. Interest in Ford Mustangs (all years) and/or other Ford products. Meets 3rd Thursday of each month at 7:30 pm at Round Table Pizza Parlor, Stony Point shopping center, Santa Rosa, CA. Monthly newsletter or bulletin. Dues: $20/year.

The West Michigan Mustang Club
3736 Parkland Ave SW
Wyoming, MI 49509
616-538-5579

Founded 1981. 160+ members. Our purpose is to preserve, restore & enjoy 1964-1/2 to current Mustangs. Monthly meetings and/or events, newsletter. We have technical advisors and sponsor an all Ford show in June. Ownership not necessary to join, only enthusiasm for Mustangs. Dues: $15/year.

Chicagoland Thunderbird Club
107 S Highland Ave
Lombard, IL 60148
630-627-2866

Founded 1982. 175 members. Thunderbird enthusiasts. Club open to cars from 1958 to present. Monthly publication: *Bird Word*. Monthly meetings. Free car shows. Dues $25 per year. Car ownership not mandatory to join.

Classic Thunderbird Club International
PO Box 4148
Santa Fe Springs, CA 90670
310-945-6836

Founded 1961. 8,000 members. Dedicated to the 1955, 1956 and 1957 Thunderbirds. Publishes magazine, *The Early Bird*. Sells manuals, posters, brochures to members only. We have 6 Regional conventions summer 1997. One International convention summer 1998 in Dallas, Texas. Works with Ford Motor Co for continuance of parts. Everyone welcome to join. Dues: $25/year plus $15 initiation fee.

Heartland Vintage Thunderbird Club of America
5002 Gardner
Kansas City, MO 64120
816-353-4061

Founded 1985. 1,400 members. National club dedicated to the preservation of all Thunderbirds 1958-69. Monthly newsletter. Dues: $20/year.

North Jersey Thunderbird Association
28 Rustic Rd
Waldwick, NJ 07463
201-670-4168

Founded 1976. 80 members. Association of T-Bird owners and enthusiasts dedicated to preservation, enjoyment and safe operation of Thunderbird automobiles. Publication: T-Bird Topics. Dues: $24/year. For information, contact at the above address: Paul Wilson, president, 201-670-4168.

Rocky Mountain Thunderbird Club
451 E 58th Ave, #1319, Box 132
Denver, CO 80216

For information, contact at the above address: Don Donahue, founder, 303-278-9043. Founded 1980. 400 members. Accept all Thunderbirds. Monthly newsletter, monthly meetings, tours and special events. "Ownership not required, but enthusiasm is." Dues: $18/year.

Thunderbird Midwest Inc
4380 245th St
Forest Lake, MN 55025
612-464-7581; FAX: 612-464-1111

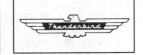

Founded 1979. 90 members. Restrictions: must be an admirer of Ford Thunderbird 58-present. Monthly meetings and newsletters. Spring, summer and fall cruises, shows. Chapter club of Vintage Thunderbird Club International. Dues: $20/year.

Tucson Thunderbird Club
3156 E President St
Tucson, AZ 85714
602-889-8634

Founded 1976. 50 members. Chapter of CTCI, #103. Membership in CTCI is not required. Ownership is not required. Dues: $10/year.

Upstate New York Thunderbird Club Inc
Box 346
Greenwich, NY 12834
518-692-7815

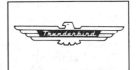

Founded 1981. 57 members. A member would benefit by meeting people across the state who are dedicated to preserving, restoring, driving and enjoying T-Birds, a monthly newsletter, meet once a month, annual general membership meeting, Syracuse, first Sunday in November. Dues: $20/year.

Vintage Thunderbird Club International
PO Box 2250
Dearborn, MI 48123-2250
716-674-7251, 8 am-8 pm EST, NY

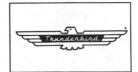

Enjoying and preserving the "personal luxury experience". Embracing all Thunderbirds, from 1958 to today. Serving Thunderbird enthusiasts for over a quarter century. Assisting over 3,000 members worldwide. Five regional/one international convention yearly. Chapters across the US and abroad. Award winning bi-monthly *Thunderbird Scoop* magazine. Send for information/application or mail $26 dues US & Canada, $45 foreign to above address.

Geo Club
PO Box 11238
Chicago, IL 60611
773-769-6262; FAX: 773-769-3240
E-mail: tnwb52a@prodigy.com

Founded 1992. 600 members. For enthusiasts of Geos: Storm, Tracker, Metro and Prizm. Quarterly publication: *The Geo World*. Annual convention. Dues: $25/year.

Gotfredson Group
15 Davis Dr
Alton, ONT Canada L0N 1A0
519-942-0436

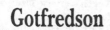

Founded 1988. 52 members. International membership. For information, contact at above address: Ed Thornton. Interest of complete historical information on the Gotfredson truck (1920-1948) and the American Auto Trimming Co (1909-1948). We offer assistance in restoration, preservation, parts location, technical and historical material. Ownership of a Gotfredson is not necessary. Newsletters published.

Graham Brothers Truck & Bus Club
9894 Fairtree Dr
Strongsville, OH 44136
216-238-4956

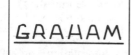

For membership information, contact at the above address: Edwin L Brinkman. Founded 1975. 215 members. Dues: none. 16 page owners's roster list available for $2 postpaid.

The H H Franklin Club
Home Office, Roy F Powers, Manager
Cazenovia College
Cazenovia, NY 13035
315-683-5376

Founded 1951. Publications, technical information, national and regional meets. For all air cooled cars of the period to 1935. 800 members. Dues: $25/year.

Hillman Commer Karrier Club
Kingfisher Ct
East Molesey
Surrey KT8 9HL England
PH/FAX: 0181-941-0604

Founded 1991. 1,000 members. Club for Hillman, Commer & Karrier vehicles and all derivatives sold under Dodge, Plymouth, etc, plus Chrysler or Talbot badged Hunters, Avengers, Sunbeams and Sunbeam Lotus. Bi-monthly publication: *HCKC News*, free to members. Dues: £8/year.

Hispano-Suiza Society
175 St Germain Ave
San Francisco, CA 94114
415-664-4378

For membership information, contact at the above address: Mr. Jules M Heumann. President. Founded 1975. 150 members. Membership for enthusiasts of Hispano-Suiza cars and/or aircraft engines. Quarterly newsletter, repro owner's manuals, shop manuals, blazer patches, membership pins, etc. Dues: $50/year US; $57.50/year overseas.

Holden-Early Holden Club of New Zealand
PO Box 47075
Ponsonby, Auckland New Zealand
PH/FAX: 64-9-444-7263

Founded 1983. 160 members. Enthusiasts of General Motors Australian designed and built Holden cars produced between 1948 to 1983. Holdens are basically the Australian Chevrolet and were sold in great numbers over the years listed. We offer assistance to owners regarding spares and service, with monthly meetings and monthly newsletter. Dues: $25/year.

Hudson-Essex-Terraplane Club
6933 Sunstrand Dr
Knoxville, TN 37924-3754
423-525-5692

Founded 1986. 50 members. Must be member of National Hudson-Essex-Terraplane Club. Bi-monthly newsletter with free classifieds, 10 meetings per year including 2 joint meets with other H-E-T Club chapters. Will also provide information on National Club. Dues: $10/year.

chapters:

Arizona *Grand Canyon Chapter*, Galen L Moon, 1650 S Arizona #7, Chandler, AZ 85248, 602-963-8168

California *California Island*, Press Kale, 8441 Ridglea, Buena Park, CA 90621, 714-523-0403

Northern California, David Houghton, 5771 Mountain Ct, Castro Valley, CA 94532, 510-582-5768

Sacramento Valley, Dennis Flint, PO Box 1967, North Highlands, CA 95660-8967, 916-332-0957

South Western Borders, Bear Frothinger, 1504 Montecito Rd #2, Ramona, CA 92065, 619-789-2553

Southern California, Ken Perkins Jr, 20543 Soledad St, Canyon Country, CA 91351, 805-298-9266

Colorado *Rocky Mountain*, John Soneff, 2165 Curtis St, Denver, CO 80205, 303-296-1688

Connecticut *Yankee*, Ed Firestone, 23 Worthington Rd, Glastonbury, CT 06033, 203-633-5001

Florida *Orange Blossom Chapter*, Joe Stinnett, PO Box 223, Ocoee, FL 34761, 407-877-1047

Georgia *Dixie*, Bob Watson, 2851 Gay Rd, Greenville, GA 30222, 770-306-1725

Idaho *Gem State*, Paul Johnson, 2503 Forest Glen, Post Falls, ID 83845, 208-773-7319

Illinois *Central Miss Valley*, Bob Hoyle, 2076 IL, Rt 26, Dixon, IL 61021, 815-288-6140

Chicago-Milwaukee, JohnVanlier, 8215 Willow Dr, Palos Hills, IL 60465, 708-974-4513

Indiana *South Central*, Harry Downing, RR 1, Underwood, IN 47177, 812-752-6390

Southern Indiana, Larry Kennedy, 9350 Vandergriff Rd, Indianapolis, IN 46239, 317-862-2020

Iowa *Central Iowa*, Jay DeJong, 8190 Main St, Reasnor, IA 50232, 515-793-2374

Kansas *Hudsonite Family Chapter*, Kathy Lawrence, 3321 Chestnut, Wichita, KS 67216, 316-529-1896

Mo-Kan Hudson Family Chapter, Jim Durand, Rt 1, Box 435, Meriden, KS 66512, 913-484-2756

Louisiana *Red River Chapter*, Erwin Sanchez Flores, 1809 S Brookwood, Shreveport, LA 71118, 318-635-3304

Maryland *Chesapeake Bay*, Lewis Mendenhall, 3513 Oxwed Ct, Westminster, MD 21157, 410-795-4992

Massachusetts *New England*, Larry Wendall, 61 Buena Vista Rd, Arlington, MA 02174, 617-648-3833

Michigan *Hudson Motor Car Co Home Chapter*, Bob Elton, 860 Edwards, Ann Arbor, MI 48103, 313-663-1020

Minnesota	*North Central,* Joan Hudson, 16741 242nd Ave, Big Lake, MN 55309, 612-263-3486
Missouri	*Gateway Chapter,* Dick Burgdorf, 1472 Oak Bluff Ln, St Louis, MO 63122, 314-822-1472
Montana	*Big Sky,* Ed Standley, 660 E Lewis, East Helena, MT 59635
Nebraska	*Iowa-Nebraska,* Bob Johnson, 110 W H St, Hastings, NE 68901, 402-462-2296
New Jersey	*Garden State Chapter,* Ted Steinmetz, 14 Forest Ave, Medford, NJ 08055, 609-983-4319
New Mexico	*Southwest,* Donald E Wustrack, 988 Rio Bravo Way, Las Cruce, NM 88005, 505-525-3393
	Zia/New Mexico Chapter, Jim Glover, 3601 Sylvia Pl SW, Albuquerque, NM 87105, 505-877-7955
New York	*Hudson Mohawk,* Bruce Smith, 42 Gilligan Rd, East Greenbush, NY 12061, 518-477-9740
	Long Island, Bob Colligan, 17 Raff Ave, Floral Park, NY 11001, 516-354-7151
	Western New York/Ontario, Ed Schmidt, 52 Bunnell St, Attica, NY 14011, 716-591-0717
North Carolina	*Dogwood Chapter,* Duke Marley, 5611 Kapp Rd, Pfafftown, NC 27040, 910-924-2951
Ohio	*North Indiana-Ohio,* Jerry Bean, 960 Eastown Rd, Lima, OH 45807, 419-331-5511
	Western Reserve, Richard Ginter, 14490 Fetterman Dr, Strongsville, OH 44136
Oklahoma	*Dust Bowl,* Jimmie Johnston, 5483 N Choctaw Rd, Choctaw, OK 73020
Pennsylvania	*Pennsylvania Dutch,* Carl Undercofler, RD Box 337A, Woodland, PA 16881, 814-857-7748
Tennessee	*Midsouth,* Billy Kemp, Rt 3, Box 172-B, Pleasant Ridge Rd, Adamsville, TN 38310
	Smoky Mountain Heartland, Wycliffe Busch, Rt 5, Box 67-2, Johnson City, TN 37601, 615-929-8449
Texas	*North Texas,* Clinton Webb, 568 Fisher St, Allen, TX 75002, 214-727-7919
	South Texas, Breckenridge Wagner, Rt 5, Box 118, Brenham, TX 77833, 713-524-0712
Utah	*Deseret,* Gert Kristiansen, 1731 S 500 E, Salt Lake City, UT 84105, 801-486-1635
Washington	*Northwest,* Steve Welzbacker, E 340 Canyon View Rd, Belfair, WA 98528
Australia	*Australia,* Les Pendlebury, PO Box 2123, N Parramatia, 215 NSW, Australia
	Australia, Phil Haxby, 216 Ryans Rd, Eltham N, 3095 Victoria, Australia
New Zealand	*New Zealand Rep,* Geoffrey Clark, 72 Scotia St, Nelson, New Zealand
South Africa	*South African Rep,* Mike Davidson, PO Box 19805, Fishers Hill, 1408 South Africa

---

Hupmobile Club
158 Pond Rd
N Franklin, CT 06254

Founded 1970. 800 members. Worldwide club for Hupmobile enthusists, currently have members in 18 countries. Publish *Hupp Herald* magazine; *Hupmobile Parts Locator Bulletin.* We reproduce parts & literature not otherwise available. Dues: $20/yr US, $25 o/s.

Iso & Bizzarini Owners Club
2025 Drake Dr
Oakland, CA 94611
PH/FAX: 510-339-8347

Founded 1980. 200 members. Founded to promote the preservation and awareness of the marques. Membership includes quarterly magazine *Griffon* and bi-monthly newsletter *Bresso Express.* No restrictions to join. Club sponsors meets and social gatherings, with an annual international meet at the Annual Monterey Historic Races. Dues: $35/year USA, $45 overseas.

Classic Jaguar Association
2860 W Victoria Dr
Alpine, CA 91901
619-445-3152

Founded 1952. 1,000 members. Dedicated to the restoration, preservation, and enjoyment of SS cars and older Jaguars. Publishes news and technical bulletins. Dues: $25/year.

Jaguar Clubs of North America Inc
Membership Dept
9685 McLeod Rd, RR 2
Chilliwack, BC Canada V2P 6H4

Founded 1954. 4,500 members who belong to 47 local clubs in the US and Canada which are affiliated with JCNA. JCNA sponsors championships in Concours d'Elegance, rally and slalom competition. The local clubs offer their own social, technical and other programs. Dues, which are paid to the local club, vary according to location and include JCNA membership, insurance and the bi-monthly *Jaguar Journal* magazine.

Jaguar Touring Club
307 Paterson Ave
East Rutherford, NJ 07073
201-438-9628 days; FAX: 201-935-4599

Founded 1978. 300 members. No restrictions, monthly publication *The Cat-A-Logue,* monthly meetings, annual Concours d'Elegance June 27, 28, 29, 1997. Club encourages using Jaguars. Dues: $45/year.

Association of Jensen Owners
140 Franklin Ave
Wyckoff, NJ 07481-3465
201-847-8549, 8-10 pm EST
FAX: 201-342-4637

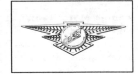

Founded 1977. 800 members. No restrictons. Communication with fellow Jensen owners, parts source, technical advice. *White Lady,* color publication, published quarterly, National meet annually. Dues: $40/year.

Jensen Interceptor Owners Club
23117 E Echo Lake Rd
Snohomish, WA 98290
206-788-0507

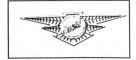

Founded 1976. International organization dedicated to the preservation, restoration and enjoyment of the Jensen Interceptor automobile. Technical assistance available to provide info on maintenance, restoration and parts location. *Gentleman's Express* newsletter lists events, club activities, technical advice, etc. Free want/for sale ads to members.

Jewett Owners Club
24005 Clawiter Rd
Hayward, CA 94545
510-785-1948

Jewett

For membership information, contact at the above address: Terrell Shelley, 510-785-1948. Founded 1982. 30 members. Open to Jewett owners. Register of Jewett cars and clubs, parts, location and literature for all Jewett models. Information on request.

Clubs & Organizations

Kissel Kar Klub
147 N Rural St
Hartford, WI 53027
414-673-7999

For membership information, write to the above address. 197 members. Membership limited to owners of cars produced by the Kissel Motor Car Company, Hartford, WI (1906-1931), also to owners of their commercial vehicles including funeral cars, taxi cabs and fire trucks, and to personnel of the old company and family members who signify interest. Dues: none. Donations accepted.

The Lagonda Club
Wintney House, London Road
Hartley Wintney
Hants, RG27 8RN England
PH/FAX: UK/125284-5451

For membership information, contact: in England, at the above address; in US and Canada, C M Salyer, 3237 Harvey Parkway, Oklahoma City, OK 73118. Founded 1951. 700 members. Should be a Lagonda owner or enthusiast. Dues: US: $60/year; Canada: $70/year; plus $18 initiation fee.

Lamborghini Owners' Club
Jim Kaminski
PO Box 7214
St. Petersburg, FL 33734

Founded 1978. 900+ members. Oldest Lamborghini club in the world. Newsletter every other month with technical tips, parts sources, meeting information, marque items for sale. Send for application form.

Dansk Lancia Register
Boserupvej 510
DK-3050 Humlebaek,
Danmark Denmark
+45-49191129

Founded 1989. 55 members. Club for owners of Lancia cars. Technical aid and information. Rallies, meetings. Dues: 150 DKK/year.

Lancia Motor Club Ltd
David Baker
Mt Pleasant, Penhros, Brymbo
Wrexham, Clwyd LL11 5LY England
01978-750631

For membership information, contact at the above address: David Baker. Founded 1947. 2,500 members worldwide. For owners and lovers of the Marque. "We cater to all models from 1911 Eta to current production models."

Continental Mark II Association
PO Box 375-VC
Reedsport, OR 97467
PH/FAX: 541-271-9235

Founded 1977 as Continental Mark II Owners Association. A fellowship of owners and enthusiasts with the goal of maintaining, restoring and enjoying 1956-57 Continental Mark II automobiles. Membership is $15 a year US, $25 foreign including four quarterly issues of The Continental newsletter. CMA also provides a marque registry service and publishes books on the history and restoration of these milestone cars.

Lincoln and Continental Owners Club
PO Box 157
Boring, OR 97009-0157
503-658-3119; FAX: 503-658-6119

Founded 1953. Over 4,000 members. Dedicated to the enjoyment, preservation and restoration of all Lincolns and

Continentals. Membership includes Continental Comments magazine, published bi-monthly, featuring articles on cars, technical tips and ads with cars and parts for sale as well as a directory issue which includes members and supplier sources. Three national meets annually with class awards and 13 major awards at each meet. 23 authorized, active regions, each with newsletters and monthly tours, dinners and social activities. National dues: $25/year US, Canada & Mexico; $35/year other countries (US funds).

regions:

Arizona	*Arizona*, Russ Upton, 8313 E Coolidge, Scottsdale, AZ 85251, 602-946-4917
California	*Western*, Wally Aiken, 1436 La Plaza Dr, Lake San Marcos, CA 92069, 619-744-8081
Colorado	*Rocky Mountain*, Keith Ritterhouse, 6759 Village Rd, Parker, CO 80134, 303-841-5614
Florida	*Florida Gulf Coast*, Jack Shea, 4604 Flagship Dr #206, Ft Meyers, FL 33919, 941-433-3642, 941-481-5770
Illinois	*Lake Shore*, Robert J Faber, 816 W 56th St, Hinsdale, IL 60521, 630-325-6861, 847-593-0707
	Mid Continent, William E LaFargue, 8455 S Damen, Chicago, IL 60620, 312-881-1339, 312-476-7357
Indiana	*Hoosier*, Jerry Flanary, 3774 Pleasant Run Pwy N Dr, Indianapolis, IN 46201, 317-356-4246
Maryland	*Chesapeake*, Bernie Wolfson, 24519 Peach Tree Rd, Clarksburg, MD 20871, 301-601-1855, 301-972-1080
Michigan	*Michigan*, Roy Lancaster, 487 Russell Woods Rd, WIndsor, ON Canada N8N 3S6, 519-979-9779; winter address: 773 Wiggins Lake Dr, Unit 205, Naples, FL 33963, 941-597-5272
Minnesota	*North Star*, Robert Gavrilescu Jr, 1520 Chelsea St, St Paul, MN 55108, 612-488-3878, 612-641-6850
New Jersey	*Philadelphia*, Lorie Rhoads, 100 Buttonwood Ln, Cinnaminson, NJ 08077, 609-829-0741
New Mexico	*New Mexico*, Maurice M Rosenthal, 8201 Rio Grande Blvd NW, Albuquerque, NM 87114, 505-898-6328
New York	*Mid-Atlantic*, Michael Simco, PO Box 188, Tivoli, NY 12583, 914-757-4448, 914-471-7430
North Carolina	*Southern*, Frederic Comlossy, 9 Ulvda Ct, Brevard, NC 28712, 704-884-5454
Ohio	*Ohio Valley*, Robert Thompson, 507 S Albright-McKay SE, Brookfield, OH 44403, 216-448-6217, 800-843-5522
	Southern Ohio, Edward G Hilton, 7640 Essington Cir, Centerville, OH 45459, 513-433-6644, 513-434-4347
Oregon	*Pacific Northwest*, Steve D'Ambrosia, PO Box 157, Boring, OR 97009, 503-658-6119, 503-658-3119
Texas	*Lone Star*, John Burge, 511 Bluff Tr, San Antonio, TX 78216, 210-490-3134
	North Texas, Douglas W Mattix, 3305 Weems Wy, Rowlett, TX 75088, 214-412-0754
	Texas Gulf Coast, Cody Gray, 1805 W Gray, Houston, TX 77019, 713-529-4850, 713-529-4859
Utah	*Bonneville*, Charles R Haskett, 603 Pioneer Ave, Tooele, UT 84074, 801-882-1628

Clubs & Organizations

Lincoln Owners Club
PO Box 660
Lake Orion, MI 48361

Organized in 1958. 500 members. Primarily interested in Lincolns built between 1920 and 1939. Specifically models L, K, KA & KB. However, ownership of such a Lincoln is not necessary for membership. Anyone interested in Lincolns is welcome. Dues: $25/year.

Lincoln Zephyr Owners Club
PO Box 422
Hazel Green, AL 35750-0422
615-433-0065

Founded 1968. 1,000 members. Bimonthly publication: *The Way of the Zephyr*. Specializing in all cars that were based on the H V12 engine.

Lincoln-Mercury Enthusiast
18376 228th St
Tonganoxie, KS 66086
913-845-3458

Founded 1990. 45 member families. Open to all enthusiasts. Many social and technical events. Free ad and info in monthly newsletter. Monthly meetings at 7 pm on the last Saturday of the month at various locations in Kansas City area. Dues: $12/year.

Road Race Lincoln Register (RRLR)
461 Woodland Dr
Wisconsin Rapids, WI 54494
715-423-9579

Founded 1972. 340 members. Must be interested in 1949 through 1957 Lincoln Premieres, Capris, Customs or Cosmopolitans and 1949 through 1951 "Baby" Lincolns on Mercury body shell, ownership not required. Deals with 1949 through 1957 Lincolns other than Mark IIs. Our quarterly newsletter, *Viva Carrera*, deals with technical matters, participation in various road races for vintage cars by club members, testimonials by owners, "want" ads or "for sale" ads, and the occasional reprint. We have several annual regional meets and have about 35 Canadian and overseas members. Dues: $19/year.

Club Elite (Lotus Type 14)
6238 Ralston Ave
Richmond, CA 94805-1519
PH/FAX: 510-232-7764

For membership information, contact at the above address: Michael Ostrov, secretary. Founded 1971. 215 members. Open to owners and enthusiasts of the original Lotus Elite and other Lotus cars. Dues: $20/year US, $25/year foreign.

Lotus Ltd
PO Box L
College Park, MD 20741
PH/FAX: 301-982-4054

Founded 1973. 1,500 members. Lotus Ltd is the largest club for Lotus car enthusiasts in the US. The club is an entirely non-profit volunteer organization with over 13 affiliated local groups. Agreed-value insurance program. Technical assistance. Monthly publication: *Lotus ReMarque*. Dues: $30/new members, $20 year renewals in US; outside US, add $5.

Marmon Club
3044 Gainsborough Dr
Pasadena, CA 91107
818-449-2325

For membership information on Marmon and/or Roosevelt, contact at the above address: Duke Marston, Secretary. Founded 1970. 400 members. Annual directory of members and their Marmon and/or Roosevelt cars. Ownership not required for membership. Worldwide membership, bimonthly publication. Dues: $20/year US, $25/year foreign. (US funds, US bank).

Maserati Club
The Paddock Old Salisbury Rd
Abbotts Ann Andover
Hampshire, SP11 7NT England
0264/710312

Founded 1971. Over 400 members. Dues: $50/year.

The Maserati Club
PO Box 5300
Somerset, NJ 08875-5300
908-249-2177; FAX: 908-246-7570

Founded 1986. 360 members. An international club with 2 US chapters and 2 Canadian chapters. Open to all Maserati enthusiasts. We publish *Il Tridente* quarterly magazine & hold events from New York to Denver & Toronto to Florida. Dues: $60/yr. Internet: http://www.themaseraticlub.com

Maserati Owners Club of North America
14220 Saddlebow Ct
Reno, NV 89511
FAX: 702-853-7212

Founded 1979. 500 members. Club founded to benefit owners and the marque. Members receive technical information, parts info, quarterly newsletter, schedule of events, decals, patches, regalia, etc. Dues: $30/year.

Mazda Club
PO Box 11238
Chicago, IL 60611
773-769-6262; FAX: 773-769-3240
E-mail: tnwb52a@prodigy.com

For information, contact at the above address: Ernest Feliciano, President. Open to all Mazda owners including the RX-7, Miata, MX-6, 626 and MX-3. Technical advice, parts discounts and newsletters. Publication: *The Only Way*. Dues: $25/year.

Mazda RX-7 Club
1774 S Alvira St
Los Angeles, CA 90035
213-933-6993, 1-6 pm

Founded 1978. 1,400 members. A technical service club aimed at the enthusiast who does some of his own maintenance and would like to improve his RX-7 with performance and cosmetic accessories. Dues: $30/year; $40/year foreign.

Mercedes-Benz 300SL Gullwing Group International
PO Box 1569
Morgan Hill, CA 95037
408-776-1788; FAX: 408-776-7488

Founded 1961. 600 members. Open to owners of 300SL gullwings and roadsters and those interested in them. Monthly publication *300 Star Letter*, tech tips, parts, projects, annual convention in different parts of USA. Dues: $55/year USA, $75/year Canada & foreign.

Mercedes-Benz 600, 6.3 & 6.9 Group
2020 Girard Ave S
Minneapolis, MN 55405
612-377-0155; FAX: 612-377-0157

M-100 Group, founded 1991. 250 members. Interest in or ownership of Mercedes-Benz 600 Model, 6.3 model and 6.9 models only. Club serves to locate fellow enthusiasts, locate service & parts resources and foster preservation. Periodic newsletters, meetings in future. Dues $30/year.

Capri Club of Chicago
7158 W Armitage
Chicago, IL 60707
733-889-5197; FAX: 630-971-2875

For membership information, contact at the above address: Wayne H. Tofel, 312-889-5197. Founded 1974. 45 members. Club functions include events, information and discounts for Capri owners. Monthly newsletter. Dues: $20/year.

Chicagoland Mercury Club
PO Box 341
Crete, IL 60417
708-672-7864, 708-532-2306

Founded 1990. Membership still growing. To encourage appreciation of the Mercury motorcar. Dues: $20/year.

Cougar Club of America
0-4211 N 120th Ave
Holland, MI 49424

Founded 1980. 1,200 members. For enthusiasts of 1967-73 Mercury Cougars. Quarterly publication. Dues: $25/year US, $30/year Canadian and foreign.

International Mercury Owners Association
6445 W Grand Ave
Chicago, IL 60707-3410
312-622-6445; FAX: 312-622-3602

Founded 1991. 700 members. Open to all Mercury enthusiasts. Quarterly publication: *Quicksilver*. Ads listed free to members (individuals only). Dues: $25/year US & Canada; $35/year international.

Mid-Century Mercury Car Club
1816 E Elmwood Dr
Lindenhurst, IL 60046
847-356-2255

Founded 1977. 400 members. Ownership not required. Dedicated to the preservation of 1949-51 Mercurys. Dues: $15/year.

American MGB Association
PO Box 11401
Chicago, IL 60611-0401
773-878-5055, 800-723-MGMG
FAX: 773-769-3240
E-mail: amgba@aol.com

For membership information, contact at the above address: Frank Ochal, President, 773-878-5055. Open to MG owners and enthusiasts. Founded 1975. 3,000 member "North America's official registry for MGBs, MG Midgets, MGB/GT V8s and MG 1100/1300s." Publication: *AMGBA Octagon*. Dues: $25/year.

Arizona MG T Roadrunners
PO Box 8641
Scottsdale, AZ 85252

Founded 1975. 53 members. Open to pre-1956 MG enthusiasts. Dues: $20/year.

Central Ohio MG Owners
10260 Covan Dr
Westerville, OH 43082-9295
614-882-6191

Founded 1983. 100 members. A group of MG enthusiasts who welcome participation of all MG owners. The club encourages the preservation and driving of MGs and the opportunity to enjoy the friendship of other families involved in the hobby. Several events are held each year including tours, car shows, picnics and an annual Christmas party. A newsletter is published 4 times a year to keep members informed. Dues: $5/year.

Connecticut MG Club
A Heady
65 Pumpkin Hill Rd
New Milford, CT 06776
203-354-9501

Founded 1988. 350 members. Welcomes all MG drivers. Holds informal but regular meetings, travels to MG events throughout New England, holds joint events with other clubs. Provides technical information and advice. Dues: $20/year with monthly newsletter.

Emerald Necklace MG Register
PO Box 81152
Cleveland, OH 44181
330-678-9394
E-mail: enmgr@newreach.net

Founded 1980. 230 members. Serving the northern Ohio area and open to all MG enthusiasts. Monthly newsletter, tech sessions, rallies, special events and support for those who are octagonally inclined. Dues: $20/year.

MG Car Club Central Jersey Centre
PO Box 435
Convent Station, NJ 07961
201-361-8314

Founded 1963. 136 members. Call phone number listed for further information regarding time and place of monthly meetings, scheduled activities, etc. Dues include monthly newsletter *Meshing Gears*. Dues: $20/year.

The MG Car Club Ltd
Kimber House, PO Box 251
Abingdon, Oxon, OX14 1FF England
01235-555552; FAX: 01235-533755
E-mail: mgcc@mgcars.org.uk.

For membership information, contact at the above address: Lyn Jeffrey. Founded 1930. Open to owners of all models of MGs. Operates throughout the world through 42 local chapters.

MG Octagon Car Club
Unit 19, Hollins Business Centre
Rowley St
Stafford ST16 2RH England
01785 51014

For membership information, contact at the above address: Harry Crutchley. Founded 1969. 2,200 members. Open to all, but full membership is given only to owners of pre-1956 MGs, so that we can give more personal service to our members. Dues: $42/year.

MG Vintage Racers Newsletter
Mark Palmer, Editor
253 Bridlepath Rd
Bethlehem, PA 18017
610-867-6014; FAX: 610-954-9489

Founded 1981. 140 members. Must actively race a vintage MG (up to 1967) to join. Publishes newsletter which consists of technical articles, letters, member profiles, competition reports, parts sources and race schedules. Joining fee: none.

New England MG T Register Ltd
PO Drawer 220
Oneonta, NY 13820
607-432-6835; FAX: 607-432-3342

For membership information, contact at the above address: Richard L Knudson. Founded 1963, 4,000 members. Regular membership is open only to owners of 1955 or older MGs powered by original type engine; all others may become associate members. Our bimonthly journal, *The Sacred Octagon*, is regarded as "the best source of MG historical material in the world." Dues: $35/year, plus $15 initiation fee. Web site: http://www.nemgt.org

North American MGC Register
Tom Boscarino, Chairman
34 Park Ave
Asheville, NC 28803
704-274-2269

Founded 1980. 500 members. A volunteer, non-profit, national register. Serving the MGC and MGC/GT 1968-1969. Annual event Challenge of Brute Agressives. Bi-monthly newsletter *C-Notes*. A register of the MGCC, England. Annual membership: $20.

North American MMM Register
Tom Metcalf, Registrar
1475 Township Rd 853
Ashland, OH 44805
419-525-0799

Founded 1990. 150 members. A volunteer, non-profit, national register. Serving the Midgets, Magnas and Magnettes 1929-1935. Annual event *Camming* and bi-monthly newsletter. A register of the MGCC, England. Annual membership, $25.

Foothills MoPar Club
PO Box 1562
Greer, SC 29652

MoPar

Founded 1992. 115 members. Membership card entitles member to discount of up to 25% at participating dealers on parts. Monthly newsletter, one annual show, different car displays throughout the year & parades. Dues $20/year.

MoPar Muscle Cars of Austin
PO Box 49829
Austin, TX 78765

MoPar

Founded 1986. 40 members. Open to all interested in the restoration, preservation and promotion of Chrysler built products. Monthly meeting and newsletter. Participates in car shows and competition drag meets. Sponsors a rally annually. Dues: $25/year.

MoPar Scat Pack Club
PO Box 2303
Dearborn, MI 48123
313-278-2240

MoPar

Founded 1981. 500+ members. Should be a Chrysler owner. Dedicated to the restoration and preservation of Chrysler high performance vehicles. Parts discount program and member super offers throughout the year. Bimonthly publication: Mighty MoPars. Dues: $25/year.

Western Ontario MoPar Owners
(WOMO Inc)
RR 3
Iona Station, ONT Canada N0L 1P0
519-764-2335

MoPar

Founded 1985. 150 members. Must own or be interested in Chrysler vehicles, open to all Chrysler/late AMC vehicles. Bimonthly newsletter, discounts at participating businesses, yearly drag, show & swap meet in June at London Motorsports Park. Meet first Tuesday of month. Open to members worldwide. Our motto, "Preservation Through Friendship." Dues: $25/year Canada, $30/year family; $30/year US, $35/year family.

WPC Club Inc
PO Box 3504
Kalamazoo, MI 49003-3504

MoPar

The WPC Club, Inc is a non-profit corporation dedicated to the preservation and enjoyment of Plymouth, Dodge, Chrysler,

DeSoto, Imperials and related cars. WPC News is a monthly publication with feature articles and want/sale ads, plus other features. Subscription rate: $23, ($27 foreign).
See our ad on this page

The 3/4 Morgan Group Ltd
c/o Vivian Wadlin
PO Box 474
New Paltz, NY 12561
914-691-2089

Founded 1971. 200 members. Three-wheeled as well as four-wheeled Morgan owners welcomed, although you need not own one to join. Northeast region covered. Informative monthly newsletter, *The Morganeer*. Promotes fellowship among Morgan enthusiasts as well as sharing technical information for maintaining the breed. Dues: $30/year.

Morgan Car Club, Washington, DC
616 Gist Ave
Silver Spring, MD 20910
301-585-0121

Founded 1959. 325 members. No restrictions to join. Gathering of Morgan enthusiasts with frequent meetings, events, competitions, worldwide communications and historical files. Monthly publication: The Rough Rider. Dues: $25/year.

Morgan Three-Wheeler Club
3708 California Ave
Long Beach, CA 90807
310-595-6179

Founded 1947. 700 members. US group of British parent club. Offers technical information, spares sources and other assistance. For membership information, contact: Alec Knight, PO Box 99, Ringoes, NJ 08551 or John Leavens in California.

Metropolitan Owners Club of North America
5009 Barton Rd
Madison, WI 53711
608-271-0457

Founded 1975. 2,300 members. Open to all Metropolitan enthusiasts and owners. National, regional and chapter meets. Monthly newsletter: *The Met Gazette*. Dues: $15/year.

The Nash Club of America
4151 220th St
Clinton, IA 52732-8943

For membership information, write to the above address. Founded 1970. 1,850 members. Should have an interest in Nashes, related automobiles and their history. Family oriented activities. Advisor service and travel assistance offered. Publishes six magazines and six ad flyers. Dues: $23/year US and $24/year Canada, $41/year foreign air, $24/year foreign surface.

regions:

Arizona	*Saguaro Region,* Tom Haney, 910 E Kaler Dr, Phoenix, AZ 85020
California	*Northern California Region,* Gordon McGregor, 1334 Mission Ave, Carmichael, CA 95608
	Southern California Region, Neil Black, 8001 Bellingham Ave, North Hollywood, CA 91605
Colorado	*High Plains Region,* Rinehold Peter, 941 W Mountain Ave, Fort Collins, CO 80521
Florida	*Sunshine Region,* Tom Larson, 11036 Eastwood Dr, Orlando, FL 32817
Georgia	*Southern Region,* Mike Wennin, 1304 Concepts 21 Dr, Norcross, GA 30092
Illinois	*Upper Mississippi River Region,* Chuck Block, 618 Lor Ann, South Elgin, IL 60177
Kansas	*Historic Trails Region,* Bill Bohrn, 1051 Ashbury, Olathe, KS 66061
Massachusetts	*Northeast Region,* Mark Chenard, 50 Cavour Cir, W Boylston, MA 01583
Michigan	*Erie Shores Region,* Carl Dawes, 3209 Erie Dr, Orchard Lake, MI 48324
Nebraska	*Central Missouri River Region,* Harvey Leners, 5426 S 185th St, Omaha, NE 68135
New York	*Niagara Frontier Region,* James Van Wyk, 7418 Boughton Hill Rd, Victor, NY 14564
	NY Metropolitan and Long Island Region, Ken Gugliucci, 249-21 88th Rd, Bellerose, NY 11426
Ohio	*Central Ohio Valley Region,* Ken Carmack, 709 Holiday Dr, Fortville, IN 46040
Oregon	*Mid-Columbia Region,* Joe Van Buren, 1141 NE 196th, Portland, OR 97230
Pennsylvania	*Mid-Atlantic Region,* Maynard Keller, 36 Younken Rd, Quakertown, PA 18951
	OH-Penn Region, George Vollmer, 2335 Dutch Ridge Rd, Beaver, PA 15009
Tennessee	*Bluegrass/Volunteer Region,* H F Houston, 710 Walter Morris Rd, Lebanon, TN 37087
Texas	*Texas Region,* Bill Downs, 5604 Oak Blvd, Austin, TX 78735-8710
Virginia	*Dogwood Region,* Jon Vanatta, 929 Jouett Dr, Newport News, VA 23602-7701
Wisconsin	*Greater Northland Region,* Terry Quesnel, Rt 2, Box 59, Cearlake, WI 54005

Clubs & Organizations

The NSU Club of America
717 N 68th St
Seattle, WA 98103
206-784-5084

For membership information contact at the above address: Jim Sykes. Quarterly 20+ page booklet. Dues: $15/year.

NSU Enthusiasts USA
c/o Terry Stuchlik
2909 Utah Pl
Alton, IL 62002
618-462-9195

Founded 1971. 100 members. Quarterly newsletter containing 24-28 pages. Annual meeting & occasional regional meetings. Dues: $15/year.

Henry Nyberg Society
17822 Chicago Ave
Lansing, IL 60438
PH/FAX: 708-474-3416 collect

Founded 1988. Nearly 50 members. Promotes and encourages the educational, research and scientific purposes or activities associated with the design, production and preservation of the Nyberg vehicles manufactured in the USA between the years 1903-1913. The name Nyberg is trademarked and we are a 501(C)3 not for profit organization with nearly 500 pieces of literature and still searching. Periodic publications. Dues: $20/year.

Curved Dash Oldsmobile Club
3455 Florida Ave N
Minneapolis, MN 55427
612-533-4280; FAX: 612-535-1421

Founded 1977. 400 members. Open to owners of 1901-07 curved dash Oldsmobiles. Offers assistance in the proper restoration and reprints of historical documents. Also promotes usage of these cars. Six newsletters per year. Dues: $14/year.

Hurst/Olds Club of America
60520 Lamplighter Dr
New Hudson, MI 48165

Founded 1983. 950 members. No restrictions. Bimonthly publication, *Thunder & Lightning*. Annual National meet at various locations across USA. Dues: $25/year. Web site: http://www.netlink.co.uk/users/spear/hurstolds/.

National Antique Oldsmobile Club
11730 Moffitt Ln
Manassas, VA 22111

Founded 1981. 5,000 members. Anyone interested in the Oldsmobile marque. Publication: *Runabouts to Rockets*, published monthly. Annual show & meet which is restricted to 1897 to 1964 Oldsmobiles. Advisors for every year 1897-1964. Dues: $20/year.

Oldsmobile Club of America
PO Box 80318
Lansing, MI 48908-0318
517-321-8825; FAX: 517-321-8770

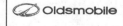

Founded 1971. 6,400 members. No restrictions. All years, no car necessary, just interest. Monthly publication, *Journey With Olds*. National meet annually, over 45 chapters. Chapter and regional meets all over the country. Dues: $30/year.

Oldsmobile Northern Lights Chapter
213 Kaskitayo Ct
Edmonton, AB Canada T6J 3T3
403-434-6335

Founded 1991. Currently 170 members worldwide. Open to everyone interested in 1897-present Oldsmobiles, affiliate

Chapter of the Oldsmobile Club of America (OCA), membership in OCA encouraged, but not required. 30 pg news magazine includes parts and cars for sale, how-to articles, events, contacts, news, technical articles, etc. Annual Oldsmobile show in the town of Olds, AB. Oldsmobile merchandise: pins, T-shirts, centennial items, etc. Dues $20/year. Write or phone Ken Pilidis for free information package.

North American Opel GT Club
1135 E Washington Blvd
Lombard, IL 60148
708-629-6792

Founded 1984. Dedicated to the preservation of the Opel GT sports car. Provides information and contacts for those interested in restoration, technical service information, parts information and location, and history. Monthly meetings held in the Chicago Metro area on the 3rd Friday of each month. Newsletter provided to members. Chapter dues: $15.

The Opel Association of North America
PO Box 9638
Richmond, VA 23228
804-262-3511
E-mail: opelprez@earthlink.net

Founded 1986. 312 members. Originally founded in 1986 as the Opel Exchange, became the Mid-Atlantic Opel Association in 1992 and in 1996 has become a full-fledged national club with 6 chapters (Mid-Atlantic, Northeast, Southern, Lone Star, Rocky Mountain and Northwest Opel Clubs). Bi-monthly newsletter, regional events, sources, ads and web site. We support all US and Canadian imported Opels and Bitters. Specializing mainly on Opel GTs, Mantas, Kadettes and Bitter SCs. Dues: $15/year US, $25(US)/year Canada. Our homepage is: http://home.earthlink.net/~opelprez/opelhome.html

Opel Kadett Coupe Club of Denmark
c/o Frank Kiessling
Mosede Kaervej 47
Greve DK-2670 Denmark
+45-42-901073, best 11 am-3 pm
US Central time

Founded 1988. 50 members. No restrictions to join. Parts locator, annual meet first weekend every August, club magazine 4 times/year, small stock of parts, library with spare parts catalogues, workshop manuals, brochures, technical data, DIY articles, videos, etc. Cooperation with other Opel clubs worldwide. Parts sold, bought, exchanged and swapped. Ask for more information. Dues: DKK 350.

Opel Motorsport Club
5161 Gelding Cir
Huntington Beach, CA 92649

For membership information, contact: OMC, Dept B, c/o Stan Harvey, 1101 Cerritos Dr, Fullerton, CA 92635; or call: 714-525-1443. Founded 1981. 265 members. Monthly meeting and annual picnics are held, including our proud monthly publication of *The Blitz*. Dues: $35/year US; $45/year Canada and International.

Pacific Northwest Opel GT Club
1007 E Princeton Ave
Spokane, WA 99307
509-292-0194

Founded 1986. 4 members. For Opel enthusiasts, especially the GT and Manta. Informal club to exchange facts and new ideas. No dues, no newsletter, just local boys and their toys. Occasional get-togethers for pizza, beer and bull. Pacific Northwest Opel GT & 1968-1973 Datsun 510 Club.

Blue Ridge Packards
BRP Membership
131 Grooms Rd
Fayetteville, GA 30215
770-461-9309

Founded 1987. 165 members. Blue Ridge Packards is a region of the Packard Club. Membership in the National Club is a pre-requisite. The purpose of Blue Ridge Packards is to serve the members in restoration, preservation and enjoyment of Packard vehicles by providing a source for exchange of information and encouraging related activities including events, tours, exhibitions and publications. BRP membership includes 6 issues of *Country Roads*. Dues: $15/year.

The Eastern Packard Club Inc
PO Box 5112
Hamden, CT 06518
914-478-1149

For membership information, contact John McCarthy, 914-478-1149. Founded 1965. Should be a Packard enthusiast, no car needed. Membership includes 8x10 commercial photograph of members' restored cars. Dues: $25/year.

Mississippi Valley Packards
602 S Franklin
Farmington, MO 63640
FAX: 314-783-5997

For membership information, contact: Ken Chapman, PO Box 681, Fredericktown, MO 63645. Founded 1976. 80 members. Ownership of a Packard is not required. Annual slide show and displays. Regional affiliate of PAC. Promotes the Packard with both social events and educational seminars or displays. Covers the St Louis area, eastern Missouri and southern Illinois. Publishes a newsletter. Dues: $10/year.

Old Dominion Packard Club
PO Box 1702
426 First St
West Point, VA 23181
804-843-3279

For information, contact at the above address: R. Tyler Bland, Jr, R.A. 125 members. 200+ Packards in club. Two meetings held each year, one spring tour in April and one in October, a judging meet. Publishes a newsletter. Dues: $10/year.

Packard Automobile Classics Inc dba The Packard Club
420 S Ludlow St
Dayton, OH 45402
214-709-6185; FAX: 214-296-7920

Membership processing and info: PO Box 28788, Dallas, TX 75228-0788. PH: 800-527-3452, FAX: 214-296-7920. Founded 1953. 3,800 members. Annual Nationwide membership meet. Monthly *Cormorant News* bulletin. Quarterly *Packard Cormorant* magazine. Dues: $35 (USA); $45 (Canada); $55 (Mexico); $95 (overseas), US funds.

Packard Truck Organization
1196 Mountain Rd
York Springs, PA 17372
717-528-4920

Founded 1981. 50 members. Open to Packard truck owners. Interested in all materials relating to 1905-23 Packard trucks. Quarterly publication. Annual meet in York Springs, PA (October). Technical assistance. For membership information, contact at the above address: David B Lockard.

Packards International Midwest Region
365 St Leger Ave
Akron, OH 44305
216-784-7155

Founded 1968. 120 members. Must be member of Packards International to join. Monthly publication: Hexagon News. Contains historical, service info and local Packard club events. Dues: $15/year.

Packards International Motor Car Club
302 French St
Santa Ana, CA 92701
714-541-8431

Founded 1963. 2,500 members. Dedicated to the preservation and driving enjoyment of the Packard automobile. Publications as well as reproduction parts and literature. Publications: *Packards International* magazine and *News Counselor*, both quarterly. Dues: $30/year US, $40/year Canada and Mexico; $55/year overseas.

regions:

Arizona	*Arizona Region*, 3008 E Cherry Lynn Rd, Phoenix, AZ 85016
California	*Northern California Region*, 1123 10th Ave, Sacramento, CA 95818
	San Diego Region, 9030 Carroll Way #1, San Diego, CA 92121
	Southern California Region, PO Box 11192, Santa Ana, CA 92711
Nevada	*Nevada Region*, 2586 Boise St, Las Vegas, NV 89121
Ohio	*Midwest Region*, 365 St Leger Ave, Akron, OH 44305
Oregon	*Oregon Region*, PO Box 42127, Portland, OR 97242
Texas	*Texas Region*, 4422 Greystone, San Antonio, TX 78233
Washington	*Northwest Region*, PO Box 88881, Seattle, WA 98138
Australia	*Australian Region*, c/o Packard Automobile Club, 152 Bannockburn Rd, Turramurra, 2074 NSW, Australia
Canada	*Alberta Region*, Box 40343 Highfield PO, Calgary, AB Canada T2G 5G7

Packards of Oregon
1240 SE Gideon St
Portland, OR 97202
503-234-8617; FAX: 503-234-8618
E-mail: hfreedman@aol.com

55 members. Specializing in Packard. Dues: $18/year.

Peerless & Warwick Register of North America
39 Ridge Rd
Lansing, NY 14882-9009
PH/FAX: 607-533-7735
(call first for FAX)

Founded 1974. 50 members. Open to anyone interested in Peerless GTs and Warwick GTs produced in England from 1958-63 (also some Gordon Keeble). Car listings, history, literature, parts references, etc. Newsletter. Dues: $10/year.

Pierce-Arrow Society Inc
135 Edgerton St
Rochester, NY 14607

Founded 1957. 1,000 members. Technical and historical information provided for all Pierce vehicles including bicycles, cars, trucks, buses, trailers and motorcycles. Dues: $25/year US. Members receive four magazines, six service bulletins, a membership roster, a technical index and free advertising privileges each year. Several regions offer local activities.

Dairyland Region Plymouth Owners Club
3026 Harriman Ln
Madison, WI 53713
608-221-1379
E-mail: jkallman@bus.wisc.edu

Founded 1994. Over 50 members. The Dairland Region (Wisconsin, Northern Illinois and Michigan's UP) of the National Plymouth Owners Club. Purpose is the preservation, restoration and promotion of Plymouth and Fargo vehicles which are 25 years of age or older. Family oriented activities include monthly auto tours, museum & antique shop visits and overnight mini-vacations. Dues: $12/year.

Plymouth Barracuda/Cuda Owners Club
4825 Indian Trail Rd
Northampton, PA 18067

Founded 1978. 800 members. Devoted to preservation/restoration of 1964-1974 Barracuda/Cuda automobiles. Annual meets. Bi-monthly publication. Dues: $16/year US, $20/year foreign (US funds).

Plymouth Owners Club Inc
(formerly Plymouth 4 & 6-Cylinder Owners Club)
PO Box 416
Cavalier, ND 58220
701-549-3746; FAX: 701-549-3744

For membership information, contact at the above address: Jim Benjaminson. Founded 1957. 3,500 members. Open to 1928-1972 Plymouth passenger and Plymouth and Fargo commercial vehicles. Recognized by Chrysler Corporation. Publishes bimonthly magazine, sample issue $2. Dues: $18/year US, (Canada and foreign must remit US funds).

Prowler Club of America
PO Box 751944
Dayton, OH 45475-1944
E-mail: orion@wspin.com

Founded 1996. 3,000 target members. Quarterly newsletters with news group privileges for those using internet. Annual meets across the USA. Publication: *Prowler Club of America*. Comprehensive newsletter regarding America's first factory turnkey hot rod. Dues: $30/year US.

Bandit Trans Am Club
PO Box 322
Cleveland, WI 53015
414-693-8355

Founded 1992. 150 members and growing. For owners and/or enthusiasts of 1976-1981 Special Edition Trans Ams (Y-81, Y-82, Y-84, Y-88 gold). Membership includes: quarterly newsletter with advertising section, club dash plaque, club decal, member shows, tech/restoration assistance, photo contests. Dues: $15/year US; $17/year Canada, $20/year international. Send business sized SASE for more information.

GTO Association of America
5829 Stroebel Rd
Saginaw, MI 48609

Founded 1979. 2,700+ members. Open to all GTO enthusiasts. Award-winning monthly magazine, National and Regional meets, local chapters. Other member benefits also. Dues: $30 US/year.

chapters:

Arizona *Cactus GTOs Inc,* Matt Luster, President, 4445 W Tierra Buena Ln, Glendale, AZ 85306, 602-883-1143

California *Inland Empire GTO Club,* Richard (Rick) Croft, President, 6936 Via Vista Dr, Riverside, CA 92506, 619-244-6647

Northern Sierra-Cascade Mountain Goats, Gary Travis, President, 878 Deercreek Ln, Paradise, CA 95969, 916-872-3923

Southern California Gathering of the Goats, Timothy Dean, President, 1307 S Ardilla Ave, West Covina, CA 91790, 714-840-1526

Tri-Valley GTOs, John Goss, President, 4455 Sherman Oaks Cir, Sherman Oaks, CA 91311, 818-784-1770

Colorado *Classic GTO Association of Denver,* Norm Warling, President, PO Box 5092, Arvada, CO 80006, 303-988-5483

Northern Colorado GTO Association, Hugh Robinson, President, 356 Glenda Dr, Loveland, CO 80537, 970-663-4532

Florida *Classic Pontiacs of Central Florida,* Bill Cocozza, President, 1434 Country Ridge Dr, Lakeland, FL 33801, 941-667-0293

Sunshine State GTO Association, Rick Hanley, President, 4376 N Mary Circle, Lake Park, FL 33410, 407-622-0228

Georgia *Southeastern GTO Association,* Bob Mohalley, President, 1150 Trailmoore Dr, Roswell, GA 30076, 770-396-5957

Idaho *Idaho Pontiac High-Performance Association Inc,* Teresa Draper, President, PO Box 1175, Meridian, ID 83680-1175, 208-888-5724

Illinois *Cruisin' Tigers GTO Club,* Randy Ray, President, PO Box 7191, Buffalo Grove, IL 60089, 708-249-1190

Indiana *Indy GTO Association,* Tom Hart, President, PO Box 53750, Indianapolis, IN 46253-0750, 317-834-1111

Northeast Indiana GTOs, Steve Hughes, President, 2105 S Main St, Goshen, IN 46526, 219-533-8945

Iowa *Pontiac Club of Iowa,* Ron Randazzo, President, PO Box 31065, Des Moines, IA 50310, 515-278-6764

Kansas *Gr-Rrr8'r Wichita GTO Club,* Mike Cooper, President, Rt 4, Box 66, El Dorado, KS 67042, 316-322-8818

Kentucky *Louisville GTO Club,* Larry Lloyd, President, PO Box 99185, Louisville, KY 40269-0185, 502-995-8802

Maine *GTO Association of Maine,* Susan Worcester, President, PO Box 717, Brownville, ME 04414, 207-965-8070

Maryland *The Royal GTOs,* John Anderson, President, 8005 Holly Ln, Clinton, MD 20735, 301-464-4322

Michigan *West Michigan Classic Pontiacs,* Kip Doyle, President, 4155 Council Crest, Battlecreek, MI 49017, 616-962-6457

Woodward GTO Tigers, Bill Schultz, President, 4677 Lockwood Dr, Washington, MI 48094-2629, 810-293-6571

Minnesota *Land of Lakes GTOs,* Dick Randall, President, PO Box 9844, St Paul, MN 55109-9844, 612-432-1741

Mississippi *Magnolia GTO Club,* Stephen Cheek, President, 513 S Natchez St, Kosciusko, MS 39090, 601-289-1198

Missouri *Gateway GTO Association,* Vic Nettle, President, 4450 Nazareth Hills, St Louis, MO 63129-1721, 314-892-3639

Montana *Big Sky GTOs,* Mark De Long, President, 4416 Harvest Ln, Billings, MT 59106, 406-656-6254

Rocky Mountain Goats, Harry Gedney, President, 5750 Meadow Vista Dr, Florence, MT 59833, 406-273-6071

New Jersey *Delaware Valley Old Goat Club,* Jim Lupo, President, PO Box 295, Hainesport, NJ 08036, 609-231-0803

Garden State GTOs, Robert J Moore Jr, President, 80 Burnt Meadow Rd, Ringwood, NJ 07456, 201-839-5150

GTO Association of New Jersey, Matty Murino, President, 52 Gettysburg Dr, Englishtown, NJ 07726, 908-536-6640

New York *Electric City GTOs Inc,* Michael Landau, President, 12 Talbot Ct, Rexford, NY 12148, 518-383-0755

GTO Association of Greater New York, David Barsky, President, 2682 Ford St, Brooklyn, NY 11235, 718-332-4479

The Hudson Valley GTO Club, Mark J Rooney, President, 43 Boniello Dr, Mahopac, NY 10541, 914-628-4903

Western New York GTO Club, Bill Brown, President, 188 Bigelow, Depew, NY 14043, 716-683-8539

North Carolina *Carolina Classic Pontiac Club,* Ms Millicent Oliver, President, 5361 Bedfordshire Ave, Harrisburg, NC 28075, 704-455-1613

Tarheel Tigers GTO Club, Gary Anderson, President, 1126 Shadyside Dr, Raleigh, NC 27612, 919-848-1928

Ohio *Buckeye GTOs,* Rick Elias, President, 4283 Abbeyville Rd, Medina, OH 44256, 216-723-1521

GTO Association of Central Ohio, Jim Evans, President, 13791 Cable Rd, Pataskala, OH 43062, 614-927-5302

Ohio Valley GTO Association, Bud Krebs, President, 10241 Snowflake Ln, Cincinnati, OH 45251, 606-635-5558

Oklahoma *Southern Plains GTO Club,* George Reaves, President, 2911 NW 122nd, #308, Oklahoma City, OK 73120, 405-721-1105

Oregon *The Goat Herd GTO Club of Oregon,* Larry Markham, President, PO Box 1071, Clackamas, OR 97015

Pennsylvania *GTO Association of Pennsylvania,* Jim Darlington, President, 1065 Buskill Dr, Easton, PA 18042, 610-258-0768

Susquehanna Valley GTO Tigers, F Fawber, President, 6 Andes Dr, Mechanicsburg, PA 17055, 717-432-3996

Texas *GTO Association of North Texas,* Larry Harbin, President, 537 Leavalley, Coppell, TX 75019, 214-462-0154

Clubs & Organizations

Gulf Coast GTOs, Mike Rynearson, President, 9746 Rocky Hollow, Laporte, TX 77571, 713-470-9394

Lone Star GTO Club, Robert Davis, President, 1501 Garnaas, Austin, TX 75758, 512-339-9312

West Texas GTO Association, Dwight Filley, President, 212 Sunset Rd, El Paso, TX 79922, 915-584-9215

Virginia *Greater Tidewater Owner's Society*, Lyndon Hamm, President, 3632 Starlighter Dr, Virginia Beach, VA 23452, 804-486-5979

Washington *Northwest GTO Legends*, Kevin Reed, President, 8101 NE 120th St, Kirkland, WA 98034, 206-821-9685

Radioactive Redskins Pontiac Club, Steven Carlson, President, PO Box 6234, Kennewick, WA 99336, 509-582-6475

West Virginia *Wild Wonderful West Virginia GTOs*, Harold Morris, President, Rt 3, Box 34A, Morgantown, WV 26505, 304-292-5056

Wisconsin *God's Country GTO Association*, Rich Rossin, President, PO Box 572, Baraboo, WI 53913, 608-847-4523

Indianhead GTO Club, Mike Champion, President, 325 W Elm Ave, Menomonie, WI 54751, 715-235-7320

Original GTO Club, Larry Lorenz, President, PO Box 18438, Milwaukee, WI 53218, 414-466-2300

Canada *Classic GTO Club of Ontario*, Peter Mazzocato, President, 1022 Weir Rd S, Lynden, ON Canada L0R 1T0, 519-647-2090

GTO Association of Alberta, Mike Walter, President, 6624 Dalcroft Hill NW, Calgary AB Canada T3A 1N4, 403-288-5762

The Judge GTO International Club
114 Prince George Dr
Hampton, VA 23669
757-838-2059

Founded 1982. 329 members. Open to owners and enthusiasts of 1969-71 Pontiac GTO Judge. Quarterly publication: *The Judge's Chambers*. Dues $20/year. Yearly convention at Virginia Beach, VA.

Land of Lakes GTO Club
PO Box 9844
St Paul, MN 55109-9844
E-mail: rrrandall@aol.com

Founded 1984. 200 members. Interest in promotion and preservation of Pontiac GTOs. We welcome all GTO enthusiasts with stock or modified vehicles. Ownership of a GTO, however, is not a membership requirement. The club sponsors cruises, technical sessions, swap meets, a charity fund-raiser for the Ronald McDonald House, the annual Muscle Car Classic™ Show, Muscle Car Shoot-Out and World of Wheels. In addition, the chapter acts as a source of information and assistance to the local GTO owner and restorer. Dues: $24/year, family.

National Firebird Club
PO Box 11238
Chicago, IL 60611-0238
773-769-6262; FAX: 773-769-3240
E-mail: firebirdclub@prodigy.com

For information, contact at the above address: Thomas Scherer, Chairman. Open to all Firebird owners. North America's official registry. Technical advice. Parts discounts and magazines. Publication: *Eagle*. Dues: $25/year.

Pontiac-Oakland Club International Inc
PO Box 9569
Bradenton, FL 34206
941-750-9234; FAX: 941-747-1341

Founded 1972. 10,000 members. Award winning 68 page monthly *Smoke Signals* magazine, yearly convention, yearly roster of members & their cars, technical advisors, club library. Dues: $25/year.

Woodward GTO Tigers
4677 Lockwood Dr
Washington, MI 48094
810-781-3130

Founded 1988. A club for GTO and Pontiac enthusiasts. Official chapter of the GTO Association of America. Sponsors annual "GTO Classic Weekend" (all GTO show/swap meet). Club activities include monthly meetings and/or special events. Publishes monthly newsletter, *Redlines*, which includes coverage of past club activities, announcements of upcoming events, feature articles, list of club discounts and swap 'n sell section. Dues: $18/year for members, $6/year for associates.

Porsche 356 Florida Owners Group
4570 47th St
Sarasota, FL 34235
813-228-2901, ext 145

Founded 1993. 100 members. Car ownership not required. Quarterly newsletter. 4-5 driving events per year. Monthly local breakfasts. Host of 356 Registry East Coast Holiday 1996. Dues: $10/year.

Porsche 914 Owners Association and 914-6 Club USA
100 S Sunrise Way
Suite 116H
Palm Springs, CA 92262
FAX: 619-325-6583
E-mail: 5010.4218@trader.com

Founded 1978. 2,000 members. An international organization with members in 20 countries. Members receive informative quarterly magazine *Mid-Engined Views* plus technical updates in the newsletter *Mid-Engined Digest*. Contains articles about 914 maintenance, restoration and history. Dues: $25/year US, $32/year overseas. Now combined with the 914-6 Club USA. Annual reunion June.

Reo Club of America
115 Cherry Rd
Chesnee, SC 29323
864-461-2894

Founded 1973. 650 members. Reo owners and enthusiasts. Dues: $18/year. Send SASE when writing to club. Worldwide group dedicated to the preservation of the works of Ransom E. Olds.

The Rolls-Royce Owners Club
191 Hempt Rd
Mechanicsburg, PA 17055
717-697-4671

Founded in 1951. 6,700 members. Dedicated to the preservation, restoration and enjoyment of of Rolls-Royce and Bentley motorcars. Dues: $45/year.

Silver Ghost Association
PO Box 737
Salina, KS 67402
913-827-9331; FAX: 913-827-9337

Founded 1986. 350 members. Newsletter, *The Tourer*, published quarterly, technical assistance by telephone or fax included with membership. Tech bible with 1,200+ pages of articles published about Silver Ghosts, club store, annual Wholly Ghost tour for Silver Ghosts only. Do not need to own a Silver Ghost to join. Dues: $35/year.

Rover Owners Club of North America
PO Box 41808
Tucson, AZ 85717

Founded 1990. 156 members. No restrictions. Unites members with newsletter. Events organized regionally. Benefits include parts and books specials, classified ad network, news and member network.

New England Sonett Club
PO Box 4362
Manchester, NH 03108
603-679-1222

Founded 1980. 300 members from all over US. Objectives include maintenance and preservation of Sonetts. Historical data, tech tips, parts info & newsletter. Dues $20/yr new, $18/yr renewal.

Saab Club of North America
7675 Bear Trap Jct
Saginaw, MN 55779
218-729-0826; FAX: 218-729-0827
E-mail:
71151.1354@compuserve.com

Founded 1973. 4,000+ members. Bi-monthly magazine features technical DIY, sources, news from Saab, history, classifieds. Dues: $34/1st year, $30/renewal.

The Sabra Connection
7040 N Navajo Ave
Milwaukee, WI 53217
414-352-8408

An organization to share interest and information about the Sabra Sport automobile produced by Autocars of Haifa, Israel and Reliant of England between 1961 and 1963. Publication: The Sabra Connection.

Saturn Owners' Car Club
14620 West 93rd St
Lenexa, KS 66215
913-541-0532

Saturn owners, all models, are invited to join us for our monthly newsletter, meetings and events for fun, social, technical. Dues: $20/12 months.

SIMCA Car Club
644 Lincoln St
Amherst, OH 44001
216-988-9104 evenings (no return calls)

Founded 1985. Dedicated to the restoration and preservation of SIMCA, Chrysler-SIMCA, and special-bodied SIMCA exotics from 1936-82. Parts inventory, information sources and European connections. Monthly newsletter: Vitesse. Dues: $20/year. Approx 100 members in 15 countries.

Squire SS-100 Registry
c/o Arthur Stahl
11826 S 51st St
Phoenix, AZ 85044-2313
602-893-9451

Founded 1989. 42 members at present. Membership is restricted to ownership or intended ownership of the Squire SS-100 manufactured in Torino, Italy, by Intermeccanica in 1971-75. Intended to find and list the owners of the fifty-odd Squire SS-100s that were produced in Italy in 1971-75 by Intermeccanica. The club is National with a possiblity of Regional or National meetings.

Intent is to aid one another in the restoration and maintenance of these vehicles. Monthly newsletter is produced and we are providing technical drawings, wiring plans, etc. Dues: $25/year, first time; $15/year thereafter.

Stevens-Duryea Associates
3565 Newhaven Rd
Pasadena, CA 91107
818-351-8237

For membership information, contact at the above address: Warwick Eastwood. Founded 1960. 100 members. Open only to owners of Stevens-Duryea automobiles. Dues: none.

50s & 60s Cruisin' Car Club
PO Box 22001
St Petersburg, FL 33742-2001

'50s & '60s

Founded 1994. 140 members. Dedicated to the preservation of 50s and 60s cars, trucks, motorcycles and all types of collectibles from the 1950s and 1960s. Including rock n' roll 45 rpm records, lps, toys, celebrity autographs, photos, posters, clothing, jewelry, furniture, appliances, etc. Special feature: the club meets every Saturday from 3 to 10 pm via our 50s and 60s Cruisin' rock n' roll radio program broadcast to 1.9 million Cruiser's in the Tampa Bay, Florida area on radio station AM 1470. Club members (cruisers) share information about 50s and 60s events and enjoy good comaraderie with phone calls to the show while enjoying their favorite 50s and 60s music. Club members buy, sell, trade cars, trucks, motorcycles, parts, services and all types of 50s and 60s collectibles during special feature segments. Dues: none. For club membership application, send a self addressed stamped envelope to the club address. Advertisers wishing to participate are invited to feature their nifty 50s & 60s goods on our Cruisin' radio show. Write for details.

The Antique Studebaker Club Inc
PO Box 28845
Dallas, TX 75228-0845
800-527-3452

Founded 1971. 1,300 members. Publishes The Antique Studebaker Review every other month. Has yearly national meet & zone meets. Dues: $23/year.

Orange Empire Chapter, SDC
7812 Vicksburg Ave
Westchester, CA 90045
310-645-3438

Founded 1969. 147 members. A chapter of the Studebaker Drivers Club. Monthly meetings and newsletter, Wheels & Deals. Purpose is sharing information on parts, tips, activities and cars. Must be a member of the Studebaker Drivers Club to join chapter. Annual LaPalma show. Dues: $15/year.

Studebaker Drivers Club
c/o CIS
PO Box 28788
Dallas, TX 75228

For membership information, contact: Membership Secretary, Studebaker Drivers Club Inc, PO Box 28788, Dallas, TX 75228, PH: 800/527-3452. Founded 1962. 13,000 members. Should have an interest in Studebakers. Monthly publication: Turning Wheels. Write for free sample of Turning Wheels to: Linda Fox, Editor, 13150 El Capitan Way, Delhi, CA 95315. Dues: $27.50/year US and Canada, $44/year foreign.

Wisconsin Region Studebaker Drivers Club
6347 Watercress Rd
Allenton, WI 53002-9782
414-629-9986; FAX: 414-629-9969
E-mail: studeacres@aol.com

Founded 1968. 240 members. A non-profit, educational organization dedicated to the preservation and operation of Studebaker vehicles, the exchange of technical information and the publication of historical research and articles pertaining to Studebaker and affiliated companies. *The Studebaker Spokesman*, published bi-monthly. Sponsor several shows and meets annually. Must be a member of Studebaker Drivers Club. Dues: $10/year.

The Stutz Club Inc
7400 Lantern Rd
Indianapolis, IN 46256
317-849-3443

Founded 1988. 300 members. Membership open to all who have an interest in Stutz vehicles (Stutz and Blackhawk autos and fire engines, HCS autos and taxicabs, Stutz Pak-Age-Car and aircraft engine) or in history of the companies producing these marques and the man responsible, Harry Clayton Stutz. Quarterly publication, *Stutz News*. Annual meeting held with Grand Stutz car meet. Provides technical information, full current directory of members and vehicles. Dues: $25/year US; $30/year outside US. Directory $5 extra.

Subaru 360 Drivers' Club
1421 N Grady Ave
Tucson, AZ 85715

Founded 1980. 350 members. Members help each other keep their Subaru 360s on the road and running on both cylinders. Quarterly newsletter. Dues: $6/year.

California Association of Tiger Owners
18771 Paseo Picasso
Irvine, CA 92612
714-854-2561; FAX: 818-541-1784

Founded 1968. 1,000 members. Alpines welcome. Worldwide membership devoted to advancing the Sunbeam marque. Extensive parts supply. Dues: $25/year US, $27/year Canada, $35/year foreign.

Midwest Sunbeam Club
Doug Ferrell
3701 NW Eric Drive
Topeka, KS 66618-3631
913-286-2987; E-mail:
rootesclub@cjnetworks.com

Founded 1986. Can also contact: Charles Marin, 1061 Harcourt Drive, Emporia, KS 66801, PH: 316-342-8814. Caters to all Rootes Group cars. Bi-monthly newsletter. Annual meet. Dues: $18/year US & Canada; $25/year overseas.

Sunbeam Owners Group of San Diego
2250 Rosecrans
San Diego, CA 92106
619-223-0496

Founded 1986. 60 members. Active enthusiasts of Sunbeams and other Rootes Group cars. Monthly activities, monthly newsletter. Dues: $20/year.

Tatra Enthusiasts
14200 New Hampshire Ave
Silver Spring, MD 20904
301-384-5856; FAX: 301-989-1866

Tatra, the only cars to have a rear-engined air-cooled ohc V8. The club specializes in information, parts, service & anything

pertaining to Tatra cars & trucks 1922 to present. Also includes earlier Nesselorfer vehicles.

Detroit Triumph Sportscar Club
13201 Common Rd
Warren, MI 48093
810-574-9394

For information, contact at the above address: Herb Hummer, 810-574-9394. Founded 1959. 250 members. Parts discounts, rallies, concours, tech info. Largest chapter of the Vintage Triumph Register and largest Triumph club in the US, Monthly publication: *Triumph Review*. Dues: $20/year.

Portland Triumph Owners Association
PO Box 5516
Portland, OR 97228-5516
503-642-1681; 503-762-1281

Founded 1972. 200 members. Dedicated to the Triumph auto marque through membership of Triumph owners and friends of Triumph. Social and auto related activities include a monthly business meeting and regular tours. Triumph and British car meets in the summer. Members are kept informed by the monthly *Triumph Trax* newsletter. Dues: $20/year.

Southern California Triumph Owner's Association
PO Box 83820
Los Angeles, CA 90083
310-322-2546

Founded 1983. 225 members. There are no restrictions to join SCTOA. We offer a club dedicated to fun and the preservation of Triumph automobiles. We are very proud of our monthly newsletter with tech tips and ways to keep our cars on the road. There are monthly meetings where you can network with other enthusiasts and we sponsor at least one event each month such as rallys, shows, racing and tours. Dues: $30/year.

TR8 Car Club of America
266 Linden St
Rochester, NY 14620
716-244-9693

Founded 1983. 350 members. Quarterly newsletter with technical data, news items, etc. Regalia & back issues of newsletters available. Dues: $15/year.

Triumph Club of The Carolinas
7300 Danay Dr
Kernersville, NC 27284
910-996-3825

Founded 1984. 200 members. The Triumph Club of the Carolinas (TCOC) encourages owners of all British car marques to join. Benefits include a monthly newsletter, monthly meetings, TSD and gimmick rallies, autocrosses, car shows, tours, technical sessions and many other opportunities to meet and socialize with other British car owners. The TCOC hosts annually each October the South Central British Car Gathering and was the 1994 host for the Vintage Triumph Register National Convention in Asheville, NC. Dues: $25/year.

Triumph International Owners Club
PO Box 6676
Holliston, MA 01746-6676
508-429-4221; FAX: 508-429-6213

Founded 1978. 2,600 members. Quarterly newsletter, patch and decal with membership. Annual rally. Founded to encourage riding, restoration and racing of Triumph motorcycles. Members worldwide. Dues: US first class mail, $18.50; US third class bulk mail, $15.50; Canada first class mail, $22 US funds; overseas airmail, $27 US funds. For memberships outside US please use postal money orders, International Reply Coupons, MasterCard or VISA.

Triumph Register of America
1641 N Memorial Dr
Suite TR3
Lancaster, OH 43130

For membership information, contact at the above address: Ron Hartley. Founded 1974. 900 members. Should be a Triumph series TR2/3/3A owner or enthusiast. Dues: $15/year.

Triumph Sports Car Club of San Diego
PO Box 84342
San Diego, CA 92138
619-484-1634

Founded 1963. 90 members, 1994 year. Owning a Triumph not necessary to join. Non-profit organization to promote the enthusiasm of the Triumph marque by rallies, slaloms, trips, concours, restorations, technical, and, of course, social events. Monthly newsletter and tech sessions. Provides information to keep members' cars running. Dues: $22/year.

Vintage Triumph Register
PO Box 36477
Grosse Pointe, MI 48236
404-475-1088

Founded 1974. 4,500 members. Dedicated to the history, preservation and enjoyment of all Triumph automobiles. Hosts annual National convention. Additional services include discount book program, technical consultants, chapter insurance and trophy programs. Publishes bimonthly newsletter and quarterly magazine. Dues: $25/year USA, $30/year Canada.

Tucker Automobile Club of America
9509 Hinton Dr
Santee, CA 92071-2760
619-390-4546; FAX: 619-573-0196
E-mail: tuckerauto@aol.com

Founded 1973. 400 members. Monthly newsletter, *Tucker Topics*. Yearly convention (1996: Nashville, TN; 1997: Ypsilanti, MI; 1998: Las Vegas, NV). The purpose of our club is to keep the legend alive. Dues: $25/year US, $40/year overseas.

TVR Car Club North America
4450 S Park Ave, Apt 1609
Chevy Chase, MD 20815
301-986-8679; FAX: 301-986-9611

Founded 1971. 1,000 members. Open to all owners & enthusiasts of TVR & Griffith hand-built sports cars. For membership information, contact at the above address: Marq J Ruben. Publication: *TVR Times*. Dues $30/year.

Vanden Plas Princess Register
14200 New Hampshire Ave
Silver Spring, MD 20904
301-384-5856; FAX: 301-989-1866

Club for Princess limousines, sedans, hearses & ambulances from 1947 to 1968. Clearinghouse for information, parts, workshop & owner's manuals, repair help, Whitworth tools. Please provide chassis number in any correspondence. Large supply of original & reproduction parts including rubber seals, brake, suspension & body parts. 12 Princess parts cars on hand.

Vespa 400 Registry
100 Prince St
Fairfield, CT 06432
203-336-1505

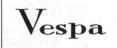

Founded 1996. 100 members. No dues, only interest in the Vespa 400 necessary. We keep a registry of cars and extra parts listings.

Victoria Registry
100 Prince St
Fairfield, CT 06432
203-336-1505

Founded 1996. 13 members. No dues, only interest in the Victoria necessary. We keep a list of owners and spare parts.

German Air Sucker Society/GASS
927 Liberty St
Salem, OH 44460
PH/FAX: 330-332-1303, 24 hrs

Founded in 1993. Over 2,500 members. Award winning *Voice of the Enthusiast* bi-monthly member/Volkswagen orientated magazine, with upcoming events, air-cooled user tech, restorations, toys and tin, insight and product articles, with free classifieds to members. Dues $25 per year. Largest non-political society of its kind in the nation.

Hudson & Mohawk Society of Volkswagen Owners
PO Box 517
Crompond, NY 10517
914-528-5376; 518-465-0477

Founded 1994. 50 members. Membership is open to any owner, former owner, admirer of Volkswagens. The club consists of members from the Hudson and Mohawk Valley regions of New York State (eastern New York), but also includes western MA, VT and CT. Membership is open to anyone. A yearly show is held within the region along w/smaller gatherings and cruises throughout the year. A quarterly newsletter is also published. Dues: $15/year.

Luchtegekoelde VW Club Nederland
Borgercompagniesterwg 64
9632 TD Borgercompagnie
Netherlands
05980-93162

For membership information, contact at the above address: H.B. Blokker. Open to air-cooled VWs. Monthly club paper: De Luchtboxer (The Air Boxer) , in Dutch. Dues: 55 Dutch guilders/year; entree fee, 25 guilders.

NEATO/Vintage VW Bus Club
PO Box 4190
Albuquerque, NM 87196
505-268-2220; E-mail:
neato@rt66.com

Founded 1986. 1,200 members. For all owners and admirers of pre-1968 VW Type 2s/Transporters, buses, Kombis, campers, etc. Newsletter, chapters & meets all across North America. Publishes member directory and old bus registry, as well. Dues: $20/year.

Society of Transporter Owners
PO Box 3555
Walnut Creek, CA 94598-0555
510-937-SOTO (7686); FAX: 510-932-2051

Founded 1983. Approximately 2,000 members. Free classified advertising in monthly newsletter, discounts at many restoration parts suppliers, quarterly meets. Open to all Volkswagen enthusiasts, newsletter/meets for 1950-1967 VW buses/trucks only. Dues: $17/year.

Volvo Club of America
PO Box 16
Afton, NY 13730
607-639-2279; FAX: 607-639-2279

For information, write, phone or FAX to the above address. National club of owners and enthusiasts of all Volvo automobiles. Magazine, parts discounts, technical information, local and national meets.

Volvo Owners' Club
34 Lyonsgate Dr
Downsview,
ONT Canada M3H 1C8
416-633-6801

Founded 1976. 250 members from US, Canada, Europe, Brazil and Australia. Covers all Volvo models, old and new.

Volvo Sports America 1800
1203 W Cheltenham Ave
Melrose Park, PA 19027
215-635-0117; FAX: 215-635-4070;
212-863-0964, NY
E-mail: bobfv1800@aol.com

Founded 1976. 2,500 members. International club devoted to the milestone/classic 1800 and other vintage Volvos. Technical service. Bimonthly magazine, parts/service discounts, national meets, concours, touring schools, rallies. Local chapters. Dues: $25/year US, $27/year Canada and $37/year foreign.

Washington Volvo Club Inc
5300 Yorktown Rd
Bethesda, MD 20816
E-mail: volvodc@aol.com

For information, contact at the above address: John E Switzer, AIA, 301/656-8053. Founded 1975. Over 400 members from California to Maine, Sweden to Puerto Rico. Open to all Volvo enthusiasts. Factory recognized. Annual meets. Monthly newsletter: Volvamus. Dues: $25/year.

Vintage White Truck Association
719 Ohms Way
Costa Mesa, CA 92627
714-645-5938 eves

Founded 1984. 150 members. Formed to supply information, guidance and assistance for those restoring vintage White commercial vehicles. Archives contain original drawings and service manuals. Semi-annual publication: *Super Power*. Contains history, photos, restoration aids. Dues: $15/year.

The Wills Club
721 Jenkinson St
Port Huron, MI 48060

For membership information, contact at the above address: Bill McKeand, 313/987-2425. Founded 1959. 100 members. Open to owners and enthusiasts of 1921-26 Wills Sainte Claire autos. Quarterly publication: Gray Goose News. Dues: $15/year.

The Willys Club
795 N Evans St
Pottstown, PA 19464
610-326-2907

For information, contact at the above address: Gordon Lindahl, manager/editor. Founded 1973. Over 1,200 members. Dedicated to the preservation and restoration of all Willys vehicles from 1933-1963. Bi-monthly publication: *Willys World*. Dues: $15 for USA and $20 for Canada and foreign (US funds).

Willys-Overland Jeepster Club News
167 Worcester St
Taunton, M A 02780-2088
PH/FAX: 508-880-6051

Founded 1964. 600 members. Willys-Overland Jeepsters 1948-1951, members around USA, Canada, Scandinavia & Europe. Annual Founders Meet, meets around USA, monthly newsletter with free classified advertisments for members. Membership available to all who own, operate, restore, collect or otherwise have interest in this vehicle. Dues: $18 US; outside USA pays extra postage.

Registries

Arnolt-Bristol Registry
PO Box 60
Brooklandville, MD 21022
410-484-1834

Founded 1964. 130 members. Recognizes the Arnolt-Bristol marque. Affiliated with the Bristol Owners Club, U.K. Ownership of marque is not required for members. Purpose of organization is to assist owners in preserving and restoring their vehicles, historic auto racing, exchange of information, memorabilia, etc. Newsletter and dues, $10/year US; $15/year Europe/Australia. For membership information, contact Lee Raskin at above address.

Classic AMX Registry
21 Creek Rd
Dauphin, PA 17018
717-921-3363

Founded 1992. 300 members. All 1968-70 AMX owners are requested to join us no matter the condition of their AMX. Historical and statistical publication planned for future. Dues: none.

Austin Series A Register (ASAR)
PO Box 9280
Marina Del Ray, CA 90295
310-827-2727; FAX: 310-306-2626
E-mail: dolphnx@aol.com

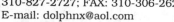

Founded 1985. 200 members, open to all British Austin owners and admirers. Quarterly newsletter: *Austin Forum*. Dues: $10/year. Founder and director: Randolph Williams.

North American Mini Moke Registry
1779 Kickapoo St
PO Box 9110
South Lake Tahoe, CA 96150
916-577-7895

Founded 1982. 70 members. Need not own a Moke to join. No meetings, newsletter provides contact between owners. In contact with Mini Moke Club of England, Moke Club of Australia and exchange letters with Mini Clubs worldwide. Dues: $15/year.

Brabham Register
1611 Alvina Ave
Sacramento, CA 95822
916-454-1115

Founded 1979. Formed to provide information to Brabham owners for use in the authentic restoration of the cars. Must own Brabham race car to join. Initiation fee: $30.

Bristol Register of New Zealand
61 Rothesay Bay Road, Rothesay Bay
Auckland, 10 New Zealand
PH/FAX: 64-9-478-7426

We maintain a register of all Bristol and Bristol engined cars in New Zealand. Limited spares for Bristol 400-406 cars and 85-100-110-BS engines.

American Bugatti Club/Register
Box 4484, Howe Hill Rd
Camden, ME 04843

For membership, register or other general information, contact: club secretary, Andy Rheault, 4484 Howe Hill Rd, Camden, ME 04843. Founded 1960, 350 members worldwide. Club promotes interest in, preservation and use of Bugattis as well as serving as an information network for those interested in the marque. The Register keeps track of Bugattis in North America. Quarterly publication: *Pur Sang*. Members' dues: $50/year.

1932 Buick Registry
3000 Warren Rd
Indiana, PA 15701
412-463-3372

Founded 1974. 325 members. Open Saturday, Sunday, 8 to 5. Open only to 1932 Buicks. Manufacture & sell reproduction parts for Buick 1925-1935. Disseminate information on 1932 model Buicks, including sales of literature. Free 1932 Buick Registry newsletter. Printed parts list available for 1925-1935 Buicks, send SASE. Dues: none.

Clenet Registry
11311 Woodland Dr
Lutherville, MD 21093
410-825-2010

A registry of this limited production luxury car listing present owners, previous owners (many custom built for celebrities), year built, color combinations, production number, maintenance tips, parts sources, etc. Information generated through personal correspondence between owners. There is no membership fee.

Datsun Fairlady Registry
c/o Les Cannaday
402 Olive Ave #A
Vista, CA 92083-3438
619-940-6365

Founded 1987. 310 members to date. Tracking all 3,148 SPL310 models sent to the US by Nissan Motor Company. Also seeking true rhd Fairladies (SR) and Fairlady "Z" in the North American Continent. This is a personal effort funded only by those who share the cost of communication. Specializing in Datsun models 1960-1970. Ownership not essential. Enthusiasm and sharing costs of communication a must. Dues: none.

The Delage Section of VSCC
c/o Peter J S Jacobs (secretary)
Cloud's Reach, The Scop
Almondsbury, Bristol, BS12 4DU
England
PH/FAX: 0154-612434

Founded 1968. 150 members and growing. Catering to owners of all models of Delage 1905 to 1954. Provides quarterly newslet-

ters, annual journal, register of surviving cars worldwide, technical advice, motoring events & free advertising for Delage sales & wants. Dues: £10 Sterling/year.

DeVaux Registry
240 Greenridge
Grand Rapids, MI 49504
616-784-6640; FAX: 616-784-0989

Registry of existing 1931-32 DeVaux automobiles.

1970 Dart Swinger 340's Registry
PO Box 9
Wethersfield, CT 06129-0009
860-257-8434 evenings

Founded 1986. 500+ members. Must own a 1970 Dodge Dart Swinger 340. Verifies and locates all 13,785 1970 Dodge Dart Swinger 340's. Free information to help restore and preserve these cars. Newsletter subscription, $10/yr for 4 quarterly issues. Dues: none.

International Viper Registry
PO Box 914
Arkadelphia, AR 71923-0914
501-246-0015; FAX: 501-246-0762
E-mail: viperjay@iocc.com

Founded 1992. 250 members. Bi-annual newsletter, registration certificate. Dues: $25/year. www.iocc.com/~viperjay

North American English Ford Registry
12 Biltmore Ave
Providence, RI 02908-3513
401-521-ENFO (3636)

Organized to unite enthusiasts of all British marques, Anglia to Zodiac, and everything in between. Central contact for parts and technical data. Source of help and encouragement. For information, contact at the above address: David Wiggins. SASE please.

Erskine Register
441 E St Clair
Almont, MI 48003

ERSKINE

For membership information, contact at the above address: Norman Hamilton. For information please send SASE.

Topolino Register of North America
3301 Shetland Rd
Beavercreek, OH 45434
513-426-0098

For information, contact at the above address: Mike Self. Founded 1969. 72 members. This is a register of Fiat 500 A/B/C, Simca 5, NSU-Fiat 500 owners and owners of Topolino-based vehicles, 1936-1955. Serves as a restoration, information and parts source exchange for owners. Register published periodically. Dues: none.

AUTO GLASS

68 Ford Torino Indy Pace Car Registry
8032 E Haynes
Tucson, AZ 85710
520-886-8004; FAX: 520-296-9525

Founded 1990. 8-12 members. Registry for 1968 Ford Torino Indy pace cars. Newsletter sometimes. Dues: none.

Fairlane Cobra Registry
1436 Exchange St
Alden, NY 14004
716-937-9257

Founded 1994. New club forming. Must own 1969 Fairlane Cobra. Bi-annual newsletter & annual copy of registry. Dues: donations.

International 7-Litre Registry
17 Verdun Dr
Akron, OH 44312
216-794-9015

Registry for the 1966 Ford Galaxie 500 7-litre hardtops and convertibles, a one-year only model. There are currently more than 160 cars on the registry.

Model T Ford Register of Great Britain
c/o Mrs J Armer
3 Riverside, Strong Close, Keighely
West Yorkshire, BD21 4JP England
01535-607978

For membership information, contact at the above address. Founded 1959. Over 400 members. Dues: £15/year; overseas members £22/year; family membership £20/year. Enrollment fee: £10.

SHO Registry
PO Box 159
Carrollton, GA 30117
770-836-1474; FAX: 770-214-8864

Founded 1990. 4,000+ members. Formed to enhance the ownership of the Taurus SHO. Perhaps the finest high-performance sedan of this generation. Only enthusiasm is required. Publishes a quarterly magazine and holds annual national convention. Annual dues: $35.

1971-73 Mustang High Performance Coupe Registry
114 Dry Ave
Cary, NC 27511
E-mail: edandsusan@aol.com

For information, send SASE to the above address, Ed Tilley. Anyone owning a 1971-73 Mustang hardtop with engine code M, R, C, J or Q is eligible for inclusion. These are the 429 CJ, 429 CJ-R, 351 CJ, 351 HO and Boss 351 engines. No cost to join.

1973 Q Code Mach I Registry
c/o Chris De Guerre
23 Eastman Crescent
Newmarket, ONT Canada L3Y 5T9
905-853-9608

Founded 1991. Over 500 members. The 1973 Q-Code Mach I Registry is dedicated to the 1973 Mach I Ford Mustangs originally equipped with the 351 4v engine (Q-code). The last of the high performance and lowest 2.9 percentage with optional 4-speed Hurst transmission in Mustang history. Complete production information on 1973 Ford Mustang Mach I, equipped with 351 4v engine.

66-67-68 High Country Special Registry
6874 Benton Ct
Arvada, CO 80003
303-424-3866

Founded 1980. over 200 members. An information source for prospective buyers and owners of 66, 67, 68 High Country Special Mustangs. Dues: none.

Boss 429 Owners Directory
S 4228 Conklin
Spokane, WA 99203
509-455-9369

Founded 1974. 800 members. Dedicated to the preservation of the history and collectibility of the 1969 and 1970 Ford Boss 429 Mustangs. Annual newsletter, registry progress reports. Boss 429 owners only. Publishing Boss 429 vehicle registry book. Dues: none.

Honda 600 Roster of Owners
c/o Bill Colford
7518 Westbrook Ave
San Diego, CA 92139
619-267-0485

No rules or regulations. A source of: reliable technical information, location of mechanics that "know" the Honda 600, restoration information and assistance, location of hard to find parts, information on the next gathering of the Honda 600 Group. No dues. No membership fee.

Jordan Register
58 Bradford Blvd
Yonkers, NY 10710-3699
914-337-5624

Founded 1980. 90 members. Offers parts and literature for sale. Quarterly parts flier. Welcomes all owners and enthusiasts of the Jordan marque to preserve and locate cars and literature. Semiannual Jordan gathering at Hershey and Carlisle meets by Jordan owners. Biannual car meet: next one to be held 1997 with Jordan cars on local daily tours. Publication: *Arrowhead Quarterly*. Dues $10/year.

North American Jowett Register
PO Box 4131
Burbank, CA 91503
818-842-5798

Founded 1976. 75 members. Dedicated to the location, preservation and restoration of Jowett cars through the exchange of historical and technical information. Quarterly newsletter and register of cars based on factory records. Open to Jowett owners and enthusiasts. Dues: $12/year.

Manx Dune Buggy Club
PO Box 1491
Valley Center, CA 92082
201-887-5808; FAX: 619-751-0610

See full listing in **Section Three** under **specialty clubs**

Mercer Associates
1380 Brinton Lake Rd
West Chester, PA 19382
215-399-3600

Founded 1949. A common denominator for all those who own or are interested in Mercer automobiles. Endeavors to instigate a Mercer reunion every few years. Dues: none.

70 Mercury Marauder X-100 Registry
18376 228th St
Tonganoxie, KS 66086
913-845-3458

Founded 1991. Dedicated to the preservation of 70 X-100s. Source of help and encouragement. Registry progress reports.

Big M Mercury Club
5 Robinson Rd
West Woburn, MA 01801
617-932-8495

Founded 1988. 124 members. Non-profit. Every member added to roster list gets date to write his story/interests in Mercury cars and send a copy to all other members on roster. SASE required. Dues: none.

California MG T Register
4911 Winnetka Ave
Woodland Hills, CA 91364

For membership information, contact at the above address: Dick Riddle, 818-883-9681. Founded 1969. 200 members. All MG owners and enthusiasts are welcome to join. Monthly newsletter, tour or event and monthly meetings in Studio City, CA. "Our purpose is to provide an association for owners of MG cars and to promote an interest in and perpetuation of these fine old cars." Dues: $20/year, $10 initiation fee. Includes jacket patch and dash plaque.

Morris Minor Registry Of North America
Tony Burgess
318 Hampton Park
Westerville, OH 43081-5723
614-899-2394

750 members nationwide and 34 regional representatives. The Morris Minor Registry is dedicated to the preservation, restoration and use of the postwar Morris Minor automobile. Bi-monthly newletter: *Minor News*, contains technical tips, feature stories on cars and related topics, meet reports, calendar of events, club and car regalia, classified ads and much more. Car registration is free. Full annual membership: $20 for the US and Canada ($30 overseas via airmail).

Morris Register
20 Chestnut Ave
Gosfield, Near Halstead
Essex, C09 1TD England
01787-473220

For membership information, contact: A Peeling, 171 Levita House, Chalton Street, London, NW1 1HR England. Founded 1959. 2,000 members. Open to all, but full membership is given only to owners of Morris vehicles designed before 1940. Dues: £14.50/first year plus £2 entry fee.

The Registry
RR 1 Box 369
Monrovia, IN 46157
317-996-2215

Founded 1984. 70 members. For 1928-29 and 30 Oldsmobiles and Vikings, not necessary to own one to join, just have the interests. Have parts and lots of info. Dues: $15 US/year.

The Orient Buckboard (& Kindred Vehicles) Roster
10917 130th St
Edmonton, AB Canada T5M 0Z4
403-452-1468; FAX: 493-455-2373

Orient Buckboard

Founded 1995. 65 members. For all owners of Orient Buckboard motorcars and other two, three and four-wheeled vehicles produced by the Waltham Mfg Co, Waltham, Mass (1901-1908). No dues.

1948-50 Packard Convertible Roster
84 Hoy Ave
Fords, NJ 08863
908-738-7859; FAX: 908-738-7625
E-mail: stellap@ix.netcom.com

Founded 1989. Seeking information on all 1948-50 Packard Super Eight and Custom Eight convertibles. Send an SASE for roster form.

The Packard V-8 Roster, 1955-56
84 Hoy Ave
Fords, NJ 08863
908-738-7859; FAX: 908-738-7625
E-mail: stellap@ix.netcom.com

Packard

For more information, contact at the above address: Stuart R Blond. Founded 1982. Roster for all 1955-56 Packards and Clippers. Send an SASE for roster form.

Jolyon Hofsted
PO Box 506
Shady, NY 12409
914-679-9601

PAIGE

Paige Registry for Paige and Jewitt cars and trucks.

1971 GTO & Judge Convertible Registry
14906 Ferness Ln
Channelview, TX 77530
713-452-0855

Founded 1989. 30 members. Registry of 1971 Pontiac GTO & Judge convertibles. Its purpose is to locate, verify and record how many of these automobiles survive today. Must own 1971 Pontiac GTO or Judge convertible and fill out registration form. Dues: none.

Firehawk Association of America
c/o W Thomas
PO Box 96
Uniontown, PA 15401
412-437-6736
E-mail: firehawk@pennet.com

Founded 1994. 350 members. Registry, quarterly newsletter, includes new products, improvements, recalls, problems & members' articles and a sell & want section. Dues: $12/year.

Powell Cycle Registry
4588 Pacific Hwy N
Central Point, OR 97502

POWELL

For information, contact at the above address: Wallace Skyrman, 503-664-2641. Founded 1982. Should have an interest in Powell motor scooters built from the late thirties through the seventies. Publishes a model description list. No dues, but long SASE requested for reply.

The Association of Rootes Vehicle Owners
3 Kingfisher Ct
East Molesey
Surrey, KT8 9HL England
0181-941-0604

ROOTES

An association of the owners of vehicles built and sold by the Rootes Group and their various subsidiary companies. Objective is to provide a means of communication and cooperation between these owners and maintain a watching brief on UK and European legislation affecting members' vehicles. Membership is open to owners and enthusiasts of Rootes vehicles. Rates: £10/year. Publication: *ARVO News*.

Clubs & Organizations

Scripps-Booth Register

c/o Scripps Downing
10 Bacon Woods Dr
Macomb, IL 61455
309-837-2593

SCRIPPS-BOOTH

Founded 1982. Current mailing list 40. Open to owners and others who can contribute to the lore and history of Scripps-Booth. Mailings occur only at 1-2 year intervals. Free.

Siata/Fiat 8V Register

PO Box 1022
Cambria, CA 93428
PH/FAX: 805-927-5802

Siata

Founded 1980. 100+ members. Register of owners of Siata, Fiat 8V, Cisitalia, Moretti, Bandini, Stanguellini, Nardi, etc, manufactured between 1946 and 1964. Dues: none.

Stephens Registry

Dick Farnsworth
1034 Henderson
Freeport, IL 61032
815-232-3825

Stephens

Sunbeam Rapier Registry of North America

3212 Orchard Cir
West Des Moines, IA 50266-2140
515-226-9475

Founded 1992. A registry and club for the identification & preservation of Sunbeam Rapiers (Series I-V, 1955-67). Publications: *Sunbeam Rapier Registry of North America* (1994) and quarterly club newsletter, *Rapier News*. Dues: $16/yr US and $19/yr Canada. Free registry publication to each Rapier owner who participates in this registry.

Connecticut Triumph Register

Wagon Wheel Ln
Portland, CT 06480
203-342-4602

Founded 1981. 190+ members. For membership information contact at the above address: Paul E DesRosiers. Promotes the ownership, restoration and use of British sports cars, especially Triumph automobiles. Dues: $20/year.

Velie Register

1811 E Stella Ln
Phoenix, AZ 85016
602-274-6049

VELIE

Founded 1993. 200 members. Open to anyone. *Velie Vehicles and Their Vitals*, 55-pg book, is the official register of Velie cars & trucks, 1909-28. Publishes 6-8 Velie newsletters per year. Dues: $10/year.

Willys-Overland-Knight Registry Inc

1440 Woodacre Dr
McLean, VA 22101-2535
703-533-0396

For membership information contact at the above address: Duane Perrin. Founded 1960. 1,300 members. An organization of people interested in the Willys-Overland family of cars to 1942 and all Knight-engined vehicles and Stearns cars. Quarterly publication: Starter. Also monthly newsletter. Dues: $24/year, US; $26/year Canada; $30/years all other countries.

Zimmerman Registry

2081 Madelaine Ct
Los Altos, CA 94024
PH/FAX: 415-967-2908
E-mail: zmrmn@aol.com

Zimmerman

Dedicated to the preservation and restoration of Zimmerman automobiles manufactured in Auburn, Indiana, from 1908-1915. Information exchanged between members by letter and FAX. No meetings, publications or dues. Founded 1989, 42 members.

Specialty Clubs

Antique Auto Racing Association Inc

Jim Witzler, Secretary
PO Box 486
Fairview, NC 28730

Founded 1973. 300 members. Open to vintage race car owners and enthusiasts. Holds five meets each year. Provides the opportunity for vintage race car owners to participate in actual dirt track racing exhibitions. Dues: $25/year.

Atlantic Coast Old Timers Auto Racing Club

PO Box 3067
Alexandria, VA 22302
703-836-2922

Newsletter address: c/o Gordon White, above address; Membership, c/o Bradley Gray, 55 Hilliard Road, Old Bridge, NJ 08857. Founded 1983. 550 members, 250 cars. Dedicated to restoring and running antique American oval-track race cars. Also has an active program of searching out and preserving records of racing history. Monthly newsletter: Pit Chatter. Dues: $14/year.

Automobile Objects d'art Club

252 N 7th St
Allentown, PA 18102
610-432-3355; FAX: 610-820-9368

For membership information, contact David K Bausch at the above address. Founded 1983. Two members. For people interested in early automobile objects d'art, paintings, prints, bronzes, etc.

Charleston British Car Club

Jack Lambert, President
1175 Mathis Ferry Rd H8
Mt Pleasant, SC 29464
803-849-9707 (home); FAX: 803-577-2061

Founded 1983. Approximately 60 members. Open to all British marques. Holds the annual British Car Day in June. Publishes *The Windscreen*, a monthly publication. Dues: $20/year.

Cobra Sport Racing Association

1915 Airport Rd, Bldg 2-C
Atlanta, GA 30341
404-843-9414; 770-458-8740

Founded 1995. 80+ members. The mission of the Cobra Sport Racing Association is to promote and perpetuate the racing heritage of the Cobra race car. CSRA brings the high-speed exuberance and nostalgia of Cobra racing back to the track. CSRA membership includes owners of original Cobras or Cobra replicas (which have been modified to race standards), corporations supplying parts to Cobra replica manufacturers, individuals and companies interested in Cobras or involved in auto racing. Dues: $50/year individual, $200/year corporate.

Cruisers of Conroe, TX

9 Springwood Dr
Montgomery, TX 77356
409-588-1448

Founded 1988. 40 members. A non-profit organization incorporated in 1994 by automobile enthusiasts to promote and preserve the hobby of collecting, restoring and preserving classic cars and trucks. Annual February car show draws over 1,000. Benefits area charities. Saturday night meet and eat at local drive-in restaurant overlooking Lake Conroe. Monthly newsletter and business meeting keep members informed. Member TVCC in good standing. Outstanding participation awards from DARE programs, 100 Club, area Kiwanis Club and Montgomery County Sheriff Dept. Dues: $36/year.

Electric Car Owner's Society
167 Concord St
Brooklyn Hgts, NY 11201
718-797-4311, ext 3262; FAX: 718-596-4852
E-mail: adc@dorsal.org

Founded 1984. 520 members. BBS, special electric car database CD Rom, electric car library & registry. $25 donation requested.

Group Ultra Van
W Christy Barden
5537 Pioneer Rd
Boulder, CO 80301-3048
303-530-1288

Founded 1981. 200 members. 360 Ultra Vans were built from 1962-69. They are 22-foot motor homes, 8 feet high and 8 feet wide. Weight from 3,200 pounds to 4,200 pounds. Club assists in preserving these classics. Quarterly publication: *Whales on Wheels.* Contains technical information on Ultra Vans. Dues: $6/year. Web site: http://www.onu.edu/~kwildman/ultravan.html

Guldstrand Racing Association
11924 W Jefferson Blvd
Culver City, CA 90230
310-391-7108; FAX: 310-391-7424
E-mail: geiauto@aol.com

Founded 1968. 160+ members. GRA (Guldstrand Racing Assoc) meets second Thursday of every month at 7:30 pm at Guldstrand Eng Inc, Culver City, CA. Solo I & II special race events. Annual dues $25.

Hoosier Model Car Association
1019 N Tuxedo St
Indianapolis, IN 46201
317-264-9387

Founded 1979. 40 members. For builders and collectors, any marque, scale or building style. Serving central Indiana area. Annual swap meet and involvement in local shows. Monthly newsletter. Dues: $12/year.

Indy Hi-Winders Car Club Inc
7565 E 300 N
Brownsburg, IN 46112
317-852-2723
E-mail: shenry51@indy.net

Founded 1962. 35 members. Events include 500 W/W, Miracle Ride, Poker Run Nationals, MoPar Nationals, various events at JRP. Yearly coordination calendar for local & Indiana events.

Lost Highways
The Classic Trailer & Motorhome Club
PO Box 43737
Philadelphia, PA 19106
215-925-2568

Founded 1993. 1,200 members and growing. A club, an archive and an award winning, glossy magazine devoted to living on wheels, teens and twenties through the sixties. You do not have to own a classic trailer or motorhome to join. Regional meets and rallies. Vintage station wagon, step van, VW bus and any other type of auto campers also very welcome. Extensive archive for research, always seeking related materials. Membership/subscription covers four issues of our magazine. Dues: $24.

Mac's Pack
306 Whitestone Cir
Cedar Park, TX 78613
512-259-5092

Founded 1987. 100+ members. To become a member you must participate in helping put on an event, showing or participating in two events. We put on an annual spring event called Mac's Pack Spring Dust-Off on the first Sunday in May. Also a fall event, a poker run with a show and shine, usually in September or October. No dues.

Manx Dune Buggy Club
PO Box 1491
Valley Center, CA 92082
FAX: 619-751-0610

Founded 1994. 420 members internationally. Open to all owners of fiberglass dune buggies and a registry for any Meyers kit car. There will be a quarterly newsletter, *Manx Mania*, with an announcement about future meets and events. Dues: $25/year. Registry: $5.

Massachusetts Antique Fire Apparatus Association
PO Box 3332
Peabody, MA 01960
FAX: 617-246-5193

Founded 1976. 200 members. Open to persons interested in the development and history of motorized fire apparatus. Monthly publication: *The Box Alarm.* Our annual parade and muster will be held Saturday, June 21, 1997, at Edgewater Park, Wakefield, MA. Dues: $10/year.

Motor Bus Society Inc
PO Box 251
Paramus, NJ 07653-0251

Founded 1948. 1,000 members. Collects and publishes the colorful and fascinating history of the bus industry. Bimonthly publication, *Motor Coach Age.* Dues: $25/year.

National Belchfire Owner's Club
Box 5502
Concord, CA 94524
510-228-7821; FAX: 510-228-1410

Five members. A national tongue-in-cheek club for professional auto writers to promote the lighter side of the automobile world. Name comes from a series of cartoons by the late George Lichty. One meeting per year at Los Angeles Auto Show. No dues.

National Historic Route 66 Federation
PO Box 423
Tujunga, CA 91043-0423
PH/FAX: 818-352-7232

Founded 1994. 1,000 members. We are dedicated to preserving America's most famous highway. Members receive a quarterly magazine and access to books, maps, guides, events, etc. Dues: $25/year. Web site: http://www.national66.com/~natl66

NZ Military Vehicle Collectors Club Inc
c/o President L Longshaw
101 Heatherington Rd, Ranui
Auckland New Zealand
09-8336576; FAX: 07-8569319

Founded 1979. 160 family members. Open to anyone interested in the collection and restoration of military vehicles. Monthly magazine. Local monthly meetings and April national meet. 11 branches throughout New Zealand. We participate in off-road events, displays, air shows, camp outs and swapping of ideas and information. Dues: NZ $40/year.

Clubs & Organizations

Pachecho, Martinea & Port Costa Sewing Circle
Book Review Society & Street Racing Association
9 Benita Way
Martinez, CA 94553
415-228-1410

Founded 1983. 1,247 members. Club meets irregularly to enjoy their automobiles and automobile business. To promote Grand Prix racing at grass roots level. No restrictions to join. Dues: none.

Pittsburgh Vintage Grand Prix Association
PO Box 2243
Pittsburgh, PA 15230
412-734-5853

Founded 1983. 1,600 members. All volunteer organization holds annual vintage races and largest collector car show in western Pennsylvania every 3rd weekend in July. All proceeds benefit Autism Society of Pittsburgh.

Red River Street Rods
PO Box 2074
Shreveport, LA 71166
318-747-0644

Founded 1973. 50 members. Meet others with same interest in cars, car shows, both local and distant. Meets 3rd Saturday of each month before our cruise night at What A Burger. Summer picnics, rod runs, dinners, etc.

Sportscar Vintage Racing Association
PO Box 489
Charleston, SC 29402
803-723-7872; FAX: 803-723-7372

Founded 1976. 1,900 members. The Sportscar Vintage Racing Association (SVRA) is the largest organization presenting vintage race events for historically-significant race cars in North America. SVRA organized its first event in 1976, and has grown into an international organization with 1,900 members in 43 states, Canada and several foreign countries. SVRA's 1996 schedule includes ten race weekends across the country. SVRA offers regular, spouse and competition memberships which include entry into spectator events and monthly publications about vintage racing. Dues: $75 & $100/year.

Steam Automobile Club of America Inc
1227 W Voorhees St
Danville, IL 61832
217-442-0268; FAX: 217-442-3299
E-mail: jreynol@aol.com

Founded 1958. 850 members. Open to all steam automobile enthusiasts. A non-profit organization dedicated to the preservation of steam auto history and to the development of modern steam automobiles. Bimonthly publication: *Steam Automobile Bulletin*. Dues: $16/year, US funds.

Tarrant County Street Rod Association
5801 Graham
Fort Worth, TX 76114
817-626-2708

Founded 1971. 25 members. You must own a 1948 or earlier model vehicle with some modifications. We meet the third Saturday of each month at Bar-B-Que, Etc on Highway 80 in West Fort Worth at 6 pm. Dues: $5/monthly.

Texas Joy Ride
2622 Micliff
Houston, TX 77068
713-444-8680; FAX: 713-443-7671

Founded 1988. Joy Williams, founder. Rod run.

Toy Car Collectors Club
33290 W 14 Mile, #454
West Bloomfield, MI 48322
810-682-0272

Founded 1993. 164 members. A club for collectors of all miniature vehicles, all manufactures, materials, scales, types, eras, etc. Services: quarterly magazine, *Toy Car Magazine*, free copy of *Model Car Directory 1992*, monthly meetings (Detroit area), annual convention, annual souvenir vehicle: 38 Hudson 112 pace car, on order. *Model Car Directory* is a book of lists: auctioneers, books, catalogs, clubs, codes, contests, conventions, dealers, dictionary, individuals, magazines, manufacturers, museums, scales, shows, videos, etc. Dues: $15/year.

United Detroit Car Modelers
13856 Roxanne Rd
Sterling Heights, MI 48312-5673
810-268-3479

Founded 1991. 12 members. Membership open to all. For builders and collectors. Monthly publication *Model Car Action*. Monthly club meetings that include model building how-to. Club located in NE Detroit suburb. Dues: $8/year.

Vehicle Preservation Society
PO Box 9800
San Diego, CA 92169
619-449-1010; FAX: 619-449-6388

Founded 1992. 200 national members. Private or commercial memberships. VPS is a hobby co-op, not for profit. We promote preservation of collectible vehicles. VPS performs appraisals, free listing service, locating, shipping, etc. Monthly publication: *Auto Truck Round-up*. Subscription rate: $14.95. Dues: none.

Vintage Kit & Custom Club
1731 Mound Rd
Jacksonville, IL 62650
217-245-0020

Founded 1992. 121 members international. Dedicated to EARLY kit, coach built and customized autos, such as Devin, Glasspar, Kellison, LaDawri, Bocar, Victress, Wildfire, Carson Top cars, Barris, Roth, etc. Major efforts at present: obtain and share information on these extremely rare cars, organize regional clubs, national meets and improving our newsletter. Benefits include: free ads in newsletter, additional knowledge, buy/sell assistance and promotion of cars most enthusiasts have never heard of. Dues $18/year.

Vixen Owners Association Inc
718 Greenland Way
Grand Prairie, TX 75050
214-262-2331

Founded 1989. 250 members. Open to those who own Vixen motorhomes, prospective owners and those who provide goods and servies but do not own Vixens. Monthly newsletter. Annual meeting plus Regional rallies every other month. Dues: $15/year.

State Clubs

Gadsden Antique Automobile Club
113 Buckingham Pl
Gadsden, AL 35901
205-547-7143

Alabama

Founded 1966. Over 100 members. Independent organization, family oriented and dedicated to preservation of antique and special interest automobiles. Annual invitational meet for over 30 years.

Clubs & Organizations

Arizona Bus Club Arizona
3121 E Yucca
Phoenix, AZ 85028-2616
PH/FAX: 602-867-7672

200+ members, monthly meetings, car shows, swap meets, largest VW club in Arizona. All VWs & family welcome.

Arizona Challenger 'Cuda Club Arizona
PO Box 41956
Mesa, AZ 85274
602-786-0485

Founded 1981. 40 members. Dedicated to the preservation, restoration and enjoyment of all Chrysler muscle cars. Monthly meetings, activites and newsletter. Dues: $25/year.

The Mid Peninsula Old Time Auto Club Inc California
PO Box 525
Belmont, CA 94002

80 members (families). Should be old car owner or enthusiast. Car must be 35 years or older. Emphasis on tours and social events. Organizer of annual Friendship Day in San Francisco Bay area. Publication: *Windshield Post*. Dues: $15/year.

Durango Old Car Club Colorado
201 Clover Pl
Durango, CO 81301
970-247-8761

For information, contact Steven Wylie at the above address. Founded 1965. 50 members. "Cars not necessary, just enthusiasm." Dues: $5/year.

Candlewood Street Rods Connecticut
c/o Mr Michael Alves
5 Mazur Dr
Danbury, CT 06811
203-790-4786

Founded 1973. 18 members. Open to owners of 1957 and older street rods. Promotes the enjoyment of and travel with modified antique cars. Dues: $20/year. All inquiries will be answered, please include phone number.

Classic Nights Car Club Connecticut
c/o Peter Kodz
1136 Capitol Ave
Bridgeport, CT 06606
203-385-4610

Founded 1984. 18 families/members. Family oriented organization created to provide a forum for individuals who enjoy sharing their interest in automobiles, primarily reflective of the cruising 50s era and who enjoy and seek the fellowship of other such individuals. Membership limited to 45 members and open to multi-make automobiles and years. Cruise nights held at Bill's Drive-In, Rt 111, Monroe, CT, every Friday night 6 to 10 pm from May-October. Yearly car show in June. As a body the club participates in other car shows and cruise nights held by local and some out of state clubs. The club also donates their time and cars for worthwhile causes. Club meetings held the 2nd Tuesday of the month, November to April, at Bill's Drive-in. Dues: $30/year.

Engine 260 Inc Connecticut
4 Flax Mill Terr
Milford, CT 06460
203-874-2605

For information, contact George A Ambriscoe at the above address. Founded 1970. 75 members. Antique fire buff organization. Sponsors annual engine 260 antique fire apparatus show and muster in September in Milford, Connecticut.

Peach State Nova Club Georgia
PO Box 724852
Atlanta, GA 31139-1852
770-921-5422

Founded 1988, 75 members. Monthly meeting 2nd Sunday of each month. Also monthly newsletter. Dues: $15 individual, $18 husband & spouse.

Pioneer Auto Club Indiana
Haynes-Apperson Chapter
PO Box 352
Kokomo, IN 46903-0352
317-457-9120

Founded 1951. 100 members. Home of the Haynes and Apperson cars. Dedicated to the preservation and restoration of antique cars. Dues: $15/year individual.

Ark-La-Tex Antique & Classic Car Association Louisiana
Box 3353
Shreveport, LA 71133-3353

For information, contact at the above address: Jan Shavers, 318-746-0159. Founded 1957. 100 members. Affiliated with MOTAA. Publication: Piston Chatter. Dues: $15/year.

Florida Parishes Vintage Car Club Louisiana
PO Box 38
Ponchatoula, LA 70454
504-386-3714

Founded 1977. 41 member families. Applicants must be voted in by members. Affiliated with Mid-America Old Time Automobile Association (MOTAA). Dues: $10/year.

Antique Motor Club of Greater Baltimore Inc Maryland
208 Brightside Ave
Pikesville, MD 21208-4806
410-484-1715

For membership information, contact Maurleen Buttery at the above address. Founded 1968. 650 members. Offers activities which every member of the family can participate in and enjoy. No judging. Activities are open to the general public. Publication: *Olde Jalopy News*. Dues: $20/year.

Branch County Antique Auto Club Michigan
717 McQueen Rd
Coldwater, MI 49036

For membership information, contact Melvin Johnson at the above address, 517-278-2053. Founded 1970. 48 members. Family social organization interested in restoring and preserving antique autos. Branch County resident must own a 25 year old or heritage car. Dues: $10/year.

Jaguar Club of Minnesota Minnesota
5610 Woodcrest Dr
Minneapolis, MN 55424
612-927-8126

Founded 1977. 100+ members. Open to owners or enthusiasts of Jaguar cars. Dues: $35/year.

St Cloud Antique Auto Club Minnesota
PO Box 704
St Cloud, MN 56302-0704

For membership information, contact Pantowners, attn: Secretary, at the above address. Founded 1971. 263 members. Our club nickname of "Pantowners" is named after the Pan automobile made in St Cloud from 1917-1919. Family centered club. Monthly meetings and newsletter, summer tours, car show and swap meet each August, always the third Sunday. Over 500 cars and 400 swappers. Smaller shows and tours throughout the year. Welcomes all antique, pioneer or collector car enthusiasts. Dues: $10/year.

Montana Street Rod Association	Montana
PO Box 991	
Livingston, MT 59047	
406-222-1084	

Founded 1976. 54 members. Meets quarterly. Purpose is to promote street rodding and other auto related activities, and provide sounding board for all clubs and interested street rodders in the state to discuss common problems. Annual picnic 3rd Sunday of August. Dues: $10/year.

Yellowstone Valley Mustang & Ford Club	Montana
PO Box 21844	
Billings, MT 59104	
406-252-3873	

Founded 1986. Open to anyone who enjoys Mustangs and Fords. Newsletters, shows, cruises, picnics. Dues: $20/year.

New Hampshire Mustang Club	New Hampshire
c/o Tom Cannon	
8 Sycamore St	
Hudson, NH 03051-4733	
PH/FAX: 603-594-0838	

Founded 1988. 182 members. Ownership not required. Nonprofit organization devoted to Ford Mustangs, past and present. Monthly meets, newsletter, shows, rallies, etc. Monthly publication: *New Hampshire Mustang*, free with membership. Dues: $25/year.

Jersey Late Greats, 58-64 Chevys	New Jersey
PO Box 1294	
Hightstown, NJ 08520	
908-291-3553	

Founded 1982. 130 members. Ownership of a car is not required, but must be sincere Chevrolet enthusiast. All restored or modified cars and trucks eligible. Dedicated to the preservation of all 1958-64 Chevrolets. Family oriented club. Monthly newsletter. Dues: $18/year. Club provides national documentation service for original 1958-64 Chevys. Send 2 stamps for information packet.

The Antique Automobile Association of Brooklyn	New York
811 Union St	
Brooklyn, NY 11215	
718-788-3400	

Founded 1962. 110 members. Dues: $20/year.

The Automobilists of the Upper Hudson	New York
398 Fillmore Ave	
Schenectady, NY 12304	
518-372-8061	

Founded 1950. 295 members. Newsletter once a month. Winter meetings January thru April at the Desmond, in Albany, NY. Summer meets and events begin May. Touring to places of interest, picnics, parades, showing cars, annual car show, Nov election of officers and awards banquet. Dues: single $15/year, joint $20/year.

Upstate New York Thunderbird Club Inc	New York
Box 346	
Greenwich, NY 12834	
518-692-7815	

See full listing in **Section Three** under **marque clubs**.

Dakota Western Auto Club	North Dakota
Ken Praus	
976 Elm Ave	
Dickinson, ND 58601	
701-225-8097	

Founded 1977. 55 members. Open to anyone with an interest and love of the automobile. Has a car show held in June at Medora, North Dakota. Dues: $10/year.

North Dakota Street Rod Association	North Dakota
PO Box 459	
Bismarck, ND 58502	
701-255-6382, 701-222-2069	
FAX: 701-222-0736	

Founded 1985. 345 members. Quarterly newsletter, annual Christmas party, co-sponsor rodding events in North Dakota. Dues: $10/year.

Buckeye Motorcar Association	Ohio
PO Box 128	
Newark, OH 43055	
614-345-1282	

Founded 1980. 65 members. Promotes interest in and ownership of vintage vehicles, antique, classic, unique, special interest and investment. Auto show consultants. Dues: $20/year.

Clinton County Antique & Classic Car Club	Ohio
662 W Locust	
Wilmington, OH 45177	
513-382-3980	

For membership information, contact at the above address: Willard Skidmore. Founded 1960. 38 members. Annual car show in September. Dues: $5/year.

The Rodfathers of Butler	Pennsylvania
4125 Oak St	
Butler, PA 16001	
412-482-4387 after 6 pm	

Founded 1991. 31 members. The club that promotes motorsports fun of all types. We have cruises, car shows, 50s dances, swap meets, etc. We also help all local charities with their fund raising. Dues: $15/year.

Now & Then Vehicles Club Inc of Southern Vermont	Vermont
RR 2, Box 552	
Putney, VT 05346	
802-257-3053	

Founded 1978. 50 families. Interest in history or preservation of autos. Family oriented club endeavoring to inform and enrich our understanding of the history and kinds of motor vehicles from the early Flivvers through the modern performance cars. The club sponsors a car show and other events to enhance the enjoyment of members of "special interest" cars and trucks. Dues: $10/year.

Skagit Old Car Club	Washington
PO Box 2147	
Mount Vernon, WA 98273	
206-293-8488 days	
FAX: 206-293-8480	

Founded 1969. 100 members. No age of vehicle restrictions, and ownership of old car not required. Mixed make general interest old car club. Family oriented, meetings monthly. Emphasis on touring and restoring all old cars. Monthly newsletter. Dues: $15/year.

Mustang Club of West Virginia
1702 Massey Cir
South Charleston, WV 25303
304-744-5540

West Virginia

Founded 1975. Approximately 50 members. Dedicated to all Ford enthusiasts, ownership is not essential, just a love of Ford autos and family fun. Done in the area around the beautiful state capitol of West Virginia. Bimonthly newsletter, yearly car show sponsored, camp outs, attend National conventions and automotive swap meets, races, etc. Dues: $12/year.

Club La Manivelle Inc
399 Lemoyne
Beloeil, QC Canada J3G 2C1

Canada

For membership information, contact at the above address: Andre LaPointe, 514-467-9453. Founded 1993. Antique car club dedicated to pre-1940 cars only. Dues: $15/year (Canadian). French bulletins only.

Dusty Wheels Auto Club
Box 1813
Rosetown, SK Canada S0L 2V0
306-882-4007, 306-882-3197

Canada

Founded 1986. 30 members. General interest car club for any car enthusiast. Holds an annual car show on the fourth weekend in September. Also holds a "Cruise Night" the 3rd Saturday of June every year. Meetings are held the second Wednesday of each month. Dues: $15/year.

Manitoba Classic & Antique Auto Club
PO Box 1031
Winnipeg, MB Canada R3C 2W2

Canada

Founded 1960. Approximately 225 members. Dues: $36/year Canadian.

Voitures Anciennes Du Quebec Inc
3155 Marcel
St Laurent, QC Canada H4R 1B3
514-337-4326; FAX: 514-331-3662

Canada

Founded 1974. 2,300 members. For information, contact Denise Bourgeois. Open to all antique car owners (15 years and older). Largest provincial club in Canada. Publishes the only French monthly publication: *"L'Auto Ancienne",* on antique cars in North America. Dues: $42/year (Canadian), $62/year United States and Europe.

Legislative Watch Organizations

National

AACA Legislative
Jack Widdel, VP
PO Box 5624
Grand Forks, ND 58206
701-746-7485; FAX: 701-775-9491

Founded 1935. Membership includes 50 states+. Interested in legislation centered around the automobile, the hobby and its preservation. Has a networking system for states to assist the hobby and club members. Publications: *Rummage Box News* and *Antique Automobile* magazine with information on state and federal automobile legislation.

American Automotive Heritage Foundation (AAHF)
PO Box 482
Carlisle, PA 17013-0482
717-240-0976; FAX: 717-240-0931

Monday-Friday, 8 am to 5 pm. Founded 1994. 501(C)(3) non-profit, tax exempt organization. Donations to the AAHF are tax deductible as permitted by federal tax laws. Mission: to protect, preserve and promote the automotive heritage of the United States through educational and other activities.

See our ad on page 514

Automotive Restoration Market Organization (ARMO)
PO Box 4910
Diamond Bar, CA 91765-0910
909-396-0289; FAX: 909-860-0184

ARMO, a council of the Specialty Equipment Market Association (SEMA), was created for the purpose of meeting the legislative, educational and communications needs of the automotive restoration industry. Through cooperative action, ARMO works to address those legislative and/or regulatory issues which may impact on the restoration industry and strives to ensure the viability of the industry/hobby. Any business or club serving the automotive industry or the collector-car hobby is invited to join. For information contact Mike Long at the above address.

Coalition for Vehicle Choice
1100 New York Ave NW, Suite 810 W Tower
Washington, DC 20005
800-AUTO-411; 202-628-5164; FAX: 202-628-5168
E-mail: cvc@his.com

Founded 1991. 40,000+ members. CVC represents more than 40,000 individuals and organizations interested in preserving safe and affordable transportation. It is a non-profit organization working to inform policymakers, the media and the public about the effects of proposed public policies on vehicle users. Dues: voluntary contributions.

Council of Vehicle Associations
10400 Roberts Rd
Palos Hills, IL 60465
708-598-7070; FAX: 708-598-4888

Founded 1992. Members: 85,000. COVA is a not-for-profit organization devoted to protecting the interests of individuals, companies and organizations involved in the collectible vehicle industry. All members receive the quarterly bulletin and applicable alerts plus a membership roster upon request. The valuable suggestion for a national license plate program originated at a COVA meeting. Dues: $25 or more/year.

members:

Alabama   *American Truck Historical Society,* Larry Scheef, PO Box 531168, Birmingham, AL 35253; 205-870-0566, 205-870-3069

Arizona   *CHVA Southern AZ Region,* Dwight Eller, 1416 E Kleindale Rd, Tucson, AZ 85719; 602-326-9952

Grand Canyon St Chap Studebaker, Chris Collins, 2410 W Freeway Ln, Phoenix, AZ 85021; 602-995-5311

Relics & Rods, John Parker, Box 1516, Lake Havasu City, AZ 86403; 602-680-6721

Tucson T-Bird Club, John Strobeck, 1517 N Wilmot Rd #144, Tucson, AZ 85712; 602-296-0519, 602-886-1184

Arkansas *Classic Chevy Club of Northern Arkansas,* Linda Coble, PO Box 56, Gassville, AR 72635

Natural State Rod & Custom, Dan Bell, Rt 9, Box 410, Lakeview, AR 72642; 501-431-8701

Twin Lakes Vintage Auto, Frank Fabrecious, PO Box 834, Mt Home, AR 72653; 501-481-5423

California *Avanti Ltd of Northern California,* Gary Croletto, 194 Strentzel Ln, Martinez, CA 94553; 510-372-7904, 510-228-9106

BAMA, Debbi Batteux, 16008 Via Descanso, San Lorenzo, CA 94580; 510-481-2634

Cadillac Drivers Club, L Wray Tibbs, 5825 Vista Ave, Sacramento, CA 95824-1428; 916-421-3193

Edsel Owners Club, Southlanders Chapter, Gerald Nash, PO Box 11232, Carson, CA 90749-1232; 310-513-6718

Golden Gate Classic Thunderbird Club, Michael Press, 124 Hollyhock Ct, Hercules, CA 94547; 510-799-0556

Gull Wing Group International, Gary Estep, 776 Cessna Ave, Chico, CA 95928; 916-345-6701

Happy Honker A's, Carson Blaydes, PO Box 1912, Porterville, CA 93258; 209-539-3815

Historical Construction Equipment, Craig Maxwell, 9451 56th St, Riverside, CA 92509; 909-681-4449, 909-822-9661

Mariposa 4 Bangers, John Jansen, 5840 Evergreen Ln, Mariposa, CA 95338; 209-742-7927

MG Owners Club, George Steneberg, 9 Pomona Ave, El Cerrito, CA 94530; 510-525-9125

North American Auto Union Register, Byron Brill, 260 Santa Margarita Ave, Menlo Park, CA 94025; 415-323-3913

North American Matra Register, Jim Duncan, 2300 A McCabe Dr, Cambria, CA 93428

Pantera Club of Northern California, Bill Santos, 948 Olympus Ct, Sunnyvale, CA 94087-5240; 408-732-6468, 415-592-9988

Santa Barbara Classic Chevy Club, Jay Peterson, 120 N La Patera, Goleta, CA 93117; 805-562-2439

Touring A's, Diane Dove, 1777 Rosswood Dr, San Jose, CA 95124; 408-266-6709

Tri-County Mustang Club, Roger Harrington, PO Box 60238, Santa Barbara, CA 93160-0238; 805-967-8324

Tucker Automobile Club of America, William Pommering, 9509 Hinton Dr, Santee, CA 90271-2760; 619-562-9644, 619-573-0196

Tulare Co Horseless Carriage Club, Ann Silva, 31511 Rd 160, Visalia, CA 93292; 209-798-1125, 209-798-1973, 209-798-1342

Colorado *AMC World Clubs Inc,* Larry Mitchell, 7963 Depew St, Arvada, CO 80003-2527; 303-428-8760

Colorado Continental Convertible Club, Keith Jackson, 960 Pennsylvania #16, Denver, CO 80203

Lincoln & Continental Owner's Club, Tom Ward, 2458 Ward Dr, Lakewood, CO 80215; 303-233-2893

Mercedes-Benz Club of America Inc, Ron Farrar, 1907 Lelaray St, Colorado, CO 80909; 719-633-6427, 719-633-9283

Rocky Mountain Jaguar Club, Bob Alder, PO Box 2923, Denver, CO 80201; 303-757-0868

Southern Colorado A's, PO Box 5221, Pueblo, CO 81002; 719-545-1774

Western Slope Cruisers, Jeanne Briska, 436 Morning Dove Dr, Grand Junction, CO 81504; 303-434-1923

Connecticut *CT Chevelle Connection,* Sharon Gregerick, PO Box 6094, Wolcott, CT 06716; 203-673-9849

Delaware *First State Corvair Club Inc,* David Ziegler III, 1002 Stonewood Rd, Wilmington, DE 19810; 302-737-3577

Historical Vintage Car Club of Delaware, Thomas Mercer, PO Box 43, Dover, DE 19903; 302-734-9912

Florida *Early Ford V8 Club,* Nancy Edwards, PO Box 12101, Lake Park, FL 33403

Florida Antique Bucket Brigade, Jim Briggs, 6855 Green Swamp Rd, Clermont, FL 34711; 904-394-8709

Florida Suncoast MG Car Club, Bruce Rauch, PO Box 0251, Tampa, FL 33601-0251; 813-576-9474, 813-576-9570

Model A Restorers Club (Crankin A's), Eric Evans, 16 Foxhunter Flat, Ormond Beach, FL 32174; 904-672-4807

Orlando Area Chapter, Studebaker, Reed Webb, 3060 Baytree Dr, Orlando, FL 32806; 407-898-9324

Palm Beach Region Model A Ford Club, Valerie Langer, 17737 122nd Dr N, Jupiter, FL 33478; 561-746-6641, 561-746-6922

Treasure Coast Vintage Car Club, Kril Jackson, PO Box 221, Palm City, FL 34991; 407-220-3021

Georgia *Vintage Thunderbird Club International,* Stephen Longaker, 9399 Kingston Crossing Cir, Alpharetta, GA 30202; 404-441-9225, 404-621-1750

Idaho *Classic T-Birds of Idaho,* Ho Nix, 408 8th Ave W, Jerome, ID 83338; 208-324-5959

Illinois *Centennial Rods and Street Machines,* Mark Schumacher, 8526 217th St N, Port Byron, IL 61275; 309-523-3918, 309-523-2710

Centerville Antique Auto Touring, Janice Newman, PO Box 33, Woodstock, IL 60098; 815-385-7048

Central Illinois Chapter of National Nostalgia, Dennis Quin, 115 Grant St, Washington, IL 61571; 309-745-5438

Chain O'Lakes Model A, Don Schreiber, 3550 Glen Flora Ave, Gurnee, IL 60031; 708-662-7502

Chicagoland Corvair Enthusiasts, Bill Harwood, 806 Monticello Pl, Evanston, IL 60201-1748; 708-864-9680

Chicagoland MGB Club, PO Box 455, Addison, IL 60101; 708-295-2753

Dekalb/Sycamore Vintage Auto Club, Keith Hill, 120 McCormick, Dekalb, IL 60115

Clubs & Organizations

Fox Valley Corvette Club Inc, Mike Hauser, 50 Pembrooke Rd, Montgomery, IL 60538; 708-892-8284, 708-892-6544

Greater Chicago Classic Chevy Club, Joe Massani, 18 S Edward, Mt Prospect, IL 60056; 708-259-0881

Illiamo Chapter of the MTFCA, Rosie Townsend, RR 51 Sunview, Quincy, IL 62301; 816-754-6666

Illinois Chapter of POCI, Laurel Von Helms, 5122 W 114th Pl, Worth, IL 60482; 708-371-8033

Illinois Valley Olds Club, Bill Wagaman, 816 13th St, Rockford, IL 61108; 815-226-4727

Midwest Model T Ford Club, Bill Soop, 7516 Little Fawn Trace, Crystal Lake, IL 60012; 815-459-6412

Naper A's Model A Ford Club, Lindell Williams, 1809 Winola Ct, Naperville, IL 60565; 708-420-0433

Northern Illinois Chapter, Late Greats, Dave Foley, 3552 S Wood, Chicago, IL 60609; 312-927-8260

Northern Mustang Corral, William Cheffer, 750 Riverside Ct, Kankakee, IL 60901-4757; 815-935-1429

Okaw Valley Classic Chevy Club, Mike Raby, PO Box 1981, Fairview Heights, IL 62208; 618-344-2950

Oldsmobile Club of America, Steve Denovi, 18650 S 76th Ave, Tinley Park, IL 60477; 708-429-5505, 708-429-5624

Packards of Chicagoland, Tony Lewandowski, PO Box 1031, Elmhurst, IL 60126

Salt Creek Chapter Model A Ford Club, Jim Ruzicka, 611 E Harding, La Grange Park, IL 60526; 708-354-9571, 708-354-0570

Shiloh Valley Mustang Association, Steven Giles, 27 Sagebrush Dr, Balleville, IL 62221; 618-234-6163

SIR AACA, William Morse, 396 May Apple Ln, Carbondale, IL 62901; 618-549-7469

Windige Stadt 356 Klub, Dale Moody, 19532 Governor's Hwy, Homewood, IL 60430-4352; 708-798-2637

Windy City Chapter ATHS, Milton Smazik, 14247 151st, Lockport, IL 60441

Indiana *Antique & Classic Auto Club,* C G Thomas, RR 4, Box 64, Clinton, IN 47842; 317-832-3049

Circle City Corvairs, Jean Allan, 50 N Main St, Southport, IN 46227-5136; 317-784-6727

Hoosier MoPar Club, Wayne Kjonaas, 2440 St Rd 26 W, West Lafayette, IN 47960-4850

Hoosier Old Wheels Inc, William Belk, PO Box 123, Plymouth, IN 46563; 219-936-9975, 219-936-5098

Michiana Antique Auto Club, Lars Kneller, 3018 W Small Rd, La Porte, IN 46350-7929; 219-324-8830, 219-325-0501

Vintage Thunderbird Club of Indiana, James Maple, 2423 S Fishers Rd, Indianapolis, IN 46239; 317-356-6672

Iowa *Hawkeye Packards,* Russell Bees, 1447 Summerset Rd, Indianola, IA 50125

Iowa Corvair Enthusiasts, Eugene Anthony, 2366 Hwy 22 W, Muscatine, IA 52761-8769; 319-263-1163

Marshalltown Area Restorers, Forrest Smith Jr, PO Box 444, Marshalltown, IA 50158

NIAPRA, Kirk Van Gundy, 455 Loomis Ave, Fort Dodge, IA 50501; 515-576-0481, 515-576-2652

Silver Wheels Car Club, Connie Bland, 1953 S 44th Ave W, Newton, IA 50208-8955; 515-792-8024

Southeast Iowa Antique Car Club, Robert Carleton, PO Box 279, Morning Son, IA 52640; 319-868-7622, 319-868-7565

Tri-State Antique & Classic Automobile, John Schloz, 2745 New Haven St, Dubuque, IA 52001

Kansas *Central Kansas Met Club,* Royal Bebermeyer, 1614 Road N, Emporia, KS 66801; 316-342-1827

Early Ford V8 Club, David Poole, 5656 Riley, Overland Park, KS 66202; 913-262-2276

Heart of America Chapter Edsel Owners, Maye Gulley, PO Box 587, DeSoto, KS 66018; 913-583-1822, 913-583-8303

Heartland Mopar Club, Tony Williams, 531 NE Twiss Ave, Topeka, KS 66616; 913-234-6912

Kansas Street Rod Association, Neal Barnhardt, 1909 NE Madison, Topeka, KS 66608-1716

Kaw Valley Studebaker Drivers Club, Charles Worthington, 2859 SW Jewell Ave, Topeka, KS 66611-1615; 913-286-0024

KC Arrowhead Chapter of POCI, Vicky Cochran, Treasurer, 3535 SE Tecumseh Rd, Tecumseh, KS 66542; 913-582-4207

Lake Garnett Cruisers, Mary K Giles, 415 N Spruce, Garnett, KS 66032; 913-448-6509, 913-448-5555

Lawrence All British Car Club, Charles Hartman, 2141 New Hampshire St, Lawrence, KS 66046; 913-841-9845

Lawrence Region Antique Club of America, Jayhawk Station, PO Box 4021, Lawrence, KS 66046

Lincoln Mercury Enthusiasts Club, Charles Hancock, 1835 E 153rd St, Olathe, KS 66062; 913-381-5679

Mo-Kan Volkswagen Club, Howard Kilgore, 6110 W 53rd St, Mission, KS 66202; 913-384-1138

Sunflower Region CHVA, Don Beck, 3140 NW 43rd St, Topeka, KS 66618; 913-843-7224

Topeka Region AACA, Tom Thomas, 3522 Thomas Rd, Silver Lake, KS 66539; 913-582-5811

Vintage Mustang Club of Kansas City, Jack Sell, PO Box 40082, Overland Park, KS 66204; 913-649-5770, 913-383-2281

Wheels of Fun Car Club, Knut Farstvedt, 325 N Minnesota, Columbus, KS 66725; 316-429-2579

Kentucky *Iron City Antique Auto Club,* Carl Virgin, 1308 Sparks St, Flatwoods, KY 41139; 606-836-5040

Mid Kentucky Antique Car Club, Bob Avery, 132 Sugartree Ln, Glasgow, KY 42121; 502-678-8932

Louisiana *Ark-La-Tex Antique & Classic Car Association*, Marilyn Wright, PO Box 3353, Shreveport, LA 71133; 318-746-0159

British Motoring Club New Orleans, Keith Vezina, PO Box 73213, Metairie, LA 70033; 504-394-3633

Maryland *1953-1954 Buick Skylark Club*, Cindy Beckley, Secretary, PO Box 1281, Frederick, MD 21702; 301-898-5137

Buick Owners of Maryland, William Anderson, 1119 Honeysuckle Ln, Annapolis, MD 21401; 410-849-3376

Catoctin Mt Street Rods Inc, Carl Callis, PO Box 4035, Frederick, MD 21705-4035; 301-831-3813

DeSoto Owner's Club of Maryland, George Sonneman, 9019 Old Harford Rd, Baltimore, MD 21234-2652; 410-665-6884

Mercedes-Benz Club America – Greater, Edward Hainke, 10755 Sawpit Cove Rd, Lusby, MD 20657; 410-326-2888

Street Cars of Desire Club, Curtis Lambdin, 9251 Furrow Ave, Ellicott City, MD 21042-1804; 410-461-0687

Massachusetts *Buick Club of America*, Minute Man Chapter, David Russo, 86 Lovell Rd, Watertown, MA 02172; 617-924-7187, 617-926-0432

Colonial Region Plymouth Club, Donald Kibbe, 456 Holyoke St, Ludlow, MA 01056; 413-589-9576

MAFCA Cape Cod, Peter Small, 43 Dartmoor Way, Yarmouthport, MA 02675; 508-362-6574, 508-771-7102

Night Cruzers of Bershire County, Glenn Roy, PO Box 672, Lanesboro, MA 01237; 413-499-8600, 413-448-6386

Power Wagons Unlimited, Kenneth Evans, 82 Coburn Rd, Tyngsboro, MA 01879; 508-649-9323

Yankee Chapter Pontiac Oakland Club, Dick Duclow, 9 June St, Peppermille, MA 01463

Michigan *Jackson Cascades VMCCA*, Ken Fish, 262 Harrington Rd, Parma, MI 49269; 517-531-3568

Lakeshore Chapter VMCCA, Norm Overpeck, 24290 Antoinette, Warren, MI 48089; 313-759-3095

Metro Detroit Chapter of NNN, Frank Miller, 18140 Tdepfer, Eastpointe, MI 48021; 313-779-4413

Misfit's Car Club, Joe Rothbauer, 1242 W Hickory Rd, Battle Creek, MI 49017; 616-966-5239

Model A Restorer's Club, Director of Regions, 24800 Michigan Ave, Dearborn, MI 48124; 313-278-1455, 313-278-2624

North American MGB Register, Jai Deagan, 11825 Columbia Hwy, Eaton Rapids, MI 48827; 800-NAMGBR-1

Minnesota *Gopher State Chevy's*, Ed Grieman, President, PO Box 120561, New Brighton, MN 55112; 612-571-8991

Itasca Vintage Car Club Inc, Harold La Frenier, PO Box 131, Grand Rapids, MN 55744; 218-328-5474

SE Minnesota Super Cars, Bruce Frondal, PO Box 261, Hayfield, MN 55940; 507-477-3170

Tall Pines Region Plymouth Club, Roger Ramberg, 10821 Russell Ave S, Bloomington, MN 55431; 612-888-9166

Mississippi *The Antique Vehicle Club of Mississippi*, Robert Jackman, PO Box 55792, Jackson, MS 39216; 601-957-2442, 601-957-7557

Missouri *Archway Olds Club*, John Palmberger, 11366 Birmingham Ct, St Louis, MO 63138; 314-355-4864

Audrain Antique Auto Association, Alan Hiles, 23 Tripoli, Mexico, MO 65265; 314-581-8544

Heart of America Corvair Owners Association, Michael Dawson, 9802 Booth, Kansas City, MO 64134; 816-763-9025

Heartland Vintage Thunderbird Club, Don Kimrey, PO Box 18113, Raytown, MO 64133

High Performance Auto Club, Dick Drake, 42 Lone Pine Dr, Cleveland, MO 64734; 816-658-7284

Hudson Essex Terraplane Club Inc, Dick Sheridan, 14644 Arpent Ln, Florissant, MO 63034; 314-921-1350

Kansas City Triumphs Club, Ann Adkins, 8002 NW 9 Hwy, Parkville, MO 64152; 816-587-2242

Mid-America Chapter BCA, Steve Hartwich, 8240 Summit, Kansas City, MO 64114-2244

Mineral Area Mustang, Donna Flieg, R #2, Box 2335, St Genevieve, MO 63670; 314-483-2266

Ozark Farm Chevys, John Woods, Rt 1, Box 757, Steelville, MO 65565, 314-775-5770

South Central Antique & Custom Car, Donald Crum, 17335 Ridge Rd, Houston, MO 65483; 417-967-3793

Nevada *Veteran Motor Car Club of America*, Art Foote, 3535 Freedom Ave, Las Vegas, NV 89121; 702-451-0026

White Pine Historical Car Club, Kevin Carnes, PO Box 153, Ely, NV 89301; 702-289-4638

New Hampshire *Keene Area Klassics Car Club*, Dave Phillips, PO Box 375, Keene, NH 03431, 603-336-7492, 603-352-8544

Profile Automobile League Inc, James Moreland, Treasurer, PO Box 1465, New London, NH 03257-1465; 603-526-6526

New Jersey *American Iron Motorcycle Club Inc*, Ed Natale Jr, Box 222, Wyckoff, NJ 07481-0222

Classic Cruizers, Frank Aadahl, 535 Church St, Bound Brook, NJ 08805; 908-469-7309

Garden State 50s Auto Club, Bob Crawford, President, 441 Esibil Ave, Nillville, NJ 08332; 609-825-0628

Jersey Lakeland Region Vintage Chevy, Ronald Panicucci, 281 Saw Mill Rd, North Haledon, NJ 07508; 201-423-0350, 201-423-5175

North Jersey Thunderbird Association, Ezra Hinkle, 7 Carol Pl, Wayne, NJ 07470; 201-694-9597

Nostalgic Automobile Society of Montclair, Tom Robinson, 92 Willowdale Ave, Montclair, NJ 07042; 201-783-4732

New York *Antique Auto Association of Brooklyn*, Michael Graff, 824 E 21 St, Brooklyn, NY 11210; 718-434-0351

Automobilists of the Upper Hudson, Kenneth Gypson, 14 Loomis Rd, Wynantskill, NY 12198; 518-283-1574

Back to the 50s Nostalgia Club, Dan Slezak, 27 Hastings St, Dix Hills, NY 11746; 516-242-0532

Capital District Chevy Club, Bob Adler, 801 NY Rt 43, Stephentown, NY 12168; 518-733-5749

Classic Mustang Long Island Region MCA, Philip Mascolo, 53 Sunset Rd, Massapequa, NY 11758; 516-798-6223

Cortland Antique Auto Club, Clifford Norte, PO Box 309, Cortland, NY 13045; 607-838-3311

Finger Lakes Chapter Buick Club, J E Dierks, 417 Westminster Rd, Rochester, NY 14607; 716-473-5508

Greater Rochester Mustangs & Fords, President, PO Box 18734, Rochester, NY 14618; 716-586-3459

Livingston Region AACA, W Russel Laidlaw, 3775 North Rd, Genesee, NY 14454; 716-243-1650

Lone Wolves Street Rd Association of Long Island, Gordon Haner, 4 Cassie Ct, Mt Sinai, NY 11766; 516-928-9399

Long Island Buick Club, Susan Heilig, 25 21st St, Jericho, NY 11753-2543; 516-931-4336

Long Island Corvair Association, Dick Downes, 88 Budenos Dr, Sayville, NY 11782; 516-567-0655

Long Island Corvette Owners Association, Ron Kober, President, PO Box 191, East Meadow, NY 11554

Long Island Ford-Mercury Club Inc, Peter Stevens, PO Box 336, Ronkonkoma, NY 11779; 516-265-4161

Long Island Late Great Chevys, William Nicholson, 17 Glen Ln, Glen Head, NY 11545; 516-531-7891, 516-531-5327

Long Island Nostalgic Car Club, Denise Miller, 959 Shelburn Dr, Franklin Square, NY 11010; 516-825-0735

Long Island Pontiac/Oakland Club, David Worthington, PO Box 226, Aquebogue, NY 11931-0226; 516-722-3784

Long Island Thunderbird Club, Barry Bruck, 737 Kearny Dr, N Woodmere, NY 11581; 516-791-4940

Metropolitan Fire Association, PO Box 050235, Staten Island, NY 10305-0003; 718-720-3415

Mohawk Antique Auto Club, Duane Dodds, 49 Puritan Dr, Schenectady, NY 12306; 518-355-8865

Mohican Model A Ford Club, Peter Winnewisser, 4508 Ridge Rd, Cazenovia, NY 13035; 315-655-2000

Mystery Cruisers of Long Island, Eddie Korth, 93 Aspen Rd, Mastic Beach, NY 11951; 516-399-5262

Northern Cruisers Car Club, John Mumford, 7649 Easton St, Lowville, NY 13367; 315-376-3411

Oldsmobile Club of LINYC, Carlyn Kompel, 35 Earl Dr, Merrick, NY 11566; 516-623-4769

Original Lost in the 50s, Bob Noto, 94 Johnsneck Rd, Shirley, NY 11967; 516-281-8718

Peconic Bay Region Antique Car Club, Margaret Vitale, President, PO Box 1254, Lake Grove, NY 11755-1254; 516-589-4779, 516-589-7969

Prison City Ramblers, Tony Marrapese, PO Box 7325, Fingerlakes Mall, Auburn, NY 13022; 315-253-4779

Schoharie Valley Region AACA, Bob Addis, 1316 Thousand Acre Rd, Delanson, NY 12053; 518-827-5112

Still Cruisin', Johnny Intrieri, 168 Main Ave, Mastic, NY 11950; 516-281-4579, 4978

Street Classics Car Club, Willie Reid, 42 Hillview Village, Hinsdale, NY 14743; 716-557-2291

Terry's Car Club, Jim Cornwell, 2360 Jericho Tpk, Green City Park, NY 11040

Upstate NY Metropolitan Club, Pamela Davis, 784 Sacandaga Rd, Scotia, NY 12302; 518-399-6817

Vanderbilt Cup Region AACA, Tom Lamans, 478 N County Rd, St James, NY 11780; 516-862-7193

Vintage Thunderbird Club International, Bob Gadra, President, 65 E Center Rd, West Seneca, NY 14224-3217; 716-674-7251

Woodstock Motor Club Inc, John Brice, PO Box 433, Saugerties, NY 12477; 914-246-0765

North Carolina *Coastal Cruisers*, Maree Smith, PO Box 15101, Wilmington, NC 28408; 910-791-5379

Fayetteville Rapid Transit System, George Barnes, 5948 Spinner Rd, Hope Mills, NC 28348; 910-424-7148

West Side Cruisers, Chuck Krauz, PO Box 17511, Asheville, NC 28816; 704-683-4472

Ohio *AMC Rambler Club*, Frank Wrenick, 2645 Ashton Rd, Cleveland, OH 44118; 216-371-0226, 216-371-5946

Buckeye GTOs, Carl Bretmersky, 4074 Tennyson Ln, North Olmsted, OH 44070; 216-777-3214

Car Coddlers Club of Ohio, Norman Abston, 3994 Bullhead Rd, Willard, OH 44890; 419-935-0286

Central Ohio Chapter, Buick Club, Tom Schoener, 4125 Ongard Dr, Columbus, OH 43204; 614-276-9713

Classic Thunderbird Club of Dayton, Glenn Forsell, 6012 Cinnamon Tree Ct, Englewood, OH 45322; 513-833-6768, 513-833-4002

Glass City Chapter of the Buick Club, David Rex, 138 E Fifth, Perrysburg, OH 43551

Mid-Ohio Austin-Healey Club, Stu Riegel, 2139 Sonora Dr, Grove City, OH 43123

Mid-Ohio Ford Club, Patricia Burgess, 220 Robinwood Ave, Whitehall, OH 43213-1712; 614-235-0381

Northwest Ohio Street Machiners, Pete Lungulow, 829 Jean Rd, Toledo, OH 43615; 419-249-5744, 419-249-5790

Ohio Valley Region Model A Ford Club, Al Duebber, 477 Happy Dr, Cincinnati, OH 45238; 513-451-3570

Penn-Ohio A Ford Club Inc, Cliff Naugle, 17502 Laverne Ave, Cleveland, OH 44135; 216-671-9917

Shenango Valley AACA, Frederick Ross, 3097 Pothour Wheeler Rd, Hubbard, OH 44425; 216-534-4188

Tri-State F 100s, Dave Cooper, 946 Old US 52, New Richmond, OH 45157; 513-553-2528

Western Lake Erie Chapter, Studebaker, Edward Costell, 5831 Balfour, Sylvania, OH 43560; 419-882-1147

Oregon *Chrysler 300 Club Inc,* Ken Smith, PO Box 1110, Boring, OR 97009; 503-658-3310

High Desert Mustangs, Phil Sledge, PO Box 7934, Bend, OR 97702-7934; 503-546-3317

Oregon Mini Society, 9765 SW Frewing, Tigard, OR 97223

Portland Area Antique Car Clubs SW, Ken Thorpe, PO Box 23722, Portland, OR 97281-3722; 503-684-3391

Portland Triumph Owners Association, Dan Johannsen, PO Box 5516, Portland, OR 97228; 503-645-6324

Rogue Valley Old Timer Car Club Inc, PO Box 695, Medford, OR 97501; 541-535-4672

Rose City Model T Club, Yvonne Townsend, PO Box 3901, Portland, OR 97208; 503-656-8648

Trick'n Racy Cars, Dennis Smith, PO Box 5185, Oregon City, OR 97045-8185

Pennsylvania *BCA Appalachian Chapter,* Gene Cunningham, Box 409, Hastings, PA 16646; 814-247-6226

Blair County Antique Auto Club, Ken Wills, 535 Bottom Rd, Ashville, PA 16613; 814-674-5301

Delaware Valley Classic T-Bird Club, David Fiedler, 5188 Judson Dr, Bensalem, PA 19020; 610-668-6543, 610-668-9318

Dream Machines Motor Club, Luanne Bittenbender, PO Box 137, Catawissa, PA 17820; 717-759-2312, 717-784-2241

Greater Pittsburgh Mustang Club, Gary White, 215 Church Ln, Pittsburgh, PA 15238; 412-767-5243, 412-782-1817

Kinzua Valley Region AACA, Deborah Ansell, 1806 Pennsylvania Ave E, Warren, PA 16365; 814-723-3633

Lanco MG Club, Dennis Blevins, 1213 River Rd, Quarryville, PA 17566; 717-872-7528

North Hills Historic Auto Club, Frank Pribanic, 100 Cherrington Dr, Pittsburgh, PA 15237; 412-487-2094

NY State Allegheny Valley Region, Clyde Johnson, RD 1, Box 481, Port Allegheny, PA 16743; 814-642-2423

Pittsburgh CARS, Joe Ciaramella Jr, 198 Firwood Dr, Bridgeville, PA 15017; 412-221-4707

Rolls-Royce Owner's Club, 191 Hempt Rd, Mechanicsburg, PA 17055

Steel City Classics Inc, Raymond Ford, 701 Prestley Ave, Carnegie, PA 15106; 412-276-0384

Vintage Car Club of America Inc, Rich Jackson, 1505 Rosalie Ave, Bensalem, PA 19020

Vintage Volkswagen Club of America, Jim Siegfried, 5705 Gordon Dr, Harrisburg, PA 17112; 717-540-9972

South Carolina *Swamp Fox Region AACA,* Charles Robinson, 4569 W Belmont Cir, Florence, SC 29501; 803-669-1474

Tennessee *Blount British Cars Ltd,* Pete Cox, 107 Navajo Dr, Maryville, TN 37801; 615-983-5893

Mid-South Region Antique, Joyce Gray, 2842 Darolyn, Bartlett, TN 38134

Mid-Tenn Classic Chevy Club, Ron Compton, PO Box 955, Madison, TN 37115; 615-824-7522, 615-824-4488

West Tennessee Chapter, Studebaker, William Schultz, 2548 Strathspey Cove, Memphis, TN 38119

Texas *Classic Thunderbird Club International,* C L Hood, Box 549, Little Elm, TX 75068

Texas Triumph Register, Leonard Myers, PO Box 40847, Houston, TX 77240-0847; 713-973-2735, 713-973-9906

Utah *Great Salt Lake Chapter of POCI,* David Johnson, 59 N Broadway, Tooele, UT 84074

Vermont *Now and Then Vehicle Club,* Margaret Fischer, RD 1, Box 172, Putney, VT 05346; 802-387-4108

Yesteryear Motor Car Club, Max Brand, 20 Bramley Way, Bellows Fall, VT 05101

Virginia *G Washington Chapter MAFCA,* Vernon Region, James Cartmill, President, 3903 Old Lee Highway, Fairfax, VA 22030; 703-369-6699

George Washington Chapter, Perry Dunn, 3903 Old Lee Hwy, Fairfax, VA 22030

National Capital Area Vintage Triumph, Charlie Brown, 2400 Stone Hedge Dr, Alexandria, VA 22306

Northern Virginia Corvair Club, George Anderson, 3019 Millstream Ct Herndon, Herndon, VA 22071; 703-391-5675

Star City Chapter of POCI, Steven Royal, 2129 Meadowbrook Rd, Roanoke, VA 24017; 540-562-2291

Washington *Bowtie Bunch,* Peggy Hesner, 12323 109th Ave Ct E, Puyllallup, WA 98374

Bremerton Auto Club, Les Parizek, 3230 View Crest Dr NE, Bremerton, WA 98310; 206-373-5358

Corsa Northwest, Bob Smith, PO Box 42093, Tacoma, WA 98442; 206-531-0438

Ford Galaxie Club of America, William Barber, PO Box 360, Salkum, WA 98582-0360; 360-377-4957

Olympic Classic Thunderbird Club, Frank Stubbs, 8331 144th Pl SE 1, Newcastle, WA 98059; 206-228-7198, 206-242-4980

Walla Walla Historical Auto Club, President, PO Box 153, Walla Walla, WA 99362

Wisconsin *Badger Wheel Studebaker Club,* Pat Knutson, 1177 Early Dr, Eau Claire, WI 54703; 715-834-4405

Chippewa Valley Model A Club, Charles Veicht, Rt 2, Box 324, Cornell, WI 54732; 715-239-6710

Cream City Chapter Buick Club, Gustave Obselka, 4581 N 60 St, Milwaukee, WI 53218-5620

NEW I Reg Group, Early Ford V8 Club, George Protogere, 519 S Buchanan St, Appleton, WI 54915; 414-739-4878

Packerland Region of VCCA, Roland Becker, 626 Vroman St, Green Bay, WI 54303; 414-497-8095

Wausau Antique Automobile Club, Rick Hunt, Editor, PO Box 104, Wausau, WI 54402-0104

Wisconsin Region Antique Auto Club, Vincent Ruffolo, 2104 Washington Rd, Kenosha, WI 53140-5335; 414-658-2600

Wisconsin Region CCCA, Warren Jensen, 2427 S 93rd St, West Allis, WI 53227, 414-545-4508

Australia
Australian Porsche 356 Register Inc, Phillip Schudmak, PO Box 7356, St Kilde Rd, Melbourne, VIC 3004, Australia; 61 39 867 2663, 61 36 866 3560

Canada
Rolls-Royce Club, Hugh Young, 1892 Cochrane St, Victoria, BC Canada V8R 3H3; 604-592-8366, 604-592-8390

state councils:

California
California Association of Four Wheel Drive, Peter Horvath, 3104 O St #313, Sacramento, CA 95816-6519; 916-332-8890, 916-332-1730

Car Club Council of Greater, Obie Oberlander, 1518 Enfield St, Spring Valley, CA 91977; 619-463-4558

Colorado
Old Car Council of Colorado Inc, Tom Ward, PO Box 280042, Lakewood, CO 80228; 303-893-8656

Georgia
Georgia Association of Motor Clubs, Vernon Peppers, President, 3819 Beya Way, Atlanta, GA 30340; 404-493-9042

Illinois
British Car Union, W Kowalski, PO Box 486, Hinsdale, IL 60522-0486; 708-852-6898, 708-852-2077

COVA of Illinois, Mark Warden, 10400 Roberts Rd, Palos Hills, IL 60465; 708-598-7113, 708-598-4888

Illinois Classic Auto Preservation Society, David Bliss, PO Box 1138, 102 W Elm, Effingham, IL 62401

Indiana
Council of Area Car Clubs, Mark Jones, 8108 Newfield Dr, Ft Wayne, IN 46815; 219-749-0490

Kansas
Kansas Council for COVA, Dave Boyd, 409 Nebraska Ave, Holton, KS 66436; 913-364-2779 (h)

Massachusetts
Mass Antique Auto Council, Robert Smith, 193 High St, Reading, MA 01867; 617-944-3447

Michigan
COVA of Michigan, Dennis Caney, 1549 Seven Mile Rd, Sanford, MI 48657; 517-687-2346

Missouri
Mid-America Association, Charles Evilsizer, PO Box 101, Raymondville, MO 65555; 417-457-6518

Nebraska
ENWI Car Council, Paul High, 12559 O St, Omaha, NE 68137-1906; 402-895-0629, 402-552-5969

New Jersey
New Jersey VORC, Jere Duffett, 17 Larsen Park Dr, Medford, NJ 08055; 609-983-8246, 609-231-7911

New York
Association of Car Enthusiasts, Art Misuraca, PO Box 636, Kenmore, NY 14217-0636; 716-627-3619

Long Island Chapter of COVA, Charles Ritschel, 135 E 25 St, Huntington, NY 11746; 516-427-9451, 516-427-2424, 516-427-2457

Long Island Chapter of COVA, John Morrison, 117 Third St, Garden City, NY 11530; 516-741-1322

Ohio
COVA of Ohio, Glenn Miller, 205 Greenfield Dr, Bryan, OH 43506; 419-636-4604

Oregon
Inter Club Council, Gary Dalton, 614 Overlook Dr, North Bend, OR 97459; 503-746-3375

Oregon Council of Vehicle Associations, Dick Larrowe, 37600 Sunset St #30, Sandy, OR 97055; 503-668-4096

Pennsylvania
Mid-Atlantic Packard, Darwin Moyer, 617 Sunset Dr, Dillsburg, PA 17019; 717-432-5762

South Carolina
Carolina Car Club Council, Jerry Brown, Rt 3, Box 1195, Manning, SC 29102; 803-473-4993

Texas
Texas Vehicle Club Council, Troy Mennis, 805 Natchez Ave, Bedford, TX 76022; 817-283-6942

Washington
Washington Car Club Council, Don Berry, PO Box 2054, Everett, WA 98203-0054; 206-347-1431

Wisconsin
Wisconsin Automobile Clubs in Association Inc, Richard Dorsey, 5114 State Rd 44, Oshkosh, WI 54904; 414-589-4652

Australia
Australia Historic Motoring Federation Inc, Terry Thompson, President, GPO Box 2862, Canberra ACT1, Australia 2601; 06-231-6060

Canada
NAAACCC (National Association of Antique Automobile Clubs of Canada), Harly Plougmann, #200, 52065, RR #210, North Cooking, AB Canada T8G 1H1; 403-922-5758

Saskatchewan Association Antique Auto Clubs, Thomas Woodhouse, 529 Princess St, Estevan, SK Canada S4A 2E8; 306-634-8178, 306-634-6234

Specialty Vehicle Association of British Columbia, WR Peigl, PO Box 47511, 1-1020 Austin Ave, Coquitlam, BC Canada V3K 6T3; 604-859-0755

Specialty Vehicle Association of Ontario, Chris Whillans, 3007 Kingston Rd, Box 142, Scarborough, ON Canada M1M 1P1; 905-649-2664

National Motorists Assn
6678 Pertzborn Rd
Dane, WI 53529
608-849-6000; FAX: 608-849-8697, 800-882-2785, information

Founded 1982. 15,000+ members. Represents the interests of American drivers. Promotes rational traffic regulation, motorist courtesy and works to eliminate abusive insurance company practices, speed traps and other infringements of motorists' rights. Strong grass roots organization. State chapter coordinators. State and national lobbying. Politcal campaign involvement. Editorials and news releases. Bimonthly national newsletter. Quarterly statewide newsletters. Dues: $29/year individual, $39/year family, $65/year business. For membership information: 800-882-2785.

Specialty Equipment Market Association(SEMA)
1575 S Valley Vista Dr
PO Box 4910
Diamond Bar, CA 91765
909-396-0289 ext 113; FAX: 909-860-0184

Founded 1963. 3,100 members including manufacturers, distributors, retailers, installers, restylers, jobbers, restorers, car dealers, race facilities, and others. SEMA is a trade association that represents the producers and marketers of specialty equipment products and services for the automotive aftermarket. SEMA's mission is to help members' businesses succeed and prosper. Web site: http://www.sema.org

---

Street Rod Marketing Alliance (SRMA)
PO Box 4910
Diamond Bar, CA 91765
909-396-0289; FAX: 909-860-0184
E-mail: mike1@sema.org

SRMA, the Street Rod Marketing Alliance, is a council of the Specialty Equipment Market Association (SEMA). SRMA is dedicated to addressing the challenges facing this segment of the

Clubs & Organizations

automotive aftermarket and to preserving and promoting the street rod industry. SRMA members are the manufacturers, builders/fabricators, dealers, car clubs and enthusiast publications that make up the street rod industry. SRMA focuses on industry-specific issues, developing effective strategies and programs that will assist members in improving their businesses. Special attention is given to addressing those legislative and/or regulatory matters which affect the rodding industry.

World Organization of Auto Hobbyists
PO Box 5624
Grand Forks, ND 58206
701-746-7485; FAX: 701-775-9491

For information contact Jack Widdel, VP Legislative Affairs, at the above address. Founded 1988. Membership includes 50 states+. Interested in legislation centered around the automobile, the hobby, and its preservation. Has a networking system for states to strengthen their own Car Club Council and its members. Publication: *WOAH News*, free quarterly publication with information on automotive legislation, state and federal. No dues.

State and Local

Citizens Against Repressive Zoning
PO Box 536
Haslett, MI 48840
517-351-6751; FAX: 517-339-4926
E-mail: malzoning@aol.com

Founded 1988. 100 members. Incorporated foundation. We publish an occasional newsletter. We are concerned with zoning zealots who abuse property and civil rights of individual collectors, salvage yards, rechrome shops, paint shops. Donations only.

Council of Vehicle Associations of Michigan
PO Box 536
Haslett, MI 48840
517-351-6751; FAX: 517-339-4926

Founded 1992. 50 member clubs. We meet bi-monthly. We are organizing all Michigan clubs and vehicle enthusiasts to resist unfair EPA laws, unfair zoning, unfair taxing. Dues: $1/year club member; $10/year individual; $50/year business.

Legislative Council of Motor Vehicle Clubs
PO Box 291
Hershey, PA 17033
717-533-9032

Founded 1977. 75 member clubs. LCMVC is a legislative watchdog organization which monitors prospective legislation relevant to antique and collectible vehicles in Pennsylvania. Dues: $35 per club, $15/associate members.

Tri River Car Club Council
1713 Eben St
Pittsburgh, PA 15226
412-341-5988; FAX: 412-341-9990

Founded 1993. 29 clubs. Open to all clubs, plus individual memberships. Bi-monthly meetings and newsletter. Sponsor socials, cruises and car show judges. Instrumental in leading opposition to central emissions testing and rfg gas. Wrote the legislation for new classic, antique and collector license plates. Dues: $40/year per club.

United Street Rods of Idaho
116 Provident Dr
Boise, ID 83706
208-336-0223; FAX: 208-377-0344
E-mail: pmartin@ipc.state.id.us

Founded 1979. 1,200 members. No restrictions joining. Legislative watch, newsletters, yearly events calendar. Dues: $5/year.

Wanderer's Car Club Central CA
Lynn & Norm Hubbard, Founders
1908 Belle Terr
Bakersfield, CA 93304-4352
805-397-7786

This is an open club with no meetings or rules. No snivelers.

Wisconsin Car Clubs Alliance (WCCA)
PO Box 562
Menomonee Falls, WI 53052-0562
414-255-5385

Founded 1989. 47 members. We are an alliance of car clubs. Each club has one vote, no matter how large or small. We are a watchdog group for legislation for and against our hobby. We also offer an individual membership. They can come to any meeting (four a year), get our newsletter, but have no vote. *WCCA Newsletter* comes with membership 4-6 times a year. It contains any information we can get on things that affect our hobby. We also list our members' car shows, swap meets and any other event they sponsor. Dues: $20/year club; $15/year individual.

Clubs & Organizations

Section Four:
Publications & Information Sources

This section contains publications for car collectors as well as sources of information, photos, technical data, restoration information, and historical data. It does not include literature dealers, which are found both in Section One under marque specialists and Section Two under literature generalists. There are five categories.

Information Sources. These are businesses or individuals offering specific or general information which may be purchased.

Books & Publications. In this category are publishers and other suppliers of books, single pamphlets, and magazine back issues.

Periodicals. Included here are magazines and other publications to which the hobbyists may subscribe. Many are also available in the form of back issues. Subscription prices were current

when the publishers submitted listings, but may have increased by the time the *Almanac* reaches you.

Newsletters ordinarily deal with investment/market condition aspects of car collecting and related fields.

Research & Reference Libraries. Includes private and public archives, libraries, specialized collections and reference sources. Many are not open to the general public and may require special arrangements to visit. Most libraries and other organizations will charge for finding and sending research material. When writing to them, be as specific as possible. Don't for instance, ask them to "send everything you have on 1951 XYZ's." The more precise you are in your request the better the response will be.

Information Sources

1958 Thunderbird Convertible Registry	book
Bill Van Ess	
2306 Post Dr NE	
Belmont, MI 49306	
616-364-1973; FAX: 616-363-2870	

See full listing in **Section One** under **Thunderbird**

AACA Library & Research Center	research library
501 W Governor Rd, PO Box 417	
Hershey, PA 17033	
717-534-2082	

See full listing in **Section Four** under **research libraries**

AARcadia Parts Locating	parts
8294 Allport Ave	
Santa Fe Springs, CA 90670	
310-698-8067; FAX: 310-696-6505	

See full listing in **Section One** under **MoPar**

All-American Auto Mags	literature
The Old Co-Op	
114 Middlewich Rd	
Clive, Winsford	
Cheshire CW7 3NT England	
01606-558252; FAX: 01606-559211	

See full listing in **Section Two** under **literature dealers**

American Automotive Heritage Foundation (AAHF)	legislative watch organization
PO Box 482	
Carlisle, PA 17013-0482	
717-240-0976; FAX: 717-240-0931	

See full listing in **Section Three** under **legislative watch organizations**

AMX Enterprises Ltd	information source
7963 Depew St	
Arvada, CO 80003-2527	
303-428-8760	

AMC performance and handling expert. Custom sway bar packages, 4-wheel disc brakes, one-piece solid axles and more. Specialty in AMX, Javelin and other AMC performance cars. Also full restoration services and restoration parts. Service and technical help on all AMC cars. Since 1974. Brokerage and finding service available. Larry Mitchell, owner.

Gary G Anderson	periodical
343 Second St, Suite H	
Los Altos, CA 94022-3639	
415-949-9680; FAX: 415-949-9685	

See full listing in **Section Four** under **periodicals**

Auto/Link	books
PO Box 460723	
Houston, TX 77056-8723	
713-973-1008	
713-973-1133 on-line service	
E-mail: alink@accesscom.net	

See full listing in **Section Four** under **books & publications**

Automotive Information Clearinghouse	information source
PO Box 1746	
La Mesa, CA 91944	
619-447-7200	
FAX: 619-447-8080, include address	

America's largest stocking warehouse for original manufacturer's publications. Shop, owner's, parts manuals, sales brochures and more. Totally computerized, 10 second quotes, 34 years' experience.

Bill Boudway	restoration info
105 Deerfield Dr	
Canandaigua, NY 14424	
716-394-6172	

See full listing in **Section One** under **Packard**

Car Club Group | book
PO Box 338
Poynette, WI 53955
608-635-7751

See full listing in **Section Four** under **books & publications**

"Check The Oil!" Magazine | periodical
PO Box 937
Powell, OH 43065-0937
614-848-5038; FAX: 614-436-4760

See full listing in **Section Two** under **petroliana**

Classic Motorbooks | books
PO Box 1/HMN | videos
729 Prospect Ave
Osceola, WI 54020
800-826-6600; FAX: 715-294-4448

See full listing in **Section Four** under **books & publications**

Coin-Op Classics Magazine | periodical
17844 Toiyabe St
Fountain Valley, CA 92708
714-756-8746; FAX: 714-963-1716
E-mail: pmovsesian@aol.com

See full listing in **Section Four** under **periodicals**

Collector Car & Truck Prices | price guide
41 N Main St
North Grafton, MA 01536
508-839-6707; FAX: 508-839-6266
E-mail: vmr@ultranet.com

See full listing in **Section Four** under **periodicals**

Publications

Cruise Consultants Group | book
PO Box 338 | consultant
Poynette, WI 53955
608-635-7751

See full listing in **Section Two** under **consultants**

DeTomaso Registry | book
Bill Van Ess
2306 Post Dr NE
Belmont, MI 49306
616-364-1973; FAX: 616-363-2870

See full listing in **Section One** under **DeTomaso/Pantera**

Eliot James Enterprises Inc | development info
PO Box 3986
Dana Point, CA 92629-8986
714-661-0889; FAX: 714-661-1901

See full listing in **Section Four** under **books & publications**

Ferraris.com | online guide
52 Payn Ave
Chatham, NY 12037-1427
PH/FAX: 518-392-7234
E-mail: editor@ferraris.com

See full listing in **Section One** under **Ferrari**

Arthur Freakes | researcher
Dept 3, Kingfisher Ct | writer
East Molesey
Surrey KT8 9HL England
PH/FAX: 0181-941-0604

Motoring writer, historian, researcher. Editor of *HCKC News* and *Rootes Group Vehicles*. Also editor of *The Mitchamian*. Research and information on Rootes Group, Hillman, Commer for motor vehicle publications.

GMC Solutions | literature
Robert English | parts
PO Box 675
Franklin, MA 02038-0675
508-520-3900; FAX: 508-520-7861
E-mail: oldcarkook@aol.com

See full listing in **Section One** under **GMC**

Leon Henry Inc | list brokers
455 Central Ave, Dept HVA | package inserts
Scarsdale, NY 10583
914-723-3176; FAX: 914-723-0205

Full service package insert/mailing list broker/manager. In our 41st year. Our brokers can place your inserts into merchandise packages, statements, co-ops, ride-alongs, card decks, sample kits, etc, to target your prospective customer. We are managers for package insert programs including Eckler's Corvette Parts, Performance Products and Summit Racing Equipment. Let us put inserts into your packages.

Hupmobile Club
158 Pond Rd
N Franklin, CT 06254

See full listing in **Section Three** under **Hupmobile**

IPTC Publishing | manuals
300 SW 12th Ave
Pompano Beach, FL 33069
800-653-4198

See full listing in **Section Four** under **books & publications**

The Italian Car Registry	information source
3305 Valley Vista Rd	
Walnut Creek, CA 94598-3943	
510-458-1163	

Mail order only. An information exchange for Italian built and coachbuilt cars on any chassis. The only worldwide registry for Italian cars of any make. Extensive production information already compiled for Abarth, Alfa Romeo, Allemano, Arnolt, ASA, Bandini, Bertone, Bizzarini, Cisitalia, DeTomaso, Dual Ghia, Ermini, Ferrari, Fiat, Ghia, Giannini, Giaur, Intermeccanica, Iso, Isotta-Fraschini, Italia, Lamborghini, Lancia, Maserati, Michelotti, Moretti, Nardi, Nash-Healey, OM, Osca, Osella, Otas, Pininfarina, Siata, Stabilimenti Farina, Stanguellini, Taraschi, Touring, Vignale, Volpini, Zagato and more. Legal SASE for information. Now available: 1994 compilation of 16,000+ cars listed by chassis numbers, 350 pages, for $35 postpaid in USA. Others, please inquire.

Jaguar Cars Inc Archives	literature sales research
555 MacArthur Blvd	
Mahwah, NJ 07430	
201-818-8144; FAX: 201-818-0281	

Mail order only. On-site research by appointment only. Provides individual vehicle research from Jaguar/Daimler build records for owners only. Fee includes JDHT certificate. Other holdings include Jaguar parts, service and owner's manuals, technical/service bulletins, paint/trim information, marketing, advertising and photographic collection. Send SASE to receive a form for vehicle or other technical research or for a list of items for sale (please specify).

Lost Highways	slide show & film presentation
Todd & Kristin Kimmell	
PO Box 43737	
Philadelphia, PA 19106	
215-925-2568	

RV and mobile home historians, Todd & Kristin Kimmell, present a history of recreational vehicles living on wheels, from auto camping in the teens and twenties to Lucy and Desi in *The Long, Long Trailer* in the fifties. The Kimmells will travel to an event for a reasonable honorarium to present the show in person or send $35 for a video tape of the complete presentation.

Main Attractions	posters videos
PO Box 4923	
Chatsworth, CA 91313	
818-709-9855; FAX: 818-998-0906	

Hot rod, classic car, drag racing, early NASCAR and biker flicks on video. *Thunder Road, Big Wheel, Drag Strip Girl, Hell on Wheels, Funny Car Summer, Stock Car Memories, Fireball 500, Hot Rod to Hell* and thousands more available.

MoPar Collector's Guide Magazine	periodical
10067 El Camino Ave	
Baton Rouge, LA 70815	
504-926-6954; FAX: 504-924-5456	

See full listing in **Section One** under **MoPar**

Peerless Co-Operator Newsletter	ads literature manuals newsletter
1094 Brookdale Dr	
Crestline, OH 44827	
419-683-3174	

See full listing in **Section Four** under **newsletters**

Petroleum Collectibles Monthly	periodical
411 Forest St	
LaGrange, OH 44050	
216-355-6608; FAX: 216-355-4955	

See full listing in **Section Four** under **periodicals**

William D Siuru Jr, PhD PE	information source
4050 Dolphin Cir	
Colorado Springs, CO 80918	
719-528-1980	

Mail order only. Research and technical consultation for all makes of cars. Also advice on collector cars as investments. Freelance automotive journalist.

Richard Spiegelman Productions Inc	photography slides
19 Guild Hall Dr	
Scarborough, ON Canada M1R 3Z7	
416-759-1644	

Photography, large slide file on old cars, color slide, 4x5 transparencies, slide shows, film productions.

Sting-Ray City	newsletter
PO Box 13343	
Scottsdale, AZ 85267	
602-314-2312	

Newsletter catering to the Schwinn Sting-Ray enthusiast. Facts, features and classified ads for Schwinn Sting-Ray bicycles manufactured from 1963 to the late 1970s. Publishes *Sting-Ray City News*. Bimonthly publication. Subscription rate: $12/year, sample issue $2. Also publishes *Klassified*. Monthly newsletter with Schwinn Sting-Ray ads only. Subscription rate: $15/year. Combo subscription special, $25.

Sunburst Technology	electronic technical consultant
PO Box 598	
Lithia Springs, GA 30057	
770-949-2979; FAX: 770-942-6091	
E-mail:10274592422@compuserv.com	

Sunburst Technology can customize your electrical, electronic and micro processor controls for auto, home and shop. A Sunburst micro parameter controller can be designed to monitor, control or adapt your machine to operate the way you want. As a technical consultant/manufacturer, Sunburst can write custom software programs to control almost any electro-mechanical powered options. Let Sunburst design your next application for engine, electrical options, alarms/monitoring and power drives. Call, we can help.

See our ad on page 524

This Old Truck Magazine	periodical
PO Box 562	
Yellow Springs, OH 45387	
800-767-5828; 937-767-1433	
FAX: 767-2726	
E-Mail: antique@antiquepower.com	

See full listing in **Section Four** under **periodicals**

Thunderbird Information eXchange	newsletter
8421 E Cortez St	
Scottsdale, AZ 85260	
602-948-3996	

See full listing in **Section One** under **Thunderbird**

University Motors Ltd	parts service technical information
6490 E Fulton	
Ada, MI 49301	
616-682-0800; FAX: 616-682-0801	

See full listing in **Section One** under **MG**

Vehicles In Motion	directory purchasing guide
1000 W Crosby #100	
Carrollton, TX 75006	
214-242-2453; FAX: 214-446-1919	

See full listing in **Section One** under **Harley-Davidson**

Publications

Vintage Parts 411 | books
PO Box 22893
San Diego, CA 92192
800-MOTORHEAD
FAX: 619-560-9900
E-mail: vp411@electriciti.com

Mail order only. *Vintage Part Sources* is updated annually. Publishing highly organized books on where to find parts for specific old cars. Different editions for different cars (full-size Chevy, GTO, Mustang, etc). Separate sections for dealers specializing in parts for body, interior, trim, engine, rubber, suspension, as well as literature. The book also contains parts restoration specialists and a nationwide listing of salvage yards specializing in old cars. Finding parts is easy because every page in the book is for your car. $12.75 plus shipping per book.

Visual Marketplace Online Inc | online auto ads
800 Silverado, Suite 324
La Jolla, CA 92037
619-459-3846; FAX: 619-459-3460
E-mail: pyoung@icreations.com

Mail order only. Visual Marketplace Online Inc is an electronic publishing clearinghouse for buyers and sellers of automobiles including classics, antiques, foreign, domestic, kit cars and replicars. Free to Internet users, 24 hours/day. Advertising fees. Web site: http://www.vmarket.com

Wolverine Video | videos
300 Stonecliffe Aisle
Irvine, CA 92715-5728
714-854-5171; FAX: 714-854-2154

"Wild, radical" says *Car and Driver* magazine of Wolverine's detailed and comprehensive coverage of the motor culture. From the 1995 International Bugatti Rally hosted by the American Bugatti Club to Bonneville Salt Flats, Muroc and El Mirage Dry Lake Speed Trials, major rod & custom events, important Concours events, unbelievable Harley runs, marque and club meets and scale model exhibitions. Its all here. See the pages of your favorite magazines come to life.

Books & Publications

1958 Thunderbird Convertible Registry | book
Bill Van Ess
2306 Post Dr NE
Belmont, MI 49306
616-364-1973; FAX: 616-363-2870

See full listing in **Section One** under **Thunderbird**

ADP Parts Services | interchange info manuals
14800 28th Ave N
Plymouth, MN 55447
800-825-0644; FAX: 612-553-0270

See full listing in **Section Two** under **car & parts locators**

All-American Auto Mags | literature
The Old Co-Op
114 Middlewich Rd
Clive, Winsford
Cheshire CW7 3NT England
01606-558252; FAX: 01606-559211

See full listing in **Section Two** under **literature dealers**

Gary G Anderson | periodical
343 Second St, Suite H
Los Altos, CA 94022-3639
415-949-9680; FAX: 415-949-9685

See full listing in **Section Four** under **periodicals**

Archway Press Inc | garage blueprints
19 W 44th St
New York, NY 10036
800-374-4766

Protect Your Vintage Beauty (and gain affordable loft/living space). Fully illustrated brochure describes 20 garage/loft plans for 2 to 5 cars. Professional building blueprints available for every plan. Call or write to order.

Auto Interchange Systems | books
Doug Johnson
PO Box 12385
Las Vegas, NV 89112
702-454-9170

Mail order. Interchange parts manuals covering 1950-65 Ford, GM, Chrysler and 1963-74 Ford products. 15-day money back guarantee.

Auto/Link | books
PO Box 460723
Houston, TX 77056-8723
713-973-1008, voice
713-973-1133 on-line service/BBS
E-mail: alink@accesscom.net

Auto/Link is an on-line system that is for the muscle car and collector car enthusiast. It is a BBS/web site combination that provides all callers access to the Internet and to auto-related resources. Auto/Link provides: 1. free Cutting Edge web browser/terminal software; 2. Telenet/web server; 3. 100s of photos for viewing; 4. on-line chat/message forum; 5. the best games including drag racing; 6. your favorite vendor's catalogs; 7. personal E-mail. Web site: http://www.alink.accesscom.net

Auto Review Publishing | publications
PO Box 510
Florissant, MO 63032
314-355-3609

Publisher of automotive restoration and historical books. Recent titles include: *Restorer's Classic Car* shop manual; *AA Truck* supplement to *Restorer's Model A* shop manual and *Selling the New Ford 1927-1931*. Upcoming books include: *Fleetwood, The Company and the Coachcraft*. Price list and information available on request. The Auto Review was established in 1906.

Auto Zone | books periodicals models videos
1895 S Woodward Ave
Birmingham, MI 48009
800-647-7288; FAX: 810-852-4070

See full listing in **Section Two** under **models & toys**

Autophile Car Books | books models
1685 Bayview Ave
Toronto, ON Canada M4G 3C1
PH/FAX: 416-483-8898

Retail store specializing in new and used car books and 1/43 scale models and kits of cars.

Autoquotes | price guide
2696 Brookmar
York, PA 17404
PH/FAX: 717-792-4936

See full listing in **Section Two** under **automobilia**

Autosport Marketing | apparel automobilia
PO Box 29033
Christ Church 4 NZ New Zealand
PH/FAX: 00-64-3-3519476

See full listing in **Section Two** under **apparel**

Publications

Robert Bentley Publishers
1033 Massachusetts Ave
Cambridge, MA 02138
800-423-4595; FAX: 617-876-9235
E-mail: sales@rb.com

books
manuals

Robert Bentley Publishers is the authoritative source for official factory service information and enthusiasts books on a multitude of automotive topics including parts identification, high-performance tuning, fuel injection, aerodynamics, engineering, vintage racing and competition driving. Bentley has books and service manuals for Volkswagen, Audi, BMW, Bosch, Saab, Volvo, Alfa Romeo, MG, Austin-Healey, Jaguar, Land Rover, Range Rover, MG, Triumph, Morris Minor, Jeep, Ford, Chevrolet and Toyota.

BritBooks
62 Main St
Otego, NY 13825
PH/FAX: 607-988-7956

books

BritBooks catalog, free. Published annually. 32-page catalog of books on British sports cars. We have a large selection of new and out of print books. Our prices are always competitive. Please write or call for our catalog.

Michael Bruce Associates Inc
PO Box 396
Powell, OH 43065
614-965-4859

publication

Corvette and Camaro publications. *Corvette Black Book, Camaro White Book.*

Cadillac Motor Books
PO Box 7
Temple City, CA 91780
818-445-1618

books

Mail order only. Publishers of *Cadillacs of the Forties, Guide to Cadillac 1950-1959, Cadillacs of the Sixties,* plus other Cadillac-LaSalle hardcover books. Also reprints of rare sales catalogs from the classic era. Send for complete list and information.

Car Club Group
PO Box 338
Poynette, WI 53955
608-635-7751

book

Mail order only. *Car Club Handbook* is a hands-on guide to starting, growing and funding a car club. Topics covered are by-laws, meetings, recruiting, public relations, fundraising and much more. Cost: $17.95.

Cars & Parts Collector Car Annual
PO Box 482
911 Vandemark Rd
Sidney, OH 45365
800-448-3611; 513-498-0803
FAX: 513-498-0808

publication

The Collector Car Annual is more than a walk down memory lane. There's lots of full-cover coverage of all the favorites, famous collector interviews, visits to restoration shops plus the most complete and up-to-date directory listings for salvage yards, antique car museums, product and service suppliers and car clubs. Published once each year. Cost $4.95.

"Check The Oil!" Magazine
PO Box 937
Powell, OH 43065-0937
614-848-5038; FAX: 614-436-4760

periodical

See full listing in **Section Two** under **petroliana**

Classic Motorbooks
PO Box 1/HMN
729 Prospect Ave
Osceola, WI 54020
800-826-6600; FAX: 715-294-4448

books
videos

Monday-Friday 8 to 4:30. The world's largest selection of automotive literature. Motorbooks is a long established publisher and mail order company offering thousands of books on repair, restoration, racing, buying, driving, and general marque studies and histories. We also offer a wide selection of videos and auto related items. Our 120-page catalog is only $3.95 or free with every order.

See our ad on this page

Cruise Consultants Group
PO Box 338
Poynette, WI 53955
608-635-7751

book
consultant

See full listing in **Section Two** under **consultants**

The Davis Registry
4073 Ruby
Ypsilanti, MI 48197
313-434-5581, 313-662-1001

periodical

Serves as a worldwide clearinghouse for information regarding history, technical background, up-keep, restoration, preservation, current events, prices and any other aspect of the aluminum bodied, three-wheeled Davis automobile built by the Davis Motorcar Co, 4055 Woodley Ave, Van Nuys, CA from 1947 to 1949. Sells authentic Davis literature, T-shirts, videos. Sample copy $2 postpaid. Quarterly publication. Subscription: $8/year. Checks payable to Tom Wilson.

Publications

DeTomaso Registry	**book**
Bill Van Ess	
2306 Post Dr NE	
Belmont, MI 49306	
616-364-1973; FAX: 616-363-2870	

See full listing in **Section One** under **DeTomaso/Pantera**

Dobbs Publishing Group Inc	**periodicals**
3816 Industry Blvd	
Lakeland, FL 33811	
941-644-0449; FAX: 941-648-1187	

Publishers of automotive magazines: *Mustang Monthly*, *Musclecar Review*, *Super Ford*, *Corvette Fever*, *MoPar Muscle*, *Ford Marketplace*, *Chevy Truck*, and *Jp*.

Dragonwyck Publishing Inc	**books**
Burrage Rd	**periodicals**
Box 385	
Contoocook, NH 03229	
603-746-5606; FAX: 603-746-4260	

Open Monday-Friday 8 to 6. Publishes *The Packard Cormorant* magazine and offers back issues.

Eliot James Enterprises Inc	**development info**
PO Box 3986	
Dana Point, CA 92629-8986	
714-661-0889; FAX: 714-661-1901	

EJE offers products and services to help hobbyists profit from their hobby as well as create and protect new ideas for their hobby and profit from them through licensing or starting a business.

The Evergreen Press	**books**
9 Camino Arroyo Pl	
Palm Desert, CA 92260	
213-510-1700; FAX: 213-510-2400	

Publisher and distributor of well illustrated hardcover books. Each is a photographic record of a specific marque. Each contains approximately 1,000 clear, sharp photos (b&w and color) illustrating model changes on a year-by-year basis.

Hemmings Motor News	**The monthly**
PO Box 100	**"bible"**
Bennington, VT 05201	**of the collector-car**
1-800-CAR-HERE ext 550	**hobby**
802-447-9550	
FAX: 802-447-1561	

See full listing in **Section Four** under **periodicals**

Hemmings Motor News	**books, videos**
Sunoco Filling Station	**HMN caps, t-shirts**
216 Main St	**HMN sweatshirts**
Bennington, VT 05201	**HMN tote bags**
HMN Customer Service:	**HMN truck banks**
1-800-CAR-HERE ext 550	**Free Vintage**
HMN Sunoco Filling Station:	**Vehicle Display**
802-447-3572	

"Old-tyme" Filling Station/Book Store/Gift Shop open daily 7 am-10 pm every day except Christmas. Offers a variety of automotive books & videos, plus *Hemmings Motor News* caps, clothing, gifts & automobilia. Located at *Hemmings Motor News* Sunoco Filling Station in downtown Bennington. Call or write for Free Mail Order Catalog of *HMN* products.

Hydro-E-Lectric Bookshelf	**literature**
48 Appleton Rd	**books**
Auburn, MA 01501	**repro manuals**
508-832-3081; FAX: 508-832-7929	

Shop manuals, parts books and interchange manuals, most US cars. Also many Jaguar manuals.

IPTC Publishing	**manuals**
300 SW 12th Ave	
Pompano Beach, FL 33069	
800-653-4198	

We are the publishers of several comprehensive automotive manuals including *The Export Manual*, *The Professional Automotive Manual*, *Rebuilding Wrecks* and *The Corvette Yellow Pages*.

See our ad on page 4

Jack Juratovic	**artwork**
819 Absequami Trail	
Lake Orion, MI 48362	
PH/FAX: 810-814-0627	

See full listing in **Section Two** under **artwork**

The Klemantaski Collection	**books**
65 High Ridge Rd, Suite 219	**photography**
Stamford, CT 06905	
PH/FAX: 203-968-2970	
E-mail: klemcoll@aol.com	

See full listing in **Section Two** under **photography**

Lamm Morada Publishing Co Inc	**books**
Box 7607	
Stockton, CA 95207	
209-931-1056; FAX: 209-931-5777	

Publishes books for auto enthusiasts. Latest: *A Century of Automotive Style*.

License Plates and Tags (Vintage)	**publications**
PO Box 369	**service**
Vashon, WA 98070-369	
PH/FAX: 206-567-4391	

Network exclusively for license plate collectors' information. All continents with international contacts. Information. Database. Anyone who has license plates or is interested in them can contact for referrals. Also tags and related items. License plates for passenger cars, trucks, motorcycles. Bought, sold, traded. Also trade-in license plate attachments and medallions.

John E Lloyd	**publication**
7480 Ellsworth Rd	
Ann Arbor, MI 48103	
313-930-9869	

Mail order only. Publishes *The International Directory of Automotive Literature Collectors*. The current issue contains the hobby interests and addresses of approximately 450 people in 25 countries, all continents, who trade, buy and sell auto literature items and automobilia. $5/per issue. Future editions will be on diskette only.

Merely Motoring	**automobilia**
153 Danford Ln	**lapel badges**
Solihull	**postcards**
West Midlands, B91 1QQ England	
0121-733-2123	
FAX: 0121-745-5256	

See full listing in **Section Two** under **automobilia**

Mid-America Auction Services	**auctions**
2277 W Hwy 36, Ste 214	
St Paul, MN 55113	
612-633-9655; FAX: 612-633-3212	
E-mail: midauction@aol.com	

See full listing in **Section Two** under **auctions & events**

Publications

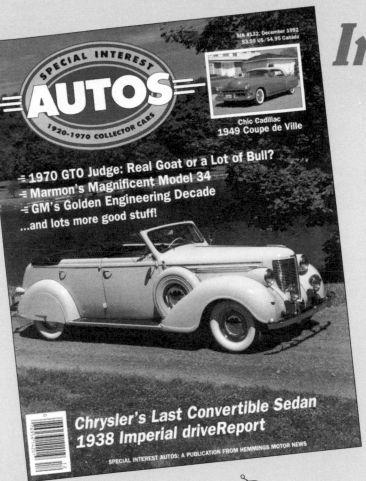

Gift Subscriptions $14.95 U.S. ONLY

Give gift subscriptions to your collector-car friends, relatives and co-workers.

Order Today!

To use MC/VISA/Discover/AmEx call ext. 550 at 1-800-CAR-HERE (toll-free) or 802-447-9550.

Subscribe to this Introductory Offer Today!

MoPar Collector's Guide Magazine	periodical
10067 El Camino Ave	
Baton Rouge, LA 70815	
504-926-6954; FAX: 504-924-5456	

See full listing in **Section One** under **MoPar**

NADA Appraisal Guides	appraisal guides
PO Box 7800	
Costa Mesa, CA 92628	
800-966-6232; FAX: 714-556-8715	

NADA Exotic, Collectible & Special Interest Car Appraisal Guide, 51 years of used values for all cars and trucks 1946-1978 including used values on exotic cars 1946-1996. The most comprehensive guide available today! Complete model listings, optional equipment, engine information, vehicle weight and three values (low-average-high) based on vehicle condition. Updated January-May-September. 1-year subscription $40.

Oil Company Collectibles	books
411 Forest St	gasoline globes
LaGrange, OH 44050	signs
216-355-6608; FAX: 216-355-4955	

See full listing in **Section Two** under **automobilia**

Petroleum Collectibles Monthly	periodical
411 Forest St	
LaGrange, OH 44050	
216-355-6608; FAX: 216-355-4955	

See full listing in **Section Four** under **periodicals**

PM Research Inc	books
4110 Niles Hill Rd	models
Wellsville, NY 14895	
716-593-3169; FAX: 716-593-5637	

See full listing in **Section Two** under **models & toys**

Portrayal Press	books
PO Box 1190	manuals
Andover, NJ 07821	
PH/FAX: 201-579-5781	

Mail order only. Publishes and sells manuals and books for older jeeps, Dodge military trucks and other military trucks (WW II to modern) and tracked military vehicles such as tanks. 48-page full size catalog mailed first class for $3 (overseas $5). Dennis R. Spence, owner.

R-Mac Publications Inc	periodical
Rt 3, Box 425	
Jasper, FL 32052	
904-792-2480; FAX: 904-792-3230	

Publication: *The Vintage Truck and Fire Engine Monthly*. Monthly magazine relating to vintage trucks and fire apparatus. Contains ads and articles of interest. $30/year bulk rate, $46/year first class and Canada. We also publish *The Packard Motor Car*, published bi-monthly, relating to anything concerning Packard, $36 annually.

Ed Rouze	painting guide book
406 Sheila Blvd	
Prattville, AL 36066	
334-365-2381	

See full listing in **Section Two** under **painting**

Samlerborsen	books
Jacobys Alle 2-4	toys
DK 1806 Frederiksberg C Denmark	
+45-33254022; FAX: +45-33250622	

See full listing in **Section Two** under **literature dealers**

Steve Smith Autosports Publications	books
PO Box 11631	
Santa Ana, CA 92711	
714-639-7681; FAX: 714-639-7941	

Mail order only. Publisher of automotive technical books such as *Street Rod Building Skills, Practical Engine Swapping, How to Build a Repro Rod, Racing the Small Block Chevy*, etc. 245 titles available. Free catalog.

Special Interest Autos	periodical
PO Box 196	
Bennington, VT 05201	
1-800-CAR-HERE, ext 550	
802-447-9550	
FAX: 802-447-1561	

See full listing in **Section Four** under **periodicals**

Spyder Enterprises Inc	accessories
RFD 1682	books
Laurel Hollow, NY 11791-9644	parts
516-367-3293 evenings	periodicals
FAX: 516-367-3260	

See full listing in **Section One** under **Porsche**

Tech-Art Publications	books
Jason Houston	
Box 753	
Ranchero Mirage, CA 92270	
619-862-1979	

Mail order only. We publish soft-bound books on promotional car models and related items. SASE required.

The Tin Type Press	auto stamp album
5313 John Thomas Dr NE	Corvette coloring
Albuquerque, NM 87111	book
505-294-4434	

Publishes *The World Automobile Stamp Album*. $19.95 + $2.05 postage. Includes old auto advertisements and maps in background. Annual update page packets available. Over 1,300 stamps illustrated. Publishes *The Corvette Coloring Book*, $6.75 postpaid.

Vehicles In Motion	directory
1000 W Crosby #100	purchasing guide
Carrollton, TX 75006	
214-242-2453; FAX: 214-446-1919	

See full listing in **Section One** under **Harley-Davidson**

Vintage Parts 411	books
PO Box 22893	
San Diego, CA 92192	
800-MOTORHEAD	
FAX: 619-560-9900	
E-mail: vp411@electriciti.com	

See full listing in **Section Four** under **information sources**

T E Warth Esq Automotive Books	books
Lumberyard Shops	
Marine on St Croix, MN 55047	
612-433-5744; FAX: 612-433-5012	
E-mail: tewarthl@aol.com	

Office open by chance or appointment and on Wednesdays 9-6. Deals in pictorial, history and technical books relating to automobiles, trucks, motorcycles, tractors, models, racing, etc; out of print and rare. No manuals, handbooks or sales literature. 8,000 title stock list available. Also operates automotive outlet book store in Stillwater, Minnesota book center.

Publications

Periodicals

911 & Porsche World
PO Box 75
Tadworth
Surrey KT20 7XF England
01737 814311
FAX: 01737 814591

periodical

See full listing in **Section One** under **Porsche**

The Alternate
PO Box 239-393
Grantville, PA 17028-0239
PH/FAX: 717-469-0777

periodical

A flea market in print with a touch of history for vintage motor racing enthusiasts. Stories by the old timers who were there during the Golden Age of motor racing. Monthly publication: *The Alternate*, $15/year; foreign $33/year (US funds).

Gary G Anderson
343 Second St, Suite H
Los Altos, CA 94022-3639
415-949-9680
FAX: 415-949-9685

periodical

Mail order and telephone only. Publishes *British Car Magazine*. The only American magazine exclusively for British car enthusiasts, devoted to the use and appreciation of classic and contemporary British cars, including marque profiles, photo essays, history, technical advice, humor, calendars and report on North American events and sources for parts and services. Subscription rate: $22.95 one year US, $26 one year Canada; $39.95 two years US, $46 two years Canada (bi-monthly).

Automobile Quarterly
15076 Kutztown Rd
PO Box 348
Kutztown, PA 19530
610-683-3169; FAX: 610-683-3287

books
periodicals
posters

Publishers of automobile history. Publishes *Automobile Quarterly* magazine, marque history books, posters, Christmas cards, calendars and the *Quatrefoil* catalog of automotive books and gifts, including books by other publishers.

**Automotive Fine Art
Society Quarterly**
PO Box 325
Dept HMN
Lake Orion, MI 48361-0325
PH/FAX: 810-814-0627

periodical

The definitive auto art journal. *AFAS Quarterly* includes trends, auctions, exhibitions & recent print releases. Browse original art by early artists including Helck, Crosby, Ham, Nockolds. Visit private museums, galleries. Profile AFAS artists each issue. Regular departments: galleries, where they are; shows & exhibitions, when & where. Collectibles, a classified buy, sell & want listing free to subscribers. Contributors include David Brownell, B S Levy, Keith Marvin, and other great auto writers and experts. $24 US; $32 Canada; $36 overseas.

Bracket Racing USA
299 Market St
Saddle Brook, NJ 07663
201-712-9300; FAX: 201-712-0990
E-mail: staff@cskpub.com

periodical

Bimonthly covering the drag racing industry from the grass roots point of view. Written and edited for the "little guy," amateur bracket racer.

British Car Magazine
PO Box 1683
Los Altos, CA 94023-1683
415-949-9680; FAX: 415-949-9685
E-mail: britcarmag@aol.com

periodical

Bi-monthly magazine dedicated to British car owners, enthusiasts, restorers and industry, with historical features on all classic marques and models, tech and restoration articles, buyers guides, how-to tips, parts and service sources, etc. Since 1985. Subscription rate: $22.95/year; $39.95/2 years.

See our ad on this page

**The Car Collector &
Car Classics Magazine**
1241 Canton St
Roswell, GA 30075
800-277-0175; FAX: 770-643-2815

periodical

A monthly magazine with features and stories on the entire spectrum of collectible cars, both foreign and domestic. Over 80 pages of color in each issue, $32/year, $60/two years, $83/three years. Enjoy *Car Collector* on line with our award winning Internet magazine. Buy, sell and talk cars with us and hobbyists worldwide via your computer.
Web site: http://www.carcollector.com

Cars & Parts Magazine
PO Box 482
Sidney, OH 45365
800-448-3611; 513-498-0803
FAX: 513-498-0808

periodical

Cars & Parts is a monthly magazine with full-color editorial features on collector cars, restoration, salvage yards, shows and swap meets, display advertising and large classified ad section with vintage cars, parts and related items for sale, and wanted. Subscription rates/year: $24 US, $35 foreign, second class; $44 US, first class; $64 foreign, airmail.

"Check The Oil!" Magazine   periodical
PO Box 937
Powell, OH 43065-0937
614-848-5038; FAX: 614-436-4760

See full listing in **Section Two** under **petroliana**

Coin Drop International   periodical
5815 W 52nd Ave
Denver, CO 80212
303-431-9266; FAX: 303-431-6978
E-mail: rbltd@crie.com

Mail order and open shop. Monday-Friday 8 am to 4:30 pm. Bi-monthly publication covering all coin-op related items. Subscription rate: $15/year.

Coin-Op Classics Magazine   periodical
17844 Toiyabe St
Fountain Valley, CA 92708
714-756-8746; FAX: 714-963-1716
E-mail: pmovsesian@aol.com

Publishes *Coin-Op Classics*. Bi-monthly publication. Covers classic coin-operated machines from slot machines, jukeboxes, arcade, Coke, gaming, pinball, peanut/gumball, scales, etc. Articles, restoration tips, classifieds, show news, etc. $39/year.

Collector Car & Truck Prices   price guide
41 N Main St
North Grafton, MA 01536
508-839-6707; FAX: 508-839-6266
E-mail: vmr@ultranet.com

Provides pricing on over 80 makes of domestics, imports & trucks. Highly detailed engine, transmission & optional equipment listings with every vehicle. Updated every issue with realistic pricing based on current market conditions. Used worldwide by appraisers, auction firms, insurance companies, investors and old car lovers everywhere. Subscription rate: $14.95, 6/yr.

Convertible Magazine   periodical
PO Box 1011-HVA
San Mateo, CA 94403
415-340-8669; FAX: 415-340-9473

Bi-monthly publication is about convertible cars, both domestic and foreign. Also covers open roadsters, sports cars, street rods and replicars. Hundreds of convertibles listed for sale plus parts, service and accessories. The magazine for the convertible enthusiast. Track the convertible market. 12 issues for only $24.00. VISA/MasterCard accepted.

Corvette Fever   periodical
3816 Industry Blvd
Lakeland, FL 33811
941-644-0449; FAX: 941-648-1187

Magazine with full color feature spreads on Corvettes of every era, Corvette lifestyle, touring and racing coverage, technical data, club news coast-to-coast, parts and service information, Corvette investment values and price guides. $24.97/year.

CSK Publishing Co Inc   periodical
299 Market St
Saddle Brook, NJ 07662
201-712-9300; FAX: 201-712-0990
E-mail: staff@cskpub.com

Specialty automotive publisher specializing in niche publications. Publications include: *Vette* magazine, Corvette enthusiast magazine featuring Corvettes from all eras, $24.97/year, 12x per year. *Muscle Mustangs & Fast Fords*, for late model Mustang and Ford enthusiasts, $27.97, 12x per year. *Bracket Racing USA*, covering all aspects of bracket racing drag racing, $18.97, 8x per year. *High Performance MoPar*, written for Chrysler and MoPar enthusiasts, $17.97, 7x per year. *High Performance Pontiac*, for Poncho enthusiasts of all eras, $16.97, 6x per year. *4x4 Mechanix*, for the do-it yourselfer 4x4 enthusiast, $16.97, 6x per year. *High Tech Performance*, for the late model EFI enthusiast, $16.97, 6x per year.

The Davis Registry   periodical
4073 Ruby
Ypsilanti, MI 48197
313-434-5581, 313-662-1001

See full listing in **Section Four** under **publications**

Deals On Wheels Publications   periodical
PO Box 205
Sioux Falls, SD 57101
605-338-7666; FAX: 605-338-5337

Monthly publication, *Deals On Wheels*. Buy/sell/trade specializing in clean, easy-to-read photo ads from across the US and Canada. All types of vehicles are for sale from Ferraris to restorable antique autos. Subscription rate: $14.95/year.

Dodge Brothers Club News   periodical
17767 Rapids Rd
Hiram, OH 44234
PH/FAX: 216-834-0233

Dodge Brothers Club News. A bi-monthly publication offering restoration & maintenance tips related to Dodge Brothers & Graham Brothers vehicles. History of these companies and the people involved. Subscription is included with membership in the Dodge Brothers Club. Subscription: $18 US & Canada, $26 foreign (US funds).

Publications

du Pont Registry
2325 Ulmerton Rd Ste 16
Clearwater, FL 34622-3371
813-573-9339; FAX: 813-572-5523

periodical

A monthly marketplace magazine presented in full color, circulated around the world. Featuring classic, luxury and exotic cars for sale. Subscription rate $49.95/year. A buyer's gallery of fine automobiles.

EWA & Miniature Cars USA Inc
369 Springfield Ave
Box 188
Berkeley Heights, NJ 07922
908-665-7811; FAX: 908-665-7814

**books
models
subscriptions
videos**

See full listing in **Section Two** under **models & toys**

Fournier Enterprises Inc
1884 Thunderbird Dr
Troy, MI 48084-5428
810-362-3722; 800-501-3722
FAX: 810-362-2866

publication

Metal Crafter's News a bi-monthly publication. Every issue: tips & techniques, new construction, tools & products, metal work history, projects & patterns and more hard to find metal work info. $19.95/6 issues.

Gameroom Magazine
1014 Mt Tabor Rd
New Albany, IN 47150
812-945-7971; FAX: 812-945-6966

periodical

Publishes monthly *Gameroom Magazine*. A valuable source of information for the pinball, jukebox, arcade, Coke, slots & more, enthusiasts. Lots of helpful articles and thousands of ads to help you find what you need. $28/year.

GN Wheels & Deals
PO Box 2138
Oroville, CA 95965
916-533-2134; FAX: 916-533-1531
E-mail: gnwd@quiknet.com

periodical

A free weekly pictorial automotive publication with circulation of over 80,000 a week, covering 24 counties of northern CA. *Wheels & Deals*. Pictures of new, used, old autos, boats, bikes and heavy equipment. A free events calendar listing and stories on auto shows, etc.

See our ad on page 531

Grassroots Motorsports
425 Parque Dr
Ormond Beach, FL 32174
904-673-4148; FAX: 904-673-6040

periodical

Glossy, colorful national publication *Grassroots Motorsports*, for amateur motor sports enthusiasts. Autocross rally vintage and road race news, events, personalities and car preparation tips. Subscription rate: $14.97. Published bi-monthly. Free sample copy. Web site: http://www.grmotorsports.com

HCKC News
Kingfisher Ct
East Molesey
Surrey KT8 9HL   England
0181-941-0604

periodical

Bi-monthly magazine for Hillman, Commer, Karrier and derivatives of these makes of vehicles, many of which were sold under Sunbeam or Dodge badges in USA and Canada. Subscriptions: £10/year.

**Hemmings Motor News
Sunoco Filling Station**
216 Main St
Bennington, VT 05201
HMN Customer Service:
1-800-CAR-HERE ext 550
HMN Sunoco Filling Station:
802-447-3572

**books, videos
HMN caps, t-shirts
HMN sweatshirts
HMN tote bags
HMN truck banks
Free Vintage
Vehicle Display**

See full listing in **Section Four** under **books & publications**

Hemmings Motor News
PO Box 100
Bennington, VT 05201
1-800-CAR-HERE ext 550
802-447-9550
FAX: 802-447-1561

**The monthly
"bible"
of the collector-car
hobby**

"The bible" of the collector-car hobby, monthly trading place, 98% paid hobby advertising with world's largest paid circulation to old car hobbyists (nearly 300,000), and publishing world's largest number of hobby advertisements (averaging over 800 pages monthly), including any-&-all antique, vintage, muscle, and special-interest collector cars, trucks, motorcycles, custom cars, &c, plus parts, literature, services, automobilia, &c, without limitations. One year subscriptions: Fourth class mail: $26.95 USA; $58.00 Canada. First class mail: $65.00 USA; $88.00 Canada; $88 Mexico. US funds only. Air mail to other countries (inquire for current rates). Wholesale terms available. Visitors welcome in Visitors' Lobby Book-&-Gift Shop, Monday-Friday 9 to 5 and HMN Sunoco Filling Station/Book Store/Gift Shop, daily 7 am-10 pm everyday except Christmas. Web Site: http://www.hmn.com

Late Great Chevrolet Association
2166 S Orange Blossom Trail
Apopka, FL 32703
407-886-1963; FAX: 407-886-7571

periodical

Mail order and open shop. Monday-Friday 8 to 5, Saturday 9 to 2. The Late Great Chevrolet Association is dedicated to the restoration and preservation of all 58-64 Chevrolets. Specializing in 58-64 Chevrolet parts & monthly magazine publication, *Late Great Chevys*, approx 32-pages, color/b&w. The magazine displays our members' automobiles along with their story. The magazine also provides restoration help, club events, general information on events around the US. The magazine also has several pages of ads, also informs members/customers of new parts available through the association. Color photos of autos. Subscription rate: $30/year second class, $40/year first class, $55/year air mail.

**The Latest Scoop - Auto
Enthusiast Calendar**
PO Box 7771
Loveland, CO 80537-0771
970-669-3277

periodical

Handy guide for automotive enthusiasts and businesses providing you with the most up-to-date information on car-related events taking place in the Rocky Mountain Region of CO, WY, NE, KS, OK, TX, NM, AZ and UT. Nine times a year. Send for sample issue and current rate.

Lost Highways Quarterly
PO Box 43737
Philadelphia, PA 19106
215-925-2568

periodical

Trailers, motorhomes, mobile homes, living on wheels. From auto camping in the teens and twenties to Lucy and Desi in *The Long, Long Trailer, Lost Highways Quarterly* explores the historical side of one night or an entire life spent on wheels. Winner of *Old Car's Weekly* Golden Quill award. Free classifieds for subscribers/members. $24/4 issues US, Canada, Mexico. Other countries $32/4 issues.

Military Vehicles Magazine	**publication**
12-H Indian Head Rd	
Morristown, NJ 07960	
201-285-0716; FAX: 201-539-5934	
E-mail: mvehicles@aol.com	

Bimonthly magazine about historic military vehicles: military jeeps, trucks, armor, etc. Features restoration, maintenance articles, advertising, swap meets. $18/year, $29/two years, sample copy $4, US only. Foreign prices higher.

Mini License Plate/Keychain Tag Collectors Newsletter	**newsletter**
Dr Edward Miles	
888 8th Ave	
New York, NY 10019	
212-765-2660	

A means for license plate collectors and mini license plate collectors (license plate key chain tags, chauffeur's badges, automotive windshield stickers, registrations, driver's licenses, etc) to exchange information. Also a means to buy and sell items relating to the hobby. $10/year.

Mobilia	**periodical**
PO Box 575	
Middlebury, VT 05753	
802-388-3071; FAX: 802-388-2215	
E-mail: mobilia@aol.com	

Marketplace for automobilia: auto art and collectibles. Magazine format. Contains news, auction results, event listings, items for sale and wanted. Monthly publication, *Mobilia*. $29/year.

Model Car Journal	**periodical**
PO Box 154135	
Irving, TX 75015-4135	
PH/FAX: 214-790-5346	

Bi-monthly publication. $16/year US, $19/year Canada (in US funds). Please write for foreign rates. Founded in 1974. Covers all types of model cars in all scales. Articles on current models as well as those out of production. Also offers a calendar of shows and a large classified section.

MoPar Collector's Guide Magazine	**periodical**
10067 El Camino Ave	
Baton Rouge, LA 70815	
504-926-6954; FAX: 504-924-5456	

See full listing in **Section One** under **MoPar**

MoPar Muscle	**periodical**
3816 Industry Blvd	
Lakeland, FL 33811	
941-644-0449; FAX: 941-648-1187	

Magazine features articles and photos on the mighty MoPars of lore and legend. From hemi, six-pack, Roadrunner and Super Bee to Darts, Demons and Dusters, plus "how-to" help, technical info, parts and service sources, restoration and repair data, buying tips, news on MoPar events nationwide and more. $16.97/year, 6 issues.

Musclecar Review	**periodical**
3816 Industry Blvd	
Lakeland, FL 33811	
941-644-0449; FAX: 941-648-1187	

Pits the latest Detroit iron against the earth-shaking muscle cars of the past, or takes readers' favorite cars to the track for "shootouts and showdowns." Plus loads of restoration, repair and maintenance information, parts and service sources, news on national muscle car events and more. $16.97/year.

Mustang Monthly	**periodical**
3816 Industry Blvd	
Lakeland, FL 33811	
941-644-0449; FAX: 941-648-1187	

America's first and only monthly Mustang magazine brings you coast-to-coast coverage on the best original and restored Mustangs in the country, with exciting full color feature articles and photos, technical and how-to help, news on all the major Mustang clubs and car shows, plus parts and service sources, classifieds and more. Monthly magazine, $24.97/year.

Old Cars Price Guide	**price guide**
700 E State St, Dept 8FT	
Iola, WI 54990	
715/445-2214; FAX: 715-445-4087	
800-258-0929 subscriptions only	

The hobby's most respected source for collector car values, featuring over 135,000 individual prices for models manufactured from 1901-1988. All values are presented according to the 1-to-6 conditional grading system, with numerous photos. Bi-monthly, $18.95/year. Subscription orders by VISA/MasterCard/Discover/AmEx.

Old Cars Weekly News & Marketplace	**periodical**
700 E State St, Dept 8FT	
Iola, WI 54990	
715-445-2214; FAX: 715-445-4087	
800-258-0929 subscriptions only	

The old car hobby's weekly source for up-to-date hobby news, restoration tips, auction reports, events calendar, plus new buy and sell opportunities in display and classified advertising for collector cars and parts. Weekly, $34.95/year. Subscription orders by VISA/MasterCard/Discover/AmEx.

Petroleum Collectibles Monthly	**periodical**
411 Forest St	
LaGrange, OH 44050	
216-355-6608; FAX: 216-355-4955	

Publication: *Petroleum Collectibles Monthly*. Most comprehensive magazine covering all aspects of collecting gas pumps, globes, signs, cans, etc. Auctions, ads, historical, discoveries, color photos, Q&A and more. Subscription rate: $29.95 US, $38.50 Canada, $65.95 international.

R-Mac Publications Inc	**periodical**
Rt 3, Box 425	
Jasper, FL 32052	
904-792-2480; FAX: 904-792-3230	

See full listing in **Section Four** under **books & publications**

Retroviseur	**periodical**
BP 67	
77301 Fontainebleau	
Cedex France	
(01) 60-71-55-55	
FAX: (01) 60-72-22-37	

Retroviseur is a monthly publication specializing in classic cars; in color, about 150 pages, news, various features, ads. Subscription: 455f/year.

Skinned Knuckles	**periodical**
175 May Ave	
Monrovia, CA 91016	
818-358-6255	

A monthly publication devoted to the restoration, operation and maintenance of all authentic collector vehicles. $18/year domestic, $21/year foreign.

Special Interest Autos | periodical
PO Box 196
Bennington, VT 05201
1-800-CAR-HERE, ext 550
802-447-9550
FAX: 802-447-1561

A bi-monthly magazine. $19.95/year US, $21.95/year foreign. Features collector cars from 1920 through 1980. In-depth, thoroughly researched articles and road tests. Over 100 photos in each issue. Authoritative information throughout. Most back issues available. Ask about our retail dealer program. Web Site: http://www.hmn.com

Specialty Car Marketplace | periodical
PO Box 205
Sioux Falls, SD 57101
605-338-7666
FAX: 605-338-5337

Monthly publication, *Specialty Car*. Buy/sell/trade publication. All types of vehicles kit cars, muscle cars, trucks, motorcycles, are available for sale in full color or black & white photos. Ads listed from across the US and Canada. Subscription rate: $12.95/year.

Super Ford | periodical
3816 Industry Blvd
Lakeland, FL 33811
941-644-0449
FAX: 941-648-1187

Magazine covers all Fords, street, strip or modified, show, vintage or classic. Get the scoop on Ford engine buildups, performance modifications, restoration, "how-to" help and parts sources, plus articles and full color photo spreads on street, track and show Fords, and the men behind the machines. $24.97/year.

The Registry | periodical
Pine Grove
Stanley, VA 22851
540-778-3728; FAX: 540-778-2402
E-mail: britregstry@aol.com

The Registry, a monthly magazine. British cars, parts, services, also club news, tech information, club calendar. Marque Spotlight each month highlights model development, history, production numbers, etc. Write or call for free sample issue. Subscription monthly, $8.95/year. Free private ads anytime.

This Old Truck Magazine | periodical
PO Box 562
Yellow Springs, OH 45387
800-767-5828; 937-767-1433
FAX: 767-2726
E-Mail: antique@antiquepower.com

Devoted to the preservation of all makes and vintages of antique trucks, station wagons, pickups and commercial vehicles. Includes color photos, restoration tips, truck company history, plus free classified ads for subscribers. Publishes *This Old Truck*, bi-monthly publication. Subscription rate: $20 US; $28 Canada; $34 overseas. Web Site: http://www.antiquepower.com

See our ad on this page

Triumph World Magazine | periodical
PO Box 75
Tadworth
Surrey KT20 7XF England
01737 814311; 01737 814591

See full listing in **Section One** under **Triumph**

Truck, Race, Cycle and Rec | periodical
PO Box 205
Sioux Falls, SD 57101
605-338-7666; FAX: 605-338-5337

Monthly publication, *Truck, Race, Cycle & Rec*. Buy/sell/trade publication. Specializing in trucks, race cars, motorcycles and repairable autos. Ads are available with photos and are placed from across the US and Canada. Subscription rate: $14.95/year.

Victory Lane | periodical
2460 Park Blvd
Palo Alto, CA 94306
415-321-1411; FAX: 415-321-4426

Monthly news magazine covering vintage auto racing in US and international. Features include race reports with results, columns by insiders, technical articles, event schedules, vintage race car classifieds, marque histories, collector car stories and more. $39.95/year.

Walneck's Classic Cycle-Trader | periodical
7923 Janes Ave
Woodridge, IL 60517
630-985-4995; FAX: 630-985-2750

Monthly magazine, *Walneck's Classic Cycle-Trader*. In print for 16 years, approx 120 pages of color and black & white classic motorcycles for sale. Also included, many old road tests for references. A free sample for the asking. Subscription: $29/year.

Walneck's Inc | motorcycles, murals, posters
7923 Janes Ave
Woodridge, IL 60517
630-985-4995; FAX: 630-985-2750

Motorcycle posters and huge murals. Call or send for free catalog.

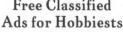

Publications

Newsletters

1929 Buick Silver Anniversary Newsletter — newsletter
75 Oriole Pkwy
Toronto, ON Canada M4V 2E3
416-487-9522; FAX: 416-322-7475
E-Mail: 75317.3253@compuserve.com

Newsletter and roster for all 1929 Buick owners, including 1929 Buick, 1929 McLaughlin Buick (Canadian) and 1929 Holden-bodied Buicks (Australian). Issued quarterly. Contact W E (Bill) McLaughlin at the above address for information.

The 60 Oldsmobile Club — newsletter
Dick Major
10895 E Hibma Rd
Tustin, MI 49688
616-825-2891; FAX: 616-825-8324

See full listing in **Section One** under **Oldsmobile**

600 Headquarters, Miles Chappell — advice / newsletter / parts / service
PO Box 1262
Felton, CA 95018
408-335-2208 shop

See full listing in **Section One** under **Honda**

Automotive Investor — newsletter
2 Madison Ave
Larchmont, NY 10538
914-834-3100; FAX: 914-834-3689
E-mail: hmatysko@aol.com

Automotive Investor. The only newsletter that covers the entire vintage car auction world, from American chrome and fins to exotic European racers. It is a financial newsletter in the vintage car business with special focus on specific market segment each month. Both European & domestic with concise buyer's guides and no-nonsense investment advice. Subscription rate: $99.50 US, $159.95 foreign, 12/year.

Behring Automotive Museum — museum / newsletter
3700 Blackhawk Plaza Cir
Danville, CA 94506
510-736-2280; FAX: 510-736-4818

See full listing in **Section Six** under **California**

Council of Vehicle Associations — newsletter
10400 Roberts Rd
Palos Hills, IL 60465
708-598-7070; FAX: 708-598-4888

See full listing in **Section Three** under **legislative watch organizations**

National Chevy Assoc — parts
947 Arcade Street
St Paul, MN 55106
612-778-9522; FAX: 612-778-9686

See full listing in **Section One** under **Chevrolet**

Peerless Co-Operator Newsletter — ads / literature / manuals / newsletter
1094 Brookdale Dr
Crestline, OH 44827
419-683-3174

Peerless restoration pictures & stories, factory history, executive personnel profiles, want list & for sale list, repro literature, repro casting of parts, repro ads for all years Peerless. Repros of original Peerless Co-Operator. Bi-monthly newsletter. $10/year.

SL Market Letter — newsletter
2020 Girard Ave S
Minneapolis, MN 55405
612-377-0155; FAX: 612-377-0157
E-mail: slmarket@aol.com

Specializes in Mercedes-Benz special models only. Especially SL Models 1954 thru 1995 and SLC, SEC. All convertibles, coupes and 6.3, 6.9 & 600. Subscription based collation of price trends, restoration & parts sources and rare M-B models offered for sale. 18 issues/year. Now in 16th year.

Research & Reference Libraries

AACA Library & Research Center — research library
501 W Governor Rd, PO Box 417
Hershey, PA 17033
717-534-2082

Library located adjacent to AACA National headquarters. Open Monday-Friday 8:30 to 3:45. Collection contains books, periodicals, sales literature, manuals, wiring diagrams, paint chips, etc, 1895-present.

Automobile Reference Collection — information source
Free Library of Philadelphia
1901 Vine St
Philadelphia, PA 19103-1189
215-686-5404

Open 12 months a year, Monday-Friday 9 to 5. Major collection of automotive literature located in one of the country's major public libraries.

Robert DeMars Ltd — appraisers / car locator / auto historians / library / resto consultants
222 Lakeview Ave, Ste 160-256
West Palm Beach, FL 33401
561-832-0171
FAX: 561-844-1493

See full listing in **Section Two** under **appraisals**

Ralph Dunwoodie Research & Information — research / information
5935 Calico Dr
Sun Valley, NV 89433-6910
702-673-3811

Pre-purchase inspection of vehicles. Early auto magazines and research material bought for reference library. Car and truck histories researched. Extensive library from 1895 to present. Research of all phases of automobile and truck information for writers, restorers, historians and enthusiasts.

Duncan F Holmes — research library
493 King Philip St
Fall River, MA 02724
508-672-0071

Automotive research library. GM, Ford, Chrysler, all independent manufacturers of 1949-1967 model years, earlier years on some cars. Over 7,000 original magazine and newspaper ads on file. Over 500 original owner's manuals, over 500 original dealer sales catalogs. New items constantly being added. Duplicate items offered for sale. Can photocopy most items at nominal cost.

Hemmings' Vintage Auto Almanac©   Twelfth Edition

Lost Highways	information source
Classic Trailer & Motorhome Archive	research library
PO Box 43737	
Philadelphia, PA 19106	
215-925-2568	

Trailers, trailer parks, motorhomes, mobile homes, auto camping, camping gadgetry, modular and experimental housing. Teens and twenties through the sixties. Archive open by appointment only. Research can be done for a reasonable fee.

Chris Smith's Creative	parts
Workshop Motorcar Restoration	restoration
118 NW Park St	service
Dania, FL 33004	
305-920-3303; FAX: 305-920-9950	

See full listing in **Section Two** under **restoration shops**

Section Five:
Salvage Yards

Sometimes the search is just as interesting as the item sought, and for those who'd like to track down a car or a needed part where it was once laid to rest, the *Almanac* presents this state-by-state listing of salvage yards. Check the individual listings for era or marque special-ties. Many of the yards will not ship parts and require a personal visit. Be sure to phone ahead or check business hours carefully before making a long drive, as some of the yards operate on irregular schedules.

Alabama

Vintage Automobiles	205-935-3649
Rt 1, Box 6	
Hackleburg, AL 35564	

Mail order. Open by appointment only. 1930-48 Ford parts; 1933-52 Dodge parts, mainly original running gear parts. Some body parts, mechanical parts, wheels, transmissions, etc.

Alaska

Binder's Auto Restoration and Salvage	907-745-4670 FAX: 907-745-5510
PO Box 1144	
1 Mile Maud Rd	
Palmer, AK 99645	

Mail order, SASE required. Salvage yard open by appointment only. Specializing in 1960 to present Cadillac cars only. Complete line of used parts and some NOS. No part too small.

Shipping worldwide. MasterCard/VISA accepted. Complete and partial restorations. Car transporting local and long distance. Please call between 6-9 pm local time for free advice.

Arizona

Canyon Classics	800-571-1488 FAX: 602-582-9141
PO Box 1111	
Black Canyon City, AZ 85324	

Mail order and open shop. Open Monday-Friday 8 to 5, Saturday 8 to 2. Specialize in used auto and truck parts for Cadillac, Ford, Mercury, Lincoln, and trucks of all makes and models. No part is too big or small.

Desert Valley Auto Parts	602-780-8024 FAX: 602-582-9141
22500 N 21st Ave	
Phoenix, AZ 85027	

Mail order and open shop. Monday-Friday 8-5:30, Saturday 8-2. Rust-free Arizona parts. 80 full acres of classic and hard to find

parts or cars for restoration projects, from the 50s to the 80s. Quality parts, dependable service and competitive prices guaranteed. New classics arrive daily to our existing inventory of thousands. Daily shipping worldwide via UPS and freight. No part too large or too small. VISA/MasterCard accepted.

See our ad on page 537

Hoctor's Hidden Valley Auto Parts 21046 N Rio Bravo Rd Maricopa, AZ 85239	520-568-2945 602-252-2122 602-252-6137 FAX: 602-258-0951

Mail order and open shop. Monday-Friday 8-5; Saturday 9-3. 80 acres of rust-free foreign and American autos and trucks. Just over 8,000 cars for parts. From 20s to 80s, mostly 50s, 60s. Also 2 other Phoenix stores for convenience. Shipping worldwide. Send specific list of needs w/SASE or call.

Wiseman's Auto Salvage 900 W Cottonwood Ln Casa Grande, AZ 85222	520-836-7960

Mail order and open shop. Monday-Friday 8-5:30, Saturday 9-1. Arizona desert salvage yard. 2,500 cars and trucks for parts. All types of auto and truck parts. Good, used, guaranteed. Twenties to seventies. Browsers welcome. Sale of used auto & truck parts. SASE please. MasterCard/VISA/Discover.

California

American Auto & Truck Dismantlers 12172 Truman St San Fernando, CA 91340	818-365-3908

Mail order and open shop. Monday-Friday 8:30-5; Saturday 9-4. Salvage yard specializing in 1955-57 Chev cars; 58-89 all GM cars and trucks; 67-89 Camaros; 64-72 Chevelles.

Buick Bonery 6970 Stamper Way Sacramento, CA 95828	PH/FAX: 916-381-5271

See full listing in **Section One** under **Buick/McLaughlin**

Downtown Auto Wrecking Steve Reich 519 E Mill St San Bernardino, CA 92408	909-889-8880 909-989-6624 evenings

Mail order and open shop. Open Mon-Fri 8 to 5:30; Sat 8 to 2:30. Auto wrecking. Old cars and trucks, complete and parts. High-performance parts and race cars, complete and parts. All cars and parts from southern California. Rust-free. Buys, sells, trades. Older, low-dollar cars and trucks. Two yards full of old parts.

Paso Robles Auto Wrecking 5755 Monterey Rd Paso Robles, CA 93446	800-549-3738 805-238-3738 805-238-3764

Mail order and open shop. Monday-Saturday 8 to 5. Specializes in American cars of the 50s-60s-70s. Some trucks. 10 acres of California rust-free cars and trucks.

Pearson's Auto Dismantling & Used Cars 2343 Hwy 49 Mariposa, CA 95338	209-742-7442

Open Friday & Saturday only, 8:30 to 5:30. A G Pearson, owner. Specializing in all cars 1959 and older. Also has some 1959 and newer used cars and parts in stock. Enclose an SASE.

Connecticut

Mostly Mustangs Inc 55 Alling St Hamden, CT 06517	203-562-8804 FAX: 203-562-4891

See full listing in **Section One** under **Mustang**

Leo Winakor and Sons Inc 470 Forsyth Rd Salem, CT 06420	860-859-0471

Open Saturday and Sunday 10 to 2. Specializing in old car parts, 1926-85.

Florida

Sunrise Auto Sales & Salvage Rt 3, Box 6 Aero Avenue Lake City, FL 32055	904-755-1810 FAX: 904-755-1855

Established 1987. Used auto and truck parts, 1940s through early 1970s. 10 acres, over 1,000 vehicles. New vehicles arriving weekly. Fair prices, honest descriptions. US and foreign visitors always welcome. VISA, MasterCard or COD. Shipping worldwide. Hours: 8 to 5:30 weekdays, Saturday 8 to 1. Located off State Road 100 East, 2-1/2 miles east of US 90 on Aero Avenue.

IPTC Automotive 300 SW 12th Ave Pompano Beach, FL 33069	800-277-3806

See full listing in **Section One** under **BMW**

Sunshine Corvettes Inc 17951 US 301 PO Box 1202 Dade City, FL 33526	352-567-4458 FAX: 352-567-4460

Corvette salvage yard. Parts, cars, sales, service 1953 and up. Florida's largest "Corvette only" recycling yard. Reproduction and used parts, rebuildables and parts cars. Nice selection of good southern cars at reasonable prices. 24-hour FAX line only.

Georgia

Bayless Inc 1111 Via Bayless Marietta, GA 30066-2770	800-241-1446 order-line (US & Canada) 770-928-1446 FAX: 770-928-1342

See full listing in **Section One** under **Fiat**

Fiat Lancia Heaven Bayless Inc 1111 Via Bayless Marietta, GA 30066-2770	800-241-1446 770-928-1446 FAX: 770-928-1342

Old Car City, USA 3098 Hwy 411 NE White, GA 30184	404-382-6141 404-974-6144 (Atlanta)

Mail order and open shop. Monday-Friday 8:30 to 5, Saturday 8:30 to noon. Call for appointment, call for trade day date. Special interest old-car advertiser bulletin board on property. Established 1931. Pre-1969 American cars. Most are restorable. List of approximately 950. Send $2.25 for inventory of restorables and parts cars. Toy car and truck collection. Elvis record collection and last car. Videos of OCC, USA and over 4,000 old cars, $19.95, add $3 s&h.

New Hampshire

Camaro-Heaven 64 River Street Rochester, NH 03867	800-CAMARO-1 FAX: 603-332-3299

See full listing in **Section One** under **Chevelle/Camaro**

Illinois

Sylvester McWorthy 6003 Illinois Rt 84 Thomson, IL 61285	**815-273-2541**

We have disposed of all automobiles. We still have a lot of older auto parts, such as, transmissions, radiators, heaters, carburetors, small parts, starters and generators 1940 through 1960. We also have some new parts, gaskets, GMC & Chevrolet truck parts, ignition parts, new mufflers and tailpipes, bottom window channels, 6-volt sealed beam conversion kits for Ford & Chev, much more. Bearings, wheelcovers in sets, large collection of original hubcaps, other chrome trim for wheels. Working alone, and may be a little slow answering your calls.

Gus Miller Rt 2 Box 217 Heyworth, IL 61745	**309-473-2979**

Open by appointment only. 10 acres of cars and parts from the forties, fifties and sixties for sale. All FOB. No mail orders.

Indiana

Webb's Classic Auto Parts 5084 W State Rd 114 Huntington, IN 46750	**PH/FAX:** **219-344-1714**

See full listing in **Section One** under **AMC**

Iowa

Van Horn Auto Parts Inc Rt 4 20966 Monroe St Mason City, IA 50401	**515-423-0655** **FAX: 515-423-2570**

Open Monday-Saturday. Over 2,000 1975 and newer cars and light trucks in stock.

Kansas

Easy Jack & Sons Antique Auto Parts Store 2725 S Milford Lake Rd Junction City, KS 66441-8446	**913-238-7541** **913-238-7161**

Open Monday through Friday 8 am to 5:30 pm CST, Saturday 8 am to 2 pm CST. Specializing in 1912-85 parts and vehicles. Over 80 different makes and brands available. Store & yard covers over twenty acres. Hundreds of restorable vehicles. Millions of parts. Buying and selling antique and collector type vehicles and parts since 1963. Located six miles west of Junction City on Interstate #70, at Milford Lake Road, exit #290. We accept MasterCard/VISA.

Bob Lint Motor Shop PO Box 87 101 S Main St Danville, KS 67036	**316-962-5247**

Mail order and open shop. Monday-Friday 8 to 5; Saturday 8 to noon. Thousands of parts, mostly Ford and Chevrolet, Plymouth, Buick, Studebaker, A & T Fords, lots of truck parts. Many 20s and 30s wire wheels, old car parts, also tires. Many old car radiators & hubcaps. Also have complete old cars and trucks, NOS tires, used transmissions, rear ends, motors, brake shoes, generators & starters, etc. In business for 43 years same location.

Louisiana

Fannaly's Auto Exchange 41403 S Range Rd PO Box 23 Ponchatoula, LA 70454	**504-386-3714**

Mail order and shop open by appointment. Approximately 400 parts cars. Cadillacs, Buicks 1939-1970, MoPar, NOS parts, obsolete marques, Blue Crown spark plugs. Antique and contemporary cars and trucks. Antique parts, both used and NOS.

Maryland

Chuck's Used Auto Parts 4722 St Barnabas Rd Marlow Heights, MD 20748	**301-423-0007** **FAX: 301-899-1535**

Open Monday-Friday 8 to 5, Saturday 9 to 1. Specializing in 88 and newer GM cars and trucks, also Corvettes. Daily UPS.

Smith Brothers' Auto Parts 2316 Snydersburg Rd Hampstead, MD 21074 410-374-6781	**410-374-6781** **410-239-8514**

Open 6 days 8 to 5. Approximately 500 cars from 1946 to 1980, some muscle cars from 1965 to 1972. Ford driveline parts 1935 and up.

TMC Publications 5817 Park Heights Ave Baltimore, MD 21215	**410-367-4490** **FAX: 410-466-3566**

See full listing in **Section Two** under **literature dealers**

Maine

Classic Ford Sales PO Box 60 E Dixfield, ME 04227	**207-562-4443** **FAX: 207-562-4576** **E-mail:** **info@classicford.com**

Mail order and open shop. Monday-Friday 9-5, closed Saturday. Ford products only 1949-1972 full size, Thunderbird, Lincoln, Mercury, Mustang, Falcon, Fairlane, Comet, Cougar, F100, parts and restorables with some NOS.

Massachusetts

Bay Road Auto Parts 588 Main, Box 746 Rowley, MA 01969	**508-948-5400**

Mail order and open shop Monday-Friday by appointment only. Specializing in mid 70s-back car and truck parts, restorable cars and trucks. Mostly GM and MoPar. We buy and sell some good, used sheetmetal. Large inventory. We ship anywhere. We find the hard-to-find items. Leave message on machine, we do return calls.

R E Pierce 47 Stone Rd Wendell Depot, MA 01380	**508-544-7442** **FAX: 508-544-2978**

See full listing in **Section One** under **Volvo**

Michigan

Bob's Auto Parts 6390 N Lapeer Rd Fostoria, MI 48435	**810-793-7500**

Mail order and open shop. 2,000 cars in yard. New and used classic and antique auto parts. Owner semi-retired. Phone for appointment or send SASE for information. Hours are 9 to 5 Monday, Wednesday, Friday; 9 to 12 Saturday. Customer may go into yard with owner or employee. Parts are removed by employees only.

Midwestern Motors & Dismantlers 19785 W 12 Mi, Bldg 404 Southfield, MI 48076	**810-559-8848**

See full listing in **Section One** under **Mercedes-Benz**

Salvage Yards

Super Auto Parts
6162 Lapeer Rd
Clyde, MI 48049

810-982-6895

Mail order and open shop. Approximately 500 cars in the yards, sells parts only. Cars are from 1950-80. In business for 50 years.

Minnesota

ADP Parts Services
14800 28th Ave N
Plymouth, MN 55447

800-825-0644
FAX: 612-553-0270

See full listing in **Section Two** under **car & parts locators**

Bill's Auto Parts
310 7th Ave
Newport, MN 55055

612-459-9733

Mail order and open shop. Monday-Friday 8 to 5:30, Saturday 8 to 12. Auto parts dismantling and recycling. Used parts only, all years, makes and models 1930 thru 1980s.

Cedar Auto Parts
1100 Syndicate St
Jordan, MN 55352

612-492-3300
800-755-3266

Mail order and open shop. Monday-Friday 8 to 6, Saturday 8 to 5. Salvage yard and used car lot with early and late model cars. Many 50s, 60s and special interest autos. Specialize in American and European cars and light trucks, 1949 to current. Although we are a full service operation, we will allow customers to browse whenever possible. Nationwide shipping and locating services.

Doug's Auto Parts
Hwy 59 N, Box 811
Marshall, MN 56258

507-537-1488
FAX: 507-537-0519

Mail order and open shop. Mon-Fri 8 am-5 pm, closed Sat. Specialize in 1932-48 Ford cars and trucks, 1937-69 Chevys.

Missouri

J & M Vintage Auto
2 Mi W Goodman on B Hwy
Goodman, MO 64843
417-364-7203

417-364-7203

Mail order and open shop. Monday-Saturday 8 to 6. 1,600 cars, 1930-1972. Customers may browse unassisted.

Trimble Farmers Salvage Inc
J E Anderson, Manager
PO Box 53
Trimble, MO 64492

816-357-2515

Open by appointment only. Specializing in Packards. We accept, and in some cases, purchase Packard cars for parts. Must have proof of ownership.

Montana

Freman's Auto
138 Kountz Rd
Whitehall, MT 59759

406-287-5436
FAX: 406-287-9103

See full listing in **Section Two** under **car dealers**

Medicine Bow Motors Inc
343 One Horse Creek Rd
Florence, MT 59833

406-273-0002

See full listing in **Section Two** under **car dealers**

Nebraska

**Roger's Foreign Auto & Recyclers
& Roger's Papio Pedal Power**
226 N Adams
Papillion, NE 68046

402-331-6666
FAX: 402-331-2867

Open Monday-Friday 8:30 to 5:30; Saturday 9 to 1 pm. Specializing in foreign cars and foreign trucks only from 1990 and older.

New Hampshire

Parts of the Past
Rt 2, Box 118A
Canaan, NH 03741

603-523-4524
FAX: 603-523-4524
*49

Mail order and open shop. Salvage yard open Monday to Friday, weekends by appointment. 1924-72 General Motors, Ford, MoPar, Hudson, Kaiser-Fraser, Edsel, Graham, Mercury, Nash, Packard, Studebaker, Lincoln, LaSalle parts. "If I don't have it, I will try to find it." Sale of parts, pieces, whole cars and restorable antiques.

New Mexico

Clovis Auto Parts
1507 US 60-84
Clovis, NM 88101

505-791-3551

Mail order and open shop. Shop open Monday-Friday 8:30 am to 5 pm, Saturday by appointment. Specializing in all types of automotive, pickup and truck salvage.

Discount Auto Parts
4703 Broadway SE
Albuquerque, NM 87105

505-877-6782

Mail order and open shop. Monday-Friday 8 to 5:30. Salvage yard. Specialist in Volkswagen and Audi.

Route 66 Reutilization
1357 Historic Rt 66 E
Tijeras, NM 87059

505-286-2222

Salvage yard. Sells vintage autos and trucks, parts and Route 66 memorabilia.

New York

Adler's Antique Autos Inc
801 NY Route 43
Stephentown, NY 12168

518-733-5749 days
518-479-4103
nights

Over 600 1935-80 Chevrolets. Specializing in 1947-55 Chevrolet advance design trucks. Parts vehicles and restoration projects, will ship UPS or truck. Browsers also welcome. Complete restoration and preservation facilities. All work and parts guaranteed. Towing available.

Elmer's Auto Parts Inc
137 Donovan St
Webster, NY 14580

716-872-4402
800-288-3883
FAX: 716-872-2519

See full listing in **Section One** under **Corvette**

Fleetline Automotive
PO Box 291
Highland, NY 12528

914-691-9228

Mail order and open shop. Open by appointment only. Specializing in Chevrolet cars and trucks and other GM makes. 1937-77 are serviced. Original low mileage engines and mechanical parts. Operator is very knowledgeable on 1937-77 GM cars. Will ship UPS or freight any destination. Dash instruments, seats, body moldings, door hardware and body parts are available. Call or write your requests.

Salvage Yards

Maffucci Sales Company Inc RD 1 Box 60, Rt 9 W Athens, NY 12015	**518-943-0100** **FAX: 518-943-4534**

See full listing in **Section One** under **Lincoln**

Reardon Enterprises Box 258A, Rt 28 Mohawk, NY 13407	**315-866-3072**

Mail order and open shop. Weekends and evenings open 24 hours. Large selection of 1928-60 GM parts cars, plus oddballs. Trucks, too. Antique motorcycles, gas pumps, oil filters, fan belts, memorabilia. Cars bought and traded.

Tucker's Auto Salvage Richard J Tucker RD 1, Box 29A Burke, NY 12917	**518-483-5478**

Open Monday-Friday, 8 to 5. Saturday, 8 to 12. Cars and parts, sandblasting, body and mechanical restoration.

North Carolina

Richard's Auto Sales & Salvage 7638 NC Hwy 49 S Denton, NC 27239	**910-857-2222** **FAX: 910-857-3222**

Mail order and open shop. Open Mon-Frid 10-5, Sat 8-1.

Thunderbird Barn 2919 Elkin Hwy 268 North Wilkesboro, NC 28659	**910-667-0837**

Specializing in 1958-68 Thunderbird cars and parts. Member of North Carolina VTCA Chapter.

Ohio

Alotta Auto Parts 8426 Upper Miamisburg Rd Miamisburg, OH 45342	**513-866-1849** **FAX: 513-866-6431**

Mail order and open shop. Mon-Fri 8:30-5, Sat 8:30-2. Six acre salvage yard with cars and parts. Specializing in 50s and 60s autos & light trucks. NOS and used parts. COD shipping available.

Del-Car Used Auto Parts 6650 Harlem Rd Westerville, OH 43081	**614-882-0777** **FAX: 614-895-1399**

Open Monday-Friday 8-5. Twelve acres, 1986 and newer American & foreign cars & light trucks. Specializes in 1986 and newer Fords and GMs. Over 1,200 units. Parts only. 26 years in business. VISA/MasterCard, your check, UPS & other shipping.

Rode's Restoration 1406 Lohr Rd Galion, OH 44833	**419-468-5182** **FAX: 419-462-1753**

See full listing in **Section One** under **Mustang**

Oklahoma

Hauf Antique & Classic Cars **& Pickups** Box 547 Stillwater, OK 74076	**405-372-1585** **FAX: 405-372-1586**

Open Tuesday-Friday 8 to 5, weekends by appointment. Specializes in classic, antique cars and pickups.

North Yale Auto Parts Rt 1, Box 707 Sperry, OK 74073	**918-288-7218** **800-256-6927 (NYAP)** **FAX: 918-288-7223**

Mail order and open shop. Monday-Friday 8 to 5. Specializes in 50-80s Chevys, Chryslers, Fords.

Oregon

Michael's Auto Parts 5875 NW Kaiser Rd Portland, OR 97229	**503-690-7750** **FAX: 503-690-7735**

Mail order. Used Mercedes parts. Monday-Friday 9 am-5 pm, Saturday 12-5 pm. Models 1960-80, body styles 108, 109, 110, 111, 114, 115, 116, 123, 2 and 4-door. Reasonable prices. Rust-free sheetmetal, glass, chrome, grilles, bumpers, a/c units, manifolds, heads, transmissions, interiors, etc. Specialize in 111 coupes. Satisfaction guaranteed.

Springfield Auto Recyclers Inc PO Box 127 Springfield, OR 97477	**503-747-9601** **FAX: 503-746-3731**

Mail order and open shop. Dismantles 1940-89 cars and trucks. Also stocks many new parts.

Pennsylvania

Corvair Ranch Inc 1079 Bon-Ox Rd Gettysburg, PA 17325	**PH/FAX:** **717-624-2805**

See full listing in **Section One** under **Corvair**

Ed Lucke's Auto Parts RR 2, Box 2883 Glenville, PA 17329	**717-235-2866**

Open Monday-Friday 9 to 5; Saturday 9 to 12. 1,200 to 1,500 vehicles, many parts already removed. Parts for 1939-56 Packards, 1939-present Chryslers and 1949 to present Fords and GMs.

Rhode Island

B & B Cylinder Head 320 Washington St West Warwick, RI 02893	**401-828-4900** **800-800-4143**

See full listing in **Section Two** under **engine parts**

South Dakota

Dakota Studebaker Parts RR 1, Box 103A Armour, SD 57313	**605-724-2527**

See full listing in **Section One** under **Studebaker**

Wayne's Auto Salvage RR 3, Box 41 Winner, SD 57580-9204	**605-842-2054**

Mail order and open shop. Monday-Saturday 9 am to 6 pm. Twenty acres of cars from the forties, fifties and sixties. A few from the thirties. Cars & pickups. Sell complete vehicles or parts. Mechanics shop.

Tennessee

Kelley's Korner 22 14th St Bristol, TN 37620	**423-968-5583**

See full listing in **Section One** under **Studebaker**

Volunteer State Chevy Parts Hwy 41 S Greenbrier, TN 37073	**615-643-4583** **FAX: 615-643-5100**

See full listing in **Section One** under **Chevrolet**

Salvage Yards

Texas

South Side Salvage Rt 2, Box 8 Wellington, TX 79095	**806-447-2391**

Open Monday-Saturday 8 to 5. Specializing in old & rebuildable vehicles and parts. Over 40 years at same location. Owner: Marshall Peters, 806-447-2490 home. Ready to retire, will sell entire business.

Vermont

Alan Hartshorn Box 18 Warren, VT 05674	**802-496-2281** **before 7:30 am**

Open by appointment only. Specializes in Ford, Chevy, Essex, Buick, Overland, Studebaker, Dodge, Chrysler, Whippet, Pontiac, Hudson. Common makes, 1925-'35 parts and parts cars, 300 fenders, 200 doors, 40 parts cars, some parts to '55. Hobby only.

Virginia

Old Dominion Mustang 509 S Washington Hwy, Rt 1 Ashland, VA 23005	**804-798-3348** **FAX: 804-798-5105**

See full listing in **Section One** under **Mustang**

Philbates Auto Wrecking Inc PO Box 28 Hwy 249 New Kent, VA 23124	**804/843-9787** **804/843-2884**

Open Monday-Friday 9 to 5; Saturday 9 to 2. Parts for 1940-82 cars. Mail order sales. Over 6,000 autos in stock at all times. Old, odd, collector autos our specialty. Browsers welcome.

Bill Thomsen Rt 4 Box 492 Moneta, VA 24121	**540-297-1200**

Mail order and open shop by appointment only. Phone hours vary, call up to 10 pm Eastern time. Small private salvage yard specializing in 1953-73 full-size Chevrolet cars. Primarily mail out shipping worldwide. Hundreds of used hard to find parts. Consistently adding to inventory.

Washington

Antique Auto Items Darrell/Donna Rosenkranz, owners S 1607 McCabe Rd Spokane, WA 99216	**509-926-0987**

Small parts specialists for all US autos. SASE requested with specific want list. Open by appointment.

Antique Auto Ranch Inc N 2225 Dollar Rd Spokane, WA 99212	**509-535-7789**

Open Monday-Friday 8 to 5; Saturday 8 to noon. Specializing in American makes 1960 and older. Large supply of used parts, plus rebuilding service for obsolete water pumps and fuel pumps.

West Virginia

Antique Auto Parts PO Box 64 60 View Dr Elkview, WV 25071	**304-965-1821**

See full listing in **Section Two** under **comprehensive parts**

Wisconsin

Ehrenreich's Corvair Service 1728 Manor Pkwy Sheboygan, WI 53083-2827	**414-458-1170**

See full listing in **Section One** under **Corvair**

Zeb's Salvage N3181 Bernitt Rd Tigerton, WI 54486	**715-754-5885**

Business hours M-F 8-5, Sat 8-3. Have about 1,000 parts cars, mid-20s to late 80s. Ship small parts only.

Australia

Old Tin Australia PO Box 26 Wendouree, Victoria 3355 Australia	**0353-36-1929** **FAX: 0353-36-2930**

Australian utilities made by Ford and Chev from 1928-52.

Canada

Richard L Mahr Box 296 Milk River, AB Canada T0M 1M0	**403-647-2477**

Specializing in 1940-80 cars, trucks and everything and anything else. Mr Mahr's place is the original home of the "Whoopeeride" and is listed in Alberta government tourism publications. Vehicles are mostly North American, numerous Canadian built Meteors, Fargo trucks, Beaumonts and Acadians also. Some foreign vehicles also to be found. Hours: 7 am-10 pm, 365 days/year.

Scotts Super Trucks Box 6772 1040 Emma St Penhold, AB Canada T0M 1R0	**403-886-5572** **FAX: 403-886-5577**

See full listing in **Section One** under **Chevrolet**

Salvage Yards

Section Six:
Museums

Auto museums are like scotch whiskey. Some are better than others, but there really are no bad ones. For the hobbyist seeking a car or auto-related exhibit close to home or on a vacation trip, museums are listed under state categories.

When planning a visit to a museum, be sure you've checked its exhibition hours as well as the months of the year when it is open. Some operate all year, but others are only open seasonally, generally in the spring, summer, and early fall. Some listed here are private museums and are open only by appointment.

Most every museum charges admission. Some, however, will offer group rates for clubs wishing to tour their collections. Many of the entries list the person in charge of the museum, and he or she should be contacted, in advance, to arrange a group visit. Some of the museums operate in conjunction with other exhibition attractions, while a few also serve as the showrooms for vintage car dealers. The latter group may be stretching the definition of a museum a bit far, but the hobbyist may find such displays interesting in their own right.

Arkansas

The Last Precinct Police Museum Rt 6, Box 345B (62 Highway West) Eureka Springs, AR 72632	501-253-4948 FAX: 501-253-4949

Open April 1 to December 31. Tuesday thru Saturday 10 am to 6 pm, Sunday by appointment. A police museum featuring 150 years of law enforcement history including: five decades of police cars and motorcycles, uniforms, badges, equipment from around the world. Movie memorabilia, old west displays. Also, large gift shop. Last one of 12 Z-28 Camaros (1979) built for CHP. Bluesmobile. Dick Tracy squad car. Propane powered police car.

The Museum of Automobiles 8 Jones Ln Morrilton, AR 72110	PH/FAX: 501-727-5427

Open daily 10 to 5. Buddy Hoelzeman, director. Exhibits include antique and classic cars on loan from private collectors. An auto fair and swap meet is held the third weekend in June with auto judging, style shows and driving events. The museum serves as national headquarters for the Mid-America Old Time Auto Assoc (MOTAA).

California

Behring Automotive Museum 3700 Blackhawk Plaza Cir Danville, CA 94506	510-736-2280 FAX: 510-736-4818

Opened in 1990. 2,700 members. Open Wednesday-Sunday 10 am to 5 pm. Presents approximately 120 of the world's truly great automobiles dating from 1890s as individual works of art. Automotive art wing presents 1,000 artifacts in various media from the mid 1800s throughout six thematic areas. The W E Miller Automotive Research Library contains the largest collection of automotive reference material west of Detroit. Membership includes exhibit previews and newsletter. Call information line above for current featured exhibitions. Blackhawk Plaza is 4 miles east of I-680 off Camino Tassajara/Sycamore Valley at Crow Canyon Rd, Danville, CA. Visit the museum's web site at: http://www.behringauto.org

Bob's Radio & TV Service/ Vintage Electronics 2300 Broad St San Lius Obispo, CA 94401	805-543-2946 FAX: 805-782-0803

See full listing in **Section Two** under **radios**

Ed Cholakian Enterprises Inc dba All Cadillacs of the Forties 12811 Foothill Blvd Sylmar, CA 91342	818-361-1147 800-808-1147 FAX: 818-361-9738

See full listing in **Section One** under **Cadillac/LaSalle**

Justice Brothers Inc 2734 E Huntington Dr Duarte, CA 91010	818-359-9174 FAX: 818-357-2550

Open all year, Monday-Friday 9 am to 5 pm. A broad collection of Midget race cars with classic street cars, a GT-40 and other unique vehicles.

Peterson Automotive Museum 6060 Wilshire Blvd Los Angeles, CA 90036	213-930-CARS (2277) FAX: 213-930-6642

Open all year. Tuesday through Sunday 10-6, and Monday holidays. A member of the Los Angeles County Natural History Museum Group. Largest, most definitive automotive museum in North America. Dedicated to the interpretive study of the automobile and its influence on American life and culture. Three levels of exhibits, secure parking and large gift shop. Venue for car shows, auctions and 3rd party special events. Features Hollywood star cars, motorcycles, petroliana and automotive themed art.

Route 66 Territory Visitors Center & Museum Thomas Winery Plaza 7965 Vineyard Ave, Suite F5 Rancho Cucamonga, CA 91730	800-JOG-RT66 FAX: 909-599-5308

Open most weekdays 10:30 to 4, most weekends 10:30 to 5. Features a growing collection of watercolor paintings of historic places along Route 66 from Rancho Cucamonga to Chicago. Also, a Route 66 photo exhibit across San Bernardino County, and a variety of watercolor paintings of nostalgic tourist attractions and facilities in Los Angeles County. Other exhibits include maps, music, gas pumps, road signs, automobilia and a video theatre. Free tourism literature and schedule of Route 66 special events. Hospitality room and Route 66 nostalgia gift shop.

San Diego Automotive Museum 2080 Pan American Plaza Balboa Park San Diego, CA 92101	619-231-2886 FAX: 619-231-9869

Open 7 days a week, year round, 10-4:30. (last admission 4 pm); summer hours, 10-5:30 pm (last admission 5 pm). A breathtaking array of rare and exotic automobiles and a world class motorcycle display with feature shows changing 2-3 times a year. Also special interest shows during the year including the annual "Motorcycles in the Park Show." Call for current show information. Full service gift shop. Museum membership available ($25 a year) providing many car enthusiast benefits, including free entry to museum and guest passes, updates on museum activities and invitations to special events.

Specialty Sales 4321 First St Pleasanton, CA 94566	**510-484-2262** **FAX: 510-426-8535** **E-mail:** specialt@ix.netcom.com

See full listing in **Section Two** under **car dealers**

Towe Ford Museum of **Automotive History** 2200 Front St Sacramento, CA 95818	**916-442-6802** **FAX: 916-442-2646**

Open daily 10 to 6 (closed Thanksgiving, Christmas and New Year's Day). The Towe Ford Museum of Automotive History houses the world's largest and most complete antique Ford collection. There are over 180 cars and trucks representing almost every year, model and body style of Ford from 1903 to 1953. We tell the story of the development of the automobile in this country. The museum also houses a number of other makes of automobiles, ie: Buick, Cadillac, Star, Chevy, etc, and other artifacts of historical significance. Library and gift shop operated by non-profit California Vehicle Foundation.

Colorado

Classical Gas Antique Auto **Museum & Sales** 245 E Collins Eaton, CO 80615	**800-453-7955** **970-454-1373** **FAX: 970-454-1368**

See full listing in **Section Two** under **car dealers**

Forney Transportation Museum 1416 Platte St Denver, CO 80202	**303-433-3643**

Open 10 to 5 Monday-Saturday, Sunday 11 to 5. Closed Thanksgiving, Christmas, New Year's Day and Easter. Motor into the past with 150 antique and classic cars from the 1890s through the early 1960s. Other exhibits include motorcycles, bicycles, carriages and three steam locomotives (including Big Boy #4005), plus several railroad cars and other railroad equipment, all housed in and around the almost 100 year old historic huge former Denver Tramway powerhouse building.

Rocky Mountain Motorcycle **Museum & Hall of Fame** 308 E Arvada St Colorado Springs, CO 80906	**PH/FAX:** **719-633-6329**

Mail order and museum. Open Monday-Saturday 10 am to 7 pm year-round. Motorcycle museum, mostly American Harley-Davidson, Indian, but many other British and Asian.

Florida

Bellm's Cars & Music of Yesterday 5500 N Tamiami Trail Sarasota, FL 34243	**813-355-6228**

Open all year, Sunday-Saturday 9:30 to 5:30. Collection of antique and special interest cars, including Rolls-Royce, Pierce-Arrow, Stutz, Moon, Cartercar, 1959 Scimitar and many more. Also large collection of over 1,800 mechanical music machines on display.

Historical Society of **Martin County** 825 NE Ocean Blvd Stuart, FL 34996	**407-225-1961** **FAX: 407-225-2333**

Open 12 months a year, 7 days a week, 11 am to 4 pm. Exhibits include antique and classic automobiles, motorcycles, bicycles, and horse-drawn vehicles. Also 1929 Phantom I Rolls-Royce Shooting Brake.

Georgia

Museo Abarth 1111 Via Bayless Marietta, GA 30066-2770	**770-928-1446**

Open Monday-Friday 9 to 5, except holidays. Admission free. Display of original Abarth, Fiat and Lancia memorabilia.

Stone Mountain Antique Car **& Treasure Museum** Stone Mountain Park Stone Mountain, GA 30087	**770-413-5229**

Privately owned collection of cars including a 1948 Tucker, Chevrolets, Fords, Oldsmobiles, and others. Also a privately owned collection of memorabilia which includes jukeboxes, player pianos, antique furniture and clocks, pedal cars, baseball cards, and other items of interest.

Illinois

Cadillac Auto Display PO Box 6732 Rockford, IL 61125	**815-229-1258** **FAX: 815-229-1238**

Future reopening to be announced. Cadillac automobiles, Cadillac parts, anything related to Cadillacs. Museum closed, but planning reopening in near future. Former display expanding to larger, more elaborate facility. Still acquiring Cadillac vehicles, literature, automobilia, etc, 1940 thru 1964 of various models. Other years considered, any condition.

Hartung's Automotive Museum 3623 W Lake St Glenview, IL 60025	**847-724-4354**

Auto museum open daily, call for hours. License plate and auto museum with over 100 antique autos, trucks and motorcycles on exhibit. Vehicles on display include 75 antique bicycles, 28 motorcycles from 1901-1941; Whizzers, sidecars and scooters; Ford Model As, Ts, V8s, panel deliveries and trucks, plus many other automobiles. License plate collection contains plates from 50 states and Canada. Also promotional model cars, auto hubcaps, radiator emblems, etc. Also police badge collection.

Volo Antique Auto Museum 27582 Volo Village Rd Volo, IL 60073	**815-385-3644** **FAX: 815-385-0703**

Open daily 10 to 5. Located 13 miles west of I-94 on Volo Village Road, one traffic light north of Route 120. Exhibits include approximately 200 restored collector cars, automobilia gift shop. Exquisite homemade food and 3 giant antique malls to browse. We buy, sell and appraise collector cars. Admission: adults, $3.95; seniors, $2.50; children ages 6 to 12, $1.50; under 6, free. Group rates by advance reservation.

Wheels O' Time Museum PO Box 9636 Peoria, IL 61612-9636	**309-243-9020**

Open Wednesday-Sunday (May-October), 12 noon to 5 pm. Also summer holidays. A hands-on museum housed in three buildings. Among displays are vintage automobiles, Austin-Healey, L-29 Cord, Glide, Packard, Pierce-Arrow, Rolls-Royce (Bentley), airplanes, bicycles, steam engines, tools, musical instruments, clocks, model trains, toys, old-fashioned barbershop with life-

size singing quartet, a miniature animated circus, tractors, gasoline engines, grain-handling machines. A replica of an early 20th century firehouse, contains fire engines. More automobiles and other displays. On a track rests a 130-ton steam engine of early 1900 vintage, Combo car, caboose, handcar and switch engine. Located 9 miles north of downtown Peoria, IL on Route 40.

Indiana

Auburn Cord Duesenberg Museum 1600 S Wayne St Auburn, IN 46706	**219-925-1444** **FAX: 219-925-6266**

Open 9 am to 5 pm daily, year round. Robert Sbarge, Executive Director. More than 100 automobiles on exhibit, featuring Auburns, Cords and Duesenbergs. The Museum is housed in the 1930 art deco factory showrooms of the Auburn Automobile Company. Autos on exhibit include the earliest Auburn known to exist and a cross section of all types of collector cars. Discount admission for any old car club member. Museum store; Auburn Cord Duesenberg festival, Labor Day weekend.

S Ray Miller Auto Museum Inc 2130 Middlebury St Elkhart, IN 46516	**219-522-0539** **FAX: 219-522-0358**

Open all year round, Monday-Friday 10 am to 4 pm, last weekend of each month 12 to 4 pm. Forty uniquely displayed antique and award winning classic autos along with miscellaneous auto memorabilia, collectibles, vintage clothing and antiques. Many National winners on display.

National Automotive & Truck Museum Of The United States 1000 Gordon M Buehrig Pl Auburn, IN 46706	**219-925-9100** **FAX: 219-925-4563**

Open all year round. Monday-Sunday 9 am-5 pm EST. NATMUS is located in the former factory buildings of the Auburn Automobile Co and is adjacent to the Auburn, Cord, Duesenberg museum. Focus is on postwar cars and trucks from all eras. There are periodical special exhibits. Over 100 cars and trucks on exhibit at any time. A large collection of toys and models.

Studebaker National Museum 525 S Main St South Bend, IN 46601	**219-235-9714**

Museum hours: Monday-Saturday, 9-5; Sunday 12-5. Admission fee. Depicts 112 years of Studebaker transportation history. Collection includes wagons, carriages, automobiles and trucks produced by Studebaker, and industrial treasures of northern Indiana. Also features X-90 Hands-On Science and Technology Center.

Iowa

National Sprint Car Hall of Fame & Museum PO Box 542 Knoxville, IA 50138	**800-874-4488** **FAX: 515-842-6177**

Open year round, weekdays 10-6, Saturdays 10-5, Sundays 12-5. The world's only museum dedicated to preserving the history of the sport of big car, super modified and sprint car racing. Handicapped accessible. Gift shop. Group tours available. All cars on loan and rotated yearly.

Van Horn's Antique Truck Museum 15272 North St Mason City, IA 50401	**515-423-0655** **office** **515-423-0550** **museum**

This unique private museum displays 65 makes of nation's oldest restored motor trucks with many displayed in settings of the era in which they were manufactured. Trucks on display date from 1930 back to 1908. Plus hundreds of other early automo-

tive items on display. Also featured is a large scale model circus that one man created over his lifetime. Open daily May 22-September 22. Admission.

Kentucky

Rineyville Sandblasting Model A Ford Museum 179 Arvel Wise Ln Elizabethtown, KY 42701	**502-862-4671**

Open year round by phone or by chance. Ernest J Pyzocha, curator and proprietor. Located off Hwy 1538 between Fort Knox and Elizabethtown, KY. 6,000 sq ft warehouse packed with nearly 40 unrestored Model A Ford cars and trucks of various body styles. Also license plate collection, signs, tools, parts, accessories, and much, much more. Admission $2.

Maine

Boothbay Railway Village Rt 27 PO Box 123 Boothbay, ME 04537	**207-633-4727**

Open daily, mid-June through mid-October, 9:30 am-5 pm. Turn of century village containing historical exhibits including Thorndike and Freeport railroad stations, Boothbay Town Hall, general store, blacksmith shop, filling station. Ride on a coal-fired, narrow gauge steam train to an exceptional antique vehicle display housing more than 50 vehicles from 1907-1949.

Cole Land Transportation Museum 405 Perry Rd Bangor, ME 04401 207-990-3600	**207-990-3600**

Open May 1 through November 11, daily 9 am to 5 pm.

Owls Head Transportation Museum PO Box 277, Rt 73 Owls Head, ME 04854	**207-594-4418 FAX:** **207-594-4410** **E-mail:** **ohtm@midcoast.com**

Open shop. Daily except Thanksgiving, Christmas and New Year's. 10 am-5 pm April-October, 10 am-4 pm November-March. Web site: http://www.ohtm.org

Wells Auto Museum Rt 1, PO Box 496 Wells, ME 04090	**207-646-9064**

Open shop only. Open weekends from Memorial weekend through Columbus weekend, 10 to 5. Open daily mid-June thru September, 10 to 5. Non-profit museum displaying automotive history from 1900-1964. Gas, electric and steam cars on display along with motorcycles and a few horse-drawn vehicles. A fine selection of nickelodeons, mutoscopes, and arcade games from the twenties and thirties. Toys, photos and paintings, and other automobilia.

Massachusetts

Beverly Historical Society & Museum Walker Transportation Collection 117 Cabot St Beverly, MA 01915	**508-922-1186**

Open all year. Wednesday evenings 7 to 10 pm; Saturday openings by appointment only. Phone 24 hours, leave message. Call or write for info. Local history and a special transportation collection featuring thousands of photos of trains, trolleys, ships, buses and automobiles. Models and displays of transportation related artifacts. Research source & library. Emphasis on New England. Admission $2.

Museums

Heritage Plantation of Sandwich
Pine and Grove Sts
Sandwich, MA 02563

508-888-3300

Mail order and open shop. Open May-October 7 days a week, 10 to 5. Museum of Americana & Gardens on 76 acres. Antique Automobile Museum with 36 vintage and classic cars. Shown in a replica of a Shaker round barn. Stars of the collection are 1930 Duesenberg, 1932 Auburn boattail speedster and 1915 Stutz Bearcat. Military museum and art museum. Picnic area. Admission.

Museum of Transportation
15 Newton St
Brookline, MA 02146

617-522-6547
FAX: 617-524-0170

Open Wednesdays-Sundays 10-5 all year. New England's premier auto museum with a changing exhibits program and full calendar of car club events.

Yankee Candle Car Museum
5 North St
South Deerfield, MA 01373

413-665-2020
FAX: 413-665-2399

Open year round, 9:30 am-6 pm daily, closed Thanksgiving & Christmas. Car museum is a world class collection of more than 70 American and European automobiles. Our 16,000 sq ft museum features an array of automobiles from the hottest sports cars to the coolest and most regal automobiles. Museum store is stocked with hats, T-shirts, model cars, books, videotapes and much more. Call for admission prices.

Michigan

Gilmore-Classic Car Club of America Museum
6865 Hickory Rd
Hickory Corners, MI 49060

616-671-5089
FAX: 616-671-5843

Open early May through late October. Daily 10 am to 5 pm. A transportation museum run in cooperation with the Classic Car Club of America Museum, dedicated to preserving and displaying the historical significance of the automobile industry. 130 cars displayed in several exquisite barns situated on ninety manicured acres. Cars featured include Packard, Cadillac, Tucker, Duesenberg, Corvette and cars made in Kalamazoo.

R E Olds Transportation Museum
240 Museum Dr
Lansing, MI 48933-1905

517-372-0422
FAX: 517-372-2901

Sunday noon to 5 pm, Monday-Saturday 10 to 5, except December 21 thru Easter, call first. Focus on Lansing's contributions to auto and transportation industry. Changing exhibits, feature 1897 Olds, 1926 Star, Indy pace cars, bicycle collection, Reo cars, Speedwagon and many other milestone vehicles.

Alfred P Sloan Museum
1221 E Kearsley St
Flint, MI 48503
FAX: 810-760-5339

810-760-1169

Open Monday-Friday 10 to 5, Saturday and Sunday 12 to 5. Major new exhibition, "Flint and the American Dream," traces the dramatic history of Flint, MI in the 20th century, from the birth of General Motors to the present. Changing automotive gallery. Automotive archives available to researchers by appointment.

Minnesota

Ellingson Car Museum
20950 Rogers Dr
Rogers, MN 55374

612-428-7337
FAX: 612-428-4370

Open daily except holidays, Monday-Sunday 10 to 5. Special focus on cars, trucks, memorabilia, set-up by decade, 1900-1980. Educational videos, a 50's lounge and a complete gift shop

featuring over 600 automotive related titles. Features 1935 Mercedes 500K, 1954 Kaiser Darrin, 1957 T-Bird, 1986 Pulse.

Mississippi

Classique Cars Unlimited
5 Turkey Bayou Rd
PO Box 249
Lakeshore, MS 39558

601-467-9633
FAX: 800-543-8691
601-467-9207 in Mississippi

See full listing in **Section One** under **Lincoln**

Missouri

Museum of Transportation
St Louis County Parks & Recreation
3015 Barrett Station Rd
St Louis, MO 63122

314-965-7998
FAX: 314-965-0242

Open daily 9 to 5; closed New Year's, Thanksgiving and Christmas. Admission: adults $4, children 5-12, $1.50, children under 5, free and senior citizens $3. Exhibits include 1935 Jaguar SS-100, 1901 St Louis, 1906 Ford Model N, 1964 Chrysler turbine, 1964 DiDia/Darrin Dream Car as well as locomotives, trains, buses, trucks, horse-drawn vehicles, aircraft, street cars and pipeline and communication devices.

Montana

Towe Ford Museum
Old Montana Prison
1106 Main St
Deer Lodge, MT 59722

406-846-3111
406-846-3114

Open daily 8 am to 9 pm in summer; shorter hours in the winter. Over 100 authentically restored Fords and Lincolns from 1903 through the fifties are on display. Guided and self-guided tours through the Old Montana Prison.

Nebraska

Chevyland USA Auto Museum
7245 Buffalo Creek Rd
Elm Creek, NE 68836

308-856-4208

World's largest display of vintage and classic Chevys from 1914 to 1975. All sport models including roadsters, convertibles, hardtops, coupes, Nomads, pickups and vintage motorcycles. All cars for sale. This beautiful collection of over 100 vehicles is open daily for your enjoyment. Open daily from Memorial Day to Labor Day, by appointment rest of the year.

Hastings Museum
1330 N Burlington
Hastings, NE 68901

402-461-4629
800-508-4629
FAX: 402-461-2379

Open Monday-Saturday 9 to 5; Sunday 1 to 5. A number of antique cars are on exhibit. Other exhibits cover a variety of interests including the natural sciences, Indian lore, pioneer history, transportation and astronomy. Giant-screen IMAX theatre open daily and evenings except Monday.

Sandhills Museum
440 Valentine St
Valentine, NE 69201

402-376-3293

Open daily 9 to 6 during the summer season. Located on W Hwy 20. Exhibits include: 1907 Cadillac roadster, 1911 Austro-Daimler, 1909 Buick, 1909 Flanders and 1916 Paterson touring.

Harold Warp Pioneer Village Foundation
Hwys 6 and 34
Minden, NE 68959-0068

308-832-1181
800-445-4447
(out of state)
FAX: 308-832-2750

Open year round, every day 8 to sundown. 50,000 historic items from every field of human endeavor. 26 buildings. Authentic originals arranged in their order of development to show visually the history of our country. 350 antique autos on display. Restaurant, motel, camping, all within walking distance. Stay overnight, come back next day, same admission fee. Write for more information.

Nevada

| Harrah National Automobile Museum
10 Lake St S
Reno, NV 89501 | **702-333-9300**
FAX: 702-333-9309 |

The museum exhibits over 200 antique, classic, vintage and special interest automobiles in 4 galleries and on 4 authentic street scenes representing each quarter of the 20th Century. Feature includes a unique multi-media theatre presentation; multi-media time lines chronicling the automobile; museum store; and riverside cafe. World-famous automotive library offers research by mail. Museum is available in the evenings for group and convention activities. Open daily 9:30 to 5:30 (closed Thanksgiving, Christmas).

| Imperial Palace Auto Collection
Imperial Palace Hotel & Casino
3535 Las Vegas Blvd S
Las Vegas, NV 89109 | **702-794-3174**
FAX: 702-369-7430 |

Open daily 9:30 am to 11:30 pm. Features over 200 antique, classic and special interest autos on display in a plush, gallery-like setting. Cited by *Car & Driver* magazine as one of the ten best auto collections in the world. Also features a unique gift shop with a wide selection of automotive memorabilia and books.

New York

| Hall of Fame & Classic Car Museum, DIRT
PO Box 240, 1 Speedway Dr
Weedsport, NY 13166 | **315-834-6667**
FAX: 315-834-9734 |

Mail order and open shop. Open April-Labor Day Monday-Saturday 10-5, Sunday 12-7; September-December Monday-Friday 10-5, Saturday & Sunday 11-4; closed January-March. Dozens of classic cars on display throughout the showroom. Our classic car finder's network assists in selling, buying and locating classic cars. A classic car corral located outdoors adds to the rare and continuously changing models already shown. Rarity can easily be found. A 1969 Dodge Charger Hemi, 4-speed, first built and ordered/owned by The Dodge News Bureau.

| The Himes Museum of Motor Racing Nostalgia
15 O'Neil Ave
Bay Shore, NY 11706 | **516-666-4912** |

Open 7 days a week, 9 to 9. Motor racing museum. Autos, boats, motorcycles. Exhibits also include Midgets, Sprints, stock cars.

| Old Rhinebeck Aerodrome
42 Stone Church Rd
Rhinebeck, NY 12572 | **914-758-8610** |

Open May 15 to October 31, 10 to 5. Living museum of old airplanes featuring WWI and earlier aircraft in weekend air shows, air museums and airplane rides. Features 1909 Renault, 1916 Packard moving van, 1918 GMC WWI ambulance, 1911 Baker Electric, 1911 International Auto Buggy, 1911 Hupmobile, 1910 Maxwell runabout, 1913 Brewster Town Car, 1916 Studebaker, 1914, 1919, 1927 Ford Model Ts, 1920 Buick, 1916 Royal Enfield motorcycle, 1917 Indian motorcycle, 1936 Indian motorcycle used in conjunction with weekend air shows. New air shows schedule: starts weekends after June 15 to October 15, Saturday and Sunday at 2:30. A great meeting place for an outing, especially for vintage car clubs.

North Carolina

| North Carolina Transportation Museum at Spencer
PO Box 165, 411 S Salisbury Ave
Spencer, NC 28159 | **704-636-2889** |

Museum open April 1-Oct 31, Mon-Sat 9-5, Sun 1-5; Nov 1- Mar 31, Tues-Sat 10-4, Sun 1-4. Museum is housed in Southern Railway's former repair facility. Visitor center, gift shop, movies, rail cars, transportation displays, steam/diesel train rides with roundhouse tour, and "bumper to bumper" antique auto exhibit. Special events include train excursions, railroad equipment show, AACA show and lectures.

Ohio

| America's Packard Museum
420 S Ludlow St
Dayton, OH 45402 | **513-226-1917**
FAX: 513-224-1918 |

Open Mon-Fri 12-5 pm; Sat-Sun 1-5 year round. Museum dedicated to Packard. Six period settings from 1930s art deco era. 21 Packards on display representing every era of production, artwork, sculpture, company artifacts. G Wolf Packard race car. Packard trucks. Web site: http://www.wspin.com/~packrd

| Canton Classic Car Museum
Market Ave S at 6th St SW
Canton, OH 44702 | **330-455-3603**
FAX: 330-456-4256 |

Open 7 days 10 am-5 pm, year round. 40 cars focusing on pre-war classics. Cars range from 1911 Model T to 1981 DeLorean. Many memorabilia items, gift shop and more. Exhibition cars include: 1914 Benham, 1922 Holmes, 1937 Packard 1508 V12 carved side hearse.

| Carillon Historical Park
2001 S Patterson Blvd
Dayton, OH 45409 | **513-293-2841** |

Open Tues-Sat 10-6, Sun 1-6 from May-Oct. 18 buildings on a 65 acre site. Auto-related exhibits include a 1908 Stoddard-Dayton, 1910 Speedwell, 1923 Maxwell, 1910 Courier, 1914 Davis and 1918 Cleveland motorcycles located in the Dayton Sales building; a 1912 Cadillac, Charles Kettering and Delco exhibits inside Deeds Barn, and a 1924 Sun Oil Company station.

| Crawford Auto-Aviation Museum
10825 East Boulevard
Cleveland, OH 44106 | **216-721-5722**
FAX: 216-721-0645 |

Open 12 months, Mon-Sun 10-5. Over 150 automobiles, airplanes, bicycles, specializing in Cleveland built automobiles. 1st Cleveland car (1898 Winton) to last Cleveland car (1932 Peerless). Special exhibition. White Motors, Crawfords' Cleveland, Cleveland air races.

| Charlie Sens Antique Auto Museum
2074 Marion Mt Gilead Rd
Marion, OH 43302-8991 | **614-389-4686**
FAX: 614-386-2521 |

Open January thru December, 7 days a week except Thanksgiving, Christmas & New Year's, 10 to 5 Monday thru Saturday, 12 to 5 Sunday. Filled with more than 120 of the most beautiful antique cars ever made from a 1903 Ford to a 1969 Corvair. These cars are all in perfect running condition. Special exhibition, 1905 Sears (only auto sold from a catalog).

| Welsh Enterprises Classic Car Museum
5th & Washington Sts
PO Box 4130
Steubenville, OH 43952 | **614-282-8649**
FAX: 614-282-1913 |

Open all year Monday-Saturday 11 to 7, Sunday 12 to 6. Twenty personal favorites of Wm Welsh surrounded by historic murals of

Steubenville and in the same complex as the Jaggin' Around Restaurant & Pub. Especially featured are Jaguars, a Ferrari and a '55 Mercedes gullwing.

Oklahoma

Mac's Antique Car Museum 1319 E 4th St Tulsa, OK 74120	918-583-7400 FAX: 918-583-3108

Open shop Saturday and Sunday 12 to 5 pm. An impressive collection of over 35 fully restored classic automobiles. The collection includes Packards (Twin Six, Super Eight and V12s), LaSalles, Cadillacs, Rolls-Royces, Fords, Chevrolets, Dodge and Chrysler and others dating primarily from the 1920s and 1930s. The 14,000 square foot facility is climate controlled, handicapped accessible, and conveniently located near downtown Tulsa. Group tours welcome.

Oregon

Tillamook County Pioneer Museum 2106 2nd St Tillamook, OR 97141	503-842-4553

Open Monday-Saturday 8 to 5; Sunday 12 to 5. Closed on Mondays from October 1 to March 15. Open all holidays except Thanksgiving and Christmas. History museum and large natural history collection. Exhibits include 1902 Holsman, 1909 Buick.

Pennsylvania

Eastern Museum of Motor Racing Williams Grove Old Timers 100 Baltimore Rd York Springs, PA 17372	717-528-8279

Founded 1975. 1,700 members. Dedicated to the preservation of motor racing history. Dues: $15/year. Call for museum tours and rates. Museum open April-October, Saturday and Sunday, 10-4. Donation. Restored fairgrounds, vintage car exhibition racing during the summer months.

Gast Classic Motorcars Exhibit Rt 896, 421 Hartman Bridge Rd Strasburg, PA 17579	717-687-9500

Open year round 9 to 5. Fifty (50) car exhibit, includes 1932 Duesenberg Model J, 1934 Packard LeBaron Sport phaeton, 1948 Tucker #24 (waltz blue), first and last MGs brought to America, 1956 Thunderbird, 1966 AC Cobra 427, 1967 Amphicar, 1967 Chevrolet Camaro SS/RS conv "Indianapolis 500 pace car," 1959 Ford Skyliner retractable hardtop, 1983 DeLorean (400 miles) and Lamborghini Countach. Write for free brochure.

Swigart Museum Box 214 Museum Park Huntingdon, PA 16652	814-643-0885 FAX: 814-643-1945

Open Memorial Day thru October. Admission: adults $4, children 6-12 $2, citizen and group rates available. William E Swigart Jr, owner. Located four miles east of Huntingdon, PA on US Rt 22. One of the foremost collections of antique cars including Duesenberg, Dupont, Scripps-Booth and Carroll. Plus a memorable collection of toys, lights, clothing and a large collection of license plates, emblems and nameplates.

Rhode Island

Pronyne PO Box 1492 Pawtucket, RI 02862-1492	401-725-1118

Founded 1970. 100 members. Open all year, 9-5. Restoration and display of historic NASCAR modifieds events, Feb thru Oct. Ole Blue (37 Chevy coupe) and the Woodchopper coupe (37 Chevrolet) on display. Dues: $15/year.

South Dakota

Old West Museum Highway I-90, Exit 260 PO Box 275 Chamberlain, SD 57325	605-734-6157

Open daily 8 to 8, April-October. Exhibits include a 1917 Oldsmobile V8 touring, a 1931 Cadillac and a 1934 Chevrolet sport sedan.

Performance Car Museum 3505 S Phillips Ave Sioux Falls, SD 57105	

Open year round, Monday-Friday 9 to 5, Saturday & Sunday 10 to 5. Specializing in performance cars, celebrity cars and exotics. Attractions include every year Shelby, low mileage muscle cars, 289 Cobra, 1955/56 Corvette prototype formerly owned by Zora Duntov, 73 Trans Am formerly owned by Clint Eastwood, many, many more.

Pioneer Auto Museum & Antique Town 503 E 5th Murdo, SD 57559	605-669-2691

Open 7 am to 10 pm, June-August; 8 to 8, March-May and September and October. Dave Geisler, manager. Located at the junction of I-90 & US Highways 16 & 83 in Murdo. Exhibits include over 250 antique and classic cars from a 1902 Oldsmobile to a 1970 Superbird. Also several other exhibits of different modes of transportation from covered wagons to trains. Motorcycles on display include Elvis Presley's motorcycle. We have added muscle cars and a 50s display. 39 buildings of exhibits. New gift shop, antique shop and food court.

Tennessee

Old Car Museum Hwy 51 S Union City, TN 38261	901-885-0700 FAX: 901-885-0440

Open Monday-Friday 8 to 5. Admission $2. Exhibits include 36 fully restored antique automobiles dating from before 1947. All are in running condition. Also thousands of automobile accessories are on display.

Texas

Alamo Classic Car Showcase & Museum 6401 S Interstate 35 New Braunfels, TX 78132	210-606-4311 FAX: 210-620-4387

Open daily 10 am-6 pm. Located on Interstate 35, just north of San Antonio, TX, between Exits 180 and 182. It features over 150 vehicles from 1911 to 1987. All vehicles are displayed inside our 35,000 sq ft showroom and also are for sale. It includes antique cars, classic cars, sports cars, Corvettes, hot rods, motorcycles, scooters, motor bikes, bicycles, tools, games, pedal cars, hubcaps, etc.

GAF Auto Museum 307 E Woodlawn St Kilgore, TX 75662	903-984-4648 800-234-0124 FAX: 903-984-6474

Open Monday-Friday 8 to 5. 60 autos from 1916-1972. Auto memorabilia. Original drawings by Herb Newport, automobile designer. Old car parts, 1920s-60s.

Pate Museum of Transportation
PO Box 711
Fort Worth, TX 76101

817-332-1161
FAX: 817-332-2340

Open daily except Monday. Jim Peel, curator. Located on Highway 377 between Fort Worth and Cresson. Exhibits include antique and special interest automobiles, aircraft and missiles and a 1,500-volume library.

Utah

Bonneville Speedway Museum
1000 E Wendover Blvd
Wendover, UT 84083

801-665-7721

Open daily May-November, 10-6. Displays Bonneville race cars, general antique cars, special interest cars and a line of general antiques. On exhibition are Bonneville World race car films.

Classic Cars International Museum
335 W 7th St S
Salt Lake City, UT 84101

801-322-5186
801-582-6883
FAX: 801-582-6112
E-mail:
JRW3989@aol.com

Open year round, Monday-Friday 9 to 4. Special hours available by phone appointment. Over 200 antique and classic cars on display. Select units for sale to rotate cars. Classics range from Rolls-Royces to Rickenbackers, Cords, Hupmobiles, Essex, LaSalles, Packards, Pierce-Arrows, V16s, V12s, 1903 to 1960 classics. Approximately 50 classics on sale year round to rotate displays.

Virginia

Glade Mountain Museum
Route 1, Box 360
Atkins, VA 24311

540-783-5678

Open May-August, Sundays 1 to 8 pm. Glade Mountain Museum, take exit #54 off I-81, west 1 mile on US 11, south 1 mile on VA 708, east 1/2 mile on VA 615 to museum. Features old cars, 1803 blacksmith shop, 1850 bear trap, 1900 washing machine, 1907 1-cylinder engine. Many more items from late 1800s. Cars are mostly Fords 1926 and later. Salvage yard operating under Jack's Garage at above address. Has over 200 vehicles from 1935 to 1970 and a few older parts.

Roaring Twenties Antique Car Museum
Route 1, Box 576
Hood, VA 22723

703-948-3744
703-948-6290
FAX: 703-948-3744

Open Sunday 1 to 6 from June to October, other times by appointment. Located in Madison County on State Route 230 between I-29 & 33. John Dudley, owner. Exhibits include cars from the 20s and 30s, trucks, stationary engines, horse-drawn equipment, farm tools, household goods and other Americana. Examples of Carter, Stephens, Cleveland, Star, Hupmobile, Paige, Essex and Nash cars are on display. Cars and parts for sale.

Washington

Dylan Bay Auto Museum
1411 4th Ave, #1430
Seattle, WA 98101

206-292-9874
FAX: 206-292-9876
E-mail:
cbayley@dylanbay.com

Mail order only. Dealing in restoration and detailing. Classic car storage. Museum by appointment. Call Dixon Schwenk, 206-587-0880.

Lynden Pioneer Museum
217 W Front St
Lynden, WA 98264

360-354-3675

Open year around Mon-Sat 10 am-4 pm. One of the largest museums of its kind in the state of Washington. Boasts 28,000 sq ft and houses some of the rarest pioneer collections anywhere.

Wisconsin

Dells Auto Museum
Richard W Tarnutzer
591 Wisconsin Dells Pkwy
Wisconsin Dells, WI 53965

414-648-2151
608-254-2008

Open daily 9 to 9 from May 15-Labor Day. An exhibition of convertibles built from 1901 to 1982 featuring Indianapolis pace cars. Also on display are 400 antique dolls and toys along with period clothing from the turn of the century through the fifties. Also license plate collection. Cars and antiques bought and sold.

Hartford Heritage Auto Museum
147 N Rural St
Hartford, WI 53027

414-673-7999

Open year round except holidays. Features Kissel automobiles, Nash, Pierce-Arrow, Locomobiles, Terraplanes and various pieces of fire fighting equipment. Also displays gasoline pumps and gasoline and steam engines. Museum houses 90 vehicles of all kinds in its 40,000 square feet of display area. Admissions: $5 adult, $4 seniors and students, $2 children 8 to 15, free to children under 8.

Zunker's Antique Auto Museum
3722 MacArthur Dr
Manitowoc, WI 54220

414-684-4005

Open May to October 10 to 5, by appointment after October. Auto museum and other displays. Doll collection and children's lunchboxes. Old gas station and cycles. Over 40 autos.

Canada

Reynolds Museum
4110 57th St
Wetaskiwin, AB Canada T9A 2B6

403-352-6201
FAX: 403-352-4666

Open daily May 15 to Labor Day. Stanley G Reynolds, President. Located on Highway 2A in Wetaskiwin. Exhibits include antique airplanes, cars, tractors, steam engines, trucks, fire engines and military vehicles museum.

Reynolds-Alberta Museum
Box 6360, 1km west on Hwy 13
Wetaskiwin, AB Canada T9A 2G1

800-661-4726
FAX: 403-361-1239

Open daily, 9 am-5 pm winter, 9 am-9 pm summer. The Reynolds-Alberta Museum interprets the history of ground and air transportation, agriculture and industry from the 1890s to the 1950s. Collection of over 1,400 vintage automobiles, trucks, aircraft & agricultural machinery. 60,000 sq ft exhibit hall with over 100 major artifacts on display. Vehicles in collection include: 1929 Duesenberg phaeton Royale Model J214, 1927 LaSalle convertible coupe, 1913 Locomobile sport phaeton, 1918 National V12 sport phaeton, 1912 Hupp-Yeats electric coach. Museum is also home to Canada's Aviation Hall of Fame.

Saskatchewan Western Development Museum
2935 Melville St
Saskatoon, SK Canada S7J 5A6

306-934-1400
FAX: 306-934-4467

Open daily 9 to 5 in summer; Saskatoon Museum open 10 to 5 in winter; North Battleford and Yorkton Museums closed in winter. Head office at above address, branches at North Battleford, Saskatoon, Moose Jaw and Yorkton. Moose Jaw Museum features exhibits on transportation theme. All museums display vintage automobiles.

Museums

Denmark

Jysk Automobilmuseum 8883 Gjern Denmark	86-87-50-50

Open April, May: Sat, Sun and holidays 10-5; June, July, August: every day 10-5; Sept, Oct: Sat, Sun 10-5. Covers 135 vehicles, most cars, but also trucks, fire engines and motorcycles.

England

National Motor Museum John Montagu Building Beaulieu, Brockenhurst, Hampshire, SO42 7ZN England	01590-612345 FAX: 01590-612624 E-mail: beaulieu@tep.co.uk

Open daily (except Christmas Day), 10-6 Easter-September; 10-5 October-Easter. The National Motor Museum is one of the finest in the world and tells the story of motoring on the roads of Great Britain from 1895 to the present day. There are over 250 vehicles on show including four land speed record breaking cars. Excellent reference, photographic and film libraries.

Ireland

Museum of Irish Transport Scotts Hotel Gardens Killarney Co, Kerry Ireland	064-34677 PH/FAX: 064-32638

Open April to October every day 10 to 6. Exhibition of veteran, vintage and classic cars, cycles, motorcycles, carriages and automobilia. Fire fighting equipment. Special exhibits including 1902 Oldsmobile, 1904 Germain, 1908 Silver Stream and 1900 Argyll. Fascinating collection of American number plates.

Museums

Section Seven:
Useful Lists and Compilations

FC: Full Classic
NC: Non-Classic
Please apply to CCCA: Call or write with specifics on the vehicle.
Note: 1925-48 Custom-bodied cars not listed should apply to CCCA.

Classic Cars 1925-1948 Classic Car Club of America

The term "classic car" is one that has been so distorted and abused over the past twenty years or so that it might be handy to those seeking a single authoritative list of Classic Cars to include this in the *Almanac*. This group of cars and no others can truly be called "Classic"; as defined and chosen through the years by the Classic Car Club of America.

Our thanks to the Classic Car Club of America, Suite 7, 1645 Des Plaines River Rd., Des Plaines, IL 60018. PH: 847-390-0443. See their free listing on page 455.

A

AC ....FC
Adler ....please apply to CCCA
Alfa Romeo...FC
Alvis, Speed 20, Speed 25 and 4.3 Litre ....FC
    Others...................................please apply to CCCA
Amilcar ....please apply to CCCA
Armstrong Siddeley...................please apply to CCCA
Aston-Martin, all 1927-39.........................FC
    Others...................................please apply to CCCA
Auburn, all 8 and 12-cyl..........................FC
Austro-Daimler ....FC

B

Ballot ....please apply to CCCA
Bentley ....FC
Benz ....please apply to CCCA
Blackhawk ....FC
BMW, 327, 328, 327/318 and 335 ....FC
Brewster, all Heart Front Fords.....................FC
    Others....................................please apply to CCCA
Brough Superior ....please apply to CCCA
Bucciali, TAV 8, TAV 30, TAV 12 and Double Huit..FC
    Others....................................please apply to CCCA
Bugatti, all except type 52......................FC
Buick, 1931-42 90 Series.............................FC
    All others ....NC
    Custom-bodied ....please apply to CCCA

C

Cadillac, all 1925-35..............................FC
    All 12s and 16s ....FC
    1936-48, all 63, 65, 67, 70, 72, 75, 80, 85, 90 Series
    ....FC
    1938-47 60 Special.................................FC
    1940-47 all 62 series ....FC
    All others ....NC
Chenard-Walcker ....please apply to CCCA
Chrysler, 1926-30 Imperial 80, 1929 Imperial L, 1931-37 Imperial series CG, CH, CL and CW...............FC
    Newports and Thunderbolts.......................FC
    1934 CX ....FC
    1935 C-3...FC
    1936 C-11..FC
    1937-48 Custom Imperial, Crown Imperial Series C-15, C-20, C-24, C-27, C-33, C-37, C-40 ....FC
    All others ....NC

Lists

Cord...FC
Cunningham, Series V6, V7, V8, V9 ....FC

D

Dagmar, 6-80 ....FC
Daimler, all 8-cyl and 12-cyl ....FC
   Others ....please apply to CCCA
Darracq, 8-cyl and 4-litre 6-cyl ....FC
   Others ....NC
Delage, Model D-8..FC
4-Cylinder cars...NC
   Others ....please apply to CCCA
Delahaye, Series 135, 145, 165.........................FC
4-Cylinder cars...NC
   Others ....please apply to CCCA
Delaunay Belleville, 6-cyl ....FC
   Others ....NC
Doble ....FC
Dorris ....FC
Duesenberg...FC
duPont ....FC

E

Excelsior ....please apply to CCCA

F

Farman......................................please apply to CCCA
Fiat ....please apply to CCCA
FN..please apply to CCCA
Franklin, all models except 1933-34 Olympic ....FC
Frazer Nash ....please apply to CCCA

G

Graham, 1930-31 Series 137 ....FC
Graham-Paige, 1929-30 Series 837 ....NC
   Custom-bodied ....please apply to CCCA

H

Hispano-Suiza, all French models, Spanish models
   T56, T56BIS, T64..FC
Horch...FC
Hotchkiss...................................please apply to CCCA
Hudson, 1929 Series L...FC
   Custom-bodied ....please apply to CCCA
Humber ....please apply to CCCA

I

Invicta..FC
Isotta Fraschini...FC
Itala ....FC

J

Jaguar, 1946-48 2-1/2 Litre, 3-1/2 Litre (Mark IV)..FC
   4-Cylinder cars...NC
Jensen.......................................please apply to CCCA
Jordan, Speedway Series 'Z'..................................FC
   All others...NC
Julian ....FC

K

Kissel, 1925-26, 1927 8-75, 1928 8-90 and
   8-90 White Eagle, 1929-31 8-126 ....FC
   All others...NC

L

Lagonda, all models except 1933-40 Rapier ....FC
Lanchester.................................please apply to CCCA
Lancia..please apply to CCCA
LaSalle, 1927-33...FC
Lincoln, all L, KA, KB and K, 1941 168 H,
   1942 268 H...FC

Lists

Lincoln Continental ....FC
Locomobile, all Models 48 and 90, 1927-29 Model 8-80, 1929 8-88 ....FC
  All others ....NC

M

Marmon, all 16-cyl, 1925-26 74, 1927 75, 1928 E75, 1930 Big 8, 1931 88 and Big 8 ....FC
  Others ....NC
Maserati..............................please apply to CCCA
Maybach ....FC
McFarlan TV6 and 8 ....FC
Mercedes ....FC
Mercedes-Benz, all 230 and up, K, S, SS, SSK, SSKL, Grosser and Mannheim............................FC
Mercer ....FC
MG, 1935-39 SA, 1938-39 WA...............................FC
Minerva, all except 4-cyl ....FC

N

NAG ....please apply to CCCA
Nash, 1931 Series 8-90, 1932 series 9-90, Advanced 8 and Ambassador 8, 1933-34 Ambassador 8 .....FC
  All others...NC

P

Packard, all Sixes and Eights, 1925-34...................FC
  All 12-cylinder models......................................FC
  1935 Models 1200 thru 1205, 1207 and 1208......FC
  1936 Models 1400 thru 1405, 1407 and 1408......FC
  1937 Models 1500 thru 1502 and 1506 thru 1508 FC
  1938 Models 1603 thru 1605, 1607 and 1608.....FC
  1939 Models 1703, 1705, 1707 and 1708............FC
  1940 Models 1803, 1804, 1805, 1806, 1807 and 1808 ....FC
  1941 Models 1903, 1904, 1905, 1906, 1907 and 1908 ....FC
  1942 Models 2023, 2003, 2004, 2005, 2055, 2006, 2007 and 2008 ....FC

1946-47 Models 2103, 2106 and 2126 ....FC
  All Darrin-bodied ....FC
  All other models...NC
  Custom-bodied ....please apply to CCCA
Peerless, 1925 Series 67, 1926-28 Series 69, 1930-31 Custom 8, 1932 Deluxe Custom 8 ....FC
  Others ....NC
Peugeot...................................please apply to CCCA
Pierce-Arrow ....FC

R

Railton ....please apply to CCCA
Raymond Mays ....please apply to CCCA
Renault, 45 hp...FC
Reo, 1931-33 8-31, 8-35, 8-52, Royale Custom 8, 1934 N1, N2, and 8-52 ....FC
Revere..FC
Riley..please apply to CCCA
Roamer, 1925 8-88, 6-54e, 4-75, 4-85e; 1926 4-75e, 4-85e and 8-88; 1927-29 8-88; 1929 and 1930 8-120 ....FC
Rochet Schneider.....................please apply to CCCA
Rohr ....please apply to CCCA
Rolls-Royce ....FC
Ruxton..FC

S

Squire ....FC
SS and SS Jaguar, 1932-40 SS 1, SS 90, SS Jaguar and SS Jaguar 100 ....FC
Stearns-Knight ....FC
Stevens-Duryea ....FC
Steyr.......................................please apply to CCCA
Studebaker, 1929-33 President, except Model 82 ....FC
  All others...NC
Stutz..FC
Sunbeam, 8-cyl and 3 Litre twin cam ....FC

Talbot, 105C and 110C ....FC
Talbot Lago, 150C ....FC
Tatra ....please apply to CCCA
Triumph, Dolomite 8 and Gloria 6 ....FC

Vauxhall, 25-70 and 30-98 ....FC
Voisin ....FC

Wills Sainte Claire..FC
Willys-Knight, Series 66, 66A, 66B custom bodied only
....please apply to CCCA

FC: Full Classic
NC: Non-Classic
Please apply to CCCA: Call or write with specifics on
the vehicle.

None of the above Classic Marques are acceptable in race car configuration.

Statement of Policy
"Race Car Configuration,"
March 10, 1993

As of March 10, 1993, the Classic Car Club of America will no longer accept any automobile which is in a "race car configuration." The race car configuration is a vehicle which is missing some or all of the following: fenders, lights, windshield, windshield wipers, bumpers, top. It may be without doors, or reverse gear or starting motor. It may not have an exhaust system other than a straight pipe, nor have proper instrumentation or upholstery. In short, it would not be considered a legal, road worthy vehicle which is licensable in a majority of the states.

Certified Milestone Cars, 1945-1972

There's also continual debate over the meaning of "Milestone" cars. Like Classics, they do have a precise meaning. Basically, they're post-WWII Classic Cars — cars of superior design or engineering or performance or innovation or craftsmanship — or a combination of these characteristics. Following is the list of Milestones courtesy of the Milestone Car Society of California Inc, 1255 La Brea Dr., Thousand Oaks, CA 91362, PH: 805-497-1955. See their free listing on page 457.

A

AC Ace	1954-61
AC Aceca	1955-61
AC Buckland Open Tourer	1949
AC (Shelby) Cobra	1962-67
Alfa Romeo Giulietta Spider	1956-64
Alfa Romeo Giulietta-Giulia Sprint Speciale	1959-61
Alfa Romeo 6C 2500 Super Sport	1949
Allard Series J2, K2, K3	1946-56
AMX, 2-seater	1968-70
Apollo	1963-66
Arnolt Bristol	1952-62
Aston Martin	1948-63
Aston Martin DB4, DB5, DB6 (all)	1964-67
Austin-Healey 100/100M	1953-56
Austin-Healey 100-6	1956-59
Austin-Healey 3000	1959-67
Austin/Morris Mini	1959-70

B

Bentley (all)	1946-67
BMW 507	1957-59
BMW 2800 CS	1969-71
Bugatti Type 101	1951
Buick Riviera	1949; 1963-70
Buick Skylark	1953-54

C

Cadillac Eldorado	1953-58
Cadillac Eldorado	1967-70
Cadillac Eldorado Brougham	1957-58
Cadillac 60 Special	1948-49
Cadillac 61 Coupe (Fastback)	1948-49
Cadillac 62 Sedanet/Convertible/deVille	1948-49
Cadillac 75 Sedan/Limo	1946-70
Chevrolet Bel Air, V8, Hardtop and Convertible	1955-57
Chevrolet Camaro SS/RS, V8 and Z-28	1967-69
Chevrolet Corvette	1953-70
Chevrolet Impala Sport Coupe/Convertible	1958
Chevrolet Nomad	1955-57
Chrysler 300 Letter Series	1955-65
Chrysler 300 Hurst	1970
Chrysler Town & Country	1946-50
Cisitalia GT (Pininfarina)	1946-49
Citroen Chapron	1960-70
Citroen DS and ID 19	1955-64
Citroen SM	1970
Continental Convertible	1958-60
Continental Mark II	1956-57
Continental Mark III	1969-70
Corvair Monza	1960-64
Corvair Monza Spyder	1962-64
Corvair Monza & Corsa	1965-69
Crosley Hotshot/SS	1950-52
Cunningham	1951-55

D

Daimler DE-36 (Custom built)	1949-53
Daimler 2.5 Special Sport Convertible	1949-53
Delage D-6 Sedan	1946-49
Delahaye Type 135, 175, 180	1946-51
DeSoto Adventurer	1956-58
Deutsch-Bonnet GT	1950-61
Devin SS	1958-62
Dodge Charger R/T and Daytona	1968-70
Dodge Coronet R/T	1967-70
Dual Ghia	1956-58

Lists

E

Excalibur II Series I................................1965-69

F

Facel Vega, V8.....................................1954-64
Ferrari, V12 (all front engined) 1947-70
Ford Crestline Skyliner.................................1954
Ford Crown Victoria Skyliner 1955-56
Ford Mustang Boss 302/Mach I...................1969-70
Ford Mustang GT/GTA, V8 1965-67
Ford Skyliner (Retractable)..........................1957-59
Ford Sportsman 1946-48
Ford Thunderbird.....................................1955-60
Frazer Manhattan 1947-50

G

Gaylord 1955-57

H

Healey Silverstone 1949-50
Hudson (all)..1948-49
Hudson Hornet 1951-54

I

Imperial...1955-56

J

Jaguar XK 120 1945-54
Jaguar Mark V Drophead 1951
Jaguar Mark VII and 1954 Mark VII M.........1951-54

Jaguar XK 140....................................1954-57
Jaguar Mark VIII...................................1956-57
Jaguar Mark IX.....................................1958-61
Jaguar Mark X......................................1962-64
Jaguar XK 150.....................................1958-61
Jaguar 3.4/3.8 Sedans 1957-64
Jaguar E-Type......................................1961-67

K

Kaiser Darrin 161.....................................1954
Kaiser Deluxe/Deluxe Virginian 1951-52
Kaiser Dragon 1951-53
Kaiser Manhattan 1954-55
Kaiser Vagabond 1949-50
Kaiser Virginian (Hardtop)..........................1949-50
Kurtis 500S & 500KK..............................1953-55
Kurtis 500M & 500X...............................1953-55

L

Lagonda, V12 1948-49
Lagonda, 2.5 Liter Drophead Coupe 1949-53
Lancia Aurelia B.20 and B.20 Coupe 1951-59
Lancia Aurelia B.24 Spyder and Convertible ..1953-59
Lancia Flaminia GT 2-Passenger Coupe or Convertible
....1961-63
Lancia Flaminia Zagato 1959-64
Lancia Flavia Coupe 1962-66
Lea Francis 2.5 Liter Eighteen Sports............1950-54
Lincoln Capri 1952-54
Lincoln Continental.................................1946-48
Lincoln Continental.................................1961-67
Lincoln Continental Custom Limos (Lehmann-
Peterson)......................................1963-67
Lotus Elite..1958-63

M

Maserati A6/1500, A6G/2000/A6GCS Berlinetta ....
....1946-57
Maserati 3500/3700 GT............................1957-64
Maserati Ghibli, Mexico, Indy, 5000 GT 1959-70
Maserati Quattroporte 1963-69

Maserati Sebring, Mistral 1965-70
MG Series TC 1946-49
MG Series TD 1950-53
MGA Twin Cam 1958-62
Mercedes-Benz 190 SL 1955-62
Mercedes-Benz 220A Coupe and Convertible..............
....1951-54
Mercedes-Benz 220S/220 SE Coupe and Convertible..
....1956-65
Mercedes-Benz 230 SL Coupe and Convertible...........
....1963-67
Mercedes-Benz 250 SE/SL Coupe and Convertible......
....1965-67
Mercedes-Benz 280 SL 1969-70
Mercedes-Benz 300S/SE/SL Coupe and Convertible...
....1952-64
Mercedes-Benz 300 SE Coupe and Convertible ....
....1965-67
Mercedes-Benz 300 SEL 6.3 1969-70
Mercedes-Benz 600 1964
Mercedes-Benz 600, SWB/LWB 1965-70
Mercury Cougar XR-7.....................................1967-68
Mercury Sportsman...1946
Mercury Sun Valley 1954-55
Morgan 4/4 1955-70
Morgan Plus Four...1950-67
Muntz Jet...1950-54

N

Nash Healey 1951-54
NSU Wankel Spyder 1964

O

OSCA MT-4 1948-56
Oldsmobile 88 (Coupe, Convertible, Holiday) ..1949-50
Oldsmobile 98 Holiday Hardtop 1949
Oldsmobile 442 1964-70
Oldsmobile Fiesta 1953
Oldsmobile Toronado......................................1966-67

P

Packard Caribbean...1953-56
Packard Custom (Clipper and Custom Eight) ....
....1946-50
Packard Pacific/Convertible................................1954
Packard Panther Daytona 1954
Packard Patrician/400 1951-56
Panhard Dyna 1946-67
Pegaso (all) 1951-58
Plymouth Barracuda Formula S 1965-69
Plymouth Fury 1956-58
Plymouth Roadrunner & Superbird 1968-70
Plymouth Satellite SS & GTX..........................1965-70
Pontiac GTO 1964-69
Pontiac Safari 1955-57
Porsche Series 356 1949-64
Porsche 356C 1965

R

Riley 2.5 (RMA, RME) 1945-55
Rolls-Royce (all) 1947-67
Rover 2000/2000 TC 1964-70

S

Shelby 350GT & 500GT...................................1965-67
Studebaker Avanti..1963-64
Studebaker Convertible (all) 1947-49
Studebaker Gran Turismo Hawk 1962-64
Studebaker President Speedster 1955
Studebaker Starlight Coupe (all)....................1947-49
Studebaker Starlight Coupe (Six and V8) 1953-54
Studebaker Starliner Hardtop (Six and V8).....1953-54
Sunbeam Tiger 1965-67

T

Talbot Lago 4.5 (all) 1946-54
Triumph TR2/TR3...1953-63
Tucker 1948

Lists

US Vehicle Makes Past to Present

One of the most fascinating lists, and one which is changing even today, is the long, long list of makes of cars built in the US during the past century. There are literally thousands of them from every corner of the nation, distilled and diminished by competition and changing markets into the small handful of volume manufacturers of motorcars left today. This list, large as it is, is not totally complete as more and more tinkerers and backyard geniuses who built cars through the decades are discovered and documented by automotive historians. But it's a hefty list nonetheless and one which we think you'll enjoy browsing through.

A

A.B.C.	1908 and 1922
Abenaque	1900
Abendroth and Root	1907
Abbott	1909-1916
Abbott-Cleveland	1917
Abbott-Detroit	1909
Abbott-Downing	1919
A.C.	1938
Acadia	1904
Acason	1915
Ace	1920-1922
A.C.F.	1926
Acme	1902-1911
Acorn	1925
Adams	1911 and 1924
Adams-Farwell	1904-1913
Adelphia	1921
Adette	1947
Adria	1921-1922
Advance	1909
A.E.C.	1914-1916
Aero	1921
Aerocar	1905-1906 and 1948
Aerotype	1921
Ahrens-Fox	1927
Airphibian	1946-1952
Air Scout	1947
Airway	1949

Ajax Electric	1901-1903
Ajax	1914 and 1923-1925
Akron	1901
Alamobile	1902
Aland	1917
Albany	1907
Alco	1909-1912
Aldo	1910
Alden-Sampson	1904-1909
All American	1919
Allegheny	1908
Allen	1914-1922
Allen and Clark	1908
Allen Cyclecar	1914
Alith	1908
Allen-Kingston	1907-1909
Allis-Chalmers	1914-1917
All Steel	1915-1916
Alma	1908
Alpena	1910-1914
Alsaca	1920-1921
Alter	1916-1917
Altha	1905
Altham	1897 and 1898
Amalgamated	1905
Ambassador	1921-1922
Amco	1920
American	
...1901, 1905-1914, 1916-1918, 1922-1925 and 1937	
American Austin	1930
American-Bantam	1937
American Beauty	1916
American Benham	1917
American Berliet	1906
American Chocolate	1903
American Coulthard	1907
American Electric	1899-1900
American Fiat	1912
American Gas	1902-1903
American-LaFrance	1910
American Mercedes	1903
American Mors	1903
American Napier	1904
American Populaire	1904
American Power Carriage	1900
American Simplex	1908
American Steam Car	1935
American Steamer	1922-1923
American Southern	1921
American Tri-Car	1912
American Underslung	1908

Lists

American Voiturette............................1900
Americar...1941
Ames ....1895, 1898 and 1912-1915
Amesbury...1898
Amex..1895
Amplex..1908-1915
Ams-Sterling......................................1917
Anchor...1909
Anderson............................1908 and 1916-1926
Anger...1913
Angus..1908
Anheuser-Busch.................................1905
Anhut..1909
Anthony...1897
Apex..1920
Apell..1911
Appel...1915
Appelo...1973
Apperson.....................................1902-1926
Apple...1917
Appleton..1922
Apollo..1906
Arbenz..1911-1919
Arcadia..1911
Ardsley..1905
Argo-Borland......................................1914
Argo-Case..1916
Argo Electric................................1912-1917
Argo-Gas..1914
Argonne...1920
Ariel..1906
Aristos...1913
Armlader..1914
Arnold Electric...................................1895
Arrow..1914
Arrow Cyclecar...................................1914
Artzberger Steamer.............................1864
Astor...1925
Astra...1920
Astre..1975-1977
Atlantic..1915
Atlas..1907-1913
Auburn.......................................1903-1936
Auglaize...1911
Aultman...1901
Aurora...1907
Austin..1903-1922
Auto-Acetylene...................................1899
Autobain..1900
Auto-Bug...1910
Autobuggy...1907
Autocar......................................1899-1911
Auto Cycle..1913

Auto Dynamic.....................................1901
Auto Fore Carriage.......................1900-1901
Auto-Go...1900
Automatic...............................1908 and 1921
Automobile Voiturette....................1900-1902
Automote..1900
Automotor...................................1901-1904
Autoplane...1947
Auto-Tricar...1914
Auto Two..1900
Auto Vehicle.......................................1903
Avanti.......................................1963-present
Avery...1921

B

Babcock......................................1909-1913
Babcock Electric...........................1906-1911
Bachelles..1901
Backhus...1925
Bacon..1925
Badger..1911-1912
Bailey...1907-1916
Baker-Electric...............................1899-1917
Baker Steam.................................1917-1924
Balboa...1924
Baldner.......................................1902-1903
Baldwin..1900
Ball..1902
Ball Steam..1900
Balzer..1900
Banker...1905
Banker Electric....................................1905
Bantam..1914
Barbarino...1923
Barley...1922-1924
Barlow...1922
Barnes..1907-1912
Barnhart...1905
Barrett & Perret..................................1895
Barrow...1896
Barrows Motor Vehicle........................1897
Bartholomew................................1901-1903
Barver...1925
Bateman...1917
Bates...1903
Bauer..1914
Bauroth..1899
Bayard...1903

Bay State	1906-1907 and 1922-1924
Beacon	1933
Beacon Flyer	1908
Beardsley	1901 and 1914-1917
Beau-Chamberlain	1905
Beaver	1920
Beck	1947
Beebe	1907
Beggs	1918-1922
B.E.L.	1921-1923
Belden	1907-1911
Belfontains	1907
Bell	1907 and 1915-1922
Bellmay	1904
Belmont	1904, 1908, 1910 and 1912-1916
Bemmel & Burham	1898
Bendix	1907
Bendix-Ames	1911
Benham	1914
Ben-Hur	1908-1917
Benner	1908-1909
Benson	1913
Bentley	1907
Benton Harbor Motor	1896
Berg	1902-1903
Bergdoll	1908-1911
Berkshire	1904-1911
Berwick Electric	1926
Bessemer	1904
Bertolet	1908-1912
Best	1900
Bethlehem	1904-1908
Betz	1919
Beverly	1904
Bewis	1915
Bewman	1912
Beyster	1910-1911
Beyster By-Autogo	1904
B.F.S.	1908
Biddle	1916-1922
Biddle-Murray	1906
Bierderman	1915
Bimel	1917
Binney-Burnham	1888-1902
Birch	1916-1923
Bird	1911
Birmingham	1921-1922
Birnel	1911
Black	1899 and 1908
Black Crow	1905 and 1909-1910
Black Diamond	1904
Blackhawk	1902-1905 and 1928-1929
Blair	1915
Blaisdell	1903
Blakeslee	1906
Blemline	1898
Bliss	1906
B.L.M.	1907-1909
Block	1905
Block Bros.	1905
Blomstrom	1904-1908
Blood	1903 and 1914
Bluebird	1910
Blumberg	1918
Bob Cat	1923
Bobbi-Car	1945
Boggs	1903
Boisselot	1901-1906
Bolte	1901
Borbein	1905
Borland	1913-1914
Boss	1903
Boston	1900 and 1903
Boston and Amesbury	1902
Boston High Wheel	1908
Bour-Davis	1916-1922
Bournonville	1914
Bouton and Bateman	1899
Bowman	1921-1922
Boynton	1922
Bradfield	1929
Bradley	1920
Bramwell	1900-1902
Bramwell-Robinson	1899
Brasie	1915
Brecht	1902-1903
Breer	1900
Breeze and Lawrence	1905
Breman	1908
Brennan	1908
Brew and Hatcher	1904-1905
Brewster	1915-1937
Bridgeport	1922
Briggs	1914
Briggs and Stratton	1920-1923
Briggs-Detroiter	1912
Brighton	1896 and 1914
Brightwood	1912
Brintel	1912
Briscoe	1914-1921
Bristol	1903 and 1908
Broc	1909-1917

Brock	1920
Brockville-Atlas	1911
Brockway	1912
Brodesser	1909
Brogan	1948
Brook	1920-1921
Brooks	1908 and 1925
Brower	1890
Brown	1898, 1914 and 1916
Brown-Burtt	1904
Brownell	1910
Brownie	1915-1916
Browniekar	1908-1910
Brunn	1906
Brunner	1910
Brunswick	1916
Brush	1907-1911
Bruss	1907
Buck	1925
Buckeye	1901 and 1906-1912
Buckeye Gas Buggy	1895
Buckles	1914
Buckmobile	1903-1907
Buffalo	1900-1907
Buffalo Electric	1901-1907
Buffington	1900
Buffman	1900
Buffum	1901-1909
Buford	11915
Buggyaut	1895 and 1908
Buggycar	1908-1909
Bugmobile	1907
Buick	1903-present
Bundy	1895
Burdick	1909-1910
Burg	1910
Burns	1910
Burroughs	1914-1916
Bus	1917-1924
Bush	1909 and 1917
Busser	1915
Buzmobile	1917
Byrider	1908-1909

C

Cadillac	1903-present
California	1902 and 1912-1914
California Cyclecar	1914

Californian	1916
Calvert	1927
Cameron	1905-1907 and 1909-1921
Campbell	1916-1921
Canda	1901
Cannon	1904
Canton	1906
Capital	1902
Capps	1908
Car Deluxe	1907
Car Nation	1913
Carbon	1902
Cardway	1923
Carhart	1871
Carhartt	1911
Carlisle	1900
Carlson	1904-1911
Carovan	1948
Carpenter	1895
Carqueville-MacDonald	1930
Carrison	1908
Carroll	1908, 1912-1918 and 1920-1922
Cartecar	1907-1911
Carter	1901 and 1903
Cartermobile	1924
Carter Twin Engine	1909
Carthage	1924
Cartone	1905
Casco	1926
Case	1909-1927
Caseler	1901
Casward-Dard	1924
Cato	1907
Cavac-Plymouth	1910
Cavalier	1927
C.B.	1917
Ceco	1914
Celt	1927
Centaur	1902
Central	1905
Century	1901, 1903 and 1911-1912
Century Tourist	1901
C.F.	1908
C.G. Gay	1915
C.G.V.	1902
Chadwick	1905-1912
Chalmers	1908-1923
Chalmers Detroit	1907
Champion	1902, 1909-1910 and 1919-1926
Champion Electric	1899-1901
Chandler	1913

Chapman	1899 and 1901
Charter Car	1904
Charter Oak	1917
Chase	1910
Chatham	1906
Checker Cab	1921
Chelfant	1906-1912
Chelsea	1901-1904
Chevrolet	1911-present
Chicago	1898, 1906 and 1914-1916
Chicago Commercial	1905
Chicago Electric	1914-1917
Chicago Motor Buggy	1908
Chicago Steam	1906
Chief	1908 and 1947
Christie	1904-1906
Christman	1901-1902
Christopher	1908
Chrysler	1924-present
Church	1903 and 1913
Churchfield	1911-1913
Cincinnati	1903
Cino	1909-1913
Cinov	1909-1912
Cistalia	1948
Clapps Motor	1898
Clark	1901-1902
Clark Electric	1906-1910
Clark Hatfield	1908-1909
Clark Steamer	1900-1909
Clarke Carter	1900-1906
Clarkmobile	1903-1906
Clarkspeed	1928
Classie	1917-1920
Clear and Durham	1905
Cleburne	1912
Clegg	1885
Clement	1903
Clendon	1908
Clermont	1903 and 1922
Cleveland	1902-1906, 1909 and 1919-1926
Climber	1919-1923
Clinton	1923
Cloughley	1902-1903
Club Car	1911
Clyde	1919
Clymer	1908
Coates	1921-1922
Coates-Goshen	1908-1910
Coey	1911
Coffon	1898

Cogswell	1912
Colburn	1906-1911
Colby	1911-1914
Cole	1910-1925
Collins	1901 and 1920
Colly	1900
Colonial	1907 and 1921-1922
Colonial Electric	1912
Colt	1908 and 1971
Columbia	1892-1913 and 1916-1925
Columbia Dauman	1900
Columbia Electric	1898-1906
Columbia Knight	1916
Columbian Electric	1915
Columbus	1903-1905 and 1906-1909
Comet	1907, 1914 and 1917-1923
Comet 3 Wheel	1947
Comet Cyclecar	1914
Commander	1921 and 1923
Commerce	1916
Commercial	1903
Commodore	1921
Commonwealth	1917-1922
Compound	1904-1906
Concord	1916
Conklin Electric	1895
Connersville	1914
Conover	1907
Conrad Steam	1900
Consolidated	1904
Continental	1907, 1909-1912, 1914 and 1933-1934
Cook	1908
Cooley	1900
Copley Minor	1917
Coppock	1907
Corbin	1903-1912
Corbitt	1907-1916
Cord	1929-1932 and 1936-1937
Cordoba	1976
Corinthian	1922
Corl	1911
Corliss	1917
Cornelian	1913-1915
Cornish	1917-1919
Correja	1911-1914
Cort	1914
Cortez	1947
Corweg	1905
Coscob	1900
Cosmopolitan	1907-1910 and 1951
Cotay	1921

Lists

Cotta...1901
Couch...1899-1900
Couch Steamer..1900
County Club..1903
Couple-Gear...1905
Courier.............................1904-1912 and 1919-1924
Covert...1902-1907
Covert Motorette...1902
Coyote..1909
C.P..1908
Craig Toledo..1906-1907
Crane..1912-1914
Crane and Breed..1912-1917
Crane-Simplex...1923-1924
Crawford...1902-1924
Crescent.......................1905-1908 and 1914-1915
Crest..1902
Crestmobile..1901-1904
Cricket..........................1913-1915 and 1971-1973
Criterion...1912
Crock..1909
Croesus Jr...1906
Crompton..1903-1905
Crosley..1940
Cross Steam Carriage.......................................1895
Crother-Duryea..1915
Crow...1915
Crowdus..1901-1903
Crow-Elkhart...1914-1925
Crown..1907 and 1915
Crown High Wheel...1897
Crown Magnetic...1907
Crowther-Duryea.......................................1915-1917
Croxton...1911-1914
Croxton Keeton..1909-1912
Cruiser..1918
Crusader..1923
Cucmobile...1907
Cull...1901
Culver...1905
Cunningham...1911
Cunningham Steamer...................................1900-1907
Curtis..1921
Custer..1921
Cutting...1910-1912
C.V.I...1907
Cyclecar..1901
Cyclemobile..1920
Cycleplane...1914-1915

D

D.A.C..1923
Dagmar...1922-1927
Daley...1893
Dalton...1911
Dan Patch...1911
Daniels...1916-1924
Darby..1909
Darling.............................1901-1902 and 1917
Darrow..1903
Dart..1922
Dartmobile..1922
Davenport..1902-1903
Davids...1902
Da Vinci...1925
Davis.................1914, 1919-1928 and 1947-1950
Dawson..1904
Day..1911-1914
Day Utility..1911
Dayton......................................1904 and 1909-1911
Dayton Electric..1911
Dayton Steam..1900
Deal..1911
Decker..1902-1903
De Cross..1914
De Dion Bouton..1888-1904
Deemaster..1923
Deemotor...1923
Deere..1906-1909
Deere Clark..1906
Deering..1915
Deering Magnetic.......................................1917-1919
Defiance...1919
Dekalb...1919
De La Vergne Motor Drag....................................1896
Delcar..1947-1949
Delling Steamer...1924-1927
Delmore...1923
Deltal..1914
De Mar..1949
De Mars Electric..1905
De Mot.................................1905 and 1909-1911
De Motte..1904
Denby..1922
Deneen...1916
De Rair..1911
Desberon Steamer......................................1901-1902
De Shaum...1908

Deshaw	1906
De Soto	1928-1960
De Tamble	1909-1912
Detroit	1900, 1905, 1916 and 1922
Detroit Air Cooled	1923
Detroit Dearborn	1909-1910
Detroit Electric	1907-1938
Detroit Steamer	1922
Detroiter	1912
De Vaux	1931-1932
Dewabout	1899
Dey Electric	1894
Dial	1923
Diamond	1907
Diamond Arrow	1909
Diamond T	1905-1911
Diana	1924-1928
Diebel	1900-1901
Diehl	1923
Differential	1921
Dile	1914-1916
Direct Drive	1907
Disbrow	1917-1918
Dispatch	1912-1922
Divco Twin	1946
Dixie	1912 and 1917
Dixie Flyer	1915-1924
Dixie Tourist	1908-1909
Dixon	1922
Doble	1914-1931
Dodge	1914-present
Dodgeson	1926
Dodo	1909
Dolson	1904-1907
Dorris	1906-1926
Dort	1915-1925
Douglas	1918-1922
Dover	1929
Dowagiac	1908
Downing	1914
Downing Detroit	1913
Dragon	1921
Dragon Steam	1906-1908
Drake	1921-1922
Drexel	1916-1917
Driggs	1915-1916
Drummond	1915-1916
Duck	1913
Dudgeon Steam	1866
Dudley	1914
Duer	1907-1909 and 1925

Duesenberg	1921-1937
Dumont	1909-1912
Dunn	1914-1917
Duplex	1909
Dupont	1915-1923
Duquesne	1913-1916
Durable	1902
Durant	1921-1932
Durocar	1908-1910
Duryea	1895-1913
Duryea Gem	1916
Dusseau	1912
Dyke	1903
Dymaxion	1933

E

Eagle	1905-1906, 1908-1909, 1914 and 1924
Eagle Cyclecar	1914-1915
Eagle Electric	1915-1917
Eagle Macaober	1917
Eagle Rotary	1917
Earl	1907-1909, 1916-1924
Eastman	1897
Eastman Steam	1900
Easton	1907
Easton Electric	1898
Eaton	1910
Eaton Electric	1898
ECK	1903-1909
Eclipse	1901-1902
Economy	1906 and 1917-1919
Economy Car	1914
Eddy Electric	1902
Edsel	1958-1960
Edwards Knight	1912-1914
E.H.V.	1903
Eichstaedt	1902
E.I.M.	1916
Eisenhuth	1896
Elberon Steam	1903
Elbert	1915
Elcar	1908-1930
Elco	1915-1916
Eldorado	1969
Eldridge	1906
Electra	1913
Electric Vehicle	1897

Electric Wagon 1895
Electrobat 1895
Electrocar 1922
Electronomic..1901
Elgin 1914-1924
Elinor 1903
Elite..1909-1919
Elite Steamer 1901
Elk...1912
Elkhart 1908-1922
Elliott...1899-1902
Ellis Electric 1901
Ellsworth 1917
Elmore...1900-1911
Elrick 1896
Elston 1895
Elwell-Parker 1909
Elysee 1926
Emancipator 1909
Emerson 1907
Emerson and Fisher 1896
E.M.F. 1909-1912
Empire.....................1898-1901 and 1910-1919
Empire State..1901
Empress 1906
Endurance Steamer.....................................1922-1923
Engelhardt...1901
Enger...1909-1917
Enterprise...1901
Entyre..1911
Entz...1914
Erie...1897 and 1916-1921
Erskine...1926-1930
Ernst 1896
Erving...1911-1913
Essex...1918-1932
Euclid 1907
Eureka...1908 and 1909-1914
Evans 1904
Evans Steam..1887
Evansville 1907-1909
Everitt 1909-1911
Everybodys 1908-1909
Ewing 1908-1910

F

Facto 1920
Fageol...1916-1917

Fairbanks-Morse 1909
Fairmont...1906 and 1978
F.A.L. 1909
Falcar....................................1908, 1910 and 1922
Falcon......................................1909-1911 and 1922
Falcon Knight 1927-1928
Famose 1909
Fanning Electric 1902-1904
Farmack 1916
Farmobile 1906-1907
Farner 1922-1924
Fauber ....1900 and 1914
Fay 1912
Fedelia 1903
Federal...1907-1909
Federal Steam...1905
Fee..1908
Felton 1914
Fergus 1915-1922
Ferris..1920-1923
Findley..1910-1912
Firestone Columbus 1906-1911
Fischer...............................1902-1904 and 1914
Fish...1908
Fisher 1914
Fitzjohn 1946
Flagler 1914
Flanders 1911-1912
Flanders Electric..1914
Flexbi 1904
Flexibel 1935
Flint....................1902-1904 and 1922-1927
Flyer 1913-1914
Foos...1913
Ford 1903-present
Forest 1908
Forest City 1906
Forster Six 1920
Fort Pitt 1908-1909
Foster Steam 1898-1905
Fostoria ....1906-1907 and 1916
Four Traction..1907
Fox 1921-1925
Frankford 1922
Franklin 1901-1934
Frayer 1905
Frayer Miller 1905-1909
Frazer 1945-1951
Fredonia..1902-1904
Fredrickson 1914
Freeman 1900-1903

Lists

Fremont	1922-1923
French	1903
Friedberd	1908
Friedman	1900-1903
Friend	1921-1923
Fritchie Electric	1907-1917
Frontenac	1909-1911, 1917 and 1922
Frontmobile	1917
F.R.P.	1915-1917
F.S.	1908
Fuller	1907-1911
Fulton	1908 and 1948
F.W.D.	1911

G

Gabriel	1912
Gadabout	1914-1915
Gaeth	1902-1906
Gaethmobile	1902
Gale	1906
Galt	1914
Gardner	1919-1931
Garford	1907-1913
Garvin	1900
Gas Au Lac	1905-1906
Gas Engine	1905
Gasmobile	1900
Gasoline Motor	1897
Gawley	1895
Gaylord	1910-1913
Gearless	1908 and 1920
Geer Steam	1900
Gem	1917
General	1903
General Cab	1929
General Electric	1899
General Vehicle	1906
Genesee	1911-1912
Geneva	1901-1909 and 1917
German American	1902
Geronimo	1917-1921
Gersix	1921
Ghent	1918
Gibbs Electric	1903
Gibson	1899
Gifford Pettitt	1907
Gillette	1916
G.J.C.	1909-1915

Gleason	1910-1912 and 1914
Glide	1902-1919
Globe	1921-1922
Glover	1921
Golden State	1928
Goldeneagle	1906
Goodspeed	1922
Gorson	1907
Graham	1903
Graham-Paige	1927-1941
Grant	1914-1923
Gray	1916 and 1922-1925
Gray-Dort	1917
Great Eagle	1911-1914
Great Smith	1911
Great Southern	1910-1914
Great Western	1909-1916
Greeley	1903
Gregory	1948
Gregory Front Drive	1922
Greyhound	1914
Griffith	1962-1966
Grinnel Electric	1910-1915
Griswold	1907
Grout Steam	1899-1912
Guilder	1922
Gurley	1901
Guy Vaughn	1912
Gyroscope	1914

H

Hackett	1916-1919
H.A.L.	1918
Hale	1917
Hall	1903
Hall Gasoline	1895
Halladay	1908-1912 and 1919-1921
Halsey	1901
Hamilton	1909
Hamilton Holmes	1920-1921
Hammer	1905
Hammer Sommer	1905
Handley	1921-1923
Handley-Knight	1921-1922
Hanger	1916
Hanover	1922-1924
Hansen	1902
Hanson	1917-1923

Lists

Harding 1916
Hardy 1904
Hare 1918
Harper 1907
Harrie 1925
Harrigan 1922
Harris Six 1923
Harrisburg 1922
Harrison 1904-1907
Harroun......................................1917-1922
Hart Kraft 1908
Hartman 1898
Harvard 1916
Harvey 1914
Hasbrouck 1900
Haseltine 1916
Hassler 1917
Hatfield 1906-1908
Hathaway 1924
Haupt 1909
Havers 1912-1914
Haviland 1895
Havoc 1914
Hawkeye 1923
Hawley 1907
Hay Berg.....................................1907-1908
Haydock 1907
Haynes 1904-1925
Haynes-Apperson 1898-1904
Hayward 1913
Hazard 1914-1915
H. Brothers 1908
H.C.S. 1920-1925
Healy 1912-1916
Heine-Velox ....1906-1909 and 1921
Henderson 1912-1915
Henley Steam..1899
Henney 1921-1931
Henrietta 1901
Henry...1911
Henry J. 1950-1954
Hercules 1914
Hercules Electric....................................1902
Herff Brooks 1915
Hermes 1915
Herreshoff....................................1909-1914
Herschell-Spillman 1904-1907
Herschmann 1906
Hertel 1895-1900
Hertz..1925
Hess Steam 1902

Hewitt..1905-1910
Hewitt Linstrom 1900
Heymann.....................................1898-1899
Hicks 1900
Highlander 1922
Hill 1907-1908
Hill Locomotor 1895
Hillsdale...1908
Hilton 1908
Hines 1908
Hobbie 1909
Hoffman 1902-1904
Hoffman Steam 1902
Hol Tan 1908
Holden 1915
Holland Steam 1905
Holley 1900-1903
Hollier 1915
Holly ....1900 and 1916-1917
Holmes ....1908 and 1918-1923
Holsman 1903-1911
Holyoke Steam...............................1901-1903
Homer Laughlin 1916
Hopkins 1902
Hoppenstand 1948
Houpt-Rockwell 1910-1912
Howard ....1901, 1903-1905 and 1914
Howard Gasoline Wagon 1895
Howey..1903
Hudson..1909-1957
Hupmobile....................................1908-1940
Hupp-Yeats 1911-1919
Hydro Carbon 1901
Hydromotor 1917
Hylander...1922

I

Ideal.........................1902, 1903, 1909-1914
Ideal Electric...1909
I.H.C. 1911
Illinois 1910-1914
Imp..1914-1915 and 1955
Imperial ....1903-1904, 1907-1916 and 1928
Ingram Hatch 1917-1918
Innes 1921-1922
International...1900
International Harvester......1907-1911 and 1961-1984
Interstate..1909-1918

Iroquois 1904-1908
Izzer 1910

J

Jackson 1903-1923
Jacquet Flyer 1921
James 1909
Janney...1906
Jarvis Huntington 1912
Jeannin 1908-1909
Jeep 1963-present
Jeffery 1914-1917
Jenkins 1907-1912
Jewel 1906-1909
Jewett 1923-1926
Johnson 1905-1912
Jones...1915-1920
Jones Corbin 1902-1907
Jonz 1908-1911
Jordan...1916-1931
J.P.L..1913-1914
Julian ....1922 and 1925

K

Kaiser 1945-1955
Kalamazoo 1922
Kankakee..1919
Kansas City 1909
Karbach 1908
Kato...1907
Kauffman 1909-1912
Kavin...1905
K.D. 1914
Kearns...1908-1916
Keasler 1916
Keating 1899
Keene Electric..................................1900-1901
Keene Steam...1948
Keeton 1908-1914
Keller Chief 1947
Keller Kar.............................1914 and 1927
Kenmore 1909-1912
Kennedy ....1898-1903 and 1915-1918
Kensington 1899-1904

Kent..1916-1917
Kenworthy 1920-1922
Kermath 1907-1908
Kermet...1900
Kessler..1921-1922
Keystone ....1909-1910 and 1915
Kiblinger...1907-1909
Kidder...1901
Kimball 1910-1912
King.............................1896 and 1910-1924
King Midget 1946-1969
King Remick 1910
Kissell...1906-1931
Kline Kar 1910-1923
Kling..1907
Klink..1907-1909
Knickerbocker 1901-1903
Knox 1900-1915
Koppin...1914
Kreuger...1904-1905
K.R.I.T. 1909-1916
Kunz..1902-1906
Kurtis 1948-1955
Kurtz..1921-1923

L

L and E..1922-1931
Laconia..1914
Lads Car..1912-1914
Lafayette...............1920-1924 and 1934-1939
Lambert...1904-1917
Lane Steamer..1899
Lanpher...1909-1912
Lansden Electric...............................1906-1908
La Petite..1905
La Salle...1927-1940
Lauth Jergens 1907-1910
Law..1905
Leach....................1899-1901 and 1920-1923
Leader 1905-1912
Lehigh...1912
Lende 1908-1909
Lenox..1911-1918
Lenox Electric...................................1908-1909
Lescina 1916
Lewis ....1899-1902, 1914-1916 and 1937
Lewis Six 1913

Lexington...1909-1928
Liberty 1916-1924
Lima 1915
Limited 1911
Lincoln.....................1908, 1914 and 1920-present
Lion 1909-1912
Little 1912-1915
Littlemac 1930-1931
Locomobile 1899-1929
Logan 1903-1908
London 1921-1924
Lone Star...1920-1922
Loomis...1896-1904
Lorraine................1907-1908 and 1920-1922
Los Angeles..1913-1915
Lowell 1908
Lozier..1905-1917
Lutz Steam 1917
Luverne 1903-1918
Luxor Cab 1920
Lyman 1903-1904
Lyman and Burnham 1903-1904
Lyon Atlas 1912-1913
Lyon Knight 1914-1915

M

MacDonald 1923
Mackle-Thompson 1903
MacNaughton 1907
Macomber...1917
Macon 1915-1917
Madison...1915-1918
Magnolia..1902
Mahoning 1904-1905
Maibohm 1916-1922
Mais...1911
Majestic 1917
Malcolm 1915
Maltby 1900-1902
Manexall..1921
Manhattan..1905
Manistee...1912
Mann...1895
Maplebay..1908
Marathon 1908-1915
Marble Swift 1902-1905
Marion...1904-1915
Marion Handley 1916-1919

Maritime 1913-1914
Mark Electric 1897
Marlboro Steam 1899-1902
Marmon..1902-1933
Marquette ....1912 and 1929-1931
Marr 1903-1904
Marsh ....1898-1899, 1905 and 1920-1921
Marshall 1919-1921
Martin.....................1920, 1926-1928 and 1931
Marvel...1907
Maryland 1900-1901
Mason 1906-1910
Mason Steamer...1898-1899
Massachusetts...1901
Massilon 1909
Master 1918
Mather 1901
Matheson 1903-1912
Maxwell Briscoe...1904-1925
Maytag...1910-1911
McCue 1909-1911
McCullough 1899
McFarlan 1910-1928
McGill 1922
McIntyre 1909-1915
McKay Steam..1900-1902
McLaughlin 1908-1922
McLean 1910
Mecca 1914-1916
Melbourne 1922
Menard 1908-1910
Menges 1908
Mercer ....1910-1925 and 1931
Merchant 1914
Mercury...............1904, 1914, 1918 and 1938-present
Merit 1920-1923
Merkel 1905-1906
Merz 1914-1915
Meteor....1898, 1902-1903, 1904-1908 and 1914-1921
Metropol 1913-1914
Metropolitan ....1922 and 1954-1961
Metz 1909-1922
Michigan...1908-1914
Middleby...1908-1913
Midland 1908-1913
Mier...1908-1909
Milburn Electric..1914-1922
Militaire 1916-1922
Miller.....................1912-1913 and 1915-1932
Miller Steam 1896
Milwaukee Steam 1900-1902

Minneapolis	1915
Mino	1914
Mitchell	1903-1923
Mobile Steam	1899-1903
Model	1903-1909
Modoc	1913
Moehn	1895
Mogul	1912
Mohawk	1903-1904 and 1914-1915
Mohler	1901
Moline	1904-1913
Moline Knight	1914-1920
Moller	1920-1921
Monarch	1908 and 1914-1917
Monarch Canada	1946-1961
Moncrieff	1901-1902
Monitor	1916
Monroe	1914-1924
Moody	1900-1903
Mooers	1900
Moon	1905-1930
Moore	1906-1907 and 1916-1921
Mora	1906-1911
Morlock	1903
Morris Salom	1895-1897
Morrison Electric	1891
Morse	1904-1909 and 1909-1916
Motorette	1910-1912
Moyea	1902-1904
Moyer	1909-1915
M.P.M.	1914-1915
Mueller	1895-1900
Multiplex	1912-1913
Munson	1899-1902
Murdaugh	1901
Murray	1902-1903 and 1916-1918
Murray Mac	1921-1928
Mustang	1948-1949

N

Napoleon	1916-1917
Nash	1917-1957
National	1900-1924
Navajo	1953-1955
Navarre	1921
Nelson	1917-1921
Neuman Electric	1922
Neustadt Perry	1902-1907
Nevada	1908

Neville	1910
Newcomb	1921
New Departure Cab	1904
New England	1898-1900
New England Electric	1899-1901
New Haven	1904
New York	1928-1929
Niagara	1903-1907 and 1915-1916
Nichols	1908
Noble	1902
Noma	1919-1923
Northern	1902-1909
Northway	1921
Norwalk	1910-1922
Novara	1917
Nyberg	1912-1914

O

Oakland	1907-1931
Oakman	1898
Oakman Hertel	1902
Obertine	1915
O'Connor	1916
Odelot	1916
Ofeldt	1899-1902
Ogren	1915-1923
Ohio	1909-1913
Ohio Electric	1910-1918
Okey	1907-1908
Oldfield	1917-1922
Oldsmobile	1897-present
Oliver	1905
Olympian	1917-1921
Omaha	1912-1913
Only	1909-1915
Orient	1901-1905
Ormond	1904-1905
Orson	1908-1909
Otto	1909-1912
Overholt	1912
Overland	1903-1929 and 1939
Overman Steam	1899-1900
O We Go	1914-1915
Owen	1910-1914
Owen Magnetic	1914-1922
Owen Schoeneck	1915-1916
Owen Thomas	1909
Oxford	1913-1915

Lists

P

Pacific 1914
Pacific Special 1914
Packard 1899-1958
Packet 1916-1917
Page ....1907 and 1923-1924
Paige 1908-1927
Pak Age Car 1935-1938
Palmer 1906
Palmer Singer 1907-1914
Pan 1918-1922
Pan American ....1902 and 1917-1922
Panda 1955-1956
Panther....................................1962-1963
Paragon ....1905-1907 and 1922
Parenti.....................................1920-1922
Parker......................................1921-1923
Parkin..1908
Parry 1910-1912
Parsons Electric....................1905-1906
Partin Palmer.........................1913-1917
Paterson 1908-1923
Pathfinder...............................1911-1918
Patriot...1922
Patterson Greenfield 1916-1918
Patton Electric 1890
Patton Gas 1890
Pawtucket Steam....................1900-1901
Payne Modern.........................1906-1909
Peabody 1907
Peck...1897
Peerless 1900-1931
Peninsular 1915
Penn...1911-1913
Pennington 1894-1902
Pennsy......................................1916-1919
Pennsylvania 1907-1911
People's 1901
Perfection 1906-1908
P.E.T..1914
Peter Pan 1914-1915
Peters 1921-1922
Petrel.......................................1908-1912
Phelps 1903-1905
Phianna 1916-1922
Philadelphia.......................................1924
Phipps 1901-1912
Pickard.....................................1908-1912

Piedmont 1917-1922
Pierce-Arrow 1901-1938
Pierce Racine 1904-1909
Piggins 1909
Pilgrim 1914-1918
Pilliod 1915-1918
Pilot..1909-1924
Pioneer 1909-1911
Pitcher 1920
Pittsburgh 1909-1911
Plass Motor 1895
Playboy.....................................1946-1951
Plymouth ....1910 and 1928-present
P.M.C..1908
Pomeroy...1902
Ponder...1923
Pontiac..................1902-1908 and 1926-present
Pope Hartford 1904-1914
Pope Robinson.........................1903-1904
Pope Toledo 1904-1909
Pope Tribune 1904-1906
Pope Waverly Electric 1904-1907
Poppy Car 1917
Porter 1919-1922
Porter Steam............................1900-1901
Port Huron...1922
Portland..1914
Postal 1907-1908
Powercar...................................1909-1912
Prado...1920-1922
Pratt 1907
Pratt Elkhart 1911-1917
Preferred 1920
Premier.....................................1903-1925
Premocar 1921-1923
Prescott Steam 1901-1905
Pridemore..................................1914-1915
Primo...1910-1912
Prince 1902
Princess....................................1914-1918
Princeton 1923-1924
Publix..1947-1948
Pullman.....................................1903-1917
Pungs Finch 1904-1910
Pup...1947
Puritan Steam 1902-1903

Q

Queen	1904-1906
Quick	1899-1900
Quinlan	1904

R

R and L Electric	1922-1928
R and V Knight	1920-1924
R.A.C.	1910-1911
Racine	1909-1911
Radford	1895 and 1903
Rae	1898 and 1902
Railsbach	1914
Rainier	1905-1911
Raleigh	1921-1922
Rambler	1902-1913
Randall Steam	1902-1903
Rand Harvey Steam	1899
Randolph Steam	1910
Ranger	1907 and 1920-1922
Ranlet	1900
Rapid	1903
Ras Electric	1898
Rauch & Lang	1905-1928
Rayfield	1911-1915
R.C.H.	1912-1916
Read	1912-1915
Reading	1913-1914
Reading Steamer	1901-1902
Real	1914-1915
Reber	1902-1903
Red Bug	1924-1930
Red Jacket	1904
Red Wing	1909
Reed	1909
Rees	1921
Reese	1887
Reeves	1896-1898 and 1905-1912
Regal	1907-1918
Regas	1903-1905
Reinertsen	1901
Relay	1903-1904
Reliable Dayton	1906-1909
Reliance	1904-1906

Remal Steam	1923
Remington	1914-1916
Reo	1905-1936
Republic	1910-1916
Re Vere	1918-1926
Rex	1914-1915
Reya	1917
Reynolds	1899-1901
Richard	1914-1919
Richards	1896-1903
Richelieu	1922-1923
Richmond	1904-1917
Rickenbacker	1922-1927
Ricketts	1909-1911
Riddle	1916-1926
Rider Lewis	1908-1911
Riess Royal	1921
Riker Electric	1897-1902
Riley and Cowley	1902
Ripper	1903
Ritz	1914-1915
R.O.	1911
Roadable	1946
Roader	1911-1912
Road Cart	1896
Roamer	1916-1929
Robe	1923
Roberts	1904 and 1915
Robie	1914
Robinson	1900-1902
Robson	1909
Roche	1924-1925
Rochester Steam	1901-1902
Rock Falls	1919-1925
Rockaway	1902-1903
Rocket	1903
Rockne	1932-1933
Rockwell	1910-1911
Rodgers	1921
Roebling	1909
Rogers	1895 and 1911-1912
Rogers and Hanford	1902
Rogers Steam	1903
Rollin	1924-1925
Rolls-Royce	1921-1935
Roman	1909
Romer	1921
Roosevelt	1929-1930
Roper Steamer	1860-1896
Ross	1915-1918
Ross Steam	1906-1909

Lists

Rotary...................................1904-1905 and 1922
Rowe...1908 and 1910
Rowena Front Drive..................................1926
Royal Electric...................................1904-1905
Royal Tourist....................................1904-1911
Ruggmobile..1922
Ruler...1917
Rumley...1920
Rushmobile...1901-1903
Russell.............................1903-1904 and 1921
Russell-Knight...1914
Rutenber..1902
Ruxton..1929-1930
Ryder..1900

S

S and M..1913
S and S Hearse...................................1924-1929
Saf T Cab...1926-1928
Saginaw...1916
Salisbury..1895
Salter...1909-1913
Salvador...1914
Sampson..1911
Samuels Electric..1899
Sandusky..1913
Santos..1902-1904
Saturn..1991-present
Savage...1914
Saxon...1914-1922
Sayers..1917-1924
Scarab..1935
Schacht..1904-1913
Schaum..1900-1903
Schebler...1908
Schleicher..1895
Schlosser..1912
Schnader..1907
Schoening..1895
Schwarz..1899-1900
Scootmobile...1947
Scott...1901
Scott Newcomb..1921
Scout..1914
Scripps-Booth......................................1912-1922
Seabury..1904-1905
Seagrave..1914

Searchmont...1900-1903
Sears Motor Buggy................................1908-1912
Sebring..1910-1912
Seely Steam...1905
Sekine..1923
Selden...1907-1914
Sellers...1908-1912
Senator...1906-1910
Seneca..1917-1924
Serpentina..1915
Serrifile..1921
Servitor..1907
Seven Little Buffaloes.................................1909
Severin...1920-1921
S.G.V...1911-1915
Shad Wyck..1917-1918
Shain...1902-1903
Sharon..1915
Sharp Arrow..1908-1910
Sharp Steam...1901
Shatwells Steam....................................1901-1903
Shavers Steam..1895
Shaw...1920-1921
Shaw Wick...1917-1919
Shawmut...1906-1908
Shelby...1903
Sheridan...1921
Shoemaker..1906-1907
Sibley...1911
Sibley Curtiss..1911-1912
Sigma...1914
Signel...1915
Silent..1912
Silent Knight..1905-1907
Silver Knight...1914-1919
Simmons Stream...1895
Simms Light Four..1920
Simplex...1907-1919
Simplex Crane.......................................1915-1919
Simplicity..1907-1911
Simplo...1908-1909
Sinclair Scott..1908
Singer..1914-1920
Single Center..1906-1908
Sintz...1902-1904
S.J.R...1915-1916
Skelton..1920-1922
Skene...1900-1901
Slater..1909
Smisor..1899
Smith..1905

Smith and Mabley Simplex	1904-1907
Smith Motor Buggy	1896
Smith Motor Wheel	1916-1919
Smith Spring Motor	1896
S.N.	1921
Snyder	1906-1908
Sommer	1904-1905
South Bend	1913-1914
Southern	1906-1908
Southern Six	1921
Sovereign	1906-1907
Spacke	1919
Spartan	1910
Spaulding	1902-1903 and 1910-1916
Special	1904
Speedway	1905-1906
Speedwell	1907-1914
Spencer	1921-1922
Spencer Steam	1862 and 1901
Sperling	1921-1923
Sperry	1899-1901
Sphinx	1914-1916
Spicer	1902
Spiller	1900
Spoerer	1908-1914
Sprague	1896
Springer	1903-1905
Springfield Electric	1908
Springfield Steam	1900-1901
Sprite	1914
Spurr	1901
Squires Steamer	1899
S.S.E.	1917
Stafford	1908-1914
Stammobile Steam	1900-1901
Standard	1900, 1902, 1904-1905, 1909-1910, 1915, 1916-1922 and 1948
Standard Electric O	1911
Standard Steamer	1900 and 1911-1915
Stanley Steamer	1897-1927
Stanley Whitney	1899
Stanton Steam	1901
Stanwood	1920-1922
Staples	1900
Star	1902-1904, 1907-1908, 1909-1911 and 1922-1928
Starin	1903-1904
States	1914-1915
Staver	1907-1914
Steam Vehicle	1900
Steamobile	1901-1902
Stearns	1901-1929
Stearns Steam Car	1898
Steco	1914
Steel Swallow	1907-1908
Stageman	1915
Stein Koenig	1926
Steinhart Jensen	1908
Steinmetz	1922-1923
Stephens	1917-1924
Sterling	1909-1911 and 1914-1916
Sterling Knight	1920-1922
Sterling Steam	1901-1902
Stetson	1916
Stevens	1899
Stevens-Duryea	1901-1927
Stewart	1895 and 1915-1916
Stewart Coates Steam	1922
Stickney	1914
Stilson	1907-1909
St. Joe	1909
St. John	1903
St. Louis	1899-1901, 1903-1907 and 1922
Stoddard Dayton	1904-1913
Storck Steam	1902
Storms Electric	1915
Stout	1946
Stout Scarab	1932-1936
Stranahan	1906
Strathmore	1899-1901
Strattan Premier	1923
Streator	1902
Stringer Steary	1899-1902
Strong and Rogers	1900
Strouse Steam	1915
Strouss	1897
Studebaker	1902-1966
Sturgis	1897
Sturtevant	1905-1907
Stutz	1911-1935
Stuyvesant	1911-1912
Suburban	1911-1912
Success	1906-1909
Sultan	1908-1912
Summit	1907-1909
Sun	1916-1917
Sunset	1900-1913
Super Cooled	1923
Super Kar	1947
Superior	1914
Supreme	1917-1922
Sweany Steam	1895

Lists

Synnestvedt..1904-1905
Syracuse Electric.......................................1899-1903

T

Tait Electric 1923
Tally Ho 1914
Tarkington...1922-1923
Tasco 1947
Taunton..1901-1903
Taylor...1895
Templar 1917-1924
Temple...1899
Templeton...1910
Terraplane 1933-1937
Terwilliger Steam 1904
Tex..1915
Texan 1920-1922
Texmobile..1920-1921
Thomas 1903-1918
Thomas Detroit......................................1906-1908
Thompson 1901-1907
Thomson Electric...1901
Thorobred..1901
Thresher Electric...1900
Tiffany 1913-1914
Tiger..1914-1915
Tiley...1904-1913
Tincher..1903-1909
Tinkham...1899
Tjaarda..1935
Toledo Steamer......................................1901-1903
Tonawanda..1900
Toquet..1905
Torbensen 1902-1906
Touraine...1912-1916
Tourist..1902-1910
Tower..1899
Trabold ....1898 and 1905
Tractobile Steam...................................1900-1902
Trask Detroit..1922-1923
Traveler...1907, 1910-1911, 1913-1914 and 1924-1925
Trebert...1907-1908
Triangle 1918
Tribune..1913
Tri Moto...1900-1901
Trinity Steam...1900-1901
Triumph 1907-1912

Trumbull 1914-1915
Tucker..1948
Tulsa 1917-1922
Turner...1900
Twin City...1914
Twombly 1913-1915
Twyford ....1899-1902 and 1904-1907

U

Ultimate..1914
Union...............................1902-1909 and 1912
United...1914
United Power 1901
Unito 1909
Universal ....1910 and 1914
University...1907
Unwin..1921-1922
Upton ....1902-1903 and 1905-1907
U.S. 1908
U.S. Electric..1899-1903
U.S. Long Distance................................1900-1904
U.S. Motor Vehicle................................1899-1900

V

Valley..1908
Van..1911-1912
Van Wagoner 1899
Vandergrift..1907
Van Dyke..1912
Vanell Steam 1895
Vanette..1946
Vaughan.....................1910-1914 and 1921-1923
V.E. Electric...1903-1904
Veerac..1905
Velie...1909-1929
Vernon...1918-1921
Verrett..1895
Vestal...1914
Victor..1913-1917
Victor Steam..1899-1903
Victoria..1900
Victory...1920-1921
Viking..........................1907-1908 and 1929-1930
Vim Cyclecar..1914

Lists

Virginian	1911-1912
Vixen	1914-1916
Vogel	1909
Vogue	1921-1922
Vulcan	1913-1915

W

Waco	1915-1917
Wagenhals	1910-1915
Wagner	1900-1901
Wahl	1913-1914
Waldron	1908-1911
Walker	1895 and 1905
Wall	1900-1903
Walter	1902-1906
Waltham	1898, 1905-1908 and 1922
Walther	1903
Walworth	1904-1905
Ward Electric	1914-1916
Ward Leonard	1903
Ware	1861
Warren	1909-1914
Warren Detroit	1910-1913
Warwick	1901-1905
Washburn	1896-1902
Washington	1908-1909, 1911-1923 and 1925
Wasp	1919-1924
Waterloo	1903-1905
Waterman	1900
Waters	1900-1903
Watrous	1905
Watt Steam	1910
Waukeshaw	1906-1910
Waverley Electric	1898-1916
Wayne	1904-1908
Webb Jay Steam	1908
Weeks	1908
Welch	1903-1911
Welch and Lawson	1895
Welch Detroit	1910-1911
West Gasoline	1895
Westcott	1909-1925
Western	1901
Westfield Steam	1901-1903
Westinghouse	1905-1907
Weston	1899-1903
W.F.S.	1912
Whaley Henriette	1900

Wharton	1922-1923
Wheeler	1900-1902
Whippet	1927-1931
White	1900-1918
White Star	1909-1911
Whiting	1910-1912
Whitney	1896-1899
Wichita	1920-1921
Wick	1902-1903
Wilcox	1910-1913
Wildman	1902
Willard	1903-1905
Williams	1905
Wills St. Claire	1921-1927
Willys	1916-1955
Willys-Knight	1914-1933
Wilson	1906
Windsor	1929-1930
Wing	1896 and 1922
Winkler	1911
Winner	1907-1909
Winther	1921-1923
Winton	1896-1924
Wisconsin	1899
Witt	1912
Wizard	1914
Wolfe	1907-1909
Wolverine	1904-1906, 1917-1919 and 1927-1928
Wonder	1907-1909
Woodruff	1902-1903
Woods	1899-1918
Woods Electric	1901
Woods Mobilette	1913-1916
Worth	1906-1910
Worthington	1904-1905
Wright	1904 and 1910-1911

X

Xenia	1914

Y

Yale	1902-1905 and 1916-1918
Yates	1914
Yellow Cab	1915-1930
York	1905

Z

Selected Index, SIA #3-#154
Is your car here?
Or the car you used to own?
Or the car you wish you had?

Enjoy detailed specs, facts and photos of your favorite cars in *Special Interest Autos* back issues!

Past issues of *SIA* give you the complete stories on over 300 marques and models including specs, diagrams, unique features, histories, photographs, marketing strategies and sales.

Plus you can select entertaining and useful articles on other topics ranging from general automotive history to restoration "how-to's."

Most driveReports average 6 to 8 pages of text and photos, and each back issue includes driveReports on two to three other marques or models plus articles on the collector-car hobby.

Special Interest Autos (a publication of *Hemmings Motor News*), has been the leading authority on collector cars since 1970. Select your back issues today and enjoy big savings when you order more than one!

AUTOMOTIVE HISTORY

This section contains diverse articles dealing with auto-related developments and events as well as certain industry personalities.

BLUEPRINTS

This section is short profiles of the history of a given car accompanied by original artwork illustrating the auto under discussion.

COMPARISON REPORTS

These are articles which test and compare competitive makes of cars from the same year of manufacture.

CAR COMPONENTS

This lists articles which have surveyed body and mechanical parts including explanations of how these components work as well as developmental histories of many components.

COACHBUILDING

This includes histories on certain body styles as well as articles on custom coachwork and large-volume body building companies such as Briggs and Fisher.

DO IT YOURSELF

This section lists SIA's articles on care, restoration and replacement of various automotive components.

EXPERIMENTALS & PROTOTYPES

This section deals with these vehicles as produced by or for recognized auto manufacturers.

NOW AND THEN

This section contains comparison reports between similar models of old and new examples of a make of car.

ONE-OF-A-KIND
(or nearly so)

This section contains one-off or extremely low-volume experimental cars which never achieved production in any form.

RACING AND COMPETITION

This includes record runs, oval track and road racing articles.

SPECIAL FEATURES

Includes photo stories, articles on oddball events and products in the industry, automotive-related events, etc.

SIA SPOTTER'S GUIDES

These Spotter's Guides from past issues of SIA come to you rolled in a cardboard tube so you can display them without creases. Each is printed on heavy, glossy paper suitable for framing. Just $3.50 per copy. We pay the postage. See order form on last page.

MGA
Includes illustrations and hand-lettered text on important features and styling. Dark green & black, 23" x 29". Item #P-6F

MG-TC, TD, and TF
Includes illustrations and hand-lettered text of facts & features. Dark green & black, 23" x 29". Item #P-1F

Jaguar XK-120, 140 & 150
Includes illustrations and hand-lettered text on features and styling changes. Dark green & black, 23" x 29". Item #P-5F

Corvette Sting Ray
Includes illustrations and hand-lettered text on changes in hoods, tops, wheels, tail lights & louvers. Red & black, 23" x 29". Item #P-2F

Town & Country
Includes important features and styling developments for the 1941-50 Town & Country, along with fact-filled text. Brown & black, 25" x 38". Item #P-3F

Cadillac Eldorado
Includes important features and styling developments for the 1953-66 Eldorado, along with fact-filled text. Blue & black 25" x 38". Item #P-4F

Please send me the back issues checked:

(Sorry, SIA back issues #1, #2, #4, #5, #6, #7, #9, #11, #13, #14, #15, #18, #19, #21, #22, #25, #27, #29, #31, #32, #33, #34, #36, #37, #38, #42, #43, #47, #49, #50, #51, #52, #53, #54, #56, #58, #59, #65, #71, #73, #75, #76, #78, #79, #84, #91, #92, #96, #102, #106 & #128 are out of print.)

❑#3	❑#35	❑#62	❑#81	❑#97	❑#111	❑#123	❑#136	❑#148
❑#8	❑#39	❑#63	❑#82	❑#98	❑#112	❑#124	❑#137	❑#149
❑#10	❑#40	❑#64	❑#83	❑#99	❑#113	❑#125	❑#138	❑#150
❑#12	❑#41	❑#66	❑#85	❑#100	❑#114	❑#126	❑#139	❑#151
❑#16	❑#44	❑#67	❑#86	❑#101	❑#115	❑#127	❑#140	❑#152
❑#17	❑#45	❑#68	❑#87	❑#103	❑#116	❑#129	❑#141	❑#153
❑#20	❑#48	❑#70	❑#88	❑#104	❑#117	❑#130	❑#142	❑#154
❑#23	❑#55	❑#72	❑#90	❑#105	❑#118	❑#131	❑#143	
❑#24	❑#57	❑#74	❑#93	❑#107	❑#119	❑#132	❑#144	
❑#26	❑#60	❑#77	❑#94	❑#108	❑#120	❑#133	❑#145	
❑#28	❑#61	❑#80	❑#95	❑#109	❑#121	❑#134	❑#146	
❑#30				❑#110	❑#122	❑#135	❑#147	

❑ Start my 1-year subscription to *Special Interest Autos* for only $14.95 (saving $5). *Offer limited to new subscribers only.*

Send the following Spotter's Guides for only $3.50 each postpaid:
❑ MG-TC, TD, & TF #P-1F   ❑ Cadillac Eldorado #P-4F
❑ Corvette Sting Ray #P-2F   ❑ Jaguar XK-120, 140 & 150 #P-5F
❑ Town & Country #P-3F   ❑ MGA #P-6F

❑ Send the full collection of 103 available SIA back issues for only $199.95, a savings of over 60% from the single back issue rate.

Complete Your Collection — and Save!

**1 issue: $5.00; 2 issues: $4.50 each; 3 issues: $4.00 each
4 issues or more: $3.50 each**

Payment enclosed for $ _____

CHARGE MY: ❑ MC   ❑ VISA   ❑ Discover   ❑ American Express

Account #_____Exp. Date_____

Signature _____

Total order $_____

   Name _____
   Address _____
   City _____
   State_____ Zip_____
   Phone # _____

For Canadian and Foreign orders please add $1.00 Shipping & Handling per copy. Vermont residents add 5% sales tax. Canadian residents add 7% GST. For faster service call ext. 550 at 1-800-CAR-HERE or 802-447-9550, or Fax your order to 802-447-1561 to charge to your MC, VISA, Discover or American Express. Prices subject to change.

Send to:

SIA Back Issues
P.O. Box 196, S20015, Bennington, Vermont 05201

Index

This index is a complete roster of all listings appearing in the *Almanac*. The page number indicated will direct you to the main listing for that supplier or organization.

Please note that numerical names (e.g. 1932 Buick Registry) and symbols (& and / for example) come before alphabetical names.

Also, vendors who use their own names are alphabetized by their last names. However, to make reading the index easier, we have printed the vendor's full name in its proper order. In addition, vendors who use a nickname or title as part of their business name are listed under that nickname or title — so that you find MoPar Jack Dyson under "M" rather than "D".

Index

B

C

D

Index

E

Index

I

M

Index

N

O

P

Q

R

S

Index

Index

X

Y

Z

Index

Is your collector-car business, club or museum listed in this Almanac?

If not, simply fill in your organization's name & address below.
You need not send detailed information now –
we'll send you a listing form right before we produce the 13th edition.
That way the information will be as accurate & up-to-date as possible!

Business/Organization Name _____

Address _____

City/State/Zip _____

Phone _____

Mail to:
Hemmings'
Vintage Auto Almanac

Thirteenth Edition • PO Box 945 • Bennington, Vermont 05201

Do you know of a business, club or museum that should be listed in this Almanac?

If not, simply fill in that organization's name & address below.
You need not send detailed information now –
we'll send them a listing form right before we produce the 13th edition.
That way the information will be as accurate & up-to-date as possible!

Business/Organization Name _____

Address _____

City/State/Zip _____

Phone _____

Mail to:
Hemmings'
Vintage Auto Almanac

Thirteenth Edition • PO Box 945 • Bennington, Vermont 05201